Brief Contents

Peter Unger/Getty Images

macmillan learning

 sapling learning
Macmillan Learning

LEARNING SCIENCE DESIGN OF

 SaplingPlus
for Economics

Features and benefits: Pre-lecture tutorials, bridge questions, embedded e-book, video tutorials, LearningCurve activities, graphing activities, a wealth of homework assignments, and refined test bank

> I found the SaplingPlus wrong answer feedback on end of chapter problems and suggested homework among the best I've seen."
> **INSTRUCTOR**

eighty-four%

Students come to class better prepared and engage more actively with SaplingPlus

84% of students report that SaplingPlus pre-lecture activities helped them prepare to participate in class

77%

Students engage in an end-to-end learning experience with SaplingPlus's integrated experience

77% of students engage with SaplingPlus before class, in class, and after class

81%

81% of students who report being less motivated in economics said that the SaplingPlus pre-lecture activities helped them to participate more in class

74%

Students enjoy their course more using SaplingPlus

74% of students report that they enjoyed their economics course more than other courses they were taking

87%

87% of students say there is more interaction in their economics classes than in other courses they are taking because of SaplingPlus

> I like that I can customize the bridge assignments and their grading is more helpful to me in class so I can go over them."
> **INSTRUCTOR**

Students increase academic performance when using SaplingPlus

Students who engaged with more SaplingPlus features achieved higher final exam scores

Level of engagement with SaplingPlus features

Final exam grade

Students who completed more pre-lecture activities achieved higher average in-class assessment grades

Aaverage final exam score

0-25%	26-50%	51-75%	76-100%
71%	77%	83%	91%

Proportion of pre-lecture activities completed

Peter Unger/Getty Images

ECONOMIC PRINCIPLES

A Business Perspective

Stephen Rubb

John F. Welch College of Business,
Sacred Heart University

Scott Sumner

Mercatus Center at George Mason University;
Professor Emeritus, Bentley University

worth publishers
Macmillan Learning
New York

Senior Vice President, Content Strategy: **Charles Linsmeier**
Program Director: **Shani Fisher**
Program Manager: **Sarah Seymour**
Development Editors: **Ann Kirby-Payne and Lukia Kliossis**
Assessment Manager: **Kristyn Brown**
Assessment Editor: **Joshua Hill**
Marketing Manager: **Andrew Zierman**
Marketing Assistant: **Chelsea Simens**
Director of Media Editorial and Assessment: **Noel Hohnstine**
Media Editor: **Lindsay Neff**
Editorial Assistant: **Amanda Gaglione**
Director of Content Management Enhancement: **Tracey Kuehn**
Senior Managing Editor: **Lisa Kinne**
Senior Content Project Manager: **Peter Jacoby**
Director of Design, Content Management: **Diana Blume**
Design Services Manager: **Natasha A. S. Wolfe**
Interior Design: **Kevin Kall**
Cover Design: **John Callahan**
Illustrations: **Network Graphics**
Illustration Coordinator: **Janice Donnola**
Photo Editor: **Kerri Wilson**
Senior Workflow Project Supervisor: **Joe Ford**
Production Supervisor: **Robin Besofsky**
Media Project Manager: **Andrew Vaccaro**
Composition: **Lumina Datamatics, Inc.**
Printing and Binding: **LSC Communications**
Cover Image: **Peter Unger/Getty Images**

ISBN-13: 978-1-4641-8249-5
ISBN-10: 1-4641-8249-3

Library of Congress Control Number: 2018952082

Printed in the United States of America

1 2 3 4 5 6   23 22 21 20 19 18

Worth Publishers
One New York Plaza
Suite 4500
New York, NY 10004-1562
www.macmillanlearning.com

Dedication

To my parents, Donald and Yolande, who instilled in me a love of knowledge. To my wife, Sue, whose support for the project was enormous. To my children, Jason and Marissa, who provided quick feedback from a student's perspective. To my sister Monique, whose genuine concern for others is inspirational. In loving memory of my sister Genevieve.

Stephen Rubb

To my wife, Bi, and my daughter, Isabella, who each made many sacrifices as I devoted many hours to this project. I will always be grateful for your support.

Scott Sumner

About the Authors

Stephen Rubb is a passionate teacher. He began his teaching career in 1994 and is currently a professor of economics at Sacred Heart University. Prior to Sacred Heart, he taught economics, finance, and statistics at a variety of business schools, including Bentley University, Stonehill College, and Bryant University. He has a master's degree in business management from Rensselaer Polytechnic Institute and a doctorate in economics from Northeastern University. Professor Rubb's research interests include migration, Social Security and retirement issues, and labor market–education issues. He has published in a variety of scholarly journals, including *Demography*, *Applied Economics*, the *Economics of Education Review*, the *Journal of Family and Economic Issues*, and *Education Economics*. Professor Rubb lives in Glastonbury, Connecticut, with his wife, Sue, his two children, Jason and Marissa, and their schnauzer-poodle mix, Jasmine.

Scott Sumner is the Ralph G. Hawtrey Chair of Monetary Policy at the Mercatus Center at George Mason University, where he is the director of the Program on Monetary Policy. He is also professor emeritus at Bentley University. In his writing and research, Professor Sumner specializes in monetary policy, the role of the international gold market in the Great Depression, and the history of macroeconomic thought. His most recent book is *The Midas Paradox: Financial Markets, Government Policy Shocks, and the Great Depression* (2015). Named by *Foreign Policy* magazine in 2012 as one of the "top 100 global thinkers," Professor Sumner has published papers in academic journals including the *Journal of Political Economy*, *Economic Inquiry*, and the *Journal of Money, Credit and Banking*. He is author of the economics blog The Money Illusion and a contributor to EconLog. Sumner received a bachelor's degree in economics from the University of Wisconsin and a master's degree and doctorate in economics from the University of Chicago.

Motivating Students with
Economic Principles: A Business Perspective

Most students in business schools are interested in seeing how economics relates to the world of business. For many students at liberal arts institutions, economics is the only business class they will take. We've each taught at both types of schools and have found that our students become more engaged with economics when they can relate theory to the types of businesses they interact with every day and to those they might envision themselves working for—if not founding—someday in the future.

Economic Principles: A Business Perspective leverages student fascination with business by drawing clear connections between fundamental economic theory and the business decisions that students—whether they are future CEOs, small business owners, managers, or independent workers—will make in their careers.

Today's students are presented with more information than any generation that came before them, but they still face the same scarcity of time. We want them to make the most of the time that they spend studying economics but struggled to find suitable course materials that present theory, examples, and applications in an efficient format and that help them to link what they're learning with what they know and with what they'll learn later on.

We crafted *Economic Principles: A Business Perspective* with the goal of striking the right balance between principles and pragmatics. Our book is designed to teach each student how to think like an economist—especially when making or evaluating business decisions. We challenge them to look at business decisions from an economist's perspective and to examine economic phenomena—ranging from supply and demand analysis to monetary policy to global trade—with an eye toward their implications for firms of all shapes and sizes. Importantly, we've stripped away the clutter that bogs down many textbooks and presented the material in a lean, efficient format that helps students get down to the business of learning and applying the fundamentals of economics.

The result is a book that gets down to the business of economics with a straightforward approach to both theory and application and a format that provides instructors with flexibility and students with practical support.

Stephen Rubb, Ph.D.
John F. Welch College of Business
Sacred Heart University

Scott B. Sumner, Ph.D.
Mercatus Center at George Mason University
Professor Emeritus, Bentley University

Getting Down to the Business of Economics

Economic Principles will motivate students by connecting economics to the business world with strong examples, a global emphasis, integrated technology, and practical pedagogy. Integrated business and policy briefs, in-depth case studies, chapter-ending business applications, thoroughly explained graphs, and a battery of simple but useful learning tools that support the intersection of theory and practice.

Business Connections

We use business examples to show students clear connections between economic concepts and the business world. To bring economic issues down to size, we periodically discuss the microeconomic decisions faced by a pair of hypothetical entrepreneurs—the owner of an established pizzeria and someone who is soon to open her own pizza place. Elsewhere, we call on real-world examples to show how big firms use the same theories to make optimal decisions on a larger, even global scale against a changing macroeconomic landscape—such as building an iPhone, developing and selling apps for it, and implementing the policies that affect Apple's bottom line, including labor, taxes, environmental regulations, and international trade.

A Global Emphasis

Roughly a fourth of all goods produced globally are exported, and even today's smallest businesses have access to the global market. With four chapters devoted to trade and the global economy, in addition to well-integrated examples from around the world integrated throughout the text, we make understanding the opportunities and challenges of the global economy a priority.

Integrated Technology

Developed alongside chapters and designed for seamless integration with the book, SaplingPlus provides students access to proven learning tools that correspond with specific text content. These resources—adaptive quizzing, tutorials, videos, activities, and a comprehensive review of math and graphing—help increase student engagement, mastery of the material, and success in the course.

Flexibility That Works for Instructors, Pedagogy That Works for Students

We know that no two instructors—or two syllabi—are alike, and so we have endeavored to organize this book in a way that offers flexibility.

Our table of contents is built for flexibility, with key concepts explained in early core chapters and a number of optional chapters provided to suit the needs of different instructors.

Each chapter is designed to be self-contained, but because some instructors will want to customize, we reinforce key terms in every chapter, cross-reference topics across chapters, and offer clear off-ramps for instructors who wish to skip specific content.

Embedded pedagogy includes the following elements:

- **Think & Speak Like an Economist.** Throughout our text, quick reminders continually reinforce the basics of economic thought to help students to contextualize new content along with material they already know and to clarify language they may encounter in the media, in other courses, and during their careers.

> ## Think & Speak Like an Economist
>
> In business, it's common for firms to use the term *increase in supply* interchangeably with an *increase in inventory*. But in economics, an increase in supply refers to a rightward shift in the supply curve.

- **Visual and Text Reinforcement.** Some readers look at the art first; others read the text first and then refer to graphs. Our clear and friendly writing style walks students patiently through each graph with detailed explanations in both the text and the caption, allowing students to work at their own pace and with their own learning styles.

- **Chapter Study Guides.** At the end of each chapter, we've integrated key terms into a cohesive Chapter Study Guide and highlighted the Top Ten Terms and Concepts, providing a useful framework for review.

- **Study Problems.** Each chapter ends with a set of Study Problems for student assignments. Complete answers are available online in the Solutions Manual.

A Business Perspective: The Intersection of Theory and Practice

Peter Unger/Getty Images

- **Real-World Business Briefs and Policy Briefs.** These succinct, highlighted examples integrate real-world data and news stories with the economic concepts that students are learning without disrupting the flow of the text. Our briefs cover both business and policy topics, with the balance shifting as appropriate in different chapters.

v Jordan Spieth misses a pricey putt.

Rich Graessle/Icon Sportswire CGV/Newscom

BUSINESS BRIEF Jordan Spieth Misses Putt, Under Armour Market Cap Falls $120 Million

In 2015, newcomer Jordan Spieth was on top of the golfing world. That year, the 22-year-old won a record $22 million. In addition, he was the youngest player to win two Majors (the Masters and the U.S. Open) in over 90 years. It was against this backdrop that the golfing world was abuzz.* Could Spieth become the first player to win all four Majors in a single year? This media attention benefited his major sponsor, Under Armour (UA), that had recently signed Spieth to a 10-year contract in an attempt to enter the golf apparel market. In the third Major of the year, the (British) Open Championship, Spieth jockeyed his way onto the top of the leader board in the final round, which due to unusual weather delays was played on a Monday when the stock market would be open.

Spieth's fortunes changed, though, when he missed a putt on the next-to-last hole. Within minutes, Under Armour's market cap fell by $120 million, as his endorsement value took a hit.† Stock prices and market caps reflect many factors, including the expected growth of earnings. When Spieth won the Master's and U.S. Open, UA's shares soared, in part due to the expectation of greater golf apparel sales. Expectations grew even higher when Spieth gave himself a chance to win the Open. When his fortunes changed, so, too, did the stock price of UA.

*Chris Chase, "Jordan Spieth's Awesome 2015 Season in 15 Unbelievable Stats," *USA Today*, September 28, 2015, http://ftw.usatoday.com/2015/09/jordan-spieth-winnings-2015-compared-to-tiger-woods-stats-record-money-grand-slam.

†Fred Imbert, "Did Jordan Spieth Hit a $120 Million Bogey?," *CNBC*, July 21, 2015, http://www.cnbc.com/2015/07/20/jordan-spieth-hits-120-million-bogey.html.

POLICY BRIEF The Surprising Benefits of Price Gouging

In the aftermath of a major natural disaster, you can expect two things: The price of certain necessities will rise, and politicians on both sides of the political aisle will claim the price increases represent "gouging." You might be surprised to learn that most economists consider price gouging to be *beneficial* to society, because it improves economic efficiency. In a survey of economists from top universities, over 60% of economists who voted disagreed with the State of Connecticut's passage of an anti-gouging law, while only 10% agreed (30% were uncertain or had no opinion).*

How does price gouging improve economic efficiency? After a natural disaster, the demand for necessities such as generators, gasoline, and water increases. At the same time, it is not unusual to see a decline in supply, as supply lines are disrupted by the disaster. Both these events cause prices to rise. These price increases ensure that the limited quantity being supplied goes where the item is most valued, as measured by willingness to pay. High prices discourage the hoarding of scarce gasoline or using it wastefully while others are in need.

Equally important, price gouging causes an increase in quantity supplied, as it provides a powerful incentive for businesses to truck in gasoline and water from regions not impacted by the disaster. Consider the actions of Bruce Garrett in the days just prior to Hurricane Irma that hit parts

Marianne Todd/Getty Images

^ Hoarding tends to occur when price gouging is prevented.

- **Case Studies.** In select chapters, we offer more thorough and in-depth analysis and application of broader economic issues in our Case Studies. These thoughtful and thought-provoking features provide students with opportunities to think critically about the economics at play in recent and historical events. Students are challenged to consider the myriad economic factors that influence both government and business decisions and, in turn, the economic implications of those decisions.

CASE STUDY The Minimum Wage Debate

Perhaps no issue divides economists more than the impact of increases in the minimum wage on the labor market. On the one hand, economists are generally believers in the benefits of using competitive markets to determine prices, unless there is a clear market failure. Raising the minimum wage to above equilibrium could create a deadweight loss and might lead to job losses or a reduction in hours worked and/or more unpleasant working conditions. It would likely have an adverse impact on business, particularly small businesses.

On the other hand, one key objective of the minimum wage is increasing the buying power of the poor—particularly the working poor—an important goal of many lawmakers. In addition, any alternative program designed to help the working poor would also have costs and result in at least some deadweight loss.

A 2013 survey asked economists from top-tier universities if they agreed that a proposed modest increase in the minimum wage "would make it noticeably harder for low-skilled workers to find employment." The responses were sharply divided: 37% of economists agreed with the statement, 34% disagreed, and the rest were uncertain or had no opinion. A similar poll conducted in 2015 asked economists if an increase the minimum wage to $15 per hour over several years would lead to a significantly lower employment rate for low-wage U.S. workers. In that survey, 30% agreed or strongly agreed with the claim, while 27% disagreed. Economists are clearly split on the issue.[*]

To complicate matters, not only is there a trade-off between equity and efficiency, but the economic impact is difficult to measure and economic studies have often reached conflicting conclusions.

- **Business Takeaways.** Each chapter ends with a quick outline of practical connections between chapter concepts and business applications. Clear and to the point, the Business Takeaways provide solid applications and examples of the ways that managers and firms routinely put economic analysis to use and help students to understand the impact of key economic indicators on the business environment.

BUSINESS TAKEAWAY

Firms benefit from trade, so it should come as no surprise that the concept of comparative advantage plays into many of the internal and external decisions that shape the activities of individual businesses, including General Electric and IBM.

Within a firm, business managers utilize the concepts of comparative advantage and specialization to increase the efficiency of their staff. Individual tasks should be assigned to those who have a comparative advantage, as when accountants keep financial records and salespeople make sales. This increases output within the firm, even without external contracts and trade. Managers are becoming increasingly aware of other ways in which they can identify and capitalize on the comparative advantage already present within their firms. IBM's pivot from computer manufacturing to consulting reflects this kind of economic decision making.

In some cases, a firm might determine that it does not have a comparative advantage in a specific area of its business. In such an instance, the firm can opt to contract out certain tasks to other companies that have more of a comparative advantage in that area of expertise. Perhaps the bookkeeping could be more efficiently done if outsourced to a firm that specializes in accounting, or maybe it makes more sense to hire a freelance event planner to manage an upcoming sales meeting than to ask the head of Human Resources to take time from her other responsibilities to coordinate the task. Likewise, individual laborers who possess a comparative advantage in a particular area can leverage those skills as well. Having a sense of your comparative advantage is useful in wage negotiations, when seeking a promotion, or when going into business on your own.

Engaging Students with Technology

The technology for this text has been developed to spark student engagement and improve outcomes while offering instructors flexible, high-quality, research-based tools for teaching this course. SaplingPlus is the first system to support and engage students at every step in the learning process.

SaplingPlus for Economics, built on learning science, is the affordable solution for improving students' skills and outcomes and saving time for instructors. With pre-lecture activities and in-class tools that help students learn key economic concepts, personalized quizzing, and a proven approach for helping students interpret, represent, and understand information in a graphical format, SaplingPlus teaches students how thinking like an economist leads to better decision making in all areas of life. Assets include the following:

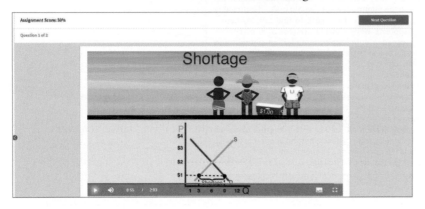

- **Pre-Lecture Tutorials.** The pre-lecture tutorials foster a basic understanding of core economic concepts before students ever set foot in a classroom. Developed by two pioneers in active-learning methods—Eric Chiang of Florida Atlantic University and José Vazquez of University of Illinois at Urbana–Champaign—this resource is part of the SaplingPlus learning path. Students watch pre-lecture videos and complete Bridge Question assessments that prepare them to engage in class. Instructors receive data about student comprehension that can inform their lecture preparation.

- **LearningCurve Adaptive Quizzing.** Embraced by students and instructors alike, this incredibly popular and effective adaptive quizzing engine offers individualized question sets and feedback tailored to each student based on correct and incorrect responses. LearningCurve questions are hyperlinked to relevant e-book sections, encouraging students to read and use the resources at hand to enrich their understanding.

Pedagogical Intent: The first questions require students to demonstrate basic comprehension of the material in the video.
According to the video, how many times has the U.S. federal government raised the federal minimum wage?

| 22 | times |

- **Video Activities.** Expand the real-world examples in *Economic Principles* with video activities powered by Bloomberg videos. These unique activities pair Bloomberg content related to key topics and examples covered in the text with an assignment built around Bloom's taxonomy. By completing these exercises, students will gain practice applying economic analysis to today's news.

- **Graphing Questions.** Powered by improved graphing, these multistep graphing questions are paired with helpful feedback to guide students through the process of problem solving. Students are asked to demonstrate their understanding by simply clicking, dragging, and dropping a line to a predetermined location. The graphs have been designed so that students' entire focus is on moving the correct curve in the correct direction, virtually eliminating grading issues for instructors.

- **Work It Out.** The Work It Out skill-building activities pair sample end-of-chapter problems with targeted feedback and video explanations to help students solve problems step by step. This approach allows students to work independently, tests their comprehension of concepts, and prepares them for class and exams.

Powerful Support for Instructors

For Assessment

Test Bank Prepared by Dixie Button and Beth Haynes, the Test Bank contains multiple-choice and short-answer questions to help instructors assess students' comprehension, interpretation, and ability to synthesize. Test Bank questions are also tagged to the standards of the Association to Advance Collegiate Schools of Business (AACSB).

Homework Assignments Each chapter contains homework of various question types, including graphing questions featuring our powerful graphing player, that provide instructors with a curated set of multiple-choice and graphing questions that are easily assigned for graded assessment.

Additional Resources

Gradebook This useful resource offers clear grading feedback to students and instructors on individual assignments and on performance in the course.

LMS integration Online homework is easily integrated into a school's learning management system so that an instructor's Gradebook and roster are always in sync.

Instructor's Resource Manual This manual, by Debbie Evercloud, offers instructors chapter objectives, chapter outlines, and teaching materials and tips for enhancing the classroom experience, and it tags concepts to AACSB standards.

Solutions Manual Prepared by the authors of the text, the Solutions Manual offers solutions to all of the text's end-of-chapter Study Problems.

Interactive Presentation Slides These brief, interactive slides are designed to hold students' attention in class with graphics and key concepts from the text.

A Guide for Planning Your Course

To help you plan your course learning objectives, and to provide an overview of our emphasis in each chapter, this chart highlights elements of business, global, and monetarism coverage. The statements provided can be used to organize your lesson plans. You will find that our text includes unique chapter coverage on organizing a firm, financial markets, personal finance, as well as four chapters on trade and the global economy.

	Chapter Highlights **B**usiness **G**lobal **M**onetarism **P**edagogical
Part I: An Introduction to Economics	
1. The Basics of Economics: *Strategies for Decision Making*	**P** Present key concepts that will be used throughout text, including opportunity cost, marginal analysis, real versus nominal values, long run versus short run, and benefit of trade.
	B Show how the language of business and economics defines words like *equity*, *investment*, *capital*, and *resources*.
1A. Appendix: *Using Graphs in Economics*	**P** Review concepts like slope and percentage change, and begin to stress that correlation does not prove causation.
2. Why We Trade: *Production, Trade, and the Global Economy*	**G** **P** Introduce an effective yet simple model showing the gains from trade and the concept of comparative advantage.
	G Introduce key terms on globalization that can be used in subsequent chapters, including *exchange rate*, *export*, and *import*.
Part II: Foundations of Markets	
3. Supply and Demand: *Determining Prices in a Changing Business Environment*	**P** Focus on how price changes cannot be evaluated without first considering whether they are caused by shifts in supply or shifts in demand.
	B Explain factors that shift supply in the context of business cost.
	G Introduce the idea that changes in exchange rates can shift the demand for goods and services.
4. Elasticity: *A Measure of Responsiveness*	**B** Demonstrate how price changes impact total revenue. Compare the business concepts of unit sales and sales revenue to quantity and total revenue.
5. Consumer Choice: *Decision Making for Consumers*	**B, P** Explain the restaurant industry's "all you can eat" concept from a business perspective (and a consumer's perspective).
	B Explain the business rationale for charging a lower price on additional items.
6. Economic Efficiency and the Power of Competitive Markets: *How Price Controls and Taxes Result in Deadweight Loss*	**P** Stress that markets maximize efficiency by allowing all mutually beneficial transactions to occur.
	B Compare the business world concept of efficiency to the economic concept of productive efficiency.
Part III: Foundations of Government and Public Policy	
7. Taxes: An Economic Analysis: *Funding Government Spending*	**B** Explain corporate inversions.

	Business **G**lobal **M**onetarism **P**edagogical
8. The Environment, Externalities, and Property Rights: *Market Failure and the Case for Government*	**P** Use a pedagogically straightforward model to show externalities, show the methods that economists advocate to fight pollution and global warming, and explain the intuition behind the Coase theorem.

Part IV: Foundations of Finance and Business

9. Organizing a Business: *Corporations and Other Legal Structures*	**B** Focus the entire chapter on business (a focus that is not commonly found in other books).
	B **G** Include a section on the advantages and disadvantages of managing a multinational business.
	B Include a section on the challenges of corporate ownership (such as the principal and agent problem and corporate social responsibility).
10. Stocks and Bonds: *Financial Markets and Personal Finance*	**B** A Focus on the stock and bond market.
	P Present the basic principles of financial investing.
10A. Appendix: *Present Value and the Time Value of Money*	**B** **P** Estimate the business concepts of net present value and internal rate of return using commonly available spreadsheet software.

Part V: Market Structure

11. The Cost of Doing Business: *Production and Economic Cost*	**B** **P** Provide the standard cost model in the context of business.
	P Introduce a character, Maria, who sets up her own business. Maria's business example is used in subsequent chapters.
12. Perfect Competition: *Maximizing Profits in Highly Competitive Markets*	**P** Introduce four market structures (coverage is not required). A similar graphic on market structures is used in four chapters to help students understand the concept.
	P Reintroduce marginal analysis (introduced in Chapter 1).
13. Monopoly and Antitrust Laws: *Businesses with Market Power*	**B** Look at antitrust policies with a focus on modern business mergers.
14. Monopolistic Competition and Price Discrimination: *When Businesses Sell Differentiated Products*	**B** Introduce a student-friendly marketing concept known as the four Ps in the context of monopolistic competition.
	B Introduce the concept of price discrimination and numerous business applications.
15. Oligopoly: *Strategic Decision Making and Game Theory*	**B** **P** Develop student-friendly examples showing the difficulties of cooperation in a duopoly setting. Explain game theory using a payoff matrix and decision tree framework to show examples related to pricing and advertising.
	B Show strategies for overcoming coordination issues.

Part VI: Special Topics in Microeconomics

16. Behavioral Economics and Strategy: *Implications for Pricing, Location, and Product Mix*	**P** Introduce a framework to explain behavioral economics and more complex business strategies.
	B Focus on location and product mix decisions. Use Hotelling's law.
	B Introduce a variation of Michael Porter's five competitive forces model called microeconomic forces that impact business profitability.

(Continued)

	Business **G**lobal **M**onetarism **P**edagogical
Part VI: Special Topics in Microeconomics (continued)	
17. Labor and Other Resource Markets: *A Supply and Demand Model for Labor and Resources*	**B P** Introduce a labor market model with a business perspective that is built around data used in the cost chapter (Chapter 13).
	P Reinforce the concept of marginal analysis used in prior chapters.
18. The Distribution of Income: *Poverty and Income Inequality*	**G** Stress the decline in global poverty rates. Explain shifting income inequalities around the globe.
19. Information, Insurance, and Health Care: *Markets with Adverse Selection and Asymmetric Information*	**B P** Introduce the concept of asymmetric information, which leads effectively to adverse selection in the insurance market, including health insurance.
	P Provide a solid framework for students to understand health care in the United States today.
Part VII: Macroeconomic Data	
20. Real GDP and the Price Level: *Measuring the Performance of the Overall Economy*	**P M** Explain inflation as a decline in the value of money.
	P Demonstrate how price indexes and real GDP are calculated.
21. Unemployment and the Business Cycle: *Measuring the Performance of the Labor Market*	**P** Show how economic data is reported to help students understand news stories on the economy.
	G Discuss how unemployment differs across many countries.
Part VIII: Long-Run Foundations of Macroeconomics	
22. Long-Run Economic Growth: *What Explains the Wealth and Poverty of Nations?*	**P** Explain the rule of 70 as a tool for predicting various growth rates over decades.
	G Discuss how inclusive and extractive institutions also impact growth, beyond the standard factors of production.
23. Saving and Investment: A Macroeconomic Perspective: *How Saving Contributes to Economic Growth*	**P G** Demonstrate the concept of foreign saving and trade deficits. Explain how investment depends on private, public, and foreign saving.
Part IX: Money and the Monetary System	
24. The Monetary System: *What Is Money and Where Does It Come From?*	**B** Present a case study of the banking crisis of 2008.
	P Explain how banks work with a simple example where a student imagines becoming a banker.
	M Discuss what makes money special.
	M Explain the concept of base money (omitted from most other books).
25. Money and the Price Level in the Long Run: *The Quantity Theory and the Fisher Effect*	**M P** Explain the intuition linking money and inflation much more clearly than other books do. Unlike other books, the ideas in this chapter are carried over to the short-run chapters.
	G M Compare money growth and inflation rates during the Great Inflation globally to illustrate the equation of exchange.

	Business **G**lobal **M**onetarism **P**edagogical
Part X: The Business Cycle and Stabilizing the Economy	
26. Aggregate Supply and Aggregate Demand: *A Model of the Business Cycle*	**P** Contrast two sources of inflation (demand and supply shocks) and two sources of recession (demand and supply shocks). Give students a better sense of how to apply the aggregate supply and aggregate demand model to a variety of real-world situations.
27. Monetary Policy: *How the Fed Tries to Stabilize the Economy*	**M** Cover quantitative easing and monetary policy after interest rates hit zero. Focus on how high interest rates can mean either tight money (liquidity effect) or high inflation (Fisher effect).
28. Fiscal Policy: *The Impact of Government Spending and Taxes on GDP*	**M** Discuss the importance of monetary policy offset when considering the size of the fiscal multiplier.
	P Provide a good commonsense explanation of the differences between the supply and demand side effects of tax cuts.
	G Present supply side ideas in an international context.
Part XI: Special Topics in Macroeconomics	
29. The Aggregate Expenditure Model: *A Fixed-Price-Level Model of the Economy*	**P** Focus on the essential aspects of the multiplier model. Discuss the intuition behind the debate between Keynesians and classical economists and the ways that they differ on saving, opportunity cost, etc.
30. The Role of Expectations in Macroeconomics: *Inflation, Unemployment, and Monetary Policy*	**P** **M** Explain the intuition behind rational expectations with simple examples from everyday life. Present the Phillips curve in a framework that identifies when it is most useful. Contrast inflation and nominal GDP targeting.
Part XII: Foundations of Global Trade	
31. International Trade: *Doing Business across Borders*	**P** **G** **B** Use many real-world examples to illustrate concepts such as comparative advantage and trade barriers.
32. The Foreign Exchange Market: *Doing Business in Multiple Currencies*	**G** **P** **B** Present an additional chapter on international economics (not commonly found in other texts) that stresses how to make payments in a foreign currency.
	P **B** Explain how exchange rates are commonly presented using a currency supply and demand model.
33. International Finance: *The Macroeconomics of Exchange Rates and the Balance of Payments*	**P** **G** Present the intuition behind purchasing power parity (PPP) with an example that asks students to look at price differences and guess the exchange rates. Use real-world examples to explain why current account deficits are a problem in some cases and not in others.
	M Discuss how long-run movements in exchange rates tend to reflect inflation differentials.

Acknowledgments

The process of writing a textbook is extremely challenging and could not be accomplished alone. As we worked on the project, we learned much from each other and from the hundreds of people who had a part in the project.

We are indebted to the many people who helped create this book. We would particularly like to thank Ann Kirby-Payne, who provided us with continual feedback on writing, especially on the ways that the material would be viewed by a student who is learning economics for the first time.

We wish to acknowledge an extraordinary team of people at Macmillan who helped us formulate, design, write, produce, and market this textbook and digital platform. This includes (but is not limited to) Lukia Kliossis, Shani Fisher, Sarah Seymour, Charles Linsmeier, Scott Guile, Thomas Digiano, Bruce Kaplan, Paul Shensa, Peter Jacoby, Kristyn Brown, Lindsay Neff, Courtney Lindwall, and Rosemary Winfield.

Finally, we are especially grateful for the reviewers listed below, who provided us with valuable feedback on every chapter:

Fatma Abdel-Raouf, *Goldey-Beacom College*

Richard U. Agesa, *Marshall University*

Fafanyo Asiseh, *North Carolina Agricultural and Technical State University*

J. Jobu Babin, *Western Illinois University*

Hamid Bastin, *Shippensburg University*

Kevin Beckwith, *Salem State University*

Susan M. Bell, *Seminole State College*

Nicholas Bergan, *Palm Beach State University*

Janine Bergeron, *Southern New Hampshire University*

Robert A. Berman, *American University*

Moiz Bhai, *University of Arkansas, Little Rock*

David Black, *University of Toledo*

Kelly Hunt Blanchard, *Purdue University*

Emily Bojinova, *University of Connecticut*

Paulo R. Borges de Brito, *Front Range Community College*

Lane Boyte-Eckis, *Troy University*

Mark Brady, *San Jose State University*

Emilio Bruna, *Santa Fe College*

Paul Byrne, *Washburn University*

Regina Cassady, *Valencia College*

Nathan W. Chan, *Colby College*

Shou Chen, *State University of New York, Geneseo*

George Chikhladze, *University of Missouri*

Lisa Citron, *Cascadia College*

Kevin Cochrane, *Colorado Mesa University*

Bradley Collins, *Asheville-Buncombe Technical Community College*

Antoinette Criss, *University of South Florida*

Jean R. Cupidon, *Berea College*

Margaret Dalton, *Frostburg State University*

Stephen Davis, *Minnesota State University*

Ribhi Muhammad Daoud, *Sinclair Community College*

Srikant Devaraj, *Bell State University*

Eva Dzialdula, *University of Notre Dame*

Barry W. Evans, *Wayland Baptist University*

William Field, *DePauw University*

Marc Anthony Fusaro, *Emporia State University*

Mary Flannery, *University of Notre Dame*

Irene Foster, *The George Washington University*

Guanlin Gao, *Indiana University, South Bend*

J. Robert Gillette, *University of Kentucky*

Deniz Gevrek, *Texas A&M Corpus Christi*

Edgar A. Ghossoub, *University of Texas, San Antonio*

Mark Gius, *Quinnipiac University*

Jerry W. Gladwell, *Marshall University*

Christian G. Glupker, *Grand Valley State University*

Terri Gonzales-Kreisman, *Delgado Community College*

Rupayan Gupta, *Roger Williams University*

Anthony G. Gyapong, *Pennsylvania State University, Abington*

John Duke Hammond, *Essex County Community College*

David Harris, *Benedictine College*

Darcy Hartman, *The Ohio State University*

Robert L Hopkins, *Georgia Perimeter College*

Dr. Yu Hsing, *Southeastern Louisiana University*

Jack Igelman, *Blue Ridge Community College*

Anisul M. Islam, *University of Houston, Downtown*

Andres Jauregui, *Columbus State University*

Janak Joshi, *Central Michigan University*

Chic Kelly, *Saint Joseph's University*

Mary Kelly, *Villanova University*

Janice Rye Kinghorn, *Miami University*

Melissa Knox, *University of Washington*

Maria Kula, *Roger Williams University*

Vicky Langston, *Columbus State University*

Peter Larsen, *Carroll College*

Nhan Le, *Alma College*

Jim Lee, *Texas A&M Corpus Christi*

Tesa E. Leonce-Regalado, *Columbus State University*

Fady Mansour, *Black Hills State University*

Victor Matheson, *College of the Holy Cross*

Robin McCutcheon, *Marshall University*

Victoria Miller, *Piedmont Technical College*

Daniel Mizak, *Frostburg State University*

Amin Mohseni-Cheraghlou, *American University*

Rebecca L. Moryl, *Emmanuel College*

James H. Murphy, *University of West Georgia*

Anna C. Musatti, *Columbia University*

John Neri, *University of Maryland*

Charles Newton, *Houston Community College*

Fola Odebunmi, *Cypress College*

Oluwole Owoye, *Western Connecticut State University*

Nataliya Pakhotina, *Texas A&M*

Cristian Pardo, *Saint Joseph's University*

Walter G. Park, *American University*

Nathan Perry, *Colorado Mesa University*

Van T. H. Pham, *Salem State University*

Ratha Ramoo, *Diablo Valley College*

Greg Randolph, *Southern New Hampshire University*

Tracy L. Regan, *Boston College*

Alfonso Rodriguez, *Florida International University*

Duane J. Rosa, *Texas A&M*

Malkiat Sandhu, *University of California*

Till Schreiber, *University of Georgia*

Angela Seidel, *Saint Francis University*

Dean Showalter, *Texas State University*

Joe Silverman, *MiraCosta College*

Modupe Soremi, *Seminole State College*

L. Mark St. Clair, *Saginaw Valley State University*

Tesa Stegner, *Idaho State University*

TaMika Steward, *Tarrant County College*

Joshua Sumner, *Miami Dade College*

Wei Sun, *Grand Valley State University*

Vera Tabakova, *East Carolina University*

Ariuntungalag Taivan, *University of Minnesota, Duluth*

Kerry M. Tan, *Loyola University, Maryland*

Eftila Tanellari, *Radford University*

Michael Tasto, *Southern New Hampshire University*

Eric Taylor, *Central Piedmont Community College*

Edward J. Timmons, *Saint Francis University*

Dosse Toulaboe, *Fort Hays State University*

Don Joseph Paredes Uy-Barreta, *Hult International Business School*

Madhavi Venkatesan, *Bridgewater State University*

Lucia Vojtassak, *University of Calgary*

Ashlie Warnick, *Northern Virginia Community College*

Bruce Watson, *Boston University*

Douglas Webber, *Temple University*

Elizabeth M. Wheaton, *Southern Methodist University*

Amanda L. Wilsker, *Georgia Gwinnett College*

Mark Witte, *Northwestern University*

Laura Wolff, *Southern Illinois University, Edwardsville*

Kelvin Wong, *University of Minnesota*

Marc A Zagara, *Georgia Perimeter College*

Sourushe Zandvakili, *University of Cincinnati*

Dima Zhosan, *Glendale Community College*

Hong Zhuang, *Indiana University, South Bend*

Contents

Peter Unger/Getty Images

∧ Economic thinking helped build a team that won as many games as the Yankees—and with a third of the payroll.

The Basics of Economics

Strategies for Decision Making

At the turn of the millennium, the Oakland Athletics were struggling. Working with a much smaller payroll than baseball teams in larger markets, they had just lost their star players to rival clubs that could afford to pay them much more than Oakland. The business decision the team faced was an economic one: how to field a playoff caliber team on a limited budget.

Oakland turned to a young economist who evaluated the productivity of available baseball players and suggested that Oakland forget about hiring glamorous superstars, focusing instead on under-the-radar players who produced a high number of runs per dollar of salary. The strategy paid off. Despite being dramatically outspent by nearly every other team in Major League Baseball, in 2002, the A's won 20 games in a row, then an American League record, and made it to the playoffs. The team's rise is captured in Michael Lewis's book *Moneyball*, which inspired the 2011 film of the same name—possibly the first sports-related film that features a hero who is not an athlete, but a statistician employing the principles of economics!

When most people contemplate business and economics, they don't think about sports. But as the Oakland A's learned, economic dilemmas arise whenever decisions involve *trade-offs*. The A's engaged in a *cost–benefit analysis*, a framework for making decisions that weighs their costs and benefits. This includes business decisions on how to spend payroll, personal decisions about whether to spend or save, and public policy decisions on how funds are allocated.

In this chapter, you will be introduced to the basic concepts of economics. We'll introduce you to the way that economists think, question, and speak, and demonstrate how economics informs decision making—in business and in life.

Chapter Learning Targets

- Define economics and the concept of scarcity. Distinguish between microeconomics and macroeconomics.

- Describe opportunity cost, marginal analysis, short run versus long run, and the benefits of markets and trade.

- Distinguish between positive analysis versus normative analysis, and between equity versus efficiency.

- Define important economic terms and understand their usage in business.

1.1 WHAT IS ECONOMICS—AND WHY DO WE FIND IT SO INTERESTING?

Economics is the study of how individuals, businesses, and governments make decisions on how to use their limited resources. A central theme of economic thought is that human wants are virtually unlimited, but *resources*—productive inputs such as labor and raw materials—are scarce. **Scarcity** is a situation that occurs when human wants and needs exceed available resources to meet those wants and needs. Time, for example, is scarce. How will you use your limited time today? Do you continue to read this chapter, study another subject, go to a party, or head to your part-time job? Scarcity forces us to make these sorts of decisions. Economists study how those decisions should be made.

A Framework to Systematically Analyze Issues

Economics is a *social science*: It examines how individual people interact within the broader society. As with other social science disciplines such as psychology and sociology, assumptions about human behavior play an important role in economics. Economics starts with the premise that most humans are rational and make decisions from which they expect to benefit.

Economics is based on the belief that *incentives* play a vital role in motivating both individuals and businesses. The notion of *rational self-interest* is fundamental to understanding economics; it enables us to predict how people will alter their behavior in response to changing incentives and circumstances. For example, if a heavy tax is imposed on gasoline, we can predict that at least some people will consume less gasoline; if a company offers a much higher wage, more people will try to secure jobs with it. Even a castaway on a desert island, with lots of time on his or her hands, must allocate that time in a rationally self-interested way, deciding whether to first build a shelter or scavenge for food.

But the idea of rational self-interest—and the drive to get the most out of limited resources—applies to entire societies as well. In a big, complex society, self-interest will push each person to concentrate on what he or she is relatively good at producing. But, of course, we'd like to also consume other products, so we engage in *trade*.

Trade leads to the formation of *markets* where people can exchange goods, services, and even financial assets. It consists of all actual and potential buyers and sellers of resources and products. Markets include everything from local flea markets to big box stores like Target, to online markets like eBay, to the New York Stock Exchange, to various job markets. In the chapters that follow, we'll learn to use economic tools and models to understand what makes each of these markets tick—and how markets evolve or change over time.

The two authors of this text became fascinated with economics when, as students, we began to examine the kinds of questions economics would enable us to answer. Why are

economics The study of how individuals, businesses, and governments make decisions on how to use their limited resources.

scarcity A situation that occurs when human wants and needs exceed available resources to meet those wants and needs.

some nations rich and some nations poor? Why can some firms raise prices much more easily than others? Why does the economy experience periods of amazing economic progress, but also massive setbacks? As we learned, economics provides models and tools that enable us to isolate *root causes* for many seemingly bewildering changes in our fast-moving society; to predict the ultimate *effect* of a sudden change in policy or economic event; and to consider how alternative policies and decisions might lead to different outcomes.

So why should you study economics? Whether you are acting as a consumer, a voter, a worker, an investor, an entrepreneur, or the manager of a baseball team, knowing how to think, question, and speak like an economist can help you make smarter decisions. After graduation, you can use economic thinking to decide between moving out of your parents' house or staying at home for another year; between paying off part of your student loan or buying a new car. If you go into business, economics will help you decide what price to charge for a product and what new products to develop. Economics will help you better evaluate government policy in areas ranging from global trade and environmental policy to taxes and health care. In fact, there are few areas of life where economics cannot help one to make more sensible decisions. So let's begin!

∧ Time for an upgrade? Economics can help you decide.

⊞ BUSINESS BRIEF Rational Self-Interest at Work in the iPhone Market

Every few years, you face a common economic decision: Should you upgrade your mobile phone—and how much should you spend to do so? For example, in 2017, Apple introduced the new iPhone 8, iPhone 8 Plus, and iPhone X with much fanfare. The new models boasted improved graphics, faster processing, and a better camera—and came at a premium price, as high as $1,149. At the same time, Apple reduced the price of its older models and continued to offer a bare-bones SE model for $349.* The differences in production cost between models were minimal, however.† What accounted for the huge differences in price?

The price of each iPhone, and the decision of countless consumers on whether to purchase a new iPhone or not, can all be explained via the basic economic concept of rational self-interest. It was in Apple's self-interest to maximize profits. The firm knew that some customers, eager for updated features, would pay a premium for the new model, and that no rational, self-interested consumer would pay the same price for an older model. Customers, meanwhile, made rational decisions about phone upgrades based on their price and features.

*Kif Leswing, "Apple's Least Expensive iPhone Quietly Got a Price Cut," *Business Insider*, September 12, 2017, http://www.businessinsider.com/iphone-se-the-cheapest-iphone-gets-price-cut-to-349-2017-9.

†Cara McGoogan, "Apple's iPhone 7 Costs Just $220 to Make," *The Telegraph*, September 23, 2016, http://www.telegraph.co.uk/technology/2016/09/23/apples-iphone-7-costs-just-220-to-make/.

Microeconomics and Macroeconomics

Both authors of this book are fascinated by economics. But one of us has focused his career on the decisions of individuals, businesses, and labor markets, while the other has devoted himself to the study of the economy as a whole. This reflects the two main branches of the field: microeconomics and macroeconomics (see Exhibit 1).

Microeconomics is the branch of economics that focuses on economic issues faced primarily by individuals and businesses in a particular segment of the overall economy.

microeconomics The branch of economics that focuses on economic issues faced primarily by individuals and businesses in a particular segment of the overall economy.

EXHIBIT 1 Microeconomics versus Macroeconomics

Issues in Microeconomics	Issues in Macroeconomics
Decision to open a new business	Gross domestic product (GDP)
Decision to work or save	Unemployment/inflation
Decision to buy a car	Recessions/depressions
Decision to expand your business	Economy of Chicago, California, or the U.S.

Microeconomics focuses on economic issues faced primarily by consumers and businesses in a particular segment of the overall economy. Macroeconomics is concerned with economic issues that impact the overall economy.

For example, a business might need to decide whether to expand, which requires additional labor and other resources. In microeconomics, we also study decision making by individuals or a household (persons who share a housing unit and pool their incomes). For example, microeconomics studies how people or households decide to spend their own scarce resources. When you choose between working overtime or enjoying your Saturday off, or between spending $30 on a night out or applying the money toward next month's credit card bill, you are making microeconomic decisions.

Macroeconomics is the branch of economics that focuses on economic issues which impact the overall economy, such as unemployment, inflation, recessions, and economic growth. Note that although the prefix *macro* usually means "large," in economics, it specifically refers to the *aggregate economy*—that is, the *total of all parts* of the economy, or the entire economy. Thus, the aggregate output of a small country such as Costa Rica is a macroeconomics issue, whereas a single industry such as the U.S. auto industry is a microeconomics issue, despite the fact that the U.S. auto industry is larger than Costa Rica's entire economy. In short, microeconomics focuses on economic decisions of specific parts of the economy, while macroeconomics zeros in on the big picture.

If you follow the news, you are probably familiar with a few macroeconomic indicators, such as *unemployment* (individuals seeking but unable to find work), and have heard of *inflation* (an increase in the overall price level). You may also know what a country's *gross domestic product* or *GDP* is (a measure of both total production and total income in that society). You have personally lived through a major *recession* (a decline in GDP often associated with an increase in unemployment), as both GDP and employment declined in 2009. You may already know that a severe recession is called a *depression*—with the most notable example being the Great Depression of the 1930s. Finally, you might have recognized that *economic growth* is an increase in total production or GDP adjusted for inflation in an economy. For those studying macroeconomics, all these terms will be covered in some detail later in the book.

1.2 THINK LIKE AN ECONOMIST

The idea that we are each, at every moment, struggling with decisions about how to allocate our scarce resources in ways that will best serve our self-interest is fundamental to understanding economics. In this section, we'll introduce you to some important steps economists take when examining how scarcity and rational self-interest motivate human behavior. We'll return to these steps, which are summarized later in Exhibit 3, throughout the text.

macroeconomics The branch of economics that focuses on economic issues which impact the overall economy, such as unemployment, inflation, recessions, and economic growth.

Determine Opportunity Cost

After graduation, you decide to take a year off to travel before starting your career. You always dreamed of exploring the world and now have the opportunity to stay with friends in Europe, Africa, and Asia. The only money you need to spend is on food and airfare. That doesn't sound too expensive. However, economists would view the cost of the trip in a completely different light—the cost would include not just travel expenses but also the income you could have earned yet forfeited by working that year instead of traveling.

Economists are very interested in the notion of *trade-offs*: how individuals, firms, and policymakers constantly make decisions using some form of cost–benefit analysis. Economists have a name for such trade-offs. **Opportunity cost** is what must be given up in order to acquire or do something else. This concept is at the heart of economics, as it applies to individuals, businesses, and entire societies. If our society hires more teachers, there will be less labor available to perform other tasks; therefore, the opportunity cost of more teachers is fewer workers producing other goods and services. Remember, all resources—including labor—are scarce.

Similarly, Mario, a pizzeria owner, is faced with a decision: Should he prepare his own taxes, or should he hire a specialist to do them? Doing them on his own, he might save money—he would not have to pay a professional tax preparer. But the decision nonetheless involves an opportunity cost: Mario must consider the many hours that he could have spent building his business *instead of* doing his taxes—hours that might have been spent perfecting recipes, training staff, building relationships with customers, and tending to other less tangible but important aspects of owning his own pizza shop. In considering opportunity cost, a business should consider foregone revenues, not just expenditures.

In contemplating the opportunity cost of an action, you need to take into account all associated foregone activities, not simply the money. The cost of obtaining an additional year of education includes not only the cost of tuition and books, but also the income that must be sacrificed because attending school means fewer hours of employment. Superstars like singer Taylor Swift and basketball player LeBron James chose not to attend college. For them, the opportunity cost to attend college would have included losing tens of millions of dollars in income. Any reasonable cost–benefit analysis of their decision would conclude that the opportunity cost of attending college was just too high.

John Salangsang/AP Images

∧ College can wait if you're Taylor Swift.

Use Marginal Analysis

Economists don't just look at the total cost and benefit of a decision. They also determine *how much* of any activity is optimal. For example, it's one thing to decide to take a job, another to decide to work overtime. When you make a decision to work extra hours, you should consider whether the *extra pay* associated with the *extra work* is worth more to you than the foregone leisure time.

Economists use the term *marginal* to refer to incremental differences, such as additional revenue, additional costs, additional taxes, and additional pay. If an individual who normally earns $15 per hour is paid double time on Sunday, then her marginal wage rate on Sunday will be $30 per hour. In this case, the individual's regular pay rate is irrelevant in the decision to work on Sunday; it is the chance to earn $30 an hour that counts.

Economics tells us that optimal economic decisions are made using **marginal analysis**, the process of comparing the additional benefits of an activity with the additional cost.

opportunity cost What must be given up in order to acquire or do something else.

marginal analysis The process of comparing the additional benefits of an activity with its additional cost.

In general, more of an activity should be engaged in whenever the marginal benefits (the additional benefits) exceed the marginal cost (the additional cost). Marginal analysis can be used in many business-related economic decisions, including how many units to produce, how much money to save or invest, how many workers to hire, and how much money to spend on advertising.

This concept is particularly important in microeconomics. *Marginal revenue* is the extra revenue earned by a business from selling one additional item—it is a marginal benefit. *Marginal cost*, in contrast, is the extra cost of selling one additional item. Suppose Mario, our pizzeria owner, currently sells 50 pizzas a day. What happens to his revenue if he sells 51? If Mario can sell one additional pizza with a marginal revenue of $12 and marginal cost of $10, then he will likely decide to produce and sell the additional pizza. Next suppose that to sell more pizza, Mario must lower his price so marginal revenue falls to $11 and marginal cost remains $10; he should also sell that pizza. The process will continue until marginal revenue equals marginal cost—in this case, when marginal revenue and marginal cost both equal $10.

Conversely, if the marginal revenue for the next pizza is $9 and the marginal cost is $10, he will likely decide not to sell the additional pizza and consider reducing production. Students studying microeconomics will use marginal analysis in many different applications and discover that the optimal amount of economic activity occurs at the level where marginal benefit (or marginal revenue) equals marginal cost.

Focus on Real Values

If your income doubled tomorrow, would you be better off? That depends: If the price of everything you spend money on triples at the same time, then you would, in fact, be worse off. In more specific terms, if you receive a 3% raise or your business observes a 3% increase in profits, but prices increase by an average of 5%, you will be worse off. In each case, the amount you can actually purchase with your income declines by 2%—the 3% raise minus the 5% inflation.

In economics, people and businesses are interested in not only the face value of income they receive but also what that income can purchase. To better understand this concept, economists measure economic variables such as GDP and wages in both nominal and real terms.

Nominal values are the face values of variables measured in current prices that have not been adjusted for inflation. Examples include nominal GDP and nominal wages. These are the numbers you encounter in your everyday life, such as the price of milk today or your weekly paycheck. In the scenario described above, you received a 3% increase in your nominal income.

As you learn more about economics, you will see that the purchasing power of money changes over time: One dollar today is not the same as one dollar next week, next year, or a decade ago. Nominal values fail to adjust for such changes. A comparison of today's nominal wages, prices, or nominal GDP with figures from 1955 would be of limited use, because a dollar nowadays has a very different value than it did in 1955.

In contrast, **real values** are the values of variables measured in prices that have been adjusted for inflation. Examples include real GDP and real wages. Using real values enables economists to compare prices, wages, and statistics such as GDP over time. Economists sometimes use the term *constant dollars* or *inflation-adjusted dollars* to indicate real values. Real values can also be expressed in physical units instead of money.

Surprisingly, people often make decisions or draw conclusions about money, income, and prices without considering the cost of living. Economists refer to this tendency to think about money in terms of nominal, rather than real, values as *money illusion*. For example, workers who agree to a contract guaranteeing a 2% annual raise for the next three years might see a nominal increase in their paychecks, but if inflation stands at the same 2%, then their real wages will not have increased at all. Similarly in macroeconomics, when measuring GDP, you might see nominal GDP increase by

nominal values The face values of variables measured in current prices that have not been adjusted for inflation.

real values The values of variables measured in prices that have been adjusted for inflation.

3% from one year to the next. However, if inflation is 3%, then society will have experienced no change in real output. Learning to think like an economist means focusing on real values—and not falling prey to money illusion.

Consider the Long Run and Short Run

Economic outcomes frequently depend on the time frame involved, and economic thinking requires taking both the long and the short view. The **long run** refers to the time necessary to make all adjustments to new economic circumstances. It is not a fixed number of months or years, as long-run adjustments take more time in some contexts than others. Thus, the long run for a food truck selling fish tacos might be a few weeks, while the long run for a jet aircraft producer might be a decade or more. When oil prices soared in the 1970s, car manufacturers lost sales at first, but recovered in the long run by adjusting to the new circumstances and producing smaller, more fuel-efficient cars. The transition to producing fuel efficient cars at automobile factories did not occur instantly—it took several years.

In contrast, the **short run** refers to a time frame that is too short to include all adjustments to new economic circumstances. The short run will also vary according to circumstances. Consider the plight of a failing restaurant with one year left on a long-term rental agreement. The rent is $12,000 a month and must be paid even if the restaurant shuts down. If the restaurant remains open, it anticipates losing $100 a month for many years into the future despite its best efforts. Should the restaurant close? The answer depends on the time period in question. Once the rental agreement expires a year from now, the restaurant should obviously close to avoid further losses. On the other hand, if the restaurant closes today, it cannot escape the rental agreement and must continue to pay $12,000 per month. In this case, the restaurant is likely to remain open and incur the smaller $100 monthly loss.

Conversely, if the restaurant wishes to expand its operations, it cannot do so in the short run as expanding or securing a new location would take significant time. In the long run, the restaurant can expand, shrink, or even close down, but this is not possible in the short run as the time frame is too short to make all adjustments to new economic circumstances.

Long-run and short-run considerations are also one of the key challenges in government policymaking: Many government policies that are good for the economy in the long run have adverse consequences in the short run, and vice versa.

Understand the Benefits of Markets and Trade

The British philosopher Adam Smith once observed, "It is not from the benevolence of the butcher, the brewer, or the baker that we expect our dinner, but from their regard to their own interest." Widely viewed as the founder of modern economics, Smith examined the concept of rational self-interest, along with the benefits of trade and the importance of markets, in his groundbreaking work *The Wealth of Nations* (1776).

When the goods and services of the butcher, brewer, and baker are bought and sold, these transactions are said to occur in a market. A **market** is a means for buyers and sellers to engage in the exchange of a good or service. Likewise, when buyers and sellers engage in a transaction to buy or sell labor, shares of stock, or a new sweater, the transactions occur in a market. Markets include *actual* buyers and sellers as well as *potential* buyers and sellers who will buy and sell if the price is right; the term also refers to the physical or virtual spaces where such exchanges take place. The beauty of markets is that they connect individuals who want a product or service with those who are willing to provide it.

There are many different types of markets, some of which are depicted in Exhibit 2. The labor market connects employees and employers, as well as potential employees

long run The time necessary to make all adjustments to new economic circumstances.

short run A time frame that is too short to include all adjustments to new economic circumstances.

market A means for buyers and sellers to engage in the exchange of a good or service.

EXHIBIT 2 Markets

A market consists of all possible buyers and sellers of resources and products. Some examples: labor markets, financial markets, online markets, and markets for natural resources.

and employers. Similarly, financial markets connect buyers and sellers of assets like stocks, bonds, foreign currencies, and many other financial assets. There are also natural resource and commodity markets, where people trade coal, oil, crops such as wheat and corn, as well as many types of metals.

The crux of Smith's thinking—which influenced the formation of the American economic system—is that even though firms act in their own self-interest, consumers benefit from their activities. The butcher, brewer, and baker might be primarily concerned with making a profit, but in the process of reaping a profit, they provide products that consumers want. Smith argued that markets were crucial for society because they incentivize self-interested actors to efficiently allocate resources and provide what society needs, as if "led by an invisible hand to promote an end which was no part of his intention."

Smith viewed unregulated markets, free from government influence, as ideal in most cases. This policy is frequently called *laissez-faire*, a term used by French businessmen who wanted the king to stay out of their commercial affairs. Today, no pure *laissez-faire* economies exist among nations. Smith himself suggested government should provide certain limited functions, such as national defense, public education, and law enforcement. Modern economists believe that government interventions are sometimes necessary because markets are not always efficient—for example, governments may promote competition, provide information on products, or manage pollution. Nonetheless, markets and free trade are often very effective ways of promoting economic development and reducing poverty.

The fact that trade is generally beneficial to both sides is a central idea in economics. Those who have not studied economics frequently have the impression that if one side benefits from a trade, then the other side will somehow be worse off—that trade is a *zero-sum game* (like baseball or poker) in which only one side can win, and every gain comes at the expense of the other side. Economists reject this oversimplification, pointing out that both sides typically benefit from trade, and that markets and trade can benefit every participant. In Chapter 2, we'll examine further why nearly all economists agree that trade is a good thing—and *not* a zero-sum game.

EXHIBIT 3 Think Like an Economist: Key Concepts to Understand

Concept	Example
Determine Opportunity Cost	The opportunity cost of society hiring more teachers is fewer workers producing other goods and services.
Use Marginal Analysis	When deciding to sell one additional product, the seller must consider both marginal revenue and marginal cost. If marginal revenue is higher than marginal cost, then the seller will likely decide to sell it.
Focus on Real Values	Economists are always aware that prices and dollar values change over time. When making calculations, they focus on real values, such as real GDP and real wages, measured in prices that have been adjusted for inflation.
Consider the Long Run and Short Run	In the long run, a firm can expand, shrink, or even close down, but this is not possible in the short run as the time frame is too short to make all adjustments to new economic circumstances.
Understand Markets and Trade Are Beneficial	The butcher, brewer, and baker provide products for his or her own benefit (or profit). In turn, this also benefits customers, who are able to obtain products they could not readily produce on their own.

An understanding of these core concepts is vital as they will continually reappear throughout the text.

POLICY BRIEF A Market Solution to Save Lives

Although humans need just one healthy kidney to survive, most are born with two of them. For individuals suffering from kidney disease, however, healthy kidneys are very scarce. While many patients receive transplants from a healthy friend or relative, thousands die each year due to the shortage of kidneys available for transplant. Is there a potential market solution that could bring kidney donors and kidney patients together?

One obvious option would be to pay kidney donors money to encourage donations, but that option is widely viewed as unethical. In recent years, however, economist Alvin Roth has been creating kidney markets that don't require the payment of money and profit motives. Instead, Roth created a market that pairs willing donors with recipients in need, and encourages trade without the use of monetary payments.

Here's how it works: Suppose a person with blood type A is willing to donate a kidney to a loved one with blood type O. This is considered a failed match. Elsewhere, a person with blood type O is willing to donate a kidney to a loved one with blood type A. Roth created a kidney market where these very scarce kidneys could be traded between these two families so that each patient would find a suitable match. This innovation continues to save hundreds of lives each year. In 2012, Roth received the Nobel Prize in Economics for creating a number of such new markets, in a variety of surprising areas where markets had never existed.[*]

[*]Susan Adams, "What Al Roth Did to Win the Nobel Prize in Economics," *Forbes*, October 15, 2012, http://www.forbes.com/sites/susanadams/2012/10/15/what-al-roth-did-to-win-the-nobel-prize-in-economics/#6dcd9127162d.

1.3 WHY ECONOMISTS DON'T ALWAYS AGREE

While economists generally agree on the basic economic principles we've discussed in this chapter, they often end up sharply divided on real-world policy issues. Sometimes, economists disagree on facts about how the economy works (Does a cigarette tax reduce smoking?). In other cases, differences in opinion may reflect differences in underlying value judgments (Should the government discourage smoking?). In this section, we will look at several of the arguments that economists are asked to address, and examine the reasons why they sometimes disagree on the answers.

Normative and Positive Analysis in Economics

Clear economic thinking requires us to consider two issues: which goals should we pursue, and which actions will best achieve those goals. **Normative analysis** is subjective and value-based; it considers questions involving goals, values, and ethics. The question of whether society should increase college aid calls for a normative analysis.

Positive analysis is objective; it considers questions involving cause and effect. For example, a positive analysis of college affordability, based on enrollment data, would likely provide insights into how the cost of college impacts who attends college. Positive analysis might show that college is becoming increasingly costly and this is discouraging some students from attending, but economists might disagree on the normative question of whether to make college more affordable.

Positive analysis examines how the world works, not what kind of world is most desirable. It tells us how we can achieve our goals, not what those goals should be. For example, how can a firm best maximize its profits? How can public policy reduce unemployment? What kind of tax system would reduce income inequality? What is the least costly way to prevent global warming?

In contrast, normative analysis takes a close look at questions involving goals, values, and ethics. What goals should public policy try to achieve? Is it desirable to have a more equal distribution of income? How much value should we place on a clean environment? Exhibit 4 lists sample questions typical of both normative and positive analysis.

To make the distinction between normative and positive, people sometimes distinguish between the words "should" and "is." What *should* be is a normative question, while what *is* true is a positive question. Consider the debate over income inequality. The statement "Incomes *should* be more equal" represents normative analysis, while the statement "Income inequality *is* increasing" reflects positive analysis.

Economists must remain objective when making a positive analysis. The world is what it is, and reality doesn't always match our preferences. You may prefer a free-market economy with no government intervention, but that doesn't mean you should assume the minimum wage causes unemployment. Alternatively, you might prefer to see companies forced to pay much higher wages, but that does not mean such a policy would have no negative side effects.

normative analysis Analysis that is subjective and value-based; it considers questions involving goals, values, and ethics.

positive analysis Analysis that is objective; it looks at questions involving cause and effect.

EXHIBIT 4 Normative Analysis versus Positive Analysis

Questions Using Normative Analysis	Questions Using Positive Analysis
Should companies pay higher taxes?	Does an increase in corporate tax rates decrease the number of start-up companies?
Should we be more concerned about high inflation or high unemployment?	How can public policy best reduce unemployment?
Should the government increase the minimum wage?	Will a higher minimum wage increase unemployment?
How much value should we place on a clean environment?	What is the least costly way to prevent global warming?

Normative analysis is subjective and value-based; it considers questions involving goals, values, and ethics. Positive analysis is objective; it considers questions involving cause and effect.

Once a normative question has been identified as important by voters or policymakers, economists might use positive analysis to determine the best way to address it. For example, society may desire to curb smokers; then economists can determine if a tax on cigarettes is the best way to accomplish that goal using positive analysis.

In the end, economists will never agree on all issues. Like everyone else, they have different values and thus may end up preferring different policies. Two economists may agree that cigarette taxes reduce smoking, but disagree as to whether discouraging smoking is any of the government's business. Two other economists might both like to see less smoking, but differ as to whether a cigarette tax will have a major impact on smoking.

Signe Wilkinson Editorial Cartoon used with the permission of Signe Wilkinson, the Washington Post Writers Group and the Cartoonist Group. All rights reserved.

Equity and Efficiency

As we've noted, most economic decisions involve trade-offs, and one of the questions on which economists often find themselves in disagreement involves the trade-off that sometimes occurs between equity and efficiency. **Equity** refers to a general sense of fairness in the distribution of income and output among members of society. Many people view equity as an important societal goal, although they may not agree on what, exactly, is fair. The entire concept of "fairness" is subjective and widely debated among religious, philosophical, and political experts. However, economists can bring something to the debate that political scientists and philosophers may not be fully aware of: the potential trade-off between equity and efficiency.

Efficiency means getting the most out of available resources. In microeconomics, business managers strive to achieve efficiency— they want their labor and capital to produce as much as possible. In business, efficiency might include obtaining the most output with a given amount of workers and machinery. In macroeconomics, efficiency requires the full employment of all available resources. Societies strive for efficiency in order to get the greatest amount of goods and services from the resources available in the economy. Inefficiency, or the lack of efficiency, is wasteful.

Some types of inefficiency are easy to understand. For example, dated technology or poorly trained labor will reduce output and drive up costs, resulting in inefficiency. If Mario's refrigerator at the pizzeria does not work properly and he frequently throws away lots of vegetables, an inefficiency occurs. But economists also explore other types of inefficiency, as when workers are idle or unemployed, despite wishing to have a job, or when rules or regulations prevent firms from producing goods in the most efficient fashion.

One way to think about both equity and efficiency is to imagine the economy as a pie—perhaps one of Mario's pizza pies. It might be a small pie, or a very large pie. In either case, the pie can be divided in many ways—eight even slices, four larger slices, or perhaps in four large slices and eight slices half as large. In economics, the way in which the pie is divided is referred to as equity.

The size of the pie, on the other hand, reflects efficiency. Improved efficiency can be thought of as increasing the size of the economic "pie." Using the best technology and all available resources will make the economic pie larger.

One way to increase the size of the *slices* is to increase the total size of the economic pie: More pie generally benefits everyone. For example, reducing the rate of unemployment may serve to increase the size of the pie through gains in efficiency as people return to work. And it might improve equity by increasing the size of the slice received by formerly unemployed individuals. We would call such a scenario a "win-win."

Unfortunately, the twin goals of equity and efficiency may also conflict, and society must strive to strike a balance between the two. A society that is mostly concerned with

equity A general sense of fairness in the distribution of income and output among members of society.

efficiency Getting the most out of available resources.

efficiency may be able to grow the economic pie, but this may not always lead to larger slices for the poor and middle class. As the U.S. economy has grown in recent decades, so, too, has the level of income inequality.

Policies to ensure that income is evenly distributed often come at a cost: If everyone earns roughly the same income, there is less incentive to work hard, or take the risk of starting a new business. One could avoid work and be almost as well off. Thus, policies that improve equity *may* come at the cost of less efficiency. Indeed, this was a major problem in many communist countries during the twentieth century. Countries that attempted to eliminate inequality (such as the former Soviet Union) typically saw reductions in efficiency as well. In response, many formerly communist regimes (such as China) have adopted some of the ideas of Adam Smith and increased their reliance on markets. Consequently, most societies today do not advocate *complete* income equality.

Nor do countries go to the other extreme, ignoring inequality and adopting a purely *laissez-faire* system of government. Instead, most governments do make some effort to redistribute income with social insurance programs and higher taxes on the rich. Indeed, the United States is said to be a *mixed economy*—with some elements of a free-market economy and some elements of an economy regulated by the government.

Consider the discussion on unemployment benefits in the upcoming **Policy Brief: How Long Should Unemployment Benefits Last?** While unemployment benefits improve equity, there is some evidence that suggests they reduce efficiency. The tension between efficiency and equity is one area where economists remain divided, as decisions are often based on not positive analysis but normative judgments about what is fair. Economists can, however, provide the sort of *positive analysis* that will help society make these difficult *normative* decisions. Economists can try to predict the efficiency costs of attempts to make society more equal, but they cannot definitively answer the question of whether the benefits of greater equity are worth the cost in efficiency. That's up to the voters and their representatives.

▲ POLICY BRIEF How Long Should Unemployment Benefits Last?

In the United States, unemployed workers in most states are typically eligible to receive unemployment insurance benefits for up to 26 weeks. But during and after the Great Recession (December 2007 to June 2009) the government extended benefits to as much as 99 weeks in states with high unemployment. There was considerable debate about this decision, which provides a useful example of the distinction between equity and efficiency.

Critics of the program worried that providing benefits for almost two years would cause some workers to search less aggressively for a new job, or be too picky about what job they would be willing to accept, knowing that they could fall back on unemployment benefits. This can reduce the efficiency of the economy. Some supporters of the program denied that unemployment would rise, pointing to studies that suggested the extra benefits would boost spending in a depressed economy. That's a positive dispute about whether unemployment benefits increase or decrease unemployment.

Using positive analysis, one academic study found a small but statistically significant effect of the program: It slightly increased the unemployment rate.[*] But economists were also mired in normative questions about whether unemployment insurance is good policy in those cases where it costs some jobs, but also boosts the living standards of workers who have lost their jobs. It is possible that both sides were partially right, but one's actual views on the policy frequently depend on how much weight one gives to efficiency versus equity.

[*]Henry S. Farber and Robert G. Valletta, "Do Extended Unemployment Benefits Lengthen Unemployment Spells? Evidence from Recent Cycles in the U.S. Labor Market," *NBER*, May 2013, http://www.nber.org/papers/w19048.

1.4 SPEAK LIKE AN ECONOMIST

Like every field of study, economics has its own unique language. Much of it may seem familiar, since economic policy is covered in both political and financial news. But it can also be challenging, because some terms you hear all the time can have very different meanings in economics. In this section, we'll preview and clarify some of the terms that you will need to use throughout the course. We will return to each of them in more detail in later chapters.

The Main Factors of Production

We've learned that economics is the study of how consumers, businesses, and governments make decisions to best satisfy virtually unlimited wants with scarce resources. **Resources** are inputs used in the production of goods and services; they are commonly referred to as *factors of production*. There are limited amounts of each of these resources, which is to say they exhibit some degree of scarcity. Economists have identified five major factors of production:

- **Labor** is the human effort used in the production of goods and services. Labor consists of physical work, such as the effort involved in making pizza, babysitting, digging a ditch, or shoveling coal, as well as the mental effort in endeavors such as teaching economics, managing a restaurant, or preparing a legal brief. Workers provide labor.

- **Natural resources** are inputs found in nature that can be used in the production of goods and services. Natural resources include land, trees, minerals, oil and gas, water, and even the airwaves over which television, radio, and some telecommunications signals are broadcast. There are limits with regard to the availability of natural resources, and these limits constrain what a society is capable of producing at any one point in time.

- **Physical capital** is durable equipment and structures used to produce goods and services; it is sometimes referred to simply as *capital* in economics. Physical capital is produced by humans, whereas natural resources are provided by nature. It includes everything from simple technologies, such as shovels, buildings, and pizza ovens, to complex equipment, such as state-of-the-art computer systems, software, cell-phone and Wi-Fi networks, and advanced robotics. Capital can be used in the production of additional goods and services, and one of the most important business decisions that firms face is whether to invest in new physical capital in order to expand production.

- **Human capital** refers to the skills acquired through education, experience, and training that allow labor to be more productive. Like physical capital, human capital allows humans to produce more output. And just as a business might decide to invest in a new factory, individuals can invest in themselves, and firms can invest in their staff, most often through education and training.

- **Entrepreneurs** are individuals who combine various resources into a business in pursuit of profit. Having natural resources, labor, physical capital, and human capital is not enough—someone must take risks and show initiative in bringing together all these other resources. These individuals don't just manage another person's business; they create and manage their own business, and risk financial loss if it fails. Famous entrepreneurs include billionaires like Mark Zuckerberg (Facebook) and Jeff Bezos (Amazon), along with your local pizza shop owner/operator, and your aunt who sells hand-crafted furniture on Etsy. There is an opportunity cost to entrepreneurship—the steady income one could earn in a more stable profession.

resources Inputs used in the production of goods and services; they are commonly referred to as *factors of production*.

labor Human effort used in the production of goods and services.

natural resources Inputs found in nature that can be used in the production of goods and services.

physical capital Durable equipment and structures used to produce goods and services; sometimes referred to simply as *capital* in economics.

human capital Skills acquired through education, experience, and training that allow labor to be more productive.

entrepreneurs Individuals who combine various resources into a business in pursuit of profit.

📊 BUSINESS BRIEF Is It Worth Going to College and Majoring in Economics?

Celebrated entrepreneurs like Zuckerberg and Bill Gates founded their companies after dropping out of college. Does this mean you should do the same? Quite the opposite. A study by the Federal Reserve Board of San Francisco showed that, on average, college graduates earn 60% more per year than those with only a high school degree. During a lifetime, this amounts to over $800,000 in average earnings.* This is partly because a college degree increases one's human capital, skills that are valuable in the labor market.

Some degrees appear to be more valuable than others, at least in monetary terms: Those with degrees in science, technology, engineering, and mathematics (often referred to as STEM fields) are among the highest-paid college graduates. In 2015–16, estimates of the mid-career earnings of full-time employees with an economics major ranged from $93,000 to $98,500, placing economics in the top 10% of all majors in terms of earnings.†

So was it a mistake for Gates and Zuckerberg to drop out of college? Probably not, as their cases were highly unusual. Having developed groundbreaking technologies while they were still students, the opportunity cost of *continuing* college for these particular computer science majors became *very* high. The extra years studying might have postponed entrepreneurship—increasing the risk that some other entrepreneur developing similar technology might beat them to the market.

*"Is It Still Worth Going to College?," *Federal Reserve Bank of San Francisco*, May 5, 2014, http://www.frbsf.org/economic-research/publications/economic-letter/2014/may/is-college-worth-it-education-tuition-wages/.

†See "Highest-Paying Bachelor Degrees by Salary Potential," *PayScale*, n.d., accessed April 20, 2017, http://www.payscale.com/college-salary-report/majors-that-pay-you-back/bachelors? page=23; and "Career Earnings by College Major," *The Hamilton Project*, September 29, 2014, http://www.hamiltonproject.org/charts/career_earnings_by_college_major/.

Ceteris Paribus

Economic questions are never really simple. Your decision to have pizza for dinner depends on countless factors: What is the price? How much do you want to spend? What are you planning to eat (and what are you planning to spend) tomorrow? Is Mario's pizza better than Maria's? Is it better than the tacos at Mike's? Because other factors are always changing, it is difficult, if not impossible, to accurately analyze cause and effect.

Faced with these questions, economists do what any scientist would do: They simplify. To do so, economists use the *ceteris paribus* assumption, Latin for "other things equal." In economics, **ceteris paribus** means other economic and business conditions are assumed not to change. *Ceteris paribus* is a critical component of economic thinking and reflects the scientific underpinnings of the discipline.

It's tempting to question the *ceteris paribus* assumption, because, of course, other things are never equal. Mario's pizza might not be as good as Maria's, and Mike's taco stand may benefit from a plum location right next to a movie theater. Nonetheless, the practice of holding other factors constant in order to understand the effect of a specific variable is a key part of the scientific method. Similarly, in physics, Newton's law of gravity allows us to predict the speed at which an apple falling from a tree will hit the ground. This theory is based on an understanding that other things are held equal—it is assumed that there are no wind and air resistance, and that no one is catching the apple. In the real world, of course, all these other factors can exist. In turn, they can change the speed at which an apple will fall—but that doesn't make Newton's law inaccurate. It simply means that physicists studying gravity and Newton's law must account for those other factors when making predictions.

In a similar vein, economists hold other things constant in analyzing economic phenomena. For example, in examining the relationship between the price of a good and the quantity of a good that buyers are willing to purchase at each price, economists

ceteris paribus The assumption that other economic and business conditions do not change.

focus only on those two factors, and assume that other factors (such as consumer preferences or consumer incomes) do not change. This allows us to zero in on the key relationship—in this case, the relationship between price and quantity demanded.

The Language of Economics versus the Language of Business

The language of economics can be challenging at times because some economic terms have different meanings in other disciplines—especially in business—and in the popular culture (see Exhibit 5). Throughout this text, we'll address these important distinctions, beginning with a few terms that regularly come up in both economics and finance.

Capital As we've learned, in economics, physical capital refers to the equipment and structures used to produce goods and services. In contrast, in business and in personal finance, the term *capital* is shorthand for "financial capital" and refers to money raised in financial markets. These two definitions of capital are loosely related: When a business sells stocks or bonds, the media reports that the firm is raising capital. But this isn't what economists mean by capital. The business may use these funds to expand by building a factory or other productive machines; the physical objects themselves are what economists refer to as capital.

Investment Similarly, the term *financial investment* refers to something very different from what economists define as investment. It is a way of employing savings, and often refers to the purchase of stocks and bonds. These transactions occur in the financial markets, such as Wall Street in New York City. In economics, however, the term **investment** refers specifically to spending on new capital goods. Investment increases the amount of physical capital in an economy. Businesses and governments often raise funds in the financial markets to purchase physical capital, including

investment Spending on new capital goods. Investment increases the amount of physical capital in an economy.

EXHIBIT 5 Speak Like an Economist: The Language of Economics and Business

Terms	What It Means in . . . Economics	Finance, Business, and the Media
Equity	*Equity* is a general sense of fairness in the distribution of income and output among members of society.	The value of a business or property minus the value of any debt obligations. Homeowner's equity is a common example.
Investment	*Investment* refers to spending on new capital goods. It increases the amount of physical capital in an economy.	Shorthand for *financial investment*, a way of employing savings, and often refers to the purchase of stocks and bonds. These transactions occur in the financial markets, such as the New York Stock Exchange.
Capital	Shorthand for *physical capital*: durable equipment and structures used to produce goods and services.	Shorthand for *financial capital*; refers to money raised in financial markets. At times, the phrase *capital* is shorthand for money. For example, a business needs capital (meaning money) to pay for new equipment.
Resources	In economics, the term *resources* generally refers to *factors of production*—that is, the inputs used in the production of goods and services. Resources include labor, land, physical capital, human capital, and entrepreneurs. Scarcity of resources limits society's productive capacity.	In business, the term *resources* also commonly includes money. Limits on the amount of money a firm or household has restricts options for business expansion and purchases. Economists do not consider money a resource.

The language of economics can be challenging at times because some economic terms have different meanings in other disciplines.

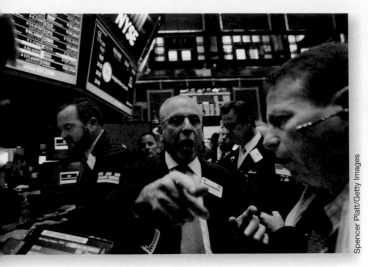

∧ The language of economics is not always the same as the language of business and finance.

rail systems, factories, and office buildings. Investment also includes a business building up its inventory for future sales.

Equity We've already learned that *equity* refers to a general sense of fairness in the distribution of income and output among members of society. That perspective is very different in the business world, where *owner's equity* refers to the value of a business or property minus the value of any debt obligations. A homeowner that holds the deed to a $500,000 property but still owes $400,000 on the loan used to purchase it is said to have homeowner's equity of $100,000.

Resources In economics, resources are inputs used in the production of goods and services. Resources include labor, land, physical capital, human capital, and entrepreneurs. The scarcity of resources limits society's productive capacity. Outside economics, resources include all these things but also commonly include money. Limits on the amount of money a firm or household has restrict the options for business expansion and purchases. Economists do not consider money a resource.

BUSINESS TAKEAWAY

Economics provides a way of analyzing business performance. It teaches us how to quantify choices, to understand relationships between resources and behavior, to systematically analyze data, and to identify emerging opportunities that others might miss. Those who master the tools and models of economics are able to "drill down" through numbers to see patterns and extract tangible solutions for business dilemmas.[1] That's exactly what the Oakland A's did to build a winning team on a shoestring budget, and it's what economic analysts in corporate and public sector careers do every day.

Students taking an introductory economics course will find that their studies provide a new way of thinking about problems, especially when it comes to analyzing information and making decisions.[2] The skills learned in the principles course are applicable in fields ranging from banking to advertising, from insurance to marketing, and from criminal justice to education.

The study of economics helps students to hone analytic, decision-making, and leadership skills, all of which are highly sought after in both the private and public sector. Terrific job prospects exist for those who choose to major in economics—but rarely will a graduate find a job posting seeking an "economist." Economics majors put their skills to work as analysts, managers, and consultants.[3] Well-known economics majors include a Super Bowl–winning NFL football coach (Bill Belichick of the New England Patriots), the NFL commissioner (Roger Goodell), the CEO at Hewlett-Packard (Meg Whitman), a former Supreme Court justice (Sandra Day O'Connor), a political and sports statistician for ESPN and FiveThirtyEight (Nate Silver), a best-selling writer (Michael Lewis, author of *Moneyball*, *The Big Short*, and *The Blind Side*), and several presidents of the United States (Donald Trump, George H. W. Bush, Ronald Reagan, and Gerald Ford). Cartoonist Scott Adams, creator of *Dilbert*, also majored in economics. Adams explained:

> I majored in economics partly because someone told me it was good preparation
> for law school, and partly because I wanted to understand how money worked.
> It seemed as though it would come in handy no matter what I did. And it did.[4]

In business, economics majors have a greater likelihood of becoming an S&P 500 CEO than any other major.[5] Those who are able to not only understand economics but also explain it to others can leverage their knowledge alongside their communications skills into careers as financial writers, reporters, and educators. Studying economics provides business majors with particularly marketable skills. A solid grounding in economic thinking gives business leaders a more thorough understanding of the economy, enabling them to better understand the way markets interact and to make optimal decisions for their firms based on economic indicators and market trends.

CHAPTER STUDY GUIDE

1.1 WHAT IS ECONOMICS—AND WHY DO WE FIND IT SO INTERESTING?

Economics is the study of how individuals, businesses, and governments make decisions on how to use their limited resources. A central theme of economic thought is that human wants are virtually unlimited and ever-changing, but resources are scarce. **Scarcity** is a situation that occurs when human wants and needs exceed available resources to meet those wants and needs. Economics starts with some basic assumptions about human behavior, the first of which is that, on average, humans are rational and make decisions from which they will benefit. Since individuals and firms are motivated by rational self-interest, economists can thus make reasonable predictions about their economic behavior. Rational self-interest leads them to engage in trade. **Microeconomics** is the branch of economics that focuses on economic issues faced primarily by individuals and businesses in a particular segment of the overall economy. **Macroeconomics** is the branch of economics that focuses on economic issues which impact the overall economy.

1.2 THINK LIKE AN ECONOMIST

Opportunity cost is what must be given up in order to acquire or do something else. **Marginal analysis** is the process of comparing the additional benefits of an activity with its additional cost. In general, more of an activity should be engaged in whenever the additional benefits (the marginal benefits) exceed the marginal cost. Optimal outcomes occur at the level where the marginal benefit equals the marginal cost. **Nominal values** are the face values of variables measured in current prices that have not been adjusted for inflation. In contrast, **real values** are the values of variables measured in prices that have been adjusted for inflation. The **long run** refers to the time necessary to make all adjustments to new economic circumstances. The **short run** refers to a time frame that is too short to include all adjustments to new economic circumstances. In both economics and business, outcomes frequently depend on the time frame involved. In *The Wealth of Nations* (1776), Adam Smith wrote about the benefits of markets and trade. A **market** is a means for buyers and sellers to engage in

the exchange of a good or service. The belief that trade is generally beneficial to both sides is a central idea in economics.

1.3 WHY ECONOMISTS DON'T ALWAYS AGREE

Normative analysis is subjective and value-based; it considers questions involving goals, values, and ethics. **Positive analysis** is objective; it considers questions involving cause and effect. **Equity** refers to a general sense of fairness in the distribution of income and output among members of society. Most people view equity as an important societal goal, although they may not agree on what, exactly, is fair. **Efficiency** means obtaining the maximum output possible with all available resources. In microeconomics, business managers strive to achieve efficiency—they want their labor and capital to produce as much as possible.

1.4 SPEAK LIKE AN ECONOMIST

Resources are inputs used in the production of goods and services; they are commonly referred to as *factors of production*. Resources include labor, natural resources, physical capital, human capital, and entrepreneurs. There are limited amounts of each resource, which is to say they exhibit some degree of scarcity. **Labor** is the human effort used in the production of goods and services. **Natural resources** are inputs found in nature that can be used in the production of goods and services. **Physical capital** (or simply *capital* in economics) is durable equipment and structures used to produce goods and services. Capital allows labor to be more productive. **Human capital** refers to the skills acquired through education, experience, and training that allow labor to be more productive. An **entrepreneur** is an individual who combines various resources into a business in pursuit of profit. *Ceteris paribus* (Latin for "other things equal") means other economic and business conditions are assumed not to change. *Ceteris paribus* is a critical component of economic thinking. **Investment** refers to spending on new capital goods and increases the amount of physical capital in an economy. Terms such as equity, investment, capital, and resources have distinct meanings in economics that may not apply in other disciplines.

TOP TEN TERMS AND CONCEPTS

(1) Economics: Microeconomics and Macroeconomics

(2) Markets

(3) Opportunity Cost

(4) Marginal Analysis

(5) Nominal Values versus Real Values

(6) Long Run versus Short Run

(7) Normative Analysis versus Positive Analysis

(8) Equity and Efficiency

(9) Resources: Labor, Natural Resources, Physical Capital, Human Capital, and Entrepreneurs

(10) *Ceteris Paribus*

STUDY PROBLEMS

1. What is economics? How is it related to the concept of scarcity?

2. State whether each of the following involves microeconomics or macroeconomics.
   a. The small state of Rhode Island experiences a spike in unemployment.
   b. Exxon, one of the worlds' largest corporations, has record profits.
   c. Economic growth of the global economy
   d. Increase in sales at Mario's pizza restaurant
   e. A consumer responds to a lower price at the market.

3. State whether each of the following is, or is not, an opportunity cost of attending college.
   a. tuition
   b. room and meals
   c. books
   d. foregone salary
   e. higher future income with a college degree

4. Which of the following is the correct use of marginal analysis? Explain.
   a. A pizzeria has more total revenue (money coming in) than total cost, so it assumes selling more pizza is a good idea.
   b. A pizzeria has less total revenue (money coming in) than total cost, so it assumes selling more pizza is a bad idea.
   c. A pizzeria is losing money. If it sells one more pizza, it will receive $15 in revenue and see its costs increase by $10. It decides to sell more pizza.
   d. A pizzeria is making money. If it sells one more pizza, it will receive $10 in revenue and see its costs increase by $15. It decides to sell more pizza.

5. Provide an example of an issue on which economists might disagree. And then discuss both the positive and normative reasons why they might disagree. Which type of disagreement can be resolved most easily by acquiring more data?

6. Why might an economist oppose a public policy that makes the economy more efficient? What other values do economists care about?

7. Suppose you paid $100 for a ticket to a Beyoncé concert. Now assume that just as you are about to enter the arena, someone offers you $500 for your ticket. As you consider whether or not to sell it, how does the concept of *opportunity cost* affect your decision? Be specific.

8. Does economics just focus on monetary costs? If not, what other types of costs must be taken into account when making a decision?

9. Describe what a market is. Provide examples. Why do economists view markets and trade favorably?

10. Why was Adam Smith an important economist? Did his ideas play more of a role in the development of capitalism or communism? Explain briefly.

11. What is human capital? Explain a rationale for attending college in terms of human capital. Look up recent data on career opportunities for various college majors with a degree.

12. Suppose two economists agreed with a study that suggested the emergency 99-week unemployment program caused the unemployment rate to rise from 8.2 to 8.6% during the recent Great Recession. Explain why they might nonetheless disagree about the desirability of the program.

13. Define each of the following, providing its meaning in economics.
    a. equity
    b. capital
    c. investment
    d. resources

14. What does *ceteris paribus* mean? Economists are examining the impact of a price change on the quantity of a product sold. For each example, state whether your feel the *ceteris paribus* assumption holds.
    a. ice cream sales in August versus December
    b. pizza sales in the morning versus dinner
    c. the price of seeing a movie in the evening versus a matinee during the day

Using Graphs in Economics

In economics, graphs are typically used to visualize models, to examine relationships between different variables, and to better understand economic phenomena. In this section, we'll introduce you to a few of the many different types of graphs you will encounter in your study of economics, as well as in the business-related media.

CALCULATING SLOPE

Most economic graphs plot data along two axes to see how the variables on each axis relate. Exhibit A1 shows a hypothetical relationship between how many pizzas are produced and the total cost of producing that number of pizzas. As more pizzas are made, the total cost of making the pizzas increases. In this example, if zero pizzas are made, then the cost is zero, and each additional pizza adds $10 to the total cost.

The **slope** describes how much one variable changes in response to changes in a different variable. In the above example, the slope describes how much *more* it costs to make each additional pizza. Often slope is defined as simply "rise over run." Slope can also be expressed mathematically:

$$\text{Slope} = \frac{\text{Rise}}{\text{Run}} = \frac{\text{Vertical change}}{\text{Horizontal change}}$$

In Exhibit A1, slope is the change in cost (the rise or vertical change) over the change in quantity of pizza (the run or horizontal change).

As in mathematics, the vertical axis is called the y-axis, the horizontal axis is called the x-axis, and the Greek letter delta (Δ) means change. In our example, the y-axis is cost and the x-axis is quantity of pizzas. Thus, the slope can also be expressed as

$$\text{Slope} = \frac{\Delta Y}{\Delta X}$$

slope Describes how much one variable changes in response to changes in a different variable.

EXHIBIT A1 Sample Graph with Positive Slope

Graphs are a visual representation of data that displays relationships found in the data. Here, we see that each additional pizza made adds $10 to the cost of making all the pizzas. That's a $10 rise over a run of 1 unit of pizza—so the slope is 10/1, or simply 10.

Either mathematical formula for slope is acceptable: They are the same formula. In Exhibit A1, it costs $10 (rise, vertical change or ΔY) for each additional pizza (run, horizontal change or ΔX). Thus, the slope in the figure is 10:

$$\text{Slope} = \frac{10}{1} = 10$$

Exhibit A1 presents a *linear relationship*—that is, a relationship with a constant slope, represented by a straight-line segment on the graph. In a linear relationship, the slope does not change. The additional cost of making the first, second, or third pizza is the same, $10.

Not all graphs contain a linear relationship. When a relationship is not linear, its slope changes along a curve. For example, suppose society must decide between the production of televisions *or* wind turbines, as shown in Exhibit A2.

The relationship between the number of televisions made and the number of wind turbines made is not constant, and thus forms a curve rather than a straight-line segment. In Exhibit A2, the slope between points *A* and *B* is

$$\text{Slope} = \frac{-1}{1} = -1$$

And the slope between points *C* and *D* is

$$\text{Slope} = \frac{-3}{1} = -3$$

Between *A* and *B*, one more turbine results in one *less* television, and between *C* and *D*, one more turbine means 3 *less* televisions.

A **positive relationship**, sometimes called a *direct relationship*, is when an increase in one variable occurs with an increase in another variable, or a decrease in one variable occurs with a decrease in another variable. A positive relationship results in a curve with a positive slope: The segment slopes upward when viewed from left to right. The relationship between number of pizzas made and total cost shown in Exhibit A1 is an example. As more pizzas are made, the total cost rises. The variables *quantity* and *cost* move in the same direction.

A **negative relationship**, sometimes called an *inverse relationship*, is when a decrease in one variable occurs with an increase in another variable, or an increase in one variable occurs with a decrease in the other variable. The two variables move

positive relationship When an increase in one variable occurs with an increase in another variable, or a decrease in one variable occurs with a decrease in another variable; sometimes called a *direct relationship*.

negative relationship When a decrease in one variable occurs with an increase in another variable, or an increase in one variable occurs with a decrease in the other variable; sometimes called an *inverse relationship*.

EXHIBIT A2 Sample Graph with Negative Nonlinear Slope

The production possibility frontier is an example of a negative nonlinear sloped curve. Between points *A* and *B*, the slope is –1. The slope changes to –3 between points *C* and *D*. Recall that slope is rise over run; here, the rise is negative.

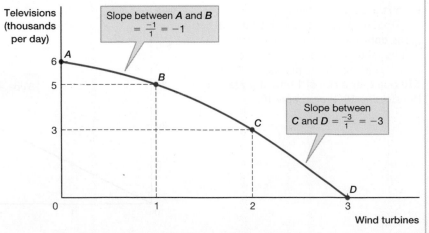

in opposing directions. A negative relationship results in a curve with a negative slope. The segment slopes downward when viewed from left to right. The relationship between the quantity of televisions and the quantity of wind turbines found in Exhibit A2 is an example. To recap:

- Positive or direct relationship: slope > 0.
- Negative or inverse relationship: slope < 0.

TIME–SERIES GRAPH

Historical data are often presented in a **time-series graph** that shows the relationship between a variable and time. Economists look at time-series graphs ranging from sales at a firm to GDP and unemployment from month to month, year to year, and even decade to decade. These graphs visualize the history of our economy. Exhibit A3 shows changes in the unemployment rate over recent decades.

CORRELATION DOES NOT PROVE CAUSATION!

Economists often comb through economic data to better understand economic relationships. On occasion, they will discover that two variables are *correlated*—that a change in one variable is consistently accompanied by a change in the other variable. Graphs can be useful for examining such relationships. But while data may suggest that two variables are related, it would be a mistake to always assume that a change in one variable *causes* the changes in the other variable.

First, what appears to be a relationship might just be mere coincidence. For example, 6 out of the last 7 times the Kentucky Wildcats won the NCAA National Basketball Championship, the New York Yankees went on to win the World Series in baseball. It would be incorrect to assume the Wildcats' success causes the Yankees' success, or that they are, in fact, related in some way. In the future, it's quite unlikely that the correlation between the two teams' records will hold. It's unlikely that the two teams' fortunes are related at all.

time-series graph A graph that shows the relationship between a variable and time.

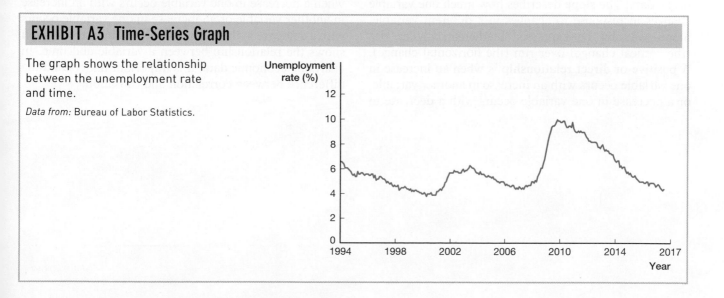

EXHIBIT A3 Time-Series Graph

The graph shows the relationship between the unemployment rate and time.

Data from: Bureau of Labor Statistics.

In other cases, two variables may actually be related, but that does not necessarily mean the relationship is causal. For example, there is a positive relationship between ice cream cone sales and drowning deaths. Of course, it would be foolish to assume that ice cream cone sales *cause* people to drown; it would be equally foolish to assume drownings *cause* ice cream cone sales. It is more likely that the relationship between these two variables is due to the existence of one or more *omitted* variables. In this case, we might note that the increases in both ice cream sales and drownings occur during warm summer months: As temperatures rise, people are more likely to eat cold ice cream and/or spend more time in or around swimming pools, lakes, and beaches. If you ignore the time of year and weather conditions, then your conclusions will be skewed by what economists call the *omitted variable bias*. Unlike the Wildcats/ Yankees correlation, ice cream sales and drownings are likely related, and the correlation between them is likely to continue in the future. However, there is no causal relationship between the two variables.

The direction of the causation is also important. Consider the correlation between average daily temperature and the number of people who drown in area swimming pools. The two are clearly positively related, yet it would be foolish to assume that more people drowning causes higher temperatures. Clearly, the causation works in the other direction, warmer weather causes more people to want to swim at a local pool, increasing the likelihood that some will drown. However, the data alone do not tell us which way the causation goes; we must bring in outside information to make that determination.

Exhibit A1 demonstrated how economic theory can be used to explain why selling more pizza increases production costs. In Exhibit A2, economic theory can be used to explain why producing more wind turbines decreases the amount of pizza made. In each case, the correlation can be explained with economic theory in conjunction with the data, but not simply by looking at raw data. Thus, *correlation by itself does not prove causation*. There must be an explanation for the correlation in order to claim causation.

APPENDIX STUDY GUIDE

Graphs are a visual representation of relationships found in the data. The **slope** describes how much one variable changes in response to changes in a different variable. Slope can also be expressed mathematically as rise (the vertical change) over run (the horizontal change). A **positive** or **direct relationship** is when an increase in one variable occurs with an increase in another variable, or a decrease in one variable occurs with a decrease in another variable. A **negative** or **inverse relationship** is when a decrease in one variable occurs with an increase in another variable or an increase in one variable occurs with a decrease in the other variable. A **time series graph** shows the relationship between a variable and time. In analyzing economic data, it is important understand the difference between correlation and causation.

STUDY PROBLEMS

1. What is the slope of the purple line? What is the slope of the blue line? What does the slope represent?

Two Nations

2. Consider the following table that shows the number of hours Max studies and his grade on his economics exams. Graph the outcome. Place grade on the *y*-axis and hours on the *x*-axis. What is the slope of the line? Does correlation exist? Does causation exist? Explain

Hours	Grade
0	50
2	60
4	70
6	80
8	90
10	100

3. What is a time-series graph? Create a time-series graph that shows the relationship between the unemployment rate in your state or country for the last 20 years.

4. In very poor countries, poorer people tend to be thinner than richer people. In wealthy countries, richer people tend to be thinner than poorer people. Why might the correlation be different in these two types of countries? *Hint*: Discuss how the causation could go in either direction.

∧ With trade, you can get the things you want without producing them yourself.

Why We Trade

Production, Trade, and the Global Economy

Every day, billions of transactions occur all over the world: Employees go to work, customers buy pizzas, landlords rent apartments, students buy textbooks, doctors provide medical services, and grocery stores sell food. Businesses ranging from huge corporations to your local pizzeria purchase materials and produce goods and services that are snapped up by customers. Why aren't people self-sufficient, producing the goods and services that they consume? The explanation is quite simple: It is usually more efficient to specialize and trade.

In markets ranging from flea markets to shopping malls to goods shipped internationally in large freight containers, people and firms regularly engage in exchanges that presumably make them better off. An important benefit of trade is that both buyers and sellers benefit from the exchange—and this is why we trade. On a global scale, this is also why nations trade with each other: When nations trade with each other, both sides of the exchange benefit.

In this chapter, we will consider the benefits of trade and examine the concepts of production and markets with the use of two economic models: the circular flow model and the production possibility frontier. You will also be introduced to some of the basic terminology describing the global economy such as imports, exports, and exchange rates.

Chapter Learning Targets

- Discuss the importance of economic models such as the circular flow model.

- Describe the production possibility frontier. Explain how it shows opportunity costs and economic growth.

- Explain how comparative advantage results in benefits from trade.

- Describe the basic terminology of the global economy.

2.1 A BASIC MODEL OF THE MARKET ECONOMY

Imagine you are planning to drive from Portland, Oregon, to Portland, Maine. It's unlikely you would begin by viewing a detailed map that showed every single road, exit, landmark, or pothole along the way. Instead, you'd begin with a GPS overview of the trip that showed the entire route on your computer or phone to get a sense of how long the trip will be and what stops you might make. Before you hit the road,

∧ The beauty of economic
models and GPS devices
are their simplicity.

circular flow model A
simplified diagram that
shows how households and
businesses interact with
one another in the product
market and in the resource
market.

you'd zoom in a bit closer to find out what specific roads to take on the first leg of the journey. When you're driving, you would likely use your GPS to provide very specific data, including a view of the road ahead and directions to places you want to visit. The GPS is programmed to provide more details as you zoom in. Thus, a *micro view* of your town will include more local details than a *macro view* on a national map.

Economic models are a sort of GPS view of the economy—they provide a simplified examination of a specific process or phenomenon. These models omit certain details in order to provide a more basic understanding of the task at hand, and allow us to analyze the effects of one factor at a time.

There is, of course, an opportunity cost to keeping things simple: Real-world complications are left out. No model can fully explain complex events like the 2008–09 global financial crisis, because a model cannot usefully accommodate all the variables behind that crisis. However, models can help us to examine the general trends in variables like unemployment or home foreclosures during the Great Recession. You will be introduced to a variety of different models throughout your study of economics.

We begin with one of the simplest: the circular flow model. Recall from Chapter 1 that a market consists of all actual and potential buyers and sellers of resources and products. Firms supply goods and services to the *product market.* These goods and services are then consumed by households, which include both individuals and family units. In order to produce goods and services, households provide resources to the firms in the *resource market.* This cyclical process is captured by the **circular flow model**, a simplified diagram that shows how households and businesses interact with one another in the product market and in the resource market (Exhibit 1).

Why do these trades and transactions occur? It all goes back to the idea of rational self-interest, also discussed in the previous chapter. For businesses, the money earned by selling goods in the product market is considered revenue. To households, this same money is considered spending, or an expenditure. Simply put, a household's expenditure is a business's revenue.

EXHIBIT 1 Circular Flow Model

The circular flow model is a simplified diagram that shows how households and businesses interact with one another in the product market and in the resource market. In the resource market, money (income to households) is exchanged for labor and other resources. To households, this money is income; to businesses, it is an expense. In the product market, money is exchanged for goods and services. To households, this money is spending; to businesses, it is revenue.

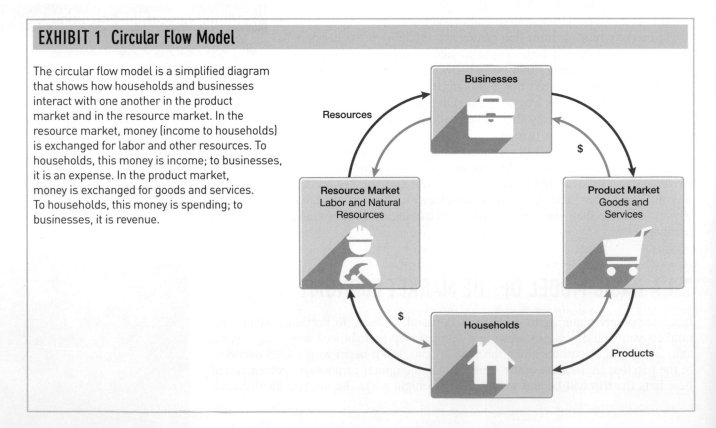

EXHIBIT 2   Production Possibility Frontier

The production possibility frontier captures the limit of what an economy can produce when all resources are used efficiently. Points *A*, *B*, *C*, and *D* reflect this limit and are considered to achieve productive efficiency. Points outside the curve (point *Y*) are not obtainable without free trade or economic growth. Points inside the curve (point *R*) are obtainable, but reflect an inefficient use of resources and possibly a recession.

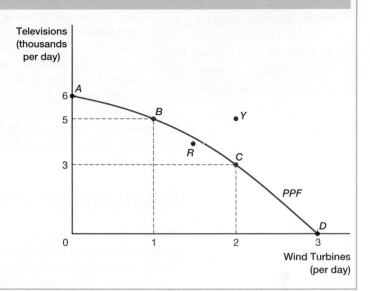

Households, of course, get money in exchange for providing resources such as labor or entrepreneurial talent. Some households may also earn money from their ownership of natural resources and physical capital. All land and capital are ultimately owned by households. To households, the money received by providing resources represents income. To businesses, this money represents an expense or cost.

You have probably noticed that many details are missing from the circular flow diagram. Financial markets and the banking system. International trade. Government spending. Each of these could be added to the model, but doing so would introduce additional layers of complexity, limiting the model's usefulness. By eliminating such factors, this very basic model illustrates one key idea: that a society's ability to generate income for its citizens will very much depend on its ability to produce output.

2.2 THE PRODUCTION POSSIBILITY FRONTIER MODEL

Recall that efficiency means obtaining the maximum output possible with all available resources. When all resources are being used efficiently, we are said to be at the boundary between what can and cannot be produced. This boundary is called the **production possibility frontier model (PPF)**, an economic model that shows the limit of what an economy can produce when all resources are used efficiently. A PPF may be drawn for individuals, businesses, or entire countries. In this section, we will use the model to explain a variety of economic concepts including economic growth and economic efficiency. In the next section, the model will be used to address the core subject of this chapter—why we trade.

Like all economic models, the PPF model is most useful when examining simplified data. Thus, we begin by examining a PPF for an economy that produces only two goods: wind turbines, which are used to generate electricity, and televisions. These goods represent physical capital and consumer goods, respectively, but any two goods could be selected.

Exhibit 2 shows the maximum possible combined output of televisions and wind turbines. Since the curve represents the limit, or frontier, of what the economy can efficiently produce with its given allotment of resources and technology, points

production possibility frontier (PPF) An economic model that shows the limit of what an economy can produce when all resources are used efficiently.

outside the curve are unattainable. While it is possible for society to produce 3 wind turbines *or* 6 televisions, it cannot produce both 3 wind turbines *and* 6 televisions, as it is outside the boundary and unattainable. Nor can it produce 5 televisions *and* 2 wind turbines (point *Y*) or any other point beyond the PPF.

Points inside the curve, such as point *R*, are attainable but inefficient. At point *R*, all resources are not being fully and efficiently utilized. When labor is not being fully utilized, the result is high unemployment and the economy is said to be operating in a *recession*. Movement from point *R* to the production possibility frontier would be akin to an economy recovering from a recession—an important topic in macroeconomics.

Opportunity Cost on the Production Possibility Frontier

The production possibility frontier model can be used to demonstrate the concept of opportunity cost (introduced in Chapter 1). What is the opportunity cost of additional wind turbines when a society operates on the production possibility frontier? If more wind turbines are produced, then the production of televisions must be reduced. The opportunity cost of more wind turbines is fewer televisions. This is demonstrated in Exhibit 3.

In general, when on the PPF, increased production of one type of good uses more resources, decreasing the production of other goods and services. If society operates at point *A*, it is producing 0 wind turbines. The opportunity cost of producing 1 wind turbine (moving from point *A* to point *B*) is 1 television (= 6 − 5). The opportunity cost of producing an *additional* turbine (moving from point *B* to point *C*) is 2 televisions (= 5 − 3). At that point, the opportunity cost of another wind turbine (going from point *C* to *D*) is 3 televisions (= 3 − 0).

This pattern is known in economics as the law of increasing cost. The **law of increasing cost** states that the opportunity cost of producing an additional item generally increases as more of the good is produced. Here, the opportunity cost of producing each additional wind turbine is higher than the opportunity cost of the preceding unit. The law of increasing cost explains the bowed-out, or concave, shape of the curve.

What is the logic behind the law of increasing cost? The answer is fairly straightforward: Not all resources are equally adaptable in the production of televisions and wind

law of increasing cost
Principle stating that the opportunity cost of producing an additional item generally increases as more of the good is produced.

EXHIBIT 3   Increasing Opportunity Cost

When society operates efficiently, the opportunity cost of more wind turbines is fewer televisions. As society produces more wind turbines, the opportunity cost of producing an additional turbine increases. For example, at point *A*, the opportunity cost of 1 turbine is 1 television as we move to point *B*. At point *C*, the opportunity cost of 1 *more* wind turbine is 3 televisions as we move to point *D*.

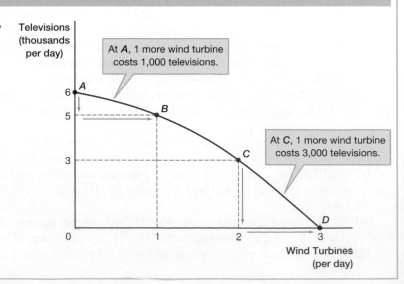

turbines. If society initially operates at point *A* (making only televisions) and shifts to point *B* (making fewer televisions but 1 more wind turbine), it is likely that the first wind turbine will be produced in green technology centers that are particularly well suited to making such products. In contrast, production of the last (third) wind turbine implies moving from point *C* to point *D*. Where will the last wind turbine be produced? It will likely occur in the areas that are the least well suited for producing turbines and best suited for making televisions. Here, the opportunity cost of making wind turbines in terms of foregone televisions is extremely high.

Clynt Garnham Renewable Energy/ Alamy Stock Photo

∧ GE found it had a comparative advantage in developing wind energy technologies.

📊 BUSINESS BRIEF GE Identifies Its Comparative Advantage

In 1927, a General Electric (GE) engineer made the first known demonstration of a television broadcast. The company would go on to become a leading producer of televisions.* But in 1985, the company stopped manufacturing televisions, selling a factory with the capacity to produce 1 million sets a year.†

General Electric is a conglomerate—a business involved in two or more distinct industries. GE determined that it no longer had an advantage in the production of televisions, but did maintain a strong one in other industries. Eventually, the company would go on to become the number two installer of wind turbines, behind Siemens, a German conglomerate.‡

In a sense, the company moved from points *A* to *D* in Exhibit 2.

*Edison Technology Center, "Television," 2014, http://www.edisontechcenter.org/Television.html.

†"GE Quits TB Production," *Chicago Tribune*, October 18, 1985, http://articles.chicagotribune.com/1985-10-18 /business/8503110462_1_ge-spokesman-sets-picture-tube.

‡"Ten of the Biggest and the Best Manufacturers," *Windpower Monthly*, June 30, 2015, http://www .windpowermonthly.com/article/1352888/ten-biggest-best-manufacturers.

Productive and Allocative Efficiency

As you will recall from Chapter 1, economics is concerned with efficiency—that is, with getting the most out of available resources. In economics, the idea of efficiency may be broken down into two distinct concepts: efficiency in production and efficiency in allocating resources to produce the goods most valued by individuals and society.

Productive efficiency is obtaining the maximum possible output with a given set of resources or obtaining output for the lowest possible cost. In the world of business, this might mean minimizing production costs per unit. Alternatively, it might also mean maximizing the output on a given budget with set inputs. It is easy to see productive efficiency on the production possibility frontier shown in Exhibit 2. Productive efficiency occurs at all points on the PPF such as points *A*, *B*, *C*, and *D*. Not surprisingly, an economy in a recession (point *R*) does *not* achieve productive efficiency.

Although an economy might produce a particular good at the lowest possible cost, if consumers do not want the good, it's hardly efficient. Thus, economists are also concerned with the combination of goods and services an economy produces—that is, finding the mixture of goods and services that society most desires among choices on the PPF. Economists refer to this optimal mix of products as allocative efficiency.

Allocative efficiency is obtaining the maximum well-being from producing the right set of goods and services. When allocative efficiency is achieved, consumers get the most out of society's productive capacity. Whereas productive efficiency refers to efficiency in the creation of goods, allocative efficiency refers to efficiency in the distribution and allotment of those goods and service. Does society desire more wind turbines or more televisions? Allocative efficiency occurs when society chooses the best point on the PPF; it will be discussed in greater detail in later in the chapter on economic efficiency.

productive efficiency
Obtaining the maximum possible output with a given set of resources or obtaining output for the lowest possible cost.

allocative efficiency
Obtaining the maximum well-being from producing the right set of goods and services.

Applying the Production Possibility Frontier: Economic Growth

The production possibility frontier can also help us to understand long-run economic growth. *Economic growth* is a sustained increase in the quantity of goods and services produced that occurs over time. Increases in real GDP, a measure of both total income and total production, are associated with economic growth. Most societies strive for economic growth because it leads to a higher standard of living. Prior to economic growth, points outside the initial curve, such as point *Y*, are unattainable, but after economic growth, society can enjoy more wind turbines and more televisions. This is shown in Exhibit 4.

Those studying macroeconomics will undertake an in-depth examination of the factors that contribute to economic growth. Here, we briefly outline the three most important sources of economic growth:

- *Innovation and new technology.* When new ways of doing things are developed, production increases. For example, a new technology may be discovered that increases the amount of electricity generated with wind turbines. Such innovations often involve new technology, but might also include new methods of using existing labor and physical capital. A classic example of innovation is Henry Ford's introduction of the rolling assembly line in 1913, which enabled his plants to turn out two cars per hour, compared to one car every 12 hours prior.[1]

- *Investments in physical capital.* Increases in physical capital are often necessary for economic growth. More machines and state-of-the-art factories and robots produced today will mean greater possible production in the future. An investment in wind farm turbines will lead to greater electricity output in the future and a higher level of total output.

- *Improvements in human capital.* A more educated and well-trained workforce will also lead to increased production and, eventually, economic growth. To operate effectively, wind farms need a workforce with the skills set to operate and repair wind turbines.

EXHIBIT 4 Economic Growth

The production possibility frontier can be used to show economic growth—a sustained long-run increase in GDP. Initially, point *Y* is unobtainable, but may become obtainable with economic growth. Sources of economic growth include innovation and new technology, investments in physical capital, and improvements in human capital.

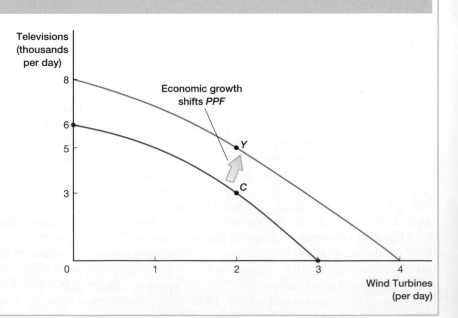

As these examples indicate, spending by individuals, businesses, and governments on the development of new technology, education, or capital expansion can foster economic growth. It is important to note that economic growth is a long-run process: It takes time for society to adapt new technology or reap the benefits of greater physical capital and improved education. Lastly, production at point *Y* is not obtainable without economic growth. But as we'll discuss in the next section, while it remains impossible to *produce* at point *Y*, it is actually possible for a society to *consume* at point *Y*—after trade!

> ### Think & Speak Like an Economist
>
> Firms discuss "growth" in terms of increased sales. But the term *economic growth* has a very specific macroeconomic meaning: It refers to a sustained increase in the quantity of goods and services produced by a society over time.

2.3 COMPARATIVE ADVANTAGE AND THE GAINS FROM TRADE

Economists believe that trade usually benefits all participants. It turns out that this occurs at both the individual level and for entire economies. In this section and in the chapter on international trade, we address why economists favor free trade.

Specialization and Trade

To understand why we trade, let's examine a parable between two individuals: Mario and Taylor. To keep things simple, let's assume they can make only two goods: pizza and shirts. This allows us to derive their *individual* production possibilities. To further simplify our analysis, it is assumed that both Mario's and Taylor's production possibility frontiers are linear (a straight line) and ignore the law of increasing cost.

In Panel A of Exhibit 5, we see the production possibility frontier for each person. Mario can produce 4 pizzas and no shirt *or* 2 pizzas and 1 shirt *or* some other combinations on the frontier. Since Mario wants some pizzas and some shirts, he produces (and *consumes* (which in economic terms means to "use up") 2 of each. The same analysis applies to Taylor, who can produce 2 pizzas and 3 shirts *or* 0 pizzas and 6 shirts *or* some other combinations on the frontier. Since Taylor wants some pizzas and some shirts, she produces and consumes 2 pizzas and 3 shirts.

Suppose that Taylor determines that Mario is better at making pizza, and she is better at making shirts. She encourages Mario to specialize in pizzas, while she specializes in shirts. **Specialization** means concentrating on the production of a single good. In this case, Mario is encouraged to focus his talents on producing only pizza. Taylor tells Mario that if he specializes accordingly, she will trade him 2 shirts for 2 pizzas. Mario is skeptical, but agrees to give the proposal a try as he views obtaining 2 shirts for 2 pizzas as a real bargain. Mario produces 4 pizzas and no shirts, while Taylor focuses on shirts, producing 6 of them. Notice that the combined production of shirts increases from 4 without specialization to 6; this is shown in Panel B.

Mario thinks he is getting a bargain by trading away only 2 pizzas for 2 shirts, but Taylor also believes she is about to get a bargain. In Panel C, you can see that *after trade* both Mario and Taylor are able to consume more goods than they could have possibly produced on their own. Mario can now consume 2 shirts *and* 2 pizzas. Without trade, if he had produced 2 shirts, he would have ended up with no pizza at all. Taylor also benefits. This is the beauty of trade; *both* participants can benefit from it.

Determining Comparative Advantage

The parable of Mario and Taylor is a useful demonstration of how individuals can leverage their unique talents to find a comparative advantage in the market. **Comparative advantage** is the ability to produce a product at a lower

specialization Concentrating on the production of a single good.

comparative advantage The ability to produce a product at a lower opportunity cost than a trading partner.

EXHIBIT 5 Why We Trade

Without trade, Mario and Taylor's consumption is limited to the production possibility (Panel A). If Mario and Taylor specialize in what they do best and trade, both will be able to consume more than otherwise possible (Panel B). If Mario specializes in pizzas by making 4 pizzas and trades away 2 pizzas in exchange for 2 shirts (Panel C), he will end up with 2 shirts and 2 pizzas—a point beyond his PPF. The ability to produce a product at a lower opportunity cost than a trading partner results in a *comparative advantage* in the production of the product. Output is given in units per day.

Panel A: Without Trade, Both Consume What They Produce

Mario

Mario produces and consumes 2 pizzas and 1 shirt.

Taylor

Taylor produces and consumes 2 pizzas and 3 shirts.

Panel B: With Trade, Both Specialize . . .

Mario

Mario specializes in pizza, producing 4 pizzas.

Taylor

Taylor specializes in shirts, producing 6 shirts.

Panel C: . . . and Both Consume More Than They Produce

Mario

Mario trades away 2 pizzas for 2 shirts consuming 2 pizzas and 2 shirts.

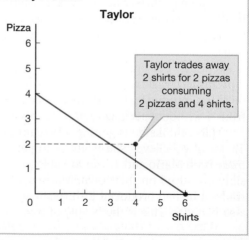

Taylor

Taylor trades away 2 shirts for 2 pizzas consuming 2 pizzas and 4 shirts.

opportunity cost than a trading partner. The concept was first written about in 1817 by British economist David Ricardo who attempted to explain why countries trade.

Comparative advantage is a *relative* concept, measured in terms of opportunity cost. For both Mario and Taylor, the opportunity cost of more shirts is less pizza. But because Mario and Taylor have different skills and interests, they have a different opportunity cost for producing each product: Taylor has a comparative advantage in making shirts, and Mario has a comparative advantage in making pizza.

Because of comparative advantage, both Taylor and Mario are able to benefit from trade after specialization expands their combined production. But how does one estimate comparative advantage? To begin, we need to compute the exact opportunity cost of each good for each person.

Step 1: Compute Opportunity Costs Mathematically, the opportunity cost represents how much less of one good is produced when 1 more unit of another good is produced. The previous wind turbine and television example showed us how to calculate opportunity cost from a PPF. In the current example, calculating opportunity costs merely requires a little division. As you will discover, the person (or country) with the steeper slope has a comparative advantage in the production of the good on the *y*-axis. This is shown in Exhibit 5.

If Mario specializes, he can produce 4 pizzas *or* 2 shirts. This means he gives up 2 pizzas for each shirt (dividing both 4 pizzas and 2 shirts by 2). For Mario, the opportunity cost of 1 extra shirt is 2 fewer pizzas. The analysis is similar for Taylor; if she specializes, she can produce 4 pizzas *or* 6 shirts. For Taylor, the opportunity cost of 1 shirt is 2/3 of a pizza (dividing both 4 pizzas and 6 shirts by 6 and simplifying 4/6 to 2/3).

In summary,

Opportunity cost of 1 shirt for Mario: 1 shirt costs 2 pizzas

Opportunity cost of 1 shirt for Taylor: 1 shirt costs 2/3 of a pizza

What is their respective opportunity cost for making a pizza? Recall that Mario can produce 4 pizzas or 2 shirts. Dividing both sides of this equation by 4 leads to 1 pizza = 1/2 shirt. A similar analysis may be conducted for Taylor. Since she can produce 4 pizzas or 6 shirts, we simplify the equation by dividing by 4. This leads to 1 pizza = 1 1/2 shirts.

Opportunity cost of 1 pizza for Mario: 1 pizza = 1/2 shirt

Opportunity cost of 1 pizza for Taylor: 1 pizza = $\left(1\frac{1}{2}\right)$ shirts

Step 2: Compare Opportunity Costs To determine comparative advantage, we must compare opportunity costs. Given the opportunity cost data presented in Exhibit 6, who should produce shirts? Would you rather give up 2 pizzas for 1 shirt (with Mario) or 2/3 of a pizza (with Taylor)? For most, the answer is Taylor, because she has a lower opportunity cost.

In a similar vein, Mario has a comparative advantage in making pizzas. After all, to make 1 pizza would you rather give up half a shirt (with Mario) or $\left(1\frac{1}{2}\right)$ shirts (with Taylor)? The answer is, of course, Mario.

Markets and trade are usually beneficial because the participants are able to specialize in their area of comparative advantage and trade for other goods. When both Mario and Taylor specialize in their comparative advantage, both sides can consume beyond the limit of their respective production possibility frontier. Comparative advantage is the reason why people can gain from trade after specialization.

EXHIBIT 6 Determining Comparative Advantage

	Opportunity Cost of 1 Pizza	Opportunity Cost of 1 Shirt
Mario (4 pizzas = 2 shirts)	1/2 of a shirt	2 pizzas
Taylor (4 pizzas = 6 shirts)	$1\frac{1}{2}$ shirts	2/3 of a pizza

To determine comparative advantage, first compute the opportunity cost of each good for each trading partner. Simple division leads to the results presented. Second, recognize that comparative advantage results from a lower opportunity cost.

Absolute Advantage versus Comparative Advantage

It is important to remember that comparative advantage is a *relative* concept measured in terms of opportunity cost. In contrast, **absolute advantage** is the ability to produce more of a product than a trading partner with an equivalent amount of resources. Taylor, for example, has an absolute advantage in shirt making. She can produce more shirts with an equivalent amount of labor.

It may surprise you to learn that absolute advantage is *not* the basis for trade or specialization. In our example, neither Mario nor Taylor has an absolute advantage in producing pizza, as they can both produce 4 pizzas with an equivalent amount of labor. Yet, an exchange can occur that benefits both parties.

The basis for the gains from trade is the expansion in total production that occurs from individuals specializing in what they do relatively well—that is, where they have a comparative advantage. In turn, the increase in *combined* production to 4 pizzas and 6 shirts allows for mutually beneficial trades to take place. As you will see in **Business Brief: Why Does Kansas Produce More Wheat Than California?**, the combined production of wheat and other crops is greatest when California *does not* specialize in wheat, in which it has an *absolute advantage*. Instead, California specializes on the basis of comparative advantage. Later in the international trade chapter, you will discover why *comparative advantage* leads to specialization and gains from international trade, whereas absolute advantage does not.

absolute advantage The ability to produce more of a product than a trading partner with an equivalent amount of resources.

∧ Kansas grows what it can; California grows what Kansas can't.

BUSINESS BRIEF Why Does Kansas Produce More Wheat Than California?

Kansas is famous as the breadbasket of America, the leading producer of wheat. Each year, it produces far more wheat than Illinois, which produces far more wheat than California. Why is this? You might assume that the soil, weather, and land in Kansas are extremely well suited to growing wheat, but in fact just the opposite is true: Conditions in Illinois are better suited to growing wheat, and California has better conditions than either state. In other words, California has an absolute advantage in the production of wheat. So why is wheat grown on land that is not particularly productive (in Kansas) and not in California?

Although Kansas is not an especially suitable environment for producing wheat, it's even less suitable for growing most other crops. Wheat happens to be a very hardy crop, which will thrive in dry places where other crops would not survive, like Kansas. Illinois can also produce corn and soybeans, which yield higher profits. California, meanwhile, is capable of producing some of the most lucrative crops of all, including fruits, nuts, and vegetables. Remember, comparative advantage is based on *relative* opportunity costs. California has an absolute advantage in growing most crops and could produce lots of wheat. But that would not be an efficient use of some of the world's most productive farmland. Instead, farmers in the state focus on the higher-valued crops for which they have a comparative advantage. This results in greater total production and allows for mutually beneficial trades. Thus, each state specializes and engages in trade on the basis of comparative advantage, not absolute advantage.

The Gains from Trade

The beauty of specialization and trade is that both sides can win when trade occurs on the basis of comparative advantage. Without trade, it would be impossible to consume beyond the PPF. You cannot consume more than you produce. With trade, however, individuals and entire societies *can* consume more than they produce.

As demonstrated in the circular flow model, in the real world, people usually work for money in the resource market, then use that money for goods and services in the product market. The gains from comparative advantage work in much the same way. If our example reflected the existence of money, Mario would sell pizza for money and buy shirts with that money. Likewise, Taylor would sell shirts for money and use it to buy pizza. In a sense, money merely works as a middleman—it serves as a medium of exchange that helps facilitate trade and exchange. But ultimately, it is comparative advantage that provides for the amazing gains produced by trade.

In a similar vein, professional athletes presumably play sports because it is the source of their comparative advantage, and as a consequence, it is where they can earn the most money. College graduates with an engineering degree tend to secure employment in fields where their degree gives them a comparative advantage, such as the aerospace industry.

The story of Mario and Taylor is not unusual. It applies in nearly all cases where individuals have different opportunity costs. It is for this reason that nearly all economists favor international trade; the advantages are the same as for trade between individuals. As you will discover in a later chapter, countries also tend to have different opportunity costs, and like individuals, they can benefit from specialization and comparative advantage.

Think & Speak Like an Economist

Being "self-sufficient" may sound nice to the average person, but markets enable individuals to specialize and trade, which allows them to consume more—and generally live better—than they would if they remained self-sufficient.

📊 BUSINESS BRIEF IBM Seeks a Comparative Advantage

In the early days of computer technology, IBM was the dominant mainframe computer manufacturer, controlling over half of the entire global market. By the early 1990s, IBM was the leading seller of personal computers. Indeed, the term *PC* refers to any IBM-compatible personal computer. IBM's dominance, however, did not last. Today, IBM no longer produces personal computers.

In 2005, IBM sold its personal computer business to Chinese computer maker Lenovo. At the time, IBM was losing roughly a quarter billion dollars a year selling PCs. IBM also stopped producing other computer hardware components: selling off its printer business in 1996 and its server business in 2014. And yet, the company has continued to thrive.*

IBM recognized that it had an exceedingly talented workforce with a comparative advantage in computer-related consulting services. IBM employees have won five Nobel Prizes and include innovators like future Apple CEO Tim Cook. By 2016, its workforce of 380,000 was focused on helping companies manage their information processing. In contrast, Lenovo had a workforce ideally suited for manufacturing personal computers—its comparative advantage.

*William M. Bulkeley, "Less Is More: IBM Is Likely to Gain from Sale of PC Unit," *The Wall Street Journal*, December 6, 2004, http://www.wsj.com/articles/SB110208516216290490.

Think & Speak Like an Economist

Firms such as IBM and GE can translate their *comparative advantage* into what is known in business as a *competitive advantage* by outperforming rivals on price, costs, or quality of goods and services produced.

globalization The opening of markets to foreign trade and financial investment, leading to an increasing interconnectivity of economic transactions across national borders.

exports Goods and services produced domestically but sold in a foreign country.

imports Goods and services produced in a foreign country but sold domestically.

2.4 LANGUAGE OF THE GLOBAL ECONOMY

The gains from trade as a result of comparative advantage have produced a thriving world economy: Goods can be produced in one country using raw materials and other resources from a second country and then sold in a third country. With businesses producing and selling products all across the world, conditions in one country can impact the economy in many other countries.

Globalization refers to the opening of markets to foreign trade and financial investment, leading to an increasing interconnectivity of economic transactions across national borders. For anyone doing business today, some understanding of globalization and the global economy is crucial. Concepts related to globalization will be used throughout the text. At this point, you need to understand some of the basic terminology, such as imports, exports, and exchange rates.

Imports and Exports

International trade is a vital component of the world's economy. Consider the case of bicycles made in China and sold in the United States. The United States is said to *import* bicycles produced in China, while China is said to *export* bicycles to the United States. **Exports** are goods and services produced domestically (at home) but sold in a foreign country. **Imports** are goods and services produced in a foreign country but sold domestically (at home).

Exhibit 7 demonstrates the highest-valued export for each nation in the world. As you might expect, oil is a particularly important export from the Middle East, but it is also a key export in parts of Asia, Africa, and South America.

In North America, Canada's largest export is related to the production of motor vehicles. The United States exports capital goods, equipment used to make other goods. And in Mexico, the largest export is clothing and shoes—much of which is sold in the

EXHIBIT 7 Major Exports by Country

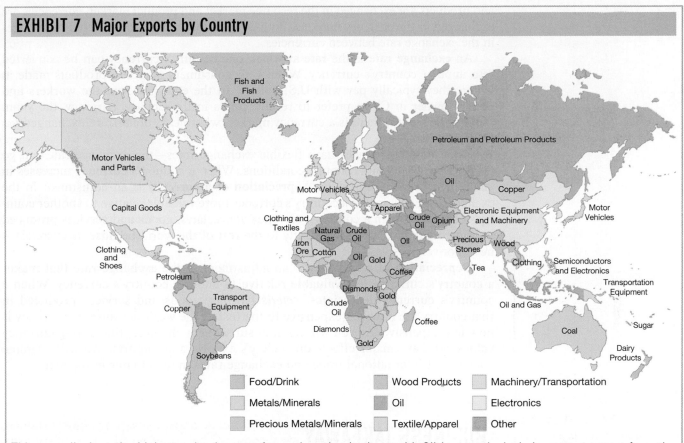

This map displays the highest-valued export for each nation in the world. Oil is a particularly important export from the Middle East as well as parts of Asia, Africa, and South America. The United States' main export is capital goods.

Data from: Simran Khosla, "This map shows which export makes your country the most money." *Public Radio International*, http://www.globalpost .com/dispatch/news/business/global-economy/140502/world-commodities-exports-map.

United States. In Europe and Japan, the focus is on manufactured goods, motor vehicles, and machinery. East Asia is very strong in electronics.

Economists often examine a country's overall trade patterns with the rest of the world. **Net exports** *(trade balance)* equal a country's exports minus its imports:

$$\text{Net exports} = \text{Trade balance} = \text{Exports} - \text{Imports}$$

A **trade deficit** occurs when a nation imports more products than it exports. Under these circumstances, net exports and the trade balance are negative. This is currently the case in the United States. A **trade surplus** occurs when a nation exports more products than it imports. Here, net exports and the trade balance are positive. This is currently the case for China.

$$\text{Net exports} > 0 \rightarrow \text{Trade surplus}$$
$$\text{Net exports} < 0 \rightarrow \text{Trade deficit}$$

Exchange Rates

One of the challenges of international trade is that when exchanges in the resource and product markets involve two or more countries, they often involve multiple currencies. The United States uses the U.S. dollar ($) and China uses the yuan (¥). Just as resources

net exports Equal a country's exports minus its imports; also referred to as the *trade balance*.

trade deficit An imbalance that occurs when a nation imports more products than it exports, resulting in negative net exports.

trade surplus The imbalance that occurs when a nation exports more products than it imports, resulting in positive net exports.

and products are exchanged in the resource market and product market, currencies are exchanged in the currency markets. Both exports and imports are affected by changes in the exchange rate between currencies.

An **exchange rate** is the rate at which one country's currency can be converted into another country's currency. When U.S. consumers purchase products made in China, they typically pay with U.S. dollars. In the end, however, the workers and factory owner in China prefer to receive funds in the Chinese currency, the yuan. Behind the scenes, there is a currency market, where U.S. dollars are exchanged for Chinese yuan.

Most major currencies have flexible exchange rates—the exchange rate can go up or down based on economic conditions. When a country's currency increases in value, it is said to appreciate. **Appreciation of a currency** is an adjustment in the exchange rate that makes a country's currency more valuable relative to another country's currency. When a country's currency appreciates, goods and services produced in that country are now more costly to the rest of the world because its currency is now more expensive.

Depreciation of a currency is an adjustment in the exchange rate that makes a country's currency less valuable relative to another country's currency. When a country's currency depreciates, *ceteris paribus*, goods and services produced in that country are now less expensive to the rest of the world because its currency is now less expensive. As you will learn in subsequent chapters, fluctuating currency values can have major effects on society's exports and imports. We will examine concepts of international trade and exchange rates in detail later in the text.

BUSINESS TAKEAWAY

Firms benefit from trade, so it should come as no surprise that the concept of comparative advantage plays into many of the internal and external decisions that shape the activities of individual businesses, including General Electric and IBM.

Within a firm, business managers utilize the concepts of comparative advantage and specialization to increase the efficiency of their staff. Individual tasks should be assigned to those who have a comparative advantage, as when accountants keep financial records and salespeople make sales. This increases output within the firm, even without external contracts and trade. Managers are becoming increasingly aware of other ways in which they can identify and capitalize on the comparative advantage already present within their firms. IBM's pivot from computer manufacturing to consulting reflects this kind of economic decision making.

In some cases, a firm might determine that it does not have a comparative advantage in a specific area of its business. In such an instance, the firm can opt to contract out certain tasks to other companies that have more of a comparative advantage in that area of expertise. Perhaps the bookkeeping could be more efficiently done if outsourced to a firm that specializes in accounting, or maybe it makes more sense to hire a freelance event planner to manage an upcoming sales meeting than to ask the head of Human Resources to take time from her other responsibilities to coordinate the task. Likewise, individual laborers who possess a comparative advantage in a particular area can leverage those skills as well. Having a sense of your comparative advantage is useful in wage negotiations, when seeking a promotion, or when going into business on your own.

Finally, economic models are becoming increasingly important in all kinds of business contexts. Firms must know how to interpret economic models to predict future market trends and to interpret data on past performance.

exchange rate The rate at which one country's currency can be converted into another country's currency.

appreciation of a currency An adjustment in the exchange rate that makes a country's currency more valuable relative to another country's currency.

depreciation of a currency An adjustment in the exchange rate that makes a country's currency less valuable relative to another country's currency.

CHAPTER STUDY GUIDE

2.1 A BASIC MODEL OF THE MARKET ECONOMY

Economic models are simplified frameworks for examining complex economic phenomena, often relying on mathematical techniques such as equations and graphs. The key characteristic of economic models is their simplicity, including only the variables needed to examine a specific process or phenomenon. The **circular flow model** is a simplified diagram that shows how households and businesses interact with one another in the product market and in the resource market. In the resource market, money (income to households) is exchanged for labor and other resources. To households, this money is income; to businesses, it is an expense. In the product market, money is exchanged for goods and services. To households, this money is spending; to businesses, it is revenue.

2.2 THE PRODUCTION POSSIBILITY FRONTIER

The **production possibility frontier model (PPF)** is an economic model that shows the limit of what an economy can produce when all resources are used efficiently. The limits to what society can produce result from the scarcity of resources such as physical capital and labor. The PPF model can be used to demonstrate the concept of opportunity cost—the opportunity cost of more of the good on one axis is less of the good on the other axis. The **law of increasing cost** states that the opportunity cost of producing an additional item generally increases as more of the good is produced. Economic efficiency is how effectively resources are used in the production and allocation of goods and services. **Productive efficiency** is obtaining the maximum possible output with a given set of resources or obtaining output for the lowest possible cost. This occurs at points on the PPF. **Allocative efficiency** is obtaining the maximum well-being from producing the right set of goods and services. Economic growth is a sustained increase in the quantity of goods and services produced that occurs over time. When economic growth occurs, the PPF shifts outward. Some important sources of economic growth are innovation and new technology, investments in physical capital, and improvements in human capital.

2.3 COMPARATIVE ADVANTAGE AND THE GAINS FROM TRADE

Specialization means concentrating on the production of a single good. Individuals and countries benefit from trade as it allows them to specialize in the area where they have a comparative advantage. **Comparative advantage** is the ability to produce a product at a lower opportunity cost than a trading partner. Comparative advantage is a *relative* concept defined in terms of opportunity cost. **Absolute advantage** is the ability to produce more of a product than a trading partner with an equivalent amount of resources. Comparative advantage, not absolute advantage, is the basis for trade and specialization. By taking advantage of comparative advantage and trade, one is able to consume beyond the production possibility frontier. There are two steps to determine comparative advantage. First, compute the opportunity cost of each good for each trading partner. Second, compare opportunity cost and recognize that comparative advantage results from a lower opportunity cost.

2.4 LANGUAGE OF THE GLOBAL ECONOMY

As a consequence of the gains from trade as a result of comparative advantage, the world economy is increasingly interconnected. **Globalization** refers to the opening of markets to foreign trade and financial investment, leading to an increasing interconnectivity of economic transactions across national borders. **Exports** are goods and services produced domestically but sold in a foreign country. **Imports** are goods and services produced in a foreign country but sold domestically. **Net exports (trade balance)** equal a country's exports minus its imports. A **trade deficit** occurs when a nation imports more products than it exports. Under these circumstances, net exports and the trade balance are negative. A **trade surplus** occurs when a nation exports more products than it imports, and net exports and the trade balance are positive. A currency is a unit of money in general use in a country or region. An **exchange rate** is the rate at which one country's currency can be converted into another country's currency. **Appreciation of a currency** is an adjustment in the exchange rate that makes a country's currency more valuable relative to another country's currency. **Depreciation of a currency** is an adjustment in the exchange rate that makes a country's currency less valuable relative to another country's currency. Fluctuating currency values can have major effects on society's exports and imports.

TOP TEN TERMS AND CONCEPTS

(1) Circular Flow Model

(2) Production Possibility Frontier (PPF)

3 The Law of Increasing Cost

4 Productive Efficiency versus Allocative Efficiency

5 Specialization and Comparative Advantage

6 Absolute Advantage

7 Exports and Imports

8 Net Exports (Trade Balance)

9 Exchange Rates

10 Appreciation and Depreciation of a Currency

STUDY PROBLEMS

1. Why do economists leave out some factors when they create a model of the economy? Do economists omit more details from models in microeconomics or macroeconomics?

2. Draw a circular flow model of the economy. Where do businesses obtain the factors of production needed to produce their products? How do they pay for these factors of production? Be specific.

3. Describe how the circular flow model shows why total income equals total expenditures.

4. Each year, American consumers spend trillions of dollars on goods and services. Is there any danger that eventually all this money will end up owned by businesses, and none at all by households? Explain your answer.

5. Discuss the relationship between the slope of the PPF and opportunity cost of the good on the *x*-axis. How about the good on the *y*-axis?

6. What is the *law of increasing cost*? How does this law relate to the shape of the PPF?

7. Discuss three factors that cause the PPF to shift outward. What is this shift called? How does an outward shift in the PPF affect average living standards in a country? Explain.

8. Draw two PPFs: one for Kansas and one for California. Assume Kansas can grow 10 units of oranges or 80 units of wheat. California can grow 100 units of oranges or 100 units of wheat. For both states, points in between these limits are possible. Show how the total production of wheat and oranges could be greater with specialization than with self-sufficiency. Assume the states trade 40 units of wheat for 20 oranges.

9. In Boston, a worker can produce either 4 pairs of red socks or 4 pairs of white socks per hour. In Chicago, a worker can produce either 2 pairs of red socks or 6 pairs of white socks per hour. The workers can also produce combinations in between.

   a. Draw the PPF for a worker in Boston and one in Chicago. Assume the PPF is linear.

   b. If specialization occurs, what will each worker produce?

   c. What is the basis for this specialization?

   d. Assume the workers in Boston and Chicago trade 2 pairs of red socks for 3 pairs of white socks. What is the consumption of each worker? Where is this point relative to the workers' PPF?

10. Suppose that Maria could produce both more pizzas and more shirts in a given workday. Does that mean she has a comparative advantage in both products? What determines Maria's comparative advantage?

11. Suppose the value of the dollar increases in foreign exchange markets. Other things equal, what happens to the price that Americans have to pay for imported goods? What happens to the price that foreigners have to pay for American goods?

12. Describe the difference between an import and an export in terms of the flow of goods and the flow of money. What is the difference between currency appreciation and currency depreciation?

13. In choosing a major, describe why it is often better to focus on an area where you have a comparative advantage, rather than an absolute advantage.

Justin Sullivan/Getty Images

∧ Consumers demand wireless headphones, and Beats supplies them.

Supply and Demand

Determining Prices in a Changing Business Environment

Imagine that you are heading out to the Apple Store to shop for a new pair of headphones. Along the way, you pass several gas stations, each boldly displaying their prices; you notice that regular gas costs a dollar more than it did last month. You pass by billboards promising great deals on everything from fast food to wireless phone plans. At the Apple Store, you select a pair of headphones and decide to use your phone to compare prices. You find that Amazon sells the headphones for a similar price.

If you drive to the store secure in the knowledge that you will be able to purchase those headphones at a competitive price, you are relying on what Adam Smith called the "invisible hand" of market forces to effectively allocate resources and set prices. In this chapter, you will examine how the two basic market forces—supply and demand— work together to produce the invisible hand of the market. We'll introduce you to a simple supply and demand model that helps explain how prices and quantities are determined. Later on in the chapter, we'll use the model to examine *changes* in prices—that is, why gas suddenly costs a dollar more.

The supply and demand model does not explain all prices in the economy. But every firm—from large corporations down to individuals running their own small businesses—must evaluate consumer demand when determining how much to charge for a product or service. The supply and demand model introduced in this chapter is a cornerstone of both economics and business.

Chapter Learning Targets

- Identify the concepts underlying a demand curve and a supply curve.

- Describe how market supply and market demand determine equilibrium.

- Recognize the key factors that shift demand.

- Recognize the key factors that shift supply.

- Determine what happens when both the supply curve and demand curve shift.

3.1 SUPPLY AND DEMAND IN COMPETITIVE MARKETS

As you will discover, the forces that determine prices are fairly simple: Buyers want to purchase goods and services and sellers want to sell them. Actual and potential buyers as a group determine demand, while actual and potential sellers as a group determine supply.

The model introduced in this chapter applies to **competitive markets**: markets that have many buyers and many sellers. Prices are determined collectively by the interaction of all buyers and all sellers. In a competitive market, no one person or company controls the market price.

Consider the market for pizza. If Mario owns a pizza shop in a town with competition from many other pizzerias, then his business is in a relatively competitive market: Neither Mario nor any other single pizza seller or buyer can alone determine the market price. However, if Mario owns the only pizza shop in town, he has considerably more influence on the prices he can charge.

In this chapter, we introduce a supply and demand model to analyze what determines prices where many buyers and sellers interact, say, a town with a dozen pizzerias. In most markets, there is at least some degree of competition; thus, the insights gained in this chapter apply to a wide variety of business settings. We begin by examining consumer demand.

> **Think & Speak Like an Economist**
>
> Competitive markets have many buyers and many sellers; thus, no one firm sets the market price. In contrast, a market with a single seller (a monopoly) is not competitive.

Demand

It is important to recognize that *demand* and *quantity demanded* have two distinct meanings in economics. The **quantity demanded (Q_d)** is the amount of a particular good that buyers are willing and able to purchase at a specific price. In contrast, when economists use the more general term *demand*, they are referring to the amount consumers would buy at *each and every* hypothetical price and not just at one *particular* price.

The Law of Demand: Lower Prices Motivate Buyers Have you ever come upon a cool new gadget that was priced so high you held back on buying it—even though you really wanted it? Perhaps you opted for a less expensive, but similar item. Or maybe you told yourself, "I'll wait until the price falls, then I'll buy one." In either case, your thought process reflects a fundamental idea of economics known as the law of demand.

The **law of demand** states that a negative relationship exists between price and quantity demanded, *ceteris paribus*. It states that, other things equal, as the price of a given item increases the quantity demanded of that item decreases, and as price falls the quantity demanded increases. This negative relationship reflects what many people see as just common sense (or, in economic terms, *rational behavior*): As the benefit from doing something increases, people and firms do more of it, and as the cost of doing something increases, people and firms do less of it. From a consumer perspective, increasing the price of a product makes it more costly to buy, and people will respond by purchasing less, other things equal. The law of demand can be summarized as

$$\downarrow P \text{ results in } \uparrow Q_d$$

$$\uparrow P \text{ results in } \downarrow Q_d$$

The law of demand results from the income effect and the substitution effect. The **income effect** is the change in the quantity demanded of a good when price changes alter the purchasing power of consumers. For example, as the price of pizza falls, consumers have more total purchasing power, which they could use to buy more pizza and/or more of other goods as well. A higher price has the reverse effect. The income effect is especially important when the product makes up a significant portion of the consumer budget: A two-fold increase in the cost of rent, for example, will have a much larger income effect than doubling the price of a pizza.

Of course, if the price of pizza doubles, consumers may choose to purchase other goods instead of pizza. The **substitution effect** is the change in the quantity demanded of a good

competitive markets Markets that have many buyers and many sellers.

quantity demanded (Q_d) The amount of a particular good that buyers are willing and able to purchase at a specific price.

law of demand The economic principle stating that a negative relationship exists between price and quantity demanded, *ceteris paribus*.

income effect The change in the quantity demanded of a good when price changes alter the purchasing power of consumers.

substitution effect The change in the quantity demanded of a good when price changes result in consumers switching from relatively high-priced products to relatively low-priced products.

EXHIBIT 1 Individual Demand Schedule and Demand Curve

Panel A: Ann's Demand Schedule

Price (per pizza)	Quantity (of pizza)
$30	1
25	2
20	3
15	4
10	5

Panel B: Ann's Demand Curve

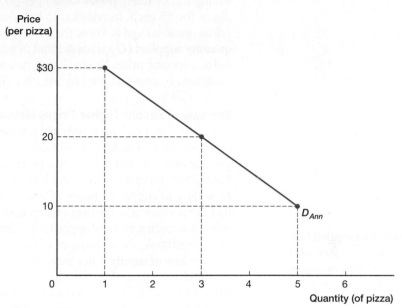

Data in the demand schedule (Panel A) are used to graph the demand curve (Panel B). Both demonstrate how many pizzas one individual (Ann) is willing to purchase at each price. As price falls, the quantity of pizza Ann demands increases. The law of demand states that a negative relationship exists between price and quantity demanded, *ceteris paribus*.

when price changes result in consumers switching from relatively high-priced products to relatively low-priced products. As the price of an item falls, it becomes relatively cheaper than an alternative product. The opposite occurs when an item increases in price.

Constructing the Demand Curve Suppose you ask your friend Ann how many pizzas she would buy each week at a price of $10 per pizza. Then you ask how many she would purchase if the price were $15, $20, $25, and $30. If you list her answers to all those questions, you end up with what is called a **demand schedule**, a table showing the quantity demanded of a good at each possible price.

Panel A of Exhibit 1 shows that Ann is willing to buy 1 pizza per week if they are priced at $30, but when the price of pizza falls to $10, Ann would purchase 5 pizzas per week. This demand schedule makes it clear how many pizzas Ann is willing to buy per week at each price.

The **demand curve** is a graph showing the quantity demanded of a good at each possible price and is a graphical representation of the demand schedule. You can think of either the demand schedule or the demand curve as describing the quantity demanded at each price. The data shown in Ann's demand schedule for pizza are used to graph Ann's demand curve for pizza in Panel B. In the downward-sloping demand curve for pizza, we see that as the price of pizza falls, Ann is willing to purchase greater quantities of pizza.

As is usually the case in economics, this relationship assumes *ceteris paribus:* We presume that Ann doesn't suddenly get a big raise, or find herself unable to cook meals at home, or develop an unexpected allergy to gluten—any of which would obviously change the way Ann feels about pizza. It is crucial to recall that only price varies along a given demand curve.

But what if other things *aren't* equal? Suppose one day the price of pizza rises to $30 *and* Ann gets a raise? Since *ceteris paribus* has been violated due to her higher salary, the existing demand curve no longer applies. These factors will change Ann's demand for pizza, and a new curve will need to be drawn. We will explore changes such as this later in the chapter.

demand schedule A table that shows the quantity demanded of a good at each possible price.

demand curve A graph showing the quantity demanded of a good at each possible price and is a graphical representation of the demand schedule.

Supply

Demand alone cannot determine the market price of a product. After all, Ann may be willing to buy many pizzas for $5 per pizza—but that doesn't mean Mario would sell his pizzas for $5 each. In addition to knowledge of consumer willingness to buy at different prices, we also need to know the quantity sellers are willing to supply at various prices. The **quantity supplied (Q_s)** is the amount of a particular good that sellers are willing and able to sell at a specific price. How will that vary as the price changes? If we assume that firms are motivated by profits, then a higher price should make sellers willing to supply more goods.

The Law of Supply: Higher Prices Motivate Sellers What do you think the labor supply would be for a *one-time* summer job cleaning the beach when the Summer Olympics come to town? Think of individuals as supplying labor and treat the hourly wage as the price of labor. At a very low price (wage), say, $1 per hour, individuals would supply very little labor. In contrast, at a very high price, say, $10,000 per hour, individuals will likely be willing to supply 15 hours of labor a day (or more), 7 days a week. For someone offered that much pay, the opportunity cost of *not* working is $10,000 per hour! Moreover, this is a once in a lifetime opportunity. Unfortunately for most of us, including the authors of this textbook, the quantity of labor demanded at such a high price is close to zero.

The **law of supply** states that a positive relationship exists between price and quantity supplied, *ceteris paribus*. This means that as the price of a given item increases the quantity supplied of that item increases, and as the price falls the quantity supplied decreases. Translated for our beach-cleaning example: When the wage (or price) rises, workers (or sellers of labor) are motivated to supply a larger quantity of labor, other things equal.

The law of supply can be summarized as

$$\uparrow P \text{ results in } \uparrow Q_s$$
$$\downarrow P \text{ results in } \downarrow Q_s$$

quantity supplied (Q_s) The amount of a particular good that sellers are willing and able to supply at a specific price.

law of supply The economic principle stating that a positive relationship exists between price and quantity supplied, *ceteris paribus*.

EXHIBIT 2 Individual Supply Schedule and Supply Curve

Panel A: Mario's Supply Schedule

Price (per pizza)	Quantity (of pizza)
$30	5
25	4
20	3
15	2
10	1
5	0

Panel B: Mario's Supply Curve

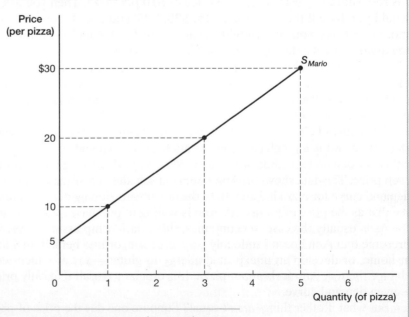

Data in the supply schedule (Panel A) are used to graph the supply curve (Panel B). Both demonstrate how many pizzas one seller (Mario) is willing to supply at each price. As price increases, the quantity of pizza Mario supplies increases. The law of supply states that a positive relationship exists between price and quantity supplied, *ceteris paribus*.

For instance, if the city cannot find enough workers to clean the beaches at $10 per hour, it can raise the wage to $15 per hour. The quantity of labor supplied at $15 per hour will be greater than the quantity supplied at $10 per hour. The supply curve is upward-sloping because at a higher price sellers supply a larger quantity (Q_s). The reason is simple: It is more profitable to do so.

Constructing the Supply Curve The distinction between supply and quantity supplied mirrors the distinction between demand and quantity demanded: When economists use the term *supply*, they are referring to the amount firms would sell at *each and every* hypothetical price and not at one *particular* price. Suppose you ask Mario how many pizzas he is willing to supply at various price points. The set of answers you receive is called a **supply schedule**, a table showing the quantity supplied of a good at each possible price.

As with the law of demand, the law of supply for a given item is more commonly expressed by a supply curve. The **supply curve** is a graph showing the quantity supplied of a good at each possible price and is a graphical representation of the supply schedule. When economists talk about "supply," they are referring to the entire supply curve—*not* the specific quantity supplied at any point on the curve.

Mario's supply schedule and supply curve are presented in Exhibit 2. Notice that as the price increases, the number of pizzas Mario is willing to sell rises. The opposite occurs as the price falls. In both circumstances, a change in price leads to a change in "quantity supplied" in the same direction. This reflects the positive relationship—depicted graphically as an upward-sloping curve—between price and quantity supplied.

Bloomberg/Getty Images

∧ Millions of buyers and sellers come together.

3.2 MARKET DEMAND, MARKET SUPPLY, AND EQUILIBRIUM

In the previous section, we learned how to derive Ann's demand curve and Mario's supply curve. But how do we bring Ann and Mario together in the marketplace? What determines the actual price of pizzas and the quantity bought and sold? To answer these questions, we need to understand how supply and demand interact. And to do this, we must consider three key concepts: market demand, market supply, and market equilibrium.

Markets Reflect All Buyers and All Sellers

When all buyers are considered, we obtain the demand for the entire market. **Market demand** is the sum of all buyers' quantity demanded at each price. Let's simplify the math by assuming the market for pizza consists of three buyers: Ann, Bill, and Chris. The demand schedule for each of these individuals is shown in Exhibit 3. To estimate the market demand, we simply add up the quantity each individual is willing to purchase at each price. This addition generates the market demand schedule in Exhibit 3.

Notice that the market demand curve has a negative slope to reflect the negative relationship between price and quantity demanded. As price falls, the quantity demanded by the market rises, reflecting the law of demand. When compared to individual demand, the market demand has similar prices on the *y*-axis (vertical), but much larger quantities on the *x*-axis (horizontal). Demand can be estimated for many different-sized markets, from small towns, which might produce 100 pizzas a day, to large cities, which might produce 100,000.

supply schedule A table that shows the quantity supplied of a good at each possible price.

supply curve A graph showing the quantity supplied of a good at each possible price and is a graphical representation of the supply schedule.

market demand The sum of quantity demanded for all buyers, at each price.

EXHIBIT 3   Market Demand Schedule and Market Demand Curve

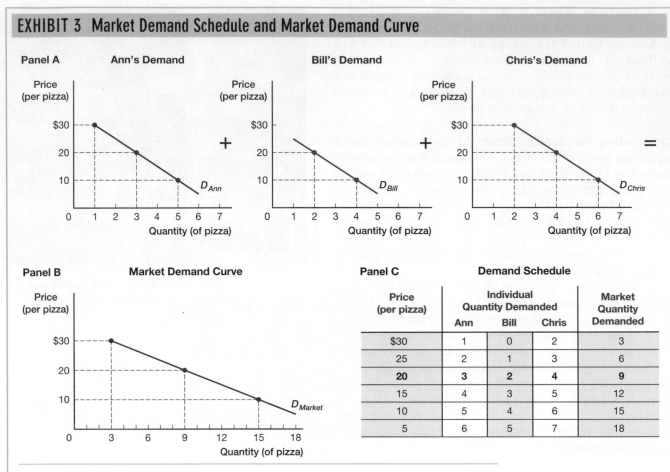

Data in the market demand schedule are used to graph the market demand curve. Market demand is calculated by summing the quantity demand by all individuals at each price. At a price of $20, Ann demands 3, Bill demands 2, and Chris demands 4 pizzas— thus, the quantity demanded by the market demand is 9. Market demand curves are generally negatively sloped.

Just as all buyers as a group determine market demand, all sellers as a group determine market supply. **Market supply** is the sum of all the sellers' quantity supplied at each price. Suppose a market consists of three pizza sellers: Mario, Tony, and Celia. To estimate the market supply, we simply add up the quantity each pizza seller wishes to produce at each price. The addition generates the market supply schedule. Notice the positive slope of the market supply curve, as shown in Panel B of Exhibit 4: As price rises, the quantity supplied by the market also rises, reflecting the law of supply.

Unless otherwise indicated, we use market supply and market demand curves throughout this book. The basic principles of the supply and demand model don't change when we generalize to markets with millions of consumers and thousands of firms: Lower prices continue to encourage consumers to buy more, and higher prices continue to encourage producers to sell more.

Equilibrium: Where Supply Meets Demand

market supply The sum of quantity supplied for all sellers, at each price.

Just as a pair of scissors needs both of its blades in order to work correctly, the supply and demand model requires both curves to determine price and quantity. If we plot the market supply and market demand curves on the same graph, we can determine the point where quantity supplied equals quantity demand.

EXHIBIT 4 Market Supply Schedule and Market Supply Curve

Panel A

Mario's Supply   Tony's Supply   Celia's Supply

Panel B Market Supply

Panel C Supply Schedule

Price (per pizza)	Individual Quantity Supplied			Market Quantity Supplied
	Mario	Tony	Celia	
$30	5	4	6	15
25	4	3	5	12
20	3	2	4	9
15	2	1	3	6
10	1	0	2	3

Data in the market supply schedule are used to graph the market supply curve. Market supply is calculated by summing the quantity supplied by all businesses at each price. At a price of $20, Mario supplies 3, Tony supplies 2, and Celia supplies 4 pizzas—thus, the quantity supplied by the market is 9. The technique used to estimate market supply is analogous to the technique used to estimate market demand. Market supply curves are generally positively sloped.

At this point, a balance occurs as the quantity consumers want to buy equals the quantity producers wish to sell, and the market is said to be in equilibrium. **Equilibrium** is the quantity and price at which quantity supplied equals quantity demanded; graphically, it is the point where the market supply curve intercepts the market demand curve. Equilibrium tells us two things: the *equilibrium price* and the *equilibrium quantity*. On a pair of scissors, equilibrium would be where the two blades meet.

For example, Panel A of Exhibit 5 combines our market supply and market demand curves for pizza. The point where the two curves intersect determines the equilibrium price ($20) and the equilibrium quantity (9 pizzas). Later in this chapter, we will return to this graph to show what happens to market price and quantity when market conditions change.

How Price Adjusts When the Market Is Not at Equilibrium

As you may have guessed, markets are not always in equilibrium: If pizza sellers find themselves with a lot of unsold pizzas at the end of the day, or not enough pizzas, they have been assessing demand for their pizza inaccurately and charging the wrong price.

equilibrium The quantity and price at which quantity supplied equals quantity demanded, it is the point where the market supply curve intercepts the market demand curve.

EXHIBIT 5   Equilibrium, Surplus, and Shortage

Panel A: Markets in Equilibrium

Panel B: Markets Moving Toward Equilibrium

At a price of $30, $Q_s = 15$ while $Q_d = 3$, a surplus of 12 units.

At a price of $10, $Q_d = 15$ while $Q_s = 3$, a shortage of 12 units.

At equilibrium, the quantity supplied equals the quantity demanded. In Panel A, the equilibrium price is $20 and the equilibrium quantity is 9. In Panel B, at a price of $30, a surplus (excess supply) of 12 units exists because the quantity supplied (15) is greater than the quantity demanded (3). This puts downward pressure on the price, which increases the quantity demanded and decreases the quantity supplied. At a price of $10, a shortage (excess demand) of 12 units exists because the quantity demanded (15) is greater than the quantity supplied (3). This puts upward pressure on the price, which increases the quantity supplied and decreases the quantity demanded. When price is not at equilibrium, it is moving toward it.

Items that sell out very quickly, such as tickets to concerts or championship sporting events, may also reflect charging the wrong price—this time one that is too low for the event.

In a competitive free market, the price moves to balance quantity supplied and quantity demanded, at least when enough time elapses to allow for price adjustments to occur. This is shown in Panel B of Exhibit 5. While market forces move prices toward equilibrium, the price may not *always* be at equilibrium. If the price being charged—which we'll refer to as the *going price*—is too high or too low, the market will not be at equilibrium.

A Surplus Occurs When the Going Price Is Too High Consider what will happen if the going price is too high (i.e., if the going price is above equilibrium). This occurs in our hypothetical pizza market when the going price is $30. Here, the quantity demanded is 3 while the quantity supplied is 15, a surplus of 12 units ($= 15 - 3$). A **surplus** is an excess of quantity supplied over quantity demanded that occurs at prices above equilibrium, which creates an unstable situation for the market. A surplus is sometimes called *excess supply*.

The high price results in many potential sellers with few potential buyers. When the market price is $30, we have 12 more units supplied than demanded. That's a lot of unsold pizza. If the price is $25, there will be a smaller surplus of 6 units because price is closer to equilibrium.

What is likely to occur under such circumstances? In general, prices fall. This is because businesses eventually make a decision that the only way to sell their surplus of goods is to lower price to entice more customers. This is usually a better option than throwing away the surplus goods. A lower price increases the quantity demanded.

surplus An excess of quantity supplied over quantity demanded that occurs at prices above equilibrium, which creates an unstable situation for the market; also called *excess supply*.

Mario, for example, might lower his prices during the last few hours of the evening in order to sell the last few pizzas. Other businesses selling more durable goods might opt to lower prices in order to move surplus merchandise. You frequently see this kind of price cutting occur in "after holiday" sales, or at the end of a season, when clothing retailers need to make room for new stock.

A Shortage Occurs When the Going Price Is Too Low

What will happen if pizza sellers start charging less than the equilibrium price? If the going price is too low, they will likely experience a shortage. A **shortage** is an excess of quantity demanded over quantity supplied that occurs at prices below equilibrium, which creates an unstable situation for the market. A shortage is sometimes called *excess demand*.

As shown in Panel B of Exhibit 5, if the price of pizza is $10, the quantity demanded will be 15 units while the quantity supplied will be 3 units, a shortage of 12 units (= 15 − 3). If the price is $15, there will be a smaller shortage of 6 units because price is closer to equilibrium.

What is likely to occur under such circumstances? In general, prices rise. This is because businesses eventually realize they can sell all their products at a higher price. In general, market forces will push the price up, lowering the quantity demanded and increasing the quantity supplied.

Hardout/Getty Images

∧ When a popular artist like Kendrik Lamar goes on tour, StubHub snaps up tickets at face value—and sells them to fans at the equilibrium price.

BUSINESS BRIEF StubHub Steps into the Concert Market

Have you tried to get tickets to a concert or sporting event where not enough tickets were available to meet demand? As we've noted, a shortage creates an unstable situation for the market. In economic terms, the reason there is a shortage is not that Beyoncé just doesn't perform at enough shows—it's that she's pricing her tickets below the equilibrium price.

Ticket resellers like StubHub are happy to gobble up tickets quickly and earn a profit by charging a price higher than the original face value of the ticket. On January 18, 2017, ticket resellers bought any remaining seats for a U2 concert in Cleveland—and started reselling them the same day. The concert was not scheduled until July.*

Such resellers would not exist if tickets were always priced at equilibrium, because they would be unable to resell them at higher prices. The fact that resellers appear in markets out of equilibrium shows how market forces are continually probing for an equilibrium price, especially when the initial price is not at equilibrium. When resellers guess wrong about the equilibrium price, they may lose money, as when a concert is less popular than expected or when an artist adds additional performances to meet demand.

*Troy L. Smith, "U2's FirstEnergy Stadium Show Sells Out, Resale Demand Soars," *Cleveland.com*, January 18, 2017, http://www.cleveland.com/entertainment/index.ssf/2017/01/u2s_firstenergy_stadium_show_s.html.

shortage An excess of quantity demanded over quantity supplied that occurs at prices below equilibrium, which creates an unstable situation for the market; also called *excess demand*.

Prices Move Toward Equilibrium In free markets, prices are generally at or moving toward equilibrium. When the going price is too high, a surplus occurs; this tends to put downward pressure on the price, pushing it toward the equilibrium price. When the going price is too low, a shortage exists; this tends to put upward pressure on the price, pushing it toward the equilibrium price. When the going price is the equilibrium price, the price is stable and unlikely to change until some event causes either the supply curve or demand curve to shift.

📊 BUSINESS BRIEF Want to See *Star Wars* for $320?

In 1977, 20th Century Fox released the first *Star Wars* film. The movie was hugely successful, ultimately securing the second-highest inflation-adjusted box office receipts of any movie. Meanwhile, a new technology was emerging that allowed individuals to watch their favorite movies at home: videocassettes. 20th Century Fox knew it had a popular film on its hands, but did not know what price to charge as the demand curve for any new product is something of a mystery until companies actually see how much consumers will purchase at various prices. At the time, many other videocassettes sold in the $40 range—most frequently to video rental stores. But this was *Star Wars*! Clearly, the demand for *Star Wars* would be higher. In June 1982, 20th Century Fox released the film on videocassette at $125, primarily to video rental stores. Adjusted for inflation, this equates to over $320 in 2018. The movie initially failed to make Billboard's Top 40 Video Cassettes list. In September 1982, the $125 price was lowered to $80 and the film quickly hit number two on the Billboard charts despite still being priced noticeably higher than its rivals.* Discovering the demand curve for a new or unique product is usually educated guesswork. Demand for *Star Wars* was strong, but not as strong as the movie studio originally estimated.

*Billboard Magazine Archive, n.d., accessed May 04, 2017, http://www.billboard.com/magazine-archive; "Star Wars on Home Video: A History," *Calameo.com*, n.d., accessed May 04, 2017, http://en.calameo.com /read/0002479280fd15fbfe411.

3.3 SHIFTS IN DEMAND: CAUSES AND CONSEQUENCES

Equilibrium is a good starting point, but the supply and demand model is most useful as a tool when a change in underlying market conditions affects equilibrium. The most important use of the supply and demand model is to explain what causes those changes, and how they affect the marketplace. Let's start with the demand side.

Changes in Quantity Demanded versus Changes in Demand

It is crucial to remember that *demand* is consumer willingness to buy a product at every possible price: It is the entire relationship between price and quantity demanded, the entire demand curve on the graph. In contrast, we saw that *quantity demanded* is the amount that people want to buy at one specific price—just one point on the line. Why is this distinction important? Because *quantity demanded can change without any change in overall demand*.

The demand curve in Exhibit 6 shows what quantity of pizzas will be demanded at each price. If price is the only factor that changes, we simply move along the curve and there is a change in quantity demanded. There is no change in demand (no curve shift) but quantity demanded changes. It's easy to remember that price is the only factor that moves you along the demand curve, because it is the only factor shown on the *y*-axis.

EXHIBIT 6 Changes in Quantity Demanded

Price changes result in changes in quantity demanded and movement along the demand curve. In this case, a price decrease from $30 to $20 increases quantity demanded from 3 to 9 pizzas.

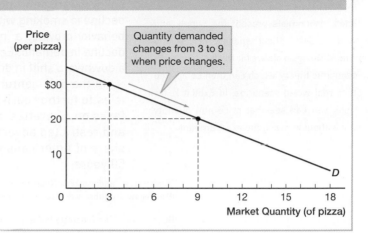

When there is a price change:

- It leads to a *change in quantity demanded* (not demand).
- There will be a movement along the demand curve.
- *Ceteris paribus* holds: Other economic and business conditions do not change demand.

What happens if other economic and business conditions do change in a manner that impacts buyers, violating the *ceteris paribus* assumption? For example, what will result should the media report a link between the mozzarella cheese used in pizza and an outbreak of *E-coli* bacteria, which causes severe gastrointestinal illness? Or what happens to the demand for pizza in a college town when students return from summer break? Both of these cases indicate a change in market conditions: The market will obviously demand less pizza if people believe it will make them ill, and likely demand more pizza when the student population increases.

When buyers are affected by a change in something other than price, the prior demand curve is no longer relevant. Instead, the curve will shift, creating a new demand curve. When demand decreases as shown in Panel A of Exhibit 7, the demand curve shifts leftward. As a result, the equilibrium price and quantity decrease. Conversely, when demand increases, as shown in Panel B, the demand curve shifts rightward, while both equilibrium price and quantity increase.

When something *other than a price change* impacts the amount that buyers wish to purchase:

- It is called a *change in demand* (and not a change in quantity demanded).
- The demand curve shifts to the left if demand decreases.
- The demand curve shifts to the right if demand increases.
- It results in a new equilibrium price and quantity.

POLICY BRIEF Cancer Warning Shifts the Demand for Cigarettes

In 1964, the U.S. Surgeon General released a report that linked cigarettes smoking to cancer.* Consumers clearly found the Surgeon General report credible: Cigarette sales quickly declined by 11 billion to 514 billion from 1963, with non-filtered cigarettes seeing a particularly steep decline. Economist George Hay of Cornell University called

Think & Speak Like an Economist

At times, economists present the supply and demand model without specific prices and quantities. Doing so allows for the focus to be on the economic theory, which can then be applied to other real-world scenarios. In Exhibit 7, for example, you can see that price and quantity change without knowing the exact amount.

the 1964 report "a watershed," noting that it marked a significant change in policy toward smoking and the tobacco industry, and prompted a long-term decline in smoking within the United States. The sudden change in consumer behavior provides a "natural experiment" demonstrating the effects of a decline in demand: Economists were able to examine real data and detected a downward shift in demand and no shift in supply.[†]

In the half-century since, lawmakers have enacted numerous policies to further curb the demand for cigarettes, including additional taxes on cigarettes, age restrictions on sales, public health campaigns, and restricted advertisements by cigarette sellers. As a result, the share of Americans who smoke has continued to decline over the past 50 years.

[*]"Cigarettes—and the 1964 Report of the Surgeon General's Advisory Committee," n.d., accessed May 04, 2017, http://www.druglibrary.org/schaffer/library/studies/cu/cu26.html.

[†]George Hay, "The Cigarette Industry," in *The Structure of American Industry*, ed. James W. Brock (Upper Saddle River, NJ: Pearson/Prentice Hall, 2009).

Factors That Can Shift the Demand Curve

When the price of the good itself changes, we simply move along an existing demand curve and quantity demanded changes. However, when factors other than price change, such as income, exchange rates, and buyers' expectations, the entire demand curve will shift. In this section, we'll examine some of the factors known to shift the demand curve.

EXHIBIT 7   Decrease and Increase in Demand

If demand decreases, the demand curve shifts to the left from D_1 to D_2. The result is a lower equilibrium price and a lower equilibrium quantity. Demand may decrease if an item is found to create a health risk or for a variety of other reasons. If demand increases, the demand curve shifts to the right (Panel B). Here, the demand curve shift from D_1 to D_2. The result is a higher equilibrium price and a higher equilibrium quantity. Demand may increase if the population increases or for a variety of other reasons.

Changes in Income and Macroeconomic Conditions As incomes increase, the demand for most goods and services increases. A **normal good** is a good for which demand increases as incomes increase, and demand decreases as incomes decrease. You can see this in your own budget all the time—as your income increases, you spend more money on many goods and services, such as clothes, dining out, or video-streaming subscriptions such as HBO Now, Hulu, or Netflix. All these products are normal goods that see an increase in demand when incomes rise during an economic boom.

In contrast, consider how you might respond if your boss cuts work hours or if you lose your job: You might eat out at restaurants less frequently, cancel your premium TV channels, or start making your own coffee at home instead of buying it at Starbucks. Consumers demand less of normal goods when average incomes decline, such as during a recession.

Panel B of Exhibit 7 shows what happens to the demand for ocean cruises as incomes rise. In this case, the demand for cruises increases: Because cruises are popular with more affluent consumers, demand for cruises rises rapidly as a country gets richer. In fast-growing China, the number of cruise passengers soared from 216,000 in 2012 to 1 million in 2015, as Chinese incomes rose. The results are a higher price and quantity for these products. To summarize:

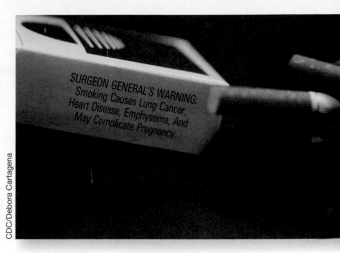

∧ Cigarettes can cause cancer, but do cancer warnings shift the demand for cigarettes?

↓ incomes *decreases* demand of normal goods

↑ incomes *increases* demand of normal goods

Not all goods are normal goods; there are some goods for which demand actually *decreases* as incomes increase. An **inferior good** is a good for which demand decreases as incomes increase, and demand increases as incomes decrease. Examples of inferior goods include frozen pizza, public transportation, and prepaid cell phones. Demand for these products would be expected to fall as incomes rise.

Consider the market for coffee. Takeout coffee from Starbucks is a normal good—the opening of a Starbucks shop, in fact, is often pointed to as an indicator of rising incomes in a particular neighborhood. In contrast, Folgers ground coffee sold at most supermarkets is an inferior good, as those with lower incomes are more likely to brew their own coffee at home. Coffee sales are also frequently indicative of the overall economy: In 2008 and 2009, in the midst of the Great Recession, Starbucks closed more than 900 stores and laid off 18,000 employees. Market demand for normal goods typically declines during a recession. During this same time period, Procter & Gamble, makers of Folgers, saw their coffee sales increase 55%.[1] To summarize:

↓ incomes *increases* demand of inferior goods

↑ incomes *decreases* demand of inferior goods

📊 BUSINESS BRIEF Market Segmentation at Gap

Many businesses diversify with multiple product lines. The apparel corporation Gap operates several brands, including the down-market Old Navy, mid-range Gap stores, and high-end retailer Banana Republic. The benefit of this strategy is two-fold. First, it allows Gap to capture sales at a variety of income levels. This combination of inferior and normal goods enables the company to compete in different market segments.

Second, it protects Gap sales in a variety of macroeconomic environments—particularly recessions. In 2009, in the depths of the Great Recession, Old Navy saw a 4% overall increase in its sales from the prior year, even as the unemployment rate crept up to 10%. Increased sales of inferior goods at Old Navy helped to offset a decline in sales

normal good A good for which demand increases as incomes increase, and demand decreases as incomes decrease.

inferior good A good for which demand decreases as incomes increase, and demand increases as incomes decrease.

at Gap and Banana Republic, and allowed the company to increase its profits.* In 2017, sales at Old Navy remained stronger than at its higher-end siblings, as many consumers' incomes remained flat; this suggests that the market for inferior goods remained robust.† Gap realized that more than one market existed for apparel and tailored its business strategy to capture each market segment.

*Gap Annual Report, 2009, http://media.corporate-ir.net/media_files/IROL/11/111302/GPS_AR_09.pdf.

†Phil Wahba, "Gap Inc Stock Soars After Strong Holiday Season Sales Results," *Fortune.com*, January 5, 2017, http://fortune.com/2017/01/05/gap-sales/.

Changes in Price of Related Goods Recall that a change in the price of a product simply moves us along the demand curve for that specific product. But sometimes, the price of one good can affect the demand for *another* product. In that case, a price change for one good will *shift* the demand curve of a second good.

Complements are products that are usually consumed together, and for which an increase in the price of one good reduces the demand for another good, and vice versa. Economists define two goods to be complements if and only if the lower price of one good increases (shifts) the demand for the other (complement) good. Printers, for example, are often sold at very low prices, because companies that make printers know they will be able to sell more toner cartridges in the future by doing so. In fact, ink is among printer maker Hewlett-Packard's (HP) biggest moneymakers. Similarly, shaving razors and replacement blades manufactured by Gillette and Schick are also complements: Lowering the price of the razor tends to increase the demand for the blades. Additional examples of products that are complements include gaming consoles and video games; e-book readers and e-books; smartphones and data plans; tablet computers and chargers, covers, and other accessories.[2] To summarize:

↑ price of another good *decreases* demand when goods are complements

↓ price of another good *increases* demand when goods are complements

In other cases, one product is an *alternative* to another. **Substitutes** are products that serve the same purpose, and for which an increase in the price of one good increases the demand for another good, and vice versa. For example, if McDonald's cuts the price of Big Macs, they will become a more attractive alternative for consumers of pizza—thus, some consumers will buy Big Macs instead of pizza. As they do so, the demand for pizza will decline, shifting the demand curve for pizza to the left. The end result is a lower price and lower sales of pizza, as shown in Panel A of Exhibit 7. The opposite happens if McDonald's raises its price for a Big Mac. The demand for pizza will increase.

↑ price of another good *increases* demand when goods are substitutes

↓ price of another good *decreases* demand when goods are substitutes

complements Products that are usually consumed together, and for which an increase in the price of one good reduces the demand for another good, and vice versa.

substitutes Products that serve the same purpose, and for which an increase in the price of one good increases the demand for another good, and vice versa.

∧ With three major brands at different price points, Gap Inc. protects its sales from a variety of economic conditions.

Not all goods are complements or substitutes; more often than not, other goods are *unrelated* in any meaningful way. A change in the price of roses would have almost no impact on the demand for pizza, for example, nor would a change in the price of pizza affect the demand for ocean cruises.

Changes in Buyers' Expectations Buyers form expectations of where prices and incomes are likely to go in the future, and changes in those expectations can affect demand for goods and services. If consumers expect dealers to lower prices on new cars at the end of the year, they are less likely to purchase a car in July; demand would decrease during the summer, causing a decline in both quantity and price, as shown in Panel A of Exhibit 7. Conversely, if buyers expect a product to cost more at some point in the future, it would increase demand today (Panel B). Price expectations are especially important for major purchases, such as cars and homes, and for financial assets such as stock.

Demand is also affected by buyers' income expectations. Even a consumer with a steady income may be reluctant to take out a six-year car loan if he or she is concerned about a reduction in income in the future. Such fears can be based on macroeconomic trends (such as rising unemployment rates), anecdotal evidence (the recent layoff of a friend or colleague), or personal factors (e.g., anticipated unpaid parental leave after the birth of a child).

The reverse occurs when incomes are expected to increase. College seniors fortunate enough to land a job prior to graduation often expect an increase in their future income. Even before their actual income has changed, the expectation of higher future income will increase their demand for normal goods, such as spring break vacations.

Changes in Tastes and Preferences Tastes and preferences often change over time, and an entire industry is devoted to making those changes happen. When firms advertise, they are attempting to increase demand, that is, to shift the demand curve for their products outward. Products that become suddenly fashionable—whether due to advertising or other market trends—see an increase in demand, as shown in Panel B of Exhibit 8. The results are a higher price and higher sales. Conversely, products that become unfashionable see a decline in demand (Panel A).

Changes in Population and Demographics An increase in population results in higher demand for most goods. But, of course, not all members of the population are potential buyers for any given product. Demographic factors—that is, the way a population breaks down by age, gender, socioeconomic status, culture, languages spoken, and so on—also affect the demand for a good or service. As the huge baby boomer generation hits retirement age, the percentage of Americans aged 65 and older is rising dramatically, which will increase the demand for products aimed at older consumers. Nursing home providers such as HCR ManorCare, Golden Living, and Life Care Centers of America each offer over 30,000 beds to seniors and continue to add more. As our society gradually ages, businesses need to anticipate the direction in which demand is likely to shift.[3]

Changes in Taxes and Subsidies Governments can create disincentives by taxing the buyers of items such as cigarettes and grocery bags. When a buyer is taxed on a purchase, demand decreases because the buyer must now pay both the seller and the tax. The intent of policymakers of such a tax is frequently to reduce demand. We will discuss taxes in detail in a later chapter.

Similarly, governments can provide incentives by offering subsidies to buyers of goods such as electric cars. A *subsidy* is the opposite of a tax; the government gives you money to encourage you to buy a product. It is an attempt by the government to incentivize certain behaviors—and thus increase demand. Subsidies are important in health care, the environment, education, and other areas where the government believes that more output would benefit society.

Change in Exchange Rates Recall from Chapter 2 that exchange rates are the rate at which you can trade one country's currency for another. If the U.S. dollar *depreciates*, American-made goods, priced in dollars, will be less expensive for consumers outside the United States—which will increase demand for U.S. goods abroad.

For example, how will a depreciating dollar impact the global demand for Florida orange juice? Foreign consumers will perceive all U.S. products to be less expensive (in their own money) due to the decline in the value of the U.S. dollar and demand more orange juice. The demand for Florida orange juice will shift to the right. The change in exchange rates reflects a change in something other than the dollar price for Florida orange juice, so the entire curve shifts. Conversely, if the dollar *appreciates*, the demand for Florida orange juice will decline as American goods priced in dollars will become more expensive for foreigners.

To sum up, when the price of the good itself changes, we move along an existing demand curve and quantity demanded changes (not demand). However, other factors such as income, exchange rates, and buyers' expectations do not appear on either axis of the supply and demand model. A change in any of these factors requires shifting the demand curve, essentially creating a new demand curve. A change in price will change quantity demanded and result in movement along an existing demand curve. A change in other factors will change demand and shift the demand curve.

> ### Think & Speak Like an Economist
>
> The distinction between a change in *demand* and a change in *quantity demanded* is crucial. An increase in quantity demanded is associated with the *falling* price of a good and represented by movement along an existing demand curve. In contrast, an increase in demand means the entire demand curve shifts to the right and results in a *rising* price.

⊞ BUSINESS BRIEF Chrysler Sales Fall to Lowest Level Since 1962!

In 2009, in the midst of the Great Recession, automobile sales in the United States fell to 10.4 million units from 16.1 million units two years earlier. Particularly hard hit were SUVs and other automobiles categorized as "light-duty vehicles," which saw a decline of 42% in unit sales during the same time period. Chrysler and General Motors were hit especially hard, with their sales declining by roughly 50%.

Chrysler failed to sell 1 million cars for the first time since 1962. The company had sold over 2 million vehicles every year for the previous 15 years.[*] This sales slump can be explained if we assume that most automobiles are normal goods. As we've learned in this chapter, the demand for normal goods declines when incomes decline. The Great Recession also reduced consumer expectations of future income. While most workers remained employed, many of them nonetheless feared that they *might* lose their job. Consumers, on the whole, cut back on spending in an effort to save more, just in case. As the economy recovered and incomes increased, the demand for automobiles rebounded strongly.[†]

[*]Michelle Krebs, "The Auto Industry 2009 Wrapup: Apocalypse Now," *AutoObserver.com*, December 22, 2009, https://www.edmunds.com/autoobserver-archive/2009/12/the-auto-industry-2009-wrapup-apocalypse-now.html.

[†]Aaron M. Kessler, "2014 Auto Sales Jump in U.S., Even With Recalls," *The New York Times*, January 5, 2015, https://www.nytimes.com/2015/01/06/business/us-auto-sales-jump-for-2014.html.

3.4 SHIFTS IN SUPPLY: CAUSES AND CONSEQUENCES

We have seen that demand shifts occur frequently in our rapidly changing society. Now we need to consider the forces that affect supply. When we are finished, we will have arrived at the complete supply and demand model. Once again, it's important to distinguish between changes in *supply*, which is a shift in the entire supply curve, and *quantity supplied*, which is the amount supplied at a particular price.

Changes in Quantity Supplied versus Changes in Supply

Recall that along any given supply curve the only factor that changes is price. Changes to any other supply-related factor will shift the supply curve. The law of supply implies that when price rises, quantity supplied also rises.

In Panel A of Exhibit 8, the supply curve shows the quantities suppliers are willing to sell at various prices. Note that when price changes, the change in quantity is associated with movement along the supply curve. This results in a change in *quantity supplied*. It's easy to remember that price is the only factor that moves you along the supply curve, because it's the only factor shown on the *y*-axis.

To summarize, when a price change occurs:

- It leads to a change in *quantity supplied* (not supply).
- There will be a movement along the supply curve.
- *Ceteris paribus* holds. Other economic and business conditions do not change supply.

Of course, other economic and business conditions do change, and often. But before we can look at the factors that cause market conditions to change and shift the supply curve, we must first consider what it means for there to be a change in supply, where the old supply curve no longer applies. And we must consider the direction of the change.

EXHIBIT 8   Change in Quantity Supplied versus Change in Supply

Panel A: Quantity Supplied Changes When Price Changes

Price

Quantity supplied changes when price changes.

S

P_2

P_1

Q_1 Q_2 Quantity

Panel B: Change in Supply Shift Curve to the Left or Right

Price

Decrease in supply shifts curve to the left.

Starting Supply

$20

Increase in supply shifts curve to the right.

Quantity

In Panel A, price changes result in changes in quantity supplied and movement along the supply curve. In this case, a price increase results in an increase in the quantity supplied. In Panel B, a decrease in supply shifts the supply curve to the left (not down). An increase in supply shifts the supply curve to the right (not up). For example, at the price of $20, the supply curve on the left results in the lowest quantity supplied and the supply curve on the right results in the highest quantity supplied.

Decrease in Supply Shifts the Supply Curve to the Left We begin with the case of a sudden increase in production cost. Since it is more costly to make an item, businesses typically reduce supply. This is because the good being produced is less profitable. A decrease in supply shifts the supply curve to the left. Students often expect it to shift down—but in fact, a *decrease* in supply shifts the supply curve to the *left* (not down). A way to visualize this is to always consider which supply curve leads to the lowest quantity supplied at any given price. Panel B of Exhibit 8 shows that a decrease in supply will lead to fewer units (quantity) being sold when the price is $20. Panel A of Exhibit 9 also shows a decrease in supply (from S_1 to S_2), but also includes a demand curve. The result is a higher equilibrium price and a lower equilibrium quantity.

Increase in Supply Shifts the Supply Curve to the Right An *increase* in supply will shift the supply curve to the *right* (not up). Supply may increase if new technology lowers production cost, which increases the profitability of the good being produced. Once again, it is important to think in terms of right and left shifts, not up and down. Visualize which supply curve leads to the highest quantity supplied at any given price. In Panel B of Exhibit 9, shifting the supply curve to the right increases quantity supplied when the price is $20. Panel B of Exhibit 9 also shows an increase in supply (from S_1 to S_2), but includes a demand curve. The result is a lower equilibrium price and a higher equilibrium quantity.

When something other than price changes in a way that impacts supply:

- It is called a change in *supply* (not a change in quantity supplied).
- The supply curve shifts to the left if supply decreases.
- The supply curve shifts to the right if supply increases.
- Results in a new equilibrium price and quantity.

EXHIBIT 9 Decrease and Increase in Supply

Panel A: Decrease in Supply

Panel B: Increase in Supply

If supply decreases, the supply curve shifts to the left from S_1 to S_2 (Panel A). The result is a higher equilibrium price and a lower equilibrium quantity. Supply may decrease due to an increase in production cost or for a variety of other reasons. If supply increases, the supply curve shifts to the right from S_1 to S_2 (Panel B). The result is a lower equilibrium price and a higher equilibrium quantity. Supply may increase if new technology lowers production cost or for a variety of other reasons.

Factors That Can Shift the Supply Curve

When the price of the good itself changes, we simply move along an existing supply curve and quantity supplied changes. However, when factors other than price change, such as those that impact the cost of doing business, the entire supply curve will shift (a change in supply). In this section, we'll examine some of the factors that are known to shift the supply curve.

New Production Technology and Automation New technologies generally lower production cost and increase supply. Some innovations are easily identified—the effects of the printing press, the steam engine, and the Internet were palpable for most consumers. Other technological innovations are invisible to consumers, but they can have a huge impact on supply. Automated assembly lines, genetically modified crops, and advanced computer systems allow manufacturers and farmers to produce goods using fewer resources than ever before. For instance, one study showed that genetically modified cotton increased output per acre in India by as much as 63%, while the associated production costs (such as the use of insecticides) were cut by 82% when compared to those of nonmodified cotton.[4]

When production costs decrease, supply increases by shifting the supply curve to the right because it is more profitable for a business to make the products that buyers demand. This results in an increase in supply, increasing quantity and lowering price, as shown in Panel B of Exhibit 9.

Changes in Resource Cost Resource costs play a major role in the profitability of businesses. Higher resource costs reduce profitability and decrease supply, while lower resource costs increase profitability and increase supply. Consider what happens when there is a sizable increase in the legal minimum wage. Businesses that employ large numbers of minimum wage workers, such as fast-food restaurants, will see an increase in the cost of doing business. This would lead to a decrease in supply, shifting the supply curve to the left. The results are higher price and lower quantity, as shown in Panel A of Exhibit 9. A similar process occurs when the cost of cheese rises for Mario's pizzas or the price of crude oil rises for gasoline producers (oil is used to make gasoline). Producers will supply less pizza and gasoline under these circumstances. And if Mario's pizzeria delivers its pies, the higher gas prices will also reduce the supply of delivered pizza.

In contrast, lower resource costs increase the supply of products. Why? Because lower costs make it more profitable for a business to produce more at any given price. It also lowers the price for consumers. For example, in recent years, innovations in "fracking"—a technique for extracting oil or gas from underground rock—have significantly lowered the price of natural gas in the United States relative to prices in other countries. Because natural gas is an important resource in chemical manufacturing, foreign-owned companies such as BASF, Braskem and Royal Dutch Shell began building chemical plants in the United States. This increased the supply of chemicals manufactured in the United States.[5]

Changes in Profitability of Alternative Products What if salads became more profitable than pizza—for example, if the cost of ingredients in salads went down relative to those for pizza, or if consumers were suddenly willing to pay much more for salads than pizza? In that case, Mario may choose to supply less pizza (while supplying salads instead). This results in a reduction in the supply of pizzas and an increase in the price of pizza, as shown in Panel A of Exhibit 9. Note that what changed initially is the profitability of salads; pizza was indirectly affected. In contrast, if the profitability of calzones or oven-baked sandwiches decreases, pizza makers may switch to selling less of these products and supply more pizzas.

Entry and Exit of Sellers The entry of other sellers generally increases the amount of competition and lowers price. Graphically, this is equivalent to an increase in supply, as shown in Panel B of Exhibit 9. For example, consider what happens to Mario's pizzeria if Domino's and Papa John's enter the local market. More sellers, *ceteris paribus*, increase market supply, shifting the supply curve to the right. This puts downward pressure on price.

Earlier in the chapter, market supply was determined by adding together the output of all the sellers at each price point. This is why the entry of a new firm or expansion of the capacity of an existing firm results in greater market supply. Conversely, a reduction in the number of sellers decreases supply and puts upward pressure on price.

Supply Shocks In 2005, Hurricane Katrina devastated communities on the Gulf of Mexico and forced the shutdown of oil rigs and shrimping operations. Five years later, the *Deepwater Horizon*, an oil rig owned by BP, spilled vast quantities of oil into the Gulf of Mexico, and shrimp operations and oil rigs were again shut down. Economists refer to such unforeseeable events as supply shocks. A *supply shock* is a major unexpected disruption in production, often the result of natural disasters such as earthquakes, floods, and disease or extreme weather that affects farm output. However, man-made problems can also disrupt production—especially war, political instability, and labor strikes.

In the aftermath of both of these disasters, the supply of Gulf shrimp decreased, shifting the supply curve to the left and causing the price of shrimp to increase: In the weeks after the *Deepwater Horizon* oil spill, the price of shrimp increased by 50% in places as far away as South Carolina. Likewise, the supply of oil decreased, shifting the supply curve to the left and causing the price of oil to increase.[6]

Changes in Sellers' Expectations Sellers' expectations of future prices will play a role in supply. Suppose the sellers of newly constructed homes expect that in a few months the price of their homes will drop, perhaps due to a banking crisis making headline news. What will happen to their willingness to supply new homes *today*? Sellers will wish to get rid of their inventory of houses prior to the price decline and do so by increasing the amount they are *currently* willing to supply at each price. Note that what changed here is not price, but the sellers' expectation of the price in the future. This increases supply and reduces price, as shown in Panel B of Exhibit 9. The opposite occurs when sellers expect a higher price in the future.

To summarize:

- Current supply increases when sellers expect a lower price in the future.
- Current supply decreases when sellers expect a higher price in the future.

Thus, expectations of future price changes will cause current prices to change in the same direction. As we saw earlier, this is also true on the demand side. Price expectations are a major factor affecting the prices of financial assets such as stocks and bonds.

Changes in Regulations, Subsidies, and Taxes on Sellers When a seller is taxed, he or she tends to supply less of a product. This causes the price of the product to increase as the supply curve shifts to the left, as shown in Panel A of Exhibit 9. Conversely, if the government provides subsidies to sellers, supply will increase, the supply curve will shift to the right, and the price of the good will decline. For example, for many years, the U.S. government has subsidized the production and sale of ethanol, a gasoline substitute manufactured from crops such as corn, and more recently introduced subsidies to encourage the development of solar electricity and electric cars.

Regulations are rules enforced by government agencies restricting business practices. For example, Mario must make his pizzas in a manner that conforms with local food safety standards. Proponents argue that such regulations protect consumers, but they also impose extra costs on Mario, as he may need to buy more modern equipment (for instance, a better refrigerator), or provide expensive food safety training for his staff. These higher costs would decrease the amount of pizza he is able to supply at each price. The higher cost imposed on businesses through regulations results in a decline in supply and a higher price for output.

Think & Speak Like an Economist

The distinction between a change in *supply* and a change in *quantity supplied* is crucial. An increase in quantity supplied is often associated with a *rising* price and represented by movement along an existing supply curve. In contrast, an increase in supply means the entire supply shifts to the right and is associated with a *falling* price.

To sum up, when the price of the good itself changes, we move along an existing supply curve and quantity supplied changes (not supply). However, other factors such as production cost do not appear on either axis of the supply and demand model. A change in any of these factors requires shifting the supply curve, essentially creating a new supply curve. A change in price will change quantity supplied and result in movement along an existing supply curve. A change in other factors will change supply and shift the supply curve.

3.5 UNDERSTANDING AND PREDICTING MARKET CHANGES

We have seen how markets reach equilibrium and how market forces can change that equilibrium over time. To fully understand markets, however, it is essential to avoid the common mistake of reasoning from price changes. In addition, we explore more complex cases where *both* the supply and demand curves shift simultaneously.

Exhibit 10 reviews the four different ways in which changes in supply and demand can impact the market equilibrium. Note that there are two reasons price can fall: a decline in demand (Panel A) or an increase in supply (Panel D). Moreover, there are two reasons price can increase: an increase in demand (Panel B) or a decrease in supply (Panel C).

> Warning: Never Reason from a Price Change

When analyzing economic phenomena, where should you start? Many individuals—from students to financial reporters to businesspeople—begin by looking at price changes. This is a crucial mistake. In order to assess changes in a market, you should never reason from a price change, but always start one step earlier by asking what caused the price change? Was it due to a shift in supply, or to a shift in demand?

To better understand this concept, consider how you would answer the following question on an exam: Use the theory of supply and demand to explain why 100 people might go to the movies when the price is $6, and 300, might go when the price is $12.

Many students, perhaps you, would struggle to explain this in economic terms: Doesn't the law of demand say that people will buy fewer movie tickets when the price is high? Not exactly. If students are able to take a step back and consider why the price changed, the picture becomes clearer: High price might be *caused* by a shift in demand. Indeed, most theaters charge a lower "matinee" price in an attempt to draw in customers when demand is lower. Since many people are at work or school during the day, 100 people go to the movie when the price is $6. During the evening, the demand for movies increases, so more people attend movies at night (300), even though the price is higher ($12). Try it yourself. Draw a supply and demand curve for movies and show a shift in demand to the right, representing higher demand for movies in the evening than in the afternoon. It will look like Panel B of Exhibit 10.

There are two ways to avoid reasoning from a price change:

1. Try to identify the cause of the price change. Was it primarily a factor that is likely to affect the supply curve, or the demand curve?

2. Alternatively, observe both the change in price and the change in quantity. Draw a supply and demand diagram, look at how price and quantity change, and observe which curve shifted. For example, if both price and quantity increase, it must result from higher demand.

EXHIBIT 10 Market Effects of Changing Supply and Demand

Panel A: Decrease in Demand Decreases Price

- Lower income (recession) with normal goods
- Higher income with inferior goods
- Higher price of complements
- Lower price of substitutes
- Buyers' expectations of a lower price or lower income for normal goods in the future
- Buyers are taxed
- Goods become unfashionable
- Currency appreciates for exported goods

Panel B: Increase in Demand Increases Price

- Higher income with normal goods
- Lower income with inferior goods
- Lower price of complements
- Higher price of substitutes
- Buyers' expectations of a higher price or higher income for normal goods in the future
- Buyers are subsidized
- Goods become fashionable
- Currency depreciates for exported goods

Panel C: Decrease in Supply Increases Price

- Higher resource cost
- Lower profitability of products in joint supply
- Higher profitability of alternative products
- Exit of other sellers or a reduction in productive capacity
- Adverse supply shock
- Increased taxes or regulations on sellers
- Sellers' expectations of higher prices in future

Panel D: Increase in Supply Decreases Price

- New production technology lowers cost
- Lower resource cost
- Higher profitability of products in joint supply
- Lower profitability of alternative products
- Entry of other sellers or an increase in productive capacity
- Sellers' expectations of lower prices in future
- Decreased taxes or regulations on sellers
- Sellers' expectations of higher prices in future
- Sellers are subsidized

There are four different ways that changes in supply and demand can impact the market equilibrium. Price can fall from a decline in demand (Panel A) or an increase in supply (Panel D). Price can increase from an increase in demand (Panel B) or a decrease in supply (Panel C).

Unfortunately, even some experts occasionally reason from a price change. Here's an example from an article in the *Wall Street Journal* titled "Oil's Plunge Could Help Send Its Price Back Up":

> If something is cheaper, people will likely buy more of it. That core principle of economics is proving to be especially true with oil after its recent plunge.[7]

At first glance, this assertion sounds reasonable. But it is not completely accurate. If you take a closer look, you'll see that people would buy more only if the lower oil prices were caused by an increase in the supply of oil, such as a new discovery of oil (see Panel D of Exhibit 10). What if the price fell because of a decrease in the demand for oil, perhaps due to an economic slowdown? In this case, there would actually be lower prices *and* less oil purchased at the same time (Panel A of Exhibit 10).

Let's take another example. In 2017 just prior to hurricanes Harvey and Irma, gas prices spiked in many areas. Does this mean less quantity of gasoline was consumed? No, in fact the opposite occurred. As people evacuated and stocked up the demand for gasoline rose sharply, resulting in both higher prices and a larger quantity of gasoline sold. Many stations ran out of gas prior to the storms despite the price hike. See Panel B of Exhibit 10. If you learn to avoid reasoning from a price change, you will be far ahead of most economics students, and even some financial reporters.

Simultaneous Shifts in Both Supply and Demand

For simplicity, the effects of a shift in demand and a shift in supply are often analyzed separately. While focusing on one shift at a time makes it easier to learn the supply and demand model, in the real world, both curves frequently shift at the same time.

Increase in Supply and Decrease in Demand Consider the case where an economy goes into a recession. This reduces both labor costs (a supply factor) and incomes (a demand factor). In the automobile industry, lower incomes reduce the demand for automobiles, while lower labor costs increase supply, as shown in Exhibit 11.

Notice that we've presented three different possible outcomes: Quantity might have decreased (Panel A), increased (Panel B), or showed no change (Panel C). When the two curves shift in opposite directions (with one increasing and one decreasing), you *may not* be able to predict what will happen to quantity, but you can predict in which direction price will change. In all three panels, price decreases—this is because both an increase in supply and a decrease in demand lower price.

In Exhibit 11, for example, we cannot determine what happens to quantity without knowing the relative magnitudes of the two shifts. In the real world, when both labor costs and incomes decline, it is common to observe a large decrease in demand and a small increase in supply, as shown in Panel A. In that case, both shifts push prices lower, but we can now expect quantity to decline because the decline in demand is assumed to be larger than the increase in supply.

What if both curves change in the same direction? This is shown in Panels B and C of Exhibit 12. In that case, we know what happens to quantity. If both supply and demand increase, quantity will increase. And if both supply and demand decrease, quantity will decrease. But in each instance, it is unclear what happens to price. In general, when both curves shift, we can determine what happens to one variable, but not both.

EXHIBIT 11   Increase in Supply and Decrease in Demand

Panel A: Demand Shifts More Than Supply

Quantity decreases

Panel B: Supply Shifts More Than Demand

Quantity increases

Panel C: Equal Shifts

Depends on size of shifts

A recession causes a decline in labor cost and buyers' income. The result is an increase in supply and a decrease in the demand for normal goods. Both shifts cause price to decrease. What happens to quantity depends on the relative size of the shifts. Panel A shows a large decrease in demand, which results in a decrease in quantity. Panel B shows a large increase in supply, which results in an increase in quantity.

More Examples of Shifts in Both Supply and Demand Here are a few examples where the supply and demand curves change at the same time:

- **A major oil discovery near Mario's pizzeria** Assume a huge new oilfield is discovered near the town where Mario's shop is located. This will increase the demand for pizza, as oilfield workers head to Mario's for lunch, *and* reduce pizza supply, as Mario must now pay his workers much higher wages in order to prevent them from deserting him for better-paying jobs in the oilfield. Remember, if Mario has higher costs, his supply curve shifts to the left. The effects can be seen in Panel A of Exhibit 12. The price of pizza will increase, but what happens to the quantity of pizza sold cannot be determined with the information provided.

- **The switch from DVD to downloadable movies** Movies purchased on DVD and movies purchased via digital download are substitutes in the same market. As consumer preferences tilt toward the convenience and quality offered by downloaded video, the demand increases. At the same time, streaming technology reduces the marginal cost of allowing one more paid download to nearly zero, increasing supply. In Exhibit 12, Panel B, you can see an increase in the quantity of movies sold and an indeterminate change in price. When this happened in the real world, the size of the supply shift was larger than the increase in demand. The result was a higher quantity of movies sold at a lower price.

- **The impact of mad cow disease on beef** Back in the 1990s, an outbreak of mad cow disease in Britain led to the death of many cattle and caused severe illness in people who had consumed infected beef. The supply of beef declined, but prices did not rise because demand decreased as well—consumers were afraid to purchase beef. The result was a decline in both supply and demand, as shown in Panel C in Exhibit 12. In cases like this, quantity will definitely decline, but what happens to price depends on the magnitude of the shifts. Here, we see that price stayed about the same, but quantity decreased sharply; thus, we can infer that demand and supply each decreased by roughly the same amount.

EXHIBIT 12 Shifts in Both Supply and Demand

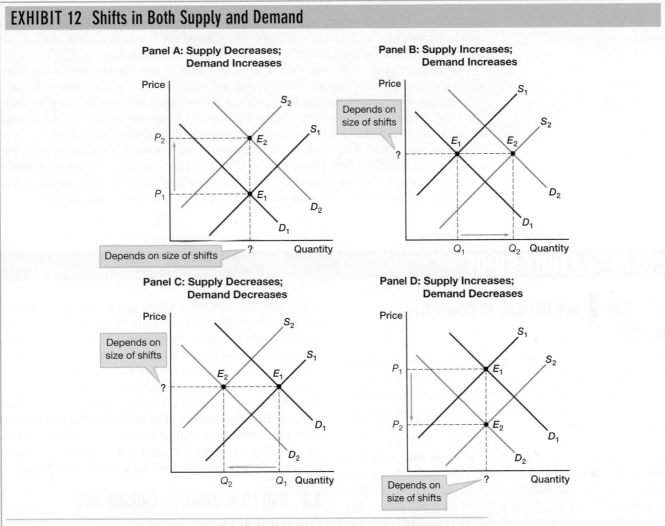

In Panel A, supply decreases while demand increases, resulting in an increase in price and an indeterminate change in quantity. In Panel B, supply and demand both increase, resulting in an increase in quantity and an indeterminate change in price. In Panel C, both supply and demand decrease, resulting in a decrease in quantity and an indeterminate change in price. In Panel D, supply increases while demand decreases, resulting in a decrease in price and an indeterminate change in quantity.

BUSINESS TAKEAWAY

The supply and demand model is one of the most powerful tools in economics—providing very useful insights for businesses. For example, one key decision for any firm is product mix: A firm that offers both inferior and normal goods can thrive in a number of different economic environments. Gap, for example, has been able to segment its market and diversify against the risks associated with a recession by offering a number of brands at different price points. An auto company that offers a variety of vehicles will appeal to more consumers, with high-end cars for wealthier buyers and economy models for the less affluent. Diversity in the product mix also enables firms to respond to changes in the price of complement goods more nimbly: If the price of fuel skyrockets, for example, an automaker can shift its focus from gas-guzzling SUVs to more efficient hybrids and compact cars, often within a single factory.

The ability to react to market conditions quickly is becoming even more important in the age of e-commerce. The taxi industry has traditionally been plagued by surpluses and shortages, because it charged a fixed price regardless of demand. Uber and Lyft came along and set up business models that minute by minute adjust the price of a ride based on demand conditions; both have experienced great success while challenging the traditional taxi industry.

A key assumption of the supply and demand model is that markets are competitive, which those of you studying microeconomics will soon discover is not always the case. Determining what price to charge for a product is often a key business decision for many firms that have some price-setting ability. The concept of consumer demand for a product, and how that demand is impacted by other competing or alternative products, is an important part of marketing strategy and business decision making. To assist in this effort, economists at digitally driven firms, such as Uber and Lyft, examine vast troves of data to estimate the shape of demand curves. These marketing ideas and pricing strategies will be developed in more realistic business settings in later chapters on microeconomics.

CHAPTER STUDY GUIDE

3.1 SUPPLY AND DEMAND IN COMPETITIVE MARKETS

The supply and demand model is the basic economic model that determines equilibrium price and quantity in competitive markets. The model assumes **competitive markets** that have many buyers and many sellers, so no single seller or buyer able to control the price. **Quantity demanded** is the amount of a particular good that buyers are willing and able to purchase at a specific price. The **law of demand** states that a negative relationship exists between price and quantity demanded, *ceteris paribus*, and is expressed graphically in the demand curve. The law of demand results from the income effect and the substitution effect. The **income effect** is the change in the quantity demanded of a good when price changes alter the purchasing power of consumers. The **substitution effect** is the change in the quantity demanded of a good when price changes result in consumers switching from relatively high-priced products to relatively low-priced products. Economists use **demand schedules** to analyze demand and generate models called **demand curves**. **Quantity supplied** of any particular good is the amount that sellers are willing and able to sell at a specific price. The **law of supply** states that a positive relationship exists between price and quantity supplied, *ceteris paribus*. The law of supply is reflected in the **supply schedule** and expressed graphically in the **supply curve**.

3.2 MARKET DEMAND, MARKET SUPPLY, AND EQUILIBRIUM

Market demand is the sum of all buyers' quantity demanded at each price. **Market supply** is the sum of all the sellers' quantity supplied at each price. **Equilibrium**
is the quantity and price where quantity supplied equals quantity demanded. Graphically, this occurs where the market supply curve intercepts the market demand curve. A **surplus** is an excess of quantity supplied over quantity demanded that occurs at prices above equilibrium. A surplus is sometimes called excess supply. A **shortage** is an excess of quantity demanded over quantity supplied that occurs at prices below equilibrium. A shortage is sometimes called excess demand. Both create an unstable situation for the market. In free markets, prices are generally at or moving toward equilibrium.

3.3 SHIFTS IN DEMAND: CAUSES AND CONSEQUENCES

A *change in quantity demanded* occurs when price changes and represents a movement along an existing demand curve. A *change in demand* occurs when something that impacts buyers other than price changes and results in a shift in the demand curve. When price changes, it leads to a change in quantity demanded (not a change in demand). A change in demand may occur due to changes in income. An increase in income increases the demand for **normal goods** but reduces the demand for **inferior goods**. Changes in the price of related goods also shift the demand curve. Demand increases when the price of a **substitute** increases but decreases when the price of a **complement** increases. Demand can also shift due to changes in buyers' expectations, changes in exchange rates, advertising, changes in taste and preferences, and for a variety of other reasons. An increase in demand shifts the demand curve to the right and results in a higher equilibrium price and quantity. A decrease in demand shifts the demand curve to the left and results in a lower equilibrium price and quantity.

3.4 SHIFTS IN SUPPLY: CAUSES AND CONSEQUENCES

A *change in quantity supplied* occurs when price changes and represents a movement along an existing supply curve. A *change in supply* occurs when something other than price impacts sellers and is presented as a shift in the supply curve. When price changes, it leads to a change in quantity supplied (not a change in supply). A change in supply often occurs due to changes in the cost of production that may result from new production technology or changes in resource cost. Supply can shift due to changes in the profitability of alternative products, entry and exit of sellers, *supply shocks* such as natural disasters, regulations, taxes on sellers, substitutes, changes in sellers' price expectations, and for a variety of other reasons. An increase in supply shifts the supply curve to the right and results in a lower equilibrium price and higher equilibrium quantity. A decrease in supply has the opposite effect.

3.5 UNDERSTANDING AND PREDICTING MARKET CHANGES

In analyzing a price change, it is important to understand the reason why the price change occurred in the first place. Never reason from a price change. The supply and demand curves often shift at the same time. When there is an increase in supply and decrease in demand, we know that price falls but cannot determine what will happen to quantity. The impact on quantity will depend on which curve shifts the most. Conversely, if both supply and demand increase, we know that quantity will increase but cannot determine price without knowing which curve shifts the most.

TOP TEN TERMS AND CONCEPTS

1. Quantity Demanded
2. Law of Demand
3. Quantity Supplied
4. Law of Supply
5. Equilibrium
6. Surplus versus Shortage
7. Changes in Quantity Demanded versus Demand
8. Normal Goods versus Inferior Goods
9. Complements versus Substitutes
10. Changes in Quantity Supply versus Supply

STUDY PROBLEMS

1. Use the following supply and demand schedule for a normal good:

Price	Quantity Demanded	Quantity Supplied
$10	100	80
20	90	90
30	80	100
40	70	110
50	60	120
60	50	130

   a. At what price does equilibrium occur? What is the equilibrium quantity?

   b. What occurs when the price is $10?

   c. What occurs when the price is $60?

   d. Suppose demand increases by 20 units at each price. What is the new equilibrium price and quantity?

2. Without using a supply and demand graph, explain the difference between an increase in demand and an increase in quantity demanded.

3. Using a supply and demand model, draw a shift in the demand curve for Mario's pizza based on each of the following events. Explain what happens to price and quantity.

   a. A new KFC opens across the street.

   b. The price of frozen pizza falls.

   c. Incomes fall and pizza is a normal good.

   d. A new movie theater opens across the street.

4. In recent years, the Chinese government has allowed many automobile factories to be built in China by companies such as the state-owned Shanghai Automotive Industry using foreign technology. Many of these cars were intended for the Chinese market. At the same time, incomes in China rose.[8] Draw a supply and demand model and explain what you expect to see with regard to both price and quantity.

5. Compare and contrast the following sets of words:

   a. Increase in supply and increase in quantity supplied

   b. Substitutes and complements

   c. Normal goods and inferior goods

   d. Surplus and shortage

6. 🏛 In the car market, expectations are important. Suppose both buyers and sellers expect higher automobile prices in a few months. Draw a supply and demand model and use it to explain what will happen *this month*. Be sure to explain what happens to quantity and prices.

7. In San Francisco, housing prices have been rising fast, with medium home prices recently exceeding $1 million. Some people say that almost no one can afford to live in this city at such prices. Use *never reason from a price change* to critique this view. Draw a supply and demand diagram to show why you think San Francisco home prices rose so high.

8. 🏛 Draw a supply and demand diagram for movies seen in a theater, and show the effects of each of the following changes on the supply and demand of movie tickets:

   a. The price of popcorn rises.

   b. The price of movie downloads rises.

   c. The movie theater reduces the price of candy.

   d. Big screen, high-definition TVs just got cheaper.

   e. Incomes rise, and seeing a movie at the theater is a normal good.

9. 📊 You drive by a trendy new restaurant and see a long line outside. Is the price of food at that restaurant above equilibrium, below equilibrium, or right at equilibrium? Discuss quantity supplied and quantity demand.

10. Americans make far more long-distance phone calls now than back in the twentieth century. Suppose you had to determine whether the increase in phone calls represented a shift in supply or a shift in demand. What variable would you evaluate to identify which curve shifted (the most)?

11. Taxes on gasoline in many European countries are roughly 10 times higher than in the United States. Discuss the likely impact of these very high taxes on

   a. The type of cars Europeans drive.

   b. How close Europeans live to work.

   c. Frequency with which Europeans use mass transit.

   d. The number of small shops that are within easy walking distance.

12. Explain how the appreciation and depreciation of a currency can impact global demand for a product.

13. In western North Dakota, companies have had trouble finding enough workers for drilling and pipeline work in the booming oil sector. High wages are offered to attract workers to a remote area, where temperatures can fall to 40 degrees below zero in the winter. How would the oil boom affect the supply and demand for ordinary plumbing services in North Dakota? *Hint:* Think about both the supply and demand side of plumbing services, particularly the price of plumbing services.

14. The ride-sharing apps Uber and Lyft allow for easy access to transportation using smartphones. Traditional taxi companies have asked local governments to restrict or even ban these competitors.[9] Explain the opposition of traditional taxi owners, and use a graph showing the impact of these new companies on just the supply and demand for traditional taxis (excluding the new companies).

15. New York City is building a new subway line on the east side of Manhattan. Assume the remaining phases of subway construction will be complete in five years. How will the *anticipation* of this new subway line impact the market for condos near future subway stops? Illustrate your answer with a supply and demand curve.

16. Use the supply and demand model to graph each of the following scenarios. Note that both the supply curve and demand curve shift in each example.

   a. During the summer, the demand for watermelons increases, yet the price declines.

   b. During the summer, the demand for lobster increases, yet the price declines.

17. Consider the following report from an economist on the beef market in *Livestock Weekly*:

   The economist warned against using demand and consumption interchangeably. "While total meat consumption has trended upward over time, it should not be concluded that demand is increasing."

   During the early 1970s, consumers appeared willing to pay more for progressively larger quantities of beef, suggesting an increase in demand. From 1979 to 1986, per capita consumption was generally stable in the 77 to 79 pound range, but retail prices plummeted, The economist further noted, "Consumers were willing to take the same quantity of beef, only at progressively lower prices. In fact, it took 30 percent lower retail prices in 1986 to move about the same quantify of beef into consumption as in 1979—a classic definition of declining demand," he told the crowd.[10]

   a. Explain the passage's first paragraph with a supply and demand graph. How could beef consumption rise without beef demand increasing?

   b. Use a supply and demand graph to illustrate the 1979–86 beef market change. Did one curve shift, or two? What must have happened to supply?

∧ How expensive could gasoline get before you stop buying it?

Elasticity

A Measure of Responsiveness

Imagine that the price of gasoline doubled tomorrow. Some drivers might cut back a little, and those in the market for new cars might opt for more fuel-efficient models. But people still need to get to work or to school, and switching to a more fuel-efficient car is expensive. So in the short run consumers would grudgingly continue to buy almost as much gasoline even after prices spike, and cross their fingers in the hope that prices will come back down soon.

On the other hand, what would happen if the price of books sold on Amazon were to suddenly double? It's likely even avid readers would buy fewer books from the website. Some would look for discounted books at places like Costco and Target; others might start shopping at local used bookstores; and some would simply check out books for free from their local library.

None of this is surprising. As we learned in Chapter 3, the law of demand suggests that when price decreases, quantity demanded increases. But just *how much* will quantity demanded change when price changes? Executives at Coca-Cola know that they'll sell less Coca-Cola if they raise the price—but how much less? And how much less Coca-Cola would they sell if alternatives like bottled water or iced tea suddenly became less expensive? Economics provides a way to measure market response to changes in variables such as price, income, and the price of alternatives. That measure, called *elasticity,* is the focus of this chapter.

Chapter Learning Targets

- Define the concept of price elasticity of demand.

- Demonstrate how price elasticity of demand is calculated.

- Recognize the links between price changes, the price elasticity of demand, and total revenue.

- Identify the concepts of cross-price elasticity and income elasticity.

- Explain the concept of price elasticity of supply and how to calculate it.

4.1 THE PRICE ELASTICITY OF DEMAND

The first three chapters looked at how people respond to changing incentives; this chapter looks at *how much* they respond. **Elasticity** is a measure of responsiveness to a change in market conditions. Economists use it to determine the degree to which one economic variable, such as quantity, responds to changes in other economic variables. There are a variety of measures of elasticity. We begin by analyzing how a price change impacts quantity demanded.

How Much Quantity Demanded Changes When Price Changes

At its heart, elasticity is a measure of *responsiveness*, of how much quantity will be impacted by economic events such as price changes. As noted earlier, consumers are generally not very responsive to changes in the prices of gasoline—at least in the short run. Demand for some items—such as medicine, cigarettes, coffee, and air travel for business—tends to change only slightly in response to fluctuations in price. These products are said to be price inelastic with respect to demand. Demand for other items, like Coca-Cola, automobiles, or fast food, is elastic—quantity demanded tends to be relatively more responsive to changes in price.

elasticity A measure of responsiveness to a change in market conditions.

price elasticity of demand **(E_d)** A measure of how responsive quantity demanded is to price changes; it equals the percentage change in quantity demanded divided by the percentage change in price.

The **price elasticity of demand (E_d)** is a measure of how responsive quantity demanded is to price changes; it equals the percentage change in quantity demanded divided by the percentage change in price. That is,

$$E_d = \frac{\text{Percentage change in } Q_d}{\text{Percentage change in } P}$$

We'll get into the mathematics used to estimate the price elasticity of demand (E_d) later in this chapter. For now, understand that the larger E_d is (in absolute value), the more responsive quantity demanded is to a given price change. To begin, consider the two demand curves in Exhibit 1. Both curves are downward-sloping, which is consistent with the law of demand. Yet, the impact of a given price change in Panel A is considerably different than the impact of the same price change in Panel B. There are very different price elasticities of demand in the two curves.

EXHIBIT 1 Elastic and Inelastic Demand Curves

Panel A: Price Elastic Demand

- Relatively responsive to price change
- Large measure of price elasticity of demand ($E_d > 1$)
- Examples: automobiles, fast food

Panel B: Price Inelastic Demand

- Not very responsive to price change
- Small measure of price elasticity of demand ($E_d < 1$)
- Examples: medicine, coffee

Panel A shows a price elastic demand curve. Quantity demanded is very responsive to price changes. The price elasticity of demand is greater than 1. Panel B shows a price inelastic demand curve. Quantity demanded is not very responsive to price changes. The price elasticity of demand is less than 1.

The demand curve in Panel A is relatively responsive, or *price elastic*. Quantity demanded is very responsive to a price change, moving by a larger percentage than price. Its measure of responsiveness E_d is greater than 1 because the percentage change in quantity is greater than the percentage change in price. The demand for luxury goods and a *specific brand* of a good tends to be price elastic as consumers respond to price increases by foregoing consumption or switching brands.

When compared to the demand curve in Panel A, the demand curve in Panel B is relatively unresponsive to price changes. This means the demand curve in Panel B is *price inelastic*. Quantity demanded is not very responsive to a price change, with quantity moving by a smaller percentage than price. Its measure of responsiveness E_d is less than 1 because the percentage change in quantity is less than the percentage change in price. For example, the demand for gasoline (when all stations raise their prices) and life-saving medicine tends to be price inelastic.

Factors That Influence Price Elasticity of Demand

A number of factors influence the price elasticity of demand. Let's consider a few of them, and see how basic economic theory can help us to understand why the price elasticity of demand varies so much from one product to the next.

Availability of Substitutes In general, demand for products with a lot of substitutes is price elastic: If peaches become 10% more expensive, consumers will switch to other fruits. The demand for Chevrolets and Rice Krispies is highly elastic. Consumers can easily switch to substitute products (such as Fords or Kellogg's Corn Flakes). Likewise, if one gas station charges 10 cents more per gallon than a nearby competitor, the high-priced station will likely experience sharply lower sales, *ceteris paribus*.

In contrast, when few substitutes are available, consumers are less responsive to price changes and the price elasticity of demand is lower (more inelastic). Here, we are assuming that *all* gasoline stations change their prices, not just a specific brand or station. That's why demand for gasoline as a whole is relatively price inelastic: Most consumers won't immediately stop using gas if the price goes up across all brands and at all gas stations.

Definition of the Market As you may have noticed, how a market is defined will impact how responsive consumers are to price changes. There is a big difference in the price elasticity of a broad category like "food" and that of a single item, like peaches, Coca-Cola, or potato chips. The demand for food, in general, is quite price inelastic—most of us would be hard pressed to identify substitutes (if you don't consume food, what would you eat?). But the demand for specific foods is much more price elastic. If the price of peaches, Coca-Cola, or potato chips increases, customers will opt for apples, iced tea, or pretzels. Branded potato chips, like Lay's or Pringles, have an even narrower market than "chips" in general, so their price elasticity of demand will be higher. Likewise, the price elasticity of demand will be higher for Coca-Cola than for all carbonated beverages. The more narrowly a product is defined, the more substitutes are likely to be available—and the more price elastic demand will be.

Time to Adjust We've discussed how gasoline is price inelastic in the short run, but as we noted in Chapter 1, economic outcomes frequently depend on the time frame involved. That's because when consumers have

▾ The availability of substitutes makes demand for specific brands highly price elastic.

Richard Levine/Alamy

more time to adjust to price changes, they can be more responsive to any price change. As a result, the price elasticity of demand is often higher in the long run than in the short run. For example, if gas prices spike, a commuter who drives a gas-guzzling SUV will likely continue to fill up for a while, but if the price of gas remains high for several weeks, he or she might start to look at alternative modes of transportation, such as carpooling or public transportation. In the long run, the driver might even consider switching to a more efficient or an electric vehicle.

Share of Budget If rents in your town suddenly doubled, chances are you'd start looking for a smaller apartment. But what would you do if the price of milk doubled? Or salt? The percentage change in price is the same in all three cases, and all three items are basic necessities. But the price increase for rent will have a much larger impact on your overall budget: Spending twice as much on rent will likely cost you thousands of additional dollars each year, while spending twice on a carton of milk will only cost you a few more dollars per week, and salt will only cost you a few more dollars per year, even at twice the current price. Demand for more expensive items tends to be more price elastic because they take up a larger share of consumer budgets: This puts more pressure on consumers to cut back and thus they are much more responsive.

Necessities, Luxuries, and Addictive Goods Consumers tend to be less responsive to the price changes of items they deem *necessities* than those they consider luxuries. In other words, changes in the price of necessities tend to have a fairly small impact on the quantity demanded. Products like emergency health-care services, business travel, groceries, and addictive items like coffee, cigarettes, beer, and narcotics are price inelastic, indicating that many consumers consider these products to be necessities, and will thus not reduce their consumption very much when prices rise. Demand for *addictive goods* can be very price inelastic. Demand for *luxuries* like fine restaurant meals, vacations, spa treatment services, and designer clothing, on the other hand, tends to be relatively price elastic: When the price of such a product rises, consumers may choose a cheaper option or simply go without it.

Advertising and Brand Loyalty Most non-economists are aware that businesses advertise to increase demand. But advertisers have an additional motive—to lower the price elasticity of demand for their product. Brands like Nike and Ralph Lauren spend huge amounts of money in advertising, in hopes of convincing consumers that other brands are not good substitutes. If they are successful, demand for their product will become less price elastic (more price inelastic).

4.2 MEASURING THE PRICE ELASTICITY OF DEMAND

We've seen that the price elasticity of demand is a measure of how responsive the quantity demanded is to price changes, other things equal. We've also examined factors that determine the price elasticity of demand. We will now examine how we compute the price elasticity of demand and why it is important to never reason from a price change when doing so. We will also look at real-world estimates of the price elasticity of demand.

Computing the Price Elasticity of Demand (E_d)

Recall that the price elasticity of demand is equal to the percentage change in quantity demanded divided by the percentage change in price. Earlier, this was shown as

$$E_d = \frac{\text{Percentage change in } Q_d}{\text{Percentage change in } P}$$

This equation can also be expressed as

$$E_d = \frac{\%\Delta Q_d}{\%\Delta P}$$

where the Greek letter Δ (delta) means change, $\%\Delta Q_d$ thus means percentage change in quantity demanded, while $\%\Delta P$ means percentage change in price.

How does one calculate percentage change $(\%\Delta)$? The *standard* way to calculate a percent change in price is the change in price over the initial price, expressed as a percentage. Such calculations are familiar to most consumers: When a North Face fleece jacket is marked down from $100 to $75, shoppers will say the jacket is 25% off. Likewise, when a large pizza once priced at $30 now costs $20, you can say the pizza is one third, or roughly 33%, off. That is,

$$\%\Delta P = \frac{\text{Change in price}}{\text{Initial price}} = \frac{\$20 - \$30}{\$30} = \frac{-\$10}{\$30} = -33.3\%$$

Unfortunately, this standard formula for calculating percentage change is problematic in that it depends on the direction of the change. For example, if the price of the large pizza rises by the same amount—that is, from $20 to $30—the percentage change in price is *not* 33.3%. Rather, it is 50%.

$$\%\Delta P = \frac{\text{Change in price}}{\text{Initial price}} = \frac{\$10}{\$20} = 50\%$$

Since the direction of the price change impacts the estimate of percentage change using the standard formula, it also affects estimates of price elasticity of demand. That is to say, using the standard formula for calculating percentage change would result in different values for the price elasticity of demand for price increases and decreases. To avoid this ambiguity, economists use an alternative measure of percentage change.

Using the Midpoint Method to Estimate the Price Elasticity of Demand To overcome ambiguity related to the direction of the price change, economists use what is known as the *midpoint method* to estimate percentage changes when calculating elasticities.

A midpoint is simply the *average* of the two end points: Rather than divide by $20 or $30 in the above pizza example (the two initial prices), economists divide by $25, the midpoint (or average) of $20 and $30. Using the midpoint method to calculate percentage change in price, we get

$$\%\Delta P_{\text{midpoint}} = \frac{\text{Change in price}}{\text{Midpoint price}} = \frac{10}{(20 + 30)/2} = \frac{10}{25} = 40\%$$

Using the midpoint formula ensures that we arrive at a single estimate of the price elasticity of demand for both price increases and price decreases. Remember, percentage change using the midpoint method is simply change over the average value. The basic idea is still the same.

$$E_d = \frac{\%\Delta Q_d}{\%\Delta P} = \frac{\dfrac{\Delta Q}{\text{Midpoint } Q}}{\dfrac{\Delta P}{\text{Midpoint } P}} = \frac{\left(\dfrac{\Delta Q}{(Q_1 + Q_2)/2}\right)}{\left(\dfrac{\Delta P}{(P_1 + P_2)/2}\right)}$$

Using the midpoint method, price elasticity of demand is the change in Q_d over average (midpoint) quantity, divided by change in P over the average (midpoint) price.

Expressions of Price Elasticity of Demand The price elasticity of demand is technically a *negative* number, as demand curves have a negative slope due to the law of demand (i.e., $E_d = < 0$). However, business analysts and economists often express the price elasticity of demand values as a *positive* number. To keep things simple, price elasticity is frequently expressed in terms of *absolute value* (i.e., how far it is from zero in either direction). The law of demand is so widely recognized that it's understood that a demand price elasticity of 0.75 is actually shorthand for −0.75. In this book, we use the shorthand technique and refer to price elasticity of demand estimates in terms of absolute value. Keep in mind that in other places, you may occasionally come across an expression of demand elasticity that includes a negative sign.

Estimating Price Elasticity of Demand Suppose Mario is the only pizza seller in town. In addition, suppose that if the price of Mario's large pizza is $20, the quantity of large pizzas demanded is 1,500, and that only 900 are demanded if the price of a large pizza increases to $30:

Price of a Large Pizza

Price	Quantity
$20	1,500
$30	900

In this case, the price of elasticity of demand for Mario's pizza is

$$E_d = \frac{\%\Delta Q}{\%\Delta P} = \frac{\dfrac{\Delta Q}{\text{Midpoint } Q}}{\dfrac{\Delta P}{\text{Midpoint } P}} = \frac{\left(\dfrac{600}{1{,}200}\right)}{\left(\dfrac{10}{25}\right)} = \frac{0.50}{0.40} = 1.25$$

In estimating the price elasticity of demand for pizza, we first estimate the percentage change in quantity. This is the change in quantity (an absolute value of 600) over the midpoint quantity (1,200), which equals (1,500 + 900)/2, which equals 0.50 (or 50%). Next, we calculate the percentage change in price, which is the change in price (10) over the midpoint price (25). This equals 0.40 (or 40%). Finally, we divide the percentage change in quantity (50%) by the percentage change in price (40%), which leads to the result that the $E_d = 1.25$.

Alternatively, consider the price elasticity of demand for toppings:

Price of Toppings

Price	Quantity
$2	1,100
$3	900

$$E_d = \frac{\%\Delta Q}{\%\Delta P} = \frac{\left(\dfrac{\Delta Q}{\text{Midpoint } Q}\right)}{\left(\dfrac{\Delta P}{\text{Midpoint } P}\right)} = \frac{\left(\dfrac{200}{1{,}000}\right)}{\left(\dfrac{1}{2.50}\right)} = \frac{0.20}{0.40} = 0.5$$

Once again, the price elasticity of demand is estimated as the percentage change in quantity over the percentage change in price. Here, the absolute value of the percentage change in quantity is 0.20 (or 20%) and the percentage change in price is 0.40 (40%). The elasticity of demand is 0.20 over 0.40, which leads to the result that $E_d = 0.50$.

What Price Elasticity of Demand (E_d) Means What does a price elasticity of demand equal to 1.25 mean? For starters, it means the price elasticity of demand for a large pizza is *elastic,* as it is greater than 1: Quantity demanded changes by relatively more than price. It also means that consumers are somewhat flexible; they can shift to alternative products if the price rises. The higher the price elasticity of demand, the more price elastic a good is. A price elasticity of 1.25 means if price changes by 1%, quantity will change by 1.25%.

Alternatively, the price elasticity of demand for toppings is 0.50. Individuals who want specific toppings on their pizza—pepperoni, onions, or mushrooms—are often not very responsive to price changes in these toppings. You would probably notice if your local pizzeria increased the price of its pie, but you might pay little attention to changes in the price of toppings. That is to say, the price elasticity of demand of toppings tends to be *inelastic,* with a price elasticity less than 1, meaning the percentage change in quantity (in the numerator) is less than the percentage change in price (in the denominator). In this example, toppings on pizzas are price inelastic, with each 1% increase in price reducing quantity demanded by 0.5%. As a result, if Mario raises the price of toppings by 10%, he can expect topping sales to decline by only 5%. Likewise, in the auto industry, consumers are very sensitive to the base price of cars, but often pay less attention to the price of fancy options like alloy wheels.

Thomas Padilla/Newscom

∧ A better burger, with a slice of inelastic cheese.

 BUSINESS BRIEF Five Guys: How Much Would You Pay for a Slice of Cheese?

The fast-food chain Five Guys dominates what is known as the "better burger" category of casual dining. In 2018, it had over 1,000 locations and was one of the fastest-growing fast-food restaurant in the United States.* Prices at Five Guys are, on average, higher than those found at other fast-food burger places, in part due its high-quality ingredients.

Management at Five Guys appears to have considered price elasticities when designing its menu. The price of its "Little Hamburger" jumps from $4.99 to $5.69 when cheese is added, and to $6.69 when both cheese and bacon are added. Similarly, the price of its hot dogs increases from $4.69 to $5.39 when customers add cheese.† That's 70 cents for 1 slice of cheese! Remember, items that are a small share of one's budget tend to be less responsive to price changes—that is to say, they tend to be price inelastic. The demand for that extra slice of cheese on a burger is probably price inelastic. Savvy business owners can—and do—capitalize on these elasticities.

*Monte Burke, "Five Guys Burgers: America's Fastest Growing Restaurant Chain," *Forbes*, July 18, 2012, https://www.forbes.com/forbes/2012/0806/restaurant-chefs-12-five-guys-jerry-murrell-all-in-the-family.html.

†"Five Guys Prices," *FastFoodMenuPrices.com*, 2018, http://www.fastfoodmenuprices.com/five-guys-prices/.

Real-World Estimates of Price Elasticity of Demand

The law of demand tells us that price increases reduce quantity demanded, while the concept of elasticity tells us by *how much*. In this section, we look at real-world estimates of the price elasticity of demand for various products and discuss these values in the context of factors that influence price elasticity of demand.

Exhibit 2 shows real-world price elasticity of demand estimates for various products. In these examples, you will notice some patterns consistent with factors that determine the price elasticity of demand. First, due to the *availability of substitutes,* demand for a specific seller like Coca-Cola, Kellogg's, Walmart, Amazon, or Chevrolet is generally more price elastic than for broad product categories like food, cars, or retailers. Due to having more *time to adjust,* demand for both gasoline and automobiles is less price elastic in the short run than in the long run. Due to being a small *share of a budget,* inexpensive items such as salt tend to have less price elastic demand than expensive goods like foreign air travel and automobiles. Food is a broad *definition of a market* and has a less price elastic demand than Coca-Cola and Rice Krispies. Demand for *luxury* goods like foreign travel is price elastic, while demand for *necessities* like food and some health-care services is price inelastic. Demand for *addictive goods* and *necessities* such as cigarettes, coffee, alcohol, and narcotics is typically price inelastic.

EXHIBIT 2 Real-World Estimates of Price Elasticity of Demand

Inelastic Goods ($E_d > 1$)	Price Elasticity of Demand	Elastic Goods ($E_d < 1$)	Price Elasticity of Demand
Health Care (appendectomy)	<0.1	Air Travel (general)	1.1
Health Care (arm cast)	< 0.1	Breakfast Cereal (all)	1.3
Salt	0.1	Fast Food	1.7
Gasoline (short-run)	0.2–0.3	Retail Products (Walmart)	1.9
Coffee	0.3	Health Care (psychologist visit)	2.1
Beer	0.3	Automobiles (all, long-run)	2.2
Gasoline (long-run)	0.6–0.9	Kellogg's Rice Krispies	2.2
Illicit Drugs (cocaine)	0.3	Online Products (at Amazon)	3.2
Cigarettes	0.4	Automobiles (Chevrolet)	1.8–2.1
Air Travel (business)	0.5	Air Travel (long-run)	2.1
Food	0.6	Foreign Travel (long-run)	4.1
Lottery Ticket (large jackpot)	0.8	Coca-Cola	4.1

Estimates of the price elasticity of demand for a variety of products.

Data compiled by the authors; see chapter notes (p. R-1) for list sources.

Ranges of Price Elasticity of Demand and Extreme Cases

The price elasticity of demand can range from zero to infinity. The larger the value of the price elasticity of demand, the more elastic the item is. These values are summarized in Exhibit 3. Most goods are either price elastic or price inelastic. On occasion, the price elasticity of demand is categorized as *perfectly inelastic* ($E_d = 0$), *unit elastic* ($E_d = 1$), or *perfectly elastic* ($E_d =$ infinity). We discuss each of these possibilities in turn.

Perfectly Inelastic Demand ($E_d = 0$) Panel A of Exhibit 3 shows a *perfectly inelastic* demand curve. It is a vertical line, meaning the quantity demanded never changes. In this case, the $\%\Delta Q$ is zero.

While this example is theoretically possible, it is very unlikely. One example that people often cite is medicine needed to survive—a consumer, it is assumed, will demand the same quantity of a life-saving medication, regardless of increases (or decreases) in price. However, even life-saving medicine does not have a *perfectly* inelastic demand: At unaffordable prices, quantity demanded falls and the price elasticity of demand is no longer zero.

Inelastic Demand ($E_d < 1$) Panel B demonstrates a relatively price inelastic demand curve. In most cases, a change in price will change quantity demanded. The question is by how much. When demand is price inelastic, the percentage change in quantity demanded is smaller than the percentage change in price. Consumers are not very responsive to price changes. Since $E_d = \%\Delta Q / \%\Delta P$ and the numerator is smaller than the denominator, E_d must be less than 1 when demand is inelastic. As we've discussed, the demand for gasoline and medicine tends to be price inelastic.

Unit Elastic ($E_d = 1$) Panel C shows an interesting case occurs when the price elasticity of demand equals 1. In this instance, the percentage change in quantity equals the percentage change in price. This is referred to as unit elastic demand. In the E_d equation, the numerator ($\%\Delta Q$) must equal the denominator ($\%\Delta P$).

Elastic Demand ($E_d > 1$) Panel D shows the case where demand is relatively price elastic. Here, the percentage change in quantity demanded is greater than the

EXHIBIT 3 Graphical Summary of the Price Elasticity of Demand

Estimates of the price elasticity of demand can range from zero (perfectly inelastic) to infinity (perfectly elastic).

percentage change in price, and the price elasticity of demand is greater than 1. In this case, consumers will respond to a price increase by sharply cutting back on purchases. As we've learned, the demand for a specific brand of gasoline, food item, or automobile tends to be price elastic.

Perfectly Elastic Demand (E_d = Infinity) Panel E also shows a perfectly elastic demand curve. It is a horizontal line. The quantity demanded for such an item falls to zero if the price rises by even 1 cent. This is approximately the demand curve that faces small firms in perfect competition. Consider a small egg farmer that produces between 100 and 200 dozen eggs a month. If monthly egg production is 625,000,000 (as it was in the United States in October 2016), the small farmer's impact on market price is likely very close to zero. This farmer takes the market price as given and simply sells as many as she chooses to produce at the current market price. The demand for an individual farmer's eggs is (almost) infinitely elastic. If she raised her price, quantity demand would fall to almost zero, as many other producers will be willing to sell at a lower price.

Think & Speak Like an Economist

When demand is price elastic, it means the price elasticity of demand is greater than 1, thus the percentage change in quantity is greater than the percentage change in price. When demand is price inelastic, it means the price elasticity of demand is less than 1.

BUSINESS BRIEF Is Demand for Life-Saving AIDS Drug Perfectly Price Inelastic?

Perfectly inelastic demand is rare and may not even apply to life-saving medicines. For example, the first successful treatments for AIDs were developed in the late 1990s. These drugs were very expensive and thus out of reach for many AIDS patients—particularly those in the developing world. In 2001, British pharmaceutical company GlaxoSmithKline reduced the price of its AIDS drugs in the 63 poorest countries of the world (by varying amounts) in response to competitive pressure from generic "copycats" in countries where such substitutes were legally sold. Subsequently, sales tripled from 2 million people treated to 6 million.* This increase in sales indicates that even the demand for life-saving drugs is not *perfectly* inelastic: The lower price increased the quantity demanded.

*Sarah Boseley and Tim Radford, "Glaxo Cuts Price of AIDS Drugs in Poor Countries," *The Guardian*, April 28, 2003, http://www.theguardian.com/uk/2003/apr/28/sciencenews.globalisation.

>Measuring Elasticity: Never Reason from a Price Change

Businesses are very concerned with how supply changes might impact the price of goods that they sell, and how this impacts the quantity sold. To answer these questions, businesses need to know the price elasticity of demand.

You might think it would be easy to calculate price elasticity of demand. Simply see what happens to sales when the price changes. But remember: Economists should *never reason from a price change*. If the price of a good rises, the quantity purchased could go up or down, depending on whether the price increase was caused by lower supply or higher demand.

Elasticity measures responsiveness to price changes along a *given* demand curve. But what if price changes *because demand has shifted*? When calculating demand elasticity, economists seek to avoid cases where the price changed because the demand curve itself shifted. For this reason, economists look for price changes caused by shifts in supply. The goal is to find two points along a given demand curve, before and after supply shifts.

For example, the government raising taxes on cigarettes paid by sellers will reduce supply and result in a shift along the demand curve. The change in consumer quantity demanded after the tax increase will help us determine the price elasticity of demand for cigarettes. For instance, if a 10% price rise caused by higher taxes leads to a 5% drop in cigarette sales, then the price elasticity of demand would be 0.5.

Alternatively, you could look at the price and quantity of coffee before and after a crop failure that caused the supply of coffee to decrease. Neither crop failures nor tax paid by sellers increases are likely to change the public's underlying demand for the product; rather, price changes along a given demand curve. Those events allow you to see how consumers respond to price change holding the demand curve constant.

Today, researchers use *econometrics* (advanced statistical models) that attempt to control for other real-world changes, allowing economists to focus on the key relationships between price and quantity demanded.

4.3 HOW A PRICE CHANGE AFFECTS UNIT SALES AND SALES REVENUE

Once a business has developed a good estimate of the price elasticity of demand for its product, it is a straightforward mathematical calculation to use this number in estimating the impact of price changes on sales. Price changes can affect what businesses refer to as *unit sales*—or more commonly what economists refer to as quantity demanded. Price changes can also affect *sales revenue,* the amount of money received by selling these units. Each of these measures of sales is significantly impacted by the price change and the price elasticity of demand for the firm's product.

How a Price Change Affects Quantity Demanded

In deciding whether to change prices, businesses often consider the impact of price changes on quantity demanded (unit sales). Recall the formula to estimate price elasticity of demand:

$$E_d - \frac{\%\Delta Q_d}{\%\Delta P}$$

There are three variables (E_d, $\%\Delta P$, and $\%\Delta Q$). If two of these variables are known, it is simple to find the third. Let's assume that the price elasticity of demand for Mario's pizzas has previously been estimated and Mario wants to know how a price increase will affect his sales. In that case, the above equation can be rewritten as

$$\%\Delta Q_d = E_d \times \%\Delta P$$

For example, if Mario knows the price elasticity of demand for his pizza is 2, and he is considering raising prices by 5%, what impact will that increase have on his sales? They will decline by 10%. Once again, remember that a negative relationship exists between price and quantity demanded.

How a Price Change Affects Total Revenue

In deciding whether to change prices, businesses also consider the impact of price changes on sales revenue or what economists refer to as total revenue or simply revenue. **Total revenue** (revenue) is the money a business receives from the sale of a product, calculated as the price of the good times the quantity sold. That is,

$$\text{Total revenue } (TR) = \text{Price} \times \text{Quantity}$$

For example, if Mario can sell 10 pizzas for $15, his total revenue will be $150. Since demand curves are downward-sloping, the impact of price increases on total revenue is uncertain because higher prices lower the quantity demanded. Thus, if price increases by 5% and quantity falls by 5%, total revenue will change very little. In general, higher prices increase total revenue, while the reduced quantity decreases total revenue. A trade-off occurs. Because P and Q move in opposite directions, the net effect on total revenue is unclear. It depends on the relative size of the percentage change in quantity and the percentage change in price:

$$? \text{ Total revenue } (TR) = \uparrow \text{Price} \times \downarrow \text{Quantity}$$

Can you have more total revenue with fewer unit sales? Earlier, we considered the case of Mario selling 1,100 pizza toppings for $2 each. In that case, his total revenue for selling toppings would be $2,200 ($2 × 1,100). We also noted that Mario could sell 900 toppings for $3 each. In that case, his total revenue for selling toppings would be $2,700 ($3 × 900). Mario receives more revenue when he sells fewer toppings! The relationship results from the fact that the price elasticity of demand for toppings is inelastic. As you will soon discover, this is not the case when the price elasticity of demand is elastic, as is the case for e-books.

> ### Think & Speak Like an Economist
>
> Businesses commonly use terms such as *unit sales* and *sales revenue*. The equivalent terms in economics are *quantity demanded* and *total revenue*. When economists use the term *revenue*, they typically are referring to *total revenue*.

📊 BUSINESS BRIEF Amazon Defends Its e-Book Pricing Strategy

Books—and particularly e-books sold on Amazon.com—compete in markets where many substitutes are available: Readers can opt to purchase print books sold on Amazon and elsewhere; they can buy used books; or they can borrow print books or e-books for free from their local library. So, it should not surprise you that books, and e-books especially, have highly price elastic demand. In 2014, Amazon became embroiled in a lawsuit with the Hachette Book Group: Hachette argued that publishers should be able to determine the price of e-books sold on Amazon. The online giant asserted that a retailer like itself should be able to offer discounts. In defending its strategy, Amazon acknowledged the high price elasticity of e-books. Specifically, Amazon's data showed that the firm could sell 1.74 times as many copies of a book if it lowered the price from $14.99 to $9.99:

> [E]-books are highly price-elastic. . . . [W]e've quantified the price elasticity of e-books. . . . If customers would buy 100,000 copies of a particular e-book at $14.99, then customers would buy 174,000 copies of that same e-book at $9.99. Total revenue at $14.99 would be $1,499,000. Total revenue at $9.99 is $1,738,000.*

total revenue The money a business receives from the sale of a product, calculated as the price of the good times the quantity sold; also called *revenue*.

The two sides eventually came to an agreement that allowed publishers to still determine the prices for their titles. In return, Amazon was granted the right to provide Hachette with incentives to keep their prices low in order to take advantage of the fact that when demand is elastic, lower prices actually lead to higher total revenue.[†]

*"Update Regarding Amazon/Hachette Business Interruption," *Amazon.com* Kindle Forum, July 29, 2014.

[†]"Frozen Conflict," *The Economist,* November 14, 2014, http://www.economist.com/news/business-and-finance/21632802-deal-between-two-firms-unlikely-end-dispute-over-prices-and-profits-e-books-frozen.

Price Increase with Inelastic Demand Increases Total Revenue Consider the demand curve for inelastic goods such as pizza toppings, health care, certain pharmaceuticals, gasoline, or coffee. Compare the previous equation with the one below, in which differently sized arrows are used to reflect the magnitude of the changes (with a small arrow ["↓"] indicating a small change, and a large arrow ["↑"] indicating a bigger change).

When the price elasticity of demand is less than 1 (inelastic):

$$E_d < 1 \text{ (inelastic) if } \frac{\downarrow\%\Delta Q_d}{\uparrow\%\Delta P}$$

$$\uparrow \text{Total revenue } (TR) = \uparrow \text{Price} \times \downarrow \text{Quantity}$$

Remember that when demand for an item is price inelastic, the percentage change in quantity is smaller than the percentage change in price ($\%\Delta Q < \%\Delta P$). When a business sells a product for which its own brand is price inelastic, it can raise prices by a significant amount without much impact on quantity demanded. In that case, total revenue will rise. Similarly, a really popular restaurant or Broadway play can increase its prices and also increase revenue. Lowering prices has the opposite effect.

Price Increase with Elastic Demand Decreases Total Revenue If Mario's pizzeria is located in a town with numerous restaurants, he will likely face demand for his pizza that is price elastic. This means the percentage change in quantity is greater than the percentage change in price ($\%\Delta Q > \%\Delta P$). Consider a neighborhood with four pizza shops, one with a price $1.00 higher than the others. What happens to sales at the pizza shop with a slightly higher price, if other things are held equal? Are sales a lot lower, or just a little bit lower? Since the product demand at any single pizza shop is typically price elastic, the quantity sold at the restaurant that raises prices will be a lot lower.

When the price elasticity of demand is greater than 1 (elastic),

$$E_d > 1 \text{ (elastic) if } \frac{\downarrow\%\Delta Q_d}{\uparrow \%\Delta P}$$

$$\downarrow \text{Total revenue } (TR) = \uparrow \text{Price} \times \downarrow \text{Quantity}$$

This means that increasing the price of elastic goods such as pizza will result in lower total revenue. Conversely, lowering the price will actually increase total revenue, as Amazon discovered in the case of e-books.

Exhibit 4 demonstrates the impact of a price increase on total revenue when demand is price elastic and price inelastic. In both cases, price increases by 20% using the midpoint method. When demand is price elastic, quantity changes by 40% and E_d is 2.0 (= 40%/20%). As a consequence, total revenue declines from $1,080 to $880. In contrast, when demand is price inelastic, quantity changes by 2% and E_d is 0.1 (= 2%/20%). As a consequence, total revenue increases from $909 to $1,089.

In summary, firms must consider the price elasticity of demand for their specific product when determining the impact of a price change on total revenue.

EXHIBIT 4 Price Increases, Total Revenue, and Price Elasticity of Demand

Panel A: Higher Price Decreases Total Revenue

Total revenue = $11 × 80 = $880

Total revenue = $9 × 120 = $1,080

Relatively Elastic
Total revenue decreases because % ΔP < % ΔQ

Panel B: Higher Price Increases Total Revenue

Total revenue = $11 × 99 = $1,089

Total revenue = $9 × 101 = $909

Relatively Inelastic
Total revenue increases because % ΔP > % ΔQ

In both panels, price increases by 20% using the midpoint method. In Panel A, demand is price elastic, quantity decreases by 40%, and total revenue decreases. In Panel B, demand is price inelastic, quantity decreases by 2%, and total revenue increases.

In general, *price increases*:

- Increase total revenue when the firm is facing demand that is price inelastic
- Decrease total revenue when the firm is facing demand that is price elastic

In contrast, *price decreases*:

- Decrease total revenue when the firm is facing demand that is price inelastic
- Increase total revenue when the firm is facing demand that is price elastic

Use Firm-Specific Price Elasticity of Demand Estimates Remember that even though demand for a product category might be price inelastic, the demand for an individual firm selling that good is often price elastic. For instance, a rise in the overall market price of gasoline will likely cause only a small reduction in quantity demanded by consumers (in Exhibit 2, $E_d = 0.2 - 0.3$). Revenue to the industry would rise. But if only *one* gas station raises its price, some consumers will switch to other sellers, often one just down the street. Revenue to that individual seller will thus fall.

Likewise, the demand for food is, in general, price inelastic—but if only one pizza seller were to increase its price, the quantity sold by that seller will decline relatively sharply. In pricing its e-books, Amazon had to consider the price elasticity of demand for its specific product, *not* the price elasticity of demand for all books, or even all e-books. In business, it's very important to distinguish between the price elasticity of demand for the overall market and the individual firm's price elasticity of demand, which is generally much more elastic.

Price Elasticity and Total Revenue Along a Linear Demand Curve

In general, the price elasticity of demand changes as one moves along the demand curve. In most cases, higher prices lead to a higher elasticity of demand. Indeed, such is always true for linear (straight) demand curves drawn as shown in Exhibit 5. This is, in part, due to the mathematics of a linear demand curve (the percentage change from $2 to $4 is larger than from $6 to $8) and, in part, due to the fact that

EXHIBIT 5   Elasticity and Total Revenue Along a Linear Demand Curve

Panel A: Total Revenue at Various Prices

Points	Price	Quantity	Total Revenue
a	$8	2	$16
b	6	4	24
c	**5**	**5**	**25**
d	4	6	24
e	2	8	16

Panel B: Price Elasticty Varies Along Demand Curve

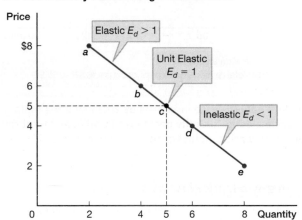

Panel C: Total Revenue Corresponds to Points on Demand Curve

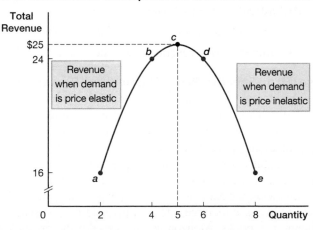

Panel A shows total revenue at various price points and various estimates of the price elasticity of demand. Notice that demand tends to be more price elastic at higher prices and price inelastic at lower prices. Raising the price from $2 to $4 increases total revenue as demand is price inelastic, while raising the price from $6 to $8 decreases total revenue as demand is price elastic. Panel B displays the corresponding linear demand curve and Panel C the corresponding total revenue curve. Total revenue is maximized where the demand curve is unit elastic. At a price of $5, 5 units are sold and total revenue is $25 (point e).

higher-price items take up a larger share of consumers' budgets. At a high enough price, all demand curves eventually become elastic, including life-saving drugs. *On a linear demand curve, the top half of the demand curve is price elastic, while the bottom half is price inelastic.*

Total Revenue Is Maximized at Unit Elasticity By now, you should recognize that businesses can increase total revenue whenever their product is price inelastic. Along a linear demand curve, however, higher prices can only raise revenue up to the point where the product is unit elastic. Raising price above $5 lowers total revenue. This means that total revenue is maximized at the point of unit elasticity. If we look at the midpoints of the price and quantity for which unit elasticity occurs (price of $6 and

$4; quantity of 4 and 6), we find a price of $5 and a quantity of 5. At this point, total revenue equals $25 ($5 × 5). No other point would lead to a higher total revenue.

The Goal of Firms Is to Maximize Profits, Not Total Revenue While revenue is important, the goal of firms is to maximize *profit,* which is equal to total revenue minus total cost. Selling more units typically involves increasing the cost of doing business. The marginal analysis introduced in Chapter 1 suggests that it is foolish for Mario to sell one more pizza at $5 if it cost $15 to make; revenue might increase, but at the end of the day, he would be spending more money than he will get in return. Although there are some cases where revenue maximization is completely consistent with profit maximization—Amazon, for example, can sell additional e-book downloads with virtually no additional costs for producing, warehousing, or shipping—in most cases firms do incur extra costs, and thus profit maximization is not the same as revenue maximization. We will discuss profit maximization further in the chapter on perfect competition.

4.4 OTHER DEMAND ELASTICITIES

In addition to understanding the responsiveness of their customers to price changes, businesses must understand the responsiveness of their customers to other variables, including changes in consumers' income and changes in the price of other products. In this section, we'll examine how the concept of elasticity can be used to estimate the degree to which factors other than price affect the quantity demanded.

Income Elasticity of Demand

Income elasticity of demand is a measure of how responsive quantity demanded is to changes in consumers' income; it equals the percentage change in quantity demanded divided by the percentage change in income. Mathematically, it is

$$E_{income} = \frac{\text{Percentage change in } Q_d}{\text{Percentage change in income}}$$

or

$$E_{income} = \frac{\% \Delta Q_d}{\% \Delta income}$$

The main difference between this formula and the formula for the price elasticity of demand is that we are analyzing the impact of changes in income. Note that in the case of income elasticity, the positive (+) or negative (−) sign is important.

As we discussed in Chapter 3, *inferior goods* are goods for which demand decreases as incomes increase and demand increases as incomes decrease. Because income and quantity demanded move in opposite directions, inferior goods have a negative income elasticity of demand. When incomes increase, the sign of the denominator (%Δincome) is positive, and since quantity demanded decreases, the sign of the numerator (%ΔQ_d) is negative. Foods like potatoes and hot dogs tend to be inferior goods—more likely to be consumed as incomes decline and by the poor rather than the affluent.

Most goods, however, are not inferior goods. As discussed in Chapter 3, most goods see an increase in demand when incomes increase and vice versa. A *normal good* is a good for which demand increases as incomes increase, and demand decreases as incomes decrease. Because income and quantity demanded both move in the same direction, normal goods have a positive income elasticity of demand. When incomes increase, the sign of the denominator (%Δincome) is positive, and since quantity demanded also increases, the sign of the numerator (%ΔQ_d) is also positive. Goods ranging from apples to automobiles to airplanes tend to be normal goods.

income elasticity of demand A measure of how responsive quantity demanded is to changes in consumers' income; it equals the percentage change in quantity demanded divided by the percentage change in income.

Among normal goods, income elasticities can vary greatly. Luxuries like cruises, fine wine, and yachts tend to be more income elastic than necessities like food and televisions. **Income elastic demand** means the income elasticity of demand is greater than 1. Luxury goods are said to be income elastic. For a good to be income elastic, the numerator ($\%\Delta Q_d$) must be greater than the denominator ($\%\Delta\text{income}$). This means the quantity demanded of luxury goods increases more rapidly than incomes. As incomes rise, the average spending on such goods goes from essentially zero to a steadily larger percentage of the budget. To be a luxury good, it's not enough for people to buy more as incomes rise; they must spend a bigger *percentage* of their income on the good as income rises.

Normal goods can also be income inelastic. **Income inelastic demand** means the income elasticity of demand falls between 0 and 1. As we discussed earlier in this chapter, price changes have little impact on the quantity of necessities (such as gasoline or milk) sold—necessities tend to be price inelastic. Likewise, such necessities are often *income inelastic*. As incomes change, spending on basic groceries and gasoline tends to rise, but by a smaller percentage. As such, these goods become a smaller share of one's budget.

 POLICY BRIEF Public Transportation in Singapore

In 2011, economists in Singapore conducted a study to examine the effect of income on the demand for different transportation options in that city. They found that when incomes fall by roughly 4%, the use of public transportation increases by 1%. Mathematically, the income elasticity of demand is

$$E_{\text{income}} = \frac{.01}{-.04} = -0.25$$

This suggests that public transportation is an inferior good. That same study estimated the income elasticity of automobile ownership in Singapore to be 0.59; the positive number suggests automobiles are a normal good, as one might expect. They are also income inelastic. When Singaporeans get a 10% raise, they tend to spend an extra 5.9% on cars and 2.5% less on public transport. Such economic studies provide policymakers with useful data for setting transportation policy. Here, the income elasticities suggest that a booming economy may reduce the use of public transportation and increase congestion on roadways. Singapore responded with a heavy tax on cars, to reduce traffic congestion.[*]

[*]Michael Z. F. Li, Daren C. B. Lau, and Daniel W. M. Seah, "Car Ownership and Urban Transport Demand in Singapore," *International Journal of Transport Economics = Rivista Internazionale di Economia dei Trasporti,* January 31, 2011, http://trid.trb.org/view.aspx?id=1102691.

BUSINESS BRIEF Income Elasticity and U.S. Auto Sales

Consider three automobiles: the Ford Focus (a compact car), the Toyota Camry (a family sedan), and the Porsche 911 (a luxury sports car). Can you guess which car was hardest hit by the Great Recession (2007–2009), during which median incomes fell roughly 4%? Sales data along with income elasticity estimates (based on raw data) are presented in Exhibit 6.

It is not surprising that the Porsche 911 was very responsive to income changes. But as you can see, the sales of the Focus fell 7%, suggesting an income elasticity of roughly 1.75. This suggests that, even an economy car like the Ford Focus was considered a luxury good during the severe downturn of the Great Recession, as its income elasticity was greater than 1.

income elastic demand An income elasticity of demand that is greater than 1.

income inelastic demand An income elasticity of demand that is between 0 and 1.

Recall that economists apply the *ceteris paribus* assumption when analyzing data. In the real world, other things are not always equal, and many changes occur almost all the time. For example, you may recall from Chapter 3 that sales of the Ford Focus rose in 2008 due, in part, to increases in gasoline prices. However, in 2009, gasoline prices fell back to 2007 levels of roughly $3 a gallon, but auto sales did not recover. By 2009, the dominant factor affecting car sales was falling incomes during a severe recession. Not only were incomes falling, many potential consumers across all income levels feared *potential* losses in income: Unemployment was rising and those with investments in stocks or real estate saw sharp losses. With all of these changes occurring at once, it is often difficult to arrive at precise income elasticity estimates. However, most studies suggest that automobile sales are a normal good ($E_{income} > 0$).*

EXHIBIT 6	Rough Estimates of Income Elasticities of Select Cars (2007–2009)		
	Ford Focus	**Toyota Camry**	**Porsche 911**
2007 U.S. Sales	173,213	473,108	12,497
Percentage Change by 2009	−7%	−25%	−45%
Income Elasticity	1.8	6	11

Between 2007 and 2009, incomes fell by roughly 4%, while automobile sales dropped dramatically. Presented here are sales data for the Ford Focus, Toyota Camry, and Porsche 911. Gasoline prices started and finished at roughly the same price. Thus, the price of gasoline was not a major factor in determining sales during this period.

*Timothy Cain, "Ford Focus Sales Figures" and "Toyota Camry Sales," *GoodCarBadCar.com*, January 2, 2011, http://www.goodcarbadcar.net/2011/01/toyota-camry-sales-figures.html.

Cross-Price Elasticity of Demand

As you'll recall from Chapter 3, some products are related: When the price of one item changes, the demand for a related good changes as well. **Cross-price elasticity of demand** is a measure of how responsive quantity demanded is to changes in the price of another product; it equals the percentage change in quantity demanded of one product divided by the percentage change in price of another product. Mathematically, it is

$$E_{cross\ price} = \frac{\text{Percentage change in } Q_d}{\text{Percentage change in price of another product}}$$

or

$$E_{cross\ price} = \frac{\%\Delta Q_d}{\%\Delta P_{another\ product}}$$

As with income elasticity, the estimated value of the cross-price elasticity of demand can be positive or negative. An increase in the price of a secondary good can increase, decrease, or have no impact on the quantity of the primary good sold.

Recall that *complements* are a pair of products that are usually consumed together, and for which an increase in the price of one good reduces the demand for the other good, and vice versa. Thus by definition, complements have a cross-price elasticity that is negative. For example, if the price of pizzas falls, then the demand for toppings increases (as more pizzas are sold).

Conversely, substitute goods have a positive cross-price elasticity: An increase in the price of a secondary good can have a positive impact on the sales of the primary good. Recall, *substitutes* are defined as a pair of products for which an increase in the price of one leads to an increase in the demand for the other, and vice versa. Substitutes can be viewed as two products that are alternatives to each other. Substitute goods have a cross-price elasticity that is positive.

cross-price elasticity of demand A measure of how responsive quantity demanded is to changes in the price of another product; it equals the percentage change in quantity demanded of one product divided by the percentage change in price of another product.

EXHIBIT 7 Income and Cross-Price Elasticities for Different Types of Goods

Panel A: Income Elasticities

Type of Good	Values	Examples
Inferior	$E_{income} < 0$	Potatoes, basic wireless phones
Normal (necessity)	$0 < E_{income} < 1$	Basic groceries and medicine
Normal (luxury)	$E_{income} > 1$	Cars such as a Bentley or Ferrari

Panel B: Cross-Price Elasticities

Type of Good	Values	Examples
Complement	$E_{cross-price} < 0$	Pizza and toppings
Unrelated Goods	$E_{cross-price} = 0$	Roses and chalk
Substitute	$E_{cross-price} > 0$	McDonald's and Pizza Hut

Inferior goods have a negative income elasticity of demand, while normal goods have a positive income elasticity of demand. Complement goods have a negative cross-price elasticity of demand, while substitute goods have a positive cross-price elasticity of demand.

For example, data suggest that when prices go up by 10% at McDonald's, sales at Pizza Hut increase by 0.7%. The cross-price elasticity is 0.07. Ten percent price increases at Subway, Burger King, Wendy's, and KFC result in an approximate 0.2% increase in Pizza Hut sales. These positive cross-price elasticity estimates suggest that various fast-food restaurants are indeed substitute products. Note, however, that a 10% price increase at Pizza Hut has a considerably smaller impact on the sales of its larger rivals, because cross-price elasticity estimates are not symmetrical.

The fact that the cross-price elasticity estimates are relatively small suggests that price changes at one particular fast-food restaurant do not have a significant impact on sales at another *particular* restaurant, as there are many other alternatives. Cross-price elasticity measurements would tend to be larger if localized within specific towns and cities, as opposed to across an entire nation.[1]

Key values of income and cross-price elasticities of demand can be found in Exhibit 7.

📊 BUSINESS BRIEF Cross-Price Elasticity of Demand Between Natural Gas and Coal

Natural gas prices fell by two thirds between 2008 and 2013 as fracking increased supply. This prompted many electric power companies to switch from burning coal—traditionally, the cheapest fuel—to natural gas, a substitute that was now less expensive. This switch reduced the demand for coal by 17.5% between 2008 and 2013.[*] In this case, the cross-price elasticity of demand can be estimated as

$$E_{cross-price} = \frac{\% \Delta Q_d}{\% \Delta P_{another\ product}} = \frac{-17.5\%}{-67\%} = 0.3$$

The increased use of natural gas and decreased use of coal in the generation of electricity contributed to a 10% decrease in the greenhouse-gas emissions from U.S. power plants between 2010 and 2012.[†] This resulted because natural gas emits far fewer greenhouse gases than coal. It is now estimated that natural gas will be used to produce a third of all U.S. electricity by 2020, compared with just over 20% in 2008.

[*]"From Sunset to New Dawn," *The Economist,* November 18, 2013, http://www.economist.com/news /business/21589870-capitalists-not-just-greens-are-now-questioning-how-significant-benefits-shale -gas-and.

[†]U.S. Energy Information Administration, "Annual Energy Review," 2011, http://www.eia.gov/totalenergy/data /annual/index.cfm.

4.5 PRICE ELASTICITY OF SUPPLY

Businesses are also responsive to price changes. Recall from Chapter 3 that the supply curve shows us that when the price of a product increases (due to an increase in demand), so, too, does the quantity supplied. This is because sellers respond to higher prices with increased output. But *how much* does output increase? For example, suppose the hourly price of a Web design service increases by 10% due to an increase in demand—the quantity of hours supplied will increase. Price elasticity of supply tells us how large the increase will be.

Price elasticity of supply (E_s) is a measure of how responsive quantity supplied is to price changes; it equals the percentage change in quantity supplied divided by the percentage change in price. In Exhibit 8, the good in Panel A is relatively responsive to price changes and is considered elastic. The supply of pizzas is fairly price elastic, especially in the long run. The good in Panel B is not very responsive to price changes and is considered inelastic. For example, in the short run, raw materials like crude oil have a steeply sloping supply curve.

price elasticity of supply (E_s) A measure of how responsive quantity supplied is to price changes; it equals the percentage change in quantity supplied divided by the percentage change in price.

EXHIBIT 8 Elastic and Inelastic Supply Curves

Panel A: Price Elastic Supply

Panel A: $E_S > 1$

Panel B: Price Inelastic Supply

Panel B: $E_S < 1$

In Panel A, the supply curve is price elastic. Here, quantity is responsive to a price change: Small price changes lead to large changes in quantity. Conversely, in Panel B, the supply curve is price inelastic: Quantity is not very responsive to price changes.

How Much Quantity Supplied Changes When Price Changes

The formula for calculating price elasticity of supplied is similar to other elasticity formulas presented earlier in the chapter. Mathematically, it is the percentage change in quantity supplied divided by the percentage change in price. That is,

$$E_s = \frac{\text{Percentage change in } Q_s}{\text{Percentage change in } P}$$

or

$$E_s = \frac{\%\Delta Q_s}{\%\Delta P}$$

The equation is similar to that of the price elasticity of demand, except price elasticity of supply uses data from the supply curve. Estimates of the price elasticity of supply can range from zero to infinity:

- $E_s = 0 \rightarrow$ perfectly inelastic supply
- $E_s < 1 \rightarrow$ inelastic supply
- $E_s = 1 \rightarrow$ unit elastic supply
- $E_s > 1 \rightarrow$ elastic supply
- $E_s = $ infinity $\rightarrow$ perfectly elastic supply

Exhibit 9 shows the range of values for the price elasticity of supply. Panel A shows a perfectly inelastic supply curve. It is a vertical line. In contrast, Panel E shows that a perfectly elastic supply curve is a horizontal line.

EXHIBIT 9 Graphical Summary of the Price Elasticity of Supply

Estimates of the price elasticity of supply can range from zero (perfectly inelastic) to infinity (perfectly elastic).

BUSINESS BRIEF The $1 Million Parking Space

Occasionally, an item has an almost perfectly inelastic supply: The supply of land, for example, is often drawn as a vertical line, as it is generally fixed by nature and hence perfectly inelastic. When supplies are fixed, the primary determinant of price is demand: The quantity supplied cannot change. Consider parking spaces near a ballpark or arena. The number of parking spots available nearby is the same, whether there is an event occurring or not. But as you may have guessed, prices change quite a bit, depending on what's ongoing at that venue. Near Fenway Park in Boston, parking can cost upward of $50 during a Red Sox game, and as little as a few quarters in a parking meter at other times.* The high price of parking stems from the limited supply of land near the ballpark, and high demand for parking on game nights.

But what happens when demand for parking *always* outpaces supply? In some parts of New York City, for example, parking spaces are scarce around the clock. Commuters seeking to park for a few hours on any given day will pay as much as a Red Sox fan looking for a spot near Fenway on game night. As such, some very wealthy New Yorkers are willing to *buy* parking spots—for as much as a million dollars. Why? Once again, supply is limited and highly inelastic—and when this occurs, the primary determinant of price is demand.

Finally, the lucky buyer of the million dollar spot does have the option of increasing supply. As the *New York Post* pointed out, "The spot could be 'duplexed' if the buyer decides to install an elevator lift so he or she can slide both the Maserati and the Lamborghini in at the same time."† What a deal!

*"Fenway Park: Parking," *MLB.com*, n.d., accessed May 11, 2017, http://boston.redsox.mlb.com/bos/ballpark /directions/index.jsp?content=parking.

†Annie Karni, "The $1 Million Parking Space," *New York Post*, May 20, 2012, http://nypost.com/2012/05/20 /the-1-million-parking-space/.

Factors That Influence Price Elasticity of Supply

Several factors determine the price elasticity of supply. These include the time it takes businesses to adjust their inputs and how much it costs to increase output.

Time to Adjust Inputs The short- and long-run distinction is even more significant on the supply side than the demand side. In general, the more time businesses have to adjust, the greater the price elasticity of supply. Three distinct time frames exist:

- *Immediate future or market day.* In the very short run, the supply may be almost perfectly inelastic. For example, consider a fisherman who fishes every morning and sells his catch in the afternoon. A change in the price of fish has no impact on the quantity of fish supplied that day, which must be sold before they spoil. Likewise, if Mario makes 1,000 slices of pizza for a carnival later that night, he cannot change his quantity supplied if demand is higher than expected.

- *The short run.* If slightly more time elapses—say, a couple of days—the higher price of fish or pizza will encourage the fisherman to work more hours or Mario to make more pizza. In the short run, however, Mario will still be constrained by the number of ovens he has available and the fisherman by the number of his boats.

- *The long run.* Remember that the long run refers to the length of time necessary to make *all* adjustments to economic circumstances. Over time, Mario can respond to higher prices by hiring more staff and expanding his pizza shop, or he might open another restaurant. The fisherman can buy additional boats

∨ Looking for a place to park? It will cost you.

Kit Leong/Shutterstock.com

and hire additional crew. More importantly, the long run is enough time for new firms to enter the industry. Most industries have an extremely elastic supply in the long run.

Marginal Cost of Increasing Output When the marginal costs to make an additional few units is rising as output rises, supply will tend to be less price elastic (more inelastic). This is typically the case when a business is at capacity. Consider the example of an automobile manufacturer such as General Motors or Ford. Once a factory is built and running at capacity, it is expensive to manufacture a few more automobiles, because if the process runs overtime, the wages paid will generally be higher.

In contrast, when the marginal cost to make an additional few units is stable, the supply will tend to be more price elastic. This will likely be the case when there is spare capacity. A Ford factory running below capacity will not find it overly expensive to operate a few more hours per day, and a Dunkin' Donuts franchise not at capacity can quickly bake extra donuts when demand is growing.

Fixed Quantity Supplied Some items such as collectibles and land have a fixed quantity supplied that cannot be changed easily, even in the long run. In this case, the price elasticity of supply is perfectly inelastic. Consider the case of a Stradivarius violin. The supply curve for such a violin is a vertical line, as shown in Exhibit 9 as $E_s = 0$. Why? Because Antonio Stradivari died in 1737—no more can be made. Similarly, land also has a fixed quantity supplied. The previous Business Brief explains how such a scenario can result in seemingly exorbitant prices for parking spaces.

CASE STUDY Why Are Gas and Oil Prices So Unstable?

During 2008 and 2009, the price of crude oil fluctuated wildly, from about $40 per barrel to $147 per barrel. Consumers were bewildered as gasoline prices soared to $4 per gallon in 2008, then plunged to $2 in 2009, then recovered to the $3 to $4 range over the next few years, before falling back to the $2 range in 2015 to 2017. Why are crude oil prices so unstable? The underlying causes are all related to the price inelastic nature of supply and demand of crude oil.

Although alternative sources of energy such as wind and solar appear promising, oil remains the primary source of energy in the world economy. The price of gasoline typically follows the price of oil, as crude oil is the most important input into gasoline. According to the economist James Hamilton who studies energy economics, a gallon of gasoline in the United States costs, on average, roughly 84 cents plus 2½% of the price of a barrel of crude oil (or Brent crude oil). If you hear a business reporter saying that crude oil is $100 per barrel, you can expect gasoline to soon cost *about* $3.34 per gallon ($0.84 + $2.50). Basically, it costs a relatively constant 84 cents per gallon to cover fairly constant transportation, refining, and distribution cost. The 2.5% covers the cost of crude, which changes on a regular basis. The actual price you pay will vary depending on factors such as state and local taxes and the degree of competition.

As we discussed at the beginning of this chapter, the demand for oil and related products like gasoline is relatively price inelastic, particularly in the short run. In the immediate aftermath of an increase in the price of oil, automobiles are still driven, homes are still heated, and electricity is still generated. But in the long run, consumers are more responsive to changes in the price of oil and gasoline—that is, price elasticity of demand is higher in the long run. In response to continually higher fuel prices, consumers will gradually find ways to conserve energy. They'll walk, bike, carpool, or use public transportation more often. When practical, they will opt for more fuel-efficient cars; some might move closer to work, or to public transportation hubs.

The supply of oil is also price inelastic. Large and easily accessible crude oil reserves are quite limited. There are relatively low-cost supplies in the Persian Gulf region of the Middle East, where nearly half of the world's conventional oil reserves are located. When demand for oil rises, however, new production must take place in areas where it is often more difficult and costly to produce oil. Sometimes the difficulty stems from political instability, as is frequently the case with oil from the Middle East and Africa. In other regions, the difficulty is often technical, as is the case in remote areas of Alaska and Canada, and with offshore oil reserves located far below the Gulf of Mexico and North Sea. However, when these expensive wells are functioning, the cost of continuing to produce oil is low, compared to the cost of drilling a new well. This means that when oil prices fall, companies tend to keep producing from existing wells but are less likely to drill new wells. All these factors make the supply of oil relatively price inelastic at current output levels.

The key characteristics of the oil market include:
- Price inelastic demand in the short run
- Price inelastic supply in the short run
- Oil often produced in areas that are politically volatile or difficult to access
- Supply subject to disruptions

Price Inelastic Supply and Demand Result in Large Price Swings

With both supply and demand being price inelastic, relatively small shifts in the supply or demand for oil can have a very large impact on prices. Motorists notice this instability every time they fill up at the gas pump. For example, in 2007 and 2008, rapid growth in developing countries such as China led to a sharp increase in oil demand. The global demand curve for oil shifted to the right. This raised price sharply, but quantity supplied only increased by a very small amount because the supply of oil in the short run is very inelastic. So even though producers earned much higher prices in 2008, they only

were able to slightly increase production. When the demand for oil suddenly declined in late 2008 as a result of the Great Recession, the price of oil fell sharply (70%).*

Exhibit 10 demonstrates a price inelastic supply and demand curve and the effects of a decline in demand. Likewise, Exhibit 11 shows how even a small decrease in supply shifts the supply curve to the left can result in a relatively large increase in the price of oil. Such supply "shocks" can result from natural or man-made disasters, from political instability or political maneuvering. In 1973, for example, the Organization of the Petroleum Exporting Countries (OPEC) slashed oil production, in retaliation for the United States' support of Israel in a military conflict in the Middle East, dramatically raising the price per barrel overnight. Soon thereafter, OPEC instituted an embargo that cut off the supply of Middle Eastern oil to the United States entirely. In three months, the price of oil tripled.†

Finally, recall that the long-run supply and demand price elasticities are greater than the short-run price elasticities. In the short run, the oil price hike of 2008 did not produce an immediate increase in global oil output. However, over the next few years, American producers responded to higher prices by investing in new technologies and alternative energy sources.

As noted earlier, increased use of fracking technology boosted the output of oil and natural gas. Alternative energy sources—such as solar and wind—have also begun to gain some traction in recent years. In 2013, over $200 billion was invested globally in renewable energy, with over half of that total pumped into solar. So intense was the expansion that more

EXHIBIT 10 Decrease in the Demand for Oil

Since the supply and demand curves for oil are both inelastic, a decrease in demand can lead to a large price change.

EXHIBIT 11 Decrease in the Supply of Oil

Since the supply and demand curves for oil are both inelastic, a decrease in supply can lead to a large price change.

solar capacity was developed between 2010 and 2014 than in the previous four decades combined. However, even at this breakneck pace, solar is expected to make up just 2 to 3% of the global electricity market in coming years.‡ Similarly, consumers can and do eventually switch to more fuel-efficient cars and insulate their homes more efficiently when prices remain high. Remember, time to adjust is a critical factor in determining the price elasticity of demand. The demand for oil is more elastic in the long run than in the short run.

*See James D. Hamilton, "Understanding Crude Oil Prices," *The Energy Journal* 30, no. 2, 2009: 179–206; and James D. Hamilton and Menzie Chinn, "Gasoline Prices Coming Down," *econbrowser.com,* June 24, 2012, http://econbrowser.com/archives/2012/06/gasoline_prices_7.

†OPEC, U.S. Energy Information Administration, http://www.opec .org/opec_web/static_files_project/media/downloads/publications /ASB2013.pdf, http://www.eia.gov/dnav/pet/hist/LeafHandler .ashx?n=pet&s=emm_epm0_pte_nus_dpg&f=w.

‡Shawn Tully, "The Shale Oil Revolution Is in Danger," *Fortune.com,* January 9, 2015, http://fortune.com/2015/01/09/oil-prices-shale-fracking/; and "We Make Our Own," *The Economist,* January 15, 2015, http://www.economist.com/news/special-report/21639020-renewables-are-no-longer-fad-fact-life-supercharged-advances-power.

BUSINESS TAKEAWAY

As demonstrated in our examination of Amazon's dispute with Hachette, the economic concept of elasticity has clear applications in business: Amazon demonstrated that its customers were highly responsive to changes in the price of e-books, and that lower prices could and did result in higher revenues. As firms become increasingly data-driven, they will be able to access vast troves of information on quantities sold at different prices, which they can then analyze to determine real-world elasticities and to set optimal prices.

Many firms employ economists to estimate demand elasticities and calculate cross-elasticities to find out which goods are substitutes and complements with sometimes surprising results. A firm selling a product for which there are no good substitutes can take advantage of price inelastic demand: Because consumers are relatively unresponsive to price changes when demand is price inelastic, such firms can easily increase price, without seeing a large decline in sales. Such a price increase is particularly appealing to the firm, as not only does total revenue increase, the firm also sells slightly fewer units, and thus has slightly lower costs. This increases profitability, even as fewer units are sold.

Most businesses, however, sell products that have *a lot* of substitutes—they compete with other brands, and with similar or alternative products. Although the overall demand for milk is price inelastic, the demand for any specific brand of milk is highly elastic. This means that individual firms usually face a demand curve that is highly elastic. In such cases, even a modest price increase will lead to a comparatively large decrease in sales and a decrease in total revenue.

When measuring price elasticities, it's important to distinguish between the demand curve facing a single product line, or a single firm, and the demand curve facing an entire industry. An independent farmer understands that the demand for her organic milk will be more price elastic than the demand for organic milk in general. In turn, this specific type of milk will be more price elastic than the overall market demand for milk.

That same farmer, of course, might seek ways to change the demand curve for her organic milk. Firms big and small advertise in hopes of both increasing the demand for their product and changing the price elasticity of demand for the goods or services they offer. A successful marketing and advertising plan can make consumers less responsive to price changes. A firm might convince consumers that certain products are necessities rather than luxuries, or that alternative products are not good substitutes, making demand less elastic.

ʌ Got milk? Consumer demand for milk is generally price inelastic, but specific brands of milk are highly elastic.

Firms benefit when they are able to capitalize on the income elasticity of goods in different market segments. A firm that sells both inferior and normal goods appeals to a wider range of customers at different income levels. Such firms will also be better positioned to weather recessions, when incomes typically fall, and consumer spending shifts toward inferior goods.

Firms can increase revenues if they make strategic decisions related to cross-elasticities among the goods and services they offer. For example, Hewlett-Packard or Brother might sell printers at a loss, in order to lock in future sales on more profitable complement goods, such as printer drums and toner cartridges. Cross-elasticities also occur between different firms: Every time Apple or Samsung releases a new device, for example, a bevy of small firms that sell complement goods such as chargers, cases, earbuds, and applications are also likely to see an increase in demand.

CHAPTER STUDY GUIDE

4.1 THE PRICE ELASTICITY OF DEMAND

Elasticity is a measure of responsiveness, with price elasticity of demand being a measure of how responsive quantity demanded is to price changes. The **price elasticity of demand (E_d)** depends on the availability of substitutes, the amount of time to adjust, the share of budget spent on the product, and whether the good is a necessity, a luxury, addictive, or heavily advertised with brand loyalty. In general, demand is more elastic and consumers are more responsive to price changes the greater the number of substitutes, the more time to adjust, the larger the share of one's budget spent on the item, and when goods are luxuries.

4.2 MEASURING THE PRICE ELASTICITY OF DEMAND

Price elasticity of demand is measured as percentage change in quantity over percentage change in price. Percentage changes are measured using the midpoint formula—change in value over average value. Thus,

$$E_d = \frac{\%\Delta Q_d}{\%\Delta P} = \frac{\left(\dfrac{\Delta Q}{(Q_1 + Q_2)/2}\right)}{\left(\dfrac{\Delta P}{(P_1 + P_2)/2}\right)}$$

Depending on the source, price elasticity of demand is expressed as a positive or negative number. When demand is price elastic, that is, $E_d > 1$, consumers are relatively responsive to price changes, and thus any given change in price will lead to a proportionally larger change in quantity demanded. When demand is price inelastic and $E_d < 1$, consumers are not very responsive to price changes.

4.3 HOW A PRICE CHANGE AFFECTS UNIT SALES AND SALES REVENUE

Price changes impacts both unit sales and sales revenue. Elasticity values can be used to make estimates of price and quantity changes. When the price elasticity of demand and the price change are known, quantity changes can be estimated as

$$\%\Delta Q_d = E_d \times \%\Delta P$$

Total revenue is the money a business receives for selling a product; also called *revenue*. It equals the price of the item times the quantity sold. When demand is price inelastic, increases in price increase total revenue, as the increase in price is proportionately larger than the decrease in quantity demanded. When demand is price elastic, an increase in price lowers total revenue. Total revenue is maximized at the point where demand is unit elastic.

4.4 OTHER DEMAND ELASTICITIES

Income elasticity of demand is a measure of how responsive quantity demanded is to changes in income. It equals

$$E_{d,\text{income}} = \frac{\%\Delta Q_d}{\%\Delta \text{income}}$$

If $E_{d,\text{income}} < 0$, the item is considered an inferior good. If $E_{d,\text{income}} > 0$, the item is considered a normal good. **Income elastic demand** means the income elasticity of demand is greater than 1. Luxury goods are said to be income elastic. In contrast, **income inelastic demand** means the income elasticity of demand falls between 0 and 1. Necessities are often income inelastic. **Cross-price elasticity of demand** is a measure of how responsive quantity demanded is to changes in the prices of another product. It equals

$$E_{d,\text{cross-price}} = \frac{\%\Delta Q_d}{\%\Delta P_{\text{another product}}}$$

If $E_{d,\text{cross-price}} < 0$, the items are considered complement goods. If $E_{d,\text{cross-price}} > 0$, the items are considered substitute goods.

4.5 PRICE ELASTICITY OF SUPPLY

Price elasticity of supply (E_s) is a measure of how responsive quantity supplied is to price changes. It is

$$E_s = \frac{\%\Delta Q_s}{\%\Delta P}$$

If $E_s = 0$, the item is said to have a perfectly inelastic supply. This may occur in the very short run, such as a single day. $E_s < 1$ suggests an inelastic supply, and $E_s > 1$ suggests an elastic supply.

TOP TEN TERMS AND CONCEPTS

1. Elasticity
2. Midpoint Method
3. Perfectly Elastic and Perfectly Inelastic
4. Total Revenue
5. Cross-Price Elasticity
6. Price Elasticity of Demand
7. Price Elastic versus Inelastic Demand
8. Determinants of Price Elasticity of Demand
9. Income Elasticity
10. Price Elasticity of Supply

STUDY PROBLEMS

1. A local Wendy's franchise owner Jim wants to increase the revenue he receives by selling Frosties in July. He already knows that when he prices the dessert at $1.59, he sells 400 per day, and when he sets the price at $1.99, he sells 300 per day. What is the price elasticity of demand for the dessert? What happens to total revenue after the price increase? Are there any other factors Jim should consider?

2. Between 2007 and 2009, sales of the Hyundai Sonata fell 17% from 145,568 to 120,028, while incomes dropped by 4% (Cain, 2011).[2] Estimate the income elasticity of demand using the midpoint method. Is the good an inferior good, income elastic, or income inelastic?

3. According to a Web posting by Amazon, if customers will buy 100,000 copies of a particular e-book at $14.99, then they would purchase 174,000 copies of that same e-book at $9.99.[3] Use this data to estimate the price elasticity of demand.

4. Live Nation, America's largest concert promoter, hires an economist to determine how to maximize total revenue for concert events with limited seating. The economist suggests that for one currently popular artist, the price elasticity of demand is 0.5. For another artist, the price elasticity of demand is 2. Based on this information, what pricing strategies do you suggest that Live Nation adopt?

5. Assume that for a certain product the price elasticity of demand is 2 and the price elasticity of supply is 3.

   a. What impact will a 10% increase in price have on quantity demanded?

   b. What impact will a 10% increase in price have on quantity supplied?

   c. Explain the differences (or similarities) between your answers to a and b.

6. List and explain the factors that help determine the price elasticity of demand. List and explain the factors that help determine the price elasticity of supply.

7. In recent decades, incomes in China have been rising at about 10% per year. Suppose you are told that Chinese consumption is changing at the following rates:

   a. Rice: −2% per year

   b. Beef: +3% per year

   c. Seafood: +12% per year

   In each case, describe the income elasticity and also the general category to which the good belongs. Are these elasticities likely to be exactly the same in the United States?

8. Consider the following list of modes of transportation. Rank them in terms of income elasticity of demand. Explain your reasoning.

   • The Gulfstream G550, the best-selling private jet

   • A cross-country trip on a Greyhound bus, a public bus company

   • A Toyota Corolla, a basic automobile

   • A Maserati, a luxury sports car

9. Retailers commonly refer to the day after Thanksgiving as Black Friday. Assume one retailer, GameStop, that sells video games sees its sales increase by 20% after reducing prices by 10%. Discuss the price elasticity of demand in the video game market. Use this example to discuss complications in making such estimates.

10. Explain why perfectly inelastic demand is rare.

11. Taxes on products typically result in higher prices and lower sales. Based on what you have learned thus far, why might taxes on products that are price inelastic such as cigarettes or pharmaceuticals not have a major impact on sales, while taxes on products that are elastic such as cruises will have a major impact on sales.

12. Explain the relationship between total revenue and price along a linear demand curve. Use separate graphs showing demand and total revenue to demonstrate your answer.

13. Business software maker Oracle produces software that firms use to effectively manage their inventories up to the minute.[4] This allows the companies to instantly prioritize what products need to be manufactured when sales on the product start to pick up, without having to hold excessively large product inventories. This technique reduces costs and allows retailers to quickly supply more product. Explain what impact such techniques have on the relative price elasticity of supply.

14. When the price of pizza sold by Mario's rival fell by 10% last summer, Mario saw a 5% decline in his sales. What was the cross-price elasticity of demand between Mario and his rival?

15. In 1916, Henry Ford made the following statement to a newspaper reporter:

There are many men who will pay $360 for a car who would not pay $440. We had in round numbers 500,000 buyers of cars on the $440 basis, and I figure that on the $360 basis we can increase the sales to possibly 800,000 cars for the year—less profit on each car, but more cars, more employment of labor, and in the end we get all the total profit we ought to make.[5]

a. If Ford's estimate was correct, what was the price elasticity of demand for his cars?

b. By how much did total revenue increase?

∧ How much pizza will customers really eat?

CHAPTER 5

Consumer Choice

Decision Making for Consumers

Mario is considering an "all you can eat Tuesdays" promotion, which would invite consumers to eat all the pizza they wish for one fixed price. He knows that the promotion would lure hungry customers to his shop, but he is concerned that customers would literally eat into his profits—he could even lose money.

Like all economic actors, Mario's customers are rational. They want to get the most pizza for their money. Hungry customers will really enjoy the first few slices, but relish each additional slice less as they start to become full. Some customers will eat three or four slices, and some even more than that. But for all customers, there will come a point where eating one more slice is not rational—even on "all you can eat Tuesdays."

In this chapter, we examine *consumer choice,* or how customers make decisions on what to buy given their limited budget. Understanding consumer choice is crucial for business owners like Mario, who must understand what their customers want, and how they will respond to pricing and promotions.

Chapter Learning Targets

● Describe the concept of utility and its applications.

● Demonstrate how consumers maximize utility given a fixed budget and explain how this concept relates to the law of demand.

● Use indifference curves and the budget constraint to determine optimal consumption.

5.1 UTILITY: A MEASURE OF CONSUMER SATISFACTION

Imagine you win a $2,500 shopping spree at the mall. You need to decide how to spend your limited budget. Would you buy only clothing and footwear? Perhaps only the latest smartphone and other electronics? Would you simply choose at random? Presumably not. Instead, you would use your money to make yourself as well off as possible—that is to say, you would attempt to maximize your satisfaction.

Undoubtedly, you would buy a mixture of goods. Just as each additional slice of pizza at Mario's brings less additional satisfaction each additional pair of Air Jordans brings less additional satisfaction than the first pair. Likewise, a second or third iPhone brings about less satisfaction than the first phone. The consequence of this is that while the first pair of Jordans may bring you the greatest amount of satisfaction, the second pair may *not* do so. The implication of this and how consumers choose to spend a limited budget is the focus of this chapter.

Utility

Economists are interested in the level of satisfaction that consumers experience from their purchases. **Utility** is a hypothetical measure of satisfaction that people get from consuming goods and services. The concept was formulated by British economist and philosopher Jeremy Bentham (1748–1832), who believed that society should strive to maximize utility. In economic terms, consumers make purchasing decisions with the goal of maximizing their utility—or satisfaction—subject to their limited budget. In simpler terms, consumers want to get the most bang for their buck.

Economists measure utility in *utils,* which are hypothetical units of satisfaction. Despite Bentham's hope that science would one day invent a machine that could measure utils, we do not have any way of deriving a precise measurement. However, most economists believe we can make inferences about utility by looking carefully at consumer behavior. For example, if consumers are willing to pay more for a new pair of Air Jordans than for a different athletic shoe, we can infer that they derive more utility from the Jordans. Similarly, if consumers eventually stop eating additional slices of pizza even on "all you can eat Tuesdays," then we can infer that at some point, the additional utility of one extra slice must be less than the utility derived from each of the first few slices.

Marginal Utility versus Total Utility

Because the third or fourth slice of pizza is often less satisfying than the first, economists find it useful to measure the additional satisfaction from consuming an additional slice of pizza. **Marginal utility** is the additional utility gained from consuming an additional unit. That is,

$$\text{Marginal utility} = \frac{\Delta \text{Total utility}}{\Delta Q}$$

utility A hypothetic measure of satisfaction experienced by consumers.

marginal utility The additional utility gained from consuming an additional unit.

total utility The overall amount of satisfaction a consumer obtains from consuming a given total of a particular good.

where the Greek letter Δ (delta) means change, and ΔQ refers to a change in quantity when an additional unit is consumed.

Do not confuse marginal utility with **total utility**—the overall amount of satisfaction a consumer obtains from consuming a given total of a particular good. It is quite likely that the total utility derived from owning two pairs of Jordans is greater than the total utility derived from one pair. But it is also likely that the second pair will *not* increase his or her level of happiness as much as did the first. Marginal utility refers to the *extra* satisfaction of the second pair, the additional unit. Exhibit 1 shows the relationship between the quantity of pizza slices consumed, total utility, and marginal utility. As you can see, the concepts of total utility and marginal utility are interrelated.

For the first nine slices, total utility increases with each slice at a decreasing rate. Total utility increases from 0 to 36 utils for the first slice and increases from 36 to 60 for the second slice. Thus, the marginal utility of the first slice is 36 (= 36 − 0) and the marginal utility for the second slice is 24 (= 60 − 36).

EXHIBIT 1 Total Utility and Marginal Utility

Panel A: Total Utility

Total Utility (utils)

Total utility increases by 5 when consuming 6 rather than 5 slices.

101
96

60

36

Quantity
1   2   5   6

Panel B: Marginal Utility

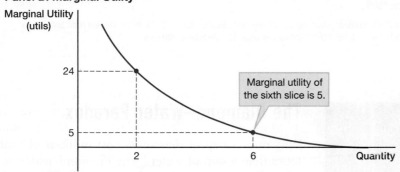

Marginal Utility (utils)

24

Marginal utility of the sixth slice is 5.

5

Quantity
2   6

Panel C: Utility Table

Quantity	Total Utility	Marginal Utilty
0	0	—
1	36	36
2	60	24
3	76	16
4	88	12
5	96	8
6	101	5
7	103	2
8	104	1
9	104.4	0.4
10	104	−0.4

Panel A shows the total utility a consumer receives by consuming various amounts of pizza. Panel B shows the marginal utility associated with each additional slice. Consistent with the law of diminishing marginal utility, marginal utility declines with each additional slice. Data for the graphs come from the table in Panel C.

The Law of Diminishing Marginal Utility

Since consumers receive less additional satisfaction from consuming their sixth slice of pizza than they do from their first slice, marginal utility is said to be diminishing. The **law of diminishing marginal utility** states that increasing consumption of a good decreases marginal utility over a given period of time. Consistent with the law of diminishing marginal utility, marginal utility for the first slice is 36 utils and just 24 utils for the second slice. As consumers become full, they value each additional slice by an ever-smaller amount. This explains why the total utility curve in Exhibit 1 (Panel A) increases at a decreasing rate and why the marginal utility curve (Panel B) is downward-sloping.

Could total utility actually fall with more consumption? It's possible. As shown in Exhibit 1, Panel B, the marginal utility of the 10th slice is negative—the consumer is so full that and the 10th slice leads to stomach pains. Economists would consider consuming this slice of pizza irrational behavior. With a utility curve like the one shown in Exhibit 1, a consumer at Mario's pizzeria for "all you can eat Tuesdays" will consume nine slices. It is this amount by which the consumer gets the most for his or her money—maximizing total utility (104.4 utils). In this example, each of the first nine slices adds to total utility but does not add to the price consumers pay because the price is fixed at an all-you-can-eat.

law of diminishing marginal utility The principle that, during a given period of time, increasing consumption of a good decreases marginal utility.

Think & Speak Like an Economist

In economics and business, it is necessary to differentiate between *marginal* and *total*. A marginal value captures a change in the total value. *Total utility* is the overall amount of satisfaction a consumer receives from consuming a given total of a particular good, while *marginal utility* is the additional total utility from each extra unit consumed.

BUSINESS BRIEF Miscalculating Marginal Utility at Red Lobster

In 2003, the seafood chain Red Lobster ran an "Endless Crab" promotion offering patrons all the crab legs they could eat for $20 to $25. Consumers were delighted: Crab legs are fairly expensive (about $5 per pound wholesale at the time), but with this offer, the price for *each additional* crab leg was zero. And because they are not particularly filling, consumers were refilling their plates as long as the marginal utility continued to be positive. One group reportedly ate 18 pounds of crab legs; another boasted that it had enjoyed 30 refills.

The end result was a sharp decline in profits for Darden Restaurants, owners of the Red Lobster chain. In a corporate conference call on the matter, one Darden executive reported, "It wasn't the second helping, it was the third one that hurt." Another chimed in, "Yeah, and maybe the fourth."* In response, Darden fired the Red Lobster president who initiated the promotion. The chain has since tweaked its all-you-can-eat formula: Its annual "Endless Shrimp" promotion continues to draw customers seeking to maximize their seafood utility, and the firm has managed to price that promotion profitably.†

*Quoted in Paul Ziobro, "Restaurants Push 'Value' Meals," *The Wall Street Journal*, October 1, 2008, http://www.wsj.com/articles/SB122282672330793007. Benita D. Newton, "All-You-Can-Eat Was Too Much," *St. Petersburg Times*, September 26, 2003.

†"Red Lobster Brings Back Endless Shrimp," *redlobster.com*, September 6, 2016, https://www.redlobster.com/news-press/press/article/2016/08/30/red-lobster-brings-back-endless-shrimp.

∧ Red Lobster got into hot water when it offered an all-you-can-eat deal on pricey, not-too-filling crab legs.

The Diamond–Water Paradox

Why does a cup of diamonds cost millions of times more than a cup of water? The *diamond–water paradox*, first presented by Adam Smith in *The Wealth of Nations* (1776), is the name given to the puzzling fact that some goods with great value to society, such as water, have a much lower value in the marketplace than other goods, such as diamonds. "Nothing is more useful than water: but it will purchase scarce anything," wrote Smith. "A diamond, on the contrary, has scarce any use-value; but a very great quantity of other goods may frequently be had in exchange for it." Smith and other early economists tried to distinguish between "value in use" (utility) and "value in exchange" (market price). Water is useful as it is necessary to survive, but diamonds command a much greater price.

Modern economists explain the diamond–water paradox by distinguishing between total utility and marginal utility. The price an individual is willing to pay for an item is not determined by total utility; rather, the willingness to pay is determined by marginal utility. Although a person cannot survive if his or her total use of water is zero, there is so much water in most parts of the world that the value of 1 additional cup is rather small. Economists would say that the total utility of water is very high, but the marginal utility of 1 extra cup of water is quite low. That is to say, the value of an extra 5 seconds in a 10-minute shower is near zero. In contrast, diamonds are so scarce and glamorous that a single cup of diamonds yields a lot of marginal utility—perhaps several thousand wedding rings with great sentimental value. Ultimately, value in exchange is based on marginal utility. So the early economists were wrong; the exchange value in the marketplace (market price) equals the value in use *at the margin*.

In the next section, we continue to assume that consumers maximize utility, but change the analysis so that each additional slice has a price (no more "all-you-can-eat" deals), there are alternative goods to choose from, and consumers have a limited budget. Not surprisingly, when consumers have a budget and must pay for each additional slice, they will likely purchase fewer than the nine slices they would have consumed with the all-you-can-eat promotion.

 POLICY BRIEF Superstars Are Like Diamonds; Teachers Are Like Water

The diamond–water paradox doesn't just apply to product markets. It also applies to the supply and demand for labor services. One often hears commentators discussing the extremely high pay of professional athletes, and wondering whether society's priorities aren't mixed up. Why do baseball players make so much more than teachers? Isn't education more valuable to society than sports?

Overall (or in total), education is indeed much more valuable than sports. But salaries reflect the marginal value to society of *one* extra teacher, in a market that has many potential teachers available. One extra teacher can typically only teach a few dozen students at a time, and hence the market value of the teacher's service is not as high as the market value of a great athlete, who can entertain tens of millions of fans. Highly talented athletic superstars are like diamonds—they are rare. The service they provide is not highly valuable in total (compared to teaching), but they are so scarce that 1 additional unit is highly valuable. In comparison, teachers are like water: Extremely valuable in total, but each teacher has only a modest additional benefit to society.[*]

[*]See Jeffrey Brown, "How Teachers Can Be Both Undervalued and Overpaid," *Forbes*, January 26, 2012, http://www.forbes.com/sites/jeffreybrown/2012/01/24/how-teachers-can-be-both-undervalued-and-overpaid/.

5.2 MAXIMIZING UTILITY WITH A LIMITED BUDGET

If consumers could maximize utility without any constraints, we would all likely buy more stuff—we'd immediately upgrade to the latest tech gadget, outsource tasks like preparing meals and housekeeping, and purchase a new wardrobe each season. But, in fact, the amount of goods we consume, regardless of utility, is constrained by how much money we have to spend on them. This is known as a limited budget or **budget constraint**, the limit of all combinations of goods and services that can be afforded within a given budget. In order to maximize utility, consumers with a set budget and multiple products to select from will purchase products that give them the most marginal utility per dollar. **Marginal utility per dollar** is marginal utility divided by price.

Consumer Decision Making and a Rule for Maximizing Utility

Let's return to Mario's pizza shop. Exhibit 2 adds to our earlier analysis by introducing prices and an alternative product: soda. Suppose the price of a slice of pizza is $2 and that of soda is $1 per can. Assume a customer, Zoe, has $2 to spend. How should Zoe spend her money to maximize utility? Purchase one slice of pizza *or* two sodas? Would Zoe buy two sodas just because she can afford a higher quantity of soda? Probably not. Zoe's total utility from consuming one slice of pizza (36) is higher than the total utility from consuming two cans of soda (16). The first slice of pizza has a higher marginal utility per dollar than would be obtained by purchasing two sodas. Pizza gives Zoe the most bang for her buck (or two bucks in this case).

Now assume Zoe has a fixed budget of $10. Zoe's first purchase will give her the most marginal utility per dollar, and her second purchase will provide the second most marginal utility per dollar. With each additional dollar she spends, Zoe searches for the purchase that gives her the highest marginal utility per dollar she spends.

budget constraint The limit of all combinations of goods and services that can be afforded within a given budget.

marginal utility per dollar Marginal utility divided by price.

EXHIBIT 2 Maximizing Marginal Utility per Dollar

Pizza (price = $2)					Soda (price = $1)				
Quantity	Total Utility	MU	$\frac{MU}{P}$	Order	Quantity	Total Utility	MU	$\frac{MU}{P}$	Order
1	36	36	18	←a	1	10	10	10	←c
2	60	24	12	←b	2	16	6	6	←e or f
3	76	16	8	←d	3	21.6	5.6	5.6	
4	88	12	6	←e or f	4	27	5.4	5.4	
5	96	8	4		5	31.1	4.1	4.1	

Note: Budget is $10.

Consumers with a fixed budget will spend in such a way as to get the most they can for their money. This entails making purchases with the highest marginal utility per dollar. In this example, a slice of pizza costs $2 and a can of soda $1, and the consumer has a $10 budget. The consumer will first purchase two slices of pizza (*a*, *b*) then one can of soda (*c*), then a third slice of pizza (*d*), followed by a fourth slice of pizza and a second can of soda (*e* and *f*). Here, the consumer's optimal consumption is achieved as the marginal utilities per dollar on the last purchases are equal (at 6).

To maximize her utility within her budget, the process continues until her $10 is spent. Using this approach, consumers maximize their utility given their budget. For Zoe, the order of purchases will be:

- 1st slice of pizza (*MU/P* = 18 vs. 1st soda *MU/P* = 10). Spent $2 total.
- 2nd slice of pizza (*MU/P* = 12 vs. 1st soda *MU/P* = 10). Spent $4 total.
- 1st soda (*MU/P* = 10 vs. 3rd slice of pizza *MU/P* = 8). Spent $5 total.
- 3rd slice of pizza (*MU/P* = 8 vs. 2nd soda *MU/P* = 6). Spent $7 total.
- Indifferent between 4th slice of pizza or 2nd soda (*MU/P* = 6). If Zoe buys both, then all $10 will be spent.

In this example, Zoe's total utility is 104: 88 from four slices of pizza and 16 from two cans of soda. The $10 could have been spent buying just five slices of pizza, *or* alternatively four sodas for $4 and three slices of pizza for $6. Either of these options, however, *reduces* total utility as compared to Zoe's best option.

Marginal utility analysis is consistent with the concept of marginal analysis found in Chapter 1. To maximize utility, consumers repeatedly make consumption choices where the marginal benefit (marginal utility) per dollar spent is greater than or equal to the *opportunity* cost of the item—the marginal utility per dollar spent on the alternative good.

Consumers attempt to get the most value for each dollar they spend. **Optimal consumption** is the bundle, or combination, of goods that maximizes a consumer's utility, subject to a budget constraint. Optimal consumption is reached by spending in such a way that the marginal utilities per dollar on the last purchases are approximately equal. The condition results from consumers approaching every purchase in a manner that gives them the most marginal utility per dollar. Mathematically,

$$\frac{MU_{\text{Good A}}}{P_{\text{Good A}}} \cong \frac{MU_{\text{Good B}}}{P_{\text{Good B}}} \cong \cdots \cong \frac{MU_{\text{Good Z}}}{P_{\text{Good Z}}}$$

If the equation was not equalized, then consumers could boost their total utility by switching their spending from low-valued items (low marginal utility per dollar) to higher-valued items (high marginal utility per dollar).

Think & Speak Like an Economist

Part of marginal analysis involves computing the change in benefits from an additional activity. In this case, marginal benefit is called marginal utility. To maximize total utility, consumption choices are made that maximize marginal utility per dollar spent.

optimal consumption
The bundle of goods that maximizes a consumer's utility subject to a budget constraint.

BUSINESS BRIEF Diminishing Marginal Utility at SeaWorld

In October 2017, adult admission to SeaWorld in San Diego was just $89.99 for a one-day pass. On the same webpage, a special deal offered an annual pass, which would allow unlimited visits, for just $99.99.* How could the price of a year's worth of additional visits be as little as $10? The answer lies in the diminishing marginal utility of the second visit. Once consumers enjoy the major attractions during the first visit, the second visit is likely to garner less additional satisfaction.

In response to diminishing marginal utility, SeaWorld determined that in order to attract repeat customers, it must lower prices dramatically to equalize the marginal utility per dollar. Given diminishing returns, the failure to reduce price would result in a situation where $MU_{2nd\ visit}/P_{2nd\ visit}$ is too high to generate repeat customers. But by offering the opportunity to visit the park a second (or third or fourth) time at a low price, SeaWorld is able to increase the total number of visitors, most of whom are likely to spend additional money on items like food and drink when they return to the park. This generates additional revenue that would have been lost if the price of a second visit were the same as the first.

∧ Will a second day be as fun as the first? Sea World's pricing suggests not.

*Sasha Foo, "SeaWorld in San Diego Unveils New Attractions for 2018." KUSI.com. September 27, 2017, http://www.kusi.com/story/36471112/seaworld-in-san-diego-unveils-new-attractions-for-2018.

Deriving a Demand Curve with Utility Analysis

Knowing that consumers spend in such a way as to maximize utility provides insight into the shape of demand curves and the law of demand. Suppose the price of pizza increases to $3 per slice. You already know from the law of demand that the quantity of pizza slices demanded should decline. Marginal utility analysis gives us the same answer.

Exhibit 3 demonstrates the impact of a price change on quantity demanded. Originally, with a price of $2 per slice, 4 slices are sold (see Exhibit 2). This is point *a* on

---

EXHIBIT 3 Maximizing Marginal Utility per Dollar and Deriving the Demand Curve for Pizza

Panel A: A price increase alters the optimal consumption . . .

Panel B: . . . and reduces the quantity of pizza demanded.

	Pizza (price = $3)				Soda (price = $1)			
Quantity	Total Utility	M.U.	$\frac{MU}{P}$	Order	Quantity	Total Utility	M.U.	$\frac{MU}{P}$	Order
1	36	36	12	←a	1	10	10	10	←b
2	60	24	8	←c	2	16	6	6	←d
3	76	16	5.3		3	21.6	5.6	5.6	←e
4	88	12	4		4	27	5.4	5.4	←f
5	96	8	2.7		5	31.1	4.1	4.1	
Budget is $10								

As shown in Exhibit 2, when the price of pizza is $2, the optimal consumption for a consumer with a $10 budget consists of four slices. This corresponds to point *a* on the demand curve in Panel B. In Panel A, that same consumer purchases two slices when the price of pizza is $3; point *b* on the demand curve. The result is consistent with the law of demand.

the demand curve. But what happens when the price of pizza increases to $3? Under such a circumstance, utility analysis shows that our consumer will purchase 2 slices of pizza and 4 cans of soda. This is point *b* on the demand curve.

Finally, note that you will not always be able to receive *exactly* the same marginal utility per dollar on the last items purchased (as was the case in Exhibit 2). In the real world, the marginal utility per dollar spent will be approximately equal, but not exactly equal (as is the case in Exhibit 3).

Advanced Topic: Income Effect and Substitution Effect

In Chapter 3, we learned that the law of demand has its foundation in the income effect and substitution effect. Recall that the **income effect** is the change in the quantity demanded of a good when price changes alter the purchasing power of consumers. As the price of an item rises, consumers can afford less as the consumer's purchasing power is reduced. When the good is a normal good, such as pizza, less of it will be purchased.

The **substitution effect** is the change in the quantity demanded of a good when price changes result in consumers switching from relatively high-priced products to relatively low-priced products. As the price of an item rises, it becomes relatively more expensive than a substitute product. Thus, when the price of pizza increases to $3, consumers cannot afford as much pizza (income effect) and soda becomes *relatively* cheaper, leading to less pizza being purchased (substitution effect). The end result is a lower quantity demanded of pizza, at the higher price.

If our consumer Zoe wishes to purchase the original bundle of goods—4 slices of pizza and 2 cans of soda—at the higher price for pizza, she will now need a *hypothetical* budget of $14 ($3 × 4 slices + $1 × 2 cans = $14). In reality, of course, this is unlikely to occur, but we make this assumption in order to isolate the income and substitution effects: By assuming a budget of $14, we are able to factor out the income effect as the consumer is now able to afford the same bundle as before.

However, with a $14 budget, Zoe would not purchase the same bundle as before. Exhibit 4 demonstrates that, with the increased $14 budget, Zoe would buy 3 slices of pizza and 5 sodas. Prior to the price change and budget adjustment, Zoe purchased 4 slices of pizza. Since we factored out the income effect by assuming a $14 budget, we see how the higher price of pizza leads Zoe to substitute away from 1 slice of pizza, *even though she could afford just as much pizza as before.* This is the substitution effect at work.

Income effect The change in the quantity demanded of a good when price changes alter the purchasing power of consumers.

Now let's isolate the income effect of a price change. The income effect can be identified by removing the assumed $4 budget increase and resetting the budget constraint back to $10. At that budget, only two slices of pizza are purchased at the new price of pizza, as shown in Exhibit 3. The income effect is also 1 slice: the difference between the 3 pizza slices purchased at the higher $3 price with the hypothetical $14 budget, and the two slices consumed with the actual $10 budget, also at $3 per slice. In other words, the impact of increasing the price of a slice of pizza from $2 to $3 is 1 less slice due to the substitution effect and 1 less slice due to the income effect. In total, the higher price reduces consumption by two slices.

substitution effect The change in the quantity demanded of a good when price changes result in consumers switching from relatively high-priced products to relatively low-priced products.

Most goods are *normal goods,* a good for which demand decreases as incomes decline. This means the income effect and substitution effects work in the same direction. In contrast, an *inferior good* is a good for which demand increases as incomes decline. Similar to a decline in income, an increase in the price of a good reduces what a consumer can afford. The result of a price increase for an inferior good is an *increase*

EXHIBIT 4 Demonstrating the Income Effect and Substitution Effect

Pizza (price = $3)					Soda (price = $1)				
Quantity	Total Utility	MU	$\frac{MU}{P}$	Order	Quantity	Total Utility	MU	$\frac{MU}{P}$	Order
1	36	36	12	←a	1	10	10	10	←b
2	60	24	8	←c	2	16	6	6	←d
3	76	16	5.3	←g	3	21.6	5.6	5.6	←e
4	88	12	4		4	27	5.4	5.4	←f
5	96	8	2.7		5	31.1	4.1	4.1	←h

Note: Budget is assumed to be $14.

When the price of pizza increases to $3 per slice, the consumer purchases 2 slices (Exhibit 3). This makes pizza *relatively* more expensive. If our consumer wishes to purchase the original bundle of 4 slices of pizza and 2 cans of soda (Exhibit 2), a budget of $14 is needed. By assuming a hypothetical $14 budget, we are able to factor out the income and substitution effects as the consumer is now able to afford the same bundle as before. In this example, the substitution effect is 1 slice of pizza because the consumer would purchase 3 slices of pizza—not 2—with a $14 budget. The income effect is also 1 slice: the difference between the 3 slices purchased at the higher $3 price with the hypothetical $14 budget and the 2 slices consumed with the actual $10 budget when the price of pizza is $3 per slice.

in quantity demanded because of the income effect that is offset by a *decrease* in quantity demanded because of the substitution effect.

Typically, the substitution effect is larger than the income effect for inferior goods. As a result, price increases lead to a decline in quantity demand and a downward-sloping demand curve. But as you will see in the next **Business Brief**, apparently this is not always the case.

BUSINESS BRIEF Giffen Goods: When Higher Prices Increase Quantity Demanded

Is it possible that the positive income effect from a price increase of an inferior good could be large enough to more than offset the negative substitution effect? Economists refer to goods for which quantity demanded actually rises as prices go up as *Giffen goods*.

Until recently, economists were only able to find examples of Giffen goods from the nineteenth century. In 2008, however, Robert Jensen of Brown University and Nolan Miller of Harvard reported that they had discovered a modern example of such a good: In very poor regions of China, the quantity demanded of rice actually rose when rice became more expensive.*

People need a certain number of calories to survive, and China's poor depend on rice to make up the bulk of theirs. These consumers tended to eat a diet that paired inexpensive rice with some more expensive meat, fish, or vegetables. But when the price of the cheapest option—rice—increased, meat became even less affordable.

Johwanna Alleyne/Alamy

∧ If the price of rice increases, will low-income consumers buy more? Apparently yes, in rural China.

Thus, the easiest way for the poor to eat the minimum number of calories was to eat *more* rice, which was still cheaper than meat.

In economic terms, the negative income effect of the inferior good (rice) was so large that higher prices actually resulted in an increase in quantity demanded, despite the offsetting substitution effect. This type of situation is most likely to occur in very low-income areas. Giffen goods are so rare that it's safe to assume that the demand for almost all goods you will encounter in everyday life is downward-sloping.

*"As Price Goes Up, So Does Demand," *The Economist*, July 18, 2007, http://www.economist.com/blogs/freeexchange/2007/07/as_price_goes_up_so_does_deman.

5.3 ADVANCED TOPICS: INDIFFERENCE CURVES AND BUDGET CONSTRAINTS

The utility analysis presented in this chapter provides useful insights into consumer decision making. However, these examples assume a purely hypothetical estimate of utility, which cannot be directly measured. Fortunately, economists have created an alternative model describing how consumers make decisions that does not require exact measurements of utility. We begin by analyzing what consumers can afford.

What Consumers Can Afford: Budget Constraint Line

Recall that Zoe made a decision on how many cans of soda and slices of pizza to purchase subject to a budget constraint. In our example, Zoe's budget is $10 and the price of a can of soda is $1. Zoe could purchase as much as 10 cans of soda, but this would mean she could buy no pizza slices. Alternatively, when the price of pizza is $2, she could purchase 5 slices—and no soda. Zoe can also use her $10 budget to purchase alternative bundles, such as 8 cans of soda and 1 slice of pizza, or 4 slices of pizza and 2 cans of soda. The **budget constraint line** is a graphical representation of the limit of all combinations of goods and services that a consumer can afford within a given budget. We present Zoe's budget constraint line in Panel A of Exhibit 5. In some respects, the budget constraint line is similar to the production possibilities frontier (PPF) introduced in Chapter 2 with one important difference: It shows the maximum allowable combination of *purchases*.

When Zoe's budget decreases to $8, the budget constraint line shifts inward. She can now afford eight cans of soda and no pizza, or four slices of pizza and no soda, or a variety of other combinations, as demonstrated in Panel B. When the price of *one product*—say, pizza—increases, the budget line rotates inward. Zoe can still afford the same number of cans of soda if no pizza is purchased, but she can no longer afford five or even four slices if the price is $3. This is demonstrated in Panel C. In contrast, a price decrease would rotate the budget constraint line outward.

When faced with a purchase decision and budget constraint, consumers can select any option on or inside of the budget constraint line. You can probably guess what option most consumers will choose—the one that maximizes utility!

budget constraint line
A graphical representation of the limit of all combinations of goods and services that a consumer can afford within a given budget.

EXHIBIT 5 The Budget Constraint Line

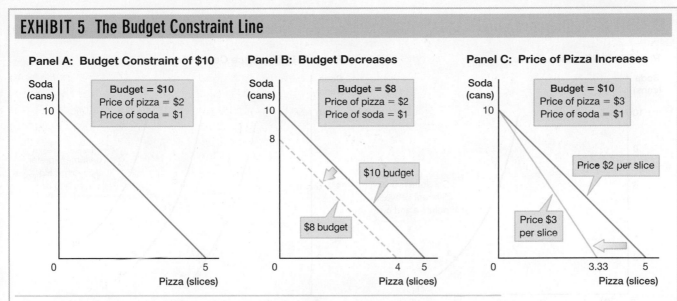

With a $10 budget, Zoe can afford 5 slices of pizza priced at $2 each or 10 cans of soda priced at $1 each, or a variety of other combinations. Panel A demonstrates these combinations. Consumers can also purchase combinations inside the budget constraint line. If Zoe's budget decreases to $8, the budget constraint line shifts inward, as shown in Panel B. If the price of pizza increases to $3, the curve rotates inward, reflecting a reduction in purchasing power. This is illustrated in Panel C.

Indifference Curves

Earlier in the chapter, we analyzed consumer choice within the context of a measure of utility or satisfaction known as utils. While the use of utils simplifies our analysis, they cannot be directly measured. In this section, we no longer assume utils can be measured, but rather that consumers can *rank* various bundles (combinations of goods and services) according to their preferences. That is to say, consumers believe that some bundles of goods and services provide more utility than others, even if the exact amount of utility cannot be measured. We also assume there are various combinations of goods and services that consumers value equally, or are *indifferent* toward, as they provide equal amounts of utility or satisfaction.

An individual's utility is determined by many factors—all of which also affect demand and quantity demanded. Chief among these factors are personal tastes and preferences. Although consumers may not consciously think in terms of utility, they regularly choose between various bundles of goods as if they were trying to maximize utility. In doing so, they indirectly demonstrate their preferences, essentially *ranking* those consumption bundles in terms of preference. Consumers demonstrate a preference regarding various bundles of goods.

These preferences and indifferences are expressed graphically using indifference curves. An **indifference curve** shows all the alternative combinations of products that give the consumer the same level of utility.

Mapping Indifference Curves Exhibit 6, Panel A, demonstrates a single indifference curve. It shows that our consumer is indifferent between points *a* and *c* because all points give the consumer the same level of satisfaction. Panel B shows an **indifference curve map**, an infinite set of indifference curves, each depicting a

indifference curve
Shows all the alternative combinations of products that give the consumer the same level of satisfaction.

indifference curve map
An infinite set of indifference curves, each depicting a unique level of utility.

EXHIBIT 6   Indifference Curves and the Indifference Curve Map

Panel A: Indifference Curve

Panel B: Indifference Curve Map

An indifference curve shows the alternative combinations of products that give consumers the same level of satisfaction. In Panel A, a consumer receives equal satisfaction consuming bundles *a* and *c*. Panel B shows an indifference curve map—an infinite set of indifference curves, each depicting a unique level of utility. Greater satisfaction is realized on I_2 than the other two indifference curves. The slope of an indifference curve expressed as a positive number is the marginal rate of substitution.

unique level of utility. Three indifference curves are shown (though many more are possible):

- The initial indifference curve (I_1). The consumer is indifferent between all points on this curve.

- A superior indifference curve (I_2). All points on this curve result in higher utility than all points on the initial curve (I_1).

- An inferior indifference curve (I_0). All points on this curve result in lower utility than all points on the initial curve (I_1).

In order to maximize utility, consumers try to reach an indifference curve as high and far to the right as possible.

Key Characteristics of Indifference Curves There are four important facts about indifference curves:

1. Indifference curves have a negative slope. If Zoe consumes more pizza, she can forego some quantity of soda and still have the same level of utility.

2. Indifference curves are said to be "convex to the origin." This means that the curve flattens as more of the good on the *x*-axis (pizza slices) is consumed. This is the direct result of the law of diminishing marginal utility. As we consume more of a product, the additional satisfaction obtained diminishes. This explains why consumers don't spend all their income on a single good.

3. Indifference curves never intersect each other. Since each indifference curve represents a different level of satisfaction, they can not intersect each other.

4. Higher indifference curves provide more satisfaction than lower indifference curves. As such, consumers prefer to be on the highest indifference curve they can afford.

Marginal Rate of Substitution Is the Slope of the Indifference Curve The slope of the indifference curve expressed as a positive number is the marginal rate of substitution. The **marginal rate of substitution (MRS)** is the rate at which consumers are willing to exchange one good for another while maintaining the same level of utility. It refers to the *MRS* of the good on the *x*-axis (horizontal axis), which is pizza in this case. Due to the convex shape of the indifference curves and the law of diminishing marginal utility, *MRS* declines as more pizza is consumed.

Optimal Consumption Using Indifference Curves

At *optimal consumption,* consumers will maximize their utility by being on the highest indifference curve possible given their budget constraint. Exhibit 7 shows that when the price of pizza is $2 per slice, the consumer chooses to be at point *a* on curve I_1, the highest indifference curve possible given his or her available funds, because it maximizes utility.

The marginal rate of substitution will equal the slope of the budget constraint line at the optimal consumption level. The budget constraint line and the highest indifference curve are tangent to each other. In Exhibit 7, point *a* is the point of tangency on indifference curve I_1, and point *b* is the point of tangency on indifference curve I_0. That is to say the highest indifference curve touches but does not cross the budget constraint line.

Price changes alter the budget constraint line. When the price of pizza rises, consumers purchase fewer slices and the budget constraint line rotates inward. A new consumer's optimal consumption is achieved at point *b* on indifference curve I_0.

marginal rate of substitution The rate at which consumers are willing to exchange one good for another while maintaining the same level of utility.

EXHIBIT 7 Indifference Curves, Budget Constraints, and the Consumer's Optimal Consumption

Panel A: Changing Prices and Indifference Curve

Panel B: Individual Demand Derived from Indifference Curves

At the consumer's optimal consumption, the consumer will be on the highest indifference curve possible given his or her budget constraint. When the price of a slice of pizza is $2, this occurs at point *a* in Panel A. Here, the consumer purchases 4 slices of pizza. When the price of pizza is $3 a slice, optimal consumption occurs at point *b*. Here, the consumer purchases 2 slices of pizza. Panel B graphs these points out on a corresponding individual's demand curve.

Notice that the higher price reduces the quantity of pizza slices demanded from 4 to 2. Consistent with the law of demand, the consumer purchases fewer slices at the higher price.

Income and Substitution Effects Revisited Recall that the substitution effect can be determined by factoring out the income effect of a price change. In the simplified example (in Exhibit 4), this was accomplished with a hypothetical consumer budget so that he or she is able to afford the same bundle of pizza and soda as originally purchased.

Indifference curves present a more precise method of examining the income effect and the substitution effect. When the price of pizza rises from $2 to $3, the consumer moves from point *a* to point *b*. To determine the income effect, we begin by creating a new *hypothetical* budget constraint line that maintains the slope of the original budget constraint line (the budget constraint line prior to the price change), but leaves the consumer on the *same indifference curve* that resulted after the price change (at point *d*). This leaves the consumer on the same indifference curve as point *b*. Creating a new budget constraint line shifts the original budget constraint line in a manner similar to Panel B in Exhibit 5.

This approach is analogous to the utility analysis presented earlier in this chapter, with one major difference: While the new *hypothetical* budget constraint line has the same slope as the original budget constraint line, it *does not* allow the consumer to purchase the original bundle. The new altered budget line shifts the budget constraint so the consumer is able to afford a bundle of goods of equal utility—but not necessarily the *same* bundle.

The key to determining the substitution effect is to remain on the same indifference curve, but to factor out the income effect by shifting the budget constraint line to reflect the change in relative prices. At points *b* and *d*, the consumer is equally satisfied but consumes a different combination because the relative prices are different.

In Exhibit 8, going from point *b* to point *d* on the same indifference curve is the substitution effect. In contrast, the income effect is determined by looking at point *d* on a *hypothetical* budget constraint and point *a* on the original budget constraint. In total, the price change results in 2 fewer slices of pizza consumzed: 1 fewer slice is purchased

EXHIBIT 8 Income Effect and Substitution Effect

As shown in Exhibit 7, when the price of a slice of pizza increases to $3, the consumer reduces his or her consumption of pizza from 4 slices to 2 slices. To determine the income effect and substitution effect, we create a new altered budget constraint line that maintains the slope of the original budget constraint line (the budget constraint line prior to the price change) but leaves the consumer on the same indifference curve. The substitution effect is the 1 slice of pizza between points *b* and *d*, both on indifference curve I_0. The income effect occurs between points *a* and *d*.

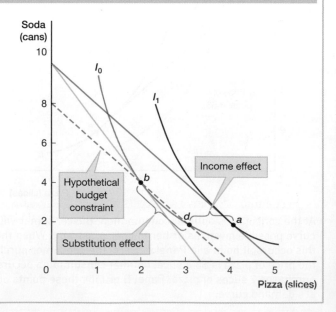

as a result of the substitution effect and 1 fewer slice is purchased as a result of the income effect.

Marginal Utility Analysis Revisited The consumers' optimal consumption occurs when consumers are on the highest indifference curve possible given their budget constraint. Here, the marginal rate of substitution equals the slope of the budget constraint line expressed as a positive number. Covering utility analysis, we also discovered that optimal consumption maximizes total utility by spending so that the marginal utilities per dollar on the last purchases are equal. In our pizza and soda example, the following must occur:

$$\frac{MU_{pizza}}{P_{pizza}} \cong \frac{MU_{soda}}{P_{soda}}$$

Are these two descriptions of optimal consumption equivalent? In fact, they are. To show this, let's begin by rearranging the above equation:

$$\frac{MU_{pizza}}{MU_{soda}} \cong \frac{P_{pizza}}{P_{soda}}$$

Although you may not recognize it at first, the right-hand side of the equation is simply the absolute value of the slope of the budget constraint line. It is the price of the good on the x-axis (price of pizza) divided by the price of the good on the y-axis (price of soda).

In Exhibits 7 and 8, when the price of pizza is $2, the absolute value of the slope of the budget constraint line is 2, $(= P_{pizza}/P_{soda} = \$2/\$1)$. With a $10 budget, the maximum amount of soda that can be purchased is 10 and the maximum amount of pizza that can be purchased is 5. Thus, rise over run (in absolute value) is 10 over 5, which equals 2. When the price of pizza is $3, the absolute value of the slope of the budget constraint line is 3 $(= \$3/\$1)$. More generally, the maximum number of the good on the y-axis that a consumer can buy is Budget/P_Y, and the maximum number of the good on the x-axis that a consumer can buy is Budget/P_X. Thus, the absolute value of the slope of the budget line is $(\text{Budget}/P_Y)/(\text{Budget}/P_X) = P_X/P_Y$. In our case, $P_X/P_Y = P_{pizza}/P_{soda}$.

The left-hand side of the rearranged equation is equal to the marginal rate of substitution. Remember, the level of utility on each indifference curve is constant: As we consume more pizza, the marginal utility we gain is exactly offset by the marginal utility we lose by consuming less soda.

Specifically, the gain from consuming more pizza is $\Delta Q_{pizza} \times MU_{pizza}$. The loss from consuming less soda is $\Delta Q_{soda} \times MU_{soda}$. Since these two must offset each other at the consumer's optimal consumption, it must be the case that

$$\Delta Q_{pizza} \times MU_{pizza} = -\Delta Q_{soda} \times MU_{soda}$$

Recall that slope equals rise over run. In Exhibit 7, it equals the change in soda over the change in pizza. Rearranging the last equation, we get

$$\frac{-\Delta Q_{soda}}{\Delta Q_{pizza}} = \frac{MU_{pizza}}{MU_{soda}} = MRS$$

In summary, for any two goods x and y on their respective axis, at the optimal consumption point, the ratio of marginal utilities equals the price ratio:

$$\frac{MU_x}{MU_y} \cong \frac{P_x}{P_y}$$

- P_x/P_y equals the absolute value of the slope of the budget constraint line.
- MU_x/MU_y equals the marginal rate of substitution.

At optimal consumption, the *MRS* equals the slope of the budget constraint line, which is the price ratio. Thus, optimal consumption can be found by using either the indifference curve approach presented in this section, or the marginal utility analysis presented earlier in the chapter.

BUSINESS TAKEAWAY

While theoretical in nature, utility analysis can provide valuable insights for firms seeking to influence consumer behavior. For example, firms can often entice consumers to make *additional* purchases by lowering the price of additional units. Thus, shoe stores like Famous Footwear and Rack Room Shoes commonly promote "buy-one, get-one-half-off" deals to entice shoppers to buy an additional pair, movie theaters offer 50% more popcorn or soda for a small increase in price to maximize sales at their concessions, and SeaWorld allows their patrons to have an unlimited number of additional visits for a few extra dollars.

When developing such sales strategies, it's crucial that firms pay close attention to costs. For a theater, offering twice the popcorn for a small increase in price works primarily because the added cost of popcorn is extremely low, and the charge for the *first* unit of popcorn at a theater is usually quite high. Firms must also be able to accurately estimate the customer's maximum consumption (there is only so much popcorn a person or even a group of people can eat during a single movie).

At some point, additional consumption, even if the price is free, leads to a reduction in consumption. If a Disney theme park, for example, determines that the typical family takes three days to enjoy all the attractions at its park, it will price its three-day pass at a premium. But the firm can capture additional sales—at little additional cost—by offering a fourth day at a deep discount.

Such pricing strategies do carry some risks, which come into sharp focus when examining "all-you-can-eat" or "pay-one-price" offers. A restaurant promoting an "all-you-can-eat" meal must pay careful attention to costs and how much the average customer eats during a single seating in order to make such a strategy work. Red Lobster failed to do so in its "Endless Crab" promotion and paid the price.

A restaurant also needs to make sure that some limitations exist in an "all-you-can-eat" strategy; a buffet that allows hungry customers to fill takeout containers with food would quickly lose money. In order to turn a profit, an "all-you-can-eat" that allowed takeout would require a price so exorbitantly high, there would likely be few or no buyers.

CHAPTER STUDY GUIDE

5.1 UTILITY: A MEASURE OF CONSUMER SATISFACTION

Utility is a hypothetical measure of satisfaction experienced by consumers. It is measured in terms of utils, imaginary units of satisfaction. **Marginal utility** is the additional utility gained from consuming an additional unit. Marginal utility captures changes in **total utility**—the overall amount of satisfaction a consumer obtains from consuming a given total of a particular good. Since consumers receive less additional satisfaction from consuming a sixth slice of pizza than the first slice, marginal utility is said to be diminishing. The **law of diminishing marginal utility** is the principle that, during a given period of time, increasing consumption of a good decreases marginal utility. The diamond–water paradox reflects the idea that while water is more useful for survival, diamonds command a higher value in terms of market price. The paradox can be explained by noting that the marginal utility of a little more water is small, while the total utility gained from water is enormous.

5.2 MAXIMIZING UTILITY WITH A LIMITED BUDGET

Consumers attempt to maximize utility subject to a **budget constraint**, the limit of all combinations of goods and services that can be afforded within a given budget. In order to do so, consumers will purchase products that give them the most **marginal utility per dollar**, the marginal utility divided by price. **Optimal consumption** is the bundle of goods that maximizes a consumer's utility subject to a budget constraint. It maximizes total utility by spending in such a way that the marginal utilities per dollar on the last purchases are approximately equal. This analysis can be used to explain the law of demand. As the price of an item falls, consumers can afford to buy more of a normal good due to the **income effect**, the change in the quantity demanded of a good when price changes alter the purchasing power of consumers. A lower price also results in a **substitution effect**, the change in the quantity demanded of a good when price changes result in consumers switching from relatively high-priced products to relatively low-priced products. In contrast, when the price of pizza increases, consumers cannot afford as much pizza (income effect)

and other food items become relatively cheaper, thus leading to consumers to buy less pizza (substitution effect). The end result is a lower quantity demanded of pizza, at the higher price.

5.3 ADVANCED TOPICS: INDIFFERENCE CURVES AND BUDGET CONSTRAINTS

Demand curves can also be estimated with the use of indifference curves and a budget constraint line. The **budget constraint line** is a graphical representation of the limit of all combinations of goods and services that a consumer can afford within a given budget. An **indifference curve** shows all the alternative combinations of products that give the consumer the same level of satisfaction. These can be demonstrated on an **indifference curve map**, an infinite set of indifference curves, each depicting a unique level of satisfaction. Consumers attempt to be on the highest possible indifference curve subject to their budget constraint. This outcome is the consumer's optimal consumption. The **marginal rate of substitution (MRS)** is the rate at which consumers are willing to exchange one good for another while maintaining the same level of utility. MRS equals the slope of the indifference curve. At the consumer's optimal consumption, MRS also equals the slope of the budget constraint line.

TOP TEN TERMS AND CONCEPTS

1. Utility
2. Marginal Utility
3. Law of Diminishing Marginal Utility
4. Marginal Utility per Dollar
5. Optimal Consumption
6. Income Effect
7. Substitution Effect
8. Budget Constraint Line
9. Indifference Curves and Indifference Curve Map
10. Marginal Rate of Substitution (MRS)

STUDY PROBLEMS

1. In your own words, describe the differences between marginal utility and total utility.

2. What is the law of diminishing marginal utility?

3. Complete the following table:

Q	Total Utility	Marginal Utility
1	100	
2		90
3		80
4	340	
5	400	
6		50

4. Suppose you go to "all you can eat Tuesdays" at Mario's. How do you determine the number of slices to consume? If the price of the special is $12, do you stop eating when you consume $12 worth of pizza? What happens to the marginal utility you receive from each additional slice of pizza?

5. Suppose a product existed that did not experience diminishing marginal utility, but rather increasing marginal utility. If consumers started consuming that product, at what point would they stop? Can you think of any goods the government has deemed illegal that might experience increasing marginal utility (at least for some people)?

6. Explain the diamond–water paradox. Use it to explain why star athletes often earn 100 times more than nurses and schoolteachers.

7. Suppose the price of a burger is $3 and the price of an order of fries is $1. Complete the following table. What will a consumer purchase if he or she has $10 to spend?

Burgers

Quantity	Total Utility	Marginal Utility	MU/P
1	50		
2	90		
3	120		
4	140		
5	150		

Fries

Quantity	Total Utility	Marginal Utility	MU/P
1	10		
2	19		
3	27		
4	34		
5	40		

8. Suppose the price of a burger increases to $5 and the price of an order of fries remains $1. Complete the following table. What will a consumer purchase if he or she has $13 to spend?

Burgers

Quantity	Total Utility	Marginal Utility	MU/P
1	50		
2	90		
3	120		
4	140		
5	150		

Fries

Quantity	Total Utility	Marginal Utility	MU/P
1	10		
2	19		
3	27		
4	34		
5	40		

9. Bill goes to a local amusement park and purchases unlimited rides for $40. When will Bill stop taking rides?

10. Can two different indifference curves ever intersect? Why or why not?

11. While at camp, Jason has $20 to spend on slices of pizza that cost $4 a slice and ice cream cones that costs $2 a cone.

   a. Draw Jason's budget constraint line.

   b. Suppose we observe Jason purchase 3 slices of pizza and 4 ice cream cones. Graph the indifference curve Jason is on. Label this as purchase point *a*.

   c. Assuming that the price of ice cream doubles, show how the budget constraint line shifts.

12. Using budget constraint lines and indifference curves, graph the effect of a price increase. Use it to explain the income effect and substitution effect.

∧ TJ Maxx invites you to maximize your consumer surplus.

CHAPTER 6

Economic Efficiency and the Power of Competitive Markets

How Price Controls and Taxes Result in Deadweight Loss

A shopper is browsing the aisles at TJ Maxx when a Michael Kors handbag catches her eye. She has seen the exact same bag priced at $299 in department stores, much more than the $200 she is willing to pay for it. When she looks at the tag, she finds the bag is priced at only $149 and immediately transfers the handbag to her cart. The reason why this transaction will take place—and the reason why a sale at the upscale department store did not—is one of the subjects discussed in this chapter. More generally, this chapter illustrates how markets can maximize our collective well-being.

In competitive markets, buyers and sellers are motivated by what Adam Smith called *rational self-interest*: Smith argued that when people freely interact in the marketplace without government interference, their self-interest often leads them to behave in a way that benefits society as a whole. Today, economists describe this behavior as *maximizing economic efficiency*. The power of markets is that they guide sellers to produce products that consumers value most highly.

As we will learn in later chapters, there are some instances in which government can usefully intervene in competitive markets, by protecting the environment and preventing monopolies from forming. But before we explore those cases, it will be useful to develop an understanding of how competitive markets usually maximize economic efficiency and how government price controls and taxes can reduce economic efficiency.

Chapter Learning Targets

- Describe the concepts of consumer surplus and producer surplus.

- Discuss how competitive markets maximize economic efficiency and how deadweight loss occurs when economic efficiency is not realized.

- Determine the effects of taxes and government price controls.

6.1 CONSUMER SURPLUS AND PRODUCER SURPLUS

The power of markets is that they bring together buyers and sellers to make mutually beneficial trades, transactions where the marginal benefit to the consumer exceeds the marginal cost of producers. Billions of such transactions occur each year. Economists assume that these transactions are generally mutually beneficial because it would be odd for a rationally self-interested person to voluntarily engage in a transaction that he or she didn't view as at least slightly beneficial. The notion that voluntary exchange makes both sides better off is a fundamental idea in economics. The next question is how much better off do these exchanges make buyers and sellers?

Consumer Surplus, Willingness to Pay, and the Demand Curve

Consider the following example. You walk by Mario's pizza, and the pies on the countertop look and smell so delicious and you're so hungry that you would be willing to pay $10 for a slice. Its actual price is $2. Do you say to Mario, "I am willing to pay $10 for 1 slice, so keep the change"? Probably not. **Willingness to pay** is the maximum price a buyer is willing to pay for a good or service. At this maximum price, consumers are indifferent about buying the item, as the price of the item equals the value the consumer puts on it.

In this case, your maximum willingness to pay is $10, but the price you pay is $2. As such, you experience a net gain of $8 ($10 − $2). This gain to the buyer from a purchase is referred to as **consumer surplus**: the buyer's gain from a purchase, measured as the difference between the buyer's willingness to pay and the actual price paid.

Assume the actual price for a large pizza is $20, and there are four potential buyers, each willing to buy only 1 pizza: Abe, Betsy, Calvin, and Dolly. Exhibit 1 illustrates the willingness to pay of each of the four consumers. It also shows the consumer surplus for each consumer if the price of pizza is $20—determined by both market supply and market demand, as discussed in Chapter 3.

Exhibit 1 and Exhibit 2 show each consumer's willingness to pay and the corresponding demand curve for a large pizza based on our four consumers' willingness to pay. At the price of $20, *consumer surplus* is:

- $10 for Abe, who buys the first pizza for $20 and is willing to pay $30.
- $5 for Betsy, who buys the second pizza for $20 and is willing to pay $25.
- $15 is total consumer surplus (= $10 + $5).

Think & Speak Like an Economist

In business, a *surplus* refers to an excess of unsold goods; this corresponds to the economic definition of surplus meaning "excess supply." Though the term *consumer surplus* sounds similar, it has a very different meaning in economics, referring to the buyer's gain from a purchase.

willingness to pay The maximum price a buyer is willing to pay for a good or service.

consumer surplus The buyer's gain from a purchase, measured as the difference between the buyer's willingness to pay and the actual price paid.

EXHIBIT 1   Willingness to Pay and Consumer Surplus

Buyer	Willingness to Pay	Consumer Surplus (price = $20)
Abe	$30	$10
Betsy	25	5
Calvin	20	0
Dolly	15	No purchase

Consumer surplus is measured as the difference between the buyer's willingness to pay and the actual price paid. Betsy has a consumer surplus of $5 because she is willing to pay $25 and the price is $20.

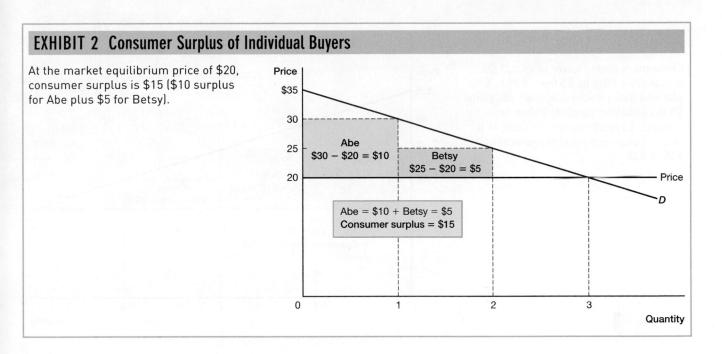

EXHIBIT 2 Consumer Surplus of Individual Buyers

At the market equilibrium price of $20, consumer surplus is $15 ($10 surplus for Abe plus $5 for Betsy).

In total, consumer surplus is $15: $10 for Abe plus $5 for Betsy, with zero consumer surplus for Calvin and Dolly. Several simplifying assumptions are made in Exhibit 2. First, Calvin may or may not purchase the pizza. If he makes the purchase, it results in zero consumer surplus because his willingness to pay ($20) matches the price he actually pays. In the real world, there may be no unit with a consumer surplus of *exactly* zero when a sale occurs. Second, we assumed that there were only four potential buyers. Third, we assumed that each buyer wishes to purchase 1 pizza. As these assumptions are unlikely to hold in the real word, we look at a more general case in the analysis that follows.

How Changing Prices Affect Consumer Surplus

As you might expect, price changes affect consumer surplus. Consumers like lower prices. When prices fall, consumer surplus increases for two reasons: the consumer surplus of the original customers increases and new paying customers enter the market.

A Lower Price Increases the Consumer Surplus of Existing Customers First, a lower price increases the consumer surplus of existing buyers. In Exhibit 3, if the price of pizza falls by $5 to $15, Abe and Betsy each receive an *additional* $5 in consumer surplus. Calvin now receives $5 in consumer surplus. As a result, consumer surplus increases by $15 to $30.

A Lower Price Increases the Consumer Surplus of New Buyers Lower prices also increase total consumer surplus by increasing the number of buyers in the market. To analyze this, it is useful to examine consumer surplus based on *market demand* (not individual demand). How might consumer surplus be depicted for thousands of potential consumers who are able to buy more than 1 pizza?

In Exhibit 4, Panel A demonstrates such a scenario. At the price of $20, 3,000 large pizzas are purchased. Consumer surplus is the area below the demand curve and above

EXHIBIT 3 A Lower Price Increases Consumer Surplus of Existing Customers

Consumers prefer lower prices. If the actual price falls by $5 from $20 to $15, Abe and Betsy each receive an additional $5 in consumer surplus. Calvin now receives $5 in consumer surplus. As a result, consumer surplus increases by $15 to $30.

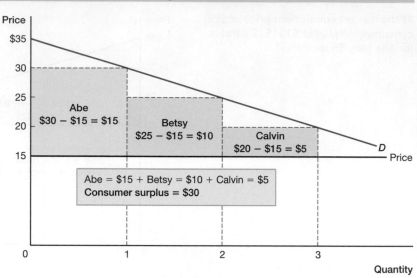

Abe
$30 − $15 = $15

Betsy
$25 − $15 = $10

Calvin
$20 − $15 = $5

Abe = $15 + Betsy = $10 + Calvin = $5
Consumer surplus = $30

∧ How much would you pay for that "free" app?

Bloomberg/Getty Images

the actual price. With thousands of consumers, the discrete steps shown in the previous figure are eliminated and the demand curve appears smooth.

In Exhibit 4, Panel B also shows the number of pizzas purchased increased from 3,000 to 4,000. Buyers who sat on the sidelines at the higher price had zero consumer surplus. Now with the price cut, a few extra buyers have some consumer surplus (shown in light blue). Panel B also shows that the consumer surplus of the original buyers increases when the price decreases.

Of course, the opposite is also true: A price increase is not welcomed by consumers as it reduces their consumer surplus. If we review Panel B in reverse and examine the price increase from $15 to $20, the consumer surplus declines for two reasons. Some consumers stop buying, and those who continue to buy pay a higher price.

📊 BUSINESS BRIEF Measuring Consumer Surplus of the Internet

What is your maximum willingness to pay for Internet services? If you are like most consumers, you also know your monthly charges for accessing data on your laptop at home or on your smartphone—and what most companies normally charge. You may also know many "hot spots" where you can access the Internet for free. But unless providers start to raise their rates substantially, it's unlikely that you've ever considered the maximum price you would be willing to pay for access to the Internet. And it's even less likely that you've considered how much you would be willing to pay for some of the Web-based services you use every day, such as Instagram, Snapchat, or Google, because you don't pay for them at all.

Measuring consumer surplus in the real world is extremely complex. Nonetheless, Shane Greenstein of Northwestern University and Ryan McDevitt of Duke University estimated that broadband (Internet and data transmissions) generated $8.7 billion in consumer surplus in 2006—that number is no doubt a lot higher in today's world.[*] The consumer surplus of a Google search is even greater. Noted economist Hal Varian of Google estimates that the value of a Google search is roughly $1.37 per day per person (over $100 billion in the United States per year) but points out that such an estimate is based on a "rough approximation" of the demand curve.[†]

[*]Shane Greenstein, "Measuring Consumer Surplus Online," *The Economist*, March 11, 2013, http://www.economist.com/blogs/freeexchange/2013/03/technology-2.

[†]Hal Varian, "The Value of the Internet Now and in the Future," *The Economist*, March 10, 2013, http://www.economist.com/blogs/freeexchange/2013/03/technology-1.

EXHIBIT 4 Consumer Surplus of a Market

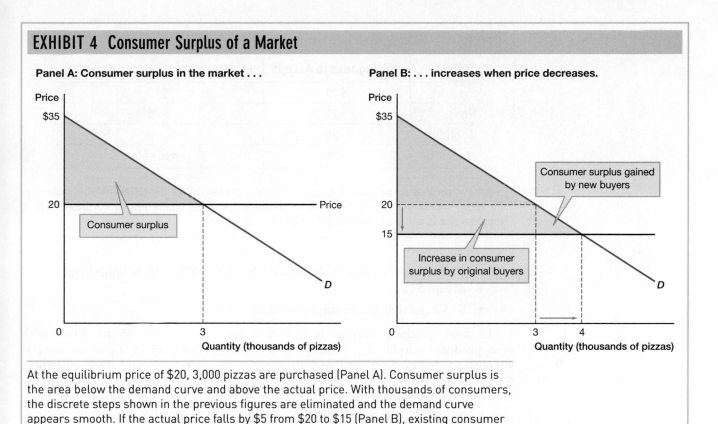

Panel A: Consumer surplus in the market . . .

Panel B: . . . increases when price decreases.

At the equilibrium price of $20, 3,000 pizzas are purchased (Panel A). Consumer surplus is the area below the demand curve and above the actual price. With thousands of consumers, the discrete steps shown in the previous figures are eliminated and the demand curve appears smooth. If the actual price falls by $5 from $20 to $15 (Panel B), existing consumer will each receive an additional $5 in consumer surplus. In addition more purchases occur; which also increases consumer surplus.

Producer Surplus, Willingness to Accept, and the Supply Curve

Have you ever listed an item for sale on eBay? If so, you may know that you can set a hidden "reserve" price, below which you will not be willing (or obligated) to sell the item. Such prices are what economists refer to as a willingness to accept. **Willingness to accept** is the minimum price a seller is willing to accept for a good or service. At this minimum price, sellers are indifferent about selling the item. On eBay, this might be the reserve price, as the price of the item equals the value the seller places on the item. **Producer surplus** is the seller's gain from a sale, measured as the difference between the seller's willingness to accept and the actual price received. On eBay, producer surplus is often the difference between the selling price and the reserve price. Likewise, the seller of a used car might be willing to accept any amount over $6,000. If a buyer offers $7,000 for the car, then the producer surplus is $1,000.

Let's return to our pizza transaction. Assume the actual equilibrium price for a large pizza remains $20 and there are four potential sellers, each willing to sell 1 (and only 1) pizza: Lincoln, Ross, Coolidge, and Madison. Exhibit 5 illustrates the willingness to accept of the four sellers of pizza. The exhibit also shows the producer surplus for each seller if the price of pizza is $20.

Panel A of Exhibit 6 shows a supply curve for pizza based on our four sellers' minimum acceptable price. In that case, at the price of $20, the *producer surplus* is:

- $10 for Lincoln who sells the first pizza for $20 and is willing to accept $10.

willingness to accept The minimum price a seller is willing to accept for a good or service.

producer surplus The seller's gain from a sale, measured as the difference between the seller's willingness to accept and the actual price received.

EXHIBIT 5 Willingness to Accept and Producer Surplus

Seller	Willingness to Accept	Producer Surplus (price = $20)
Lincoln	$10	$10
Ross	15	5
Coolidge	20	0
Madison	25	No sale

Producer surplus is the seller's gain from a sale, measured as the difference between the seller's willingness to accept and the actual price. Ross has producer surplus of $5 because she is willing to accept $15 and the price is $20.

- $5 for Ross who sells the second pizza for $20 and is willing to accept $15.
- $15 in total producer surplus (= $10 + $5).

In total, producer surplus is $15: $10 for Lincoln plus $5 for Ross, with zero producer surplus for Coolidge and Madison. Once again, there are several simplifying assumptions designed to explain the basic concept. First, producer Coolidge may or may not make a sale as the price of $20 matches exactly his willingness to except, but either way his producer surplus is zero. In the real world, there may be no unit with a producer surplus of exactly zero when a sale occurs. Second, we assumed that there were only four potential sellers. Third, we assumed that each

EXHIBIT 6 Producer Surplus of Individual Sellers

At the market equilibrium price of $20, producer surplus is $15 (Panel A). Sellers prefer higher prices. If the actual price increases to $25, Lincoln and Ross each receive an additional $5 in producer surplus. Moreover, Coolidge now receives $5 in producer surplus. As a result, producer surplus increases to $30 (Panel B).

business wishes to sell only 1 pizza. As these assumptions are unlikely to hold in the real world, we look at a more general case in the analysis that follows.

How Changing Prices Affect Producer Surplus

Similar to the manner price changes impact consumer surplus, price changes also affect the amount of producer surplus. Of course, sellers like *higher* price prices; when prices rise producer surplus increases for two reasons; the producer surplus of the original sellers increases and there are new sellers.

A Higher Price Increases the Producer Surplus of Existing Sellers In Panel B of Exhibit 6, the price increases from $20 to $25 and this increases the producer surplus of the existing sellers. Lincoln and Ross each receive an *additional* $5 in producer surplus. In addition, Coolidge now receives $5 in producer surplus.

A Higher Price Increases the Producer Surplus of New Sellers Higher prices also increase total consumer surplus by increasing the number of sellers in the market. To analyze this, it is useful to examine producer surplus based on market supply (and not the supply of a few individuals).

As shown in Panel A of Exhibit 7, producer surplus can also be depicted with thousands of pizzas being sold by hundreds of sellers. At the price of $20, 3,000 pizzas are sold and producer surplus becomes the area above the supply curve and below the actual price. By having more sellers and allowing them to sell multiple pizzas, the discrete steps shown in the previous exhibit are eliminated and the supply curve appears smooth.

EXHIBIT 7 Producer Surplus of Market

Panel A: Consumer surplus in the market . . .

Panel B: . . . increases when price increases.

At the equilibrium price of $20, 3,000 pizzas are sold (Panel A). Producer surplus is the area above the supply curve and below the actual price. With thousands of consumers, the discrete steps shown in the previous figures are eliminated and the supply curve appears smooth. If the actual price increases to $25 (Panel B), existing sellers will each receive an additional $5 in producer surplus. In addition new sales occur, which also increases producer surplus.

Higher price increases total producer surplus by generating more sales (from 3,000 to 4,000), which also creates additional producer surplus and new sellers. These are sellers who refused to sell the item at the lower price and previously had zero producer surplus. At the higher price, additional sales now occur and generate some additional producer surplus. The total increase in producer surplus is summarized in Panel B of Exhibit 7.

📊 BUSINESS BRIEF Walmart's Expansion Disrupts Consumer and Producer Surplus

Perhaps no company demonstrates the economic trade-offs associated with competitive markets better than retail giant Walmart, which is known for its low prices. In the 1990s and early 2000s, the company engaged in a massive expansion effort. The firm transitioned from a regional retailer to one that could be found across the country and around the globe. This allowed economists to compare the prices of many products and also wages for workers before and after the retailer expanded.

On the one hand, the data suggest that when Walmart lowers prices, this increases consumer surplus. According to a 2005 paper by Jason Furman (who went on to become the chief economic advisor to President Obama), the benefit to consumers was enormous—some $263 billion a year. This amounted to a savings of over $2,300 per household. Moreover, Walmart's low prices disproportionately benefited low-income consumers.

On the other hand, when Walmart opens up a store in a new location, it disrupts existing firms and labor markets, as lower prices reduce producer surplus. In this case, Walmart's expansion put downward pressure on wages. It was estimated that Walmart's expansion lowered retail wages by $5 billion. That's a lot of money, to be sure—but still less than one fiftieth of the increase in consumer surplus.*

*Jason Furman, "Wal-Mart: A Progressive Success Story," Center for American Progress, November 28, 2005.

6.2 ECONOMIC EFFICIENCY AND DEADWEIGHT LOSS

As we have seen, in a competitive market, equilibrium price is generally determined by where quantity supplied equals quantity demanded. In most cases, it is at this price where total surplus is maximized. **Total surplus** is the sum of consumer surplus and producer surplus, plus any tax revenue. In the current example, we ignore tax revenue. Total surplus is the total benefit to society from having a market to buy and sell goods. As you will see, the equilibrium price and quantity typically maximizes total surplus.

What if the market is not in equilibrium? That is, what happens when the market is not really "free"—when, for example, the government intervenes with a tax or regulation on price, or when a single company dominates the market. Economists call such factors *market distortions*. Markets not in equilibrium fail to maximize total surplus because of a market distortion that prevents the price from reaching equilibrium; economists refer to this reduction in total surplus as deadweight loss.

Deadweight loss (DWL) is the reduction in total surplus that results from a market distortion. The concept of deadweight loss is a very important tool used by economists to evaluate whether government policies are beneficial. In this section, we will look at markets that are in equilibrium and those that are not and show how economists measure efficiency and deadweight loss in both situations.

total surplus The sum of consumer surplus and producer surplus, plus any tax revenue.

deadweight loss (DWL) The reduction in total surplus that results from a market distortion.

Earlier, you learned that efficiency is how effectively resources are used in the production and allocation of goods and services. When people in the business world apply the term *efficiency*, they are generally referring to what economists call productive efficiency, which means minimizing production costs for any given output. **Productive efficiency** is obtaining the maximum possible output with a given set of resources or obtaining output for the lowest possible cost.

Here, we focus on another type of efficiency: how competitive markets absent government interference can maximize what economists refer to as allocative efficiency. **Allocative efficiency** is obtaining the maximum well-being from producing the right set of goods and services.

Markets in Equilibrium Often Maximize Total Surplus

Markets in equilibrium typically achieve allocative efficiency by maximizing total surplus, resulting in no deadweight loss. Total surplus is the area below the demand curve and above the supply curve. Exhibit 8 illustrates total surplus. In competitive markets absent government interference, the equilibrium price tends to maximize allocative efficiency.

It may help to think in terms of the marginal analysis first introduced in Chapter 1. In a competitive market, consumers will continue buying marginal (additional) units as long as the price is lower than the willingness to pay, which can be determined from the demand curve. That means they buy right up to the equilibrium point. Sellers will keep selling additional units as long as the price exceeds the willingness to accept, which is the supply curve and determined by the marginal cost of producing products. That means they sell right up to the equilibrium quantity. Once equilibrium is reached, no further units can be bought and sold at a mutually beneficial price. The possibilities for mutually beneficial trades have been exhausted and total surplus is maximized.

In a competitive market, actual price is typically determined by the equilibrium where quantity supplied equals quantity demanded. This is demonstrated in Exhibit 8.

productive efficiency
Obtaining the maximum possible output with a given set of resources or obtaining output for the lowest possible cost.

allocative efficiency
Obtaining the maximum well-being from producing the right set of goods and services.

EXHIBIT 8 Total Surplus Is Maximized at Equilibrium

Total surplus is consumer surplus plus producer surplus: the area below the demand curve and above the supply curve. In the figure, consumer surplus is Area *A*, producer surplus is Area *X*, and total surplus is Area *A* + *X*; there is no deadweight loss.

At this price, allocative efficiency is achieved because total surplus is maximized (Areas $A + X$). This occurs because at the equilibrium price all mutually beneficial transactions that can occur do occur. In other words, there is no other price or quantity that would result in a higher level of total surplus.

Markets Not in Equilibrium Often Result in Deadweight Loss

The best way to see how markets generally maximize economic efficiency is to analyze cases where total surplus is *not* maximized. Therefore let's consider what happens when markets are not in equilibrium. This frequently occurs when a government intervention keeps the price above or below the free market equilibrium, but can also occur when markets are not competitive, for instance, when a monopoly exists. As you will see, the result is a deadweight loss.

Suppose that concerns about obesity prompt the government to intervene in the pizza market. One option would be to artificially restrict pizza sales to a quantity of 2,000. Alternatively, the government could fix the price of pizza at $25—in which case, only 2,000 pizzas will be demanded. Or the government could fix the price of pizza at $15—in which case, only 2,000 pizzas will be supplied. In all three cases, the quantity of pizzas sold will be 2,000 and a deadweight loss will occur.

Exhibit 9 shows the deadweight loss that occurs when government policy reduces the pizza market to 2,000 units: far fewer than the equilibrium quantity. DWL represents the reduction in total surplus that results from such a policy, that is, the deadweight loss. Since the area of a triangle is $1/2 \times$ base $\times$ height; thus, the value of the deadweight loss is $5,000 = 1/2 \times (3,000 - 2,000) \times (\$25 - \$15)$. A deadweight loss typically occurs when markets fail to reach equilibrium.

Here's the basic idea behind the deadweight loss in this example. Output declines from 3,000 to 2,000 after the government intervenes. So, the public no longer gets to consume the other pizzas, and the sellers no longer get to sell the other pizzas. The two sides of the market lose producer and consumer surplus by not engaging in *all* possible mutually beneficial trades.

At 2,000 pizzas, the marginal benefit to consumers from buying pizza is greater than the marginal cost to make the pizza. Such exchanges are mutually beneficial and the sale of additional pizzas would add to total surplus—but these sales cannot occur due to a government policy. There are transactions that no longer occur despite the fact that the buyer is willing to pay a price greater than what the seller is willing to accept. The deadweight loss is the potential gains from trade that *do not occur due to government intervention*.

In the supply and demand model, a price and quantity at market equilibrium efficiently maximize total surplus and minimize deadweight loss. In contrast, government policies

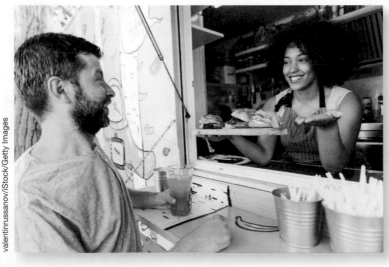

▲ Both buyers and sellers benefit from this transaction.

that mandate a different quantity or price generally result in a reduction in total surplus.

EXHIBIT 9 Deadweight Loss Results from Government Intervention

If government intervention restricts quantity to 2,000 units, deadweight loss occurs. Deadweight loss is the reduction in total surplus that results from a market not in equilibrium. Society's well-being is not maximized because transactions where the marginal benefit to consumers exceeds the marginal cost to producers cannot occur.

6.3 PRICE CONTROLS AND TAXES

In Chapter 1, we learned that in economics there is often a trade-off between efficiency and equity. Absent market failure, market equilibrium prices are efficient—they maximize total surplus. Although maximizing total surplus is efficient, cases exist in which policymakers might have priorities other than efficiency, such as equity, fairness, or changing consumer behavior. For these reasons, governments occasionally intervene in markets. In this section, we will examine several such interventions, and how they affect efficiency.

Price Ceilings Result in Shortages and Deadweight Loss

We begin by examining cases where policymakers pass laws that artificially hold down prices. A **price ceiling** is a law that sets a maximum price, generally below equilibrium. Examples of price ceilings include rent controls, energy price controls, and maximum interest rates on loans. In each example, the government attempts to help demanders: renters in the case of rent control, the consumers of gasoline and electricity in the case of energy price controls, and borrowers in the case of interest rate ceilings.

When a price ceiling is binding—that is, when it pushes price below equilibrium—the price ceiling distorts the market. This is shown in Panel A of Exhibit 10. The equilibrium price is $20. A price ceiling of $15 results in a shortage of 2,000 pizzas, which is the difference between the new and higher quantity demanded (4,000 pizzas) at the controlled price and the new and lower quantity supplied (2,000 pizzas). The price ceiling leads to a reduction in quantity supplied to 2,000, as the actual quantity bought and sold is based on the quantity supplied, not the higher quantity demanded. As you can see, a price ceiling also creates deadweight loss.

In Chapter 3, we learned that markets without price controls adjust to shortages by increasing prices to the equilibrium price. Higher prices increase quantity supplied and decrease quantity demanded. This eliminates the shortage. With a price ceiling, however, prices *cannot* increase; thus, the shortage persists.

price ceiling A law that sets a maximum price, generally below equilibrium.

EXHIBIT 10 Price Ceiling

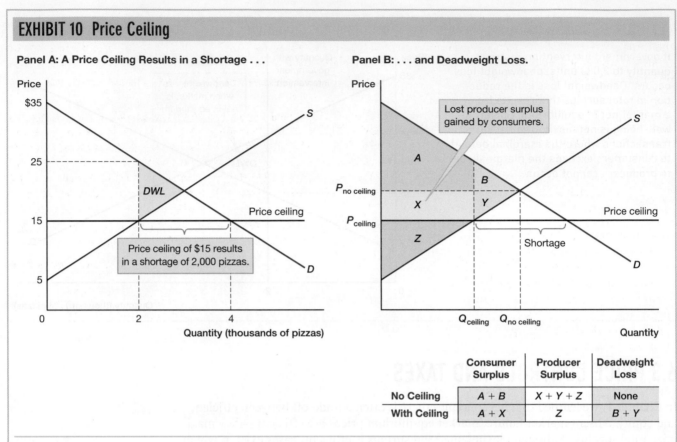

Panel A: A Price Ceiling Results in a Shortage . . .

Price ceiling of $15 results in a shortage of 2,000 pizzas.

Panel B: . . . and Deadweight Loss.

Lost producer surplus gained by consumers.

	Consumer Surplus	Producer Surplus	Deadweight Loss
No Ceiling	$A + B$	$X + Y + Z$	None
With Ceiling	$A + X$	Z	$B + Y$

A price ceiling of $15 results in a shortage of 2,000 pizzas (Panel A). This is the difference between the new and higher quantity demanded (4,000) at the controlled price and the new and lower quantity supplied (2,000 pizzas). A price ceiling results in deadweight loss (DWL) of areas $B + Y$ (Panel B). Examples include rent control, energy price controls, and interest rate controls.

Panel B of Exhibit 10 demonstrates the impact of a binding price ceiling on consumer and producer surplus. Without a price ceiling, the market would be at equilibrium. Consumer surplus would be Areas $A + B$; producer surplus would be Areas $X + Y + Z$. Producer surplus decreases to Area Z alone. As expected, producers lose as a result of lower prices. Consumer surplus loses Area B but adds Area X. Consumer surplus may increase as buyers like lower prices, but this is not always the case. But both producer surplus and total surplus will always decline. The price ceiling leads to a deadweight loss of Areas $B + Y$.

While a price ceiling will always reduce producer surplus, it is also possible that a price ceiling could decrease consumer surplus due to its impact on quantity supplied. In Panel B, the loss in consumers from the lower quantity (Area B) is less than the gain by consumers remaining customers (Area X). Consumers thus seem to be better off with the price ceiling.

This is, however, not always the case as it is possible that Area B is greater than Area X, resulting in consumers being worse off. To visualize such a circumstance, consider what happens if the government sets a price ceiling so low that there are no sellers. In this case, there would be no consumer surplus at all and both buyers and sellers will be worse off. The deadweight loss from this price ceiling would be the entire amount of total surplus that would have existed except for the price ceiling.

Finally, *price ceilings have no effect when they are nonbinding*. A price ceiling above equilibrium has no impact on market price; it stays at equilibrium. For example, a $1,000 price ceiling on a gallon of gasoline would have no effect on the gasoline market. That's because a price ceiling represents a legal maximum: Producers are free to charge a lower price. As an analogy, the impact of a highway speed limit of 400 miles per hour (mph) would be the same as having no speed limit at all. In contrast, a speed limit of 65 mph tends to reduce the driving speed of at least some drivers.

🏛 POLICY BRIEF Shortages and Long Lines at the Gas Pump

Twice during the 1970s (1973 and 1979), geopolitical events led to a spike in the global price of oil, which in turn caused a dramatic increase in gasoline prices. In response to complaints by the public, the government imposed price controls, which pushed the price of gasoline below equilibrium. According to Harvard University economist Joseph Kalt, consumers saved as much as $12 billion a year in gasoline costs in the 1970s.* A shortage ensued as the quantity of oil supplied fell as much as 1.4 million barrels a day due to lower production.

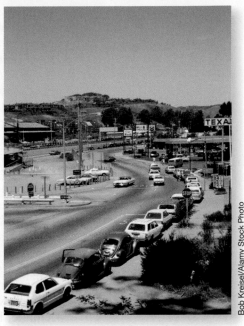

∧ Long lines at the pump were commonplace when there was a price ceiling on gasoline.

The gasoline shortage had tangible effects across the country: Gas stations backed up with enormously long gas lines, and some stations only remained open for a few hours a day. A black market developed for gasoline, and occasional fistfights broke out at the pump. In response to the shortage, policymakers attempted a variety of methods to ration gasoline to consumers. One such scheme was odd/even day of the month rationing, whereby consumers could only purchase gasoline on designated days determined by their license plate number.

Most economists believe that the best way to eliminate shortages is to remove price controls and let the price rise to equilibrium. In 1981, President Reagan took office and removed price controls on oil. The gasoline shortage disappeared almost immediately.

*"How Gas Price Controls Sparked '70s Shortages," *The Washington Times*, May 15, 2006, http://www.washingtontimes.com/news/2006/may/15/20060515-122820-6110r/?page=all.

Price Ceilings in Practice: Rent Control

Rent control is a classic example of a price ceiling found in a number of major cities all over the world. In the United States, rent control laws were particularly prevalent in the decades following World War II. During the war and in the prior decade (the Great Depression), very little apartment construction had taken place. At the war's conclusion, many citizens, including returning GI's, found themselves in need of a home of their own. As a consequence, rents soared. Local governments attempted to help renters by holding down the rent of many apartments to below equilibrium. Most economists are deeply skeptical of rent control laws. In a 2012 survey of leading economists, more than 80% of respondents affirmed their belief that rent control laws have an adverse economic impact.[1]

Rent control results in winners and losers similar to those shown in Exhibit 10. Those fortunate enough to obtain a rent-controlled apartment are the winners. The losers are landlords who receive lower rents, and those who cannot find affordable apartments due the shortage. Rent control often results in a shortage of available apartments and deadweight loss as some would-be renters are unable to rent at all.

The shortage tends to grow progressively worse over time. This is because the short-run supply of rental units is difficult to change; a fixed number of apartments exist. In the long run, the supply of rental units is considerably more flexible—but apartments are only going to be built if landlords see the potential for profit. Developers will therefore opt to build the kind of housing that will command the highest rents, resulting in a smaller and smaller percentage of lower-priced available rentals over time. Moreover, some existing apartments are converted into condominiums or cooperative units to be sold rather than rented, thereby circumventing local rent control laws.

In addition to creating deadweight loss, rent control results in two other problems. First, how do landlords decide who gets an apartment when a housing shortage exists? Landlords tend to favor tenants who have high-paying, stable jobs, who promise to spend money to maintain their property, and perhaps those who are willing to pay a "bribe" to the landlord to rent an available apartment (a practice known as *key money*). An unfortunate side effect of this situation is that the winners from rent control are often *not* the poor. In addition, the shortage makes it easier for landlords to successfully rent their units while discriminating on the basis of race or lifestyle, particularly against families with children.

Second, a shortage reduces the incentives of landlords to update, modernize, and maintain properties. Under rent control apartments can be rented easily without expensive renovation as there is frequently a housing shortage. Without rent control, some landlords would update their units to attract better tenants and justify raising rents.

Allowing a property to go a year or two without proper upkeep may not be problematic, but a decade or two without maintenance can be devastating. According to economist Paul Niebanck, in the United States 29% of rent-controlled housing was in disrepair compared to 8% of non-rent-controlled housing.[2] Similar findings led one economist, Sam Bowman, to conclude that "in many cases rent control appears to be the most efficient technique presently known to destroy a city—except for bombing."[3]

🏛 POLICY BRIEF The Surprising Benefits of Price Gouging

In the aftermath of a major natural disaster, you can expect two things: The price of certain necessities will rise, and politicians on both sides of the political aisle will claim the price increases represent "gouging." You might be surprised to learn that most economists consider price gouging to be *beneficial* to society, because it improves economic efficiency. In a survey of economists from top universities, over 60% of economists who voted disagreed with the State of Connecticut's passage of an anti-gouging law, while only 10% agreed (30% were uncertain or had no opinion).[*]

Marianne Todd/Getty Images

∧ Hoarding tends to occur when price gouging is prevented.

How does price gouging improve economic efficiency? After a natural disaster, the demand for necessities such as generators, gasoline, and water increases. At the same time, it is not unusual to see a decline in supply, as supply lines are disrupted by the disaster. Both these events cause prices to rise. These price increases ensure that the limited quantity being supplied goes where the item is most valued, as measured by willingness to pay. High prices discourage the hoarding of scarce gasoline or using it wastefully while others are in need.

Equally important, price gouging causes an increase in quantity supplied, as it provides a powerful incentive for businesses to truck in gasoline and water from regions not impacted by the disaster. Consider the actions of Bruce Garrett in the days just prior to Hurricane Irma that hit parts of Florida hard in 2017. The Florida real estate agent and businessman secured hundreds of generators that he then sold on the streets of Brunswick, Florida. At the same time, Florida's attorney general issued stern warnings against gouging.[†] While Garrett's actions may have been motivated by a desire to profit on the misfortune of others, most economists would view his actions as socially beneficial.[‡] They would regard the anti-gouging laws as actually making a natural disaster even worse, by reducing the incentives for others to act as Garrett did. If price gouging is banned then there will be fewer goods available, and those goods that are available will not go to those with the greatest need.

[*]"Price Gouging," Chicago Booth School of Business, IGM Economics Experts Panel, May 2, 2012, http://www.igmchicago.org/igm-economic-experts-panel/poll-results?SurveyID=SV_cGhnqM71sWPaoHa.

[†]L. Hobbs, "Generator Sales a Breeze with Irma's Approach," *The New Brunswick News,* September 7, 2017, http://thebrunswicknews.com/news/local_news/generator-sales-a-breeze-with-irma-s-approach/article_59ea7062-46d2-5432-be2f-a4210f53edb2.html.

[‡]"Price Gouging After a Natural Disaster Could Actually Help People," *Business Insider,* November 14, 2012, http://www.businessinsider.com/in-defense-of-price-gouging-2012-11.

Price Floors Result in Surpluses and Deadweight Loss

Just as policymakers might use ceilings to prevent prices from becoming too high, at times they determine that the market price is *too low* and pass laws that prevent prices from falling below a certain level. A **price floor** is a law that sets a minimum price, generally above equilibrium. Examples of a price floor include minimum wage laws and farm price supports. These laws are typically aimed at benefiting suppliers, just the opposite of price ceilings.

Advocates of price floors often point to the issue of equity, or fairness. The minimum wage is aimed at helping the working poor earn more money, whereas farm price supports establish a minimum price for agricultural products such as wheat with the goal of boosting the income of farmers. In the United States, agricultural price floors were instituted in the early 1900s in order to maintain food production at a time when many Americans were leaving the farm to pursue more lucrative opportunities in rapidly industrializing cities.

Exhibit 11 shows the impact of a price floor. First, a binding price floor results in a surplus. This is because the higher price results in an increase in quantity supplied and a decrease in quantity demanded. Without price controls, markets adjust to price floors with a decline in prices. With price controls, prices cannot fall below the floor and the surplus becomes permanent.

In Panel A, a price floor of $25 results in a surplus of 2,000 pizzas. This is the difference between the new and higher quantity supplied (4,000 pizzas) at the controlled price and the new and lower quantity demanded (2,000 pizzas).

In addition to creating a surplus, a price floor that is binding also results in a deadweight loss. Absent a price floor, the market will be at equilibrium. In Panel B, consumer surplus is Areas $A + B + C$ without price controls. Producer surplus is Areas $Y + Z$. When the government sets up a price floor, it results in the deadweight loss of Areas $C + Z$ as some mutually beneficial transactions no longer occur. Consumer surplus decreases to Area A. As expected, consumers lose from higher prices. Producer surplus adds Area B but loses Area Z. Producer surplus usually increases as sellers like higher prices, but may decrease due being able to sell less product. But both consumer surplus and total surplus decline and deadweight loss results. This explains why the majority of economists tend to be very critical of most price floors, such as agricultural price supports.

Finally, *price floors have no effect when they are nonbinding.* For example, a price floor of $1 on a new automobile would be nonbinding because no one would want to sell a car for $1.

price floor A law that sets a minimum price, generally above equilibrium.

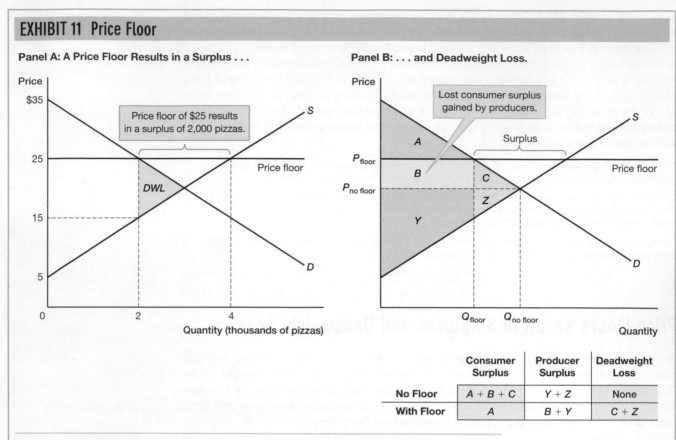

EXHIBIT 11 Price Floor

Panel A: A Price Floor Results in a Surplus . . .

Price floor of $25 results in a surplus of 2,000 pizzas.

Panel B: . . . and Deadweight Loss.

Lost consumer surplus gained by producers.

	Consumer Surplus	Producer Surplus	Deadweight Loss
No Floor	A + B + C	Y + Z	None
With Floor	A	B + Y	C + Z

A price floor of $25 results in a surplus of 2,000 pizzas (Panel A). This is the difference between the new and higher quantity supplied (4,000) at the controlled price and the new and lower quantity demanded (2,000 pizzas). A price floor results in deadweight loss (DWL) of Areas C + Z (Panel B). Examples include minimum wage laws and farm price supports.

Taxes Result in Deadweight Loss

Taxes are the government intervention with which you are probably most familiar. Governments impose taxes on transactions for a wide variety of reasons: including discouraging certain types of behavior (such as smoking) as well as raising funds (as with a gas tax and payroll taxes). Taxes will be discussed in depth in the next chapter. For now, we look at the effects of taxes on total surplus and deadweight loss. You will find that the impact mirrors that of other market distortions—taxes generate deadweight loss as they prevent some transactions from occurring.

Earlier in the chapter, we showed how deadweight loss results when the government imposes a *quantity restriction* on the number of pizzas sold, limiting it to 2, and also from a *price control*. Instead of showing a quantity restriction or price control, in Exhibit 12 there is a $10 tax on pizzas paid by sellers. This shifts the supply curve to the left, reducing the quantity of pizza sold to 2,000 and increasing the price the buyer pays to the new equilibrium of $25. The price the seller receives after paying the tax is reduced to $15 (= $25 − $15).

Recall that total surplus is the sum of consumer surplus and producer surplus, *plus any tax revenue*. While both consumer surplus and producer surplus decrease, taxes result in tax revenue for the government ($10 per pizza on 2,000 pizzas). This is shown in green in Exhibit 12. Since this value is retained by society it is part of total surplus, and not part of the deadweight loss.

DWL represents the reduction in total surplus that results from such a policy, that is, the deadweight loss. Once again, the value of the deadweight loss is

EXHIBIT 12 Deadweight Loss Results from a $10 Tax on Pizza

A $10 tax on sellers reduces supply, results in higher prices for buyers and creates a deadweight loss.

$5,000 = 1/2 \times (3,000 - 2,000) \times (\$25 - \$15)$. A deadweight loss typically occurs when markets fail to reach the free market equilibrium.

When output declines from 3,000 to 2,000, the public no longer gets to consume the other 1,000 pizzas, and the sellers no longer get to sell the other pizzas. The two sides of the market lose producer and consumer surplus by not engaging in *all* possible mutually beneficial trades. There are transactions where the buyer is willing to pay a price less than $25, say, $21 or $22 which the seller would accept, that no longer occur because of the tax.

The next chapter explores many other implications of taxes, such as tax revenue for the government and why it does not matter whether buyers or sellers legally pay the tax. You will also discover that the size of the tax combined with the price elasticity of supply and demand impacts the amount of deadweight loss and tax revenue.

CASE STUDY The Minimum Wage Debate

Perhaps no issue divides economists more than the impact of increases in the minimum wage on the labor market. On the one hand, economists are generally believers in the benefits of using competitive markets to determine prices, unless there is a clear market failure. Raising the minimum wage to above equilibrium could create a deadweight loss and might lead to job losses or a reduction in hours worked and/or more unpleasant working conditions. It would likely have an adverse impact on business, particularly small businesses.

On the other hand, one key objective of the minimum wage is increasing the buying power of the poor—particularly the working poor—an important goal of many lawmakers. In addition, any alternative program designed to help the working poor would also have costs and result in at least some deadweight loss.

A 2013 survey asked economists from top-tier universities if they agreed that a proposed modest increase in the minimum wage "would make it noticeably harder for low-skilled workers to find employment." The responses were sharply divided: 37% of economists agreed with the statement, 34% disagreed, and the rest were uncertain or had no opinion. A similar poll conducted in 2015 asked economists if an increase the minimum wage to $15 per hour over several years would lead to a significantly lower employment rate for low-wage U.S. workers. In that survey, 30% agreed or strongly agreed with the claim, while 27% disagreed. Economists are clearly split on the issue.*

To complicate matters, not only is there a trade-off between equity and efficiency, but the economic impact is difficult to measure and economic studies have often reached conflicting conclusions.

EXHIBIT 13 U.S. Federal Minimum Wage (in 2017 prices)

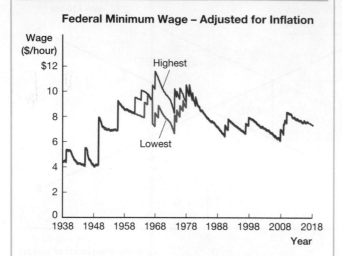

Federal Minimum Wage – Adjusted for Inflation

In the United States, the first federal minimum wage was introduced in 1938 at $0.25 per hour, which was the equivalent of $4 in 2015. Between 1961 and 1978, multiple minimum wages were mandated that depended on a worker's industry, occupation, and age.

Data from: U.S. Department of Labor and authors' calculations.

In the United States, state-level minimum wage laws have been in existence since 1912. In 1938, the Fair Labor Standards Act established the first national minimum wage of $0.25 per hour (around $4 per hour in today's prices). Exhibit 13 demonstrates the federal minimum wage law since 1938, adjusted for inflation.

The current national minimum wage of $7.25 per hour is considerably higher than when first introduced, but considerably lower than when the minimum wage (adjusted for inflation) peaked in 1968. As of 2017, U.S. cities such as San Francisco, Seattle, Washington, and Los Angeles had enacted laws to gradually increase the minimum wage to as high as $15 per hour for select occupations. Similar laws had been enacted in two states.

Why are economists split on the issue? We begin by showing an economic analysis of the minimum wage law similar to that presented for other price controls. We then consider the limits of this theoretical analysis.

Exhibit 14 illustrates the impact of the minimum wage on those workers most likely to earn it—the unskilled. Note that the price in the model is the price of labor, which is the hourly wage rate. It is important to recognize that the minimum wage is intended to help low-skilled individuals with hourly earnings close to the minimum wage—usually workers with relatively little education and work experience. It generally does not impact highly skilled workers like doctors or accountants, earning far above the minimum.

If there were no minimum wage, then the low-skilled labor market would be at equilibrium of $10. Here, the "consumers" are employers (who demand labor), and consumer surplus is Areas $A + B + C$. Producer surplus (the benefit to workers who sell their labor) is Areas $Y + Z$. When the government imposes a minimum wage, it results in the deadweight loss of Areas $C + Z$. Consumer surplus decreases to just Area A. As expected, consumers lose from higher prices. Producer surplus (the surplus benefit to workers who sell their labor) adds Area B but loses Area Z. In total, producer surplus may well increase (labor likes higher prices in the form of wages), but both consumer surplus and total surplus decline. The economy becomes less efficient as a result of lower employment levels.

As shown in Exhibit 14, the minimum wage also reduces the number of hours worked to below the equilibrium level. In the graph, the quantity of labor

EXHIBIT 14 Minimum Wage

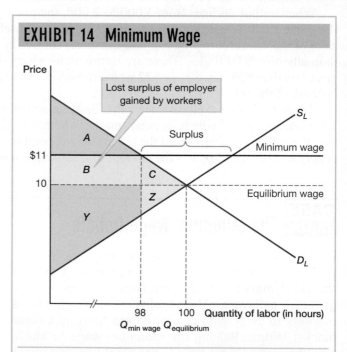

Analysis of the minimum wage is similar to that of other price floors; it creates deadweight loss of Areas $C + Z$. From labor's perspective (producers), workers gain overall as Area B is greater than Area Z. For the employers' perspective (consumers), they lose areas B and C. The figure is drawn to capture the consensus price elasticity of demand for low-skilled workers of 0.2, meaning that a 10% increase in wages decreases the quantity of labor demanded by 2% (from 100 to 98).

employed falls from 100 to 98. Moreover, the minimum wage results in a surplus of labor, which is the difference between the new quantity supplied at the above equilibrium legal minimum wage and the new, lower quantity demanded (98). This occurs because higher wages encourage people to work more hours, but wanting more work is not the same as getting more hours.

The amount of *job loss* is smaller than the surplus, for two reasons. First, the surplus *also* captures increases in quantity supplied, as more people are willing to supply more labor at higher wages. Second, the surplus may capture a reduction in hours worked and not necessarily a loss of employment.

The economic impact of the minimum wage may not be as straightforward as presented in Exhibit 14. Here are some real world complications:

The Quantity of Labor Demanded May Not Be Very Responsive to Changes in the Wage Rate Economists believe that, other things equal, a higher price will cause quantity demanded to decrease. However, the more important question often is: "How much will quantity change?" Such an estimate is known as the price elasticity of demand. Economic research suggests that the price elasticity of demand for labor centers around 0.2, although the estimates are not precise. This means that if the minimum wage increases by 10%, the quantity of labor demanded will fall by roughly 2%, as shown in Exhibit 14. Changes in wages probably have a relatively small impact on the quantity of labor demanded in the short run. After all, an established business with a given capital stock typically requires a set number of workers; thus, many firms are unwilling or unable to reduce their workforce in the short run. Over a longer period of time, companies will find ways to substitute away from the now more expensive workers, and employment will fall by a larger amount.

The Benefit to Low-skilled Workers May Outweigh Deadweight Loss In the survey mentioned above, 47% of economists agreed that the deadweight loss of raising the minimum wage was "sufficiently small compared with the benefits to low-skilled workers who can find employment." Only 11% disagreed with the statement. This means that about half of economists believed the benefits of the minimum wage to low-wage workers (Area B) were clearly greater than the costs in terms of possible job loss. They believed that producer surplus (gain to workers) would increase as wages rise, as the demand for labor is price inelastic. In Exhibit 14, a minimum wage increases the overall pay of workers from $1,000 (= 100 units of labor × $10) to $1,078 (= 98 × $11). Yes, the quantity of labor is

2 out of 3 LIKE a Minimum Wage HIKE

reduced and deadweight loss occurs, but the total pay to these workers is higher, even allowing for the quantity reduction.

Few Workers Earn the Minimum Wage In 2017, fewer than 3% of workers earned the minimum wage. Moreover, nearly half those earning the minimum wage were under the age of 25, and about a fifth were teenagers.[†] Consequently, the impact of changes to the minimum wage on the overall economy is likely to be small, though meaningful to those who pay or earn the minimum wage.

Better Ways Exist to Help the Working Poor Some economists contend that even if the job loss that results from higher minimum wage laws is insignificant, any job destruction is unacceptable. These economists frequently argue that a better way to help the poor is through programs such as the Earned Income Tax Credit or EITC. Under the EITC, if you are employed and have low earnings, the government will not require you to pay taxes, but rather will subsidize you with a tax credit. That is to say, the government will give you money to work, even at private businesses. Since this program doesn't affect the wage paid by businesses, employment will not be reduced. Some economists believe that the EITC program can increase the total income of poor workers, but without costing any jobs.

Disagreements on Economic Outcome Abound You might have noticed in this section that words such as "some," "likely," and "may" are used to describe the economic impact of increases in the minimum wage. This is because great uncertainty exists about the outcomes. One problem is that it's difficult to estimate the price elasticity of demand for labor—the measure of "how much" the quantity of labor demanded will change in response to wage changes. While most estimates of price elasticity of demand for labor center around 0.2, the range of estimates varies from 0 to 1. This means that a 10% increase in the minimum wage might have no impact on labor demanded, or it might result in a 10% decrease. We simply cannot be sure.

One reason why the impact of the minimum wage on jobs is so difficult to estimate is that any adverse impact is likely to be greater in the long run than in the short run. Faced with a higher minimum wage, firms may be more inclined to introduce labor-saving technologies such as self-checkout at retailers, electronic toll collection devices, kiosk machines at restaurants, and self-dispensing soda machines at fast-food establishments. However, these changes take time. Any adverse effects of increases in the minimum wage may not show up in the short run.

How Much the Minimum Wage Changes Matters The adverse impact on employment and the associated deadweight loss is likely very small for minor increases in the minimum wage and very large for major increases in the minimum wage. Increasing the minimum wage by half a dollar per hour would probably create an adverse impact on employment too small for economists to accurately measure. A government-mandated increase in wages to $25 per hour could well have a devastating impact. For example, when the first national minimum wage law was passed in the United States, the U.S. territory of Puerto Rico saw its minimum wage increase to a level well above prevailing wages at the time. The unemployment rate on the island increased to nearly 50%. Two years later, the U.S. law was rewritten to exclude Puerto Rico.

One early study funded by the city of Seattle by economists at the University of Washington found that when then minimum wage was increased to $13 per hour (from $11) in 2016, earnings by low wage workers in restaurants decreased by $125 per month as a consequence of employees working fewer hours. In contrast, when the minimum wage was increased to as much as $11 per hour (from $9.47) a year earlier, the impact was modest as the amount of job loss was near zero.[‡]

Some economists believe that deadweight loss and job losses—however small—should be avoided at all cost. These economists oppose minimum wage laws and often advocate alternative approaches, such as increasing the Earned Income Tax Credit. Other economists believe that since the adverse impact on employment appears sufficiently small, low-income workers would benefit from some increase in the minimum wage. These economists tend to favor increasing the minimum wage. As state and local governments experiment with $15 per hour minimum wages, we may soon learn more about the effect of these policies on low-wage workers.[§]

[*]"Minimum Wage," Chicago Booth School of Business, IGM Economics Experts Panel, February 26, 2013, http://www.igmchicago.org/igm-economic-experts-panel/poll-results?SurveyID=SV_br0IEq5a9E77NMV.

[†]"Characteristics of Minimum age Workers, 2016," BLS.gov, https://www.bls.gov/opub/reports/minimum-wage/2016/home.htm.

[‡]Ekaterina Jardim, Mark C. Long, Robert Plotnick, Emma van Inwegen, Jacob Vigdor, Hilary Wething, "Minimum Wage Increases, Wages, and Low-Wage Employment: Evidence from Seattle," online access to NBER Working Papers, NBER Working Paper No. 23532 (issued in June 2017, revised in October 2017).

[§]See also: Card and A. B. Krueger, *Myth and Measurement: The New Economics of the Minimum Wage* (Princeton, NJ: Princeton University Press, 1995). D. Neumark and W. Wascher, "Minimum Wages and Employment: A Case Study of the Fast-Food Industry in New Jersey and Pennsylvania: Comment," *American Economic Review* 90 (2000): 1362–1396. D. Neumark and W. Wascher, *Minimum Wages* (Cambridge, MA: MIT Press, 2008). A. Dube, T. William Lester, and M. Reich, "Minimum Wage Effects Across State Borders: Estimates Using Contiguous Counties," *Review of Economics and Statistics* 92, no. 4 (2010): 945–964. T. Rustici, "A Public Choice View of the Minimum Wage," *Cato Journal* 5, no. 1 (Spring/Summer 1985): 103–131.

BUSINESS TAKEAWAY

Retailers make pricing decisions based on their perceptions of customers' maximum willingness to pay. A high-end retailer like Nordstrom is able to capture the sales of clients who are willing to pay a premium for an item; the following season, the same item might find its way to a discount chain like TJ Maxx or Nordstrom Rack, where it is priced lower, capturing additional sales among consumers with a lower willingness to pay. In both cases, efficiency is maximized: Consumers got what they wanted for the price they were willing to pay at the time, resulting in a surplus for the consumer and for the producer.

However, market efficiency is often disrupted by taxes and price controls, and this has consequences for most firms. Price ceilings such as rent control, for example, may lead businesses to begin competing by adjusting the quality of their product: Landlords may reduce the upkeep of rent-controlled apartments. Similarly, price floors such as the minimum wage may lead employers to find alternative inputs; for instance, to take orders, fast-food restaurants may replace minimum wage staff with kiosk machines. Or they may reduce fringe benefits for employees.

CHAPTER STUDY GUIDE

6.1 CONSUMER SURPLUS AND PRODUCER SURPLUS

Markets bring together buyers and sellers to make mutually beneficial trades. They also generate consumer surplus and producer surplus. **Consumer surplus** is the buyer's gain from a purchase, measured as the difference between the buyer's willingness to pay and the actual price paid. **Willingness to pay** is the maximum price a buyer is willing to pay for a good or service. Graphically, consumer surplus is the space between the demand curve and the equilibrium price line. A decrease in price increases the consumer surplus of existing buyers and generates consumer surplus for new buyers. **Producer surplus** is the seller's gain from a sale, measured as the difference between the seller's willingness to accept and the price received. **Willingness to accept** is the minimum price a seller is willing to accept for a good or service. Graphically, producer surplus is the space between the supply curve and the equilibrium price line. A price increase increases the producer surplus of existing sellers and generates producer surplus for new sellers.

6.2 ECONOMIC EFFICIENCY AND DEADWEIGHT LOSS

Total surplus is consumer surplus plus producer surplus, represented by the space between the demand curve and the supply curve. This is the total benefit to society from having a market. Market equilibrium typically maximizes total surplus and economic efficiency. Economic efficiency is how effectively resources are used in the production and allocation of goods and services. It includes productive efficiency and allocative efficiency. **Productive efficiency** (or *efficiency* in the business world) is obtaining the maximum possible output with a given set of resources. **Allocative efficiency** is obtaining the maximum well-being from producing the right set of goods and services. When a market is not in equilibrium, it frequently results in **deadweight loss**, a reduction in total surplus that results from a market distortion such as price controls, a monopoly, or taxes. Markets in equilibrium often maximize total surplus and result in no deadweight loss.

6.3 PRICE CONTROLS AND TAXES

Policymakers occasionally set minimum or maximum prices, which are called price controls. A **price ceiling** is the maximum legally allowable price, generally below equilibrium. A binding price ceiling creates a shortage and results in deadweight loss. Examples of price ceilings include rent controls, energy price controls, and interest rate ceilings on loans. A **price floor** sets a legal minimum price, generally above equilibrium. A binding price floor creates a surplus and generates deadweight loss. Examples of a price floors include minimum wage laws and farm price supports. Both price ceilings and price floors create deadweight losses when binding and do not achieve economic efficiency. Most economists are opposed to price controls, except for minimum wage laws, on which economists remain divided. Nonbinding price controls have no impact. Taxes also generate deadweight loss and a reduction in total surplus.

TOP TEN TERMS AND CONCEPTS

1. Willingness to Pay
2. Consumer Surplus
3. Willingness to Accept
4. Producer Surplus
5. Total Surplus
6. Deadweight Loss
7. Productive Efficiency
8. Allocative Efficiency
9. Price Ceiling
10. Price Floor

STUDY PROBLEMS

1. 📊🏃 Why is it difficult to measure consumer surplus in the real world? What technical difficulties do you expect when estimating the consumer surplus of wireless spectrum, estimated at $5 trillion to $10 trillion.[4]

2. Assume that the banning of a product reduces supply, but has no impact on demand. Use a supply and demand graph to illustrate such a scenario. Demonstrate what happens to consumer surplus, producer surplus, and deadweight loss.

3. 🏛 Graph a binding price ceiling. Illustrate any shortage or surplus that results. Demonstrate the impact of the price ceiling on total surplus.

4. 🏛 Explain the difference between a binding price ceiling and a nonbinding price ceiling.

5. 📊🏃 Explain what happens to consumer surplus when new firms enter a market. What happens to the producer surplus of *existing* firms?

6. 🏛 What is price gouging? Explain how laws banning price gouging are similar to a price ceiling.

7. Explain how minimum wages are a form of a price floor. Use a graph in your explanation.

8. Many economists believe that an increase in the minimum wage creates minimal deadweight loss and is an effective way to help the working poor. Drawing two graphs, compare and contrast the impact of a minimum wage with a labor demand curve that is elastic versus one that is inelastic. Which of the two graphs results in the highest amount of unemployment?

9. Assume there are 4 people willing to pay to have their lawns cut. Their willingness to pay is as follows:

Al	$25
Steve	$45
Bob	$30
Scott	$50

Also assume there are 4 landscaping services, each willing to cut only one lawn. Their willingness to accept is as follows:

A-1 Lawns	$25
Lawns Cheap	$15
Best Yards	$35
Green Greens	$30

   a. How many lawns will be cut?

   b. What will the price be?

   c. Who will cut the lawns? What is producer surplus?

   d. Who will have their lawns cut? What is consumer surplus?

   e. What is total surplus?

10. Using the data from Question 9, assume the government passes a price control on lawn services. How many lawns will be cut? Does total surplus increase, decrease, or stay the same?

   a. a price floor of $20

   b. a price ceiling of $20

   c. a price floor of $49

   d. a price ceiling of $49

11. During the twentieth century, there were often shortages in Russian and Soviet bloc countries, with long lines of customers at the grocery store. This was much less true in low-income nations in Asia and Africa. Why might food shortages have been more common in a middle-income country like Russia than a low-income country like India? Why do you think long lines at grocery stores no longer exist in Russia?

∧ All you need is love . . . and low marginal tax rates.

David Redfern/Getty Images

Taxes: An Economic Analysis

Funding Government Spending

In 1966, the Beatles released the hit song "Taxman" in which a tax collector proclaims, "Let me tell you how it will be. There's one for you, nineteen for me." These lyrics referred to the decision by the British government to set the top (marginal) tax rate at 95%—taking $19 out of every $20 earned for income above a certain threshold for high earners like the Beatles. Were there ways for the foursome to avoid paying the tax? Does a marginal tax rate that high maximize tax revenue for the government? Does it distort the economy? Economists have developed a framework to help answer questions such as these.

Modern governments require enormous amounts of revenue. Thus, nearly every financial transaction in which you take part involves some form of taxation. Some taxes are added directly to the price (as when the tax is added at the register when you pay for an item). In other cases, the tax is already included in the selling price (as with gasoline and cigarettes). Most transactions generate wages and profits, which are also taxed.

In this chapter, we focus our attention on the economic impact of taxes. We analyze the difficult question of who *really* bears the burden of a tax (the buyer or the seller?). We'll also examine the link between tax rates and tax revenue, and explore how taxes affect economic efficiency and equity. We begin by examining the major taxes and types of government spending in the United States.

Chapter Learning Targets

- Identify the major expenses and sources of revenue for governments in the United States.

- Explain tax incidence, tax revenue, and deadweight loss from taxation.

- Determine how price elasticity of demand impacts tax incidence, deadweight loss, and tax revenue.

- Describe the U.S. tax system and define equity issues related to taxation.

- Identify strategies businesses employ to reduce their tax liability.

7.1 PUBLIC FINANCE: GOVERNMENT SPENDING AND TAXES IN THE UNITED STATES

Loren Fishman

"Mind if I go in first?"

As Benjamin Franklin wrote in 1789, "In this world nothing can be said to be certain, except death and taxes." In the United States, political debates over taxes have been heated since at least the days of the Boston Tea Party, a protest over the taxes Great Britain had imposed on its American colonies. While few individuals enjoy paying taxes, the reality is that modern governments require enormous amounts of money in order to operate. In the United States, government spending is roughly 36% of all economic activity.

In this chapter, we turn our attention to **public finance**, a branch of economics which studies how governments raise and spend money. We begin by analyzing the major areas of government spending.

Major Areas of Government Spending: "An Insurance Company with an Army"

Every government program, from the military to public education, must be paid for by taxpayer dollars. For the U.S. federal government, the largest expenditure categories are pensions, health care and insurance, national defense, and welfare (public assistance programs). In addition, the government must pay interest on its debt, which is money previously borrowed.

Social insurance programs provide social insurance against the risk of hardship due to poverty, unemployment, retirement, and health-care expenditures. One example is *Social Security*, a government pension program that primarily insures retired elderly people against loss of income. *Medicare* and *Medicaid* are social insurance programs designed to provide health insurance and disability benefits to the elderly (Medicare) and the poor (Medicaid). *Unemployment insurance* provides short-term income to individuals who recently lost their job.

When military spending is combined with expenditures on social insurance programs, you can see why an economist once famously described the federal government as "an insurance company with an army." Together, these programs represent roughly three fourths of total federal expenditures.[1] For state and local governments, the largest expense is education. Government spending data are shown in Exhibit 1.

Major Sources of Tax Revenue

In order to finance government spending, the federal, state, and local governments of the United States levy taxes. The federal government gets most of its revenue from the following three sources. **Personal income taxes** are taxes on personal and household income. **Social insurance taxes** are taxes primarily on wages and salaries paid by employers and employees to fund social insurance programs. Social

public finance A branch of economics which studies how governments raise and spend money.

social insurance programs Government programs that provide social insurance against the risk of hardship due to poverty, unemployment, retirement, and health-care expenditures.

personal income taxes Taxes on personal and household income.

social insurance taxes Taxes primarily on wages and salaries paid by employers and employees to fund social insurance programs; also called *payroll taxes*.

EXHIBIT 1 Federal Spending, 2016; State and Local Government Spending, 2015

Social insurance programs (pensions, health care, and welfare) and national defense make up three fourths of the federal budget. The largest expense for states is education. State and local welfare payments include vendor payments to providers of medical care through Medicaid.

Data from: U.S. Federal Budget (Washington, DC: U.S. Government Printing Office), Historical Tables 2.1 and 5.1; U.S. Census Bureau, Table 1, State and Local Government Finances.

Expense	Federal Spending (in billions of $)	State and Local Spending (in billions of $)
Pensions	$1,071	$274
Health Care	1,120	265
Education	110	937
Welfare	372	653
Interest on Debt	240	106
Defense	788	NA
Other	272	1,166
Total	$3,973	$3,401

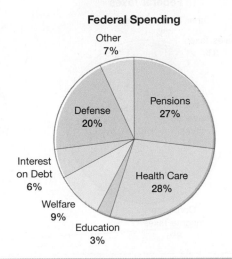

Federal Spending

Other 7%
Defense 20%
Pensions 27%
Interest on Debt 6%
Welfare 9%
Education 3%
Health Care 28%

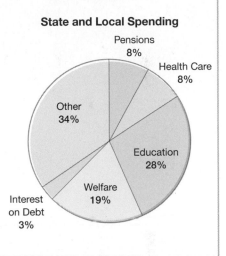

State and Local Spending

Pensions 8%
Health Care 8%
Other 34%
Education 28%
Welfare 19%
Interest on Debt 3%

---

insurance taxes are sometimes called *payroll taxes.* In the United States, the social insurance tax is commonly referred to as FICA (which stands for the Federal Insurance Contribution Act), a tax paid by *both* employees and employers (with independent contractors paying the entire tax). Finally, **corporate income taxes** are taxes on corporate profits. Exhibit 2 shows the relative importance of the major taxes.

State and local governments obtain most their revenue from several *additional* sources. **Property taxes** are taxes on owners of properties such as real estate and motor vehicles based on the value of such properties. **Sales taxes** are taxes on the sale of goods expressed as a percentage of the selling price of an item. Interestingly, the United States is one of the few developed countries that does not have a comprehensive national sales tax (called the *Value Added Tax* or *VAT* in Europe). However, in the United States, the federal government does tax specific products, such as gasoline, alcohol, and cigarettes. States also raise revenue with personal income taxes, social insurance taxes, and corporate income taxes. The largest category of state and local government taxes is labeled "other." This category includes utility and liquor store taxes, transportation taxes (gasoline tax), and license fees.

States and local governments vary widely in their sources of revenue. Some states have no state income tax at all. States like Texas and Florida use the lack of a state income tax as an inducement to attract high-income residents and businesses from other areas. States with the highest state income taxes, such as Hawaii,

corporate income taxes Taxes on corporate profits.

property taxes Taxes on owners of properties such as real estate and motor vehicles based on the value of such properties.

sales taxes Taxes on the sale of goods expressed as a percentage of the selling price of an item.

EXHIBIT 2 Federal Taxes, 2016; State and Local Government Taxes, 2015

Most federal tax revenue is collected from personal income taxes, social insurance taxes, and corporate income taxes. Most state and local tax revenue is collected from personal income taxes, social insurance taxes, sales taxes, and property taxes.

Data from: U.S. Federal Budget (Washington, DC: U.S. Government Printing Office), Historical Tables 2.1 and 5.1; U.S. Census Bureau, Table 1, State and Local Government Finances.

Tax	Federal Taxes (in billions of $)	State and Local Taxes (in billions of $)
Individual Income Taxes	$1,628	$368
Corporate Income Taxes	293	57
Social Insurance Taxes	1,101	323
Sales Taxes	97	545
Property Taxes	0	488
Other Taxes and Fees	217	1,139
Total	$3,336	$2,920

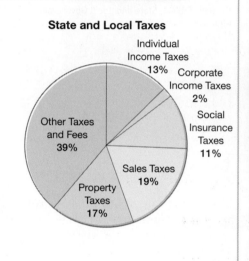

California, and New York, believe they can hold onto wealthy individuals due to factors such as a favorable climate, a competitive high-paying labor market, and/or cultural amenities. However, because it's easier to move between states than to another country, even the highest state income tax rates are much lower than the top federal income tax rate.

The Budget Deficit and National Debt

You might have noticed that in Exhibit 1 the federal government spends $3,973 billion, whereas in Exhibit 2 it only collects $3,336 billion. This $637 billion shortfall is known as the **budget deficit**, government spending minus net tax revenue when government spending exceeds net tax revenue. The government funds the budget deficit by borrowing in the financial markets. In rare cases where tax revenue exceeds spending, the government is said to have a *budget surplus*.

Keep in mind that the government already has large debts from the money borrowed in previous years. The **national debt** is the total amount of money owed by the federal government. It is the total stock of debt accumulated over the years. Those studying macroeconomics explore the effect of the national debt and budget deficit on the economy.

budget deficit Government spending minus net tax revenue when government spending exceeds net tax revenue.

national debt Total amount of money owed by the federal government.

7.2 THE IMPACT OF TAXATION ON CONSUMERS AND PRODUCERS

Imagine a situation where gasoline sold for $3 per gallon. Then the government decided to add a tax on gasoline equal to $1 per gallon. What would happen to the price of gasoline? Many people might assume the price would rise to $4 per gallon, the original price plus the tax. As you will soon discover, the supply and demand model predicts that the price of gasoline will likely rise by *less* than $1 per gallon.

Throughout the rest of this chapter, we will consider several interrelated questions: What would determine the new price of gasoline, after a $1 tax was added? How would the burden of the tax be shared between buyers and sellers? What would the tax do to the quantity of gasoline sold? What would the tax do to economic efficiency? How would the tax impact government revenue? As we will see, the answers to all these questions depend on the price elasticity of supply and demand for gasoline.

A tax levied on a particular good such as gasoline is called an **excise tax**, a tax on the sale of a specific good or service. Excise taxes are applied to items such as gasoline, alcohol, cigarettes, and hotel rentals. Though a relatively minor source of tax revenue in the United States, excise taxes are the easiest tax to analyze because they are a fixed dollar amount per unit.

 POLICY BRIEF   How High Are Excise Taxes on Gasoline in Your State?

Gasoline is one of the most heavily taxed products sold in the United States. The federal government imposes an excise tax of 18.4 cents per gallon. In addition, combined federal and state excise taxes run as high as 78 cents per gallon in Pennsylvania. This excise tax is over 30 cents per gallon higher than in neighboring Ohio. In July 2017, 19 states had a total excise tax of 50 cents per gallon or more on gasoline (see Exhibit 3). At the time, gasoline prices (which included both state and federal taxes) averaged $2.23 a gallon.

The tax paid by drivers goes toward the construction and maintenance of roads used by drivers. The more one drives, the more one pays in gas taxes. However, these taxes alone are not adequate, as state and local spending on roads is more than double the amount collected from the gasoline tax. Furthermore, the shortfall is likely to worsen with increased fuel efficiency, especially with greater use of hybrid and electric cars.

Tax Incidence and the Effects of Taxes

We begin with two simple questions. Can businesses pass along the *full* cost of the tax to consumers, and does it matter who actually writes the check to the government? As you will see, the answer to both questions is generally no. **Tax incidence** is a measure of who bears the economic burden of a tax once prices have adjusted. Note that tax incidence differs from the issue of who bears the *legal tax obligation*, that is, who actually makes the tax payment to the government. Thus, if a 30 cent tax caused the price of gasoline to rise by 20 cents, then we'd say that consumers bear two thirds of the economic burden of the tax, in the form of higher prices. Sellers, for example, may be legally obligated to pay a tax, but they can (and often do) pass on much of the cost, or burden, of the tax to buyers.

excise tax A tax on the sale of a specific good or service.

tax incidence A measure of who bears the economic burden of a tax once prices have adjusted.

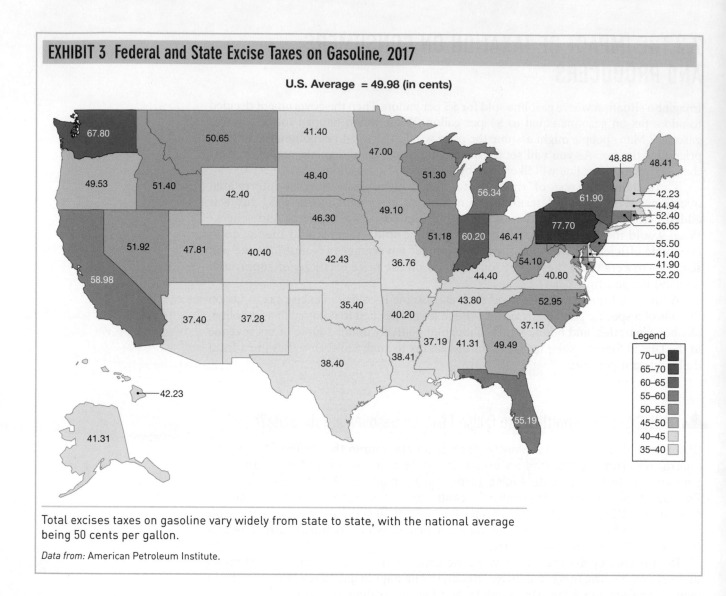

EXHIBIT 3 Federal and State Excise Taxes on Gasoline, 2017

U.S. Average = 49.98 (in cents)

Legend

| 70–up |
| 65–70 |
| 60–65 |
| 55–60 |
| 50–55 |
| 45–50 |
| 40–45 |
| 35–40 |

Total excises taxes on gasoline vary widely from state to state, with the national average being 50 cents per gallon.

Data from: American Petroleum Institute.

Suppose a simple $10 excise tax has been imposed on the purchase and sale of every pizza sold at Mario's. Exhibit 4 demonstrates that the tax incidence is the same regardless of whether the buyers or sellers have the legal obligation to pay the tax. Initially, the equilibrium price of pizza is $20 and the equilibrium quantity is 9. In Panel A, Mario (our seller) pays a $10 tax to the government on each pizza sold. This tax represents an increase in the cost of supplying pizzas. In response to the tax, the supply of pizza decreases, shifting up and leftward by the amount of the tax, $10 in this case. As a result, fewer pizzas are now sold (6 instead of 9). Buyers pay part of the tax in the form of a higher equilibrium price of $25. Of the $25 price, a total of $10 in tax goes to the government and Mario keeps the remaining $15.

Panel B shows a similar $10 tax per pizza, but this time the buyers have the legal obligation to pay the tax, not Mario. Demand decreases when buyers are forced to also pay a tax with each purchase. Since consumers care about the total cost, including the tax, the demand for pizza decreases by the exact amount of the tax. The result of the tax is that fewer pizzas are now sold (6). As in the previous case, Mario bears part of the burden of the tax and receives a new equilibrium price of $15. Since buyers must pay the seller the $15 price *and* pay an additional $10 tax, the total "after-tax" price to buyers for a pizza is $25, including the tax—just as in Panel A. Once again, tax incidence does not depend on who has the legal obligation to pay the tax.

Finally, in both cases, the government collects $60 in taxes. To see this, one needs to understand the difference between *tax rates* and *tax revenue*. **Tax rates** are the tax

tax rates The tax per unit, expressed as an exact dollar amount or a percent of sale price or income.

EXHIBIT 4 Tax Results in Lower Quantity and Higher After-Tax Prices

In Panel A, an excise tax is placed on sellers. This decreases supply. The result is an equilibrium quantity of 6 pizzas and an equilibrium price of $25. The seller receives $15 per pizza after taxes. In Panel B, an excise tax is placed on buyers. This decreases demand. The result is an equilibrium quantity of 6 pizzas and an equilibrium price of $15. The buyer pays $15 pizza to the seller and another $10 in taxes. The "after-tax" price the buyer pays is $25. Thus, tax incidence does not depend on who legally pays the tax. Moreover, the government collects $60 in tax revenue (= $10 × 6) in both cases.

per unit, expressed as an exact dollar amount or a percent of sale price or income. Conversely, **tax revenue** is the total amount of money the government collects from a tax. For an excise tax, the total tax revenue is simply the tax rate times the number of units sold, or $T \times Q$. In the above case, it is $10 times the number of pizzas sold (6). As with tax incidence, the amount of tax revenue does not depend on who legally pays the tax.

In comparing Panel A and Panel B, you will notice that economic outcomes are the same regardless of who legally pays a tax:

- 6 pizzas are now sold.
- The price the buyers pay is $25 per pizza—either all $25 goes to the seller, or $15 goes to the seller and $10 goes to taxes.
- The price the seller keeps is $15 per pizza.
- Tax revenue is $60: $10 per pizza on 6 pizzas.

The key insight here is that the question of who is legally responsible for paying the tax is irrelevant in an economic sense. Consequently, for the remainder of the chapter, we will simply draw a "tax wedge" equal to the tax rate to the left of the pre-tax equilibrium similar to those shown in Exhibit 4. That tax wedge means the price that consumers pay exceeds the amount producers receive by the amount of the tax rate.

Deadweight Loss from Taxation Revisited

Although most people don't like paying taxes, governments cannot function without them. Unfortunately, taxes don't just transfer money from the public to the government, they often reduce economic efficiency. Since taxes raise the after-tax price of the good being taxed, taxes reduce quantity demanded, which results in fewer mutually

tax revenue The total amount of money the government collects from a tax.

EXHIBIT 5   Economic Impact of Taxation

The tax creates a tax wedge between the price the buyer pays and the price the seller receives. It also creates tax revenue of Areas $B + X$ and deadweight loss of Areas $C + Y$.

	Consumer Surplus	Producer Surplus	Tax Revenue
No Tax	$A + B + C$	$X + Y + Z$	None
With Tax	A	Z	$B + X$

beneficial transactions occurring. As discussed in the previous chapter, this leads to a **deadweight loss (DWL)**, the reduction in total surplus resulting from a market distortion. While taxes do generate tax revenue for governments, they also move markets away from free-market equilibrium, which is usually the more efficient position.

Exhibit 5 shows the tax incidence, deadweight loss, and tax revenue associated with an excise tax. We begin by first drawing a tax wedge equal to the tax rate (remember, with whom the legal obligation to pay the tax rests is irrelevant to the current discussion). The tax revenue collected by the government equals Areas $B + X$, which represents the tax rate times the number of units sold. The tax incidence of the buyers is Area B, whereas that of the sellers is Area X. However, this does not represent the total loss to consumers and producers.

Consumer surplus at the no tax equilibrium is the difference between the demand curve and the no tax price of $P_{no\ tax}$, which is Areas $A + B + C$. Since the price the buyer pays with the tax (P_{buyers}) is higher than $P_{no\ tax}$, consumer surplus falls to Area A. Consumers lose Areas $B + C$, which includes *both* the tax incidence of consumers and the lost value of transactions that no longer occur.

Producer surplus at the no tax equilibrium equals Areas $X + Y + Z$. Since the tax reduces what the seller receives (P_{seller}), producer surplus falls to Area Z. Producers lose Areas $X + Y$, which includes *both* the tax incidence of producers and the lost value to sellers of transactions that no longer occur.

Lost from consumer surplus and producer surplus is Areas $B + C + X + Y$. However, Areas $B + X$ is not lost to society—it is collected in the form of tax revenue and goes to the government. Recall that total surplus is the sum of consumer surplus (Area A with the tax) and producer surplus (Area Z) plus tax revenue (Areas $B + X$). Tax revenue is not part of deadweight loss.

Who gets Areas C and Y? No one! The deadweight loss from a tax equals Areas $C + Y$. It is the loss in consumer *and* producer surplus that does not generate tax revenue for the government. Area $C + Y$ is lost to society. It is the loss in consumer and producer surplus from goods that are no longer even being produced.

The total incidence of a tax is sometimes called the *tax burden* (Areas $B + C + X + Y$). The deadweight loss portion is often called an *excess burden* ($C + Y$),

deadweight loss (DWL) The reduction in total surplus that results from a market distortion.

because it is a burden above and beyond the actual taxes collected $(B + X)$. All taxes result in fewer mutually beneficial transactions between buyers and sellers: Fewer pizzas are bought and sold than otherwise would be the case. This is why taxes generally result in a deadweight loss.

The concept of deadweight loss might be easier to visualize if you imagine a tax that is set so high that no one buys any pizza—let's say a tax of a million dollars per pizza. In that case, you'd have lots of disappointed customers, unable to eat their favorite dish, and lots of disappointed pizza shops, unable to finds any buyers for their pizzas. Producers and consumers would thus both clearly suffer losses. In a way, the government experiences a loss, too: No pizza being purchased means that no tax on pizza is being paid. Governments are mindful of this kind of scenario developing, of course, so in the real world taxes are generally not set so high that they prevent any sales from occurring. But any tax will reduce output somewhat, compared to untaxed equilibrium. It is this loss of output that explains the deadweight loss to society.

The Economic Impact of Changing Tax Rates

Higher tax rates would always increase tax revenue if sales did not decrease. However, taxes almost always result in some reduction in quantity sold. If the impact on sales is relatively small, the higher tax rates will generate increased revenue. However, if the impact on quantity sold is unusually large, it is possible that a higher tax rate could actually reduce tax revenue.

Exhibit 6 builds on our previous example by expanding the size of the market by 100-fold. It demonstrates the impact of five possible tax rates on pizza: $5, $10, $15, $20, and $30. In Panel A, pizzas are untaxed, resulting in an equilibrium price of $20 with 900 pizzas being sold. In Panel B, a $5 tax on pizza results in 750 pizzas being sold. Since each pizza generates $5 in taxes, tax revenue equals $3,750 (= $5 × 750). In Panel C, the tax rate doubles to a $10 tax on pizza, which results in 600 pizzas being sold. Tax revenue less than doubles: It increases to $6,000 (= $10 × 600). In Panel D, a $15 tax on pizza results in 450 pizzas being sold. Since each pizza generates $15 in taxes, tax revenue equals $6,750 (= $15 × 450). At this point, further increases in tax rates *lower* tax revenue. In Panel E, a $20 tax on pizza results in 300 pizzas being sold. Since each pizza generates $20 in taxes, tax revenue equals $6,000 (= $20 × 300). Finally, a $30 tax on pizza results in no tax revenue at all, because the quantity of pizza demanded falls to zero. This is shown in Panel F.

In Exhibit 6, when the tax rate doubled from $5 to $10, tax revenue less than doubled. Then when tax rates increased by 50% from $10 to $15, tax revenue increased by only 12.5%. Increases in tax rates almost never result in a proportionate increase in tax revenues. Thus, a 10% increase in tax rates may result in a 2, 4, or 6% increase in tax revenues, or possibly no additional tax revenues at all. However, it will generally not result in a 10% increase in tax revenues, because the higher tax rate almost certainly reduces quantity purchased. If you think of tax revenue as a rectangle on the supply and demand diagram, then as you make the box taller (representing a higher tax rate), you also make it narrower (fewer units sold).

In Exhibit 6, when the tax rate climbed from $15 to $20, total tax revenue actually fell. When tax rates are already relatively high, a further increase in tax rates may result in a decline in tax revenues. In this particular example, we are levying a $20 tax on a pizza with a no tax equilibrium price of $20. In that case, the negative impact on sales overwhelms the positive increase in tax rates.

Most taxes are like those in Panel B, a relatively small percentage of the total price. Consider sales taxes, which are expressed as a percentage of the price of goods sold. In the United States, sales taxes are usually less than 10% of the sales price. In that case, an increase in the tax rate will usually lead to more revenue. Doubling a sales tax from 5 to 10% might reduce sales a little bit, but it won't result in total sales falling by half, so tax revenue increases. The goal of a sales tax is generally not to maximize tax

EXHIBIT 6 Impact of Changing Tax Rates on Tax Revenue and Deadweight Loss

Panel A: No Tax

Panel B: $5 Tax

Panel C: $10 Tax

Panel D: $15 Tax

Panel E: $20 Tax

Panel F: $30 Tax

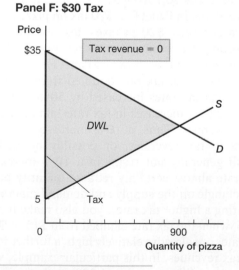

In Panel A, there is no tax and no tax revenue. In Panel B, the tax rate is $5 and tax revenue is $3,750 (= $5 × 750). In Panel C, the tax rate is $10 and tax revenue is $6,000 (= $10 × 600). In Panel D, the tax rate is $15 tax and tax revenue is $6,750 (= $15 × 450). In Panel E, the tax rate is $20 and tax revenue is $6,000 (= $20 × 300). Finally, in Panel F, the tax rate is $30 and there is no transactions or tax revenue. Also note that increasing tax rates increases the amount of deadweight loss (shaded in yellow), with no DWL in Panel A, and the most DWL in Panel F.

revenue, but rather to raise some money while *not* generating a significant amount of deadweight loss by discouraging economic activity.

What about Panel D, which yields the highest revenue? A good example might be state lottery tickets, which are often sold at a price of $1 each. About 40 cents of that dollar is a tax imposed by the state, which helps to fund programs like education. Unlike what occurs with the sales tax, states usually do set tax rates on lottery tickets at the level expected to maximize revenue. They aren't too concerned about deadweight loss from fewer tickets sold, because gambling is often viewed as a frivolous activity that should not be encouraged.

Panels E and F are the most unusual examples. Here, taxes are set above the revenue-maximizing point. This leads to both less revenue and a bigger deadweight loss—a lose-lose situation. In the rare cases where this occurs, the government is usually trying to intentionally discourage consumption. For instance, some cities place extremely high taxes on cigarettes. In such instances, a large reduction in smoking would be viewed as a benefit by anti-smoking advocates, not a cost.

Finally, note that as the tax rate becomes higher, the deadweight loss triangle (shaded in yellow) grows much larger. This is because taxes tend to discourage the production of whatever is taxed, reducing the overall efficiency of the economy. With no tax, there is no DWL. With a tax of $5 or even $10, the amount of DWL is fairly modest. As tax rates increase, however, the DWL can grow to be as large as the amount of tax revenue collected as happens to be the case with a $20 tax in Panel E. Finally, a $30 tax on pizza in Panel F will only result in deadweight loss and no tax revenue, as no transactions occur.

7.3 PRICE ELASTICITIES AND TAXES

In Chapter 4, we learned that elasticity is a measure of responsiveness to a change in market conditions. Here, we will focus on how economists use the price elasticity of supply and the price elasticity of demand to measure "how much" quantity changes in response to taxes. These concepts also help economists determine how much deadweight loss is generated by taxes, and who bears the burden of a tax. As you will discover, a tax on an item with a demand curve that is price inelastic (such as gasoline, cigarettes, or coffee) will tend to have a different impact than a tax on an item with a demand that is price elastic (such as pizza, sneakers, or soft drinks).

How Price Elasticities Impact Tax Incidence

The price elasticity of supply relative to the price elasticity of demand determines who bears the burden of a tax. In general, the group with the more price inelastic (least price elastic) curve bears the largest burden of a tax.

Suppose you spend $100 per month on gasoline and $100 per month on pizza, and the government imposes a 30% tax on these two products. On paper, it might seem as if a 30% tax on either product would hurt you equally. But in reality, the gas tax would be tough to avoid, while the pizza tax could be avoided by switching to an alternative, such as making your own pizza at home or purchasing instead (untaxed) hamburgers. Governments often consider such alternative behaviors on the part of consumers, which is why it's much more likely you'll see a big tax imposed on gasoline rather than pizza.

We know that the demand for goods with lots of close substitutes are price elastic. The pizza example suggests that consumer behavior would change dramatically in response to a tax on goods with price elastic demand, but consumers would be hurt more significantly by a tax on necessities with price inelastic demand, like gasoline.

If a tax is fully passed onto consumers in the form of higher prices, then economists would say that 100% of the tax incidence falls on consumers. In

Think & Speak Like an Economist

Economists describe supply and demand in terms of price elasticity—not slope. Demand for products like gasoline, cigarettes, and coffee is price inelastic as quantity is not very responsive to price changes. Demand for products like pizza, sneakers, and soft drinks is price elastic as quantity is relatively responsive to price changes.

Think & Speak Like an Economist

Economists are generally unconcerned with who has the *legal obligation* to makes tax payments; rather, they focus on *tax incidence*— who bears the burden of a tax. While tax incidence is shared, it mostly falls on buyers when demand is less price elastic (more price inelastic) than supply.

reality, the burden of the tax is usually split between buyers and sellers. For example, in the United States, it is usually cigarettes sellers who are legally obligated to make the payment for the excise tax. They pass much of that cost on to buyers in the form of higher prices, but they cannot pass all of it along.

Tax incidence depends on the relative price elasticity of supply and demand. In this case, demand for cigarettes is relatively price inelastic, much more so than supply. When demand is price inelastic, buyers are not very responsive to price changes, including price changes that result from taxation. If demand is less price elastic (more inelastic) than supply, then buyers bear the largest share of the tax.

In contrast, if supply is less price elastic (more inelastic) than demand, then sellers bear most of the tax burden. For example, labor supply is often viewed as relatively price inelastic (though estimates vary). Thus, the burden of a wage tax falls on the sellers of labor (the workers). Likewise, the supply of land is price inelastic, and hence taxes on land are mostly absorbed by the landowner, who is the supplier.

For most products the supply is much more price elastic than demand, and hence consumers usually bear most of the burden of sales and excise taxes. This scenario is demonstrated in Panel A of Exhibit 7. The tax burden is greatest on buyers when demand is price inelastic and supply is elastic; most of the tax revenue and DWL is coming from a reduction in consumer surplus. In contrast, the tax burden is greatest on sellers when supply is price inelastic and demand is price elastic; most of the tax revenue and DWL is coming from a reduction in producer surplus.

To recap:

- When price elasticity of demand is:

  - *inelastic*, this tends to *increase* the portion of the tax paid by *buyers*.

  - *elastic*, this tends to *decrease* the portion of the tax paid by *buyers*.

EXHIBIT 7 Tax Incidence Is Impacted by Price Elasticities

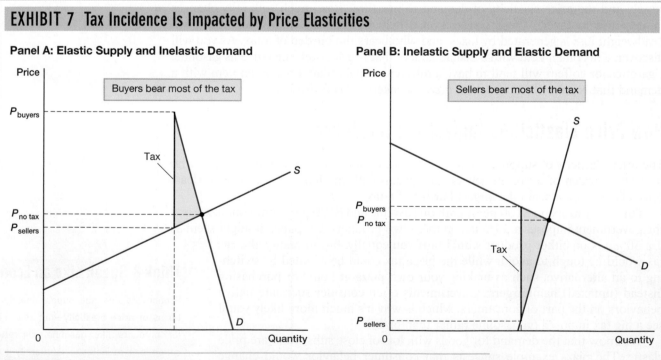

Tax incidence depends on the relative values of the price elasticity of supply and demand. The tax burden is greatest on buyers when demand is price inelastic and supply is elastic (Panel A). This is the case for an excise tax on gasoline. In contrast, the tax burden is greatest on sellers when supply is price inelastic and demand is price elastic (Panel B). This is often the case for taxes on labor and land.

- When the price elasticity of supply is:
  - *inelastic*, this tends to *increase* the portion of the tax paid by *sellers*.
  - *elastic*, this tends to *decrease* the portion of the tax paid by *sellers*.

 BUSINESS BRIEF Marlboro Pays a Larger Share of Taxes on Cigarettes Than Discount Sellers

The demand for cigarettes is more price inelastic than supply. As a result, smokers pay the bulk of excise taxes on cigarettes. This is consistent with the Panel A of Exhibit 7. According to a 2014 Chicago area study by Lesley Chiou of Occidental College and Erich Muechlegger of Harvard University, cigarette companies paid about 20 cents of every dollar through which cigarettes are taxed.

Moreover, the price elasticity of demand varies by cigarette type. When cigarettes are taxed, some buyers switch from premium brands such as Marlboro to discount brands. When discount cigarettes are taxed, buyers do not have a lower-priced alternative. In this situation, discount cigarettes tend to have a price elasticity of demand which is more inelastic (less elastic) than that of branded cigarettes. Consistent with the economic theory of taxation, Phillip Morris, the seller of premium brand cigarettes such as Marlboro, paid roughly 30 cents of every dollar of cigarettes taxed. In contrast, sellers of discount cigarettes paid only 10 cents of every dollar of cigarettes taxed.*

*See Lesley Chiou and Erich Muehlegger, "Consumer Response to Cigarette Excise Tax Changes," *SSRN*, October 17, 2010, https://papers.ssrn.com/sol3/papers.cfm?abstract_id=1693263.

 POLICY BRIEF "No Damn Politician Can Ever Scrap My Social Security Program"

You've probably noticed that a portion of your paycheck goes to FICA, a social insurance tax (payroll tax) which funds Social Security and other government benefits. The tax rate is currently set at 15.3% of income.* For most employees, the tax is shared, with workers paying half (7.65%) and employers paying the other half. This 50-50 split in the legal burden of the tax has more to do with politics than economics. Commenting on the payroll tax, President Franklin Roosevelt stated in 1941:

> We put those pay roll contributions [taxes] there so as to give the contributors a legal, moral, and political right to collect their pensions. . . . With those taxes in there, no damn politician can ever scrap my social security program. Those taxes aren't a matter of economics, they're straight politics.†

Roosevelt was obviously interested in how the program would appear to the public. But does the actual burden of the tax depend on how it is legally shared by the employee and employer? Clearly not; the economic outcome is the same regardless if the legal obligation of the tax falls on the employee, the employer, or is evenly split (as in this case). What matters are the relative price elasticity of labor supply and the price elasticity of labor demand. It turns out the labor supply is highly inelastic, particularly among those who work full-time. For such workers, modest changes in tax rates have relatively little impact on the quantity of labor they supply. Most economists believe that the suppliers of labor, that is, the employees, pay the lion's share of Social Security taxes, similar to Panel B of Exhibit 7.

*"Congress and the New Deal: Social Security," *National Archives and Records Administration*, n.d., https://www.archives.gov/exhibits/treasures_of_congress/text/page19_text.html.
†Larry DeWitt, "Research Note #23: Luther Gulick Memorandum re: Famous FDR Quote," Social Security Administration Historian's Office, July 21, 2005, https://www.ssa.gov/history/Gulick.html.

∧ A monthly check for retirees, funded by payroll taxes—the biggest tax most Americans pay.

EXHIBIT 8 Elasticity, Tax Revenue, and Deadweight Loss

Panel A: Inelastic Supply and Inelastic Demand

Panel B: Elastic Supply and Elastic Demand

The amount of tax revenue collected is smaller, and the amount of deadweight loss from a tax is greater, when both supply and demand are price elastic than when one or both curves are inelastic.

How Price Elasticities Impact Deadweight Loss and Tax Revenue

Just as elasticity affects tax incidence, it also affects the size of deadweight loss and the amount of tax revenue. Recall that the key factor in determining the extent of deadweight loss is the change in quantity that occurs as the result of a tax. The more output that gets eliminated by a tax, the bigger the deadweight loss and the smaller the amount of tax revenue.

This is demonstrated in Exhibit 8. The DWL is smaller in Panel A. When either the supply or demand is price inelastic, the impact on quantity is relatively small. As a result, the deadweight loss will be smaller. In contrast, if both supply and demand are price elastic, the impact of a tax on quantity will be larger and the amount of deadweight loss will be larger.

The preceding analysis suggests that government policies that impact quantity the least tend to generate the smallest deadweight loss. Consequently, governments often tax items with an inelastic demand such as gasoline, or an inelastic supply such as land and labor. These taxes have a smaller impact on quantity and total surplus than taxes on goods where the supply and demand are elastic.

Elasticity doesn't just affect tax incidence and the deadweight loss; it also affects the total amount of revenue collected by the tax (green area). When both buyers and sellers are responsive to price changes, sales fall sharply in response to a tax, which reduces overall tax revenues. Governments are often disappointed to find they collect less revenue than expected when taxing items that have *both* a price elastic demand curve and a price elastic supply curve (Panel B in Exhibit 8). The amount of tax revenue collected by the government in this instance is smaller than in the case where supply and demand are both inelastic (Panel A).

 POLICY BRIEF Taxing Broadband in San Francisco

What happens when the government puts a tax on broadband Internet service? Economist Austan Goolsbee, former economic advisor to President Barack Obama, analyzed those factors in 70 cities. At the market price of $40, he estimated the price elasticity of demand to be about 2.65 in San Francisco: highly elastic. This occurred in part because individuals were able to find alternative means to access the Internet, and in part because Internet access was viewed as more of a luxury to many. Similar estimates of the price elasticity of demand were found in other cities. The price elasticity of supply was also determined to be elastic.

As shown in Panel B of Exhibit 9, when both the supply and demand of broadband are price elastic, taxes creates a very large deadweight loss and less tax revenue than if demand were inelastic. In the case of San Francisco, Goolsbee estimated that the loss in consumer and producer surplus totaled $136 million, but the government collected only $23 million in revenue. The remaining $113 million burden to consumers and producers was simply a deadweight loss. That's a relatively inefficient tax.*

*Austan Goolsbee, "The Value of Broadband and the Deadweight Loss of Taxing New Technology," *NBER*, February 2006, http://www.nber.org/papers/w11994.

7.4 TAXES AND PUBLIC POLICY

Americans pay a lot of taxes. Thus far, our analysis has mostly focused on the simplest of them—excise taxes such as taxes on gasoline and cigarettes, as well as the hypothetical $10 tax on pizza. These taxes are the easiest tax to analyze in terms of tax incidence and economic efficiency, as they are a fixed dollar amount. However, the U.S. income tax system is much more complex than excise or sales taxes.

The Language of Tax Systems

Analyzing the income tax system is complicated partly because the federal income tax, and many state income taxes, incorporate lots of tax credits and tax deductions (sometimes called *loopholes*).

Tax Credits versus Tax Deductions A **tax credit** is a tax rule that allows taxpayers to reduce the amount they owe in taxes by exactly the amount of the credit. Some individuals receive tax credits for child care, college tuition, or the purchase of an electric car. Many low-income individuals might receive the Earned Income Tax Credit. These credits are received regardless of the amount of taxes owed, allowing for the possibility of an individual having a negative tax obligation—which means getting money back from the government.

A **tax deduction** is a tax rule that allows taxpayers to reduce their taxable income by the amount of the deduction. For example, individual taxpayers can deduct amounts they donate to charities, interest they pay on home mortgages, money spent on health insurance, and tax payments. Similarly, small businesses can deduct usage of a vehicle and utilities.

Since a tax deduction reduces one's taxable income, it reduces a person's tax bill by less than an equal tax credit. For instance, a $1,000 tax credit reduces your tax bill by $1,000. In contrast, a $1,000 tax deduction with a 24% marginal tax rate reduces your tax bill by $240.

In the United States, there are thousands of tax deductions and tax credits. As a consequence, completing a tax return is time-consuming and often involves the services of companies like H&R Block, Pricewaterhouse Coopers (PwC), and Deloitte—the three largest tax preparers in the country. Many economists view such expenses as wasteful and favor a simpler income tax system with far fewer tax deductions and credits.

"Sorry, but under-the-table donations aren't tax deductible."

Loren Fishman/Cartoon Stock

tax credit A tax rule that allows taxpayers to reduce the amount they owe in taxes by exactly the amount of the credit.

tax deduction A tax rule that allows taxpayers to reduce their taxable income by the amount of the deduction.

Marginal Tax Rates versus Average Tax Rates It is also important to distinguish between marginal tax rates and average tax rates. The **marginal tax rate** is the amount of additional taxes one pays from an additional dollar of income. The Beatles faced a marginal tax rate of approximately 95%. However, it did not apply to all their income, only to the portion of their income above a certain threshold. In contrast, the **average tax rate** is the total taxes paid divided by total income.

In general, it is the marginal tax rate that has the greatest impact on decisions such as whether to work extra hours or a second job. Marginal tax rates are particularly important because people tend to determine how much additional income they will receive after taxes with additional work—consistent with the idea of marginal analysis.

In 2018, the United States had seven federal income tax marginal rates or brackets. Exhibit 9 displays these rates for a single taxpayer and married couples in

marginal tax rate The amount of additional taxes one pays from an additional dollar of income.

average tax rate Total taxes paid divided by total income.

EXHIBIT 9   U.S. Federal Marginal Tax Rates, 2018

Higher marginal tax rates on higher levels of income are a common feature of a progressive tax. Note that there is an additional "surtax" of 3.8% on high earners, primarily to fund the ACA, making the effective top federal rate 40.8%. When other federal, state, and local taxes on income are included, it is not uncommon for the top marginal tax rate to be close to 50%.

Marginal Tax Rate	Income where Tax Rate Begins	
	Individual	Married Couple*
10%	$0	$0
12	$9,525	$19,050
22	$38,700	$77,400
24	$82,500	$165,000
32	$157,500	$315,000
35	$200,000	$400,000
37	$500,000	$600,000

*Filing jointly.

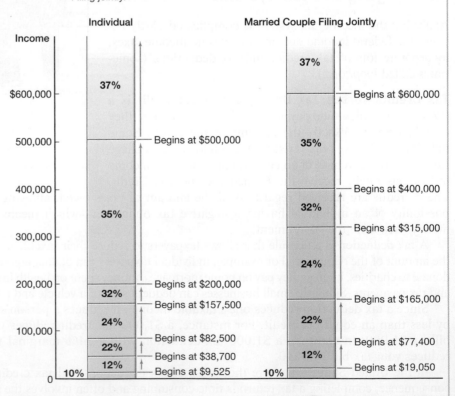

2018, based on taxable income, which is income after tax deductions. Individuals paid a tax rate of 10% on their first $9,525 earned that year. Earnings over $9,525 were taxed at a variety of rates with the maximum rate of 37% applying to every dollar of taxable income over $500,000.

We now simplify our examination by assuming the government imposes only the two tax rates shown in Exhibit 10 (rather than the seven outlined in Exhibit 9): an initial marginal rate of 10% for the first $25,000 in income and a second marginal rate of 50% for all income above $25,000. We'll also assume that there are no tax deductions. Suppose Susan earns $25,000. She pays 10% in taxes, or $2,500 (= 0.10 × $25,000). Her marginal tax rate equals the average tax rate of 10%.

Now consider Jason who has $40,000 in income. He pays $10,000 in taxes: $2,500 in taxes on the first $25,000 in income and $7,500 or 50% of the *next* $15,000 in income ($10,000 = 0.10 × $25,000 + 0.50 × $15,000). His marginal tax rate is 50%, but his average tax rate is 25%, which equals $10,000 in taxes paid divided by $40,000 in income. Finally, consider Marissa with $100,000 in income. She pays $40,000 in taxes: $2,500 in taxes on the first $25,000 in income and $37,500 or 50% of the *next* $75,000 income ($40,000 = 0.10 × $25,000 + 0.50 × $75,000). For Marissa, the marginal tax rate is 50%, but the average tax rate is 40%, which equals $40,000 in taxes paid divided by $100,000 in income. A tax system where average tax rates increase with income, such as the U.S. income tax system in Exhibit 9 and the simple two rate tax system in Exhibit 10, are considered *progressive*.

Evaluating the Tax System

Ultimately, any discussion on taxes evolves into a question on how to split the tax burden among those with different levels of income. The discussion often centers around two principles: the *benefits-received principle* versus the *ability-to pay-principle*.

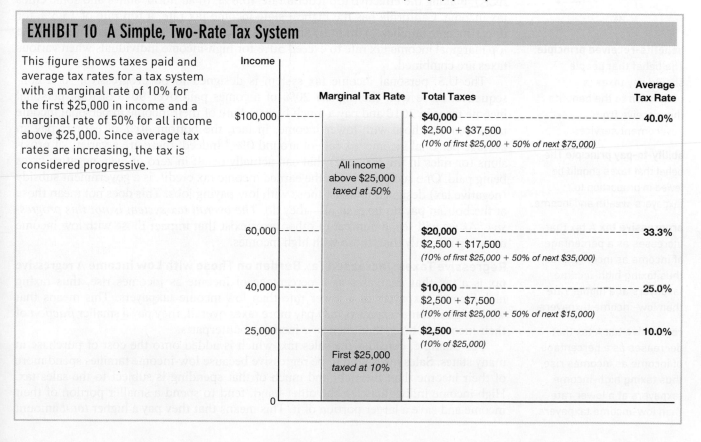

EXHIBIT 10 A Simple, Two-Rate Tax System

This figure shows taxes paid and average tax rates for a tax system with a marginal rate of 10% for the first $25,000 in income and a marginal rate of 50% for all income above $25,000. Since average tax rates are increasing, the tax is considered progressive.

Think & Speak Like an Economist

Economists focus on marginal, not average, tax rates. Marginal tax rates are the tax rate on *additional* income. The marginal tax rate for a specific individual is referred to as their tax bracket. In contrast, average tax rates are the fraction of one's total income that is paid in taxes.

The **benefits-received principle** of taxation states that people should pay taxes in proportion to the benefits they receive from government services. For example, individuals who drive on a road should pay a tax in the form of a toll to support the building and maintenance of the road. Thus, many view the gasoline excise tax (discussed in our earlier **Policy Brief: How High Are Excise Taxes on Gasoline in Your State?**) as reasonable. Likewise, excise taxes on plane tickets are often used to fund airport operations in accordance with the benefits-received principle.

The **ability-to-pay principle** of taxation states taxes should be levied in proportion to taxpayers' wealth and income. In most countries, citizens accept the notion that the wealthy pay more in taxes than the poor because the wealthy can do so without a severe reduction in their standard of living. Furthermore, in most countries, the wealthy pay income taxes at a higher rate.

Progressive Taxes: Increased Tax Burden on Those with High Income A **progressive tax** is a tax that increases as a percentage of income as incomes rise, thus taxing high-income taxpayers at a higher rate than low-income taxpayers. This means that those with higher incomes don't just pay more taxes; they also pay a *higher average tax rate* than those with lower incomes. Although the details of income tax systems vary from country to country and from year to year, most national (federal) income tax systems are progressive, meaning marginal tax rates increase as incomes increase. Marginal tax rates are higher than average tax rates in a progressive system, such as those shown in Exhibit 9.

As noted above, in the United States in 2018, the top marginal tax rate on ordinary income was 37%. In contrast, the lowest federal income tax rate was 10%. When other taxes on income are considered, the top tax rate actually exceeds 37%. There is an additional "surtax" of 3.8% on high earners, primarily to fund the Patient Protection and Affordable Care Act (often simply referred to as the Affordable Care Act or ACA), making the effective top federal rate 40.8%. In addition, states and some cities tax income. California has the highest state income tax rate, a top rate of 13.3% for upper-income families. With these additional income taxes, it is not uncommon for the top marginal income tax rate to exceed 50% for high-income individuals when various taxes are combined.

The U.S. personal income tax system is designed to be progressive. As a consequence, those with the highest 20% of incomes paid over 90% of total personal income taxes in 2010 and pay a much higher share of their income in personal income taxes than do those with lower income. In fact, the bottom 40% of earners pay an average personal income tax rate of around 0%.[2] Indeed, there are a variety of provisions (or rules in the tax code) that can actually result in zero or even negative taxes being paid. One such provision, the earned income tax credit, is a government subsidy (negative tax) designed to assist those with low-paying jobs. This does not mean those at the bottom pay no taxes at all—they do. *The overall tax system is not this progressive.* As we will see, a number of other taxes exist that impact those with low income more significantly than those with high incomes.

Regressive Taxes: Increased Tax Burden on Those with Low Income A **regressive tax** is a tax that decreases as a percentage of income as incomes rise, thus taxing high-income taxpayers at a lower rate than low-income taxpayers. This means that while high-income taxpayers may pay more taxes overall, they pay a smaller *fraction* of their income in taxes than their low-income counterparts.

For example, consider the sales tax, which is added onto the cost of purchase in many states. Sales taxes tend to be regressive because low-income families spend more of their income than the rich, and much of that spending is subject to the sales tax. High-income individuals, on the other hand, tend to spend a smaller portion of their income and save a larger portion of it. This means that they pay a higher *total* amount

benefits-received principle The belief that people should pay taxes in proportion to the benefits they receive from government services.

ability-to-pay principle The belief that taxes should be levied in proportion to taxpayers' wealth and income.

progressive tax A tax that increases as a percentage of income as incomes rise, thus taxing high-income taxpayers at a higher rate than low-income taxpayers.

regressive tax A tax that decreases as a percentage of income as incomes rise, thus taxing high-income taxpayers at a lower rate than low-income taxpayers.

of sales tax (having spent more money overall), but a smaller *proportion* of their income is subject to sales taxes. Europe's Value Added Tax (VAT) is also regressive. Many states attempt to work around the regressive nature of a sales tax by exempting necessities like groceries and low-priced clothing.

In the United States, part of the FICA payroll tax used to fund Social Security is also regressive. This is partly because payroll taxes only tax income from labor up to a certain threshold, about $128,700 is 2018. The logic was to tax just enough to provide for each person's future retirement. In addition, income from inheritances, financial investments, profits on businesses are mostly excluded from the payroll tax. The most regressive tax of all is probably the cigarette tax. Of course, saying that a tax is "regressive" does not necessarily imply it is bad.

Proportional Taxes A **proportional tax** is a tax that remains a constant percentage at all levels of income; also called a **flat tax**. As one's income increases (or decreases), the share of one's income paid in taxes remains constant. Some countries have a 15 or 20% "flat tax" *applied to all income* without tax deductions, which would be considered a proportional tax. With a proportional tax rate of 20%, a person who earns $10,000 per year would pay $2,000 in taxes, a person making $100,000 per year would pay $20,000, and a person earning $1 million would pay $200,000 in taxes. In this case, marginal tax rates and average tax rates are equal.

Tax Incidence and Equity Revisited As we learned earlier in the chapter, it matters less who pays a tax than who bears the ultimate burden of it. For example, the corporate income tax might be very progressive if it comes out of profits, but is less progressive if corporations pass on the tax to consumers in the form of higher prices. Similarly, taxes on rental properties legally fall on property owners; however, most economists believe that at least part of the property tax is passed on to renters in the form of higher rent. Since low-income households typically pay a larger share of income on housing than high-income households, property taxes are generally considered regressive. Unfortunately, the exact burden of many taxes is difficult to estimate, and thus all statistics on tax burden should be regarded as estimates only. No one knows precisely how much of the tax burden falls on the rich, poor, and middle class.

∧ Calculating taxes is complex in any language.

7.5 TAX AVOIDANCE AND CORPORATE INVERSIONS

Businesses and consumers always look for ways to lower their tax burden, and in some cases seek to avoid paying taxes altogether. To avoid high taxes, all four members of the Beatles moved out of their home country and created their own music company, Apple Records, to manage their taxes more effectively.

In Indonesia, imported cars were taxed much more heavily than motorcycles. As a consequence entrepreneurs found creative ways to transform motorcycles into taxis by customizing the frames and adding benches for additional passengers. Noted tax economist Arnold Harberger of the University of Chicago wrote of taxi service during his travels to the nation:

> Three-wheel cycles were converted, by artful additions, into virtual buses, or at least taxis. Sometimes a single bench was added, with the passenger looking backward. Other times the cycle was stretched at the back. . . . I was truly astounded when I saw my first eight passenger motorcycle.[3]

Like the Beatles, taxi owners in Indonesia were trying to minimize their tax burden—or avoid paying taxes—without breaking any laws. **Tax avoidance** is any effort by taxpayers to legally reduce tax obligations. These techniques can be simple: An individual might stop smoking to avoid paying taxes on cigarettes, or turn down

proportional tax A tax that remains a constant percentage at all levels of income; also called a **flat tax**.

tax avoidance Any effort by taxpayers to legally reduce their tax obligations.

Ed Rooney/Alamy

extra work to avoid high tax rates on additional income. More complex tax avoidance techniques include taking advantage of details in the tax law, such as allowable *tax deductions* and *tax credits.*

In recent years, many multinational corporations have resorted to a very complex tax avoidance strategy known as a tax inversion. A **corporate inversion** (or **tax inversion**) is a tax avoidance strategy whereby a business establishes its corporate headquarters in a low-tax nation, even as a significant part of its operations remains in a nation with very high corporate tax rates. The most common method for doing so is to acquire or merge with a foreign entity, and to claim the foreign headquarters as the new corporate headquarters. For example, in 2014, Burger King acquired Canadian-based Tim Hortons, allowing the fast-food restaurant to claim its headquarters is in Canada, which had lower corporate tax rates than the United States. Similarly, Pfizer acquired Allergan in order to "move" its corporate headquarters to low-tax Ireland in 2016. Other inversions have taken place to relocate firms' bases to Finland, the United Kingdom, the Netherlands, Bermuda, Denmark, the Cayman Islands, Israel, and Australia. This method of avoiding taxes is legal, as long as it is done in compliance with existing U.S. tax code. As of 2016, more than $2 trillion of profits by American corporations were moved outside the United States.[4] In 2018, corporate tax rates in the United States were lowered, in part to limit the benefit of corporate inversions.

Of course, many individuals—and some firms—have been known to avoid taxes using illegal means. **Tax evasion** is any effort by taxpayers to pay fewer taxes by illegal means. These techniques range from smuggling cigarettes from low-tax states into high-tax states, to failing to report income, to falsely claiming tax deductions on income tax returns. A small business that pays workers off the books may save some money in payroll taxes, but it also risks hefty fines and a potential prison sentence for its owner.

Both tax avoidance and tax evasion result in an additional distortion in the economy. In an ideal world, individuals and corporations would make decisions that are economically efficient. In the real world, however, minimizing tax payments is often an important objective for taxpayers and can sometimes lead to inefficient business practices.

🔲 BUSINESS BRIEF Tesla Plays the Field to Minimize Taxes

In 2014, Tesla Motor Company announced that it planned to build a gigantic car battery factory, 20 times larger than any other such facility in the world. CEO Elon Musk knew that many states would be very interested in becoming home to this high-profile project—along with 6,500 manufacturing jobs. He shrewdly negotiated with five different Western states, to see which one would offer the best deal.

In the end, Nevada won the competition, but at a fairly substantial cost: Tesla would pay no sales tax for two decades and no state payroll and property taxes for a decade. To further sweeten the deal, the state offered tax subsidies to encourage job creation, discounted electricity for eight years, and guaranteed millions of dollars of road repair near the new factory. The total value of the package was estimated at more than $1.25 billion over 20 years.*

Nevada policymakers calculated that the state would gain in the long run, even with such tax concessions. However, some economists question the value of this sort of tax competition between states, which often then requires them to raise taxes in other sectors of their economy.

*Matthew L. Wald, "Nevada a Winner in Tesla's Battery Contest," *The New York Times,* September 4, 2014, https://www.nytimes.com/2014/09/05/business/energy-environment/nevada-a-winner-in-teslas-battery -contest.html?_r=0.

---

corporate inversion A tax avoidance strategy whereby a business establishes its corporate headquarters in a low-tax nation, even as a significant part of its operations remains in a nation with very high corporate tax rates; also called **tax inversion**.

tax evasion Any effort by taxpayers to pay fewer taxes by illegal means.

BUSINESS TAKEAWAY

We've seen that even if a tax is legally imposed on sellers, businesses may be able to pass along *part* of the additional cost of the tax to buyers. Companies need to make a careful decision about how much of the tax to shift to buyers, as a higher price will tend to reduce sales. Businesses selling goods with a price elastic demand must recognize that passing on a higher tax may sharply reduce their sales.

Although no business likes seeing its products taxed, sellers of cigarettes and gasoline are less concerned with taxes on their products than sellers of goods such as pizza and sneakers, where demand is more elastic. Of course, businesses are keenly aware of how taxes impact their bottom line. U.S. tax policy provides legal means of reducing a firm's tax burden, including making deductible investments and moving to foreign countries with more favorable tax policies. When a company decides to invest in a new factory, careful consideration of the role of taxes must be taken. Sometimes firms are able to negotiate favorable tax treatment from state and local governments.

Businesses also need to decide whether the "sticker price" of their product or service will include taxes, or that tax will be added at the cash register. For instance, you may have noticed that some of your local movie theaters choose to include the state sales tax in the $5 price for a bag of popcorn, while another theater across town may add the sales tax to the price at the cash register.

CHAPTER STUDY GUIDE

7.1 PUBLIC FINANCE: GOVERNMENT SPENDING AND TAXES IN THE UNITED STATES

Public finance is a branch of economics which studies how governments raise and spend money. In total, three fourths of federal government spending is for social insurance programs or national defense. **Social insurance programs** provide social insurance against the risk of hardship due to poverty, unemployment, retirement, and health-care expenditures. For state and local governments, the largest two expenses are education and health care. The federal government obtains most of its revenue from personal income taxes, social insurance taxes, and corporate income taxes. **Personal income taxes** are taxes on personal and household income. **Social insurance taxes** (also called *payroll taxes*) are taxes primarily on wages and salaries paid by employers and employees to fund social insurance programs such as Medicare, Social Security, and unemployment insurance. **Corporate income taxes** are taxes on corporate profits. **Property taxes** are taxes on owners of properties such as real estate and motor vehicles based on the value of such properties. **Sales taxes** are taxes on the sale of goods expressed as a percentage of the selling price of an item. Finally, the **budget deficit**, government spending minus net tax revenue when government spending exceeds net tax revenue. In rare cases where tax revenue exceeds spending, the government is said to have a budget surplus.

The **national debt** is the total amount of money owed by the federal government.

7.2 THE IMPACT OF TAXATION ON CONSUMERS AND PRODUCERS

An **excise tax** is a tax on the sale of a specific good or service. When sellers have a legal obligation to pay a tax, the impact is similar to what occurs when buyers have that same legal obligation. A tax on sellers results in a decrease in supply, a lower quantity, and a higher after-tax price. A tax on buyers results in a decrease in demand, a lower quantity, and a higher after-tax price. **Tax incidence** is a measure of who bears the economic burden of a tax once prices have adjusted. Who has the legal obligation of paying a tax does not impact tax incidence. **Tax rates** are the tax per unit, expressed as an exact dollar amount or a percent of sale price or income. **Tax revenue** is the total amount of money the government collects from a tax. Tax revenue from an excise tax equals the tax rate times the number of units sold. **Deadweight loss (DWL)** is the reduction in total surplus resulting from a market distortion. DWL is the *excess burden* from taxation. Taxes generate tax revenue but create deadweight loss. Increases in tax rates almost never result in a proportionate increase in tax revenue. Moreover, increasing tax rates that are already at very high levels may reduce tax revenue. Increasing tax rates always increase deadweight loss at an increasing rate, regardless of where the tax rate is set.

7.3 PRICE ELASTICITIES AND TAXES

Tax incidence depends on price elasticity—a measure of responsiveness to a change in market conditions—of both the supply and demand curves. The relative price elasticity of supply and demand determines tax incidence. The tax burden falls mostly on buyers when demand is more price inelastic (less elastic) than supply. In contrast, the tax burden is greater on sellers when supply is more price inelastic than demand. When either the supply or demand is price inelastic, the impact of taxes on quantity is relatively small. As a result, the deadweight loss will be smaller when either supply or demand is relatively inelastic. Conversely, when both demand and supply are price elastic, the amount of tax revenue collected is relatively small and the deadweight loss is large.

7.4 TAXES AND PUBLIC POLICY

A **tax credit** allows taxpayers to reduce the amount they owe in taxes by exactly the amount of the credit. A **tax deduction** allows taxpayers to reduce their taxable income by the amount of the deduction. A $1,000 tax credit reduces your tax bill by $1,000. In contrast, a $1,000 tax deduction with a 24% marginal tax rate reduces your tax bill by $240. The **marginal tax rate** is the amount of additional taxes one pays from an additional dollar of income. The **average tax rate** is the total taxes paid divided by total income. Marginal tax rates are particularly important because people tend to determine how much additional income they will receive after taxes with additional work—consistent with the idea of marginal analysis.

Economists have developed a basic framework to analyze the burden of a tax. The **benefits-received principle** of taxation states that people should pay taxes in proportion to the benefits they receive from government services. Under the benefits-received principle, those who benefit from government-provided goods and services should pay the taxes needed to offer them. The **ability-to-pay principle** of taxation states that people

should pay taxes in proportion to taxpayers' wealth and income. A **progressive tax** is a tax that increases as a percentage of income as incomes rise, thus taxing high-income taxpayers at a higher rate than low-income taxpayers. Personal income taxes are usually progressive. A **regressive tax** is a tax that decreases as a percentage of income as incomes rise, thus taxing high-income taxpayers at a lower rate than low-income taxpayers. Sales taxes and many social insurance taxes are regressive. A **proportional tax** is a tax that remains a constant percentage at all levels of income; also called a *flat tax*.

7.5 TAX AVOIDANCE AND CORPORATE INVERSIONS

Tax avoidance is any effort by taxpayers to legally reduce their tax obligations. A **corporate inversion** (or *tax inversion*) is a tax avoidance strategy whereby a business establishes its corporate headquarters in a low-tax nation, even as a significant part of its operations remains in a nation with very high corporate tax rates. **Tax evasion** is any effort by taxpayers to pay fewer taxes by illegal means.

TOP TEN TERMS AND CONCEPTS

1. Public Finance in the United States
2. Tax Incidence
3. Tax Rates versus Tax Revenue
4. The Impact of Changing Tax Rates on Tax Revenue and Deadweight Loss
5. Price Elasticity of Supply and Demand and the Economic Impact of Taxation
6. Tax Credit versus Tax Deduction
7. Marginal Tax Rate versus Average Tax Rate
8. Benefits-Received versus Ability-to-Pay Principles
9. Progressive, Regressive, and Proportional Taxes
10. Tax Avoidance versus Tax Evasion

STUDY PROBLEMS

1. What is an excise tax? Name a product that is subject to an excise tax by both states and the federal government.

2. Using two supply and demand graphs, show how a tax on buyers has the same economic impact as a tax on sellers.

3. Graph and explain the relationship between tax rate and tax revenue.

4. Explain in your own words the impact of increasing tax rates on deadweight loss.

5. Taxes result in a reduction of both consumer surplus and producer surplus. What happens to this surplus?

6. Explain the logic of the discussion on tax rates and tax revenue as it applies to state-run lotteries.

7. For each of the following scenarios, explain whether buyers bear the largest tax incidence, sellers bear the largest tax incidence, or the tax incidence is shared roughly equally:

a. a product with a price elastic demand and price elastic supply

b. a product with a price inelastic demand and price elastic supply

c. a product with a price elastic demand and price inelastic supply

d. a product with a price inelastic demand and price inelastic supply

8. Which of the following scenarios is likely to generate the most deadweight loss for a given tax rate? The least deadweight loss? The most tax revenue? The least tax revenue?

a. a product with a price elastic demand and price elastic supply

b. a product with a price inelastic demand and price elastic supply

c. a product with a price elastic demand and price inelastic supply

d. a product with a price inelastic demand and price inelastic supply

9. Suppose the government increases taxes on gasoline by $2 a gallon. Would such a tax likely generate more tax revenues (per day) after one week or one year? Would such a tax likely generate a bigger deadweight loss next week or next year?

10. In Vietnam in 2014, the then Ministry of Health proposed a tax on cigarettes of over 150%.[5] Is it possible a lower tax rate would have yielded more tax revenue? Why would such a tax be proposed?

11. Explain whether the fact the payroll tax is equally shared by buyers and sellers is economically important. Using a supply and demand analysis, show the tax incidence of a payroll tax. Assume the supply of labor is price inelastic.

12. Which of the following taxes are progressive? Which are regressive? Explain.

a. sales taxes

b. income taxes

c. payroll taxes for Social Security

d. a tax on low-income apartments

e. a tax on first-class airline tickets

13. The U.S. federal government has been referred to as "an insurance company with an army." Explain this statement.

14. Rank the following federal government spending programs from highest to smallest:

a. interest payments on the national debt

b. defense

c. health care

d. pensions

15. What is tax avoidance? How do large corporations avoid paying taxes in making location decsions?

Ray Pfortner/Photolibrary/Getty Images

8

CHAPTER

∧ Who pays the economic costs of pollution?

The Environment, Externalities, and Property Rights

Market Failure and the Case for Government

On October 27, 1948, in Donora, Pennsylvania, a small town outside Pittsburgh, smog from a nearby steel mill and zinc plant filled the air. Charles Stacey, then in high school, later remembered that "the smog created a burning sensation in your throat and eyes, but we still thought that was just normal." Smog was not unusual in Donora, but this time, an unusual weather pattern had trapped toxins in the air for five straight days. The worst air pollution disaster in U.S. history ensued: Half the town fell ill, and 20 people died as a result. It also made the American public painfully aware of the costs of pollution.[1]

In Chapter 6, we examined how competitive markets maximize economic efficiency and showed that government interference with markets often generates deadweight loss. There are some cases, however, in which unregulated markets fall short of economic efficiency. Pollution is one such case. Left to their own devices, industries have few incentives to reduce pollution, because the costs of pollution, as illustrated in Donora in 1948, are not borne by the polluting firms, but rather by members of the public who had little or no role in the decisions that led to the pollution. In such examples, most economists agree that at least some government intervention might be necessary. In this chapter, we examine some of the ways in which markets may fail to achieve economic efficiency, and what role government can play in improving the situation.

Chapter Learning Targets

▪ Describe positive and negative externalities. Show how free markets fail to reach social equilibrium when externalities occur.

▪ Identify how market-based environmental policies can help realize the social equilibrium.

▪ Describe Coase's theorem and how property rights limit issues related to negative externalities.

▪ Define public goods and common resources.

8.1 EXTERNALITIES AND THE SOCIAL EQUILIBRIUM

One of the basic tenets of economics is that, in competitive markets, total surplus is *often* maximized at the market equilibrium price. As shown in Chapter 6, government interference often leads to a reduction in total surplus and results in deadweight loss. But *often* does not mean *always* as markets occasionally fail to achieve economic efficiency.

Market failure is a circumstance in which free, unregulated markets fail to maximize economic efficiency. When a factory pollutes, for example, society often bears costs not fully paid for by either the firm or by the firm's customers: The private costs of production incurred by the factory are different than the total cost to society. This results in a market failure as economic efficiency is not realized. The firm's pricing and output decisions do not reflect the full costs of production—specifically, the cost to people impacted by the production who had no involvement in the firm's decisions. Economists call these side effects *externalities*.

Externalities

▼ Vaccinations have positive externalities, but don't bother to explain.

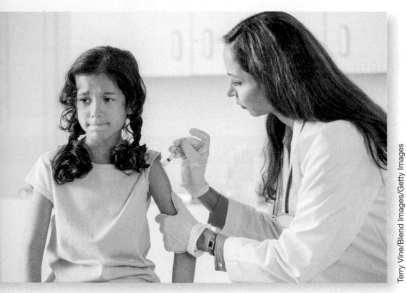

Terry Vine/Blend Images/Getty Images

An **externality** is a side effect of a transaction that affects someone not directly involved in the transaction. Externalities are sometimes referred to as *spillovers,* and they can be positive or negative. Consider the case of an outdoor concert venue located in a densely populated part of town. Local fans of artists who perform there might view the ability to hear the artists' music from the comfort of their home a positive outcome even if they do not attend the show—a spillover benefit. Others, those who do not enjoy the performers' music, may view things very differently.

A *negative externality,* sometimes referred to as an *external cost,* occurs when someone not directly involved in a transaction is harmed by it. Being forced to endure the sound of music you can't stand from a venue down the road is an example of a negative externality; likewise, a person smoking a cigarette might create a negative externality for nearby nonsmokers.

Some transactions produce a *positive externality* (or *external benefit*), as when someone benefits from a transaction in which they are not directly involved. Vaccination programs, for example, produce external benefits by reducing the spread of disease even among those who are not vaccinated. On a lighter note, the use of deodorant also produces external benefits.

market failure A circumstance in which free, unregulated markets fail to maximize economic efficiency.

externality A side effect of a transaction that affects someone not directly involved in the transaction.

marginal private costs (*MPC*) Marginal costs borne by sellers.

marginal social costs (*MSC*) Marginal private costs plus additional external costs.

Social Equilibrium: When Marginal Social Costs Equal Marginal Social Benefits

When individuals and businesses engage in transactions, they frequently fail to account for externalities. When a factory pollutes the water, the costs to society are different from the costs to the firm. This means that the marginal private cost of production borne by the factory is different than the marginal social cost. **Marginal private costs (*MPC*)** are marginal costs borne by sellers. For the most part, these are traditional business costs that would show up on an accounting statement; being private they typically do not consider external costs. **Marginal social costs (*MSC*)** are marginal private costs plus additional external costs. These include costs that show up on accounting statements plus *external* costs that are often more difficult to measure, involving factors like increased cancer risk to another person or decreased home values of neighbors. They are the costs from society's perspective.

Marginal private benefits (*MPB*) are marginal benefits received by buyers. As is the case with *MPC*, marginal private benefits exclude externalities. **Marginal social benefits (*MSB*)** are marginal private benefits plus additional external benefits. For example, the marginal private benefit of going to college might consist of the higher salary you will likely earn upon graduation. The marginal social benefit would include your *MPB* plus the external benefits that society receives from having a well-educated population that results in, among other things, better-informed voters. To recap:

$$MSC = MPC + \text{Marginal external cost}$$

$$MSB = MPB + \text{Marginal external benefits}$$

Consistent with marginal analysis, economic efficiency occurs when marginal social costs equal marginal social benefits. This point is the optimal outcome, referred to as the social equilibrium. Notice that this looks like a supply and demand diagram, except that we use social costs and benefits, not private costs and benefits. The **social equilibrium** is the quantity and price at which quantity supplied equals quantity demanded absent a market failure:

$$MSC = MSB$$

at the social equilibrium

Recall the concept of marginal analysis, introduced in Chapter 1. For a market without any externalities, the socially optimal output occurs when marginal cost equals the marginal benefit. When externalities exist, it is socially optimal to produce up to the point where *MSB* = *MSC*, as demonstrated in Exhibit 1. To see why this social equilibrium is optimal, notice what happens at quantities other than Q_{social}. At quantities greater than Q_{social}, *MSC* is greater than *MSB*. It's not efficient to produce something where the cost exceeds the benefit, and thus this output would not be economically efficient. It would be the equivalent of spending $10 for a product that gives you only $5 in benefits.

Conversely, if production stopped short of the optimal point (Q_{social}), then *MSB* would be greater than *MSC*. This is also not economically

marginal private benefits (*MPB*) Marginal benefits received by buyers.

marginal social benefits (*MSB*) Marginal private benefits plus additional external benefits.

social equilibrium The quantity and price at which quantity supplied equals quantity demanded absent a market failure.

Think & Speak Like an Economist

Optimal economic decisions are usually made using marginal analysis—by comparing the marginal benefits of an activity with the marginal costs. However, when an externality exists, the market equilibrium based on marginal private costs and benefits may differ from the social equilibrium.

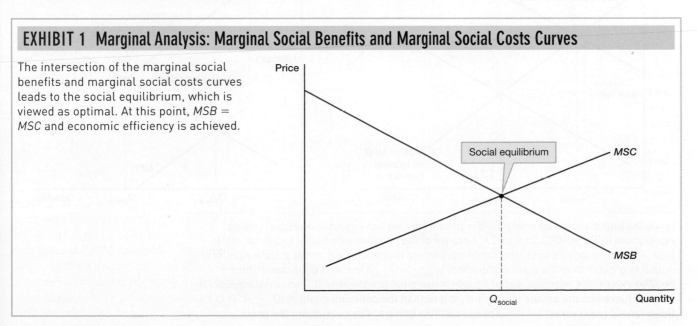

EXHIBIT 1 Marginal Analysis: Marginal Social Benefits and Marginal Social Costs Curves

The intersection of the marginal social benefits and marginal social costs curves leads to the social equilibrium, which is viewed as optimal. At this point, *MSB* = *MSC* and economic efficiency is achieved.

efficient, as you would be foregoing valuable output. It would be the equivalent of *not* buying a product for only $5 that would provide you with $10 in benefits.

Negative Externalities Result in Overproduction In free markets, people make decisions based on *private* benefits and cost, which leads to an equilibrium where $MPC = MPB$. When externalities exists, however, this is no longer the social equilibrium, as MSC no longer equals MSB. When negative externalities exist, a free market often leads to excessive output relative to the social equilibrium. Consider a steel mill that pollutes a nearby stream, killing valuable fish. In Panel A of Exhibit 2, the true cost of production to society, the MSC, includes the external cost of fish killed, and hence is higher than the private cost paid for by the firm, the MPC.

If the buyer and seller of steel only consider *private* cost and not the total social cost, we can expect to end up at the private equilibrium. Since the negative externality from pollution causes the marginal social cost to be higher than the marginal private cost, society produces more than the optimum quantity of steel ($Q_{private} > Q_{social}$). The inefficiency occurs because at the private equilibrium, buyers and sellers only consider private costs, not the total social cost of the steel. In the section on environmental policies that follows, we consider actions that can be taken to overcome this inefficiency.

Positive Externalities Result in Underproduction Now consider the case where a positive externality exists. As noted above, vaccinations reduce the spread of disease and benefit even those who have not been vaccinated. This means that the social benefit of vaccinations is greater than the private benefits, and thus the private (free-market) equilibrium output is too low, as the public may not consider the external benefits that their own vaccination would provide to society. Think about your own situation: Are you more motivated to get a flu shot because it will keep you healthy, or because you think it will keep other people healthy? In the end, when there are positive externalities, the output of the good is less than the social equilibrium ($Q_{private} < Q_{social}$), as Panel B

EXHIBIT 2   Externalities and the Social Equilibrium

Panel A: Negative Externalities Result in Overproduction

Panel B: Positive Externalities Result in Underproduction

Since the buyer and seller only consider private cost we can expect to end up at private equilibrium ($MPB = MPC$). In Panel A, because of the negative externality, marginal social cost > marginal private cost. The social equilibrium is not achieved as the private equilibrium output is greater than the optimum quantity ($Q_{private} > Q_{social}$). In Panel B, because of the positive externality, marginal social benefit > marginal private benefit. The social equilibrium is not achieved as the private equilibrium is less than the optimum quantity ($Q_{private} < Q_{social}$). Government may correct for the lack of economic efficiency by subsidizing the good.

demonstrates. This means that, when left to their own devices, too few people would be vaccinated relative to the social equilibrium and the flu would be more likely to spread. The inefficiency occurs because at the private equilibrium people only consider their own private benefits, not the total social benefits of the product.

Governments can correct for positive externalities with a subsidy for buyers, which would shift demand (*MPB*) toward the social marginal cost. Ideally, the government would provide a subsidy for the good that is exactly equal to the amount of the positive externality. In the end, the government tries to provide a large enough subsidy so that output rises to the social equilibrium quantity. Alternatively, the government could subsidize sellers or provide the good for free, reducing *MPC*, moving the equilibrium quantity toward Q_{social}.

8.2 ENVIRONMENTAL POLICIES AND THE ROLE OF GOVERNMENT

What is the optimal amount of pollution? Many people's gut response to this question is an unequivocal "none"! But economists believe that this answer is far too simple. Economics teaches us that there are lots of trade-offs, in both private life and public policy, and that it is important to weigh both costs and benefits *at the margin* when making any decision. A clean environment is certainly a very important societal goal, but we are not willing to spend an infinite amount of resources to achieve it, as high levels of employment and a comfortable standard of living are also important societal goals. When faced with such trade-offs, economics can help us weigh the costs and benefits in order to make more intelligent decisions.

There is generally an opportunity cost associated with reducing pollution. Pollution-generating activities include transportation, industrial production, farming, and heating the buildings in which we live, work, attend school, and receive medical care. Zero pollution would imply none or at least far fewer of these activities. Because societal benefits are associated with many pollution-generating activities, economists suggest that rather than reducing pollution to zero or some other arbitrary number, we reduce pollution to the point where the marginal benefit of less pollution (a cleaner environment, reduced health-care costs) equals the marginal cost of reducing pollution, which might be the cost of pollution-control equipment and/or foregone output of the goods and services. Clearly, pollution is harmful, but it is a consequence of activities that society values.

To understand this, reconsider Panel A of Exhibit 2. At the private equilibrium, too much of the good with a negative externality is produced. Negative externalities such as pollution result in an allocation of resources that is not economically efficient. But, Exhibit 2 also demonstrates that at the social equilibrium, some quantity of the good with a negative externality is still produced: Pollution levels do not fall to zero; rather, they fall to the point where marginal benefits equal marginal costs.

Thus, policymakers can potentially improve economic efficiency by enacting laws that limit pollution and move us toward the social equilibrium (not to zero of the negative externality). Economists overwhelmingly favor market-based environmental policies to correct for negative externalities. However, although governments sometimes use such policies, the more traditional approach historically has been command-and-control environmental policies—and that is where we begin.

Command-and-Control Environmental Regulations

One method to address pollution is the use of **command-and-control environmental regulations**, direct government regulation of business by setting strict pollution limits or requiring the use of pollution-control devices. The government establishes the

command-and-control environmental regulations
Direct government regulation of business by setting strict pollution limits or requiring the use of pollution-control devices.

regulations as to how much pollution a firm can emit or what specific pollution-control technologies will be required. All businesses are required by law to meet the regulations, or they must pay heavy fines.

One of the most common command-and-control policies involves environmental standards. **Environmental standards** are rules to protect the environment through government regulations. They include federal and state limits on the amount of carbon monoxide an automobile can emit, or of sulfur dioxide power companies can emit. Local governments might also enforce environmental standards. For example, some towns prohibit burning piles of autumn leaves or ban the use of single-use disposable bags.

In some cases, command-and-control policies are almost inevitable. For instance, the government now bans smoking in most public buildings. When dealing with some of the largest environmental problems, however, finding the correct command-and-control policy is a daunting task. In those cases, most economists prefer market-based solutions to environmental policies.

Internalizing the Externality with Market-Based Policies

If generating electricity at power plants creates pollution, shouldn't we simply tax electricity? A tax on electricity would increase the firm's private cost and decrease the private equilibrium quantity. Less electricity might be produced, but the electricity that is produced would continue to be generated in a manner that generates the negative externality—a great deal of pollution. Economists believe we can do much better by directly attacking the externality (pollution), rather than focusing on the end product (electricity).

Market-based environmental policies aim to force polluters to pay for the damage they cause; in economics, this is referred to as internalizing the externality. **Internalizing an externality** is the act of altering private costs or benefits so that they fully account for external effects. In other words, when a firm pollutes, the external cost of the pollution to society is added to the firm's private cost. In this section, we'll discuss a few market-based solutions that force producers to internalize the externality, and evaluate them from an economic standpoint.

Taxing Activities That Generate Pollution One way to force polluters to internalize the externality is to simply tax pollution at a level equal to the exact size of the external cost from the pollution. A **corrective tax** is a tax levied on activities that generate a negative externality so that the externality is considered in decision making. Such a tax will raise the production cost and shift the *MPC* by the amount of the tax. Businesses have an incentive to respond to the tax by polluting less. Less pollution can occur by producing fewer products, by developing alternative products, or by more environmentally friendly ways of producing products.

The private cost of producing electricity with existing technologies (ignoring externalities) from sources such as wind and solar is considerably higher than the cost of producing electricity from coal. Coal is abundant and relatively cheap to convert into power. Wind, the least expensive alternative fuel, costs 60% more per unit of electricity than coal when the external cost of carbon emissions is not factored in. However, when the cost of carbon emissions is accounted for, the cost of producing electricity with coal and wind is roughly equal.[2]

Taxing the pollution resulting from the generation of electricity from coal gives power plants an incentive to find alternative methods of generating electricity such as wind or solar. In contrast, if you simply taxed electricity, then the power plant would *not* have an economic incentive to find clean methods of producing electricity. It would continue to produce electricity at the lowest private marginal cost, which is often *not* the most environmentally friendly technology.

environmental standards Rules to protect the environment through government regulations.

internalizing an externality The act of altering private costs or benefits so that they fully account for external effects.

corrective tax A tax levied on activities that generate a negative externality so that the externality is considered in decision making.

EXHIBIT 3 Corrective Tax Can Achieve Social Equilibrium

A negative externality results in overproduction. A corrective tax can remedy this and achieve the social equilibrium by requiring firms to internalize the externality. Essentially, this requires a tax exactly equal to the negative externality, which shifts *MPC* leftward.

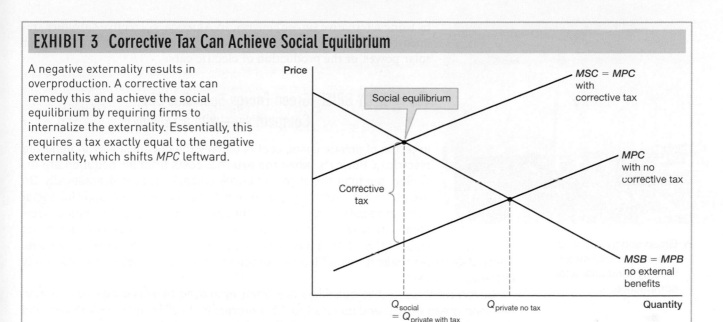

A corrective tax means higher costs are associated with activities that generate pollution. A portion of these costs will be passed onto consumers in the form of higher prices. Although that may be politically unpopular, it is economically appropriate, because economic efficiency requires that the prices paid by end consumers reflect the true social cost of producing the product: If electricity prices rise either because of the tax or because of the use of alternative energy sources such as wind, then consumers will likely use less electricity. The optimal environmental policy requires sacrifices from both producers and consumers. Otherwise, more than Q_{social} will be bought because the price does not reflect the full cost of producing electricity.

Exhibit 3 demonstrates how a corrective tax works. Since the buyer and seller only consider private cost, we can expect to end up at private equilibrium ($MPB = MPC$). This leads to overproduction when a negative externality occurs, as discussed earlier. A corrective tax can remedy this and achieve the social equilibrium by requiring firms to internalize the externality. This requires a tax *exactly* equal to the negative externality, which shifts the *MPC* curve upward and to the left. The market price of the output will also increase to reflect the external cost; however, the price that sellers receive after taxes will be reduced (see Chapter 7 for more details).

In practice, finding the tax rate that gets society *exactly* to Q_{social} is difficult because determining the exact amount of the negative externality is hard. For example, how does one measure health care and other costs associated with polluted air and water? Nonetheless, corrective taxes can move us closer to Q_{social} than would otherwise occur.

Subsidizing Activities That Do Not Generate Pollution

Another approach to reducing pollution is for the government to subsidize methods of producing electricity that do not result in pollution. Although this approach is not always as efficient as a pollution tax, it is an easier sell politically and has been used increasingly in recent years. Recall from Chapter 3 that a subsidy is the opposite of a tax; the government gives you money to encourage you to buy a product. A **corrective subsidy** is a subsidy on activities that generate a positive externality or a smaller negative externality than a comparable activity so that the externality is considered in decision making. Often, a corrective subsidy provides an economic incentive for firms to pollute less, perhaps

corrective subsidy A subsidy on activities that generate a positive externality or a smaller negative externality than a comparable activity so that the externality is considered in decision making.

∧ Green energy subsidies make electricity generated by wind and solar competitive.

by using alternative (green) energy. In America, corrective subsidies frequently take the form of financial aid to industries installing wind or solar power, or the production of electric cars.

⛪ POLICY BRIEF Green Energy Subsidies Get Competitive—with a Subsidy

In terms of private costs, coal is usually the cheapest way to generate electricity. However, when the external costs from air pollution are included, the total social cost of burning coal increases dramatically. On the other hand, although wind and sunshine are free, and the social costs associated with them might seem low, the private costs associated with converting these resources into energy for consumers is—at least at this point in their technological evolution—relatively expensive. These differences make it very difficult for green energies to compete with fossil fuels in the open market.

Government corrective subsidies are often employed to encourage competition between green energy and its fossil fuel counterparts. In 2014, governments around the world spent over one quarter of a trillion dollars on subsidizing emerging renewable energy technology, including wind, solar, biomass, waste-to-water, geothermal, and other green energy sources. Taken together, these sources contributed just under 10% of the world's electricity (this figure excludes hydroelectricity). China, the world's largest polluter in 2014, spent over $80 billion on green energy, most notably on offshore wind and solar. The United States and Japan each spent slightly less than $40 billion on green energy sources. Even with such high levels of government investment, renewable energy faced fierce competitive pressures in 2014 and 2015 as the price of oil fell by more than 60% as oil-producing nations increased productivity.[*]

[*]Data from "Green Energy Subsidies Surge to $270 Billion in 2014," *Science 2.0,* March 31, 2015, http://www.science20.com/news_articles/green_energy_subsidies_surged_to_almost_300_billion_worldwide_last_year-154467.

Creating a Market of Tradable Pollution Permits There is an alternative method of internalizing externalities: Governments can place a limit on the amount of pollution each firm produces, and then allow firms to trade the unused portion of their pollution limit on an *open market*. **Tradable pollution permits** assign pollution rights for a strictly limited amount and type of pollution. The program is often called **cap and trade** because the maximum allowable amount of pollution is "capped" or limited, and the permits can be traded between firms. With the "supply" of pollution limited, tradable pollution permits become valuable property rights. As will be shown in the next section, negative externalities associated with pollution result from a lack of property rights for resources such as the climate, rivers, and oceans.

The markets for some tradable pollution permits is now so well developed that they are sold on the Chicago Board of Trade. In the United States in the 1990s, a cap-and-trade system successfully reduced sulfur dioxide and acid rain. In the northeastern United States, the system is being used to reduce greenhouse gases—primarily carbon dioxide. Likewise, in Europe, the European Union Emission Trading Scheme is the world's largest greenhouse gas emissions trading scheme. China has also adopted policies aimed at trading carbon dioxide in select cities.

Allowing the pollution permits to be traded puts the free market to work attacking pollution. In industries where it is relatively expensive to reduce pollution, firms will buy the permits, but the increased cost of polluting will exert pressure on those firms to reduce pollution as well. In industries where it is inexpensive to reduce pollution, firms

tradable pollution permits. A government policy that assigns pollution rights for a strictly limited amount and type of pollution; also called **cap and trade**.

will sell their permits and, in doing so, become incentivized to reduce pollution emissions even further if the sale of those permits is profitable. Should a firm already own a pollution permit, it would be inclined to sell the permit if the price is higher than the cost of reducing pollution. Furthermore, environmental advocates purchase permits and choose *not* to use them—effectively reducing the supply of permits and increasing the cost of pollution to others. Finally, putting a price on pollution provides an incentive for firms to develop or invest in new pollution-reducing technologies. Firms are now willing to pay for cleaner technologies, which is often expensive, instead of the price of the pollution permit.

Critics of tradable pollution permits believe that business will purchase the permits rather than attempt to reduce pollution. But proponents of cap and trade point out that the program allows the government to strictly control the number of permits available on the market: If the cost of permits is so low that it encourages firms to simply buy more permits and continue to pollute, the government can respond by reducing the number of permits available, thus raising their price.

POLICY BRIEF China Adopts an "All of the Above" Approach to Emissions

By 2015, China had become the world's largest greenhouse gas producer: The country's rapid economic growth, combined with a population 4½ times larger than that of the United States, required more energy and produced more pollution. The Chinese government decided to tackle the problem by adopting several measures.

First, the government introduced a nationwide cap-and-trade program to limit greenhouse gas emissions. At the time, Chinese electricity plants were required by the government to run 5,000 hours a year, regardless of economic cost and the amount of pollution. So, highly inefficient electricity plants were required to operate by law. The introduction of tradable permits would mean that new, highly efficient plants would be the first to provide electricity to the public because they pollutes less, thus requiring fewer costly permits than the older plants that pollute more.

However, China still needed more energy, from additional sources, to feed the country's rapid growth. Thus, the government paired the cap-and-trade program with subsidies for renewable energy sources. China has recently become the largest investor in wind and solar electricity sources, investing over $100 billion in such technologies in 2015.*

*See Steven Mufson, "With Cap and Trade Plan China Adopts Emissions Plan That Couldn't Get Through U.S. Congress," *Washington Post*, September 28, 2015, http://www.washingtonpost.com/news/energy-environment /wp/2015/09/28/with-cap-and-trade-plan-china-adopts-emissions-policy-that-couldnt-get-through-u-s -congress/.

8.3 THE IMPORTANCE OF PROPERTY RIGHTS: COASE THEOREM

It is not a coincidence that the worst pollution problems tend to involve commonly owned resources, such as the climate, rivers and oceans, which are shared by all and in a sense owned by no one. Property rights ensure that when an individual's privately owned land is damaged by another, he or she can legally recoup the cost of such damage. Likewise, if an individual owns a lake and someone dumps toxins into it, the owner of the lake can legally recoup the damage. In a sense, property rights provide a means of internalizing the damage to the property. In this section and in the one that follows, we will examine the relationship between property rights, externalities, and public goods.

Ronald Coase Reframes the Externality Problem

Up until 1960, economists thought they had figured out the externality problem. Externalities such as pollution were a market failure, and the solution was either government regulation or corrective taxes. But that year, an economist named Ronald Coase took a fresh look at the issue and identified the important role that property rights play in environmental issues such as externalities. Coase later won a Nobel Prize in Economics for his work in this area.

The **Coase theorem** states that if property rights are clearly defined and transaction costs are low, then private individuals should be able to negotiate an efficient solution to the problem of external costs (or benefits). To better understand the Coase theorem, consider a simple example: A property developer plans to build 200 homes on a large piece of land just downwind from a pig farm. Unfortunately, the smell from the pig farm is unpleasant and would substantially reduce the value of the new houses. This is a classic externality problem, in which the bad smell imposes external costs on nearby neighbors.

Prior to 1960, economic theory suggested that the solution was government regulation: A law should exist that forced the pig farmer to reduce the smell. But, of course, the farmer could reasonably object that he had created his pig farm in the area long beforehand, and if the developer wanted to construct houses in the community, he and any buyers would have to adjust to its rural conditions. Should the farmer be held legally liable for the harm done by unpleasant odors? Maybe city folk with delicate noses were the problem.

Coase was able to demonstrate something quite surprising: To achieve an efficient solution, it did not matter who was legally liable for the bad smell. The farmer and property developer had an overriding incentive to negotiate the optimal solution—that is, the most efficient outcome—regardless of whether the pig farmer was legally liable for the bad smells or not.

For instance, suppose the unpleasant smells would reduce the value of the developer's land by $500,000, because the new houses will likely sell for a lower price. In that case, the developer should be willing to pay up to $500,000 to the farmer to stop raising pigs and instead devote his farm to a crop or livestock that would not produce an odor. If the cost to the farmer of switching to a different good is less than $500,000, then these two parties should be able to negotiate a mutually advantageous agreement.

On the other hand, if it cost $2 million to switch from pig farming to an alternative, no agreement could be reached. Coase pointed out that in such a case, it would be efficient to allow the pig farm to continue operating, because the benefits from pig farming exceeded the cost in terms of reduced property values for the developer.

The Complexity of Transaction Costs

Coase showed that externality problems do not necessarily require government intervention such as regulation or corrective taxes. In some cases, both parties could negotiate a mutually beneficial outcome. But Coase didn't stop there. He went on to show that when *many* people are affected by negative externalities, it becomes difficult to negotiate the sort of mutually beneficial outcome exemplified in the pig farm example. Coase called the expense of complex negotiated settlements *transaction costs* and explained that the real root of the externalities problem is not external costs alone, but rather externalities *combined with transaction costs*. Government regulates pollution from factories because it's too costly for thousands of nearby residents to get together and negotiate with the factory.

Coase theorem The theory that if property rights are clearly defined and transaction costs are low, then private individuals should be able to negotiate an efficient solution to the problem of external costs (or benefits).

Now let's suppose that high transaction costs make a negotiated solution impractical. For instance, suppose that hundreds of homeowners, not just one property developer, are affected by unpleasant smells from the pig farm. Does that mean Coase's ideas are irrelevant? No, because Coase also suggested that government should assign legal liability in a way that makes it easiest to achieve the most efficient outcome. If the cost to pig farmers of reducing unpleasant odors is relatively low, the government might want to make them legally liable for the harm caused by these smells. On the other hand, if suburban developers could just as easily have built homes in some other area, not close to existing pig farms, then the government may want to give pig farmers the right to continue operating without facing continual lawsuits. Today, Coase's work plays a big role in the fields of law and economics. His ideas have influenced policy decisions regarding property rights over the airwaves, where TV, radio, and cell-phone signals might interfere with each other.

Coase's findings are applicable to small settings as well as large ones. For example, suppose a large office employs both smokers and nonsmokers. What sort of smoking policy should this company adopt? Should smoking in the workplace be banned? Coase would have approached the issue from a practical perspective: Which outcome is the most efficient? Would smokers be willing to pay, perhaps in the form of lower wages, to continue to smoke in the office? Conversely, how much would the nonsmokers be willing to pay, perhaps in the form of lower wages, to not have to breathe secondhand smoke?

If the company wishes to maximize profits, it should adopt the smoking policy that maximizes the combined welfare of both smokers and nonsmokers. If smokers really want to be able to smoke during the workday and nonsmokers wouldn't be bothered very much by that behavior, then a ban on smoking would force the company to pay significantly higher wages to hire workers who do smoke. On the other hand, if the negative effects of smoking on nonsmokers are substantial, exceeding the benefits to smokers, then a company ban on smoking would actually reduce its wage costs by making it much easier to hire nonsmokers.

Thus, Coase's insights show that the owner of any enclosed space, whether it be an office, a factory, or a restaurant, would have an incentive to adopt the most efficient smoking policy. In theory, government regulation of indoor smoking is not needed. Nonetheless, governments around the world have sought to reduce smoking for public health reasons; included in such efforts are smoking bans at places of employment as well as in public spaces.

📊 BUSINESS BRIEF Are Free Markets for Bees "Sweet Like Honey"?

Beekeeping is a surprisingly big business. Many agricultural crops must be pollenated to bear fruit, and bees can do a lot of the pollenating. In 2014, President Barack Obama issued a statement noting that "honeybee pollination alone adds more than $15 billion in value to agricultural crops each year in the United States."*

The beekeeping business is also an example of positive externalities, particularly for beekeepers and apple growers. The relationship was first noted in 1952 by Nobel Prize–winning economist James Meade, who suggested that if an apple farmer considered increasing the size of his or her orchard, part of the social benefit would be that nearby bees could produce more honey.† That increased honey production is an external benefit—a positive externality. Similarly, if a beekeeper were to increase his or her supply of bees, this would provide an external benefit in the form of increased apple production for nearby orchards. Because the Coase theorem had not yet been developed, Meade simply assumed that this positive externality was a market failure. Recall that positive externalities are every bit as much market failures as negative externalities, because the free market will otherwise produce too little of the product and not have an incentive to reach the social equilibrium.

Today, both beekeepers and apple growers are fully aware of this externality problem. To overcome the externality, they take a page out of Coase's theorem and treat the bee market as a private good, negotiating a mutually beneficial transaction. Orchard owners actually pay beekeepers to set up bee colonies next to their orchards, to facilitate the pollination process. In this case, the private sector was able to overcome an externality problem without corrective taxes or subsidies.

*Data from "Presidential Memorandum—Creating a Federal Strategy to Promote the Health of Honey Bees and Other Pollinators," *White House,* June 20, 2014, https://www.whitehouse.gov/the-press-office/2014/06/20 /presidential-memorandum-creating-federal-strategy-promote-health-honey-b.

†James Meade, "External Economies and Diseconomies in a Competitive Situation," *Economic Journal* 62, no. 245 (March 1952): 54–67.

8.4 PUBLIC GOODS AND COMMON RESOURCES

It should not be surprising that the most problematic forms of pollution tend to affect not private property, but resources commonly owned by society as a whole, such as water and air. The Coase theorem suggests that negative externalities occur, in part, because of a lack of property rights. In contrast, you usually don't see companies dumping huge piles of garbage in your front yard, because they would be violating your private property rights. Thus, economists are especially concerned with distinctions between private property and commonly owned resources.

In order to think like an economist, it is important that you consider two important factors when evaluating goods. The first factor is **rivalry**—whether one person's consumption of a good reduces the availability of that good to others. If you eat a slice of pizza, others cannot eat the same slice of pizza. A rival good is a good that can only be consumed or used by one consumer; thus, one person's consumption of a rival good (like pizza) diminishes the ability of others to consume the same good. On the other hand, when you listen to a particular radio station, it in no way prevents a friend of yours from listening to the same radio station. Radio is a non-rival good, as it can be consumed by many people at once, and one user's consumption does not in any way reduce the ability of others to consume the good.

The second factor is **excludability**, whether it is possible to exclude people who don't pay for a good from benefiting from that good. Excludable goods are goods that can be denied to individuals who do not pay. Pizza, for example, is an excludable good, because the seller won't provide pizza to someone who does not pay. In contrast, anyone can listen to an over-the-air radio station, even if he or she doesn't pay. So, the radio is considered a non-excludable good. However, satellite radio by SiriusXM is excludable. Likewise, news found online can be non-excludable or excludable depending on whether the outlet requires a subscription. Non-excludable goods are those goods for which it is impossible to exclude nonpayers.

Using the characteristics of rivalry and excludability, economists are able to divide goods into four distinct categories, as shown in Exhibit 4:

1. **Private goods** are goods that are rival in consumption and excludable. Pizza, smartphones, and haircuts are examples.

2. **Non-rival private goods** are goods that are non-rival in consumption and excludable. Wi-Fi, cable TV, and watching a movie on Netflix are examples.

rivalry Whether one person's consumption of a good reduces the availability of that good to others.

excludability Whether it is possible to exclude people who don't pay for a good from benefiting from that good.

private goods Goods that are rival in consumption and excludable.

non-rival private goods Goods that are non-rival in consumption and excludable.

3. **Public goods** are goods that are non-rival in consumption and non-excludable. Examples include flood control, over-the-air radio, and national defense.

4. **Common resource goods** are goods that are rival in consumption and non-excludable. Examples include fish in the ocean, the climate, and public non-toll roads. There is no price for catching fish in the ocean, but one person catching a fish prevents another from catching the same fish. As more fish are caught, fewer fish remain. When an individual drives on a public road and increases congestion, the benefits to others are diminished. You might not think of the situation this way, but whenever you are caught in a traffic jam, *you have helped to cause it.*

In this section, we focus on the last two types of goods: public goods and common resources. Both types of goods are non-excludable—you can't exclude nonpayers. They are often produced by the public sector, but not always.

public goods Goods that are non-rival in consumption and non-excludable.

common resource goods Goods that are rival in consumption and non-excludable.

EXHIBIT 4 Four Types of Goods

	Rival	Non-Rival
Excludable	**Private Goods** Pizza, Smartphones, Haircuts	**Non-Rival Private Goods** Wi-Fi, Cable TV, Movies
Non-Excludable	**Common Resource Goods** Fish and Wildlife, Climate, Public (non-toll) Roads	**Public Goods** National Defense, Flood Control, Over-the-Air Radio

The four types of goods are private goods, non-rival private goods, common resource goods, and public goods. These goods vary in terms of whether they are excludable and/or rival. Excludable goods are goods that cannot be received by individuals who do not pay. Rival goods are goods that the use by an individual diminishes the ability of another to use the same good.

Public Goods and the Free-Rider Problem

As explained above, when economists refer to "public goods," they mean goods that are non-rival and non-excludable. It is important to bear in mind that the term *public good* does not mean such goods are produced by the government: Commercial radio is a public good produced by the private sector, and K–12 education is a private good often produced by the public sector. It would be possible to exclude nonpaying first graders; indeed, private schools do so.

Because it's not possible to exclude nonpayers, public goods frequently end up being provided by the government. If the government provides national defense, it protects all individuals in society, even those who pay no taxes. If the government builds a dam to reduce flooding, everyone who lives downstream from the dam is protected. If the government provides mosquito control to a neighborhood, everyone benefits. There is no way to exclude individuals from the benefits of the mosquito control, the dam, or national defense.

The production of public goods is akin to an activity that generates positive externalities—some people may benefit from the production of a good they do not pay for. As shown earlier in the chapter, private equilibrium may not be the socially optimal equilibrium when externalities exist. In the case of many public goods, there are external benefits enjoyed by the public, regardless of whether they pay for them. In that case, the marginal social benefit curve would be considerably higher than the private marginal benefit curve.

Without mandatory payments for public goods, a market failure often occurs, as some individuals do not pay. Economists refer to such individuals as free-riders. A **free-rider** is an individual who receives benefits from a public good without paying. Due to the free-rider problem, private markets may not provide the public good at all—another example of a potential market failure.

In Chapter 3 you discovered that the *market demand for a private good* was determined simply by adding up the quantity each individual is willing to purchase at each price. Using data found in that chapter, at a price of $20, Ann demands 3, Bill demands 2, and Chris demands 4 goods—thus, the quantity demanded by the market demand is 9 goods.

In contrast, to determine the marginal social benefit of a public good, add the price each consumer is willing to pay for a specific overall quantity. This is equivalent to the *market demand for a public good.* Exhibit 5 shows each individual's willingness to pay to purchase two goods: Ann is willing to pay $25, Bill is willing to pay $20, and Chris is willing to pay $30. This amount is the value each buyer places on the good, and this benefit occurs regardless of who pays for the product. Thus the value to society of 2 goods—the marginal social benefit—is $75 ($25 + $20 + $30). Yet, in our example, no individual consumer is willing to purchase the good at $75. That means the optimal quantity of the good would not be produced as the social equilibrium is not achieved by private markets.

While the free-rider problem is usually associated with public goods, it affects some private goods as well. For example, imagine that four college students share an apartment. They all agree to help keep the place clean. But over time they get very busy, and each one relies on the other three to do the cleaning. They are "free-riding" on the good will of their roommates. If all four free-ride in this way, the apartment gradually gets dirtier and dirtier.

Solving the free-rider problem for the student apartment example is relatively easy: Simply assign each student one room to clean, and kick out any roommate who fails to cooperate. In the case of public goods that are non-excludable, solving the free-rider problem is more complex and usually involves government. If the government can recognize the marginal social benefit and marginal social cost of the public good, it can provide the economically efficient quantity of that good. To pay for the good, the government will need to collect taxes.

free-rider An individual who receives benefits from a public good without paying for them.

EXHIBIT 5 Public Goods

The marginal social benefit is the price each consumer is willing to pay for a specific quantity. In this example, to purchase 2 goods Ann is willing to pay $25, Bill is willing to pay $20, and Chris is willing to pay $30; thus the *MSB* is $75. At that price, however, no consumer is willing to privately purchase any of the good and the social equilibrium is not obtained.

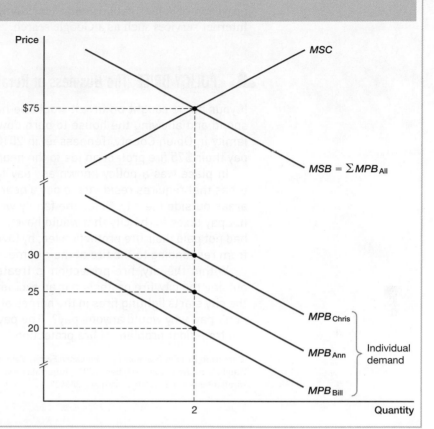

Inevitably, government involvement in providing public goods brings politics to the fore. Some individuals and groups of individuals will benefit more than others from each type of public good. A new interstate highway from Los Angeles to Las Vegas will benefit tourists from California, highway builders, and casino owners in Las Vegas. The highway is less likely to benefit a pizza maker in New Jersey. Determining the correct amount of public goods, and which taxpayers should pay for them, is complex and controversial.

To aid in such decisions, governments often do a *cost–benefit analysis* that weighs the costs and benefits of a project. Such analysis is used in the private sector as well. For example, suppose Mario is considering opening a second pizzeria in a new town. Mario would evaluate all potential costs and compare them with expected benefits, which are the revenues from selling pizza. If total costs are greater than total benefits, Mario should not expand.

Ideally, governments make decisions on a similar basis, but the process is more complex because benefits are difficult to measure. Mario can't always determine future revenues, but the value of national defense or space exploration is even harder to estimate. Governments can only make educated guesses, especially on the benefit side. For example, how much do you value national security? Can you put a dollar amount on it? How much do you think your neighbor values national security? In modern democracies, the political system makes these kinds of decisions based on a *rough* estimate of costs and benefits.

As noted above, public goods do not necessarily need to be provided by the government. Broadcast television and radio are examples of goods that are non-rival and non-excludable that are often provided by private firms (such

Think & Speak Like an Economist

It is common for governments and businesses to engage in *cost–benefit analysis* when deciding to do or not do projects. This entails considering both the added cost and added benefits of a project, measured in dollar terms. In economics, this is the functional equivalent of *marginal analysis*.

as ABC, CBS, and NBC). Revenues from advertising can support the private sector provision of some "public goods," including broadcast radio and television, as well as Internet services such as a Google search.

 POLICY BRIEF   The Business of Rural Fire Departments: Pay to Spray

If your home caught on fire, it would be hard to imagine firefighters refusing to respond and allowing the house to burn down. But that is exactly what happened to a family in Obion County, Tennessee, in 2010. Apparently, the family had neglected to pay their $75 fire protection fee to the nearby city of South Fulton.

In place was a policy known as "pay to spray," a common policy in many rural areas that requires residents to pay a nearby fire department to respond to blazes in areas outside the city. Since the family was not a resident of South Fulton, they did not pay taxes to the city that would have included fire services. And, since the family had not paid their fire protection fee, by law, South Fulton firefighters were prohibited from responding to the fire at their home.

Within the city, fire protection is treated as a public good funded by taxes, but outside the city, fire protection is an excludable private good. As one official noted, "If the city starts fighting fires in the homes of people outside the city (South Fulton) who don't pay, why would anyone pay?" The pay to spray policy is thus a way to overcome the free-rider problem of fire protection.[*]

[*]Data from Bradley Blackburn, "Tennessee Family's Home Burns to the Ground as Firefighters Stand and Watch," *ABC News.com,* October 5, 2010, http://abcnews.go.com/US/tennessee-familys-home-burns-ground -firefighters-stand-watch/story?id=11806407.

 POLICY BRIEF   Easing Traffic by Internalizing the Externality

Public road use is rival in nature: Each car on the road diminishes the ability of other cars to fully use that road. When you decide to take a busy road, you indirectly slow down other drivers. If you are not charged any price for road use, you will only take into account your private costs, such as time and gasoline, and not the total social cost of your driving. Thus, highways are a commonly owned resource that can be overused unless the proper incentives are provided.

Many cities are beginning to experiment with such incentives. In 2003, London began charging drivers roughly $20 to enter the congested area of central London.[*] The congestion tax reduced traffic congestion by encouraging people to use other forms of transport, such as buses and subway trains. Similar systems have been implemented in Singapore and Stockholm.[†]

On Interstate Highway 91 in Orange County, California, the toll paid by drivers depends on the amount of traffic congestion at that time of day.[‡] The more congested the road, the higher the toll. These congestion charges are a way of forcing drivers to internalize an externality caused by their decision to enter a crowded highway—an effective way to reduce traffic congestion.

[*]Charles Komanoff, "Lessons from London After 10 Years of the Congestion Charge," *StreetsblogNYC,* February 15, 2013, http://www.streetsblog.org/2013/02/15/lessons-from-london-after-10-years-of-the-congestion -charge/.

[†]Todd Litman, "London Congestion Pricing: Implications for Other Cities," *Victoria Transport Policy Institute,* November 24, 2011, http://www.vtpi.org/london.pdf.

[‡]"Congestion Charge," *Transport for London,* n.d., https://tfl.gov.uk/modes/driving/congestion-charge.

EXHIBIT 6 Common Resource Goods

Common resource goods are goods that are rival in consumption and non-excludable. The non-excludable nature of these goods makes the marginal private cost relatively low as they exclude the direct cost of the resource. This results in overuse. The social equilibrium is not achieved as the private equilibrium is greater than the optimum quantity ($Q_{private} > Q_{social}$). The overuse of common resource goods is known as the tragedy of the commons.

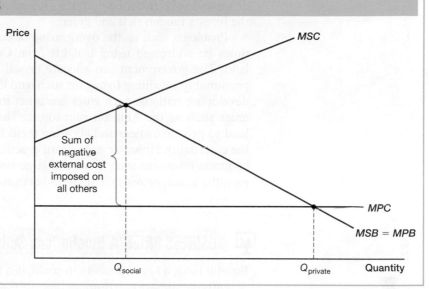

Sum of negative external cost imposed on all others

MSC

MPC

MSB = MPB

Q_{social} $Q_{private}$ Quantity

Price

Common Resources and the Tragedy of the Commons

Just as public goods provide positive externalities, common resource goods such as fishing areas often generate negative externalities when consumed. Unfortunately, the negative externality is frequently ignored by the public when they determine how much to consume. Too much of the good is then consumed. In that case, the marginal social benefit of the good ends up being less than the marginal social cost.

Recall that common resource goods are rival in consumption and non-excludable. There is no price to use a non-toll road or to catch fish in the ocean—that is to say, the marginal private cost is simply the private cost of driving or catching fish. Yet as more people drive, the road becomes congested, and as more people catch fish, there are few fish left for others to catch. Notice that these examples involve external costs imposed on others due to the fact that a commonly owned resource is overutilized.

This is demonstrated in Exhibit 6. The marginal private costs are relatively low, including the indirect cost of obtaining the resource (such as renting a boat and hiring labor), but excluding the direct cost of the common resource, which is non-excludable. This results in overuse. The social equilibrium is not achieved as the private equilibrium is greater than the optimum quantity ($Q_{private} > Q_{social}$).

In 1968, ecologist Garrett Hardin noted the tendency of society to overuse shared resources in a well-known essay entitled "The Tragedy of the Commons."[3] **Tragedy of the commons** refers to the tendency to overuse common resources. Hardin described the open grazing of livestock in public lands without assigned property rights, or "commons" as they were once known. Since livestock owners could graze their animals for free, they tended to overgraze, and in the process they depleted the resource. Each owner had an incentive to just look at his or her marginal private benefit and ignore the cost imposed on others. Common lands are indeed often overused until no grass remains—that is the tragedy of the commons to which Hardin called attention.

Hardin's example may be a parable, but the tragedy of the commons has real effects. Satellite images of the border between Haiti and the Dominican Republic dramatically show the effects that common ownership can have on the environment: The Haitian side of the border is

tragedy of the commons
The tendency to overuse common resources.

∨ The border between Haiti (left) and the Dominican Republic. Which country is experiencing a tragedy of the commons?

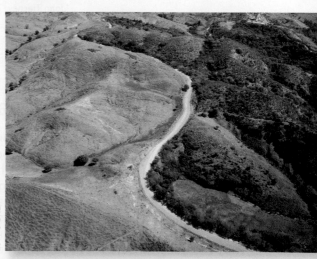

2011 © UNEP

marred by severe deforestation, as trees on commonly owned land are continuously cut down and sold. In contrast, in the Dominican Republic, where land is privately owned, the forests remain rich and green.

Problems such as the overgrazing of common lands and deforestation can sometimes be addressed using insights from Coase—by assigning property rights to the land. The government can allocate or sell the land to the livestock owner, who will presumably be willing to pay for such land if free grazing is no longer available. In poor developing nations, such rules are often inadequately enforced, especially in remote areas such as the Amazon rain forest. The Coase theorem suggests that selling the land to private owners and allowing them to enforce property rights could internalize the externality. However, significant practical obstacles exist in granting ownership of common resources such as air and large bodies of water. In the early twenty-first century, the ocean provides a modern-day example of the tragedy of the commons.

📊 BUSINESS BRIEF A Bluefin Tuna Sells for $1.76 Million

Bluefin tuna, a key ingredient in sushi, is a type of fish found only in the Pacific Ocean. Scientists estimate that the population of Pacific Bluefin tuna has declined by over 96% in the last few decades. They have become so rare that in 2013 a single fish, weighing nearly 500 pounds, sold for $1.76 million to Kiyoshi Kimura, the owner of a Japanese sushi restaurant chain. That's more than $3,600 per pound—providing a strong business incentive for fishing boats to target tuna.[*]

The Coase theorem suggests that assigning property rights serves as an effective solution to the tragedy of the commons. But the oceans are the most vast commons on earth, which makes assigning property rights less practical. Individual countries do have exclusive ownership of ocean resources up to 200 miles offshore, and in those coastal regions it is possible to regulate commonly owned resources.

In Australia, for example, each fishing company is given property rights to catch a specified number of fish in coastal waters. This amount is limited to prevent overfishing. As a result, fish stocks have remained at a healthy level, year after year. In contrast, in areas of the world where anyone is allowed to freely catch as many fish as they wish—frequently more than 200 miles offshore—there is often so much overfishing that the stock of remaining fish has fallen to dangerously low levels.[†] The Australian example shows how assigning property rights can help solve the tragedy of the commons.

[*]Data from Bryan Walsh, "The Pacific Bluefin Tuna Is Going, Going. . . ," *TIME Magazine*, January 11, 2013, http://science.time.com/2013/01/11/the-pacific-bluefin-tuna-is-almost-gone/.

[†]John Tierney, "A Tale of Two Fisheries," *The New York Times Magazine*, August 27, 2000.

CASE STUDY Global Climate Change and Carbon Dioxide

Climate change is one of the most important environmental issues facing the world today. Scientists have identified links between increases in the amount of carbon dioxide in the atmosphere and global climate change. The use of oil, coal, and natural gas to generate electricity and power automobiles results in the emission of carbon dioxide and other greenhouse gases, which most scientists believe increase global warming. Atmospheric concentrations (or levels) of carbon dioxide and other greenhouses gases are over 50% higher

than they were prior to the Industrial Revolution, and average global temperatures have increased over the past century.[*] Carbon dioxide emissions have been increasing, particularly in developing economies such as China, which in recent years accounts for roughly half of the global increase in emissions.[†]

Economists are concerned not merely with the reduction of pollution, but with ensuring that any reduction in pollution is achieved in the most economically efficient way possible. Consequently, economists

EXHIBIT 7 Average Global Temperatures, 1880–2012

Differences from Period Average

Average global temperatures relative to historic norms in degrees Celsius.

Data from: NASA.

EXHIBIT 8 Atmospheric CO$_2$ LEVELS, 1958–2013

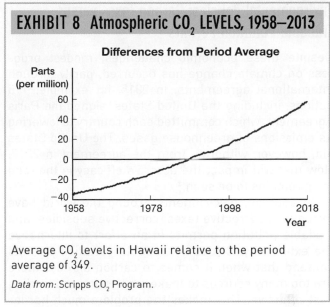

Differences from Period Average

Average CO$_2$ levels in Hawaii relative to the period average of 349.

Data from: Scripps CO$_2$ Program.

typically favor using market-based solutions to reduce CO$_2$ emissions and to assign property rights where possible. However, even market-based policies impose costs on society. Therefore, such policies only make economic sense if society has correctly estimated the impact of CO$_2$ in the first place.

Exhibit 7 presents data from NASA on the average global temperature since 1880 relative to historic averages. It shows that since 1880 average global temperatures have climbed over 1 degree Celsius. Each change of 1 degree Celsius is equivalent to a change of 1.8 degrees Fahrenheit. The Scripps CO$_2$ Program at the University of California–San Diego has been tracking atmospheric CO$_2$ levels at a station in Hawaii since 1958. Its tracking is the oldest continuous real-time documentation of CO$_2$ levels; earlier measurements are based on frozen ice core data.

Exhibit 8 presents seasonally adjusted monthly average CO$_2$ levels from that station relative to the period average of 349 parts per million. As discussed in the Appendix to Chapter 1, correlation does not prove causation. Historically, global temperatures have gone through a variety of periods of warming and cooling that often last hundreds of years. Recently, however, most scientists have concluded that causation exists, and activities that increase the levels of carbon dioxide in the atmosphere appear to be a contributor to global warming.

Economic Complexities in Setting Environmental Polices

Climate change presents three big challenges, which make it an especially difficult problem for policymakers to address. First, although most scientists are convinced

the problem is real, the issues are very complex and the worst effects will occur far into the future. Thus, it's difficult for economists to precisely estimate the cost of climate change. This has led some people to be skeptical about the size of the problem and the role of human activity in causing it.

Second, because fossil fuels are such an important part of the global economy, which is developing rapidly in places such as Asia, the cost of limiting greenhouse gases is quite high. Developing and implementing green technologies will require large sums of money, and will draw resources (including labor and innovation) away from other endeavors. These costs have made it difficult for political leaders to address the problem aggressively.

Third, the external costs related to climate change are especially widespread and severe. The effects of many other types of pollution are primarily local: Although some air pollution drifts across international boundaries, the people most negatively affected by pollution generally live near its source. In contrast, greenhouse gas emissions impact the entire world, and thus a country that refuses to reduce emissions is mostly hurting other countries. There is no international agency with the power to force all countries to produce fewer greenhouse gases. In a sense, climate change is a tragedy of the commons—the ultimate externality and the one that is the most difficult to address.

Given the global nature of climate change, corrective policies done on a nation-by-nation basis might prove ineffective as they may not fully account for external costs. Many people believe that effective action requires an international agreement among all major countries to reduce greenhouse gas emissions.

Environmental Policies: Carbon Taxes versus Tradable Pollution Permits

Despite these economic challenges, modest progress on climate change has occurred, partly through international agreements. In 2015, for example, 195 nations, including the United States, signed the Paris Agreement, which committed each country to lowering its emissions of greenhouse gases. The United States did, however, withdraw from the agreement in 2017. How that will impact the accord's efficacy in the long term remains to be seen.[‡]

In addition, governments around the world have introduced corrective taxes, corrective subsidies, and tradable pollution permits in an effort to internalize the externality. Critics of tradable pollution permits contend that when it comes to carbon dioxide, there are too many sources to make monitoring and trading cost-effective. This makes the problem much harder to address than sulfur dioxide, for which tradable permits were introduced in 1990 in the United States and other countries in the years that followed (most sulfur dioxide pollution derived from a limited number of well-known coal-burning electric power plants). Many economists believe that a simple corrective tax on carbon dioxide—called a "carbon tax"—would address the externality more effectively than tradable permits, and may be more difficult to evade. Unfortunately, taxes are politically unpopular, which explains why tradable permits are often used, even when less efficient.

All proposed solutions to climate change have potential trade-offs, and this issue will continue to be the focus of policymakers for many decades to come. We can expect more experiments with corrective taxes, subsidies, and tradable pollution permits.[**]

[*]"Getting Warmer," *The Economist*, December 3, 2009.

[†]"Tepid, Timid," *The Economist*, June 29, 2013. http://www.economist.com/node/14994872.

[‡]"No Cooling: Trumps Indifference to Climate Change has not Changed China's View," *The Economist*, April 20, 2017, https://www.economist.com/news/china/21721227-once-foot-dragger-it-now-wants-lead-trumps-indifference-climate-change-has-not-changed.

[**]For further reading, see Nicholas Stern, *The Economics of Climate Change* (Cambridge, UK: Cambridge University Press, 2006).

BUSINESS TAKEAWAY

Firms typically focus on their own private costs when deciding what quantity of output to produce and what prices to charge. But society often has broader concerns. For example, the competitive nature of business often prevents firms from developing socially optimal policies with regard to the environment, unless some government intervention takes place. Firms committed to environmental sustainability might find it difficult to compete with firms that ignore environmental problems. Yet, environmentally friendly policies do emerge in the business world from time to time.

Such initiatives are labeled *corporate social responsibility* (see the chapter on organizing a business), business policies that foster environmental and social benefits. For example, in 2008, IKEA became the first major retailer in the United States to stop providing customers with free, single-use plastic bags, in an effort to reduce the firm's environmental impact.[4]

Most iPhones are made in China, a country that struggles with a severe pollution problem. Thus, Apple Corporation decided to invest in a Chinese wind power company that is set to construct a massive wind farm to generate electricity.[5] Companies such as Google and Facebook are also moving toward renewable energy. Indeed, Microsoft now relies 100% on renewable energy. These policies also sow a bit of good public relations along the way.

Policymakers often try to address the problem of pollution by forcing businesses to internalize the externalities. For example, a corrective tax on pollution gives firms an incentive to behave in a socially beneficial fashion. Alternative ways to internalize the externality include tradable pollution permits and a clearer assignment of property rights.

As society becomes increasingly environmentally focused, there will be more and more business opportunities in areas such as green energy. Businesses that anticipate the future direction of regulatory policies will be better able to meet the new challenges as they materialize. This may explain some of the examples cited earlier, such as tech companies doing more for green energy than the law currently requires.

CHAPTER STUDY GUIDE

8.1 EXTERNALITIES AND THE SOCIAL EQUILIBRIUM

In free competitive markets, total surplus is often but not always maximized at the market equilibrium price. **Market failure** is a circumstance in which free, unregulated markets fail to maximize economic efficiency. An example of a market failure is an **externality**, a side effect of a transaction that affects someone not directly involved in the transaction. There are two types of externalities: a negative externality (external cost) and a positive externality (external benefit). To see why externalities result in a market inefficiency, it is useful to do marginal analysis. **Marginal private costs (MPC)** are marginal costs borne by sellers. **Marginal social costs (MSC)** are marginal private costs plus additional external costs. As such, *MSC* is greater than *MPC* when there is a negative externality. **Marginal private benefits (MPB)** are marginal benefits received by buyers. **Marginal social benefits (MSB)** are marginal private benefits plus additional external benefits. *MSB* is greater than *MPB* when there is an external benefit. The **social equilibrium** is the quantity and price at which quantity supplied equals quantity demanded absent a market failure. The social equilibrium may not equal the private equilibrium because people tend to only consider marginal private benefits and marginal private costs. As a result, negative externalities such as pollution result in overproduction relative to social equilibrium, while positive externalities result in underproduction.

8.2 ENVIRONMENTAL POLICIES AND THE ROLE OF GOVERNMENT

Command-and-control environmental regulations are the direct government regulation of business by setting strict pollution limits or requiring the use of pollution-control devices. Most economists view these as less efficient ways to limit pollution. **Environmental standards** are rules to protect the environment through government regulations. Several market-based policy options are available to governments to address market failure that results from pollution. One option is to simply limit the production of the good that results in pollution. In most cases, however, there is a more effective way to reduce pollution. **Internalizing an externality** is the act of altering private costs or benefits so that they fully account for external effects. This means making polluters pay for the damage they cause. This can be accomplished by restricting pollution with corrective

taxes: A **corrective tax** is a tax levied on activities that generate a negative externality so that the externality is considered in decision making. It will raise the private production cost and shift the *MPC* by the amount of the tax. Alternatively, a **corrective subsidy** is a subsidy on activities that generate a positive externality or a smaller negative externality than a comparable activity so that the externality is considered in decision making. **Tradable pollution permits** assign pollution rights for a strictly limited amount and type of pollution. The program is often called **cap and trade** because the maximum allowable amount of pollution is "capped" or limited, and the permits can be traded between firms. The more traditional approach toward environmental policies is command-and-control environmental regulations.

8.3 THE IMPORTANCE OF PROPERTY RIGHTS: COASE THEOREM

The **Coase theorem** says that if property rights are clearly defined and transaction costs are low, then private individuals should be able to negotiate an efficient solution to the problem of external costs (or benefits). According to Coase, the real problem is not external costs alone, but rather externalities combined with transaction costs, as transaction costs can be prohibitive for common resource goods.

8.4 PUBLIC GOODS AND COMMON RESOURCES

It is important that you consider two important factors when evaluating goods. **Rivalry** is whether one person's consumption of a good reduces the availability of that good to others. **Excludability** is whether it is possible to exclude people who don't pay for a good from benefiting from that good. **Private goods** are goods that are rival in consumption and excludable. **Non-rival private goods** are goods that are non-rival in consumption and excludable. **Public goods** are goods that are non-rival in consumption and non-excludable. **Common resource goods** are goods that are rival in consumption and non-excludable. A **free-rider** is an individual who receives benefits from a public good without paying for them. Due to the free-rider problem, private markets may not provide the public good at all. **Tragedy of the commons** refers to the tendency to overuse common resources. Open grazing of livestock in public lands, or "commons," is one such example.

TOP TEN TERMS AND CONCEPTS

1. Market Failure
2. Externality
3. Marginal Private Cost and Benefit Versus Marginal Social Cost and Benefit
4. Command-and-Control Environmental Regulations and Environmental Standards
5. Internalizing an Externality: Corrective Tax, Corrective Subsidy, and Tradable Pollution Permits
6. Coase Theorem
7. Rivalry and Excludability
8. Private Goods and Public Goods
9. Free-Rider
10. Common Resource Goods and Tragedy of the Commons

STUDY PROBLEMS

1. Classify each of the following as a positive externality or negative externality:

   a. pollution that occurs from dumping toxins in a stream

   b. pollution that occurs from sitting next to a smoker in a public space

   c. vaccination

   d. repair of a house that is an eyesore in the neighborhood

   e. a golf course that may look beautiful but has resulted from the application of a fertilizer that is entering a nearby body of water

   f. an expanding apple orchard, which is, in turn, increasing honey production from bees

   g. single-use plastic bags

2. Explain and graph the differences between marginal social cost and marginal private cost. Use examples of electricity generation.

3. A corrective subsidy increases the supply of a technology that doesn't pollute. Explain this statement using a graph. How does this compare to a corrective tax?

4. Does a free market overproduce or underproduce goods that generate a negative externality? Use a graph in formulating your answer.

5. Start with Panel A of Exhibit 2 and in a graph show how a corrective tax internalizes the externality.

6. What is a corrective subsidy? How does this impact the marginal private cost a potential producer faces?

7. What is a tradable pollution permit? Give examples. Explain how tradable pollution permits internalize an externality.

8. Occasionally, private businesses take environmental corrective policies. In your own words, describe some.

9. What is the Coase theorem? When does it apply? When is it limited?

10. Years ago, smoking was allowed at restaurants. Some individual restaurants banned smoking at their own establishments. Explain what impact this has had on the demand for restaurant meals of smokers? Non-smokers? How does this apply to the Coase theorem?

11. Describe the free-rider problem. What does it say about the need for government to provide public goods?

12. For each of the following, state whether the good is rival or non-rival:

    a. public radio

    b. highway during rush hour

    c. public grasslands for cattle grazing

    d. pizza

    e. fish caught in open bodies of water

    f. Wi-Fi

    g. national defense

13. For each of the following, state whether the good is excludable or non-excludable:

    a. public radio

    b. highway during rush hour

    c. public grasslands for cattle grazing

    d. pizza

    e. fish caught in open bodies of water

    f. Wi-Fi

    g. national defense

14. What is the tragedy of the commons? Give examples.

15. In your own words, explain the tragedy of the commons as it applies to tree cutting in Haiti.

16. Explain how climate change relates to negative externalities. What does economics tell us about the most efficient approach to address climate change?

∧ Kraft and Heinz merged in 2015 to create a single, multinational corporation.

Organizing a Business

Corporations and Other Legal Structures

Kraft Heinz is a multinational corporation valued at over $100 billion in 2017. The company sells an assortment of food products in over 100 countries under a variety of brands, including Oscar Mayer, Jell-O, Planters, Kool-Aid, and Grey Poupon–and, of course, Kraft and Heinz. The corporate giant obtained its global reach with over a 100-year history of successful deal making and product development, including the 2015 merger between Kraft and Heinz.

The company also had its share of missed opportunities. In 2005, for example, Hamdi Ulukaya bought a food-processing plant Kraft was closing and hired several former Kraft employees. Eventually, he formed Chobani, which quickly grew to become the top seller of Greek yogurt in the United States. Unlike Kraft, Chobani was not a corporation, but rather a partnership owned primarily by Ulukaya and other investors, with employees owning 10% of it.

In this chapter, we explore how businesses are organized: from small-town pizza shops with a single owner to partnerships like Chobani to large multinational corporations like Kraft Heinz. We then take a detailed look at the economic issues corporations face. We examine how they raise funds and what happens when stockholder's interests are not aligned with those of management. Finally, we explore both the economic challenges and opportunities of being a multinational business.

Chapter Learning Targets

- Describe the different legal structures of firms.

- Examine how corporations raise funds.

- Discuss the principal–agent problem and ways to minimize it.

- Explain the main advantages and disadvantages of being a multinational corporation.

9.1 THE LEGAL STRUCTURES OF BUSINESSES

Henry Ford, Sandra Lerner, and Mark Zuckerberg all needed to make important decisions when establishing their business. All three eventually decided to create corporations: Ford Motor Company, Cisco, and Facebook. A **corporation** is a business that exists as a separate legal entity from its owners. In the United States, corporations account for the majority of business *revenues* and *profits*. Recall that

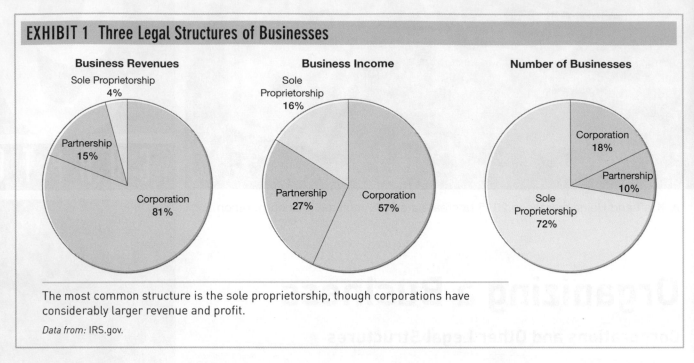

EXHIBIT 1 Three Legal Structures of Businesses

Business Revenues

Sole Proprietorship 4%

Partnership 15%

Corporation 81%

Business Income

Sole Proprietorship 16%

Partnership 27%

Corporation 57%

Number of Businesses

Corporation 18%

Partnership 10%

Sole Proprietorship 72%

The most common structure is the sole proprietorship, though corporations have considerably larger revenue and profit.

Data from: IRS.gov.

revenue (or total revenue) is the money a business receives from the sale of a product; profit is business income equal to a firm's total revenue minus its total costs.

Most businesses, however, are not corporations; they are sole proprietorships. A **sole proprietorship** is a business owned by one individual. It is easy to find sole proprietorships on any commercial street in the United States, including locally owned pizza restaurants, small retailers, general contractors, and many local real estate agencies. This structure is also increasingly common among small online merchants, such as those who sell on eBay and Etsy. Sole proprietorships tend to be small and have substantially lower average profit and revenue than other business structures.

Finally, a **partnership** is a business owned by more than one individual, not formed as a corporation. Partnerships are commonly found among groups of professionals like accounting firms, law firms, consulting agencies, and medical clinics. In the United States, there are fewer partnerships than corporations and sole proprietorships. Typically, they enjoy larger revenues and profits than found in sole proprietorships, but lower revenues and profits than found in corporations.

Exhibit 1 displays the three major types of business structures by business revenue, profit, and number of firms in the United States. In this chapter, we take a detailed look at factors that determine how entrepreneurs decide among the three major legal classifications of businesses. Each has its own strategic advantages and disadvantages.

Starting Small: Sole Proprietorships

corporation A business that exists as a separate legal entity from its owners.

sole proprietorship A business owned by one individual.

partnership A business owned by more than one individual, not formed as a corporation.

The simplest and easiest type of business to establish is a sole proprietorship. Owners of sole proprietorships are self-employed and have complete control over their businesses. This structure gives businesses tremendous flexibility in decision making compared to corporations and partnerships. If business conditions warrant a change in strategy, only one person needs to agree with the decision to change—the owner. In addition, profits are only taxed once, at the personal income level. (In contrast, the profits of corporations are taxed twice.)

Sole proprietorships also have several major disadvantages. A sole proprietorship is not recognized as a "separate legal entity." In practical terms, this means the owner is legally responsible for all contracts he or she enters, even if the business fails. The owner has unlimited legal liabilities. When lawsuits are brought against the firm, it is the owner of the sole proprietorship who is being sued, not the business itself. The business ends upon the death of the owner. Furthermore, sole proprietorships have limited ability for expansion. Financing is limited to what the owners have or can borrow. There are limits on the size a business can achieve when one owner needs to effectively control the entire business. After all, the owner faces unlimited personal legal liability and will need to control all aspects of the business to limit potential risks.

Teaming Up: Partnerships

A business owned by more than one individual, not formed as a corporation, is a partnership. From a legal entity standpoint, partnerships differ from sole proprietorships only in the fact that partnerships are jointly owned. In general, partnerships have a greater ability to raise money, as more than one person is able to secure loans. Since each partner is an owner and maintains a vested interest in the success of the business, less monitoring of partners is necessary. In contrast, sole proprietors must carefully monitor employees who have no ownership stake and thus less vested interest in the business's success. Each partner can focus on a specific aspect of the business, without the other partners needing to fully understand every area of the business. This allows for greater specialization. As with sole proprietorships, profit is taxed just once, as personal income. Because partnerships have multiple owners, decision making is more complex. When more than one person is involved in any decision, there will be differences of opinion that need to be resolved. In addition, many partnerships also have unlimited personal legal liabilities. Each partner is fully at risk for actions and debt incurred by *any* partner. The mistakes of one partner could expose all partners to enormous liabilities.

Scaling Up: Corporations

As noted above, Kraft Heinz, Ford Motor Company, Cisco, and Facebook are all corporations. A corporation is a business that exists as a separate legal entity from its owners. Being a separate legal entity provides the corporation with the rights of an individual. As a consequence, corporations provide owners limited liability, which is perhaps the most important feature of a corporation. **Limited liability** means the owners of a business are not personally responsible for the debt and other financial obligations of a firm beyond what they put into it.

A corporation can legally enter into contracts with others. With most partnerships and sole proprietorships, owners enter contracts as *individuals* and not as a separate business. A corporation can sue and be sued for breach of such contracts, among other circumstances. However, the *owners* of the corporation cannot be sued for its actions. Since owners of corporations face limited legal liabilities, the most they can lose is their investment in the corporation.

Corporations have an ability to raise the enormous sums needed for expansion in industries such as auto manufacturing, aerospace, and business computers. They can do so by issuing stocks, taking out loans, issuing bonds, or retaining their earnings. Another advantage of corporations is that a share in their ownership (stocks) has a perpetual existence. Since stocks are easily exchanged in the world's major stock markets, when a stockholder dies or otherwise wishes to end his or her ownership stake, the stocks can simply be sold to a new owner and the corporation continues with business as usual.

The major disadvantage of a corporation is that its profit is often taxed twice. Profit is first taxed at the corporate level, through the corporate income tax. Remember, corporations are a separate legal entity from their owners, and can be taxed as if they were a person. As the owners of the corporation, stockholders are also typically taxed

limited liability When the owners of a business are not personally responsible for the debt and other financial obligations of a firm beyond what they put into it.

EXHIBIT 2 Advantages and Disadvantages of Three Business Legal Structures

	Sole Proprietorship	Partnership	Corporation
Advantage	Easy to establish and manage	Access to partner's funds	Limited legal liability
	Complete flexibility	Less monitoring and greater specialization	Tremendous ability to raise money
	Income taxed as personal income	Income taxed as personal income	Perpetual existence
Disadvantages	Unlimited personal legal liability	Unlimited personal legal liability	Complex to organize and manage
	Limited ability for expansion	More complex decision making	Possible double taxation of income
Common Examples	Local pizza restaurant	Accounting and law firms	Ford Motor Company
	Small retailers	Consulting agencies	Cisco
	Small online merchants	Medical clinics	Kraft Heinz

Sole proprietorships, partnerships, and corporations vary in terms of the ease with which they can be managed and formed, and their ability to raise funds, their tax treatment and legal liabilities.

when they eventually receive their share of the corporate profits. Such income is subject to the personal income tax.

In the United States, there are far fewer corporations than proprietorships, but these corporations are often quite large. They generate the bulk of business revenues and the bulk of businesses profits. Exhibit 2 summarizes key aspects of a corporation and other legal structures.

Other Options: Limited Liability Companies and Franchises

Other hybrid legal structures of businesses exist that attempt to provide benefit of single taxation of a sole proprietorship or partnership with the benefit of limited liability or name recognition of a large corporation. These hybrid legal structures have been used to organize businesses in many states and countries in recent decades.

A **limited liability company (LLC)** is a partnership whereby *some* partners enjoy limited liabilities. Chobani, for example, legally formed as a LLC. In an LLC, some partners will not be at risk if another partner makes costly mistakes (similar to owners of a corporations). Although such partners have limited liabilities, they typically also have limited management control. Since the LLC is a partnership, profits are taxed only once.

In addition, many large corporations allow others to operate under their name. Domino's Pizza Inc., for example, owns and operates many but not all Domino's restaurants. However Domino's Pizza Inc. also sells Domino's franchises to sole proprietors, partnerships, and even other smaller corporations. A **franchise** is a purchased right to operate under an established brand name. Franchises are especially common in the fast-food industry. Franchise owners typically have access to the trademark and proprietary knowledge of the main business. However, franchise owners are not simply employers; they have an ownership stake in their local business (not the national chain), and thus Domino's Pizza Inc. allows owners of its franchise to operate Domino's restaurants in select areas—for a fee, of course!

limited liability company (LLC) A partnership whereby some partners enjoy limited liabilities.

franchise A purchased right to operate under an established brand name.

▣ BUSINESS BRIEF Top Franchise Opportunities

Franchises are common in the business world of fast food. For a few million dollars, you can establish your own KFC, Wendy's, McDonald's, or Taco Bell. A franchise for Moe's Southwest Grill is only about half as expensive, and a SUBWAY franchise is even less.

Franchises are not limited to fast food. If you wish to own a hotel, Hampton Inn, Days Inn, and Super 8 all offer franchise opportunities. If operating a hotel is not your thing, perhaps you'd prefer to open your own Ace Hardware or Aaron's Automotive. Are you more interested in retail clothing? Then maybe you'd like to own a Plato's Closet. Hair styling? How about opening a Supercuts, Great Clips, or Sport Clips store?

Each year, *Entrepreneur* magazine lists its top 500 franchise opportunities. In 2017, the top five franchise opportunities were 7-Eleven, McDonald's, Dunkin' Donuts, the UPS Store, and Jimmy John's gourmet sandwiches.* Buyers of a franchise typically gain access to the trademark and proprietary knowledge of the main business, and sellers are able to expand at a rapid pace while gaining a consistent source of revenue—a potential win-win situation. And the parent company knows that franchise owners will be highly motivated to do well, because they get to keep the profits earned after they have paid the franchise fee.

"I'd like to inquire about franchise opportunities."

Scott Nickel/Cartoon Stock

*"2017 Top Franchises from Entrepreneur's Franchise 500 List," *Entrepreneur*, accessed October 29, 2017, http://www.entrepreneur.com/franchise500.

9.2 CORPORATE FINANCE: HOW CORPORATIONS RAISE FUNDS

A vital requirement of any business is the ability to raise funds necessary for expansion and current operating expenses. Since corporations are often much larger than other business-related legal structures, they may need to raise more money than can be provided by any one individual. **Corporate finance** is the study of the financial activities of a corporation. Corporations have three primary ways to raise money for expansion: issuing new stocks, retaining earnings, and borrowing through bank loans and bonds.

Issuing New Stocks

Corporations are unique in their ability to raise funds by selling stock to many different investors. Partnerships and sole proprietorships do not have this option. A **stock** is a share of ownership in a corporation. When a corporation sells *new* shares of ownership, it is said to issue stocks or equities. **Stockholders** are the owners of a corporation. If a large corporation has 1 million shares of stock outstanding and you own one share of that company's stock, then you own 1 millionth of the corporation—congratulations!

People often are confused on this point. A retired schoolteacher with a few shares of General Motors stock is an owner of GM. The CEO of General Motors, who may earn millions of dollars per year and make major business decisions, is actually an *employee* of GM. The CEO technically works for the schoolteacher with GM stock and, of course, many other GM stockholders. That's not to say CEOs can't own stocks; they frequently do, but

corporate finance The study of the financial activities of a corporation.

stock A share of ownership in a corporation.

stockholders The owners of a corporation.

such a stock portfolio is separate from their role as a company employee. It is important to note that stocks only generate funds for corporations when they are first issued. Shares of existing stocks traded in financial markets, which have been previously issued, do not raise additional funds for the corporation. We will look more closely at the stock market from the viewpoint of those making personal financial investments in Chapter 10. Here, we focus on how corporations raise funds.

v When the corporation that owns the world's best-selling beer needed funds, it issued new shares of stock.

 BUSINESS BRIEF Owner of the World's Best-Selling Beer to Issue New Shares

In 2016, China Resources Beer, owner of the world's best-selling beer brand Snow, announced its plan to issue as much as 800 million additional shares to raise over $1.2 billion. The ability to raise enormous sums of money to pay for expansion and other ventures is a unique characteristic of corporations such as China Resources Beer. Earlier that same year, the giant beer maker had agreed to buy out SABMiller's stake in China. The brewer also used the proceeds to fund expansion by buying smaller rivals and microbreweries. On the announcement, the company's stock price fell by over 4%.* A number of factors could have caused the stock price to fall upon this announcement, but one possibility is what economists call the *principal–agent problem*—the difficulty of making the CEO act in the best interest of the stockholders. Perhaps investors worried that the expansion was too ambitious, and that the CEO was more concerned with presiding over a larger company than maximizing shareholders' wealth.†

*Donny Kwok, "China Resources Beer Plans $1.2 Billion Rights Issue to Buy SABMiller's JV Stake," *Reuters*, July 6, 2016, http://www.reuters.com/article/us-china-res-beer-equity-idUSKCN0ZM04O.

†Daisuke Harashima, "World's Biggest Beer Market Keeps Getting Smaller," *Nikkei Asian Review*, February 22, 2017, http://asia.nikkei.com/Business/Trends/World-s-biggest-beer-market-keeps-getting-smaller.

Dividends and Retaining Earnings

When corporations earn a profit, they must decide how much of the profit to return to stockholders and how much to invest to try to generate higher future profits. When corporations decide to return some of the profit to stockholders, they usually do so by paying dividends. **Dividends** are the portion of profits paid to stockowners per share of stock. Other times, they will actually buy back stock from shareholders. This may allow stockholders to benefit by selling their shares at a higher price than they originally paid for the stock.

Corporations generally do not return all profits to stockholders with dividends and stock buybacks. They generally retain some of their earnings for future use. **Retained earnings** are profits the corporation does not immediately return to stockholders. Retaining earnings is often a good way for profitable corporations to fund new investments. Rapidly growing corporations will typically retain earnings and pay little or no dividends because the owners (stockholders) prefer to reinvest the profit in the growing business. This may be combined with other sources of money to fund business expansion.

dividends The portion of profits paid to stockowners per share of stock.

retained earnings Profits the corporation does not immediately return to stockholders.

bond A tradable legally binding obligation to repay borrowed money and interest.

Borrowing Through Bank Loans and Bonds

Corporations are also able to borrow money to fund current operations or new investments. This is done either through loans from banks and other financial institutions or by issuing bonds. A **bond** is a tradable legally binding obligation to repay borrowed money and interest. Bondholders have no claim of ownership of the business. In many ways, bonds are a type of loan. The crucial difference between bonds and other types of loans is that bondholders may sell their bonds in the financial markets. Corporations are able to borrow money by selling new bonds. By law, bondholders are paid before owners (stockholders) in the unfortunate event of bankruptcy.

When corporations borrow directly from banks and other financial institutions, they pay back the loan along with an interest payment. This is similar to consumers borrowing to buy a home or car. As is the case with bonds, lenders to corporations such as banks do not have an ownership claim of the corporation. And as is also the case with bonds, by law, lenders must also be paid before owners (stockholders) in the event of bankruptcy.

9.3 THE CHALLENGE OF CORPORATE OWNERSHIP

Stockholders of major corporations typically do not directly run the business. Instead, they hire managers who usually have at most a small ownership stake in the corporation. How can stockholders be sure that their managers will make decisions and pursue strategies consistent with the goals of the owners?

When a business is structured as a sole proprietorship or partnership, then the managers are also the owners. Thus, if a project is expected to be profitable, it will generally get done. But what happens if a corporate manager is making decisions about a project where her goals conflict with those of the stockholders?

The Principal–Agent Problem

Consider the following business anecdote based on an actual event. In the 1970s, Kodak was by far the world leader in film and photography. A Kodak engineer named Steve Sasson developed an idea—digital cameras. This was a novel concept for the time period. He brought his idea to management; their response: "That's cute, but don't tell anyone about it."[1]

The Kodak manager to whom this invention was pitched could have spent millions of dollars developing a product that, if successful, would earn Kodak billions of dollars in profits. Unfortunately, if unsuccessful, the manager would have just spent millions of dollars and might have well lost his job. Although the corporation's owners would likely benefit from risking millions to make billions, the manager might not. In hindsight, Kodak should have pursued the digital camera project when it was first proposed. In 2012, Kodak was forced to declare bankruptcy in large part because its reliance on profits generated by selling film, which disappeared in the digital age.[2]

A similar story may be told about IBM. Once the world leader in computer technology, IBM stumbled when businesses such as Microsoft and Apple (then startup companies) developed software and computers for everyday use. Ironically, in the 1980s, Microsoft had offered to sell its company to IBM, which was not interested at the time. By 2000, Microsoft had become the most valuable company in the world, and IBM undoubtedly regretted its decision. The process repeated itself a few years later. However, Microsoft was now the slow-moving giant, a late and reluctant entrant into the world of Internet search. Internet search was soon dominated by a new firm on the scene—Google.

The **principal–agent problem** refers to the difficulty of making agents act in the best interest of the principals that they serve. The goal of the principal is to maximize profit, whereas the goal of the agent is likely to maintain employment or enhance his or her career potential, or enjoy lots of vacation time. When the stock price of China Resources Beer fell after announcing the company was going to raise $1.2 billion by issuing new stocks, it may have been an indication that the principals were concerned

principal–agent problem
The difficulty of making agents act in the best interest of the principals that they serve.

the agent (the CEO) was more concerned with presiding over a large company than maximizing shareholders' wealth.

The principal–agent problem is an extremely important issue that can create conflict in many other areas of life where one person is hired to help another, both in a corporate and noncorporate setting:

- An automobile mechanic (agent) may have different goals (expensive repairs) than the owner of the automobile (principal) being repaired.

- A real estate broker (agent) might have better information as to why to not buy a specific home than the buyer (principal), but may attempt to sell the property to earn a commission.

- A CEO (agent) may attempt to acquire another firm because of a personal aspiration to manage a larger company, rather than basing his or her decision on evidence that the acquisition will benefit the firm and its shareholders (principal).

Information is the key advantage of the agent. In the above examples, the mechanic, the real estate broker, and the CEO all had more information than the principals. In economics, this disparity is known as asymmetric information. **Asymmetric information** occurs when one party in a transaction has better information than the other. The mechanic knows more about the repairs your car needs than you do, for example, and the real estate broker likely knows more about the local real estate market (and about the specific house you're looking at). Principals often attempt to overcome the information disadvantage—they might attempt to learn about needed car repairs and the local real estate market online. Online services like Yelp provide ratings for businesses and help to reduce the problem of asymmetric information.

Businesses have developed several methods to overcome the principal–agent problem and the related problems associated with asymmetric information. For example, franchise owners have "skin-in-the-game." If the location they choose is successful, they can reap enormous profits. If their location is unsuccessful, they can incur losses. Thus, they have an interest in furthering many of the goals of the parent corporation.

Monitoring the agent is another way to overcome the principal–agent problem. Stockholders try to monitor the performance of its CEO, other senior managers, and employees by requiring a board of directors to evaluate their performance.

Establishing the right incentives also seems to help. This can be accomplished by rewarding employees who develop profitable business lines and not rewarding CEOs who make poor decisions. In practice, it is not always easy to create the right incentive system. Many companies offer managers and executives stock in the corporation or an option to buy the stock at a discounted price in the future. These stocks and options tend to be more valuable if managers pursue the principal's goal of maximizing profit. This is similar to why Chobani gave its employees a 10% stake in the business in 2016.

But even profit sharing doesn't completely eliminate the principal–agent problem, because most of the gains from improved efficiency go to other shareholders, not the manager who is responsible for the profitable innovation. Overcoming the principal–agent problem is one of the central challenges in the field of business management.

Think & Speak Like an Economist

The notion of *rational self-interest* enables us to predict how people change their behavior in response to changing incentives and circumstances. To overcome the principal–agent problem, a rational agent must be provided with incentives that align with the goals of the principal.

asymmetric information An exchange where one party has better information than the other.

stakeholders Any group that is impacted by corporate policy decisions.

Managing Conflicting Goals: Corporate Social Responsibility

Not everyone agrees that profit maximization is, or should be, the only corporate goal. Many people have argued that corporations should not just focus on profits, but rather on the well-being of all their **stakeholders**, any group that is impacted by corporate policy decisions. These include stockholders, employees, lenders, customers, governments (to which they pay taxes), and residents who live nearby (and who might be impacted, e.g., by pollution).

In recent years, a movement advocating corporate social responsibility has evolved. **Corporate social responsibility** refers to the idea that corporations have a broader responsibility to society, not just maximizing profits. Recall that Adam Smith had pointed out that businesses would often end up acting in society's best interest, even when pursuing the selfish goal of reaping a profit. Advocates of corporate social responsibility don't deny that the market often produces outcomes that benefit society, but also suggest that there are many cases where profits and ethics may conflict. In such an instance, they argue, corporations have an ethical obligation to behave responsibly. For instance, they may oppose corporations seen as exploiting cheap labor, polluting the air, or evading taxes. Others suggest that corporations should donate some of their profits to worthy causes.

Not surprisingly, a lively debate has ensued over exactly where to draw the line between the goal of enriching shareholders and meeting broader societal goals. Skeptics say that governments should set the rules on minimum wages, or pollution limits, or appropriate taxes, and that corporations should merely abide by the rules established by society. They argue that corporations do the greatest amount of good by maximizing profits within the rules of the game, and that the shareholders (owners) should decide where to donate money, not the agents (CEOs) who work for them.

Others point out that government policies can never deal with all societal problems, and because corporations are often quite rich and powerful, encouraging corporate social responsibility will make it easier to address society's challenges. Thus, it may be difficult to get Congress to pass legislation addressing global warming, and hence activists will instead directly lobby privately owned utilities to burn less coal.

A third group suggests that corporate social responsibility may actually be in the best interests of a company's bottom line. There is some evidence of companies with aggressive corporate responsibility policies doing well, even in terms of profit growth. These advocates suggest that "doing good" is also good for business. Donating money to communities and supporting other worthy causes such as a clean environment may give a big corporation a more positive image, leading to more receptive government regulators and more eager customers, and making it easier to hire idealistic employees.

To summarize, there is no uniform agreement on exactly where to draw the line on corporate social responsibility. However, it will almost certainly continue to be an issue in the decades to come, and even skeptical corporations cannot afford to completely ignore public opinion on this issue.

John M. Heller/Getty Images

∧ Corporate giving—not advertising—created buzz around Toms Shoes.

📊 BUSINESS BRIEF Toms's "One for One" Model

In 2006, Blake Mycoskie founded Toms, a company that sells shoes and eyewear. What makes Toms unusual is the business's approach to corporate social responsibility. When Toms sells a pair of shoes, it gives away a pair of shoes to a poor child. When Toms sells a pair of glasses, part of the profit is used to help the vision of a person in a developing country. In a similar vein, the company now sells coffee—donating water with each cup of java sold. By 2015, the company had given away 35 million pairs of shoes and helped improve the vision of 300,000.

According to Mycoskie,* the business model is hugely successful:

> For many retailers, their profit margins are low. They spend lots of money on advertising. . . . Toms doesn't have any ad spend. A big portion of our spend goes on giving. But by giving, we build a community and people recommend through word of mouth and on social media. (quoted in Anderson, 2015)

*Elizabeth Anderson, "How Toms Made Hundreds of Millions of Dollars by Giving Shoes Away," *The Telegraph*, May 3, 2015, http://www.telegraph.co.uk/finance/enterprise/11580387/How-Toms-made-hundreds-of-millions-of-dollars-by-giving-shoes-away.html.

corporate social responsibility The idea that corporations have a broader responsibility to society, not just maximizing profits.

9.4 MULTINATIONAL CORPORATIONS

Businesses have an incentive to go international, as this opens up many more market opportunities. However, international business also raises many complex issues that do not exist for purely domestic firms, such as working in an environment with very different laws, cultural practices, and technical development. A **multinational corporation (MNC)** is a corporation that produces and sells goods and services in more than one country. For example, Sony Corporation produces and sells a wide range of consumer electronics products. Sony employs over 130,000 people worldwide. American automakers General Motors and Ford produce many cars in Europe, Canada, Mexico, and China. MNCs have a variety of economic challenges and opportunities to consider.

📊 BUSINESS BRIEF Forbes Global 2000 List of Multinational Corporations

Each year, using data on sales, profits, assets, and market value, Forbes ranks multinational corporations. Although Sony Corporation is a large company, it only ranked 449th on Forbes 2017 Global 2000 list of the largest multinational corporations. Kraft Heinz ranked 117th. The top 20 multinational corporations are listed in Exhibit 3. The largest two firms were Chinese banks owned by the Chinese government. General Electric, a U.S.-based conglomerate (a firm in multiple different industries), also produces a wide range of products, including aircraft engines, power-generation equipment, household appliances, medical imaging machinery, television content, and both consumer and business financing. General Electric employs nearly 300,000 people and was ranked 14th on the Forbes 2017 Global 2000 list. Walmart employed 2.3 million people and ranked 17th.*

*For a complete list, see Forbes, "The Global 2000." https://www.forbes.com/global2000/#225e9ccd335d.

Risks of Global Expansion

Multinational corporations face many risks. When firms seek to expand, they are often welcomed by foreign countries, particularly when they will bring new technology or capital. However, this does not mean they are *always* welcome. Expansion into foreign markets can lead to conflicts with the local culture and there is also the risk of a sudden change in exchange rates.

Country Risk Multinational firms must be aware of political issues, social attitudes, cultural differences, and religious norms in the countries where they decide to expand. They must also be familiar with the different tax laws, as well as the risk that the host countries might change their tax rules. **Country risk** refers to the risk that the business environment in a foreign country unexpectedly changes. Typically, unexpected changes are political (i.e., a sudden change in the country's leadership). In a few cases, a company might be nationalized, which means taken over by the foreign government.

Currency Risk In addition, expanding into a new country exposes companies to the risk of fluctuating exchange rates. **Currency risk** is the risk that the values of financial obligations change as the result of currency fluctuations. For example, a U.S. firm buys products with an obligation to pay for the items in a specific foreign currency two months into the future. If during the intervening two months the foreign currency appreciates, the U.S. firm will need *more* U.S. dollars to convert into the recently appreciated foreign currency to meet its financial obligation. A similar risk occurs when borrowing or lending in foreign currencies or when a firm acquires assets or incurs liabilities (debts) denominated in a foreign currency.

When a firm *owes* money in a foreign currency, it runs the risk that the foreign currency appreciates. For a U.S. firm, it will take more dollars to convert into the same

multinational corporation (MNC) A corporation that produces and sells goods and services in more than one country.

country risk The risk that the business environment in a foreign country unexpectedly changes.

currency risk The risk that the values of financial obligations change as the result of currency fluctuations.

EXHIBIT 3 Top 20 Multinational Corporations on Forbes Global 2000 in 2017

Rank	Company	Country	Industry
1	ICBC	China	Banking
2	China Construction Bank	China	Banking
3	Berkshire Hathaway	United States	Investment Services
4	JPMorgan Chase	United States	Banking
5	Wells Fargo	United States	Banking
6	Agricultural Bank of China	China	Banking
7	Bank of America	United States	Banking
8	Bank of China	China	Banking
9	Apple	United States	Computer Hardware
10	Toyota Motor	Japan	Auto Manufacturers
11	AT&T	United States	Telecommunications
12	Citigroup	United States	Banking
13	ExxonMobil	United States	Oil and Gas
14	General Electric	United States	Conglomerate
15	Samsung Electronics	South Korea	Semiconductors
16	Ping An Insurance Group	China	Diversified Insurance
17	Walmart Stores	United States	Discount Stores
18	Verizon Communications	United States	Telecommunications
19	Microsoft	United States	Software and Programing
20	Royal Dutch Shell	Netherlands	Oil and Gas

Each year, using data on sales, profits, assets, and market value, Forbes ranks multinational corporations. In 2017, Sony Corporation, a consumer electronics firm, ranked 449th, while Kraft Heinz ranked 117th.

Data from: Forbes, https://www.forbes.com/global2000/list/#tab:overall.

amount of a foreign currency that appreciates. Of course, the opposite can occur. If a U.S. firm that owes money in a foreign currency sees the foreign currency depreciate, the company will need fewer dollars to pay off the money it owes.

Advantages of Global Expansion

While being a multinational corporation entails risks, it also brings opportunities. This is why General Electric, Sony Corporation, Walmart, and many other firms operate in multiple countries. Multinational firms have grown more important in recent decades and this trend is likely to continue. The rewards include expanded opportunities to sell in new markets, diversification benefits, currency opportunities, access to resources, a reduced threat of tariffs, and potentially lower borrowing costs.

Expanded Business Opportunities and Customer Base Multinational firms often attempt to expand into areas with few competitors. This allows them to earn above-normal profit. Other multinationals may choose to expand into highly competitive markets for strategic reasons. For example, a firm may wish to expand into a competitive market to prevent a rival from dominating it, or to increase sales so the firm's factories operate closer to capacity.

Diversification Benefits Firms may not want to "put all their eggs into one basket." Multinationals can often reduce such risk by diversifying the location of their consumer markets. For example, a multinational firm may have poor sales in one region of the world, but remain profitable because of profits made in other parts of the world.

Currency Opportunities and Risk Reduction When a specific country's currency depreciates, business operations in that country become less expensive. A multinational firm has an opportunity to expand its production into such countries to take advantage of the cost savings associated with the depreciated currency. In addition, currency risk (mentioned above) can be reduced when firms *both* produce and sell in multiple countries. Japanese automakers built many American factories to reduce the risk of an unfavorable change in exchange rates. Similarly, currency risk can be reduced by having assets (such as any money a firm is owed) in one currency partially offset by liabilities (debts) denominated in the *same* currency.

Access to Resources Firms often expand to gain access to raw materials (e.g. oil, copper, etc.) or to low-cost labor in countries such as China, India, and Mexico. Multinational mining companies may possess technology that is lacked by low-income countries with mineral reserves. **Outsourcing** occurs when a business obtains products or services from another firm, one frequently located in a foreign country. For example, it is common for automakers to outsource the production of certain parts to another firm. Also, many firms have call centers located in foreign countries. In both cases, firms determine that they can obtain these products or services at a lower cost by outsourcing.

From a business perspective, outsourcing lowers costs; thus, most economists believe outsourcing improves overall economic efficiency. From society's perspective, outsourcing to foreign firms often displaces domestic workers, but society gains overall as the result of improvements in economic efficiency. In short, outsourcing results in a trade-off analogous to the gains from free trade discussed in Chapter 2.

Reduced Threat of Tariffs A *tariff* is a tax on imports imposed by the country where products are being imported. If a multinational corporation has production facilities and hires workers in a foreign country, the foreign country is less likely to impose a tariff. This is because the multinational corporation is contributing to domestic production and employment.

Lower Borrowing Costs Multinational corporations are often able to take advantage of global financial markets and to borrow where the interest rate is lowest. They frequently bring new technology and capital to poor and underdeveloped countries. Living standards in such countries typically improve as a result. At the same time, products are produced more efficiently, allowing for lower-priced goods and services worldwide. Overall, multinational corporations provide a benefit to society similar to the benefit created by increased free trade. Not everyone benefits, but overall society is better off.

BUSINESS TAKEAWAY

Every business, from self-employed craftsmen to huge multinational corporations, operates within a specific legal structure. For many entrepreneurs, a sole proprietorship provides flexibility, independence, and creative and practical control. While the dream of being one's own boss is appealing, the sole proprietorship model provides limited opportunities for businesses to grow. Many businesses also establish themselves as a partnership, in which the risks and rewards of business ownership are shared by two or more people. Partnerships range from mom-and-pop stores with a few employees to large law firms and medical practices.

Most large businesses choose a corporate structure, which provides them with much greater ability to raise money, limits the legal liability of their owners, and provides for a perpetual existence beyond the life of the founder. Although

outsourcing When a business obtains products or services from another firm, one frequently located in a foreign country.

corporations are less common than smaller business structures, they are far larger and more profitable, in part because the rules that govern corporations allow them to raise money and expand.

The principal–agent problem is an issue for any business with employees. While this problem can never be entirely eliminated, it is important for firms to encourage managers to operate in the best interests of their owners (stockholders). Techniques to overcome the principal–agent problem involve both "carrot" and "stick" approaches. Careful monitoring ensures that bad managers can be removed, whereas incentives such as stock options can motivate good managers to do an even better job.

Multinational corporations must be aware of country risk, especially the laws and cultural norms of the countries where they operate. This is why it is often helpful to hire local managers who understand the culture and laws. These corporations must also pay attention to exchange rates in order to effectively manage currency risk. Multinational operations additionally provide corporations with some unique opportunities. These include the opportunity to expand their customer base, diversification benefits, ways to benefit from changes in exchange rates, access to additional resources, reduced threats of tariffs, and potentially reduced borrowing costs.

CHAPTER STUDY GUIDE

9.1 THE LEGAL STRUCTURE OF BUSINESSES

A **corporation** is a business that exists as a separate legal entity from its owners. Owners of corporations have limited legal liability, a tremendous ability to raise money, perpetual existence, complex management issues, and possibly experience the double taxation of their income. A **sole proprietorship** is a business owned by one individual. Sole proprietorships are easy to establish and manage, offer complete flexibility in decision making, and their earnings are taxed only once as personal income. The owner of a sole proprietorship faces unlimited legal liability and has limited ability for expansion. A **partnership** is a business owned by more than one individual, not formed as a corporation. It provides access to partners' funds, involves less need for monitoring, means its income is taxed only once, has unlimited legal liability, and results in more complex decision making than with a sole proprietorship. **Limited liability** means the owners of a business are not personally responsible for the debt and other financial obligations of a firm beyond what they put into it. A **limited liability company (LLC)** is a partnership whereby some partners enjoy limited liabilities. A **franchise** is a purchased right to operate under an established brand name.

9.2 CORPORATE FINANCE: HOW CORPORATIONS RAISE FUNDS

Corporate finance is the study of the financial activities of a corporation. Corporations have three primary ways to raise money for expansion: issuing new stock,

retaining earnings, and borrowing through bank loans and bonds. A **stock** is a share of ownership in a corporation. When a corporation sells *new* shares of ownership, it is said to issue stocks or equities. **Stockholders** are the owners of a corporation. **Dividends** are the portion of profits paid to stockowners per share of stock. Earnings not distributed in the form of dividends are often retained. **Retained earnings** are profits the corporation does not immediately return to stockholders. A **bond** is a tradable legally binding obligation to repay borrowed money and interest. Bondholders have no claim of ownership of the business.

9.3 THE CHALLENGE OF CORPORATE OWNERSHIP

The **principal–agent problem** refers to the difficulty of making agents act in the best interest of the principals that they serve. The essence of the principal–agent problem is disparity in available information. **Asymmetric information** occurs when one party in a transaction has better information than the other. The principal–agent problem can be overcome with incentives or through monitoring. The term **stakeholder** refers to any group that is impacted by corporate policy decisions. These include stockholders, employees, lenders, customers, governments (to which they pay taxes), and residents who live nearby (and who might be impacted, e.g., by pollution). **Corporate social responsibility** refers to the idea that corporations have a broader responsibility to society, not just maximizing profits.

9.4 MULTINATIONAL CORPORATIONS

A **multinational corporation (MNC)** is a corporation that produces and sells goods and services in more than one country. Multinational corporations involve added risks and opportunities. **Country risk** refers the risk that the business environment in a foreign country unexpectedly changes. **Currency risk** is the risk that the values of financial obligations change as the result of currency fluctuations. The opportunities of a multinational corporation include expanded business opportunities, diversification benefits, currency opportunities and risk reduction, access to resources, reduced threat of tariffs, and lower borrowing costs. **Outsourcing** occurs when a business obtains products or services from another firm, one frequently located in a foreign country.

TOP TEN TERMS AND CONCEPTS

1. Corporations
2. Sole Proprietorships
3. Partnerships and Limited Liability Company (LLC)
4. Franchises
5. Corporate Finance
6. Stocks and Bonds
7. Dividends and Retained Earnings
8. Principal–Agent Problem
9. Corporate Social Responsibility
10. Multinational Corporation

STUDY PROBLEMS

1. Julia is considering setting up a small flower business. Explain the advantages and disadvantage of each legal structure available to her. Also discuss how she can raise funds.

2. Julia is also considering forming her business as a franchise. Explain what a franchise is.

3. Compare and contrast a limited liability company with a partnership. With a corporation.

4. Which is the most common type of business structure? Which legal structure has the greatest share of business income? The greatest share of business revenues?

5. For each of the following, identify if the organization described is a sole proprietorship, partnership, or corporation. More than one answer may apply.

   a. allows you to make your own decisions

   b. limits your risk to the amount of your original investment

   c. reduces the monitoring cost of other owners

   d. is capable of raising large amounts of funds

   e. is subject to the principal–agent problem

   f. is the easiest to establish

   g. experiences the double taxation of its profits

   h. results in unlimited legal liability

   i. continues beyond the death of the original owners

6. Explain the difference in the tax treatment of the dividends of a corporation and profits on a sole proprietorship.

7. Explain why asymmetric information can be a problem. Is it more likely to be a bigger problem in small businesses or large businesses?

8. List three ways a corporation can raise funds.

9. What is a share of stock? Do partnerships and sole proprietorships issue stock?

10. Describe the principal–agent problem. How can owners reduce it?

11. Suppose you are the CEO of a corporation. Should you operate the company in the best interest of the owners, or the best interest of all stakeholders? Discuss the pros and cons of each point of view.

12. Explain the difference between country risk and currency risk.

13. What is a multinational corporation? Name the advantages and disadvantages of being a multinational corporation.

14. Search for a news story on corporate social responsibility. Describe what occurred.

∧ Is buying shares of Snapchat's stock a good financial investment?

Stocks and Bonds

Financial Markets and Personal Finance

In March 2017, Snap Inc.—better known as Snapchat—raised $3.4 billion by selling 200 million new shares of stock at $17 per share. It was the first time shares could be purchased by the public on the New York Stock Exchange. Over the next twelve months, Snapchat's stock rose as high as $23, and sank as low as $12; in March 2018 it was close to its initial price of $17 per share. Companies like Snapchat sell shares in order to raise money to fund operations and expansion. In this chapter, we consider why individuals wish to purchase stocks and bonds as a financial investment: a part of economics known as personal finance.

You may have read a headline proclaiming that the Dow fell 200 points or heard that interest rates were expected to increase and wondered what this meant for financial investors. Television networks such as CNBC, Fox Business, and Bloomberg offer extensive coverage of both the stock and bond markets, which bring together savers and borrowers. Businesses and governments go to these markets to raise enormous sums of money. The funds are raised from individuals who wish to place their savings in assets that will provide a return on their financial investment. This chapter gives insights into stocks and bonds from the perspective of personal finance and also a few simple guidelines that may prove useful to you in the future.[1]

10.1 THE STOCK MARKET

In Chapter 1, we learned that a **financial investment** is a way of employing savings and often refers to the purchase of stocks and bonds. We begin with an introduction to the stock market from the perspective of a buyer. Even if you don't pay close attention to the business world, you probably know that the news media focuses obsessively on the ups and downs of markets such as the New York Stock Exchange (NYSE), the London Stock Exchange, and the Stock Exchange of Hong Kong.

Chapter Learning Targets

- Explain the basics of the stock market and factors that impact the value of a stock.

- Describe bonds and factors that impact the value of a bond.

- Identify basic concepts in personal finance including the trade-off between risk and return and the importance of diversification.

What, exactly, is being exchanged in these markets? A **stock** is a share of ownership in a corporation. Corporations raise funds by selling new shares of stock. If a large corporation has 1 billion shares of stock outstanding and you own one share of that company's stock, then you own 1 billionth of the corporation—a pretty small fraction! The major stock exchanges are *secondary markets,* in which existing shares of stocks are exchanged between two financial investors, rather than being directly sold by the company itself. From the perspective of those investing in stocks, the ability to easily buy and sell stocks on a secondary exchange is an appealing attribute.

Major Stock Market Indices in the United States

The words "Wall Street" now symbolize the U.S. financial markets in much the same way that "Broadway" symbolizes American theater. Individual investors can track the performance of specific stocks; as you will soon discover, the price of each *individual* stock reflects the expected future earnings of that company. However, many economists and financial investors gain a sense of how the stock market is performing overall by looking at stock market indices. A **stock market index** is an aggregate value of a set of representative stocks. In the sections that follow, we'll examine some of the best-known American stock indices.

Standard & Poor's 500 The Standard & Poor's 500 (S&P 500) is a U.S. stock index consisting of 500 large company stocks. The index is calculated in a manner that weights large companies more heavily than other companies, a process known as market cap weighting. The term *cap* is short for "capitalization," the total value of all shares of a given stock. The largest market cap in March 2018 applied to Apple, valued at $900 billion. Thus, the S&P 500 is considered a large cap stock market index.

NASDAQ Composite Index The National Association of Securities Dealers Automated Quotations (NASDAQ) is a U.S. stock exchange focused on the technology sector. The NASDAQ Composite Index contains more than 3,000 technology stocks, including those of big players that are also in the S&P 500 such as Apple, Facebook, Google, and Microsoft; as well as a number of newer, smaller companies. The focus on technology and its many startups makes the NASDAQ more volatile than the S&P 500. Like the S&P 500, the NASDAQ is a market cap–weighted index.

Dow Jones Industrial Average The Dow Jones Industrial Average (or Dow) is a U.S. stock index consisting of 30 leading companies. It is perhaps the world's most well-known stock market index and was first calculated in 1896. Each of the 30 companies in the index counts equally. While the Dow is reported regularly in financial news, industry experts consider the fact that large companies and small companies in the Dow have an equal weight in the index to be a design flaw and prefer to track the S&P 500.

📊 BUSINESS BRIEF Facebook Goes Public

financial investment A way of employing savings; often refers to the purchase of stocks and bonds.

stock A share of ownership in a corporation.

stock market index An aggregate value of a set of representative stocks.

Facebook first became a publicly traded company on May 18, 2012, when shares were first made available to the general public in what is known as an initial public offering (IPO). Since then Facebook has traded in the NASDAQ secondary market under the ticker symbol "FB." The closing stock price on that first day of trading was just over $38, making Facebook founder and CEO Mark Zuckerberg a multibillionaire.

The stocks of new companies are often especially risky, particularly stocks that trade on the NASDAQ. Many early buyers of FB stock saw the value of their financial investment slashed by more than half. Someone who had bought $10,000 in stock witnessed its value plummet below $5,000. By early September 2012, the stock price had fallen to under $18 (see Exhibit 1). At the time, some began to question if the company was simply a fad and sold their shares, fearing the stock's price would drop even further.

Nonetheless, with risk comes the *potential* for rewards—and Facebook ultimately has proven to be a good financial investment for those who could stomach the volatility. By the time the five-year anniversary of its IPO rolled around in May 2017, Facebook stocks were routinely trading at prices above $140 per share. In July of that same year, Facebook reached a milestone market cap of half a trillion dollars ($500 billion), with a stock price above $170 per share.* You can search the current stock price, market cap, and P/E ratio of Facebook by searching under "FB stock." It should be noted that not all IPOs experience this level of success, as risk does not *always* mean reward.

*Matt Egan, "Facebook and Amazon Hit $500 Billion Milestone," *CNNMoney*, http://money.cnn.com/2017/07/27/investing/facebook-amazon-500-billion-bezos-zuckerberg/index.html.

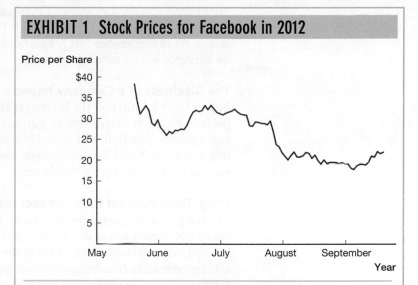

EXHIBIT 1 Stock Prices for Facebook in 2012

Facebook (FB) stock was somewhat volatile at first, then grew substantially in value over the first five years as the company reached a valuation of over half a trillion dollars.

Data from: NASDAQ (http://www.nasdaq.com/symbol/fb).

Price Earnings (P/E) Ratio: One Measure of a Stock's Value

The price of a stock by itself tells us very little. This is because stock prices reflect both the value of the corporation and the number of shares outstanding. If a large corporation has only a few shares outstanding, it will have a much higher stock price than if *the same corporation* has billions of shares outstanding. Facebook, for example, has 3 billion shares outstanding. The number of shares outstanding should not change the underlying total value of the corporation. Therefore, the price of an individual share of stock can vary enormously based on the number of shares outstanding.

Consider a company that offers each shareholder two *new* shares of stock in exchange for one *old* share of stock. This is referred to as a "two for one split." Such an action would double the number of shares. However, because the total value underlying the company should not be affected by doubling the number of shares, the value of each share will fall by roughly 50%.

Financial experts often look at a company's P/E ratio when evaluating the value of a stock, though other measures exist. The **P/E ratio** is the price of a stock divided by its earnings per share. The P/E ratio is sometimes called the **price/earnings ratio** as the "P" refers to the price of the stock, while the "E" corresponds to its earnings per share:

$$P/E \ ratio = \frac{Price \ of \ stock}{Earnings \ per \ share}$$

Stock prices are strongly influenced by expected future earnings per share. However, higher earnings do not necessarily translate into a lower P/E ratio. When earnings increase over an extended period of time, the price of the stock often increases by roughly a corresponding amount. P/E ratios (and stock prices) are primarily determined by the expected growth of a company's earnings, the perceived riskiness of the company, and long-term interest rates.

Expected Earnings Growth Impacts the P/E Ratio A corporation with earnings that are expected to grow over time will have a higher P/E ratio (and a higher stock

P/E ratio The price of a stock divided by its earnings per share; also called the **price/earnings ratio.**

price) than a stable or declining company. Investors are willing to pay more in anticipation of higher future profits. High P/E ratios frequently occur in the technology sector. As of September 2017, Facebook had a very high P/E ratio of 38 based largely on expected future earnings growth.

The Riskiness of a Company Impacts the P/E Ratio The less risky a company, the higher its P/E ratio and the higher its stock price. This is because financial investors prefer safety over risk, *ceteris paribus*. In other words, if a financial investor has two options, one that will earn 10% per year with certainty and one that will earn 0% some years and 20% in others, investors prefer the more predictable earnings stream over the less predictable one.

Long-Term Interest Rates Impact the P/E Ratio The P/E ratio can also be affected by changes in long-term interest rates, which reflect the rate of return in alternative investments such as bonds. Since bonds are a substitute investment for stocks, higher interest rates on bonds tend to lower the appeal of stocks. In other words, high interest rates increase the opportunity cost of owning stocks. This leads to lower average P/E ratios in stocks. In contrast, when long-term interest rates are low (as in recent years), P/E ratios tend to be high.

📊 BUSINESS BRIEF   Jordan Spieth Misses Putt, Under Armour Market Cap Falls $120 Million

▼ Jordan Spieth misses a pricey putt.

Rich Graessle/Icon Sportswire CGV/Newscom

In 2015, newcomer Jordan Spieth was on top of the golfing world. That year, the 22-year-old won a record $22 million. In addition, he was the youngest player to win two Majors (the Masters and the U.S. Open) in over 90 years. It was against this backdrop that the golfing world was abuzz.* Could Spieth become the first player to win all four Majors in a single year? This media attention benefited his major sponsor, Under Armour (UA), that had recently signed Spieth to a 10-year contract in an attempt to enter the golf apparel market. In the third Major of the year, the (British) Open Championship, Spieth jockeyed his way onto the top of the leader board in the final round, which due to unusual weather delays was played on a Monday when the stock market would be open.

Spieth's fortunes changed, though, when he missed a putt on the next-to-last hole. Within minutes, Under Armour's market cap fell by $120 million, as his endorsement value took a hit.† Stock prices and market caps reflect many factors, including the expected growth of earnings. When Spieth won the Master's and U.S. Open, UA's shares soared, in part due to the expectation of greater golf apparel sales. Expectations grew even higher when Spieth gave himself a chance to win the Open. When his fortunes changed, so, too, did the stock price of UA.

*Chris Chase, "Jordan Spieth's Awesome 2015 Season in 15 Unbelievable Stats," *USA Today*, September 28, 2015, http://ftw.usatoday.com/2015/09/jordan-spieth-winnings-2015-compared-to-tiger-woods-stats-record-money-grand-slam.

†Fred Imbert, "Did Jordan Spieth Hit a $120 Million Bogey?," *CNBC*, July 21, 2015, http://www.cnbc.com/2015/07/20/jordan-spieth-hits-120-million-bogey.html.

Two Ways Stockholders Profit: Dividends and Capital Gains

stockholders The owners of a corporation.

Stockholders are the owners of a corporation. There are two ways in which a stockholder can realize a gain from his or her financial investment. Either the stock price can increase or the corporation can pay owners a portion of the profits. When a business is highly successful, the price of its common stock will often increase. When stockholders sell their stock at a higher price than they paid for it, they will receive a capital gain. A **capital gain** is the profit from the sale of a property or financial asset resulting from a price increase between the time of purchase and the time of sale. Capital gains are also common for people who sell a home they have owned for many years.

Alternatively, owners of stocks can realize gains from a financial investment by receiving dividends. **Dividends** are the portion of profits paid to stockowners per share of stock. Dividends can be a fixed amount or vary based on a variety of factors, such as the level of profit and the extent to which the corporation chooses to hold onto profits to be used for corporate expansion. The profits they hold on to are called retained earnings. When earnings are retained, it is often reflected in a capital gain that results from a higher share price.

10.2 THE BOND MARKET

Financial investments can also be made in the bond market. Both governments and businesses raise money in the bond market. A **bond** is a tradable legally binding obligation to repay borrowed money and interest. It is a promise to pay a specified amount of money at specific dates in the future. Unlike the owner of stocks, bondholders have no claim of *ownership* of the business or government. In the event of bankruptcy, bondholders are more likely to receive payment (or partial payment) than stockholders. In general, owning a bond entails less risk.

From the perspective of a buyer, purchasing a bond is equivalent to making a loan. The crucial difference between bonds and other types of loans is that bondholders may easily sell their bonds in the financial markets. As is the case with stocks, only newly issued bonds raise money for corporations and governments—nonetheless, many bonds trade regularly in the secondary markets.

Although the specifics vary from bond to bond, most bonds have some general attributes. The typical bond has a specified date of *maturity;* the date by which the principal on a bond must be paid in full. The *principal* (or *par value*) is the face value of the bond that is repaid at maturity. The principal often (but not always) equals the initial amount borrowed. Bondholders essentially make loans to the government or corporation in exchange for being paid interest. Interest payments are often (but not always) made on a regular basis. The **coupon** is the annual interest payment on a bond. Typically, in exchange for lending money to the bond issuer (seller), the bondholder is paid the coupon interest annually and receives back the principal at the date of maturity.

Government and Corporate Bonds

Governments and corporations often borrow money in the bond market. The U.S. federal government is a particularly large borrower in the bond market, the world's largest during most years. This is how the government finances the national debt (see Chapter 7). There are two major types of bonds issued by the federal governments in the United States: Treasury bonds and Treasury bills. In addition, state and local governments and corporations issue bonds. Exhibit 2 summarizes the four main types of bonds.

Treasury Bonds: Federal Government Bonds with Maturity over One Year A *Treasury bond* is a bond issued by the U.S. federal government with maturity dates from 1 to 30 years. Treasury bonds are commonly referred to as "Treasuries," and bonds with a maturity between 1 and 10 years are also called "Treasury notes" (or T-notes).

capital gain The profit from the sale of a property or financial asset resulting from a price increase between the time of purchase and the time of sale.

dividends The portion of profits paid to stockowners per share of stock.

bond A tradable legally binding obligation to repay borrowed money and interest.

coupon The annual interest payment on a bond.

EXHIBIT 2 Four Main Types of Bonds in the United States

	Treasury Bills	Treasury Bonds	Municipal Bonds	Corporate Bonds
Issuer	Federal Government	Federal Government	State and Local Governments	Corporations
Maturity	Up to 1 year	Over 1 year	Typically, more than 1 year	Typically, more than 1 year
Default Risk	Near zero	Near zero	Some, but varies	Some, but varies
Nicknamed	T-bills	Treasuries	Munis	Corporates

In the United States, there are four main types of bonds: Treasury bills, Treasury bonds, municipal bonds, and corporate bonds.

Treasury Bills: Federal Government Bonds with Maturity up to One Year A *Treasury bill* is a bond issued by the U.S. federal government with a maturity date up to one year and no coupon payment. Treasury bills are commonly referred to as "T-bills." The buyer typically benefits by purchasing the T-bill at a price less than the principal due at maturity.

Municipal Bonds: Bonds Issued by State and Local Governments A *municipal bond* is a bond issued by a state or local government, often to fund specific projects. For example, a municipal bond may be issued to pay for a new school, rail system, or roads. In the United States, interest income received by municipal bond owners is frequently exempt from federal income taxes. Consequently, municipal bonds typically pay a lower interest rate than otherwise equivalent bonds. This is because bond buyers prefer to receive interest payments that are not taxable and are willing to accept a lower interest rate to avoid paying taxes. Municipal bonds are commonly called "Munis."

Corporate Bonds: Bonds Issued by Corporations Corporations and other businesses are also able to borrow money in the bond market. A *corporate bond* is a bond issued by a corporation. Corporations issue bonds to raise funds to pay bills or expand. Such bonds are often referred to as "Corporates."

The Determinants of Interest Rates and Bond Prices

Since bondholders are legally entitled to interest payments, they are paid before stockholders. As a result, bond prices are usually more stable than stock prices, which fluctuate with changes in the expected earnings of the associated firm. This makes bonds an attractive financial investment option for those who wish to minimize the risk of losses. On the flip side, not having an ownership stake also reduces upside potential if the corporation is more successful than expected. There are three key determinants of bond prices: the underlying interest rate, risk, and time to maturity.

A Negative Relationship Between Interest Rates and Bond Prices Interest rates frequently change. When interest rates go *down,* the price of previously issued bonds goes *up,* and when interest rates go *up,* the price of previously issued bonds goes *down.*

Consider the following example, with an infinite maturity to make the math easier to follow. A bond pays $5 in interest payments a year forever. In the future, the bond can be sold to someone else at its current price. The $5 is the annual coupon payment. If the going interest rate is 5%, the price of the bond will be $100. Why? Because a bond buyer will pay $100 to receive back $5 in interest every year, as $5 is 5% of $100. Now, if the going market interest rate increases to 10%, the price of the bond will fall to $50. Why? This happens because if market interest rates rise to 10%, then other bonds will offer a 10% rate of return. In that case, no one would be willing to pay more than $50 for a bond with an annual coupon payment of $5, as $5 is 10% of $50. This illustrates an extremely important concept: There is a negative relationship between bond prices and market interest rates. As you will see in the Appendix, the actual mathematics of bond prices is somewhat more complicated when the bond has a specific maturity date.

The Positive Relationship Between Interest Rates and Risk Any attribute of bonds that makes them less desirable will also tend to reduce their price and raise the interest rate buyers receive. Because there is more risk of default on corporate bonds, they pay higher interest than Treasury bonds.

Consider the following example. Two companies are issuing bonds with a $5 coupon: "Safe AAA" and "Unsafe Junk." Which company's bonds would you be willing to pay a higher price for? Since Safe AAA is less risky, many financial investors would be willing to pay more for its bonds than the riskier Unsafe Junk bonds. Since the price of Safe AAA company's bonds is higher, the interest rate it pays is lower. In other words, financial institutions are willing to lend at a lower interest rate to companies with a low default risk. However, don't be fooled by terms like *junk bonds*. Although they might have a higher risk of default, they also offer a higher interest rate to compensate you for that risk. Thus, because an investment is called "junk" does not necessarily make it a poor choice, just one with greater risk.

∧ Traders busy at work.

The Positive Relationship Between Interest Rates and Maturity Interest rates are typically higher when governments or corporations issue bonds with a longer time to maturity. This is to compensate lenders for added risk that occurs when they lend out their money for a longer period of time. However, on rare occasion, longer-term rates can be lower than short-term rates. That happens when investors expect market interest rates to fall over time.

Credit-Rating Agencies

The **default risk** on a bond is the likelihood that a borrower will fail to make the required payment on debt. You have just seen that the greater the default risk on a bond, the higher the interest rate a borrower must pay and the lower the price of the bond. But how does one measure *default risk*?

Estimating default risk is difficult. It involves taking a detailed look at the financial statements and economic outlook of the borrower. To simplify matters, there are several rating agencies that evaluate the default risk on bonds. The three largest rating agencies are Moody's, Standard & Poor's, and Fitch; Exhibit 3 lists the bond rating categories for each agency.

In general, bonds with a credit rating of Aaa or AAA have the lowest risk of default. To illustrate the bond ratings and their meaning, we'll examine the ratings format that both Fitch and Standard & Poor's use. "AAA" and "AA" are high credit-quality investment grade with the lowest risk of default. "A" and "BBB" are medium credit-quality investment grade and represent a low risk of default. "BB," "B," "CCC," "CC," and "C" are low credit-quality and non-investment grade. Since these bonds have a greater

default risk The likelihood that a borrower will fail to make the required payment on debt.

EXHIBIT 3 Major Credit Risk Agencies and Various Ratings of Default Risk

Moody's Investor Services	Standard & Poor's (S&P) and Fitch	Meaning
Aaa	AAA	Highest credit quality
Aa	AA	Lowest default risk
A	A	Medium credit quality
Baa	BBB	Low default risk
Ba	BB	Low credit quality
B	B	Non-investment grade
Caa	CCC	"Junk bonds"
Ca	CC	
C	C	
	D	Bonds in default

The default risk on a bond is the likelihood that a borrower will fail to make the required payment on debt. There are three major credit-rating agencies that rate bonds based on their default risk.

Data from: Jeff Jewell and Miles Livingston, "A Comparison of Bond Ratings from Moody's S&P and Fitch IBCA," *Financial Markets, Institutions and Instruments* 8, no. 4 (November 1999): 1–45; "Bond Ratings," *Investopedia,* May 5, 2016, http://www.investopedia.com/exam-guide/series-7/debt-securities/bond-ratings.asp.

chance of default, they are sometimes referred to as "speculative bonds" or "junk bonds." Finally, "D" are bonds already in default.

Why would a financial investor purchase a B-rated bond over an AAA-rated bond? The B-rated bond pays a higher rate of interest and has a lower price. As you will see in a subsequent section, there is a trade-off between risk and expected return. The lower-rated bonds will pay a higher return *if* (emphasis added) one gets paid back in full.

📊 BUSINESS BRIEF Bond-Rating Agencies Understate Default Risk

Bond-rating agencies such as Moody's, Fitch, and Standard & Poor's have been around since the early part of the twentieth century, with their ratings widely used by government regulators and financial investors. In 2008, these agencies were assigned the job of rating a type of security backed by payments on home loans, known as mortgage-backed securities.

Rating agencies seldom change their ratings—and when they do, it is usually big news. In the months prior to the summer of 2008, the rating agencies collectively lowered their ratings on nearly $2 trillion of securities backed by home mortgages from AAA (highest quality) to CCC (junk). Suddenly, bondholders around the globe who had only months earlier believed they owned some of the safest financial investments available found themselves holding junk bonds. To compound the problem, in some instances, holders of these securities were required by law to sell their position because government regulations did not allow them to hold risky assets. This meant the immediate forced sale of such investments at the exact time others were being forced to take the same action. The default of many of these securities and the corresponding credit downgrade—combined with changes in macroeconomic conditions, a collapse in housing prices, and sharp decline in stock prices—contributed to what is now commonly called the Great Recession.*

*James Surowiecki, "Ratings Downgrade," *The New Yorker,* May 9, 2017, http://www.newyorker.com /magazine/2009/09/28/ratings-downgrade.

10.3 FINANCIAL INVESTMENTS AND PERSONAL FINANCE

In 1973, Burton Malkiel wrote a seminal financial investment strategy book entitled *A Random Walk Down Wall Street*. Malkiel made this controversial claim: "A blind-folded monkey throwing darts at a newspaper's financial pages could select a (stock) portfolio that would do just as well as one carefully selected by experts."[2] In 2013, an examination of 48 years of stock market data confirmed what numerous previous studies have found: When comparing the gains of randomly chosen stocks—as might be selected by a monkey throwing darts—to stocks chosen by paid financial professionals, the contest is not even close. It turns out Malkiel was being generous to the financial professionals. The *monkey* won![3]

Of course, the monkey example is just an analogy. The real point is that it's hard for even the experts to beat the *overall average* stock market return, or a group of those stocks picked at random. The reason why is interesting. If most experts were able to see that one group of stocks was superior to another, then the demand for this group of stocks would increase. This would raise the price of the desirable stocks high enough until they were no longer considered above-average investments. Success in the stock market isn't merely about figuring out which companies will be successful; it involves determining which companies will do *better than the market consensus*. And that's quite difficult. Indeed, when the business media relays information on corporate earnings or macroeconomic conditions, it often reports both the actual data and the *expected values* (consensus). The few investors who have "beaten the market" fairly consistently, such as Warren Buffett, often become rich and famous.

Trade-Off between Risk and Potential Return

Making a financial investment involves deciding how best to address the trade-off between risk and return. Recall that high-quality investment grade bonds have a lower default risk but, *on average*, pay bondholders a lower interest rate than non-investment grade bonds with a higher default risk. This also applies when comparing stock and bond investments. In the event of a bankruptcy, bondholders are more likely to receive payments or partial payments than stockholders. In the long run, risky assets such as stocks offer higher average returns than safer assets such as bonds (or money kept in the bank). It is not uncommon for stocks to lose half of their value or more in short periods of time. With risk comes the potential for large gains, but also for major losses.

Research in behavioral finance has shown that average investors often panic during stock market crashes. Losing enormous amounts of money puts fear into the hearts and minds of even very experienced investors. Major stock market declines frequently result in average investors selling at low prices and incurring losses. Of course, every sale is also a purchase, so presumably the smarter and more experienced investors buy shares when their price is low.

It is useful to have a basic understanding of how risk and returns are estimated. One measure of risk is the standard deviation of returns. *Standard deviation* is a statistical measure of variability. A standard deviation of 20% (for stocks) means that stocks will do 20 percentage points worse than average roughly once every six years.

Average returns of a financial asset are calculated by estimating the *geometric mean*, which is used when averaging rates of return. While the mathematics of calculating geometric means go beyond the scope of this textbook, they can be estimated easily on Google Sheets or Microsoft Excel. To see the importance of using geometric means, consider a $100 investment that increases in value by 50% one year, then decreases in value by 33.3% the next year. In this case, the simple mathematical average return would be +8.7% ((50 − 33.3)/2). However, such a financial investment would see no change in

EXHIBIT 4   Return and Risk by Asset Class and the Benefits of Diversification, 1928–2016

Stocks typically have higher returns than Treasury bonds; however, they also entail greater risk. A portfolio of one third of each asset (T-bills, Treasury bonds, and stocks) shows the benefits of diversification. Such a combination has a higher return and lower risk than a portfolio of Treasury bonds alone. In general, owning different asset classes is an effective tool to reduce but not eliminate risk.

Data from: Authors' calculations using data from the NYU Stern School of Business.

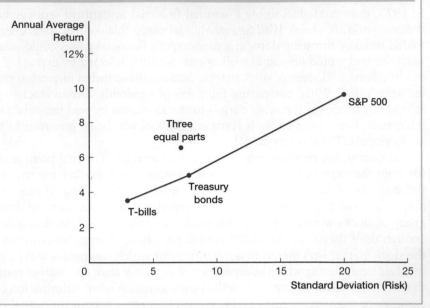

value over the two-year period. The $100 would first grow to $150, but then decline by 33.3% back to $100. As a consequence, the geometric return would be zero.

The trade-off between risk and return is demonstrated in Exhibit 4 using annual return data for stocks, Treasury bonds, and Treasury bills from 1928 to 2016. When compared to Treasury bonds and bills, stocks have both higher average returns and higher risk. Moreover, due to their longer date to maturity, Treasury bonds are riskier than Treasury bills. As a result, Treasury bonds have higher risk and higher returns, on average, than their Treasury bill counterparts.

A Few Simple Guidelines for Financial Investing

There are a few simple guidelines for personal finance (buying stocks and bonds) that can be very useful in the long run:

- Maximize diversification to help manage risk.
- Make financial investments early in life and often.
- Minimize the costs of making financial investments.

Maximize Diversification One key to successful financial investing is to diversify. **Diversification** is an investment technique that reduces risk by putting funds into unrelated assets and asset classes.

You may have heard people say, "Avoid putting all your eggs in the same basket." This means that if you drop the basket, you will end up with no eggs. Consider the following quote from the Talmud (ca. 1200 B.C.–500 B.C.):

> Let every man divide his money into three parts, and invest a third in land, a third in business and a third let him keep by him in reserve.

A modern equivalent would be to stay diversified by owning many different assets and asset classes. If you owned nothing but Internet stocks in the year 2000, then you lost most of your fortune over the next few years. Google and Facebook stocks did not exist in 2000, and many early Internet companies went bankrupt.

Diversifying a portfolio of stocks lowers risk when compared to only owning a single company's stock. By owning many stocks in different sectors of the economy, or even different countries, investors can reduce the risks associated with any *one* sector or *one* country. It is important to note that this strategy does not eliminate risk. Although owning a cross section of stocks is considerably less risky than owning an individual stock, even stock market indexes occasionally lose a sizable portion of their value. Indeed, there are times when most stock market indexes around the globe fall sharply, such as during the 2008 global financial crisis.

Modern financial markets have made it easy to diversify. A variety of financial products or "funds" allow investors to purchase hundreds of different stocks at the same time. An individual who invests in one of these funds will indirectly own many different financial assets. Examples include mutual funds and exchange-traded funds.

A **mutual fund** is a financial investment fund that pools money from multiple investors to purchase a portfolio of stocks, bonds, or other financial assets. Mutual funds do not trade on a stock exchange. Investors need to be aware that *some* funds own stocks in closely related firms, such as a technology fund or a health-care fund. For optimal diversification, one should own stocks in many different industries and many different countries.

An **exchange traded fund (ETF)** is a fund that pools money from multiple investors and trades on a stock exchange. The first ETF was introduced in 1993. It traded the entire S&P 500 index as a single share under the stock ticker (name) "SPY." In 2018, there were over a billion shares of SPY outstanding valued at over $300 billion.

Even greater diversification can be achieved by including other assets such as real estate or bonds, especially Treasury bonds. Historically, Treasury bonds have performed relatively well during sharp stock market declines. For instance, Treasury bonds rose in price during the severe financial crisis of 2008, when most stocks declined. Indeed, Treasury bond prices often rise during recession years, when many other investments fall in price. Owning both stocks and bonds is less risky than owning only stocks.

Owning a mixture of different types of stocks and bonds is an important way to reduce risks. Exhibit 4 shows the benefits of diversification with a simple portfolio of one third of each asset (T-bills, Treasury bonds, and stocks). This combination of assets has historically produced a higher return and lower risk than a portfolio of Treasury bonds alone. In general, owning different asset classes is an effective tool for reducing risk. Even in this example, however, some risk remains.

Make Financial Investments Early in Life and Often A second key to successful financial investing is to start early in life. If one hopes to become a multimillionaire, wealthy, or even just secure a comfortable retirement, then it is commonsense to begin making financial investments at a young age. Many people underestimate the importance of **compound interest**, interest earned on previously earned and reinvested interest. If you earn a 7% rate of return on your investments, the value of your assets roughly doubles every 10 years. Over long periods of time, that makes a big difference. An individual who saves $5,000 a year starting at age 20 will amass over $2.2 million by retirement (age 66) if his or her financial investments rise at an 8% annual rate (which is somewhere between the historical returns on stocks and Treasury bonds).

Minimize the Costs of Making Financial Investments Earlier in the section, it was claimed that a monkey throwing darts could outperform a financial expert in picking stocks. Because the monkey picks stocks at random, the expected return should equal that of a representative group of all stocks. One popular low-cost diversification method is an **index fund**, a mutual fund or ETF that automatically invests in all of the stocks in a particular stock index. The SPY S&P 500 ETF mentioned earlier is an example of this approach. The return on this index fund will be almost identical to the *average* return of investors who buy stocks in the S&P 500 index. Since all stocks in the index are included, it is very easy for mutual funds to set up this kind of fund.

In contrast, "managed" mutual funds have a variety of extra costs that are ultimately borne by the buyer. They require hiring financial managers and paying for a great deal of expensive research by Wall Street experts on which stocks to include: all of which adds to the costs. When such extra costs are factored in, it

diversification An investment technique that reduces risk by putting funds into unrelated assets and asset classes.

mutual fund A financial investment fund that pools money from multiple investors to purchase a portfolio of stocks, bonds, or other financial assets.

exchange trade fund (ETF) A fund that pools money from multiple investors and trades on a stock exchange.

compound interest Interest earned on previously earned and reinvested interest.

index fund A mutual fund or ETF that automatically invests in all of the stocks in a particular stock index.

becomes difficult for even highly skilled fund managers to consistently surpass the returns of index funds. Our hypothetical monkey comfortably beats the average expert after these costs are included.

Some index funds have annual expenses as low as one half of one tenth of 1% of the amount invested (0.05%). Such index funds allow holders to own a diversified basket of stocks at a very low cost. In contrast, it is not uncommon for actively managed mutual funds to have annual expenses 20 or 40 times higher (above 1 or 2%).

To understand the importance of administrative fees, consider the following. Earlier we noted that an individual who saves $5,000 per year starting at age 20 will amass over $2.2 million dollars by age 66 if average annual returns are 8% per year. Suppose that instead of using low-cost index funds, a manager was hired, and as a result of administrative fees the average returns are 6% per year. In this case, the individual will end up with $1.2 million dollars at age 66—a full $1 million dollars less!

Efficient Market Hypothesis and the Randomness of Financial Investments

One reason why the "dartboard" theory of investing does surprisingly well is that financial asset prices tend to move somewhat randomly. Unless one has "inside information" not available to other investors, it is difficult to know which way stock prices are likely to move. If you do have inside information, it may be illegal to trade stocks using that knowledge.

Many economists believe that financial asset prices already incorporate all the publicly available information that is relevant. Thus, if it were widely known that a company was likely to do much better in the future, its price would have already been bid up to a level where the expected rate of return was comparable to that of similar alternative investments. Because all publicly available information is already factored into the price by both the buyers and sellers of a stock, it is exceedingly difficult for financial professionals to consistently do better than the market average.

Those who follow professional sports may find the following analogy helpful. Even if you know which team participating in the Super Bowl is likely to win, it is difficult to make money betting on the Super Bowl. This is because the point spread already incorporates the views of bettors as to the relative strength of the two teams. To win a bet on the favorite, they must do better than expected. In a similar way, a very profitable company must do even better than expected, to outperform the market average.

The **efficient market hypothesis (EMH)** is the theory that financial asset prices incorporate all relevant publicly available information. This theory implies that one would have to be very lucky to consistently achieve above-average returns *on a risk-adjusted basis.* In other words, if you think a stock will increase in price due to a recent news event, chances are that the stock price already reflects such information. In general, economists believe markets are at least somewhat efficient, but there is some disagreement among them on the extent of financial market efficiency.

The EMH implies that the current stock price captures the collective wisdom of all buyers and sellers of the stock. The idea that the market as a whole is smarter than any individual is sometimes called "the wisdom of the crowd." Consider the following analogy. Studies have shown that if you ask an individual how many jellybeans are contained in a large glass jar, the estimates are often very inaccurate, as you'd expect. However, if you ask several hundred people the same question, the average prediction of the entire group is frequently very close to correct. This is the very concept that underlies the EMH—the wisdom of the crowd. Each individual knows a little bit about the market. But according to the EMH, when thousands of individuals trade a stock, they collectively move the price close to its fundamental value.

If one combines the view that markets are efficient (and not all experts agree on this point) and the fees charged by investment managers for their research, the implication is that even an expertly managed mutual fund would be unlikely to outperform an index fund that has very low expenses (or even a monkey throwing a dart at the stock page of the morning newspaper).

Stock index funds cannot outperform the overall market as the index fund owns that market. In contrast, owning individual stocks or a fund of select stocks has the *potential* to outperform. Likewise, a stock fund manager may outperform the market by owning riskier than average stocks. However, recall that there is a trade-off between risk and return. The efficient market hypothesis merely claims that it is difficult to outperform the market *on a risk-adjusted basis*. Those who take great risks will occasionally do much better than the market average. But they also risk doing much worse.

One criticism of the EMH is that people are not always as rational as economic theory assumes them to be. A stockholder who sells in a panic is one example of irrational behavior. When many investors behave irrationally at the same time, a market "bubble" may emerge. A **bubble** is a period of time when prices rise above their true fundamental value as investors get swept up in enthusiasm that prices will rise ever higher. Perhaps the first recorded bubble occurred in 1637 when rampant speculation drove the price of a single tulip higher than the annual income of skilled craftsmen. Some experts believe that bubbles occurred during the Internet stock boom of the late 1990s and subsequent bust of 2000, and with the rise in U.S. housing prices that peaked in 2006 before falling.

 BUSINESS BRIEF Active Fund Managers Tend to Underperform in the Long Run

In 2008, Warren Buffet made a million dollar bet that the S&P 500 would outperform a basket of actively managed "hedge" funds over the next decade.* Hedge funds are private financial investment accounts that only the wealthy are allowed to invest in. The fees in hedge funds are considerably higher than those in stock index funds and other mutual funds.

Not surprisingly, Buffet comfortably won his bet, as the S&P 500 easily beat the alternative group of hedge funds. Indeed, very few active fund managers are able to beat the overall average return in the stock market over a 10-year period. Even worse, the best performers may not be the best performers over the *next* 10-year period, which is what really matters.† The efficient markets hypothesis is the basis of Burton Malkiel's controversial claim that a blindfolded dart-throwing monkey does better at picking stocks than most experts.

For this reason, many economists suggest that average investors consider owning index funds rather than actively managed funds. These funds have lower costs, and average investors have almost no way of knowing which of the very few managed funds will end up outperforming the market. Even experts have great difficulty doing so. Buffett—one of the world's most successful stock pickers—famously (and

efficient market hypothesis (EMH) The theory that financial asset prices incorporate all relevant publicly available information.

bubble A period of time when prices rise above their true fundamental value as investors get swept up in enthusiasm that prices will rise ever higher.

publicly) advised trustees of his will to put 10% of the cash in short-term government bonds and 90% in a very low-cost S&P 500 index fund.[‡]

[*]Roger Lowenstein, "Why Warren Buffett Is Winning His $1 Million Bet Against Hedge Funds," *Fortune.com,* May 11, 2016, http://fortune.com/2016/05/11/warren-buffett-hedge-fund-bet/; Jeff Cox, "Your Mutual Fund Manager Has Probably Failed for the Past 15 Years," *CNBC,* April 12, 2017, http://www.cnbc.com/2017/04/12/bad-times -for-active-managers-almost-none-have-beaten-the-market-over-the-past-15-years.html.

[†]Roger Lowenstein, "Why Warren Buffett Is Winning His $1 Million Bet Against Hedge Funds," *Fortune.com,* May 11, 2016, http://fortune.com/2016/05/11/warren-buffett-hedge-fund-bet/.

[‡]Berkshire Hathwaway, shareholder letter, 2013, http://www.berkshirehathaway.com/letters/2013ltr.pdf.

BUSINESS TAKEAWAY

Businesses ranging from small startups to large firms like Snapchat, Facebook, and Under Armour use financial markets to raise enormous amounts of financial capital. Of course, financial firms operating in the stock and bond markets are often themselves big businesses. This chapter, however, provides economic insights into these markets from the perspective of personal finance.

Economists focus on trade-offs, an idea that is very useful when considering what sort of financial investments to make. Stocks and bonds give financial investors an opportunity to grow their money over time but doing so entails risk. In general, higher risk is associated with higher potential returns. A wise investor must decide how much risk he or she is willing to take, in order to seek higher rates of return in the long run. Diversifying financial investments—that is, owning a variety of different financial assets—is one way of managing both long- and short-term risk.

Economists also emphasize that it is important to consider management fees and other expenses associated with financial investment when estimating the potential return. They argue that it is nearly impossible for even the most knowledgeable and experienced stock pickers to consistently beat the market over a long period of time; thus, they often recommend low-cost index funds. Indeed, the increasing popularity of low-cost index funds partly reflects the growing influence of economic ideas in the investment world. Taxes are also an important consideration, and many financial strategies—such as buying municipal bonds—reflect a desire to minimize tax liabilities.

CHAPTER STUDY GUIDE

10.1   THE STOCK MARKET

A **financial investment** is a way of employing savings and refers to the purchase of stocks and bonds. A **stock** is a share of ownership in a corporation. Previously issued stocks trade on secondary stock exchanges around the world. A **stock market index** is an aggregate value of a set of representative stocks. The S&P 500 is a U.S. stock index consisting of 500 large company stocks. The NASDAQ Composite Index is a U.S. stock index of over 3,000 technology companies that trade on the NASDAQ stock exchange. The Dow Jones Industrial Average (Dow) is a U.S. stock index consisting of 30 leading companies. The S&P 500 and NASDAQ are cap-weighted indices, meaning they are based on

the market capitalization of the companies included in the index. Financial experts often look at a company's P/E ratio when evaluating the value of a stock, though other measures exist. The **P/E ratio** or **price/ earnings ratio** is the price of a stock divided by its earnings per share. Three factors that impact the P/E ratio are the expected growth of a company's earnings, the perceived riskiness of the company, and long-term interest rates. There are two ways **stockholders**, the owners of a corporation, can realize a gain from their financial investment. A **capital gain** is the profit from the sale of a property or financial asset resulting from a price increase between the time of purchase and the time of sale. **Dividends** are the portion of profits paid to stockowners per share of stock. Dividends can be a fixed amount or vary based on a variety of factors, such as the level of profit and the extent to which the corporation chooses to hold onto profits to be used for corporate expansion.

10.2 THE BOND MARKET

A **bond** is a tradable legally binding obligation to repay borrowed money and interest. Unlike the owner of stocks, bondholders have no claim of ownership of the business or government. Most bonds have some general attributes. The typical bond has a specified date of *maturity;* the date by which the principal on a bond must be paid in full. The *principal* (or *par value*) is the face value of the bond that is repaid at maturity. Bondholders essentially make loans to the government or corporation in exchange for paid interest. The **coupon** is the annual interest payment on a bond. A *Treasury bill* is a bond issued by the U.S. federal government with a maturity date up to one year and no coupon payment. A *Treasury bond* is a bond issued by the U.S. federal government with a maturity date from 1 to 30 years. A *municipal bond* is a bond issued by a state or local government, often to fund specific projects. A *corporate bond* is a bond issued by a corporation. A negative relationship exists between interest rates and bond prices. Interest rates are usually higher on riskier bonds and those with greater time to maturity. The lowest interest rates occur on short term government bonds (*Treasury Bills*). The **default risk** is the likelihood that a borrower will fail to make the required payment on debt. Default risk is estimated by credit rating agencies such as Moody's Investor Services, Standard & Poor's, and Fitch.

10.3 FINANCIAL INVESTMENTS AND PERSONAL FINANCE

It is difficult for even the experts to beat the overall average stock market return. In general, there is a trade-off between risk and potential return. Riskier assets such as stocks have the potential for greater returns but also the potential for greater losses. Some generally accepted guidelines for buying and selling stocks include maximizing diversification to manage risk, making financial investments early in life, and minimizing the costs of making financial investments. **Diversification** is an investment technique that reduces risk by putting funds into unrelated assets and asset classes. Modern financial markets have made it easy to diversify with mutual funds and exchange traded funds. A **mutual fund** is a financial investment fund that pools money from multiple investors to purchase a portfolio of stocks, bonds, or other financial assets. An **exchange traded fund (ETF)** is a fund that pools money from multiple investors and trades on a stock exchange. Starting to invest early in life takes advantage of **compound interest**, interest earned on previously earned and reinvested interest. An **index fund** is a mutual fund or ETF that automatically invests in all of the stocks in a particular stock index. The **efficient market hypothesis (EMH)** is the theory that financial asset prices incorporate all relevant publicly available information. A **bubble** is a period of time when prices rise above their true fundamental value as investors get swept up in enthusiasm that prices will rise ever higher.

TOP TEN TERMS AND CONCEPTS

(1) Financial Investment

(2) Stock and Stock Market Index

(3) P/E Ratio

(4) Capital Gains

(5) Dividends

(6) Bonds

(7) Coupon

(8) Mutual Funds and Exchange Traded Funds (ETF)

(9) Index Fund

(10) Efficient Market Hypothesis

STUDY PROBLEMS

1. Look up the price, P/E ratio, and market cap of five stocks.

2. Which of the following financial investments do you expect will pay a higher interest rate?

   a. a U.S. government bond with 30 years to maturity, or a U.S. bond with 5 years to maturity

   b. the corporate bond of a company rated A, or the corporate bond of a company rated C

   c. a U.S. government bond, or a bond with equivalent maturity from Greece

3. Compare and contrast stocks and bonds.

4. In 2016, Volkswagen (VW) was sued by the U.S. Justice Department for allegedly installing devices on their autos designed to "dupe emissions tests" on over half a million vehicles. In this scenario, would you rather be a stockholder or bondholder? What do you expect happened to the value of VW stocks and bonds once the government initiated this lawsuit?

5. 📊 Under each of the following scenarios, would you rather be a stock or bondholder? Explain your responses.

   a. A company expects to see a sharp increase in earnings.

   b. A company is facing bankruptcy.

   c. A company's earnings are on the decline due to a recession.

   d. A small company is about to be purchased by a larger firm at a high price.

6. The economy of South Africa is a heavy exporter of mined commodities. In 2015, the prices of commodities such as gold and silver plummeted. In turn, this reduced government tax revenue. Credit agencies decided to subsequently downgrade the debt of South Africa. What does this mean in terms of the borrowing cost for the government of South Africa? What impact will this development have on the price of South African bonds?[4]

7. 📊 Explain the efficient market hypothesis.

8. Are market bubbles such as the tech bubble of 2000 consistent with the efficient market hypothesis? Why or why not?

9. Describe what happened in 2007 when major credit-rating agencies suddenly lowered the default risk rating of many mortgage-backed securities.

10. 📊 Suppose your friend tells you about a drug company that has just found a cure for cancer. He suggests that the company's stock will be a great investment. Why might you be skeptical?

11. Back in 2001, many employees of Enron Corporation had their retirement plans invested in Enron stock. Even if you don't know anything about the Enron case, discuss why such an investment decision might not be a good idea.

10

CHAPTER APPENDIX

Present Value and the Time Value of Money

If someone were to offer you $1 million today or $1 million in 20 years, which would you choose? Most people would choose the money today. This example underlies one of the cornerstones of financial analysis, the concept known as the **time value of money**, the idea that the value of having money today is better than receiving the same amount of money in the future. The money one has today can be invested and earn interest, boosting the future value of your money holdings.

Present value is the discounted current value of a future sum of money. Discounting typically occurs at a prevailing interest rate. Financial analysis involves discounting future *cash flows,* the total amount of money going into and coming out of a business. Cash flow is a central component of modern finance and accounting. One million dollars received in 20 years needs to be discounted to determine its present value.

For example, a business may need to spend a large sum of money today to purchase a factory and machines that will generate cash flows (income) in future years. To assess whether building a factory is worthwhile, that business must discount the future cash flows (net profits) the new factory will generate and compare that amount with the dollar amount needed to build the factory. If the present value of the sum of the discounted future cash flows *is greater than* the amount needed to build the factory, then the project is worthwhile. In the same way, bond prices are determined by discounting future interest payments (coupons) and the principal received at maturity.

For instance, a factory that costs $100 million and generates $5 million per year in profits for 50 years might seem highly profitable at first glance. After all, $5 million in profits for 50 years adds up to $250 million, which is much more than the cost of the factory. But such an analysis fails to account for the time value of money. Suppose you could buy a corporate bond paying 6% interest. In that case, the business should invest the $100 million in the bond rather than the factory. Doing so will result in $6 million in interest per year, which is more than the $5 million in profit per year generated by the factory. The bond offers a higher rate of return.

The Mathematics of Calculating Present Value

While businesses typically estimate present value by discounting future cash flows, we begin by reversing the process, to better understand the mathematics involved. Suppose an individual has $100 in a bank. The bank pays an interest rate of 10%. How much is the *future value,* in one year, of $100 today? The answer is $110. Specifically, the money grows by the $10 in interest received:

$$FV = PV + \text{Interest received} = PV \times (1 + \text{Interest rate})$$

The present value is multiplied by (1 + the interest rate) to get the future value. The "1" allows the saver to receive back the initial deposit, while the "+ interest rate" is the interest the saver receives expressed as a decimal:

$$FV = PV \times (1 + \text{Interest rate}) = \$100 \times (1 + \text{Interest rate}) = \$100 \times 1.10 = \$110$$

What if the money remains in the bank for two years? In this case, the $100 needs to be multiplied by "1 + interest rate" twice. When the interest rate is 10%, $100 grows to $110 in one year; then the $110 grows by 10% or $11 to $121 in Year 2. This can be calculated as $100 times 1.10^2, which equals $121.

time value of money
The idea that the value of money today is greater than receiving the same amount of money in the future.

present value The discounted current value of a future sum of money.

213

More generally, if the money is kept in the bank for t years, the present value ($100) needs to be multiplied by "1 + interest rate" t times. In the following formula, i is the nominal interest rate and t is the number of years money remains in the bank (or is discounted):

$$FV = PV \times (1 + i)^t \tag{A1}$$

As noted above, businesses are primarily concerned with present value. Therefore, they need to discount a future anticipated cash flow. Dividing both sides of equation (A1) by $(1 + i)^t$, we get:

$$PV = \frac{FV}{(1 + i)^t} \tag{A2}$$

Calculating PV simply reverses the process of calculating FV. If the one-year future value of $100 at 10% interest is $110, then the present value of $110 received a year from today, discounted at 10%, is equal to $100:

$$PV = \frac{FV}{(1 + i)} = \frac{\$110}{(1 + 0.10)} = \$100$$

We are now able to discount $1 million received in 20 years. If the prevailing discount rate (interest rate) is 10%, the present value is $148,644. To see this in worked-out form, in equation (A2), replace FV with $1,000,000, $(1 + i)$ with 1.10, and t with 20:

$$\$148,644 = \frac{\$1,000,000}{1.10^{20}}$$

Understanding the Present Value Formula

For many, understanding how money grows is easier than discounting future values. However, estimating present value is the more useful concept in business. Fortunately, the two concepts are mathematically related. We start with the formula for future value [equation (A1)]:

$$FV = PV \times (1 + i)^t$$

Dividing both sides by $(1 + i)^t$, we get:

$$\frac{FV}{(1 + i)^t} = PV \times \frac{(1 + i)^t}{(1 + i)^t}$$

Since $\frac{(1 + i)^t}{(1 + i)^t} = 1$, the above expression can be rearranged:

$$PV = \frac{FV}{(1 + i)^t}$$

Calculating the Present Value of a Bond One can think of a bond as a financial asset that promises to pay a fixed amount of money at specified dates in the future. The present value of a bond is essentially the price of the bond for a given rate of interest. Suppose a bond has a five-year maturity, $50 coupon, and $1,000 principal payment due in five years. What is the present value of the bond if the interest rate is 5%? If the interest rate is 10%?

In this scenario, we need to discount five future payments:

- $50 for each of the next 4 years.
- $50 for the fifth year's coupon plus $1,000 for the principal payment. This totals $1,050.

Calculating the present value of the bond at an interest rate of 5% entails making five present value calculations and summing the result:

$$PV = \frac{\$50}{(1.05)^1} + \frac{\$50}{(1.05)^2} + \frac{\$50}{(1.05)^3} + \frac{\$50}{(1.05)^4} + \frac{\$1,050}{(1.05)^5}$$

$$\$1,000 = \$47.62 + \$45.35 + \$43.19 + \$41.14 + \$822.70$$

The present value of the bond is $1,000 (which happens to be the principal of the bond). Now suppose the interest rate *doubles* to 10%. Recall that earlier in the chapter, we saw that higher interest rates depress bond prices. Now let's see by how much. Once again, we need to calculate the value of the bond by making five present value calculations—this time with the interest rate at 10%—and summing the results. The answer indicates that the price falls to $810.46:

$$PV = \frac{\$50}{(1.10)^1} + \frac{\$50}{(1.10)^2} + \frac{\$50}{(1.10)^3} + \frac{\$50}{(1.10)^4} + \frac{\$1,050}{(1.10)^5}$$

$$\$810.46 = \$45.45 + \$41.32 + \$37.57 + \$34.15 + \$651.97$$

Calculating the Present Value of a Lottery Prize You have just won a lottery prize of $100 million! Congratulations. Actually, the lottery is for 25 payments of $4 million: one immediate payment and 24 additional payments of $4 million each year.

The lottery offers you a deal. You can either collect the $100 million prize in installments *or* receive $50 million immediately. How would you go about making such a decision? The answer involves a present value calculation. You first must decide what rate of interest to use in discounting future payments. The calculations below discount the annual $4 million payments at 5% and at 10%:

$$PV = \$4,000,000 + \frac{\$4,000,000}{(1.05)^1} + \frac{\$4,000,000}{(1.05)^2} + \cdots + \frac{\$4,000,000}{(1.05)^{23}} + \frac{\$4,000,000}{(1.05)^{24}}$$

$$= \$59,194,567 \text{ (when discounted at 5\%)}$$

$$PV = \$4,000,000 + \frac{\$4,000,000}{(1.10)^1} + \frac{\$4,000,000}{(1.10)^2} + \cdots + \frac{\$4,000,000}{(1.10)^{23}} + \frac{\$4,000,000}{(1.10)^{24}}$$

$$= \$39,938,976 \text{ (when discounted at 10\%)}$$

Which rate of discount should one use? That's a rather difficult question, but in principle you'd look at various investment alternatives to estimate the rate of return you could earn if you invested the net winnings today, for a period of 24 years.

As with the inverse relationship between interest rates and bond prices, the present value of the lottery prize is lower when discounted at a higher interest rate. In the above example, the $50 million up-front payment offer from the lottery is a good deal if you discount at a 10% interest rate. This is because the present value of the 25 payments when discounted at 10% is $39,938,976, while the present value of the lottery's offer of immediate payment is (of course) $50 million. In other words, if you can expect a return of 10% on your financial investment, the option of $4 million per year is not a good one because you could take $50 million and make financial investments that pay $5 million every year (10% of $50 million). In contrast, the lottery's offer of immediate payment is not a good deal at a 5% interest rate as the present value of the future cash flows is $59,194,567, which is greater than the $50 million offer.

Using a Spreadsheet to Calculate Present Value

Calculating present value can be very tedious. Fortunately, spreadsheets such as Google Sheet or Microsoft Excel make it much easier; they do all the hard calculations. The following demonstration on how to perform present value calculations assumes that you are familiar with the basics of a spreadsheet. Begin by creating a table of future payments, which is the amount received in the future and the number of years until each sum is received. Exhibit A1 demonstrates two approaches to calculate the present value of a bond at a 10% interest rate using Google Spreadsheet. The two processes are identical for Microsoft Excel.

The first approach mirrors the technique discussed above. You calculate the present values of all future cash flows and sum the total in a multistep process. Column C converts the values in Column B into their present value equivalent. Column D shows the command found in column C (which presents the results). Keep in mind the following details on notation. First, a 10% interest rate is "0.10"; thus, 1 + the interest rate equals 1.10. Second, the symbol "^" means raised to the power. Third, A6 = 5 and B6 = $1,050. Thus, in Cell C6 "1.10^A6" is 1.10^5 and "=B6/1.10^A6" is $\$1,050/1.10^5$. Finally, after making the line-by-line calculation, you simply sum the total.

Making things even easier, both Excel and Google Sheets have a *built-in* present value function called NPV (net present value). Simply type "=NPV(interest rate, range of future payment cells)," as demonstrated in Cell C9 of Exhibit A1. Recall that the interest rate is expressed as a decimal (0.10). Row 11 calculates the net present value of a bond paying a 5% (.05) interest rate; which is $1,000 as shown above. Also, do not discount any payments received immediately, such as an immediate lottery payment.

The lottery calculation is also easier to do on a spreadsheet. Exhibit A2 demonstrates. In the "NPV" function, the first payment discounted is the one received a year from today. Notice that the formula in Column C separately adds in the initial $4 million payment. This occurs because that payment is received immediately and is not discounted. In Cell C6, the NPV function calculates the present value of future cash flows and adds in another $4 million which is not discounted.

Internal Rate of Return

Instead of estimating the present value of future cash flows, a business can estimate an interest rate equivalent of all cash flows. This is one way of accounting for the fact that a mix of *both* cash outflows and cash inflows take place over time. In business, cash

---

EXHIBIT A1   Present Value of a Bond on a Spreadsheet

	A	B	C	D
1	Year	Payment	Present Value	Function in Column C
2	1	$50.00	$45.45	=B2/1.10^A2
3	2	$50.00	$41.32	=B3/1.10^A3
4	3	$50.00	$37.57	=B4/1.10^A4
5	4	$50.00	$34.15	=B5/1.10^A5
6	5	$1,050.00	$651.97	=B6/1.10^A6
7			$810.46	=sum(C2:C6)
8				
9	Alternatively:	at 10%	$810.46	=npv(.10,B2:B6)
10				
11		at 5%	$1,000.00	=npv(.05,B2:B6)

Estimating present values is easier on a spreadsheet such as Google Sheets or Microsoft Excel. Begin by creating a table of future payments. These values are discounted at a 10% interest rate (0.10) in Column C (using the formula shown in Column D) and then added together. Alternatively, the net present value (NPV) function can be utilized.

EXHIBIT A2 Twenty-Five Payments of $4 million: Net Present Value and Internal Rate of Return

	A	B	C	D
1	Year	Payment	Notes	Function in Column C
2	0	-$46,000,000.00	First payment less $50,000,000 (payout) for IRR calculation.	
3	1	$4,000,000.00		
4	2	$4,000,000.00	Net Present Value (NPV) at 5% Interest Rate	
5	3	$4,000,000.00		
6	4	$4,000,000.00	$59,194,567.18	=NPV(0.05,B3:B26) + 4000000
7	5	$4,000,000.00	Immediate payment ($4,000,000) is added seperately for NPV calculation.	
8	6	$4,000,000.00		
9	7	$4,000,000.00	Net Present Value (NPV) at 10% Interest Rate	
10	8	$4,000,000.00		
11	9	$4,000,000.00	$39,938,976.08	=NPV(0.10,B3:B26) + 4000000
12	10	$4,000,000.00	Immediate payment ($4,000,000) is added seperately for NPV calculation.	
13	11	$4,000,000.00		
14	12	$4,000,000.00	Internal Rate of Return (IRR)	
15	13	$4,000,000.00		
16	14	$4,000,000.00	6.97%	=IRR(B2:B26)
17	15	$4,000,000.00		
18	16	$4,000,000.00		
19	17	$4,000,000.00		
20	18	$4,000,000.00		
21	19	$4,000,000.00		
22	20	$4,000,000.00		
23	21	$4,000,000.00		
24	22	$4,000,000.00		
25	23	$4,000,000.00		
26	24	$4,000,000.00		

Using the net present value function on a spreadsheet is an easy way to discount the value of future cash flows. Simply type "= NPV (interest rate, range of future payment cells)" as demonstrated in Cell C6. In this particular example, since $4 million is received immediately, it is not discounted and added in separately. Estimating the internal rate of return (IRR) of a project can also be done on a spreadsheet. Simply type "=IRR (range of all payment cells)" as demonstrated in row 16. It is important to note that all payment cells include outflows at the start (year zero). This project has an IRR of 6.97%.

outflows often occur when a business expansion project begins, with inflows occurring subsequently. The lottery example involved only cash inflows, but a business equivalent would be $46 million *outflow* now (the difference between a $50 million lump sum payment or $4 million now) and 24 annual *inflows* of $4 million. Suppose an entrepreneur is considering such a project. Should she opt to *pay* $46 million now to receive $4 million a year for 24 years?

The answer depends on how much it costs to borrow money. An investment that looks profitable if a business can borrow at 5% might well prove unprofitable if the business must pay 10% to borrow money. In general, businesses are more inclined to borrow at lower interest rates, *ceteris paribus.*

An internal rate of return calculation helps firms decide which projects are worth doing. The **internal rate of return (IRR)** is the percentage annual rate of return on the amount invested. The IRR then helps to determine whether a project is profitable. If a firm can borrow money at an interest rate below the IRR, then the project will be profitable. If the cost of borrowing exceeds the IRR, then the project is not worth pursuing.

Although the mathematics of an IRR calculation go beyond the scope of this text, estimating an IRR is easy with a spreadsheet. Exhibit A2 demonstrates the calculation

internal rate of return (IRR)
The percentage annual rate of return on the amount invested.

of IRR using Google Sheets. Simply type "=IRR(range of all payment cells)," as demonstrated in Row 16. It is important to note that all payment cells include outflows at the start (Year 0). In this case, Year 0 is an outflow of $46 million; this is the "−$46,000,000" in Cell B2. Unlike the present value, the IRR cannot be calculated with *only* cash inflows. Unless you also have cash outflows, the IRR would be infinite. Exhibit A2 shows that the IRR on this investment project is 6.97%.

The economic implication of IRR calculations is straightforward. Assume that to pay for the project, a business must borrow the initial $46 million. If the firm can borrow money at interest rates lower than 6.97%, say, 5%, then the project is worth pursuing. Otherwise, the project should not be considered. As a consequence, when firms can borrow at lower interest rates, they are inclined, other things equal, to find more investment projects worth doing. This finding will be important when you study macroeconomics. As a way of combating recessions, monetary policymakers often try to reduce interest rates in order to boost borrowing for investment.

Earlier in the section, we estimated how to compute the *price* of a bond. Suppose we know the price of the bond, but instead wish to estimate its *interest rate*. This is the equivalent of an IRR calculation. Suppose we want to know the rate of return on two bonds with the following characteristics:

- They have prices of $810.46 and $1,000. These values represent outflows.
- Both bonds pay a $50 coupon for each of the next four years. These values represent inflows.
- Both bonds pay $50 for the fifth year's coupon plus $1,000 for the principal payment.

These bonds are the equivalent to those analyzed above. Thus, the rates of return on the bonds *should be* 10% and 5%, respectively. These rates of return are exactly what would be estimated using the IRR function on Google Sheets, as demonstrated in Exhibit A3. Note that the purchase of a bond represents an outflow and is entered as a negative number (Cells B3 and B12).

EXHIBIT A3 Interest Rates on a Bond—Internal Rate of Return (IRR)

	A	B	C	D
1	**Bond 1**			
2	**Year**	**Payment**	**Notes and IRR:**	**Function in Column C**
3	0	-$810.46	Cash outflows	
4	1	$50.00		
5	2	$50.00	10.00%	=IRR(B3:B8)
6	3	$50.00		
7	4	$50.00		
8	5	$1,050.00		
9				
10	**Bond 2**			
11	**Year**	**Payment**	**Notes and IRR:**	**Function in Column C**
12	0	-$1,000.00	Cash outflows	
13	1	$50.00		
14	2	$50.00	5.00%	=IRR(B12:B17)
15	3	$50.00		
16	4	$50.00		
17	5	$1,050.00		

The IRR function on a spreadsheet can be used to estimate the interest rate on a bond. The bonds in question are identical to those presented in Exhibit A1. Here, we know the price of the bond (outflow at time of purchase), but wish to learn the interest rate the bond is paying.

APPENDIX STUDY GUIDE

PRESENT VALUE AND THE TIME VALUE OF MONEY

The **time value of money** is the idea that the value of money today is greater than receiving the same amount of money in the future. The money one has today can be invested and earn interest, boosting the future value of your money holdings. **Present value** is the discounted current value of a future sum of money. Discounting typically occurs at a prevailing interest rate. Financial analysis involves discounting future *cash flows,* the total amount of money going into and coming out of a business. Cash flow is a central component of modern finance and accounting. Mathematically, $PV = FV/(1 + i)^t$. Present values can also be calculated on a spreadsheet. The **internal rate of return (IRR)** is the percentage annual rate of return on the amount invested. An internal rate of return calculation helps firms decide which projects are worth doing.

STUDY PROBLEMS

1. A seven-year bond has a payment stream of $50 for each of the next six years, with a payment of $50 for the seventh year's coupon plus $1,000 for the principal payment. This totals $1,050. Mathematically, calculate the present value of the bond if the going interest rate is each of the following. (Show your work.)

   a. 3%

   b. 5%

   c. 7%

2. Verify your answers to the previous question using a spreadsheet.

3. Using the data in Exhibit A3 from the chapter, what is the internal rate of return of such an investment if the initial investment is each of the following?

   a. $900

   b. $1,000

   c. $1,200

4. What do the answers to the previous three questions demonstrate about the link between higher interest rate and bond prices?

^ Entrepreneurs must consider all costs when starting a business.

The Cost of Doing Business

Production and Economic Cost

Maria knows a thing or two about the hospitality business. She worked her way through college at her brother Mario's pizzeria and then accepted a high-paying job at Hilton Hotels & Resorts after graduating near the top of her class with a major in accounting. Now Maria is exploring the possibility of leaving the corporate world to become her own boss, running a restaurant of her own.

Having kept the books for a number of Hilton's dining rooms, Maria knows the costs of doing business in the food service industry and lists all her projected expenses on a spreadsheet. She also realizes that some costs (such as ingredients and labor) will vary with unit sales, whereas other costs (such as her rent at a great location near the mall) will not change with the level of production. She won't pay herself a salary, but understands that forfeiting her annual salary of $140,000 represents an opportunity cost, and that this, too, must factor into her decision making.

In this chapter and subsequent ones, we will follow Maria's story as we develop a basic framework to examine how businesses maximize profits. Understanding the role of cost in business is an essential first step in profit maximization, and it is where we begin.

Chapter Learning Targets

- Distinguish between economic profit and accounting profit.

- Describe the production function and the law of diminishing returns.

- Distinguish between various measures of costs, including variable costs, fixed costs, average cost, and marginal cost.

- Define long-run average total cost, economies of scale, minimum efficient scale, diseconomies of scale, and economies of scope.

11.1 ECONOMIC COST AND ECONOMIC PROFIT

Maria doesn't just want to be her own boss and own her own restaurant—she also wants to run a profitable business. But what is profit? Here is the most basic definition:

$$\text{Profit} = \text{Total revenue} - \text{Total cost}$$

It seems simple enough, but as the old saying goes, the devil is in the details.

When Maria calculates profit, she tends to think like an accountant, tallying up expenses and potential revenue on a spreadsheet. It turns out that economists and accountants look at costs and profits somewhat differently.

Calculating Accounting Profit

Maria expects revenues of $500,000 per year. She anticipates that her expenses will be as follows: $100,000 to rent a space with a brick pizza oven, $100,000 for ingredients and materials, and $200,000 for her staff—a total of $400,000. To calculate profit, an accountant simply deducts the expenses (or accounting costs) from total revenue. Thus, **accounting profit** equals total revenue minus accounting costs. That is,

$$\text{Accounting profit} = \text{Total revenue} - \text{Accounting costs}$$

Maria would add up all revenues and subtract all costs paid to determine profit:

$$\$100,000 = \$500,000 - \$400,000$$

In this case, her restaurant would make $100,000 in profits—not bad!

Maria's spreadsheet includes her out of pocket expenses, every dime she will spend to start her restaurant and keep it running. These are her **explicit costs**, input costs that involve actual payments of money. Maria must pay the rent, the workers, and the utilities. **Accounting costs** are the explicit costs of production. Maria's accounting profit is reviewed in the middle column of Exhibit 1. But are those her only costs? An economist would say "no."

accounting profit Total revenue minus accounting costs.

explicit costs Input costs that involve actual payments of money.

accounting costs Explicit costs of production.

EXHIBIT 1   Accounting Costs and Profit versus Economic Costs and Profit

	Accounting Costs and Profit	Economic Costs and Profit
Total Revenue	$500,000	$500,000
Explicit Costs		
Building and pizza oven rentals	$100,000	$100,000
Ingredients, materials, and utilities	$100,000	$100,000
Labor and staff	$200,000	$200,000
Implicit Costs		
Opportunity cost of owner's time	—	$140,000
Opportunity cost of owner's money	—	$10,000
Total Cost		
Accounting Costs	$400,000	—
Economic Costs	—	$550,000
Profit		
Accounting Profit	$100,000	—
Economic Profit	—	−$50,000

Accounting costs are the explicit costs of production. Economic costs are explicit costs plus implicit costs. Consequently, economic costs are generally higher than accounting costs. Zero economic profit implies a normal accounting profit and is not bad. To an economist, the term "profit" generally refers to economic profit.

Calculating Economic Profit

Maria projects that if she opens a restaurant, she will earn an accounting profit of $100,000. But is opening a restaurant a good economic decision? Remember, Maria would also be quitting a lucrative job in order to run her restaurant: the $140,000 she currently earns per year working for Hilton.

To answer this question, an economist would look at Maria's spreadsheet of explicit costs and insert a number of implicit costs. **Implicit costs** are input costs that do not involve the payment of money. They are implied; the opportunity cost of inputs not calling for payments. Maria's former salary of $140,000 is an example of an implicit cost. In addition, she also plans to use money she has saved for her retirement to pay for many of the restaurant's startup expenses, such as furniture, fixtures, and construction costs. Withdrawing that money means foregoing $10,000 in interest income per year. An economist would view each of these as important, even though none of them would be entered on an income tax statement. **Economic costs** are explicit costs plus the implicit costs of production. In this instance, economists would measure Maria's $400,000 in expenses (her explicit costs) plus *additional* opportunity costs of $150,000: the salary and interest income she must give up to open the restaurant. As illustrated in the second column of Exhibit 1, her total *economic costs* are $550,000.

Economic profit equals total revenue minus economic costs. In order to calculate economic profit, Maria needs to consider both explicit and implicit costs, that is, she needs to consider economic cost:

$$\text{Economic profit} = \text{Total revenue} - \text{Economic cost}$$

Maria's *economic profit* equals

$$-\$50,000 = \$500,000 - \$550,000$$

A negative economic profit is called an economic loss. Although in an accounting sense her profit is $100,000, in an economic sense she will experience a loss of $50,000.

Is opening the restaurant a good economic decision? Economic formulas don't always provide easy answers, but they are useful tools. If one considers the economic loss of $50,000, it seems that opening the restaurant would be a poor decision. However, it is possible that the satisfaction one will derive from doing a certain job over another is worth the pay cut one might take to do so. It is also possible one expects to see greater profits in the future. Thus, there are no easy answers in determining the best course of action.

Zero Economic Profit Means a Normal Accounting Profit

The key difference between economic profit and accounting profit is how each treats costs. Come tax time, Maria would love to use implicit opportunity costs such as her foregone salary as an expense—it would mean she incurred a loss and could expect a nice tax refund. Unfortunately, Maria cannot deduct her implicit costs, at least not without risking time in jail. Accountants follow a strict set of rules governed by groups such as the Financial Accounting Standards Board (FASB) as well as the tax laws of various government agencies. Economists, on the other hand, are not bound by such rules; they seek a more complete picture of the costs involved in any decision. Thus, when implicit costs exist, economic costs are greater than accounting costs. In summary:

- Accounting costs = Explicit costs
- Economic costs = Explicit costs + Implicit costs = All opportunity costs

implicit costs Input costs that do not involve payment of money.

economic costs Explicit costs plus the implicit costs of production.

economic profit Total revenue minus economic costs.

Because economic costs are generally greater than accounting costs, economic profits are generally lower than accounting profits. To an economist, "profit" generally refers to economic profit, and that's the context in which we'll use the term in this textbook.

It is important to note that although the term "zero economic profit" seems to have a negative connotation, it implies that a business is operating about "normal," or roughly as well as the owner would be doing if his or her labor and capital were allocated to the next best use. It may be helpful to think of zero economic profit as the point where a business earns a "normal accounting profit." For example, zero economic profit would occur *if* Maria's restaurant instead generated an accounting profit equal to her former salary and interest earnings: $150,000, instead of the $100,000 assumed in the above example.

For economists, the zero economic profit point is an important benchmark. It's the dividing line between success and failure, and we will see that it has important consequences when considering whether entry into a particular industry is desirable. In the business world, it is common to view zero profit as a bad thing, but that is because in business profit is usually measured as "accounting profit." However, when using economic analysis, this is *not* the case. Zero economic profit is a *normal* rate of return, not at all indicative of failure.

Think & Speak Like an Economist

Since economic costs are generally greater than accounting costs, economic profits are lower than accounting profits. Moreover, zero economic profit entails a normal accounting profit and is an important benchmark in economics.

11.2 PRODUCTION IN THE SHORT RUN

Once Maria finds a location for her restaurant and determines how much she will have to spend on rent and equipment, she must decide how many workers to hire. If she hires too many, she will have excessive labor expenses, and if she later has to fire unneeded workers, staff morale would suffer. But if she hires too few workers, she won't be able to meet customer demand and will fall short of her revenue potential.

In this section, we will look at the link between labor and output in the *short run*—a time frame that is too short to make all adjustments to changing business conditions. For simplicity, we assume that Maria cannot change her rental agreements, but can alter how many workers she keeps on staff. We also assume she has no other costs. Although this assumption is obviously not realistic (pizza does need cheese), it makes demonstrating the critical economic relationship between additional labor and output much easier.

The Production Function and Marginal Physical Product

production function
An expression of the technological relationship between different combinations of inputs and maximum output.

marginal physical product of labor (*MPP*$_L$) The additional output from an additional unit of labor, holding the amount of physical capital and other inputs fixed.

The **production function** expresses the technological relationship between different combinations of inputs and maximum output. Panel A of Exhibit 2 presents a production function. It demonstrates the relationship between various amounts of labor and output. If Maria hires no labor, she produces no pizza. Maria needs to hire 2 units of labor (workers) to produce 150 pizzas per month and 5 units of labor to produce 300 pizzas.

The production function tells us how much output can be produced with various levels of inputs, given current technology. In this case, it reveals how many pizzas will be produced with various amounts of labor and a fixed amount of physical capital—for Maria, that means the amount of seating in her restaurant and the capacity of her pizza oven. The production function in Exhibit 2 is simplified by only varying the amount of labor. More complex production functions vary the amount of labor, capital, and other inputs.

The **marginal physical product of labor** (*MPP*$_L$) is the additional output from an additional unit of labor, holding the amount of physical capital and other

EXHIBIT 2 Marginal Physical Product of Labor and Diminishing Returns

Panel A: Production Function Data

Labor (L)	Total Product (Q)	Marginal Physical Product ($\Delta Q/\Delta L$)
0	0	–
1	70	70
2	150	80
3	210	60
4	260	50
5	300	40
6	330	30
7	350	20
8	360	10

Panel B: Marginal Physical Product Curve

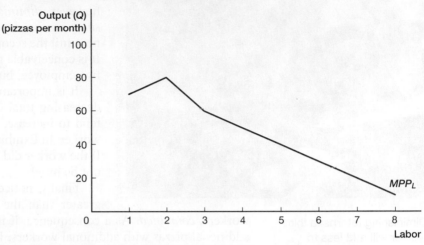

The production function expresses the technological relationship between different combinations of inputs and maximum output and is shown in Panel A. Panel B displays the marginal physical product of labor (MPP_L); the additional output from an additional unit of labor, given a fixed amount of physical capital and other inputs. The declining MPP_L beyond the second worker exhibits the law of diminishing returns.

inputs fixed. It tells us how much output increases with each extra unit of labor. Mathematically,

$$\text{Marginal physical product of labor} = \frac{\text{Change in output}}{\text{Change in labor}} = \frac{\Delta Q}{\Delta L}$$

where the Greek letter Δ (delta) means change. ΔQ thus means the change in output, while ΔL means the change in labor. Panel B in Exhibit 2 offers a graphical representation of the MPP_L data found in Panel A. The second worker, for example, increases output by 80, from 70 to 150. Thus, the MPP_L of the second worker is 80. The third worker increases output by 60 from 150 to 210. The MPP_L of the third worker therefore is 60.

The Law of Diminishing Returns

Notice that the marginal physical product of labor declines for each unit of labor (worker) after the second worker, exhibiting what economists call diminishing returns. The **law of diminishing returns** states that, in the short run, the marginal physical product of labor declines as more labor is employed, with other inputs held fixed. This means that each additional worker adds less to total output than the previous worker, when the amount of physical capital is fixed.

To understand the basics of the theory behind the law of diminishing returns, consider the simple example of a local suit maker with only two sewing machines. The MPP_L of the 3rd and 4th workers will clearly be less than the MPP_L of the 1st and 2nd workers—after all, there are only two machines; thus, these workers will presumably produce fewer additional suits. Other workers can help in other ways: perhaps cutting fabric or packing and delivering the finished suits. But they are not likely to be as productive as those using the machinery.

law of diminishing returns
Theory stating that in the short run the marginal physical product of labor declines as more labor is employed, with other inputs held fixed.

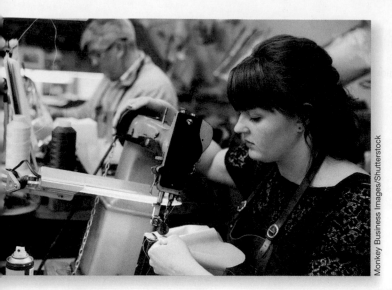

∧ Diminishing returns: a third worker will add less to output with the number of machines fixed at two.

Similarly, at Maria's, there is only so much space at her restaurant. Thus, additional workers may not add as much to total output as her first few workers. Diminishing returns do not always take place with the first few workers; however, *diminishing returns eventually set in for every short-run production function.* At Maria's restaurant, it is not until the second worker that MPP_L becomes maximized. It is conceivable that the first employee is the most productive employee, but this need not be the case.

It is important to not confuse diminishing returns with decreasing total output. When labor is added, output will tend to increase, but at a slower rate with each additional worker. In Exhibit 2, the eighth worker adds to total output. If the worker did not add to output, he or she would simply not be hired.

Finally, notice that the MPP_L of the second worker is greater than the MPP_L of the sixth, seventh, and eighth workers, *combined.* As a consequence, it is increasingly costly for Maria to produce additional pizzas with additional workers. Later in the chapter, you will discover that the *law of diminishing returns results in increasing marginal cost.* For now, it is important to recognize that the MPP_L and cost of doing business (the chapter's primary focus) are linked.

11.3 COSTS IN THE SHORT RUN

Maria is looking at a great location for her restaurant. Rent on the property, which comes furnished with tables, chairs, and a fully equipped kitchen, is $10,000 per month. She's also considering leasing a custom pizza oven, which will cost her another $2,000 a month. Maria knows that if she signs these lease agreements, she will be obligated to pay $12,000 per month even if she sells zero pizzas. This is considerably more than she anticipated on her original spreadsheet. In addition, Maria will take on expenses that vary, like payroll, utilities, and perishable ingredients. These costs will vary with the number of pizzas sold. In this section, our focus is identifying various types of costs.

Total Costs Include Fixed Costs and Variable Costs

The cost of doing business is an important factor that must be considered when making business decisions. Some costs have to be paid no matter how many products are sold as they do not vary with the level of production. **Fixed costs (*FC*)** are short-run costs that do not change with the quantity of output. Maria, for example, has two rental agreements: one for her building and one for her brick pizza oven. Each of these would be considered a fixed cost. If Maria has insurance, this amount is also typically a fixed cost; as a business owner, she carries insurance no matter how many pizzas are produced. In the business media, fixed costs are sometimes referred to as *overhead*. These costs do not vary as Maria sells more pizza.

Note that it doesn't matter whether Maria leases or borrows money to pay for the pizza oven (or the building)—in either case, the monthly payments will be considered part of her fixed costs. Similarly, if Maria withdraws money from her bank account to pay for the oven, then the implicit cost of the foregone interest is also a fixed cost. This means that regardless of how the oven is obtained, *the costs associated with physical capital are fixed costs.* The requirement to make fixed payments on a lease contract implies the business has monthly costs that cannot be changed in the short run; thus, these payments are considered fixed costs.

fixed costs (*FC*) Short-run costs that do not change with the quantity of output.

In contrast, some of Maria's other costs will vary with the level of output. If Maria sells more pizza, then she needs more cheese and workers; if she sells less pizza, then she would need less of these inputs. **Variable costs (VC)** are short-run costs that change with the quantity of output. We've seen that in the short run there are two types of costs: fixed costs and variable costs. **Total costs (TC)** are the cost of all inputs in production, which equal fixed costs plus variable costs:

$$\text{Total costs} = \text{Fixed costs} + \text{Variable costs}$$

Finally, note that both fixed costs and variable costs are defined as short-run costs. In the long-run, when the rental agreements expire Maria can decide to not renew the contracts. This means that *fixed costs only exist in the short run.* Any distinction between fixed and variable costs implicitly reflects a short-run perspective.

Average Cost Is the Cost per Unit

Businesses also need to know production cost expressed *per unit cost*—what economists refer to as *average cost*. For example, if it costs a total of $60 to make 6 pizzas, the average total cost is $6 per pizza.

There are three different types of average cost:

- **Average fixed cost (AFC)** is fixed costs per unit; $AFC = \dfrac{FC}{Q}$.

- **Average variable cost (AVC)** is variable costs per unit; $AVC = \dfrac{VC}{Q}$.

- **Average total cost (ATC)** is total costs per unit; $ATC = \dfrac{TC}{Q}$.

Average total cost is often referred to as just *average cost.* Just as total costs are the sum of fixed and variable costs, average total cost is equal to the sum of average fixed cost and average variable cost:

$$\text{Average total cost} = \text{Average fixed cost} + \text{Average variable cost}$$

Marginal Cost

In Chapter 1, you learned that optimal economic decisions are made using marginal analysis: A business should pursue certain activities only if the marginal benefit equals or exceeds the marginal cost. This means that the concept of marginal cost is especially important. **Marginal cost (MC)** is the additional costs a business incurs from 1 additional unit of output. Mathematically,

$$\text{Marginal costs} = \frac{\text{Change in total cost}}{\text{Change in output}} = \frac{\Delta TC}{\Delta Q}.$$

If the total cost of 2 units is $18 and the total cost of 3 units is $21, then marginal cost will equal $3. This means that to make 1 more pizza, Maria must spend $3 more on additional variable costs such as cheese and labor.

The data points in Exhibit 3 are designed to keep the mathematics simple. Let's make the analysis a bit more realistic so that Q is in units of 1,000 and fixed, variable, and total costs are also in units of $1,000. Then Maria's fixed costs are $12,000, as described in the example above. It is important to note that marginal cost is additional cost over additional quantity. Consequently, the marginal cost is $3 (= $\Delta TC/\Delta Q$ = $3,000/1,000 = $3). *Additional quantities may not always be in 1-unit increments* (as presented in Exhibit 3).

variable costs (VC) Short-run costs that change with the quantity of output.

total costs (TC) Cost of all inputs in production, which equals fixed costs plus variable costs.

average fixed cost (AFC) Fixed costs per unit.

average variable cost (AVC) Variable costs per unit.

average total cost (ATC) Total costs per unit; also called *average cost.*

marginal cost (MC) The additional costs a business incurs from one additional unit of output.

EXHIBIT 3 Short-Run Cost Schedule for Maria's Restaurant

Quantity Q	Fixed Cost (rent)	Variable Cost (cheese, labor)	Total Cost TC = FC + VC	Marginal Cost MC = $\Delta TC / \Delta Q$	Average Fixed Cost AFC = FC/Q	Average Variable Cost AVC = VC/Q	Average Total Cost ATC = TC/Q
0	$12	$0	$12	—	—	—	—
1	12	4	16	$4	$12	$4	$16
2	12	6	18	2	6	3	9
3	12	9	21	3	4	3	7
4	12	16	28	7	3	4	7
5	12	28	40	12	2.40	5.60	8
6	12	48	60	20	2	8	10

In the short run, there are fixed costs and variable costs. These costs sum to total costs. Each of these can also be expressed as a per unit average. Marginal cost is the additional cost of an additional unit.

Note: We will return to these identical cost values in several places over the next few chapters.

Quantity and total, fixed and variable costs are expressed in increments of 1,000.

Understanding the Short-Run Cost Curves

Exhibit 3 demonstrates Maria's various costs at different levels of output. If she sells no pizza she has fixed costs of $12 as she must pay her rent; but since she needs no cheese or workers her variable costs are zero. As she sells more pizza, her variable costs and total cost increase but her fixed cost do not. In this example, if she sells 4 pizzas, her fixed costs are $12, her variable costs are $16, and her total costs are $28. Consequently, her AFC is $3(= $12/4), AVC is $4(= 16/4), and ATC is $7 (28/4 or $3 + $4). Her marginal cost for the fourth unit of pizza is $7. This is because in order to make 1 more pizza, her total costs increase from $21 at 3 units of output to $28 at 4 units of output.

Note that average fixed cost is a fixed number ($12 in the current example) divided by quantity. At 1 unit of output, AFC = 12, at 2 units of output AFC = 6, and at 6 units of output AFC = 2. Average fixed cost declines with any increase in output. This is the direct result of dividing a fixed amount of costs by larger numbers of output—division by larger numbers always results in smaller average number. To better understand how businesses make decisions in an attempt to maximize profit, it is useful to graph the various average and marginal cost curves. Exhibit 4 presents Maria's average total cost, average variable cost, and marginal cost curves based on the data from Exhibit 3. Consistent with the above discussion, at 4 units of output Maria's AVC = $4, ATC = $7, and MC = $7. Cost curves identical to these will be used in several places over the next few chapters.

Note that in Exhibit 4, each curve has a distinct shape. Although the exact dollar amounts of each cost vary from firm to firm, the general shape of various cost curves is consistent.

Marginal Cost Curve Is Upward-Sloping in the Relevant Range As shown in Panel A of Exhibit 5, the MC curve may initially slope downward, but a competitive firm would rarely want to produce in that range. The upward slope of the marginal cost curve results from the *law of diminishing returns*: As firms hire additional workers with a fixed amount of capital (buildings, pizza ovens, etc.), each additional worker adds a little less to output than the previous worker, causing the marginal cost of additional output to rise. If Maria's restaurant is near capacity, then each additional pizza produced costs more than the previous one.

EXHIBIT 4 Short-Run Cost Curves for Maria's Restaurant

The marginal cost (MC), average variable cost (AVC), and average total cost (ATC) for Maria's restaurant using the data in Exhibit 3. At 4 units of output, $ATC = \$7$, $MC = \$7$, $AVC = \$4$, and $AFC = \$3$.

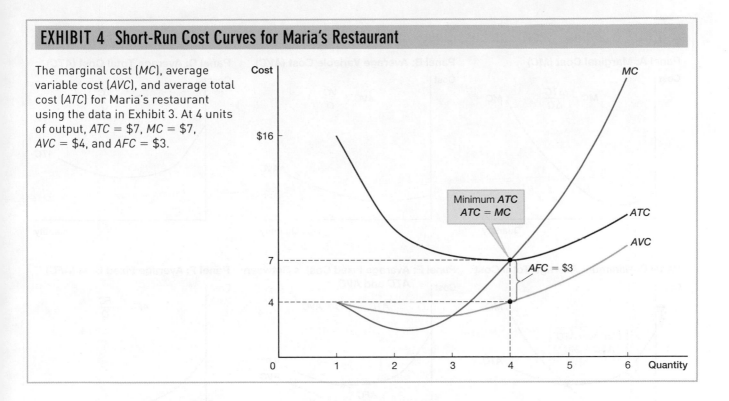

Average Variable Cost Curve Is Upward-Sloping in the Relevant Range As shown in Panel B, after the first few units of output, average variable cost increases as output expands. This results from increasing marginal cost. If it costs more to make 1 additional unit (marginal cost), the average variable cost of making each unit must increase. Maria's projected costs reflect this: Her AVC increases after the third unit of pizza is produced. After the third unit, the marginal cost of each additional unit is higher than the AVC.

Average Total Cost Curve Is U-Shaped As shown in Panel C, the average total cost curve is U-shaped. Recall average total cost is average fixed cost plus average variable cost. Since average fixed cost declines rapidly with initial output, it drives down average total cost. The average total cost for the first unit of pizza is expensive. As more units are produced, there is a rapid decline in average fixed cost. At some point, AFC declines at a slower rate and the decline in AFC is offset by the steady increase in marginal cost that result from diminishing returns.

In general, whenever marginal cost is less than average total cost, average total cost is decreasing. This typically occurs at small quantities. Conversely, when marginal cost exceeds average total cost, average total cost is increasing. This typically occurs at large quantities. The end result is a U-Shaped ATC curve. For instance, suppose the average total cost of a product is $50. If making 1 additional unit costs less than $50, say, $10, what will likely happen to the average as 1 more unit is produced? It decreases because marginal cost is less than the average total cost. In contrast, if making 1 more unit costs more than $50, say $100, the average total cost would increase.

As an analogy, imagine you measured the height of every student in your economics class and found that the average height is 5 feet, 6 inches. What would happen to the average height in the room if a 7-foot-tall basketball player enrolled? It will increase because the height of the marginal student (7 feet) exceeds the average height in the class. Similarly, if a 2-year-old child walks into the room, the average height in the room would decline. The same logic also explains why average variable cost is upward-sloping at levels of output where MC is greater than AVC.

$ATC = MC$ at Minimum of Average Total Cost As shown in Panel D, the marginal cost curve intercepts the average total cost curve at the minimum point on the average total cost curve. The logic here is the same as for the U-shape of the ATC curve. When

EXHIBIT 5 Typical Short-Run Cost Curves and Formulas

Panel A: Marginal Cost (*MC*)

$$MC = \frac{\Delta TC}{\Delta Q}$$

Cost / Quantity — *MC*

Panel B: Average Variable Cost (*AVC*)

$$AVC = \frac{VC}{Q}$$

Cost / Quantity — *AVC*

Panel C: Average Total Cost (*ATC*)

$$ATC = \frac{TC}{Q}$$

Cost / Quantity — *ATC*

Panel D: Minimum Average Total Cost

Minimum *ATC*
ATC = *MC*

Cost / Quantity — *MC*, *ATC*

Panel E: Average Fixed Cost Is Between *ATC* and *AVC*

ATC = *AFC* + *AVC*

Cost / Quantity — *ATC*, *AVC*, *AFC*

Panel F: Average Fixed Cost (*AFC*)

$$AFC = \frac{FC}{Q}$$

Cost / Quantity — *AFC*

Typical short-run average cost curves.

MC is lower than *ATC*, *ATC* is declining and has not reached its minimum point which occurs when *MC* equals *ATC*. Finally, when *MC* is greater than *ATC*, *ATC* is increasing and is past the minimum point.

To summarize:

- *ATC* must be decreasing whenever $MC < ATC$.
- *ATC* is at its minimum where $MC = ATC$.
- *ATC* must be increasing whenever $MC > ATC$.

Distance Between *ATC* and *AVC* Curves Is *AFC* Since average total cost equals the average fixed cost plus the average variable cost, the vertical distance between the average total cost and average variable cost must be average fixed cost. At 1 unit of output, *ATC* equals 16 and *AVC* equals 4, so *AFC* equals 12. At 6 units of output, *ATC* equals 10 and *AVC* equals 8, so *AFC* equals 2. This is shown in Panel E.

Average Fixed Cost Curve Is Downward Sloping Finally, Panel *F* shows that the *AFC* curve is downward sloping. As mentioned before, this is the direct result of dividing a fixed amount of costs by larger numbers of output.

📊 **BUSINESS BRIEF The Cost of Producing a Mobile App**

You have a multimillion dollar idea for a great new app. What costs are involved? There are a few fixed costs to consider. First, you will need to develop and market the app, either on your own (which will carry an opportunity cost) or by paying a third party to do so. You will likely want to sell your app on several platforms, most of which charge an annual fee (the Apple App Store charges $100 per year; Google Play $25). You might sell 1 app or 1 million, but your annual fee remains fixed.*

However, once your app is developed, marketed, and made available for download, the marginal cost of selling one additional app is typically 30% of the selling price. Thus, for an app that sells for $10, the marginal cost is a constant $3 up to the point where additional servers are needed. The marginal cost of 1 extra unit is often much lower in newer industries that rely on information technology than in older industries that require expensive inputs such as raw materials and labor. In such industries, it is often the case that the average total cost curve is downward-sloping while marginal cost is constant. This is because the ATC will always be at least a little more than MC.

*Based on Isha Kasliwal, "What Goes into the Cost of a Mobile App?," *The Huffington Post,* December 26, 2013, http://www.huffingtonpost.com/fueled/what-goes-into-the-cost-of-a-mobile-app_b_4493998.html; Tim Mackenzie, "App Store Fees, Percentages, and Payouts: What Developers Need to Know," *TechRepublic,* n.d., accessed May 5, 2017, http://www.techrepublic.com/blog/software-engineer/app-store-fees-percentages -and-payouts-what-developers-need-to-know/.

Sunk Costs Don't Change

Some costs have already occurred or been legally agreed to. Once a payment is made, getting it back is usually difficult. This means that previously contracted expenses are irrelevant in most economic analysis. **Sunk costs** are costs that are not avoidable, and thus they should not affect economic decision making. Here are some examples of why sunk costs should not affect decisions:

- The fact that Maria spent $100,000 on her accounting degree is a sunk cost and irrelevant in her decision to open a pizza restaurant.

- A highly paid professional athlete loses motivation and becomes a liability on the field. The millions of dollars the team spent signing the superstar are a sunk cost and irrelevant—you should play your most effective athletes.

- Your automobile lease expires. You have the option to now buy the car or return it. The payments you made while holding the lease are sunk costs and irrelevant in future decisions.

- Maria pays $100,000 for a non-recoverable option to buy the building she is considering renting, at a set price, in the future. Since Maria will not receive a refund for her $100,000 if she does not buy the building, the option is a sunk cost.

Think & Speak Like an Economist

When you sell an asset—be it a car, a home, or a stock—don't get hung up on how much you paid for it. Economists view how much you paid for an asset as irrelevant: It's a sunk cost. What matters is the price you can sell it for today.

📊 BUSINESS BRIEF Star Athlete, Sunk Costs, and the Business of Baseball

During his professional baseball career, Ken Griffey Jr. hit 630 home runs and won the Home Run Derby three times. He was also admitted into baseball's Hall of Fame, receiving a record 99.3 percent of the vote. Nike sold "Air Griffey Max," a line of turf trainers, for decades.

Griffey played most of his career with the Seattle Mariners, but signed a nine-year contract with the Cincinnati Reds for over $116 million in 2000. According to the contract, the Reds retained an option to extend the contact for a 10th season for $12.5 million or pay Griffey a $4 million buyout (payment not to play). Just after signing the contract, Griffey suffered a string of injuries; he never returned to play at the level at which he had previously performed. For the next nine seasons, Griffey continued to play baseball when he was healthy, as the contract was a sunk cost. The marginal

sunk costs Costs that are not avoidable, and thus they should not affect economic decision-making.

cost of playing him was zero; he was paid regardless of his performance. Griffey did not play for the tenth season of his contract. Instead, he was paid the $4 million buyout, a sunk cost. The marginal cost of him playing that year would have been $8.5 million ($12.5 million less the $4 million buyout). Given that his level of play had declined so much, the Reds decided it was better for the team to absorb the $4 million loss.[*]

[*]See "Griffey Notebook: Contract Is Richest Ever—Or Is It?," *Cincinnati Enquirer,* February 11, 2000, http://reds .enquirer.com/2000/02/11/red_griffey_notebook.html.

How Diminishing Returns Results in Increasing Marginal Cost

As a firm hires more workers, each additional worker adds a smaller amount to output; that is to say marginal physical product declines. This is a consequence of the law of diminishing returns that results in an upward-sloping marginal cost curve.

To understand the basics of this concept, let's return to the simple example of our local suit makers with two sewing machines. Assume the firm pays a wage of $200 and there are no other costs. The second worker produces 2 suits ($MPP_L = 2$). Since the worker is paid $200 to produce 2 suits, the MC of each suit is $100. Mathematically, the MC is the additional cost of $200 divided by the additional quantity of 2, which equals $100 (= $200/2$).

Due to the law of diminishing returns, the third worker produces less as there are only 2 sewing machines. The MPP_L of the third worker is 1 suit. Since the third worker is paid $200, the marginal cost of the last suit is $200 (not $100). The law of diminishing returns results in increasing marginal cost as output rises. In other words, when more workers produce fewer additional units of output but are paid the same wage, the marginal cost of additional output *must* be increasing.

A similar logic can be applied to Maria. Based on Exhibit 2, the second worker increases output by 80, the third worker increases output by 60, the fourth worker increases output by 50, and the fifth worker increases output by 40. The lower marginal product of additional workers drives up marginal cost. To see this, suppose Maria pays all workers $240 per week and there are no other costs.

Her corresponding *marginal costs* are:

- $3 by hiring the second worker. The change in total cost of $240 divided by the change in output of 80.

- $4 by hiring the third worker. The change in total cost of $240 divided by the change in output of 60.

- $4.80 by hiring the fourth worker. The change in total cost of $240 divided by the change in output of 50.

- $6 by hiring the fifth worker. The change in total cost of $240 divided by the change in output of 40.

As you can see, diminishing returns results in increasing marginal cost.

📊 **BUSINESS BRIEF Marginal Cost of One Instagram Post**

Have you ever considered the marginal cost of posting a photo on Instagram when you're not connected to Wi-Fi? If you are like most consumers, probably not, because most mobile phone plans have data buckets, such as 10 or 50 GB. Consumers tend to consider how much data they expect to use each month and then find a plan that best matches their expectation. As long as you don't go over your monthly data limit, your wireless bill remains the same. This means that the marginal cost of each individual post is effectively zero, until you reach your monthly limit. After that, the marginal cost of uploading one additional photo moves you into a new data bucket—posting just one additional photo could cost $10 or more.

From the perspective of the wireless carriers, the marginal cost of providing that additional data is close to zero.* Once the phone carriers have built their network, they typically do not incur additional cost for additional use when below capacity. Yes, building the infrastructure needed to provide wireless data is expensive, but once the infrastructure is in place, one more customer using the data costs Verizon and AT&T very little extra. In general, the marginal cost of digital content such as music and videos is very low and has resulted in the falling prices of such content over the years.

B Christopher/Alamy stockphoto

∧ How much is one more post worth?

*See Mark Rogowsky, "Mobile Wars: AT&T Goes Whale Hunting, But Verizon, Sprint Bite Back as Data Prices Continue to Fall," *Forbes*, October 2, 2014, http://www.forbes.com/sites/markrogowsky/2014/10/02/mobile-wars-att-goes-whale-hunting-but-verizon-sprint-bite-back-as-data-prices-continue-to-fall/.

11.4 AVERAGE COST IN THE LONG RUN AND ECONOMIES OF SCALE

Up to this point, we have looked only at short-run costs. In the long run, however, there are no fixed inputs or costs, giving businesses much more flexibility. In the long run, Maria can shut down an unprofitable restaurant, open a new restaurant or several, or expand in her existing location. Recall that the long run refers to the time necessary to make all adjustments to economic circumstances; it could be 1 month or 10 years, depending on the type of costs. Since all costs can change in the long run, all costs are variable in the long run.

How do firms make long-run production decisions? How does Maria decide how many restaurants to operate? She needs to forecast the level of output that will maximize profits in the future, and then find a combination of inputs (labor, capital, etc.) that minimize costs to produce such a level of output.

Long-Run Average Total Cost Curve

In the long run, there is a combination of inputs that minimizes costs for each level of output. The cost-minimizing combination is expressed graphically as the long-run average total cost curve. The **long-run average total cost curve (*LRATC*)** represents the lowest average total cost at which a business can produce various levels of output when all inputs are allowed to vary.

Exhibit 6 demonstrates a long-run average total cost curve. When deciding how much "fixed cost" to commit to (and corresponding short-run *ATC* curve), a business expecting to maximize profit by selling 1,000 units per month in the future will do so in a way that minimizes costs. Each *ATC* curve reflects a different business plan. In that case, it would select short-run ATC_1. This is because other short-run average total cost curves with different amounts of fixed expenses result in higher costs. The firm could choose to be larger and produce 1,000 units on *a different ATC* curve; however, this would result in higher average costs.

Alternatively, if the business expects its profit-maximizing quantity to be 5,000 units per month, it will select short-run ATC_3. Operating smaller on ATC_2 or larger on ATC_4 would result in higher average cost. Businesses make such decisions based on

long run average total cost curve (*LRATC*) Curve that represents the lowest average total cost at which a business can produce various levels of output when all inputs are allowed to vary.

EXHIBIT 6   Deriving the Long-Run Average Total Cost Curve from Short-Run Average Total Cost Curves

The long-run average total cost curve (*LRATC*) in orange represents the lowest costs at which a business can produce various levels of output, when all inputs are allowed to vary. If a firm expects to maximize profit by producing 1,000 or 5,000 units in the future, it will select the short-run average total cost curve (*ATC*) that minimizes costs. Operating on an alternative short-run average total cost curve such as ATC_2 would result in higher average costs. The diagram depicts five *ATC* curves from which to select in purple. In reality, businesses have an almost infinite number of short-run average total cost curves from which to operate.

the objective of minimizing costs for an expected future quantity that maximizes profit. They make the best forecast they can, but inevitably will sometimes guess wrong.

Exhibit 6 demonstrates five possible short-run average total cost curves in purple, each one representing a different business plan. Those on the right side of the graph reflect companies that expect to produce a larger level of output and have built their companies in such a way as to minimize costs when output is high. They typically have lots of physical capital. Those on the left side (lower output) have planned the size of their company on the assumption that output will remain low. They do not expect to produce a large output and have avoided significant expenses. In the long run, businesses have an almost infinite number of short-run average cost curves from which to choose. In the short run, they are stuck on the short-run *ATC* they previously choose.

Economies of Scale: The Benefit of Mass Production

If Maria were to expand to multiple locations, and her expertise and skills could manage these additional locations at relatively little added expense, Maria would be experiencing economies of scale. **Economies of scale** occur when the long-run average total cost declines as output increases. They reflect the benefits of mass production.

To be clear, whenever output expands, total costs increase; but it is often the case that average cost declines. For example, total costs rise when automakers produce more cars, but it is entirely possible that the per car cost declines. If so, the firm is experiencing the benefits of mass production known as economies of scale.

For instance, in 2018, Tesla completed construction of a massive factory to produce car batteries, far more than needed worldwide only a few years earlier. Because of the company's fast growth, it was planning ahead to build the capital needed for a company that (upper management hoped) would grow much larger in the future. Obviously, this increases total cost. However, Tesla expected that this new factory would reduce its ATC in the long run by achieving economies of scale.[1]

economies of scale

A condition occurring when long-run average total cost declines as output increases.

Two Sources of Economies of Scale

- *Increased specialization:* As businesses get larger, each unit of labor can specialize in more narrowly defined tasks. In the automobile business, with increased specialization salespeople can focus on sales, accountants and finance experts on financial matters, engineers on automobile technology and design improvements, while plant workers focus on production. For Maria, increased specialization might mean hiring a restaurant manager to handle inventory, staff scheduling, and marketing.

- *Increased efficiency in use of physical capital:* Economies of scale also come into play when making capital investments. It would make little sense for Maria to invest in an expensive, high-end color printer to create her menus. However, suppose the print center at Staples has invested in a high-end printer that cost upward of $20,000, and it will print Maria's menus at relatively low cost. That's because Staples is spreading the cost of the printer over thousands and thousands of copies made in its shop. Economies of scale are the reason why automakers are willing to spend millions on state-of-the-art robots, and why Tesla is investing in a battery plant: Economies of scale allow costs to be spread out over a very large number of units.

Minimum Efficient Scale: When Economies of Scale Are Exhausted Economies of scale are not endless; average cost (per unit cost) does not fall to zero. At some point, all economies of scale are exhausted. The point at which businesses have taken advantage of every known benefit of mass production is called the minimum efficient scale. The **minimum efficient scale (MES)** is the smallest level of output at which all economies of scale have been fully utilized. Beyond this point, the long-run average total cost curve no longer declines. The minimum efficient scale is shown in Exhibit 7. Note that not all firms produce at the minimum efficient scale. Exotic and elite carmakers such as Ferrari produce high-end performance and luxury cars almost entirely by hand. The cost of producing each unit is extremely high, and relatively few of these cars will be sold, at very high prices. Ferrari is an example of a company that has not reached MES. Ferrari remains viable primarily because it is able to charge high prices due to its exclusivity.

The typical shape of the LRATC curve is that of a flat bottom bowl, as seen in Exhibit 7. The first part of the curve reflects economies of scale. These are exhausted at the minimum efficient scale. The typical LRATC curve is flat at outputs just beyond the minimum efficient scale.

Think & Speak Like an Economist

Remember: The concept of diminishing returns is a short-run concept assuming a fixed input—each additional worker adds less to output with a fixed store or factory size. In contrast, the concept of economies of scale is a long-run concept that assumes all inputs can change, including buildings and machines.

minimum efficient scale (MES) The smallest level of output at which all economies of scale have been fully utilized.

EXHIBIT 7 Typical Long-Run Average Total Cost Curve

A typical long-run average total cost curve exhibits economies of scale at low levels of output. When all economies of scale are exhausted, a business reaches its minimum efficient scale. Beyond this point, firms typically experience constant returns to scale and then, beyond some other point, diseconomies of scale. Businesses often find their optimal firm size to be in the region of constant returns to scale.

Λ Economies of scale can result from use of robotics and other forms of physical capital.

Constant Returns to Scale: A Flat LRATC Curve

Once economies of scale have been fully utilized, long-run average total cost no longer declines. At the same time, average total cost may not immediately increase with additional output. **Constant returns to scale** occur when long-run average total cost does not change as output increases. Maria's pizza restaurant is an example of constant returns to scale. Once she reaches the minimum efficient scale, twice as many pizzas mean twice as much flour, cheese, ovens, and pizza shop locations. Therefore, it's quite likely that average total cost neither declines nor increases. As a result, Maria only needs to reach the minimum efficient scale to have costs similar to those of large chains like Pizza Hut and Papa John's. Yes, pizza giants have thousands of stores, but the average cost at each store is roughly the same as what Maria's restaurant will incur.

Businesses in competitive industries find the optimal firm size to be in the region of constant returns to scale. Smaller firms will have a higher average cost than their larger rivals. These companies would find it difficult to compete with the lower average total cost of their larger rivals.

Diseconomies of Scale: An Upward-Sloping LRATC Curve

If a business expands even further, it *may* run into a situation where its average cost starts increasing. **Diseconomies of scale** occur when the long-run average total cost increases as output increases. Here, the firm has become so large that it is difficult to effectively manage: The business has become a complex bureaucracy in which assets and tasks become overly complicated or duplicated. For example, a local call center manager may spend resources developing a more efficient way to handle customer service calls. At the same time, *another* call center manager at the same firm engages in the exact same task. Since neither call center is aware of the ongoing effort of the other, work is being duplicated, increasing the overall costs of the firm. In short, bigger is not always better.

Generally, businesses will not knowingly expand to the points of diseconomies of scale as they will have a cost *disadvantage* over there smaller rivals. There are at least two main sources of diseconomies of scale: the principal–agent problem and the fact that input costs tend to increase with expansion.

- *Principal–agent problem.* It is increasingly difficult to maintain motivation and enthusiasm among workers and low-level managers as firms get larger. This is part of the *principal–agent problem*—the difficulty of making agents act in the best interest of the principals that they serve. As described in Chapter 9, the goal of the principal is to maximize profit, while the goal of the agent is likely to maintain employment to enhance career potential, or enjoy lots of vacation time. As companies grow, they hire more and more managers, and each manager gets a smaller and smaller share of the profits that result from hard work. This is why hired managers in big companies have less incentive to work hard than an entrepreneur who owns a smaller company. It is also why some companies offer profit sharing to their employees.

- *Input costs increase.* As firms become larger, they tend to bid up their own costs. An automobile factory in a small town might expand to the point where it can only hire additional workers by bidding up wages or paying people to relocate from outside the town, increasing overall cost.

constant returns to scale
A condition occurring when long-run average total cost does not change as output increases.

diseconomies of scale
A condition occurring when long-run average total cost increase as output increases.

POLICY BRIEF Betting on Electric Car Batteries

In an effort to offset the high price of gasoline and reduce the environmental damages of fossil fuels, governments around the world have subsidized the production of electric cars. But whether economies of scale can be reached in large car batteries is uncertain. If economies of scale can be reached, building a massive battery factory might prove very lucrative.

On the other hand, increases in input costs are often a major obstacle in achieving economies of scale. In the case of car batteries, some 30% of the cost derives from nickel, manganese, and cobalt. If the prices of such raw materials increase as the demand for car batteries increases, as some experts predict they will, diseconomies of scale may be present.

Nissan put its money where its mouth is, taking advantage of government subsidies and building a large-scale battery plant in Smyrna, Tennessee. Battery manufacturer A123 Systems also opened new battery plants, noting that it expects battery costs to decrease by a factor of two or more. Likewise, electric car maker Tesla made a huge investment in battery production. These businesses believe that mass production will lower overall average cost.[*]

[*]See Mike Ramsey, "High Battery Cost Curbs Electric Cars," *The Wall Street Journal*, October 17, 2010, http://www.wsj.com/articles/SB10001424052748703735804575536242934528502.

Long Run Average Total Cost in Select Industries

Let's see how the LRATC curve determines industry characteristics by considering three industries: dry cleaners, automakers, and fast-food providers. The dry cleaner industry is dominated by small firms; many are family-owned businesses. This means the output level at which diseconomies of scale set in is fairly low. The auto industry, on the other hand, is dominated by very large companies, as there are enormous economies of scale from mass production on assembly lines. This means the LRATC slopes downward for quite a large range of output. The minimum efficient scale might be several million cars per year.

The fast-food industry is perhaps the most interesting case. It's an industry where huge corporations, mom-and-pop take-out restaurants, and tiny food trucks compete side by side. The most likely explanation for this diversity is that the constant returns to scale range in the restaurant industry is quite large. The LRATC curve is relatively flat. The advantages of scale for the large firms are roughly offset by the tighter quality control and efficiency of small restaurants, which position the owner directly onsite to oversee operations. That's why large chains like McDonald's often use a franchise structure (see Chapter 9): Giving the local manager partial ownership helps him or her overcome the principal–agent problem. As a general rule, large fast-food chains do better when the product line remains simple, and it's easy to delegate authority to others. One rarely sees large corporations in the high end of expensive fine dining, which requires careful oversight by the owner.

Economies of Scope

When a business expands into a *different* product line, it often is able to further reduce long-run average cost by taking advantage of economies of scope. **Economies of scope** are reductions in costs associated with a business expanding into multiple product lines. A pizzeria might choose to also produce calzones, as the two foods use many of the same ingredients. When economies of scope exist, the combined costs of a *single* business producing multiple products are lower than if *multiple* businesses produce the same products.

economies of scope
Reductions in costs associated with a business expanding into multiple product lines.

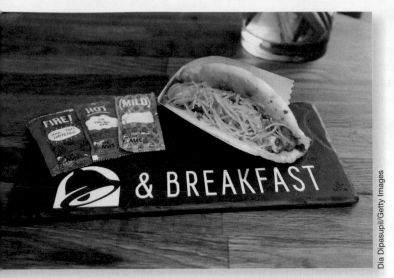

Dia Dipasupil/Getty Images

∧ Taco Bell takes advantage of economies of scope by serving breakfast.

Economies of scope are different from economies of scale. Economies of scale decrease average costs by expanding production in the *same* product line. Economies of scope occur when a business expands into a *different* product line. For example, cable television companies provide cable television, telephone, and Internet service at a lower combined cost than if three separate companies offer the same services. Likewise, General Motors manufactures automobiles and trucks at lower costs than if two separate firms made only cars and only trucks. That's because certain components which it produces can be used in both products.

📊 BUSINESS BRIEF Breakfast at Taco Bell?

Taco Bell is best known for its low-cost Mexican menu. Beginning in 2014, however, the fast-food giant began to sell breakfast. Why? The opportunity to be open more hours to increase revenue was certainly one reason. Economies of scope was another. At the time, the fast-food breakfast industry did over $50 billion worth of business.

The marginal cost of remaining open additional hours was relatively low: It would involve hiring some additional staff and purchasing various other food ingredients, but important fixed costs such as the cost of renting, and heating and cooling, locations were already covered by the chain's lunch and dinner operations. Adding breakfast service thus allowed Taco Bell to take advantage of economies of scope: One franchise location serving both breakfast and a daytime menu needs only one building. Why do so in 2014? According to one source, millennials prefer items like breakfast tacos that they "can hold in one hand and cellphones in the other."*

Such a firm will clearly have lower costs than if two firms providing the same dining options existed separately: one open in the morning and one open during the day and at night, each operating out of its own location.

*Bruce Horovitz, "Taco Bell Thinking Outside the Breakfast Bun," *USA Today.* February 24, 2014, http://www.usatoday.com/story/money/business/2014/02/24/taco-bell-fast-food-breakfast/5704107/.

BUSINESS TAKEAWAY

Since a firm's profit is revenue minus costs, business managers must keep a watchful eye on all types of costs. One key step is understanding the differences between long- and short-run costs, and utilizing optimal approaches for managing both. Businesses that sign long-term contracts to rent buildings must pay the amount of any lease even if their business proves unsuccessful. Such costs are referred to as fixed costs. On the other hand, variable costs are easier to manage. Businesses that are booming will have more variable costs than firms whose business is lackluster. A pizzeria in a college town that expects to sell a lot of pizzas during the school year will buy more cheese when school is in session than it will when students return home for the summer.

In the long run, however, firms can adapt to changing circumstances, and long-run costs thus require a different analysis. Expanding a business can allow firms to take advantage of economies of scale, the benefit of mass production. Should firms *always* attempt to expand to take advantage of economies of scale? Absolutely not. Businesses need to consider if expansion will lead to managerial slack or drive up input costs.

If either problem occurs, the firm may be experiencing diseconomies of scale. In such cases, expanding to capture economies of scale may not be prudent. Furthermore, businesses must consider their ability to sell more products at a profitable price if they should expand. An important point made in the coming chapters is that the goal of a business is generally to maximize profits and not simply to minimize costs.

Firms occasionally downsize in an effort to reduce their average total cost. General Motors, for example, eliminated many nameplates, such as Pontiac and Saturn, during the Great Recession (2007–09). Some firms will outsource certain functions to smaller specialized firms that are more efficient at doing specific tasks. Remember, businesses in competitive industries seek the optimal firm size to be in the region of constant returns to scale. The goal is to keep costs as low as those of your competitors.

Most competitive firms tend to operate in a range of constant returns to scale. Furthermore, businesses must also be concerned with sales. Profits may fall if managers expand in order to lower average total cost at a time when they cannot sell additional output. On the other hand, if businesses are able to easily sell additional output, expanding the firm's production capacity likely makes sense, particularly when economies of scale are present.

CHAPTER STUDY GUIDE

11.1 ECONOMIC COST AND ECONOMIC PROFIT

Economists and accountants use different measures of cost and consequently have different measures of profit. **Accounting profit** equals total revenue minus accounting costs. **Explicit costs** are input costs that involve actual payments of money. **Accounting costs** are the explicit costs of production. In addition to explicit costs, economists also consider **implicit costs**, input costs that do not involve the payment of money. **Economic costs** are explicit costs plus the implicit costs of production. **Economic profit** equals total revenue minus economic costs. Finally, zero economic profit means a normal accounting profit.

11.2 PRODUCTION IN THE SHORT RUN

The **production function** expresses the technological relationship between different combinations of inputs and maximum output. The **marginal physical product of labor (MPP_L)** is the additional output from an additional unit of labor, holding the amount of physical capital and other inputs fixed. Mathematically,

$$\text{Marginal physical}\atop\text{product of labor} = \frac{\text{Change in output}}{\text{Change in labor}} = \frac{\Delta Q}{\Delta L}$$

The **law of diminishing returns** states that, in the short run, the marginal physical product of labor declines as more labor is employed, with other inputs held fixed. This means that each additional worker adds less to total output than the previous worker, when the amount of physical capital is fixed. This is due to short-run limitations on technology and the amount of capital.

11.3 COSTS IN THE SHORT RUN

In the short run, costs can be categorized in two ways: as variable costs and as fixed costs. **Fixed costs (FC)** are short-run costs that do not change with the quantity of output. **Variable costs (VC)** are short-run costs that change with the quantity of output. Finally, **total costs (TC)** are the cost of all inputs of production, which equals fixed costs plus variable costs: $TC = VC + FC$. It is often useful to know the average cost, the cost per unit of production. There are three different types of average cost. **Average fixed cost (AFC)** is fixed costs per unit; $AFC = FC/Q$. **Average variable cost (AVC)** is variable costs per unit; $AVC = VC/Q$. **Average total cost (ATC)** is total costs per unit; $ATC = TC/Q$. Just as total costs are the sum of fixed and variable costs, average total cost is equal to the sum of average fixed cost and average variable cost. **Marginal cost (MC)** is the additional cost a business incurs from 1 additional unit of output; $MC = \Delta TC/\Delta Q$. Some costs have already occurred or been legally agreed to. **Sunk costs** are costs that are not avoidable; and thus they should not affect economic decision making. It is often useful to graph various cost curves. Each curve has a distinct shape. The AFC curve is downward-sloping. The MC and AVC curves are upward-sloping in the relevant range. The ATC curve is U-shaped, with a minimum point occurring where $MC = ATC$. The marginal cost curve is upward-sloping due to the law of diminishing returns.

11.4 AVERAGE COST IN THE LONG RUN AND ECONOMIES OF SCALE

The **long-run average total cost curve (*LRATC*)** represents the lowest average total cost at which a business can produce various levels of output when all inputs are allowed to vary. A downward-sloping *LRATC* curve represents economies of scale. **Economies of scale** occur when long-run average total cost declines as output increases. Economies of scale reflect the benefits of mass production that occur due to increased specialization or increased efficiency in the use of capital. At some point, all economies of scale are utilized. The **minimum efficient scale (*MES*)** is the smallest level of output at which all economies of scale have been fully utilized. Beyond this point, the long-run average total cost curve no longer declines. *LRATC* may also exhibit constant returns to scale or diseconomies of scale. **Constant returns to scale** occur when the long-run average total cost does not change as output increases. **Diseconomies of scale** occur when the long-run average total cost increases as output increases. Diseconomies of scale might occur due to the principal–agent problem or increases in input costs. Finally, when a business expands into a *different* product line, it often is able to further reduce long-run overall average cost by taking advantage of economies of scope. **Economies of scope** are reductions in costs associated with a business expanding into multiple product lines.

TOP TEN TERMS AND CONCEPTS

(1) Explicit Costs and Implicit Costs

(2) Accounting Profit and Economic Profit

(3) Marginal Physical Product

(4) Law of Diminishing Returns

(5) Variable Costs, Fixed Costs, and Total Costs

(6) Average Variable, Average Fixed, and Average Total Cost

(7) Marginal Cost

(8) Economies of Scale and Minimum Efficient Scale

(9) Constant Returns to Scale and Diseconomies of Scale

(10) Economies of Scope

STUDY PROBLEMS

1. Describe the difference between economic profit and accounting profit.

2. 📊 According to *The Economist,* "The marginal cost of wind and solar power is zero."[2] Nevertheless, the average cost of electricity generated from coal or oil is often lower. Explain how this might be the case.

3. Based on the figure below,

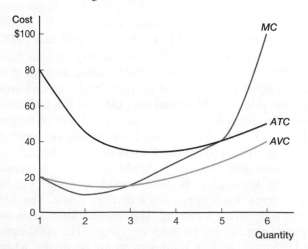

   a. what is the *ATC* at 3 units of output?

   b. what are the total costs at 3 units of output?

   c. what are the average total, average variable, and average fixed costs at 6 units of output?

   d. what level of output minimizes *ATC*? How can you tell that this point minimizes *ATC*?

   e. what are the fixed costs at 3 units of output?

   f. Explain the differences in the answers to parts c and e.

4. 🏛 What is the minimum efficient scale? How will a firm know when it reaches this "minimum"?

5. 📊 Describe diminishing returns. Is the concept a short- or long-run concept?

6. What is higher: the marginal cost of a book publisher printing one additional book or the marginal cost of a book publisher allowing for one additional download?

7. 📊 Which of the following is an example of a sunk cost?

   a. a long-term contract for a star athlete

   b. hot dogs sold at a stadium

   c. a lease agreement on a new car

   d. workers hired on a daily basis

8. 🏛 Describe economies of scale. What are their sources? Describe diseconomies of scale. What are their sources?

9. Consider the following table. Show the link between total output and labor.

Labor	Output
1	10
2	30
3	45
4	55
5	60
6	62

a. What is the marginal physical product of the 2nd, 4th, and 6th worker?

b. Where do diminishing returns occur?

c. What happens to marginal cost when diminishing returns occur?

d. A worker costs $100 a day. There are no other variable costs. Fixed costs are $1,000. What are the total costs of 55 units of output?

e. What are the total costs of 60 units of output?

10. Consider the impact on cost curves of two tax proposals with regard to pizza and pizza sellers. One calls for a tax of $1 per pizza to be paid by the seller. The other calls for a $100 tax to be levied on pizza sellers each week.

a. Which tax will have no impact on marginal cost?

b. Which tax will have no impact on fixed costs?

c. Which tax will have no impact on average variable costs?

11. Marissa is a local florist. She is considering doubling the size of her flower shop when her current rental agreement expires. Is she making a short- or long-run decision?

12. ▲ Laura is considering doubling the size of her clothing store. Determine whether each of the following expansion results exhibits economies of scale, constant returns to scale, or diseconomies of scale:

a. Her average total costs remain unchanged.

b. Her average total costs decline.

c. Her total costs increase but less than double.

d. Her total costs more than double.

e. Her total costs exactly double.

13. Complete the following table:

Q	FC	VC	TC	MC
0			100	—
1		50		
2				60
3		180		
4			360	

14. Complete the following table (*Hint:* You may need to separately estimate total costs and variable costs):

Q	AFC	AVC	ATC	MC
1	100	100		
2		200		
3			300	
4				500
5			400	

15. In each of the following cases, describe if the firm is likely to experience economies of scale or diseconomies of scale:

a. a small automaker that is starting to use robots and modern manufacturing techniques

b. a jewelry manufacturer that specializes in rare diamonds

c. a large automaker with multiple managers for each employee

16. 📊 Describe economies of scope. How are they different ✖ from economies of scale?

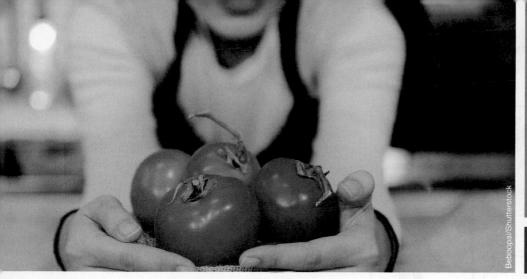

Beboopai/Shutterstock

∧ Sellers of tomatoes encounter stiff competition.

Perfect Competition

Maximizing Profits in Highly Competitive Markets

Maria is moving one step closer to opening her restaurant, putting together a business strategy where she'll detail her plans for its menu and pricing. But before she can determine what to serve and how much to charge for it, Maria needs to think very carefully about the business environment she will be entering: How many restaurants are nearby? What do they charge? And why do the local restaurants vary in price, while the farmers she's contacted as potential suppliers charge almost the same exact price for tomatoes? Maria must consider what economists refer to as market structure—the business composition of a specific industry, especially the size and number of competing firms.

This chapter focuses on businesses with no pricing power at all, such as Maria's possible tomato suppliers, who compete in a market structure known as *perfect competition*. Although perfect competition is not very common, it serves as a useful benchmark for understanding other market structures examined in subsequent chapters.

12.1 THE FOUR MARKET STRUCTURES

Maria knows that she will have limited ability to set prices due to stiff competition from nearby pizza shops. This is even more true of the farms that supply her tomatoes. Pricing and output decisions are largely determined by the business environment in which a firm operates— what economists refer to as market structure. **Market structure** is the business composition of a specific industry or product market, including the size and number of competing firms. The market characteristics of an industry impact degree of competition, pricing power, and long-run profitability. We'll begin by looking at the four major market structures, the first of which, perfect competition, is the main subject of this chapter.

Chapter Learning Targets

- Compare and contrast the four market structures.

- Identify the key market characteristics of perfect competition.

- Determine the profit-maximizing behavior of firms in perfect competition.

- Describe profit-maximizing behavior when losses occur and the links between marginal cost and supply curves.

- Discuss the long-run supply curve and how perfect competition results in productive and allocative efficiency.

243

Mark Lynch/Cartoonstock.com

CartoonStock.com

Market structures range from highly competitive (lots of sellers selling the exact same product) to completely uncompetitive (one seller completely dominating the entire industry), with a great deal of variation in between. For simplicity, economists think of industries as falling into one of four basic structures:

- *Perfect competition* is a market structure with a very large number of sellers of a standardized product. Perfect competition is relatively rare, but Maria's tomato sellers are a good example—most customers see little difference between Farmer A's plum tomatoes and Farmer B's plum tomatoes. Examples include many agricultural products, like tomatoes, eggs, and milk, as well as raw materials and commodities like copper, aluminum, and rubber.

- *Monopolistic competition* is a market structure with many firms selling similar but differentiated product. If Maria chooses to establish her business on a crowded downtown street with lots of restaurants that sell similar but not quite the same products, she will be entering a monopolistic competition structure. Other examples include smartphone apps, toothpaste, and services such as those a hair salon might provide.

- *Oligopoly* is a market structure with a few dominant firms that are highly interdependent. For example, chances are that the phone in your pocket is running on AT&T, Verizon, T-Mobile, or Sprint's mobile network. These firms control 98% of the cellular services market in the United States; while fiercely competitive with one another, they don't face much competition from other firms.[1]

- *Monopoly* is a market structure with high barriers to entry in which a single seller supplies a product that has no close substitutes. Examples include patented medicine and electricity delivery. In each of these examples, one firm dominates a market as it is extremely difficult for new rivals to enter the market.

The most obvious difference between the four market structures is the number of competing firms. Exhibit 1 summarizes the four market structures in terms of the number of firms in each structure. The number of sellers in a market can vary significantly: At one extreme is a monopoly, a market structure with a single firm, and at the other, perfect competition, a market structure in which a very large number of firms operate.

As you will discover, the four market structures depend on the number of sellers, entry conditions, price-setting ability, price elasticity of demand that each firm faces, potential for positive long-run economic profit, and degree of product differentiation. Bear in mind that not every business or industry will fit precisely into one of these four categories. There are many examples of industries that have some characteristics of multiple market structures.

The characteristics of each market structure are often interconnected. In perfect competition, for example, a very large number of competing firms exist in part because of the low barriers to entry. This means that other firms can easily enter a competitive market if profits are being made. Such a scenario keeps economic profits to a minimum, as more competition tends to put downward pressure on market price. In perfect competition, each firm is a *price taker*. With a large number of firms selling identical products, each firm loses the ability to control price.

market structure The business composition of a specific industry or product market, including the size and number of competing firms.

EXHIBIT 1   Four Market Structures and the Number of Firms

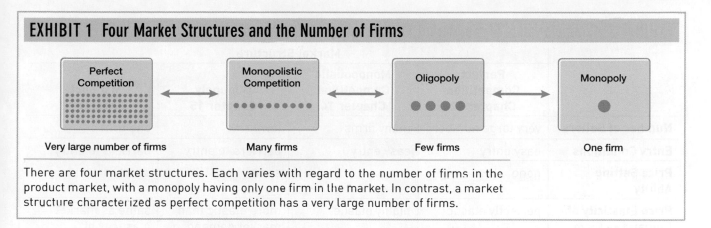

Perfect Competition	Monopolistic Competition	Oligopoly	Monopoly
Very large number of firms	Many firms	Few firms	One firm

There are four market structures. Each varies with regard to the number of firms in the product market, with a monopoly having only one firm in the market. In contrast, a market structure characterized as perfect competition has a very large number of firms.

In sharp contrast, the key characteristic of a monopoly is the fact that there is *one firm.* That is because high barriers to entry prevent potential rivals from entering the market. With zero rivals, a monopolist has far more control over price than firms in other market structures, and is more likely to earn positive long-run economic profits.

In an oligopoly, there are only a few dominant firms, entering the market is difficult, and long-run profits are possible. The key characteristic of oligopolies is that firms are *highly interdependent,* and therefore each firm's actions have a big impact on its rivals. For example, when Apple changes the price or features on a smartphone, rival firm Samsung will be affected and will frequently want to respond. Since barriers to entry exist, firms like Apple and Samsung can make larger than normal profits.

In monopolistic competition, there are many firms selling products that are similar but not perfect substitutes for each other. Economists call these close substitutes *differentiated products.* For example, pizza from Domino's is different than pizza sold by other pizza sellers, but all the businesses are part of the same industry. Nonetheless, firms have only a limited ability to set price due to competitive pressures. As with perfect competition, other firms can easily enter a competitive market if profits are being made. This keeps economic profits at a minimum.

In the pages that follow, we will explore each of these structures in depth. We begin now with perfect competition, the focus of this chapter, which is highlighted in Exhibit 2.

BUSINESS BRIEF   A Tale of Two Tablet Markets

The market for premium tablet computers is not an example of perfect competition. It is dominated by Apple, which set the standard for tablet computing with the iPad, iPad Air, and iPad Mini. Entry is extremely difficult, though several manufacturers have tried. Competitors ranging from Samsung to Nokia to Amazon have spent enormous amounts of money developing premium products to compete with the iPad, but few have even made dent. Many potential buyers are already entrenched in the Apple ecosystem and resistant to change. Such barriers to entry are similar to those that may be observed in oligopolies or monopolies.

In contrast, entry into the market for budget tablets is considerably easier and highly competitive. These models often have a 7- or 8-inch screen, use Google's Android operating system (which is free), and sell for as little as $100. In many ways, budget tablets are similar to other standardized products like tomatoes and computer chips.

The Economist magazine notes, "Entry at the bottom is as easy as it is hard at the top, with (profit) margins that reflect perfect competition rather than near-monopoly."* As such, economic profit in the budget tablet market is close to zero, but Apple's profits in the premium market are considerably higher.

*Quoted in "Overdose," *The Economist,* October 26, 2013, http://www.economist.com/news/business/21588377 -market-tablets-has-already-split-two-overdose.

EXHIBIT 2   Characteristics of the Market Structures: Perfect Competition

	Market Structure			
	Perfect Competition Chapter 12	**Monopolistic Competition** Chapter 14	**Oligopoly** Chapter 15	**Monopoly** Chapter 13
Number of Sellers	very large number	many firms	few firms	one firm
Entry Conditions	easy entry	easy entry	barriers to entry	barriers to entry
Price Setting Ability	none	some	some	some
Price Elasticity of Demand — Firm Level	perfectly elastic	highly elastic	more elastic than market demand	same as market elasticity of demand
Long-Run Profit	zero economic profit	zero economic profit	potentially	potentially
Product Differentiation	standardized product	differentiated product	varies by product market	unique product with no close substitutes
Key Characteristic	firms price takers	differentiated product	firms highly interdependent	one firm
Examples	tomatoes copper lumber	delivered pizza smartphone apps toothpaste	search engines wireless service mobile phones	patented medicine first-class mail electricity delivery

Each market structure varies in the number of sellers, entry conditions, price-setting ability, price elasticity of demand that the firm's product faces, potential for long-run profits, and product differentiation. In perfect competition, there are a large number of sellers and every firm is a price taker.

12.2 CHARACTERISTICS OF PERFECT COMPETITION

In perfect competition, products are essentially *standardized*: Copper is copper, oil is oil, and tomatoes of a certain type are much the same. As noted at the beginning of this chapter, **perfect competition** is a market structure in which a very large number of sellers supply a standardized product. Of course, some buyers may still express preferences—Maria may be looking for organic tomatoes, or local tomatoes, or a particular type of heirloom tomato, or just a tomato vendor with whom she likes to do business. For these reasons, truly "perfect" perfect competition is somewhat rare. But despite the fact that perfect competition is relatively uncommon, the tools used to make sense of business decision making in perfect competition are powerful and help us understand decision making in more complicated market structures.

Firms in Perfect Competition Are Price Takers

perfect competition A market structure in which a very large number of sellers supply a standardized product.

Because of the large number of firms, and because the product is standardized, each individual seller tends to have very little say on price in a perfectly competitive market. A family farmer who sells tomatoes, for example, cannot charge more for his tomatoes than other farmers with a similar product. In economic terms, the tomato farmer is a price taker.

A **price taker** is a firm that does not have the ability to impact the market price. Businesses are price takers because they are small relative to the overall market. Each year, U.S. farmers produce over 25 billion pounds of tomatoes (about 80 pounds per person)—and that figure, according to the U.S. Department of Agriculture, does not even include tomatoes grown in home gardens by end users. What impact does a small local farmer thus have on the market price of tomatoes in the United States? Economists believe the answer to this question is almost none.

Consider Exhibit 3. In Panel A, we graph the market supply and market demand for fresh tomatoes. For simplicity, we assume 80 billion one-pound boxes of tomatoes are sold each year and the equilibrium price is $7 per box. In Panel B, we graph the demand a single firm—in this case, a small local farmer—faces. Whether our small local farmer sells 100 or 200 or even 300 one-pound boxes, he does not impact the price in a market of several billion boxes. Since the farmer can sell all the tomatoes he wants at $7 a box, he has no reason to lower his price. Conversely, if the farmer attempts to increase the price of tomatoes, he will sell no tomatoes at all. Buyers have thousands of other farmers from which to choose.

In perfect competition, there are a very large number of competing firms, and no barriers to entry. This means firms in perfect competition are price takers, and also that new firms can easily enter a competitive market if economic profits are being made. Thus, each farmer faces a demand curve that is perfectly elastic, which means the demand curve each firm faces is a horizontal line. As we will see, this lack of pricing power simplifies the decision making for firms in perfectly competitive industries—they don't have to decide what price to change, the market tells them.

price taker A firm that does not have the ability to impact market price.

Think & Speak Like an Economist

In market structures other than a monopoly, the demand curve that a firm faces is not the same as the market demand curve. In perfect competition, the demand curve facing the firm is perfectly elastic as all firms are price takers.

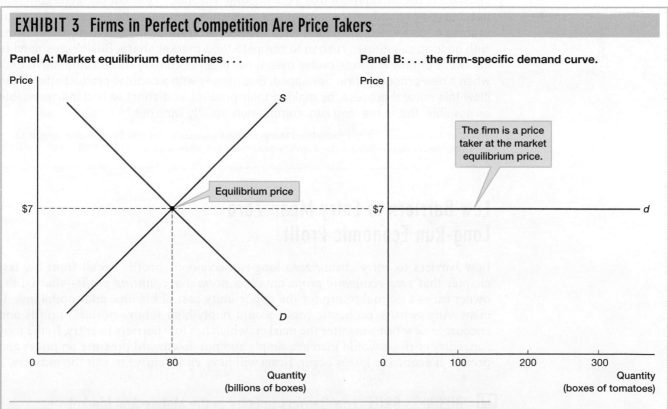

EXHIBIT 3   Firms in Perfect Competition Are Price Takers

Panel A: Market equilibrium determines . . .

Panel B: . . . the firm-specific demand curve.

The price of tomatoes is determined by market supply and market demand (Panel A). Here, the equilibrium price is $7. Firms in perfect competition take this price as given. The firm's demand curve is perfectly price elastic (Panel B).

Firms Sell Standardized Products

Products in perfect competition are standardized and often called *commodities,* standardized goods such as metals (copper, iron), energy (coal, oil, and natural gas), and agricultural products (eggs, tomatoes, and milk). In such markets, competing firms' products are roughly equivalent: One tomato is as good as another. In contrast, products such as pizza, cars, and smartphones have different attributes from one maker to the next. Not every commodity business is perfectly competitive. Oil, for example, is a commodity dominated by a few large producers. In Chapter 15, we will look at the OPEC oil cartel, which does retain some pricing power.

Nonetheless, in the modern business world, the term "commodity" is so closely associated with price takers that it is now often used as a metaphor for highly competitive product markets that are fairly close to perfect competition. For example, the *budget* tablet market is viewed as a commodity because of the intensity of the competition. Similarly, a stock market analyst might say, "Computer memory chips are becoming a commodity." What she actually means is that the computer memory chip market is becoming so competitive that firms have no pricing power and profits are low.

📊 BUSINESS BRIEF Do You Still Need Microsoft Office?

Some 1.1 billion people use Microsoft Office products such as Word, Excel, and PowerPoint. Recently, however, Google, Apple, and others have started to offer similar products for free. These products include Google Docs, Sheets, Slides (all free) and Apple iWork (included with Apple hardware).

With so many substitutes, a logical question to ask is: "Does anyone really need Microsoft Office?" If the answer is "no," then economic theory suggests that office software is becoming more like a commodity. The industry is not perfectly competitive, but it is certainly more competitive than when dominated by Microsoft. A similar process occurs when the patent for a medical drug runs out, and many other firms with generic substitutes rush in to compete for a market share. Businesses need to be aware of how markets evolve over time, often becoming more competitive than when a new product is first developed. Businesses with a popular product often try to slow this natural process, by making their product as distinctive and indispensable as possible. But in the long run, competition usually wins out.*

*Based on Joanna Stern, "Do You Really Need Microsoft Office Anymore?," *The Wall Street Journal,* August 12, 2014, http://www.wsj.com/articles/do-you-really-need-microsoft-office-anymore-1407873198.

Low Barriers to Entry Mean Zero Long-Run Economic Profit

Low barriers to entry ensure zero long-run economic profit. Recall from the last chapter that *zero economic profit* entails a *normal accounting profit*—that is, the owner earns a normal return for the opportunity cost of his time and capital investment. Any *positive* economic profit would imply high (above-normal) profits and encourage new firms to enter the market, which has low barriers to entry. In the long run, entry of rivals would increase supply and put downward pressure on prices and profits. If economic losses occur, firms will have an incentive to exit the industry.

📊 BUSINESS BRIEF Low Barriers to Entry in the Mobile App Market

In 2013, Australian entrepreneur Stuart Hall spent a few hours researching and coding a smartphone app called *7 Minute Workout.* He uploaded it to the App Store, where it became an immediate hit, earning Hall more than US$50,000 the first year. Hall states, "I put very little work into an app and launched it into a huge market."* The app development world was in the midst of what was then referred to as the "Mobile Gold Rush"—the lure of large profits in a promising new market.†

Entry into the app market is relatively quick and easy; the barriers to entry are low. But that means the enormous economic profits made by Hall and other like him can stop just as quickly. A year later, a study by VisionMobile found that 2% of developers made more than the other 98% combined—and most developers made relatively little. Even apps that launch success-fully will quickly find themselves facing competition from similar products. The wildly successful *Angry Birds*, for example, eventually faced competition from copycats: First came *Flappy Birds*, followed by clones *Flappy Wings*, *Snappy Bird*, *Flappy Flyer*, and *The Impossible Flappy Game.* The low bar-riers to entry in this profitable market tend to put downward pressure on prices and profits, and while a successful app might make a lot of money when it first launches, in the long run, economic profits fall due to the intense competition.

∧ *Angry Birds* was followed by a flock of competitors.

*Quoted in Tim Bradshaw, "Apps: Growing Pains," *Financial Times*, August 19, 2014, http://www.ft.com/intl/cms/s/2/d72f0e14-27ab-11e4-be5a-00144feabdc0.html#axzz3eT7tIRSB.

†See Arden Pennell, "The Mobile Gold Rush Is Not Even Close to Peaking," *Business Insider,* March 12, 2012, http://www.businessinsider.com/ignitionwest/2012/mobile.

12.3 PROFIT MAXIMIZATION

We start our analysis of a business in perfect competition by looking at a firm's deci-sion on how much to produce in order to reach its objective of maximizing profits. To do so, we consider the case of one of Maria's possible tomato suppliers: Tom. We assume Tom's market is one of perfect competition, meaning he is a price taker. Here we will assume Tom can sell large boxes of tomatoes for $12. For simplicity, we also assume his production costs are similar to those faced by Maria in the previous chapter. As shown in Exhibit 4, Tom maximizes his profits at a quantity of five units, as no other level of output results in higher profits.

As we proceed, we will further explore two implications of profit maximization. First, we will explain why the marginal cost of selling the fifth box ($12) exactly equals the price he charges. Second, we will examine why Tom's profit of $20 equals his total revenue ($60) minus his total cost ($40) and equals his profit per unit ($4) times the number of units sold (5).

Marginal Revenue

Why does Tom stop at selling only five boxes? Why not sell the sixth box to increase sales and total revenue? Tom compares the additional revenue of selling the sixth box ($12) with the additional cost ($20) and recognizes selling that final box will *lowers* his profit by $8 (to $12 in Exhibit 4). Given this situation, Tom would not sell more tomatoes. This is the essence of marginal analysis described in Chapter 1.

When a firm sells an additional product, it will usually see its revenue increase. This increased revenue is known as **marginal revenue (MR)**, the additional revenue a business receives from one additional unit of output: $MR = \Delta TR / \Delta Q$. This is easiest to visualize in the case of perfect competition, where selling one more unit doesn't impact the market price.

marginal revenue (MR)
The additional revenue a business receives from one additional unit of output.

EXHIBIT 4   Profit Maximization by the Numbers (Price = $12)

Quantity (Q)	Price and Marginal Revenue (P)	Total Revenue (TR)	Total Cost (TC)	Marginal Cost (MC)	Average Total Cost (ATC)	Profit per Unit (P − ATC)	Profit TR − TC (P − ATC) × Q
1	12	12	16	4	16	−4	−4
2	12	24	18	2	9	3	6
3	12	36	21	3	7	5	15
4	12	48	28	7	7	5	20
5	**12**	**60**	**40**	**12**	**8**	**4**	**20**
6	12	72	60	20	10	2	12

To maximize profits, 5 units should be sold. Here profits equal $20, which equals total revenue ($60) minus total cost ($40); but also profit per unit ($4) times the number of units (5). Since the market structure is that of perfect competition, price ($12) equals marginal revenue. At the profit maximizing quantity, marginal cost also equals $12.

In perfect competition, marginal revenue equals price. It is simply the price at which the extra unit is sold ($MR = P$, with P = Price). Tom can sell each box he produces at the market price of $12 each. If he sells 100 boxes of tomatoes, his total revenue is $1,200. If he sells 101 boxes, his total revenue increases by $12 to $1,212. However, as you will discover in subsequent chapters, *marginal revenue does not equal price in other market structures.*

$$MR = \frac{\Delta TR}{\Delta Q}$$

$$MR = \text{Price (in perfect competition only)}$$

The concept of marginal revenue mirrors that of marginal cost (previous chapter). Recall marginal cost is the additional cost of producing an additional unit with $MC = \Delta TC / \Delta Q$.

Marginal Analysis

Marginal analysis entails comparing marginal revenue to marginal cost. All firms maximize profits at the quantity where marginal revenue equals marginal cost:

$$MR = MC$$

at the profit-maximizing level of output

The logic is incredibly simple. As long as marginal revenue is higher than marginal cost, a firm benefits from increasing production. Selling one extra unit brings in more revenue than it costs to produce one extra unit. Increased production is profitable. So firms will keep increasing production until they reach the point where MR is just equal to MC. In Exhibit 4, this occurs at five units. Here price, marginal revenue, and marginal cost all equal $12.

Previously, you learned that marginal cost curves are upward-sloping (beyond the first few units). Under perfect competition, MR = Price. That means the MR curve is a horizontal line—the demand curve facing the firm in perfect competition. Thus,

$$P = MC$$

at the profit-maximizing level of output when $MR = P$

Tom's cost curves are shown in Exhibit 5. The price is $12 and sellers take that price as given. Consequently, MR equals $12. This is the demand

Think & Speak Like an Economist

Economists believe that businesses maximize total profit and not necessarily market share, unit sales (Q), sales revenue (P × Q), or profit margin (P − ATC or the firm's profit per unit).

EXHIBIT 5 Three Simple Steps to Calculate Maximum Profit in Perfect Competition

A firm maximizes profits at a level of output where $MR = MC$. In this example, the market price of the product is $12. Each additional sale generates $12 of marginal revenue. Marginal cost equals $12 at 5 units of output (Step 1). At this level of output, average total cost (ATC) is $8 per unit (Step 2). Firms selling output at $12 with an ATC of $8 experience an economic profit of $4 per unit. Profit is $20 or $4 per unit on 5 units (Step 3). Additional output will decrease profit. Selling 6 units, for example, will lead to a profit of $12 (= $2 per unit × 6 units).

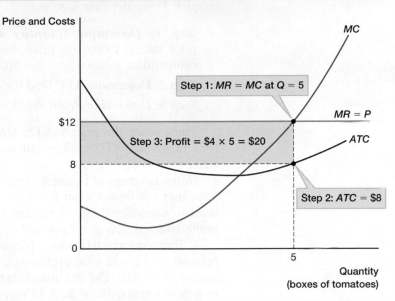

Step 1: $MR = MC$ at $Q = 5$

$MR = P$

ATC

Step 3: Profit = $4 × 5 = $20

Step 2: $ATC = 8

Quantity
(boxes of tomatoes)

curve facing Tom: the firm. The profit-maximizing number of units is 5. At *smaller* levels of output, $MR > MC$; thus, at these levels of output, producing 1 more unit adds more to revenue than to cost. For example, selling the third unit of output adds $12 to revenue but only $7 to cost. Selling extra units adds to profits. Conversely, at *larger* levels of output, $MR < MC$; at these levels of output producing additional units adds more to cost than to revenue, which lowers profit.

Three Simple Steps to Calculate Maximum Profit

Profit equals total revenue minus total costs:

$$\text{Profit} = \text{Total revenue} - \text{Total costs}$$

In our example, Tom is a price taker who sells 5 boxes of tomatoes for $12 each; thus, he has total revenue of $60 (= $12 × 5). Each box costs Tom an average of $8 to produce; thus, he has total costs of $40 (= $8 × 5). Tom's profits are $20. Maximizing profits entails finding the biggest possible difference between total revenue and total cost. And this occurs precisely at the point where $MR = MC$.

Total profit also equals profit per unit multiplied by the number of units. Since Tom experiences a profit of $4 per box (= $12 − $8) and sells 5 boxes, his profit is $20 (= $4 × 5):

$$\text{Profit} = (\text{Price} - \text{Average total cost}) \times \text{Quantity}$$
$$\text{Profit} = (P - ATC) \times Q$$

Mathematical Equivalence of Two Profit Formulas

$$\text{Profit} = TR - TC$$

Since $TR = P \times Q$ and $TC = ATC \times Q$, the equation can be rewritten as

$$\text{Profit} = (P \times Q) - (ATC \times Q)$$

Isolating Q, the equation can be rearranged as

$$\text{Profit} = (P - ATC) \times Q$$

Exhibit 5 demonstrates how to calculate the profit-maximizing quantity and the level of profit using marginal analysis, using the cost curves developed in the previous chapter. Three steps are involved:

Step 1: Determine Quantity and Price In perfect competition, firms are price takers. Using this price, find quantity (Q) at which $MR = MC$; in perfect competition, this is where $P = MC$.

Step 2: Determine ATC Find the average total cost (ATC) at this quantity.

Step 3: Determine Profit Profit $= (P - ATC) \times Q$

Thus, when the price is $12, MR is equal to MC at 5 units of output. At this level of output, $ATC = \$8$, profit *per unit* is $4 ($12 − $8), and total profit equal $20 (= $4 × 5).

In the language of business, profit per unit is sometimes called the *profit margin*. Note that you do not want to achieve the largest possible profit margin. Nor do you want to maximize the total number of units you sell. The goal is to maximize *total profit, which equals profit per unit times quantity.*

If Tom were to sell 6 units, ATC would increase to $10, the firm would have a profit per unit of $2, and total profits would decline to $12. This is because at 6 units of output $MC > MR$. The last unit costs more to produce than the extra revenue it earns. In fact, at 6 units, $MC = \$20$; $8 more than MR which is $12, so profit falls by $8 (to $12). Similarly, if you only produced 3 units, your profit per unit would be larger but total profit smaller.* Five is optimal.

12.4 BUSINESS DECISIONS TO SHUT DOWN OR EXIT

Of course, businesses do not always earn economic profits. At times, businesses earn zero economic profits, or even negative economic profits (i.e., economic losses). **Breakeven** occurs when economic profit equals zero. This results from price equaling average total cost.

Assume that as a result of other firms entering the market, the market price of a box of tomatoes falls to $7 (from $12). This is shown in Exhibit 6. Here, the profit-maximizing quantity of output is 4, as it is the quantity where $P = MC$. At this level of output, both price and average total cost equal $7, the firm has zero economic profit and is breaking even.

Remember, zero economic profit implies a normal accounting profit, which means it is not a bad performance, just average. For example, in the prior chapter, we considered what would happen if Maria quit her job to open a restaurant with an *accounting profit* of $150,000; equal to her former salary ($140,000) and forgone interest income ($10,000). When these opportunity costs are factored in, she is said to break even and has zero *economic profit.*

When price falls below the breakeven point, economic losses *must* occur, as the price will be lower than the average total cost for any level of output. Maria might unexpectedly see economic losses, and if such a pattern were to continue, she would have to make the difficult decision on whether to close her restaurant or not. It turns out that in the *long run,* a business incurring losses will cease operations. However, as you will soon discover, in the *short run,* there are times when the best decision is to continue operating—even at a loss. Such a decision is more complex in the short run, and that is where we begin.

The Short-Run Decision to Shut Down or Operate

The decision to shut down is a short-run decision; and is more complex due to the existence of fixed costs. When a firm shuts down, it will have zero revenue and presumably no variable costs. For Maria, there would be no reason to continue buying cheese if she

---

breakeven Occurs when economic profit equals zero.

*Due to the mathematical simplification of the example, profit also equals $20 at 4 units of output. Profit can never be higher than at the profit-maximizing quantity.

EXHIBIT 6 Breakeven Occurs When $P = ATC$

Breakeven is the level of output where economic profit equals zero. When the market price is $7, the profit-maximizing quantity of output equals 4 units, ATC equals $7, and the firm has zero economic profit. If market price is lower than $7, $P < ATC$ and an economic loss will occur.

does not plan on selling more pizza. For Tom, there would be no reason to pay people to pick tomatoes if he does not plan on selling them.

Unfortunately, when a business shuts down, it will continue to have fixed costs in the short run, such as a long-term land rental agreement of $12 per month. In that case, shutting down will mean a loss of the fixed cost of $12. Of course, in the long run, all costs are variable; for example, when the rental agreement expires, the firm can decide not to renew it and avoid paying the rent. But the focus for this analysis is the short run, and Tom cannot get out of the rental agreement.

Because of fixed costs, there are times when firms must decide whether to operate at a loss for a period of time, or to shut down completely. In such cases, "maximizing profits" actually means "minimizing losses." How can we use the cost and price information to determine whether a business should continue operating at a loss in the short run? If the business is losing money, how can it minimize these losses? To answer these questions, we need to consider the firm's variable costs.

If Tom can sell boxes of tomatoes for $2 when his average variables costs are $3 per box for items such as fertilizer and labor, then continuing to sell more tomatoes will only *add* to his losses. In this example, the price of tomatoes is less than the average variable cost, and it would be foolish to continue selling them. On the other hand, if Tom can sell tomatoes for more than his average variable cost of $3 per box, then each box sold will add to profits—or at least minimize the losses.

In Exhibit 7, AVC is allowed to change with output. In Panel A, the price of a perfectly competitive good (tomatoes) is assumed to be $2. Thus, $MR = P = $2. If the tomato farm were to operate where $MR = MC$, it would produce 2 units. However, this is below the average variable cost. The average total cost to produce the tomatoes is $9. There would be a loss of $7 per box, even at the optimal quantity. Continuing to operate would mean the business incurs a total $14 loss (a loss of $7 per unit on 2 units). In the short run, the business would be better off simply shutting down and losing the $12 in fixed costs.

If the price is $5, $MR = $5 and profit maximization occurs at 3.5 units, where $MR = MC$. Since the average total cost to make 3.5 units is $7, Tom would experience a loss of $2 per unit ($7 − $5). Total profit is a loss of $7 (a loss of $2 per unit on 3.5 units). This is better than the $12 loss that would be incurred if the firm shuts down; therefore, it should continue to operate. The decision on whether to shut down hinges

EXHIBIT 7   Business Decision to Shut Down: Short Run

In the short run, firms must consider fixed and variable costs in deciding to shut down. In our example, fixed costs are $12. In Panel A, the market price is $2. The firm should shut down in the short run as $P < AVC$. If the firm were to remain open, it would lose $14 rather than $12 if it shuts down. In Panel B, the market price is $5. The firm should remain open in the short run as $P > AVC$. If $P = AVC$, the firm is indifferent between operating and shutting down in the short run.

on whether the business is able to cover its variable cost. When the price is $5, total revenue is more than total variable cost, and price exceeds AVC.

The **shutdown price** is the minimum price at which a profit-maximizing firm will choose to operate; this price equals the minimum average variable cost. At a lower price, the firm should shut down immediately as $P < AVC$ and total revenue is lower than total variable cost. At a higher price, a profit-maximizing firm should continue to operate at least in the short run because $P > AVC$ and total revenue is higher than total variable cost. If price equals the shutdown price, the firm is indifferent between operating and shutting down in the short run. The decision to operate or shut down can be summarized as follows:

- Shut down in the short run when (Panel A):
  - $P < AVC$
  - Total revenue < Total variable cost
- Continue to operate in the short run when (Panel B):
  - $P > AVC$
  - Total revenue > Total variable cost

shutdown price The minimum price at which a profit-maximizing firm may choose to operate; this price equals the minimum average variable cost.

It should be noted that in each case the top and bottom equations are equivalent: We simply multiply P and AVC in the top equation by Q. The result is $P \times Q$ and $AVC \times Q$, which equal total revenue and total variable cost, respectively. The analysis is similar. A firm should operate if its total revenue is high enough to cover all variable costs. When the opposite occurs, the firm should shut down.

When firms are able to produce output in two different locations, the AVC curve can help them decide which unit to shut down when sales are weak. For instance, some utilities produce electricity with both large hydroelectric dams and oil-fired power plants. The dams have very low *AVC* because the energy comes from "free" water flowing downhill and powering turbines. The oil-fired plants have higher *AVC*, as the oil they burn is expensive. When demand for energy is low, these same utility companies will keep operating the dams with low *AVC* and shut down the more expensive oil-fired power plants (with high *AVC*).

Kristina Blokhin/Alamy Stock Photo

∧ Persistent losses can lead firms to exit the market in the long run.

The Long-Run Decision to Exit or Enter

The decision to exit or enter a market is a long-run decision; and is more straightforward. If a firm is persistently operating at a loss, it should exit the market. This occurs when total cost is greater than total revenue, or when average total cost is greater than price. For example, Tom should exit in the long run if the average cost to make a box of tomatoes is $8 and he is only able to sell a box of them for $7. He would exit the industry when he is able to get out of his fixed cost, such as when a rental agreement expires.

Alternatively, a business should continue to operate as long as it remains *at least* able to break even. When $P = ATC$ the firm is breaking even as total revenue equals total cost. For simplicity, we assume that the firm will continue to operate. Something interesting happens when $P > ATC$. Not only is the firm profitable, but these profits are likely to entice *entry* from other firms. In the case, the industry will expand as new firms enter the market.

- Exit in the long run when:
  - $P < ATC$
  - Total revenue < Total cost
- Enter in the long run when:
  - $P > ATC$
  - Total revenue > Total cost

In each case, the top and bottom equations are equivalent: We simply multiply P and ATC in the top equation by Q. The result is $P \times Q$ and $ATC \times Q$, which equal total revenue and total cost, respectively.

Finally, the decision rules we have discussed don't just apply to companies, they also apply to units and plants within large companies. Radio Shack, for example, had closed most but not all its stores by the end of 2017. For the units that closed, this is the equivalent of the long-run decision to exit despite the company remaining in operation.

During a severe recession large automaker like GM or Ford may permanently close poorly performing factories and sell off their assets; consistent with the long-run decision to exit. Other factories will be shut down, but only in the short run. When the recession is over, they may be brought back into production. The automakers are willing to pay the (fixed) cost of maintaining these facilities until they are needed again, but don't actually produce anything at them because price cannot cover *AVC*. And then a third group of factories will continue producing, as price exceeds *AVC*. Even during recessions, there is some demand for cars. The management team at GM and Ford needs to calculate *MC*, *AVC*, and *ATC* in order to make the best use of each factory.

Think & Speak Like an Economist

Economists draw an important distinction between *shutting down* and *exiting*. A *shutdown* is a short-run decision to cease operations when price falls below average variable cost. In contrast, *exiting* an industry is a long-run decision that occurs when losses take place and a firm is able to free itself from all long-term contractual obligations.

The Firm's Short-Run Supply Curve—and Other Cost Curves

If the marginal cost curve, average variable cost curve, and average total cost curve in Exhibits 5, 6, and 7 look like a plate of spaghetti, don't worry. We can simplify the analysis by recognizing each curve as a tool. The average variable cost curve has one purpose: to help firms determine when to shut down in the short run. Firms will always be better off producing output when price is greater than *AVC*, and firms are always better off shutting down when price falls below the minimum *AVC*.

The average total cost curve also only has one purpose, to determine profitability, and thus whether to stay in business in the long run. Recall that profit equals $(P - ATC) \times Q$. Note we use *ATC* to estimate profits (not *MC* or *AVC*). This is why the *ATC* is used to determine whether firms should exit or enter the industry. If price is above the *ATC*, profit is positive and other firms may want to consider entering the industry. If price is below *ATC*, then firms will tend to exit the industry in the long run.

Finally, the marginal cost curve is used for one important purpose—deciding how much to produce. Firms maximize profits by producing at the *Q* where *MR* = *MC*. If this firm happens to be in a perfectly competitive industry, then *MR* is the same as price, so *P* = *MC* at the profit-maximizing level of output.

In Chapter 3, you learned that the positive relationship between the price of an item and the quantity a business is willing to supply is the firm's supply curve. It turns out that the firm's supply curve is also the firm's marginal cost curve—more specifically, the upward-sloping part of the *MC* curve that lies above the *AVC* curve in the short run. Consider these data points from the example developed earlier in the chapter:

- At *P* = $12, *MC* = *MR* at 5 units. The quantity supplied equals 5.
- At *P* = $7, *MC* = *MR* at 4 units. The quantity supplied equals 4. This is the breakeven price.
- At *P* = $5, *MC* = *MR* at 3.5 units. The quantity supplied equals 3.5 in the short run because *P* > *AVC*.
- At *P* = $2, the firm will shut down and quantity supplied equals zero.

Exhibit 8 shows the short-run supply curve of a firm. All points on the *MC* curve at or above the minimum point on the *AVC* curve represent the firm's short-run supply curve.

EXHIBIT 8 Marginal Cost and the Individual Supply Curve

The marginal cost curve above the minimum point on the average variable cost curve is the firm's short-run supply curve. When the market prices fall below this point, zero quantity is supplied as firms shut down.

Recall that *market supply* is the sum of all individual sellers' quantity supplied at each price. This means it is the sum of all *individual supply curves* at each price. As we saw in Chapter 3, to estimate the market supply, we simply add up the quantity that all the firms are willing and able to produce at each price.

12.5 THE LONG-RUN COMPETITIVE EQUILIBRIUM

In the long run, perfectly competitive industries are highly sensitive to profits and losses. Each firm is a price taker because there are many buyers and many sellers. In addition, entry and exit are possible. In the previous section, we learned that in the long-run firms exit when economic losses occur $(P < ATC)$. Conversely, when economic profits do occur $(P > ATC)$, new firms will enter the industry.

Profits and Losses Shift Market Supply

If Tom experiences an economic profit of $20, potential rivals will see an opportunity and enter the market. When new firms enter the market, what happens to the short-run market supply? Supply increases, gradually shifting the short-run supply curve to the right. This decreases market price.

Such a scenario is demonstrated in Exhibit 9. Panel A shows the firm making an economic profit. In the long run, these profits attract new firms and increase market supply, as illustrated in Panel B. This puts downward pressure on the price that the firm faces (Panel A), *but does not change the firm's cost curves*.

> ### Think & Speak Like an Economist
>
> Because economists believe that it is easy for firms to enter the market in perfect competition, they also believe that it is unlikely that in the long run an individual firm in perfect competition will make an economic profit. Remember, zero economic profit usually implies a positive accounting profit.

EXHIBIT 9   Industry Adjustments to Economic Profits

Panel A: Profits result in rivals entering the market . . .

Panel B: . . . increasing market supply and decreasing price.

Panel A shows a business initially making an economic profit $20 when the price of a product is $12. In the long run, economic profit encourages entry of rivals, shifting the short-run supply curve to the right as shown in Panel B. This puts downward pressure on the price facing the firm (Panel A) but does not change the firm's cost curves. In the long run, equilibrium occurs at a price of $7, quantity of 4 and zero economic profit.

EXHIBIT 10   Industry Adjustments to Economic Losses

Panel A: Losses result in rivals exiting the market . . .

Panel B: . . . decreasing market supply and increasing price.

Panel A shows a business with an economic loss of $7 when the price of a product is $5. In the long run, economic losses encourage some firms in the industry to shut down, shifting the short-run supply curve to the left as shown in Panel B. This puts upward pressure on the price facing the firm (Panel A) but does not change the firm's cost curves. In the long run, equilibrium occurs at a price of $7, quantity of 4 and zero economic profit.

Of course, the opposite can occur: If the market price is $5, firms in this industry will see losses, and in the long run some firms will exit the market. Short-run supply decreases, pushing the market equilibrium price up to $7. The end result is zero economic profit in the long run. This is demonstrated in Exhibit 10.

Long-run competitive equilibrium occurs when businesses in a competitive industry have zero economic profit because price equals average total cost at the profit maximizing level of output. In Exhibits 9 and 10, this occurs at the price of $7. The possibility of entry and exits pushes the market toward this equilibrium.

When the market price of an item is below average total cost and businesses incur losses, some firms eventually exit the market. This decreases the short-run supply and increases price. In contrast, when profits exist, firms find it lucrative to enter the market. This increases short-run supply and decreases price. In both scenarios, economic profits move toward zero.

Long-Run Market Supply

long-run competitive equilibrium Occurs when businesses in a competitive industry have zero economic profit because price equals average total cost at the profit maximizing level of output.

constant cost industry An industry where the entry of new firms does not change average total cost, resulting in a flat long-run supply curve.

To understand long-run market supply, consider what happens to quantity supplied when demand increases or decreases. For simplicity, we'll return to the industry Maria is considering entering—the pizza industry. We assume this industry is perfectly competitive and at long-run equilibrium with zero economic profit. Then we observe what happens in the short and long run when demand shifts.

Constant Cost Industry A **constant cost industry** is an industry where the entry of new firms does not change average total cost, resulting in a flat long-run supply curve. In a constant cost industry, all new firms enter with the same minimum *ATC* as existing firms, and the long-run supply curve is perfectly elastic.

When the price of pizza rises as a result of an increase in demand, profits will increase, as Exhibit 11 demonstrates. We see equilibrium price rise from P_1 to P_2 and short-run equilibrium will occur at point *b*. As profits rise, new firms will enter the pizza industry and the short-run supply curve will shift to the right.

EXHIBIT 11 Short- and Long-Run Effects of an Increase in Demand

Panel A: Constant Cost Industry

Outcome in short run before new firms enter.

Outcome in long run after new firms enter.

$S_{short\ run}$

$S_{long\ run}$

Price

P_2

P_1

a

b

c

Increase in demand

D_2

D_1

Quantity

Panel B: Increasing Cost Industry

Outcome in short run before new firms enter.

Outcome in long run after new firms enter.

$S_{short\ run}$

$S_{long\ run}$

Price

P_2

P_3

P_1

a

b

c

Increase in demand

D_2

D_1

Quantity

In both panels, the analysis begins at point *a*, the initial long-run equilibrium, where firms are breaking even. In the short run, an increase in demand creates a new equilibrium at point *b*. The higher price results in economic profits. In the long run, the economic profit results in some firms entering the industry, shifting the short-run supply curve to the right (not shown) and establishing a new equilibrium at point *c*. In Panel A, the industry is a constant cost industry (such as bags of ice). Increased industry output will not change average total cost and price will settle at the original equilibrium price (point *c*). In Panel B, the industry is an increasing cost industry (tomatoes). Increased industry output will increase average total cost and price will settle above the original equilibrium price (point *c*).

Let's initially assume that the entry of new firms does not drive up input prices. So the basic cost of production stays the same. If the minimum *ATC* was $7 before new firms enters, it is still $7. In that case, new firms will keep entering until the price gets driven back down to point *c*, which is the breakeven point. Because price will be continually driven back down to the breakeven point, in the long run, the pizza industry can supply an almost unlimited quantity of pizzas at a constant price—the minimum *ATC*. Thus, big cities have many more pizza restaurants than small cities, but each restaurant may be roughly the same size in both large and small cities. That is why the long-run supply curve in Panel A is perfectly elastic (completely flat) in a constant cost industry.

Consider the market for bags of ice. Bagged ice is a constant cost industry: The primary natural input in ice is water, and an increase in the demand for ice does not change the cost of making ice or the global availability of water.

During a prolonged power outage, there is likely to be increased demand for bagged ice, as consumers buy more of it in order to prevent food from spoiling.

The increase in the demand for bags of ice puts upward pressure on the price of ice. Stores with existing bags of ice (and working refrigeration) may be able to temporarily raise prices. Yet, when such events occur, rival icemakers from nearby locations not impacted by the natural disaster quickly enter the market. Once new firms enter, the market price of a bag of ice is quickly pushed back toward the constant long-run supply curve. Not all industries are constant cost industries, as some will see costs go up as the industry expands. This is not, however, the case for ice.

Increasing Cost Industry Now let's consider how the tomato industry would be affected by an increase in demand. As with the bags of ice example, the price would initially

∧ Access to oil is easy in some places like Saudi Arabia, but increasingly costly in others.

increase, higher profits would be earned, and this would cause new firms to enter the industry. However, unlike what happens in the bags of ice example, an increase in demand for tomatoes might raise prices, even in the long run. The key difference is that a rising demand for tomatoes pushes up the cost of inputs used in producing tomatoes, even in the long run.

An **increasing cost industry** is an industry where the entry of new firms increases average total cost, resulting in an upward-sloping long-run supply curve. This results from the fact that important inputs like fertile land have somewhat inelastic supplies. In Panel B, the price initially rises, just as in the case of a constant cost industry. However, the higher price of tomatoes will tend to push up the price of fertile farmland, and this will increase the *ATC*, even in the long run. In addition, tomatoes may have to be grown in less fertile and more costly areas. Thus, price will no longer fall back to the original level, as the breakeven point will have increased.

Increasing cost industries are most likely to occur in areas where an important input is restricted by nature. It might be scarce natural resource inputs (fertile land, oil wells), or it might be a highly specialized talent for sports or acting. In this case, expansion tends to increase costs in two ways.

- The price of the resource increases. Industry expansion means the demand for the resource increases; in turn, this raises its price.

- Less productive resources are used. Expansion may result in tomatoes being grown on less fertile land or in greenhouses. This makes it more expensive to produce tomatoes, even in the long run.

Panel B shows the effect of higher demand in the tomato industry. After the demand for tomatoes rises, price rises and new firms enter. The new firms will increase short-run supply (not shown), just as in the constant cost industry case. As supply increases, the price of tomatoes will tend to fall back somewhat, but not all the way back to the original level. The price will fall back to the breakeven point, point *c* in this case. But the breakeven point *will now be higher*, perhaps $8 instead of $7, as the cost of land to produce tomatoes has risen or less fertile land is used. Thus, an increase in demand will cause the price of tomatoes to rise, even in the long run.

📊 BUSINESS BRIEF An Increasing Cost Industry and a Constant Cost Industry in Energy

Oil provides an excellent example of an increasing cost industry. Over the past few decades, the number of people driving cars in developing countries like China increased sharply. This drove up the global demand for gasoline. It also increased the demand for crude oil, a key input in making gasoline. This resulted in efforts to increase the quantity of crude oil supplied. However, new crude oil supply was often more expensive (involving techniques like fracking) than oil found in more accessible locations, such as Saudi Arabia.

In North America, the oil industry expanded at a rapid pace in response to higher prices. But the oil market is an increasing cost industry.* Drilling rig rental rates and wages of specialized workers all increased. Although the use of new technology somewhat offset these cost increases, the average cost in the oil industry increases as the industry expands.

Oil prices fell sharply in late 2014 and early 2015. This resulted in over a thousand wells being shut down. It also resulted in reduced costs for oil production inputs such

increasing cost industry An industry where the entry of new firms increases average total cost, resulting in an upward-sloping long-run supply curve.

as rig rentals. These events are also consistent with an increasing cost industry: Average cost rises as production expands, but falls as production declines.

Compare this example to energy from wind. What impact will a more high-tech windmill known as wind turbines have on the price of one key input, wind? Obviously, wind has no price. It has other associated costs, such as buying or renting land, but these costs are also fairly low. The main cost is building the wind turbines. More production of wind turbines tends to have little impact on the price of inputs used to make windmills (steel for the body, glass or carbon fiber reinforced with plastics for the blades); thus, wind energy is closer to a constant cost industry, as is solar energy.

*See Edward Lotterman, "Shale Oil's Complex Cost of Production," *Twin Cities*, October 25, 2015, http://www
.twincities.com/business/ci_27077567/shale-oils-complex-cost-production.

Decreasing Cost Industry While *most* industries experience constant or increasing costs, not *all* industries do. In a very few cases, industries experience decreasing costs. A **decreasing cost industry** is an industry where the entry of new firms decreases average total cost, resulting in a downward-sloping long-run supply curve. The most familiar examples occur in the tech sector, where economies of scale are often realized in the resource and other input markets. For example, in the early days of personal computing, critical components such as memory chips and the CPU were expensive. As the industry expanded, firms were able to achieve economies of scale in producing computer chips. Over time, the price of personal computers fell sharply as their input costs declined. A similar process occurred with computer software and smartphone apps.

A decreasing cost industry also results in *higher* average total cost as output *contracts*. For instance, costs may rise in dying industries that are no longer able to obtain economies of scale, such as the television or watch repair industries. Since decreasing cost industries usually involve large firms with economies of scale, they seldom occur in perfect competition.

Economic Efficiency of Perfect Competition in the Long Run

decreasing cost industry
An industry where the entry of new firms decreases average total cost, resulting in a downward-sloping long-run supply curve.

Long-run competitive equilibrium occurs when businesses in an industry have zero economic profit, as shown in Exhibit 12. This occurs as a result of entries and exits that occur over time. It also results in two important sources of economic efficiency.

EXHIBIT 12 Long-Run Equilibrium and Economic Efficiency

In perfect competition, long-run equilibrium results in productive efficiency as the average total cost of producing items is minimized (minimum *ATC*). It also results in allocative efficiency as the price consumers are will to pay for the item equals the marginal cost to make it ($P = MC$).

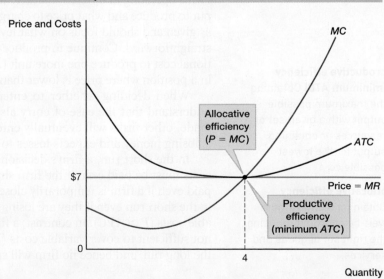

As you will learn over the next few chapters, these efficiencies do not occur in other market structures.

Productive efficiency (minimum *ATC*) is obtaining the maximum possible output with a given set of resources, or obtaining a given level of output at the lowest possible cost. This occurs when the production of goods and services is at the lowest possible average total cost, as seen in Exhibit 12. It is the entry and exit of firms that pushes competitive industries toward minimum *ATC* in the long run. For example, if new technology is developed that lowers the minimum average total cost to $6, firms will adapt the technology in the pursuit of higher profits. The profits they earn will encourage others to follow suit, increasing short-run supply and pushing price down to $6. Ironically, as all firms struggle to earn above-normal profits, the forces of competition relentlessly help minimize production costs in the long run.

Allocative efficiency is obtaining the maximum well-being from producing the right set of goods and services. Whereas productive efficiency refers to efficiency in the creation of goods, allocative efficiency refers to efficiency in the distribution and allotment of those goods and services as they are *allocated* to their highest-valued use. To achieve allocative efficiency, firms continue to produce additional units of output up to the point where the price of the output equals marginal cost ($P = MC$).

Free markets tend to maximize allocative efficiency and a deadweight loss occurs when output is not at the competitive equilibrium. Recall from Chapter 6 that allocative efficiency implies we don't want to produce too little, where consumers value goods more than the marginal cost to produce them ($P > MC$). Doing so would imply that some mutually beneficial transactions do not occur, resulting in a deadweight loss. Allocative efficiency also implies that we don't produce too much, where consumers value goods at less than the cost of production. Perfect competition prevents this from occurring as no firm wants to produce where $P < MC$.

This is why many economists consider perfect competition to often be an ideal market structure. Perfect competition automatically pushes firms to maximize productive and allocative efficiency. Put simply, under perfect competition, the industry should produce the right amount of output and do so in the most efficient way possible. As such, it is the benchmark by which other more common market structures will be compared, such as oligopoly, monopolistic competition, and monopoly, where price is not always equal to marginal cost or the minimum average total cost.

BUSINESS TAKEAWAY

Firms operating in different market structures face different decisions on what level output to produce and what price to charge. In perfect competition, firms must take the price as given and should focus on what level of output to produce. The decision on output is straightforward: Continue to produce output until the price no longer exceeds the additional cost to produce one more unit ($MR = MC$). If a profit-maximizing firm finds itself in a position where price is lower than marginal cost, it should decide to reduce sales.

When deciding whether to enter a perfectly competitive market, firms need to understand that the ease of entry also limits profits in the long run. If profits can be made, other firms will eventually enter the market. A firm should exit an industry if it is losing money and expects losses to continue in the long run.

In the short run, a firm's decision to shut down is based on variable costs, as fixed costs must be paid even if the firm shuts down temporarily. Rent, for example, must be paid even if a firm is temporarily closed. As a consequence, firms should keep operating in the short run even if they are losing money, as long as they are able to cover their variable costs ($P > AVC$). In contrast, a firm should shut down immediately if its revenue is not sufficient to cover variable costs ($P < AVC$). Of course, all costs become variable in the long run, and hence no firm will stay in business forever if it is losing money.

productive efficiency (minimum *ATC*) Obtaining the maximum possible output with a given set of resources or obtaining output for the lowest possible cost.

allocative efficiency Obtaining the maximum well-being from producing the right set of goods and services.

CHAPTER STUDY GUIDE

12.1 THE FOUR MARKET STRUCTURES

Market structure is the business composition of a specific industry or product market, including the size and number of competing firms. The market characteristics of an industry impact the degree of competition, pricing power, and long-run profitability. There are four market structures: perfect competition, monopolistic competition, oligopoly, and monopoly. They vary on the basis of the number of sellers, ease of entering or exiting a product market, price-setting ability, elasticity of demand that each firm faces, potential for long-run profits, and level of product differentiation and similarity.

12.2 CHARACTERISTICS OF PERFECT COMPETITION

Perfect competition is a market structure with a very large number of sellers of a standardized product. Due to the large number of firms, and because the product is standardized, each individual seller tends to have very little say on price and is considered a **price taker.** As a consequence of each firm being a price taker, in perfect competition, the firm's demand is assumed to be perfectly elastic. Firms in perfect competition sell standardized products. Commodities are standardized goods such as metals (copper, iron), energy (coal, oil, and natural gas), and agricultural products (eggs, tomatoes, and milk). Low barriers to entry ensure zero long-run economic profit. Any positive economic profit would imply high (above-normal) profits and encourage new firms to enter the market.

12.3 PROFIT MAXIMIZATION

Marginal revenue (MR) is the additional revenue a business receives from one additional unit of output; $MR = \Delta TR / \Delta Q$. In perfect competition *only*, $MR =$ Price. All firms maximize profits at the quantity where marginal revenue equals marginal cost; $MR = MC$. Profits can be calculated as Total revenue − Total cost. This also equals profit per unit multiplied by the number of units. That is,

Profits = (Price − Average total cost) × Quantity

12.4 BUSINESS DECISIONS TO SHUT DOWN OR EXIT

Breakeven occurs when economic profit equals zero. This results whenever price equals average total cost. When price falls below the breakeven point, economic losses *must* occur, as the price will be lower than average total cost for any level of output. Firms will have to make the difficult decision on whether to exit the industry. In the long run, firms operating with a persistent loss should exit the industry. The decision to shut down in the short run is somewhat more complex due to the existence of fixed costs, which must be paid regardless of the level of sales. Firms should continue to operate (even if at a loss) provided they can cover their variable costs ($P > AVC$) and shut down when they cannot ($P < AVC$). **Shutdown price** is the minimum price at which a profit-maximizing firm may choose to operate; this price equals the minimum average variable cost. At a lower price, the firm should shut down immediately. At a higher price, the firm should continue to operate in the short run.

12.5 THE LONG-RUN COMPETITIVE EQUILIBRIUM

Profits result in new firms entering the market and losses result in some firms exiting the market. Both shift the market supply curve and change market price. In addition, when rivals enter or exit the market, the demand curve that existing firms face shifts, but not their cost curves. **Long-run competitive equilibrium** occurs when businesses in a competitive industry have zero economic profit because price equals average total cost at the profit maximizing level of output. The long-run market supply curve can take on several forms. A **constant cost industry** is an industry where the entry of new firms does not change average total cost, resulting in a flat long-run supply curve. An **increasing cost industry** is an industry where the entry of new firms increases average total cost, resulting in an upward-sloping long-run supply curve. A **decreasing cost industry** is an industry where the entry of new firms decreases average total cost, resulting in a downward-sloping long-run supply curve. The long-run competitive equilibrium results in productive efficiency and allocative efficiency. **Productive efficiency (minimum ATC)** is obtaining the maximum possible output with a given set of resources, or obtaining a given level of output at the lowest possible cost. **Allocative efficiency** is obtaining the maximum well-being from producing the right set of goods and services.

TOP TEN TERMS AND CONCEPTS

(1) Market Structure

(2) Perfect Competition

(3) Price Taker

(4) Marginal Revenue

(5) $MR = MC$ at Profit Maximization

(6) Profit = $(P - ATC) \times Q$ and Breakeven

⑦ Shutdown Price

⑧ Long-Run Competitive Equilibrium

⑨ Increasing and Constant Cost Industries

⑩ Productive and Allocative Efficiency

STUDY PROBLEMS

1. What are the four market structures? Describe each.

2. In which three of the following examples would a firm likely be considered a price taker?

   a. Porsche selling its cars

   b. Joe selling 100 shares of Facebook stock

   c. A farmer selling 100 bushels of corn

   d. An art collector selling a Picasso

   e. Apple selling a new watch

   f. A local dairy farmer selling milk

3. In which three of the following examples would a firm likely face many rivals due to low barriers to entry?

   a. A calendar app on a smartphone

   b. A top-of-the-line Tesla automobile

   c. A local dairy farmer selling milk

   d. A premium tablet market

   e. Generic office suite software

4. Describe the term "commodity" in the context of the modern business world. Describe the term "standardized." How does it relate to perfect competition?

5. Explain the demand curve facing a firm in perfect competition. What is the price elasticity of demand? How is it different from the market demand curve?

6. Consider the data in the following graph. If the market price is $60,

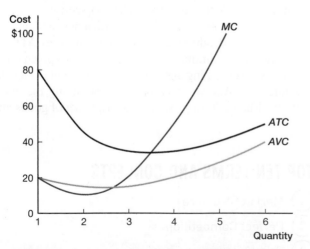

   a. what is the profit-maximizing level of output?

   b. what is ATC at that level of output?

   c. what is profit per unit and overall profit at that level of output?

   d. what is total revenue?

7. Consider the data in the graph in Problem 6. If the market price is $36,

   a. what is the profit-maximizing level of output?

   b. what is ATC at that level of output?

   c. what is profit per unit and overall profit at that level of output?

   d. how low would price need to fall so that the firm would shut down in the short run?

8. A firm in perfect competition has total revenue of $10,000 and marginal revenue of $10. What is the selling price of the item and how many units are sold?

9. A firm in a perfectly competitive market is currently producing 1,000 units and selling its product for $5 each. The average total cost of producing the product is $4. Fixed cost is $1,000. The firm is maximizing profits. What are

   a. its profits?

   b. its average variable cost?

   c. its marginal cost?

   d. Is this a long-run equilibrium? Explain.

10. Describe a firm's decision to shut down in the short run. How is this different than a firm's decision to exit an industry in the long run?

11. In 2015, automobile customers began to switch from standard cars to sports utility vehicles and trucks. Profits per unit on these products are higher than on automobiles. According to the *Financial Times*, "General Motors reported second-quarter profits four times higher than last year's level . . . (with) revenues of $36.7bn, down 4.7 percent."[2] Explain how this might occur. Given that profits were rising as sales were falling, what does the story suggest about marginal cost relative to price?

12. When the price of Mario's pizza price rose by $5 last summer, he suddenly began to face competition. What are the short- and long-run outcomes of an increase in the price of pizza?

13. In response to falling gold prices, Barrick Gold, the world's largest gold producer, began closing mines in 2013. In gold production, different mines have a different average total cost of production. Over half of Barrick's gold output derived from five mines with accounting production costs less than $700 an ounce and another 18% was produced at an accounting cost below $1,000. When gold prices fell to around $1,300 an ounce, some mines were no longer able to earn an economic profit (a normal accounting profit). According to Barrick Gold CEO Jamie Sokalsky, "If you have a number of assets that aren't making money

at a certain gold price, then you have to deal with them, and, that does mean less production."[3] Describe the shutdown decision that Barrick faced.

14. In the long run, firms in perfect competition achieve productive efficiency and allocative efficiency. In which two of the following cases are both conditions met?

   a. *ATC* is minimized, $P = MC$

   b. $ATC = MC = P$

   c. *ATC* is minimized, $P > MC$

   d. *AVC* is minimized, $P = MC$

   e. *AVC* is minimized, $P > MC$

15. Describe an increasing cost industry. What factors lead to increasing cost? Are professional sports an increasing cost industry? Explain.

16. A major storm hits the New York City area and electricity is out for days. What happens to the demand for ice? The price of ice in the short run? How does such a price change impact supply? What happens to price in the long run? Do you think making ice is an increasing cost industry or a constant cost industry?

Michael Conroy/AP Images

∧ Only the local utility company can keep your lights on.

Monopoly and Antitrust Laws

Businesses with Market Power

After careful consideration, Maria decides to open a pizza restaurant and begins to pour all her energy into her newest endeavor. She has identified the cheapest seller for ingredients and supplies. But there's one expense for which she cannot find a better deal: her electricity delivery. Electricity in her town is supplied by just one company, Duke Energy. Maria must pay the price set by Duke if she wants to keep her lights on and her food fresh. Her electricity company is in a market structure known as a monopoly.

Maria wishes her pizza restaurant could also be a monopoly—she observed the higher profits for Hilton hotels in cities with no serious rivals. Of course, she also knows that a pizza monopoly is unlikely, even in her small town. There are already several pizzerias and other casual restaurants in town. She also knows that there is nothing to prevent new firms from entering the market in the future. Her business is definitely not capable of becoming a monopoly. In this chapter, we'll examine businesses that face no serious competition, such as Duke Energy. Fortunately, insights gained in this chapter can be applied to businesses in other market structures described in the chapters ahead.

Chapter Learning Targets

● Identify the characteristics of a monopoly and the importance of barriers to entry.

● Determine the profit-maximizing level of output and profit for a monopoly.

● Compare economic outcomes of perfect competition versus a monopoly.

● Explain government policy option for natural monopolies.

● Describe key antitrust legislation in the United States.

13.1 CHARACTERISTICS OF A MONOPOLY

The term "monopoly" literally means one seller. **Monopoly** is a market structure with a single seller of a product with no close substitutes and high barriers to entry. Unlike firms in perfect competition, a monopolist has no rivals. With little competitive pressure and high barriers to entry, long-run economic profits can occur.

Examples of monopolies include sellers of patented medicine with no close substitutes, first-class mail delivery of letters, and the delivery of electricity. The major characteristics of monopolies are compared with those of other market structures in Exhibit 1.

Monopolies Exist Because of High Barriers to Entry

monopoly A market structure with a single seller of a product with no close substitutes and high barriers to entry.

barriers to entry Obstacles that prevent other firms from entering an industry.

patent The temporary exclusive right to sell a product granted to its inventor.

copyright The temporary exclusive right to sell books, films, and music.

In a monopoly, there is only one firm in the market due to **barriers to entry**, obstacles that prevent other firms from entering an industry. It is important to note from the onset that *barriers to entry exist in both monopoly and oligopoly market structures*.

Legal Barriers Businesses that supply unique goods and services benefit from laws that protect their creations from copycat competitors. A **patent** is the temporary exclusive right to sell a product granted to its inventor. The protections offered by patents provide an incentive for inventors and firms to develop new technology and products. A typical patent lasts 20 years. Similar protections exist for intellectual property such as books, films, music, and computer software. A **copyright** is the temporary exclusive right to sell books, films, and music. Copyrights last 70 years and even longer in some cases. Patents and copyrights are extremely important barriers in many tech industries such as computer technology and biotech, as well as in creative industries such as entertainment and software design.

EXHIBIT 1   Characteristics of Market Structures: A Monopoly

	Market Structure			
	Perfect Competition Chapter 12	**Monopolistic Competition Chapter 14**	**Oligopoly Chapter 15**	**Monopoly Chapter 13**
Number of Sellers	very large number	many firms	few firms	one firm
Entry Conditions	easy entry	easy entry	barriers to entry	barriers to entry
Price Setting Ability	none	some	some	some
Price Elasticity of Demand—Firm Level	perfectly elastic	highly elastic	more elastic than market demand	same as market elasticity of demand
Long-Run Profit	zero economic profit	zero economic profit	potentially	potentially
Product Differentiation	standardized product	differentiated product	varies by product market	unique product with no close substitutes
Key Characteristic	firms price takers	differentiated product	firms highly interdependent	one firm
Examples	tomatoes copper lumber	delivered pizza smartphone apps toothpaste	search engines wireless service mobile phones	patented medicine first-class mail electricity delivery

A monopoly is a market structure with a single seller of a product with no close substitutes and high barriers to entry. Unlike firms in perfect competition, a monopolist has no rivals. Thus, the demand the monopolist faces is the same as the market demand.

Sometimes, governments create legal barriers that give one firm the exclusive right to sell a product. For example, in many countries, there are laws that give a single postal service a monopoly over first-class mail delivery of letters. Likewise, the government often imposes licensing requirements for radio stations, taxis, and street cart food vendors.

Economies of Scale As you'll recall from Chapter 11, when economies of scale exist, long-run average total cost declines as the output of a firm expands. The flip side of this benefit of mass production is that it can pose a substantial barrier to entry: It is often difficult for a new business with higher average total cost to compete with a large established business with lower costs. It is for this reason that there are only two jumbo jet makers in the world: Boeing and Airbus. A new firm entering either market will often be too small to compete on cost. Economics of scale create barriers to entry that limit competition in both a monopoly and an oligopoly market structure.

When economies of scale are extremely large and there are very high fixed costs, a monopoly may occur because it is less costly to have only one firm produce the product. This is because smaller firms will frequently be too small to take full advantage of the economics of scale. Sometimes a single firm can supply a product at lower costs than would happen with two or more competing firms; a situation known as a *natural monopoly*. One example is the case with utilities: Because of economics of scale, it is cheaper to have one firm deliver water with one network of pipes than for many firms with multiple networks of pipes to do so. We will discuss natural monopolies and government policy options to address them later in this chapter.

Control of a Resource Another barrier to entry occurs when a firm (or in some cases, a government) controls the supply of an important natural resource. For example, the Chinese government controls the mining and production of most of the rare earth metals used in many tech products. Overall, however, natural resource monopolies are less common than other types of monopoly.

Brand Loyalty One barrier to entry for potential rivals is that customers may be loyal to the existing brand. That's one reason why Pepsi and Coke advertise heavily and pay large sums for exclusive selling rights at schools, theme parks, and sports arenas: They hope to establish brand loyalty with younger customers.

Network Externalities The more individuals who use Snapchat, the more value Snapchat has to users. Likewise, the more buyers and sellers on eBay, the more value eBay has for its users. **Network externalities** are the benefits a consumer receives from a good or service as a result of others using the same product. Network externalities are a barrier to entry—they make entering the self-destructing picture market or online auction market difficult for potential rivals. Consumers prefer to use the most popular firms in these industries.

Patrick Allard/REA/Redux

∧ "Monopoly" has copyright protections, but Parker Brothers doesn't have a monopoly on board games; it competes with many other sellers.

📊 BUSINESS BRIEF Network Externalities at the Bell Telephone Company

Alexander Bell invented the telephone in 1876 and formed the Bell Telephone Company the next year after receiving a patent for his invention. After the patent expired, several companies competed for customers in the fledgling home telephone market. However, each company was limited in terms of the customers it could connect: At the time, people were only allowed to call others in the *same* network. This gave the largest network, Bell Telephone (later AT&T), a substantial

network externalities
The benefits a consumer receives from a good or service as a result of others using the same product.

TRUNK LINES OF THE BELL TELEPHONE SYSTEM
Connecting over 70,000 Cities, Towns and Rural Communities

PUT A TACK IN YOUR HOME TOWN

For Alan/Alamy

∧ Being able to call 70,000 cities and towns was a significant network externality for Bell Telephone.

advantage over its much smaller rivals. Consumers were inclined to join the phone network that allowed them to call the most people, and Bell Telephone became more useful as more people signed up for the largest phone network—a classic example of a network externality. Smaller companies with fewer customers (and thus smaller networks) simply could not compete with Bell Telephone.*

*Ofgang, Erik, "CT Files: New Haven Was Home of World's First Telephone Exchange," *Connecticut Magazine*, May 23, 2017, accessed December 03, 2017, http://www.connecticutmag.com/the-connecticut-story/ct-files-new-haven-was-home-of-world-s-first/article_bef57208-3a4e-11e7-9176-a7aa002e4aad.html.

Demand Is Market Demand and Potential Long-Run Economic Profits

Since there is only one firm selling a product (with no close substitutes), the monopolist faces no serious competition. Monopolies have more power to set prices than firms in other market structures. This is because the monopolist is able to choose a price anywhere along the market demand curve.

In the previous chapter, you discovered that in perfect competition each firm was a price taker and faced a horizontal demand curve that was perfectly elastic ($e_d = \infty$) at the market price. A monopoly, in contrast, faces the *entire* market demand curve, which is downward-sloping. In a monopoly, customers cannot switch to a competing firm's product because there are no rivals in the industry, nor do any close substitutes exist for the monopolist's product. Thus the demand curve facing the monopolist is less price elastic than one for a firm in perfect competition.

While being a monopoly does not guarantee an economic profit, it certainly doesn't hurt. In perfect competition, economic profits encouraged new firms to enter, and this resulted in lower prices and ultimately zero economic profit. With little competitive pressure in a monopoly, if profits in an industry are high, new firms will almost certainly *want* to enter but barriers to entry prevent them from doing so. As a result, monopolies have the potential to earn economic profits, even in the long run.

13.2 OUTPUT AND PRICING DECISIONS FOR A MONOPOLY

In the last chapter, we discussed how firms in perfect competition calculate marginal revenue, total revenue, and maximum profits. Many of these calculations also apply to monopolies, for instance, profit maximization occurs where $MR = MC$. However, there is one important distinction: Price no longer equals marginal revenue in a monopoly because the demand curve for the monopolist is no longer perfectly elastic. A monopolist is not a price taker.

The Demand and Marginal Curves for a Monopoly

Since the monopolist *is the entire market,* the demand curve facing the firm is the same as the demand curve facing the market. This means the demand curve a monopolist faces is downward-sloping. As a consequence, the monopolist has considerable pricing power, but it is not unlimited. If a monopolist wishes to sell more units, *it must lower its price.* Even a monopolist cannot force consumers to pay a price above the market demand curve. This has an important implication for the concept of marginal revenue.

EXHIBIT 2 Demand and Marginal Revenue

Panel A: Demand and Marginal Revenue Schedule

Price (P)	Quantity (Q)	Total Revenue TR = P × Q	Marginal Revenue ΔTR/ΔQ
11	0	–	0
10	1	10	10
9	2	18	8
8	3	24	6
7	4	28	4
6	5	30	2
5	6	30	0

Panel B: Demand and Marginal Revenue Curves

Determine price from demand curve.

Due to the downward-sloping demand curve a firm must lower price to sell more units. As shown in Panels A and B, a firm can sell 2 units for $9 or 3 units for $8, but marginal revenue on the third unit is $6 (not $8). As a result, price is greater than marginal revenue (except for the first unit). In Panel B, the marginal revenue curve lies below the demand curve.

Note: This demand and marginal revenue curve will be used in several places in next few chapters.

Consider the data in Panel A of Exhibit 2. The monopolist can sell 1 unit at $10 or 2 units at $9. Surprisingly, selling the second unit for $9 does *not* increase revenue by $9. The marginal revenue of the second unit sold is only $8. To understand this important point, let's review the mathematics of calculating marginal revenue. Recall that *marginal revenue* is the additional total revenue (*TR*) from selling 1 additional unit:

$$MR = \frac{\Delta TR}{\Delta Q}.$$

When selling only 1 unit, the total revenue is $10. When selling 2 units, total revenue rises to $18 ($9 for each unit × 2 units). Total revenue increases by only $8; thus, *MR* = $8. This occurs because we assume that the only way to sell 2 units instead of 1 is to lower the price. The monopolist does not know which of the two consumers is willing to pay $10 once the price is set at $9 (and if the customer is asked, "What is the most you are willing to pay?" it's not likely the monopolist would get an honest answer!).

Notice that in order for the monopolist to sell 3 units, the price must fall to $8. Here, total revenue increases from $18 to $24 ($8 each × 3 units). The marginal revenue of the third unit is only $6, as in order to sell 3 units, the price must be reduced to $8 on all 3 units. Kim Kardashian might be willing to pay $5,000 for an iPhone, but if Apple wants to sell millions of iPhones, it must charge a reasonable price, which applies even to Kim.

If we assume all consumers pay the same price, then *price is greater than marginal revenue* for all units after the first one is sold. This is true for monopolies and more generally in all market structures other than perfect competition. Notice in Exhibit 2 that the marginal revenue curve lies below the demand curve.

To see the importance of marginal revenue being less than price, consider the following hypothetical example. Mega Monopoly sells a product with the demand curve illustrated in Panel B of Exhibit 2. For simplicity, we assume Mega's marginal cost and average total cost are both $7 (not shown for brevity). Should Mega sell the third unit for a price of $8 when it costs $7 to produce? It is tempting to answer "yes," because price is above both average total cost and marginal cost. However, the correct answer is "no," because selling the third unit only increases revenue by $6. Mega would receive an additional $6 in revenue, but would incur an extra $7 in production cost. This is why a profit-maximizing monopolist needs to use marginal analysis to determine the profit-maximizing quantity.

Three Simple Steps to Calculate Maximum Profit

Now that we have developed an understanding of the demand and marginal revenue curves for a monopolist, we can determine its profit-maximizing output. As with firms in perfect competition, the output and price that maximize profits for a monopolist can be determined using marginal analysis. There is a crucial difference: we need to determine the price the monopolist will charge.

Exhibit 3 relaxes the assumption of constant cost for a monopolist. In this figure, marginal and average total cost curve are identical to those used in the previous two chapters. The demand and marginal revenue curves are identical to the one depicted in Panel B of Exhibit 2. Grounded in marginal analysis, the following three simple steps are used to calculate maximum profit:

Step 1: Determine Quantity and Price Profit-maximizing quantity occurs where $MR = MC$. This is at "3.5" units, which equals 3,500 because Q is in increments of 1,000. Price is found on the demand curve at the profit-maximizing quantity. In this case, it is $7.50.

Step 2: Determine ATC At this quantity, average total cost is $7.

Step 3: Determine Profit Recall $Profit = (P - ATC) \times Q$. Thus the firm makes $0.50 per unit (or $7.50 − $7.00) on each of 3,500 units and has a total profit of $1,750 (= $0.50 × 3,500).

Price Is Found on the Demand Curve When learning material for the first time, it is not uncommon to see students wrongly find the *price* where $MR = MC$; in Exhibit 3, that occurs at just over $4. But remember, marginal analysis gives us the profit-maximizing *quantity* ($Q = 3,500$). Thus, the profit-maximizing monopolist must take one

---

EXHIBIT 3 Profit Maximization Decision of a Monopolist

Businesses maximize profits at the quantity where $MR = MC$. This occurs at 3,500 units. The firm can sell 3,500 units for $7.50. Each of these units costs an average of $7.00 to make ($ATC$). Thus, the firm earns $0.50 per unit on each of 3,500 units and has a profit of $1,750 (= $0.50 × 3,500).

additional action—price must be found on the demand curve *at this quantity*. The profit-maximizing price lies on the demand curve, directly above the point where $MR = MC$.

Quantity Where $MR = MC$ Maximizes Profits, Other Levels of Output Do Not Let's review the rationale for the $MR = MC$ rule rooted in marginal analysis. If instead of making 3,500 units, the firm considers producing 4,000 units, what would the marginal cost be? At 4,000 units, $MC = \$7$. What would the marginal revenue be? At 4,000 units, $MR = \$4$. It makes little sense to sell this number of units because marginal cost exceeds marginal revenue. Doing so will *lower* profit. Similarly, it makes little sense to reduce output to 3,000 units. Here, marginal cost is roughly $3 ($MC = \$3$), but marginal revenue is $6 ($MR = \$6$). Since selling these units adds to profit, a profit-maximizing firm will choose to do so. It will continue to increase sales until marginal revenue equals marginal cost.

Being a Monopoly Does Not Guarantee an Economic Profit When firms earn a profit in perfect competition, this induces other firms to enter the market. When a monopolist earns a profit, however, other firms that would *want* to enter the market but cannot do so due to the existence of barriers to entry. This allows the monopolist to earn economic profits in the long run. Thus, monopolists differ from competitive firms in two important ways: They are price setters, and they often earn positive economic profits in the long run. However, even monopolies are not always profitable.

Monopolists attempt to maximize profits, but there are occasions in which the maximum profit is actually a loss. Some monopolists produce goods and services where demand is declining over time, such as first-class mail delivery of letters. These firms might exit the industry, or may survive as subsidized government entities, due to their perceived social value. For instance, demand for train travel declined sharply after the invention of cars and airplanes. Amtrak is a government company created out of failed private railroads. It has a monopoly on intercity train travel in many parts of the United States, yet the company frequently loses money, relying on government subsidies for survival.

Exhibit 4 demonstrates what happens if demand falls sharply, while costs remain unchanged. Here, $MR = MC$ at 3,000 units. The highest price a monopolist can charge for 3,000 units is $5, but each unit costs an average of $7 to make. The monopolist will lose $2 on each of 3,000 units, or $6,000 in total. As in a competitive industry, a

EXHIBIT 4 Monopolist with Economic Losses

Being a monopolist does not guarantee an economic profit. At the profit-maximizing quantity of 3,000, price ($5) is less than average total cost ($7).

Step 3: Profit = ($5 − $7) × 3,000 = −$6,000

Step 2: ATC = $7

Step 1: MR = MC at Q = 3,000; P = $5.00

profit-maximizing monopolist suffering an economic loss will always exit the industry in the long run. In the short run, the firm will remain open as long as the firm can cover its variable cost; that is if $P > AVC$.

Finally, note that it is technically possible for marginal revenue to be negative; however, a profit-maximizing monopolist will never want to sell at the point where $MR < 0$. It makes no sense to sell an additional unit that reduces total revenue. Profit maximization occurs at the quantity where MR equals MC, and marginal cost cannot be negative.

POLICY BRIEF New York's Fading Taxi Medallion Monopoly

The yellow taxi cab is an icon of New York City, but you can't just paint your car yellow and go into business driving people around the five boroughs. City law restricts the number of yellow cabs—also known as "medallion cabs" after the city-issued placards they bear. In 2016, the total number of medallions was just 13,587. Given the number of firms, the market is not considered a monopoly; however, its barriers to entry have an effect similar to that of a monopoly.

In 1937, when the city first issued medallions, they sold for $150 in today's prices; by 2012, they often sold for more than $1 million.* Why so much? Because the fixed number of medallions means limited competition and the potential for long-run economic profit.

Recently, however, ride-sharing services such as Uber and Lyft have challenged the status quo in New York and elsewhere, weakening yellow cabs' near monopoly position by eliminating a key barrier to entry. While these drivers cannot pick up customers hailing them on the street, smartphone applications have made it possible for businesses like Uber to pick up passengers on request—effectively reducing the barrier to entry posed by the medallion law. Medallion prices declined quickly as the taxi market became less of a monopoly: In 2017, a New York medallion sold for just $245,000.†

*Jeff Horwitz and Chris Cumming, "The Taxi Medallion System in New York and Other Cities Raises Fares, Impoverishes Drivers, and Hurts Passengers. So Why Can't We Get Rid of It?," *Slate,* June 6, 2012, http://www.slate.com/articles/business/moneybox/2012/06/taxi_medallions_how_new_york_s_terrible_taxi_system_makes_fares_higher_and_drivers_poorer_.html.

†Danielle Furfaro, "Taxi Medallion Owners Find Their Dreams Dashed by Uber, Lyft," *New York Post,* July 5, 2016, http://nypost.com/2016/07/05/city-lets-uber-and-lyft-cannibalize-the-american-dream/.

13.3 MONOPOLY VERSUS PERFECT COMPETITION

How does a monopoly compare to perfectly competitive markets in terms of output, pricing, and economic efficiency? Should society be concerned about monopolies? To answer these questions, we will draw on our analysis of economic efficiency in Chapter 6 and the previous chapter.

Lower Output and Higher Prices in Monopoly

For simplicity, we begin our analysis by assuming the monopolist is in a constant cost industry, such as the production of a patented drug. This is a reasonable assumption, as once a drug is invented, the marginal cost of producing extra units is roughly constant. Because the supply curve depends on the marginal cost curve, the long-run market supply curve is also flat. Market demand is downward-sloping; thus, the marginal revenue curve lies below the market demand curve. Panel A of Exhibit 5 demonstrates this scenario.

If the market is *perfectly competitive* and in a constant cost industry (thus having a horizontal long-run supply), market output would be determined by where the long-run market supply intercepts demand—here, output is Q_C and price is P_C. A profit-maximizing *monopolist* produces at the level of output where marginal revenue equals marginal cost (Q_M) and charges a price read off the demand curve (P_M). In general, monopolies charge higher prices and sell a lower quantity of output than occurs under perfect competition.

Deadweight Loss Results in Monopoly

As you might expect, the combination of higher prices and reduced quantity results in a deadweight loss. This is because a monopoly does not simply move money from the pockets of consumers to producers; it also reduces the quantity of output below the competitive level. In other words, the gains to producers in the form of higher profits are smaller than the loss to consumers in the form of a reduction in consumer surplus.

Panel B shows the consumer surplus and deadweight loss that result from lower output levels. In a competitive industry, the price of the product is P_C and consumer surplus equals Areas $A + B + C$. If price increases to P_M, consumer surplus declines. Recall from Chapter 6 that consumer surplus is the area above the price line and below the demand curve. Consumer surplus decreases when the price of the product increases. In this case, the higher monopolist price of P_M results in consumer surplus being reduced to Area A. Consumer surplus declines by Areas $B + C$.

Area B captures the producer surplus and represents the monopolist's economic profit. Therefore, Area B is not lost from society. Rather, it is simply transferred from consumers to producers. The deadweight loss is Area C, which is lost by consumers and not captured by producers. It is a net loss in the overall well-being of society, due to less output being produced. This is one of the primary reasons why our society implemented laws to prevent monopolies.

Notice that the deadweight loss that results from a firm being a monopoly does *not* exist because the monopoly has profits, but instead because the high price and reduced

EXHIBIT 5 Monopoly Results in Higher Prices and Deadweight Loss

Panel A: A Monopoly Charges a Higher Price . . .

Panel B: . . . Creating Deadweight Loss

If this constant cost industry is competitive, price is P_C and quantity is Q_C. At that price, consumer surplus is Area $A + B + C$. Panel A shows that a profit-maximizing monopolist produces at the level of output of Q_M where $MR = MC$ and charges a price of P_M read off the demand curve. Panel B shows that at this higher price and smaller quantity, consumer surplus is reduced to Area A, Area B is producer surplus (monopolist profit), and Area C is deadweight loss.

output required to achieve such profits cause a loss in consumer surplus (loss of Areas $B + C$) not fully captured by producers. This means that the problem with a monopoly is not just that the metaphorical pie is being redistributed from consumers to producers, the total pie (output) is *actually smaller* under a monopoly.

Allocative and Productive Efficiency May Not Occur in a Monopoly

In perfect competition, the outcome is *allocatively efficient* ($P = MC$). It delivers the maximum well-being from producing the right set of goods and services. Panel A of Exhibit 6 demonstrates a perfectly competitive market. To achieve allocative efficiency, additional units of output are produced up to the point where the price of the output (what consumers value the product at) equals marginal cost.

Allocative efficiency implies we do *not* want to produce too little, where consumers value goods more highly than the marginal cost to produce the goods ($P > MC$). However, this is exactly what occurs in a monopoly, as shown in Panel B. The outcome for a monopolist is not *allocatively efficient* ($P > MC$) as the monopolist produces too little output.

In addition, the monopolist will rarely produce output at the point of minimum average total cost, even in the long run. In Panel A, the firm is in a perfect competition market structure, where average total cost is minimized; *productive efficiency* occurs. Economic forces push toward $MR = MC = ATC$ in perfect competition. Firms that do not produce in the least costly manner will suffer economic losses and be forced out of business.

In contrast, Panel B demonstrates a monopolist profit-maximizing decision. In a monopoly, $MR = MC$ leads to profit maximization, but not generally at an output level with minimum ATC. There are cases where large economies of scale cause a *natural monopoly* and one big firm is more efficient than many smaller firms. Later in the chapter, you will discover that productive efficiency may be maximized by monopolies in those instances.

EXHIBIT 6   Productive and Allocative Efficiency Do Not Occur with a Monopoly

Panel A: Productive and Allocation Efficiency in Perfect Competition

Panel B: Neither Productive nor Allocative Efficiency in Monopoly

Perfect competition (Panel A) achieves both productive efficiency (minimum ATC) and allocative efficiency ($P = MC$) in the long run. In a monopoly (Panel B), neither productive efficiency nor allocative efficiency necessarily occurs.

Rent Seeking Can Lead to a Monopoly

Firms and industry groups often try to influence public policy in order to reduce competition, a process known as rent seeking. **Rent seeking** refers to activities such as lobbying the government with the goal of obtaining barriers to entry, subsidies, and other special privileges. It is especially common with monopolies, or firms attempting to become monopolies by restricting competition. In other cases, a group of firms may collectively engage in rent seeking, trying to keep new competition from entering their industry. This includes attempts by taxi medallion holders to thwart competition by Uber and Lyft, or when the steel industry attempts to block imports.

Economists generally consider rent seeking aimed at obtaining a legal barrier to entry to be highly inefficient, because the activity imposes an opportunity cost on society as resources used rent seeking could be used in alternative ways. Nevertheless, rent seeking is big business, especially in Washington, D.C. Special interest groups spend enormous sums lobbying Congress, as well as state and local governments, for special treatment. Most economists are highly skeptical of barriers to entry that do not have a clear social purpose (such as encouraging innovation through patents and copyrights).

POLICY BRIEF Casinos Opposed by . . . Other Casinos

Casino gambling has been legal for decades in New Jersey, but only in Atlantic City, which is located in the southern part of the state. In 2014, state lawmakers considered allowing gambling in northern New Jersey—just across the river from New York City. The sought-after location would be in the Meadowlands, a huge sports complex that is home to the New York Giants and Jets. Indeed, one casino developer was willing to spend in excess of $4 billion for a 95-story casino, hotel, and motor sports stadium. The Atlantic City casinos, understandably, saw this proposal as a threat. It was rejected by New Jersey voters in a 2016 referendum.*

Previous efforts to allow casino style gambling at the Meadowlands had been obstructed by the lobbying efforts of already existing casinos. These attempts to use the political process to lessen competition are what economists consider rent seeking. Atlantic City casino owners frequently spoke of the greater public good, but in fact they simply did not wish to see additional competition.

*See Brent Johnson, "N.J. Voters Overwhelmingly Reject North Jersey Casino Proposal," *NJ.com*, November 8, 2016, http://www.nj.com/politics/index.ssf/2016/11/nj_voters_reject_north_jersey_casino_proposal_by_a.html; Associated Press, "Hard Rock Not Giving Up on Idea of Meadowlands Casino," *NJ.com*, November 16, 2016, http://www.nj.com/bergen/index.ssf/2016/11/hard_rock_will_wait_patiently_to_open_meadowlands.html.

rent seeking Activities such as lobbying the government with the goal of obtaining barriers to entry, subsidies, and other special privileges.

Innovation Can Lead to a Monopoly

Much of our discussion has focused on the harmful effects of a monopoly on consumers: higher prices, lower output, and economic inefficiencies. But the incentive to become a monopoly provides a powerful incentive to create new products. These incentives would be far smaller without the potential to earn monopoly profits. Copyrights and patents encourage people to generate valuable new ideas, inventions, and works of art by giving individuals and firms a temporary monopoly on the production and sale of the products they create.

There's an old saying, "If you build a better mouse trap, the world will beat a path to your door." Businesses often spend enormous amounts of money researching and developing new products in hopes of obtaining a monopoly and then earning

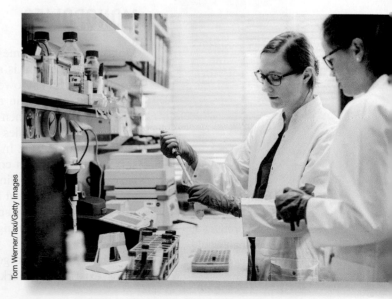

▼ Patents on medicine create monopolies. When patents expire, competition and lower prices follow.

Tom Werner/Taxi/Getty Images

monopoly profits. For example, Google has a near monopoly on Web searches. Some contend that the firm remains dominant because Google's search engine is simply a superior product—so good, it drove some predecessors out of business and continues to stave off competitors (like Yahoo! Search and Microsoft Bing). The process of new businesses supplanting an older business is known as *creative destruction* (a term coined by Harvard economist Joseph Schumpeter in his 1942 *Capitalism, Socialism, and Democracy*). Makers of outmoded mouse traps and search engines suffer from creative destruction, but society benefits overall as firms provide them with new and better products.

📊 BUSINESS BRIEF Eli Lilly Sees Drugs Come Off Patent

When a pharmaceutical company has a patent on a drug, it creates a monopoly for that product, especially if there are no close substitutes. But once the patent expires, other pharmaceutical firms are permitted to manufacture close substitutes. This competition puts downward pressure on the price of the drug and increases the quantity sold. In 2014, when Cymbalta (an anti-anxiety drug) and Evista (a drug that treats osteoporosis) came off patent, the impact on revenue for Eli Lilly, their manufacturer, was predictable: Much cheaper generic substitutes quickly flooded the market. While it is extremely difficult to invent new drugs, copying existing drugs is relatively easy for generic drug makers. More of a drug is sold at a lower price.

In reality, when a patent expires, the market *does not* become perfectly competitive. This is because the pharmaceutical company still maintains *some* market power due to another barrier to entry discussed earlier in the chapter—brand loyalty.

Finally, how do firms like Lilly respond to new competition as drugs come off patent? As you would expect, they continue to develop new drugs, to hopefully obtain new patents. Between 2009 and 2012, Lilly increased its research and development budget by more than 20% to over $5 billion, or roughly one fourth of its total sales revenue.*

*Michael Calia, "Lilly Sales Hit by Patent Expirations, Currency," *The Wall Street Journal,* January 30, 2015, http://www.wsj.com/articles/eli-lilly-sales-hit-by-patent-expirations-currency-1422618597; Peter Loftus, "Eli Lilly, Unlike Rivals, Isn't Pulling Back on R&D," *The Wall Street Journal,* October 20, 2013, http://www.wsj.com/articles/SB10001424052702304500404579125440699770948.

13.4 GOVERNMENT POLICY OPTIONS FOR NATURAL MONOPOLIES

Monopolies often come about because they have enormous economies of scale. When this occurs the firm is said to be a **natural monopoly**; when a single firm is able to supply a product at lower costs than would happen with two or more competing firms. Economies of scale in a natural monopoly are so large that consumers may benefit from lower prices when a monopoly is allowed.

Natural monopolies are common in the distribution of utilities such as natural gas, electricity, and water. In each case, there are enormous costs associated with the necessary infrastructure. If competition existed, then each firm would be forced to install a very costly set of pipelines or transmission wires, running side by side. A single firm is able to produce output at lower average total costs to society, because the costs of all this infrastructure are spread over the entire customer base of the market. The average total cost of distributing natural gas, water, and electricity is usually lower if there is only one firm.

The benefits of large economies of scale are demonstrated in Exhibit 7. If several firms exist in the market, each firm will produce less output and therefore have a

natural monopoly What occurs when a single firm can supply a product at lower costs than would happen with two or more competing firms.

EXHIBIT 7   Average Total Cost in a Natural Monopoly

A natural monopolist typically has high fixed costs and enormous economies of scale. Average total cost can be reduced by having a single firm in the market make a large quantity to take advantage of the economies of scale (a monopolist), as opposed to multiple firms that would presumably be smaller and unable to take advantage of the economies of scale.

higher average total cost. Competition leads to firms that are too small to capture all the benefits of economies of scale and reach the minimum efficient scale. In contrast, having a single firm in the market will allow that firm to capture the economies of scale, thus maximizing *productive efficiencies*.

However, this means society faces a trade-off as a single firm in the market also gives that firm enormous pricing power. Policymakers have several options when addressing natural monopolies, with costs and benefits corresponding to each option.

Allow the Natural Monopoly to Maximize Profits

At times, the government allows natural monopolist to exist and does *not* regulate the firm involved. This is the case in the satellite radio market, with one dominant firm, SiriusXM. The company is not heavily regulated, in part, because policymakers believe there is sufficient competition from close substitutes, such as local and Internet radio. In cases like this, the monopolist will then maximize profits using the $MR = MC$ rule explained earlier in the chapter. Panel B of Exhibit 8 demonstrates this scenario. Marginal revenue (MR) intersects marginal cost (MC) at Q_M and the monopolist charges a price P_M. Profits equal $(P_M - ATC) \times Q_M$. Since there are barriers to entry, this level of profit may be sustainable in the long run.

Curtail the Natural Monopoly with Competition

Allowing the natural monopolist to maximize profits often results in relatively high prices for consumers. Consequently, policy makers may attempt to curtail the monopolist. In some local cable TV markets, lawmakers have decided to break up the monopoly and allow competitors to enter the market, even though such a circumstance can lead to somewhat higher ATC. In this case, competition would lead to several smaller firms, which may not be able to take full advantage of economies of scale. On the other hand, the added competition might put downward pressure on prices, spur innovation, and provide consumers with more choice.

Panel A of Exhibit 8 illustrates a market with multiple firms. It shows the demand curve facing each firm. Notice the curve is below the average total cost curve, though

EXHIBIT 8   Policy Options for a Natural Monopoly

Panel A: Forcing Competition

Price and Costs

Demand curve facing a firm with competitors

Losses occur because price is less than average total cost ($P < ATC$)

P_{firm}

$ATC_{Long\ run}$

D_{firm}

$Q_{each\ firm}$

Quantity

Panel B: Profit Maximization and Price Regulation

Price and Costs

D_{Market}

Unregulated monopolist results in economic profit ($P > ATC$).

P_M

Average cost pricing results in zero economic profit ($P = ATC$).

Marginal cost pricing results in economic loss ($P < ATC$).

P_{ATC}

MC $ATC_{Long\ run}$

P_{MC}

MR

0

Q_M

Quantity

An unregulated profit-maximizing natural monopolist finds the quantity (Q_M) where $MC = MR$. As shown in Panel B, this will result in a price P_M and economic profit. In part due to relatively high prices on consumers, policy makers may attempt to curtail the monopoly. One option is to allow competition. This, however, may push firms out of business as shown in Panel A. This is because each firm's demand curve, which reveals price, is below the average total cost curve ($P < ATC$), though this need not be the case. Price regulation is another option. As shown in Panel B, regulators can attempt to minimize deadweight loss by requiring the firm to set price equal to marginal cost ($P = MC$), which results in an economic loss. The more common approach is average cost pricing (or rate of return regulation), a policy that require a business to set price equal to ATC ($P = ATC$), resulting in zero economic profit for the natural monopolist and lower prices for consumers than if unregulated.

this need not be the case. In this case, creating competition by enforcing laws will push firms out of business. Even if the smaller firms can remain profitable, the average total cost of producing the item for society will be higher than if there were only one firm.

Price Regulation of a Natural Monopoly

As an alternative to breaking up a natural monopoly or allowing it to charge a high price and make enormous profits, governments often regulate the price that the natural monopolist can charge. Most electric utility companies are price regulated. But how should the regulators determine a "fair" price? Should the government set the regulated price equal to marginal cost or average total cost?

In general, setting price equal to marginal cost will minimize deadweight loss. From society's perspective, the cost of making the last unit (marginal cost) should equal what the last buyer is willing to pay. This would minimize deadweight loss and achieve allocative efficiency, just as setting price at the equilibrium of supply and demand minimizes deadweight loss in competitive markets. Unfortunately, setting price equal to marginal cost would result in economic losses for a natural monopoly, as marginal cost is below the average total cost. This can be seen in Panel B of Exhibit 8.

In the utility industry, regulators usually try to set price equal to average total cost so that monopolies can earn a normal *accounting* profit (which you'll recall is the equivalent of zero economic profit). **Average cost pricing regulation** (also referred to as *rate of return regulation*) are policies that require the monopolist to set price equal to *ATC* (*P* = *ATC*), resulting in zero economic profit. This allows the owners of the firm to earn a reasonable rate of return on the capital investment. In Panel B, the regulated monopolist under average total cost pricing is required by regulators to set price equal to average total cost (*P* = *ATC*). Since *P* equals *ATC*, the economic profit of the monopolist is zero.

Average cost pricing regulation is not without its disadvantages. Regulated firms have little incentive to minimize cost. If costs go up, their regulated prices increase in proportion and economic profit remains unchanged. For example, costs may rise as a result of the firm hiring incompetent friends of the manager, spending lavishly, or working inefficiently. Such costs are less likely to occur if the business has a profit-maximization motive. Unfortunately, it is frequently difficult for regulators to determine the difference between *legitimate* costs and wasteful expenditures. Despite this drawback, average cost pricing is commonly viewed as the least bad option for natural monopolies.

> ### Think & Speak Like an Economist
>
> Regulators allow utilities to charge a price equal to average total cost so that they can provide their investors with a "normal return." Remember, when we say that a firm has made zero economic profit, that usually implies that the firm has earned a positive accounting profit.

Government Ownership of a Natural Monopoly

Another option for natural monopolies is for the government to own and operate them. In the United States, ordinary mail delivery is provided by the quasi-public USPS (United States Postal Service), and many water companies are owned by local governments. This way, the government can instruct the firm to produce the optimal amount and offer subsidies if losses occur. The drawback is similar to that sometimes experienced by regulated firms; without the profit motive, a government-owned firm may become somewhat inefficient, with excessively high production costs.

13.5 ANTITRUST LAWS AND MERGERS

Since monopolies charge high prices to customers and create both allocative and productive inefficiencies, lawmakers have enacted antitrust laws to limit the ability of firms to monopolize an industry. **Antitrust laws** are laws designed to limit behavior that substantially lessens competition. Antitrust laws apply to not just monopolies, but also any business engaged in actions that make industries less competitive.

A Brief History of Trusts

In the United States, antitrust laws date back to the decades following the Civil War, which ended in 1865. During this time period, business leaders in a variety of industries formed **trusts**—organizations of rival firms that conspired to acquire monopoly power in an industry. Perhaps the most famous example was John D. Rockefeller's oil trust, which consisted of 40 different oil firms that agreed to work together and behave like a monopoly, dominated by Rockefeller's own Standard Oil Company.

Similar trusts emerged in the steel industry (dominated by Andrew Carnegie and later J. P. Morgan) and in the railroad industry (dominated by Cornelius Vanderbilt). Rockefeller, Carnegie, Vanderbilt, and others like them became known as "robber barons," having built huge empires via business practices that were widely seen as unfair. However, their legacies are more complicated than this name would imply. Some built business empires that played an important role in developing the U.S. economy. Rockefeller contended, for example, he was bringing order to an otherwise chaotic industry.

average cost pricing regulation Policies that require the monopolist to set price equal to *ATC* (*P* = *ATC*), resulting in zero economic profit; also called *rate of return regulation*.

antitrust laws Laws designed to limit behavior that substantially lessens competition.

trusts Organizations of rival firms that conspired to acquire monopoly power in an industry.

Sherman Antitrust Act of 1890

Prior to 1890, some of the most egregious activities of trusts were completely legal. Facing mounting pressure from the public, lawmakers began to pass a series of laws to thwart such abuses. The *Sherman Antitrust Act* of 1890 was the first antitrust law in the United States. This law, sometimes referred to simply as the Sherman Act, prohibits actions that restrain trade or encourage monopolies. Its most important sections include the following provisions:

- **Section 1:** "Every contract, combination in the form of trust or otherwise, or conspiracy, in restraint of trade . . . is declared to be illegal."

- **Section 2:** "Every person who shall monopolize, or attempt to monopolize . . . shall be deemed guilty. . . ."

One activity clearly outlawed by the Sherman Act is *price fixing*, whereby several firms agree to all charge the same high price by forming a *trust*. This rule is especially applicable to oligopolies today. Unfortunately, the language in the act was rather vague, with no clear explanation of what it means to engage in "restraint of trade" or to "monopolize" an industry. This partly explains why the government did not win a major case under the law until 1911, when the law was successfully employed in breaking up both Standard Oil (see **Business Brief: John D. Rockefeller and Standard Oil**) and American Tobacco into numerous smaller companies.

📊 BUSINESS BRIEF   John D. Rockefeller and Standard Oil

John D. Rockefeller (1839–1937) was co-founder of the Standard Oil Company. At the time of his death, he was by far the richest person up to that point in U.S. history and its first billionaire. Rockefeller donated much of his wealth to various charities and foundations.*

Standard Oil was relentless in its attempt to monopolize the U.S. oil market. The firm would buy out a competitor, or convince the rival to join its trust so that Standard Oil could jointly determine prices—a practice known as price fixing. Firms that failed to do so would soon see Standard Oil sell its oil at a loss in their local market to drive them out of business—a practice now known as predatory pricing. Standard Oil would only agree to use railroads that charged their rivals higher shipping prices—a practice known as price discrimination. Eager to sign a contract with the dominant Standard Oil, railroads would often agree to terms that were anticompetitive.

At its peak, Standard Oil controlled 90% of the U.S. oil market. Public outcry over such practices led to the 1890 Sherman Antitrust Act, which was ultimately used to break up Rockefeller's oil empire into smaller companies. Today, major corporations such as Exxon and Chevron are merely pieces of the old Standard Oil trust.

*"The Wealthiest Americans Ever," *The New York Times,* July 15, 2007, http://www.nytimes.com/ref/business/20070715_GILDED_GRAPHIC.html#; "Financier's Fortune in Oil Amassed in Industrial Era of 'Rugged Individualism,'" *The New York Times,* May 24, 1937.

Clayton Act of 1914 and Subsequent Antitrust Laws

While the Sherman Act successfully broke up Standard Oil, other monopolies seized on numerous loopholes in the law and the law eventually needed to be reinforced. The *Clayton Act* of 1914 is an antitrust law that strengthens the Sherman Antitrust Act by banning specific practices that substantially lessen competition. Today, the Clayton Act and its subsequent amendments are the focal point of U.S. antitrust policy. The key mandates of the Clayton Act are:

- **Section 2** prohibits *price discrimination* when it substantially lessens competition. As you will discover in the next chapter, price discrimination is the business strategy of selling essentially the same product at different prices to different consumers. At times, price discrimination is done primarily to thwart competition; for example, the railways were encouraged to price-discriminate against oil companies competing with Standard Oil.

- **Section 3** makes two specific actions illegal if either of them substantially lessens competition. The first is *exclusive dealings*, wherein one company forces buyers or sellers to not deal with the company's rivals, if these exclusive deals substantially lessen competition. For example, it would be illegal for the manufacturer of X-Box to insist that retailers avoid selling PlayStation. The second is *tying sales*—that is, requiring the buyer to purchase an additional product, often from the same firm, if the agreement substantially lessens competition. One example of a tying sale occurred in 2007 when consumers of Apple's first iPhone were required to only use the AT&T phone network. Today, an iPhone can operate on competing networks.

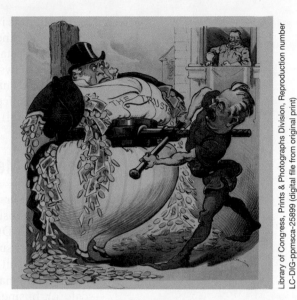

∧ Squeezing the trusts.

- **Section 7** makes stock mergers and acquisitions illegal when the merger substantially lessens competition. A recent application of Section 7 of the Clayton Act occurred when the U.S. government blocked a proposed merger between AT&T and T-Mobile in 2012.

- **Section 8** makes it illegal for any person to be a director of two or more competing corporations.

It is important to note that many actions covered by the Clayton Act are illegal only if they substantially lessen competition. Such provisions are not what lawyers call *per se violations* (automatic violations). As you will discover in the next chapter, the airline industry remains highly competitive despite extremely widespread use of price discrimination. It is also important to note there are some key exemptions to the Clayton Act. Labor unions (Chapter 17), agricultural organizations, and Major League Baseball are exempt.

Like the Sherman Act, the Clayton Act has evolved over the years. The following three amendments to the Clayton Act were enacted to address weaknesses in the original law:

- The *Robinson–Patman Act* of 1936 bans certain types of price discrimination that substantially lessen competition. In particular, the act bans predatory pricing. Predatory pricing involves selling a product below cost with the intent of driving out a rival.

- The *Celler–Kefauver Act* of 1950 plugs a loophole in the Clayton Act that allowed firms to effectively merge by buying nonstock assets of rivals.

- The *Hart–Scott–Rodino Act* of 1976 strengthens the Clayton Act by applying it to sole proprietorships and partnerships.

Some economists are skeptical of the Robinson–Patman Act and the concept of predatory pricing. This law has often been used to protect less efficient firms against competition from more efficient firms. For instance, when large supermarkets were first developed, they posed a competitive threat to small grocery stores. The small stores tried to claim that the large supermarkets were engaged in predatory pricing, when their lower prices, in fact, simply represented production efficiencies.

Finally, it is important to realize who is responsible for the enforcement of the Clayton Act and other antitrust laws in the United States. The *Federal Trade Commission Act* of 1914 established the Federal Trade Commission (FTC) to investigate violations of antitrust laws and other anticompetitive business practices such as predatory pricing. The FTC enforces antitrust laws, reviews proposed mergers, and investigates other business practices that may reduce competition. Today, both the FTC and Department of Justice (DOJ) enforce antitrust policies.

Types of Mergers

A **merger** refers to the combining of two companies into a single firm. Mergers are one of the most difficult—and important—issues that antitrust regulators such as the FTC and DOJ must contend with. The government often attempts to prevent mergers that substantially lessen competition, even if a pure monopoly does not form as a result.

Mergers may allow for greater economic efficiencies due to economies of scale or business synergies. These factors allow a combined firm to have lower costs than two separate firms. This type of merger is generally considered good for society. On the other hand, when two or more rivals merge, it reduces competition, which may harm consumers and society. The federal government weighs the various costs and benefits of a proposed merger, and then allows some mergers and blocks others. There are three primary types of mergers.

Conglomerate Merger A **conglomerate merger** is a merger between firms in unrelated industries. A merger between an airline and a pizza chain would be an example. Conglomerate mergers may improve economic efficiency by lowering costs, and are unlikely to substantially lessen competition. As a consequence, the FTC and DOJ seldom challenge these kinds of mergers.

Vertical Merger A **vertical merger** is a merger between firms at different stages of production. A merger between a clothing maker and a retail clothing store would be one such example. Vertical mergers also have the potential to improve economic efficiency by lowering cost, and are seldom challenged by the FTC and DOJ. However, in a few rare cases such mergers are of interest to regulators when the merger gives the acquiring firm a dominant position in the market of a critical input. The concern is that this could potentially allow the firm to charge higher prices to rivals, who also need the critical input higher prices. An airline would likely be allowed to merge with a jet fuel refinery. Such was the case in 2012 when Delta bought a refinery. However, if the merger gave an airline a dominant position in the jet fuel market the merger would be carefully scrutinized.

Horizontal Merger A **horizontal merger** is a merger between firms in the same industry. A merger between two wireless phone companies would be an example. While such mergers can potentially improve economic efficiency and lower costs, they also have the greatest potential to substantially lessen competition. As a consequence, the FTC and DOJ are far more likely to challenge a horizontal merger than the other types of mergers. Accordingly, we will examine regulations involving horizontal mergers in greater depth.

Antitrust laws do not ban monopolies outright. Rather, they attempt to ban anticompetitive behavior. Antitrust laws are typically *not* aimed at businesses that become a monopoly because the firm makes a better product than its rivals or firms that have a genuine cost advantage, such as a natural monopoly. Nor are the laws aimed at firms that become a monopoly because they invent and patent a new product.

It is also important to note that antitrust laws do not *only* apply to monopolies and businesses attempting to become monopolies. Antitrust laws more generally apply to firms that attempt to gain market power by engaging in practices that substantially lessen competition. In 2012, the government prevented a merger between AT&T and T-Mobile not because the combined firm would result in a monopoly (Verizon and

merger The combination of two companies into a single firm.

conglomerate merger A merger between firms in unrelated industries.

vertical merger A merger between firms at different stages of production.

horizontal merger A merger between firms in the same industry.

Sprint would still exist), but rather, because the combined firm would substantially lessen competition and boost prices for consumers.

Measuring Industry Concentration: The Herfindahl–Hirschman Index (HHI) It is difficult to determine if a merger will substantially lessen competition. In evaluating whether a merger will be harmful, it is useful to begin by looking at how concentrated an industry is. To do this, DOJ uses a measure of sales concentration known as the **Herfindahl–Hirschman Index (HHI)**, a measure calculated by summing the square of the percentage market share of each and every firm in an industry. That is to say,

$$HHI = \sum_{\text{All firms}} (\text{Market share})^2$$

Consider a market with four firms with market shares of 40%, 30%, 20%, and 10%, respectively:

$$HHI = \sum_{\text{All firms}} (\text{Market share})^2 = (40)^2 + (30)^2 + (20)^2 + (10)^2$$
$$= 1,600 + 900 + 400 + 100 = 3,000$$

In the extreme case of a monopoly with one firm having 100% market share,

$$HHI = 100^2 = 10,000.$$

It is useful to see other estimates of the HHI and how mergers may change the index.

- 3 firms with 33.3% market share each:
  - $HHI = 33.3^2 + 33.3^2 + 33.3^2 = 3,333$
  - If 2 firms merge, the result will be 1 firm with 33.3% market share and 1 with 66.7% market share.
  - Postmerger $HHI = 66.7^2 + 33.3^2 = 5,555$
- 20 firms with 5% market share each:
  - $HHI = 5^2 + 5^2 \ldots + 5^2 = 500$
  - If 2 firms merge, the result will be 1 firm with 10% market share and 18 firms with 5% market share each.
  - Postmerger $HHI = 10^2 + 5^2 + 5^2 \ldots + 5^2 = 550$

Exhibit 9 demonstrates the two proposed mergers. The government is likely to *challenge* the first merger, as it would be viewed as substantially lessening competition. The second merger would likely be allowed.

In general, mergers are likely to be allowed if the postmerger HHI remains below 1,000 *or* the merger increases the HHI by less than 50 points. In contrast, the merger is unlikely to be allowed if the postmerger HHI is above 1,800 *and* the merger increases the HHI by 100 points.

📊 POLICY BRIEF Government Blocks Merger Between AT&T and T-Mobile

In 2011, AT&T offered to buy T-Mobile for nearly $40 billion. If the deal had gone through, AT&T and T-Mobile would have merged into a single company. The merger, however, was blocked by the government. In cities across America, the merger would have given the combined company immense market power. In New York City, Chicago, and Seattle, the HHI would have increased by over 900 points, to more than 3,000. This is well above the government guidelines stipulating an increase of no more than 50 and a postmerger HHI below 1,800.[*]

[*]James B. Stewart, "Antitrust Suit Is Simple Calculus," *The New York Times*, September 9, 2011, http://www .nytimes.com/2011/09/10/business/att-and-t-mobile-merger-is-a-textbook-case.html?pagewanted=all&_r=0.

Herfindahl–Hirschman Index (HHI) A measure of concentration calculated by summing the square of the percentage market share of each and every firm in an industry; $HHI = \sum_{\text{All firms}} (\text{Market share})^2$

EXHIBIT 9   A Tale of Two Mergers

Panel A: Merger will be Challenged

3 Firms 33.3% market share each	⟷	2 Firms 66.7% and 33.3% market share
HHI = 3,333		HHI = 5,555

Panel B: Merger will be Allowed

20 Firms 5% market share each	⟷	19 Firms 18 with 5% and one with 10% market share
HHI = 500		HHI = 550

In general, a proposed merger is likely to be challenged if the postmerger HHI is above 1,800 and the merger increases the HHI by 100 points. Therefore, the merger in Panel A is likely to be challenged. In contrast, a merger is likely to be allowed if the postmerger HHI remains below 1,000 or the merger increases the HHI by less than 50 points. The merger in Panel B is likely to go unchallenged.

Merger with Remedy In some cases, the government may allow a merger to occur, but only if the firms involved also agree to a specific remedy that would prevent a monopoly. For example, in 1999, the two oil giants Exxon and Mobil were permitted to merge into a single company. The estimated value of the combined company was over a quarter of a trillion dollars. As large as these companies were, a merger among the largest petroleum companies would result in little overall industry concentration as the HHI remained well under 1,000. From an aggregate standpoint, industry concentration was not a problem.

However when considering the merger, the FTC and DOJ took a comprehensive look at local gasoline stations to determine the impact such a merger would have on the towns and communities served. They found that the new entity would have an effective monopoly on gasoline sales in some markets. The government proposed a remedy: It would allow the merger *only* if Exxon and Mobil sold over 2,400 gasoline stations to rivals. In a similar fashion, European regulators allowed the same merger if Mobil first sold Aral (a large chain of gasoline stations). Exxon and Mobil also needed to sell oil refineries and pipelines.

Contestable Markets and Evolving Markets The concentration index (HHI) is not the only factor at which regulators look. Another important factor is contestability. A **contestable market** is a market that is easy for rival firms to enter. Perhaps the most famous example is the airline industry, which is highly concentrated in certain local markets. However, airline profits tend to remain quite low, as an attempt by one airline to raise prices excessively in one market causes other airlines to enter—or contest—that market. Hence, mergers are sometimes allowed in the airline industry that would not be permitted in less contestable industries, where entry is more difficult.

To summarize, there are many complex issues associated with a monopoly. Our antitrust laws mirror that complexity, by differentiating between a variety of situations and practices. Our legal system continues to evolve as economic research provides a better understanding of the costs and benefits of different types of monopoly and oligopoly.

contestable market A market that is easy for rival firms to enter.

BUSINESS TAKEAWAY

Entrepreneur Peter Thiel once said that competition is for losers and "monopoly is the condition of every successful business."[1] In one sense, Thiel's remarks sound anti-social, as a monopoly can hurt consumers and overall economic efficiency. But he argued that monopolies are built when firms provide better products than their rivals, citing the Google search engine as a prime example.

Thiel, who founded PayPal, is a tech entrepreneur who focuses on innovative firms. His advice to young entrepreneurs is that the only way to make persistent economic profits, year after year, is to create a product that no one else is producing. This is what he meant when suggesting that all firms should try to be monopolies. Firms are legally allowed to operate as monopolies, if it is a result of innovation leading to patented or copyrighted products. Nonetheless, entrepreneurs following Thiel's advice always need to be aware of antitrust laws.

Once established, a monopolist needs to decide what quantity to sell and what price to charge. These are not two separate decisions, as the price the monopolist charges depends on the level of sales. In order to boost sales, the monopolist must reduce prices. However, lower prices from higher sales also decrease marginal revenue; indeed, MR declines even faster than price. Barriers to entry allow some monopolists to earn sizable economic profits. And, the desire to earn monopoly profits may lead a monopolist to create barriers to entry.

A firm may gain monopoly power by developing a new product that it patents, or by creating a product with significant network externalities. These activities add value to society. Two rival firms may also decide to gain monopoly power by merging. However, mergers that significantly lessen price competition are often blocked by government antitrust enforcement, even if they do not result in a pure monopoly. This is what stopped the proposed merger between AT&T and T-Mobile.

CHAPTER STUDY GUIDE

13.1 CHARACTERISTICS OF A MONOPOLY

A **monopoly** is a market structure with a single seller of a product with no close substitutes and high barriers to entry. **Barriers to entry** are obstacles that prevent other firms from entering an industry. In market structures with high barriers to entry, such as oligopolies and monopolies, other firms facing serious obstacles entering the market even when the potential for profit is large. These barriers include patents and copyrights. A **patent** is the temporary exclusive right to sell a product granted to its inventor. A **copyright** is the temporary exclusive right to sell books, films, and music. Another barrier is economies of scale, which often result in a natural monopoly. Additional barriers include control of a resource, brand loyalty, and **network externalities,** the benefit a consumer receives from a good or service from other users of the same product. Monopolists face the market demand curve and have the potential for long-run economic profit.

13.2 OUTPUT AND PRICING DECISIONS FOR A MONOPOLY

Since the demand curve a monopolist faces is downward-sloping, selling more units requires lowering prices. As a result, marginal revenue is less than price ($MR < P$). As is the case in perfect competition, firms maximize profits at the quantity where marginal revenue equals marginal cost, with profit equal to $((P - ATC) \times Q)$. Since $P > MR$, the profit-maximizing price is generally not equal to MC. Price is found on the demand curve at the profit-maximizing quantity. Being a monopoly does not guarantee an economic profit and marginal revenue can be negative.

13.3 MONOPOLY VERSUS PERFECT COMPETITION

Economists generally prefer competition because it naturally leads to lower prices, higher output, productive efficiency, and allocative efficiency. When compared to perfect competition, a monopolist charges higher prices and sells less output. The lower output generates a dead-weight loss. At times, monopolies engage in **rent seeking**, which refers to activities such as lobbying the government with the goal of obtaining barriers to entry, subsidies, and other special privileges. Rent seeking is especially common with monopolies, or firms attempting to become monopolies by restricting competition. Alternatively, monopolies can be regarded as positive if they encourage new product development.

13.4   GOVERNMENT POLICY OPTIONS FOR NATURAL MONOPOLIES

Natural monopolies occur when a single firm can supply a product at lower costs than would occur with two or more competing firms. This is the result of economies of scale (the benefit of mass production). In such a case, society may benefit from lower prices if a monopoly is allowed to exist. Policymakers who favor competition have several options when addressing natural monopolies. In this case, competition will mean smaller firms with higher costs. Simply allowing the natural monopoly to exist and maximize profits will lead to higher prices for consumers and a deadweight loss. Alternatively, policymakers could regulate the price a natural monopoly can charge. One such option is setting price equal to marginal cost, but this may result in an economic loss. A more common option is to set price equal to average total cost. This is known as **average cost pricing** or *rate of return regulation*. It results in zero economic profit for the monopolist and relatively low prices for consumers. Alternatively, the government can choose to take ownership of the natural monopoly.

13.5   ANTITRUST LAWS AND MERGERS

Antitrust laws are designed to limit behavior that substantially lessens competition. In the United States, the first antitrust laws were the Sherman Antitrust Act of 1890 and the Clayton Act of 1914. Antitrust laws are enforced by the Federal Trade Commission (FTC) and Department of Justice (DOJ). A **trust** is an organization of rival firms designed to acquire monopoly power in an industry. A **merger** refers to the combining of two companies into a single firm. A **vertical merger** is a merger between firms at different stages of production. A **conglomerate merger** is a merger between firms in unrelated industries. Finally, a **horizontal merger** is a merger between firms in the same industry. When deciding to allow a merger, policymakers often look at the **Herfindahl–Hirschman index (HHI)**, a measure of concentration calculated by summing the square of the percentage market share of each and every firm in an industry:

$$HHI = \sum_{\text{All firms}} (\text{Market share})^2$$

Regulators also consider if a market is a **contestable market,** one that is easy for rival firms to enter.

TOP TEN TERMS AND CONCEPTS

① Monopoly

② Barriers to Entry

③ Patent

④ Network Externalities

⑤ Rent Seeking

⑥ Natural Monopoly

⑦ Average Cost Pricing (Rate of Return Regulation)

⑧ Trust and Antitrust Laws

⑨ Horizontal, Vertical, and Conglomerate Mergers

⑩ Herfindahl–Hirschman Index (HHI)

STUDY PROBLEMS

1. What are barriers to entry? Why are they important? Name five such barriers. What impact do such barriers have on the potential for long-run economic profit?

2. In the following table, fill in the data for total revenue (*TR*) and marginal revenue (*MR*) that represent the demand curve for a monopolist. Assuming that marginal cost is a constant $40, how many units should the monopolist sell? What price should the monopolist charge?

P	Q	TR	MR
100	1		
90	2		
80	3		
70	4		
60	5		

3. The Los Angeles Dodgers have five seats to sell behind home plate. They can sell all five seats for $1,800 or four seats for $2,500 each.

   a. What is the marginal revenue of the fifth seat? Based on this, should the Dodgers sell four or five seats?

   b. Suppose the Dodgers could sell all five seats for $2,000 each. What would the marginal revenue of the fifth seat be?

   c. Suppose the Dodgers could sell all five seats for $2,200 each. What is the marginal revenue of the fifth seat? Based on this, should the Dodgers sell four or five seats?

4. Consider the demand curve for a monopolist given below. What is the profit-maximizing quantity? What price should the monopolist charge? What is the monopolist's profit?

5. What is a natural monopoly? What problems exist when forcing a natural monopolist to compete? What problems occur with price regulation when attempting to achieve allocative efficiency? What price results with average cost pricing?

6. Consider the headline of a 2015 *Wall Street Journal* article "As Mergers Multiply, U.S. Antitrust Cops Raise Their Game."[2] What government agencies are the "cops"? What factors do these government agencies consider?

7. The following figure represents a market that switches from perfect competition to a monopoly. When perfect competition exists, what is consumer surplus? What happens to consumer surplus when the market becomes a monopoly? What does Area *B* capture? What is the deadweight loss? Overall, what happens to society's well-being?

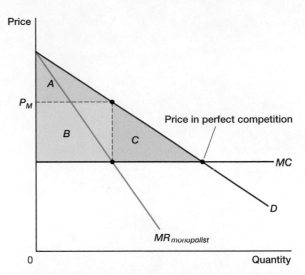

8. Nexium is a medicine used for the treatment of acid reflux. In 2014, AstraZeneca's patent on the drug expired and the firm was forced to compete with generic substitutes.[3] What do you think happened to the former monopolist's profits? What impact did the patent's expiration have on the prices consumers paid?

9. Suppose several pizza restaurants on an island combine into one company. Using a diagram, show what happens to the price of pizza, consumer surplus, producer surplus, and total surplus. Who benefits from such a combination?

10. What is rent seeking activity? Is it helpful for consumers? Who engages in rent seeking?

11. New York City taxi medallions allow their owners to operate a taxi cab. In recent years, the owners of such medallions have lobbied lawmakers and mounted legal challenges to prevent government plans to create a fleet of "green cabs." These kinds of activities are considered rent seeking by economists.[4] Why do medallion owners engage in rent seeking?

12. To what does the term "robber barons" refer?

13. Briefly describe the main provisions of the Sherman Antitrust Act of 1890. What companies did the law break up? What flaws existed in the original law?

14. What is the Clayton Act of 1914? What are the key sections of the law? Name several subsequent laws designed to strengthen the Clayton Act. Who is exempt from the Clayton Act?

15. What government agencies review mergers between similar companies? What types of mergers may arouse antitrust concerns? What is the Herfindahl–Hirshman index, and how is it used to evaluate mergers?

14

CHAPTER

∧ Maria decides to go upscale! Product differentiation is a key characteristic of monopolistic competition.

Monopolistic Competition and Price Discrimination

When Businesses Sell Differentiated Products

Maria knows that her restaurant will face intense competition on several fronts: There are other pizzerias in the area, as well as fast-food joints and casual dining restaurants. But unlike her tomato suppliers, Maria has some pricing power. Her pizzas are different from—and she's betting, better than—those of her rivals, and she knows that with the right location, décor, service, and atmosphere, she can probably attract customers. Maria's business background tells her that her marketing mix—product, price, placement, and promotion (the four Ps)—will play an important role in differentiating her restaurant from every other one in town.

This chapter examines businesses, such as Maria's, that operate in *monopolistic competition,* a very common market structure in which many firms compete, selling slightly different products. The chapter also examines how businesses benefit by selling similar products at different prices to different segments of their market.

Chapter Learning Targets

- Recognize the key characteristics of monopolistic competition.

- Describe economic efficiency and other characteristics of monopolistic competition in the long run.

- Explain the economic role of advertising.

- Define price discrimination.

- Compare and contrast perfect and imperfect price discrimination.

14.1 CHARACTERISTICS OF MONOPOLISTIC COMPETITION

As a consumer, you are already quite familiar with markets in which many firms compete: Every time you choose one brand over another, or drive a bit further to get a better price or slightly different product, you are likely participating in a market with monopolistic competition. **Monopolistic competition** is a market structure with many firms selling similar but differentiated products. Unlike a monopoly, firms in monopolistic competition face fierce competition. Unlike firms in a perfectly competitive market structure, a monopolistic competitor sells a product that is differentiated from its rivals. In this section, we'll examine the distinctive characteristics of this very common market structure, and also how firms differentiate their products in order to compete.

Product Differentiation and Non-Price Competition

Maria faces price competition from Domino's and Papa John's pizza, both of which are relatively close substitutes. She would lose many of her customers if she charged prices that were far above those of her rivals. Maria may not have a monopoly on pizza, or dining, or takeout food—but only Maria can make Maria's pizza. Likewise, only Domino's can sell pizza with the Domino's brand name. Maria can charge a slightly higher price than Domino's and other rivals if her product is perceived as more desirable by at least some consumers.

In order to have some pricing power, Maria's product must be clearly different from those of her competitors in the eyes of her customers. **Product differentiation** is a real or perceived difference among products that are close substitutes. Unlike in perfect competition, the substitutes are close but not perfect substitutes. Maria and Domino's are both selling pizza, but not the exact same pizza. Some consumers might like Maria's pizza better, or prefer the atmosphere at her restaurant, or wish to support a small local business rather than a large corporation. Others might opt for Domino's because it is fast or more convenient.

Honey, honey, always honey:
We'll never get rich unless we can
differentiate ourselves from the competition...

Hagen/Cartoon Stock

All these factors, unrelated to price, can affect sales at both Maria's and Domino's. **Non-price competition** occurs when businesses try to distinguish their products from rivals without changing the price. Businesses engage in many types of non-price competition in an effort to boost sales. Product differentiation and non-price competition exist in both oligopoly and monopolistic competition market structures. There are several strategies that a firm can use to differentiate its business.

Location Some firms differentiate simply by making their products more convenient. For brick-and-mortar retailers such as gas stations and convenience stores, location is key. Lots of gas stations sell the same exact gasoline, but those with prime locations (such as near expressway exits) and no rivals may charge more. Geographical dispersion can be a source of product differentiation.

In a few cases, consumers actually benefit from geographical concentration. For instance, multiple car dealers are frequently located on a single major street or highway. That's because consumers prefer to do comparison shopping for cars (differentiated product) more than for regular gasoline (standardized product), and hence like to quickly go from one dealer to the next.

Product Quality and Design Products often vary in terms of reliability and other measures of quality. Maria may choose to use fresh tomatoes and homemade mozzarella on her pizzas, while the shop around the corner uses canned tomatoes and processed cheese. Automobiles are a good example of a product in which quality differs from one model to the next. Likewise, an iPhone has a unique operating system and design characteristics that differentiate it from other smartphones. Variations in style, flavor, color, texture, and other features can differentiate a product.

Service Maria's pizzeria might offer table service, while competitors offer only counter service and takeout; customers who want a more formal, sit-down dinner are more

monopolistic competition
A market structure with many firms selling similar but differentiated products.

product differentiation
A real or perceived difference among products that are close substitutes.

non-price competition What occurs when businesses try to distinguish their products from rivals without changing the price.

likely to choose Maria's. In a similar way, many Apple customers prefer to stick with the brand because of the firm's excellent customer service and the ease with which they can get their device serviced at a local Apple store.

Perception Products may have differences that only exist in the minds of consumers. Often, this is the result of brand loyalty, effective marketing, clever packaging, or public relations. Maria knows that establishing her business as a member of the community will create positive perceptions of her restaurant. She may thus choose to support a neighborhood soccer team or school drama club production.

Brand Name and Advertising Products often differentiate themselves in terms of recognition by consumers. This is frequently the direct result of establishing a brand name and identity through advertising. Consumers, for example, can quickly differentiate a burger from Five Guys, McDonald's, and Burger King. We will have more to say on the economics of advertising later in the chapter; for now, it is enough to recognize advertising as a source of product differentiation.

📊 BUSINESS BRIEF Selling Donuts—and Cronuts

What is your favorite donut? Perhaps a Boston cream donut from Dunkin' Donuts, a glazed donut from Krispy Kreme, or a jelly-filled donut at Tim Hortons? Maybe you fancy one from a local donut shop. Product differentiation is an extremely important element in this monopolistically competitive market and a key to selling donuts. Donut shops can be found everywhere: from local street corners to airports and rail stations. Donuts can be bought at supermarkets, convenience stores, and even gas stations. Some donuts are sold with a brand name as a signal of quality or with a friendly face at the counter; others are not.

Consumers clearly have preferences, and many donut businesses have found it advantageous to differentiate their products. For example, in 2013, pastry chef Dominique Ansel created what appeared to be a better donut, the "Cronut," a cross between a croissant and a donut. For months, lines stretched around the corner from his bakery in NYC's Soho neighborhood. While the fad waned, demand has remained high as Ansel's shop is the only place where you can find the original Cronut.[*]

[*]Brendan O'Connor, "The Mysterious Persistence of the Cronut," *The New York Times*, May 8, 2015, https://www.nytimes.com/2015/05/08/magazine/the-mysterious-persistence-of-the-cronut.html?_r=0.

Low Barriers to Entry, Highly Elastic Demand, and Zero Economic Profit

Entry is relatively easy in monopolistic competition. This leads to three outcomes. First, there are many sellers. Examples include pizza restaurants, convenience stores, and clothing retailers. In fact, many of the small businesses that you would observe on Main Street fall into the monopolistic competition category.

Second, due to product differentiation, demand is less price elastic than in perfect competition, where all firms are price takers facing a demand that is perfectly elastic ($e_d = \infty$). The demand curve facing a firm in monopolistic competition has some slope, but because there are many substitutes, the demand curve these firms face is *highly elastic* as consumers can be quite responsive to price changes by firms in monopolistic competition.

Finally, as with perfect competition, low barriers to entry prevent firms from having long-run economic profits. This occurs because profits encourage rival firms to enter the market, putting downward pressure on prices and profits. The characteristics of monopolistic competition are compared with those of other market structures in Exhibit 1.

EXHIBIT 1   Characteristics of Market Structures: Monopolistic Competition

	Market Structure			
	Perfect Competition Chapter 12	**Monopolistic Competition Chapter 14**	**Oligopoly Chapter 15**	**Monopoly Chapter 13**
Number of Sellers	very large number	many firms	few firms	one firm
Entry Conditions	easy entry	easy entry	barriers to entry	barriers to entry
Price Setting Ability	none	some	some	some
Price Elasticity of Demand—Firm Level	perfectly elastic	highly elastic	more elastic than market demand	same as market elasticity of demand
Long-Run Profit	zero economic profit	zero economic profit	potentially	potentially
Product Differentiation	standardized product	differentiated product	varies by product market	unique product with no close substitutes
Key Characteristic	firms price takers	differentiated product	firms highly interdependent	one firm
Examples	tomatoes copper lumber	delivered pizza smartphone apps toothpaste	search engines wireless service mobile phones	patented medicine first-class mail electricity delivery

Monopolistic competition is a market structure with many firms selling similar but differentiated products. Unlike a monopoly, firms in monopolistic competition face fierce competition. Unlike firms in a perfectly competitive market structure, a monopolistic competitor sells a product differentiated from its rivals.

14.2 THE LONG-RUN COMPETITIVE EQUILIBRIUM IN MONOPOLISTIC COMPETITION

Monopolistic competition is a cross between perfect competition and monopoly. In order to determine the long-run equilibrium in monopolistic competition, we need to focus on two concepts. First, we use the demand and marginal revenue curves, as well as marginal analysis, to determine the profit-maximization output. Second, we need to recognize that barriers to entry and exit are low, which pushes the industry toward zero economic profits in the long run.

Demand and Marginal Revenue Curves

Due to product differentiation, the demand curve facing any firm in monopolistic competition is downward-sloping. On the other hand, the demand curve facing Maria's or Domino's is flatter (more elastic) than the entire market demand curve for pizza. In general, the demand curve is highly elastic when there is a considerable amount of competition from rivals. However, because the product is differentiated, the demand curve facing a firm in monopolistic competition is not perfectly elastic, as is the case in perfect competition. Pizza from Maria's is not exactly the same as pizza from Domino's.

EXHIBIT 2 Typical Demand Curve for a Firm

Panel A: Monopolistic Competiton

Price

Highly price elastic demand, but not perfectly price elastic

D_{MC}

MR_{MC}

Quantity

Panel B: Perfect Competition

Price

Perfectly price elastic demand

D_{PC}

$P = MR$

Quantity

Panel C: Monopoly

Price

Less price elastic demand of overall market

D_M

MR_M

Quantity

The existence of competition from close substitutes make the monopolistic competitor's demand curve more elastic than it would be if the market structure is a monopoly, but less elastic (steeper) than if the market structure is perfect competition due to product differentiation. Since the monopolistic competitor's demand curve is downward-sloping, the marginal revenue curve lies below the demand curve ($P > MR$).

Exhibit 2 shows the demand curve a firm faces in perfect competition, monopolistic competition, and monopoly. Due to the existence of greater competition, the demand curve facing a firm in monopolistic competition is *more* price elastic than the demand curve facing a monopolist; however it is *less* price elastic than in perfect competition with a (flat) demand curve that is perfectly elastic ($e_d = \infty$).

As with any downward-sloping demand curve, the marginal revenue curve lies below the demand curve for a firm in monopolistic competition and monopoly. If the monopolistic competitor wishes to sell more units, it must lower its price, *ceteris paribus*. Since the monopolistic competitor's demand curve slopes downward, the marginal revenue curve lies below the demand curve ($P > MR$). This is similar to monopoly and accounts for the monopolistic part of the phrase "monopolistic competition."

Profit Maximization in the Long Run and Short Run

The marginal analysis used to determine the short-run profit maximization of a firm in monopolistic competition is similar to the marginal analysis used by a monopoly and firms in perfect competition. Thus, it is useful to recall the *three simple steps to calculate maximum profit*:

Step 1: Determine Quantity and Price Find the quantity (Q) at which MR equals marginal cost. At this quantity, price (P) is read off the demand curve.

Step 2: Determine ATC Find the average total cost at this quantity.

Step 3: Determine Profit Finally, (total) profit equals profit per unit times the number of units. This equals price minus average total cost times the profit-maximizing number of units (Profit = $(P − ATC) \times Q$).

Exhibit 3 demonstrates this process. In the two graphs on the left, the profit-maximizing quantity is Q_{MC}. This is where $MR = MC$. Since price is greater than marginal revenue, price is read off the demand curve (P_{MC}). In Panel A on left, since $P_{MC} > ATC$, the firm is profitable. In Panel B on left, $P_{MC} < ATC$ and a loss occurs.

Think & Speak Like an Economist

In monopolistic competition, the firm's demand curve is less price elastic than a firm in perfect competition that faces a (flat), perfectly elastic demand ($e_d = \infty$). The market demand curve is even less price elastic. As a consequence, the firm's demand curve has some slope and price is greater than marginal revenue—a feature that also occurs in a monopoly.

As in perfect competition, there are low barriers to entry in monopolistic competition. It is easy to enter and exit the industry. To see this, consider what happens when a firm in monopolistic competition is profitable. As a result of such profitability, rival firms are likely to enter, shifting the demand curve facing the *existing* firm to the left (as shown in Panel A on right) and the cost curves remain the same. If a Wendy's opens up across the street from a McDonald's and Burger King, the demand facing the existing fast-food restaurants declines. As a result, profits at the existing firms decline. Ultimately, entry lowers price and results in zero economic profit in the long run (a normal accounting profit), just as under perfect competition.

EXHIBIT 3 Profit Maximization in Monopolistic Competition

Panel A: Economic Profit Reduces Firm Demand When Rivals Enter

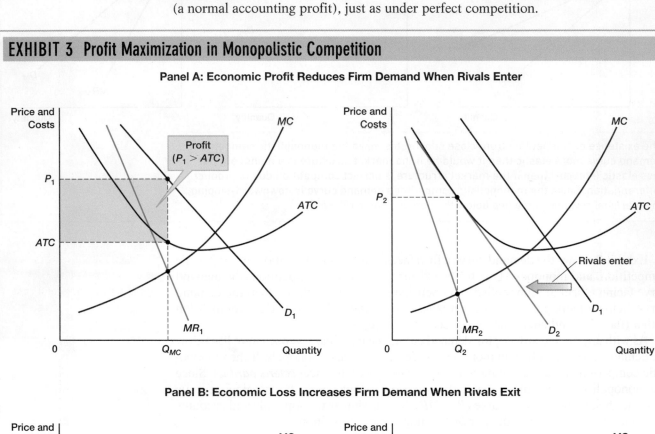

Panel B: Economic Loss Increases Firm Demand When Rivals Exit

Firms in monopolistic competition determine the profit-maximizing level of output by finding where $MR = MC$ and reading price off the demand curve. In Panel A, the firm is profitable. This causes other firms to enter, shifting the demand curve facing the firm to the left. The opposite occurs when there is an economic loss (Panel B). Note that only the demand curve facing the firm changes when rivals enter or exit the market; the firm's cost curves do not change. In the long run, firms earn zero economic profit.

The opposite occurs when there is an economic loss, as in panel B. Here, economic losses encourage rivals to exit, shifting the demand curve of the remaining firm to the right, as shown in Panel B (right). This is what would happen if a fast-food restaurant located across the street closes.

The long-run equilibrium for both perfect competition and monopolistic competition occurs at the output level where firms just break even and earn zero economic profit. This is because profits encourage new firms to enter and losses encourage some of the existing firms to exit the market. Note that the firm's cost curves do not change as rivals enter or exit the market; only the firm's demand curve and marginal revenue curve shift.

Monopolistic Competition versus Perfect Competition

Notice that entry and exit cause firms in both monopolistic competition and perfect competition to earn zero economic profits in the long run. However, there are differences between the two. As shown in Exhibit 4, these market structures vary in terms of excess capacity, productive efficiency, allocative efficiency, and product differentiation in the long run.

Excess Capacity in Monopolistic Competition In perfect competition, firms minimize average total cost. This is shown in Panel A. In monopolistic competition, however, ATC is *not* minimized as shown in Panel B. Firms in monopolistic competition have **excess capacity**; the amount by which output would need to increase in order to minimize average total cost.

In other words, if the firm expands by increasing output, it will lower average total cost. In the figure, the firm needs to increase output to $Q_{\min ATC}$ to minimize average total cost. Selling more units, however, requires the firm to lower price and incur

excess capacity The amount by which output would need to increase in order to minimize average total cost.

EXHIBIT 4 Long-Run Competitive Equilibrium in Perfect and Monopolistic Competition

In Panel A, firms in perfect competition break even in the long run, achieving both productive efficiency (*minimum ATC*) and allocative efficiency ($P = MC$). In Panel B, firms in monopolistic competition break even in the long run ($P = ATC$). At this equilibrium, productive efficiency is not achieved (not at minimum *ATC*). Excess capacity exists, as the firm could increase output to $Q_{\min ATC}$ and lower average total cost. Allocative efficiency is also not achieved ($P > MC$). On the other hand, monopolistic competition provides product differentiation.

"GIVEN THE DOWNWARD SLOPE OF OUR DEMAND CURVE, AND THE EASE WITH WHICH OTHER FIRMS CAN ENTER THE INDUSTRY, WE CAN STRENGTHEN OUR PROFIT POSITION ONLY BY EQUATING MARGINAL COST AND MARGINAL REVENUE. ORDER MORE JELLY BEANS."

Harris, S/Cartoonstock.com

CartoonStock.com

economic losses. This occurs because profits are maximized at the quantity where $MR = MC$, but average total cost is minimized at the quantity where $ATC = MC$ (which is a higher quantity). It is important to note that excess capacity does not imply that companies are producing the *current level* of output in an inefficient fashion. Economic incentives encourage all businesses to produce a given level of output (Q_{MC}) in the least costly manner possible.

Differences in Productive and Allocative Efficiency

Monopolistic competition results in a lack of productive efficiency because ATC would be lower if firms produced *a different level of output (more units)*. In perfect competition, ATC is minimized. No level of output would reduce ATC. In perfect competition, allocative efficiency is also achieved when the firm's price equals marginal cost ($P = MC$). All mutually beneficial transactions that can occur do take place under perfect competition. This is not the case in monopolistic competition, as $P > MC$. This means that there is a price mark-up over marginal cost. As with monopoly, consumers value goods more than the marginal cost of production, and thus too few goods are produced relative to what is required to achieve allocative efficiency.

Product Differentiation in Monopolistic Competition

We've just seen that monopolistic competition does not lead to either productive efficiency or allocative efficiency. However, monopolistic competition offers society something else it desires: product differentiation. In perfect competition, society may be able to produce a product such as toothpaste at a lower price and lower production cost, but it would mean few choices of toothpaste. A trip down the toothpaste aisle indicates that consumers prefer a variety of options for toothpaste brands, flavors, and features. Similarly, students may save on prom dresses if all dresses were the same, but producers know that most people would prefer to choose their own style.

Consumers often prefer differentiated products even when a cheaper generic version is available. Similarly, some college students choose to go to more expensive private universities instead of state schools. Society benefits with differentiation, as some schools are better suited for some students than others. In certain cases, the very same consumer will prefer to occasionally shift to a new and different product. The old saying "variety is the spice of life" describes consumer preferences for product differentiation.

◫ BUSINESS BRIEF Economic Profit in the Real Estate Brokerage Business

A good example of excess capacity in monopolistic competition occurs in the real estate brokerage industry after a housing price boom. In any local community, there are often dozens of agents to choose from, and barriers to entry are relatively low.

Real estate brokers tend to earn standardized sales commissions of about 6% of the home price. When the price of homes rises sharply during a housing price boom, such brokers earn many more dollars for each home they sell. These economic profits cause new brokers to enter the industry. Each broker sells fewer houses but earns more for each house sold. Economic profits return to the breakeven point.

Housing prices vary widely from community to community. Does this mean brokers in high-priced communities are rich? Not exactly. Austan Goolsbee, former economic advisor to President Barack Obama, points out that agents in Steubenville,

Ohio, see roughly similar profits as those in pricey San Francisco, where a home sells for almost six times as much money:

> [T]he average full-time agent working in Steubenville sells more than 22 houses per year, whereas the same agent in San Francisco sells less than one-fifth as much. The average income for real-estate work in the two locales is virtually identical.[*]

Low barriers to entry in the real estate brokerage business result in entry; thus, brokers in high-value markets don't earn much more than in ordinary towns. The competition from new firms entering drives economic profit toward zero, even in the wealthiest towns.

[*]Austan Goolsbee, "Why Real-Estate Agents Aren't Rich," *Slate*, August 26, 2005, http://www.slate.com/articles/business/the_dismal_science/2005/08/bubblelusions.html.

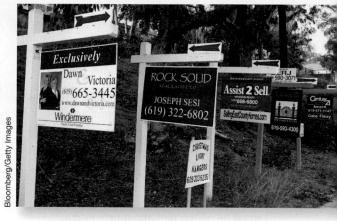

∧ Low barriers to entry result in intense competition in the real estate brokerage business.

14.3 MARKETING AND ADVERTISING DECISIONS

Maria knows it's not enough to just make the best pizza, deliver outstanding service, and create an appealing atmosphere at her restaurant. If she wants to be successful, she needs to ensure that she's delivering the product customers want, at the right price, and the customers can trust her product is different from those of competitors. A large part of Maria's business plan must thus be devoted to marketing.

Marketing Mix and the "Four Ps"

Marketing refers to all the activities and strategies that businesses use to sell products. The many decisions involved in marketing products are often referred to as the marketing mix, and can be categorized into four basic categories known in business as the *four Ps*[1]:

- *Price.* Putting a price on a product or service is a crucial step in the marketing process. A business must be concerned with what price it can charge customers, what price its rival charges for similar products, and any possibility for price discrimination (discussed later in the chapter).

- *Product.* Product differentiation is often a key component of the offering; other factors include product quality, design, and selection.

- *Placement.* A firm needs to determine how and where a consumer will gain access to its product. The focus here is on product distribution, which may include both retail and online stores.

- *Promotion.* Promotion refers to the techniques a business uses to communicate with potential customers. It includes not only paid advertising but also social media campaigns, public relations, and other strategies that are utilized to increase brand awareness, customer loyalty, and, ultimately, sales.

Product, placement, and promotion are all forms of non-price competition—an essential feature of monopolistic competition and oligopoly. Marketing professionals are concerned with each of the four Ps. Maria, for example, will need to consider them when launching her restaurant, as detailed in Exhibit 5.

Economics of Advertising

Advertising refers to paid activities that businesses and other organizations use to sell products. Advertising is only a small portion of a firm's marketing mix, yet it shows up nearly everywhere: You can't watch a television show, click on a Web link, ride a bus,

marketing All the activities and strategies that businesses use to sell products. The many decisions involved in marketing products are often referred to as the marketing mix.

advertising Paid activities that businesses and other organizations use to sell products.

EXHIBIT 5 The Four Ps and Maria's Marketing Decisions

Maria must establish a competitive pricing structure based on what the pizza market in her community will accept. She also needs to engage in various forms of non-price competition. She must decide what kind of product she will offer, and how she can make her pizza unique and distinctive. Placement is an especially important decision. She needs to locate where target customers will have easy access to her restaurant. Finally, she must be concerned about promotion.

- How much can she charge for pizza?
- How much can she charge for soda?
- How much can she charge for wine?

- What kind of food to serve?
- How many types of pizza?
- What kinds of beverages?
- What kinds of service(s)?

Price **Product**

Placement **Promotion**

- What's the best location for her pizzeria?
- Will she offer delivery?
- Counter service or table service?

- Should she advertise in the local papers?
- Should she offer coupons or customer loyalty cards?
- Should she start a website?

or even pump gas without being exposed to a paid advertisement. Businesses spend large amounts of money on these ads; indeed, advertising accounts for roughly 2% of all economic activity in the United States. Firms advertise to boost demand for their product—selling more units and/or charging a higher price.

Some economists argue that advertising provides useful information to consumers, such as product prices and the existence of new products, enabling them to make more informed choices. In addition, advertising may help encourage competition from existing firms and new firms. This is why the Federal Trade Commission (FTC), which tries to promote competition, opposes most bans on advertising.

Other economists insist that advertising increases cost (as shown above) and does little more than manipulate consumers into unwise decisions. Perhaps it encourages consumers to eat too much junk food. Why does it matter if there is beautiful scenery and glamorous people in an automobile commercial? On the other hand, most people seem to think it is *other people* who are manipulated by ads, not themselves. Of course, this cannot be true for everyone! Businesses advertise because it works—advertising does often boost demand. Next, we consider some of the economic issues surrounding advertising.

Advertising in Monopolistic Competition and Oligopoly Advertising primarily takes place in monopolistic competition and oligopoly market structures. Businesses in these market structures advertise because it helps consumers recognize the firm's existence, as well as any product differentiation.

Panel A of Exhibit 6 demonstrates two potential impacts of advertising on the demand curve facing a firm. First, advertising increases demand. Think of an increase in demand as "more people wanting to buy the product" as the demand curve shifts to the right.

Second, advertising lowers price elasticity of demand of the firm's product, meaning consumers become somewhat less responsive to price changes. This allows businesses to charge higher prices. Think of this as "buyers are less resistant to price increases," thus willing to accept price increases. Effective advertising generates product differentiation and brand loyalty, which tend to decrease the price elasticity of demand (and steepens the demand curve). Consumers may start to believe that a rival's brand is inferior. This allows a firm to raise price above that of its rivals.

Advertising is one way to influence those trends and build brand loyalty. When a firm builds customer loyalty, it essentially becomes a single seller of its own brand.

EXHIBIT 6 Economic Impact of Advertising

Panel A: Impact of Effective Advertising on Firm's Demand

Advertising increases demand and lowers price elasticity of demand.

D_2

D_1

Panel B: Impact of Advertising on Average Total Cost

Advertising shifts up ATC curve.

Advertising may increase cost or advertising may decrease ATC by allowing the firm to realize economies of scale.

ATC without advertising

ATC_2

ATC_1

When effective, advertising will increase demand and reduce the price elasticity of demand (steepens the demand curve) as shown in Panel A. Advertising also increases total cost and shifts the average total cost curve upward as shown in Panel B. If advertising is not effective at increasing demand, it will result in higher costs and lower profits. On the other hand, if advertising is effective, it may increase profits. In addition, ATC may decrease if economies of scale are realized.

The stronger the customer loyalty, the greater the firm's monopoly power. For example, there are lots of brands of cosmetics, beer, and running shoes for sale, but many consumers are very loyal to one brand or another. This mirrors the progression of demand curves becoming less elastic (steeper) with greater monopoly power, as shown earlier in the chapter (Exhibit 2).

Advertising May Increase or Decrease Average Total Cost Advertising costs money. Spending more money on advertising will shift the firm's average total cost curve upward. Surprisingly, this does not necessarily mean higher average cost. How can that be? A successful advertising campaign may increase sales by a significant enough amount to allow the firm to achieve economies of scale and/or spread out fixed cost over more units. This could lead to lower average total cost. Many automobile manufacturers advertise in order to maintain sufficient sales to spread out fixed costs and thus take advantage of economies of scale. Likewise, auto insurers advertise heavily. This allows them to insure a sufficient number of drivers and obtain economies of scale. Of course, advertising may also increase average total cost. Both scenarios are depicted in Panel B of Exhibit 6. In this case, if sales remain at 50 units, average total cost increases from $15 to $20. But if sales increase to 150 units, *ATC* decreases to $10.

Advertising as a Signal of Quality Advertising can also provide a signal of quality—even when it provides little actual product information. Some economists suggest that spending large amounts of money on a celebrity to promote a product or service provides a powerful signal of quality to consumers. Or consider an ad aired during the Super Bowl. The expense of this ad might signal that the company has enormous resources, which it would be unlikely to risk by selling a defective product.

∧ Brand names are common in monopolistic competition and provide a signal of quality.

An appealing ad or alluring social media campaign can entice customers to give Maria's new restaurant a try. If her product is only fair, she may not see those customers again. On the other hand, if Maria's pizza is great, and her restaurant is inviting and its service outstanding, her marketing outreach is likely to lead to a lot of repeat customers. Advertising—whether in the form of paid advertising or social networking campaigns that primarily cost only Maria's time—is more likely to be worthwhile when it leads to repeat customers, which is why advertising generally must be combined with product quality to be effective.

Brand Names as a Signal of Quality

A brand name can also be a signal of quality. Teen and young adult apparel companies like American Eagle Outfitters, Forever 21, Abercrombie & Fitch, and Urban Outfitters spent years developing and cultivating their brands. Abercrombie & Fitch, for example, has been around since 1892. When companies survive for very long periods, consumers are more likely to view their merchandise as being reliable. The brand is a signal of that quality.

Could a successful company change its product mix and start selling low-quality items of clothing and save on production costs? Yes, it could. And because costs will be lower, this might even lead to higher profits in the short run. However in the long run, the company's sales could decline. Switching its product line to low-quality items could destroy the brand, a brand that the firm spent decades cultivating. Its brand would no longer be a signal of quality and would be less likely to command a premium price.

Do Firms in Perfect Competition Advertise?

Firms in perfect competition rarely advertise, because products are standardized and consumers recognize this. With identical products, firms in perfect competition have no reason to engage in non-price competition—they strictly compete on the basis of price. In perfect competition, advertising may boost market demand, but will not increase the demand a small individual firm faces. Therefore, no single firm has any incentive to bear the cost of advertising.

But then again: What about those "Got Milk?" ads that seemed to be everywhere when you were growing up? Milk is fairly close to perfect competition, so why would dairy farmers pay for advertising? Note that these commercials were designed to encourage consumers to purchase more milk in general, *not* a specific brand of milk. In fact, they were launched not by a single firm, but by the California Milk Processing Board, a nonprofit organization representing that state's many dairy farmers. Such campaigns are designed to increase *market* demand—in this case, they wanted you to drink milk instead of substitutes like soda, iced tea, and juice.[2]

Of course, many firms do spend a great deal of money on advertising despite a lack of meaningful product differentiation. An aspirin is an aspirin, but that doesn't stop Bayer from spending millions on ad campaigns. The goal of such advertising is to convince consumers that their brand is somehow superior to rivals—the firm is attempting to create product differentiation in a market structure that would otherwise be considered perfect competition. In short, the firm is trying to change the market structure, moving it toward monopolistic competition.

From a business perspective, there is a major risk that such a strategy will not succeed. If consumers view similar products as perfect substitutes *no matter what*, then advertising will increase cost but not increase demand and price. Since the long-run

Bloomberg/Getty Images

equilibrium in perfect competition occurs at breakeven, any increase in cost without a corresponding increase in price will result in an economic loss.

On the flip side, the firm may be successful in creating product differentiation by convincing consumers its product is better. In doing so, the market structure will change from perfect competition to monopolistic competition or oligopoly. Historical examples of such a shift are peanuts (Planters), cola (Coca-Cola), chocolate candy bars (Hershey's), aspirin (Bayer), and toothpaste (Crest/Procter & Gamble). Recent interest in healthy foods has led to more brands of organic milk, chicken, and eggs showing up in grocery stores, and at a premium price.

📊 BUSINESS BRIEF How Frank Purdue Changed an Industry

The chicken market was once considered perfect competition—chicken was an identical product sold by thousands of corporate and family farms. Frank Perdue changed all that by differentiating his chicken. He developed his product, branded it, and advertised it heavily; informing consumers that Perdue chickens were better fed, more tender, meatier, and never frozen. His marketing strategy not only grew his family's backyard egg business, but he also changed the entire industry. Purdue's chicken business grew to be one of the world's largest, employing 20,000 associates and partnering with 7,500 family farms prior to his death in 2005. In the process, Frank Purdue made the Forbes list of the richest 400 Americans.[*]

Through advertising and product differentiation, Purdue was able to increase the demand for his product, make the demand for his product less price elastic, and move an industry from perfect competition to monopolistic competition. As *The New York Times* noted, "A Purdue chicken became more than a mere chicken. It became a brand. That's no small feat."[†]

[*]"Chicken Magnate Frank Perdue Dies at 84," *NBCNews.com,* April 1, 2005, http://www.nbcnews.com/id /7356605/ns/business-us_business/t/chicken-magnate-frank-perdue-dies/#.VY8Y__vbKM9.

[†]Joseph Nocera, "Chicken Hawker," *The New York Times,* December 25, 2005, http://www.nytimes .com/2005/12/25/magazine/chicken-hawker.html.

14.4 PRICE DISCRIMINATION

So far, we have assumed that a business will sell its product at a single price to all customers. In perfect competition, this was at the market equilibrium price as all businesses were price takers—they simply took the market price as given. In other market structures (including monopolistic competition, oligopoly, and monopoly), a firm may be able to charge different prices to different customers. After all, consumers are different and some are willing to pay more than others.

Consider the hypothetical case of two fathers, each buying a car for his daughter upon graduation. The first dad asks the dealer for the "best price" on the car his daughter wants. He indicates to the dealer that he has been checking out consumer websites and has already priced the same-model car at two other dealers in neighboring towns. As he is price sensitive, his demand is relatively price elastic.

The second father also asks the dealer for the price of the *exact same* car, as he pulls up a sleeve on his Brooks Brothers custom suit to look at his Rolex and check the time. He then announces to the dealer he has to meet an important client in an hour. The dealer quickly recognizes the father as rich, less price sensitive and presumably has a less price elastic demand. Which father will get a better price for the same-model car?

Price discrimination is the business strategy of maximizing profits by selling essentially the same product at different prices to different consumers. The phrase "essentially the same product" means that any price differences are not justified by minor cost differences to businesses. Price discrimination does *not* occur if cost differences are *not* minor. Yes, the car dealer would like to charge a high price to all customers, but he also recognizes that he will likely only be able to negotiate a higher price with the wealthy dad wearing the expensive suit. The maximum price he can charge the price conscious father is somewhat lower. As long as this price exceeds the dealer's cost, it is still in the dealer's interest to sell the car at a somewhat lower price to the first dad.

Since changes in price tend not to change costs, price discrimination can increase profits by increasing total revenue. Exhibit 7 demonstrates this scenario. Panels A and B show the *market* demand for consumers with a relatively price elastic demand (i.e., the price conscious father) and less price elastic consumers (i.e., the rich father). For simplicity, we assume a constant marginal cost equal to average total cost.

If the profit-maximizing firm were to engage in price discrimination, it would apply marginal analysis twice: once for each market segment. If the firm were to charge a single price, profits from at least one segment would *not* be maximized and overall profits would be reduced. The result is that the group with the relatively more price elastic demand pays a lower price of $20,000 and the group with the relatively price inelastic demand is charged a higher price of $24,000.

price discrimination
The business strategy of maximizing profits by selling essentially the same product at different prices to different consumers.

EXHIBIT 7 Marginal Analysis and Price Discrimination

Panel A: More Price Elastic Demand Results in a Lower Price

Panel B: Less Price Elastic Demand Results in a Higher Price

Price discrimination is the business strategy of maximizing profits by selling essentially the same product at different prices not justified by different costs. Profit maximization with price discrimination entails applying marginal analysis separately: once for each group. Doing otherwise would result in profits not being maximized in both segments. The result is that the group with the relatively more price elastic demand is charged a lower price. In this case, the more price conscious consumer in Panel A pays $20,000, while the consumer in Panel B pays $24,000.

When Can Businesses Price-Discriminate?

The automobile dealership example is hypothetical. In practice, the man wearing the expensive suit and Rolex might be able to hide his ability to pay more. Nonetheless, subtle examples of price discrimination are commonplace. Let's consider the conditions necessary for price discrimination to occur and how businesses in the real world price-discriminate.

Firms Must Have Some Price-Setting Ability Price discrimination can occur in all market structures except perfect competition. After all, the key characteristic of perfect competition is that firms are *price takers*.

Firms Must Have Some Ability to Differentiate Buyers The firm must be able to differentiate between different groups of buyers. Vending machines, for example, cannot price-discriminate because they are unable to discriminate between buyers. When buyers can be segmented, price discrimination is often done on basis of the different price of price elasticities of demand (as shown in Exhibit 7).

Firms Must Have Some Ability to Prevent Resale and Arbitrage In the auto example, price discrimination will be more difficult if one dad can easily turn around and sell the car to the other. The process of buying a good in a single market, and immediately selling the same good at a higher price in another market with little or no risk, is called *arbitrage*. Price discrimination generally does not occur in markets where arbitrage is easy to accomplish. You might be able to resell groceries purchased with coupons, for example, but any accounting profit would likely be small—and it would not outweigh the full economic costs involved in terms of time and hassle. In other cases, firms can prevent arbitrage by making resale difficult or impossible. Airline tickets, for example, are non-transferable.

BUSINESS BRIEF Price Discrimination at Colleges and Universities

Look around your classroom. You are receiving the same education as all your classmates, but chances are that you and your fellow students are not paying the same price for it. If you are at a state school, you know that nonresidents pay a higher tuition than residents. And at both private and public colleges and universities, scholarships, grants, and financial aid (outside of loans) lower tuition costs for many students by varying amounts. What determines the amount of financial aid a student receives? It's complicated. Financial aid is determined based on detailed information with regard to a student's family income and the cost of the school attended. Applying for financial aid requires divulging a great deal of personal information; it's unlikely you would provide a car dealership, for instance, with similar details about your family finances.

Colleges and universities meet all three conditions for price discrimination to occur: First, they have price-setting ability; second, they can differentiate buyers based on financial aid information; and finally, resale of their product is not possible (a student cannot sell her discounted education to someone else). Exhibit 8 presents the sticker price (both out of state and in state), average net price, and average net price for low-income families at five select colleges: Claremont McKenna College, Dartmouth College, University of Notre Dame, University of Central Florida, and Texas A&M University.

EXHIBIT 8   Price Discrimination at Colleges and Universities

Colleges and universities typically charge different students different prices. This figure compares sticker prices with average net prices paid at several college and universities in 2016. Schools are able to price-discriminate by offering in-state tuition discounts, varying amounts of scholarships, grants, and financial aid outside of loans.

Data from National Center for Education Statistics, 2017. https://nces.ed.gov/.

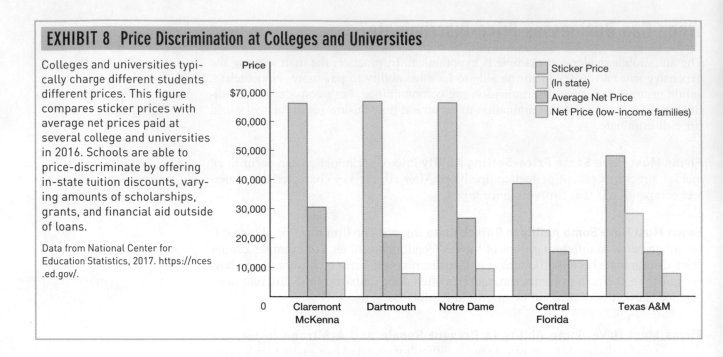

How Do Businesses Price-Discriminate?

A pure form of price discrimination occurs when selling the *exact same* product at different prices to different customers. Examples of this include offering discounts to members of specific groups (veterans, students, members of fraternal organizations, etc.) and charging different customers different prices for the exact same car. As we've seen, such price discrimination also occurs at most colleges and universities.

Increasingly in the modern business world, firms use *product differentiation* as an alternative way to engage in price discrimination. Essentially, this entails charging different customers different prices for *slightly* different products. An airline ticket booked days ahead of time is different from a ticket booked months ahead of time, even if it's for the exact same flight. A movie attended at night is very similar to the same movie seen during the day, but not exactly the same. A concert ticket four rows from the stage may cost five times as much as a concert ticket on the side of the upper level. Yes, there is some product differentiation, but is one ticket five times better? In these cases, the price discrimination involves slight product differentiation.

As a consumer, you encounter price discrimination all the time. Coupons are widely used to discriminate among consumers—those with more elastic demand typically seek out discount coupons. In other cases, businesses slightly alter the nature of their products in a way that allows them to charge higher prices to some customers, such as hardcover versus paperback books and e-books. Often, doing so involves a complex mixture of both price discrimination and product differentiation. The following are a few familiar examples.

Pricing by Age When a child turns 12, does he or she take up more space? When an adult turns 65, does he or she take up less? Probably not, but movie theaters usually offer discounts for senior citizens and children, even though they are watching the same film as those paying full price. Each age group has a different demand for seeing the movie. Offering children a discount indirectly provides a discount to families—the cost of attendance for a family of five seeing a movie can get quite expensive. Kids frequently watch popular films multiple times and hence are more price sensitive. Similarly, many senior citizens have limited income. On the other hand, busy working couples often combine dinner and a film. For them, the price of the film is less of an issue and their demand is less elastic. Discounts are *not* typically provided on concessions for children and senior citizens (who receive discounts for the tickets). Why? To prevent "resale." Otherwise, children could buy concession snacks for their parents (who, of course, pay for the popcorn in the first place).

College students attending school near ski resorts are frequently offered substantial discounts on ski lift tickets. Similar discounts are offered to students for travel during spring break or computer software. Some businesses verify one's age, others do not. Either way, differentiating by age provides a "close enough" way for businesses to segment their potential customers.

"It says the cost of the flight went up because we acknowledged its existence."

Zachary Kanin/Conde Nast/The Cartoon Bank

Sales, Specials, and Coupons Many retailers have found creative ways to price-discriminate. We've seen that coupons allow supermarkets to segment their price conscious consumers and those who are less price conscious. Similarly, sales provide opportunities to take advantage of these two market segments. For example, price savings for consumers on "Black Friday" can be enormous, but generally entail shoppers arriving very early and waiting in line for hours to get the best deals. Those are generally the consumers with more elastic demand.

Mail-in rebates are another mechanism by which retailers can price-discriminate. Consider a $8 mail-in rebate on office supplies, such as a printer, or a $200 rebate on a state-of-the-art computer system. Such rebates are often limited to "one per household," and this effectively limits the number of businesses that can apply for the rebate. Wealthier consumers with a higher willingness to pay may not even bother with the paperwork for a $8 rebate; their time is too valuable. Firms can also discriminate between customers through loyalty card discounts issued to regular patrons, or by offering "first timers" a special price to get them in the door.

Online coupon providers such as Groupon allow businesses to price-discriminate by offering lower prices to customers who may not have heard of a product previously. Yes, a few customers who might otherwise have been willing to pay more are able to obtain a great deal, but users of Groupon, on average, are more price sensitive than non-Groupon users. In other words, Groupon users typically have more price elastic demand.

By Location A chain of gas stations may charge higher prices at some stations than others. The product is slightly differentiated, but often the price difference cannot be justified on the basis of cost. This practice is known as price discrimination by location.

Branding and Generics Retailers also engage in product differentiation, offering similar products—including generics and "house brands"—at different price points. By differentiating their products in this way, stores are able to price-discriminate between buyers who are willing to pay more for a brand-name product and those who are not.

Bundling Disney charges one admission price for all its amusement rides at its theme parks in Florida and around the word. The rides at the theme park are sold in a *bundle,* which means the rides are purchased as part of a package. Why do firms like Disney do this? It turns out that bundling is a subtle yet sophisticated form of price discrimination.

Consider two families going to Disney World. One family has children in elementary school and the other has teenagers. Assume the family with young children is willing to pay $30 for easy rides like merry-go-rounds and only $20 to ride roller coasters. The family with teenagers is willing to pay $30 to ride roller coasters and only $20 for the easy rides. Without bundling, Disney could charge $20 for each "type" of ride and collect $20 from each family. By bundling, Disney can charge each family $50. It allows Disney to charge $30 for the rides each family desires the most *and* charge $20 for the rides each family desires the least.

Bundling is common. For example, your cable television provider knows that some customers would pay more for sports channels and less for news channels, while others would spend more for news channels and less for sports channels. By bundling the channels, the cable is able to price-discriminate: offering different customers the opportunity to buy different "tiers" of service. Other examples of bundling include option packages on new cars and Microsoft Office, which includes Word, Excel, and PowerPoint.

Pricing by Gender Some businesses price-discriminate on the basis of gender. At popular nightclubs, it is common to see reduced drink prices and a low cover or no charge at all for women on ladies' night. The nightclub owners realize that women's demand for drinks is somewhat more elastic than that of males. Some studies suggest that women often pay more than men for a variety of personal care products, although it's not always easy to distinguish between price discrimination and quality differences. There may be some of each.

📊 BUSINESS BRIEF Patents, Prescriptions, and Price Discrimination

When American firms sell drugs in a foreign market at a lower price than in the United States, it is illegal for someone to sell those same drugs back in America. One purpose of such laws might be product safety. A government cannot assure the quality of secondhand products. Such laws, however, are also useful tool for pharmaceutical companies to segment their buyers by country. As a result, Americans typically pay more for medications patented in the United States than do consumers in other nations: A recent three-year study revealed that prices for the 68 best-selling brand-name prescription drugs ranged anywhere from 5% to 198% higher in the United States than in other developed countries. These drugs included Nexium (prescribed for acid reflux, manufactured by AstraZeneca), Lipitor (lower cholesterol, Pfizer), Plavix (heart disease, Bristol-Myers Squibb), and Advair Diskus (asthma, GlaxoSmithKline). Moreover, in regions such as Africa, the prices of such drugs were particularly low. This is the result of African consumers having a more elastic demand for such drugs, due to much lower incomes.[*]

[*]Panos Kanavos, Alessandra Ferrario, Sotiris Vandoros, and Gerard F. Anderson, "Higher U.S. Branded Drug Prices and Spending Compared to Other Countries May Stem Partly from Quick Uptake of New Drugs," *Health Affairs* 32 (April 2013): 4753–4761, http://content.healthaffairs.org/content/32/4/753.

14.5 ADVANCED TOPIC: PERFECT AND IMPERFECT PRICE DISCRIMINATION

perfect price discrimination
A form of price discrimination whereby a firm charges each customer the maximum price the buyer is willing to pay; also called *first-degree price discrimination*.

To understand the economics of price discrimination, it is helpful to consider the practice in its most extreme form. Assume a business knows the highest price that every single customer is willing to pay and also has the ability to prevent resale. In this special case, the business is able to engage in perfect price discrimination. **Perfect price discrimination** (also called *first-degree price discrimination*) is a form of price discrimination whereby a firm charges each customer the maximum price the buyer is willing to pay. Although perfect price discrimination is uncommon, it provides a useful benchmark for examining the economics of more common types of price discrimination.

Economics of Perfect Price Discrimination

Would you ever honestly reveal to a seller the absolute most you are willing to pay for something? Probably not. That is why perfect price discrimination rarely occurs. Nonetheless, something close to this occurs at auctions for one-of-a-kind goods such as rare baseball cards, signed guitars, or famous paintings. On eBay, for example, each bidder has an incentive to bid up to his or her maximum willingness to pay for a good. The actual sale price is slightly more than the second highest bid, or the second highest maximum willingness to pay.

Total Revenue and Marginal Revenue with Perfect Price Discrimination
Exhibit 9 demonstrates how being able to perfectly price-discriminate alters total revenue and marginal revenue. The first four columns reproduce data for "Mega Monopoly" first presented in Exhibit 2 of Chapter 13 (Monopoly). The monopolist can sell 1 unit at $10 or 2 units at $9. Selling the 2nd unit increases total revenue by $8, from $10 for the 1st unit to $18 for the 2nd unit (= 2 × $9). The marginal revenue of the 2nd unit sold is $8. Similarly, in order for the monopolist to sell 3 units, the price must fall to $8. As a consequence, total revenue from selling 3 units is $24 and marginal revenue equals $6. Notice that $P > MR$, except for the 1st unit.

With the exception of the 1st unit, both total revenue and marginal revenue are higher when a firm can perfectly price-discriminate. In that case, a firm that sells 3 units will charge $10 for the 1st unit, $9 for the 2nd unit, $8 for the 3rd unit, and $7 for the 4th unit. Total revenue for all units is $34 with price discrimination, as opposed to $28 (= $7 × 4) without price discrimination. Firms price-discriminate because it increases total revenue but does not change the total cost of making 4 units.

EXHIBIT 9 Perfect Price Discrimination

Price (P)	Quantity (Q)	No Price Discrimination		Perfect Price Discrimination		
		Total Revenue TR = P × Q	Marginal Revenue ΔTR/ΔQ	Add Price Each Customer Will Pay	Total Revenue	Marginal Revenue ΔTR/ΔQ
$11	0	$0	—			
10	1	10	10	10 =	$10	$10
9	2	18	8	10 + 9 =	19	9
8	3	24	6	10 + 9 + 8 =	27	8
7	4	28	4	10 + 9 + 8 + 7 =	34	7
6	5	30	2	10 + 9 + 8 + 7 + 6 =	40	6
5	6	30	0	10 + 9 + 8 + 7 + 6 + 5 =	45	5

Price discrimination is the business strategy of maximizing profits by selling essentially the same product at different prices not justified by different costs. An extreme version is perfect price discrimination whereby a firm charges each customer the maximum price he or she will pay. This very rare form of price discrimination leads to higher prices, revenue, and profits for businesses, but also allows more consumers to purchase the product than might otherwise be the case.

In addition, perfect price discrimination increases marginal revenue. In the very rare instance of perfect price discrimination, *MR* equals price. In that case, the marginal revenue curve *is the demand curve*. This is demonstrated by the last column (*MR* with perfect price discrimination) equaling the first column (price).

Because price discrimination increases marginal revenue, it typically increases the number of units the firm will sell at profit maximization. Returning to Mega Monopoly, Mega's demand curve is replicated in Exhibit 9. Mega has marginal cost and average total cost of $7 ($7 = $MC = ATC$). When Mega *does not* price-discriminate, it made little sense to sell the 3rd unit for a price of $8, because marginal revenue was only $6 for that unit (thus, $MR < MC$).

Now consider what happens when Mega is able to engage in perfect price discrimination. Since Mega is able to sell to each customer at the maximum possible price, the *MR* curve is identical to the demand curve, as shown in Exhibit 9. This means that *MR* for any quantity is equal to the price. Since *MC* is constant at $7, Mega will not only sell the 3rd unit for $8, it will sell the 4th unit for $7. At this point, $MR = MC = \$7$ and the firm will be maximizing profit. This development is highlighted in Exhibit 9.

No Deadweight Loss or Consumer Surplus with Perfect Price Discrimination
Perfect price discrimination allows more consumers to purchase the product than might otherwise be the case. This improves allocative efficiency as price equals marginal cost. In turn, this eliminates deadweight loss. To see this, consider the Mega example in Exhibit 9. Mega now sells the 3rd and 4th units. Since all mutually beneficial transactions that can occur do occur, deadweight loss is eliminated.

Eliminating deadweight loss does not necessarily mean consumer surplus increases. Recall that for an individual, consumer surplus is the difference between the maximum price that the consumer is willing to pay and what he or she actually has to pay. Under the very rare case of perfect price discrimination, there would be no consumer surplus *at all*. Each consumer pays the most he or she is willing to pay. In essence, the reduction in consumer surplus shows up as an increase in total revenue for the business that is able to perfectly price-discriminate.

Economics of Imperfect Price Discrimination

While perfect price discrimination is virtually nonexistent in the real world, some of the same *general outcomes* also occur with imperfect price discrimination, which is very common. **Imperfect price discrimination** is a form of price discrimination whereby a firm charges different groups of customers different prices based on either purchasing volume or differences in the price elasticity of demand. From the perspective of business, price discrimination:

- Increases total revenue by reducing consumer surplus. One reason why businesses price-discriminate is to capture some of the consumer surplus.

- Reduces deadweight loss by increasing unit sales. This allows more customers to purchase the product. It also increases profits for the business.

Consider the following example. A firm is able to devise a way to separate its consumers into three groups: "high-price customers," "mid-price customers," and "low-price customers." The firm also finds a way to prevent customers from reselling the item. Pharmaceutical companies do this by selling the same drug for different prices in different countries.

Exhibit 10 shows how this type of price discrimination allows businesses to increase total revenue and reduce the deadweight loss for society. Panel A shows what happens if price discrimination does not occur. The firm maximizes profits at the quantity where $MR = MC$ and reads price on the demand curve. In this case, the firm will sell 200 units for $3 each and have total revenue of $600 (= 3×200).

imperfect price discrimination A form of price discrimination whereby a firm charges different groups of customers different prices based on either purchasing volume or differences in the price elasticity of demand.

EXHIBIT 10 One Price versus Price Discrimination with Three Prices

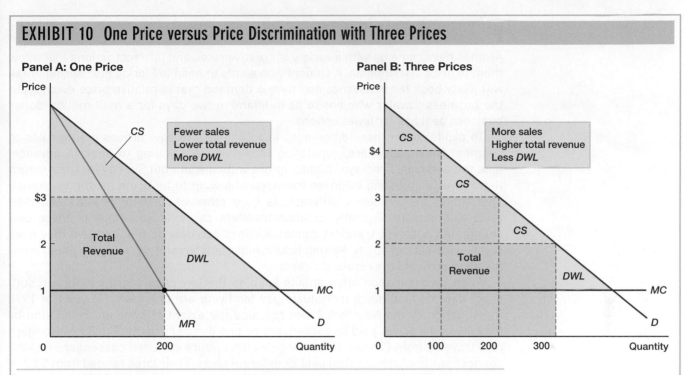

In Panel A, a firm charging a single price maximizes its profits by selling 200 units at $3. Total revenue is $600 (= $3 × 200). In Panel B, a price-discriminating firm charging 3 prices is able to increase total revenue to $900 (= ($4 × 100) + ($3 × 100) + ($2 × 100)). A comparison between the panels reveals that price discrimination reduces deadweight loss and improves overall economic efficiency.

Panel B demonstrates what happens if the firm is able to differentiate customers into three groups. In this case, the firm will sell the *first* 100 units for $4, the *second* 100 units for $3, and the *last* 100 units for $2. This will increase the firm's total revenue to $900, as the firm receives $400 from its high-price customers (= $4 × 100), $300 from mid-price customers (= $3 × 100), and $200 from low-price customers (= $2 × 100). Total revenue increases from only $600 with no price discrimination to $900 (= $400 + $300 + $200) with price discrimination. A comparison between Panels A and B reveals that price discrimination reduces deadweight loss and improves overall economic efficiency. And notice that although perfect price discrimination completely eliminates consumer surplus, imperfect price discrimination benefits consumers willing to pay just under $3 who can now pay $2.

Let's go back to those two dads, each planning to buy his daughter a car. Obviously, the dealer cannot perfectly price-discriminate: Neither of the fathers will truthfully reveal to car dealers the most he's willing to pay. If the dealer only charges one price (such as in Panel A), the dealer will choose a price that maximizes profits. This price might be too high for the less wealthy dad to purchase the car. By price discriminating, the dealer sells more cars while maximizing overall profits. This also reduces deadweight loss, as both dads are now able to purchase the car.

The question of whether charging different customers different prices for the same goods is fair is a normative question, which involves complex ethical issues that are beyond the scope of this course. However, it is important for both businesses and consumers to be aware of the practice, as it's an important part of our economic system, and almost certainly growing more common. By understanding how and why businesses price-discriminate, voters and policymakers will be able to make more intelligent decisions about how to regulate the practice.

📊 BUSINESS BRIEF Price Discrimination by Airlines

Airlines have come up with a variety of creative rules and fare restrictions that allow them to price discriminate. A student who wants to head to Florida next spring break will likely book far in advance and have a demand that is relative price elastic, but the business traveler who has to be in Miami in two days for a multimillion-dollar business deal has far fewer options.

To capitalize on these differences in willingness to pay, airlines create rules to segment their customers, separating those who are willing to book in advance, take the overnight "red-eye" flights, or are willing wait until Sunday for their return flight (thus eliminating business travelers who want to be home for the weekend). This allows the airlines to differentiate their otherwise similar product and then price-discriminate. Typically, vacation travelers can take advantage of these discounts, but business travelers cannot. Airlines can only do this because they have some price-setting ability. Making tickets non-transferrable by requiring photo identification prevents the resale of tickets.

Price discrimination often entails keeping the low price secretive. As a result, exact data on how much individuals pay for flying are unknown. However, a 1998 investigation by the *New York Times* revealed the extent of price discrimination by examining the prices paid by passengers on one domestic flight. The 33 passengers who traveled from Chicago to Los Angeles (this figure excluded passengers making connections from other cities) paid 27 different fares. Their fares ranged from $1,249 for a business-class ticket purchased on the day of the flight, to $108 for a coach ticket purchased the same day. The *New York Times* reporter found that people who bought their tickets early often got better deals, but this was not always the case.[*]

[*]Matthew L. Wald, "So, How Much Did You Pay for Your Ticket?," *The New York Times,* April 11, 1998, http://www.nytimes.com/1998/04/12/weekinreview/so-how-much-did-you-pay-for-your-ticket.html.

BUSINESS TAKEAWAY

Monopolistic competition is a more common market structure than perfect competition and monopoly. It is also more complex. In addition to making decisions on quantity and pricing, firms in monopolistic competition must make decisions on product differentiation, location, and other forms of non-price competition. A restaurant or store, for example, may try to find a better location or carry unique items. In the long run, however, vigorous competition with close but not perfect substitutes ensures zero long-run economic profit (a normal accounting profit).

Marketing and advertising are common forms of non-price discrimination. Effective advertising can help consumers recognize that a product exists. This is particularly important for new products—if Apple had not actively promoted the first iPhone, consumers would never have known that this revolutionary technology was available. Advertising also allows firms to maximize their profits by increasing demand for a product and reducing price elasticity of demand if consumers become convinced that substitute products are inferior. This was certainly the case for the iPhone, as Apple was able to achieve a strong foothold long before Android-based competitors arrived on the scene.

When a business has some market power, it may be able to increase profitability by charging higher prices to customers willing to pay more and lower prices to other customers, a practice known as price discrimination. In order for price discrimination to be an effective strategy, a firm must have some price-setting ability, be able to differentiate buyers who are willing to pay more, and be able to prevent resale by customers who buy the item at a lower price. Without these preconditions, it is difficult to engage in price discrimination.

CHAPTER STUDY GUIDE

14.1 CHARACTERISTICS OF MONOPOLISTIC COMPETITION

Monopolistic competition is a market structure with many firms selling similar but differentiated products. Unlike a monopoly, firms in monopolistic competition face fierce competition. Unlike firms in a perfectly competitive market structure, a monopolistic competitor sells a product that is differentiated from those of its rivals. The key characteristic of monopolistic competition is **product differentiation**, the real or perceived difference among products that are close substitutes. **Non-price competition** is an attempt by a business to distinguish its products from its rivals without changing the price. Differences can occur due to location, quality, design, and service. Differences can also reflect perception, not reality. The demand curve a firm faces in monopolistic competition is highly elastic because there are some substitutes, but not perfectly elastic because there is some product differentiation. Firms in monopolistic competition determine the profit-maximizing level of output by finding where $MR = MC$, and reading price off the demand curve.

14.2 THE LONG-RUN COMPETITIVE EQUILIBRIUM IN MONOPOLISTIC COMPETITION

In the long run, economic profits encourage the entry of rivals, shifting the demand curve facing the existing firm to the left. Economic losses have the opposite impact. This ensures that long-run economic profits equal zero (a normal accounting profit). At the long-run equilibrium, price is greater than marginal cost and thus allocative efficiency is not achieved. Moreover, productive efficiency does not occur as ATC is not minimized. **Excess capacity** is the amount by which output would need to increase in order to minimize average total cost. However, society appears to prefer some product differentiation, even at the cost of allocative and productive inefficiency.

14.3 MARKETING AND ADVERTISING DECISIONS

Marketing refers to all the activities and strategies that businesses use to sell products. The many decisions involved in marketing products are often referred to as the marketing mix. The marketing mix is often called the "four Ps": product, price, placement, and promotion. **Advertising** refers to paid activities that businesses and other organizations use to sell products. It is an essential component of marketing and common in monopolistic competition. Effective advertising can help consumers recognize the existence of a product, increase demand, and reduce the price elasticity of demand for the firm's product. All this allows firms to sell more, charge a higher price, or both. It may also allow a firm to realize economies of scale.

14.4 PRICE DISCRIMINATION

Price discrimination is the business strategy of maximizing profits by selling essentially the same product at different prices to different customers. Doing so successfully allows firms to increase their revenue. In order for price discrimination to occur, firms must have some price-setting ability, be able to differentiate buyers and prevent resale. This is done with different pricing by age, sales and specials, location, branding and generics, bundling, and pricing by gender. Businesses often use minor forms of product differentiation to price discriminate.

14.5 ADVANCED TOPIC: PERFECT AND IMPERFECT PRICE DISCRIMINATION

Perfect price discrimination (also called *first-degree price discrimination*) is a form of price discrimination whereby a firm charges each customer the maximum price the buyer is willing to pay. With perfect price discrimination, $P = MR$, businesses increase their revenue, and there is thus no consumer surplus or deadweight loss Perfect price discrimination is uncommon, as businesses seldom know the highest price each customer is willing to pay. In contrast, **imperfect price discrimination** is relatively common. It is a form of price discrimination whereby a firm charges different groups of customers different prices based on either purchasing volume or differences in the price elasticity of demand. From the perspective of business, price discrimination increases total revenue by reducing consumer surplus, does not change production costs for a given number of units, and increases unit sales. It also reduces deadweight loss.

TOP TEN TERMS AND CONCEPTS

(1) Monopolistic Competition

(2) Product Differentiation

(3) Non-Price Competition

(4) Excess Capacity

(5) Productive and Allocative Efficiency in Monopolistic Competition

(6) Marketing and the "Four Ps"

⑦ Advertising

⑧ Price Discrimination

⑨ Perfect Price Discrimination

⑩ Imperfect Price Discrimination

STUDY PROBLEMS

1. How is monopolistic competition similar to and different from monopolies? How is monopolistic competition similar to and different from perfect competition?

2. Maria is one of many pizza sellers in her local market.

   a. Is the price elasticity of demand for Maria's pizza elastic or inelastic?

   b. Graph Maria's demand curve and marginal revenue curve.

   c. Graph Maria's marginal cost curve.

   d. What are Maria's expected profits in the long run?

   e. Graph Maria's average total cost curve. Be sure to consider your answer to the previous question.

   f. Does the outcome obtain productive efficiency?

3. What is the short-run profit-maximization rule for firms in monopolistic competition? Does price equal marginal cost? Does price equal marginal revenue? Explain.

4. Name and explain the various ways in which firms differentiate their products from those of their rivals.

5. Consider the market for ibuprofen, a pain reliever and nonsteroidal anti-inflammatory drug (NSAID). Ibuprofen is sold under the brand names Motrin and Advil, and by a large number of generic manufacturers. Compare and contrast the demand curves for the brand-name versions of ibuprofen and its generic versions.

6. When a rival goes out of business, how do the cost curves of a firm shift? How does the demand curve facing a firm shift?

7. What factor eliminates the long-run profitability of firms in monopolistic competition? Is the long-run outcome found in monopolistic competition productively efficient? Allocatively efficient? Explain your responses. Why does excess capacity exist?

8. For each pair of businesses, state which firm is more likely to advertise. Explain your answers.

   a. a dairy farm selling milk or an elastic ice cream vendor selling milk shakes

   b. a monopolist selling electricity or a seller of cars that use electricity

   c. the seller of gourmet mozzarella cheese for pizza or the seller of mozzarella cheese

   d. the seller of sneakers or the seller of socks

   e. the generic makers of ibuprofen or the manufacturer of Advil

9. Does advertising make the price elasticity of demand for a product more elastic or less elastic?

10. Is it possible for advertising to lower a firm's average total cost? Explain your response.

11. How does the advertising of a product once thought to be perfectly competitive make the market monopolistically competitive?

12. The Huffington Post recently reported the price various artists charge to perform at a private party. "According to the research, acts like Dave Matthews Band, Bruce Springsteen, Justin Bieber (ugh), Justin Timberlake, and Taylor Swift are the most expensive to book, with an estimated rate of $1 million-plus per performance, while it'll run you around $125,000–$175,000 for 'Happy' singer Pharrell."[3] In contrast, a Dave Matthews *tribute band* will perform for under $10,000. Are such price differences an example of product differentiation? Price discrimination? Explain your answers.

13. It is not uncommon for ski mountain resorts to charge students lower prices for lift tickets. Crotched Mountain in New Hampshire, for example, recently offered a special price called "Youth Pay Their Age Day."[4] Explain such a promotion in terms of price discrimination.

14. The development of dating apps is a lucrative business. According to the *Wall Street Journal*,

    Dating sites in the United States are expected to make $1.17 billion and dating apps are expected to log $628.8 million this year, up from $1.08 billion for dating sites and $572 million for dating apps in 2014, according to IBISWorld.[5]

    Note that the figures represent economic profits. The *Wall Street Journal* also reports that Apple's iTunes store offers more than 500 dating apps. How do these products differentiate themselves? What do you expect the economic profits of dating apps to be in the long run?

15. What conditions are necessary for a firm to successfully price-discriminate? Does price discrimination increase or decrease consumer surplus? Explain your responses.

15

CHAPTER

∧ With only a few nationwide wireless networks—the market structure is an oligopoly.

Oligopoly

Strategic Decision Making and Game Theory

T-Mobile is considering reducing the price of its all-in-one shared data plan for families. One executive suspects that if the firm lowers the price, it may gain market share from its competitors AT&T and Verizon. But another executive is skeptical, noting that if it cuts the price, its two rivals will likely do the same, and T-Mobile will not gain market share. The wireless communication market is a classic example of an oligopoly, an industry dominated by a few very large firms. As a consumer, you are already very familiar with oligopolies, regularly deciding between just a few major soft drink brands, wireless phone carriers, or Internet search engine platforms. Some of the most intense rivalries in business are oligopolies.

In an oligopoly, the competition is fierce and the stakes are high. The outcome of a decision by T-Mobile to lower price depends on the antici-pated response of Verizon and AT&T. Oligopolies not only compete on the basis of price, they also engage in tremendous non-price competi-tion such as product features and advertising. If T-Mobile develops a new data package, its competitors will likely respond. Such decisions don't just apply to big firms that dominate huge markets: If only two competing restaurants are located nearby Maria's, she must carefully consider how her rivals will respond to any price change. Likewise, if Maria advertises heavily, her rivals may do the same. Economic models developed in previous chapters do not account for the response of com-petitors. In this chapter, we analyze the strategic decision making of firms using a new framework that captures the actions of rival firms. This framework is known as game theory.

Chapter Learning Targets

● Identify an oligopoly as a market structure where firms are highly interdependent.

● Derive profitability of various output levels and describe collusion.

● Use simultaneous and sequential move games to analyze various business strategies.

● Describe strategic pricing decisions and price fixing.

● Identify implicit cooperation strategies such as price leadership, low-price guarantees, and the tit-for-tat strategy.

● Apply game theory to advertising.

15.1 CHARACTERISTICS OF AN OLIGOPOLY

An **oligopoly** is a market structure with a few dominant firms that are highly inter-dependent. Unlike a monopoly, firms in an oligopoly face considerable competition. Unlike perfect competition and monopolistic competition, an oligopoly has only a few dominant firms. The actions of one firm impact all other firms in the industry. Examples of oligopolies range from video game consoles (Microsoft Xbox and Sony PlayStation) to jumbo jets (Boeing and Airbus) to soda (Coke and Pepsi) to major hotel chains in large cities (Hilton and Marriott) to wireless phone service providers. The simplest form of oligopoly is a **duopoly**, an oligopoly with exactly two firms. Because a duopoly is the simplest form of an oligopoly to model and analyze, and because the insights gained from analyzing a duopoly apply to oligopolies with more than two firms, we'll focus primarily on duopolies in this chapter.

An oligopoly sells products that can be either standardized, as found in perfect competition (paper or light bulbs), or differentiated, as found in monopolistic competition (smartphones or automobiles). As is the case in a monopoly (Chapter 13), firms have *some* price-setting ability: They are not price takers. Verizon, for example, can change prices, but it must anticipate the response of its rivals. The existence of competitors means the demand facing the firm is more price elastic than the market demand. In addition, firms engage in considerable non-price competition, such as advertising and product differentiation. This feature is similar to that found in monopolistic competition (Chapter 14).

oligopoly A market structure with a few dominant firms that are highly interdependent.

duopoly An oligopoly with exactly two firms.

A Few Highly Interdependent Firms with Potential Long-Run Economic Profits

The key characteristic of an oligopoly is that it contains a few firms that are highly interdependent. What Verizon does impacts AT&T, and what Apple does with its iPhone impacts Samsung (and vice versa). Thus, when making any decision, a firm

EXHIBIT 1 Characteristics of Market Structures—Oligopoly

	Market Structure			
	Perfect Competition Chapter 12	**Monopolistic Competition Chapter 14**	**Oligopoly Chapter 15**	**Monopoly Chapter 13**
Number of Sellers	very large number	many firms	few firms	one firm
Entry Conditions	easy entry	easy entry	barriers to entry	barriers to entry
Price Setting Ability	none	some	some	some
Price Elasticity of Demand—Firm Level	perfectly elastic	highly elastic	more elastic than market demand	same as market elasticity of demand
Long-Run Profit	zero economic profit	zero economic profit	potentially	potentially
Product Differentiation	standardized product	differentiated product	varies by product market	unique product with no close substitutes
Key Characteristic	firms price takers	differentiated product	firms highly interdependent	one firm
Examples	tomatoes copper lumber	delivered pizza smartphone apps toothpaste	search engines wireless service mobile phones	patented medicine first-class mail electricity delivery

An oligopoly is a market structure with a few firms due to high barriers to entry and the potential for long-run economic profit. The key characteristic of an oligopoly is that competing firms are highly interdependent on the actions of their rivals.

must anticipate the reactions of its rivals. If Coca-Cola, for example, decides to lower prices, it must anticipate that Pepsi will in some way respond.

In oligopoly, as in monopoly, barriers to entry make it difficult for a new firm to enter the market. The most common barrier is economies of scale, the benefit of mass production. Thus, there are usually only a few firms in an oligopoly, and these firms are typically large.

As is the case in a monopoly, barriers to entry give oligopolists the *potential* to earn economic profits in the long run. While the potential for profits will attract new firms that *want* to enter the oligopolistic market, barriers to entry prevent new firms from doing so successfully. The characteristics of an oligopoly are highlighted in Exhibit 1.

Measuring Market Concentration

To identify an oligopoly, economists rely on a variety of measures of market (industry) concentration. One common measure is the **concentration ratio**, the percentage of market sales accounted for by the largest few (usually, 4, 5, or 8) firms in an industry.

Exhibit 2 presents the concentration ratios for highly concentrated industries in the United States. In the search engines market, for example, the largest four firms account for roughly 99% of all searches, with Google accounting for nearly two thirds of all searches. In wireless telecommunication, the largest four firms have 95% of market sales. Among satellite television service providers, two firms account for 95% of market sales.

The examples presented in Exhibit 2 are *highly concentrated*. That is to say, sales in the industry are captured by only a few firms. These are obvious cases of an oligopoly market structure. Less clear are industries that are less concentrated than those presented. Such industries may be viewed either as an oligopoly or as monopolistic competition market structure (see Chapter 14). There is no sharp dividing line between these two market structures that all economists accept. Thus, economists use

concentration ratio The percentage of market sales accounted for by the largest few (usually, 4, 5, or 8) firms in an industry.

EXHIBIT 2 Concentration Ratios of Highly Concentrated U.S. Industries

Product	Concentration Ratio (%)	Largest Firms (more than 10% market share)
Search Engines	99	Google (64), Yahoo! (18), Microsoft (14)
Arcade, Food & Entertainment	96	Chuck E. Cheese (52), Dave & Buster's (35)
Sanitary Paper Products	93	Kimberly-Clark (36), Proctor & Gamble (30), Georgia Pacific (27)
Wireless Telecommunications	95	Verizon Wireless (37), AT&T (32), Sprint Nextel (15), T-Mobile (11)
Satellite TV Provider	95	DirecTV (58), Dish Network (37)
Soda	94	Coca-Cola (41), Pepsi (34), Dr. Pepper Snapple Group (15)
Food Service Contractors	93	Compass Group (33), Aramark (28), Sodexo (26)
Lighting & Bulb Manufacturing	92	General Electric (33), Koninklijke Philips Electronics (32), Siemens AG (27)
Tire Manufacturing	91	Goodyear (39), Michelin (28), Cooper Tire & Rubber (13), Bridgestone (12)
Major Household Appliances	90	Whirlpool (44), Electrolux (21), General Electric (17)

The concentration ratio is the percentage of market sales accounted for by the largest few firms in an industry. Here, the concentration ratios of four firms within select industries in the United States are provided.

Data from Andrea Alegria, Agata Kaczanowska, and Lauren Setar, "Highly Concentrated: Companies That Dominate Their Industries," *IBISWorld*, February 2012, http://www.themarketworks.org/sites/default/files/uploads/charts/Highly-Concentrated-Industries.pdf.

∧ Fierce competition in the duopoly between the world's biggest plane makers.

a variety of market concentration measures, including the Herfindahl–irshman index (HHI) introduced in Chapter 13. The HHI plays a major role in antitrust and merger policy: Recall that the U.S. Federal Trade Commission blocked a proposed merger between AT&T and T-Mobile that would have made the wireless communication market even more concentrated and did so on the basis of the HHI.

Measuring market concentration is complicated by the fact that it is often difficult to fully measure the relevant market. Even if firms have a high market share in their narrowly defined industry, they may face competition from related industries. Do satellite TV providers such as DIRECTV and Dish Network compete only with each other? Not exactly. They also compete with cable TV providers, streaming video content, and broadcast television stations. Relevant markets are also complicated by geographic considerations. Does an airline flying between New York and Florida compete with an airline flying between California and Hawaii? Probably not. This complicates any measurement. Moreover, in some markets, firms must compete with international rivals for customers around the globe. The rivalry between airplane manufacturers Boeing and Airbus is a classic example of an international duopoly, as their finished product can easily be flown to customers anywhere in the world.

15.2 STRATEGIC DECISION MAKING ON OUTPUT

Analyzing the profit-maximizing behavior of an oligopoly is complicated by the fact that the firms are highly interdependent. In both perfect competition and monopolistic competition, rivals are considered small, thus largely irrelevant in output decision making. In a monopoly setting, in contrast, there are no rivals. But what happens if rivals enter the market of a (former) monopoly? Suppose additional firms enter the market, as when Samsung and others began offering smartphones (without keyboards) to compete with Apple's iPhone. The market structure is now characterized as an oligopoly. As noted earlier, when *exactly one* new firm enters a monopolistic market, a duopoly is formed. In this section, we'll use the example of a hypothetical duopoly as a model for analyzing firm behavior in an oligopoly.

Decisions, Decisions—How Much to Produce?

Suppose that two firms sell pizza in a small town located on an isolated island. The market is too small to support a third pizzeria, and there is no real competition elsewhere for pizza, because there is limited ferry service off the island. The two pizzerias, Romeo's Pizza and Juliet's Pizza, are operating in an oligopoly—specifically, a duopoly.

One might assume that Romeo and Juliet could come to an agreement about price or quantity, but, as is the case in Shakespeare's play, Romeo and Juliet are strictly forbidden from getting together. That's because in most countries (including the United States), antitrust laws (see Chapter 13) prohibit collusion among firms.

Collusion is an agreement among rivals to cooperate by limiting price and non-price competition. So, if Romeo and Juliet form an agreement to divvy up the market (e.g., by setting delivery boundaries that don't overlap), they'll be breaking the law.

When a *group* of firms become involved in collusion, they form what is called a **cartel**, an organization of rival firms with agreements among members to collude, often by restricting output and increasing prices. If Romeo and Juliet were to openly engage in collusion, then the cartel would have complete control of production and the power to choose the price and output that maximize profits for the entire industry. In this case, the cartel is the industry and will behave like a monopoly: Nobody sells pizza on that island other than Romeo's and Juliet's.

Cartels result in higher prices for consumers and deadweight loss for society that is similar to the deadweight loss that occurs under a monopoly market structure. For this reason, antitrust laws in the United States and many other countries prohibit cartels. Most economists believe that a competitive market structure is preferable to a monopoly or cartel.

The hypothetical scenario between Romeo and Juliet provides a useful model for examining the profit-maximizing behavior of firms in oligopoly. To begin, it is useful to recall the profit-maximizing behavior of a monopoly with an ordinary downward-sloping market demand curve, as shown in Exhibit 3. For simplicity, we assume marginal cost and average total cost each equal $2.

The profit-maximization output for the combined industry is realized if the market is a monopoly. This is the level of output a cartel would desire because the combined profits in a market *cannot* be higher than those obtained by a profit-maximizing monopoly. In Exhibit 3, marginal analysis suggests that industrywide profit maximization occurs at 6 units ($MR = MC$ at 6 units) with industrywide profits of $36 ($6 per unit on 6 units). As such, the combined profits of the cartel *cannot* be higher than $36.

Using similar data, Exhibit 4 also shows that the profit-maximizing level of output occurs at 6 units. Here, total revenue is $48, total cost is $12, and profits equal $36 ($48 − $36). No other level of output results in higher profits. This is the industry's maximum profit. It is also the maximum profit attainable if a cartel is formed.

collusion An agreement among rivals to cooperate by limiting price and non-price competition.

cartel An organization of rival firms with agreements among members to collude, often by restricting output and increasing prices.

EXHIBIT 3 Profit Maximization of Industry Using Marginal Analysis

The combined profit maximization for the industry (market) is realized if the market is a monopoly. Using marginal analysis, $MR = MC$ at 6 units and industry profits are $36. A profit-maximizing cartel will make pricing and output decisions as if it is a monopoly. This figure approximately represents data found in Exhibit 4.

EXHIBIT 4 Profit Maximization with Collusion

Price (P)	Quantity (Q)	Total Revenue TR = P × Q	Total Cost $2 per unit	Profit
$14	0	$0	—	$0
13	1	13	2	11
12	2	24	4	20
11	3	33	6	27
10	4	40	8	32
9	5	45	10	35
8	**6**	**48**	**12**	**36**
7	7	49	14	35
6	8	48	16	32
5	9	45	18	27

Given the demand data in the first two columns and average total cost of $2, the highest possible profit in this industry occurs at 6 pizzas per hour with profit of $36.

In these circumstances, how might Romeo and Juliet respond to the industry data in Exhibit 4 (representing pizzas per hour)? Assume for a moment that Romeo and Juliet are willing to ignore antitrust laws and form a cartel. Clearly, they would choose to produce 6 pizzas per hour and sell them for $8 each. They might agree to divide up the market by agreeing to each limit their production to 3 pizzas per hour. Since each pizza costs $2 to make, selling 3 pizzas each at a price of $8 allows each firm to make $6 per pizza for a total profit of $18 each. In this case, the firms evenly split the highest potential profit of $36.

From the perspective of the cartel, of course, it is unfortunate that collusion is illegal: Romeo and Juliet would benefit from collusion because it results in higher prices. From a public policy perspective, however, higher prices harm consumers. Although we teach children that cooperation is a good thing, in the business world, collusion between firms can harm the economy—and lead to time in prison for the managers who engage in it.

Possible Outcomes in a Duopoly

In addition to collusion, there are other possible outcomes. To explore these possibilities, we continue with the example of Romeo's Pizza and Juliet's Pizza using the demand schedule as shown in Exhibit 4, with an average total cost of $2. For simplification, we add an additional assumption: Each firm's output choices are limited to either 3 or 4 units. Several outcomes are possible:

- **Successful collusion occurs when both firms cooperate.** To collude and maximize profits, the two firms must behave as if they were a monopoly. In an attempt to earn monopoly-level profits for the industry, each firm agrees to limit output so that the industry produces 6 units, which results in a market price of $8. If each firm limits its output to 3 units, profit per unit is $6 ($8 − $2) and each firm's profit is $18. Since this outcome occurs when firms cooperate, it is often referred to as a *cooperative solution.*

EXHIBIT 5 Profit Possibilities for Duopoly—With and Without Collusion

Quantity				Profit		
Total	Romeo	Juliet	Price	Total	Romeo	Juliet
6	**3**	**3**	**$8**	**$36**	**$18**	**$18**
7	4	3	7	35	20	15
7	3	4	7	35	15	20
8	**4**	**4**	**6**	**32**	**16**	**16**
9	4	5	5	27	12	15
9	5	4	5	27	15	12

If a duopoly exists in the market similar to the one shown in Exhibit 4, a cooperative solution occurs when both Romeo and Juliet make 3 units (6 total) and have a profit of $18 each. If both firms cheat on the collusion agreement, they both make 4 units (8 total) and have a profit of $16 each. Since $ATC = \$2$, Profit $= (Price - \$2) \times$ Quantity.

- **One firm cheats on collusion agreement.** If either Romeo or Juliet cheats on the agreement by making 4 units, the market will now be producing 7 units, the market price falls to $7 and profit per unit is $5 ($7 − $2). In this case, the cheater has a *higher* profit of $20 ($5 per unit on 4 units). The possibility of higher profits incentivizes the cheating. The other firm has a *lower* profit of $15 ($5 per unit on 3 units). When cheating occurs, it is generally done by a firm attempting to maximize its *own* profits.

- **Both firms cheat on collusion agreement—or no collusion occurs.** If both Romeo and Juliet break the collusion agreement by producing 4 units, the market will now be producing 8 units, the market price falls to $6, and profit per unit is $4 ($6 − $2). Each firm's profit is $16 ($4 per unit on 4 units). Note that the firm that did not cheat initially *increases* profit from $15 to $16. The outcome of this unsuccessful collusion is the same as if no collusion occurred at all.

When both firms make 4 units, there is no incentive for either firm to further increase output, as doing so would lower profits for *both* firms. Suppose we change the above simplifying assumption and allow one firm to make 5 units and the other 4 units. The market will now be selling 9 units and the market price will fall to $5. Under this scenario, profit per unit falls to $3 and total profits decline for both firms.

Exhibit 5 summarizes these possible outcomes. Both Romeo and Juliet are better off if collusion occurs (the cooperative solution that occurs when price is $8 and total quantity is 6), rather than without collusion (when price is $6). Later in the chapter, we will take a more detailed look at how firms make decisions on pricing and output using new economics models that focus on strategic decision making by business managers.

📊 BUSINESS BRIEF OPEC—An Oil Cartel

The Organization of the Petroleum Exporting Countries (OPEC) is an oil cartel that attempts to fix the price of oil. It does this primarily by adjusting oil production to agreed upon quotas, the quantities of oil each member may produce. Key members of OPEC include several Middle Eastern nations (including Saudi Arabia, Iraq, Kuwait, and Iran) as well as other oil-producing countries like Venezuela and Nigeria. Because it is an organization of sovereign countries, United States and other country-specific antitrust laws do not apply. This allows member nations to openly talk about prices and production quotas. Agreements can be explicit.

Nonetheless, collusion remains very difficult: The lack of international laws to enforce such contracts makes OPEC susceptible to the same problem faced by other cartels—cheating. Moreover, the fact that there are 12 rivals in OPEC and even more oil producers outside of OPEC makes collusion difficult for members of the cartel.

In its heyday, OPEC was enormously successful at raising the price of oil. In 1973, in retaliation for the United States' support of Israel during the Arab-Israeli War in the Middle East, OPEC slashed oil production and dramatically raised its price per barrel overnight, soon thereafter instituting an embargo that cut off the supply of oil to the United States entirely. In three months, the price of oil almost quadrupled. Oil revenue among OPEC nations approached nearly $300 billion by 1981, much more than the competitive outcome.* At other times, however, collusion has proven more difficult. In 2014, the price of oil was halved due to new oil sources being discovered in non-OPEC countries. This made an agreement among all oil-producing countries, whether an OPEC member nation or not, increasingly difficult.†

*Laurie Watson, "The Organization of Petroleum Exporting Countries May Soon Lose. . . ," *United Press International (UPI)*, October 19, 1982, https://www.upi.com/Archives/1982/10/19/The-Organization-of-Petroleum-Exporting-Countries-may-soon-lose/1013403848000/.

†"Leaky Barrels," *The Economist,* February 22, 2014, https://www.economist.com/news/finance-and-economics/21596986-higher-production-elsewhere-undermining-cartel-leaky-barrels?zid=298&ah=0bc99f9da-8f185b2964b6cef412227be.

15.3 AN INTRODUCTION TO GAME THEORY

In 2000, Chris Ferguson, became the first player to win a tournament prize of over a million dollars in the World Series of Poker. Ferguson credits his win to his knowledge of game theory.[1] **Game theory** is the study of strategic behaviors, and the ways in which individuals (or other entities) make optimal decisions by anticipating how rivals will respond to their actions. It has applications that range from actual games like poker and chess to military strategy, international diplomacy, strategic nuclear arms negotiations, and in particular businesses operating in an oligopoly.

Simultaneous Move Games

The economic models developed thus far are not equipped to handle situations where a firm's profits depend on the actions of another firm. A new framework therefore needs to be developed; one that is rooted in game theory.

A **simultaneous move game** involves all firms making their strategic decisions at the same time, without full knowledge of the actions of their rivals. The children's game of rock-paper-scissors is a good example of this type of game. Players must choose a rock or paper or a scissors *at the same time*, without any prior knowledge of what their competitors will choose. If this game were played sequentially, the player who goes second could win every time.

Since the models used in earlier chapters are no longer appropriate, a somewhat different framework is needed. Simultaneous move games make use of a **payoff matrix**, a graphical representation of a simultaneous move game that demonstrates different actions and their potential payoffs.

Exhibit 6 demonstrates a payoff matrix for the Romeo and Juliet duopoly example developed earlier in the chapter. Romeo must decide if he wants to produce 3 or 4 pizzas per hour. He also has no control over what Juliet does. Nor does Romeo have knowledge of Juliet's decision. Likewise, Juliet does not maintain control or knowledge of Romeo's actions.

game theory The study of strategic behaviors, and the ways in which individuals (or other entities) make optimal decisions by anticipating how rivals will respond to their actions.

simultaneous move game A game that involves all firms making their strategic decisions at the same time, without full knowledge of the actions of their rivals.

payoff matrix A graphical representation of a simultaneous move game that demonstrates different actions and their potential payoffs.

EXHIBIT 6 Simultaneous Move Game—Quantity Decision

It is useful to demonstrate simultaneous move games using a payoff matrix. Juliet must decide whether to make 3 or 4 units. At the same time, Romeo makes a similar decision. If Romeo decides to make 4 units, Juliet maximizes profits by making 4 units based on data found in Exhibit 5. If Romeo decides to make 3 units, Juliet maximizes profits by making 4 units. Juliet's dominant strategy is to make 4 units as this decision will always be more profitable regardless of the actions of Romeo. Romeo also has a dominant strategy to make 4 units. A non-cooperative solution occurs when both players follow their dominant strategy and each player receive a payoff of $16. A cooperative solution occurs with each player receiving a payoff of $18.

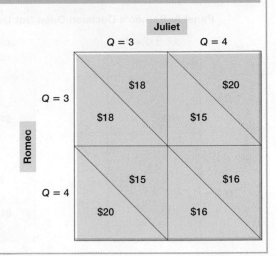

The Language of Game Theory

Since Romeo does not have knowledge of Juliet's actions, it is helpful to separately analyze Romeo's best response for each of Juliet's two possible actions. This is done in Panel A of Exhibit 7. If Juliet decides to produce 3 pizzas per hour, Romeo can either have a payoff of $18 if his $Q = 3$ or a payoff of $20 if his $Q = 4$. Notice that these values correspond to the two boxes on the left of Exhibit 6. On the other hand, if Juliet makes 4 units, Romeo can either have a payoff of $15 if his $Q = 3$ or a payoff of $16 if his $Q = 4$. These values correspond to the two boxes on the right of Exhibit 6.

While Romeo is unaware of Juliet's decision, he is *always* better off making 4 pizzas, regardless of what she does. This is known as a **dominant strategy**, a strategic decision that is best regardless of the strategic decision made by a rival. Regardless of the actions of Juliet, Romeo's best action is making 4 units. Dominant strategies occur in simultaneous move games and other games.

Panel B demonstrates Juliet's strategic decision. Juliet must decide if she wants 3 or 4 pizzas per hour with no control over what her rival Romeo chooses. Since Juliet does not have knowledge of Romeo's decision, it is useful to analyze each possibility separately. She realizes that if Romeo decides to make 3 pizzas (top two boxes in Exhibit 6), she is better off making 4 pizzas. Furthermore, if Romeo decides to make 4 pizzas (bottom two boxes in Exhibit 6), she is still better off making 4 pizzas. Juliet is *always* better off making 4 units, regardless of what her rival does. Her dominant strategy is to make 4 units. Moreover, Juliet's strategic decision making will involve her anticipating Romeo's most likely decision ($Q = 4$).

If both Romeo and Juliet follow their dominant strategy, the end result will be a non-cooperative solution. The **non-cooperative solution** is the outcome that occurs when players do not collaborate, with each pursuing their own self-interest. In this example, a non-cooperative solution results when both Romeo and Juliet make 4 units and have a payoff of $16 each. This corresponds to the lower-right box in Exhibit 6.

This particular non-cooperative solution also leads to a result where no player has an incentive to change strategy on his or her own. A **Nash equilibrium** is an outcome in which no player can improve through a unilateral change in strategy. In a sense,

dominant strategy A strategic decision that is best regardless of the strategic decision made by a rival.

non-cooperative solution The outcome that occurs when players do not collaborate, with each pursuing their own self-interest.

Nash equilibrium An outcome in which no player improves through a unilateral change in strategy.

EXHIBIT 7   Solving a Simultaneous Move Game

In solving a simultaneous move game, it is helpful to separately analyze each player's best decision for their rival's two possible actions because neither player has knowledge of the decision of their rivals. In Panel A, Romeo must decide between 3 or 4 units. If Juliet decides to make 3 units, Romeo maximizes profits ($20) by making 4 units. If Juliet decides to make 4 units, Romeo maximizes profits ($16) by making 4 units. In Panel B, Juliet must decide between 3 or 4 units. If Romeo decides to make 3 units, Juliet maximizes profits ($20) by making 4 units. If Romeo decides to make 4 units, Juliet maximizes profits ($16) by making 4 units. For both players, the dominant strategy is to make 4 units as this decision will always be more profitable regardless of their rival's actions.

cooperative solution The outcome that occurs when collaboration leads to a situation where both players are better off than under the non-cooperative solution.

each player is doing the best he or she can given the actions of a rival. This is called an "equilibrium" because once reached, neither player has an incentive to change strategies on his or her own. If Juliet selects $Q = 4$, Romeo cannot do better than selecting $Q = 4$; thus, Romeo has no incentive to change strategies. Likewise, if Romeo selects $Q = 4$, Juliet cannot do better than selecting $Q = 4$ and has no incentive to change strategies. Later in this chapter and the next one, we will show Nash equilibrium in games on pricing, advertising, entry deterrence, product mix, location, and even the decision to confess to a crime.

Note that *both* Romeo and Juliet would be better off if they *both* changed strategies to $Q = 3$. To get to this point, they would have needed to cooperate with each other. A **cooperative solution** is the outcome that occurs when collaboration leads to a situation whereby both players are better off than under the non-cooperative solution. In our example, the cooperative solution is for each duopolist to make 3 units and have profits of $18 each instead of $16 under the non-cooperative solution. This corresponds to the upper-left box in Exhibit 6. The cooperative solution is *not* a Nash equilibrium as each firm can do better selecting $Q = 4$ when its rivals select $Q = 3$.

The Dilemma of Duopolists . . . and Prisoners

Each firm has an incentive to cheat on the agreement and select $Q = 4$. In this case, the cheating firm's profit will increase to $20. This is what makes reaching a cooperative solution so elusive. It is also the crux of what is known as the *duopolists' dilemma*.

The **duopolists' dilemma** is a condition in which both duopolists are jointly better off under a cooperative solution than the non-cooperative solution, but have difficulties cooperating because individually they gain by cheating. Specifically, if they *attempt* to cooperate but one firm cheats, the firm that does so will see an increase in its profits to $20. Moreover, public policy makes formal attempts to cooperate illegal.

The duopolists' dilemma can be seen in the simultaneous move game shown in Exhibit 6, although it can also be found in other games. The box on the top left demonstrates what happens when the two firms successfully collude and are able to share the sort of profits earned in a monopolistic industry. It is the *cooperative solution*. They split the $36 in monopoly profit ($18 each).

In the boxes on the lower left and upper right, one of the two firms cheats. The cheater's profits *increase* to $20, which incentives cheating. Now look at the bottom-right box, where each firm produces $Q = 4$ and earns $16. Why is that number lower than in the top-left box? Because both firms each tried to pursue their own self-interest and maximize their own profit, without considering the interest of the cartel. They both follow their dominant strategy and cheat. This is the *non-cooperative solution*. They produce a higher output, which lowers the price of pizzas. They share a total industry profit that is now less than what could be shared if they had behaved like a monopoly (top-left box). Unfortunately for the duopoly, if one firm cooperates and produces $Q = 3$, the other firm has an incentive to produce $Q = 4$. This incentive to cheat is the essence of the *duopolists' dilemma*.

The duopolists' dilemma is a variation of a classic game called the **prisoners' dilemma**, a condition in which two prisoners are jointly better off under a cooperative solution than the non-cooperative solution, but have difficulties cooperating because individually they gain by cheating. The prisoners' dilemma is often explained in terms of two suspects facing questioning by the police.

The suspects—we'll call them Bonnie and Clyde—are brought in for interrogation. The police *only* have enough evidence to convict them of the lesser crime of "resisting arrest." Yet, the officers strongly suspect the couple is guilty of a bank robbery. In search of such evidence, they call Bonnie and Clyde to the station house and place them in *separate* interview rooms. Each is faced with a decision as to whether or not to provide evidence to the police. Doing so cuts one's jail time in half if convicted of robbery. The payoffs for Bonnie and Clyde are as follows:

- Each will be sentenced to 1 year in jail for resisting arrest if neither provides evidence.

- Each will receive 6 years in jail if both provide evidence.

- If one provides evidence but the other does not, the suspect who provides evidence goes home, while the other serves 12 years in jail.

This scenario is illustrated using a payoff matrix in Exhibit 8. The decision making for both Bonnie and Clyde is similar, so we will only focus on Bonnie's decision. She must decide if she wants to provide evidence or not. She has no control over what Clyde does. Nor does Bonnie have knowledge of Clyde's actions

duopolists' dilemma A condition in which both duopolists are jointly better off under a cooperative solution than the non-cooperative solution, but have difficulties cooperating because individually they gain by cheating.

prisoners' dilemma A condition in which two prisoners are jointly better off under a cooperative solution than the non-cooperative solution, but have difficulties cooperating because individually they gain by cheating.

EXHIBIT 8 The Prisoners' Dilemma

In this prisoners' dilemma, each player can benefit by providing evidence at the expense of the other player. The goal of each player is assumed to be minimizing jail time. If both players provide evidence, the outcome (a non-corporative solution) results in a worse outcome than would occur with cooperation. The prisoners' dilemma is analogous to the duopolists' dilemma—they are better off cooperating but find cooperation elusive.

Think & Speak Like an Economist

The prisoner's dilemma can be applied to a variety of economic or business decisions in which each player individually benefits by not cooperating with the group—even though both players would be better off cooperating.

because they are in separate rooms. If Clyde decides to not provide evidence, Bonnie can either go home by providing evidence or do 1 year in jail by holding out. Conversely, if Clyde provides evidence (again, she has no control over Clyde), her jail time will be cut in half if she also offers evidence, from 12 years to 6. She has a dominant strategy to provide evidence. And because Clyde is in exactly the same situation, he has the same dominant strategy. A non-cooperative solution occurs when both players follow their dominant strategy, each providing evidence and doing 6 years in jail. This is the lower-right box in the payoff matrix. Yet, as a group, they would both be better off if neither provides evidence to the police.

Does this mean prisoners never cooperate? Clearly not. Bonnie and Clyde were lovers. Some crime gangs are made up of family members, who find it easier to cooperate because of their strong family ties. Members of some crime organizations may go free by providing evidence to the police but run the risk of death; others may believe that if they "take the fall" for the organization, their family will be compensated for their "sacrifice." This substantially changes the payoff matrix.

What does the prisoners' dilemma between Bonnie and Clyde have in common with the duopolists' dilemma between Romeo and Juliet in Exhibit 6? As it turns out, a lot! In both cases, cooperation is beneficial, resulting in either reduced jail time or higher profits. In both cases, however, cooperation is elusive because of the rules of the game. And in both cases, Nash equilibrium occurs under the non-cooperative solution. Given that Romeo makes $Q = 4$ or Bonnie confesses, the best Juliet or Clyde can do is follow suit.

sequential move game A game that involves all firms making their strategic decision with full knowledge of the prior actions of their rivals.

decision tree A graphical representation of a sequential move game that demonstrates different actions and payoffs.

Sequential Move Games

Although it is possible to envision games where both players make a decision at the same time, it is also possible to envision a scenario where one player makes a decision and then the next player decides. For example, what happens if Juliet gets to make her decision *after* Romeo makes his? To see this, it is helpful to view the earlier Romeo and Juliet example as a *sequential move game* using a *decision tree*.

A **sequential move game** involves all firms making their strategic decision with full knowledge of the prior actions of their rivals. In sequential move games such as chess, one player moves and then the next player moves. A **decision tree** is a graphical

EXHIBIT 9   Strategic Quantity Decision in a Sequential Game

It is useful to demonstrate sequential move games using a decision tree. First, Romeo must decide whether to make 3 or 4 units. In turn, Juliet makes a similar decision. If Romeo decides to make 4 units, Juliet maximizes profits by making 4 units. As a consequence, Romeo's payoff will be $16. Romeo's dominant strategy is to make 4 units as this decision will always be more profitable regardless of the actions of Juliet. A non-cooperative solution occurs when both players make 4 units and receive a payoff of $16. A cooperative solution occurs with each player receiving a payoff of $18.

representation of a sequential move game that demonstrates different actions and pay-offs. The use of decision trees is commonplace for businesses making strategic deci-sions. Exhibit 9 illustrates such an example. In a decision tree:

- A player (a duopolist in this case) makes a decision, represented with *arrows*.
- In sequence, the other player makes a decision.
- Optional: Additional decisions may be made by alternating players.
- Payoffs (profits in this case) are realized at the end of the game (in *green boxes*).

Romeo is the first to act. He must decide whether to make 3 or 4 units. Once Romeo makes his decision, Juliet makes a similar decision. Suppose Romeo selects $Q = 3$. At this point in time, Juliet can select $Q = 3$ units and have a payoff of $18. This corresponds to the upper-left box in Exhibit 6. The problem with this solution is that if Romeo selects $Q = 3$, Juliet can select $Q = 4$ units and have a higher payoff of $20. Absent col-lusion, Juliet will likely decide to maximize her profits by producing 4 units.

The key is to analyze all decision trees by using backward induction (working backward); figuring out the best move is to always carefully consider how your rival

Understanding How to Analyze Decision Trees—An Overview

It is easier to analyze all decision trees by using *backward induction* (working backward).

- Since Juliet is the *last* to decide, it is easier to analyze her decision *first*.
  - If Romeo makes 3 units, Juliet is better off making 4 units (payoff of $20 rather than $18).

  - If Romeo makes 4 units, Juliet is better off making 4 units (payoff of $16 rather than $15). Notice Juliet's best response is always to make 4 units.

- Since Romeo is the *first* to decide, it is easier to analyze his decision *last*.
  - Romeo assumes that Juliet will produce 4 units because it is always her best response. Thus, Romeo can earn $15 by making 3 units or $16 by making 4 units. Therefore, he makes 4 units.

will respond. This is the essence of strategic decision making; it involves anticipating the move of your rival. In this case, Romeo should anticipate that if he selects $Q = 3$, Juliet will select $Q = 4$ because it is her best response. As a consequence, Romeo's profit will be $15. If Romeo selects $Q = 4$, his profit will be *higher,* either $20 or $16. As a result of strategic decision making, Romeo is inclined to select $Q = 4$. This is a dominant strategy.

When Romeo selects $Q = 4$, Juliet can select $Q = 3$ units with a profit of $15 or select $Q = 4$ units with a profit of $16. When Romeo selects $Q = 3$, Juliet can select $Q = 3$ units with a profit of $18 or select $Q = 4$ units with a profit of $20. Juliet is likely to decide to maximize her profit by producing 4 units. In the end, if Romeo selects $Q = 3$ *or* if Romeo selects $Q = 4$, Juliet's best response is producing 4 units. She, too, has a dominant strategy of $Q = 4$.

As was the case in the simultaneous move game (Exhibit 6), each player has a dominant strategy to produce 4 units, the two players end up at the non-cooperative solution absent collusion. Both players would be better off if they *both* selected $Q = 3$. This is the essence of the duopolists' dilemma.

15.4 STRATEGIC DECISION MAKING ON PRICING

Business decision making is not limited to deciding how much quantity to produce. Businesses often make strategic decisions based on what price to charge. Once again, the effectiveness of such a decision depends on the actions of your rival.

Decisions, Decisions—What Price to Charge?

Assume that Target and Walmart would like to underprice their rivals and capture additional sales. Yet, if *both* firms were to price slightly higher, then their profit per unit would be higher than if both firms price low. Both firms pricing high could potentially maximize their collective profits. This is another example of the duopolists' dilemma.

Exhibit 10 demonstrates a sequential move game with a decision on pricing. We assume that if a firm underprices its rival, it will see an increase in both sales and profits. For the individual firm, the best outcome of all is its rival pricing high and its price remaining low. As you can see, pricing low ends up being a dominant strategy, even though both firms would be better off if they cooperate and charge a higher price.

Walmart first decides whether to price high or low. If Walmart prices high, Target can underprice with a payoff of $40 or price high with a payoff of $30. Since Target is likely to price low, Walmart expects that pricing low will result in a payoff of $10. In contrast, if Walmart prices low, its lowest payoff is $20. As a result, Walmart chooses to price low. In turn, Target must decide whether to price high or low with the knowledge that Walmart prices low. In this case, Target will choose to price low (with a payoff of $20 rather than $10).

Both Walmart and Target have a dominant strategy to price low. A non-cooperative solution occurs with each firm receiving a payoff of $20 (the bottom green box in Panel A). This solution is a Nash equilibrium because neither Walmart nor Target has an incentive to change strategies. Yet as a group, the two firms would actually be better off under a cooperative solution with both pricing high. This is yet another example of the duopolists' dilemma. In the next section, we explore possible

EXHIBIT 10 Strategic Decision on Pricing

Panel A: Sequential Move Game

Panel B: Simultaneous Move Game

Walmart and Target must separately decide whether to price high or low. Panel A is a sequential move game. First, Walmart must decide, then Target makes a similar decision. Since both Walmart and Target have a dominant strategy to price low, a non-cooperative solution occurs when both players price low and receive a $20 payoff. Panel B presents the decision as a simultaneous move game. The non-cooperative solutions occur in the lower-right box of the payoff matrix. In both panels, a cooperative solution occurs with each player pricing high and receiving a higher $30 payoff. This is another example of the duopolists' dilemma.

ways for the two duopolists to overcome this dilemma without a formal price-fixing agreement.

Often, these firms must make strategic decisions at the same time or without any real knowledge of the actions of their rivals. With that in mind, let's examine their options with a payoff matrix, as depicted in Panel B. Both Target and Walmart have a dominant strategy to lower price. Walmart is better off pricing low if Target prices low ($20 > $10) and better off pricing low if Target prices high ($40 > $30). Likewise, Target has a dominant strategy to price low. A non-cooperative solution occurs in the lower-right box of the payoff matrix, with each firm obtaining a $20 payoff. A cooperative solution involves both firms charging a high price and is found in the upper-left box of the payoff matrix, with each firm obtaining a $30 payoff.

Price Fixing

One commonly observed type of collusion is **price fixing**, collusion achieved by rivals agreeing to a set price. Based on the example from earlier in the chapter, Romeo and Juliet might find it easier to simply agree to both charge one price: $8 (rather than each agreeing to only sell 3 pizzas). While price fixing is seldom overt and open, over the years, law enforcement agents have uncovered a variety of firms engaged in this practice, a direct violation of public policy. Price fixing and other forms of collusion involve cooperation.

price fixing Collusion achieved by rivals agreeing to a set price.

EXHIBIT 11 Examples of Price Fixing

Industry	
Ivy League Colleges	Prior to the 1990s, eliminated price competition by offering identical financial-aid packages to each student in a given category who qualified for assistance.
Lasers for Eye Surgery	The manufacturers of lasers used in laser eye surgery were charged with price fixing in 2006. It is estimated that the price fixing raised the price of such surgery by $500 per eye. The companies involved included Summit and VISX.
Computer Chip Makers	The manufacturers of large memory chips admitted to price fixing and paid fines totaling over $300 million in 2014. These chips were used in video game consoles and computers made by Sega, Microsoft, Nintendo, Apple, Dell, IBM, and others. The companies involved included Samsung, Toshiba, Micron, Mitsubishi, NEC, Elpida, Hitachi, Hynix, Infineon, Mosel, Nanya, and Winbond.
LCD Panel Makers	The manufacturers of LCD panels agreed to pay $553 million in a price-fixing settlement in 2011. The companies involved included Sharp and Samsung.
Auto Part Makers	In 2013, several auto part makers were fined $740 million for fixing the price of parts sold to major car manufacturers such as Toyota, Ford, and General Motors. The companies involved included Hitachi, Mitsubishi, and Panasonic.
German Beer Makers	In 2014, Germany imposed a $146 million fine on five beer makers for price fixing. The breweries fined included Krombacher, Bitburger, Veltins, Warsteiner, and Privatbrauerei Ernst Barre. Anheuser-Busch was also involved, but not fined because it was the first to admit to and report the cartel's activities.

Price fixing is collusion achieved by rivals agreeing to a set price and a direct violation of public policy.

Compiled by the authors from the sources noted.[2]

Antitrust laws make cooperation difficult because agreements are necessarily secretive and unenforceable or implicit. In contrast, agreements that are legal can be recorded in writing and are enforceable through the court system. Since collusion agreements are not legal, no legal enforcement mechanism exists. It would be foolish to sue someone for not engaging in an action (collusion) that involves both parties breaking the law. This reduces the amount of collusion, but does not eliminate collusion entirely. Evidence of price fixing can be found in Exhibit 11.

As the number of sellers in an oligopoly increase, price fixing and other forms of collusion become increasingly difficult and the market structure looks more and more like monopolistic competition. Collusion is nearly impossible if there are a large number of firms involved, because it is difficult to negotiate an agreement and difficult to tell which firms are cheating. It would be difficult to engage in price fixing with all the pizza restaurants in New York City or Chicago. Likewise, it would difficult for collusion to occur in the wide-open paperback book market, but somewhat easier in the e-book market due to the limited number of sellers.

Finally, it is frequently difficult to prove that a price-fixing agreement has occurred. You might wonder why antitrust officials don't simply check to see if each firm is charging the same price. The problem is that while such an activity might represent price fixing, it's also true that firms tend to change the same price in highly competitive industries where each firm is a price taker. For example, many pizzas in New York City sell for roughly the same price, yet it is unlikely that price fixing is occurring due to the number of sellers.

BUSINESS BRIEF Throwing the Book at iBooks

When Apple launched its iPad in 2010, it sought to create a new market for e-books—and new competition for e-book sellers like Amazon and Barnes & Noble. A few years later, the firm was found guilty of price fixing. Apple settled the lawsuit in 2016, agreeing to pay up to $400 million in damages to consumers. Five publishers had previously agreed to settlements in 2014. A contemporaneous *New York Times* story attributed the following e-mail statement to Apple's founder Steve Jobs:

> Throw in with Apple and see if we can all make a go of this to create a real mainstream e-books market at $12.99 and $14.99.[*]

According to the Department of Justice (DOJ), in an effort to maximize its own profits, Apple coordinated efforts to reach a cooperative solution. Specifically, Apple sought to undercut book companies from attempting to underprice its rivals. DOJ claimed that Jobs's e-mail showed Apple was the "ringmaster" in a price-fixing conspiracy in the e-book market. In the end, the courts ordered Apple to modify its publisher contracts to prevent price fixing and to hire external monitors to ensure that it was not violating antitrust laws.[†]

[*]Quoted in Edward Wyatt and Nick Wingfield, "U.S. Now Paints Apple as 'Ringmaster' in Its Lawsuit on E-Book Price-Fixing," *The New York Times,* May 14, 2013, http://www.nytimes.com/2013/05/15/technology/us-now -paints-apple-as-ringmaster-in-its-lawsuit-on-e-book-price-fixing.html?_r=0.

[†]See Brett Molina, "Apple Settles E-books Price-Fixing Suit for Up to $400M," *USA Today,* July 16, 2014, http ://www.usatoday.com/story/tech/2014/07/16/apple-ebooks-prices/12734921/.

BUSINESS BRIEF "Raise Your Airfares. I'll Raise Mine."

In the 1980s, American Airlines and Braniff Airways were fierce competitors when they discussed the idea of collusion in a recorded phone call. Both airlines were in the midst of an unprofitable fare war—with each airline attempting to underprice its rival. To overcome this dilemma, a senior executive at American Airlines, Robert Crandall, came up with the following idea:

> Raise your goddamn fares 20 percent. I'll raise mine the next morning. . . .
> You'll make more money and I will too.[*]

The suggestion amounted to price fixing. However, this sort of clear-cut case of price fixing is relatively rare. Today, legal experts contend that in order to prove price fixing, prosecutors need unmistakable evidence because it is possible for two competing airlines to simultaneously raise fares in response to higher costs or an increase in demand. Moreover, airlines constantly monitor each other's prices, so their exhibiting similar price movements is to be expected.

Nonetheless, decades later, over 20 international airlines were found guilty of, once again, price fixing. Between 2000 and 2006, the heads of various airlines held secret meetings at airports to discuss pricing for passenger and cargo fees. The cartel included British Airways, Korean Air, and Air France-KLM. In total, some $1.7 billion in fines were paid and several executives went to prison. The smoking-gun evidence in this case? Two airlines turned on their rivals and provided even more compelling evidence.[†] Yet, the transgressions appear to continue. In 2015, separate allegations of price fixing in the United States (involving American Airlines, Delta Airlines, Southwest Airlines, and

United Airlines) and in Europe (a dozen cargo airlines) resulted in a significant number of court cases.[‡]

*"U.S. Probe into Airline Collusion Needs More Than Circumstantial Evidence," *PBS NewsHour,* July 3, 2015, http://www.pbs.org/newshour/rundown/us-airline-probe-need-proof-beyond-business-usual/.

[†]Alicia A. Caldwell, "21 Airlines Fined for Fixing Passenger, Cargo Fees," *The Washington Post,* March 5, 2011, http://www.washingtonpost.com/wp-dyn/content/article/2011/03/05/AR2011030501365.html.

[‡]David Koenig, Scott Mayerowitz, and Eric Tucker, "US Probes Possible Collusion Among Airlines to Keep Fares Up," *Associated Press,* July 2, 2015, https://apnews.com/fbe53033dd424612974b0c0f8c19910e.

15.5 IMPLICIT PRICING STRATEGIES TO OVERCOME THE DUOPOLISTS' DILEMMA

Antitrust laws prohibit explicit written contracts between two firms to coordinate prices, so collusion agreements are neither legal nor binding. Price fixing is illegal. Moreover, horizontal mergers between similar businesses are often blocked by government regulators. Even so, duopolists frequently figure out creative ways to work around the dilemma.

In some product markets, *implicit collusion*—that is, cooperation between firms without any formal or written agreement—does appear to occur over time. For example, firms can achieve cooperation with subtle and often merely implied agreements, such as simply accepting the price set by the industry leader.

Price Leadership Model

Price leadership is an implicit pricing agreement in which one firm in the oligopoly (often the largest) establishes a price that the other firms then adopt. Recall the example of two pizza sellers on an island: Romeo and Juliet. Now suppose Romeo sells more pizza than Juliet and is the price leader. Over the years, the two firms have come to recognize they are in a local duopoly. In the past, Juliet would frequently attempt to underprice Romeo. Each time, Romeo swiftly responded by lowering his price.

Eventually, Juliet realized that it was beneficial to match each and every price change of Romeo, to the penny. As a consequence, Romeo evolved as the price leader and now decides how to best price his pizza with full (but implicit) knowledge of how his smaller rival will respond. Although no formal agreement has been entered, the two firms are operating cooperatively.

price leadership An implicit pricing agreement in which one firm in the oligopoly (often the largest) establishes a price that the other firms then adopt.

📊 **BUSINESS BRIEF General Mills Takes the Lead on Cereal Prices**

Sometimes, the price leadership model breaks down or a new price leader emerges. For many years, Kellogg's was the price leader in the ready-to-eat breakfast cereal market. During the summer of 2010, cereal sales were sluggish as Americans continued modifying their eating habits. As a result, a price war broke out when Kellogg's and its key competitor General Mills each aggressively lowered prices. Profits at Kellogg's slid, while profits at General Mills increased, primarily due to increases in the sales of General Mills' most popular cereal brand, Cheerios. Remember, these firms also engage in various types of non-price competition such as product differentiation. By December 2010, General Mills announced it would increase its price the following year. A few months later, Kellogg's announced it would do the same.* There is no evidence of an explicit agreement between General Mills and Kellogg's, but General Mills appears to have assumed the role of price leader.

*See Matt Andrejczak and William Spain, "General Mills to Raise Prices," *MarketWatch*, December 16, 2010, http://www.marketwatch.com/story/general-mills-profit-rises-on-tax-benefit-2010-12-16; Matt Andrejczak, "Kellogg Profit Hurt by Cereal-Price War," *MarketWatch*, November 2, 2010, http://www.marketwatch.com/story/kellogg-profit-hurt-by-cereal-price-war-2010-11-02; and "Kellogg Co. Announces Price Increases," *Natural Products INSIDER*, February 7, 2011, http://www.foodproductdesign.com/news/2011/02/kellogg-co-announces-price-increases.aspx.

Low-Price Guarantees

Firms know that their rivals are better off underpricing, so they seek to avoid being underpriced. One way they do this is by offering a guarantee to match (or beat) any competitor's price. Low-price guarantees sound like something that is consumer friendly, yet economic analysis shows that they are a creative way for a business to overcome the duopolists' dilemma and reach a cooperative solution. As you will learn, a low-price guarantee eliminates the risk of being underpriced by one's rivals.

A low-price guarantee is modeled in Exhibit 12. For simplicity, we begin by assuming that if Walmart prices low, Target will also price low. This is the non-cooperative solution depicted in Panel A of Exhibit 10. Now consider how Target responds to Walmart pricing high with a low-price guarantee. If Target attempts to underprice, Walmart will match the lower price and both firms will have a payoff of $20. On the other hand, if Target matches Walmart's high price, then both firms will have a payoff of $30. Exhibit 12 re-creates the Walmart/Target sequential move game, but adds an option for pricing high with a low-price guarantee. Unlike in Exhibit 10, the duopolists end up at a cooperative solution even though they have not entered any formal agreement.

Consumers might assume that a "low-price guarantee" encourages firms to price low to avoid paying out refunds. Economic analysis shows, however, that such a guar-

---

EXHIBIT 12 Low-Price Guarantee

A low-price guarantee eliminates the risk of underpricing by one's rivals. As shown in Exhibit 13, if Walmart prices low, Target prices low, and each firm receives a $20 payoff. If Walmart prices high with a low-price guarantee, Target has an option to price low and receive a $20 payoff, or price high and receive a $30 payoff. A low-price guarantee results in a cooperative solution and overcomes the duopolists' dilemma.

Walmart price low or high?

High (with low price guarantee) →

Target price low or high?

High → Walmart $30 Target $30

Low → Walmart will honor low price. → Low → Walmart $20 Target $20

Low →

Target Target will price low. → Low → Walmart $20 Target $20 antee typically results in both firms achieving a cooperative solution—in this case, by charging a high price. A low-price guarantee results in each having an incentive to price *high,* as cutting prices is pointless if you know that your rival will match any price cut. This is a clever way of attaining the cooperative solution and overcoming the duopolists' dilemma. For example, such guarantees are common in various local tire markets. Economists Maria Arbatskaya, Morten Hviid, and Greg Shaffer took a detailed look at these kinds of guarantees and found them to be an effective way to discourage price cutting.[3]

Finally, since no player has an incentive to unilaterally change strategy, the outcome once it is reached is also a Nash equilibrium—an outcome where no player can improve through a unilateral change in strategy. A firm that attempts to underprice its rival when a low-price guarantee is in effect will find itself worse off.

Duopolists' Dilemma in the Long Run—Repeated Games

Game theory can be a powerful tool in understanding strategic decision making. The models developed thus far provide useful insights on strategic decision making, the benefits of cooperation, and why cooperation may be elusive. But we also know that simple models can leave out important real-world complexities, and game theory is no exception. In the real world, businesses are involved in a repeated game situation: They play a game over and over again. Repetition enables each player to learn from the behavior of its rivals and seek ways to implicitly reach a cooperative solution without entering a formal agreement. The price leadership model that we have just examined is one such example.

In 1980, Robert Axelrod and W. D. Hamilton ran simulations to determine if an optimal strategy exists in repeated games. It is important to remember that a player (firm) can *only* control its own strategy; the firm cannot control the strategy of its rivals and prevent them from attempting to underprice. The winning strategy in many of these simulations (and subsequent simulations) is a relatively simple copy-cat method called the **tit-for-tat strategy**, a game theory strategy whereby a player cooperates on the first move and then copies what the other player(s) previously do on all subsequent moves. If *both* players adopt the tit-for-tat strategy, a cooperative solution will occur. On the other hand, if a rival attempts to underprice, a non-cooperative solution quickly results. This non-cooperative solution remains until the *rival* raises its price and allows the other firm to raise its price the *next* period. Once a cooperative solution is reached (again), the firms remain there if (and only if) neither firm attempts to underprice again.[4]

tit-for-tat strategy A game theory strategy whereby a player cooperates on the first move and then copies what the other player(s) do on all subsequent moves.

▼ In the video game console market, Microsoft and Sony are in a repeated game; constantly introducing new product lines at similar prices.

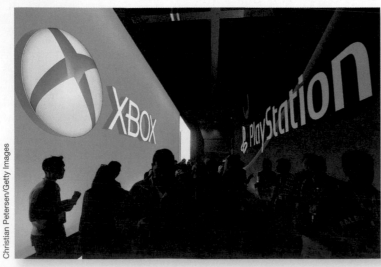

Christian Petersen/Getty Images

Exhibit 13 demonstrates the tit-for-tat strategy. Maria initially prices high and hopes her rival follows suit. From then on, Maria merely copies the strategy played by her rival in the prior period. Alternative strategies, such as *always* pricing high, allow the firm's rivals to underprice. Conversely, a strategy where one always prices low (fearful that if you price high, your rival will underprice) misses any opportunity for cooperation.

In many ways, claims by a business that "we will not be undersold" or other forms of low-price guarantees are a kind of tit-for-tat strategy. They announce to one's rivals that their prices will be matched. If the rival prices high, the firm can subsequently price high. If the rival prices low, the firm will subsequently price low to avoid being

EXHIBIT 13 Tit-for-Tat (TFT) Strategy in Repeated Games

Cooperative Pricing	Underpricing Pricing	Non-Cooperative Pricing	Underpricing Pricing	Cooperative Pricing
TFT begins with cooperation. This pattern can potentially last for several periods.	Rival attempts to underprice. This pattern will last only one period.	TFT requires Maria to copy rival's low price. This pattern can potentially last for several periods.	Firm that initiated the underpricing attempts to regain cooperative pricing. This pattern will last for only one period.	TFT requires Maria to copy rival's high price. This pattern can potentially last for several periods.

Tit-for-tat strategy (TFT) is a game theory strategy whereby a player cooperates on the first move and then copies what the other player(s) do on all subsequent moves. Here, Maria initially prices high and from then on, merely copies the strategy played by her rival in the prior period. It is important to note that Maria cannot control the strategy adopted by her rival. Researchers have found the tit-for-tat strategy effective in repeated games.

undersold. The price leadership model also appears to occur over time and is a form of the tit-for-tat strategy by the follower.

Finally, it is important to note that these subtle forms of cooperation evolve in some instances and not in others. Reaching a cooperative solution implicitly is difficult and explicit collusion is illegal.

15.6 STRATEGIC DECISION MAKING ON ADVERTISING

The Super Bowl may be the biggest game in football, but it's an even bigger game for advertisers. Coke and Pepsi alone spent over $160 million advertising during the five Super Bowl games from 2009 to 2013. In 2014, the price of a 30-second advertisement topped out at over $4 million.[5] Suppose these two companies believed that advertising did not cause more people to drink soda, but merely shifted sales from one firm to another. In that case, a cooperative solution would be for each firm to agree not to spend millions of dollars on advertising. However, both firms know that the firm that advertises may be able to capture market share if its rival does not advertise. Alternatively, if the rival does advertise, it is often in the other firm's best interest to also advertise to avoid losing market share.

Panel A of Exhibit 14 demonstrates a sequential move game involving a decision on advertising. Pepsi first decides whether to advertise or not advertise. If Pepsi does not advertise, Coke can advertise with a payoff of $125 or not advertise with a payoff of $100. Since Coke is likely to advertise, Pepsi anticipates that not advertising will result in a payoff of only $50 and it will lose market share to Coke.

In contrast, if Pepsi advertises, its lowest payoff is $75. Therefore, Pepsi makes a strategic decision to advertise. At this point, Coke must decide whether to advertise with the knowledge that Pepsi has already decided to advertise. In this instance,

EXHIBIT 14   Strategic Decision on Advertising

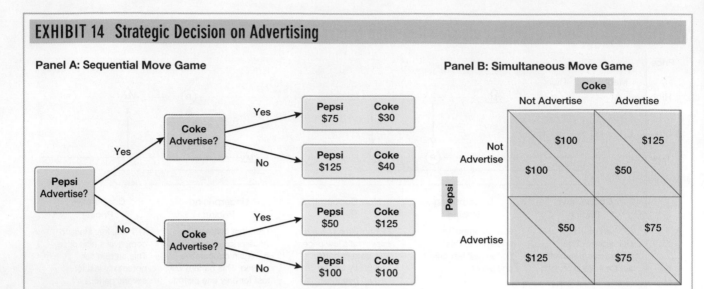

Panel A: Sequential Move Game

Pepsi Advertise?
- Yes → Coke Advertise?
  - Yes → Pepsi $75 | Coke $30
  - No → Pepsi $125 | Coke $40
- No → Coke Advertise?
  - Yes → Pepsi $50 | Coke $125
  - No → Pepsi $100 | Coke $100

Panel B: Simultaneous Move Game

	Coke Not Advertise	Coke Advertise
Pepsi Not Advertise	Coke $100 / Pepsi $100	Coke $125 / Pepsi $50
Pepsi Advertise	Coke $50 / Pepsi $125	Coke $75 / Pepsi $75

Pepsi and Coke must separately decide whether to price high or low. Panel A is a sequential move game. First, Pepsi must decide, then Target makes a similar decision. Since both Pepsi and Coke have a dominant strategy to advertise, a non-cooperative solution occurs when both players advertise and receive a $75 payoff. Panel B presents the decision as a simultaneous move game. The non-cooperative solutions occur in the lower-right box of the payoff matrix. In both panels, a cooperative solution occurs with each player pricing not advertising and receiving a higher $100 payoff. This is another example of the duopolists' dilemma.

Coke will choose to advertise (with a payoff of $75 rather than $50). Both firms make a strategic decision to advertise based on the expectation that their rival is likely to advertise.

Both Pepsi and Coke have a dominant strategy to advertise. This may be either to gain market share if their rival *does not* advertise or to prevent losing market share if their rival does advertise. A non-cooperative solution occurs, with each firm receiving a payoff of $75 (top green box). This outcome is a Nash equilibrium as neither firm has an incentive to not advertise when their rival advertises. Yet, both firms would be better off under a cooperative solution by not advertising. This is another example of the duopolists' dilemma.

As is often the case, firms might make strategic decisions at the same time or without any real knowledge of the actions of their rivals. As such, Panel B examines their options as a simultaneous move game with a payoff matrix. Pepsi is better off advertising if Coke advertises ($75 > $50) and better off advertising if Coke does not advertise ($125 > $100). Likewise, Coke has a dominant strategy to advertise. Since both firms have a dominant strategy to advertise, a non-cooperative solution occurs in the lower-right box of the payoff matrix, with each firm obtaining a $75 payoff. A cooperative solution involves both firms *not advertising* and is found in the upper-left box of the payoff matrix, with each firm obtaining a $100 payoff.

POLICY BRIEF A Policy Banning Cigarette Advertisements

Occasionally, the government provides solutions to the duopolists' dilemma in advertising. Cigarette makers were the largest product advertisers on television prior to passage of a law that banned such ads in 1970. The ban was designed to discourage smoking for health reasons. Prior to the ban, cigarette companies often advertised to capture market sales from their rival and to help establish brand names. After the ban, advertising costs fell significantly with little impact on sales. Brands that were already established at the time became entrenched as new potential brands lost a key method of reaching new customers. Although clearly not the intent of the advertising ban, the law helped well-established cigarette companies reach a cooperative solution on advertising. The ban boosted the profits of existing cigarette companies.*

*See George A. Hay, "The Cigarette Industry," in *Structure of American Industry*, 13 ed. James Brock (Long Grove, IL: Waveland Press Inc, 2016).

BUSINESS TAKEAWAY

When a market is dominated by just a few rivals, competition is intense. Business managers in an oligopoly must anticipate key rivals' responses to every action they take. Lowering the price of a product might boost sales initially, but rivals will likely respond with their own price cut. This kind of "race to the bottom" ultimately lowers profit per unit and overall profitability for both firms. This is the essence of the duopolists' dilemma, and it's the reason why many rival products—Xbox and PlayStation, Coke and Pepsi, Nikes and Reeboks—are often sold at similar prices.

Of course, one way to maximize profits would be for rival firms to collude—that is, to make agreements about price or quantity, essentially divvying up the market among themselves. But such agreements would run afoul of antitrust law, and without legal standing, such agreements would be unenforceable. If Romeo backs out of his illegal arrangement with Juliet, Juliet doesn't have any legal recourse.

There is little honor among thieves or illegal cartels. But that doesn't mean firms can't make implicit arrangements: Juliet might just follow Romeo's lead on pricing, without making any formal arrangement to do so. In a similar fashion, movie studios might avoid releasing a film on the same weekend when the latest Marvel blockbuster hits the screen, effectively ceding territory to a competitor without any sort of collusion.

The process of anticipating rivals' behaviors is the underlying theme of game theory, which has useful applications in business and economics. Economists have developed tools such as payoff matrixes and game trees that firms can use to analyze a rival's likely response to a given decision. Like most economic tools, these are simplified models designed to explain basic economic theory by eliminating real-world complexity. Nonetheless, the basics of strategic decision making provide useful insights for firms in oligopolistic competition. Working out a payoff matrix can help firms make better decisions about pricing, advertising, and marketing.

CHAPTER STUDY GUIDE

15.1 CHARACTERISTICS OF AN OLIGOPOLY

An **oligopoly** is a market structure with a few dominant firms that are highly interdependent. A **duopoly** is an oligopoly with exactly two firms. An oligopoly has a high degree of market concentration as measured by the **concentration ratio,** the percentage of market sales accounted for by the largest few firms in an industry. Since firms in an oligopoly are highly interdependent, the decisions of one firm impact the others.

15.2   STRATEGIC DECISION MAKING ON OUTPUT

If an oligopoly is to maximize industrywide profits, it will price like a monopolist. This is difficult due to the fact that cooperation from competing firms is required. To have the industry behave like a monopolist will involve **collusion**, an agreement among rivals to cooperate by limiting price and non-price competition. Collusion involves cooperation. Cooperation is made difficult by antitrust laws, the lack of international law, and the fact that in most oligopolies there are more than two sellers. A **cartel** is an organization of rival firms with agreements among members to collude, often by restricting output and increasing prices. When cheating occurs, cooperation falls apart. Successful collusion occurs when both firms cooperate; however, this is frequently not the case.

15.3   AN INTRODUCTION TO GAME THEORY

Game theory (in economics) is the study of strategic behaviors and the ways in which individuals (or other entities) make optimal decisions by anticipating how rivals will respond to their actions. The use of game theory helps to model the behavior of oligopolists. **Simultaneous move games** involve all firms making their strategic decisions with full knowledge of the prior actions of their rivals. Simultaneous move games make use of a **payoff matrix,** a graphical representation of a simultaneous move game that demonstrates different actions and their potential payoffs. A **dominant strategy** is a strategic decision that is best regardless of the strategic decision made by a rival. A **non-cooperative solution** is the outcome that occurs when players do not collaborate, with each pursuing their own self-interest. A **Nash equilibrium** is an outcome in which no player can improve through a unilateral change in strategy. A **cooperative solution** is the outcome that occurs when collaboration leads to a situation where both players are better off than under the non-cooperative solution. The **duopolists' dilemma** is a condition in which both duopolists are jointly better off under a cooperative solution than the non-cooperative solution, but have difficulties cooperating because individually they gain by cheating. The duopolists' dilemma is a variation of a classic game called the prisoners' dilemma. The **prisoners' dilemma** is

a condition in which two prisoners are jointly better off under a cooperative solution than the non-cooperative solution, but have difficulties cooperating because individually they gain by cheating. A **sequential move game** involves all firms making their strategic decision with full knowledge of the prior actions of their rivals. In sequential move games such as chess, one player moves and then the next player moves. A **decision tree** is a graphical representation of a sequential move game that demonstrates different actions and payoffs. The use of decision trees is commonplace for businesses making strategic decisions.

15.4   STRATEGIC DECISION MAKING ON PRICING

Sequential and simultaneous move games can also be used to show a duopolist's dilemma in pricing. **Price fixing** is collusion achieved by rivals agreeing to a set price. While price fixing is seldom overt and open, over the years, law enforcement agents have uncovered a variety of firms engaged in the practice.

15.5   IMPLICIT PRICING STRATEGIES TO OVERCOME THE DUOPOLISTS' DILEMMA

Several strategies exist to help overcome the duopolists' dilemma. **Price leadership** is an implicit pricing agreement in which one firm in the oligopoly (often the largest) establishes a price that the other firms then adopt. A low-price guarantee is an implicit strategy. Economic analysis shows that such a guarantee typically results in both firms achieving a cooperative solution—in this case, by charging a high price. **Tit-for-tat strategy** is a game theory strategy whereby a player cooperates on the first move and then copies what the other player(s) do on all subsequent moves. If both players adopt the tit-for-tat strategy, a cooperative solution will occur.

15.6   STRATEGIC DECISION MAKING ON ADVERTISING

Game theory can be also used to show a duopolists' dilemma in advertising. Cooperation entails rival firms agreeing to not advertise; however, each firm independently finds that advertising is in its best interest.

TOP TEN TERMS AND CONCEPTS

(1) Oligopoly

(2) Concentration Ratio

(3) Cartel and Collusion

(4) Game Theory

(5) Sequential versus Simultaneous Move Games

(6) Dominant Strategy and Nash Equilibrium

(7) Cooperative versus Non-Cooperative Solution

(8) Prisoners' Dilemma

(9) Price Fixing

(10) Price Leadership and Tit-for-Tat

STUDY PROBLEMS

1. 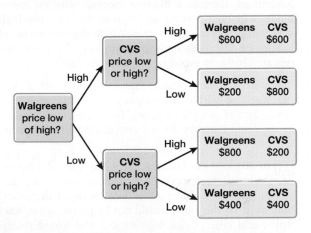 Describe each of the following methods for overcoming the duopolists' dilemma. Discuss the implication of price cuts and price increases.

   a. price leadership

   b. low-price guarantees

   c. tit-for-tat strategy

2. Suppose there are five firms in a market, each with an equal market share. What is the four firm concentration ratio? Suppose two of the firms merge. What is the market share of the largest firm? What is the four firm concentration ratio after the merger?

3. In 2011, Bank of America announced its plan to charge customers $5 a month for the use of a debit card. Previously, there had been no monthly fees. An article in *The Wall Street Journal* at the time noted that "other big banks are *expected* to follow suit." [6] The other big banks such as JPMorgan Chase and Wells Fargo did not follow suit.[7] A month later, Bank of America cancelled the fees due to mass customer cancellations. Explain this scenario in terms of price leadership and the difficulty of enforcing cooperation.

4. Assume Bank of America's (BofA) main rival is Wells Fargo. Consider the payoff matrix below in answering the following questions:

   a. What is each firm's dominant strategy?

   b. What is the cooperative solution?

   c. What is the non-cooperative solution?

5. During the five Super Bowls between 2009 and 2013, Hyundai and Chrysler each spent around $65 million on advertising.[8] Assume, for the sake of simplicity, that the industry is a duopoly, and if each firm advertises, it will each earn profits of $100 million. If they both do not advertise, each firm will earn profits of $120 million. If one advertises and one does not, the firm that advertises will capture market share and earn $140 million, while the rival will earn $80. Draw a payoff matrix. Describe each

firm's dominant strategy and the likely outcome absent cooperation.

6. In November 2013, Sony released PS4 and Microsoft Released Xbox One. Each is considered the eighth generation of a video game system; each was priced at $399.99 at launch. Use game theory to explain why both firms are reluctant to attempt to underprice their rivals. Do you suspect these firms engage in non-price competition?

7. Answer the three questions below using the following data. Suppose CVS and Walgreens are the only two pharmacies in town. Also assume that they are making pricing decisions on select products and these decisions can be modeled as a sequential move game using the following decision tree:

   a. What is each firm's dominant strategy?

   b. What is the cooperative solution?

   c. What is the non-cooperative solution?

   d. Why is reaching a cooperative solution difficult?

8. In the United States, Major League Baseball (MLB) imposes a surcharge called a luxury tax on teams with what each league views as excessive payrolls.[9] Teams with a payroll in excess of the limit, $197 from 2014 to in 2018, must pay a luxury tax ranging from 17.5 to 50%. The belief among league officials is that this will help promote parity so that games will be more competitive. In 2013, the New York Yankees paid the tax for the 11th time, forking over a total of more than $250 million. That same year, the Los Angeles Dodger also paid the tax. MLB is exempt from many antitrust laws.

   a. Draw a decision tree to explain this situation absent a payroll tax. Assume for simplicity this is a duopoly, with the two teams being the Yankees and the Chicago Cubs. The Yankees move first. Assume that if both teams pay low salaries, they will earn $200. If both teams pay high salaries, they will earn $100 as neither will have a competitive edge. But, if one team pays high salaries (buys a good team) while a rival pays low, the team paying high will have a competitive edge and earn $300 while the rival will earn 0.

b. Draw another decision tree with a payroll tax. Assume the payroll tax will lower the profits of firms pricing high by $150 (from $300 to $150 or from $100 to −$50). What outcome will now occur?

9. In North Jacksonville, Florida, a new hospital operated by the University of Florida was cleared for construction and expected to open in 2017. Government regulations exist that make it difficult to enter the hospital industry. Discuss how these regulations impact the ability of hospitals to engage in collusion.[10]

10. What are some examples of price fixing? How are they examples of collusion?

11. When state governments build highways, they often contract out the work to a private construction firm. Sometimes, there is a bidding process, with the lowest bidder winning the contract. Suppose there are two highway contractors in a given state. Would they be able to collude more effectively on a single project, or if there were repeated highway projects, one after another?

12. Economists believe that society is better off if people working within a company cooperate with each other, and if people working for different companies in the same industry do not cooperate with each other. Explain why.

13. In 2013, at the biennial Paris Air Show, Boeing and Airbus fiercely competed to secure orders for their planes.[11] Assume that neither was aware of the other's bids and that the game would not be played again. Each firm could either price high or low and would receive the following payoffs (in billions of dollars):

a. What is each firm's dominant strategy?

b. What is the cooperative solution?

c. What problems might arise in trying to reach a cooperative solution?

d. What is the non-cooperative solution?

e. How do the cooperative solution and the non-cooperative solution compare?

f. How realistic is the assumption of the game not being played again? How might outcomes change if the game is played sequentially?

14. What is OPEC? Describe it in the context of a cartel and collusion. Why does OPEC often find collusion elusive?

David Franklin/Alamy

∧ Maria's success will depend on strategic decisions involving pricing, location, and product mix.

Behavioral Economics and Strategy

Implications for Pricing, Location, and Product Mix

Maria is moving forward with her business plan. She has done her homework—determining how to legally set up her firm, figuring out costs and potential profits, and researching the market in which her restaurant operates. Right now, she's looking for the perfect location, which is not as simple as finding a beautiful space in a nice part of town. Maria needs to think about where her restaurant will be situated in relation to its rivals. If she opens in an established part of town with a lively restaurant scene, will she be able to compete? If she is the first to open in an edgier, up-and-coming neighborhood, will she be able to lure customers? If she finds success in this new location, how long will it be before other restaurants enter the market? In addition, Maria must face some important pricing decisions. How much can she charge for her pizzas, drinks, and salads?

In this chapter, we will examine business strategies that can help an entrepreneur like Maria make optimum decisions. You will discover that Maria needs to think not just like an economist, but also like a psychologist—she must anticipate how her competitors and her customers will react to her decisions. For that reason, we will begin this chapter with a discussion of the role that human psychology plays in economic decision making, a subject known as behavioral economics. As you will soon discover, behavioral economics provides useful insights for businesses and consumers alike.

Chapter Learning Targets

● Identify several behavioral factors affecting decision making.

● Describe the first-mover advantage and other business strategies related to location and product mix.

● Explain entry deterrence strategies and when their use is appropriate.

● Summarize the microeconomics forces that impact business profitability using insights from Porter's five competitive forces model.

16.1 BEHAVIORAL ECONOMICS: ARE PEOPLE ALWAYS RATIONAL?

Economists and psychologists both study the choices that people make. Economics is built on the principle that decisions are reached on the basis of rational economic self-interest, often viewed in monetary terms. Psychology, on the other hand, involves examining a complex mixture of economic and psychological factors to explain human behavior. In the 1960s and 70s, psychologists Daniel Kahneman and Amos Tversky merged applied economic modeling to their study of human behavior, creating the hybrid field of behavioral economics. Despite never having taken an economics course, Kahneman won the 2002 Nobel Prize in Economics for his work.[1]

Their work, and that of others, show that humans don't always make economically rational decisions. They argued that the sort of rational decision making assumed in economics models may require complex mathematical calculations that the average person likely does not have the time, inclination, or intellectual capacity to consider.

Behavioral economics is the study of how economic decisions are impacted by psychological factors beyond rational economic self-interest. Factors including emotional states, personal ethics and values, processing errors, mental shortcuts, and social pressures all affect economic decision making. Behavioral economics has important implications for business—most notably for pricing strategies.

People Often Care About Fairness

Game theory methodologies introduced in the last chapter are useful to illustrate several key ideas of behavioral economics. Consider the following variation of what is commonly referred to as the *ultimatum game*. The first player is given 6 one dollar bills and told he *must* split the money with a second player. The second player knows each player's payoffs, but can only accept or reject the offer. The second player is not allowed to provide any input into the first player's decision. If the second player rejects the offer, neither player keeps any of the money. Here are some possible outcomes:

- The first player splits the $6 evenly, with each player receiving $3. Then the second player accepts the offer.

- The first player claims $4. The second player accepts $2.

- The first player claims $5. The second player accepts $1.

- The second player rejects the first player's offer and each player receives $0.

Exhibit 1 demonstrates the ultimatum game. According to the game theory model presented in the previous chapter, the second player's dominant strategy is to accept the split no matter what. Even a small amount of money is better than zero. Moreover, the first player has an advantage: being the first to act (we'll discuss the *first-mover advantage* in depth later in the chapter). Recognizing this, the first player has an incentive to offer the second player a less than even split, perhaps only a dollar, as shown in Exhibit 1. The first player's best strategy is to claim $5 of the $6, because he knows that the second player has a dominant strategy to accept any offer above zero. The resulting solution of a $5 − $1 split is a Nash equilibrium, which you'll recall occurs when neither player can improve his or her outcome through a unilateral change in strategy.

behavioral economics The study of how economic decisions are impacted by psychological factors beyond rational economic self-interest.

Think & Speak Like an Economist

In a Nash equilibrium, no player can improve through a unilateral change in strategy; each player is doing the best he or she can given the actions of a rival. It is an equilibrium because once reached, neither player has an incentive to change strategies on his or her own.

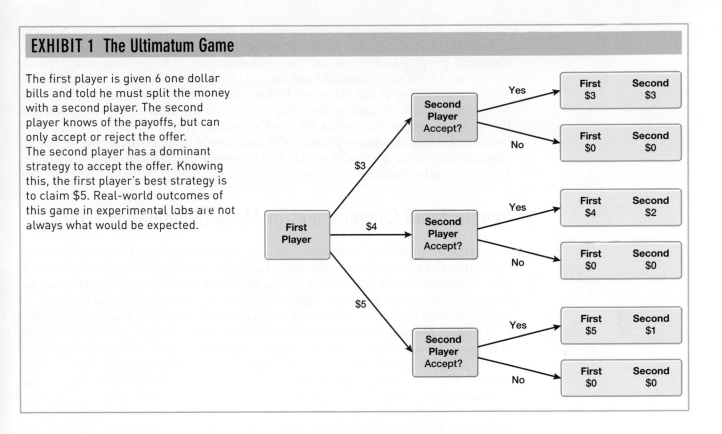

EXHIBIT 1 The Ultimatum Game

The first player is given 6 one dollar bills and told he must split the money with a second player. The second player knows of the payoffs, but can only accept or reject the offer. The second player has a dominant strategy to accept the offer. Knowing this, the first player's best strategy is to claim $5. Real-world outcomes of this game in experimental labs are not always what would be expected.

Suppose you are the second player and the first player claims $5. Would you accept the $1? Or, might you become so upset by the "unfair" offer that you say "no"? If you are inclined to say "no," you are not alone. When the ultimatum game is played in experimental labs with varying dollar amounts, the second player often rejects "unfair" splits (less than 50%), despite being worse off by doing so. In general, the more unfair the split, the more likely that the second player rejects the offer.

Another interesting pattern is that the first player frequently offers a fair split or nearly fair split, perhaps due to either a sense of fairness or fear of being rejected by the second player. In fact, there is evidence that the primary concern of the first player is indeed a sense of fairness. In a variation of the ultimatum game known as the *dictatorship game,* the decision of the first player to act is binding (hence, application of the word "dictator"). Suppose the payoffs are similar to those in Exhibit 1, but the second player cannot reject the offer. In this case, the dictator (first player) will maximize his or her well-being by taking $5, leaving the second player with only $1. However, in experimental labs, the dictator most often does *not* take the maximum payoff. This suggests that many players do have a sense of fairness.

Another variation of the dictatorship game requires both players to *earn* money by doing a routine task rather than simply be given money. In this case, the dictator is even more likely to offer an even split (and less likely to maximize his or her own payment), presumably due to concerns over fairness. It seems especially unfair for a person not to be paid for work he or she has done.

Traditionally, economists stress maximizing payoffs in making economic decisions, which means the second player should accept any offer in the ultimatum game that makes him or her better off. Similarly, in the dictatorship game, the first player should claim as much as allowed. But the experiments described above have convinced many economists to embrace ideas from behavioral economics.

Critics of behavioral economics contend that experimentally observed behavior misses an important aspect of the real world. For example, how might the outcome change if the players were to split $6 million in million dollar increments? Would the second player really reject $1 million out of a sense of fairness or spite? Recent studies suggest that as the stakes get higher, people behave more rationally. That is, they offer a smaller fraction to the other player, and the other player is less likely to turn down a smaller share when the sums of money involved are large. Nonetheless, behavioral economics does provide us with some useful insights that people, to varying degrees, care about fairness. And this has important implications when formulating pricing and other business strategies.

People Avoid Computations or Make Computation Errors

According to traditional economics, rational decision making often implies doing detailed analysis and making mathematical calculations. People struggle to make complex computations in a limited time frame, and often avoid doing such analysis at all. Frequently, they do not have enough information to make an informed decision. As a result, human behavior is not always consistent with traditional economic models.

Consider games of chance such as lottery tickets, slot machines, carnival games, and claw machines. Upon reflection, most people realize the odds of winning the Powerball lottery are slim, but this does not stop some of them from purchasing tickets. Some people, of course, enjoy playing the lottery whether they win or lose; for them, it is simply a form of entertainment. But many players also engage in games of chance based on a hope of winning—and more often than not, they greatly overestimate their chances of doing so based on misperceptions about the probability of winning. In addition, few people who buy lottery tickets take the time to calculate their probability of winning, or the expected payout.

People Often Fail to Think Long Term

In a similar vein, optimal economic decisions often require thinking about the long term, rather than focusing on the short term. For someone in their twenties or thirties, saving for retirement means sacrificing now for benefits that won't be reaped until far into the future. That seems entirely rational. But the temptation is, of course, to spend the money today and worry about retirement later. This behavioral temptation frequently results in too little being saved, even among those with stable incomes. It also helps to explain government policies designed to encourage certain behaviors, such as offering tax breaks to those who save for retirement.

A classic psychology experiment illustrates the ways in which individuals often behave irrationally, if given choices between an immediate or long-term benefit. Psychologists offered a group of 4-year-olds the following choice: They could have one marshmallow immediately or they could have two marshmallows if they were willing to wait for just 15 minutes. Some two thirds of the children studied couldn't wait, and grabbed the one marshmallow before 15 minutes had expired. Those who did wait were rewarded with two marshmallows. The researchers then followed these children throughout their lives, and found that those who had waited for the two marshmallows tended to achieve more education and also amassed greater retirement savings, suggesting we are not all equally inclined to make rational decisions in the long term.[2]

📊 BUSINESS BRIEF How Credit Cards Capitalize on Impatience

Credit card companies know that people lack patience when it comes to more than just marshmallows. As that experiment showed, when offered the opportunity to make purchases today and defer the payment until later, many consumers will opt for immediate gratification—even though they know they could save money by thinking long term. Often, consumers wind up paying high interest rates on credit card purchases, and future payments can significantly exceed the amount of the original purchase. Sure, those interest payments can be avoided if you pay the balance in full each month—but your credit card bill will usually only ask for the minimum required payment, typically about 2% of the balance. This is a form of framing (discussed shortly), designed to nudge consumers to stretch out payments, adding interest to the bill each month along the way.

Those payments add up quickly: A customer who has an $8,000 credit card balance at 19% interest and makes only minimum monthly payments would need more than 45 years to pay off the balance, with total payments including the initial amount owed equaling $34,897. To offset the potential computational error and behavioral biases, credit card statements are required by law to include a "minimum payment warning."* Websites such as creditcards.com and bankrate.com provide calculators that show exactly how long it will take consumers to pay off a balance, factoring in the amount of their monthly payments.

*Paul Katzeff, "Credit Card Debt: Hot to Tame It, How to Avoid Carrying a Costly Balance," *Investor's Business Daily*, September 29, 2017, http://www.investors.com/etfs-and-funds/personal-finance/credit-card-debt-how -to-tame-it-how-to-avoid-carrying-a-costly-balance/.

Business Strategies on the Way Choices Are Presented

People are often influenced by the way choices are presented. This is because rather than conducting a thorough analysis of all available information, people frequently rely on personal preferences and prejudices, or take mental shortcuts rather than engaging in complicated computations of costs and benefits. Behavioral scientists in both economics and psychology have identified specific behaviors, sometimes referred to as *cognitive biases,* and demonstrated how they affect decision making. In this section, we'll introduce just a few of them and examine their applications in business, especially in terms of pricing and purchasing decisions.

Framing and Anchoring As just noted, credit card companies present their product in a manner that entices consumers to use the credit card and to stretch out payments. This is known as framing; the way a price, or an option, is framed can have a profound influence on customer behavior.

Framing refers to the idea that the way in which a decision is presented to customers, which often affects behavior. For example, you've probably noticed that many items are priced at slightly below a round number, say, $8.99 or $8.95. This practice, known as *odd* pricing, is a form of framing. It works because consumers tend to have a *left digit bias*: Studies show that a one penny difference in price has a disproportionately large impact on sales when the left digit changes. Of course, most consumers understand that $8.99 was closer to $9 than $8, but this cognitive bias persists. If almost every gas station charged $2.99 and 9/10 cents per gallon, then consumers driving by a sign proclaiming "3.00/gallon" will assume it represents $3.00 and 9/10 cents. Thus, no company has an incentive to break from the practice of framing prices.

One form of framing that has proven particularly effective for retailers is anchoring. The **anchoring effect** means framing economic decisions based on irrelevant information. Here, consumers base economic decisions on the first piece of information offered (the "anchor")—regardless of its relevance. For example, prices are often framed in a way to provide consumers with misleading information such as a "list price" in making their decision. For example, a sweater at Kohl's may have a retail price sticker of $100 but be marked down 60% to $40. What a deal! It's frequently the

framing The idea that the way in which a decision is presented to customers often affects their behavior.

anchoring effect The concept of framing economic decisions based on irrelevant information.

case that no one ever buys the sweater for $100. The $100 list price is actually irrelevant, merely used as a framing device to make the current price seem cheaper. This is a common example of anchoring.

Anchoring can also be effective when used to offer similar products with slightly better features—say, a deluxe model—at much higher prices. While businesses hope to sell both models, introducing a deluxe model suddenly makes the regular model feel like a bargain. Upscale kitchen outfitter Williams-Sonoma offered a bread maker for $279, but observed sluggish sales. When it added a $429 "deluxe" model, sales of the new model flopped, but sales of the $279 model doubled.[3]

Presenting Goods with Leaders When Maria opens her restaurant, she will want to figure out ways to draw customers in, so she decides to launch a happy hour special, selling select appetizers at cost. In doing so, she is presenting *other* goods as part of a package. **Leader pricing** is a strategy whereby businesses reduce the price of a popular item in order to attract customers who will likely purchase other goods. Maria knows that while she'll make less profit on appetizers, most of her happy hour customers will want other goods such as a glass of wine, beer, or soda to enjoy—and those are items that are highly profitable.

Maria might even set her appetizer prices lower than her costs, effectively selling them at a loss. This practice is known as *loss leader* pricing, and it can be effective if other goods are highly profitable. Some discount movie tickets, for example, are a loss leader. In this case, popcorn and food items are effectively presented as part of a package, which includes the movie.

Status Quo Bias Behavioral economists have demonstrated that loyal customers view price increases as a loss. For example, Fred has been a regular customer of Maria's lunch special for $8. If Maria raises her price to $9 or $10, Fred may consider this a loss and stop buying lunch at her restaurant. A change from the status quo is viewed as a loss by many consumers. The **status quo bias** is a consumer preference to maintain the current situation. This is particularly true of products that individuals purchase very frequently. Because consumers seek to avoid losses, they may not continue purchasing a product that increases in price, even if the price increase is justified on the basis of cost, or in line with rising consumer incomes.

The status quo bias is not limited to price. One perplexing finding is known as the *paradox of choice,* which indicates that when consumers are offered too many choices, they are less likely to change their minds—or make any purchase at all. In one study, researchers showed that consumers were more likely to purchase jam when they were offered fewer flavors than when they were offered many flavors.[4] Their conclusion— that less choice can be good for sales—is valuable in business. Maria, for example, may be able to sell more wine if her wine list is limited. Moreover, consumers are more likely to stick to their old choices even if more (and potentially better) choices become available; this is a form of the status quo bias.

leader pricing A strategy whereby businesses reduce the price of a popular item in order to attract customers in an effort to sell other goods.

status quo bias A consumer preference to maintain the current situation.

Many large companies offer voluntary retirement plans (such as a 401k or 403b). Typically, employees make contributions that the employer will match to a certain percentage; the taxes on the funds contributed are deferred until retirement. For example, an employer may put $1,000 into an employee's retirement plan if (and only if) the employee also contributes $1,000. Financial experts (and economists!) strongly advise their clients to take advantage of such a program, as it is close to free money. And yet, many employees do not enroll—even when they are very aware of the benefits and have expressed an interest in doing so. Studies by behavioral economists suggest that status quo bias is behind this decision; that is, individuals simply accept the "default" option. This means that the way options are framed influences whether or not individuals enroll.

Consider the two ways to frame the enrollment process:

- *Opt in.* Employees will participate in the retirement benefit plan if and only if they sign up.

- *Opt out.* Employees will automatically participate in the benefit plan unless they ask not to be enrolled.

From a purely rational point of view, the economic decision should be based on the needs of the employee and the quality of the matching program. However, enrollment rates were 86% when employees had to opt out, but only 37% when employees had to opt in.[5] Also consistent with the status quo bias, once enrolled in a retirement plan, participants tended to remain enrolled.

Similarly, when consumers obtain services like Netflix or membership at a gym, they tend to be heavy users at the onset. As time fades, use of these services frequently wanes. So why do people simply not cancel memberships? The answer is the status quo bias.

"So what's it going to be? The same size as last year or the same price as last year?"

Frank Modell/Conde Nast/Cartoon Bank

BUSINESS BRIEF   Same Price, Less Chocolate: Hershey Caters to Status Quo Bias

The first Hershey chocolate bar was produced in 1900. The price was only 5 cents. Over the years, the cost of manufacturing chocolate bars changed, yet the price of the candy bar remained 5 cents into the 1950s. Hershey feared that raising the price of the chocolate bar would alienate consumers. Consumers would view such a price increase as a loss and thus might be discouraged from purchasing the candy bar.

Instead, Hershey simply changed the size of the candy bar, making it smaller when input costs rose and larger when input costs fell. They wished to avoid having consumers view the company as unfair, or the price increase as a loss. In reality, consumers faced implicit price increases via smaller packages. In terms of price per ounce of chocolate, consumers actually saw prices rise over the period. However, they may not have recalled the previous size of the candy bar, or did not care enough to calculate the price per ounce on such a small transaction.[*]

[*]See Hershey Community Archives, "Hershey's Milk Chocolate: Bar Wrappers over the Years," n.d., accessed May 6, 2017, http://www.hersheyarchives.org/exhibits/default.aspx?ExhibitId=20&ExhibitSectionId=42.

16.2 BUSINESS STRATEGIES ON TIMING, LOCATION, AND PRODUCT MIX

Even if everyone were rational, strategic decision making would be very complex. In this section, we continue our use of game theory and decision trees from the prior chapter, but will relax some of the simplifying assumptions to address a richer set of examples. We begin by showing that being the first person to decide often, but not always, provides an advantage in sequential move games. With this insight, we can better understand business decisions on location and product mix.

The Timing of Decisions: First-Mover Advantage and Disadvantage

Strategic decisions are often made sequentially, which may give one player an advantage. Consider the ultimatum game presented in Exhibit 1, where the player who goes first has an advantage. The **first-mover advantage** occurs when the first player to act has a strategic advantage. In business, it is often an advantage to be the first firm to act. For example, a first-mover advantage can be found if the first firm attempts to dominate the market. The second must then decide how to respond given that the first firm has already produced a large quantity. This gives the first firm a distinct advantage.

To understand this scenario, let's reconsider the Romeo and Juliet example from the last chapter. In Exhibit 2, Panel A presents identical market demand and total revenue data. Some modifications are needed to enrich our example. First, we change the average total cost from $2 to $2.10. Increasing ATC complicates the mathematics (slightly), but eliminates the possibility of a player having to decide between equal payoffs. It also slightly reduces profit payoffs. Second, in the last chapter, choices were limited to $Q = 3$ or $Q = 4$. We now allow Romeo and Juliet to select *any* output level. With these two modifications, we are now able to complete a more thorough analysis.

As was the case in the last chapter, the highest level of profit in the industry occurs at a market price of $8 and a market output of 6 units per hour. If Romeo and Juliet cooperate by each producing 3 units per hour ($Q = 3$), they can split the monopoly profit of $35.40 and make $17.70 each. This is highlighted in Panel A and shown in Panel B.

Now let's consider whether moving first allows one firm to receive a *higher* payout. Assume that Romeo is the first to act and can produce a variety of units of output. Romeo's profit depends on what Juliet subsequently does. As shown in Panel B, if Romeo decides to make 6 units, for example, his payoff will be $23.40 if Juliet makes 2 units, and $11.40 if Juliet makes 4 units. Likewise, if Romeo decides to make 7 units, his payoff will be $27.30 if Juliet makes 1 unit, and $13.30 if Juliet makes 3 units.

To arrive at a strategic decision, Romeo will analyze the effect of Juliet's likely response. For example, Romeo recognizes that if he makes 8 units, Juliet will maximize her profits by making 2 units (her profit will be $3.80). In this case, Romeo's profit will be $15.20. Juliet's highest payout for *each of Romeo's possible outputs* is highlighted in Panel B.

Strategic thinking involves anticipating your rival's subsequent decisions. Some of Romeo's expected payoffs are:

first-mover advantage
Occurs when the first player to act has a strategic advantage.

- If Romeo produces 6 units, Juliet's highest payoff will occur if she makes 3 units. Romeo's expected payoff is $17.40.

- If Romeo produces 7 units, Juliet's highest payoff will occur if she makes 2 units. Romeo's expected payoff is $20.30.

EXHIBIT 2 Production Possibilities for a Duopolist

Panel A: Profits for the Market and the Cooperative Solution

Price (P)	Quantity (Q)	Total Revenue TR = P×Q	Total Cost $2.10 per unit	Profit
9	5	45	$10.50	$34.50
8	**6**	**48**	**12.60**	**35.40**
7	7	49	14.70	34.30
6	8	48	16.80	31.20
5	9	45	18.90	26.10
4	10	40	21.00	19.00
3	11	33	23.10	9.90
2	12	24	25.20	−1.20

Panel B: Profits for Each Firm

Quantity			Profit	
Romeo	Juliet	Price	Romeo	Juliet
3	3	8	17.70	17.70
6	2	6	23.40	7.80
6	3	5	17.40	8.70
6	4	4	11.40	7.60
7	0	7	$34.30	$0
7	1	6	27.30	3.90
7	2	5	20.30	5.80
7	3	4	13.30	5.70
8	1	5	23.20	2.90
8	2	4	15.20	3.80
8	3	3	7.20	2.70
9	1	4	17.10	1.90
10	1	3	2.70	0.90
11	0	3	9.90	0.00
11	1	2	−1.10	−0.10

As presented in Panel A, the maximum profits for the market is $35.40. This is the cooperative solution and is highlighted. This occurs when 6 units are sold for $8 each and is the cooperative solution. Panel B shows the profits for each firm for a variety of plausible outcomes with Romeo first to act. Since ATC = $2.10, Profit = (Price − $2.10) × Quantity. Highlighted is Juliet's profit-maximizing choice given the quantity selected by Romeo.

- If Romeo produces 8 units, Juliet's highest payoff will occur if she makes 2 units. Romeo's expected payoff is $15.20.

Under these circumstances, Romeo would make 7 units as he has the *first-mover advantage*. If Juliet responds by maximizing her profits by producing 2 units, Romeo will be better off than under the cooperative solution. In addition, because Juliet is also maximizing her profit—the result is a Nash equilibrium—neither Romeo nor Juliet has an incentive to unilaterally change strategies.

EXHIBIT 3   Sequential Move Game: A Quantity Decision with More Options

First, Romeo must decide how many units to make. In turn, Juliet arrives at a similar decision. As is the case with all decision trees, it is best to do the analysis using backward induction. If Romeo makes 6 units, Juliet's highest payoff will result when she makes 3 units. If Romeo makes 7 or 8 units, Juliet's highest payoff will result when she makes 2 units. Thus, Romeo can expect a payoff of $17.40 if he selects $Q = 6$, $20.30 if he selects $Q = 7$, and $15.20 if he selects $Q = 8$. Profit maximization suggests that Romeo will select 7 units and Juliet 2 units. The first-mover advantage only applies in sequential move games.

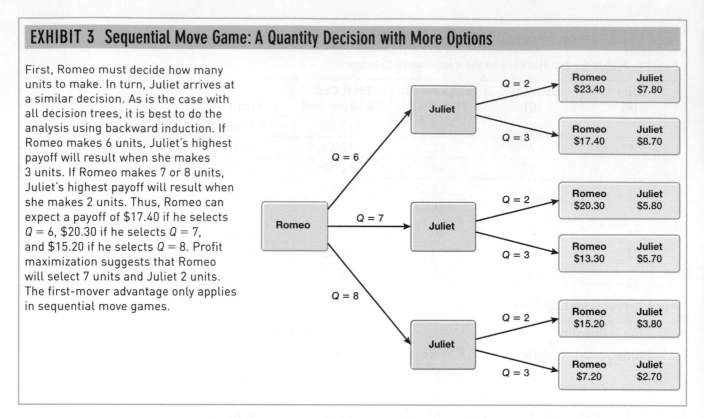

Romeo's first-mover advantage can also be expressed in a decision tree, as shown in Exhibit 3. To simplify the analysis, only three of the many options for each player are shown. As with all decision trees, it is best to analyze the options working backward—that is, using backward induction. If Romeo makes 6 units, Juliet's highest payoff will result when she makes 3 units. If Romeo makes 7 or 8 units, Juliet's highest payoff will result when she makes 2 units. Thus, Romeo can expect a payoff of $17.40 if he selects $Q = 6$, $20.30 if he selects $Q = 7$, and $15.20 if he selects $Q = 8$. Romeo likely opts to make 7 units, with Juliet choosing to produce 2 units. This increases Romeo's payoff to $20.30.

Keep in mind that the first-mover advantage only applies in sequential move games such as the one presented here. In simultaneous move games presented in the previous chapter such as rock-paper-scissors, neither player moves first. Clearly in simultaneous games, a first-mover advantage cannot exist as both players make decisions simultaneously.

Moreover, the first-mover does not always have an advantage. The **first-mover disadvantage** occurs when the first player to act has a strategic disadvantage. The first moving player does worse than if given the opportunity to act second. Imagine if the game of rock-paper-scissors were played *sequentially*: The first-mover would lose every time, unless the other player were especially incompetent!

In business, second-movers may be able to use an alternative version of the (expensive) technological advances developed by the first-mover. In addition, the second-mover *may* be able to better understand customer needs in a new groundbreaking product line. New product development is often very expensive and developing similar products (while avoiding the violation of patent laws) is frequently less expensive. Moreover, first-movers *may* need to advertise heavily to make consumers aware of a new product market that previously did not exist. In essence, late movers *may* be able to free-ride off the first-mover. Some economists note that the first-mover in the smartphone business was Blackberry. Not only did the company develop extensive technological insights, it also advertised extensively in order to create a market for smartphones that previously had not existed. This helped *others* develop an understanding of what features customers wanted. Second-mover Apple—and later, Google with its Android platform—were able to capitalize on Blackberry's success and eventually overcome them in the smartphone market.

first-mover disadvantage

Occurs when the first player to act has a strategic disadvantage.

Location, Location, Location!

Consider Maria's decision on location in the chapter introduction. It *may be* advantageous for her to be the first to open shop in an edgier, up-and-coming neighborhood. In this case, she would have a first-mover advantage: She could establish her business in a new hotspot and lock in a lower rent than she would pay in a more established area.

Now consider a small suburban town, in which the town zoning board has tentatively approved two new convenience stores at locations to be determined. Two competing chains, 7-Eleven and Circle K, are in the process of deciding where to open up shop. Both firms know that location is key for any convenience store—if potential customers will have to travel too far, they'll choose a cheaper big box retailer instead—so choosing the right location is a critical decision.

The population of the suburb is split into two clusters: one at the east end and the other at the west end. The east end of town is more populated. As a consequence, a convenience store there will have a payoff of $300, while a convenience store in the west end of town will have a payoff of $200 if no other firm enters the area. If both firms enter the same area, then each firm will experience zero economic profit as a result of the competition.

In this example, the first-mover advantage must be modeled as a sequential game. Exhibit 4 demonstrates the scenario with a decision tree. If Circle K makes

EXHIBIT 4 First-Mover Advantage in a Location Decision

If Circle K is the first to act (Panel A), it will select "east," leaving its rival 7-Eleven's best option to select "west." Circle K's payoff will be $300. If Circle K is the second to act (Panel B), its rival will select "east," leaving its best option to select "west." Circle K's payoff decreases to $200. In this case, a first-mover advantage exists.

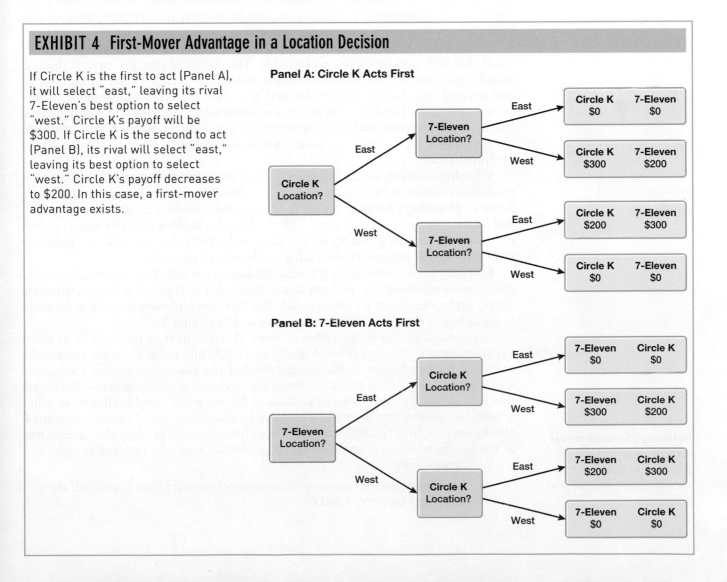

a decision first, it will be inclined to locate its store in the east end of town. This is demonstrated in Panel A. Once it has set up shop, 7-Eleven is better off selecting a location at the west end of town. This outcome is a Nash equilibrium. In contrast, if 7-Eleven makes a decision first, then it will want to locate in the east end of town. This is demonstrated in Panel B. In that case, Circle K is better off selecting a location in the west end of town. Such a result is also a Nash equilibrium. Notice that both firms have an incentive to cooperate once the first player decides on its location. As a consequence, there are two Nash equilibria—neither firm has an incentive to unilaterally change the decision to locate at the opposite end of town.

Needless to say, there is often a race among rival firms to be the first to obtain a zoning permit in an ideal location. This is a direct result of the first-mover advantage. Indeed, it might be worth locating in a growing neighborhood for a short time before consumer demand could justify a new business—this gives the first-mover an advantage in locking down a prime location.

Why Does Clustering Occur? Hotelling's Location Model

Does the previous convenience store example prove that firms should *always* locate away from each other to avoid price competition? Not at all. In fact, Maria's best decision may well be to locate in a well-established restaurant scene. That's because while there's some advantage to being the only firm in an area, an economic rationale also exists for similar firms to cluster near each other.

In the Circle K and 7-Eleven example above, the market at each location is so small that *only* one firm can be profitable. This is not always the case in the real world. For example, you've likely seen car dealerships located close to each other, and noticed that Lowe's is often located near Home Depot, Burger King on the same street as McDonald's, and so on. Furniture stores are also commonly located in clusters; restaurants and clothing stores compete side by side in malls and downtown shopping areas. That's because consumers frequently prefer to shop in a concentrated area.

Why do businesses cluster? In 1929, Harold Hotelling demonstrated that the most profitable location is often right next to a competitor, despite increased price competition. **Hotelling's location model** is an economic model that illustrates the optimal location strategy of businesses.[6] This model is particularly effective when product differentiation occurs primarily on the basis of location, but can also be applied to show why similar businesses often sell a similar mix of products.

Consider an ice cream stand at a crowded beach. For simplicity, assume the beachgoers are evenly dispersed (uniform distribution—not in clusters) and that customers simply prefer the closest ice cream stand. The first firm will want to position its stand in the center of the beach. This is seen as point A in Exhibit 5.

A second firm can locate either at point B (right next to point A) or at point C (the midpoint between point A and point E). While point C would reduce the commute for beachgoers in the eastern third of the beach, the goal of the second ice cream stand is not to minimize the walking distance of consumers—the objective is to maximize the number of customers for whom its stand is closest. In other words, the second firm wants to maximize its customer pool. Locating at point B allows the new firm to capture nearly the entire customer pool on the eastern half of the beach, which is a larger customer pool than would be realized at point C.

For the new firm:

- Locating at point C captures all customers between C and E, and half the customers between A and C.

Hotelling's location model
An economic model designed to illustrate the optimal location strategy of businesses.

EXHIBIT 5 Hotelling's Location Model

Ideally, the first ice cream stand is located in the middle of a crowded beach, at point *A*. An entrant will capture more customers by locating close to point *A* (such as point *B*), rather than locations further away from point *A* (such as point *C*).

Based on: http://ingrimayne.com/econ/International/Hotelling.html.

- Locating at point *B* captures all customers between *E* and *B*, and half the customers between *A* and *B*. Locating at point *B* captures more customers.

Hotelling's location model has several other interesting implications. Suppose the firm at location *A* can relocate without cost—let's say that its ice cream stand is actually an ice cream cart. Will the first firm move? Probably not. If the first firm were to relocate, it would locate near point *B*, on the side that maximizes the customer pool. In Exhibit 5, this occurs at point *A*—exactly where the first firm started! Remember that most businesses are not so portable: Once a Lowe's, a McDonald's, or a car dealership establishes its location, the costs of moving the business to a different spot are enormous. These relocation costs further reduce a firm's incentive to move.

In Hotelling's location model, there is no significant first-mover advantage or disadvantage. Unlike in our earlier Circle K/7-Eleven scenario, the second firm is successfully able to split the potential pool of customers with the first firm. This is because customers on the beach were evenly distributed; in the convenience store example, customers lived in clusters and neither cluster was large enough to support two convenience stores.

This type of analysis can be applied to the location decision for a vast array of other examples, including a firm's location near a highway exit or train station. Although there are some limits on its application, the basic location model can help to explain the frequent clustering of similar types of merchants.

🖳 BUSINESS BRIEF Drugstore Location Wars: CVS and Walgreens

On York Avenue in Edina, Minnesota, a CVS and Walgreens are separated only by a narrow grass median. According to a news report, their stores are so close that people working in the drive-through windows can wave to their competition. In the nearby town of Brooklyn Park, there are two CVS stores and two Walgreens, all less than 5 miles apart.[*]

This pattern occurs across the United States. Why? The answer may be found in Hotelling's location model. Once a rival is established, it is often best for a new firm to locate close to its soon-to-be rival. According to the model, doing so will result in the greatest number of potential customers. So while townspeople may want drug store locations spread across various population areas, it often makes the most sense for businesses to locate next to their rivals.

*Susan Feyder, "Nation's Biggest Pharmacies Sidle Right Up to Each Other," *Star Tribune*, October 29, 2012, http://www.startribune.com/nation-s-biggest-pharmacies-sidle-right-up-to-each-other/176188911/.

v Hotelling's location model in action.

Product Mix Decisions

Insights from Hotelling's location model also shed light on why firms often try to match, rather than differentiate from, the product mix of their rivals. **Product mix** refers to the assortment of products a business offers its customers. You may have noticed that competing movie chains usually feature the same films on any given weekend, and often start films at roughly the same times. Hotelling's location model helps explain why. Rather than product differentiation on the basis of location, product differentiation occurs on the continuum of time. A theater showing a movie at 8 p.m. will likely lose customers wanting to see the movie at 7 p.m. to a theater that starts the movie at 6:45 p.m. Rather than start the movie at 8 p.m. the theater could capture customers wanting to see the movie at 8 p.m. by starting a little later than 6:45 p.m. (say, 7:10 p.m.) and *also* capture some customers wanting to see the movie closer to 7 p.m.

Hotelling's location model also illustrates the more abstract concept of *product space*. In this case, products differentiate themselves on the basis of product attributes. For the same reason that firms often locate close to a rival or theaters start a movie at a similar time, businesses have an incentive to create similar products. For example, Coca-Cola and Pepsi both sell sports drinks and lemon-lime soda in addition to their main product. Yes, Gatorade (owned by Pepsi) dominates the sports drink market, but Powerade (owned by Coke) captures some of the same customer pool. Likewise, Sprite (owned by Coke) dominates the lemon-lime soda market, but Sierra Mist (owned by Pepsi) captures some of the same customer pool. Because neither company wishes to concede a product space to its rival, they have both developed many similar products over the years.

16.3 BUSINESS STRATEGIES ON ENTRY DETERRENCE

product mix The assortment of products a business offers its customers.

contestable market A market that is easy for rival firms to enter.

strategic entry deterrence An action taken by an existing business that discourages rivals from entering the market.

If Maria opens her restaurant in a newly gentrifying neighborhood, it may be the only restaurant in town, but if she is successful, her location advantage will not last long. When a monopoly exists in a market that rivals can easily enter, the market is considered contestable. A **contestable market** is a market that is easy for rival firms to enter.

When a market is contestable, existing businesses can limit the effects of competition by engaging in actions that deter rivals from entering the market in the first place. **Strategic entry deterrence** is an action taken by an existing business that discourages rivals from entering the market. By virtue of being the incumbent, the existing firm has a first-mover advantage. This advantage is a crucial component of strategic entry deterrence. Suppose a firm gains a monopoly because it is first to market (and not because

EXHIBIT 6 Strategic Entry Deterrence

The incumbent has the ability to deter entry, but doing so lowers profit below the short-run profit-maximization level. If the incumbent does not try to deter entry, its profits will be $1,000 if no other firm enters the market, but only $400 if a rival enters the market. If the market is contestable, it may be more profitable in the long run to engage in limit pricing or in other forms of entry deterrence to keep the rival out of the market. Doing so successfully results in a profit of $500.

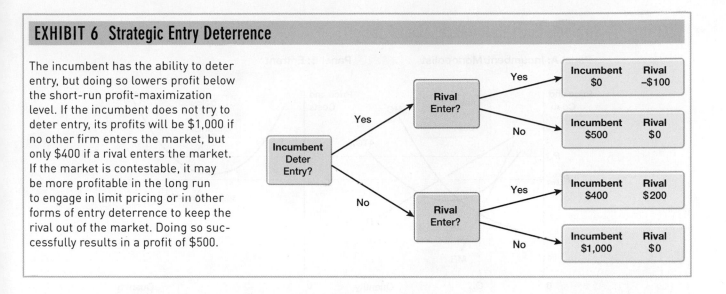

it has high barriers to entry). We will call this firm the incumbent. It *may* be prudent for the incumbent firm to find a price that is both profitable yet low enough to deter a second from entering.

In Exhibit 6 the incumbent firm—an existing monopoly in this case—has the ability to deter entry, but doing so lowers the incumbent's profit below the profit-maximization level based on *MR = MC in the short run*. Specifically, if the firm does not try to deter entry, its profits will be $1,000 if no rival enters the market but only $400 if a rival does enter the market. Alternatively, if the incumbent realizes that the market is contestable, it may be more profitable to engage in actions that deter the entry of a potential rival. In this example, the firm will make $500 in profits if it takes actions that successfully deter entry. Taking actions to deter entry often lowers profit in the short run. In the long run, however, it may be worth sacrificing some profits in order to keep a rival out of the market.

Limit Pricing

Limit pricing is a strategic entry deterrence policy of setting price low enough to deter entry while remaining profitable. Consider the graph in Exhibit 7. The potential rival has higher costs than the existing firm, perhaps due to a combination of being relatively small and not realizing economies of scale. While a monopoly exists, the market is contestable. Attempts by the incumbent firm to profit-maximize by pricing at P_M will mean it is profitable for a potential rival to enter the market. This is because price is greater than the minimum average total cost of the entering rival ($P_M >$ minimum ATC_R).

Instead, the incumbent firm may choose a *lower price*. Wouldn't this mean the firm will *not* be profit-maximizing? Perhaps. However, if the barriers to entry are low enough so that rivals can enter, then strategic decision making may try to prevent the market structure from becoming monopolistically competitive in the long run—an outcome that would mean zero long-run economic profit for the incumbent.

limit pricing A strategic entry deterrence policy of setting price low enough to deter entry while remaining profitable.

EXHIBIT 7   Strategic Entry Deterrence: Limit Pricing

Since the incumbent firm has greater economies of scale and lower average total cost, it has the ability to deter entry by selecting a price just below the minimum ATC of its potential entrant. In this case, the firm may not be maximizing profits in the short run, but will remain profitable and able to deter entry.

In Exhibit 7, the incumbent may price at or just below the minimum ATC_E of the potential entrant, but above its own average total cost (ATC_M). Recall that the potential rival has higher average total cost. This is limit pricing, which makes it difficult for a rival to enter the market and be profitable. Some observers claim that online retailer Amazon has held its prices below the profit-maximizing point in order to deter online competitors.

Excess Capacity and Economies of Scale

As an alternative to limit pricing, an incumbent may engage in strategic entry deterrence by expanding to the point where the business has excess capacity. Consider a gasoline station that is a local monopoly with no nearby competitors. The firm might deter others from entering the market by expanding the existing station: let's say installing more pumps and tanks. This provides the owner with economies of scale and sends a signal to potential competitors: "If you enter my market, I have the capacity to sell large amounts of gasoline at a deep discount." Having an unusually large gas station increases operating costs and lowers profits in the short run, but deterring entry has potential long-run benefits. This strategy deters possible entrants, while continuing to allow the existing firm to charge high prices. Examples of this form of strategic deterrence may occur in manufacturing (where a large factory with economies of scale can deter entry) and among hardware superstores (like Home Depot and Lowe's).

Entry Deterrence Is Not Always Optimal

Many economists are skeptical of entry deterrence strategies in the long run as the cost of such a strategy can be excessive. Moreover, entry deterrence is *not* always optimal even in the short run: At times, a business is better off allowing a rival

EXHIBIT 8 Deterrence Is Not Always Optimal

Romeo has the ability to deter entry by selecting $Q = 11$ and to make a profit of $9.90 if Juliet does not enter the market as expected. Note that if Juliet enters the market, both firms will experience a loss. Conversely, if Romeo does not deter entry, he may select $Q = 7$ and make a higher expected profit of $20.30 if Juliet enters the market and maximizes her profit by selecting $Q = 2$.

to enter rather than price so low as to deter entry. Exhibit 8 considers additional possibilities for the Romeo and Juliet example depicted in Exhibit 2. Recall that Romeo is first to act. Could Romeo produce such a large quantity and drive price so low that Juliet will stay out of the market? The answer is "yes," he can, but he may not want to.

To deter entry, Romeo needs to select $Q = 11$ as Juliet has the potential to be profitable if he selects a smaller quantity. If Romeo selects $Q = 11$ and Juliet *does not enter* the market, $P = 3$. Romeo's profit per unit will be $0.90 and his overall profit $9.90. Juliet will experience zero economic profit. Romeo has successfully deterred Juliet's entry because if she enters the market, she will incur a loss as her entry requires the price of her output to fall to $2 (below ATC of $2.10). Even so, Romeo can do better by producing 7 units. In that case, he can expect Juliet to enter the market and make 2 units, leaving Romeo with an economic profit of $20.30. It would thus be foolish for Romeo to block Juliet's entry, as he'd have to price so low that he'd be worse off than if the two shared the market.

Output and Pricing in Various Competitive Landscapes

While each industry is unique, it is useful to compare pricing and output for a cartel with other industry structures such as a competitive duopoly that has no collusion. Exhibit 9 helps to demonstrate. In general:

- *Cartel (or monopoly).* Lowest quantity and highest price.
- *Duopoly with no collusion.* Lower prices and higher market quantity than those of a cartel or monopoly. Price remains higher than found under more competitive circumstances or with entry deterrence.
- *Entry deterrence.* Price is usually sufficiently low and/or quantity is sufficiently high to deter potential rivals from entering the market. Price and quantity are typically not at monopolistically competitive levels.
- *Monopolistic competition.* Highest quantity and lowest price of any possible market with product differentiation.

EXHIBIT 9 Output and Pricing of Cartel, Duopoly, Entry Deterrence, and Monopolistic Competition

Prices are highest when the industry is a monopoly or cartel and lowest when the industry is a monopolistic competition. Prices determined with an entry deterrence strategy are typically lower than they would otherwise be, but higher than under monopolistic competition.

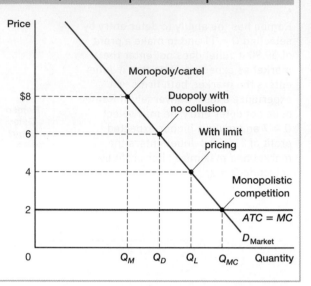

16.4 PROFITABILITY AND THE ECONOMICS OF THE FIVE COMPETITIVE FORCES

In 1980, Michael Porter of the Harvard Business School developed a model that draws extensively on microeconomic concepts in evaluating the intensity of competition in an industry. Since that time, Porter's *five competitive forces model* has become an important tool for analyzing industry structures and strategy. The parallels of Porter's model and concept related to market structure are striking. Exhibit 10 presents a variation of Porter's model with a focus on the microeconomic forces that impact the profitability of a business, rather than the industry.

Business profitability depends on, among other factors, the number of firms in a market (i.e., whether the market structure is perfect competition, a monopoly, or something else). This microeconomic force is called the "intensity of rivalries." Others include the threat of new entrants, the threat of substitute products, the bargaining power of suppliers, and the bargaining power of buyers.

Intensity of Rivalries

In most market structures, the degree of competition is a major determinant of business profitability. Recall that the potential for profitability is highest in an unregulated monopoly with no rivals. For simplicity, we focus here on oligopolies (Chapter 15) with just a few firms. In this case, when firms do not cooperate, they ultimately end up in a less profitable environment. This is especially true when the intensity of the rivalry is strong. Conversely, some oligopolies are able to obtain an implicit cooperative outcome and greater profits.

Here are a few factors that determine the intensity of business rivalry:

- *Market concentration.* The more firms, the less likely a cooperative solution will be realized.

- *Growth of the market.* When a market grows, firms can expand profitability by simply expanding along with the market.

EXHIBIT 10   Microeconomic Forces That Impact Business Profitability

The profitability of a business depends significantly on these microeconomic forces.

Adapted from: Michael E.Porter *Competitive Strategy: Techniques for Analyzing Industries and Competition* (New York: The Free Press, 1980), p. 300.

- *Level of advertising.* Generally speaking, markets with greater advertising observe a greater intensity of rivalries.

- *Buyer switching cost.* Rivalries are more intense when customers can easily switch their purchases from one firm to another. Brand loyalty increases customers' switching costs and lowers the intensity of the rivalry (see Chapter 14).

Threat of New Entrants

The threat of new entrants also affects profitability for incumbent firms. Businesses often respond to the threat of new entrants with limit pricing and the other forms of strategic entry deterrence discussed earlier in the chapter. When entry occurs, the entrants often drive down prices while attempting to secure market share. Here are a few factors that determine the threat of new entrants:

- *Barriers to entry.* If barriers to entry are high, the threat of a new entrant is low. Recall that with perfect competition and monopolistic competition, there are low barriers to entry.

- *Access to distribution.* If it is difficult for entrants to obtain distribution, the likelihood of a new entrant is reduced. For example, it is difficult for a new entrant in the soft drink market to gain shelving space in most supermarkets.

- *Economies of scale.* In any industry, most firms have reached a level of production known as the minimum efficient scale (see Chapter 11). This is the output level where economies of scale have been fully utilized. If a firm entering the market produces less than this level of output, it will be at a strategic disadvantage and thus less likely to enter the market.

- *Buyer switching cost.* If there is a cost imposed on customers switching to a new firm, new firms are less likely to enter the market. This is what keeps iPhone users from switching to an Android and vice versa.

Threat of Substitutes

A product's price elasticity (see Chapter 4) is related to the availability of substitute products, including those *from different markets.* A seller of lemonade, for example, may have to compete with other sellers of lemonade and seller of different beverages and food products. Goods with a lot of substitutes tend to have a more price elastic demand. In perfect competition, the demand curve facing the firm is perfectly elastic and the seller has no pricing power. In contrast, if there are few substitutes, the firm has more pricing power. Here are a few factors that determine the threat of substitutes:

- *Price of the substitute.* The lower the price of the substitute, the greater the threat created by the substitute.

- *Degree of product differentiation.* The lower the degree of product differentiation, the more similar products are perceived to be and the greater the threat of substitutes.

- *Network externalities.* As you learned in Chapter 15, network externalities occur when the value of using an item increases by others using similar technology. These are an effective barrier to entry. For example, the more people who use Facebook, the greater the value to those who do. Using another website or technology adds little value if there are few people using the alternative technology with which to interact. Products with network externalities face a smaller threat from substitutes.

- *Buyer switching cost.* The higher the cost imposed on customers switching to a new product, the lower the threat posed by substitutes.

Bargaining Power of Suppliers

The bargaining power of suppliers of resources, including labor and raw material, can impact a firm's profitability. The greater the bargaining power of suppliers, the lower the industry's profitability. Here are a few factors that determine the bargaining power of suppliers:

- *Uniqueness of suppliers.* The relative scarcity of highly talented CEOs or software engineers gives them tremendous bargaining power. Likewise, labor unions (discussed in Chapter 17) increase the bargaining power of workers.

- *Number of suppliers.* If supplies are competitively priced, the industry may be more profitable.

- *Supplier switching cost.* Is it costly to switch from one supplier to another? If "yes," the bargaining power of suppliers is high.

- *Substitute inputs.* Both corn syrup and sugar can be used as a sweetener. Switching from one input to another is usually not expensive. This lowers the bargaining power of suppliers.

Bargaining Power of Buyers

The bargaining power of buyers affects the profitability of businesses. For example, Chinese semiconductor maker Foxconn once made 90% of Apple's iPhones. Although this allowed Foxconn to rapidly grow, it also created problems for the tech manufacturing giant, because the buying power of its main client was enormous.[7] Situations like this result in buyers having tremendous leverage, a situation known as a *monopsony* (see Chapter 17). Here are a few factors that determine the bargaining power of buyers:

- *Market concentration.* The more firms, the more choices buyers have.

- *Concentration of buyers and buyer volume.* Boeing and Airbus have substantial bargaining power over the makers of jumbo jet engines; firms like Amazon, Costco, and Walmart have some bargaining power over toy makers.

- *Buyer information.* If buyers are unaware of the existence of substitutes or unaware of the price of substitutes, they will have less bargaining power.

- *Buyer switching cost.* If there is no cost imposed on customers switching to a new firm, buyers have greater bargaining power.

Microeconomic Forces at Work—Profitability of Two Businesses

Consider two businesses: One is a pharmaceutical company selling patented medicine and the other sells pizza, like the restaurant Maria plans to open. Can you guess which business has the highest profits? (*Hint:* It does not sell food!)

For the pharmaceutical company, the intensity of rivalries is relatively low. The threat of new entrants is minimal, because developing new drugs is extremely costly, and every product developed comes with a significant risk of failure. Patent protections give established firms a monopoly on their discoveries for a set period of time, after which competition for substitute products remains limited because new companies lack the distribution channels of established firms and the name recognition of their established brands. Moreover, the pharmaceutical company has bargaining power over suppliers as chemical inputs and compounds come from multiple sources. And finally, the bargaining power of buyers is relatively low, particularly for medicines consumers need.

In contrast, in Maria's pizza restaurant, the intensity of rivalries is high. She likely faces multiple competitors and the threat of new entrants is high. Barriers to entry are low. There are many substitutes available, including competing restaurants, as well as meals from nearby convenience stores and take-out restaurants, and of course customers can also choose to cook their own food at home. The bargaining power of some of her suppliers is frequently high: Only one firm makes Coca-Cola products and only one firm makes each specific brand of beer. Finally, the bargaining power of her buyers is high, since so many substitutes are available.

BUSINESS TAKEAWAY

Behavioral economics and strategic decision making have practical applications for businesses ranging from Maria's startup to pharmacies to large pharmaceutical companies. Each decision requires making the best decision you can given your knowledge of facts on the ground and the anticipated actions of others. It is important to bear in mind that consumers don't always behave rationally. Maria, for example, needs to factor in the status quo bias before changing prices—she may lose business if she raises her prices, even if her costs have increased. In a similar vein, cable companies know that they can raise their prices with little push back from their customers, because the non-monetary costs of switching to another carrier are high: Customers who switch providers must take off time from work the day of installation and reconnect countless devices to new home networks, and then figure out the new channels for their favorite stations or programs. Even though the second firm might charge less for the same service, many will opt to stick with the status quo.

Knowledge of such biases has tremendous value. Research has shown that when presented with a choice between two options, most people simply opt not to decide, effectively choosing the default option. Firms seeking to encourage one option over another can nudge consumers toward their preference by making it the default option. Demand can be affected by such psychological phenomena as framing effects, anchoring effects, and a status quo bias. Savvy businesses take advantage of these cognitive biases when setting prices, choosing locations, and determining their product mix. Maria may use loss leaders on appetizers to get customers in the door, knowing that she will likely sell more of her other goods such as wine, beer, or soda. Furthermore, research suggests that Maria may be able to sell more wine if the wine options she offers are limited.

At other times, behavior is more predictable, and firms can use game theory to predict outcomes of particular scenarios. In some cases, the first-mover has a distinct advantage: Maria, for example, can gain an advantage if she locates her restaurant in an up-and-coming neighborhood, effectively capturing the market before rivals enter. At other times, the first-mover has a disadvantage, as rivals can learn from the experience of the firm that acts first. In certain instances, it makes sense to engage in strategic entry deterrence strategies such as limit pricing. In other situations, entry deterrence is either impossible or too costly: It might be more profitable to allow a rival to enter than to price so low that rivals stay out.

At times, finding a remote location away from rivals makes the most sense; as we learned in this chapter, such was the experience of a convenience store in a small suburb. However, in businesses such as a pharmacy, car dealership, or clothing store, firms often prefer to locate in clusters. Since no single rule of thumb applies to all cases, the key takeaway from this chapter is that strategic decision making requires a lot of careful analysis of the specific real-world circumstances surrounding each decision.

CHAPTER STUDY GUIDE

16.1   BEHAVIORAL ECONOMICS: ARE PEOPLE ALWAYS RATIONAL?

Behavioral economics is the study of how economic decisions are impacted by psychological factors beyond rational economic self-interest. Factors including emotional states, personal ethics and values, processing errors, behavioral biases, and social pressures all affect economic decision making. For example, insights from the ultimatum game and the dictatorship game suggest people care about fairness, not just income maximization. Behavioral economics also provides insights into people failing to consider the importance of time and, in particular, the long-term consequences of their choices. Furthermore, people's decisions are often influenced by the way their choices are presented. **Framing** refers to the idea that the way a decision is presented to customers often affects behavior. In particular, individuals can be swayed by the "original" list price for an item, even though such a price never actually existed, a process known as anchoring. The **anchoring effect** is the framing economic decisions based on irrelevant information. In other cases, people tend to default to the easiest or most familiar option: **Leader pricing** is a strategy whereby businesses reduce the price of a popular item in order to attract customers in an effort to sell other goods. While the company may earn a smaller profit or no profit on the leader, it expects to sell other merchandise. The **status quo bias** is a consumer preference to maintain the current situation, and it leads people to stick with particular products or brands, and to accept "default" options rather than actively seek the option that is most beneficial to them.

16.2   BUSINESS STRATEGIES ON TIMING, LOCATION, AND PRODUCT MIX

The **first-mover advantage** occurs when the first player to act has a strategic advantage. In business, it is often, but not always, an advantage to be the first firm to act. For example, a first-mover advantage occurs if one firm attempts to dominate the market in terms of quantity. At times, there is a first-mover advantage in determining location. Typically, this occurs in small markets best served by one firm. Other times there is a **first-mover disadvantage**; when the first player to act has a strategic disadvantage. The first moving player does worse than if given the opportunity to act second. **Hotelling's location model** is an economic model designed to illustrate the optimal location strategy of businesses. It shows why firms may prefer to cluster. Clustering also occurs in product mix. **Product mix** refers to the assortment of products a business offers its customers.

16.3   BUSINESS STRATEGIES ON ENTRY DETERRENCE

A **contestable market** is a market that is easy for rival firms to enter. When a market is contestable, existing businesses can limit the effects of competition by engaging in actions that deter rivals from entering the market in the first place. **Strategic entry deterrence** is an action taken by an existing business that discourages rivals from entering the market. By virtue of being the incumbent, the existing firm has a first-mover advantage. **Limit pricing** is a strategic entry deterrence policy of setting price low enough to deter entry while remaining profitable. Firms may also be able to signal entry deterrence with excess capacity. A business might be better off allowing its rival to enter rather than price so low as to deter entry.

16.4 PROFITABILITY AND THE ECONOMICS OF THE FIVE COMPETITIVE FORCES

Business profitability depends significantly on several microeconomic forces, including intensity of rivalries, threat of new entrants, threat of substitute products, bargaining power of suppliers, and the bargaining power of buyers.

STUDY PROBLEMS

1. What is behavioral economics? What field of study does behavioral economics draw from? What are common mistakes people make while reaching economically rational decisions?

2. Describe the ultimatum game and the dictatorship game. What does the outcome of such games suggest about the goal of maximizing income?

3. What are framing and the anchoring effect? Provide examples of each.

4. What is the status quo bias?

5. Indicate whether each of the following reflects the anchoring effect or status quo bias:

   a. Joe always orders the same value meal listed on the menu at his favorite restaurant.

   b. Sue is considering buying a new coffee maker. The deluxe model sells for $300, so she views the $150 price of the regular model as a terrific deal.

   c. David goes to Kohl's and finds a sweater marked 70% off the suggested retail price. He realizes the suggested retail price is high, but figures the sweater is a great value because of the markdown.

   d. Bill's monthly gym membership fee is automatically deducted from his credit card. He chooses to continue his membership despite having moved closer to a different gym.

   e. Ice cream sellers reduce the size of their standard container of ice cream to avoid changing the price of their product.

6. Which type of business is more likely to cluster in one part of a town: car dealers or grocery stores? Explain why, using consumer preferences in your answer.

TOP TEN TERMS AND CONCEPTS

1. Behavioral Economics
2. Framing and Anchoring Effect
3. Leader Pricing
4. The Status Quo Bias
5. First-Mover Advantage and Disadvantage
6. Hotelling's Location Model
7. Product Mix
8. Contestable Market
9. Strategic Entry Deterrence and Limit Pricing
10. Five Competitive Forces Model

7. Several years back, various fast-food restaurants began to sell a small order of french fries for $1, marketed as part of their "Dollar Extra Value Menu." Over time, the number of fries included in a $1 order got smaller and smaller. Using insights from behavioral economics, explain why such fast-food chains might have been reluctant to simply raise their price.

8. Describe economic issues related to behavioral aspects with regard to time.

9. Indicate whether the following situations have a first-mover advantage or disadvantage:

   a. child's game of rock-paper-scissors
   b. location of a new superstore in a small town
   c. introduction of a new groundbreaking product that consumers are not aware of
   d. limit pricing to deter entry

10. Which of the following would be considered a contestable market?

    a. the market for generating electricity, with plants that have enormous economies of scale
    b. a fast-food restaurant in a town with only one such establishment
    c. a current monopoly selling a product with no known barriers to entry

11. What is strategic entry deterrence? What are two potential ways to deter entry? Is this strategy always effective? Is it always optimal?

12. Two ice cream stands are making location decisions along a 1-mile stretch of the local beach. Potential ice cream buyers are evenly distributed along the beach, but may not end up purchasing ice cream if the stand is more

than a half mile away. Using insights from Hotelling's location model:

a. Where should the first ice cream stand locate if the seller expects no competition?

b. After the first stand sets up shop, where should the second stand locate?

c. Where should the first ice cream stand locate if the seller fully anticipates a second seller?

d. In this situation, is there a first-mover advantage?

13. Consider the previous question, but now the potential ice cream buyers are located in two clusters. A smaller cluster is located to the right end of the 1-mile beach. This cluster will purchase approximately 1,000 cones a day. A 10% larger cluster is located to the left end of the beach. This cluster will buy 1,100 cones a day. No buyer will walk more than a half mile (one way) to purchase ice cream. Consider this question from the perspective of the first-mover.

a. Where should the first ice cream stand locate if the seller fully anticipates a second seller?

b. In this scenario, does a first-mover advantage exist?

c. Where should the second seller locate?

d. Assume that each potential customer generates $1 in profit and that if two firms are located in the same cluster, the market will be evenly split. Draw an extended game tree and explain the thinking behind it.

14. Describe each of the five competitive forces.

15. In each of the following scenarios, describe which of the five competitive forces is most involved:

a. Taco Bell enters the fast-food breakfast market.

b. Amazon enters the subscription-based video on demand market to compete with Netflix.

c. A pharmaceutical company develops and patents a new miracle drug.

d. Competition develops between Apple and Samsung in the smartphone market.

e. A strike occurs at a mine that extracts the material needed to make lithium batteries.

Tiziana Fabi/Getty Images

∧ Maria must now decide how many workers to hire and what to pay them.

Labor and Other Resource Markets

A Supply and Demand Model for Labor and Resources

One of Maria's many important decisions will be how to mobilize resources to make pizza as cost effectively as possible. How many workers should she hire, and what sort of machinery and technology is optimal? Fortunately, Maria can use the same basic marginal analysis that is used in other areas of economics. For example, suppose an additional worker can generate $1,000 in additional revenue per week. Should Maria hire another worker? As you might expect, the answer depends on how much this worker adds to cost. Just as a firm will want to sell one more unit if the marginal revenue exceeds the marginal cost, Maria will want to hire one more worker if the employee produces more value for the firm than it costs to employ him or her.

Roughly 150 million people are employed in the United States, a category that includes everyone from the workers Maria might hire to the CEOs of major corporations. This chapter uses marginal analysis to examine different types of resource markets. We begin by taking a close look at labor markets because wages and earnings comprise roughly two thirds of all income in the United States.

Chapter Learning Targets

- Use marginal analysis to determine the profit-maximizing quantity of labor.

- Determine the profit-maximizing quantity of physical capital and other resources.

- Describe factors that impact the quantity of labor supplied.

- Explain how labor unions impact wages and worker productivity.

- Use a supply and demand framework to explain differences in wages and the price of labor.

17.1 MARGINAL REVENUE PRODUCT AND THE DEMAND FOR LABOR

The demand for labor is ultimately based on both the demand for the products that labor produces and also worker productivity. In other words, the demand for labor is a derived demand. A **derived demand** is a demand for a resource (such as labor) that depends on the demand for the final product. The higher the demand for products that labor produces, the higher the demand for that type of labor.

365

Marginal Physical Product

Suppose Maria wishes to hire workers for her pizza restaurant. As you learned in Chapter 11, the **marginal physical product of labor (MPP_L)** is the additional output from an additional unit of labor, holding the amount of physical capital and other inputs fixed. Mathematically,

$$MPP_L = \frac{\Delta Output}{\Delta L}$$

Because other inputs are being held fixed, MPP_L is a short-run concept. Think of a pizza restaurant with a single oven that can seat 60 customers. Because the restaurant's capacity is fixed in the short run, labor is the variable factor. MPP_L exhibits diminishing returns. Recall the *law of diminishing returns* states that an additional worker adds less to output than the previous worker, when the amount of physical capital is fixed. Here, an additional worker adds to output, but beyond some point, the MPP_L tends to decline.

Exhibit 1 presents a *production function* similar to those examined in Chapter 11. Total product (output) of the first worker is 70 pizzas per week, so as output increases from 0 to 70 pizzas, the MPP_L of the first worker is 70. Total output from the second worker goes from 70 to 150, thus the marginal output of that worker (MPP_L) is 80. Consistent with diminishing returns, the MPP_L of the third worker falls to 60 pizzas, and the MPP_L of the fourth worker is 50 pizzas.

Marginal Revenue Product Is the Demand for Labor

Although the MPP_L is important, Maria needs more information before deciding how many workers to hire. The problem is that MPP_L is measured in units of pizza but workers are paid in dollars. Maria would like to know the benefit of hiring a fourth

derived demand A demand for a resource that depends on the demand for the final product.

marginal physical product of labor (MPP_L) The additional output from an additional unit of labor, holding the amount of physical capital and other inputs fixed.

EXHIBIT 1   Marginal Physical Product and Marginal Revenue Product

Labor (L)	Total Product (Q)	Marginal Physical Product (MPP_L)	Total Revenue Price = $10 ($TR = P \times Q$)	Marginal Revenue Product $MRP_L = \Delta TR / \Delta L$ $MRP_L = MPP_L \times P_{output}$
1	70	70	700	700
2	150	80	1,500	800
3	210	60	2,100	600
4	**260**	**50**	**2,600**	**500**
5	300	40	3,000	400
6	330	30	3,300	300
7	350	20	3,500	200

The marginal physical product of labor (MPP_L) is the additional output from an additional unit of labor, holding the amount of physical capital fixed. The marginal revenue product of labor (MRP_L) is the additional revenue from an additional unit of labor, holding the amount of physical capital fixed. The MRP_L is the demand for labor and is derived from the productivity of the worker and the demand for the final output.

The exhibit is based on data provided in Chapter 11.

worker in dollar terms. Yes, the fourth worker has a MPP_L of 50 pizzas, but how much are those pizzas worth?

Demand for Labor in Perfectly Competitive Product Markets ($P = MR$) The demand for labor depends on both the productivity of workers and the demand for the final product that the workers produce. To start, we simplify things by assuming that Maria faces a competitive product market where firms are price takers. This assumption implies that changing the number of workers does not affect the market price of the output; that is the price is constant. For instance, let's assume that pizza sells for $10 regardless of how many workers Maria hires. This price would then be equal to marginal revenue. We will later relax this assumption.

Marginal revenue product of labor (MRP_L) is the additional total revenue (TR) from an additional unit of labor, holding the amount of physical capital and other inputs fixed. Because other inputs are held constant, MRP is a short-run concept. Mathematically, MRP equals MPP times the price of the output in *competitive product markets*. It is the amount of extra stuff produced by an additional worker times the price at which that stuff sells:

$$MRP_{L, (P=MR)} = \frac{\Delta TR}{\Delta L} = MPP_L \times P_{output}$$

(in perfect competition only)

Exhibit 2 demonstrates the marginal revenue product of labor based on MPP_L data found in the previous exhibit and the additional assumption of pizza priced at $10. Thus, the marginal revenue product of the second worker is measured two ways:

- the change in total revenue from the third to the fourth worker ($500 = $2,600 − $2,100)

- the MPP_L of the fourth worker times the price of the output ($500 = $50 × $10)

Either way, the MRP_L of the fourth worker is $500. The fifth worker adds 40 pizzas to our production, and these can be sold for $10 each. Thus, the fifth worker generates $400 (or $10 × 40 pizzas) in extra revenue for Maria's restaurant.

Equilibrium in the Labor Market We've seen that the demand for labor depends on the marginal revenue product. However, to determine how many workers Maria should hire, we also need to know about wages and the price of labor.

A **wage (W)** is the monetary payment for labor, which excludes the cost and value of benefits. Wages can be expressed in hourly, daily, weekly, monthly, or annual terms. A worker's total compensation includes monetary payments (wages) and other job benefits, such as health insurance. The **price of labor (P_l)** is the total compensation an employee receives from working. It includes the wages paid to workers, the cost of any benefits the worker receives, and other expenses related to employing a worker. If we assume that workers are compensated in money wages with no additional benefits, then $W = P_l$. As shown in the next Business Brief, however, this usually is not the case. As a consequence, we denote the cost of labor as P_L (not W).

Assume that the price of labor is $500 per week and Maria can hire as many workers as she chooses at that price. In other words, we assume that Maria hires workers in a competitive labor market where both she and her workers take the price of labor as a given. Should Maria hire a second worker at a price of labor of $500 when that worker generates $800 in additional total revenue? Should Maria hire a third worker at a price of labor of $500 when that worker generates $600 in additional revenue? Should Maria hire a fifth worker for $500 when that worker generates only $400 in revenue? The principle of marginal analysis is that you keep adding units as long as the marginal benefit exceeds the marginal cost. In this case, the second and third workers are profitable, but the fifth is not. So Maria should hire the first four workers at this

marginal revenue product of labor (MRP_L) The additional total revenue from an additional unit of labor, holding the amount of physical capital and other inputs fixed.

wage (W) The total payment for labor, which excludes the cost of benefits.

price of labor (P_l) The total compensation that an employee receives from working. It includes the wages paid to workers, the cost of any benefits the worker receives, and other expenses related to hiring a worker.

EXHIBIT 2 Supply and Demand for Labor Facing a Business in Competitive Markets

The marginal revenue product of labor (MRP_L) is the demand for labor. We assume that a firm can hire as many workers as needed at a going price of labor (P_L) of $500. At equilibrium, $MRP_L = P_L$.

Think & Speak Like an Economist

Marginal analysis is the process of comparing the additional benefits of an activity with the |additional cost. It is a key foundation of economic thinking with clear business applications—from deciding whether to hire an additional worker to determining whether to close one hour earlier or later.

point her additional labor cost would exactly equal the marginal revenue product of the last worker hired.

In other words, the marginal revenue product of the fourth worker equals the prevailing price of labor. In total, firms will hire workers up to the point where $MRP_L = P_L$. In this case, the fourth worker will be hired, but the fifth worker will not. It would not be profitable to hire workers if their MRP_L is less than their wage, which is the cost of hiring them.

Exhibit 2 graphically displays the marginal revenue product for labor. *The MRP curve is the demand for labor.* It shows the number of workers that Maria will choose to hire at each possible wage rate. To understand this, let's calculate the quantity of labor demanded when the price of labor is $500. Because only the first four workers produce (MRP) at least what they cost (P_L), four is the quantity demanded.

Because the demand for labor slopes downward, higher wages will decrease the quantity of labor demanded. If the price of labor increases to $800, the second worker will be hired ($MRP = \$800$), but the third worker would not be hired ($MRP = \$700$). Conversely, if the price of labor is lower, more workers will be hired. In short, the MRP_L tells us how many workers will be hired at a given wage.

In Exhibit 2 equilibrium occurs where the price of labor intercepts the labor demand curve—that is, where $MRP_L = P_L$. At this point, businesses will employ the profit-maximizing amount of labor. This key point is utilized throughout the chapter:

$$MRP_L = P_L$$

Note that this equilibrium condition applies to workers with all types of skills. At equilibrium, for example, the $MRP_{doctor} = P_{L, doctor}$, and the $MRP_{engineer} = P_{L, engineer}$. As is shown in the next section, equilibrium in the physical capital markets (K) will equal the price of capital (P_K), and more generally, the marginal revenue product of any input equals the price of that input.

📊 **BUSINESS BRIEF The True Price of Labor: It's Not Just Wages and Salary**

The price of labor is not the same thing as wages. Although wages and salary usually make up the bulk of employee compensation, benefits are an increasingly important component of the cost of labor. In 2017, the average hourly wage was $24.33. But this figure does not include the additional benefits workers received, including paid vacation and sick time, health insurance, retirement benefits, and their employers' share of payroll taxes. On average, those additional benefits add up to an additional $11.31 per hour—46% of the average wage. Thus, the average price of labor and total employee compensation in 2017 was $35.64 per hour, not $24.33.* For comparison, in 1970, benefits were only about 20% of employees' wages and salary—less than half of today's figure.†

These figures demonstrate that although wages have been stagnant in recent decades, total compensation has grown steadily due to fast-rising benefits. This trend means that when businesses make decisions about how many workers to hire, they are looking at total compensation packages and not just hourly wages.

*"Employer Costs for Employee Compensation—September 2017," U.S. Bureau of Labor Statistics, accessed January 11, 2018, https://www.bls.gov/news.release/pdf/ecec.pdf.

†William J. Wiatrowski, "Tracking Changes in Benefit Costs," *Compensation and Working Benefits* (Spring 1999): 32–37, accessed May 6, 2017, http://www.bls.gov/opub/mlr/cwc/tracking-changes-in-benefit-costs.pdf.

Demand for Labor When Firms Are Not Price Takers

Initially, we assumed Maria was a price taker and faced a demand curve that is perfectly elastic. As a consequence, price equals marginal revenue ($P = MR$). We now relax that assumption and consider the case where price is greater than marginal revenue ($P > MR$). This occurs when firms face a downward-sloping demand curve, such as in monopolistically competitive markets (like pizza restaurants) but also in oligopoly and monopoly. In other words, what happens if hiring additional workers and producing more output lead to a lower price for the output?

To incorporate this new outcome, our previous analysis requires only one change. Without competitive product markets, MRP_L equals MPP_L times the marginal revenue generated from the additional output, not the price:

$$MRP_L = \frac{\Delta \text{Revenue}}{\Delta L} = MPP_L \times \text{Marginal revenue}_{\text{output}}$$

Without perfectly competitive product markets, $P > MR$. Thus, when Maria hires additional workers, she must consider that increasing her output will put downward pressure on the price of pizza. If she hires more workers and output expands, she can sell the additional output only by at least slightly lowering the price. This means that Maria also must consider the impact of hiring more workers on the price of her output.

We saw that when the product market is perfectly competitive, then price (P) equals marginal revenue (MR). Both formulas apply equally well in this case: $MRP_L = MPP_L \times P$ or $MRP_L = MPP_L \times MR$. In other words, the above formula using MR applies for both perfectly competitive and other markets. And when markets are not perfectly competitive, then the formula using MR is the only one that applies.

The demand for labor is downward sloping for two reasons. First, *diminishing returns* results in a downward-sloping labor demand curve. As more workers are hired, the marginal physical product of additional workers declines. Second, in all market structures other than perfect competition, *marginal revenue declines* with additional output. As more workers are hired and output increases, firms that are not in perfect competition must lower the price of their output to sell more units. In short, the demand for labor is the marginal revenue product of labor, and MRP_L equals marginal physical product times marginal revenue. Both *MPP* and *MR* decline as output rises.

Shifts in the Demand for Labor

Now let's consider factors that will cause the labor demand curve to shift. Exhibit 3 demonstrates shifts in the demand for labor, which is based on *MRP*. Because the marginal revenue product is related to both the worker's productivity and the marginal revenue from additional output, changes in either MPP_L or *MR* will shift the demand for labor. When labor demand increases, Maria tends to hire more workers, *ceteris paribus*. The opposite occurs when labor demand decreases.

Changes in Labor Productivity Shift the Labor Demand Curve Labor productivity directly impacts the demand for labor. More productive workers have higher marginal physical product and as a result have higher marginal revenue product. Labor may become more productive by acquiring additional human capital, adding physical capital (machines), or benefitting from new technology. Workers who master new technologies will be in particularly high demand. For instance, the demand for engineers and computer scientists has been particularly high in recent decades. In the United States, the average worker is more productive than workers in many other nations, partly due to the high levels of physical capital found.

Changes in the Price of Output Shift the Labor Demand Curve The price of output also can impact the demand for labor. When the price of the firm's product increases, marginal revenue obtained from selling additional units increases, which increases MRP_L. When the price of oil rose above $100 barrel, the demand for petroleum engineers rose significantly. In contrast, if the price of output declines, the demand for related labor declines. If tomatoes were found to be unhealthy, for example, the demand for those who pick tomatoes would suddenly decline.

The Effects of New Technology and Physical Capital on Labor

If physical capital becomes less expensive, we can expect increased use of physical capital. Likewise, if new technology reduces production costs, we can expect new technology to be used. But does the use of more capital and new technology increase or decrease the use of labor?

EXHIBIT 3   Shifts in the Demand for Labor

Because marginal revenue product $MRP_L = MPP_L \times MR$, changes in either MPP_L or *MR* will shift the demand for labor.

Other resources can be viewed as *substitutes* for labor. A machine that picks tomatoes will replace (substitute for) workers who pick tomatoes. In this case, the machine will be considered labor-saving and reduce the demand for labor. Likewise, machines that collect tolls on highways replace the need for toll collectors, and phones can be used to purchase tickets to movies and other events, replacing the need for human ticket sellers.

History suggests that physical capital and technology are often *labor augmenting*—that is, they complement labor. Individuals who maintain and develop the machines that pick tomatoes, those who manage the E-ZPass toll-collection system, and tool and die makers who manufacture these kinds of machines find that the physical capital complements their skills. These workers will see an increase in the demand for their labor because they will be more productive.

It often is not always apparent how technology will impact the demand for certain labor. For example, it was widely believed that the expanded use of ATM machines would reduce the number bank teller jobs. In fact, the opposite happened. Because each branch requires fewer tellers, banks have found it more affordable to open up branches, and as they expand in an effort to gain market share, they hired more tellers.[1] Recently, smartphones have increased the number of online banking transactions. How this impacts the labor market is also not apparent. On the one hand, it will likely mean more technology-related jobs and fewer teller positions. On the other hand, it may simply mean fewer ATM transactions.

Stuart Ramson/AP Images

∧ What is the impact of physical capital like kiosks on the demand for labor?

BUSINESS BRIEF DIY Ordering at Customer Kiosks

In recent years, fast-food restaurants like Panera Bread, McDonald's, and Wendy's have begun experimenting with self-serve kiosks where customers can place their own orders. The trend is expected to continue because the rental rate of capital—that is, the cost of the machines—has declined.* But are these machines actually replacing workers?

The business opportunities provided by technology are often more complex than simply offering a substitute for labor. Although the machines reduce the number of cashiers at each store, they also free up workers to do other tasks, enabling fast-food restaurants to offer new products like table service and delivery. And as was seen with banks, the reduced cost of labor can lead to the opening of more restaurants. In this case, the machines will be labor augmenting. As Panera executive Blaine Hurst notes, "The consumer-facing technology results in labor savings for Panera; these hours are redeployed in the cafe. In fact, in most cases, Panera increases the number of associate hours in our cafes; and they see increases in overall guest satisfaction."†

The bottom line is that the machines increase productivity, and this increased productivity results in a wide range of possibilities going forward—from reduced demand for labor to increased demand for labor.

*Shan Li, "Wendy's Adds Automation to the Fast-Food Menu," *Los Angeles Times*, February 27, 2017, http://www.latimes.com/business/la-fi-wendys-kiosk-20170227-story.html; Hayley Peterson, "McDonald's Shoots Down Fears It Is Planning to Replace Cashiers with Kiosks," *Business Insider*, June 23, 2017, http://www.businessinsider.com/what-self-serve-kiosks-at-mcdonalds-mean-for-cashiers-2017-6.

†Quoted in Hollis Johnson, "Fast Food Workers Are Becoming Obsolete," *Business Insider*, May 16, 2016, http://www.businessinsider.com/self-service-kiosks-are-replacing-workers-2016-5.

17.2 THE DEMAND FOR OTHER FACTORS OF PRODUCTION

We've seen that concepts such as marginal revenue product help firms to decide how many workers to hire. Fortunately, the same sort of marginal analysis applies to other resources purchased by firms, such as physical capital and land. It is the additional total revenue (*TR*) from an addition input. We can calculate the marginal revenue product and marginal physical product of capital or any other input in much the same way that we did for labor:

$$MPP_{input} = \frac{\Delta Output}{\Delta Input}$$

$$MRP_{input} = \frac{\Delta TR}{\Delta Input} = MPP_{input} \times Marginal\ revenue_{output}$$

The MRP_{input} is the demand for that input. The analysis of how much of an input to acquire is similar to the analysis of how many workers to hire. If the *MRP* of a machine is $1,000,000 and the machine costs $1,100,000, then this machine should *not* be purchased.

To simplify our analysis, we assume that the machine is rented because a purchased machine may well be in use for a decade or more, so we would need to derive an annual cost of using the machine. Thus, the rental cost plays exactly the same role as the price of labor. Economists define the price of capital as *R* for the "rental" price of physical capital; or P_K, for the rental "price" of physical capital. Similarly, the price of labor is often expressed as *W*, for wages, but it also can be expressed as P_L, for the price of labor. For simplicity, in this text we denote the price of labor as P_L and the price of physical capital as P_K.

The Cost-Minimization Rule

When a business must choose among multiple inputs, it does so in a way that minimizes the cost for a given level of output. Because most businesses choose between hiring additional labor (*L*) or acquiring additional physical capital (*K*), we will focus on these two inputs.

Suppose Maria must choose between hiring an additional worker or renting a machine that will make pizza twice as fast as the worker. Although it may appear obvious that Maria should rent the machine, we cannot jump to this conclusion without knowing the price of the labor and machine. The machine might cost 100 times more per hour than additional workers, or it might cost the same per hour.

When a firm is attempting to minimize the cost of production, it should choose among additional inputs based on which input provides the most additional output per dollar spent on the input and gives the most "bang for the buck." The **cost-minimization rule** suggests that the costs of producing a given level of output are minimized when the marginal physical product per dollar spent on every input is equalized. That occurs when

cost-minimization rule
The costs of producing a given level of output are minimized when the marginal physical product per dollar spent on every input is equalized. This occurs when $MPP_L/P_L = MPP_K/P_K$.

$$\frac{MPP_L}{P_L} = \frac{MPP_K}{P_K}$$

In other words, cost minimization requires the same marginal physical product per dollar to be spent on all resources. This means that an extra dollar spent on labor has the same benefit as an extra dollar spent on physical capital.

To see this, let's examine what happens when the rule is violated. Suppose the MPP_L per dollar spent on labor is 20 units per dollar. Further suppose the MPP_K per dollar spent on physical capital is 10 units per dollar. That is,

$$\frac{MPP_L}{P_L} = 20 \text{ units per dollar and } \frac{MPP_K}{P_K} = 10 \text{ units per dollar}$$

Since $MPP_L/P_L > MPP_K/P_K$, cost minimization would push the business to hire more workers and use fewer machines. When more workers are hired, the MPP_L will decrease. Eventually, this causes MPP_L/P_L to equal MPP_K/P_K and the cost-minimization rule to hold.

These same rules can be used to explain why more productive labor is paid more money than less productive labor is paid. Suppose that Maria must choose between two workers—Ann (who is highly productive) and Ben (who is less productive). Let's initially assume that Ann and Ben are paid the same, even though Ann is more productive. In this case, the ratio of MPP to price of input would not be equal, that is:

$$\frac{MPP_A}{P_{L,A}} > \frac{MPP_B}{P_{L,B}}$$

Under this circumstance, Maria and other firms will wish to hire more workers like Ann and fewer like Ben. This increases the demand for Ann's labor and increases her wages. Ann's wages increase until the marginal revenue product of Ann's labor equals her price of labor. At the same time, the demand for Ben's labor may decrease, reducing his wages. This results in:

$$\frac{MPP_A}{P_{L,A}} = \frac{MPP_B}{P_{L,B}}$$

In the end, both Ann's wages and Ben's wages adjust until they equal their respective marginal revenue product. That is,

$$MRP_A = P_{L,A}$$
$$MRP_B = P_{L,B}$$

Differences in pay can result from producing either higher marginal physical products or products with higher output prices. If Ann is a highly productive worker, she's not limited to working at Maria's. She might take her highly productive self to a more profitable restaurant or to an entirely different industry (e.g., one that is developing software instead of pizza).

The Marginal Revenue Product and the Price of Resources

A firm should produce a *given level of output* in the least costly manner, but it also must decide which level of output maximizes profits. Recall that in monopolistic competition, for example, firms produce an output where profits are maximized, not where average total cost is minimized.

Earlier in the chapter, we showed that equilibrium in the labor market requires equating the marginal revenue product of labor to the price of labor. This condition is necessary for profit maximization. If $MRP_L > P_L$, a business could increase profits by hiring more labor. Doing so will decrease MRP_L. Conversely, if $MRP_L < P_L$, a business could increase profits by laying off some workers. The same analysis can be applied to other resources. The demand for any resource is the marginal revenue product of that resource. A profit-maximizing combination of resources will lead to all of the following conditions:

$$MRP_{land} = P_{land}$$
$$MRP_K = P_K$$
$$MRP_{input} = P_{input}$$

Profit maximization involves equating the marginal revenue product of each resource to the price of that resource. At the profit-maximization point, $MRP_{input} = P_{input}$ for every resource, including every different type of labor, physical capital, and land.

17.3 THE SUPPLY OF LABOR

We've looked at what determines the demand for labor at any given wage rate. But what determines the equilibrium wage? To answer this question, we need to add the supply of labor to our model. As with other supply curves, we can analyze labor supply from the perspective of either the market or an individual worker. In addition, we can analyze the supply of labor facing an individual business. We begin by looking at the individual's supply of labor.

The Individual's Supply of Labor

There's a reason we call it work: most people would rather do something else. This means that there is an opportunity cost to an individual who is supplying labor. Think about what you give up when you work more hours. What is the best alternative use of your time? Although there are many answers to this question, economists view forgone leisure as the primary opportunity cost of hours spent working. This means that at the margin, the opportunity cost of leisure is the price of labor—the wage rate. If your job pays $20 per hour, then each hour of leisure means that you have forgone the chance to earn another $20 in wages.

Suppose you earn $10 an hour as a lifeguard and suddenly your pay is boosted to $20 per hour. Would you want to work additional hours or fewer hours? The answer is not immediately obvious, is it? You might work more hours to take advantage of the higher wage. Alternatively, you might have a goal of making $200 and can now do so working half as many hours as before. Economists call these two ways that a wage change can impact the quantity of labor supplied by an individual the substitution effect and the income effect.

Ralph Hagen/www.cartoonstock.com

A train station is where a train stops. A bus station is where a bus stops. This is a work station.

substitution effect on labor supply An effect that occurs when workers supply more labor at higher wages because the opportunity cost of leisure increases.

income effect on labor supply An effect that occurs when workers supply less labor at higher wages because the additional income increases the demand for leisure.

The Substitution Effect on Labor Supply Recall from Chapter 3 that the *substitution effect* is the tendency of consumers to replace relatively high-priced products with relatively low-priced products. In this case, a higher wage rate will increase the opportunity cost of leisure, which will cause workers to substitute away from the now more expensive leisure and toward more time spent working. Thus, the quantity of labor supplied increases. The **substitution effect on labor supply** occurs when workers supply more labor at higher wages because the opportunity cost of leisure increases. For example, once basic needs are met, workers may only work additional hours if paid a higher "overtime" rate. For such workers, leisure becomes quite valuable. In contrast, when wages fall, leisure becomes cheaper, and people work fewer hours.

The Income Effect on Labor Supply Higher wages also can have a powerful income effect. Recall that the *income effect* occurs when there is a change in purchasing power resulting from a price change. The **income effect on labor supply** occurs when workers supply less labor at higher wages because the additional income increases the demand for leisure. When wages rise, individuals can earn the same income while working fewer hours. Consider people who collect a pension and Social Security and want a little more income to maintain their desired lifestyle. If they find a job with a high hourly wage rate, they will be able to hit their income target while working fewer hours.

In Chapter 3, we consider a hypothetical one-time summer job cleaning the beach for a very high wage during the Olympics. If you could earn $10,000 per hour to do this job, you probably would work as much as possible because taking an hour off would cost you $10,000! This highlights the substitution effect: leisure becomes more expensive as wages rise. But suppose we relax the assumption, and rather than being a one-time job, this $10,000 hourly wage becomes a salary you could earn anytime you want (for life). Now both the income effect and substitution effect come into consideration. Some might respond by working a few hours a week—say, 5—figuring they could survive comfortably on $50,000 per week. Others might work for a year or so then retire. At some point, individuals have enough income to afford time off. This is the essence of the income effect.

Consider the labor supply decision of a star baseball player who has earned tens of millions of dollars. As his skills begin to fade near the end of his career, he could work a few more years to increase his bank account by a few million dollars, or he might prefer to stop working and enjoy the extra leisure. Successful people in other careers (such as doctors, lawyers, and investment managers) who are nearing retirement face a similar situation. Working a few more years could increase their lifetime earnings, but they may prefer the extra leisure. Likewise, some musicians can make enormous sums of money each night they perform and therefore may choose to work only a few months in every year.

Panel A of Exhibit 4 shows an ordinary upward-sloping labor supply curve of an individual where the substitution effect is larger than the income effect. For these individuals, a higher price of labor (wages) results in an increase in hours worked. Panel B shows the unique case of a backward-bending labor supply curve, which occurs at a price of labor above P_L. For these individuals, higher income allows the individual to *afford* more leisure and decreases work effort.

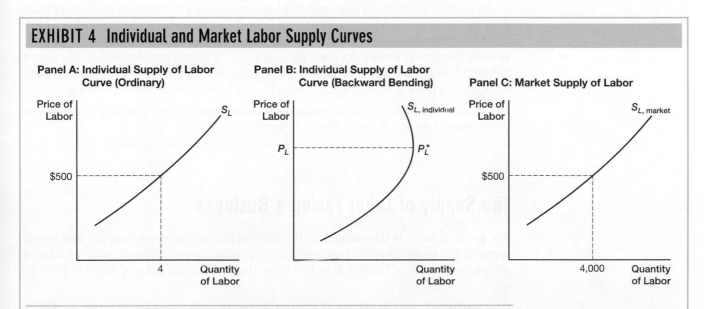

EXHIBIT 4 Individual and Market Labor Supply Curves

Panel A: Individual Supply of Labor Curve (Ordinary)

Panel B: Individual Supply of Labor Curve (Backward Bending)

Panel C: Market Supply of Labor

A higher price of labor typically increases the quantity of labor supplied by an individual (Panel A). It is possible that higher wages encourage some individuals to work fewer hours when the income effect from higher total compensation exceeds the substitution effect, resulting in a backward-bending labor supply curve (Panel B). Market labor supply curves are upward sloping, reflecting a positive relationship between the price of labor and the quantity of labor supplied in the market, *ceteris paribus* (Panel C).

The Market Supply of Labor

We now turn from individual workers to the market supply curve. Here, we do not have to worry much about the income effect; while a higher wage might make some want to drive fewer hours, it also will lead others to seek employment. Thus, at the market level, the supply of labor generally slopes upward—just like any other supply curve.

An increase in the wage rate or employee benefits tend to increase the quantity of labor supplied in the market, other things being equal. Considerable evidence suggests that the higher the total compensation from employment in one industry, the higher the *total* amount of labor supplied to that industry. This represents all labor being supplied within a given labor market—that is, a given set of skills. A market labor supply curve is demonstrated in Panel C of Exhibit 4. At higher wages and benefits, the total market quantity of labor supplied increases.

 BUSINESS BRIEF   Can Drivers Have a Backward-Bending Labor Supply Curve?

Determining an individual's labor supply is a daunting task for economists; in large part because after receiving a change in pay many workers cannot alter their hours worked without changing where they work or adding a second job. In addition, it is difficult to measure the total wage and benefit package that employees are offered.

Orley Ashenfelter, Kirk Doran, and Bruce Schaller found a creative way around these technical issues by studying New York City taxicab drivers when the city altered the regulated taxi fares. With such information, they were able to estimate the elasticity of labor supply for taxicab drivers at −0.23. A 10% increase in total compensation *decreased* the quantity of labor supplied by 2.3%. This means they found a backward-bending labor supply curve: the income effect of a fare increase dominates the substitution effect.[*]

As companies such as Uber and Lyft (which use apps to connect riders and private drivers) gain market share, economists expect to see an increasing number of jobs where self-employed workers determine the number of hours they will supply in what is becoming known as the "gig economy." If these drivers have a backward-bending labor supply curve that is similar to New York's taxicab drivers, those who work during peak (premium) hours may decide to work fewer hours overall.

[*]Orley Ashenfelter, Kirk Doran, and Bruce Schaller, "A Shred of Credible Evidence on the Long-Run Elasticity of Labour Supply," *Economica* 77, no. 308 (October 2010): 637–650.

The Supply of Labor Facing a Business

The price of labor is determined by the intersection of the *market supply* and *market demand* for labor. These curves intersect to produce an equilibrium price of labor as shown in Panel A of Exhibit 5. In this case, the equilibrium price of labor is $500 per week.

Competitive Labor Markets In Exhibit 5, Maria must decide how many workers to hire at an $500 wage rate. The supply of labor facing Maria's firm is perfectly price elastic (as seen in Panel B).

When deciding how many workers to hire, many businesses are price takers in the labor market. This situation is similar to the demand curve that is facing a firm in perfect competition, which is also perfectly price elastic. But in this case, we focus on the supply of labor facing a firm. After the price of labor is established, firms essentially

EXHIBIT 5 Labor Supply Curve Facing a Business in Competitive Labor Markets

Panel A: Equilibrium in the Labor Markets Determines the . . .   **Panel B: . . . Labor Supply Facing a Competitive Business.**

Markets determine the equilibrium price of labor (Panel A). Firms takes the market price of labor as a given and decides how many workers to hire at that price of labor (Panel B). In competitive labor markets, firms can hire additional labor without impacting the market price of labor.

take this as a given and offer employees the equilibrium level of wages and benefits. This horizontal line is considered the labor supply curve facing a firm. In competitive labor markets, firms can hire additional workers without impacting the market price of labor.

Monopsony: Upward Sloping Labor Supply Facing a Business Labor markets encountered by firms need not always be competitive. At times, large firms can have a sizable impact on the labor markets, just as a monopoly can have a sizable impact on the product markets. Consider the labor market faced by a large firm that is the only employer in an isolated small town. Alternatively, consider the "company towns" of the late nineteenth century, such as Pullman, Illinois (Pullman Palace Car Company), Hershey, Pennsylvania (Hershey Chocolate Company), or Steinway Village, New York (Steinway & Sons). In these cases, the labor market was not competitive because each town had essentially only one employer.

A **monopsony** is a market with a single buyer. As the only buyer of labor, the firm has a big impact on wages. When a monopsony hires more workers, it bids up the price of labor it pays all workers, thus moving up and to the right on the market supply curve for labor. To attract more workers, the firm must bid up its own price of labor, whereas the monopsony would prefer to pay a lower wage if possible. This means the labor supply curve facing a monopsonist is upward sloping, similar to the market supply of labor shown in Panel C of Exhibit 4.

As with a monopoly, firms need not be a pure monopsony to have some influence on wages. Market power is often a matter of degree, and the more market power a firm has, the more influence it has. Many cities, for example, have a limited number of hospital and medical facilities where health-care professionals can work. This gives a large employer some bargaining strength but not unlimited market power. When firms with monopsony power face a rising supply of labor, they are forced to pay higher wages as they hire more workers. These companies often seek out methods of hiring

Think & Speak Like an Economist

A monopsony is almost a mirror image of a monopoly. In a monopoly, prices tend to be higher than the competitive price, benefitting the seller. In contrast, when a monopsony occurs, prices tend to be lower, benefiting the buyer.

monopsony A market with a single buyer.

EXHIBIT 6 Increase in Market Labor Supply

Increases in the market labor supply put downward pressure on the price of labor. An increase in market labor supply can occur with an increase in population and for a variety of other reasons.

new workers without boosting the pay of existing workers. One way to do this is to offer one-time hiring bonuses.

Shifts in the Market Supply of Labor

Exhibit 6 demonstrates an increase in the *market supply* of labor. As with any supply increase, this shift puts downward pressure on the equilibrium price. In this case, an increase in the market supply of labor reduces the equilibrium price of labor to $400 and increases the quantity of labor demanded. Labor supply can shift over time in response to a variety of changing economic circumstances.

Immigration and Population Growth Population growth has a big impact on the supply of labor. Increases in the working-age population tend to increase the supply of labor.

Taste and Preferences People have different preferences for work in different industries, and this affects the supply of labor. There are probably fewer workers who are willing to work on steel beams hundreds of feet above the ground than there are workers willing to work in a store or restaurant.

Nonlabor Income Including Social Insurance Program Benefits Income not related to a job also impacts the supply of labor. When nonlabor income is high—say, from a pension or financial investments—the demand for leisure increases, thereby reducing the supply of labor. In a similar vein, benefits from social insurance programs reduce labor supply, particularly in low-income jobs.

Taxes In the end, what motivates individuals is take-home pay—that is, their income after taxes have been paid. Taxes on income reduce the price of leisure and increase the quantity of leisure demanded. This reduces labor supply, although the effects vary from one person to another. People who are supporting families, for example, may work full-time regardless of small changes in income tax rates. In contrast, the supply of labor for second earners in a family or workers in semi-retirement can be impacted by after-tax income. Higher taxes in Europe may partly explain why labor supply tends to be lower in Europe than the United States.

17.4 LABOR UNIONS

labor union An organization through which workers bargain collectively for wages, benefits, and work conditions; also called a **union**.

collective bargaining The negotiation of wages, benefits, and working conditions between an employer and a labor union.

Although we tend to think of economic decisions as individual decisions, sometimes individuals find it in their best interests to act collectively. A **labor union** (often referred to simply as a **union**) is an organization through which workers bargain collectively for wages, benefits, and work conditions. Unions usually are formed within specific trades or professions to advocate for and protect members' rights and interests.

Collective Bargaining and the National Labor Relations Act

Labor unions are permitted by law to negotiate wages as a group. This gives them greater bargaining power than individual workers have. **Collective bargaining** is the negotiation of wages, benefits, and working conditions between an employer and a labor union. When unions are successful in collective bargaining, they negotiate an employment agreement that is better than what workers could achieve on their own. Economic studies suggest that, on average, union workers earn 10% to 20% more than workers with similar skills and experience who are not unionized.

Unions often are able to negotiate higher wages by exercising their best bargaining chip—the threat of a strike. A **strike** is a refusal to work by members of a labor union, which often happens in order to gain some concession from employers. Workers first gained the legal right to unionize and strike in the United States during the depths of the Great Depression. The National Labor Relations Act of 1935 (NLRA, also known as the Wagner Act) is a law that allows workers to form labor unions through democratic elections, allows unions to strike, and requires employers to bargain in good faith with unions. Similar laws exist in other countries.

Richard Levine/Alamy

∧ Do unions increase workers' productivity?

An Economic Analysis of Unions

From a union worker's perspective, unions provide appealing incentives including better wages, job security, and additional health benefits and protections for workers. From employers' perspectives, these incentives are costs, and so businesses usually resist workers' efforts to unionize. But from the perspective of society as a whole, do unions improve aggregate well-being? Economists are split on this issue. If unions increase wages by increasing worker productivity, unions add real value to society. On the other hand, the benefit of unions to society is less clear if they increase wages by restricting labor supply and especially if they impose restrictive work rules that lower productivity.

Unions May Counter the Market Power of a Monopsonist Economists are most supportive of unions when the employer has monopsony power. When a firm has some monopsony power, wages are often driven below competitive levels. Unions provide a useful way to counteract the market power of monopsonist employers.

A union is essentially a cartel of workers and thus has some monopoly power. You may recall from Chapter 13, that labor unions are exempt from antitrust laws. This means that the market power of a firm with some monopsony power is pitted against a union with some monopoly power. The bargaining power of the union will depend on many factors, including whether the industry also contains competing firms with nonunion employers. The bargaining power of the firm, in contrast, will depend on the degree of its market (monopsony) power in hiring workers.

A classic example of the monopoly/monopsony face-off is collective bargaining agreements in professional sports. Although many players are able to negotiate their own wages, limits on such contracts are decided after intense negotiations between sports team owners (the buyers of labor) and the players' union (the sellers). In this case, the owners have monopsony power because they form a cartel and are the only industry where these athletes can earn large incomes. The players have monopoly power, as well, because they control the limited supply of highly talented athletes.

Unions May Lead to Some Productivity Gains Some economists contend that union workers earn more because they are *more* productive. These economists suggest that by reducing worker turnover (which can be costly) and increasing job satisfaction, unions may increase worker productivity. In addition, some unions may sponsor training programs and apprenticeships that increase the productivity of their members. To the extent that all these claims are true, the wage premium paid to union workers might be beneficial to society.

Unions May Restrict the Labor Supply Other economists point out that by restricting labor supply, unions reduce the quantity of labor demanded and that this may have adverse consequences for both employers and perspective employees. Unions may

strike A refusal to work by members of a labor union, which often happens in order to gain some concession from employers.

EXHIBIT 7 Labor Unions and Higher Wages

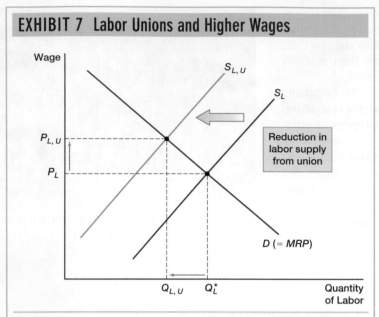

Labor union workers have higher average earnings than non-union workers, *ceteris paribus*. As a result, a smaller quantity of labor is demanded ($Q_{L,U}$). One way that a union can increase wages is by reducing the supply of labor.

engage in policies that restrict membership, such as charging high union dues or creating rules that limit who can join the union, effectively limiting work options for nonmembers. In addition, when unions negotiate higher-than-market wages, the quantity of labor demand is reduced, and there are fewer jobs for everyone. In essence, through negotiations with an employer, the union is basically picking a wage along the demand curve for labor. Because this wage is generally above equilibrium, a smaller quantity of labor is demanded. This is the equivalent of a leftward shift in labor supply.

This shift is presented in Exhibit 7. Those who have a union job earn more. However, the higher wages also reduce the quantity of labor demand: fewer workers are demanded ($L_u < L^*$). The higher wages mean employers do not hire some workers who otherwise would be hired. To the extent that union workers earn more by restricting supply, unions may benefit *only* members of the union and not society as a whole. This results in a deadweight loss, as some mutually beneficial transactions that could occur do not occur. In this case, those harmed by unions are workers who would be willing to work at the competitive wage rate but are unable to find employment at the higher union wage rate.

Unions May Engage in Featherbedding In an effort to combat the loss of work associated with higher wages, unions also work to protect members from loss of employment, often by engaging in practices that limit production. **Featherbedding** is the practice of requiring businesses to hire more workers than needed to perform a specific job, which reduces productivity. The practice deliberately limits production and requires excess staff to create additional jobs or protect workers from losing jobs.

Perhaps the area where economists are most critical of unions is when featherbedding occurs. Although some examples of featherbedding have roots in worker safety measures, many are clearly designed solely to protect worker jobs and consequently reduce productivity. Dockworkers, for example, fought for many years to prevent the adoption of shipping container systems that would render the jobs of many members obsolete. Similarly, a New York City painters' union restricted workers from using paintbrushes that exceeded a certain width, effectively slowing them down and reducing productivity. Even Broadway plays are impacted by unions: they are required to have a permanent carpenter and electrician on site for every performance, even though construction work was completed before the show opened.

These rules are designed to protect members' jobs. Ordinarily, the lower productivity due to union rules would lower demand for workers and reduce the number of workers hired. But with featherbedding, the opposite occurs: the union threatens to strike if more workers are not hired. As a consequence, featherbedding is an example of a labor market inefficiency that may help some workers but the reduction in productivity is not beneficial to society as a whole.

featherbedding The practice of requiring businesses to hire more workers than needed to perform a specific job, which reduces productivity.

The Decline in Union Membership Rates

After the National Labor Relations Act was passed in 1935, the percentage of wage and salary workers who belonged to a labor union (referred to as the rate of unionization) increased dramatically. Exhibit 8 shows labor union membership rates since 1948. In the late 1940s and early 1950s, unionization rates peaked at nearly 35% of workers.

EXHIBIT 8 Union Membership Rates in the United States from 1948 to 2015

The share of wage and salary workers who belong to labor unions has declined since the 1950s. Today, most unionized workers have government jobs.

Data from: U.S. Bureau of Labor Statistics; and Gerald Mayer, "Union Membership Trends in the United States," Cornell University ILR School, August 31, 2004, accessed May 6, 2017, http://digitalcommons.ilr.cornell.edu/cgi/viewcontent.cgi?article=1176&context=key_workplace (data for 1982 is not included).

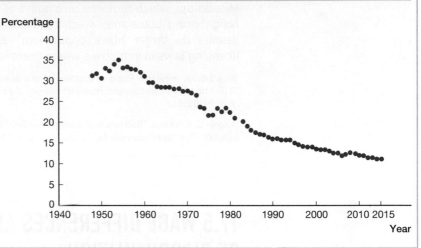

In 1947, the Labor Management Relations Act (better known as the Taft-Hartley Act) restricted some union activities. Unions, for example, were required to bargain in good faith (as were employers under the NLRA) and were no longer allowed to strike in support of a strike by another union. Taft-Hartley banned *closed shops* (workplaces that require workers to join a union before being hired) and permitted states to enact *right-to-work* provisions that allow states to prevent unions from compelling nonmembers to pay union dues. In the decades since Taft-Hartley was passed, there has been a marked decline in unionization rates, particularly in right-to-work states. More recently, unionization rates have declined in large part due to structural changes in the U.S. economy. Most notably, there has been a decline in the fraction of jobs in manufacturing, a sector that often is unionized.

The decline in unionization rates has occurred mostly in the private sector, where unions now represent less than 7% of workers. The public sector has seen the opposite trend. Prior to 1962, government sector employees such as teachers, police officers, and firefighters were prohibited from organizing, but today more than 35% of government workers are unionized. Most union members in the United States now work for the government.[2]

 ## POLICY BRIEF Restricting Competition through Licensing

Although union membership has declined since the early 1950s, an increasing number of workers have found similar protections to those provided by unions through occupational licensing regulations. These rules are enacted by state governments, often after a request by professional organizations that lobby state legislators on behalf of their members. The resulting regulations often create onerous barriers to entry into these professions. The outcome is similar to what occurs when labor unions restrict competition; some workers (braiders) are protected while others cannot enter the market.

For example, several states require anyone who wishes to work as a hair stylist to obtain a cosmetology license—often at a cost of more than 2,000 hours of training and $20,000. This requirement creates a high barrier to entry that is particularly onerous for stylists who wished to practice only a few specific services, such as natural hair styling, which involves braiding, twisting, and weaving hair without the use of any dyes or chemicals. In order to operate legally in these states, such stylists—many of them entrepreneurs and most of them African American women—would have to be trained in many services that they would never perform for their customers.*

There is little evidence that such regulations protect public health. They do, however, appear to have a chilling effect on the labor supply. A study of 12 states and the District of Columbia showed an inverse relationship between the number of hours required for licensing and the number of hair braiders working in different states: "In 2012, Mississippi, which requires zero hours of training, had over 1,200 registered braiders. Neighboring Louisiana, which requires 500 hours, had only 32 licensed braiders— despite its larger black population."[†] Economists generally oppose occupational licensing laws in industries where there is no clear health or safety rationale.

[*]Nick Sibilla, "How Hair Braiding Explains What's Gone Wrong with America's Economy," *Forbes*, January 29, 2015, https://www.forbes.com/sites/instituteforjustice/2015/01/29/hair-braiding-and-occupational-licensing /#57c703855dbd.

[†]Angela C. Erickson, "Barriers to Braiding: How Job-Killing Licensing Laws Tangle Natural Hair Care in Needless Red Tape," Institute for Justice, Arlington, VA, July 2016, http://ij.org/wp-content/uploads/2016/07/Ba.

17.5 WAGE DIFFERENCES AND THE ECONOMICS OF DISCRIMINATION

So far, we have examined how the supply and demand model can be used to explain equilibrium prices of resources. The demand for labor is based on workers' marginal revenue product. The total supply of labor depends on factors such as immigration and population growth, as well as taste and preferences for work and non labor income. To understand why wages differ between professions and how that affects the distribution of income, we need to focus on the supply and demand for workers in each industry.

Factors That Contribute to Differences in Earning

We begin by examining the economic factors that explain why some workers earn more than others. As you will discover, much of the inequality in pay between professions can be explained by the basic labor supply and demand model.

Education and Human Capital Education and human capital directly impact the productivity of workers. Workers with greater job experience tend to earn more than workers with less job experience. On average, college graduates earn more than non-college graduates. Even among college graduates, those with engineering degrees earn more than those with a less quantitative major, reflecting differences in productivity measured as marginal revenue product. For the same reason, those with degrees from elite universities tend to earn more than those with degrees from less selective institutions.

Talent and Ability Within industries, top performers earn considerably more than most other workers. Best-selling authors like J. K. Rowling and John Grisham make more money than most other writers, and the same is true for highly talented people in many other fields, such as entertainment, sales, finance, and software engineering. These superstars have a high marginal revenue product and see a high demand for their services.

Compensating Differentials and Favorable Job Characteristics You might be surprised to know that the fewer people who are willing to do a job, *the more it pays*. This might seem counterintuitive because it is commonly believed that high-paying jobs are the best jobs. Here it is important to hold other things equal and never reason from a price change.

A **compensating differential** is additional income given to workers in a job with less desirable characteristics. For example, construction workers who do dangerous work (such as building bridges, tunnels, or skyscrapers) tend to command higher salaries than other construction workers. Because fewer individuals are willing and able to do risky work, firms seeking to build such projects must compete for workers—driving up their wages. Similarly, any business that must be staffed 24 hours a day—such as hospitals, public safety organizations, and some factories—will typically offer additional incentives, such as higher pay or extra time off to those who work the night shift.

In contrast, jobs with flexible hours, work locations near (or in) one's home, or perks such as free travel (airlines) are especially desirable. The supply of workers applying for these jobs is high, decreasing wages. In essence, workers accept lower pay in exchange for jobs with favorable characteristics.

Unions As was shown earlier, union workers typically earn more than nonunion workers in the same occupations. This occurs for a variety of reasons, including by restricting the supply of labor and by countering the monopsonist power of some employers.

The Labor Supply and Labor Demand Model Revisited

Why are wages in some occupations more lucrative than others? In a competitive market, the price is determined by supply and demand, and the price of labor is no exception. The demand for labor is determined by labor's marginal revenue product, and some workers produce output that is more highly valued in the marketplace than the output of others. The marginal revenue product of surgeons is higher than it is for teachers, for example, because their output is more highly valued.

The demand side, however, does not fully explain salary differences between professions. A teacher who wants to earn more cannot simply start working as (and getting paid like) a surgeon. To explain why everyone doesn't switch into higher-paying jobs, we must examine the supply side of this profession. A surgeon must invest in years of extensive and costly education at medical school to earn a medical degree and then spend years in intensive internships, residencies, and fellowships during which they train on the job, working long hours for relatively little pay. This arduous and expensive career path tends to limit supply of surgeons and raise the wage rate for those who are able to make it through to the end of their education and training. It also makes surgeons more productive, which boosts demand by increasing their marginal revenue product.

Exhibit 9 demonstrates the supply and demand curve for surgeons and teachers. According to the U.S. Bureau of Labor Statistics, in 2015 there were 41,600 surgeons with an average salary (annual wage) of $247,520. In contrast, there were 2,027,280 elementary and middle school teachers with an average salary of $58,060. The forces of supply and demand explain why surgeons earn roughly four times more than teachers.

An Economic Analysis of Discrimination in the Labor Market

Not all differences in pay are the result of market forces. In some instances, employers treat workers differently on the basis of things unrelated to productivity; discriminating on the basis of race, age, gender, or sexual orientation. Lawmakers have attempted to address issues related to workplace discrimination with a series of laws, including

compensating differential
Additional income given to workers in employment with less desirable job characteristics.

EXHIBIT 9 Salaries of Surgeons and Teachers

Salaries (annual wages) are determined by the combination of supply and demand. On the demand side, the marginal revenue product of surgeons is higher than the marginal revenue product of teachers. On the supply side, the number of individuals with the education and other credentials to be a surgeon is relatively limited. The result is that surgeons earn roughly four times more than teachers.

Data from: U.S. Bureau of Labor Statistics.

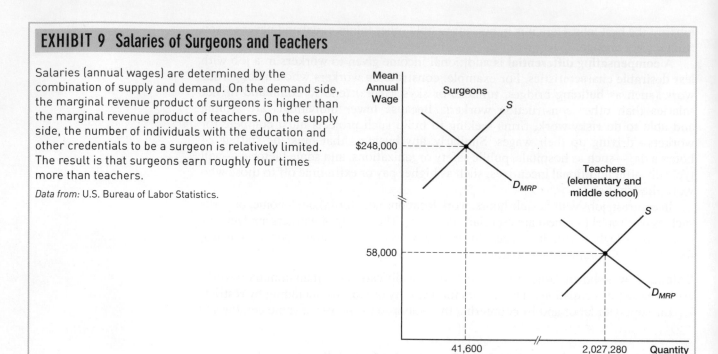

the Equal Pay Act of 1963, the Civil Rights Act of 1964, and the Lilly Ledbetter Fair Pay Act of 2009.

A truly free labor market would match the best employees with the best opportunities, but when employers discriminate, they remove potentially valuable human capital from their prospective labor pool—a deadweight loss to society. **Discrimination in labor markets** is the offering of different job opportunities or pay to different employees on the basis of characteristics such as race, age, gender, or sexual orientation.

Much of the early economic research on discrimination in the labor market can be attributed the Nobel Prize–winning economist Gary S. Becker, whose 1957 book *The Economics of Discrimination* came at a time where race- and gender-based discriminations were not prohibited in the United States. Becker criticized the then common belief that discrimination *benefits* the business that discriminates. Instead, he showed that discrimination usually hurts firms as well as the people who are discriminated against.

Consider Major League Baseball prior to 1946. By hiring only white players, teams in the National and American Leagues were missing out on a pool of highly talented professional players playing in what was then known as the Negro Leagues, many of whom might have accepted lower wages than white players. *Not hiring* African American players carried a cost, in terms of payroll and performance, for owners. The owners (and by extension their fans and players) paid a cost for their discriminatory behavior because they missed out on highly productive human capital—and perhaps a winning team.

But discrimination does occur in the real world, despite these costs. Major League Baseball owners prior to 1946 did not hire black players. When Jackie Robinson joined the Brooklyn Dodgers in 1946, he contended with racism in the locker room and the stands, but conditions improved when he started batting in runs and stealing bases and the Dodgers started winning games. As Becker notes, market forces tend to push

discrimination in labor markets The offering of different opportunities and pay to different employees on the basis of characteristics such as race, age, gender, or sexual orientation.

against discrimination over time. Robinson's success soon prompted other owners to hire players from the Negro Leagues.

Marginal analysis can be used to show why discrimination is often counterproductive from the perspective of a business attempting to maximize profits. Recall from earlier in this chapter that profit maximization requires using all resources until the marginal revenue product (*MRP*) equals the price of that resource. Here we use two hypothetical examples of Ann and Ben. Profit maximization requires

$$MRP_A = W_A$$
$$MRP_B = W_B$$

Non-profit-maximizing discrimination behavior of firms entails *one* of the following two conditions:

$$MRP_A > W_A$$
$$MRP_B < W_B$$

If Ann is being discriminated against, then it must be the case that $MRP_A > W_A$. Not only will Ann be underpaid, but the discriminating firm will not be profit maximizing. Nondiscriminating firms could hire Ann to boost profits, and this would bid up her wage. Furthermore, if Ben is overpaid, it must be the case that $MRP_B < W_B$. But in this case, profit-maximizing firms would have an incentive to reduce the quantity of Ben's labor that is demanded, putting downward pressure on his wage.

A word of caution is needed here. Just because labor market discrimination is inconsistent with profit maximization does not mean that discrimination does not occur. Rather, if labor market discrimination occurs in a free market, then it probably is *not* the result of *profit maximizing* behavior because market forces appear to work against employment discrimination.

Finally, businesses often do not know the marginal physical product and the marginal revenue product of their perspective employees before they are hired. This can be particularly problematic when an employer must select interviewees based on hundreds of résumés and applications, which is often when discrimination can occur. Employers with a lack of perfect information on perspective applicants may rely on the perception that one group is more productive than another.

 BUSINESS BRIEF Is It Easier for Greg and Emily to Get a Job Than Jamal and Lakisha?

In a field experiment that focused on hiring practices, Marianne Bertrand of the University of Chicago and Sendhil Mullainathan of Harvard University sent out nearly 5,000 résumés in response to posted job openings in Boston and Chicago in 2001 and 2002. The résumés were identical except for one key component—the applicant's name.

The study found that résumés with white-sounding names (such as "Greg Baker" and "Emily Walsh") were more likely to generate calls for interviews than were résumés with African American–sounding names (such as "Jamal Jones" and "Lakisha Washington"). Call backs occurred 6.45% of the time for African American–sounding names and 9.65% of the time for Caucasian-sounding names. The study found that discrimination occurred in all types of occupations, including federal contractors and employers who listed "Equal Opportunity Employer" in their advertisements. The researchers concluded that in the United States, "differential treatment by race still appears to still be prominent."*

*Marianne Bertrand and Sendhil Mullainathan, "Are Emily and Greg More Employable Than Lakisha and Jamal? A Field Experiment on Labor Market Discrimination," *American Economic Review* 94, no. 4 (2004): 991–1013.

An Econometric Analysis on the Gender Wage Gap

Since the pioneering work by Gary S. Becker in the 1950s and 1960s, economists have sought to explain differences in pay between genders. One data point commonly cited in the news media is the pay gap between men and women using data from an annual Bureau of Labor Statistics (BLS) report called *Highlights of Women's Earnings*. According to this report, women have earned 80 to 83 cents of what men earn every year between 2004 and 2015.* According to another large study by PayScale, women earned 76 cents for every dollar that men earned.

Differences in earnings, even when they appear drastic, do not tell the whole story and are not necessarily evidence of broad discrimination by employers. Even in a labor market that is completely free from discrimination, some wage differences would be expected. If more men choose dangerous or undesirable work (with compensating differentials), men's salaries would be higher than women's. For example, a high school graduate who works as a coal miner in West Virginia will typically earn more than a classmate who becomes a cashier at Walmart. To understand the gender pay gap or to find evidence of discrimination, one would need to compare the salaries of male and female coal miners (or male and female cashiers) who are working in the same market, for the same firm, and with similar experience and seniority on the job. To economists, the *ceteris paribus* assumption is paramount: to see differences in wages, *all other attributes must be held equal*.

To make these kinds of analyses, economists use a statistical technique known as *econometrics*, which uses statistical methods to control for all measurable factors that impact wages. In layman terms, this means comparing apples to apples rather than apples to oranges. In examining the gender pay gap, these studies attempt to hold constant all factors (other than discrimination) that impact earnings equality. This is done by comparing men and women who have the same job, the same experience, the same current job tenure, the same education, the same skill set, the same hours, the same occupation, the same job attributes, the same union or nonunion status—the same *everything*.

So what happens when these differences in career choice are controlled for—that is, when the salaries of middle managers at similar firms, with similar job requirements, and with similar experience and education are parsed out by gender only? The previously

EXHIBIT 10 Annual Full-Time Earnings by Gender, 2016

	Men	Women	Women's Earnings as a Percentage of Men's
Simple Average (Uncontrolled)	58,000	44,300	76%
Controlled (Similar skills and jobs)	58,000	56,600	98%

Men have higher median full-time pay than women, with women earning 76 cents for every one dollar earned by men. Nearly all economists caution against using this simple summary statistic, however, and instead use statistical models that hold constant all other factors.

Data from: "What Is the Gender Pay Gap?," PayScale, accessed November 8, 2017, https://www.payscale.com/data-packages/gender-pay-gap.

mentioned study by PayScale allows for such an analysis because it has many control variables. These findings can be found in Exhibit 10.

The PayScale study found that women earned 98 cents per each dollar that men make when all such controls are made. This is considerably larger than the 76 cents without such controls. The annual Bureau of Labor Statistics study does not control for factors that can explain the earning differences by gender, but other studies using BLS data also find the gender pay gap exists, but is considerably smaller than the simple average before controlling for other factors.

The differences between the uncontrolled and controlled pay gaps raise many important questions that are of interest to economists. One of the many factors economists wish to control for is differences in occupations. The demand for labor is a derived demand: it is derived from the demand for such services. For example, over 90% of hairdressers, daycare providers, and preschool teachers are females, and the demand for their services is quite price sensitive. If the price of daycare increases, for example, fewer parents send their children to a daycare provider. In contrast, over 90% of computer engineers, electrical engineers, and pilots are male. These occupations are in high demand and have a much more limited supply of labor. As a result, those who work in these occupations tend to earn more than those working as preschool teachers or hairdressers.

There does appear to be some evidence that some management opportunities are not being offered to women. As noted in the PayScale study, women are

Clay Bennett/Cartoonist Group

significantly less likely to hold management roles by midcareer. The study notes that the uncontrolled gap shows "that women are less likely to hold high-level, high-paying jobs than men. The more stubborn gap is one of opportunity rather than 'equal pay for equal work.' When we compare men and women who hold the same jobs, the median salaries are significantly closer."[†]

Differences in occupational opportunities create another set of questions that interest economists. To what extent do these differences reflect workplace discrimination? To what extent do occupational differences reflect differences in personal choices? And to what extent do occupational differences reflect unequal opportunities and bias? On the one hand, far more men than women obtain a degree in engineering, for example. The relatively few female engineers may represent choices made by women while in college, or it may reflect a subtle bias that steers young women away from classes in math and science. The gender pay gap may represent bias at a societal level, but it may or may not occur at the point where hiring decisions are made.

In addition, studies have found that there are implicit gender differences in job performance evaluations. Women were far more likely to be described as supportive or helpful in team efforts, and men had far more references to their technical expertise or specific business outcomes. The direct consequence of these differences is fewer promotion opportunities for women. But experts note a secondary consequence: women focus on how they are perceived, which is often counterproductive.[‡]

Pay differences between men and women also can be partially explained by the higher likelihood that women will experience career interruptions, most often between the birth of a child and the time the child enters school. Career interruptions reduce earnings at the time of the interruption, and econometric studies show that they also have an adverse impact on earning for many years afterward, due to reduced labor market experience. According to one study, women who have never been married or had children earn 17% *more* than their male counterparts.[**]

In addition, women have historically had lower labor force attachment. Decades ago, fewer females worked outside the home than do today. As a consequence, the average female worker is younger and less far along in her career than the average male worker, which lowers average wages for woman overall.

Economic studies also show that women often place higher value on factors other than wages when choosing their work than do men. Female workers may be willing to accept lower pay in exchange for favorable job characteristics, such as flexible hours, a shorter commute, or childcare benefits. In contrast, men are more likely to accept work that is dangerous or requires a great deal of time away from home. These job characteristics command a compensating differential (pay premium).

Finally, although the controlled studies show that the differences in earnings between men and women are

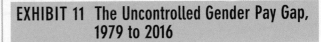

EXHIBIT 11   The Uncontrolled Gender Pay Gap, 1979 to 2016

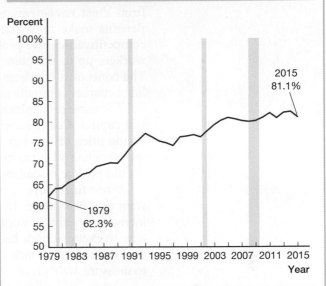

Women's full-time earnings as a percentage of men's earnings have been increasing since the 1970s as factors that explain the gender pay gap have been addressed. Note that shaded areas indicate periods of economic recession.

Data from: U.S. Bureau of Labor Statistics.

significantly less than the uncontrolled gap, there is also evidence that shows the *uncontrolled* gap is narrowing in recent decades. This is occurring as factors that explain differences in earnings by gender are being minimized. In recent decades, the share of females in college and graduate school has risen and currently outpaces men. In addition, women are making an increasingly larger share (though usually still a minority) in fields of study such as engineering, physics, business, and computer science. Accordingly, women have found increased levels of employment in high-paying occupations where they previously had been underrepresented.[††] This has resulted in a gradual narrowing of the uncontrolled gender pay gap, as is shown in Exhibit 11 using data from the annual Bureau of Labor Statistics' *Highlights of Women's Earnings* report.

[*]U.S. Bureau of Labor Statistics, *Highlights of Women's Earnings in 2015*, Report 1064, November 2016, https://www.bls.gov/opub /reports/womens-earnings/2015/pdf/home.pdf.

[†]"What is the Gender Pay Gap?" PayScale, accessed May 6, 2017, http://www.payscale.com/data-packages/gender-pay-gap.

[‡]R. E. Silverman, "Gender Bias at Work Turns Up in Feedback," *Wall Street Journal*, September 30, 2015, https://www.wsj.com/articles /gender-bias-at-work-turns-up-in-feedback-1443600759.

[**]Warren Farrell, *Why Men Earn More: The Startling Truth behind the Pay Gap—and What Women Can Do about It* (New York: AMACOM, 2005).

[††]Belinda Luscombe, "Workplace Salaries: At Last, Women on Top," *Time*, September 1, 2010, accessed August 13, 2017, http://content. time.com/time/business/article/0,8599,2015274,00.html.

BUSINESS TAKEAWAY

Business decisions on how many workers to hire are based on simple principles. First, firms must pay attention to the real price of labor and not just wages and salaries. Benefits make up a significant share of total employee compensation. Second, in competitive markets profit maximization dictates that firms should continue to hire workers up to the point where marginal revenue product equals the price of labor. The concept is consistent with marginal analysis. Furthermore, discrimination in the labor market is usually not consistent with profit maximization.

The same principles apply when deciding how to use other resources, such as physical capital. Cost minimization suggests that the marginal physical product divided by the price of that input is equal for all inputs. If not, the firm should use more of the resources with the highest marginal physical product per dollar. In addition, firms should pay for resources up to the marginal revenue product of that resource.

When firms have monopsony power, they may not able to hire all the workers they want at a fixed wage. In order to hire more, firms must raise wages, forcing wages to increase for existing workers. To avoid this, some firms offer signing bonuses to attract new workers without boosting the wages of existing workers. Workers are ultimately paid on the basis of their marginal revenue product, although it is often difficult for firms to measure MRP precisely.

CHAPTER STUDY GUIDE

17.1 THE MARGINAL REVENUE PRODUCT AND THE DEMAND FOR LABOR

A **derived demand** is a demand for a resource such as labor that depends on the demand for the final product. What determines the demand for labor is ultimately the demand for the products labor produces. The **marginal physical product of labor (MPP_L)** is the additional output from an additional unit of labor, holding the amount of physical capital and other inputs fixed. Mathematically, $MPP_L = \Delta Output/\Delta L$. Because another input is being held fixed, marginal physical product is a short-run concept that exhibits diminishing returns and is measured in terms of units of output. **Marginal revenue product of labor (MRP_L)** is the additional revenue from an additional unit of labor, holding the amount of physical capital and other inputs fixed. MRP is measured in terms of money. Mathematically, MRP equals MPP times the marginal revenue of the output or times the price of the output in competitive product markets. More generally, $MRP_L = \Delta Revenue/\Delta L = MPP_L \times Marginal\ revenue_{output}$. A **wage** is the total payment for labor, which excludes the cost of benefits. The **price of labor** is the total compensation that an employee receives from working. It includes the wages paid to workers, the cost of any benefits the worker receives, and other expenses related to hiring a worker. Firms should hire workers up to the point where $MRP_L = P_L$. Two factors cause the labor demand curve to be downward sloping—diminishing returns and declines in the price of

output as more workers are hired. Shifts in the labor demand curve occur with changes in labor productivity (MPP) and, changes in the price of output. Physical capital can be viewed as a substitute for labor or as labor augmenting.

17.2 THE DEMAND FOR OTHER FACTORS OF PRODUCTION

When a business must choose among multiple inputs such as labor, land, and physical capital, it will do so in a way that minimizes the cost for a given level of output. The **cost-minimization rule** suggests that the costs of production for a given level of output are minimized when the marginal physical product per dollar spent on every input is equal—that is, when $MPP_L/P_L = MPP_K/P_K$. Profit maximization entails equating the marginal revenue product of each resource to the per dollar spent on that resource. Thus, at the profit-maximization point, $MRP_{input} = P_{input}$ for every resource.

17.3 THE SUPPLY OF LABOR

Market labor supply curves are upward sloping. This reflects a positive relationship between the price of labor and the quantity of labor supplied, *ceteris paribus*. When examining an individual's labor supply, the opportunity cost of labor is leisure. The **substitution effect on labor supply** occurs when workers supply more labor at higher wages because the opportunity cost of leisure increases. The **income effect on labor supply** occurs when workers supply less labor at higher wages because the additional income increases the demand for leisure. An individual's labor supply curve may be backward bending when the income effect from higher wages exceeds the substitution effect. When the labor market is competitive, the labor supply curve facing a firm is perfectly elastic: firms can hire additional labor without impacting the market price of labor. Labor markets encountered by firms need not always be competitive. A **monopsony** is a market with a single buyer. In this case, if a firm hires more workers, it will increase the price of labor. Several factors will shift the market labor supply curve, including immigration and population growth, changes in taste and preferences, non-labor income (including social insurance program benefits), and taxes.

17.4 LABOR UNIONS

A **labor union (union)** is an organization of workers that legally bargains collectively for wages and work conditions. **Collective bargaining** is the negotiation of wages, benefits, and work conditions between an employer and a labor union. On average, union workers earn 10 to 20% more than workers with similar skills and experience who are not unionized. Unions can counter the market power of a monopsonist. Some economists believe that union workers earn more because of gains in productivity. Other economists believe that union workers earn more by reducing supply or featherbedding, often through the threat of a **strike** (a refusal to work by members of a labor union, which often happens in order to gain some concession from employers). **Featherbedding** is the practice of requiring businesses to hire more workers than needed to perform a specific job.

STUDY PROBLEMS

1. 📊 Describe difference between wages and the price of labor. At the website of the U.S. Bureau of Labor Statistics, find updated data on wages and the price of labor (total compensation). What has been happening to the gap between the price of labor and the average wage rate?

2. 📊 Why is the demand for labor considered a derived demand? What factors impact the demand for labor?

3. 📊 Name two factors that could cause the demand for labor to increase. Explain.

4. 📊 Describe the income effect on labor supply and the substitution effect on labor supply.

17.5 WAGE DIFFERENCES AND THE ECONOMICS OF DISCRIMINATION

Workers with higher-than-average earnings tend to have greater amounts of education, human capital, talent, and ability. Individuals in less desirable jobs earn more, while individuals in jobs with favorable characteristics tend to earn less, other things equal. A **compensating differential** is additional income given to workers in employment with less desirable job characteristics. Finally, individuals in unions tend to have higher earnings. **Discrimination in labor markets** is the offering of different opportunities and pay to different employees on the basis of characteristics such as race, age, gender, or sexual orientation. Economist Gary S. Becker has concluded that discrimination often conflicts with the profit-maximization behavior of a firm.

TOP TEN TERMS AND CONCEPTS

1. Derived Demand
2. Marginal Physical Product of Labor
3. Marginal Revenue Product of Labor
4. Wage and Price of Labor
5. Cost-Minimization Rule
6. Substitution Effect and Income Effect on Labor Supply
7. Monopsony
8. Labor Union (Union), Collective Bargaining, and Strike
9. Compensating Differential
10. Discrimination in Labor Markets

5. Consider data from the following table:

Quantity of Labor	Mega Pizzas
0	0
1	10
2	19
3	27
4	34
5	40
6	45
7	48

Mega Pizza is a price taker that sells its large pizzas for $20 and pays its workers $120.

   a. What is the marginal physical product of each worker?

   b. What is the marginal revenue product of each worker?

   c. How many workers should Mega Pizza hire if it is attempting to maximize profits?

6. Using data from question 5, suppose that the price of pizza doubles to $40 and workers are paid $120.

   a. What is the marginal revenue product of each worker?

   b. How many workers should Mega Pizza hire if it is attempting to maximize profits?

   c. Assume that the price of labor also doubles to $240 per day. What is the marginal revenue product of each worker?

   d. How many workers should Mega Pizza hire?

7. 📊 For each of the following, describe the impact on the equilibrium quantity and price of labor. State how the demand for or the supply of labor shifts.

   a. A machine that is labor augmenting and increases workers' productivity becomes cheaper.

   b. A person's job hours move from the 8 a.m. to 4 p.m. shift to the midnight to 8 a.m. time slot.

   c. The price of a product that labor produces declines.

   d. Five workers at a firm split a winning lottery ticket and share the $100 million prize.

   e. A machine that replaces workers become cheaper.

8. Look up the current unionization rates of U.S. workers. Are most union jobs now in the public or private sector?

9. Discuss the pros and cons of labor unions from the perspective of society as a whole.

10. Surgeons earn more than teachers. State if each of the following is or is not a rationale.

   a. The marginal revenue product of surgeons is higher.

   b. Teachers add tremendous value to the lives of children.

   c. There are more teachers than surgeons.

11. Summarize the findings of advanced statistical analysis known as econometrics on the gender pay gap.

12. South Africa used to have laws banning blacks from certain types of work. The southern part of the United States also had laws that restricted the employment of African Americans. Did these laws help or hurt owners of white-owned businesses? Explain briefly.

Hoang Dinh Nam/AFP/Getty Images

∧ Income inequality and poverty remains today, despite much economic progress since the days of the world's first billionaire.

The Distribution of Income

Poverty and Income Inequality

Would you trade places with one of the world's first billionaires? Before you answer the question, consider this: A century ago, John D. Rockefeller (1839–1937) was the wealthiest person in the world. Although he lived almost like a king, in some ways most Americans today are richer. The first antibiotics were not widely used until the 1940s, and during most of Rockefeller's lifetime, care for people who were sick or injured was terrible by today's standards. Women were 70 times more likely to die in childbirth, and roughly 10% of infants died in their first year.[1] Rockefeller had a sister and a daughter who died during infancy. The most successful industrialist of the age lacked many of the goods and services that even low-income Americans enjoy today. Even his in later years, air conditioning and air travel were in their infancy, and television and the Internet were decades away.[2]

A hundred years ago, there were very few government services to help the needy. People who were poor were far hungrier, less educated, and less healthy that than most of our impoverished citizens today. As a consequence of the remarkable economic progress that has occurred since the days of Rockefeller, as well as government programs to help the poor, living standards in the United States have greatly improved.

But many citizens still have relatively low incomes. Globally, billions of people have incomes so low that they live in poverty, while others earn millions annually. This chapter examines the distribution of income. We introduce an official definition for poverty, review several ways that poverty is measured, and look at the separate issue of income inequality.

Chapter Learning Targets

- Define poverty and explain the ways it is commonly measured.

- Discuss the concepts related to income inequality and the ways it is commonly measured.

- Use marginal analysis to evaluate the economic efficiency of antipoverty programs.

18.1 POVERTY

In 1964, President Lyndon B. Johnson asked the U.S. Congress to declare an "unconditional war on poverty." This led to the enactment of a number of **social insurance programs** that provide social insurance against the risk of hardship due to

Gabriel Bouys/AFP/Getty Images

∧ The war on poverty has improved but has not eliminated poverty—even on Hollywood Boulevard.

poverty, unemployment, retirement, and health-care expenditures (see Chapter 7). Twenty-five years later, President Ronald Reagan stated, "We fought a war on poverty, and poverty won." In 2014, on the 50th anniversary of the war on poverty, President Barack Obama stated, "If we hadn't declared unconditional war on poverty in America, millions more Americans would be living in poverty today." Even today, it's not entirely clear which president was most accurate in his assessment of the war on poverty. Government programs provide benefits to millions of low-income Americans, yet poverty has not been eradicated.

Since the 1960s, the average income per person in the United States has increased substantially. At first glance, one might assume that this sort of economic growth would have helped reduce poverty. Although this economic growth has probably boosted some individuals above the poverty line, the overall progress has been disappointing.

We begin by examining the ways in which poverty is measured and explore trends in the poverty rate in the United States and around the globe. When measuring poverty, economists examine income, not wealth. *Income* measures money received from employment or other activities on a daily, weekly, monthly, or annual basis. *Wealth* is the net value of all assets at a point in time (including the value of houses, stocks, and automobiles), less any debts owed. In the official data, it is possible to be counted as poor even if one owns a home, car, and stocks.

Measuring Poverty

social insurance programs Government programs that provide social insurance against the risk of hardship due to poverty, unemployment, retirement, and health-care expenditures.

poverty line (threshold) The minimum level of income, including certain government benefits, below which an individual, a family, or a household is considered poor.

poverty rate The percentage of the population with incomes below the poverty line.

Every year, the U.S. Census Bureau publishes a report titled *Income and Poverty in the United States*. The Census Bureau estimates a poverty line, and people with income below that line are officially counted as poor. The **poverty line (threshold)** is the minimum level of income, including certain government benefits, below which an individual, a family, or a household is considered poor. In 2016, the Census Bureau's poverty line for an adult living alone was $12,486 and for a typical family of four it was $24,339 (in the 48 contiguous states and the District of Columbia). These levels are set at roughly three times the amount needed to buy an adequate amount of food. In the official measurement of poverty, cash received from government programs are included as part of income. This includes social insurance payments in the form of unemployment benefits and social security (see Chapter 7). Noncash benefits (such as food stamps and health insurance) are excluded. The **poverty rate** is the percentage of the population with incomes below the poverty line.

All measurements of poverty should be viewed with caution and need to be examined in context with other economic data. Economists point to several shortcomings in measuring the poverty rate. First, although cash benefits are included, many government assistance programs that provide noncash (in-kind) benefits are not. Most notably, the benefits received through the Supplemental Nutrition Assistance Program (SNAP) (commonly referred to as *food stamps*) are not considered income in determining the poverty rate. If such benefits are included, the poverty rate would be lower than the official figures suggest. Second, when calculating income, various government benefits and subsidies to low-income workers—most notably, a government subsidy known as the earned income tax credit (discussed later in this chapter)—are not factored in. Third, the poverty line attempts to apply a single standard to a very diverse population. It does not account for variations in the cost of living, for example, or for other kinds of support that impact individuals' quality of life. Earning the median national income has different implications in Fort Wayne, Indiana, than it does in San Francisco or New York City. Many contend that setting the poverty line at "three times" the amount needed to buy an adequate amount of food is not a magic number but is only an estimate of the income needed for a very basic living standard.

Measuring the poverty rates is also flawed because it fails to account for the life-cycle of earnings. Young adults typically have lower earnings than workers in their early 50s, which is when earnings, on average, peak. For example, the town of Athens, Ohio, has the second-highest poverty rate in America at 56%.[3] But this rate is misleading because the town has a very large population of college students, who typically have low incomes when young but much higher incomes later in life. They may be poor in terms of income but not in terms of lifestyle.

Poverty Rates in the United States

Despite these shortcomings, there is fairly broad agreement among economists about the *general* trend in poverty in the United States. The official poverty rate has remained roughly constant since 1970, after a period of steady decline. This is demonstrated in Exhibit 1.

Demographic factors play a role in poverty and income inequality. Poverty rates vary by age, race, and ethnicity. In the United States, the poverty rate of African Americans and Hispanics, for example, is roughly double that of whites and Asians. The poverty rate among select demographic groups in the United States is presented in Exhibit 2.

In recent decades, increasing numbers of women have entered the workforce, boosting the household income of married couples and lowering their poverty rates. We also have seen an increase in the number of single-parent households, which appears to have the opposite effect because the demands of working at a job and parenting often conflict. Female households with no partner present have particularly high rates of poverty. Children of female-headed households are five times more likely to live in poverty than children of two-parent households.

The data also suggest that economic conditions have an important impact on poverty. Not surprisingly, those who do not work are over 10 times more likely to be in poverty than those who work full time. Indeed, not working during the year is the best predictor of household poverty.

EXHIBIT 1 Poverty Rates in the United States, 1970–2016

Poverty rates declined during the 1950s and 1960s. Since 1970, however, the official poverty rate has remained roughly constant. Note that annual data for the consumption poverty rate began in 1984. Since that time period, alternative measures of poverty have shown a steady decline.

Data from: U.S. Census Bureau.

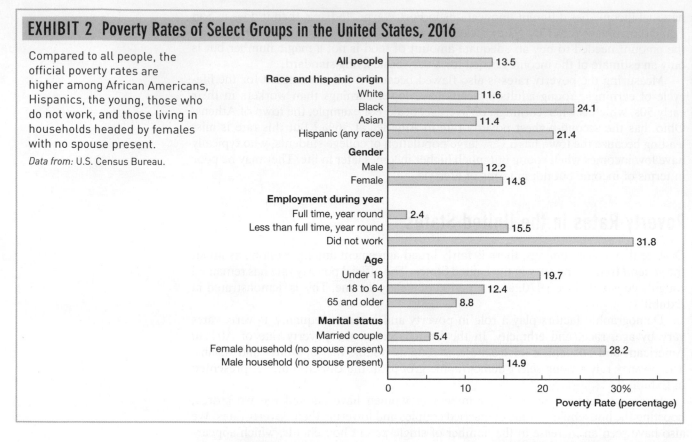

EXHIBIT 2 Poverty Rates of Select Groups in the United States, 2016

Compared to all people, the official poverty rates are higher among African Americans, Hispanics, the young, those who do not work, and those living in households headed by females with no spouse present.

Data from: U.S. Census Bureau.

All people — 13.5

Race and hispanic origin
White — 11.6
Black — 24.1
Asian — 11.4
Hispanic (any race) — 21.4

Gender
Male — 12.2
Female — 14.8

Employment during year
Full time, year round — 2.4
Less than full time, year round — 15.5
Did not work — 31.8

Age
Under 18 — 19.7
18 to 64 — 12.4
65 and older — 8.8

Marital status
Married couple — 5.4
Female household (no spouse present) — 28.2
Male household (no spouse present) — 14.9

Poverty Rate (percentage): 0   10   20   30%

🏛️ **POLICY BRIEF Is America's Actual Poverty Rate Lower Than Reported?**

As noted above, the poverty line set by the U.S. Census Bureau does not include the value of programs designed to alleviate the effects of poverty. A study by economists Bruce D. Meyer and James X. Sullivan found that if the value of antipoverty programs such as SNAP and the federal earned income tax credit (a subsidy) are included as income, far fewer Americans would be counted as poor. Exhibit 1 presents the poverty rate, using three different measures of poverty—the official poverty rate, the poverty rate for after-tax income, and the consumption poverty rate.

The study begins by adjusting income for taxes and subsidies, which provides a better measure of the money actually available for spending. Notice that after-tax poverty declined much more than the official poverty rate. The study also looked at the consumption (that is, the use) of goods and services, which accounts for in-kind benefit programs such as food stamps and housing subsidies that affect living standards. Here, the decline in poverty-level consumption was even more impressive. The authors note that "by this measure, the poverty rate almost reaches zero percent in 2007, before the Great Recession."*

*Bruce D. Meyer and James X. Sullivan, "Annual Report on US Consumption Poverty: 2016," September 13, 2017, American Enterprise Institute. http://www.aei.org/publication/annual-report-on-us-consumption-poverty-2016/.

The Decline in Global Poverty Rates

Although poverty is a significant problem in rich nations such as the United States, it is a much larger problem in less developed countries, particularly in Africa and South Asia. The World Bank and United Nations measured "extreme" poverty using a poverty threshold of roughly $1.90 per day (in 2015 prices). As with the U.S.

EXHIBIT 3 World Population Living in Extreme Poverty, 1820 to 2015

The absolute number of extremely poor people began declining around 1970 (red area), even as the world's population roughly doubled from 3.7 billion to 7.3 billion. As a result, only about 10% of the world's population still lived in extreme poverty in 2015, as compared to 60% in 1970 and over 90% in earlier centuries.

Data from: OurWorldinData (https:// ourworldindata.org/extreme-poverty); World Bank; Bourguignon and Morrison (2002).

Population (billions)

7

6

5

4

Number of people not in extreme poverty

3

2

Number of living in extreme poverty

1

0

1820 — 94% lived in extreme poverty

1890 — 86% lived in extreme poverty

1970 — 60% lived in extreme poverty

2015 — 10% lived in extreme poverty

poverty line, there is nothing special about $1.90 per day (someone is not significantly better off at $1.91 per day); yet even using that relatively low threshold the rate of poverty is higher in many developing countries than in the United States using a higher poverty threshold.

Global poverty is a challenging issue. Living standards in some areas are almost unimaginably low in comparison with affluent regions such as the United States and Western Europe. In addition, poor countries such as India often have very large populations so the absolute number of poor people is quite large. Poverty also contributes to other problems such as poor health and perhaps even military conflict.

Fortunately, developing countries as a whole have seen a remarkable decline in extreme poverty in recent

∧ Globally, extreme poverty rates have fallen in recent decades.

decades. This is demonstrated in Exhibit 3. Notice that the absolute number of extremely poor people began declining around 1970 (red area) even as the world's population roughly doubled from 3.7 billion to 7.3 billion. As a result, only about 10% of the world's population still live in extreme poverty, as compared to 60% in 1970 and over 90% in earlier centuries. This sharp decline in extreme poverty is largely due to economic growth in places like China and India because there is a strong correlation between economic growth, higher incomes, and increased living standards. Those studying macroeconomics examine the causes of economic growth in greater detail.

18.2 INCOME INEQUALITY

Suppose that all Americans were placed on a giant ladder with those with the highest income placed on the top and those with the lowest income placed on the bottom. Over the period since 1970, the top of the ladder has moved significantly higher—reaching extraordinary heights—while those at the bottom of the ladder have stayed fairly close to the ground. Low- and middle-income Americans are somewhat better off than they were in 1970, but their gains are quite small relative to the gains made by those in the upper-income brackets. Income inequality has risen, and poverty has remained a problem despite significant economic growth. **Income inequality** is the unequal distribution of income among members of society that occurs when some individuals or households earn more than others.

The Lorenz Curve and the Gini Coefficient

One commonly used technique for describing income inequality is to rank the income of households from lowest to highest and then separate earners into five quintiles. A *quintile* is a statistical unit that represents one fifth (20%) of a given population. The five quintiles have equal numbers of households.

Panel A of Exhibit 4 demonstrates the share of *income* of the five quintiles of the population. In 2016, the lowest quintile (the bottom 20% of households) had 3.1% of the money income in the United States. In contrast, the highest quintile (the top 20% of households) received 51.5% of the total income of society. Note that the figure excludes in-kind government benefits (which typically help the poor), excludes taxes (which lower the income of the rich), and does not adjust for family size (each quintile

income inequality The unequal distribution of income among members of society that occurs when some individuals or households earn more than others.

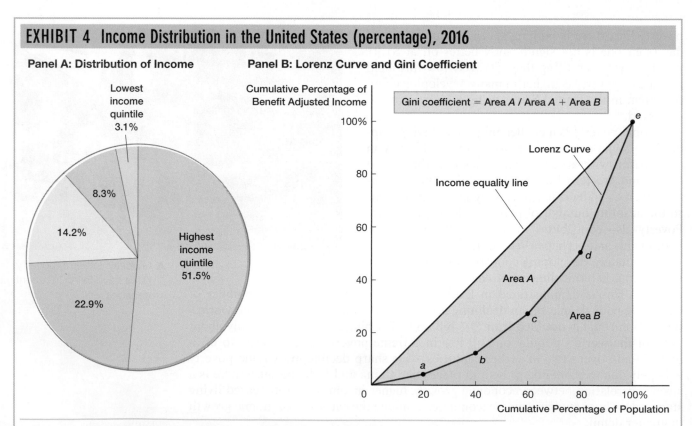

EXHIBIT 4   Income Distribution in the United States (percentage), 2016

Panel A: Distribution of Income

Lowest income quintile 3.1%

8.3%

14.2%

22.9%

Highest income quintile 51.5%

Panel B: Lorenz Curve and Gini Coefficient

Cumulative Percentage of Benefit Adjusted Income

Gini coefficient = Area A / Area A + Area B

Lorenz Curve

Income equality line

Area A

Area B

Cumulative Percentage of Population

In 2016, the lowest quintile of households received 3.1% of money income, and the highest quintile received 51.5% of income (Panel A). The Lorenz curve is a graphical presentation of the cumulative distribution of income or wealth (Panel B). The Gini coefficient captures the extent which the Lorenz curve deviates from the income equality line. In 2016, the Gini coefficient in the United States was .464.

Jessica L. Semega, Kayla R. Fontenot, and Melissa A. Kolar, *Income and Poverty in the United States: 2016*, Current Population Reports, September 2017, U.S. Census Bureau, https://www.census.gov/content/dam/Census/library/publications/2017/demo/P60-259.pdf.

does not have the same number of individuals or workers). These programs as well as various taxes are discussed in Chapter 7.

Exhibit 4 presents the quintiles as a pie chart. If there were complete income equality, each quintile would receive 20% of the income, and each segment of the pie graph would be equal in size. The data in the pie chart also can be expressed graphically with a Lorenz curve (Panel B). A **Lorenz curve** is a graphical presentation of the cumulative distribution of income or wealth. Panel B shows a Lorenz curve for income. The vertical distance from the axis represents the cumulative share of income earned. Point *a*, for example, shows that the bottom 20% of the income distribution receives 3.1% of income. Point *d* shows that the bottom 80% of the income distribution receives 48.5% of all income. The Lorenz curve is a useful way to compare complete equality with the actual distribution of income or wealth. If there were complete income equality, the Lorenz curve would lie on top of the income equality line (the 45 degree line).

The **Gini coefficient** is a convenient summary measurement of relative income or wealth inequality. It is perhaps the most widely used measure of income inequality. The Gini coefficient is a measure of the *relative* income and wealth distribution. It compares incomes among groups in a given society but doesn't provide an absolute measure of poverty. For example, if a recession and a stock market crash hit the highest quintile harder than the other four quintiles (perhaps because stock ownership is concentrated among the highest quintile), income equality will improve, and yet each quintile would actually be worse off as national income falls.

The Gini coefficient captures the extent to which the Lorenz curve deviates from the diagonal income equality line. Exhibit 4 can be used to demonstrate how the Gini coefficient is calculated. Mathematically, the Gini coefficient is the area between the Lorenz curve and the income equality line (Area *A*) divided by the total area (Area *A* + *B*). The Gini coefficient can be expressed either on a zero to 1 scale or on a percentage basis. Because Area *A* + *B* is half or .5 (50%) of the overall area of 1 (100%), the Gini coefficient equals 2 times Area *A* (= *A*/.5):

$$\text{Gini coefficient} = \frac{\text{Area } A}{\text{Area } A + \text{Area } B} = 2 \times \text{Area } A$$

A Gini coefficient of zero means perfect income equality because the Lorenz curve *is* the income equality line (Area *A* is zero). Maximum income inequality occurs when one household receives all the income in a society. In that case, the Gini coefficient equals 1 (or 100%) because Area *B* is zero (so the numerator in the Gini coefficient formula equals the denominator). In 2016, the money income Gini coefficient in the United States was .464. This means that the area between the Lorenz curve and the income equality line (Area *A*) was 46.4% as large as the entire triangular area under the income equality line (Area *A* + *B*). As is the case with all measurements of poverty and income inequality, the Gini coefficient needs to be evaluated with other data to see a complete picture.

Gini Coefficients Around the Globe

Gini coefficients represent income inequality within a nation. They do not compare income levels across countries. Exhibit 5 shows recent Gini coefficients from around the globe. High income inequality does not always mean low incomes. Families in the lowest two quintiles in the United States, for example, have higher average incomes than those in the top two quintiles in some countries with greater income equality (such as Kenya and Ukraine). Some high-income countries (such as Canada, Germany, Japan, and Australia) have greater income equality than the United States. Some emerging economies (such as Brazil and South Africa) have relatively high income inequality, and others (such as India and Russia) have somewhat greater equality.

> ### Think & Speak Like an Economist
>
> Many non-economists confuse wealth and income. Wealth is the net value of all assets less any debts owed. Income, on the other hand, measures money received from employment or other activities. Economists study the distribution of both wealth and income.

Lorenz curve A graphical presentation of the cumulative distribution of income or wealth.

Gini coefficient A convenient summary measurement of relative income or wealth inequality. It is perhaps the most widely used measure of income inequality.

EXHIBIT 5 Gini Coefficient Estimates of Income Inequality around the Globe

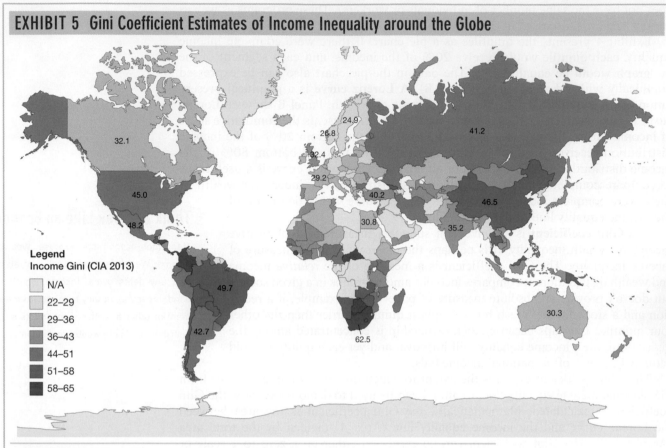

Legend
Income Gini (CIA 2013)

- N/A
- 22–29
- 29–36
- 36–43
- 44–51
- 51–58
- 58–65

The United States has higher income inequality than is commonly found in Europe, Asia, Australia, and Canada. Higher levels of income inequality can be found in Africa and South America.

Data from: Central Intelligence Agency.

Increasing Income Inequality in the United States

Many people find it easier to visualize inequality by considering the average income at different levels of society. In Exhibit 6, Panel A shows the median income levels of the lowest, middle, and highest quintiles from 1970 to 2016. This figure is in real terms, meaning it adjusts for the effects of inflation. Although all quintiles have seen at least a small increase in incomes since 1970, the increase has been considerably more pronounced for the highest 20% of earners. The figure shows that for the last several decades, median incomes in the lowest and middle quintiles have been stagnant.

Panel B demonstrates the corresponding Gini coefficient in the United States during the same time period. Notice that the level of income inequality in the United States has been increasing since 1970. Much of this reflects a significantly higher share of income going to the top quintile; particularly very high-earning households (the top 1%). The United States has a slightly lower poverty rate and higher income inequality than other large, highly developed economies such as Germany and Japan.

Causes of Increasing Income Inequality

Some inequality in terms of income and wealth is to be expected because individuals differ in terms of their productivity, willingness to work long hours, and propensity to save and invest. However, the recent *increase* in inequality is of interest to economists. The following factors explain at least part of the trend toward greater inequality.

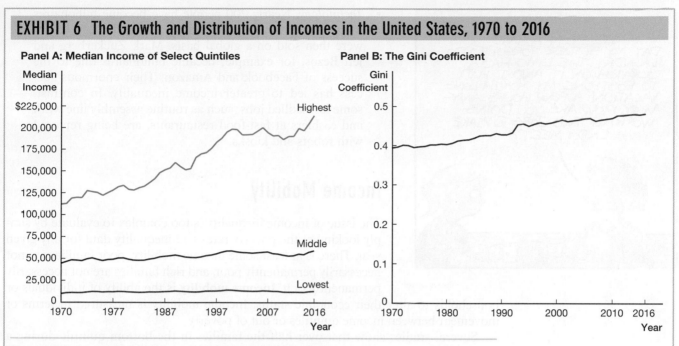

EXHIBIT 6 The Growth and Distribution of Incomes in the United States, 1970 to 2016

Panel A: Median Income of Select Quintiles

Panel B: The Gini Coefficient

Since 1970, the median income of the highest quintile of earners has steadily increased, and the median income of other quintiles has remained stagnant (Panel A). As a consequence, the Gini coefficient has been increasing (Panel B). Note that in Panel A the figures attempt to measure actual living standards by removing the effects of inflation. Actual incomes in current dollars have risen substantially for all groups, but much of that gain has been offset by inflation.

Data from: U.S. Census Bureau.

- *Higher Education.* The gap between the earnings of those with only a high school diploma (or no high school diploma) and those with a college or advanced degree has widened. As the number of individuals with a college degree has increased, those without a degree are often left behind.

- *Skill-Based Economy.* In recent decades, human capital has become increasingly important in our economy. As the economy has focused on service businesses that include scientific research and professional skills, workers with highly specialized skills have done remarkably well, while those without such skills have fallen behind.

- *Globalization.* Increased international trade has increased the demand for highly skilled workers in the United States because some U.S. exports are made using cutting-edge technology. At the same time, globalization has decreased the demand for U.S. low-skilled workers, who now complete directly or indirectly with low-skilled workers around the globe.

- *Dual-Income Households.* In earlier decades, the spouse of a high earner often stayed at home doing unpaid child care and housework. Today, high-income households are increasingly likely to be families with two earners. The growth in the number of two-income households has widened the gap between low quintiles and high quintiles. In addition, high-income people are more likely to marry and increasingly tend to marry other individuals with high levels of education.

- *Single-Parent Households.* There has been an increase in the number of households with children headed by a single parent. As noted above, poverty rates are particularly high among female heads of households with no partner present.

Nate Fakes/cartoonstock

CartoonStock.com

- *Technology.* Nearly 200 people have become billionaires because they were able to master new technologies that were then sold on a global basis. Mark Zuckerberg and Jeff Bezos, for example, became billionaires due to the success of Facebook and Amazon. Their enormous success has led to greater income inequality. In contrast, some low-skilled jobs, such as routine assembly line work and cashiers at fast-food restaurants, are being replaced with robots and kiosks.

Income Mobility

The issue of income inequality is too complex to evaluate by simply looking at the poverty rates and inequality data for any given year. There is at least some income mobility: poor families are not necessarily permanently poor, and rich families are not necessarily permanently rich. **Income mobility** is the ability of individuals or households to alter their economic status. Income mobility is measured in terms of movement between income quintiles or out of poverty.

Several studies show that over half the families in the bottom quintile during a given year move up to a higher quintile 10 years later. This is partly due to lifecycle effects: average earnings typically peak for individuals in their 50s. One study conducted by the Internal Revenue Service divided families into quintiles in 1996 and then observed their rankings in 2005. Although 42.6% of families in the lowest quintile remained there in 2005, over half moved out of that quintile, with nearly 3 in 10 moving to the middle quintile or above. Another study showed that 73% of Americans spend at least one year in the top quintile.[4] Thus, there is substantial income mobility in the United States, and not all who are poor today will remain poor throughout their lives.

Other evidence of income mobility can be found by looking at the ability of households to move out of poverty. A 2014 U.S. Census Bureau report analyzes households for a 36-month period between January 2009 and December 2011.[5] Note that in 2009, the economy was in a severe recession. During this period of time,

- For at least 2 months, 31.6% of the population was in poverty, an increase from 27.1% between January 2005 and December 2007.
- Only 3.5% of the population was in poverty for all 36 months.
- About 35.4% of the population that was in poverty in 2009 was not in poverty in 2011.
- About 5.4% of the population that was not in poverty in 2009 was in poverty in 2011.

Although there is substantial income mobility in our society, there also appears to be a group of individuals who remain in poverty throughout much of their lives. Some of these individuals are unable to work due to disability or other issues. Many single mothers struggle to earn money while also taking care of small children. These and other factors make it difficult to eliminate poverty, which is one reason that most governments offer programs aimed at boosting the living standards of low-income households.

 POLICY BRIEF Thomas Piketty and the Top One Percent

income mobility The ability of individuals or households to alter their economic status.

In 2013, Thomas Piketty of the Paris School of Economics drew attention to the issue of income inequality with his book *Capital in the Twenty-First Century.*[*] Most of the countries he examines experienced a dramatic drop in the share of income

EXHIBIT 7 The Share of Income Going to the Top One Percent and the Bottom 50 Percent in United States, 1962 to 2014

The share of pretax income going to the top one percent of income earners declined for many decades prior to 1976, at which time the pattern reversed. The share of income going to the bottom 50% of earners has decreased since 1969.

Data from: World Wealth & Income Database.

going to top earners around the time of the Great Depression and World War II. As shown in Exhibit 7 starting around 1976, the share of income going to the top earners began to increase in the United States, and since 1969, the share of income going to the bottom half of earners has declined sharply. A similar pattern was experienced in Canada and the United Kingdom but was *not* seen in France, Germany, and Japan, where inequality has increased only modestly or not at all.

In his analysis, Piketty uses data from income tax records. Critics contend that such data can be problematic particularly for years prior to World War II because not everyone completed tax returns. For this reason, data on the bottom half of earners is not available prior to 1962. Nonetheless, Piketty's data is useful in spotting general historic trends.

Two facts stand out when examining earners in the top one percent. First, their share of national income has more than doubled—from 10% in the mid-1970s to 20% today. Second, and perhaps more important, the *extremely rich*—the top one percent of the top one percent—did particularly well. The share of income going to this group, which represents 0.01% of the population, quadrupled from roughly 1% to over 4%. Currently, the extremely rich earn about a fifth of the share of income going to the top one percent and are largely driving recent trends in income inequality.

*Thomas Piketty, *Capitalism in the Twenty-First Century*, trans. Arthur Goldhammer (Cambridge, MA: Harvard UP, 2013).

18.3 THE BASIC ECONOMICS OF INCOME REDISTRIBUTION

The persistence of income inequality has led to various government policies to address the issue, including antipoverty programs and progressive income taxes (see Chapter 7). Recall that a progressive tax system puts a higher tax rate on individuals with higher incomes both to reduce income inequality and to fund government programs. This raises an important question: What does economics tell us about ways to reduce inequality?

In Chapter 1, you learned that there is often a trade-off between *equity* (which is a general sense of fairness in the distribution of income) and *efficiency* (which is an attempt to maximize output). Efforts to achieve greater equity may result in less efficiency, and economists are divided on the normative questions that surround these issues.

To help policymakers to understand the trade-offs between equity and efficiency, economists have introduced *marginal analysis* into the discussion of ideal antipoverty programs and developed the concept of the *implicit marginal tax rate* (implicit MTR). To understand this concept, let's first review the *marginal tax rate*—the amount of additional taxes one pays from an additional dollar of income. If the marginal tax rate is very high, then the incentive to work harder is reduced. Very high tax rates on labor or products also generate enormous deadweight loss (see Chapter 7).

This disincentive effect applies not only to taxes but also to government benefits that people might *lose* if they earn more income. The implicit marginal tax rate is the amount of additional taxes that are paid and benefits that are forgone from an additional dollar in income. Suppose that a low-income worker is offered a chance to work a few extra hours and increases his or her income by $100 per week. But also suppose that this higher income leads to another $20 dollars in taxes and a reduction of $50 in government benefits such as food stamps. In this case, earning an extra $100 would make the worker only $30 per week better off. Because $70 of the extra income is lost through higher taxes and reduced benefits, economists would say that this worker faces an implicit marginal tax rate of 70%. Such a rate reduces economic efficiency in much the same way as an ordinary tax rate of 70% reduces economic efficiency.

A rate of 70% is considered a relatively high implicit marginal tax rate, but in the real world, the implicit MTR occasionally exceeds 100%. In such cases, an increase in income results in the loss of so many benefits that people are actually *worse off* when they earn more money. These high implicit MTRs typically occur for individuals at the poverty line or slightly above—the point at which government programs are phased out. An extremely high implicit MTR can generate a large deadweight loss by reducing workforce participation.

When economists use marginal analysis to create antipoverty programs, the goal is to provide assistance while also incentivizing low-income people to improve their economic situation. To do this, economists have played a role in designing public policies such as the **earned income tax credit (EITC)**, a tax credit that is designed to supplement the earnings of low-income workers by providing a subsidy for working. Economists widely believe the EITC is an extremely effective tool for reducing poverty among the working poor. Instead of taxing income at low-paying jobs, the government subsidizes it, so many workers in low-wage jobs receive money from both an employer and the government. The effect is to reduce the implicit marginal tax rate associated with the reduction in other government benefits that occurs at the same time. This increases the incentive to continue to work because workers are able to keep more of their pay.

In 2016, more than 26 million working families received the earned income tax credit. The credit begins with the first dollar of earned income and *increases* with greater earnings until the maximum benefit is reached. The disincentive to work is less severe because the loss of government benefits is partly offset by the wage subsidy provided by the EITC program.

Exhibit 8 shows the earned income tax credit for a married family with three children in 2017. Initially, the EITC *phases in* by providing a tax credit of 45 cents for

earned income tax credit (EITC) A tax credit that is designed to supplement the earnings of low-income workers by providing a subsidy for working.

Think & Speak Like an Economist

People rely on marginal analysis when deciding how much labor to supply. When implicit marginal tax rates are excessively high, the marginal benefit from working additional hours is low. This reduces the incentive to work additional hours.

EXHIBIT 8 Design of the Earned Income Tax Credit, 2017

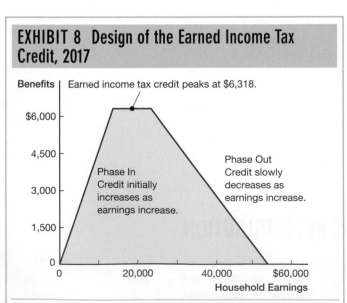

The earned income tax credit reduces the implicit marginal tax rate by providing a subsidy for the working poor.

every dollar earned. As a consequence, an individual with a job that pays $14 per hour receives over $20 per hour with the EITC. This occurs until earnings reach $14,040. At this point, the credit peaks at $6,318, where it remains until earnings reach $23,930. Those with higher earnings have their credit *phased out* at a rate of 21 cents for every dollar earned. The phaseout is designed to be slow, which keeps the implicit MTR as low as possible, and the benefit is not completely phased out until earnings exceed $53,930 (just under the median income). A smaller EITC exists for families with fewer children and for singles, but the basic design element remains the same.

In recent years, other economists and business leaders have looked at the complicated categories of antipoverty programs and advocated a simpler *universal basic income*. In 2017, for example, Facebook CEO Mark Zuckerberg called for such a program in a commencement address he delivered at Harvard University.[6]

Under this plan, all Americans would receive a basic income from the government, perhaps $10,000 per year, and this program would replace many other poverty programs, which are costly to administer. Proponents say this plan would give the poor an incentive to work hard because they would not lose this benefit even if they take a job or marry. Under current poverty programs, taking a job or marrying can result in a loss of benefits.

Critics of a universal basic income program tend to fall into one of three camps. Some people worry that the poor would not spend this money wisely, and they tend to favor in-kind programs (like food stamps, housing subsidies, and Medicaid) to ensure that government benefits address basic necessities. Others worry that giving all Americans a basic income would be very expensive and require higher taxes, which could slow the economy. Finally, some oppose giving benefits to able-bodied people who choose not to work.

 POLICY BRIEF An Experiment with Universal Basic Income

In 2016, GiveDirectly, a nonprofit organization, began giving 95 people in Kenya a universal basic income of roughly $22 per month for 12 years.[*] For nearly half the participants, this amounted to largest sum of money they ever had. According a survey by GiveDirectly conducted in the early months of the experiment, participants used the money to purchase food, fishing equipment, livestock, and health care; to pay for school tuition; and to start their own businesses. Moreover, they appeared to decrease their consumption of tobacco and alcohol.[†]

Perhaps most important from an economics perspective, people did not use the money to stop working, in part because the benefit does not decrease with additional income as is often the case with many government-run programs. In effect, the program is designed with an implicit marginal tax rate of zero.

[*]Dylan Matthews, "This Kenyan Experiment Seeks to Dispel an Insidious Myth About Poor People," *Vox*, March 6, 2017, accessed November 9, 2017, https://www.vox.com/policy-and-politics/2017/3/6/14007230/kenya-basic-income-givedirectly-experiment-village.

[†]Joe Hutson and Caroline Teti, "What It's Like to Receive a Basic Income," Give Directly (blog), February 23, 2017, https://www.givedirectly.org/blog-post?id=1423924916713458127.

BUSINESS TAKEAWAY

A free-market system can lead to considerable income inequality. A century ago, men like John D. Rockefeller and Henry Ford grew rich over many decades, but today, tech entrepreneurs such as Mark Zuckerberg and Jeff Bezos have become billionaires at relatively young ages due the success of their business ventures. Unusually large profits earned in fields like technology and finance have recently led to an increase in income inequality, especially at the top.

Since the days of Adam Smith, economists have widely believed in the benefits of markets and trade because few people engage in transactions from which they do not receive some benefit. Today, most economists support the basic capitalist framework as a spur to innovation and economic growth. This growth has produced so many new products that today, Americans of modest means enjoy better health, more access to information, and even many everyday luxuries that were unavailable to wealthy men like Rockefeller and Ford a century ago.

There is fairly widespread support for *some* redistribution of income, either by providing government benefits to the poor or through a progressive tax system. However, economists do not agree on specifics. One key issue to be mindful of in designing an antipoverty program is the importance of the implicit marginal tax rate. Another key issue is how far redistribution can go without discouraging business investment, entrepreneurship, and the hard work that fosters economic growth. At the international level, economic growth spurred by international trade has reduced extreme poverty in countries such as China and India, although poverty in many developing countries remains much more severe than it is in the United States.

CHAPTER STUDY GUIDE

18.1 POVERTY

Due to concerns about poverty, the government has passed numerous **social insurance programs**; government programs that provide social insurance against the risk of hardship due to poverty, unemployment, retirement, and health-care expenditures. The **poverty line (threshold)** is the minimum level of income, including certain government benefits, below which an individual, a family, or a household is considered poor. The **poverty rate** is the percentage of the population with incomes, including certain entitlement benefits, that are below the poverty line. In the United States, official poverty rates have been roughly constant since 1970 after a period of steady decline. If noncash government benefits are included, then poverty rates have continued to decline. Developing nations have recently seen a significant reduction in poverty.

18.2 INCOME INEQUALITY

Income inequality is the unequal distribution of income among members of society that occurs when some individuals or households earn more than others. One method of measuring income inequality is to rank the income of households from lowest to highest and then separate earners into five quintiles and observe differences in income levels. A **Lorenz curve** is a graphical presentation of the cumulative distribution of income or wealth. The **Gini coefficient** is a convenient summary measurement of relative income or wealth inequality. It captures the extent to which the Lorenz curve deviates from the diagonal income equality line. In the United

States, income inequality has increased because of differing levels of higher education, the shift to a skill-based economy, globalization, the increase in dual-income households and single-parent households, and technology. **Income mobility** is the ability of individuals or households to alter their economic status. Income mobility is measured in terms of movement between income quintiles or out of poverty. Not everyone who is poor today will remain poor throughout his or her life.

18.3 THE BASIC ECONOMICS OF INCOME REDISTRIBUTION

There are no easy answers for addressing income inequality and poverty. To help policymakers with such issues, economists use marginal analysis and the concept of the *implicit marginal tax rate*. One method of assisting those with low earnings that is popular with economists is the **earned income tax credit (EITC)**, a tax credit that is designed to supplement the earnings of low-income workers by providing a subsidy for working. The program reduces implicit marginal tax rates of low income workers.

TOP TEN TERMS AND CONCEPTS

(1) Social Insurance

(2) Poverty Line

(3) Poverty Rate

(4) Income Inequality

STUDY PROBLEMS

1. Which is more unequal—the incomes earned by the public or the consumption levels of the public?

2. Explain which government policies are included as income in estimating poverty rates. Which are excluded?

3. What is the lifecycle effect on poverty rates? Why are so few elderly people living in poverty in the United States?

4. What has happened to the rate of extreme poverty in the world? Using data from the World Bank and the United Nations, update the summary findings.

5. What are Lorenz curves? What is the Gini coefficient? Graph a sample Lorenz curve, and use it to explain how the Gini coefficient is determined.

6. Some people have argued that although inequality is worsening in the United States and most other countries, there is less inequality globally. How could inequality worsen within most countries but be less of a problem globally? (*Hint:* What must be true of the growth rate of developing countries for this to be occur?)

7. Describe what share of income has been going to the top one percent and to the top 1/100th of one percent in recent decades in the United States.

8. What are the causes for the recent increase in income inequality in the United States?

9. Since 1980, average incomes in China have risen very rapidly, and income inequality has increased. Do these facts tell us how the poor have fared in China? Why or why not?

Rawpixel.com/Shutterstock

∧ What makes the markets for used cars, healthcare and insurance different from other markets?

Information, Insurance, and Health Care

Markets with Adverse Selection and Asymmetric Information

If you've ever shopped for (or even considered shopping for) a used car, you know that the process can be daunting. You might set certain criteria (e.g., a particular model, year, and mileage limit) and consult websites like Kelley Blue Book or Edmunds to get a sense of what you should expect to pay. But even if you find a car that satisfies all the boxes on your list, you won't know the whole story. How well has the car been maintained? Was it driven primarily on highways or on congested city roads? Has it ever been in an accident? Does it have a history of mechanical problems?

Simple economic models often come up short when buyers and sellers of products do not have equal information about a product or service. In economics, this imbalance is referred to as asymmetric information, and it affects more than just used cars. Asymmetric information is prevalent in markets like health care, used cars, and insurance. This chapter examines the ways that these markets are distorted when there is an information imbalance. We also examine health care in the United States. Because it is easier to envision the economics of asymmetric information by examining the market for used automobiles, we begin by looking at this market.

Chapter Learning Targets

- Explain the concept of asymmetric information and adverse selection.

- Identify adverse selection in the insurance market.

- Discuss the health-care system of the United States.

19.1 THE PROBLEM OF ASYMMETRIC INFORMATION AND ADVERSE SELECTION

Throughout the text, we usually assume that buyers and sellers have the same information. In reality, one participant is often less informed about a product's quality than another participant. Consider the following examples:

- The seller of a used automobile often knows more about the car's problems and history than a potential buyer does.

407

- Candidates at job interviews often know more about their actual skills than does the potential employer.

- Individuals buying health insurance often know more about their likelihood of making an insurance claim than does the insurance company.

- A borrower applying for a car loan or home mortgage often knows more about his or her ability to repay a loan than do lenders.

- Doctors may know more about various treatment options than do their patients.

In each of these instances, buyers and sellers do not have access to the same level of information about a product or service. When this problem of unequal information occurs, basic economic models need to be revised.

Asymmetric information refers to an exchange where one party has better information than the other. In some cases (such as selling a used car, hiring a new employee, or prescribing medical treatments), the buyer (the car buyer, employer, or patient) is often less informed than the seller (the car seller, job applicant, or doctor). The reverse is often true for lending and insurance. Borrowers and insurance buyers are often better informed than banks or insurance companies are about their ability to repay loans or probability of collecting on an insurance policy. We began by analyzing asymmetric information in the market for used automobiles. Later in the chapter, we explore how asymmetric information impacts the markets for insurance and health care.

Adverse Selection in the Market for Used Automobiles

Exhibit 1 demonstrates the market for used automobiles. For simplicity, we assume two types of cars, lemons and plums. Lemons are cars with hidden defects that are known by the seller but are not apparent to buyers at the time of purchase. A plum is a highly desirable car that is free from defects.

It will help to begin our analysis by assuming that information is symmetrical (both sides have equal information) and then to look at the impact of asymmetric information. If everyone knows the exact quality of each car, then a separate equilibrium price will be reached in each market for each quality level of cars. The demand for lemons will reflect the full knowledge, among both buyers and sellers, that the car is a lemon. Likewise, the demand for plums will reflect the fact the car is a plum. In Exhibit 1, we can see that the equilibrium price of a lemon is $6,000 in Panel A and the equilibrium price of a plum is $10,000 in Panel B.

The problem is that buyers of a plum have no way of knowing whether the car they are buying is a lemon or a plum, and the buyers are aware that their lack of knowledge puts them at risk. They also know that sellers of lemons have an incentive to present their cars as plums. The risk of buying a lemon when the buyer wants a plum has the effect of lowering the demand for plums. This is shown in Panel B of Exhibit 1 as $D_{\text{asymmetric information}}$. Suppose you were the buyer. Would you offer full price, not knowing the car's actual condition? The greater the risk of receiving a lemon, the greater the decline in demand.

As the probability of buying a lemon approaches 100%, the demand for plums approaches the demand for lemons. This equilibrium is like buying a so-called Rolex watch on the street in New York City. Most people know that these watches are usually fake and will pay only a price that reflects the assumption they are fake.

A risk that a car is a lemon reduces—but does not eliminate—the demand for plums. If the price is right, someone will buy a lemon knowing that it is likely to need repairs. The lower price offsets the buyer's risk of purchasing a lemon. Nonetheless, the equilibrium in the plum market *with perfect or identical information* cannot be reached. Fewer plums are sold, and the price is lower than would be the case with

asymmetric information An exchange where one party has better information than the other.

EXHIBIT 1 Asymmetric Information in the Used-Car Market

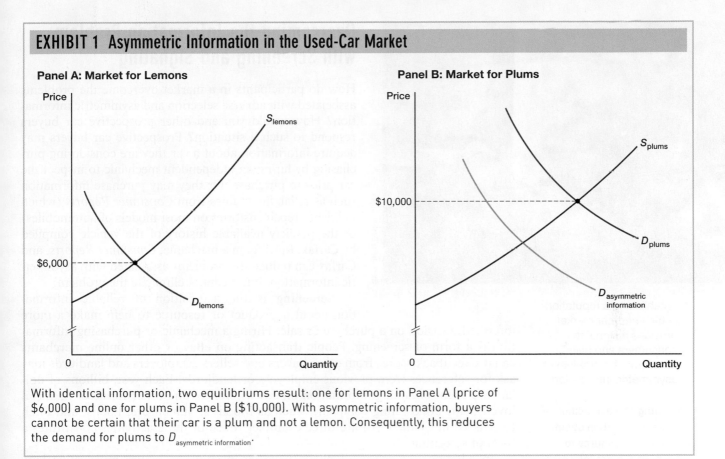

Panel A: Market for Lemons

Panel B: Market for Plums

With identical information, two equilibriums result: one for lemons in Panel A (price of $6,000) and one for plums in Panel B ($10,000). With asymmetric information, buyers cannot be certain that their car is a plum and not a lemon. Consequently, this reduces the demand for plums to $D_{asymmetric\ information}$.

perfect information. Asymmetric information prevents mutually advantageous trades from occurring.

The end result is that uninformed buyers have a less than ideal selection of automobiles—a phenomenon that economists refer to as adverse selection. **Adverse selection** is the tendency of asymmetric information to result in a less desirable selection of goods and services in the marketplace due to uninformed buyers or sellers. For instance, the buyer might think, "Why would he be selling that one-year-old car unless it has problems?" The potential for a car thought to be a plum actually to be a lemon is so pervasive that cars that are only a few months old and have been driven only a few thousand miles often sell at a substantial discount over new cars. Because nearly new cars sell at a sizable discount, consumers most likely to sell their recent-year model are precisely those drivers who know their car has problems and hence are willing to sell at a discounted price.

In extreme cases, the asymmetric information problem can decrease the demand for plums to a point where no plums are supplied. This occurs because the lower price that comes with lower demand discourages owners of plums from selling their car. At the same time, owners of some lemons remain willing to sell their cars at even lower prices. When plums exit the market completely (a situation that does not always occur), equilibrium price becomes the equilibrium price for lemons ($6,000), and only lemons are supplied.

Finally, adverse selection results in a *deadweight loss*. Because some owners of plums would like to sell their cars at a higher price and some consumers prefer to buy a plum at a higher price (and not buy a lower-priced lemon), some mutually beneficial transactions that might occur with full information do not occur.

adverse selection The tendency of asymmetric information to result in a less desirable selection of goods and services in the marketplace due to uninformed buyers or sellers.

∧ Establishing a reputation in the used-car market provides a signal to consumers and helps overcome the problem of asymmetric information.

screening The acquisition of reliable information about a product or resource to help make a more informed decision on a purchase or sale.

Overcoming the Information Problem with Screening and Signaling

How do participants in a market overcome the problems associated with adverse selection and asymmetric information? How would you and other prospective car buyers respond to such a situation? Prospective car buyers may acquire information about a car they are considering purchasing by hiring an independent mechanic to inspect the car prior to purchase. Or they may purchase information such as reliability studies from *Consumer Reports* (which publishes repair histories on most models of automobiles) or the publicly available history of the vehicle compiled by Carfax. Relying on a mechanic, *Consumer Reports*, and Carfax can reduce the problems associated with asymmetric information, but it cannot eliminate the problem.

Screening is the acquisition of reliable information about a product or resource to help make a more informed decision on a purchase or sale. Hiring a mechanic or purchasing information is a form of screening. People transacting on eBay or other online merchants can use feedback scores from other buyers and sellers. Employers and landlords may ask for references from previous employers or landlords. Each year, billions of dollars are spent obtaining information on stocks, bonds, and other forms of financial investment. Bond rating companies such as Moody's, Standard & Poor's, and Fitch (discussed in Chapter 10) are three examples. Each of these activities constitutes a form of screening.

In addition, the sellers of plums have an incentive to assure prospective buyers of the car's quality. Doing so allows them to charge a higher price as shown in Exhibit 2. Without signaling, the equilibrium price is $8,000; with signaling, it is $9,000.

EXHIBIT 2   Overcoming Asymmetric Information with Signaling

Signaling increases demand from where demand would be with asymmetric information absent signaling. In this case, demand increases $D_{asymmetric\ info}$ to $D_{with\ signaling}$; increasing the equilibrium price.

Signaling is the providing of reliable information about a product or resource to help another party make a more informed decision on a purchase or sale. It is not uncommon for sellers of quality used automobiles to provide a free Carfax vehicle history report for their cars. Likewise, signaling of quality can occur by developing a reputation. CarMax, for example, is the largest seller of used cars in the United States and, as of 2017, had sold over 6 million used cars.[1] By doing a rigorous certified quality inspection on each of its cars, CarMax has built a reputation for quality used cars. Signaling can increase demand above what would occur in a market with asymmetric information and no signaling, and this allows the firm to charge a higher price.

Companies also can signal by offering customers a warranty. If dealers know that a car is a plum, then they know that warranty service is unlikely to be needed. Nonetheless, the warranty provides a powerful signal to prospective buyers. The buyer knows that warranties are costly to service if a car is a lemon and thus that the seller probably will not offer a warranty on a car that is likely to need repairs. Some automobile manufactures now sell certified preowned versions of their cars. This signal boosts demand by reducing the adverse selection problem.

📊 **BUSINESS BRIEF Overcoming Adverse Selection on eBay with Screening**

Adverse selection exists in online eBay auctions of vintage baseball cards. High-quality (excellent condition) baseball cards generally sell below their book price (Beckett Media publishes a price guide for sports collectibles). In this example of adverse selection, there is a risk that the card is not in as good condition as advertised.*

How do buyers and sellers overcome the problem of adverse selection? On eBay, buyers and sellers screen each other through rating tools. Sellers have an economic incentive to maintain a high rating, which allows them to get top dollar for the items they sell. One study showed that card sellers received a higher price when they had a good reputation and when they provided insurance to buyers.

*Lee Van Scyoc and M. Ryanb Haley, "Adverse Selection, Seller Reputation and Buyer Insurance in Online Auctions for 1960s-Era Collectible Baseball Cards," *Applied Economics Letters*, January 1, 1970, accessed May 7, 2017, http://ideas.repec.org/a/taf/apeclt/v17y2010i14p1341-1345.html.

The Value of a College Degree: A "Sheepskin Effect" or Productivity Gains?

On average, college graduates earn substantially more than individuals with only a high school diploma. One common explanation for this discrepancy is that education increases one's human capital and productivity (see Chapter 17).

But is this really all that college represents? Some Harvard University students were asked whether they would want to take four years of Harvard classes for free if they would not be able to get the degree itself. Most said they would not take the offer because the signaling from a Harvard degree was more valuable than the roughly $280,000 cost of attending classes for four years.

Although reading this textbook and moving toward a degree undoubtedly increases your knowledge and human capital, a college degree also serves as a powerful signal to prospective employers. Consider a job interview and screening process from the prospective of a potential employer. Because prospective employers rarely truly know a candidate's ability, they can screen prospective job candidates by reviewing their work experience and education.

Although most colleges now issue diplomas on paper, sheepskin was the material of choice for centuries because it was strong enough to be rolled and unrolled as evidence

signaling The providing of reliable information about a product or resource to help another party make a more informed decision on a purchase or sale.

of a scholar's education. Today, the **sheepskin effect** refers to the increase in earnings that is obtained from earning higher credentials as opposed to developing higher levels of human capital. In college education, the sheepskin effect is wage increases *above* what would normally be expected from an additional year of education. As discussed in Chapter 17, each additional year of schooling adds to a person's potential earnings via increases in human capital. That said, the increase in average earnings from a third year of college is less than the increase in earnings from the fourth year of college when a degree is earned. In fact, the fourth year of college adds relatively little to one's expected earnings if a degree is not earned. Empirical studies suggest that both signaling and increases in human capital contribute to one's expected wages by earning a degree. Employers may view the completion of a degree as a signal of skills often sought by employers (such as self-motivation and determination).

📊 BUSINESS BRIEF   Signaling and Screening with Gifts while Dating

Gift giving is a big business in the United States. For Valentine's Day, nearly $2 billion dollars is spent on candy, another $2 billion on flowers, and over $4 billion on jewelry. In 2016, about $19 billion was spent celebrating the holiday, and the average amount spent per person was just over $150 (men spent just over $200).*

The theory of signaling and screening also can be applied to dating and the business of gift giving. For simplicity, assume that the objective of dating is to find a long-lasting meaningful relationship. Initially, there is an adverse selection problem because the only things known about the other person are some physical attributes and generic personality traits. While dating, people regularly signal (by providing information about themselves) and screen (by obtaining information about their dates).

When a relationship develops, signaling and screening usually continue. Perhaps one partner is insecure and unsure of the true feelings of the other. Under this scenario, words or perhaps gifts may serve as signals of continued interest. For one's partner, words or gifts may provide a useful signal and screening tool.

Gift giving can be tricky, however. The thoughtfulness of the gift serves as yet another signal and screening tool. A college student who receives a gift of cash from a parent may greatly appreciate the monetary gift but might be offended to receive a cash gift from someone he or she is dating. Choosing the right gift rather than a gift card or money can show you are thinking about the other person and trying to imagine the gift they might enjoy. Money doesn't send that signal.

*Anne-Marcelle Ngabirano, "On Valentine's Day, Here's How Much We're Willing to Spend for Love," *USA Today*, February 14, 2017, https://www.usatoday.com/story/money/2017/02/13/more-expensive-year-show-your -love/97766678; David J. Neal, "How Men and Women See Themselves on Valentine's Day," *Miami Herald*, February 14, 2017, http://www.miamiherald.com/news/local/community/miami-dade/article132576964.html.

19.2 THE INSURANCE MARKET: LESS INFORMED SELLERS

The problems associated with asymmetric information do not always occur when the buyer has less information than the seller. The buyer often has *more* information. A good example occurs in the market for insurance. Consider the case of automobile or health insurance, where buyers may know more about their driving ability and their health than an insurance company knows, particularly if they are newly insured.

To be profitable, an insurance company must take in more revenue by selling insurance policies than it spends in paying claims. These companies realize that they will not make a profit on every policy. For example, it will lose money by insuring a home that later is damaged in a fire. But insurance companies attempt to make a profit *on average*. Using advanced statistical techniques and actuarial science, they attempt to predict the amount of insurance claims likely to be paid over the next year. Two factors

sheepskin effect The increase in earnings from obtaining higher credentials as opposed to higher levels of human capital.

make this difficult to predict. First, the people who purchase insurance are more likely than nonbuyers to have a problem (such as illness or accident) that causes them to file a claim. This situation is similar to the *adverse selection* problem confronting buyers of used cars. Second, the existence of insurance may change human behavior in a way that increases the likelihood that a claim will be filed. This situation is known as a *moral hazard* and is discussed in depth at the end of the section.

Adverse Selection in the Insurance Market

Who knows more about the driving skills of the insured—the insurance company or the driver? The insurance company can do screening of individual driving records, but those records can reflect good or bad luck. In the end, the buyers are the best judge of their own tendency to speed, drive while texting, drive while drunk, or engage in other types of risky behavior.

Insurance companies will likely end up with an *adverse selection* of insurance customers, particularly for their premium products, which provide complete coverage. This is demonstrated in Exhibit 3. With perfect information, an equilibrium price of $10,000 is established. Because the sellers of automobile insurance are aware of the adverse selection process, they reduce the supply of the premium product, which increases its price to $12,000. As a consequence, fewer people buy the insurance product.

Once again, adverse selection results in deadweight loss. There are some "low cost to insure" individuals (meaning they are unlikely to file expensive claims) who would buy a policy at $10,000 but not $12,000. As a consequence, some mutually beneficial transactions that might occur with full information do not occur. In an extreme case, the market may fail, and insurance companies may completely stop selling the insurance.

Moral Hazard in Insurance Markets

Insurance can actually *change* human behavior. **Moral hazard** is a situation where there is an increased tendency to take risks because some of the potential costs associated with taking such risks will be paid by others. As is shown in the following example, moral hazard tends to change behavior, not morals.

moral hazard A situation where there is an increased tendency to take risks because some of the potential costs associated with taking such risks will be paid by others.

EXHIBIT 3 Adverse Selection and Asymmetric Information in the Insurance Market

From the insurance company's perspective, asymmetric information in the insurance market results in an adverse selection of customers. In turn, this reduces supply and increases price.

Suppose someone gives you a Ferrari with two stipulations: you cannot sell it or insure it. Because you are not able to insure the Ferrari, you might drive it extremely carefully as damage to the car is costly. Now suppose you are allowed to insure the Ferrari so that if the car is damaged in an accident, you get a new Ferrari. Economic theory related to moral hazard suggests that you might drive it faster. After all, the car is a Ferrari!

Many other examples of moral hazard can be found. Homeowners who purchase insurance have reduced incentives to keep smoke detectors or fire extinguishers on hand. Users of illicit drugs are unlikely to pay the full cost of treatment should they become addicted. Individuals with health insurance may be more inclined to eat unhealthy foods and ski on icy mountains than if they were uninsured. Each of these scenarios is an example of the moral hazard problem.

Of course risky behavior may occur with or without insurance. The owner of an uninsured Ferrari may still drive too fast. The point is that moral hazard increases the *tendency* to drive fast. In most cases, the moral hazard problem is not severe enough to prevent insurance markets from forming. Even when they are insured, most people don't want to be in accidents or suffer from illness, accidents, or addiction.

Although in many cases, the moral hazard problem is not severe, it has caused major distortions in the field of banking. You may have noticed that banks advertise that "Deposits are insured by the Federal Deposit Insurance Corporation (FDIC) up to $250,000." Perhaps you have never thought about bank deposit insurance. If so, that is precisely the moral hazard problem. Due to the insurance, risky banks can attract deposits just as easily as safe banks. Without the insurance, individuals would want a higher interest rate (return) to put their money in the riskier bank. Since riskier banks *do not* have to pay a higher rate, the insurance changes the bank's behavior as banks are more inclined to make riskier loans.

Think & Speak Like an Economist

Many people confuse adverse selection with moral hazard. Adverse selection occurs prior to entering into a transaction. Buyers of insurance have more information than sellers, and thus insured people are riskier from the perspective of the insurance company. In contrast, moral hazard occurs after the transaction, when buyers of insurance have less incentive to minimize the likelihood of needing to file a claim.

BUSINESS BRIEF Moral Hazard and the 1980s S&L Crisis

In the 1980s, many savings and loan banks (S&Ls) that specialized in real estate loans made lots of risky loans to real estate developers. In a market that did not have deposit insurance, people would have to be very careful about where they placed their life savings. Before the Federal Deposit Insurance Corporation (FDIC) (1933) and the Federal Savings and Loan Insurance Corporation (FSLIC) (1989) were created, banks had to work hard to reassure people that their money was safe. The creation of the FDIC removed one problem (the fear of losing one's life savings in a bank failure) at the cost of creating another—a moral hazard. Instead of being concerned about whether banks were taking excessive risks, customers worried about the interest rate that banks paid on deposits.

This change in focus allowed banks to make speculative loans. If the loans were repaid, bankers could become wealthy. But if the loans failed, most of the cost of paying off depositors would fall on the deposit insurance fund. By the end of the 1980s, taxpayers had spent more than $100 billion bailing out these deposit insurance funds. To some extent, these risky real estate loans were a game of "Heads, the banks win. Tails, the taxpayer loses"—an excellent example of moral hazard.*

*Kenneth J. Robinson, "Savings and Loan Crisis: 1980–1989," Federal Reserve History, November 22, 2013, accessed May 19, 2017, https://www.federalreservehistory.org/essays/savings_and_loan_crisis.

The Language of Insurance: Overcoming Moral Hazard and Adverse Selection

Although they cannot completely eliminate the problems associated with moral hazard and adverse selection, insurance companies attempt to *minimize* them. To understand how, one must first be familiar with the basic terminology used in the market for automobile, home, health, and other types of insurance. Insurance policies often vary significantly from company to company and from policy to policy, even for essentially similar products, but most use similar terminology to describe the coverage and benefits.

High Deductibles A **deductible** is the amount that a consumer must pay before the insurance provider will pay any claims on the policy. Typically (but not always), deductibles must be met each year. For example, an individual who has a home insurance deductible of $5,000 and suffers from $20,000 in water damage must pay $5,000 toward the repair before the insurance company will pay any claims for the remaining balance. If another claim is made during the same year, some policies (especially homeowner's and automobile insurance) require the payment of another deductible, but health insurance generally requires only one deductible per year.

Buyers of insurance who are most likely to file a claim tend to prefer low-deductible policies. In general, higher deductibles result in lower prices on the insurance policy, *ceteris paribus*. To some extent, insurance companies can minimize the problem of adverse selection by charging very high prices on low-deductible options. The high price of insurance policies with low deductibles encourages some individuals to buy the cheaper high-deductible policies, which reduces the moral hazard problem.

Consider the above Ferrari example, but now assume that your insurance policy has a big deductible that requires you to pay for the first $10,000 in repairs. This high deductible would tend to make you more careful, especially in avoiding fender benders where you'd have to pick up the full repair cost (if less than $10,000). This reduces but does not completely eliminate moral hazard as long as you still have insurance that covers the accident costs that exceed $10,000.

High Copayments Some insurance policies, particularly health insurance, require the insured individual to make a partial payment for each insured event. For example, when visiting the emergency room, those with insurance often have to pay a set amount (perhaps $250), and their insurance provider pays the rest. In this example, the $250 is referred to as a copayment. A **copayment** is individual's share of the cost on a claim with the insurance provider paying the rest. Copayments can be expressed as a percentage (such as 20%) or a fixed dollar amount ($250). A second emergency room visit in the same year typically results in *another* copayment.

Health insurance providers typically use high copayments to discourage certain consumer practices and low copayments to encourage other types of behavior. Emergency room visits, for example, are very expensive when compared to doctor or clinic visits. A high copayment discourages people from using the emergency room for nonurgent care, another example of moral hazard. Although for many policies the high copayment is waived when insured people are admitted to the hospital, people run the risk that they will not be admitted and have to make the high copayment. This allows health insurance providers to manage costs and overcome the moral hazard problem of using the emergency room when a routine doctor visit will suffice.

In contrast, low copayments (or no copayments) are often used to encourage certain behaviors, like physical exams. These exams often help detect certain ailments early before they become extremely costly to treat.

deductible The amount that a consumer must pay before the insurance provider will pay any claims on the policy.

copayment An individual's share of the cost on a claim with the insurance provider paying the rest.

Copayments are similar to deductibles in that copayments usually involve money that comes out of the insured's pocket when claims are filed. Unlike deductibles, however, copayments tend to be smaller dollar amounts and are applied on a per claim basis. Deductibles, in contrast, usually are applied on a per period (such as per year) basis. Some insurance policies have an annual limit on the amount of money that the insured is asked to pay. This *out-of-pocket maximum* limits the copayments that must be paid by an insured individual.

Experience Rating and Screening One popular screening device used by insurance providers is an experience rating. An **experience rating** is a method used to determine the price of insurance based on a group's or an individual's history of claims. With this form of *screening*, those who file a claim on their insurance may see an increase in the price of their insurance policies in the future because they are seen as a greater risk to insurance companies. The same applies to groups of insured. A company that employs many older workers and files many claims might have to pay more to provide health insurance for its workforce.

Other types of insurance also have issues with asymmetric information. Those who buy flood insurance to protect their property against flood damage are presumably more likely to be at risk of having their property flooded. Those who protect their home or apartment against burglary are seen as being more prone to need such insurance. Similarly, those who borrow money have better information than a lender might on their ability to pay back the loan.

As is usually the case, the insurance companies counter the asymmetric information problem with screening. They may look at the addresses of the people purchasing flood insurance and analyze the likelihood of a flood. They may look at crime statistics in a given neighborhood prior to selling a policy that insures against burglary. Health exams are often required prior to buying a life insurance policy. Lenders screen potential borrowers by paying for their credit score and checking on the borrower's employment history.

Mandated Insurance In many places, having automobile insurance is *mandated* by law, and this offsets the problem of adverse selection. Even safe drivers *must* buy at least the minimum amount of required insurance. The automobile insurance company no longer must select customers from an adverse pool of customers. Instead, the tendency of their customers to be in an accident will be roughly equal to the tendency of the entire population to be in an accident.

In 2010, lawmakers passed the Patient Protection and Affordable Care Act (ACA) to address issues related to the lack of health insurance among people who were not able to buy it from their employer and were not eligible for other government-provided health insurance programs. This law had attempted to overcome the adverse selection problem by requiring individuals to purchase insurance and imposing a penalty on anyone who does not purchase health insurance. In 2018, the mandatory purchase provision was rescinded. In addition, the ACA mandated that employers with 50 or more full-time employees provide health insurance to such employees. More details on the ACA can be found in the next section.

A Limited Open Enrollment Periods Another method for reducing the problem of adverse selection in the insurance market, particularly the health insurance market, is to limit the period in which people can buy an insurance policy; this is known as an *open enrollment period*. For example, people who buy insurance at work might select their coverage in November during an open enrollment period, and their insurance coverage would begin in January of the following year. Buyers of insurance would need to know at the time of purchase that they are more likely than average to use the insurance, which may not always be the case.

experience rating A method used to determine the price of insurance based on a group's or an individual's history of claims.

19.3 THE U.S. HEALTH-CARE SYSTEM: STRUCTURE AND OUTCOMES

In September 2004, the world's smallest baby girl was born prematurely in a Chicago area hospital. The baby was 8.6 ounces—about the weight of an iPad Mini. When she was discharged a few months later, doctors expected her to develop normally.[2] This tiny success story is one of many due to modern medical advances. The daughter of one of the authors of this textbook was born 2 months premature at a weight just over 4 pounds. After a month in the hospital, she came home and has been healthy ever since.

Stephen Rubb

∧ Marissa Rubb (daughter of an author) was born two months premature and is healthy today—a modern medical miracle with a high price tag.

We all have heard astonishing success stories that are the result of medical advances. Yet the ability to save lives does not change the fundamental laws of economics: health care involves the use of resources that have a significant opportunity cost that must be paid for by someone—most often by someone with health insurance. Success stories such as these premature deliveries also involve a large financial cost. The typical cost of a hospital stay for a premature baby is more than $5,000 a day and can last many months.

Health care today is the largest and perhaps the most important industry in the United States and many other developed countries. It affects people's lives and well-being and uses an enormous amount of resources. In many societies, health care is viewed as a basic right. In the United States, health-care spending accounts for more than 1 out of every 6 dollars spent in the entire economy, as measured by GDP. This is far more than what is spent in other countries. Moreover, the cost of health insurance explains a large part of the difference between wage rates and the price of labor faced by employers (Chapter 17). At General Motors, for example, providing health insurance for employees accounts for up to $2,000 in the price of every car that the company sells.

Most Americans have *health insurance* that pays for a variety of routine and major medical expenses. The U.S. health-care system is different from that in other countries in three major areas:

1. Health-care spending in the United States is extremely high compared to spending in other countries and has been increasing in recent decades. Even U.S government spending on health care alone (i.e. excluding private spending) exceeds the total spending on health care in most other developed countries.

2. Tens of millions of Americans do not have health insurance. This number has declined somewhat since the 2010 passage of the Patient Protection and Affordable Health Care Act.

3. Life expectancy, infant mortality, and other outcome-based measures of well-being do *not* provide evidence that the overall health-care system in the United States is more effective than the systems in other countries.

To understand the U.S. health-care system requires understanding how health insurance evolved in the United States and how it is handled in other countries. Nearly all developed (high-income) countries except for the United States have universal health coverage. **Universal health coverage** is a health-care system that ensures that health-care benefits are provided to all citizens. Under such a system, everyone receives some insurance coverage, but not every medical procedure is covered.

Many developed countries, such as Canada and the United Kingdom, provide universal coverage through a single-payer health insurance system. A **single-payer health-care system** is a health-care system where the government pays for most

universal health coverage
A health-care system that ensures that health-care benefits are provided to all citizens.

single-payer health-care system A health-care system where the government pays for the vast majority of health-care costs.

health-care costs. Under such a system, the government either provides medical services or provides health insurance. Funding comes from the government (the single payer), but some single-payer countries also allow a small role for the private sector.

When the government pays for health care, questions often arise about how much to spend and how best to spend a limited budget. Economic theory suggests that there are no easy answers to these questions. On the one hand, health care is often viewed as a right, particularly in high-income countries. On the other hand, if health care is given away with no cost controls, spending will rise rapidly, leaving fewer resources for other important goals. In countries with universal coverage, the government often rations certain medical services either by requiring long wait periods or by not paying for services when regulators believe that the benefits do not justify the costs.

The U.S. Health-Care System

Instead of universal coverage or a single-payer system, the United States has a complex mixture of public and private health insurance that covers most but not all citizens. Many Americans rely on private-sector health insurance, which people often obtain through their (or a family member's) employer. Employer-based health insurance emerged during World War II at a time when wages and other prices were controlled by the government as part of the war effort and there was a very tight labor market. Ordinarily, wages rise in this scenario, but the wartime wage controls were essentially price ceilings that prevented them from doing so. Because companies were not allowed to pay higher wages, they used the extra benefit of free health insurance to attract new workers.

With employer-provided health insurance, individuals receive their health insurance through a plan that is *partially* paid by their employer and *partially* paid by the employee. Because an employer provides the insurance company with a large group of people to sell insurance to, the insurance company can sell its product at a discounted price (based on the experience rating of the employer). From an insurance company's perspective, enrolling an entire company's workforce tends to overcome the adverse selection problem because most workers are likely to be relatively healthy. Today, employers offer health insurance for a complex mixture of reasons, including an increased ability to attract workers, government mandates, and the advantage of compensating workers in untaxed benefits rather than heavily taxed wages and salaries.

After private health insurance became widely available from employers, many people argued that it was unfair to deny health insurance to those without employment, those whose employers did not offer it, and those who could not afford it. This led to government programs such as Medicare (which provides health insurance for the elderly) and Medicaid (for the disabled and those with low incomes) (see Chapter 7).

Despite the complex mixture of Medicare, Medicaid, and private health insurance, 10s of millions of Americans had no health insurance in 2010. To reduce the number of uninsured Americans, lawmakers passed the Patient Protection and Affordable Care Act, commonly referred to as the Affordable Care Act (ACA). The following key provisions of the ACA are designed to help reduce the number of uninsured:

- *An Employer Mandate.* Businesses with 50 or more full-time employees are required to offer health insurance to all full-time employees.

- *State Health Insurance Exchanges.* Each state is required to establish a health insurance exchange where health insurance companies provide insurance to individuals and small businesses with fewer than 50 employees.

- *Government Subsidies.* To help make health insurance less expensive to low-income consumers, the government provides subsidies that pay part of the price of health insurance.

- *Medicaid Expansion.* Medicaid, which provides insurance to the disabled and low-income individuals (and their families), was expanded. States are allowed to provide Medicaid to individuals and households with incomes as high as 138% above the poverty line.

- *Protection for Preexisting Conditions.* Under the ACA, health insurance companies cannot refuse to cover patients with *preexisting conditions*—medical conditions for which the patient or insured has already received care. Previously, some insurance plans used preexisting conditions as a screening device to overcome the problem of adverse selection.

According to census data in the Current Population Survey, the percentage of individuals without health insurance *for the entire year* fell from 13.3% in 2013 to 10.4% in 2014, when the ACA law was first implemented.[3] In 2017, roughly 9% had no health insurance at all for the entire year.

Although the ACA met its objective of reducing the number of Americans without insurance, the law has remained controversial and been the target of repeated repeal attempts. Opponents of the ACA fall into two camps. Some feel that the law did not go far enough: millions of Americans still do not have health insurance, and those who purchase insurance on the state exchanges often have very high deductibles that need to be met and paid before coverage kicks in. These opponents typically advocate universal health coverage.

Others point to the overall rising cost of health insurance in the United States after the law's passage, particularly the increase in government spending to pay for the subsidies and the expansion of Medicaid. Critics contend that because the ACA allows individuals to buy insurance any time of the year and bars insurance companies from denying coverage based on a preexisting condition, some individuals delay buying coverage until it is absolutely needed. By allowing people to buy insurance *after* they need care, the law results in issues related adverse selection and raises premiums (similar to what is shown in Exhibit 3). The debate over health care and health insurance is likely to continue for years to come.

Health-Care Spending in the United States and Other Developed Nations

Health-care spending is extremely high in the United States compared to other developed countries and has increased in recent decades. First, we examine where money is spent in the United States and how U.S. spending compares to other countries. Later, we address the question of *why* the United States spends so much on health care.

The biggest share of health-care spending goes to hospital care, which accounts for roughly a third of all medical spending in the United States. This is demonstrated in Exhibit 4. In 2017, the average cost of a 3-day hospital stay was around $30,000.[4] In contrast, doctors and medical clinics accounted for roughly a fifth of health-care spending.

The United States spends far more per person on health care than every other country in the Organization for Economic Cooperation and Development (OECD). In fact, the United States spends roughly 25% more on health care than the second-biggest spender (Switzerland) and roughly 2½ times the OECD average. Data on the average health-care spending for all OECD nations can be found in Exhibit 5. Compared to

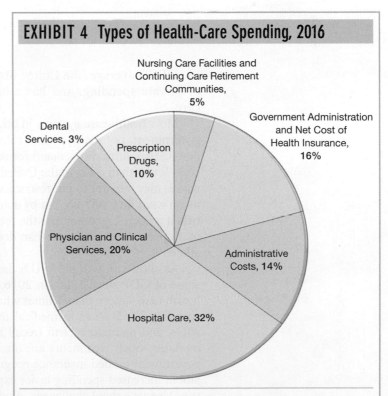

EXHIBIT 4 Types of Health-Care Spending, 2016

A third of health-care spending in the United States is for hospital care, and a fifth is for doctors and clinics account.

Data from: Centers for Medicare and Medicaid Services, Office of the Actuary, National Health Statistics Group.

EXHIBIT 5   Health-Care Spending per Person around the World

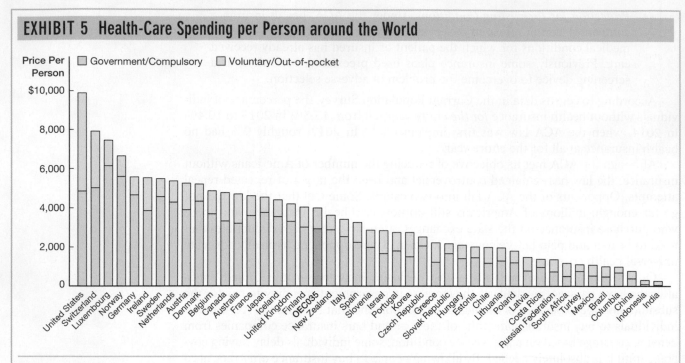

The United States spends more per person on health care than any other developed nation. The United States spends roughly 25% more than the second-biggest spender on health care, Switzerland. Note that the share of private spending is much higher in the United States than in other countries and that government spending on health care in the United States is also high.

Data from: OECD Health Statistics 2017, WHO Global Health Expenditure Database.

the OECD average, the United States spends much more in total, has a higher share of private spending, and has a higher amount of government spending on health care.

Most health-care systems in other countries have strict price controls (prices set by government, not markets) and rules about who can and cannot have expensive procedures. They limit the demand for services with rationing, which helps keep health-care costs lower than costs in the United States. In the United States, private insurance companies may attempt to put restrictions on expensive procedures by stating they have limits on what they will pay, but by doing so will run the risk of lawsuits. This is particularly true if a doctor recommends the procedure. Moreover, U.S. doctors tend to recommend more procedures and tests than doctors do in other countries for patients with similar ailments.

As shown in Exhibit 5, U.S. health-care spending has accounted for an increasing share of GDP since 1960. In 2016, the United States spent nearly 18% of its GDP on health care—more than 3 times what it spent in the 1960s. One source of the increased spending is advances in medical treatment. Many conditions—such as kidney failure, AIDs, and premature birth (recall the stories in the opening of this section)—are now treatable. Such treatments are often expensive and usually are paid for by private or government-funded insurance programs. Furthermore, due to the country's aging population, increased spending is not expected to reverse in the near future. But other countries also face these challenges. As discussed earlier, the key difference is that the United States does not have the strict price controls (i.e. price ceilings) and rationing that are used in most countries that offer universal coverage.

Uninsured in the United States

Despite the high level of spending on health care in the United States, tens of millions of Americans have no health insurance. Exhibit 7 demonstrates how Americans obtained health insurance in 2016 (although people sometimes have more than one form of insurance). Over half the population received some form of insurance from their employer at some point during the year. Others bought health insurance in the private market rather than through an employer. Directly purchased health insurance plans are often very expensive, a result that stems from an inability to control for adverse selection (which can be done by insuring groups of people through employers). Still others receive health insurance from various government programs.

In 2016, roughly 9% of the population had no health insurance. About half of the uninsured were from families headed by someone who worked full time at a low-paying job. Such individuals are considered the working poor: they have low-paying jobs that do not provide health insurance, but their incomes are too high for them to receive Medicaid and social insurance benefits (welfare). Many Americans have health insurance in multiple categories.

Lack of health insurance does not always mean a complete lack of health-care services. Some people pay for their own health-care services out of pocket—that is, without using insurance. In some cases, those without health insurance and without an ability to pay are provided with health-care services at free city or county hospitals and walk-in clinics or through charity provided by private hospitals and government mandates on hospitals. Hospitals cannot collect payments from some patients who receive care. In extreme cases, patients can file for bankruptcy, which allows them to avoid paying medical expenses.

Some contend that when a hospital is unable to collect payments from patients who receive care, prices are raised for those with insurance, which raises the price of

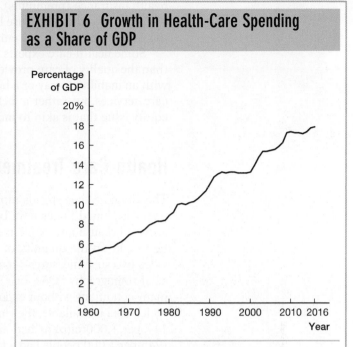

EXHIBIT 6 Growth in Health-Care Spending as a Share of GDP

In the United States, health-care spending is now roughly 18% of GDP, triple what it was in the 1960s. Medical advances account for much of the growth.

Data from: Centers for Medicare & Medicaid Services.

EXHIBIT 7 Types of Health Insurance in the United States (Percentage of the Population), 2016

Over half of the people in the United States received health insurance from an employer at some point in 2016. Over 9% of the population had no health insurance for the entire year. The percentages do not add up to 100 because many Americans have two types of insurance coverage.

Data from: U.S. Department of Census.

health insurance (premiums). This exacerbates the adverse selection problem noted in the previous section because healthy consumers figure they will receive care anyway in the case of an unexpected emergency and so they buy less insurance.

Some health-care experts also worry that the quality of care given for free is lower than the quality of care provided to those with insurance. In other words, one problem with an inability to pay or a lack of insurance is not so much a complete lack of health-care services but rather a lack of *high-quality* care. Such critics see health care as an equity issue that is akin to income inequality and poverty (discussed in Chapter 18).

Health-Care Treatments and Outcomes in the United States

The United States spends more on health care than all other developed countries, but does the United States have better health-care outcomes? This is a difficult question to answer because any single measure may be misleading. One plausible measure would be to add up the quantity of health-care treatments that are provided. Exhibit 8 provides two such measures—magnetic resonance imaging (MRI) scans and computerized axial tomography (CAT or CT) scans per person. These scans help doctors diagnose many conditions without exposing patients to radiation. Among all OECD countries for which data is available, the United States has the third-most MRI scans per person (over 117 per 1,000 citizens had an MRI scan in 2015) and the most CT scans per person (245 per 1,000 people had a CT scan in that year). These figures are roughly double the OECD average. According to an OECD report, there has been a substantial increase in the number of such examinations since 2000, particularly in the United States.[5]

There are at least two problems with relying on this sort of data. First, the data may pick up medical care provided to nonresidents. Second, most medical experts would prefer to measure the *quality* of health care and not the *quantity* of health-care services. In other words, more MRIs and CT scans may add to the overall cost of providing health care but may or may not add to the overall quality.

Exhibit 8 also looks at two other widely used measures of health-care outcomes— life expectancy and infant mortality rates—which are widely used to measure the health

EXHIBIT 8 Health-Care Spending, Treatments, and Outcomes in the United States and Developed Nations, 2015

	Spending		Treatments		Outcomes	
	Per person (U.S. dollars)	Share of GDP (percentage)	MRI Exams (per 1,000 population)	CT Exams (per 1,000 population)	Life Expectancy (years)	Infant Mortality (deaths per 1,000 live births)
United States	$9,892	17.2%	117.8	245.3	78.8	5.8
Germany	5,551	11.0	131.3	143.8	80.7	3.3
Japan	4,519	10.9	112	230.8	83.9	2.1
Canada	4,753	10.6	56	152.8	81.7	4.8
OECD median	4,003	9.0	65	143.1	80.6	3.9

The United States has the most CT scans and the third-most MRI scans per 1,000 citizens in all developed countries. Most medical experts would prefer to measure health-care quality and not the quantity of services. Despite higher spending levels, the United States lags other OECD nations in life expectancy and infant mortality. Such data, however, only partially reflects the quality of health care.

Data from: OECD.

of the population. The data suggests that despite higher spending on health care per person in the United States, outcomes are not better than those found in other developed countries. The U.S. infant mortality rate is nearly 50% greater than the median rate for other OECD nations. At the same time, life expectancy in the United States is lower.

The use of life expectancy and infant mortality rates may also be a flawed measure of health-care performance. To some extent, this data measures factors beyond the control of the health-care system. Illicit drug use, alcohol, and cigarettes, for example, contribute to both a lower life expectancy and a higher rate of infant mortality. Traffic accidents, murder, and suicide rates also vary among nations. Nonetheless, the data we do have fails to provide any solid evidence that the high level of spending in the United States leads to significantly better health outcomes.

🏛 POLICY BRIEF Are an Extra Two Months of Life Worth $100,000?

Medical science is an exciting industry that continues to develop new techniques and medications, but it is also an industry with very high costs. Developing new drugs, for instance, can cost hundreds of millions of dollars in research and testing. Drugs to treat cancer often cost more than $100,000 per year per patient. Dr. Vinay Prasad, who is a cancer specialist, has said that the average life extension from new cancer drugs is 2.1 months and that even this may overestimate the drugs' usefulness because it includes only the most effective types of cancer drugs.[*]

Every society faces painful decisions about which sorts of medical treatments are worth the cost. Wealthy countries like the United States tend to spend more on expensive new technologies than less developed countries spend, but even in the United States there is increasing pressure to hold down medical costs. After drugs come "off patent" and are no longer subject to patent restrictions, new generic competitors are allowed into the market, and prices often fall sharply.

Policymakers face a difficult dilemma. Cost controls can discourage new medical innovations by reducing the profit motive. But a lack of cost controls can put tremendous pressure on government budgets and on the ability of firms to provide health insurance.

[*]Allen Frances, "Why Are Most Cancer Drugs So Expensive and So Ineffective?," *Huffington Post*, October 15, 2015, accessed May 8, 2017, http://www.huffingtonpost.com/allen-frances/why-are-most-cancer -drugs_b_8294392.html.

Why Does the United States Spend So Much on Health Care?

Neither government nor private health insurance plans are exempt from the laws of economics. Society faces an economic trade-off between health-care spending and spending on other societal goals. Regardless of whether health care is paid for by the government or by an employer-provided plan, the public ultimately bears the cost. Furthermore, health care is increasingly expensive. An advanced magnetic resonance imaging (MRI) machine, for example, can cost over $2 million. Hospital buildings and highly skilled health-care workers are also expensive. All of these costs must be paid for somehow.[6]

Although there are numerous reasons why U.S. health care is expensive, many relate to the design of our health-care system. Health care differs from most other industries in that consumers usually pay out of pocket for only a relatively small share of the total cost. Economists have identified the following major reasons that health care costs in the United States are higher than what is paid in other developed nations.

Insurance Boosts the Demand for Health-Care Services Health insurance can lead to the overuse of medical services. We've seen the problem of moral hazard— which occurs when insurance leads people to engage in risky lifestyles. But there is also a problem with the overuse of services for any given condition. We've seen that most costs are covered by private insurance or government programs and are not paid by consumers out of pocket. Because consumers directly pay only a relatively small share of the costs, the demand for health care is higher than if they paid out of pocket. Although all costs are ultimately borne by the public, when you decide whether to have an extra MRI scan, you probably don't think about the impact on other people who buy insurance or other taxpayers across the country.

Health care is almost a perfect storm of incentives to push costs ever higher. Let's begin with a thought experiment. Say you have a middle-income job and are deciding whether to buy a Ford Fusion or a Honda Accord. Each costs about $25,000. How would your decision be different if someone offers to pay for whatever car you buy and you merely have to pay a 5% copayment for the car? Perhaps that offer would lead you buy something nicer, like a BMW or Mercedes. Similarly, when insurance pays for a large portion of health care, consumers might consume more health care.

The preceding analogy is not perfect. Most people don't order heart surgery just because they have to pay a relatively small share of the cost. Unlike car purchases, medical expenditures are much more dependent on health. But the analogy may be at least partly valid. For instance, health-care experts call very generous health insurance plans "Cadillac plans" because they cover a wide range of expenses. And studies show that the more generous the health-care plan, the more services that people will consume, on average. So not all health expenditures are 100% based on medical condition. Price also plays a role.

When one of the authors of this text had a sore shoulder, his insurance company was willing to provide weekly physical therapy. Even though he did not have to pay for the weekly therapy, he stopped going because the exercises he did at home were just as effective and he was too busy writing this book. But what if he had not been busy? It's easy to see how medical treatments occasionally might be overused if provided for free.

The economics of cosmetic surgery is particularly interesting. Over recent decades, the cost of cosmetic surgery has risen much less than for other types of surgery. Because cosmetic surgery often is paid for by the patient, without insurance or government funding, consumers are price conscious, and providers must work much harder to hold down costs. In contrast, other types of surgery are often paid for with insurance, so customers are less likely to complain about high prices (or even know about them).

To discourage the overuse of medical services, most insurance plans have deductibles and copayments that require the patient to bear part of the cost of each medical procedure. A high copayment discourages individuals from using the emergency room when a cheaper visit to their doctor would be adequate. Recall that the high copayment often is waived when an emergency room visitor is admitted to the hospital but is not waived when the visitor is discharged. This encourages people to think carefully about whether an emergency room visit is needed or whether a regular office visit is all that is necessary. In contrast, these copayments are often waved for basic check-ups, prenatal care, and some cancer screenings because these medical services may reduce long-run costs. Many illnesses are much easier to treat if caught early.

Subsidies and Tax Benefits Increase the Demand for Health Insurance Another important factor that drives up the costs of health insurance are government subsidies and the various tax benefits that are received by those who purchase health insurance. The cost of health insurance can be deducted against both personal income taxes and payroll taxes. This means that the government implicitly subsidizes health care paid for by insurance. Consider a middle-class worker who has a $20,000 health insurance plan that is provided by his or her employer. The worker's tax bill is about $8,000 lower than if the employer had paid the extra $20,000 in salary and required the employee buy health care privately. This means that roughly 40% of the cost of health insurance is implicitly paid by the government in the form of lower taxes.

Here's an analogy. After a new car warranty runs out, most people don't buy insurance (in the form of an extended warranty) to cover major auto repairs. That's partly because the government does not subsidize auto repair insurance with tax deductions.

If it did, people would be more likely to buy insurance for ordinary repairs like a new muffler because the government would be absorbing part of the cost with tax deductions. Because health insurance is heavily subsidized with tax deductions, people are much more likely to use health insurance to pay for routine medical expenses than to use auto insurance to pay for routine car repairs.

Demand Is Relatively Price Inelastic Most people view health care as a necessity, which makes demand relatively price inelastic. As shown in Chapter 4, the price elasticity of demand for services like an appendectomy and an arm cast is less than 0.1. The demand for a routine doctor's office visit for a cold or treatment for a minor ailment is also relatively price inelastic. In addition, customers appear to have tremendous "brand loyalty" to their preferred doctor, whom they may have been seeing for many years. Because people are reluctant to switch doctors, the demand for the services of any given doctor is often relatively price inelastic.

Recall from Chapter 4 that when an item has a price inelastic demand, businesses (in this case, health-care providers) can raise prices and increase total revenue. This puts upward pressure on medical prices. In countries that provide universal coverage and a single payer, governments often negotiate prices with providers in an attempt to hold down health-care costs.

Each year, more and more new medical technologies are developed. Some provide great benefits, and others are of doubtful utility. If expensive new procedures are not always cost-effective, then why are patients willing to pay for them? Again, because most patients pay relatively little out of pocket, they do not show the sort of consumer resistance that would occur in other industries if costs rose rapidly. As a result of the demand for health care being relatively price inelastic, a sharp rise in price associated with slightly improved technology causes only a small decrease in quantity demanded.

The Principal–Agent Problem Increases Demand Most people are perfectly capable of deciding when they need a new car, but they rely on the expertise of doctors when deciding whether to purchase an expensive operation. Doctors face a different set of incentives than patients do, however. Their incomes positively depend on the amount of medical services that they provide, which means that they may have a financial incentive to recommend more medical procedures. This is an example of the principal–agent problem, discussed in Chapter 9.

The **principal–agent problem** refers to the difficulty of making agents act in the best interests of the principals that they serve. The principal (the patient) hires the agent (the doctor) to perform services that benefit the principal. Because the self-interest of the principal and agent do not coincide exactly, the agent may not always act in the best interests of the principal. Moreover, there is asymmetric information with doctors typically knowing more about various treatment options.

Defensive Medicine Increases Demand Even if doctors don't benefit directly from extra medical procedures, they may face other conflicts of interest. For example, doctors may fear malpractice lawsuits in which they have to defend a decision *not* to order various diagnostic tests.

These extra tests are known as defensive medicine. **Defensive medicine** is the practice of recommending a diagnostic test or treatment that is not normally required but is done to protect doctors against potential malpractice lawsuits. In fact, doctors often provide screening for some types of cancer even when scientific studies suggest that such tests

principal–agent problem
The difficulty of making agents act in the best interest of the principals that they serve.

defensive medicine The practice of recommending a diagnostic test or treatment that is not normally required but is done to protect doctors against potential malpractice lawsuits.

"AND NOW SOME EXPENSIVE TESTS TO SEE IF THE CHEAP ONES WE RAN WERE ACCURATE ..."

Harley Schawadron/Cartoonstock

EXHIBIT 9 Diminishing Returns on Health-Care Spending

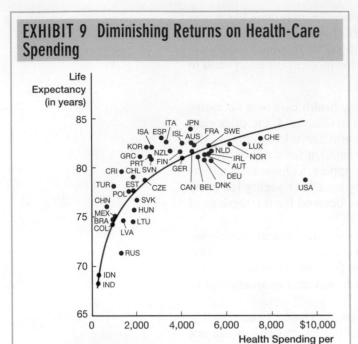

Health-care spending also appears to have diminishing returns (see Chapter 11). The marginal benefit from additional health care in a measurable health-care output decreases with additional spending. The figure shows that additional spending on health care has diminishing returns on life expectancy.

Data from: OECD

may do more harm than good. Most economists agree that defensive medicine and malpractice lawsuits add to the overall cost of health care, although there is disagreement on the extent of such costs.

End-of-Life Care Is Expensive End-of-life health care is particularly expensive. As one *60 Minutes* news report noted, "Every medical study ever conducted has concluded that 100 percent of all Americans will eventually die. This comes as no great surprise, but the amount of money being spent at the very end of people's lives probably will." Medicare alone spends some $50 billion dollars on patients during the last two months of life. This accounts for roughly 25% of Medicare's hospital spending and 10% of Medicare's overall spending.[7] For example, 40.3 percent of Americans with cancer were admitted to an intensive care unit during the last six months of life, a rate more than double that of any other nation.[8]

Cutting-Edge Medical Technology Can Lead to Diminishing Returns Not only does health insurance make patients less cost conscious when deciding where to spend their health-care dollars, but it also has given the medical industry an enormous incentive to innovate—to create new techniques and new drugs that provide some benefit, no matter how slight. Unfortunately, there is evidence of rapidly diminishing returns beyond a certain level of expenditure.

As health-care spending increases, the marginal benefit from an additional dollar spent falls sharply, as Exhibit 9 demonstrates. In the typical OECD nation, the first $2,000 per person spent on health care increases life expectancy by over 12 years on average, the second $2,000 spent on health care adds roughly 6 years, and the third $2,000 spent on health care adds even less to life expectancy. This may overstate the benefits of health care because death rates in richer countries also fall for other reasons, like better diet and fewer accidents.

Even worse, there is some evidence that the excessive use of medical services can actually reduce health in some cases. Each year, many people die from infections picked up while they are in a hospital. There is no solid evidence that Americans receive any benefit at all from spending twice as much on health care as most other developed countries spend. There might be a slight benefit, but it is difficult to prove.

Barriers to Entry Restrict Supply and Reduce Cost-Effectiveness There are many barriers to entry in health care, which makes it difficult for new, more cost-effective firms to enter the industry and hold down costs. The number of doctors is restricted by government laws that require doctors to have a medical license, and the American Medical Association (AMA) restricts the number of medical students. As is the case in other businesses, when supply is limited, imperfect competition exists. This raises the salaries of American doctors far above the average level in other developed countries.

In many cases, foreign medical providers could produce medical services at dramatically lower costs, but Medicare won't pay for their services. Regulations make it difficult to open a new hospital. Americans are not allowed to buy pharmaceuticals from other countries, where prices are often dramatically lower. Residents of one state are not allowed to buy health insurance from companies in a neighboring state, where prices may be far lower. Regulations often prevent nurses from providing certain routine medical services. A pharmacist cannot prescribe drugs. And there are many, many more such examples.

Much of this problem is related to *rent seeking*—activities such as lobbying the government with the goal of obtaining subsidies, barriers to entry, and other special privileges (see Chapter 13). For instance, when groups like the AMA lobby politicians to restrict entry into the medical profession, the net effect is to make the supply of health care much less price elastic than it could be.

BUSINESS BRIEF SmartShopper Overcomes Asymmetric Information in Health Care

Consumers tend to shop for the best price for everything from apples to airplane tickets but not for MRI scans. One investigation revealed that in Pensacola, Florida, the prices for an MRI range from $400 to $800—even though the location with the best equipment had the lowest price. Because of the nature of health insurance, consumers tend not to be price conscious.*

In 2010, a small company called SmartShopper was formed to allow consumers to compare both prices and the quality of care. Insurers pay for the site, which helps more than 150 million people a year to overcome the problem of asymmetric information.†

Better still, the company uses a system of rebate checks to encourage consumers to choose a lower-cost health-care provider for services ranging from routine lab work to non-life-threatening surgeries. This puts downward pressure on the price of these items. The savings typically add up to a few hundred dollars a year for each user—enough to motivate consumers to focus on the price of the health-care services they are receiving. It also reduces cost for health insurance companies.‡

*"Episode 655: Pay Patients, Save Money," Planet Money, NPR, October 2, 2015, http://www.npr.org/sections /money/2015/10/02/445371930/episode-655-pay-patients-save-money.

†"About SmartShopper," Vitals SmartShopper, accessed May 8, 2017, https://www.vitalssmartshopper.com /About.

‡Tom Murphy, "Employers Offer Cash to Push Shopping Around for Health Care," *Cleveland Jewish News*, February 8, 2017, accessed May 8, 2017, http://www.clevelandjewishnews.com/features/health/employers -offer-cash-to-push-shopping-around-for-health-care/article_e2efd6da-ee3b-11e6-ba8c-7775fe674d42.html.

BUSINESS TAKEAWAY

Effective business decision making entails understanding the economics of information and insurance. Even if you sell a high-quality product, you will not be able to achieve a premium price if buyers have doubts about quality. Businesses have a strong incentive to overcome asymmetric information through effective product signaling. Similarly, if you are providing a product such as insurance or lending, you need to take steps to overcome the adverse selection and moral hazard problems. Otherwise, your business may face an adverse selection of individuals who are buying insurance plans or applying for loans.

Health care touches almost every aspect of the American economy. It is the largest industry in the United States and includes some of its most dynamic companies, such as biotech companies that are creating new treatments for diseases. Health-care costs affect almost all businesses and all levels of government. General Motors, for example, spends more than $2,000 per car on health insurance for its employees. Because health-care costs are rising rapidly and insurance coverage is a major part of employee wages and benefits, employers are continually looking for insurance plans that are cost effective. To reduce health-care costs, companies have experimented with ideas such as higher deductibles to discourage workers from overusing medical services. At the same time, as new research leads to expensive new treatments for health conditions, employees expect to have access to all treatments if they get sick.

CHAPTER STUDY GUIDE

19.1 THE PROBLEM OF ASYMMETRIC INFORMATION AND ADVERSE SELECTION

Asymmetric information refers to an exchange where one party has better information than the other. **Adverse selection** is the tendency of asymmetric information to result in a less desirable selection of goods and services in the marketplace due to uninformed buyers or sellers. **Screening** is the acquisition of reliable information about a product or resource to help make a more informed decision on a purchase or sale. **Signaling** is the providing of reliable information about a product or resource to help another party make a more informed decision on a purchase or sale. Screening and signaling provide buyers and sellers with ways to overcome problems associated with asymmetric information. The **sheepskin effect** refers to the increase in earnings from obtaining higher credentials as opposed to higher levels of human capital.

19.2 THE INSURANCE MARKET: LESS INFORMED SELLERS

The buyer often has more information than sellers. A good example occurs in the market for insurance. Insurance companies need to be concerned about ending up with an adverse selection of insurance customers, particularly for their premium products, which provide complete coverage. **Moral hazard** is a situation where there is an increased tendency to take risks because some of the potential costs associated with these risks will be paid by others. A **deductible** is the amount that a consumer must pay before the insurance provider will pay any claims on the policy. A **copayment** is an individual's share of the cost on a claim with the insurance provider paying the rest. High deductibles and copayments reduce the moral hazard problem. An **experience rating** is a method used to determine the price of insurance based on a group's or an individual's history of claims. Mandated insurance is insurance required by law. Such a requirement tends to minimize adverse selection because everyone must have insurance. Another way to limit the problem is to limit the period of time in which people can buy an insurance policy; this is known as an open enrollment period.

19.3 THE U.S. HEALTH-CARE SYSTEM: STRUCTURE AND OUTCOMES

Health care is the largest industry in the United States and in many other developed countries. Health-care spending is much higher in the United States than in other countries and has been increasing in recent decades. Even so, tens of millions of Americans lack health insurance, although the recent Patient Protection and Affordable Care Act (ACA) has reduced that number somewhat. Most measures of well-being, such as life expectancy and infant mortality, do not provide evidence that the overall health-care system in the United States is more effective than in other countries. **Universal health coverage** is a health-care system that ensures that health-care benefits are provided to all citizens. A **single-payer health-care system** is a health-care system where the government pays for most health-care costs. Instead of universal coverage or a single-payer system, the United States has a complex mixture of public and private health insurance plans. Health-care spending in the United States is high for several reasons, include the following: (1) Insurance boosts demand for health-care service; (2) subsidies increase the demand for health insurance; (3) there is a price inelastic demand for health care; (4) the **principal–agent problem** refers to the difficulty of making agents act in the best interest of the principals that they serve; (5) **defensive medicine** is the practice of recommending a diagnostic test or treatment that is not normally required but is done to protect doctors against potential malpractice lawsuits; (6) end of life care is expensive; (7) there is a high cost for cutting-edge medical technology and diminishing returns; and (8) barriers to entry reduce supply.

TOP TEN TERMS AND CONCEPTS

1. Asymmetric Information
2. Adverse Selection
3. Screening and Signaling
4. Sheepskin Effect
5. Moral Hazard
6. Deductible and Copayment
7. Experience Rating
8. Universal Coverage and Single Payer
9. Patient Protection and Affordable Care Act of 2010 (ACA)
10. Principal–Agent Problem and Defensive Medicine

STUDY PROBLEMS

1. In each of the following markets, state whether the buyers or sellers have an informational advantage.

   a. The used boat market

   b. The life insurance market

   c. The used appliance market

   d. A website collectibles market

2. Why might sellers of collectible goods command higher prices when they have a high seller rating on eBay?

3. A cash gift may be welcome from a parent or relative. A similar gift received from a dating partner may be problematic. Use the concept of signaling to explain why.

4. List a few ways that insurance companies can overcome the moral hazard problem.

5. In the 1980s, many savings and loan banks failed. Prior to failure, these institutions often paid higher-than-average interest rates to lure in depositors. Explain this in the context of moral hazard.

6. Graph a supply and demand model for quality preowned boats used primarily in fresh water and problematic preowned boats used primarily in salt water. Assume that buyers are unable to identify which type of preowned boat is being purchased. Explain what happens to the price of the preowned boat.

7. In 2013, prior to the implementation of many of the provisions in the Affordable Care Act, 13.3% of people were without insurance for the entire year. Using online census data, what the most recent estimate?

8. In what ways does asymmetric information impact the demand for medical care? Provide an example.

9. In what ways does moral hazard impact the demand for medical care? Provide an example.

10. In what ways does restricted supply impact the demand for medical care? Provide an example.

11. For each of the following, state which demand is more price inelastic.

    a. A routine physical covered by insurance versus one not covered by insurance

    b. A CT scan when there are symptoms of a life-threatening disease versus a scan to detect a broken rib.

    c. Cosmetic surgery versus life-saving surgery

12. Discuss the pros and cons of allowing very high prices on new cancer drugs. Do so by considering the pros and cons of price controls to hold down drug prices. How does the existence of health insurance impact the market for cancer drugs?

13. How does the U.S. health-care system differ from single-payer systems such as the one in Canada?

14. Since 1960, health-care costs in the United States have risen sharply. Provide three reasons for the sharp increase in costs.

15. Some people compare the effectiveness of health care in different countries by looking at life expectancy. In average, what happens to life expectancy as spending on health care rises? Also discuss why life expectancy data might provide a misleading indicator of the quality of health care.

^ Measuring the economy is a vital first step in macroeconomics.

Real GDP and the Price Level

Measuring the Performance of the Overall Economy

Every couple of months, the news cycle is dominated by at least one announcement about the economy. Analysts might express concern that the economy expanded by only 0.2% in the second quarter or that the inflation rate is rising. Perhaps you have seen a spokesperson for the president promise economic growth of 4% from the White House lawn. But what do these terms mean? How do economists measure the economy—and what does it mean to say that the economy is growing? How does this growth affect you?

The state of the economy matters to just about everyone—businesses trying to figure out whether to expand or invest, families trying to balance their budgets, recent college graduates seeking employment, nations deciding if they can afford a public works project or a military buildup, and politicians at every level seeking to be elected or reelected. In order to make intelligent decisions, each of these actors must understand how economists evaluate the overall performance of the economy. As you'll recall from Chapter 1, that's what macroeconomics is all about—economic issues that impact the overall economy. In this chapter, we begin with two vital macroeconomic measures—the rate of inflation and the gross domestic product (GDP). We start with the broadest measure of the economy, GDP.

20.1 GROSS DOMESTIC PRODUCT (GDP)

Gross domestic product (GDP) is the market value of all final goods and services produced in a country during a given time period. GDP is the broadest measure of the economy and captures all economic activity—from the development of apps to the production of airplanes,

Chapter Learning Targets

● Define gross domestic product (GDP), and explain what it measures.

● Describe how GDP is measured, and identify other measures of national income.

● Define inflation, deflation, and disinflation, and explain how the inflation rate is calculated.

● Compare and contrast the major price indices.

● Distinguish between the differences between nominal GDP and real GDP.

zinc cream, and zucchini bread. It also includes services like haircuts, taxi rides, and economic lectures. In the United States, GDP is measured in trillions of dollars. To put this in perspective, a trillion dollars is a million *million*—enough to give a million people a million dollars each. Here we investigate each element of the definition of GDP in greater detail.

"the market value ..." GDP is measured in terms of market value based on prices, not quantity. Combining a million units of apples and airplanes would not be useful because one apple is very different from one Boeing 787 Dreamliner. Because the price of one apple or one app is only a small fraction of the price of an airplane, the production of an airplane adds more to a country's GDP than the production of an apple or app does. GDP is measured in monetary terms, so U.S. GDP is measured in U.S. dollars, Japanese GDP is measured in Japanese yen, and German GDP is measured in euros.

"... of all final goods and services ..." GDP attempts to measure the entire production of all finished goods and services. Finished goods and services are only those things that are sold to end users. GDP excludes intermediate goods. **Intermediate goods** are products used as an input in the production of final goods. For example, the pizza you buy at Mario's is part of GDP, but the inputs that Mario purchased to make the pizza—the ingredients, the labor, and so on—are not. On the other hand, when you buy ingredients to make pizza at home, those transactions are included as part of GDP. GDP focuses on final goods in order to avoid *double counting*: If we count the value of the Mario's inputs and also count the value of his final sales of pizza, then we would be counting the intermediate goods twice, making GDP seem larger than it actually is.

GDP includes the value of using housing. For apartments and other rental units, this value is simply the rents paid to landlords. But many people own their own homes and do not pay rent. To account for this, GDP includes "owner's equivalent rent," an estimate of rents homeowners would need to pay to rent an equivalent housing unit. Essentially, it is the value of homeowners' use of their own homes.

Although economists would like to know the value of *all* final goods and services, as a practical matter GDP excludes a great deal of production. GDP fails to capture production that occurs outside of markets. GDP excludes things (like mowing one's own lawn or caring for one's own children) that, if purchased from paid professionals, would be included in GDP. It also excludes the sale of illegal goods and services.

"... produced in a country ..." GDP captures *domestic* production, which is production within a single country, and excludes items made outside the country. A German-made Mercedes sold in Chicago is produced outside the United States, and thus the production cost of the car is excluded from U.S. GDP. However, GDP does include services, so although the wholesale price of the imported Mercedes is part of the German GDP, the cost of trucking it from the dock to the Chicago dealership and the retail markup charged by the dealer are part of the U.S. GDP.

"... during a given time period" GDP measures total production within a country during a specific time frame. It includes items made during the current period, even if unsold, and excludes items made during prior periods. Items such as homes and cars often are not sold in the same year they are built and are considered **inventory**—a stock of unsold goods and raw materials.

The value of the *retailing services* (as opposed to the production cost) on the sale of older goods (such as inventory and used goods) are counted as part of GDP in the year the goods are sold. For example, if a new Ford pickup truck produced in the United States in 2018 is not sold until 2019, then the production cost of the Ford is part of U.S. GDP for 2018, and the retail markup on the truck is part of the 2019 GDP.

GDP is typically measured in both annual (12-month) and quarterly (3-month) increments. Note that U.S. quarterly growth rates are often annualized in news reports, which means they are multiplied by four. If you hear that U.S. GDP rose by 2% in

gross domestic product (GDP) The market value of all final goods and services produced in a country during a given time period.

intermediate goods Products used as an input in the production of final goods.

inventory A stock of unsold goods and raw materials.

EXHIBIT 1 Unpacking the Definition of GDP

"The market value . . .	of all final goods and services . . .	produced within a country . . .	during a given period of time"
GDP is measured in terms of market value based on prices, not quantity.	GDP attempts to measure the entire production of all finished goods and services.	GDP captures domestic production—that is, production within a country.	GDP is total production within a country in a given time period. It excludes items made during prior periods.

The definition of GDP packs a powerful punch. Each component carries a specific meaning.

the most recent quarter, it actually rose by 0.5% above the previous quarter's level, a 2% annual rate if continued for a full year. Note that the quarterly GDP figures for many other areas, such as Europe and Japan, typically are not annualized by the news media, which can lead to confusion. Exhibit 1 summarizes the key elements of the definition of GDP.

20.2 IT'S NOT EASY TO MEASURE GDP

As you might imagine, measuring something as big as the U.S. economy is complicated. Economists use several different approaches. The most widely understood method of measuring GDP is to add up all *expenditures*. There are several other methods as well. Recall that every dollar spent by one person is another person's income. Suppose that Amelia purchases a pizza from Mario's for $20. The $20 expenditure by Amelia (money spent) is revenue (money received for selling products) to Mario. If Mario has no expenses related to the pizza, he receives $20 in income (earnings).

In reality, Mario almost certainly has some expenses. If he has $18 in expenses—$6 for labor and $12 for raw materials and ingredients—then Mario will have income in the form of profits of $2 ($20 in revenue minus $18 in costs and expenses). But notice that Mario's expenses then become *someone else's* income. Mario's workers have income of $6, and the producers of the raw materials and ingredients have income of $12. Thus, the purchase of a $20 pizza leads to $20 in expenditures and $20 in income for Mario and various producers ($2 for Mario, $6 for his workers, and $12 for his suppliers). Alternatively, if Mario buys raw materials and ingredients for $12, then he and his employees *add* $8 to the value of the materials, and the suppliers *add* $12 in value by producing raw materials. Once again, this adds up to $20.

This example illustrates the three most common ways of measuring GDP—adding all expenditures in a country, adding all income in a country, or adding the value that is added at each step of production. To see how the three approaches relate to each other, let's review the circular flow model from Chapter 2 as shown in Exhibit 2. Products flow from firms through the product market to households. Simultaneously, resources flow from households through the resource market to firms. These resources are used to produce the goods and services that firms sell in the product market. In exchange for providing resources, households receive income: They are paid wages for their labor, rent for their land, interest for their capital, and profits for their entrepreneurship. The circular flow model demonstrates that expenditures equal total income and that total income equals total production.

Think & Speak Like an Economist

When discussing GDP, *production* refers only to goods and services that are bought and sold in legal markets. Personal production—for example, growing your own food or changing the oil in your car—has real value but doesn't contribute to measured GDP.

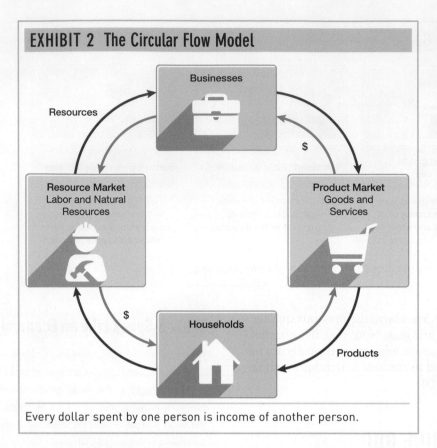

EXHIBIT 2 The Circular Flow Model

Businesses

Resources

Resource Market
Labor and Natural
Resources

Product Market
Goods and
Services

$

$

Households

Products

Every dollar spent by one person is income of another person.

Four Expenditure Components of GDP

There are four major expenditures that, when added together, equal GDP. The **expenditure approach equation** calculates GDP by adding all expenditures for consumption (C), investment (I), and government purchases (G), and net exports (NX):

$$GDP = C + I + G + NX$$

In essence, the equation calculates total spending on domestically produced products, including all final goods and services. Understanding the expenditure approach equation is vital as we move through the chapters on macroeconomics, so let's look at each component more closely.

Consumption Expenditures (C) The largest expenditure in GDP is consumption. **Consumption expenditures** include household purchases of goods and services other than new housing. It includes *durable goods* (goods expected to last more than a year, like appliances and cars), *nondurable goods* (like food and clothing), and services (like haircuts and Internet connections). It does not include goods used to produce additional goods and services or the purchase of a home. Instead, the use of housing (measured as rent) is included in consumption.

Investment Expenditures (I) Spending on goods and services used in the production of other goods and services makes up the second part of the expenditure approach equation. As is shown in Chapter 1, **investment** refers to spending on new capital goods. Also recall that **physical capital** is durable equipment and structures used to produce goods and services; it is sometimes referred to simply as *capital* in economics. Examples including spending on new office buildings, new residential structures, and new machines.

There are three major categories of investment:

- *Business fixed investment.* Spending by businesses on physical capital. Examples include new factories, new office buildings, new restaurant buildings, and machinery.

- *Residential investment.* Spending by households and businesses on new homes and apartments buildings. Although the use of an existing home is considered a consumption expenditure, the production of a new home is considered a residential investment. The sale of an existing home was already included in GDP when the home was constructed.

- *Inventory investment.* Changes in stockpiles of final goods, raw materials, and other components used by businesses to meet the anticipated future needs of customers. Even if these are consumer goods, they are treated as an inventory investment until the year they are sold.

From a business perspective, the decision to stockpile goods and make an inventory investment is similar to the decision to build a new factory with the hope that it

Think & Speak Like an Economist

Remember that economists use the term *capital* to refer specifically to physical capital and *investment* to describe spending on new physical capital. In business and finance, both terms generally refer to money: *Financial capital* is money raised in financial markets, and *financial investment* is a way of employing savings such as buying stocks.

expenditure approach equation An equation that calculates GDP by adding all expenditures for consumption (C), investment (I), government purchases (G), and exports (NX). Mathematically, this is $GDP = C + I + G + NX$.

consumption expenditures Household purchases of goods and services other than new housing.

will be profitable in the future. Walmart and toy stores may stockpile merchandise in October with the hopes of making a profit in December. Note that inventory investment represents *changes* in the stockpile of goods. The existing inventory was already included in GDP estimates for prior periods.

Government Purchases (G) **Government purchases** are spending by federal, state, and local governments on goods, services, and investments. These purchases exclude transfer payments. Government spending on law enforcement, firefighting, the legal system, national defense, infrastructure, and education is all included in GDP.

Not all government spending is considered a government purchase. **Transfer payments** are payments made by a government when no goods and services are currently supplied. Examples include Social Security, unemployment benefits, and interest payments on government debt. Because these do not involve the current production of any goods and services, they are not included in GDP.

Net Exports (NX) If we stop after $C + I + G$, we have total final sales in the economy—all goods and services sold in a given year. But GDP measures total domestic *production*, not sales. What if U.S. automobile manufacturers sell U.S.-made cars in Canada? That is U.S. production, but it's not domestic (U.S.) consumption. We add exports and subtract imports in order to convert total domestic sales into total domestic production. **Net exports** equal a country's exports minus its imports and are also referred to as the *trade balance*. Because U.S. exports are produced inside the United States, they should be included as part of U.S. GDP. But they don't show up as part of U.S. consumption, investment, or government output.

Conversely, when an American purchases a $30,000 Volkswagen Jetta imported from Germany, it is *not* included in the U.S. GDP. The Jetta appears positively as a consumption expenditure (*C*) *and* is subtracted as an import (recall that $NX = \text{Exports} - \text{Imports}$). The positive consumption and negative imports exactly cancel out each other, and thus imported goods are not included in the GDP total. By including net exports in the expenditure approach equation, we are able to include domestically produced items sold in another country (exports) and not include foreign-made items sold domestically (imports).

investment Spending on new capital goods. Investment increases the amount of physical capital in an economy.

physical capital Durable equipment and structures used to produce goods and services; sometimes referred to simply as *capital* in economics.

government purchases Spending by federal, state, and local governments on goods, services, and investments. Government purchases exclude transfer payments.

transfer payments Payments made by a government when no goods and services are currently supplied.

net exports Equal a country's exports minus its imports; also referred to as the *trade balance*.

📊 BUSINESS BRIEF What Is an "American" Car?

In the 1950s, identifying a U.S.-made car was easy: People could just look for a Ford, General Motors, or Chrysler nameplate. If a car had the nameplate of a foreign automaker, it was an import. Today, it can be difficult to identify the country of origin on most mass-produced cars. Exhibit 3 shows the "domestic content"—roughly the percentage of final value that comes from U.S. firms—of some of the best-selling cars in 2017.* The domestic content is the share of the total cost of a car that leads to income for American workers and companies.

Notice that many cars manufactured by foreign automakers are actually more "American" in terms of domestic content than some popular Ford and GM products. Does this matter? Americans seem to think so. A recent *Consumer Reports* survey found that, given the choice between a U.S.-made product and an identical product made elsewhere, 78% of Americans would rather buy American. But as these figures imply, it's not always easy to "buy American" when buying a new car.†

EXHIBIT 3 Made in America Auto Index, 2017

Make	Model	Approximate Domestic Content
Toyota	Camry	78.5%
Honda	Accord	76.0
Nissan	Altima	61.5
Infinity	QX 60	45.0
Buick	Encore	20.5
Ford	Fusion	48.5
Ford	Fiesta	15.5
Jeep	Renegade	38.0
Chevrolet	Captiva	12.5

The approximate domestic content of select automobile models in 2017.

This also complicates the measurement of GDP. Exports are produced within a country, and imports are not. To gauge an automobile's contribution to GDP, estimates of a car's domestic content are required. Roughly 78.5% of a 2017 Toyota Camry is produced in the United States—and so 78.5% of its final selling price is included in the U.S. GDP. The other 21.5% is imported and included in the GDP of other countries.

*Frank DuBois, "Made in America Auto Index 2017," Kogod School of Business, American University, accessed November 11, 2017, http://www.american.edu/kogod/research/autoindex.

†"Knowing Which Products Are Truly Made in America," Consumer Reports, February 2013, accessed May 14, 2017, http://www.consumerreports.org/cro/magazine/2013/02/made-in-america/index.htm.

Breaking Down GDP by Expenditure Categories Exhibit 4 shows the values of the major expenditure components of U.S. GDP for the first quarter of 2018. These are the key findings:

- Consumption expenditures make up 69.0% of GDP. Services account for the majority of consumption expenditures.
- Investment expenditures make up 16.9% of GDP. Business fixed investment accounts for the majority of gross private domestic investment.

EXHIBIT 4 GDP Expenditures, 2018

Expenditure Approach Measure of GDP for U.S. 2018 in dollars and percent of GDP

Category	Billions of U.S. Dollars	Percentage of GDP
Consumption Expenditures	**$13,776**	**69.0%**
Durable Goods	1,502	
Nondurable Goods	2,915	
Services	9,359	
Gross Private Domestic Investment	**3,378**	**16.9**
Business Fixed Investment	2,577	
Housing and Residential Investment	779	
Change in Private Inventories	22	
Government Purchases	**3,443**	**17.3**
Federal	1,297	
State and Local	2,146	
Net Exports of Goods and Services	**−641**	**−3.2**
Exports	2,468	
Imports	3,109	
Gross Domestic Product	**$19,957**	**100.0%**

Gross domestic product (GDP) can be measured using the expenditure approach, which adds all spending for final goods and services by households, firms, and governments. GDP = Consumption (C) + Investment (I) + Government (G) + Net exports (NX). The largest category is consumption expenditures. Consumption accounts for most of GDP, and net exports (exports minus imports) is negative. This is annualized data from Q1 2018.

Data from: U.S. Bureau of Economic Analysis, http://www.bea.gov.

- Government purchases make up 17.3% of GDP.

- Net exports account for −3.2% of GDP. The United States had a trade deficit, so this figure is a negative percentage. But this is simply accounting. It does *not* mean that the U.S. economy would be bigger if we had no trade deficit because other categories (like *C* and *I*) would also change if we imported fewer goods.

Value Added and Income Approaches to Measuring GDP

In addition to using the expenditure approach, GDP also can be estimated using the value added approach and the income approach. Using the expenditure approach equation, we add the value of all final goods and services produced in the economy and exclude the value of intermediate goods to avoid double counting.

Another way to avoid double counting is to use the *value added approach*—counting only the increases in the market value of the product made at each stage of production. In our example, Mario sells pizza for $20 and buys raw materials and ingredients for $12, which is paid to the producers of the raw goods. In making the pizzas, Mario and his employees add $8 to the value of the raw materials and ingredients. Instead of counting only the final value of the pizzas, we could simply add the value added at each stage of production. The producers of raw materials (farmers) also add $12 in value, and so the total contribution to GDP is $20.

In most products, there are many stages of production. For instance, coal and iron are used to make steel, and steel is used to make cars. But no matter how many stages, by calculating the value added at each stage of production *once*, we end up with the final value of the product. Carrying this out for every product produced in the economy should result in an identical result for GDP. Outside the United States, the value added approach is especially important because most developed countries have value added tax (VAT) systems.

The *income approach* calculates GDP by adding all income earned by all resources in the economy. This includes wages paid to workers, interest earned by savers and lenders, rent earned by property owners, and profits earned by business owners. In the pizza example, the seller has profits of $2 and pays workers $6 per pizza, and the producers of various raw materials (such as farmers) have a total income of $12, presumably shared with their workers. The total contribution to GDP is $20 ($2 + $6 + $12).

Other Measures of Income and Federal Reserve Economic Data (FRED)

Although measuring production in an economy is important, particularly in macroeconomics, other measures of income are also important. For example, a business may be less concerned with total production in society and more concerned with the income of its customers.

Gross domestic product is somewhat higher than the income that the public actually receives. This is because some of the nation's capital depreciates and often needs to be replaced. **Depreciation of capital** is the loss of value that occurs when physical capital wears out with use or becomes obsolete. Subtracting capital depreciation from GDP results in net domestic product. **Net domestic product (NDP)** is gross domestic product adjusted for capital depreciation. NDP is the income that society actually sees.

In addition, indirect business taxes (such as sales taxes) are part of the price of goods and services but are not part of anyone's income. So we also subtract indirect

depreciation of capital The loss of value that occurs when physical capital wears out with use or becomes obsolete.

net domestic product (NDP) Gross domestic product adjusted for capital depreciation.

business taxes to obtain national income. **National income** is gross domestic product minus depreciation and indirect business taxes.

Business are particularly concerned with the income of their customers. **Disposable personal income** is earned and unearned income minus taxes. Disposable income is income available to be spent or saved by households. Because some social insurance transfer payments (such as Social Security and unemployment benefits) are a form of household income, they are combined with earned income in the calculation of disposable income.

This text emphasizes GDP measured using the expenditure approach. This is a gross measure of income, which is somewhat larger than net domestic product, national income, and disposable personal income. Fortunately, these measures track each other relatively closely over time.

Businesses do not need to gather their own economic data on the state of the economy, including the various measures of income presented above. Federal Reserve Economic Data (FRED) compiles U.S. and international data for each of these statistics and numerous others (http://research.stlouisfed.org/fred2/). Half a million time series data sets from 87 sources from around the world are hosted on a single website that allows for economic data to be downloaded and viewed graphically at no cost to the public. FRED data is used extensively throughout macroeconomics, including reports on GDP, unemployment, inflation, and the level of current business activity.

national income Gross domestic product minus depreciation and indirect business taxes.

disposable personal income Earned and unearned income minus taxes.

GDP Is Not a Perfect Measure

GDP per capita (per person) is one of the most widely used macroeconomic concepts for measuring living standards. Exhibit 5 demonstrates GDP per capita for 12 major economies in 2016, measured in U.S. dollars and adjusted for cost of living

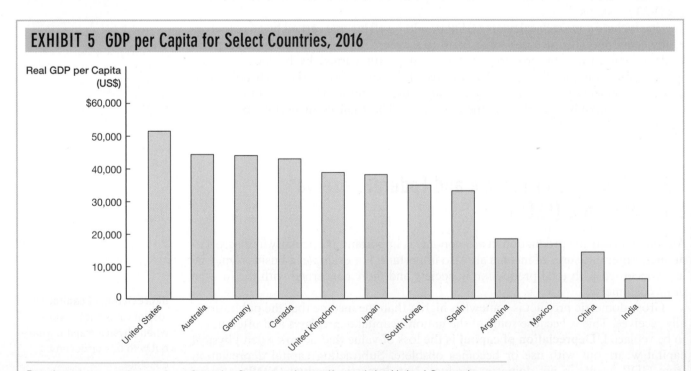

EXHIBIT 5   GDP per Capita for Select Countries, 2016

Developed economies such as Canada, Germany, Australia, and the United States have larger GDP per capita than developing economies such as Mexico, China, and India, even after adjusting for cost of living differences.

Data from: World Bank.

differences. Developed economies such as Canada, Germany, Australia, and the United States have larger GDPs per capita than developing economies such as Mexico, China, and India.

Although GDP per capita data is useful, the estimated values ignore some factors that also affect living standards. These omissions may not be important when we examine short-run changes during recessions and economic expansions. But they are very important if we are trying to use GDP per capita as an estimate of living standards.

The Value of Leisure Is Not Considered Leisure represents time away from work and is an economic "good" that is not included in GDP. Suppose you were offered two jobs with equal pay. In one job, you work 4 days a week, and in another job, you work 7 days a week. Which job would you prefer? Clearly, leisure has a positive value, but because it does not involve producing goods and services, it is not included in GDP.

Americans now have more leisure time than they had in 1900, when a six-day workweek was standard.[1] Since 1900, the average workweek has dropped from 53 hours to about 36 hours. This demonstrates that our living standards have improved by even more than the increase in goods and services available—and thus more than the increase in GDP would indicate.

Nonmarket Transactions and Illegal Activities Are Not Considered Earlier we saw that GDP excludes nonmarket transactions and illegal activities. Cooking your own meals and caring for your own children are not counted as part GDP, but when you are paid to provide such services to others, it is. Likewise, vegetables from your garden don't count, but those purchased at your local farm stand do. Illicit activities (like illegal drug sales) and unreported earnings (money earned "off the books" in part to avoid paying taxes) are not included in measured GDP. Accurately measuring the value of these transactions—often referred to as the "underground economy"—is difficult, although a few rough estimates have been made. One study has estimated the underground economy to be 13% of GDP in developed countries and 36% in developing countries. In the United States, estimates range from 7.2 to 12% of GDP.[2]

Environmental and Health Issues Are Not Considered Suppose that two companies produce tires—one in an environmentally friendly manner and the other in a factory that emits a lot of pollution. The market value of the tires reflects only the quality of the tire to the buyer. It does not reflect differences in how "green" the production process is. GDP fails to capture the value to society of clean water, clean air, and health-related outcomes (such as increased life expectancy and decreased infant mortality rates resulting from improved sanitation, education, and healthcare).

There Are Limits to International Comparisons The actual gap between high-income and low-income countries may be different than what GDP per capita (per person) estimates suggest. On the one hand, poor nations typically have more production in nonmarket transactions. People in very poor nations, for example, often grow and prepare their own food and build their own houses. Including this sort of production would lower the gap

▼ The size of the underground economy in developing countries complicates measuring GDP.

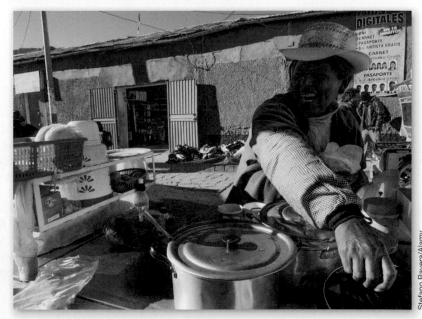

Stefano Ravera/Alamy

between rich and poor nations. On the other hand, poor nations often have greater environmental problems, lower life expectancies, higher crime rates, and less leisure time. Including these factors would widen the gap.

Putting a clear and consistent value on things like leisure, health outcomes, and environmental quality is difficult and would involve a great deal of guess-work. And nonmarket transactions—especially illegal activities—are typically unreported, making them difficult to quantify. Despite its shortcomings, GDP per capita is viewed as a useful indicator of economic well-being and economic activity.

📊 BUSINESS BRIEF   The Informal Economy in Latin America

In most developing countries, many people work in what is called the informal or unreported economy. Their small family enterprises are not regulated, and they often lack property rights to their place of business. In Mexico and Brazil, the informal economy is estimated to be roughly 28% of GDP, and in several smaller economies (Honduras, Ecuador, Paraguay, and Nicaragua), the share is over 50%. In Bolivia, it is estimated that the informal economy accounts for 65% of measured GDP.

The informal economy is a part of the underground economy that engages in mostly otherwise legal economic activity. Most people in this sector work in small, often family-run businesses and have relatively low incomes. Why is there such a large share of business activity in the informal economy? One reason is that joining the formal economy often means paying taxes. In addition, complex and costly regulations make it difficult to start new businesses in the formal economy.

As an experiment, economist Hernando De Soto attempted to legalize a small, one-employee garment shop near Lima, Peru. It took his team nearly 300 days at a cost over 30 times higher than the *monthly* minimum wage. De Soto concluded that "Inevitably (workers and small business owners) do not so much break the law as the law breaks them—and they opt out of the system."* For this reason, GDP data in many Latin American countries significantly underreports otherwise legal economic activity due to the existence of the informal economy.

*Hernando De Soto, quoted in John Otis, "Informal Economy Swallows Latin American Workers," *GlobalPost*, Public Radio International, July 3, 2012, http://www.globalpost.com/dispatch/news/regions/americas/120702 /informal-economy-swallows-latin-american-workers.

20.3 INFLATION

GDP measures the total size of the economy in dollar terms. But this can be a misleading measure when prices are unstable. If prices are increasing, for example, the dollar value of GDP may rise even as the amount of goods and services being produced remains the same. This leads to the second key macroeconomic variable that economists must consider when analyzing the economy—the overall average price level of goods and services.

If you've already studied microeconomics, you know that when demand for a product increases or supply decreases, then its price will increase. But this is very different from a change in the *overall price level*, which affects thousands of goods. Recall from Chapter 1 that **inflation** is an increase in the overall price level that results in a decline in the value or purchasing power of money. On the other hand, **deflation** is a decrease

inflation An increase in the overall price level that results in a decline in the value or purchasing power of money.

deflation A decrease in the overall price level that results in an increase in the value or purchasing power of money.

in the overall price level that results in an increase in the value or purchasing power of money.

Such changes in overall prices are generally reported as the **inflation rate**—the annual percentage change in average prices. Inflation occurs when there is a positive inflation rate, and deflation occurs when there is a negative inflation rate. The inflation rate captures changes in *average* prices, but individual price changes vary widely. When the overall inflation rate is 2%, some prices will be rising much more rapidly, and some prices will actually be declining. When economists talk about inflation, they generally are talking about the inflation rate.

Inflation Leads to a Decline in the Value of Money

The value of money reflects its *purchasing power*. This means that the value of a dollar bill declines with inflation, which decreases the purchasing power of money. For instance, if the price level doubles, then each dollar bill buys only half as many goods and services as before.

Consider the hypothetical example of the price of a dozen eggs in 1820, 1920, and 2020 as shown in Exhibit 6. The dollar price of a dozen eggs doubled from 1820 to 1920 and increased 10-fold from 1920 to 2020. Although in dollar terms, a dozen eggs cost 20 times what they used to cost, eggs probably are not 20 times more valuable than they were 200 years ago. It is more likely that the value of the U.S. dollar has declined.

To see this, let's look at the same transaction from the opposite direction. Rather than consider how much eggs cost, we can consider the value of a dollar in terms of eggs. In 1820, a farmer would have to produce 120 eggs (10 dozen eggs) to earn a dollar. In 1920, a farmer needed only 60 eggs to earn a dollar. Thus, the value of a dollar was essentially cut in half from 1820 to 1920, in terms of eggs. By 2020, a farmer needed only 6 eggs to earn a dollar. Over 200 years, the value of the dollar fell sharply, and the purchasing power of money declined. In 1820, one dollar purchased 120 eggs, but in 2020, one dollar purchased only 6 eggs. Most Americans think of inflation as rising prices, but inflation also can be seen as a decline in the value of the dollar.

EXHIBIT 6	Decline in the Value of Money		
	Value of 12 Eggs (in dollars)	**Value of Dollar**	
		(in dozens of eggs)	**(in eggs)**
1820	$0.10	10 dozen	120 eggs
1920	0.20	5 dozen	60 eggs
2020	2.00	1/2 dozen	6 eggs

When the dollar price of a dozen eggs rises, the value of a dollar in terms eggs declines.

Measuring Inflation and a Price Index: A Simple Example

Economists use price indices to gauge the price level. A **price index** is a measure of average prices of a fixed basket of goods or services. The fixed basket is determined during a base year, which serves as a starting point for comparison with all other years. Exhibit 7 shows how a price index is estimated and demonstrates why we need to fix the quantity of items in the basket and follow the same basket of goods through time. To see why this is crucial, we begin by looking at what happens if the basket is not held constant.

inflation rate The annual percentage change in average prices.

price index A measure of average prices of a fixed basket of goods or services.

∧ Has the value of the
burger increased, or has
the value of the dollar
declined?

As shown in Exhibit 7, in year one (2018), the economy produces and sells 2,001 items—2,000 pizzas at a price of $10 each and 1 auto at a price of $20,000. The total amount of money spent on pizzas and autos is $40,000—$20,000 for pizzas and $20,000 for the auto. The average price per item is approximately $20 (about $40,000/2,001 items).

In year two (2019), prices do not change, so the price index should not change. Suppose that society now produces 2,000 pizzas and 2 autos. The total amount of money spent on pizzas and autos is now $60,000—$20,000 for pizzas and $40,000 for autos. The average price per item is approximately $30 (about $60,000/2,002 items). *Yet not a single price changed!*

The problem with the above analysis is that it fails to fix the quantity of items in the basket. To isolate the effects of price changes, we select a group of items in the base year and then calculate the price of *this same basket of goods* in each subsequent year. The base year chosen can be any year but typically is the first year in the analysis. After a base year is chosen, we calculate the cost of the same fixed basket for all other years. Notice that in year two, if we continue to buy 2,000 pizzas and 1 auto, the price of the basket does not change. In year three (2020), prices change to P_{pizza} = $11 (an increase) and P_{autos} = $22,000 (an increase); that year the basket costs $44,000. In year four (2021), prices are P_{pizza} = $10 (a decrease) and P_{autos} = $22,000 (no change); that

EXHIBIT 7   Simplified Estimates of a Price Index and Inflation

Year	Production Quantities	Prices	Base Year's Basket in Current Prices	Price Index	Notes
2018 (base year basket)	**2,000 pizzas 1 auto**	$10 $20,000	$20,000 $20,000 $40,000	$\frac{\$40,000}{\$40,000} \times 100$ = 100	Base year price index = 100.
2019	2,000 pizzas 2 autos	$10 $20,000	$20,000 $20,000 $40,000	$\frac{\$40,000}{\$40,000} \times 100$ = 100	No change in prices or price index. Ignore new quantity.
2020	2,000 pizzas 2 autos	$11 $22,000	$22,000 $22,000 $44,000	$\frac{\$44,000}{\$40,000} \times 100$ = 110	Price level rises. Inflation rate = 10%.
2021	2,200 pizzas 2 autos	$10 $22,000	$20,000 $22,000 $42,000	$\frac{\$42,000}{\$40,000} \times 100$ = 105	Deflation: Inflation rate = −4.5%.

A price index is estimated using a fixed basket of goods and services of 2,000 pizzas and 1 auto. This allows us to focus on changing prices. Then the price of the basket is converted into a price index. The inflation rate is the percentage change in the price index from one year to the next.

year the basket costs $42,000. In summary, the prices of the base year basket of 2,000 pizzas and 1 auto for each year are as follows:

- In 2018 and 2019, the basket cost $40,000 ($20,000 for 2,000 pizzas + $20,000 for 1 auto).

- In 2020, the basket cost $44,000 ($22,000 for 2,000 pizzas + $22,000 for 1 auto).

- In 2021, the basket cost $42,000 ($20,000 for 2,000 pizzas + $22,000 for 1 auto).

Measuring a Price Index To simplify the analysis, the price index is mathematically adjusted to assume the value of 100 in the base year. This enables economists to see at a glance how fast prices have risen since the base year. If an index goes from 100 to 110 in consecutive years, the price level went up by 10%, and there was 10% inflation.

The formula for estimating a price index is

$$\text{Price index}_{year\ y} = \frac{\text{Price of basket}_{year\ y}}{\text{Price of basket}_{base\ year}} \times 100$$

In our simplified example, when 2018 is the base year, the index equals 100. To calculate the index, $40,000 is divided by $40,000 (which equals 1) and then multiplied by 100. Price indexes are scaled to 100 in the base year. In 2019, the index also equals 100 because prices did not change. The corresponding price index measurements are

$$\text{Price index}_{2018\ \&\ 2019} = \frac{\$40,000}{\$40,000} \times 100 = 100$$

$$\text{Price index}_{2020} = \frac{\$44,000}{\$40,000} \times 100 = 110$$

$$\text{Price index}_{2021} = \frac{\$42,000}{\$40,000} \times 100 = 105$$

Measuring Inflation As noted above, the inflation rate is the annual percentage change in average prices. The inflation rate can be computed as follows:

$$\text{Inflation rate} = \frac{(\text{Change in price index from prior year})}{(\text{Price index in prior year})} \times 100\%$$

with

$$\text{Change in price index from prior year} = \text{Price index current year} - \text{Price index prior year}$$

Now let's assume that the price index in 2017 (the year prior to 2018) is 90.9. In this case, the inflation rates in 2018, 2019, 2020, and 2021 are

$$\text{Inflation rate}_{2018} = \frac{100 - 90.9}{90.9} \times 100\% = \frac{9.1}{90.9} \times 100\% = 10\%$$

$$\text{Inflation rate}_{2019} = \frac{100 - 100}{100} \times 100\% = \frac{0}{100} \times 100\% = 0\%$$

$$\text{Inflation rate}_{2020} = \frac{110 - 100}{100} \times 100\% = \frac{110}{100} \times 100\% = 10\%$$

$$\text{Inflation rate}_{2021} = \frac{105 - 110}{110} \times 100\% = \frac{-5}{110} \times 100\% = -4.5\%$$

Notice that the change in the price index is divided by the *prior year* price index, not the base year price index. In 2018, we divide by 90.9, and in 2021, we divide by 110. The inflation rate is the percentage change in the overall price index from one year to the next.

The Costs of Inflation

Economists tend to agree that high rates of inflation (and deflation) are best avoided, but their concerns are somewhat different from those of the average consumer. Although consumers must pay higher prices when there is inflation, economists know that every dollar spent by one person is a dollar received by another. Recall the circular flow model (Exhibit 2), which illustrates how money spent on goods and services flows back in the form of higher incomes: We pay much higher prices than people did 100 years ago, but we also receive much higher incomes than people did 100 years ago. So inflation doesn't directly make us poorer, at least as a society. But that's not to say that inflation doesn't have costs. Economists have identified four costs of inflation.

Unexpected Inflation Redistributes Incomes and Wealth When prices rise unexpectedly, it can take time for wages and contracts to catch up. If Mario's 10-year rental agreement for his pizza restaurant has a fixed payment, he will come out ahead if inflation suddenly and unexpectedly skyrockets. Although he will see higher revenues and some increases in costs, his biggest cost—rent—will remain stable.

Recall from Chapter 1 that **nominal values** are the face values of variables measured in current prices that have not been adjusted for inflation. In contrast, **real values** are the values of variables measured in prices that have been adjusted for inflation. In Mario's case, the nominal value of his rent is constant during the rental agreement, but inflation decreases its real value. As a result, he needs to sell fewer pizzas at higher prices (due to higher price levels) to cover his rent.

Note the role played by expectations here. If the property owner anticipates high inflation in the future, he likely will demand a higher rent at the beginning, and Mario would presumably be willing to pay it, expecting future increases in the price of his pizza. Thus, only *unexpected* inflation redistributes incomes and wealth because it changes the real value of rents, wages, interest rates, and other fixed payments in contracts.

Unexpected inflation also affects people who have borrowed money because the real value of the money being repaid falls as the price level rises. Here, unexpected inflation redistributes wealth from lenders and savers to borrowers. In general, higher than anticipated inflation hurts savers and lenders and benefits borrowers, while lower than anticipated inflation helps savers and lenders and hurts borrowers.

Consider how unexpected changes in inflation affect retirees, many of whom receive *fixed payments*—pensions and other sources of income that do not rise with increases in the price level. If inflation is higher than expected, they'll feel the pinch: A fixed $2,000 per month retirement pension buys less when prices rise. On the other hand, if you borrow money to buy a home at a 30-year fixed interest rate loan (mortgage) and inflation suddenly rises, over time you will wind up paying back less interest in real dollars because your dollars will be worth less than originally anticipated.

The wealth and income redistribution effects from unexpected inflation can be minimized with contracts that automatically adjust for inflation. Labor unions often negotiate contracts with a cost of living adjustment (COLA), pegging pay increases equal to the inflation plus 1 or 2%. Similarly, Social Security benefits are *indexed* to inflation—that is, they are adjusted so that they increase with the rate of inflation. Similarly, some loans have interest rates that vary based on factors heavily influenced by the rate of inflation.

nominal values The face values of variables measured in current prices that have not been adjusted for inflation.

real values The values of variables measured in prices that have been adjusted for inflation.

Menu Costs Increase Even *expected inflation* can create inefficiencies. When prices change, businesses must change price labels, update websites, reprint catalogs and menus, adjust prices at vending machines, and communicate new prices to customers often through advertising. Each of these changes carries some cost. These expenses are referred to as **menu costs**—inefficiencies associated with the labor wasted on increasingly frequent price updates during inflationary periods. Menu costs are less onerous than they once were because bar code systems and dynamic pricing in e-commerce allow sellers to adjust prices electronically, making the prices system more responsive and efficient during periods of inflation.

An Inflation Tax Reduces Purchasing Power Inflation also reduces the value of the cash in your wallet, which has less purchasing power after prices rise. This effect is sometimes called an **inflation tax**—a reduction in the purchasing power of money that occurs with inflation. A subtle reduction in purchasing power occurs over time, which is effectively a tax on everyone who holds money. No one receives an "inflation tax bill," but as we will see, inflation provides revenue for the government while holders of money see a decline in their purchasing power.

Inflation Induces Tax Distortions Inflation also can increase the amount of taxes paid on income, especially gains from financial investments. If an asset doubles in value over a 20-year period and the price level also doubles over the same period of time, you would not have made any profit in real terms. You merely would be keeping up with inflation. Yet in most countries (including the United States), you still would be required to pay taxes on that gain in value, including the part reflecting inflation. Similarly, if you own a stock that goes up by 8% when inflation is 5%, you often will be required to pay a tax on the entire 8% nominal gain, not the smaller 3% gain over inflation.

Deflation Is Also a Problem Because inflation usually is viewed as being harmful, you might think that deflation is great. It's not. In fact, most economists are even more opposed to deflation than inflation. When deflation occurred in the past, the economy often had difficulty adjusting to falling prices, and severe deflation can lead to bankruptcies and unemployment. Fortunately, deflation has been rare in recent decades. In future chapters, we evaluate why most economists favor stable prices or low and steady inflation.

20.4 THE CONSUMER PRICE INDEX (CPI) AND ALTERNATIVES

Economists use a variety of indices to measure inflation. These include the consumer price index, the producer price index, the personal consumption expenditure price index, and the GDP deflator. Each takes a slightly different approach in measuring inflation.

The Consumer Price Index and Its Biases

The **consumer price index (CPI)** measures the average prices paid by a typical urban family of four for a representative basket of goods. Calculated by the U.S. Bureau of Labor Statistics on a monthly basis, the CPI includes approximately 80,000 prices. It is the most widely cited price level measure in the United States. Exhibit 8 shows the makeup of major expenditures in the price index.

There are several sources of bias in measuring the CPI that tend to *overstate* the rate of inflation and its impact on the cost of living. This occurs because the CPI is computed using a basket that is fixed for many years.

Substitution Bias If chicken sandwiches become cheaper and hamburgers become more expensive, the typical consumer buys more chicken sandwiches and fewer

menu costs Inefficiencies associated with the labor wasted on increasingly frequent price updates during inflationary periods.

inflation tax A reduction in the purchasing power of money that occurs with inflation.

consumer price index (CPI) A measure of the average prices paid by a typical urban family of four for a representative basket of goods.

EXHIBIT 8 Major Components of Consumer Price Index

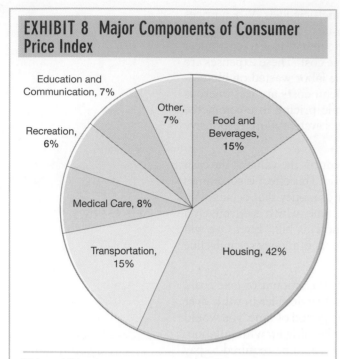

- Education and Communication, 7%
- Recreation, 6%
- Medical Care, 8%
- Transportation, 15%
- Other, 7%
- Food and Beverages, 15%
- Housing, 42%

This exhibit shows the percentage share of expenditures in the consumer price index in April 2017.

Data from: U.S. Bureau of Labor Statistics, http://www.bls.gov/cpi.

producer price index (PPI) A price index that measures the price of goods purchased by a typical producer.

v Compared to today, televisions and video game consoles from the 1980s had relatively higher prices and much lower quality.

INTERFOTO/Alamy Stock Photo

hamburgers. Because the consumer basket is assumed to be fixed, this natural substitution toward cheaper goods is not captured in the CPI. The fixed basket is based on the assumption that consumers do not respond by buying more chicken sandwiches and fewer hamburgers. Thus, the cost of living actually does not rise quite as rapidly as implied by the CPI.

New Product Bias New products—especially technology products like flat screen televisions and rooftop solar panels—commonly fall in price as technology improves and mass production lowers costs. But the fixed basket does not contain many new products that tend to fall in price, often because they hadn't been invented at the time the basket was set.

Quality Improvement Bias The next time you purchase a television, would you rather buy one made in this year or in 1980? TVs were so primitive in the 1980s that today you'd have trouble finding a TV with such a poor picture, even in a discount store. This quality improvement should command higher prices, but this is not captured when the basket is fixed. Despite their lower quality, televisions from the 1980s had higher prices than today's TVs, even when not adjusting for inflation. Similarly, for about the same inflation-adjusted price, you could purchase an Atari 2600 video game system in 1982 or the latest Xbox or PlayStation today. Thus, a fixed basket approach in creating a price index tends to *overstate* inflation because it understates the improvement in our living standards. In recent years, the Bureau of Labor Statistics has made adjustments in how it approaches the consumer price index, and it now accounts for at least some quality changes, especially when calculating prices for things like video games and televisions.

Alternatives to the Consumer Price Index

In addition to the consumer price index, the government calculates a variety of alternatives that differ in terms of the basket of goods being measured, as well as the method of estimating the price index.

The Producer Price Index (PPI) The **producer price index (PPI)** is a price index that measures the price of goods purchased by a typical producer. Some goods (such as automobiles and electricity) appear in both the CPI and PPI. However, the PPI includes raw materials and machines that the typical consumer does not purchase directly. Because raw material prices tend to change *prior* to changes in finished products, changes in the PPI often occur more rapidly than changes in the CPI.

The substitution bias is particularly problematic in the PPI, leading to an overstating of producer inflation. For example, coal, natural gas, and oil can be used at power plants to generate electricity. If one of these items becomes relatively expensive while another becomes relatively less expensive, power plants generate more electricity with the relatively less expensive fuel. Because the fixed weight approach keeps the basket of goods fixed, it misses how utilities will purchase more of the less expensive fuel source and less of the more expensive fuel source. In a similar vein, food manufacturers often switch between sugar and corn syrup based on which sweetens their products for the lowest cost. Therefore, changes in the PPI tend to slightly overstate the increase in actual producer costs.

The Personal Consumption Expenditure Price Index (PCE) Although no price index is completely accurate, two alternative price indices attempt to avoid the substitution problem that occurs when using a fixed basket. A *chain-weighted price index* measures the current prices of a basket of goods purchased in the previous period. Each year, the basket is updated. Because the basket is fixed for only one period, this allows for the continual updating of the standard basket and the capturing of changes in product quality over time.

One such chain-weighted price index is the **personal consumption expenditure price index (PCE)**—a chain-weighted price index that measures primarily prices of household consumption expenditures. In the United States, it is the preferred inflation measurement of monetary policymakers (the Federal Reserve) and often shows a slightly lower inflation than the CPI.

The GDP Deflator The **GDP deflator** (also referred to as the **implicit price deflator**) is an alternative price index that measures general price levels in the economy in aggregate. The "basket" reflects the current GDP of the economy and is updated yearly (chain weighted). There are two major differences between the CPI and the GDP deflator. The CPI covers only consumer goods and relies on a fixed basket of goods and services that includes imports. The GDP deflator covers all goods and services produced in the economy, including exports, and updates the basket each year.

Comparing Various Price Indices

As shown in Exhibit 9, the major price indexes have similar patterns when plotted in a time-series diagram, but they are not exactly the same. Differences occur because of

personal consumption expenditure price index (PCE) A chain-weighted price index that primarily measures prices of household consumption expenditures.

GDP deflator An alternative price index that measures general price levels in the economy in aggregate; also called the **implicit price deflator**.

EXHIBIT 9 Annual Percentage Changes in the CPI, the PPI, and the GDP (Implicit Price) Deflator

This exhibit shows the percentage change in three price indexes. The percentage changes are often similar but are seldom exactly the same. Deflation was common in the 1930s, and inflation was high during World War II (1941–1945) and the 1970s. Shaded areas indicate recessions.

Data from: Federal Reserve Bank of St. Louis, 2016 data, research.stlouisfed.org.

what is included in each basket. For example, the CPI and PPI include imports, the CPI contains used goods, and the GDP deflator includes items in a nation's GDP (such as exports and government services) that may not appear in either the CPI or PPI. The PPI is more volatile because it includes raw materials that have large price fluctuations.

Which price index is "best" depends on the intended use of the index. A firm concerned about business costs may look at the PPI. For society, the best overall inflation measure might be the comprehensive GDP deflator. The average person may prefer the CPI or PCE because it shows the cost of a basket of goods and services purchased by a typical consumer. The CPI is used for annual adjustments in Social Security benefits earned by retirees.

As noted earlier, no macroeconomic measurement is without its flaws. The government is now trying to do a better job of accounting for quality changes, but the value of those quality changes will always be a bit subjective, mattering more to one person than another.

20.5 REAL GDP

Suppose that after graduation you receive a job paying $100,000 per year. Congratulations! The next year, your salary (amazingly) doubles to $200,000. Are you better off? Probably. But what if prices triple, as recently occurred in Venezuela? In this case, you would be worse off. More realistically, suppose you get a $2,000 raise (or 2%) raise when inflation is 3%. Once again, you actually would be worse off.

For the same reason, the meaning of a rising GDP depends on whether it reflects higher prices or increases in the goods and services being produced. Recall that GDP is measured using market values (prices). This is known as *nominal* GDP. However, economists wish to know whether an increase in GDP reflects an increase in the physical output of goods and services or merely an increase in prices. In order for GDP to measure changes in output, we need to remove the effects of price changes.

Real GDP, Nominal GDP, and Real GDP per Capita

real GDP A measure of GDP using constant prices in order to adjust for inflation.

nominal GDP A measure of GDP using current prices that does not adjust for inflation.

Real GDP is a measure of GDP using constant prices in order to adjust for inflation. By using a constant set of prices, real GDP controls for changes in the price level that often occur from one year to the next. Real GDP is particularly helpful in determining whether the economy is in a recession. In contrast, **nominal GDP** is a measure of GDP using current prices that does not adjust for inflation. The government measures nominal GDP directly using the prevailing prices (and price level) and then estimates real GDP by taking out the effects of inflation. When output stays constant from one year to the next, real GDP is unchanged, while nominal GDP changes with prices.

Similarly, suppose that over 100-year period, a country's real GDP doubles. Is this country better off? It may appear to be: After all, it now has twice as many goods and services. But what if over the same stretch of time, the population of this country triples? In this case, society would be worse off because each person now consumes fewer goods and services than his or her ancestors did a century before. Economists refer to this as a decline in **real GDP per capita**—real GDP per person. To calculate real GDP per capita, we divide real GDP by the total population to obtain the real value of goods and services per person. Mathematically,

$$\text{Real GDP per capita} = \frac{\text{Real GDP}}{\text{Population}}$$

This conversion is necessary in order to make meaningful comparisons between countries with different populations. China, for example, has more than 4 times the population of the United States, nearly 3 times the population of the European Union, and 11 times the population of Japan. Real GDP per capita allows businesses to estimate the purchasing power of a typical individual in China, Brazil, or Germany. In per capita terms, China's real GDP is still less than one third the level of the EU and Japan and one fourth the level of the United States. We remove the effects of price changes when we estimate the growth in the total real output of a country, and we divide by population when we want to get a sense of the purchasing power of the average person in that country.

These sorts of adjustments are also necessary in order to make meaningful comparisons in living standards between different periods of time. For example, how does the current U.S. GDP compare to the U.S. GDP of 1, 5, 20, or 100 years ago? It is likely that both population and price levels have changed over time. Economists focus on real GDP per capita when analyzing long-run economic growth.

The U.S. economy has been growing for almost its entire history, although GDP did not begin to be calculated officially until the 1940s. From the first quarter of 1947 to 2017, nominal GDP rose from $243.1 billion to $19,027.6 billion, a more than 78-fold increase. But much of this increase was due to the effects of inflation, which sharply raised the prices of most goods and services. During the same time period, real GDP (in 2009 dollars) rose from $1,934.5 billion to $16,861.6 billion, nearly a 9-fold increase. That means nine times as many goods and services are now produced. Also during this period, the U.S. population more than doubled. Real GDP per capita increased from $13,513 to $51,919, a nearly 4-fold increase. On average, U.S. living standards have nearly quadrupled in 70 years. Although impressive, this figure is considerably smaller than the increase in nominal GDP. This is shown in Exhibit 10.

EXHIBIT 10 Nominal and Real GDP per Capita, 1947–2017

Due to inflation, nominal GDP grew faster than real GDP between 1947 and 2017 in the United States. Base year is 2008.

Data from: Federal Reserve Bank of St. Louis.

 POLICY BRIEF Japan's Falling Price Level

In modern times, most countries see their price levels rise gradually over time. This causes nominal GDP to rise faster than real GDP. The Japanese economy, the third-largest economy in the world, experienced an unusual situation between 1994 and 2013—deflation. Notice in Exhibit 11 that nominal GDP (blue line) hardly changed over those two decades, whereas real GDP (red line) increased significantly. This means that Japan is producing more goods and services in physical terms but the total expenditure in money terms is not changing. In 2013, the nominal income of the average Japanese person was no higher than it was in 1994, and yet living standards have risen.

real GDP per capita A measure of real GDP per person.

EXHIBIT 11 Impact of Deflation on Nominal and Real GDP in Japan

Due to deflation, nominal GDP grew slower than real GDP between 1994 and 2013 in Japan, where the GDP deflator declined by about 16%. Index values set at 100 in 1994.

Data from: Federal Reserve Board of St. Louis; Japanese Cabinet Office.

The cause of this peculiar situation is very simple: If real GDP is rising faster than nominal GDP, then the GDP deflator must be falling. And that's exactly what has happened. In Japan, the price level in 2013 was actually lower than in 1994 (green line).

Measuring Real GDP

Although the U.S. economy is enormous, measuring nominal GDP is a relatively straightforward process of measuring total expenditures at the prices that final goods sell for in the marketplace. In contrast, measuring real GDP is somewhat more complex. To measure real GDP, we need to value expenditures in real or constant dollars. To do so, we select a *base year* to serve as a basis for comparing with other years when estimating real GDP and prices. The key is to use the same *prices* in both years in order to isolate the changes in real GDP. Whenever we talk about real GDP or price level, we need to specify the base year.

We begin with a simple example that demonstrates why we need to use constant base year prices to calculate real GDP. The data can be found in Exhibit 12, which uses data from the same simple economy shown earlier in the chapter when measuring the CPI (see Exhibit 7). Assume an economy produces two goods, pizza and autos. In 2018 (the base year), the economy produces and sells 2,000 pizzas at a price of $10 each and 1 auto at a price of $20,000. Both nominal and real GDP are $40,000 ($20,000 for 2,000 pizzas at $10 each and $20,000 for the auto).

In year two (2019), real GDP and nominal GDP are $60,000 ($20,000 for 2,000 pizzas at $10 each and $40,000 for the 2 autos at $20,000 each). Society produces one *additional* automobile, and real GDP increases by the value of one auto. Real GDP captures the increase in production. In this case, nominal GDP also rises, but as we will see, increases in nominal GDP do not necessarily lead to increases in real GDP.

In year three (2020), production quantities do not change. Because society produces the same quantities of goods as in 2019, real GDP does not change. Real GDP is calculated using the output of 2020 but the prices of the base year (2018). Thus, real GDP is $60,000, reflecting $20,000 for the 2,000 pizzas priced at $10 per slice and $40,000 for the 2 autos priced at $20,000 each.

Despite no changes in product quantities, nominal GDP rises to $66,000 in 2020—$22,000 for 2,000 pizzas at $11 and $44,000 for 2 autos at $22,000 each (these are *2020's prices*). Why? Nominal GDP increases solely because of actual price increases. Real GDP needs to be calculated using constant prices of a base year because nominal GDP can increase merely when prices increase, without any increase in real output.

In year four (2021), society produces 200 more pizzas, and real GDP increases to $62,000—$22,000 for 2,200 pizzas and $40,000 for 2 autos (calculated using base year prices). Nominal GDP remains the same. How is this possible? It occurs because the increase in pizza production is offset by the price of pizza falling back to $10. In fact, it is possible for real GDP to increase while nominal GDP declines. This would be the case if the price of pizza fell below $10 in 2021 because nominal GDP then would be below $66,000.

In calculating a price index and an inflation rate, the basket of goods must be fixed in order to focus on price changes. In contrast, real GDP attempts to

EXHIBIT 12   A Simplified Estimate of Nominal and Real GDP

Year	Production Quantities	Prices	Nominal GDP (in current prices)	Real GDP (in base prices)	Notes
2018 (base year prices)	2,000 pizzas 1 auto	**$10** **$20,000**	$20,000 $20,000 $40,000	$20,000 $20,000 $40,000	In base year, nominal GDP = real GDP.
2019	2,000 pizzas 2 autos	$10 $20,000	$20,000 $40,000 $60,000	$20,000 $40,000 $60,000	Real GDP increases as society produces more autos.
2020	2,000 pizzas 2 autos	$11 $22,000	$22,000 $44,000 $66,000	$20,000 $40,000 $60,000	Nominal GDP rises strictly due to price increases.
2021	2,200 pizzas 2 autos	$10 $22,000	$22,000 $44,000 $66,000	$22,000 $40,000 $62,000	Nominal GDP unchanged; real GDP rises.

Some increases in nominal GDP occur because prices increase, and others occur because production increases. *Real GDP* is GDP adjusted for inflation and price level. Real GDP is estimated using prices from a base year (2018). *Nominal GDP* is GDP measured in current market prices and not adjusted for inflation. Notice that in 2020 nominal GDP increases without any change in production. The change occurs strictly because of price increases. Real GDP is the same in 2019 as in 2020.

capture changes in output by holding prices constant. Real GDP is also important when studying recessions and closely tracks other economic indicators such as employment.

Measuring Real GDP with a Price Index

The real world is considerably more complex than the simple two-good economy described above because many thousands of products are sold for different prices. Calculating nominal GDP is relatively straightforward: You measure total expenditures at the prices the products sell for. Calculating real GDP is more complex because it involves removing the effects of price changes. Fortunately, price indexes such as the GDP deflator can be used to convert nominal GDP into real GDP.

Real GDP can be computed using nominal GDP and a price index such as the real GDP deflator:

$$\text{Real GDP}_{\text{current year using year } z\text{'s prices}} = \frac{\text{Nominal GDP}_{\text{current year}}}{\text{Price index}_{\text{current year}}} \times \text{Price index}_{\text{year } z}$$

For simplicity, assume that the current year is 2018. Because nominal GDP is measured in year 2018 prices, when we divide it by the 2018 price index, we have factored out 2018 (current) prices. That's because year 2018 prices appear in both the numerator and denominator. Prices are then converted into year z prices, which can be any year.

For convenience, economists set the base year price index to 100. When year z is the base year, real GDP for year y can be expressed as

$$\text{Real GDP}_{\text{year } y \text{ in base year's prices}} = \frac{\text{Nominal GDP}_{\text{year } y}}{\text{Price index}_{\text{year } y}} \times 100$$

The formula now estimates year y's real GDP in the base year's prices. Notice that on the right side of the equation, year y's prices are factored out (as they appear in both the numerator and denominator). This shows year y's GDP in the base year's prices.

Real GDP can be viewed as what GDP would have been if output had changed but prices were still at the same level as in the base year (when price index equals 100). It tells us how much more or less we are producing in terms of actual physical goods and services.

It may be easier to understand these concepts with a simple example. Suppose that both real and nominal GDP are $10 trillion during the first year of an economic study. Ten years later, nominal GDP rises to $20 trillion, and real GDP is $15 trillion. How would you explain the economy's performance to someone who has never studied economics? You could say that the total market value of all goods and services produced doubled. Part of that increase, however, was due to higher prices. The physical output of goods and services rose by only 50%.

Any nominal value in economics can be converted to a real value using the following formula:

$$\text{Product price}_{\text{year } z\text{'s prices}} = \frac{\text{Product price}_{\text{year } y}}{\text{Price index}_{\text{year } y}} \times \text{Price index}_{\text{year } z}$$

This formula is often used to convert nominal income into real income or the nominal price of your house into the real price of your house. As is the case with the previous equations, year y's prices are factored out of the right side of the equation. Because the goal of this measure is to determine purchasing power, the most common price index to use in this calculation is the consumer price index.

📊 BUSINESS BRIEF New York Yankees Sign Star Baseball Player for $80,000 (in 1931)

In 1931, New York Yankees baseball star Babe Ruth earned $80,000—$5,000 more than President Herbert Hoover. When asked about the pay difference between himself and the president, Ruth famously quipped, "I had a better year."

How much is $80,000 earned in 1931 worth in 2017 dollars? The CPI in 1931 was 15.2, and the CPI in April 2017 was approximately 244.5. That's a lot of inflation!

$$\$1{,}286{,}842_{2017} = \frac{\$80{,}000_{1931}}{15.2_{1931}} \times 244.5_{2017}$$

Adjusted for inflation, Babe Ruth was paid just over under $1.3 million in 2017 prices. Notice that 1931 prices cancel each other out in the right side of the equation.

To put this number in perspective, however, Los Angeles Dodgers pitcher Clayton Kershaw earned $33 million in 2017. Indeed, many bench players today make more than Ruth did, even adjusted for inflation. That year, the average salary for a professional baseball player was $4.5 million. Part of the increase is due to inflation. But another part is real: Kershaw can buy a lot more real goods and services with his $33 million salary in 2017 than Babe Ruth could buy with his $80,000 salary in 1931. That's because Major League Baseball is more profitable today than it was in 1931, largely due to television revenues. Thinking in terms of GDP, TV allows baseball—and baseball advertisers—to reach vastly more consumers today than were reached in 1931 (via attendance at games, radio broadcasts, and newspaper articles). In that sense, modern players—even mediocre ones—are more productive than even the great Babe Ruth.[*]

[*]Gabe Lacques, "MLB Salaries 2017: Earnings Flatten Out, While Clayton Kershaw Leads Pack," *USA Today*, April 2, 2017, https://www.usatoday.com/story/sports/mlb/2017/04/02/mlb-salaries-payroll-2017/99960994.

BUSINESS TAKEAWAY

Businesses rely on macroeconomic data in order to make sound decisions about investments, production, and prices. The state of the U.S. economy can be evaluated using data on GDP, inflation, and unemployment available from the Federal Reserve, the Economic Report of the President, and many business news outlets. Finding the data is not difficult, but understanding it is more complicated.

When examining such data, businesses should pay attention to changes in real GDP per capita. Because real GDP per person factors out inflation and changes in the population, changes in this measure of GDP can provide businesses with valuable insights on the economic health of their typical consumer.

During periods of expanding real GDP, it often is profitable for a firm to expand output. Conversely, when real GDP falls, as it did in 2008 and 2009, firms may wish to delay new investment projects because sales are likely to be weak, suggesting no need to add capacity. When this occurs unexpectedly, inventories may pile up faster than desired. Firms need to watch trends in real GDP to ensure they are not caught off guard when sales decline.

In a global economy, macroeconomic data plays an even bigger role. Countries with rapidly growing real GDP per capita often offer attractive business opportunities, and firms that can identify emerging markets for their products often reap huge benefits. General Motors saw incomes rising rapidly in China and made a strategic decision to sell cars in China, establishing itself as the first U.S. carmaker with a big presence in China. Today, GM produces and sells far more Buicks in that market than it does in the United States. Identifying such markets is not simply a matter of looking at nominal GDP, however.

Consider the various ways that a business can increase its total revenue—that is, its sales measured in dollars. It can sell more products, raise prices, or do some combination of the two. Likewise, nominal GDP growth can occur from an increase in real GDP, an increase in the price level (inflation), or some combination of the two. Some countries experience a rapidly growing nominal GDP that is almost totally due to inflation. This type of GDP growth may not be a very promising market for business ventures.

CHAPTER STUDY GUIDE

20.1 WHAT GROSS DOMESTIC PRODUCT (GDP) IS ... AND WHAT IT ISN'T

Macroeconomic data is very important in analyzing the business environment. **Gross domestic product (GDP)** is the market value of all final goods and services produced in a country during a given time period. To avoid double counting, this aggregate measure of output does not include **intermediate goods**—products used as an input in the production of final goods. Goods unsold are included in GDP as part of **inventory**, a stock of unsold goods and raw materials.

20.2 IT'S NOT EASY TO MEASURE GDP

There are three ways to derive GDP. The **expenditure approach equation** calculates GDP by adding all expenditures for consumption (C), investment (I), government purchases (G), and net exports (NX). **Consumption expenditures** include household purchases of goods and services other than new housing and comprises over two-thirds of GDP. **Investment** is spending on new capital goods. **Physical capital** is durable equipment and structures used to produce goods and services; it is sometimes referred to simply as *capital* in economics. **Government purchases** are spending by federal, state, and local governments on goods, services, and investments; they exclude transfer payments. **Transfer payments** are payments made by a government when no goods and services are currently produced. **Net exports** equal a country's exports minus its imports and are also referred to as the *trade balance*. GDP also can be derived with the value added approach (adding up the value added of all firms in the economy) and the income approach (adding up all the types of income earned in the economy during a given year). **Depreciation of capital** is the loss of value that occurs when physical capital wears out with use or becomes obsolete; depreciation is considered when determining **net domestic product (NDP)**; gross domestic product adjusted for capital depreciation. Gross domestic product minus depreciation and minus indirect business taxes (such as sales taxes) determines **national income**.

Many businesses are concerned about their customers' **disposable personal income** (earned and unearned income minus taxes). All GDP measures have flaws because they tend to miss nonmarket goods (such as home production) and goods sold in the underground economy. In addition, factors such as crime, leisure time, and pollution levels need to be considered when evaluating living standards, so real GDP per capita is only an approximation.

20.3   INFLATION

Inflation is an increase in the overall price level that results in a decline in the value or purchasing power of money. On the other hand, **deflation** is a decrease in the overall price level that results in an increase in the value or purchasing power of money. The **inflation rate** is the annual percentage change in average prices. Average prices are estimated using a **price index**—a measure of average prices of a fixed basket of goods or services. When prices rise, people selling products see a corresponding increase in their income. Nonetheless, most economists believe that high inflation is something that should be avoided. **Nominal values** are the face values of variables measured in current prices that have not been adjusted for inflation. In contrast, **real values** are the values of variables measured in prices that have been adjusted for inflation. Unexpected inflation tends to redistribute wealth and income in a manner not tied to productivity. **Menu costs** are inefficiencies associated with the labor wasted on increasingly frequent price updates during inflationary periods. An **inflation tax** is a reduction in the purchasing power of money that occurs with inflation. Inflation-induced tax distortions are undesirable changes in economic activity that occur because taxation is distorted by inflation. This occurs when inflation increases the effective tax on income, especially income from financial investments.

20.4   THE CONSUMER PRICE INDEX (CPI) AND ALTERNATIVES

There are four major ways of measuring the price level. The **consumer price index (CPI)** is a measure of the average prices paid by a typical urban family of four for a representative basket of goods. The **producer price index (PPI)** is a price index that measures the price of goods purchased by a typical producer. A **personal consumption expenditure price index (PCE)** is a chain-weighted price index that primarily measures prices of household consumption expenditures. Finally, the **GDP deflator** is an alternative price index that measures general price levels in the economy in aggregate; sometimes called the **implicit price deflator**. These measures differ in terms of both goods measured and technique used to fix the basket of goods. The CPI is most often used to capture the change in the cost of living. Each index exhibits some bias because it is difficult to measure price changes when new goods are introduced or quality changes occur. In addition, consumers and producers often substitute toward goods falling in price, and this fact is missed by price indices that assume a constant basket.

20.5   REAL GDP

Real GDP is a measure of GDP using constant prices in order to adjust for inflation. By using a constant set of prices, real GDP controls for changes in the price level that often occur from one year to the next. In contrast, **nominal GDP** is a measure of GDP using current prices that does not adjust for inflation. The productivity of an economy also can be measured by looking at **real GDP per capita**, which is a measure of real GDP per person.

TOP TEN TERMS AND CONCEPTS

1. Gross Domestic Product (GDP)
2. Intermediate Goods
3. Expenditure Approach Equation
4. Durable Goods and Nondurable Goods
5. Business Fixed Investment, Residential Investment, and Inventory Investment
6. Measuring GDP with Value Added and Income Approaches
7. Inflation and Deflation
8. Price Indexes Including the Consumer Price Index (CPI)
9. Real GDP versus Nominal GDP
10. Real GDP per Capita

STUDY PROBLEMS

1. Which of the following is included in the current measurement of U.S. GDP?

   a. A used American-made automobile
   b. A new BMW made in Germany
   c. A new BMW made in South Carolina
   d. The salary of a school teacher
   e. Your grandfather's Social Security check
   f. A house built in 2014 and resold today
   g. The 6% commission a real estate broker earns selling the house in item f today

2. Describe the major components in the expenditure approach equation in estimating GDP. Which component accounts for roughly two thirds of GDP? Which component is most volatile?

3. ▲ Using data from FRED, plot the growth of real GDP and nominal GDP over the last several decades for Japan and four other countries.

4. Explain the three major ways to measure GDP.

5. In microeconomics, economists tend to measure output in terms of quantity. For example, Mario sold 250 pizzas yesterday. Why is it more difficult to measure output in macroeconomics?

6. Suppose prices rise in the economy but the level of output remains the same. What happens to real GDP? What happens to nominal GDP? Explain any differences or similarities.

7. Why is GDP an imperfect measure of economic well-being?

8. Suppose the price level rises from 100 to 120 in one year and then to 132 in the next year. During that two-year period, what has been the rate of inflation each year? What has happened to the value of money? Is this an example of inflation or deflation?

9. Which price index tends to be the most volatile over time? Explain why.

10. Suppose you bought a house for $200,000 in 1990 and sold it for $1 million in 2020. Also suppose that the CPI rises from 100 to 200 during this 30-year period. What was the real value of your house in 1990, measured in current dollars? How much did the value of your house appreciate in real terms?

11. Government expenditure on goods and services is about 18% of GDP. Yet total government spending is about 35% of GDP. Explain the difference. Discuss two types of government spending that are a part of GDP and two that are not.

12. ▲ Discuss the difference between deflation and a fall in the rate of inflation. Which of the two cases do many economists believe is more damaging to the economy?

13. Discuss three reasons that GDP per capita may not provide an accurate estimate of the differences between living standards in developed and developing countries.

14. 📊✈ Why are exports included in GDP and imports excluded? How is a car that is produced in Japan and is sold in the United States counted in U.S. GDP estimates? In Japan GDP estimates?

Jeremy Hogan/Alamy

∧ A healthy economy generates jobs.

Unemployment and the Business Cycle

Measuring the Performance of the Labor Market

Mario is considering expanding his pizza business, but he is concerned by economic forecasts predicting a recession—an economic downturn marked by rising unemployment and falling GDP. What might happen to his business if the economy enters a recession and the unemployment rate increases sharply? He also is puzzled about the current unemployment rate. His local newspaper reported a 5% unemployment rate, but he has heard political candidates saying that it is actually much higher.

Entrepreneurs like Mario must be able to decipher economic data and understand how factors such as the unemployment rate may affect their business. In this chapter, we take a closer look at the causes of unemployment and the various ways it can be measured.

21.1 UNEMPLOYMENT AND THE LABOR FORCE

The loss of a job can have devastating consequences for an individual's or a family's well-being. Because a lower income makes it harder to pay bills, the most immediate consequence is a reduction in income and standard of living. But other consequences include a diminishing of skills during periods of unemployment, increased anxiety and fear, and strained personal relationships. Divorce rates, for example, are higher among the unemployed than the employed.

High unemployment rates also make us poorer as a country. When unemployment levels are high, society is not at its *production possibility frontier*, which is the limit of what an economy can produce when all resources are used efficiently (Chapter 2). Society suffers as the potential output of its unemployed workers is lost. Those who remain employed are also impacted because their loss of confidence in the economy and fear of future job losses can prompt them to curtail their spending. Thus, profits tend to decline during times of high unemployment, and employee morale suffers.

Chapter Learning Targets

- Define the unemployment rate and the labor force participation rate.

- Describe the business cycle.

- Identify causes of cyclical, frictional, and structural unemployment.

457

Measuring Unemployment and Labor Force Participation

Measuring unemployment is not simply a matter of counting the people who are not working. The term **unemployed** describes only those individuals age 16 and over who are available to work, did not work in the past week, and actively looked for work during the previous four weeks. These criteria are very specific: To be counted as unemployed, individuals must be willing and able to work but not be currently doing so. In contrast, the **employed** are individuals age 16 and over who worked in the past week, even part-time, or are temporarily away from work (for example, due to vacation or illness).

Taken together, the unemployed and the employed make up the pool of actual workers and potential workers in the labor force. The **labor force** is the number of individuals age 16 and over who are either unemployed or employed. Mathematically, this is

$$\text{Labor force} = \text{Employed} + \text{Unemployed}$$

Those who are neither employed nor unemployed based on the definitions given above are considered to be "not in the labor force." This means they are nonemployed individuals who are *not* actively seeking employment. Those not in the labor force include full-time homemakers, full-time students, retirees, some disabled individuals, and people who are institutionalized. For a variety of reasons, members of the armed forces are not counted as part of the labor force.

Unemployment Rate It is useful to measure the extent of unemployment as a fraction of the overall labor force. The **unemployment rate** (also referred to as the **U3 unemployment rate**) is the percentage of the labor force that is unemployed (*not* the percentage of adults who are not working). It represents the percentage of people who have looked for work for the past four weeks but are unable to find a job. Up-to-date data on employment and other key labor statistics can be found on the U.S. Bureau of Labor Statistics (BLS) website at https://www.bls.gov.

The news media tends to focus on one specific unemployment rate, called U3, because the BLS uses it as the official unemployment rate. U3 is calculated as follows:

$$\text{Unemployment rate (U3 unemployment rate)} = \frac{\text{Unemployed}}{\text{Labor force}} \times 100\%$$

As shown in Exhibit 1, the U.S. U3 unemployment rate averaged 4.4% in 2017. Later in the chapter, we discuss an alternative measure of the unemployment rate, but unless

---

unemployed Individuals age 16 and over who are available to work, did not work in the past week, and actively looked for work during the previous four weeks.

employed Individuals age 16 and over who worked in the past week, even part-time, or are temporarily away from work.

labor force The number of individuals age 16 and over who are either unemployed or employed.

unemployment rate (U3 unemployment rate) The percentage of the labor force that is unemployed. U3 is considered the official unemployment rate.

EXHIBIT 1 U.S. Labor Force Data, 2017

The labor force participation rate (LFPR) is the fraction of the adult population that is either employed or unemployed. The U3 unemployment rate is the fraction of the labor force that is not employed.

Data from: U.S. Bureau of Labor Statistics. (Difference may occur due to rounding.)

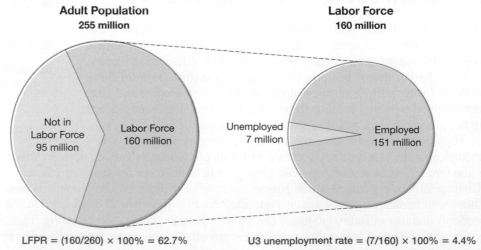

Adult Population
255 million

Not in Labor Force
95 million

Labor Force
160 million

Labor Force
160 million

Unemployed
7 million

Employed
151 million

LFPR = (160/260) × 100% = 62.7%

U3 unemployment rate = (7/160) × 100% = 4.4%

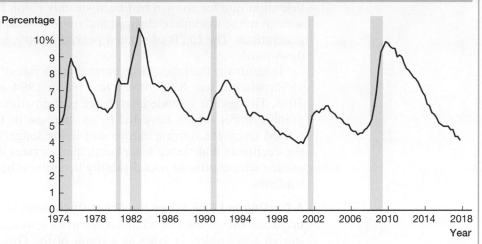

EXHIBIT 2 U.S. Unemployment Rate (U3), 1974 to 2017

The unemployment rate (U3) is the fraction of the labor force that is not employed. Unemployment rates typically increase during recessions, shown as the shaded areas.

Data from: BLS.gov and Federal Reserve Board of St. Louis.

otherwise noted, in this book, we are referring to the U3 unemployment rate when discussing the unemployment rate.

As shown in Exhibit 2, in the years since 1974, the U3 unemployment rate in the United States has ranged from 4 to 11%. This is far lower than it was during the depths of the Great Depression of the 1930s, when the U.S. unemployment rate peaked at 25%.

Labor Force Participation Rate It is also helpful to measure the labor force as a fraction of the overall population. The **labor force participation rate (LFPR)** is the percentage of the adult population that is either employed or unemployed and thus in the labor force. Mathematically, this is

$$\text{Labor force participation rate (LFPR)} = \frac{\text{Labor force}}{\text{Adult population}} \times 100\%$$

The LFPR represents those with jobs and those trying to get a job but does not include those who are not seeking paid work. The adult population denotes the civilian noninstitutional population age 16 years and over. In 2017, the U.S. labor force participation rate was 62.7% using data from the U.S. Bureau of Labor Statistics (see Exhibit 1).

The labor force participation rate has seen dramatic changes over the past century, particularly among women. Exhibit 3 shows the male and female labor force

labor force participation rate (LFPR) The percentage of the adult population that is either employed or unemployed and thus in the labor force.

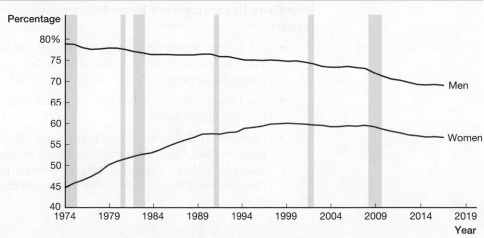

EXHIBIT 3 U.S. Labor Force Participation Rate by Sex, 1974 to 2017

The labor force participation rate (LFPR) of women has averaged between 55% and 60% since the 1980s. The LFPR of men continued to decline, from over 75 to under 70%.

Data from: BLS.gov.

participation rates since 1974. Since the late 1980s, the labor force participation rate of women has averaged slightly under 60%. Prior to then, the labor force participation rate for women had been steadily rising from 33% in 1950 as the role of women in the workforce changed and more women pursued careers than in previous generations. The LFPR of women peaked at 60% in 2000 and recently has trended downward.

In contrast, the labor force participation rate of men has steadily declined since 1950, when it was 87%. It fell to 75% in 1994 and recently has fallen to below 70%. The decline in male labor force participation is primarily the result of demographic shifts, which have led to an increase in the proportion of men who are retired (men are retiring earlier and living longer). Other factors contributing to the decline in male labor force participation rates include an increasing percentage of men who choose to take disability benefits or be either homemakers or full-time students.

A Decline in LFPR Since the Great Recession In 2015, the overall labor force participation rate in the United States fell to its lowest level since the 1970s. The decline started accelerating in 2008 as a result of the Great Recession (December 2007 to June 2009), when workers who lost their jobs were not always able to find new ones. Many workers dropped out of the labor force, often by retiring early. This trend is also partly due to demographics. After 2006, the baby boomers—the huge generation of Americans born in the years after World War II—began entering their 60s and retiring. Because boomers accounted for a relatively large share of the U.S. population, this natural attrition led to a decline in overall employment. Another factor contributing to this trend is an increase in the number of Americans who receive disability insurance and have exited the workforce permanently.

Regardless of the reasons for the decline, the fall in the labor force participation rate is a trend that seems unlikely to reverse in the near future because many more baby boomers will retire over the next few decades, and most will live longer than their parents and grandparents did.[1]

Characteristics of the Unemployed and Unemployment

As shown in Exhibit 4, unemployment rates vary greatly on the basis of education, age, race, and sex. Individuals with a high school diploma or less education are substantially more likely to be unemployed than individuals with a four-year college degree or more. African Americans and Hispanics have higher rates of unemployment than whites. Unemployment rates are also much higher for teenagers than for older adults, especially for black teenagers. In recent years, women have experienced lower rates of unemployment than men, a reversal of previous decades.

How Does Unemployment Begin? Unemployment typically *begins* for one of three reasons:

- *Job Losers.* When people who are fired or laid off begin looking for a new job, they become unemployed. This is the most common way for unemployment to begin.

- *Job Leavers.* When people quit a job and start looking for a new job, they become unemployed.

- *Entrants and Reentrants.* When people decide to enter or reenter the labor market, they are unemployed until employment can be secured. For example, college graduates are considered unemployed after receiving their degree if they are searching for employment. Some workers who exit

EXHIBIT 4 U.S. Unemployment Rate for Select Demographic Groups, 2016

The annual average unemployment rates (in percentage) in 2016 in the United States for select demographic groups.

Data from: BLS.gov.

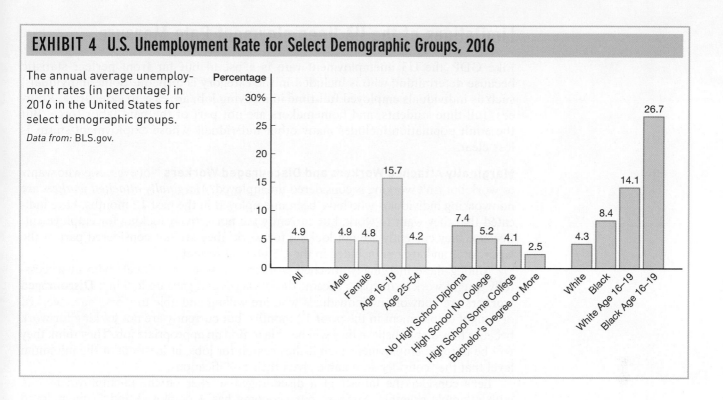

the workforce to take care of small children or aging parents are counted as unemployed when they begin to seek paid work once again.

How Does Unemployment End? In contrast, unemployment *ends* in one of two ways:

- *Securing Employment.* This occurs when people find a new job or are called back to a prior job.

- *Exiting the Labor Force.* This occurs when people stop looking for employment. For example, an individual might leave a job (or stop looking for one) in order to pursue more education or training. As noted above, some workers exit the workforce to care for small children or aging parents.

How Long Does Unemployment Last? For most people, unemployment is a relatively short-term condition. In 2007, only one in five unemployed individuals looked for work for more than half a year; that year, the median duration of unemployment was eight weeks. This is significant because in the United States unemployment insurance benefits expire after 26 weeks when the job market is healthy. **Unemployment insurance** is temporary government-provided income to individuals that partially makes up for lost income during periods of involuntary unemployment. It generally is not provided to those who quit their jobs or are fired for willful misconduct and other related circumstances. The program is designed to help those who involuntarily become unemployed and to provide a source of income during the period when the unemployed are looking for a new job.

During and for a few years after the Great Recession, nearly half of the unemployed were without jobs for over 26 weeks, and lawmakers extended unemployment benefits to as much as 99 weeks. In June 2010, the median duration of unemployment peaked at 25 weeks—*twice as long as* the highest median duration of unemployment recorded since 1967, when the BLS began tracking it. By July 2015, 1 in 4 of those unemployed had been without a job for 26 or more weeks, with a median duration of 11 weeks.

unemployment insurance
Temporary government-provided income to individuals that partially makes up for lost income during periods of involuntary unemployment.

Limitations of the U3 Unemployment Rate Measure

Like GDP, the U3 unemployment rate is a useful but far from perfect statistic because determining who is included in the category is difficult. Some individuals, such as individuals employed full-time in a paying job, are easy to categorize. Retirees, full-time students, and homemakers are not part of the paid labor force. But the adult population includes many other individuals whose employment status is less clear.

Marginally Attached Workers and Discouraged Workers Not everyone who wants to work but isn't working is considered unemployed. *Marginally attached workers* are nonworking individuals who have been unemployed in the past 12 months, have indicated that they want to work, but currently are not actively looking for employment. Because they currently are not looking for work, they are not considered part of the labor force and are not included in the U3 unemployment rate.

Among these marginally attached workers are some individuals who unsuccessfully sought work in the past, became discouraged, and gave up looking. **Discouraged workers** are nonworking individuals who are willing and able to work, have worked or sought employment in the prior 12 months, but currently are not looking for work because they do not believe they will be able to find an appropriate job. They think they will be not find employment even if they search for jobs, at least not at the minimum level that they consider acceptable given their qualifications.

Let's consider the impact of a discouraged worker on the unemployment rate with a simple example. Suppose our economy has 4 employed and 2 unemployed people. Under this circumstance, the labor force is 6, and the unemployment rate is $33.3\% = 2/6 \times 100\%$. After many months of seeking employment, 1 of our 2 unemployed workers becomes discouraged and stops looking for work, and the following occurs:

- The number of employed remains 4.
- The number of unemployed falls from 2 to 1 as the discouraged worker exits the labor force.
- The labor force falls from 6 to 5.
- The unemployment rate *falls* from 33.3% to $20\% = 1/5 \times 100\%$.

Although the unemployment rate decreases, the economy has not improved. In reality, things may even be worse because the discouraged worker may have lost hope of finding a job.

Discouraged workers are one subset of people who are marginally attached to the labor force because they believe they will not find a job regardless of how hard they try. Other reasons that people can be marginally attached to the labor force include those unrelated to the job market, such as having difficulties in securing daycare or transportation to and from work.

discouraged workers
Nonworking individuals who are willing and able to work, have worked or sought employment in the prior 12 months, but currently are not looking for work because they do not believe they will be able to find an appropriate job.

Underemployed Workers and Overeducated Workers Another problem with the U3 unemployment rate is that it fails to capture the inefficiencies that occur when the workforce is underutilized. The category of *underemployed workers* includes people who work part-time but would prefer to work full-time and people who are highly skilled but are employed in low-paying, low-skill jobs. In both cases, the workers' skills are not fully utilized, but because they are employed and part of the labor force, they are not included in the unemployment rate. Consider the above example with four individuals employed, two unemployed, and an employment rate of 33%. If one employed person takes a part-time position, the unemployment rate will not change, and yet the labor market has deteriorated.

A worker's abilities cannot be measured solely on the basis of education, but one simple way to visualize the underemployed on the basis of their skills is to look at mismatches between education and occupation. *Overeducated workers* are people who are in an occupation requiring less education than they have. Examples include someone with a Ph.D. in engineering who drives a school bus or a college graduate who works as a waiter. These workers *might* represent inefficiencies in the labor market because they have skills that are not being fully utilized. Alternatively, they might have chosen these jobs for personal reasons, might have received poor-quality schooling, or might have obtained a degree even though they received low grades.

In any case, it is difficult to measure the number of underemployed. For example, it is unclear how many part-time workers wish to work full-time. Some individuals (including many college students) prefer to work fewer than 40 hours each week. Additionally, some part-time employees prefer to work part-time if they cannot find what they view as a good full-time job that uses their education and training. The reasons behind underemployment are difficult to quantify, and the U3 unemployment rate cannot capture all the complexities of the labor market.

"I've stopped looking for work, which, I believe, helps the economic numbers."

Leo Cullum/Cartoon Bank

The U6 Unemployment Rate

In an attempt to overcome some of the shortcomings of the U3 unemployment rate, economists also look at several broader definitions of the unemployment rate, the most important of which the Bureau of Labor Statistics refers to as U6. The BLS began tracking the U6 in 1994. The **U6 unemployment rate** is an alternative measure of the unemployment rate that considers both marginally attached workers and underemployed workers. Mathematically, this is

$$\text{U6 unemployment rate} = \frac{\text{Unemployed} + \text{Marginally attached} + \text{Underemployed}}{\text{Labor force} + \text{Marginally attached}} \times 100\%$$

Persons marginally attached to the labor force are not officially considered part of the labor force and are added to both the numerator and denominator when estimating the U6 unemployment rate. In contrast, underemployed workers are already considered part of the labor force and are added only to the numerator in estimating the U6 unemployment rate.

Let's consider the impact of a discouraged worker on the U6 unemployment rate with the simplified example used above. Recall our economy has four people employed and two unemployed. The U6 unemployment rate and the U3 unemployment rate are both 33.3% = 2/6 × 100%. If after many months of seeking employment one of our unemployed workers becomes discouraged (now marginally attached) and stops looking for work, the following occurs:

- The U6 unemployment rate *remains* 33.3% = $\frac{1+1}{5+1} \times 100\%$.

When a worker becomes discouraged it does not change the U6 unemployment rate (though the U3 rate declined, as shown above). Further suppose one of the employed

U6 unemployment rate
An alternative measure of the unemployment rate that considers both marginally attached and underemployed workers. Mathematically, this is U6 unemployment rate = ((Unemployed + Marginally attached + Underemployed) / (Labor force + Marginally attached)) × 100%.

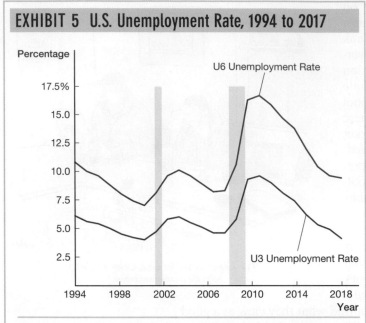

EXHIBIT 5   U.S. Unemployment Rate, 1994 to 2017

Notice that from 1994 to 2017, the U3 unemployment rate (red) and the U6 unemployment rate (blue) for the United States generally move in a similar pattern. Also notice that unemployment rates typically increase during recessions.

Data from: BLS.gov and Federal Reserve Bank of St. Louis, https://research .stlouisfed.org/fred2/series/U6RATE.

workers becomes underemployed by working part time involuntarily:

- The U6 unemployment rate increases to

$$50\% = \frac{1 + 1 + 1}{5 + 1} \times 100\%.$$

In this case, the U6 unemployment rate captures the hardship suffered by the underemployed worker; while the U3 unemployment rate would not change. In the business press, the U6 rate is often referred to as the "real" unemployment rate. The U6 unemployment rate always is higher than the traditional unemployment rate but generally is lower than what is shown in the previous example.

Exhibit 5 shows the standard U3 unemployment rate (red) and the U6 unemployment rate (blue) since 1994. During this time, the highest U6 unemployment rate occurred in October 2009, when it was 17.1%. The standard U3 unemployment rate peaked at the same time at 10% in an unusually severe recession. Over time, the two unemployment rates typically rise and fall together. Either unemployment measurement is a useful indicator for the general direction of the economy.

 POLICY BRIEF Is the Official Unemployment Rate (U3) a "Big Lie"?

Gallup is one of the most respected polling companies in the United States and around the world. Its founder, George Gallup, began successfully predicting presidential elections during the 1936 reelection campaign of Franklin D. Roosevelt. Thus, it caught many by surprise when in 2015, Jim Clifton, the chief executive officer at Gallup, wrote that the official (U3) unemployment rate "is extremely misleading" and even called it "the big lie."

Clifton focused his argument on discouraged workers and the underemployed: "If you are so hopelessly out of work that you've stopped looking over the past four weeks—the Department of Labor doesn't count you as unemployed. . . . If you perform a minimum of one hour of work in a week and are paid at least $20— maybe someone pays you to mow their lawn—you're not officially counted as unemployed."[*]

Clifton captured some flaws in the traditional U3 unemployment rate measurement, but as we've seen, the government collects several different types of unemployment data, some of which address the issues cited by Clifton. Despite its shortcomings, the U3 unemployment rate remains useful for tracking the ups and downs of the economy. Notice in Exhibit 4 how the two unemployment rates move in tandem, even if U6 is much higher than U3. All macroeconomic statistics have at least some flaws, but they can be useful if those weaknesses are kept in mind. The key is to think about which type of statistic is best for the sort of analysis that you wish to do.

[*]Jim Clifton, "The Big Lie: 5.6% Unemployment," Gallup, February 3, 2015, http://www.gallup.com /opinion/chairman/181469/big-lie-unemployment.aspx.

Think & Speak Like an Economist

The most commonly cited unemployment rate is U3, which does not adjust for marginally attached workers and the underemployed. The more comprehensive U6 unemployment rate— often referred to as the "real" unemployment rate in the media—is higher than U3.

21.2 THE BUSINESS CYCLE AND THE UNEMPLOYMENT RATE

At the beginning of this chapter, we learned that Mario, a pizza shop owner, is worried that rising unemployment is signaling a weaker economy. It's not the only measure of the economy, however. In Chapter 20 we saw the growth rate of real GDP (that is, GDP adjusted for inflation) is another important indicator. Although the United States has experienced tremendous economic growth over the past two centuries, this growth has not gone uninterrupted.

Expansions and Recessions

When the economy is growing, it is called an **expansion**—a macroeconomic condition associated with rising real GDP and falling unemployment. From a business perspective, expansions also can pose challenges because firms may find it difficult to recruit and retain qualified workers during such periods. As indicated above, periods of expansion are always eventually interrupted by periods of recession.

A **recession** is a macroeconomic condition associated with falling real GDP and rising unemployment. The term *recession* often is described by the media as two straight quarters of falling real GDP. However, the official designation is determined by the National Bureau of Economic Research, based on a more complex set of criteria. Taken together, these ups and down in the economy make up what is known in economics as the **business cycle**—short-run alternating periods of economic expansion and recession.

expansion A macroeconomic condition associated with rising real GDP and falling unemployment.

recession A macroeconomic condition associated with falling real GDP and rising unemployment.

business cycle Short-run alternating periods of economic expansion and recession.

Tracking the Business Cycle

When examining business cycles, economists typically look at two key economic indicators—real GDP growth and the rate of unemployment. Exhibit 6 shows how the economy grows in the long run, with a typical business cycle. In the long run, the trend growth in real GDP on an overall basis (not per person) has averaged roughly 3% per year in the United States. This trend line is the red dashed line. (We examine the

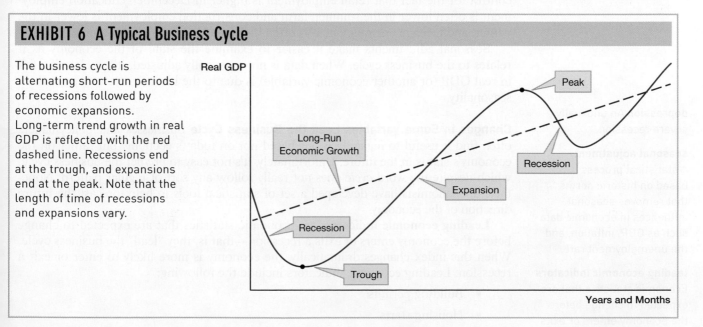

EXHIBIT 6 A Typical Business Cycle

The business cycle is alternating short-run periods of recessions followed by economic expansions. Long-term trend growth in real GDP is reflected with the red dashed line. Recessions end at the trough, and expansions end at the peak. Note that the length of time of recessions and expansions vary.

EXHIBIT 7   Recessions Since World War II

Dates	Length in Months	Peak Unemployment Rate (U3)
November 1948 to October 1949	11 mos.	7.9%
July 1953 to May 1954	10	6.1
August 1957 to April 1958	8	7.5
April 1960 to February 1961	10	7.1
December 1969 to November 1970	11	6.1
November 1973 to March 1975	16	9.0
January 1980 to July 1980	6	7.8
July 1981 to November 1982	16	10.8
July 1990 to March 1991	8	7.8
March 2001 to November 2001	8	6.3
December 2007 to June 2009	18	10.0

Since World War II, the United States has had 11 recessions. The average length of a recession is just under 1 year. In contrast, the average expansion lasts about 5 years. The exhibit also shows peak unemployment rates associated with each recession, which typically lag at the end of the recession.

Data from: National Bureau of Economic Research.

causes of this growth in Chapter 22.) However, the economy does not grow steadily along this trend line but experiences alternating periods of recessions and expansions.

The most severe recession in U.S. history was the Great Depression of the 1930s, when the unemployment rate peaked at 25%. A **depression** is an unusually severe recession. The United States has endured many recessions in the years since, but none has been as severe as the Great Depression, which saw high unemployment for over a decade in the United States and throughout much of the world. As shown in Exhibit 7, the 11 recessions that have occurred since World War II were far less severe, with the average recession lasting a little less than 1 year. The average expansion lasted about 5 years, but there are wide variations, with expansions lasting anywhere from 1 to 10 years. The highest rate of unemployment since World War II was 10.8% in 1982.

Economics Data Undergoes Seasonal Adjustments Not every brief up and down of the economy indicates an expansion or a recession. The economy typically produces more goods during certain times of the year and produces less in other periods (such as summer). Thus, quarterly macroeconomic data also undergoes a **seasonal adjustment**—a statistical process based on historic norms that removes seasonal influences in economic data such as GDP, inflation, and the unemployment rate. When looking at employment data, for example, economists need seasonal adjustments to control for the fact that retail employment is higher in December, education employment is often lower in the summer, farm and construction employment is lower in the winter, and teenage unemployment is often highest at the start of the summer.

Seasonal adjustments make it easier to examine the state of the economy as it relates to the business cycle. When data is not seasonally adjusted, it's unclear if a fall in real GDP (or another economic variable) is due to the business cycle or a result of seasonality.

Changes in Some Variables Lead the Business Cycle Businesses and policymakers often find it useful to make decisions based not on today's economy but rather on the economy's status in the future. Unfortunately, it's not easy to predict the business cycle, which despite the word *cycle* does not really follow any sort of regular pattern. Nonetheless, economists have developed a set of statistical tools to help forecast the future direction of the economy.

Leading economic indicators are economic statistics that are expected to change before the economy enters or exits a recession—that is, they "lead" the business cycle. When this index changes dramatically, the economy is more likely to enter or exit a recession. Leading economic indicators include the following:

- Building permits
- Housing starts
- Average duration of unemployment

depression An unusually severe recession.

seasonal adjustment A statistical process based on historic norms that removes seasonal influences in economic data such as GDP, inflation, and the unemployment rate.

leading economic indicators Economic statistics that are expected to change before the economy enters or exits a recession.

- Manufacturers' orders for durable goods
- Stock prices
- Interest-rate spreads (the differences between long-term and short-term rates)

For example, building permits issued by state or local governments indicate that individuals or firms have been granted permission to build. A decline in the number of permits may indicate that construction activity (and ultimately economic activity) is likely to decline. One of the most closely watched indicators is the stock market, which often turns sharply lower before a recession. This probably is because corporate profits tend to decline during a recession, and so investors who spot a recession on the horizon may sell stocks to avoid losing profits after the recession begins.

Unfortunately, sometimes there are false alarms. In October 1987, for example, the stock market crashed, but no recession occurred for three years. Nobel Prize–winning economist Paul Samuelson once joked that the stock market had predicted nine of the past five recessions. Nonetheless, stocks often fall sharply when a recession is beginning and sometimes even before professional economists are aware that a recession has begun.

From a business perspective, these indicators help to provide knowledge that allows businesses to plan ahead. If a recession is likely in the near future, firms may want to postpone undertaking a major investment project or hiring new workers. If the developers of New York's famous Empire State Building had paid more attention to leading indicators like the October 1929 stock market crash, the building might never have been built. Construction began in January 1930, and the building opened in 1931, during the depths the Great Depression. It was mostly empty for many years, earning the nickname the "Empty State Building."

📊 BUSINESS BRIEF Can Skyscrapers Predict Recessions?

The business of building a new skyscraper requires predicting future economic activity well into the future. The construction process can last many years, and rents are not collected until the project is complete. In 2005, economist Mark Thorton published a paper pointing to some interesting patterns and historical milestones in the construction of skyscrapers that begin right before major economic downturns. The Chrysler Building was started during the boom year of 1929 and completed just as the Great Depression began. The Empire State Building was finished soon after and remained the world's tallest building for the next 40 years. In 1973, the World Trade Center was completed in New York, and in 1974, the even taller Sears Tower was completed in Chicago. Both began construction during a boom and came on the market just as the late 1973 oil shock plunged much of the world into severe recession. In 1998, the record-setting Petronas Towers were completed in Malaysia, just as much of Southeast Asia plunged into severe economic crisis.*

The current record holder for height is the 2,626-foot Burj Khalifa (nearly a half mile high), which opened in Dubai in 2010, just as that dynamic Middle Eastern city-state was plunging into a financial crisis. The Dubai example is particularly interesting because it occurred after Thorton's paper was published. Once again, the building was begun while the economy was booming and was completed soon after the world faced its most severe recession since the 1930s.†

∧ Does building a skyscraper suggest overoptimism?

Are all these examples just bad luck? Or is there a sort of "overoptimism" during boom times that leads developers to produce excessively grandiose projects? Most economists agree that leading economic indicators (such as construction permits and new skyscrapers) are just that—indicators. They are not an infallible predictor of future economic activity.

*Mark Thornton, "Skyscrapers and Business Cycles," *Quarterly Journal of Austrian Economics*, 8, no. 1 (Spring 2005), 51–74, https://mises.org/library/skyscrapers-and-business-cycles-4.

†Gregory White, "The Amazing Pattern of How Skyscrapers Predict Recession," *Business Insider*, February 19, 2010, http://www.businessinsider.com/the-ten-skyscrapers-that-signaled-recessions-and-the-next-two-to-watch-out-for-2010-2#ixzz3ki21hcwU.

The Unemployment Rate Lags Behind the Business Cycle In contrast, lagging indicators change *after* a recession ends. One such lagging indicator is the unemployment rate, which is the primary focus of this chapter. Typically, real GDP increases and the economy improves *before* the unemployment rate declines. Moreover, the economy may enter a recession *before* the unemployment rate starts to increase.

The fact that the unemployment rate lags behind the business cycle is a source of confusion for the public, which often associates the word *recession* with any period generally regarded as "bad times" in terms of employment. However, economists use the term *recession* to designate a much more specific economic problem—falling output. It means the economy is getting worse.

During the early stages of a recovery, the levels of output and employment in the economy are still relatively low even though they are moving up. This can be seen in Exhibit 6 just past the point marked "Trough," a point where the economy may still be in poor health but is improving. At those times, economists will say the economy is in expansion, but to the public it still feels like a recession because unemployment remains high (remember that the unemployment rate lags behind the business cycle).

In addition, when an economy enters an expansion, discouraged workers begin to feel optimistic about their prospects of finding employment. Recall that discouraged workers are not considered unemployed or part of the labor force. The labor force participation rate rises when they return to the labor force. Consequently, the number of unemployed and the unemployment rate (U3) also increase as more people begin the process of searching for a job.

When an economy enters a recession and real GDP declines, the unemployment rate may not increase immediately. Employers often delay firing workers until they are sure the overall economy is poor. Conversely, employers are reluctant to hire new employees immediately after an economy enters an expansion. Businesses prefer to wait until they are confident that the economy is healthy enough to warrant the additional payroll expenses that come with new employees. This is why unemployment related to the Great Recession, which ended in June 2009, did not peak at 10% until October 2009—four months into the recovery. Indeed, unemployment often remains quite high for a few years after the end of a recession. So don't make the mistake of assuming that expansion means a booming economy. It just means that the economy is improving.

Think & Speak Like an Economist

There is some confusion about the definition of a recession. Although the media often says that a recession is defined as two straight quarters of falling real GDP, the actual designation comes from the National Bureau of Economic Research and involves a complex set of criteria.

21.3 THREE TYPES OF UNEMPLOYMENT AND THE NATURAL RATE OF UNEMPLOYMENT

Although the lack of a job is a hardship for the individual, unemployment is not always a sign of a dysfunctional economy. A modest level of unemployment is consistent with a dynamic, highly mobile, and healthy economy. Economists find it useful to divide unemployment into three basic types—cyclical unemployment, frictional unemployment, and structural unemployment.

Cyclical Unemployment

We begin with unemployment related to the business cycle. During the recession phase, unemployment is typically higher than usual and increasing. **Cyclical unemployment** is unemployment that results from a recession. The phrase *cyclical unemployment* is derived from the recession phase of the business *cycle*. When the economy begins to expand again, cyclical unemployment tends to go down.

From a business perspective, forecasting cyclical unemployment is especially important. A slow economy is likely to hurt sales and may result in a need for fewer workers or shorter hours. When firms fire some of their workers or go out of business completely, there are fewer employed workers and a rise in the unemployment rate. Cyclical unemployment imposes heavy economic and social costs and is the type of unemployment that the media tends to focus on the most.

Even during economic peaks with no cyclical unemployment, however, some level of unemployment persists. Since 1970, the annual average unemployment rate in the United States has never dropped below 4%, which represents millions of workers. Why is a portion of the labor force always unemployed, even when the economy is booming? Economists identify two sources of persistent unemployment that can occur at any time during the business cycle—frictional unemployment and structural unemployment.

Frictional Unemployment

In a vibrant economy, some people are temporarily between jobs, so a certain level of unemployment is due to normal worker turnover in the labor market. **Frictional unemployment** is unemployment that occurs during the time individuals spend seeking employment that is best suited to their skills. Frictional unemployment describes the status of individuals who are seeking better jobs—who change jobs in order to move up the ladder to a higher-level position or decline jobs that are far below their skill level. This type of unemployment can benefit both individuals (because they often end up in better jobs) and society (because workers eventually are assigned to jobs that better fit their skills and increase productivity). For most individuals, frictional unemployment is a short-run phenomenon, but it is a permanent part of the economy. Each month, some individuals become frictionally unemployed, and others leave the unemployment rolls to start better jobs.

For example, consider a recent college graduate with a bachelor's degree in economics who finds her first job offer is waitressing at Mario's. Should she accept? Unless she has been unable to find a job for a long period of time, she probably should decline. A job search will likely yield a better job in which she will be able to utilize her degree in economics (and most likely, earn more money). In the end, she and society will be better off if she spends some time in a job search.

Structural Unemployment

Another type of unemployment that occurs during all phases of the business cycle is structural unemployment. **Structural unemployment** is unemployment that occurs when workers lack the skills required for available jobs. Individuals may lack skills because they have inadequate education and training or because their skills have been rendered obsolete by new technology or changes in the underlying structure of the economy. Typically, structural unemployment lasts longer than other types of unemployment. Let's consider a few sources of structural unemployment.

cyclical unemployment
Unemployment that results from a recession.

frictional unemployment
Unemployment that occurs during the time individuals spend seeking employment that is best suited to their skills.

structural unemployment
Unemployment that occurs when workers lack the skills required for available jobs.

Changing Technology At times, technological changes result in a mismatch of skills and jobs. Sometimes workers find themselves replaced by technology, as when manufacturing workers are displaced because robots or other forms of automation allow products to be produced more efficiently. But unemployment also can reflect a failure to adapt to changing technology. Computer programmers must put considerable effort into keeping their skills up to date to avoid becoming become structurally unemployed when new coding languages and more advanced platforms emerge. Both of these causes of structural unemployment reflect a change in technology and can occur in both booms and recessions.

International Trade Flows In Chapter 2, we saw that free trade is generally beneficial because it expands total output. Nonetheless, free trade also leads some nations to adjust the mix of the products they produce—to increase jobs producing exports and decrease jobs producing goods the nation imports. In the United States, for example, auto and textile workers have lost jobs due to foreign competition over the past several decades, and such workers often lack the skills required to fill jobs in other sectors that are growing.

Unemployment Insurance Some economists favor unemployment insurance as a means of helping families during times of need and to stimulate the economy during recessionary periods by increasing consumer spending. However, many economists believe that this program can reduce the incentive to accept new employment and thus contributes to structural unemployment. This occurs because the marginal (additional) income received by obtaining employment would be the difference between the pay of the new job and the unemployment insurance benefits that one forgoes after obtaining employment. Simply put, high unemployment benefits reduce the financial sting of being unemployed and make the unemployed more selective about which jobs they'll accept. Unemployment insurance might also increase frictional unemployment because it makes it easier for workers to spend additional time to find the job best suited to their skill set.

When unemployment insurance benefits expire (typically after 26 weeks) or are about to expire, the probability that an individual will find a job increases. This is because *some* individuals are now willing to accept the less desirable, lower-paying jobs that they had previously declined while collecting unemployment benefits. This is an example of the tradeoff between equity and efficiency discussed in Chapter 1. Unemployment insurance can make society more equal but at a cost of less efficiency if it boosts structural unemployment.

 POLICY BRIEF Unemployment, Unemployment Benefits, and the Great Recession

During the Great Recession when the U.S. unemployment rate hit the highest level in decades, finding a job was extremely difficult, and the financial hardship on the newly unemployed was enormous. In response, Congress extended unemployment benefits from the normal 26 weeks to as much as 99 weeks between 2009 and 2012.

Prior to the Great Recession, economic studies typically showed that states with longer-lasting unemployment benefits had higher rates of unemployment. These studies generally were conducted during periods when the unemployment rate was low and finding a job was relatively easy. Economists Henry S. Farber of Princeton University and Robert G. Valetta of the Federal Reserve Bank of San Francisco examined the impact of unemployment insurance during the Great Recession and found that the extensions of unemployment benefits correlated to a 7% increase in the duration of unemployment. This suggests that without the extended benefit, the average person would have found work about 11 days sooner (in 4.55 months instead of 4.89), which would have lowered the unemployment rate by roughly 0.4 percentage points.[*]

These findings imply that unemployment insurance may have some impact on the unemployment rate but that the impact is modest (or at least it was modest during the Great Recession). Economics often involves tradeoffs: Without the unemployment insurance extension, millions of jobless people would have had struggled without income in an economy where it was difficult to find jobs.

[*]Henry S. Farber and Rogert G. Valletta, "Do Extended Unemployment Benefits Lengthen Unemployment Spells? Evidence from Recent Cycles in the U.S. Labor Market," Federal Reserve Bank of San Francisco, April 2013, http://www.frbsf.org/economic-research/files/wp2013-09.pdf.

Wages That Are Above Equilibrium Structural unemployment also occurs if wages are above equilibrium. Exhibit 8 shows that wages above the competitive equilibrium price create a surplus of unskilled workers as $Q_S > Q_D$, not a surplus of jobs. Although fewer workers are demanded by businesses at the high wage rate, the quantity of workers supplied actually increases because individuals are willing to supply more labor at the higher wage rate The result is higher wages for those who are able to earn an above-equilibrium wage rate but structural unemployment for those who are unable to secure employment as a result of the higher-than-equilibrium wage rates.

One factor that pushes wages above equilibrium is the existence of minimum wage laws, discussed in Chapter 6. Minimum wage laws may increase the aggregate income of those earning the minimum wage but also may result in some job loss among those low-skilled individuals who are not productive enough to be employable at the current minimum wage rate.

Sometimes structural unemployment can result if wages are above equilibrium because labor unions negotiate higher pay. By bargaining as a group and wielding a credible threat (workers can strike or slow down production), labor unions are able to negotiate higher wages for their members. Union workers typically earn 10 to 20% more than similar nonunion workers.[2] For those studying microeconomics, labor unions are discussed in detail when examining resource markets. The combination of relatively high minimum wage rates, strong labor unions, and generous unemployment

---

EXHIBIT 8 Nonequilibrium Wages in the Labor Market

When wages are set above the equilibrium wage rate, it results in a surplus of labor ($Q_S > Q_D$). These surplus workers are willing and able to work but are unable to find employment. Wages may be set above equilibrium due to minimum wage laws, unions, and efficiency wages.

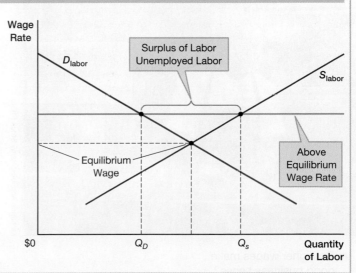

compensation is believed to be one of the reasons that the structural unemployment rate in Europe is far higher than in the United States.

On occasion, businesses choose to pay workers an above-equilibrium wage with no legal mandate or collective bargaining threat involved. **Efficiency wages** are above-equilibrium wages paid voluntarily by businesses to encourage productivity. A firm that is known to pay workers an above-equilibrium wage attracts a better pool of applicants and motivates employees to work harder to keep their high-paying jobs. Retaining workers also benefits the firm because training new employees can be costly. In addition, labor market studies of poor nations find that it is sometimes profitable for businesses to pay above-equilibrium wages because it improves the health of the workers and healthy workers are usually more productive.

Perhaps the most celebrated example of efficiency wages occurred in 1914, when Henry Ford decided to pay his workers a minimum of $5 a day, doubling the wages for most employees. At the time, the *New York Times* referred to the move as "one of the most remarkable business moves of his entire remarkable career." The move provided Ford with many of the benefits of an efficiency wage.[3]

📊 BUSINESS BRIEF Costco Pays an Efficiency Wage

Costco may be best known as a warehouse seller of giant packs of toilet paper and supersized bundles of laundry detergent. But among employees, it has another reputation—as a great place to work. In 2013, Costco paid its retail employees an average salary of $20.89 per hour, not including overtime. The national average retail worker earns $11.39 per hour. Moreover, 85% of its employees had company-sponsored health insurance where employees pay less than 10% of the cost of the insurance. In addition, employees receive paid vacation and company-matched funds for employee retirement savings. *Bloomberg Business Week* cites several employees who are very happy with their jobs and refers to Costco as the "Happiest Company in the World."*

efficiency wages Above-equilibrium wages paid voluntarily by businesses to encourage productivity.

Why does Costco pay workers such high salaries? One reason is that company founder Jim Sinegal and CEO Craig Jelinek both believe it is the right thing to do. But there may be an additional motivation—efficiency wages. Jelinek once explained the benefit of providing high pay for employees in a letter to President Barack Obama: "We know it's a lot more profitable in the long term to minimize employee turnover and maximize employee productivity, commitment and loyalty." Costco's generous wage scale had an additional benefit—a favorable contrast with its competitors and good press.

So why doesn't every retail employee work for Costco? And why doesn't every firm pay an efficiency wage? The answer to both questions is that they can't. Costco can hire only so many employees, and the benefit of efficiency wages works only when employees earn a lot more than they can earn elsewhere. If every retailer paid the same, the efficiency benefit of the higher wages would mostly disappear.

*Brad Stone, "Costco CEO Craig Jelinek Leads the Cheapest, Happiest Company in the World," Bloomberg, June 7, 2013, https://www.bloomberg.com/news/articles/2013-06-06/costco-ceo-craig-jelinek-leads-the-cheapest-happiest-company-in-the-world.

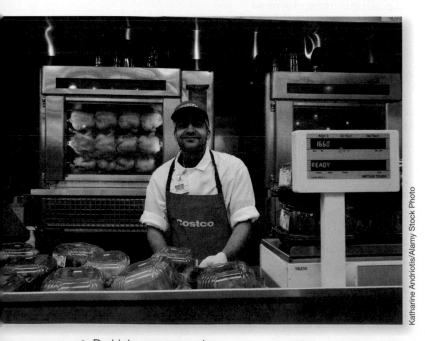

Katharine Andriotis/Alamy Stock Photo

∧ Do higher wages make good business sense? Costco thinks yes.

EXHIBIT 9   Unemployment Rate of Select Economies, 2017

In 2017, Japan and South Korea had unemployment rates below 4%. In contrast, many countries in Southern Europe (such as Italy, Spain, and Greece) had unemployment rates that were considerable higher. Cyclical unemployment can explain only part of the difference because the natural rate of unemployment is also considerably higher in Southern Europe.

Data from: OECD.

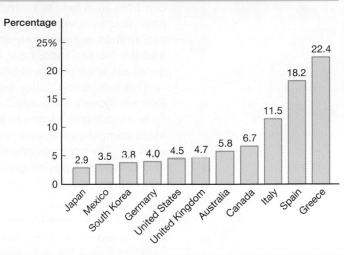

The Natural Rate of Unemployment

As we've learned, some unemployment exists during booms. When cyclical unemployment is at zero and the only remaining unemployment is frictional or structural in nature, the economy is often said to be operating at **full employment**. The term *full employment* is a bit misleading because as it does not mean that everyone is working. Rather, it represents the normal level of employment for an economy operating at potential.

The **natural rate of unemployment** is the unemployment rate that occurs when the economy is at full employment and there is no cyclical unemployment. Mathematically, this is

$$\text{Natural rate of unemployment} = \text{Frictional unemployment rate} \\ + \text{Structural unemployment rate}$$

$$\text{Natural rate of unemployment} = \text{Unemployment rate} - \text{Cyclical unemployment rate}$$

Exhibit 9 shows the rate of unemployment in 2017 for 11 economies. Unemployment rates tend to be lowest in East Asia and highest in Southern Europe. In the United States, the natural rate is currently roughly 5%, but it can move slightly higher or lower over time. In East Asia, the natural rate of unemployment is roughly 3%. Natural unemployment rates are much higher in some European countries but vary. As is shown in the Policy Brief below, the natural unemployment rate in Germany fell sharply after significant labor market reforms were introduced in 2004.

full employment An economic condition that occurs when cyclical unemployment is at zero and the only remaining unemployment is frictional or structural in nature.

natural rate of unemployment The unemployment rate that occurs when the economy is at full employment and there is no cyclical unemployment.

Think & Speak Like an Economist

The optimal unemployment rate is *not* zero. There will always be some frictional unemployment, even in a healthy economy. When economists use the term *full employment*, they're talking about the *natural rate of unemployment*—meaning that there is no cyclical unemployment.

 POLICY BRIEF   The Natural Rate of Unemployment in Europe

European unemployment has been puzzlingly high for several decades. In 2017, the Eurozone unemployment rate was over 9%, more than double the U.S. level. In 2005—a few years before the Great Recession began—Eurozone unemployment was over 9%, and in 1995 it was over 10%.* It seems as though the natural rate of unemployment in Europe is significantly higher than in the United States.

Several theories have tried to explain the high unemployment rates in Europe. Some note that government policies such as minimum wages and unemployment compensation tend to be more generous in Europe than in the United States. Others point to unions, which are stronger in Europe than in the United States. But no single explanation is completely satisfactory. Some European nations, such as Denmark and the Netherlands, have fairly low natural rates of unemployment, despite very generous unemployment benefits and strong unions.

One interesting policy experiment occurred in Germany. From 2003 to 2005, the German government enacted some labor market reforms to boost employment. They encouraged unions to seek smaller wage gains, reduced long-term unemployment compensation, and provided government subsidies to the hiring of low-wage workers. The unemployment rate, which was about 11% in 2005, began to fall sharply and remained surprisingly low even during the Great Recession. In 2015, German unemployment fell below 5% for the first time in decades.[†]

[*]Olivier J. Blanchard, "Explaining European Unemployment," NBER Reporter: Research Summary, National Bureau of Economic Research, Summer 2004, http://www.nber.org/reporter/summer04/blanchard.html.

[†]Tom Krebs and Martin Scheffel, "German Labour Reforms: Unpopular Success," VOX, CEPR's Policy Portal, September 20, 2013, http://www.voxeu.org/article/german-labour-reforms-unpopular-success.

BUSINESS TAKEAWAY

Business planning requires the careful analysis of macroeconomic data. Data sources such as the St. Louis Fed's Federal Reserve Economic Data (FRED) (https://fred.stlouisfed.org) provide historical data on thousands of economic indicators (like the unemployment rate), which can be useful for firms seeking to understand how the overall business cycle might have affected their business in the past. A firm that sells budget items (inferior goods) might actually see higher sales during a recession, whereas luxury goods makers tend to do well when the stock market is booming.

When unemployment is rising, it can be easier for firms to find highly skilled workers. During booms, on the other hand, employment is essentially a seller's market that benefits employees. To attract workers, firms need to offer higher wages and other creative techniques, such as signing bonuses, relocation costs, additional paid vacations, and in-house perks like catered lunches and employer-provided day care.

The business cycle has an especially powerful impact on business investment. Capital projects are risky when the economy is likely to go into a recession and the unemployment rate is about to increase. Conversely, firms often benefit from adopting time-consuming projects during a recession because the costs of labor and materials are lower and the project may not be completed until after the recession has ended. Decisions today also depend heavily on the economic environment that is expected in the months and years ahead. This is what makes economic forecasts valuable.

A key challenge for any business analysis is to put macroeconomic data into context and to recognize that data is often flawed. A decline in the unemployment rate, for example, may be the sign of a healthy economy, or it may indicate that unemployed individuals have given up on finding a job—which in many ways is a worse outcome than being unemployed. A simple look at the headline unemployment rate number is not sufficient to determine the health of the economy because it is often a lagging indicator. By looking at a wide range of macroeconomic indicators and factoring in the risks of error, managers are more liking to make decisions that help their businesses thrive.

CHAPTER STUDY GUIDE

21.1 UNEMPLOYMENT AND THE LABOR FORCE

When society is not at its productive capacity, unemployment levels are typically high. The **unemployed** are individuals age 16 and over who are available to work, did not work in the past week, and actively looked for work during the previous four weeks. Unemployed individuals must be willing and able to work but not be currently doing so. In contrast, the **employed** are individuals age 16 and over who worked in the past week, even part-time, or are temporarily away from work. The **labor force** is the number of individuals age 16 and over who are either unemployed or employed. Mathematically, this is Labor force = Employed + Unemployed. The **Unemployment rate (U3 unemployment rate)** is the percentage of the labor force that is unemployed (*not* the percentage of adults who are not working). U3 is considered the official unemployment rate. Mathematically, the U3 unemployment rate = (Unemployed/Labor force) × 100%. The **labor force participation rate (LFPR)** is the percentage of the adult population that is either employed or unemployed and thus in the labor force. Mathematically, the LFPR = (Labor force/Adult population) × 100%. The U.S. LFPR declined significantly after 2008. African Americans, teenagers, and those with no high school diploma tend to have a higher unemployment rate than the national average. Unemployment begins when people lose their jobs, leave their jobs, or enter the labor market. Unemployment ends when people secure employment or exit the labor force. There are several technical difficulties in determining the unemployment rate. Marginally attached workers are nonworking individuals who currently are not looking for employment but who indicate they want to work. Because they currently are not looking for work, they are not considered unemployed. Persons marginally attached to the labor force include discouraged workers. In the United States, unemployment insurance benefits expire after 26 weeks when the job market is healthy. **Unemployment insurance** is temporary government-provided income to individuals that partially makes up for lost income during periods of involuntary unemployment. **Discouraged workers** are nonworking individuals who are willing and able to work, have worked or sought employment in the prior 12 months, but currently are not looking for work because they do not believe they will be able to find an appropriate job. Underemployed workers are working part-time but want to work full-time. The **U6 unemployment rate** is an alternative measure of the unemployment rate that adjusts for both marginally attached and underemployed workers. Mathematically, the U6 unemployment rate = ((Unemployed + Marginally attached + Underemployed)/(Labor force + Marginally attached)) × 100%. U6 is often referred to as the "real" unemployment rate.

21.2 THE BUSINESS CYCLE AND THE UNEMPLOYMENT RATE

Macroeconomic conditions impact the unemployment rate. An **expansion** is a macroeconomic condition associated with rising real GDP and falling unemployment. A **recession** is a temporary macroeconomic condition associated with falling real GDP and rising unemployment. Since World War II, the United States has had 11 recessions. The average length of a recession is just under 1 year. In contrast, the average expansion lasts about 5 years. The **business cycle** refers to short-run alternating periods of recessions followed by economic expansions. A **depression** is an unusually severe recession. In the United States, the most famous example was the Great Depression, which occurred during the 1930s. Economic variables often undergo a **seasonal adjustment**, which is a statistical process based on historical norms that removes seasonal influences in economic data such as GDP, inflation, and the unemployment rate. Changes in the unemployment rate typically lag behind the business cycle. Businesses are able to make better decisions if they can forecast the business cycle. One widely used tool for forecasting is the **leading economic indicators**—economic statistics that are expected to change before the economy enters or exits a recession.

21.3 THREE TYPES OF UNEMPLOYMENT AND THE NATURAL RATE OF UNEMPLOYMENT

Cyclical unemployment is unemployment that results when real output declines in a recession. **Frictional unemployment** is unemployment that occurs during the time individuals spend seeking employment that is best suited to their skills. **Structural unemployment** is unemployment that occurs when workers lack the skills required for available jobs. At times, technological changes or shifts in international trade result in a mismatch of skills and jobs. A side effect of government unemployment benefits is that such programs also may contribute to structural unemployment. Finally, when the labor market is not in equilibrium, it results in structural unemployment. Wages can be above equilibrium due to a minimum wage law, a union contract, or efficiency wages. This results in higher pay for some and structural unemployment for others. **Efficiency wages** are above-equilibrium wages paid voluntarily by businesses to encourage productivity. **Full employment** occurs when cyclical unemployment is at zero and the only remaining unemployment is frictional or structural in nature. The **natural rate of unemployment** is the unemployment rate that occurs when the economy is at full employment and there is no cyclical unemployment. Mathematically, the Natural Rate of Unemployment = Frictional Unemployment Rate + Structural Unemployment Rate.

TOP TEN TERMS AND CONCEPTS

1. Unemployed and Employed
2. Unemployment Rate (U3 Unemployment Rate)
3. Labor Force Participation Rate
4. Marginally Attached and Underemployed Workers
5. U6 Unemployment Rate
6. Business Cycle
7. Recession, Depression, and Expansion
8. Cyclical Unemployment
9. Frictional and Structural Unemployment
10. Full Employment and the Natural Rate of Unemployment

STUDY PROBLEMS

1. Since the 1980s, the unemployment rate in Western Europe has generally been higher than the rate in the United States. Is this difference due to more frictional, structural, or cyclical unemployment? Provide two possible explanations.

2. What demographic groups have higher-than-average unemployment rates?

3. Describe the impact of each of the following events on the unemployment rate:
   a. The government doubles unemployment benefits.
   b. Labor unions demand substantial pay increases.
   c. The minimum wage is reduced.
   d. Robots are developed that can replace low-skilled labor.
   e. The government reduces how long people can collect unemployment benefits.

4. Discuss three reasons that Costco might benefit from paying its workers wages that are higher than those paid by rival retailers.

5. Using data found on the Federal Reserve Economic Data (FRED), plot the unemployment rate (U3) and the U6 unemployment rate in your state since 1994. What factors account for the differences?

6. Immediately following the Great Recession of late 2007 to mid-2009, the median duration of unemployment peaked at 25 weeks. What was the median duration of unemployment in 2007? During the Great Recession, roughly what fraction of the unemployed was unemployed for more than 26 weeks?

7. According to the "skyscraper indicator," describe how skyscraper construction is related to the business cycle. Do record-setting projects typically start during booms or recessions? Are they typically completed during booms or recessions?

8. Using data found at the website of the U.S. Bureau of Labor Statistics (BLS.gov), what are the current unemployment rate, the U6 unemployment rate, and the labor force participation rate?

9. A *Wall Street Journal* article reports that a shoe repair shop in the Empire State Building closed after being in business for decades. According to the article, "The shoe-repair business suffered the vagaries of fashion, which moved away from leather and toward rubber soles, to say nothing of sneakers."[4] What type of unemployment would shoe repairers experience when their skills cannot be used elsewhere? Explain.

10. Early in the Great Recession, in January 2008, the U.S. unemployment rate stood at 4.9%. It had been higher in the previous month, yet the number of employed also fell. Describe how this can occur.

11. Suppose that a politician running for office promises to eliminate all unemployment. Is this goal realistic? Is this goal desirable? Explain your reasoning.

12. Does the business cycle follow a regular pattern, or do recessions occur at random intervals? How does this affect the ability of economists to predict recessions?

13. Discuss why high rates of unemployment are costly to society. Consider both the effects at the individual level and the macroeconomic affects at the aggregate level.

14. What is the least harmful type of unemployment from society's perspective? Provide an example of that type of unemployment.

15. In 1914, Henry Ford decided to pay his workers a minimum of $5 a day, doubling the wages for most employees. He also introduced profit sharing. Describe an economic rationale for such a decision.

2013

∧ Shanghai then (1987) and now (2013); remarkable economic growth transformed the Chinese city in just a few decades!

22
CHAPTER

Long-Run Economic Growth

What Explains the Wealth and Poverty of Nations?

In the 1970s, visitors to Chinese cities encountered thousands of pedestrians and bicyclists and few if any skyscrapers. In the countryside, where 80% of the population lived, there was hunger and high rates of infant mortality due to diseases considered easily curable in developed nations such as the United States. Today, China's largest cities have a modern skyline, the bikes have been replaced by cars and subways, and state-of-the-art high-speed trains zip across the countryside. In short, rapid economic growth transformed China from an extremely poor country to one of the world's largest economies, all in less than 40 years.

The economic development of China is remarkable but not unique. In terms of economic growth, the past few hundred years have been the most dynamic in all of human history. For the first time ever, most of the world's population is not living in extreme poverty, currently defined an income of less than roughly $2 per person per day. How did the world experience such extraordinary economic growth? As we will see, economic policies can play an important role in deciding whether countries end up rich or poor.

Chapter Learning Targets

● Describe how economic growth can improve a country's well-being.

● Explain the major factors that determine productivity.

● Compare policies that encourage economic growth in developing versus developed economies.

● Identify the role of natural resources and financial aid in economic growth.

● Discuss diminishing returns and catch-up growth with use of a production function.

22.1 THE IMPORTANCE OF ECONOMIC GROWTH

Over the last two centuries, global economic growth has been remarkable. China is just one of many nations that have seen dramatic economic growth over that period. But what exactly is economic growth? **Economic growth** is a sustained increase in real GDP per capita that occurs over time. Both parts of this definition need to be kept in mind when thinking about growth.

First, economic growth is measured by changes in *real GDP per person*, not total GDP. In Chapter 20, we saw that real GDP per capita is frequently used as an indicator of living standards. Countries that are more productive tend to have higher incomes and higher living standards. In contrast, total GDP is not a reliable indicator of living standards because countries with large populations (such as China and India) often have larger total GDPs than small countries with much greater output per person (such as Switzerland and Belgium). China, for example, has one of the world's largest economies, but China's GDP per capita is still just one quarter of U.S. levels. In this chapter, we focus on explaining growth in output per person, not total output. Furthermore, output is measured in real terms, that is, adjusted for the effects of inflation.

Second, growth is a long-run economic phenomenon that generally occurs *over time*—over many decades. In later chapters, we examine short-term movements in real GDP (such as recessions and booms). Here we focus on economic growth such as the rapid growth experienced by China, which transformed a poor developing country into a more prosperous nation. But what is considered rapid economic growth—20 or 30% growth a year? As you will see, even growth rates of 3% per year can radically transform a society if maintained over multiple decades. Low or negative economic growth, on the other hand, can result in countries that are stuck with persistently high levels of extreme poverty.

Think & Speak Like an Economist

Economists view economic growth as a long-run change that occurs over an extended period of time. The focus is on real per capita incomes, which are seen as measuring living standards. An economic expansion after a recession is viewed differently.

Economic Growth Estimates from around the World

To understand the long-run effects of economic growth, it is useful to compare the economies of various countries over an extended period of time. Exhibit 1 shows real GDP per capita for 11 countries in 1913 and 2016. In both years, real GDP per capita levels vary significantly from country to country. Among the countries selected, South Korea (then Korea) had the lowest level of GDP per capita in 1913. But South Korea witnessed a 46-fold increase in real GDP per capita in a period of just over 100 years. The United States, in contrast, saw real incomes grow 6-fold while Germany increased roughly 8-fold.

All countries grew significantly, but even a small difference in annual growth rates can have a big impact over a century. Exhibit 1, also shows the annual economic growth rates for the 11 nations. Amazingly, South Korea went from a developing economy with relatively low income in 1913 to a relatively high-income country in 2016. This is because its real GDP per capita grew by nearly 4% per year. And even that number understates this achievement because the country was still quite poor after the Korean War ended in 1953 and then grew much faster between 1964 and 1997. Also notice that fast-growing nations such as Japan, Germany, and China had average economic growth of around 2 to 3% for the entire period. As with South Korea, they often experienced shorter bursts of much faster growth.

Economic growth in Argentina was anemic. In 1913, Argentina was a relatively high-income country whose real GDP per capita was greater than that of South Korea, Japan, and Germany. But Argentina today is considered only a middle-income country, with real GDP less than two thirds that of South Korea and less than half that of Germany. This is due to Argentina's comparatively low economic growth rate of only 1.11%.

Today even low-income countries such as India are much better off than they were in 1913, although they remain much poorer than more developed countries. In contrast, the United Kingdom was the richest country in the world during much of the 1800s. Due to its relatively modest growth rate, many of the UK's former colonies (such as Canada, Australia, and the United States) surpassed the United Kingdom by 1913.

The Miracle of Sustained Economic Growth and the Rule of 70

economic growth A sustained increase in real GDP per capita that occurs over time.

To obtain a better sense of how sustained economic growth can transform a poor nation into a high-income one, it is useful to understand the concept of *compounding*. Imagine you place $1,000 in a financial investment that pays 10% interest each year.

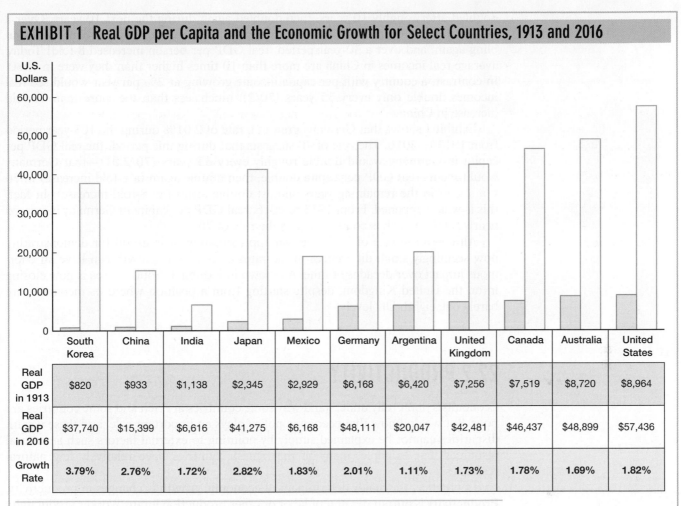

EXHIBIT 1   Real GDP per Capita and the Economic Growth for Select Countries, 1913 and 2016

	South Korea	China	India	Japan	Mexico	Germany	Argentina	United Kingdom	Canada	Australia	United States
Real GDP in 1913	$820	$933	$1,138	$2,345	$2,929	$6,168	$6,420	$7,256	$7,519	$8,720	$8,964
Real GDP in 2016	$37,740	$15,399	$6,616	$41,275	$6,168	$48,111	$20,047	$42,481	$46,437	$48,899	$57,436
Growth Rate	3.79%	2.76%	1.72%	2.82%	1.83%	2.01%	1.11%	1.73%	1.78%	1.69%	1.82%

Small differences in annual economic growth rates over more than a century can have a big impact. Between 1913 and 2016, South Korea had rapid economic growth of 3.79%, while Argentina had economic growth of 1.11%. Although real GDP per person in Argentina in 1913 was almost 8 times higher than it was in South Korea, fast economic growth allowed South Korea to increase its real GDP per person from $820 to $37,740 by 2016, while Argentina increased its real GDP per capita to just over $20,000.

Data from: the Maddison Project (1913 real GDP), World Bank, the International Monetary Fund IMF (2016), and authors' calculations.

The first year, your $1,000 grows by 10% (or $100) to $1,100. The next year, both your initial $1,000 and the interest you earned previously ($100) grow by another 10%. Thus your $1,100 grows by $110 to $1,210. In dollar terms, your money grows by a larger amount each year as you begin to earn interest on top of the interest you earned previously.

When dealing with long-term investments, it is helpful to consider roughly how long it will take your money to double—that is, how long it will take $1,000 to grow to $2,000. When interest rates are 10%, your money will double in just over 7 years. The mathematics involved in this calculation can be simplified with the rule of 70.

The **rule of 70** is an estimate of the number of years it takes a variable to double when increasing at a steady percentage rate of growth. The doubling time is calculated as 70 divided by the annual growth rate ($70/g$). In the above case, money grew by 10% a year, so $g = 10$ and $70/g = 7$ years.

The same logic applies to economic growth rates. Since 1980, some measures of China's growth in real per capita income averaged around 7%. Thus, real incomes

rule of 70 An estimate of the number of years it takes a variable to double when increasing at a steady percentage rate of growth.

doubled after roughly 10 years, then doubled again during the next 10 years. Over a 20-year period, China's real GDP per person increased 4-fold by doubling and doubling again, and over a 30-year period, real GDP per person increased 8-fold! Today, average real incomes in China are more than 10 times higher than they were in 1980. In contrast, a country with per capita income growing at 2% per year would see real incomes double only every 35 years (70/2), much less than the more than 10-fold increase in China.

Exhibit 1 shows that Germany grew at a rate of 2.01% during the 103-year period from 1913 to 2016. The rule of 70 suggests that during this period, the real GDP per capita in Germany would double roughly every 35 years (70/2.01)—that Germany would see its real GDP per capita double, then double again (a 4-fold increase) in 70 years, and in the remaining years, almost double again (an 8-fold increase). In fact, this is what happened. From 1913 to 2016, real GDP per capita in Germany increased nearly 8-fold, which is consistent with the rule of 70.

Although the rule of 70 is only an approximation, it is useful for demonstrating how seemingly small differences in the rates of economic growth can have an enormous impact over decades of time. As shown in Exhibit 1, South Korea is now closing in on the United Kingdom, despite starting from a position where its incomes were barely one eighth UK levels.

22.2 PRODUCTIVITY

Economists don't fully understand why some countries are rich and some countries are poor. But we do know that economic policy plays an important role, and these wealth disparities cannot be explained simply by pointing to external factors such as natural resources. For example, many of the richest countries have relatively few natural resources.

In practice, the major determinant of economic growth is changes in productivity. **Productivity** is output per unit of labor or other production input. Worker productivity can be measured in several different ways, but here we focus on real GDP produced per hour worked. The key to achieving higher per capita GDP is improving worker productivity.

You might wonder if a lack of jobs explains poverty in low-income countries. In theory, a country might be poor despite high worker productivity if most people are unemployed. Surprisingly, however, jobs are not the key issue. Indeed, people tend to work relatively long hours in low-income countries. The key problem is low productivity, not jobs.

Productivity and the Production Possibility Frontier

In Chapter 2, you learned that the **production possibility frontier (PPF)** is an economic model that shows the limit of what an economy can produce when all resources are used efficiently. The production possibility frontier also can be used to explain some of the factors determining worker productivity and economic growth.

Recall that economic growth is a sustained increase in GDP per capita over a long period of time. It reflects an increase in productivity. Economic growth is illustrated in Exhibit 2. In 1913, points Y or Z is unattainable with current resources. Economic growth gradually expands the potential output of capital goods and consumption goods—shifting the PPF outward. Thus, increases in productivity allow society to enjoy both more consumption goods and more capital goods.

productivity Output per unit of labor or other production input.

production possibility frontier (PPF) An economic model that shows the limit of what an economy can produce when all resources are used efficiently.

EXHIBIT 2 Increases in Productivity Shift the Production Possibility Frontier

Panel A: More Capital Goods and Rapid Growth

Panel B: Fewer Capital Goods and Slower Growth

The production possibility frontier can be used to show economic growth—a sustained long-run increase in GDP. This occurs when productivity increases. Initially, points Y and Z are unobtainable, but it may become obtainable with higher levels of productivity. One factor that encourages economic growth is the production of capital goods. The country in Panel A that starts at point A may have greater growth than the country in Panel B that starts at point B. Of course, beginning at point A requires a sacrifice of less consumption goods initially. Countries also can grow due to other factors.

Five Factors That Determine Productivity

The position of the production possibility frontier depends on productivity. Simply put, society was less productive in 1913 than it is today. As society became more productive, the production possibility frontier shifted outward. Improving productivity does *not* mean forcing workers to work harder and harder. Rather, gains in productivity result from five broad categories of factors.

Physical Capital per Worker: Machines and Buildings Workers are able to be more productive if they have access to useful tools. Imagine you are driving along a highway in the United States and see a worker using a Caterpillar excavator to dig a trench beside the road. In a low-income country, that same job might be done by 100 men using hand shovels. Thus low productivity in the developing country does not reflect a lack of work ethic. The workers with shovels are likely working harder than the American worker sitting in an air-conditioned excavator compartment. The problem is a lack of sophisticated tools—what economists call physical capital.

As is shown in Chapter 1, **physical capital** is equipment and structures used to produce goods and services. Capital is any nonhuman factor of production that was created by people rather than freely available from nature. In Exhibit 2, an economy at point A in 1913 is likely to see more productivity increases than a society at point B. The reason for this is simple: at point A, society is producing more physical capital, and more physical capital will allow the production possibility curve to shift outward. Of course, a society at point A is making more initial sacrifice by having less consumption goods than a society is initially at point B. (In Chapter 23, we will discover how society may obtain more physical capital through greater saving and investment.)

Many factors have contributed to productivity in the United States—its growing population, well-educated workforce, and abundant natural resources. But the physical

physical capital Equipment and structures used to produce goods and services.

capital stock of the United States is one of the most important. The United States has thousands of miles of railroads, superhighways, airports, and subways. That is all physical capital. Think of the skyscrapers in Manhattan or the endless tracts of suburban housing in California. That is also physical capital. So are hospitals, universities, and utilities such as electrical systems and water distribution systems. So are all the factories and the machines inside. Ships, trucks, trains, and airplanes are capital. When electric carmaker Tesla builds a massive car battery factory, it is also physical capital. Even the new technologies created in Silicon Valley are now considered a form of physical capital or simply capital.

Human Capital per Worker: Education and Skills Countries also differ greatly in terms of the level of education and skills—what economists call human capital. Recall that **human capital** refers to the skills acquired through education, experience, and training that allow labor to be more productive. A highly educated and highly skilled workforce is likely to be more productive than a less educated and less skilled workforce; and developing a highly educated workforce requires some investment.

To see how important human capital is today, imagine a United States in which no one has more than a fourth-grade education. The economy would be much less advanced, but workers would have *some* human capital because some forms of labor do not require advanced skills and some workers will develop more advanced skills on the job or on their own. But much greater skills can be gained through education and other forms of job training, such as apprenticeships.

Human capital shares many of the same characteristics as physical capital. First, the creation of both physical and human capital requires an initial investment—of time, money, or both. Second, both physical and human capital can boost productivity. Third, both physical and human capital can depreciate over time.

Technological Progress and Innovation Technological progress is another key determinant of productivity. This may help explain the economic growth of both countries in Exhibit 2, including the country at point *A*. A hundred years ago, most farmers worked behind a mule or horse that pulled a wooden plow. The plow is physical capital. Suppose that a country tries to develop by adding more and more mules and wooden plows. At some point, *diminishing returns* would set in: Each extra mule and plow would add less and less additional output. We will return to the concept of diminishing returns later in the chapter. For now, it is important to understand that in order to sustain economic growth, farmers need to do more than simply add mules and plows. The *quality* of physical and human capital also needs to be improved.

This is where technological progress comes in. Today, farming is an increasingly high-tech business that uses mechanical tractors, grain combines, irrigation, and advanced seeds to yield the maximum possible output per acre. Farming is not the only industry that has undergone technological progress. Businesses are constantly innovating, trying to create not only new products but better methods for building, distributing, and selling the goods and services they produce. Technological progress improves our capital stock and thus allows humans to be more productive.

Technological progress is the key driver of growth in countries that are already fully developed, such as the Germany, Japan, and the United States. In contrast, poor nations often need only to adapt existing technologies that already are in use in developed nations: They do not need to "reinvent the wheel." This explains how China and South Korea were able to grow faster during the latter half of the twentieth century than the United States and the United Kingdom grew during the industrial revolution a hundred years before. These late bloomers were able to adopt available technologies; they did not need to wait for another Thomas Edison to invent the light bulb.

Think & Speak Like an Economist

Economists use the term *capital* to refer to *physical capital*. In business, the term *capital* is often used to describe money raised in financial markets, that is, *financial capital*.

human capital Skills acquired through education, experience, and training that allow labor to be more productive.

BUSINESS BRIEF Innovating to Increase Productivity at UPS

When considering modern technology companies, few people envision the package delivery company United Parcel Service (UPS). At UPS, however, computers measure nearly everything its drivers do—including how many seconds it takes a driver to buckle his or her seatbelt and how many times a driver takes a left-hand turn.*

Companies have an enormous incentive to reduce the time an employee must spend on a given task. UPS estimates that saving one more minute per driver per day adds up to $14.5 million dollars in productivity gains. Thus, UPS computers determine the best way to load trucks in the morning and the best routes to make deliveries in the least time possible. One time-saving trick is avoiding left-hand turns because they often require drivers to wait longer to proceed safely.† Frequently, economic growth results from attempts by businesses like UPS to increase their own productivity. In turn, this increase in productivity at the firm level helps to increase the productive capacity of the entire economy.

*Jacob Goldstein, "To Increase Productivity, UPS Monitors Drivers' Every Move," Planet Money, NPR, April 17, 2014, http://www.npr.org/sections/money/2014/04/17/303770907/to-increase-productivity-ups-monitors-drivers-every-move.

†Shawna Ohm, "Why UPS Drivers Don't Make Left Turns," Yahoo! Finance, September 30, 2014, http://finance.yahoo.com/news/why-ups-drivers-don-t-make-left-turns-172032872.html.

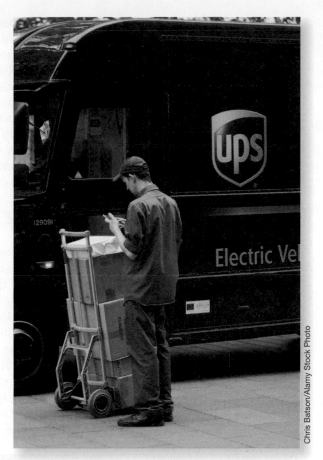

Chris Batson/Alamy Stock Photo

∧ At UPS, the use of new technology such as electric vehicles and state-of-the-art computer systems help reduce cost and increase productivity.

Inclusive Institutions For a market economy to grow and reach its potential, businesses and consumers must be protected by certain rights and rules. Economists Daron Acemoglu and James Robinson recently contrasted two types of institutions—inclusive and extractive. **Inclusive institutions** are laws, practices, or customs that allow all members of society the opportunity to create wealth. They include factors such as the rule of law, property rights, honest government officials, and openness to trade. For example, when contracts are not fulfilled, people should be able to seek legal redress in the courts. Inclusive institutions are also commonly referred to as *good institutions.*

The term *rule of law* refers to a system where people are allowed to do as they please as long as they obey clearly defined laws. That is, government officials cannot simply order people around at their whim but must obey clear laws. When contracts are not fulfilled, people should be able to seek legal redress in the courts.

Unfortunately, many countries have bad institutions. **Extractive institutions** are laws, practices, or customs that give insiders special rights, allowing them to extract wealth from the general public. A system of extractive institutions is sometimes called *crony capitalism* and usually features a high level of corruption. In many cases, only those with special political connections (the cronies) are allowed to do business. Regardless of effort, individuals in parts of the world without inclusive institutions will find it challenging to be as productive as those from parts of the world with good institutions. Development experts have suggested that many African nations failed to develop due to a lack of secure property rights and high levels of corruption, and indeed to a lesser extent this is true throughout much of the developing world. As a general rule, more productive nations tend to have better institutions.

There is some indirect evidence that inclusive institutions increase economic development. For instance, Singapore became by some measures the wealthiest and most successful economy in Asia after its government cracked down on corruption. Other evidence comes from that fact that migrants from countries with poor institutions are

inclusive institutions Laws, practices, or customs that allow all members of society the opportunity to create wealth.

extractive institutions Laws, practices, or customs that give insiders special rights, allowing them to extract wealth from the general public.

natural resources Inputs found in nature that can be used in the production of goods and services.

often far more successful after moving to free-market economies with inclusive institutions, such as Australia, Canada, and the United States.

There is an old joke that says, "In America, everything that is not explicitly forbidden is allowed. In Russia, everything that is not explicitly allowed is forbidden." This is an exaggeration but suggests an important difference. Although the United States has many regulations, businesses usually know that if they obey the regulations, they won't be punished (inclusive institutions). In contrast, in some countries, it's dangerous to enter a new industry without strong connections with key officials. The entrepreneur might be seen as a threat to existing companies that are politically well connected (exclusive institutions). There is some corruption in virtually all societies, however, and this problem is certainly not the only factor holding back productivity.

🏛 POLICY BRIEF Good and Bad Institutions on the Korean Peninsula

At the end of the World War II, the Korean peninsula was split into two nations—North Korea and South Korea. Shortly afterward, the Korean War erupted and ended in a stalemate in 1953. After the war, South Korean policymakers created a set of good institutions such as private property rights, openness to trade, and eventually political rights. In stark contrast, North Korea adopted a rigid communist system that lacked private property rights, political rights, or an independent legal system. Korea is a particularly useful case because North and South Korea are in many ways quite similar and had relatively equal natural and human resources at the time the country was divided. The North was actually slightly richer than the South during the early postwar years. This provides a natural experiment on the role of good institutions in economic growth.

The nearby photo shows the Korean peninsula at night, taken from a satellite. The northern part of the peninsula is almost completely dark, while the south blazes with light. Today South Korea is a quite advanced economy, but North Korea still suffers from severe poverty and famine. Per capita income in South Korea is an astounding 40 times higher than in the North. The lesson here is simple: Even from outer space one can see the impact of differing economic policies.[*]

[*]James Pethokoukis, "North Korea vs. South Korea: A Natural Economic Experiment," American Enterprise Institute, December 20, 2011, http://www.aei.org/publication/north-korea-vs-south-korea -a-natural-economic-experiment/.

∨ The Korean Peninsula at night. Economic growth sheds light on South Korea while the lack of progress mires North Korea in darkness. Also pictured are parts of China (top left) and Japan (bottom right).

Universal Images Group North America LLC/Alamy Stock Photo

Natural Resources per Capita Finally, natural resources play a vital role in determining productivity. Recall that **natural resources** are inputs found in nature that can be used in the production of goods and services. No matter how much effort someone puts into farming in Antarctica, that farm will not be as productive as a farm in Iowa. For much of human history, farmland was the key natural resource and even today explains much of the vast populations of India and China. But after the Industrial Revolution, minerals like iron and coal became relatively more important. Today, oil reserves are the natural resource with the biggest impact on productivity. For example, Saudi Arabia's growth has been due largely to the exploitation of the world's largest crude oil reserves.

Natural resources play an important role in productivity, but the impact of natural resources on long-run economic growth is less clear. As we will learn later in the chapter, the discovery of resources leads to a brief surge in productivity and economic growth, but this boom does not persist in the long run. Natural resources are the one productivity variable that countries have little control over.

Think & Speak Like an Economist

Economists view productivity as a key determinant of living standards. The most reliable way to raise living standards over time is to boost the average output produced by each worker.

22.3 PUBLIC POLICIES THAT FOSTER ECONOMIC GROWTH

Thus far, we have considered factors that boost an economy's potential output, shifting the production possibility frontier outward. However, not all countries produce the maximum possible output, given their labor, capital, technology, and natural resources. Because economic growth is important for living standards, economists have explored a number of options for using public policy to promote growth and development. Most economists believe that two distinct cases need examining—the catch-up growth of low-income developing countries (countries that aspire to become high-income countries) and the economic growth in high-income countries that are already developed.

Policies for Developing Countries

Economists have long struggled with the question of why some countries are rich while others are poor. You might say that poor countries lack modern technology. But why is that? Many technologies can be purchased at low cost, and descriptions of many others are freely available on the Internet and in books. Why did South Korea succeed in growing quickly while North Korea languished? There is no single, universally accepted policy for economic growth in a developing economy. In this section, we examine a few of the most often cited strategies for promoting growth in low-income countries.

Develop a Market Economy Earlier we saw that communist North Korea's institutions were very different from South Korea's. But is there evidence that communism was the deciding factor determining the lack of growth in North Korea? It turns out that similar outcomes occurred in the several other countries divided by the politics of the Cold War. From 1949 to 1978, capitalist Hong Kong and Taiwan with market-based economies quickly grew much richer than mainland China, which operated a rigid communist system. Germany also was divided into two nations after the end of World War II, and by the time the Berlin Wall came down in 1989, market-oriented West Germany was significantly richer than communist East Germany. Having a market-based economy is now widely viewed as one of the key determinants of good governance and inclusive institutions.

Encourage More Foreign Trade From the 1960s through the 1980s, many East Asian countries grew very rapidly. These "tiger economies" included Hong Kong, Japan, Singapore, South Korea, and Taiwan. There were important differences between each country, but one unifying theme was that all five focused heavily on international trade. Because these countries were not rich in natural resources and were densely populated, they initially focused on labor-intensive manufacturing. As they became wealthier, their economies switched to more capital-intensive forms of production and service-sector industries such as banking and finance.

In contrast, regions that did not encourage international trade such as parts of Africa, Latin America, and South Asia (India) did not fare as well, particularly in the late 1970s and 1980s. As a consequence, the East Asian economic model became increasingly popular. When countries are open to international trade, businesses are under more competitive pressure to boost productivity and product quality up to the levels of their competitors. In addition, international trade allows countries to specialize in goods where they have a *comparative advantage* (Chapter 2).

Encourage More Investment One way to boost productivity is to increase the amount of physical capital. But how? Developing nations are poor and often lack the funds

∧ The introduction of property rights in China was an important source of their recent economic growth.

necessary to invest in physical capital. In the short run, higher levels of investment have an opportunity cost of less production of consumer goods, and lower living standards. Therefore, even if a country is able to mobilize funds for investment, it often makes more sense to borrow the money from overseas and then pay it back when they have become more developed (this approach was used by South Korea). Thus, new physical capital in a developing nation is frequently purchased with foreign money. This may involve foreign loans or investments in the developing country's stock market. Or it may involve direct investment in new capital by foreign multinational corporations. **Foreign direct investment** is the ownership of business activities by an entity based in another country.

The purchase of physical capital also may be funded from foreign aid. **Foreign Aid** is the transfer of money, food, and other resources, often provided by high-income nations to developing countries. Such assistance comes in a variety of forms, including grants and subsidized loans. At times, foreign aid is provided for the express purpose of purchasing physical capital.

Provide Property Rights to Empower the Poor Early theories of development emphasized copying the success of rich countries, with big projects such as hydroelectric dams and steel mills. Over time, however, development economists realized that many low-income countries were wasting their most important resource—people.

Economist Hernando De Soto has studied the problems faced by members of the informal economy of Peru, especially the urban poor. In a book entitled *The Other Path: The Invisible Revolution in the Third World* (1989), he observes that the poor often built their homes on land that they *did not own*, and then operated small family businesses, perhaps out of their houses.[1] The problem with the lack of property rights was the lack of collateral, which made it difficult to take out bank loans. Because people often did not own the land under their house, they had no property to use as collateral for loans from a bank.

De Soto recommended that developing countries make it easier for small businesses to grow. Residents should be granted title to land they have occupied for many years. In rural areas, there was a push for "land reform" that would give peasants ownership over typically small plots of land that they had worked for generations, often as landless peasants on a large plantation. De Soto also pushed to simplify the process of obtaining permits to do business, which at times took many years. His ideas influenced policy in developing countries such as Peru, although much more work needs to be done.

foreign direct investment The ownership of business activities by an entity based in another country.

foreign aid The transfer of money, food, and other resources, often provided by high-income nations to developing countries.

🏛 POLICY BRIEF Peasant Farmers Take the Lead in Reforming China

Mao Zedong founded the People's Republic of China in 1949 and ruled until his death in 1976. Under Mao's strict communist leadership, China did not tolerate any private business. Most Chinese lived in the countryside, working on large communes whose output was shared by all. Unfortunately, peasants had little incentive to work hard because the benefits were spread to thousands of other peasants in the commune.

In 1978, 18 members of the village of Xiaogang met secretly and triggered what would become a revolutionary change in the world economy. Although at that time, private enterprise could lead to severe punishment in communist China, these

Kimberly Walker/robertharding/Alamy Stock Photo

villagers agreed to set up a system of private plots of land, one per family, without informing the government, and they signed the agreement in blood. They had good reason to want to reform their system: From 1958 to 1960, one fourth of the county's population starved to death during a famine.

After the profit motive became an incentive, output rose sharply, Xiaogang's idea spread to other villages, and eventually, the Chinese government approved the idea. Because China had fallen far behind much of East Asia by 1978, the new Chinese leadership decided to allow a much bigger role for private enterprise, while maintaining an important role for the state in key sectors. During the 1980s, output in the countryside soared in both farming and "township enterprises," which technically were cooperatives but acted more like private businesses. Poverty rates in China declined sharply. Along the coast, special economic zones were created where multinational businesses could set up factories and produce goods for export. This led to the greatest manufacturing boom the world has ever seen as firms from developed countries hired millions of Chinese peasants who migrated from farms to the cities.*

*Ronald Coase and Ning Wang, *How China Became Capitalist* (London: Palgrave Macmillan, 2013).

Reduce Corruption and Encourage Transparency As noted above, extractive institutions are often associated with corruption. Although no country is completely free of corruption, some are more corrupt than others. There are at least two ways to think about how corruption might slow economic development.

First, corruption is like a tax on business, and often it is a quite severe tax. In some countries, business people may have to bribe many officials in order to do business, which can lead to a strong disincentive to operate a business. Developing countries often see some of their most talented people become discouraged and move to countries with lower levels of corruption, such as Australia or Canada.

Second, corruption encourages political connections over new ideas and entrepreneurship. When well-connected insiders are given permission to have a monopoly in a lucrative industry (such as a monopoly mobile phone network), aspiring entrepreneurs may not have the political connections required to compete against established firms. This is why many economists recommend government transparency: Corruption is less likely in a country where the law clearly spells out which rules a business needs to follow and allows businesses the freedom to operate as long as they obey a clearly defined set of rules.

Improve Productivity with Better Health Care, Education, and Infrastructure Another problem faced by developing countries is low worker productivity. India has much lower wages than China, and yet despite this cost advantage, its export industries have fallen far short of their Chinese competitors. What explains this difference? Many economists point to differences in health, education, and infrastructure—all factors that tend to affect worker productivity. China has substantially better health conditions than India, as evidenced by its longer life expectancy. Healthier people are able to work harder. Hunger plays a role, too. In many low-income countries, poor workers cannot afford to consume the roughly 2,000 calories needed each day to meet the physical demands of their jobs.

Perhaps the biggest difference between India and China is infrastructure. China has very high savings rates and has invested vast sums in physical capital such as electrical power plants, roads, airports, and high-speed railroads. In India, the roads are poor, and the electrical grid is unreliable. Even though multinational firms can employ Indian workers at lower wages than Chinese workers, the lack of good infrastructure can add greatly to the total cost of production. Firms often have to produce their own electricity on site. It is no coincidence that India's biggest success story involves Internet-related industries such as software and call service centers. These industries are not as impacted by the poor quality of Indian roads and ports because digital information can be sent around the world electronically at very low cost.

Education is an important component of economic development. In India, the state schools often offer very low-quality education, so many Indians (even many poor Indians) send their children to private schools. The country would benefit from education reforms that boost the quality of the state schools and access to private schools. Some economists have suggested solutions such as offering voucher programs to expand access to private schooling in places like India and ensuring gender equality in education. Economies in which girls and women are able to get an education tend to grow faster than those where they are relegated to more traditional gender roles.

 POLICY BRIEF Economic Growth in Two Neighboring African Countries

EXHIBIT 3   Economic Growth in Botswana and Zimbabwe, 1980 to 2010

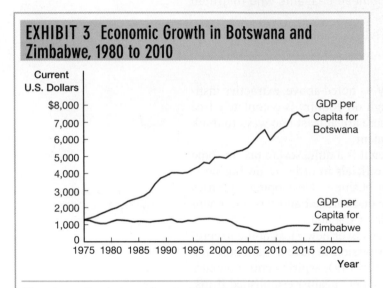

Since becoming independent in 1980, Zimbabwe has seen its GDP per capita decline due to misguided government policies. In contrast, Botswana has adopted sensible economic policies, and its GDP per capita has increased sharply since 1980.

Data from: the Federal Reserve Economic Data (FRED) and Federal Reserve Bank of St. Louis.

In 1980, Zimbabwe became an independent nation. At the time, the country had many highly productive farms that were able to feed the country and provide substantial exports. The new government, however, seized many of these farms and gave them to people with connections to the ruling party. The new owners were often much less skilled at farming than the original owners, and production plummeted. Years of economic mismanagement have resulted in negative economic growth, and Zimbabwe has gone from being one of Africa's richest countries to one of its poorest.

In contrast, neighboring Botswana, which was one of Africa's poorest countries, is now one of Africa's richest. Botswana did a better job of securing property rights, reducing corruption, and relying on free markets. As a result of better economic management since the country became independent in 1966, its economic growth has averaged 6% per year. Exhibit 3 demonstrates the recent economic growth of the two neighboring African countries.

*Marian L. Tupy, "Botswana and Zimbabwe: A Tale of Two Countries," *The American*, American Enterprise Institute, May 14, 2008, https://www.cato.org/publications/commentary/botswana-zimbabwe-tale-two-countries.

Policies for High-Income Countries

Thus far, we've examined issues faced by developing countries. Economic growth in high-income countries involves a different set of challenges. High-income countries usually are open to trade and investment and also have market-based economies, relatively inclusive institutions, secure property rights, and fairly high-quality education, health care, and infrastructure. For high-income countries to grow indefinitely, they cannot just keep adding physical capital. This is because at some point *diminishing returns* sets in; initially new capital such as more plows for farmers tends to add a lot to output, but as more capital is used it becomes less beneficial. To grow, high-income countries must innovate—that is, create technological change.

Subsidizing Research and Development It often takes a very long time for progress in basic science to trickle down to new product development. In many cases, the scientists that make a theoretical breakthrough will not benefit personally from the value that the innovation provides to future high-tech industries. For this reason, governments of developed countries subsidize basic research, often with grants to university researchers. In the United States, the National Institutes of Health (NIH) funds a great deal of basic research that is looking for the causes of and possible treatments for various diseases. This work can be seen as complementing the work of private biotech companies, which often focuses on applying new theoretical breakthroughs to the development of specific new drugs.

📊 BUSINESS BRIEF The Human Genome Project

One of the best examples of research in basic science that has had spillover benefits is the Human Genome Project, a U.S. government-funded effort to identify and sequence all 3 billion letters in the human genome. This project began in 1990, was completed in 2003, and led to the identification of more than 1,800 disease genes. As a result, more than 2,000 genetic tests have been developed for various human conditions. Private-sector firms also have benefited. By 2013, an estimated 350 biotechnology products were already undergoing clinical trials. Furthermore, companies such as 23andme and Ancestry.com allow people to order personalized genetic reports that provide insights into health, personal traits, and ancestry. Biotechnology is now one of the fastest-growing high-tech industries in America. One study found that the $3.8 billion dollar investment in the human genome project created 310,000 jobs and drove an economic impact of $796 billion.*

*Simon Tripp and Martin Grueber, "Economic Impact of the Human Genome Project," Technology Partnership Practice, Battelle Memorial Institute, May 2011, https://www.battelle.org/docs/default-source/misc/battelle-2011-misc-economic-impact-human-genome-project.pdf?sfvrsn=6.

Bringing Together Productive Workers Why does innovation tend to occur in certain locations? Many experts point to the advantages of being close to major research universities. Silicon Valley is near Stanford and Berkeley universities, and the Massachusetts cluster of biotech firms is near Harvard and the Massachusetts Institute of Technology. In many cases, a scientist develops a new idea in a university and then sets up a new firm with funding from *venture capital firms*—groups of investors who provide financial capital for startup businesses that offer high-risk, high-reward opportunities.

Other U.S. cities are homes to outstanding research universities—including Chicago, Columbia, Michigan, Duke, Cornell, Princeton, and Yale—so what makes Silicon Valley special? Economists believe that in certain industries, there are advantages to *agglomeration*—being close to others in the same industry. The **advantages of agglomeration** refers to the fact that in some industries, productivity is higher when workers are able to interact with others working in the same industry. An entire culture built around the tech industry in Silicon Valley means that a large pool of tech talent is concentrated in that area. Similar clusters exist around theater (Broadway), finance (Wall Street), and film and television (Hollywood).

Many economists believe that two key policy reforms that encourage clustering of talent in the United States could be effective in boosting growth. First, allowing more highly skilled immigrants to work in the United States would increase the overall pool of talent that feeds industries like technology and medical research. Second, economists favor policies that would make it easier for workers to relocate near productivity centers within the United States. Typically, this means developing more

advantages of agglomeration The fact that in some industries, productivity is higher when workers are able to interact with others working in the same industry.

"We realized it is an unnecessary department, but the acronym was just too cool to shut it down."

HALL OF BUREAUCRACIES

D.U.D.E. DEPARTMENT OF UNUSUAL DEVELOPING ECONOMICS

high-density housing in those cities and investing more in mass transit infrastructure.

Defending Intellectual Property Rights Many high-tech industries produce goods that have relatively low marginal costs of production but high fixed costs associated with development. This is the traditional argument for intellectual property rights such as patents and copyrights. By giving inventors a temporary monopoly on new products, intellectual property rights act as a spur to innovation. Apple, for example, invented the iPhone because it was able to secure profits through the use of patents.

Some economists believe that intellectual property rights have become too restrictive. One complaint is that patents are often given out for trivial innovations, not just for truly new inventions. Another fear is that excessively restrictive patents and copyrights can be barriers to new firms entering an industry and can slow the spread of innovative ideas across the economy. Thus, it's important to find the right balance between property rights that encourage innovation and rules that become unnecessarily burdensome.

22.4 THREE DEBATES IN DEVELOPMENT ECONOMICS

The field of development economics studies forces that lead to economic growth. But the discipline is not without its share of intellectual debates. In this section, we examine three such debates.

Are Natural Resources a Blessing or a Curse?

The United States is blessed with ample natural resources, and it has been one of the most productive countries in the world for over a century. But these two facts are not necessarily as closely linked as you might assume. The United States is *not* a typical rich nation. It is both larger and better endowed with natural resources than most other wealthy nations. Many advanced economies that experienced rapid economic growth—for example, East Asian economies like Japan, Singapore, South Korea, and Taiwan and Western European countries such as Austria, Denmark, and Switzerland—are not especially well-endowed with natural resources. And many developing countries—such as Bolivia, Congo, and Venezuela—remain underdeveloped despite abundant natural resources. This raises the question of whether natural resources are usually a blessing or a curse.

A few countries have clearly benefited from natural resources, and it's striking how important one particular resource—crude oil—is. Almost all of the countries that have high per capita incomes due to natural resources—including Brunei, Kuwait, Qatar, Saudi Arabia, and the United Arab Emirates—reached that level through the export of oil and gas.

Some economists believe that abundant natural resources can also be a curse. Countries that rely on natural resource exports may not develop the good institutions required to generate diversified growth in a wide range of industries. Indeed, a striking number of oil-rich countries—including Iraq, Libya, Nigeria, and Venezuela—have failed to develop good institutions. Others—such as Indonesia, Iran, Mexico, and

Russia—have done somewhat better but still seem to have fallen short of their potential. Norway often is regarded as having invested its oil wealth the most wisely and has generally excellent political and social institutions. It made a strategic decision to put most of its oil wealth into a sovereign wealth fund for future generations, which has allowed it to avoid a high level of corruption in allocating this wealth.

Is Foreign Aid an Effective Way to Help Developing Countries?

Foreign aid has played an important role in many developing countries. Although most people think of gifts or grants when visualizing foreign aid, the biggest flows are actually loans made by institutions such as the World Bank, often at interest rates well below market rates.

There is a lively debate over the merits of foreign aid. Proponents of more aid, such as Columbia economist Jeffrey Sachs, have argued that it is a moral imperative and point to the relative ease with which lives can be saved in developing countries through low-cost programs that provide things like clean water and anti-malaria bed nets. The public is often skeptical of foreign aid, complaining that we should first fix problems here at home. On the other hand, the problems faced in developing countries really are dramatically worse than those in rich countries, and certainly a dollar is worth much more to a starving person in Somalia than to even a poor person in the United States.

The most thoughtful critics of foreign aid, such as economist William Easterly, accept the premise that the needs are much greater in developing countries but question whether foreign aid is effective in meeting its goals. Easterly documents many cases where aid has not gone for the intended purpose but rather has been diverted to the private gain of government officials. This debate is not easy to resolve because it is not just about "following the money." For instance, suppose a donor insists that foreign aid must be spent on new schools. The receiving country might comply with this in a technical sense but not adhere to the spirit of the requirement. Thus, it might spend all the foreign aid on schools but divert tax money that it previously spent on schools to a lavish office building for government officials.

Is Economic Growth Slowing Down for High-Income Countries?

One of the most puzzling trends in recent decades has been the slowdown in the rate of productivity growth. In 1987, economist Robert Solow quipped, "You see the computer age everywhere but in the productivity statistics." Productivity growth accelerated during the 1995 to 2004 Internet boom, but since 2004, growth has again been slowing. No one is quite certain why.

One factor may be the growth of the service sector, which is an increasingly large part of the U.S. economy. In fields like teaching or cutting hair, productivity does not seem to grow very fast. For the most part, one teacher still stands in front of a class of 25 students, or one barber cuts one person's hair. In contrast, each autoworker today builds many more cars than a worker made 50 years ago. However, manufacturing workers comprise a steadily shrinking share of the economy (partly due to fast productivity growth), so this sort of progress has less and less impact on total productivity.

As with many growth issues, economists disagree about what this means. Some claim we are not properly measuring growth on the Internet, where services are often given away for free (who needs to buy a dictionary today?). Some see a period of dazzling growth ahead when computers and robots will do many of the tasks currently done by humans. Self-driving cars could replace taxi drivers, and drones might replace package delivery workers. Some even wonder how we will have enough jobs for workers in a world where robots do almost everything more cheaply than people do.

Other economists suggest that predictions that machines will replace workers have been made for nearly a century, and somehow the economy always seems to be able to create new jobs when old ones are replaced by technology. The unemployment rate in early 2018 (about 4.1%) was lower than it was in many earlier decades when there was far less automation. So perhaps we don't need to worry that robots will replace too many workers.

Some economists think the biggest challenge will be finding jobs for less skilled workers. The easiest jobs to automate are often those requiring brute force, not those requiring sophisticated reasoning and judgment. Will low-skilled workers be able to find jobs in a world full of increasingly sophisticated robots? One way or another, this may be a defining question of the 21st century.[2]

22.5 ADVANCED TOPIC: DIMISHING RETURNS AND THE CATCH-UP EFFECT

To understand changes in economic growth over time around the world, economists have developed a basic production function similar to ones used in microeconomics (Chapter 11) that encompasses many of the sources of productivity discussed earlier—such as physical capital, human capital, and natural resources. A pioneer of economics in the use of production functions to model economic growth was Nobel laureate Robert Solow from the Massachusetts Institute of Technology. We begin with a simplified production function:

$$y = f(k, h, n)$$

This simple equation says that with a *given level of technology*, total output per person (y) depends on three primary factors (f) of production—physical capital (k), human capital (h), and natural resources (n). Economists use this basic equation to create mathematical models telling how much output can be expected with varying amounts of k, h, and n. In general, greater inputs result in greater output. Natural resources (n) are a special case because the amount is fixed by nature. Little can be done to increase the amount of natural resources, so economists tend to focus on the other two factors of production—physical capital (k) and human capital (h)—as key determinants of growth.

Economists are particularly interested in the question of whether there are limits to growth. If we keep adding more and more physical capital per worker, will productivity rise without limit? As we will see, one additional assumption is necessary. Consider what would happen if we kept increasing the amount of physical capital while holding technology and other factors fixed. Initially, output would rise very rapidly as labor becomes more productive by using modern machines (such as excavators) rather than simple tools (such as shovels). But at some point, diminishing returns would set in.

The **law of diminishing returns** is a theory stating that in the short run the marginal physical product of labor declines as more labor is employed, with other inputs held fixed. Physical capital exhibits diminishing returns when we hold constant technology and other factors of production such as labor. In this case, as the amount of capital increases, the marginal product from even more capital gets smaller and smaller. Earlier in the chapter, it was noted that years ago each extra mule and plow would add less and less additional output for a farmer. Similarly, having two or three excavators for one worker does not make that worker much more productive than having a single excavator because one worker can use only one excavator at a time.

Exhibit 4 illustrates the concept of a production function and diminishing returns. Increases in the amount of physical capital per worker (k) have a much greater impact

law of diminishing returns
Theory stating that in the short run the marginal physical product of labor declines as more labor is employed, with other inputs held fixed.

EXHIBIT 4 Production Function and Diminishing Returns

The production function shows the relationship between inputs and output. In this case, real GDP per worker (y) is impacted by the level of physical capital per worker (k). Physical capital exhibits diminishing returns: As the amount of capital per worker increases, the additional output from even more capital gets smaller and smaller.

Real GDP per Worker

Production Function
$y = f(k, h, n)$

An increase in k results in a small increase in real GDP per worker

An increase in k results in a large increase in real GDP per worker

Low   High
Physical Capital per Worker (k)

on GDP per worker at low levels of physical capital (on the left) than at high levels of physical capital. As noted earlier in the chapter, when considering the prospects for economic growth, it is important to distinguish between developing economies and economies already operating near the limit of what they can produce. Recall our discussions of growth in South Korea, which went from being a very poor nation at the end of the Korean War in 1953 to a prosperous nation today—mostly by using tools and techniques already in use elsewhere.

South Korea experienced the **catch-up effect**, which is the idea that nations that start off poor have the potential to grow more rapidly than rich nations. As shown in Exhibit 4, a poor nation (on the lower left) has the opportunity to raise productivity faster than a rich nation (on the upper right), where the marginal product of capital is much lower. Thus, we need to revise the simple growth model to distinguish between these two very different situations and to determine which growth strategies are most effective.

In contrast, much of the recent growth in the United States has *not* been driven by catch-up growth, but rather by *technological change*, such as the computer chip. Technology is not a normal factor of production in the simplified production function; it results in an entirely new (higher) production function. Technological advances makes k, h, and n more productive. The new production function, however, will still exhibit diminishing returns.

Some people are confused by the differences between technological change, human capital, and physical capital. The invention of a new software language is an example of a technological change. Teaching this new software language to thousands of computer science students in college is an investment in human capital. Designing a new computer is technological change. Manufacturing 100,000 of those computers is building physical capital.

Technological advances need not involve dramatic inventions like the airplane, computer chips, or new software language. It also can reflect incremental improvements in technique. For example, a few years back, someone in the fast-food industry realized it would be more efficient to have just one size of cap for all soda cups. So the small, medium, and large cups were modified to have the same size rim. The cups differed only in height. This tiny change slightly boosted efficiency.

In a similar fashion, a road map can be used to figure out directions, but new map technology (GPS devises) do so more efficiently by allowing firms like UPS to schedule deliveries more efficiently (see previous Business Brief). In a modern economy, innovations ranging from one-sized caps to cutting edge technologies happen all the time.

Which is more important for economic growth, more physical capital or technological progress? As you might suspect, the answer depends on whether we are discussing

catch-up effect The theory that nations that start off poor have the potential to grow more rapidly than rich nations.

catch-up growth of low-income developing economies or growth in high-income countries. For low-income countries, the most important factor is increasing the amount of physical capital, as diminishing returns are not yet a major problem. For high-income countries, new technology is essential for maintaining growth.

BUSINESS TAKEAWAY

In a global economy, businesses should always be looking for opportunities that lie beyond their home country. From exporting goods to importing workers, the fates of many firms are intrinsically tied with what is happening in other countries around the globe. As GDP rises and nations become wealthier, their people become more educated and affluent, which opens new markets for businesses and increases the supply of highly educated labor.

In the decades ahead, countries with large populations and fast-growing GDPs are likely to become huge markets. This is especially true in Asia, which has almost 60% of the world's population. Both China and India are growing rapidly, and as they become richer, they will become increasingly important markets for Western businesses. Countries with low GDPs tend to offer smaller product markets, but they can provide a source of inexpensive labor for low-skilled manufacturing and are often a destination for firms that develop natural resources.

But doing business internationally poses some challenges. Companies must look critically at the institutions at work in foreign markets. Government policies that are neither protective nor hostile to business generally produce greater long-term growth. Firms also should look at institutions at home and encourage policies that will allow them to attract talent from around the country and around the globe and to ensure that the products of their labor and innovations are protected by intellectual property laws.

CHAPTER STUDY GUIDE

22.1 THE IMPORTANCE OF ECONOMIC GROWTH

Economic growth is a sustained increase in real GDP per capita that occurs over time. Between 1913 and 2016, South Korea saw its real GDP per capita increase 46-fold by growing at an annual rate of 3.79%. In contrast, Argentina was a relatively high-income country in 1913 with real GDP per capita greater than Germany, Japan, and South Korea, but due to slow economic growth, its real GDP per capita was surpassed by these nations. The **rule of 70** is an estimate of the number of years it takes a variable to double when increasing at a steady percentage rate of growth. The doubling time is calculated as 70 divided by the annual growth rate (g)—$70/g$. The rule of 70 can be used to show how seemingly small differences in the growth rate can make profound differences in the long run.

22.2 PRODUCTIVITY

Productivity is output per unit of labor or other production input. The key to achieving higher per capita GDP is improving worker productivity. The **production possibilities frontier (PPF)** is an economic model that shows the limit of what an economy can produce when all resources are used efficiently. There are several factors that determine productivity. **Physical capital** is equipment and structures used to produce goods and services. **Human capital** is the skills acquired through education, experience, and training that allow labor to be more productive. Technological progress and innovation also help determine productivity. **Inclusive institutions** are laws, practices, or customs that allow all members of society the opportunity to create wealth. **Extractive institutions** are laws, practices, or customs that give insiders special rights, allowing them to extract wealth from the general public. Countries with inclusive institutions often have greater productivity than ones with extractive institutions. Finally, **natural resources** help determine productivity and are inputs found in nature that can be used in the production of goods and services.

22.3 PUBLIC POLICIES THAT FOSTER ECONOMIC GROWTH

In determining policies that encourage economic growth, it is important to distinguish policies for high-income and low-income countries. Low-income countries need to develop a market economy, encourage more foreign trade and investment, provide property rights to empower the poor, reduce corruption and encourage transparency, and improve productivity with better health care, education, and infrastructure. Investments include **foreign direct investment**—the ownership of business activities by an entity based in another country. The purchase of physical capital may also be funded by **foreign aid**—the transfer of money, food, and other resources, often provided by high-income nations to developing countries. Such assistance comes in a variety of forms, including grants and subsidized loans. Foreign aid is often provided for the express purpose of purchasing physical capital. In contrast, policies that foster economic growth of high income countries include subsidizing research and development, bringing together productive workers (agglomeration), and defending intellectual property rights. The **advantages of agglomeration** refers to the fact that in some industries, productivity is higher when workers are able to interact with others working in the same industry.

22.4 THREE DEBATES IN DEVELOPMENT ECONOMICS

Economists are split on whether natural resources are a blessing or a curse, as some countries appear to benefit from abundant natural resources while others thrive without them. Economists debate how effective foreign aid is at helping low-income countries and whether or not we are in a new period of slower economic growth for high-income countries.

22.5 ADVANCED TOPIC: DIMISHING RETURNS AND THE CATCH-UP EFFECT

An important pioneer in the field of economic growth was Nobel laureate Robert Solow, who used a production function to model economic growth. Real GDP per person depends on the factors of production, such as natural resources, physical capital, and human capital. The production function exhibits diminishing returns. The **law of diminishing returns** is a theory stating that in the short run the marginal physical product of labor declines as more labor is employed, with other inputs held fixed. This means that increasing amounts of physical capital will have less and less impact as the amount of capital increases. The **catch-up effect** is the theory that nations that start off poor have the potential to grow more rapidly than rich nations. It results from the fact that the production function flattens with increased amounts of capital. New technology results in a new (higher) production function, so that any given level of physical and human capital will be more productive with improved technology. New technology is an important factor for the economic growth of developed economies like the United States.

TOP TEN TERMS AND CONCEPTS

(1) Economic Growth

(2) Rule of 70

(3) Productivity

(4) Production Possibility Frontier

(5) Determinants of Productivity

(6) Inclusive Institutions versus Extractive Institutions

(7) Economic Growth Policies for Developing Countries

(8) Economic Growth Policies for High-Income Countries

(9) Law of Diminishing Returns

(10) Catch-up Effect

STUDY PROBLEMS

1. Use the rule of 70 to determine how long it takes the following countries to double their real GDP and how many times real GDP will increase in the span of roughly 100 years.

   a. A country with a 0.7% growth rate

   b. A country with a 1.4% growth rate

   c. A country with a 2.1% growth rate

   d. A country with a 2.8% growth rate

   e. A country with a 3.5% growth rate

2. Name several pairs of neighboring countries that experienced considerably different rates of economic growth. Describe the sources of some of these differences.

3. List and explain five factors that help determine productivity.

4. 📊 Which of the following are likely to increase labor productivity? Explain.

   a. Decreasing infrastructure

   b. Increasing amounts of machinery

   c. Increasing access to education

   d. Increasing population

   e. Improving business efficiency

5. Which type of economic model puts more emphasis on promoting free-market policy reforms—the export-oriented East Asian model or the communist development model?

6. Assume that a country reduces consumption and makes investments to increase physical capital.

   a. What impact would this have on economic growth?

   b. Demonstrate using a production possibility frontier.

7. Describe the differences between inclusive institutions and extractive institutions.

8. Why did Chinese agricultural output soar much higher when the country's farming changed from very large communes to small plots of farmland owned by individual families?

9. Discuss the impact of natural resources on economic development. Is it more accurate to say that natural resource wealth allows countries to become high income

(a) often, (b) occasionally, or (c) never? Which natural resource was most important in ancient times?

10. In many developing countries, girls and young women attain lower levels of education than their male counterparts. How does this limit the economic growth of a developing country?

11. List and explain policies that result in greater economic growth for a developing country.

12. List and explain policies that result in greater economic growth for a high-income country.

13. Would spending considerable resources on cutting-edge technologies such as the human genome project be an effective use of resources for a developing economy?

∧ Samsung's "Digital City" near Seoul, South Korea; with nearly 400 acres of office space required an enormous amount of investment.

Saving and Investment: A Macroeconomic Perspective

How Saving Contributes to Economic Growth

As you discovered in Chapter 22, economic growth in South Korea has been nothing short of spectacular: Per capita real incomes have increased 46-fold over the span of a century, with most of the growth occurring in recent decades. Today, the streets of cities such as Seoul and Busan contain spectacular skyscrapers and ultramodern transportation systems. South Korean businesses like Hyundai, Kia Motors, LG, and Samsung played a key role in the growth story, but their growth required substantial investment in physical capital.

We have seen that physical capital is a key ingredient for increasing productivity. Physical capital does not appear by magic: It requires saving and investment. In 2017, Samsung opened a new chip factory which required an investment of $15 billion. That same year, the tech giant spent an additional $44 billion on physical capital, far more than any other company in the world invested. The latter sum is roughly equal to three times the entire GDP of South Korea in 1961, even adjusting for inflation. It took many of these sorts of investments to enable South Korea to grow especially fast.[1]

Today, the amount of physical capital in the world is vastly more than it was a century ago. This is partly because of investments made in the production of new capital goods. These investments were paid for with saving. Saving does not just give people a place to store extra money; it also provides the funds necessary to produce new capital goods. In this chapter, you will learn how the linkages between saving and investment impact the overall economy and especially how they contribute to growth.

Chapter Learning Targets

- Explain the linkages between saving, investment, and economic growth.

- Analyze how government saving and foreign saving impacts the $S = I$ relationship.

- Describe how interest rates adjust so that saving equals investment.

- Identify long-run fiscal challenges related to the net national debt.

497

23.1 SAVING, INVESTMENT, AND PHYSICAL CAPITAL

As is shown in Chapter 22, increasing the amount of physical capital in an economy can contribute to economic growth. **Physical capital** is equipment and structures used to produce goods and services. Physical capital includes equipment (like business computers, servers, software, and heavy machinery) as well as structures (like manufacturing plants, office buildings, and other facilities). In the nonbusiness sector, residential buildings also count as capital. Physical capital plays an enormous role in our economy.

∨ Financial investment is a form of saving that spurs investment.

Robert Cicchetti/Shutterstock.com

Recall that in economics, the term **investment** refers to spending on new capital goods. Investment increases the amount of physical capital in an economy. But how do homebuyers, businesses, and governments fund the purchase of physical capital? The funds to pay for or finance these investment projects come from savers. **Saving** is forgone current consumption, which equals after-tax income minus spending on consumer products. Saving can take the form of money put into a bank or the purchase of stocks, bonds, and other financial investments. One of the most important ideas in macroeconomics is that saving equals investment. In this section, we examine, one step at a time, how saving and investment are related. Later in the chapter, we use a modified version of the supply and demand model to show how saving and investment reach equilibrium through adjustments in the interest rate.

Saving Equals Investment: The GDP Expenditure Equation Approach

We begin by reviewing the major components of GDP in the expenditure equation:

$$GDP = C + I + G + NX$$

Here, gross domestic product equals consumption (C), investment (I), government expenditures (G), and net exports (NX). Recall that the circular flow of the economy implies that gross domestic product is equal to total income. Thus, by definition,

$$\text{Total income} = C + I + G + NX$$

The easiest way to see the relationship between saving and investment is to simplify our analysis by assuming an economy with no trade, no government spending, and no taxes. This allows us to set both G and NX as equal to zero. Later in the chapter, we add government and trade back into the equation, and the basic concept still holds true.

In the simple model, there are only two ways that income can be spent:

$$\text{Total income} = C + I \qquad (1)$$

Now we can think about the two ways that people can allocate their income in a simple economy with no government: They can spend it (consumption) or save it. That is,

$$\text{Total income} = C + S \qquad (2)$$

For example, suppose you earn \$20,000 on a job. If you spend \$18,000 on consumption, then saving equals \$2,000. To put it another way, saving is the part of income that is not spent on consumption.

physical capital Equipment and structures used to produce goods and services.

investment Spending on new capital goods. Investment increases the amount of physical capital in an economy.

saving Forgone current consumption, which equals after-tax income minus spending on consumer products.

Total income equals $C + S$ (equation (2)) and also equals $C + I$ (equation (1)). Setting these two equations equal to each other results in

$$C + S = C + I$$

This is saying that we can produce two types of output (consumer goods and investment goods) and that we can do two things with our income (spend it on consumption or save it). Because the consumption on both sides of the equation cancels out, saving must equal investment:

$$S = I$$

Saving is essentially the funds put into investment, and thus they are equal by definition. They are two sides to the same coin, just as the buyer's expenditure in a market equals the seller's revenue.

Capital goods are not directly consumed by the public but rather produce a flow of goods and services over time. So investment can be considered a form of "delayed gratification" that is similar to saving. Instead of producing and consuming goods that give us instant satisfaction, with investment we produce goods that will boost our future standard of living. Saving and investment requires patience, and the reward for patience is more consumption in the future.

Think about deciding either to study hard for medical or law school or to go to lots of parties in high school and college. It's easy to see how the willingness to defer gratification might lead to career success. It is an investment in one's own human capital. But it's also easy to see why not everyone would make the same decision.

One common misconception about the saving equals investment relationship is that not *all* saving leads to investment. What if I set $2,000 aside by putting it in a bank? That's considered saving. And suppose the bank loans the money to my neighbor for a new pizza oven for his business. That pizza oven is investment. So far so good. But what if the bank loans the money to a different neighbor, who spends the money on a trip to Las Vegas? The trip is consumption. Does that mean that my saving doesn't lead to more investment?

Here we need to recall that the equality between S and I holds only in the *aggregate*, which means for society as a whole. When a neighbor borrows money for a trip to Vegas, economists consider that action *dissaving*, which means negative saving. If my neighbor earns $10,000 and borrows $1,500, he may end up spending $11,500 on consumption. In that case, we say he had negative $1,500 in saving, which equals income ($10,000) minus consumption ($11,500). In total, overall saving should always equal investment, but in this case, overall saving and investment is $1,500 *less than* it would be without the dissaving needed to pay for the Vegas trip. In this case, aggregate saving and investment is $500—the initial saving of $2,000 less the $1,500 dissaving.

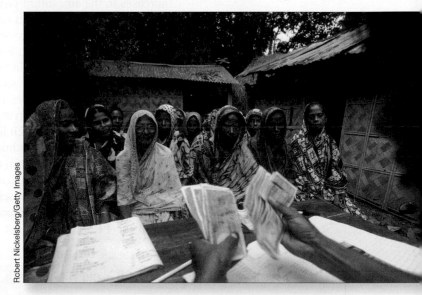

Robert Nickelsberg/Getty Images

∧ Microfinance loans like those issued by the Grameen Bank have had a positive impact on investment and economic growth.

BUSINESS BRIEF Microfinance in Bangladesh

Bangladesh's population is roughly half as large as the U.S. population, and it is squeezed into an area about the size of the state of Arkansas. Most citizens are peasant farmers who work small plots of land in the fertile delta region of the Ganges River. In 1976, economist Muhammad Yunus began researching how to provide loans to low-income peasants, which eventually led to the creation of Grameen Bank in 1983. Loan amounts from the Grameen Bank are small, averaging around $100, and they are based on trust, not written contracts. They typically are made to people who would not be able to borrow money from conventional banks. The loans often are used to make investments in physical capital, such as a phone to set up a phone service business or small solar panels to generate electricity in remote areas.

The bank focuses on groups that traditionally are underserved, such as the poor, the illiterate, and especially women, who make up over 90% of borrowers. The bank sets up small groups of people within each village and makes the group responsible for any defaults. Members agree to follow certain practices, such as ensuring that their children go to school and setting aside money each month for emergencies. If a member cannot pay, the group typically covers the debt and tries to collect the money later because a default would lead the Grameen Bank to cut off the entire group of villagers.

There is evidence that the Grameen Bank has had a positive impact on investment and economic growth. It also helped reduced poverty. Over 50% of borrowers were able to cross the poverty line as a result of their loans.* In 2006, Professor Yunus and the Bank were jointly awarded a Nobel Peace Prize.

*Grameen Support Group, Australia, "Grameen Bank: Banking on the Poor," Summary Paper, Global Development Research Center, accessed December 4, 2017, http://www.gdrc.org/icm/grameen-supportgrp.html.

Net Investment and Economic Growth

Increases in the amount of physical capital help explain many of the economic success stories around the world in recent decades, including countries such as South Korea and China. Increases in the amount of capital tend to boost worker productivity and generate economic growth, even for small farmers in Bangladesh.

But what exactly is an increase in the amount of capital? It is not as simple as producing a new factory every so often because some existing capital wears out each year. This is referred to as *depreciation of capital* (as discussed in Chapter 20). When determining the net impact of investment spending on the quantity of capital, it is helpful to subtract depreciation, which leads to what economists refer to as *net investment*. It is net investment that tells us how fast the quantity of capital is growing over time. Thus if 300,000 houses are built in a given year, and 50,000 old houses are torn down, then the quantity of houses in existence would increase by 250,000. In this case 250,000 is the net investment in houses.

Saving and net investment impact long-run economic growth. In Exhibit 1, we revisit the 11 nations that are discussed in Chapter 22, this time showing their saving

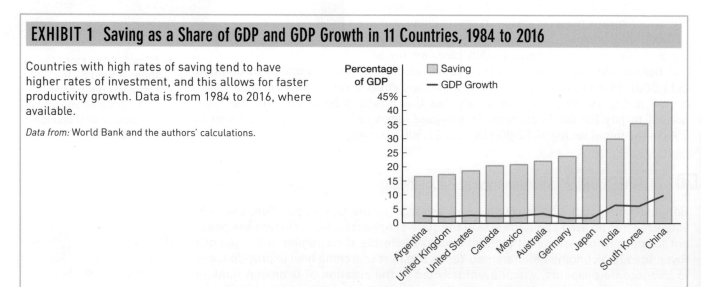

EXHIBIT 1 Saving as a Share of GDP and GDP Growth in 11 Countries, 1984 to 2016

Countries with high rates of saving tend to have higher rates of investment, and this allows for faster productivity growth. Data is from 1984 to 2016, where available.

Data from: World Bank and the authors' calculations.

rate and economic growth for the period 1984 to 2016. As shown in Exhibit 1, countries with higher saving rates (saving as a percentage of GDP) tend to have higher rates of growth in real GDP. On average, these higher savings rates lead to higher investment rates (investment as a percentage of GDP), which boost the capital stock and make workers more productive. However, it's also clear from Exhibit 1 that the relationship is far from perfect.

23.2 GOVERNMENT SAVING AND FOREIGN SAVING

In the previous section, we demonstrated that saving equals investment in an economy without government and international trade. But in the United States and in many developed economies, governments run massive budget deficits, and there are often enormous trade imbalances. How do these factors impact the saving equals investment ($S = I$) equation? To analyze this question, we extend the analysis by introducing government saving and international trade.

Government Saving and the Budget Deficit

We now add in the government sector and look at whether saving is still equal to investment. The government sector uses two concepts—government purchases (G) and net taxes (T). There are two important concepts to recall. First, as is shown in Chapter 7, government spending seldom equals the amount of money that a government collects in taxes. Governments generally collect less in taxes than they spend and run a budget deficit.

Second, G represents actual goods and services purchased or produced by the government, not transfer payments to individuals (such as those for social insurance programs). Thus, G includes road construction, education, and the military but not Social Security payments and unemployment benefits. For purposes of our analysis, transfer payments are subtracted from taxes paid. **Net taxes** equals total taxes paid to the government minus total transfer benefits received from the government. If the public pays $3 trillion in taxes and receives $1 trillion in transfer payments, for example, net taxes would be $2 trillion.

When we include government purchases and taxes, the total income equations become

$$\text{Total income} = C + I + G$$

and

$$\text{Total income} = C + S_p + T$$

The basic concept illustrated by these equations is simple. The first equation shows that output can consist of consumer goods, investment goods, or government purchases. The second equation shows that income can be spent on consumer goods, privately saved or used to pay in taxes to the government. There is no other use of income. Notice the subscript p after the saving term. This refers to private-sector saving as opposed to government-sector saving, which will be introduced shortly.

Setting these equations equal to each other,

$$C + I + G = C + S_p + T$$

We can further simplify by dropping C from both sides of the equation:

$$I + G = S_p + T$$

Rearranging the terms by subtracting G from both sides,

$$I = S_p + (T - G) \tag{3}$$

net taxes Total taxes paid to the government minus total transfer benefits received from the government.

government saving Saving by the government. It equals net taxes minus government spending.

budget surplus Net tax revenue minus government spending when net tax revenue exceeds government spending.

budget deficit Government spending minus net tax revenue when government spending exceeds net tax revenue.

"WHAT'S THIS I HEAR ABOUT YOU ADULTS MORTGAGING MY FUTURE?"

Dave Carpenter

Taxes (*T*) Minus Government Purchases (*G*) Equals Government Saving (*S_g*) At first glance, it seems that saving no longer equals investment. But they are still equal because the extra term taxes minus government purchases $(T - G)$ is equal to saving by the government sector (S_g). **Government saving** is saving by the government. It equals net taxes minus government spending. Why does $T - G$ equal government saving? Think about the government as an organization that needs to somehow balance its books, at least in an accounting sense. If it takes in more in net taxes than it spends on government output, then it ends up saving the difference. If you think of the government as being like a household, then taxes are essentially income for the government, and G is government spending on goods and services.

If net taxes exceed government output, then the difference is saved. This is called a budget surplus. The **budget surplus** is net tax revenue minus government spending when net tax revenue exceeds government spending. In this case, government saving is a positive value.

Suppose the government sector has $4 trillion in purchases and only $3 trillion in net taxes. In this case, the net saving is negative—a negative saving of $1 trillion. Negative saving is more commonly known as a **budget deficit**—government spending minus net tax revenue when government spending exceeds net tax revenue. In this case, government saving is a negative value. Because deficits are fairly common, they usually are referred to in the media with a positive number. In recent years, the United States has usually run a budget deficit.

Typically, governments run larger budget deficits during recessions. Not surprisingly, the largest U.S. deficit occurred in 2009 in the midst of the Great Recession, when it reached nearly 10% of GDP. This is shown in Exhibit 2. More details on the U.S. federal budget can be found in Chapter 7. We return to deficits in Chapter 28, where we examine the role played by budget deficits in stabilization policies known as fiscal policy. In this chapter, we focus on the fact that a budget deficit is *negative* government saving.

You might wonder how the government pays for all of its spending on output if it does not take in enough in net taxes. The answer is simple: It borrows the money, which is government dissaving. It borrows money by issuing Treasury bonds and bills (as is discussed in Chapter 10).

EXHIBIT 2   The U.S. Budget Surplus or Deficit as a Share of GDP, 1950 to 2016

The budget deficit increases during recessions. The deficit was especially large during the deep recession of late 2007 to mid-2009. The link between recessions and the budget deficit is established in Chapter 28. Note that a budget deficit is *negative* government saving. Shaded areas indicate U.S. recessions.

Data from: Federal Reserve Economic Data (FRED).

The budget deficit is the amount of extra money that the government borrows each year. Keep in mind that the government already has large debts from the money borrowed in previous years. The **national debt** is the total amount of money owed by the federal government. This debt has been accumulated over many years. The extra borrowing over a 12-month period is called the budget deficit and usually is much smaller than the entire national debt. In 2016, the U.S. budget deficit was just over half a trillion dollars, and the total national debt was about $19 trillion. To review,

- Government saving: $S_g = T - G$
- Budget surplus: $T - G$ when $T > G$ and government saving (S_g) is positive
- Budget deficit: $G - T$ when $G > T$ and government saving (S_g) is negative

Investment (I) Equals Private Saving Plus Government Saving In an economy with a government sector and no international trade, total saving equals private saving plus government saving. The total of private and government saving is sometimes called *national saving*. Mathematically, it equals $S_p + S_g$. Equation (3), $I = S_p + (T - G)$, can be rewritten as

$$I = S_p + S_g$$

This equation can help us understand why many economists worry about the federal deficit. If the government runs a budget deficit, then S_g is a negative number. This means that investment will be smaller than private saving. Not all of the money saved by the private sector funds new investment projects. The government borrows a portion of private saving to finance its budget deficit. This is government dissaving. However, any overall evaluation of the budget deficit requires that we also consider whether we are in a boom or recession. We consider these issues in more depth in Chapter 28.

Foreign Saving and the Trade Balance

Now we are ready to complete our model of saving and investment by adding foreign saving to the equation. **Foreign saving** is the saving that foreigners have invested in an economy other than their own. Total saving available to fund domestic investment equals saving in the private sector plus government saving plus foreign saving. That is,

$$I = S_p + S_g + S_f$$

The greater a country's trade deficit, the greater the amount of foreign saving *received* by that country. To illustrate, imagine that we import a Toyota Camry from Japan but do not sell any goods and services to the Japanese in return. If this is the only transaction, it results in a trade deficit because it means that we import more from Japan than we export to Japan. But surely the Japanese are not going to give us the car for free. We must give them something in return.

Initially, we pay for the car in U.S. dollars. In turn, the Japanese might use that money to purchase U.S. exports. But suppose that after the Japanese buy all the U.S. products they want, they still have dollars left over. After all, the United States usually has a trade deficit with Japan: We import more from Japan than we export to Japan. What do the Japanese do with their extra dollars? The answer is simple: They save them. They either purchase U.S. stocks, bonds, or real estate or place the dollars in a financial institution such as a U.S. bank. This is the essence of foreign saving.

national debt Total amount of money owed by the federal government.

foreign saving The saving that foreigners have invested in an economy other than their own.

Much of the money that Americans borrow to finance new homes actually comes indirectly from Japan and other foreign countries. Home mortgages, initially issued by local banks, often are combined with others into a *mortgage-backed bond* that is then sold to Japanese investors. Where did the Japanese investors get the money to buy all these bonds? By exporting lots of goods and services to the United States.

Foreign saving includes not just the trade balance but also transfers (money that workers send to their home countries) and investment income (including interest, dividends, and rental income). Here we consider a simplified model where foreign saving equals the negative of the trade balance (which equals exports minus imports):

$$S_f = -(\text{Trade balance}) = -(EX - IM)$$

📊 BUSINESS BRIEF Oil-Rich Nations Seek to Diversify: Sovereign Wealth Funds

Although some oil-rich nations are wealthy, oil wealth will not last forever. Eventually, the reserves will be exhausted or at least made less valuable as alternative energy sources are developed. Because oil-rich countries cannot assume they will be able to live off their natural resources forever, many of the better-governed and wealthier petro-states have invested a substantial share of their earnings from oil exports into *sovereign wealth funds*—government-owned financial investment funds comprised mostly of stocks and bonds. These funds, shown in Exhibit 3, are built up through government saving.

Notice that four of the world's five largest sovereign wealth funds are financed by earnings from oil exports. In these government-owned funds, the money generally is invested in a diversified set of assets, including stocks and bonds. The funds are often quite large. Because Norway has only 5.2 million people, its fund contains $192,700 per resident or about $770,000 for each Norwegian family of four. The per capita holdings of Kuwait, Qatar, and the United Arab Emirates are also extremely large. In the United States, the oil-rich state of Alaska also has a sovereign wealth fund.

EXHIBIT 3 The Five Largest Sovereign Wealth Funds, 2017

Country	Sovereign Wealth Fund	Assets (in billions of U.S. dollars)	Established	Source of Funds
Norway	Government Pension Fund Global	$1,002.8	1990	Oil
Abu Dhabi, United Arab Emirates	Abu Dhabi Investment Authority	$828	1976	Oil
China	China Investment Authority	$813.6	2007	Noncommodity
Kuwait	Kuwait Investment Authority	$524	1953	Oil
Saudi Arabia	Saudi Arabian Monetary Authority (SAMA) Foreign Holdings	$514	1952	Oil

Four of the world's five largest sovereign wealth funds are financed by earnings from oil exports.

Data from: Sovereign Wealth Fund Institute rankings, 2017.

23.3 A MODEL OF SAVING, INVESTMENT, AND THE LOANABLE FUNDS MARKET

An **interest rate** is the cost of borrowing money and also the reward for saving money, expressed as a percentage of the amount borrowed or saved. In this section, we see how interest rates adjust in the financial markets to bring about an equilibrium level of saving and investment. Fortunately, we are able to do this with a familiar supply and demand graph, where saving plays the role of supply of loanable funds, investment plays the role of demand for loanable funds, and the interest rate is the price. To be specific, the interest rate is the *price* of funds used for saving and investment purposes.

The loanable funds model helps explain what determines the interest rate. In the market for loanable funds, the interest rate must adjust so that saving equals investment, just as prices adjust in the market for goods and services so that quantity supplied equals quantity demanded.

The Saving Supply and Investment Demand Curves

People save so that they or their descendants can consume more in the future. Even if other motives are involved, such as to provide a fund to be used in case of a medical crisis, saving is still fundamentally about future consumption. Because the reward for saving is higher future consumption, you might expect that people would be willing to save more if offered a greater reward for saving. This means that, other things equal, the quantity of saving supplied should be positively related to the interest rate. The saving supply curve is shown in Exhibit 4, Panel A: People are willing to save larger amounts when offered the reward of a higher interest rate.

The effect of interest rates on desired investment is the exact opposite of the effect of interest rates on desired saving. Other things being equal, the higher the interest rate, the lower the willingness to invest in new physical capital. In essence, this is because people must either borrow to invest (pay interest) or reduce their savings to invest (earn less interest). The opportunity cost of investment is forgone interest.

interest rate The cost of borrowing money and also the reward for saving money, expressed as a percentage of the amount borrowed or saved.

EXHIBIT 4 The Saving Supply and Investment Demand Curves

Panel A: Higher Interest Rates Increase Quantity of Saving Supplied

Interest Rate — S_{saving} — Saving

Panel B: Lower Interest Rates Increase Quantity of Investment Demanded

Interest Rate — $D_{investment}$ — Investment

In Panel A, saving represents the supply of loanable funds. The reward for saving is interest. Other things equal, the quantity of saving is positively related to the interest rate. In Panel B, investment represents the demand for loanable funds. Other things equal, the quantity of investment is negatively related to the interest rate. This occurs because firms must either borrow to invest in new capital projects or give up the opportunity to earn interest with existing funds.

internal rate of return (IRR)
The percentage annual rate of return on the amount invested.

Interest rates have clear implications for businesses—from large corporations to small firms like Mario's Pizza. For example, consider all the possible investment projects that Mario could undertake in expanding his pizza business nationally. He might expand into areas where projected sales are high, such as a college campus with few competitors. Alternatively, he might expand into a more competitive (and expensive) city such as New York or San Francisco. In either case, he must decide whether to buy a small, cheap oven (that is adequate for most orders) or a large, expensive oven (that can cook many pizzas at the same time for the occasional large party order).

Now imagine that Mario consults his accountant to estimate the expected rate of return from each project. The **internal rate of return (IRR)** is the percentage annual rate of return on the amount invested (see Chapter 10). Assume that Mario has three potential projects, which offered different expected internal rates of return—3%, 5%, and 9%. Which project should he undertake? All of them? One of them? None of them?

The answer depends in part on the level of interest rates at the time. If interest rates are 6%, Mario should do the project with the IRR of 9%. The other projects would be akin to borrowing money from bank, paying 6% interest on the loan, and placing the loan money back in the bank and earning 3% or 5%. Of course, if the interest rate is 10%, Mario should do none of the projects.

Think of the interest rate as the cost of funds that Mario plans to *borrow* in order to finance the project. In that case, the project would have to earn a rate of return at least as high as the cost of funds; otherwise, the project would not be profitable. So when the interest rate is 6%, Mario would do only those projects that would earn more than the 6% interest rate on loans, and only one of the projects passes that test. What if Mario does not need to borrow money for the projects? Here, the interest rate is *still* the opportunity cost of using his own money. If he does not invest in the project, he can earn 6% interest on that money. Finally, note that in the real world, things are a bit more complicated because there are many different interest rates and different projects have varying degrees of risk.

Marginal analysis tells us that the business community will continue to invest as long as the project provides a higher expected internal rate of return than the interest rate at which the business must borrow. At a lower market interest rate of 4%, two projects are profitable—the projects with the expected rate of return greater than 4% (the 5% and the 9% projects). Thus, for any given investment demand, the quantity of investment is negatively related to interest rates. In Exhibit 4, Panel B, we see that the lower the rate of interest, the higher the quantity demanded of investment projects. That's because at lower rates, more projects are profitable.

Equilibrium in the Loanable Funds Market

If we put the saving supply and investment demand on the same graph, we will be modeling the loanable funds market and no longer have to assume a given interest rate. Now we can see how the interest rate is determined. In Exhibit 5, the equilibrium interest rate is 6%. When the rate is higher than 6% (say, 10%), then savers will want to save more than investors want to invest. There will be a surplus of saving, which causes interest rates to fall.

When the rate is too low (say, 3%), then there will be more investment demand for funds than supply of saving. In this case, there will be a shortage of saving, which causes interest rates to rise. We reach equilibrium where the amount that people want to save is exactly equal to the amount that firms want to invest. In the loanable funds market, voluntary exchange occurs between savers and borrowers for investment, and such exchanges are mutually beneficial.

Lower Investment Demand Decreases the Equilibrium Interest Rate As with our basic supply and demand model, the loanable funds model is most useful when something occurs to cause a shift in one of the curves. In the United States, the investment demand is much less stable than the saving supply, so we focus first on investment demand shifts.

EXHIBIT 5   Equilibrium in the Loanable Funds Market

The market interest rate is determined by saving supply and investment demand. This is the interest rate at which the amount that people want to save equals the demand for funds used for investment.

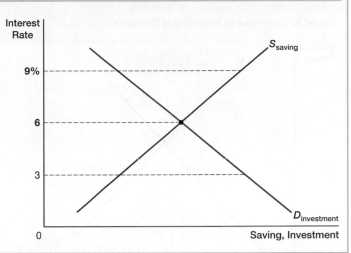

Just as a change in price causes you to move along the demand curve, a change in interest rates causes you to move along the investment demand curve. To get a shift in investment demand, something else must change. After years of rising prices, housing prices fell during 2007–09 and unemployment rose. Both of these events led to a decline in the demand for investment to finance those projects. At any given interest rate, there was less investment demand. This caused the investment demand curve to shift to the left. Panel A of Exhibit 6 shows that as investment demand declined, interest rates fell. A decline in investor confidence or higher tax rate on profits generated by investments will also decrease investment demand.

Higher Investment Demand Increases the Equilibrium Interest Rate The opposite situation occurred in the late 1990s, when the U.S. economy underwent a tech boom as the Internet emerged as a major industry and personal computers sales increased. With many good investment opportunities and much investment demand, the investment demand curve shifted to the right. At any given interest rate, the demand for investment funds increased. As the investment demand curve shifts to the right, interest rates increased, as seen in Panel B of Exhibit 6. In turn, higher interest rates increased the quantity of saving supplied. Reasons for an increase in investment demand also include sudden business optimism and the expectation of higher after tax profits, perhaps due to a tax cut on business profits as shown in the next Business Brief.

BUSINESS BRIEF   Corporate Tax Cuts and New Investment by Apple

In 2018, a major cut in corporate tax rates was enacted, reducing the tax rate from 35% to 21%, and setting up a much lower tax rate on foreign profits brought back to the United States. One purpose of the tax cut was to encourage corporations to increase investment spending on physical capital. In other words, proponents of the tax cut argued that it would shift the investment demand schedule to the right, which would tend to boost the quantity of investment.

Proponents of the tax cut pointed to an announcement made by Apple in early 2018, indicating that they would bring home several hundred billion in overseas earnings, and also invest another $30 billion in U.S. facilities. We don't know for certain how much of this new investment in physical capital was due to the tax cut, and how much would have occurred in any case. Nonetheless, lower corporate tax rates do provide some additional incentive to move production to the United States, boosting business investment and shifting the investment demand curve rightward.

*https://www.bloomberg.com/news/articles/2018-01-17/apple-expects-38-billion-tax-bill-on-overseas -repatriated-cash.

EXHIBIT 6 Shifts in Investment Demand

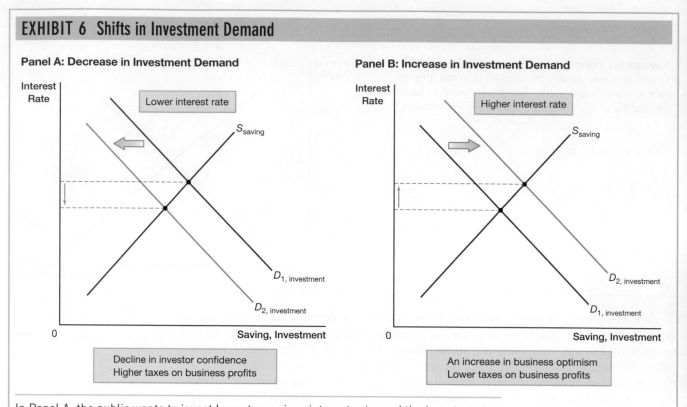

Panel A: Decrease in Investment Demand

Lower interest rate

S_{saving}

$D_{1, investment}$

$D_{2, investment}$

0   Saving, Investment

Decline in investor confidence
Higher taxes on business profits

Panel B: Increase in Investment Demand

Higher interest rate

S_{saving}

$D_{2, investment}$

$D_{1, investment}$

0   Saving, Investment

An increase in business optimism
Lower taxes on business profits

In Panel A, the public wants to invest less at any given interest rate, and the investment demand curve shifts left. This might occur during a recession. The decrease in investment demand pushes interest rates lower. In Panel B, the public wants to invest more at any given interest rate, and the investment curve shifts right. This might occur during an economic boom. The increase in investment demand pushes interest rates higher.

Lower Saving Supply Increases the Equilibrium Interest Rate Since the investment demand is much more unstable than the saving supply, the investment demand curve tends to shift more often than the saving supply curve. However, interest rates can also be affected by changes in the supply of saving. A decrease in saving will shift the saving supply curve to the left and result in higher interest rates. For example, if the government runs a large budget deficit, then government saving will be reduced. This would shift the saving supply curve to the left as shown in Panel A of Exhibit 7. Notice that as a consequence of the budget deficit, the interest rate tends to be higher than otherwise would be the case; this reduces the quantity of investment demanded. Similarly, a decrease in foreign saving will shift the saving supply curve to the left. New taxes on interest earned by savers would also shift the saving supply curve leftward.

Higher Saving Supply Decreases the Equilibrium Interest Rate Finally, if the supply of saving increases, then the saving supply shifts to the right. This tends to result in a lower interest rate and a higher level of investment. This is shown in Panel B of Exhibit 7. Suppose the government provides tax benefits to encourage more saving for retirement. In this case, there may be an increase in the saving supply from the private sector. Similarly, an increase in foreign saving will shift the saving supply curve to the right.

One of the most important issues in macroeconomics is the long downward trend in interest rates in the United States and many other developed countries. Why has the average level of interest rates been lower in the 21st century than they were in the 20th century? Lower inflation is one contributing factor, but even interest rates adjusted for inflation have generally moved lower. Economists point to a global

EXHIBIT 7 Shifts in Saving Supply

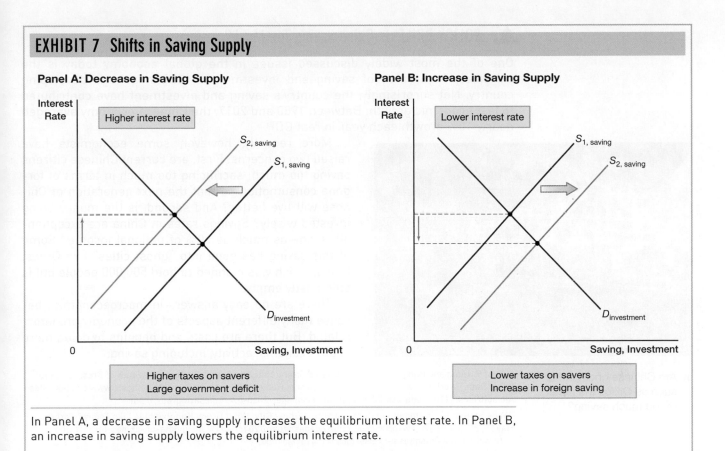

Panel A: Decrease in Saving Supply

Interest Rate

Higher interest rate

$S_{2, \text{saving}}$

$S_{1, \text{saving}}$

$D_{\text{investment}}$

0   Saving, Investment

Higher taxes on savers
Large government deficit

Panel B: Increase in Saving Supply

Interest Rate

Lower interest rate

$S_{1, \text{saving}}$

$S_{2, \text{saving}}$

$D_{\text{investment}}$

0   Saving, Investment

Lower taxes on savers
Increase in foreign saving

In Panel A, a decrease in saving supply increases the equilibrium interest rate. In Panel B, an increase in saving supply lowers the equilibrium interest rate.

"savings glut," which is partly associated with high savings rates in East Asian countries such as China (see next Policy Brief) as well as oil exporters in the Middle East. This has increased the supply of saving and lowered the interest rate.

> Quantity of Investment and Interest Rates: Never Reason from a Price Change

Many people assume that low interest rates are always a "good thing." This is faulty reasoning. As is noted in Chapter 3, one should *never reason from a price change.* Lower prices do not always mean that more goods are sold. The quantity sold depends on whether the low prices are caused by an increase in supply or a decrease in demand.

In this case, the interest rate can be considered the price of loanable funds. When considering whether low interest rates are good for business and the quantity of investment, we cannot simply look at the rates. We also must consider what has caused the rates to be low. Was it a greater supply of saving or a lower demand for borrowing? More often than not, low interest rates are caused by a drop in investment demand because the investment demand curve is considerably less stable than the saving supply curve.

During the Great Depression and the Great Recession, a low investment demand to finance various projects caused low interest rates. The investment demand shifted to the left, and both interest rates and the quantity of investment fell (Panel A of Exhibit 6). Conversely, during the economic booms of the late 1980s and late 1990s, relatively high interest rates were the result of a strong economy. Investment demand shifted right, pushing both interest rates and the quantity of investment higher (Panel B of Exhibit 6).

POLICY BRIEF Is China Saving Too Much?

One of the most widely discussed issues in the global economy today is the extremely high rates of saving and investment in China, a huge developing country. Not surprisingly, the country's saving and investment have contributed to fast economic growth. Between 1980 and 2017, the Chinese economy averaged nearly 10% growth each year in real GDP.

More recently, however, some economists have raised two concerns: First, are current Chinese citizens saving too much; sacrificing too much in terms of for-gone consumption so that the next generation of Chinese will live better? And second, is the money being invested wisely? Savings rates in China are exceptionally high—as much as 50% of national income.* Some of this saving has gone into "ghost cities" like Ordos, China, which was planned to hold 500,000 people but is still mostly empty.†

There are no easy answers in macroeconomics because many different aspects of the economy are interrelated. But there are costs and benefits to doing more of any economic activity, including saving.

∧ Are Chinese ghost cities such as Ordos the result of too much saving?

*Juann H. Hung and Rong Qian, "Why Is China's Saving Rate So High? A Comparative Study of Cross-Country Panel Data," Working Paper 2010-07, Congressional Budget Office, November 2010, https://www.cbo.gov/sites/default/files/111th-congress-2009-2010/workingpaper/2010-07-chinasavingrate_0.pdf.

†Wade Shepard, "An Update on China's Largest Ghost City: What Ordos Kangbashi Is Like Today," *Forbes*, May 28, 2016, http://www.forbes.com/sites/wadeshepard/2016/04/19/an-update-on-chinas-largest-ghost-city-what-ordos-kangbashi-is-like-today/#341a1faa1e08.

23.4 ADVANCED TOPIC: THE NATIONAL DEBT AND LONG-RUN FISCAL CHALLENGES

In recent decades, the U.S. budget balance usually has been negative because government spending has exceeded taxes. When the government runs a budget deficit, it must borrow enough money to pay for all the expenses not covered by taxes. In 2016, for example, the U.S. federal government spent $3,973 billion and collected $3,336 billion in taxes. The difference ($637 billion) represents the budget deficit for 2016. A discussion of the role of budget deficits in a recession can be found in Chapter 28. Here, we focus on long-run challenges of large accumulated national debt.

National Debt and Net National Debt

Recall that a budget deficit occurs when government saving (S_g) is negative because government spending is greater than net taxes ($G > T$). The budget deficit is often confused with the national debt. Recall from earlier in the chapter that the *national debt* is the total stock of debt or amount of money that the federal government now owes. It represents budget deficits accumulated over many years and is much larger than the budget deficit for a single year. In 2016, the national debt was $19 trillion, which was slightly higher than the United States' annual GDP.

It is difficult to grasp the size of the national debt. If $19 trillion dollars were shared by the entire U.S. population, each person would have over $60,000. Alternatively, if someone earned $1,000 each second, it would take over 600 years to earn $19 trillion. That's a lot of money. Should Americans be worried about this debt? As we will see, this is not an easy question to answer.

It might be helpful to compare the government budget to a household budget. Suppose that during one month, the family spends more than it receives in income by charging expenses on a credit card. In this case, the family will be running a deficit for that month. The family's debt is the total of all past deficits minus any monthly surpluses that reduce the debt. Similarly, the national debt is the total of all past annual budget deficits minus the occasional budget surpluses that may occur.

The government often finances national debt by the selling Treasury bonds and bills. Because the federal government and various government agencies have bought back some of their own debt, including Treasury bonds and bills, economists often focus on the net debt held outside the government by the public. For example, the Social Security Administration buys U.S. government bonds as a way to put aside money to pay future Social Security benefits. The **net national debt** is the total national debt minus debt obligations that the government owes to itself. It is the debt owed to people and institutions outside of the U.S. government.

net national debt The total national debt minus debt obligations that the government owes to itself.

debt ratio The net national debt as a share of GDP.

The Debt Ratio and Debt Ceiling

In 2017, the net national debt was roughly 77% of GDP. The **debt ratio** is the net national debt as a share of GDP. Even though this ratio is lower than it was during the late 1940s, many economists are concerned about the likely future trajectory of the debt. Unlike the late 1940s, the national debt is now trending upward, even as a share of GDP. Exhibit 8 shows the net national debt of the United States as a percentage of GDP throughout American history.

There are several noticeable patterns in the data. The debt ratio tends to rise sharply during wartime, reaching a peak of just over 100% of GDP at the end of World War II. The debt ratio also rises during economic depressions, such as the Great Depression of the 1930s and the Great Recession of late 2007 to mid-2009. The debt ratio usually declines during peacetime. This does not mean the United States pays off the national debt. The decline is often due to an increase in the

EXHIBIT 8 Debt Ratio: U.S. Net National Debt as a Share of GDP, 1790 to 2030

The national debt ratio tends to rise during wartime, major depressions, and major recessions. Normally, the debt ratio falls during peacetime, but there are now fears that the U.S. debt ratio will continue to climb.

Data from: Congressional Budget Office.

debt ceiling A legal limit on Treasury borrowing set by Congress.

nominal GDP, which is the denominator of the debt ratio. Thus, the large decline in the national debt ratio after World War II was caused mostly by rapidly rising real GDP and inflation.

There is a great deal of confusion about the national debt, especially the question of whether it is a burden on the public. The national debt is an obligation of current and future taxpayers to repay principal and interest to holders of Treasury bonds. These bonds are held by both individual and institutional investors, with roughly equal shares in the United States and in foreign countries. If the debt becomes too large, it puts a substantial burden on future taxpayers, which might lead to much higher taxes and reduce long-run economic growth.

Another area of concern is the **debt ceiling**, which is a legal limit on Treasury borrowing set by Congress. The debt ceiling limits government spending to the amount of tax revenue raised. Because spending often outpaces revenues, Congress must periodically authorize increases in the debt ceiling so that the Treasury can finance additional budget deficits.

What happens when the debt ceiling is not raised to cover these costs? One possibility is that the government will stop payments on *prior* debt. This scenario is considered a default. Historically, Congress has always agreed to an increase the debt ceiling, and the United States government has never defaulted on its debt. When other governments have defaulted, they sometimes found it more difficult to borrow in the future.

A second danger is that the debt could grow so large that it becomes unsustainable. What happens in that case? This happened in Greece in 2011 when its debt rose to unsustainable levels. Holders of Greek government bonds were forced to accept only partial repayment of the debt.

The situation in the United States is different from that in Greece in one important respect. The United States borrows in its own currency (dollars), whereas Greece borrows in euros. In this sense, Greece is more comparable to individual state and local governments in the United States, which borrow in dollars but do not control monetary policy. For instance, the city of Detroit declared bankruptcy in 2013. Many economists believe that a debt crisis in the United States would not lead to default because the federal government has the legal right to print almost unlimited quantities paper money and hence can always repay its debts in its own currency. Greece did not have that option. However, in the next few chapters, we'll see that the option to print money can create other problems.

The Challenges of Rising Health-Care Costs and an Aging Population

The debt ratio tends to increase during periods of war and severe recession. Today, many economists are concerned that the debt ratio will increase in future years even if war is avoided and recessions are modest. This is because under current law the government is projected to spend considerably more than it collects in taxes in the decades to come. Specifically, government spending is projected to grow as a percentage of GDP, but tax revenue is not expected to keep pace.

As a consequence, economic forecasts show a rising debt ratio in the United States over the next few decades. This primarily reflects demographic changes due to increases in life expectancy (people are living longer), the retiring baby-boomers (people born between 1946 and 1964), and decreases in family size (people are having fewer children than their parents and grandparents did). Taken together, these factors mean that there are relatively more older Americans than ever before. An aging population puts upward pressure on both pension costs and health-care costs, which already comprise roughly half of the federal budget. Most of the expenditures on Social Security (pensions) and Medicare (health insurance) go to retired people. As the U.S. population ages, expenditures on these government programs are likely to increase even though the taxes to fund such programs are not expected to increase as rapidly.

In the United States, Social Security benefits are paid for only *partly* with money collected and saved in the past. Most payments are made with money collected in the form of FICA (Federal Insurance Contribution Act) payroll taxes taken from the paychecks of current workers. The aging population means that the number of workers per Social Security recipient is declining. Exhibit 9 shows that by 2030, the United States is expected to have only 2.1 workers per recipient. This is a significant decrease from 1960, when there were 5.1 workers for every retiree, and 1945, when there were 41.9 workers per retiree. In an effort to maintain Social Security benefits, economists expect the government to borrow money in the future, putting upward pressure on the debt ratio. Due to these concerns, policymakers occasionally make changes such as raising the retirement age to reduce benefits paid out and reduce future government borrowing.

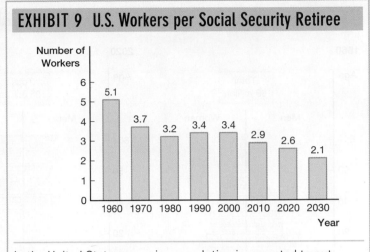

EXHIBIT 9 U.S. Workers per Social Security Retiree

In the United States, an aging population is expected to put stress on national budgets, especially pension and health-care costs. In 1945, there were 41.9 workers per retiree.

Data from: Social Security Administration.

Health care is another concern in an aging economy like the United States. Health-care costs have been rising much faster than the overall cost of living since at least the 1950s. Reasons for the increase are examined in microeconomics (Chapter 19). Furthermore, the government spends an enormous sum of money on health care through government programs such as Medicare, Medicaid, and the Patient Protection and Affordable Care Act. Spending on health care as a percentage of GDP has risen from 5% in 1960 to 17% today. Spending on health care in the United States greatly exceeds that of all other nations.

Each of these factors cause rapidly rising expenditures on federal programs. In one sense, the solution to the long-run fiscal problems of the national debt and rising pension and health-care costs is relatively simple: The federal government needs to reduce the size of the budget deficit by reducing spending and increasing taxes. Most economists believe that a reasonable series of reforms can prevent the United States national debt from rising to unsustainable levels. However, policymakers will have to make some difficult choices because tax increases and spending cuts are not politically popular.

🏛 POLICY BRIEF The Aging Populations of Europe and Japan

Many European and East Asian countries face an increase in the proportion of their population that is over age 65 that is even more dramatic than that of the United States. As shown in Exhibit 10, Japan's population is aging especially rapidly. In 1950, the largest Japanese cohort was the young. Throughout most of human history, the demographic chart has had this sort of pyramid shape. Today, the largest cohort is the working aged. And by 2050, the largest cohort of Japanese is expected to be the elderly, which reflects Japan's very low birth rate.

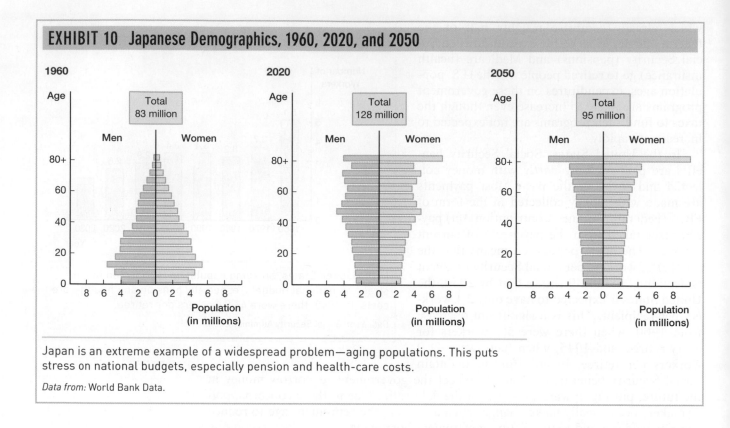

EXHIBIT 10   Japanese Demographics, 1960, 2020, and 2050

Japan is an extreme example of a widespread problem—aging populations. This puts stress on national budgets, especially pension and health-care costs.

Data from: World Bank Data.

BUSINESS TAKEAWAY

Firms benefit from a fundamental understanding of what motivates people to save, what motivates businesses to invest, and how the links between the two are connected through interest rates. Businesses also should be able to identify and predict the effects of government activity and foreign investment on interest rates.

Firms must pay attention to macroeconomic indicators. Falling interest rates, for example, may signal a lack of investment demand—meaning worthy investment projects are not plentiful. Under such circumstances, businesses should be cautious when considering investments in new physical capital, even if interest rates are low. Recall that businesses should avoid reasoning from a price change.

On the other hand, interest rates may fall due to increased government saving, meaning a budget surplus. Interest rates also may fall as a result of trade deficits because they represent an inflow of foreign saving into the country. In both cases, the lower interest rate provides a good opportunity for investment and does not necessarily reflect low investment demand or a decline in the economy.

Firms also should recognize that not all investments with a positive internal rate of return are worth undertaking. It is helpful to think like an economist when making investment decisions. Businesses need to be aware that the opportunity cost of funds spent on investment projects is the interest that could be earned in alternative investments of equal risk, such as buying stocks or bonds.

CHAPTER STUDY GUIDE

23.1 SAVING, INVESTMENT, AND CAPITAL

Physical capital (capital) is equipment and structures used to produce goods and services. **Investment** is spending on new capital goods. Investment increases the amount of physical capital in an economy and helps foster economic growth. The funds to pay for or finance these investment projects come from saving. **Saving** is forgone current consumption, which equals after-tax income minus spending on consumer products. A simple version of the expenditure equation without the government sector or international trade can be used to show saving equals investment. The $S = I$ relationship occurs only in the aggregate.

23.2 GOVERNMENT SAVING AND FOREIGN SAVING

The $S = I$ relationship can be also shown when including the government sector and foreign trade. **Net taxes** equals total taxes paid minus total transfer payments. **Government saving** is saving by the government. It equals net taxes minus government spending ($S_g = T - G$) and can be positive or negative. The **budget surplus** is net tax revenue minus government spending when net tax revenue exceeds government spending. The **budget deficit** is government spending minus net tax revenue when government spending exceeds net tax revenue. In recent years, budget deficits have been fairly common in the United States. The **national debt** is the total amount of money owed by the federal government. It represents budget deficits accumulated over many years and is much larger than the budget deficit for a single year. **Foreign saving** is the saving that foreigners have invested in an economy other than their own. Ultimately, $I = S_p + S_g + S_f$.

23.3 A MODEL OF SAVING, INVESTMENT, AND THE LOANABLE FUNDS MARKET

An **interest rate** is the cost of borrowing money and the reward for saving money, expressed as a percentage of the amount borrowed or saved. Saving represents the supply of loanable funds. Other things equal, the quantity of saving is negatively related to the interest rate. The **internal rate of return (IRR)** is the percentage annual rate of return on the amount invested. Investment creates a demand for loanable funds. Other things equal, the quantity of investment is positively related to the interest rate. Shifts in either the investment demand curve or the saving supply curve change the equilibrium interest rate. An increase (decrease) in investment demand will increase (decrease) the equilibrium interest rate. A decrease (increase) in saving supply will increase (decrease) the equilibrium interest rate.

23.4 ADVANCED TOPIC: THE NATIONAL DEBT AND LONG-RUN FISCAL CHALLENGES

The **net national debt** is the total national debt minus debt obligations that the government owes to itself. The **debt ratio** is the net national debt as a share of GDP. Many economists are concerned about the likely future trajectory of the debt ratio. The **debt ceiling** is a legal maximum on Treasury borrowing set by Congress. It limits the size of the national debt. By law, Congress must authorize increases in the debt ceiling before the Treasury can finance additional budget deficits. Not increasing the debt ceiling would limit government spending to the amount of tax revenue it collects. Many developed economies have long-run fiscal concerns due to the size of their national debt and debt ratio, the impact of an aging population on government pensions, and the increasing costs of health care.

TOP TEN TERMS AND CONCEPTS

(1) Physical Capital, Investment, and Saving

(2) Saving Equals Investment

(3) Government Saving

(4) Budget Deficit and Budget Surplus

(5) Foreign Saving

(6) Interest Rate

(7) Saving Supply and Investment Demand

(8) Internal Rate of Return

(9) National Debt and Net National Debt

(10) Debt Ratio

STUDY PROBLEMS

1. An increase in the budget deficit will increase or decrease the following, other things equal:

   a. Government saving

   b. Investment

   c. Interest rates

   d. Saving supply

2. How do microfinance loans like those in Bangladesh demonstrate the relationship between saving and investment? How might such loans contribute to economic growth?

3. Assume the government suddenly runs a budget surplus. Using the saving supply and investment demand model, demonstrate the impact on interest rates.

4. Assume businesses suddenly become optimistic about the economic future and start to expand. Using the saving supply and investment demand model, demonstrate the impact on interest rates.

5. What is private saving? What is government saving?

6. Due to a decline in the price of oil during 2015, many owners of sovereign wealth funds reduced saving to pay for spending projects. Using the saving supply and investment demand model, demonstrate the impact on interest rates.

7. Suppose the amount of national saving is stable over time. Then assume the trade deficit gets larger. What happens to total saving in the economy? What happens to investment? Does this make you less concerned about the impact of a growing trade deficit on jobs?

8. What is the relationship between investment and the amount of capital in the economy? In your answer, distinguish between the total amount of investment (which appears in the GDP equation) and the net level of investment. Why do they differ?

9. Suppose the government wants to reduce the debt ratio over time. Discuss several methods by which this could be done. Why is it often difficult for governments to address the debt issue?

10. Former Federal Reserve chair Ben Bernanke has argued that interest rates have recently been held down by a "global savings glut." What does this mean, and what factors does Bernanke think contribute to this savings glut? Illustrate your answer with a supply and demand graph.

11. Why are most of the big sovereign wealth funds held by major oil exporting nations?

12. Explain how changing demographics impact the likely future path of government spending. How might this impact the debt ratio?

13. Discuss how firms decide whether an investment project is worth undertaking. Rather than borrowing money, suppose a firm uses its own funds for a new investment. Does this mean it no longer has to worry about the interest rate in deciding whether to go forward with the project? Explain briefly.

14. When we compare countries around the world, what is the correlation between saving as a percentage of GDP and the growth rate of GDP? How strong is the correlation? Discuss the pros and cons of China's high saving rate.

15. Using the saving supply and investment demand model, demonstrate the impact on interest rates of a cut in corporate tax rates.

Izel Photography—A/Alamy

∧ Money is more than a picture of Alexander Hamilton on a green piece of paper.

The Monetary System

What Is Money and Where Does It Come From?

It would be hard to get through your day without money. Money allows you to buy a pizza at Mario's, which you might pay for with cash, debit cards, credit cards, Apple Pay, or even meal cards from a local college. Each of these methods constitutes either money or the promise of a future payment of money. Mario then uses this revenue to pay his suppliers and employees. Money is also the benchmark by which we measure the value of goods and services. All kinds of monetary payments—your weekly salary, your college tuition, your stock portfolio, and the GDP of the entire United States—are measured in terms of U.S. dollars.

It is not surprising that money plays a crucial role in our economic system. But have you ever wondered how a green piece of paper with a picture of a founding father enables you to purchase goods and services? How many Americans actually know where money comes from—or why it has value?

In this chapter, we examine the nature of money and how it is measured. We also examine the business of banking and introduce the concept of a central bank and its role in the banking and monetary system. In the United States, the central bank is the Federal Reserve System (or the Fed).

Chapter Learning Targets

- Identify the three roles of money and the concept of liquidity.

- Distinguish between the three measures of the money supply.

- Explain fractional reserve banking and the ways that banks create money.

- Describe the Federal Reserve system.

- Identify how the monetary base and broader money supplies are controlled.

24.1 WHAT IS MONEY?

Almost everyone would like to have more money, but few people understand what money actually *is*. When we say that Mark Zuckerberg "has a lot of money," we usually are thinking about the billions of dollars in Facebook stock, real estate, and other valuable assets that he owns. But economists generally don't consider assets like stocks and houses to be money because those assets typically cannot be used to make purchases. Money, it turns out, has a very specific meaning.

Money is an asset commonly used in the exchange of goods and services. It is a specific type of asset—mainly cash and bank deposits. Money is not the same as wealth. *Wealth* generally refers to a broad class of assets that include anything and everything a person or firm owns that has value, including money. Money is more than just a means to store wealth. It is an asset used to make everyday transactions such as buying pizza, paying workers, and paying rent.

In order to understand money's role in the exchange of goods and services, it is helpful to imagine what life would be like without money. An economy without money is called a **barter system**—an economic system where people directly exchange one good for another. This type of economy has two major drawbacks that make the system both impractical and inefficient.

The first drawback is that buyers and sellers find it difficult to find a *double coincidence of wants*. In order to barter, you have to find someone who is selling something that you wish to purchase and who also wants to buy what you are selling. For instance, you might want to buy a new economics textbook and be willing to wash dishes to pay for it. In this case, you could try to find someone who has a textbook to sell and wants dishes washed. A second shortcoming of the barter system has to do with setting prices. Imagine the price tags at a grocery store that operates under a barter system. Because there is no money, the price tag on pineapples might say 4 apples or 3 pears or 2 oranges or 40 grapes. The price would depend entirely on which product you are exchanging for the pineapple. Now envision how difficult this would be in a highly specialized modern economy with thousands of different goods and services.

The existence of money greatly simplifies the exchange of goods and services. In the sections that follow, we take a look at the basic functions that money serves in an economy and at several different types of money.

Three Functions of Money

Economists have identified three important functions of money—as a unit of account, a medium of exchange, and a store of value.

Money Provides a Standard Unit of Account When you work in the United States, your paycheck is likely to be in U.S. dollars, and when you spend that paycheck, the products you buy are also priced in U.S. dollars. A **unit of account** is a standard way of measuring prices. Thus, in the United States, the U.S. dollar is the unit of account. Wages and prices in the United States are almost always quoted in terms of U.S. dollars. In Germany and France, wages and prices are almost always expressed in terms of the euro, while in Great Britain, the British pound is used as the unit of account.

The unit of account function of money serves as a useful measuring rod. A day's work may be exchanged for $100, a new iPhone may cost $800, and a new car may cost $25,000. In modern economies, money is a standard unit of account, which means that prices are expressed in terms of money. Consider the analogy of measuring the distance between two cities. Americans measure such distances in miles, whereas the French measure distances in kilometers. In much the same way, America uses the U.S. dollar to measure the value of goods and services, while France uses the euro.

Money Serves as a Medium of Exchange Dollars are accepted for nearly all purchases in the United States. A **medium of exchange** is an asset that is widely used for purchasing other goods and services. Cash and checking account balances are the two assets that best fit the economic definition of money. Most purchases are made with cash (paper currency and coins) or with transfers from checking accounts via checks, debit cards, or electronic transfers.

Money Serves as a Store of Value. If you set aside $100 dollars today, the money can be used in the future to make purchases. This $100 represents a **store of value**—an asset that people can use as a place to put their savings. It is a way of holding purchasing power for use in the future.

money An asset commonly used in the exchange of goods and services.

barter system An economic system where people directly exchange one good for another.

unit of account A standard way of measuring prices.

medium of exchange An asset that is widely used for purchasing other goods and services.

store of value An asset that people can use as a place to put their savings.

Because money can be a useful way to store value, it often is confused with wealth. But other assets can also store value. For instance, stocks, bonds, and real estate are not considered to be money, but they are stores of value. Other stores of value include gold bars, silver coins, and collectibles (such as rare stamps, fine art, and first-edition, mint-in-the-box *Star Wars* action figures).

The store of value function of money is often considered to be less important than the unit of account and medium of exchange roles. People holding alternative assets such as stocks and bonds, for example, will often earn a higher rate of return than people holding cash or checking account balances.

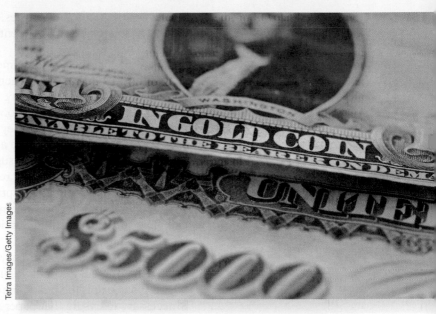

∧ A century ago, your $1 gold certificate was backed by $1 worth of gold.

Different Types of Money

A wide variety of goods—shells, beads, salt, and even cigarettes—have served as money in different times and places. All of these items can be considered money if they function as a generally agreed on unit of account, medium of exchange, and store of value.

Suppose we start with a system of barter and the community eventually decides it would be more convenient to price everything in terms of a specified amount of one particular good or "commodity." This commodity would be considered money.

Commodity Money Some forms of money have intrinsic value. **Commodity money** is money that has an underlying value apart from its role as money. In a commodity money system, the unit of account is defined in terms of a specific amount of a given commodity. For instance, during World War II, cigarettes were used as a medium of exchange by American soldiers in German POW camps, and right after the war, cigarettes were widely used as money in Germany. The most famous example of a commodity money system was the *gold standard*, where even paper money was redeemable into gold. Throughout most of history, silver was an even more important form of commodity money. Indeed, the official name of the British currency is "pound sterling," which refers to the fact that hundreds of years ago a British pound was literally one pound of sterling silver. The gold standard is discussed in Chapter 25.

Fiat Money Today U.S. paper money is no longer redeemable into gold. Modern paper money is an example of what is now known as **fiat money**—money that is not backed by a commodity and that has little or no underlying value apart from its role as money. It is believed that the Chinese first invented fiat paper money about 700 years ago.

To understand why fiat money is important, consider the fact that it costs the government only about six cents to produce a $100 bill. Producing fiat money can be highly lucrative for the government because it is a source of revenue much like taxes. At various times, this has led governments in places like Brazil and Argentina to print lots of money as a way of paying their bills, especially when the country is short of funds. As you might imagine, when something sounds too good to be true, it usually is. In Chapter 25, we will see that printing too much fiat money can lead to high rates of inflation.

In addition, fiat money is important because it gives the government greater control of the monetary system than it had when gold was used as money. Policymakers have responded to this flexibility by using control over the quantity of fiat money in circulation to influence important macroeconomic variables such as interest rates, inflation, and unemployment. This is called *monetary policy* and is explored in Chapter 27.

Despite the fact that you can no longer arrive at the U.S. Treasury and demand $20 worth of gold or silver in exchange for a $20 bill, you can use that cash to purchase

commodity money Money that has an underlying value apart from its role as money.

fiat money Money that is not backed by a commodity and that has little or no underlying value apart from its role as money.

$20 worth of goods and services. So what makes these little green pieces of paper valuable? There are several different theories about why fiat money has value, and more than one may be true.

First, people like to use some products because they know that other people prefer these products—a phenomenon known as *network externalities*. One example is the online auction website eBay. People shop at eBay because lots of other people are selling there, and people sell goods on eBay because lots of other people are shopping there. This may be true of money as well. People accept money because they know that other people are also willing to accept it in exchange for goods and services.

Second, some economists suggest that currency has value because it is a form of *legal tender*. The government requires that it be an accepted form of payment. For instance, the government accepts only U.S. dollars as payment for *taxes*. The tax bill you receive from the government specifies that you owe a certain amount of U.S. dollars. The Internal Revenue Service does not wish to be paid in apples, oranges, gold, bitcoin, or Japanese yen.

Finally, although paper money is no longer formally backed by gold, some economists believe that there is a sort of *implied backing*. As long as the government is not in danger of going bankrupt, the public may rationally believe that policymakers will do whatever is necessary to ensure that paper money has value. For instance, suppose that we adopt an all-electronic monetary system where paper currency is no longer used. The public may believe that when the changeover occurs, the paper money in circulation will be redeemed for something of equal value, such as electronic money or government bonds.

24.2 THE U.S. MONEY SUPPLY

We have seen that not all assets count as money. Money must be a medium of exchange. Even so, there are multiple ways to define and measure the **money supply**, which is the total value of financial assets that are considered money. As you will discover, each measure serves a different purpose. Before we can define the money supply, we need to introduce the concepts of liquidity and various types of bank accounts.

The Liquidity of Money and Types of Bank Accounts

One important characteristic of assets viewed as money is **liquidity**, which is the ease with which an asset can be turned into a medium of exchange. Cash is the ultimate form of liquidity, and checking accounts are also very liquid. These are both widely accepted forms of payment. Other assets—such as stocks, bonds, and real estate—can be converted to cash but usually at some cost in terms of time and transaction fees.

When a store advertises a "liquidation sale," this means that the business has assets (such as furniture or automobiles) that must be converted into money, perhaps to pay lenders or taxes. Although liquidity is useful, an opportunity cost is associated with liquidity. Businesses that maximize liquidity by carrying large amounts of cash might forgo opportunities to buy additional inventory to sell, additional capital equipment to produce more products, or stocks that might generate a higher return.

Currency and coins created by the government are only a part of the total quantity of money in circulation. For instance, many purchases are made directly from checking accounts and other bank deposits. Checks are just one method of transferring money from one person's bank account to another. When you use your debit card or a payment app on your smartphone to make a $40 purchase at Mario's, the $40 is subtracted from your checking account and added to Mario's bank account. Because the transaction depends on having the promised funds be available on demand, checking accounts are sometimes called **demand deposits**—which are accounts at the bank that are immediately

money supply The total value of financial assets that are considered money.

liquidity The ease with which an asset can be turned into money.

demand deposits Accounts at the bank that are immediately available for spending.

available for spending. Money in a checking account is convenient because it is highly liquid: You can spend it easily. Because banks must keep money available on demand, such accounts typically pay low or no interest.

Depositors who are willing to forgo some liquidity and provide their money for a longer period of time earn a higher interest rate on the deposit. **Time deposits** are accounts that hold money deposited in a bank that cannot be withdrawn for a specified period of time. The many types of time deposits include savings accounts, money market mutual funds, and certificates of deposit (CDs). Time deposits are not as liquid as demand deposits but pay higher interest rates because banks have more confidence the money will not be withdrawn after a short period of time.

Guy & Rodd/Cartoon Stock

 BUSINESS BRIEF Electronic Payments: The Business of Moving Money

All over the globe, billions of dollars are transferred electronically each day. Moving money is big business. But are the apps, debit cards, and credit cards that you use to make payments money? No, they are not—because they are not a store of value. Rather, they are tools used to access value that is stored elsewhere.

When making electronic payments, directly transferring funds between bank accounts (such as demand and time deposits accounts) is different from using a credit card. Direct bank transfers *move* money from a demand deposit account to another account almost instantly. When you swipe your debit card using your personal identification number (PIN), it is an automatic transfer from your bank account. Electronic bank transfers work in much the same way.

With credit cards, however, the bank that issues the credit card makes payments to merchants while simultaneously creating loans for the cardholder. Cardholders must repay these loans in the future and often must pay interest on the loans. As such, the transfer of funds involved with credit cards is indirect, with the bank that issues the credit card acting as a middle agent. Finally, modern technology allows for the use of mobile payment services (such as ApplePay, Venmo, and PayPal) that link directly to a bank account or a credit card.

In most cases, merchants (but not buyers) are charged a fee for transactions involving the direct transfer of funds or credit cards. Notable exceptions to these fees include using electronic methods to pay bills and loans as well as making some person-to-person bank transfers. These fees make this business highly lucrative, so much so that Visa has recently started incentivizing merchants to stop accepting cash.[*] Banks are also entering the transfer marketplace by developing systems that are designed to replace checks and cash and that do not involve credit cards. More than 30 American banks worked together to launch Zelle, a simplified direct transfer system that is designed to make cash transfers between individuals "fast, free and ubiquitous" and that allows banks to set up their own fee structure for using the service.[†] Such transfer systems are already the norm in many countries outside the United States.

[*]Teresa Rivas, "Visa, MasterCard Shares Can Charge Higher Yet," *Barron's*, October 30, 2014, http://online .barrons.com/articles/visa-mastercard-shares-can-charge-higher-yet-1414690118.

[†]Stacy Cowley, "Cash Faces a New Challenger in Zelle, a Mobile Banking Service," *New York Times*, June 12, 2017, https://www.nytimes.com/2017/06/12/business/dealbook/mobile-banking-zelle-venmo-apple-pay .html?_r=0.

time deposits Accounts that hold money deposited in a bank that cannot be withdrawn for a specified period of time.

M1 A measure of the money supply that includes all cash (including paper money and coins) in circulation, along with demand deposits and traveler's checks.

M2 A measure of the money supply that includes M1 plus time deposits.

monetary base A measure of the money supply that includes cash held by the general public plus reserves held by commercial banks.

Three Measures of the Money Supply

In the United States, there are three major measures of the overall money supply—M1, M2, and the monetary base—and each serves a distinct purpose.

M1: Money as a Medium of Exchange M1 is a measure of the money supply that includes all cash (including paper money and coins) in circulation, along with demand deposits and traveler's checks. M1 is the most liquid form of money and is easily available as a medium of exchange. M1 is the definition of the money supply that is most consistent with its medium of exchange role.

M2: Money as a Store of Value A second and broader measure of the money supply is **M2**—a measure of the money supply that includes M1 plus time deposits. M2 is less liquid than M1 because it includes savings account balances and other deposits that serve primarily as stores of value rather than a medium of exchange. For simplicity, we focus on the role of banks, but keep in mind that the actual definitions of M1 and M2 now include some deposits that are outside the commercial banking system, such as money market mutual funds.

The Monetary Base: Government-Created Money In a fiat money system, government policymakers have the ability to create money. The **monetary base** is a measure of the money supply that includes cash held by the general public plus reserves held by commercial banks. Bank reserves can be deposited at the Federal Reserve (discussed later in this chapter) or held as currency in the vault of the bank. Bank reserves are *not* part of M1 or M2.

It may surprise you to learn that cash accounts for less than half of M1 (the most liquid measure of money) and roughly 10% of the broader M2 definition of money. Exhibit 1 shows estimates of various measurements of the money supply in December 2017.

Think & Speak Like an Economist

The monetary base includes cash held by the public and bank reserves. It represents the fiat money that is created and controlled by the policymakers. When people say that the government can "print money," they are referring to the monetary base.

The Missing Cash and the Future of Money

How much cash do you think is held by the public right now? As noted in Exhibit 1, in December 2017, there was about $1.5 trillion in cash in circulation outside the banking system—in wallets, cash registers, and piggy banks and under mattresses. That's about $4,677 for each man, woman, and child in the United States. That might

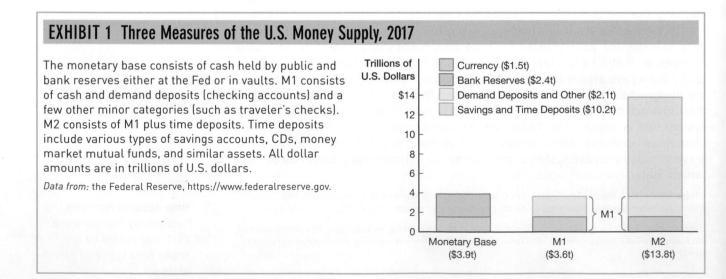

EXHIBIT 1   Three Measures of the U.S. Money Supply, 2017

The monetary base consists of cash held by public and bank reserves either at the Fed or in vaults. M1 consists of cash and demand deposits (checking accounts) and a few other minor categories (such as traveler's checks). M2 consists of M1 plus time deposits. Time deposits include various types of savings accounts, CDs, money market mutual funds, and similar assets. All dollar amounts are in trillions of U.S. dollars.

Data from: the Federal Reserve, https://www.federalreserve.gov.

Trillions of U.S. Dollars

Currency ($1.5t)
Bank Reserves ($2.4t)
Demand Deposits and Other ($2.1t)
Savings and Time Deposits ($10.2t)

Monetary Base ($3.9t)   M1 ($3.6t)   M2 ($13.8t)

not sound like much, but remember we are talking about cash, not bank deposits or other components of M1 and M2. Two explanations have been offered to explain the mystery of high levels of cash in circulation—dollarization and the underground economy.

First, some U.S. currency has flowed out of the country and is held by people in other countries. The U.S. dollar is an especially popular store of value in places with political or economic instability. Some countries (including Ecuador, El Salvador, Panama, and Zimbabwe) have completely abandoned their previous currency and switched to the U.S. dollar, a policy known as *dollarization*.

Second, some currency is held in the U.S. *underground economy*, which represents economic transactions that are not officially recorded by the government. It refers to two distinct activities. First, the underground economy includes illicit businesses (such as the illegal drug trade) that rely on cash to avoid detection by the government. Second, the underground economy also includes transactions that are legal but are not reported to the government. Small businesses and independent workers may use cash to avoid reporting their full earnings to tax collectors.

Bloomberg/Getty Images

∧ Does Bitcoin represent the future of money?

📊 BUSINESS BRIEF Bitcoin and the Rise of Cryptocurrencies

Until recently, economists assumed that money had to be based on a commodity or created by government fiat. Who would trust a money that was created by private individuals and was not redeemable into any other asset? It turns out that lots of people are willing to use private currency because (like cash) it provides an easy way to transferring funds anonymously. Bitcoin is perhaps the best-known example of a digital or cryptocurrency. Bitcoin was created in 2009 and has become an important alternative money that can be transferred over the Internet.

Bitcoin uses advanced encryption techniques to generate the currency and to verify the transfer of funds independent of government oversight. A complex computerized trading system allows the holders of bitcoins to send money anonymously to anyone else participating in the network, anywhere in the world. Users store their bitcoins on "wallets" that can be as simple as a piece of paper or a smartphone. A QR code is provided on the paper or screen, and it contains the necessary credentials required to use (or sell) the bitcoins. This code is known as the bitcoin "address," although no physical address is stored.

Although bitcoin is a convenient medium of exchange for some transactions, it is not a stable unit of account. The value of bitcoins has been very unstable in dollar terms and has often risen and fallen sharply over short periods of time. In 2013, for example, the value of a bitcoin ranged from $13 to $1,145, at times losing nearly half its value in weeks. By June 2017, it had rebounded to $3,000, and in December that same year it peaked at $19,800 and fell to $10,400 in the same week.[*]

It's too soon to know whether something like bitcoin represents the future of money. How effective will it become as a store of value? How widely will it be accepted as a medium of exchange? Will more businesses use bitcoin prices as a unit of account? One thing seems certain: The Internet will play an increasingly important role in our monetary system.

*Evelyn Cheng, "Bitcoin Plunges Below $11,000 in Volatile Trading on Coinbase as Rout Accelerates; Now down 40 Percent from Record," CNBC, December 22, 2017, https://www.cnbc.com/2017/12/22/bitcoin-plunges -below-12000-on-coinbase-as-rout-accelerates-now-down-40-percent-from-record.html.

24.3 THE BUSINESS OF FRACTIONAL RESERVE BANKING

Cash is only a small part of the overall monetary system. Much of the money we use for transactions is deposited in banks. In order to understand the entire monetary system, we need to look at the business of banking and the ways that banks create money.

Fractional Reserve Banking

Commercial banking can be pretty complicated. But the basic idea can be illustrated with a simple example. Suppose Serena lives in a high-crime area in a world without banks. She gives her friend Isabella $10,000 in cash to store for her. Because Isabella soon develops a reputation for being trustworthy, many people want to store their money with her. She soon receives a total of $1 million in deposits and is suddenly in the banking business.

Now suppose Serena wants to buy a used car from MaxCars for $7,000. She writes a note to Isabella saying, "Please pay MaxCars $7,000 from my deposit." Soon, many other customers are writing similar notes. Today, these notes are called *checks* and are one of the most important ways that money circulates throughout our economy.

Isabella, our banker, notices that on any given day, only a few people will stop by to ask for their money. So she loans half of it to borrowers and charges interest on the loans. The other half is kept in reserve in case any depositors show up looking for their money. Now, she has $1 million in deposits but only $500,000 in reserves. Is it a problem that Isabella keeps only a fraction of her deposits on reserve? Probably not. After all, only a few people ask for their money on any given day.

Eventually, others recognize the big profits Isabella is making on loan interest and decide to enter the banking business as well. But how can new banks attract new deposits? They can pay depositors a small interest rate on their deposits and then turn around and lend the money to other people at a higher rate. To compete, Isabella must do likewise. Now we have a competitive commercial banking system with all of the essentials, including deposits, loans, checks, interest rates, and reserves.

The basics of modern banking are surprisingly similar to this simple example. Commercial banks accept deposits on which they pay interest, allow the depositors to write notes (checks and electronic transfers), are competitive with other banks, and keep only a fraction of their deposits in the form of reserves.

Fractional reserve banking is the banking practice of keeping a fraction of deposits available as reserves. It is hard to imagine a vibrant commercial banking system without it. If banks simply sat on 100% of the money that was deposited, they would not be able to pay depositors interest and would not be able to provide free check writing.

In the previous example, we can see several key roles played by our commercial banking system. First, banks offer a place for savers to keep their money for safekeeping and earn interest on deposits. Additionally, banks issue loans to individuals and businesses that wish to borrow. People may borrow to buy a house or car, go to college, start a business, or pay for a variety of other purchases. But banks do not lend money for free: They charge interest.

How do banks earn profits? The key is to charge borrowers a higher interest rate than they pay savers. For example, they may pay an interest rate of 1% on deposits and then turn around and lend that money to others at an interest rate of 4%. The 3% "spread" between the interest rates allows banks to earn a profit. In converting savings into loans, banks provide extra liquidity in the economy.

Many people naively think that the money they deposit at the bank is always there. After all, they can walk in and withdraw it anytime they wish. If you think about it, however, after the bank issues loans using your deposited money, they no longer have all of your money in reserve. They have lent some of it to others. This is the essence of fractional reserve banking. Perceptive readers might have a nagging feeling that something could go wrong with this system. Stay tuned!

fractional reserve banking
The banking practice of keeping a fraction of deposits available as reserves.

A Simplified Bank Balance Sheet

To better understand fractional reserve banking, let's look at a simplified accounting statement of a bank, also known as a balance sheet. The basic premise of a balance sheet is that a business has both assets and liabilities that offset each other. A simplified balance sheet of a bank is shown in Exhibit 2.

A total of $100 million is on deposit at National University Bank. You probably think of your bank account as an "asset," but to the bank these deposits are a "liability" because the bank owes the depositor money. The bank chooses to hold $12 million in reserve and has lent out the other $88 million. To the bank, loans are assets because borrowers owe the bank money. Notice that banks hold only a fraction of deposits in the form of reserves.

The balance sheet shown in Exhibit 2 also illustrates a potential problem associated with fractional reserve banking. If you walk into a bank, you expect to be able to withdraw the money you previously deposited, and in general, you can do so. But if everyone walks into the bank at the same time, there will not be enough reserves to pay off all depositors immediately. Much of the deposit money has been lent out. And banks cannot immediately retrieve the money that they have lent to borrowers. Instead, they have to rely on the fact that it's extremely unlikely that all depositors will show up on the same day asking for their deposits.

Modern banking is made possible by the predictability resulting from the *law of large numbers*, which says that the behavior of thousands of people is, on average, more predictable than the behavior of any single individual. Banks can safely predict that no more than a certain fraction of depositors will show up on any specific day.

Why would a bank choose to hold 12% of its deposits in the form of reserves? After all, in economics we assume that businesses attempt to maximize profits, and wouldn't lending those reserves lead to even more profits? There are several factors to consider. First, in the United States, the government generally sets a minimum reserve requirement: Most banks are legally required to hold a certain percentage of deposits in the form of reserves. The **required reserve ratio** is the legally required minimum level of reserves that a bank must hold, expressed as a fraction of deposits. The required reserve ratio varies based on a variety of factors, including the size of the bank. For large banks, it is roughly 10% of demand deposits. In our example, we assume it to be 10%.

required reserve ratio The legally required minimum level of reserves that a bank must hold, expressed as a fraction of deposits.

EXHIBIT 2 A Simplified Bank Balance Sheet

University Bank of America has $100 million in deposits. To the bank, this represents a liability because the funds can be withdrawn by the depositor. Notice that the bank also has $100 million in assets. This includes reserves of $12 million and loans of $88 million. If the required reserve ratio is 10%, the bank will be required to have reserves of $10 million and thus have excess reserves of $2 million.

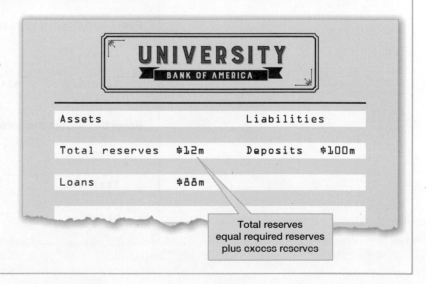

Assets		Liabilities	
Total reserves	$12m	Deposits	$100m
Loans	$88m		

Total reserves equal required reserves plus excess reserves

In addition, banks will generally choose to hold some excess reserves, which can be used when depositors come in to withdraw their money. **Excess reserves** are reserves held above and beyond the legally required minimum of reserves a bank must hold. Banks may choose to have excess reserves so they can ensure they have enough funds on hand to meet the demands of their depositors. Alternatively, banks may have excess reserves because they do not see any profitable loan opportunities. Before 2008, banks usually held only small amounts of excess reserves because reserves were not very profitable. In our example, University Bank is required to keep $10 million in reserves but has actual reserves of $12 million. Thus, the bank holds $2 million in excess reserves.

How Banks Create Money

We have seen how bank deposits form an important part of the M1 and M2 money supplies. To see how banks create money and deposits, let's look at how the balance sheet of a typical bank changes when someone deposits money into a bank account. For instance, suppose you deposit $1,000 cash into your bank—First University Bank. The bank's reserves increase by $1,000. For simplicity, we assume you are making the very first deposit at the bank. This balance sheet is shown in Panel A of Exhibit 3. This bank's total deposits are now $1,000.

Let's assume the bank prefers to hold only 10% of deposits in the form of reserves, so it loans the other 90%, or $900. This is shown in Panel B. In this scenario, what happens to the money supply? You, the depositor, had $1,000 deposited and still do. Now, however, the borrower also has $900 in cash that she borrowed from the bank. In this scenario, the money supply increases by $900. The bank creates $900 in new money by issuing a loan. Now the money supply is $900 larger than before you deposited the cash into your account.

It is important to remember that money is not wealth. Yes, the bank has created an extra $900 because the $1,000 in deposits are backed by only $100 in reserves.

excess reserves Reserves held above and beyond the legally required minimum level of reserves that a bank must hold.

EXHIBIT 3 How Banks Create Money

When First University Bank receives a deposit of $1,000, its reserves rise by the same amount. When the bank loans out some of the deposit, the money supply increases and reserves decline.

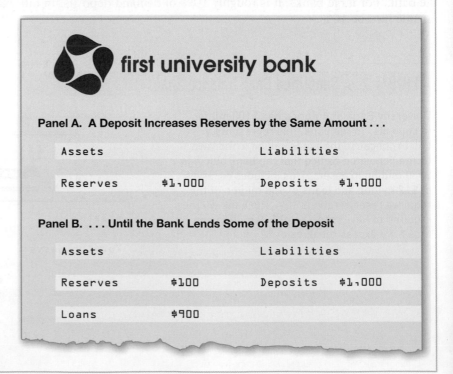

first university bank

Panel A. A Deposit Increases Reserves by the Same Amount . . .

Assets		Liabilities	
Reserves	$1,000	Deposits	$1,000

Panel B. . . . Until the Bank Lends Some of the Deposit

Assets		Liabilities	
Reserves	$100	Deposits	$1,000
Loans	$900		

But these deposits are not the bank's money: They are liabilities of the bank. The borrower has $900 in deposits that she did not have before, but the borrower is not actually wealthier because she also has incurred $900 more in debt (her loan). There's no "free lunch" when banks create money.

Money and Potential Deposit Multipliers

Suppose the customer who receives the $900 loan spends the money on a used car. Then the person who sells her the car deposits her $900 in another bank (say, Second University Bank). As with First University Bank, Second University Bank does not want to hold all of the extra $900 deposit in the form of reserves, so it lends 90% of the $900, or $810, to a borrower. This is shown in Exhibit 4.

EXHIBIT 4 Deposit Creation and the Potential Deposit Multiplier

The deposit multiplier is the maximum possible change in deposits for each dollar change in bank reserves. In this case, a deposit of $1,000 in cash initially results in $1,000 in new deposits and reserves. Subsequently, the bank lends out all but the required reserve (10%) or $900. The process continues when Second University Bank receives a deposit and issues a loan. In total, deposits can expand by a maximum of $10,000, including the initial deposit, if banks do not hold excess reserves and people do not hold on to extra cash.

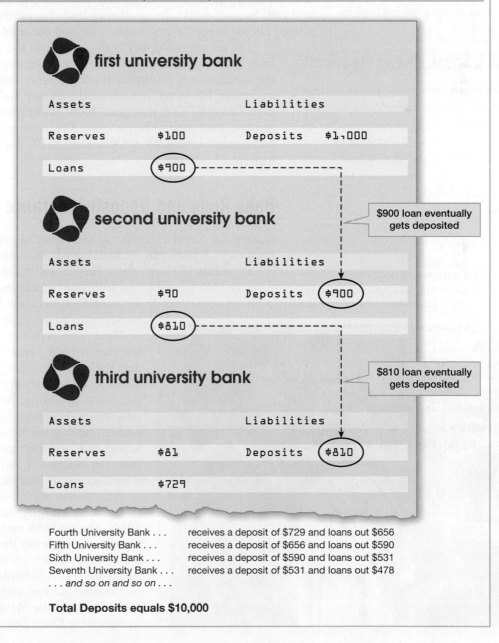

Fourth University Bank . . .	receives a deposit of $729 and loans out $656
Fifth University Bank . . .	receives a deposit of $656 and loans out $590
Sixth University Bank . . .	receives a deposit of $590 and loans out $531
Seventh University Bank . . .	receives a deposit of $531 and loans out $478
. . . and so on and so on . . .	

Total Deposits equals $10,000

potential deposit multiplier
The maximum possible change in deposits for each dollar change in bank reserves. It equals 1/Required reserve ratio.

money multiplier The change in the overall money supply resulting from a $1 increase in the monetary base.

bank run (banking panic)
An event that occurs when depositors rush to withdraw money from their bank in fear that the bank may fail. This problem can and often does spread from one bank to another.

Think & Speak Like an Economist

Economists use the word *multiplier* in a variety of contexts. Here, increases in the monetary base tend to have a ripple effect on the overall money supply. Later, we'll see that an increase in government spending also can have a multiplier effect on economic activity. Multipliers are not fixed numbers, they vary considerably over time.

As is the case with the first bank, the second bank creates new money, in this case an extra $810. The $810 loan might be deposited at a third bank—say, Third University Bank. This process continues indefinitely—a deposit is made, a portion of the deposit is held as reserves, and a portion is lent out—with each new round of deposits getting smaller. In the long run, deposits increase as shown in Exhibit 4.

The **potential deposit multiplier** is the maximum possible change in deposits for each dollar change in bank reserves:

$$\text{Potential deposit multiplier} = \frac{1}{\text{Required reserve ratio}}$$

In the example above, with a 10% reserve ratio, the deposit multiplier will be $1/.10 = 10$. Thus, when the first $1,000 is deposited, reserves change by $1,000. When this is multiplied by the deposit multiplier of 10, the end result is that total deposits rise by $10,000. This includes the initial deposit and all new subsequent deposits.

This is only the *potential* money multiplier. In practice, things are more complicated. First, some of the money loaned at each stage will go into cash held by the public and not be redeposited in banks. This reduces the amount of money that banks can lend out. Second, banks do not always lend the maximum allowed by law. They may instead choose to hold *excess reserves* beyond the legal requirement.

The **money multiplier** is the change in the overall money supply resulting from a $1 increase in the monetary base. For the two reasons cited above, the actual money multiplier is considerably smaller than the potential deposit multiplier. Moreover, the size of the money multiplier varies significantly over time. Later, we'll see that since 2008, banks have held considerably more excess reserves than used to be the case. As a consequence, the money multiplier has fallen substantially. As of December 2017, the M1 and M2 money multipliers were roughly 1 and 4.

Bank Runs and Deposit Insurance

During the Great Depression, the financial system suffered from a series of bank runs. A **bank run** (or **banking panic**) is an event that occurs when depositors rush to withdraw money from their bank in fear that the bank may fail. This problem can and often does spread from one bank to another. A series of bank runs can lead to a loss of confidence in the banking system and long lines of depositors outside banks trying to get their deposit money back.

Bank run behavior was memorably illustrated in the classic 1946 film *It's a Wonderful Life* when angry depositors rush to George Bailey's bank to demand their deposits. Bailey tells his customers, "You're thinking of this place all wrong. As if I had the money back in a safe. The money's not here. Well, your money's in Joe's house … and in the Kennedy house, and Mrs. Macklin's house, and, and a hundred others. Why, you're lending them the money to build, and then, they're going to pay it back to you as best they can."[1]

The movie scene was inspired by the bank runs that occurred throughout the United States in the early 1930s. During bank runs, the multiplier effect works in reverse—by reducing the money supply and magnifying the adverse impact on the economy. The multiplier fell during the 1930s as banks that did not experience a bank run became cautious and held onto greater reserves. This further reduced the M1 and M2 money supply and likely worsened the Great Depression.

∨ "The money is not here." A bank run, as depicted in *It's a Wonderful Life.*

Liberty Films, Inc./ RKO Radio Pictures/Ronald Grant Archive/Alamy Stock Photo

In response to this severe banking crisis, the U.S. government created the Federal Deposit Insurance Corporation (FDIC) in 1934. You might notice a sign in the window of your bank saying "Deposits FDIC insured up to $250,000." This means that if the bank fails, then depositors will be guaranteed to get back the first $250,000 of any deposit. For example, in 2008, Washington Mutual (WaMu), with over $300 billion in assets, became the largest commercial bank failure in U.S. history. In part due to FDIC insurance, depositors received their money from the bank.

An interesting consequence of FDIC was that it changed the image of banks. Prior to 1934, banks often looked like fortresses. Their huge, intimidating buildings with grand architecture were intended to reassure depositors that their money was safe and available on demand. After FDIC, depositors no longer feared losing their savings because they knew that the bank was insured. Banks became less inclined to create the impression of security and opted instead for more accessible (and inexpensive) locations, like strip malls and, eventually, online.

Although FDIC essentially eliminated the problem of bank runs among small depositors, it did not completely solve the problem of banking instability. Later in the chapter, we will see that the creation of deposit insurance may have increased moral hazard by encouraging some banks to make riskier loans.

Most people are familiar with commercial banks, but there is also a vast *shadow banking system* that includes financial intermediaries (such as investment banks, money market funds, and hedge funds) that provide some of the services provided by traditional banks but are outside the scope of normal banking regulations. For instance, instead of relying on lots of small depositors, investment banks borrow lots of money from large institutions and lend the funds to riskier businesses.

Because these institutions do not offer deposit insurance, they are particularly vulnerable to bank runs. In 2008, Lehman Brothers, then one of the world's largest investment banks, collapsed in the largest bankruptcy in history; Lehman was not a commercial bank. The event triggered memories of bank runs during the Great Depression and led to the controversial decisions to bail out some banks that were not FDIC insured as a way to prevent the collapse of the entire system.

Today the Fed monitors the activities of all systemically important institutions—that is, any firm whose failure could lead to a loss of confidence in the entire financial system. Financial capital requirements have been raised so that there is less risk that a bank's liabilities will exceed its assets. However, the problem of financial stability has not been completely solved and may reoccur at some point in the future.

∧ FDIC changed the face of banking and assured Washington Mutual depositors they would get their money back when the bank failed.

24.4 CENTRAL BANKS AND THE FEDERAL RESERVE SYSTEM

All countries now use fiat money issued by institutions called central banks. A **central bank** is an institution that determines the quantity of fiat money in circulation. In most countries, the central bank also regulates the banking system. The term *central bank* is a bit misleading because a central bank does not provide banking services to the public. Rather, a central bank is considered a banker's bank that provides important services to ordinary commercial banks but not to individuals. Most central banks are at least partly controlled by the governments of the countries in which they operate and assist in government policies.

central bank An institution that determines the quantity of fiat money in circulation. In most countries, the central bank also regulates the banking system.

The Federal Reserve System (the Fed)

The central bank of the United States is formally called the Federal Reserve System and is commonly referred to as *the Federal Reserve* or more often simply *the Fed*.

The Structure of the Fed The Fed includes a seven-member Board of Governors (often referred to as the Federal Reserve Board) that includes the Fed chair, currently Jerome Powell. The chair and other members of the Board of Governors are appointed by the U.S. president and must be confirmed by the U.S. Senate. Governors serve a 14-year term, and the chair serves a four-year term and can be reappointed when his or her term ends. The Board has a large research staff of economists who analyze the current condition of the economy and make suggestions about the types of Fed policy that they think will be most effective.

The structure of the Fed reflects the fact that it was created in 1913, when the United States was far less centralized than most other countries. Unlike other central banks, such as the Bank of England (in London) or the Bank of Japan (in Tokyo), the Fed's power is not all concentrated in one city. There are 12 regional Federal Reserve banks in major cities throughout the United States. The regional bank in New York is especially important.

The most important part of the Fed is the Federal Open Market Committee (FOMC), which makes key decisions that affect the quantity of fiat money as well as the rate of interest. The committee has 12 members, including the seven-member Board of Governors, the president of the New York Fed, and four other regional bank presidents who serve on a rotating basis. The FOMC meets in Washington, DC, usually every six weeks, and formulates Fed monetary policy. When you hear on the news that "the Fed" changed its policy, the reporter is almost always referring to the FOMC.

Decisions by the FOMC are designed to affect the overall economy in what is called **monetary policy**—changes in the money supply and interest rates by the central bank, often with the goal of influencing employment and inflation. Such actions are discussed in detail in Chapter 27. For now, we focus on the mechanics of the Federal Reserve—in particular, how the Fed injects new money into the economy.

The Fed as Lender of Last Resort The United States has always had a more unstable banking system than countries like Canada. In the 1800s and early 1900s, the United States experienced banking panics (bank runs) every decade or so. In part, this was due to the fact that most states used to restrict "branch banking," which led to tens of thousands of individual banks that were mostly very small and not well diversified. In contrast, during the same time period, Canada had only about a dozen large and well-diversified banks with branches all across the country and has largely avoided banking panics.

The Fed was created in 1913 to be a lender of last resort that could step in and lend money to banks in the event of a banking panic. Other roles, such as influencing inflation and unemployment, were added to its mandate after the United States moved off the gold standard and the Fed had more control over the size of the money supply.

The European Central Bank (ECB)

The Eurosystem was created in 1999 by the members of the European Union that adopted the euro as their currency. Its structure is similar to the Federal Reserve System in the United States because it represents 19 (originally 12) countries. The original central bank of each country using the euro became a regional bank in the Eurosystem, very much like the regional Fed banks. The headquarters of the Eurosystem is called the European Central Bank (ECB) and is located in Frankfurt, Germany. Although technically the acronym ECB refers only to the Eurosystem headquarters, it is now commonly used to refer to the entire Eurosystem. The ECB serves as the lender of last resort in countries that use the euro as their currency.

monetary policy Changes in the money supply and interest rates by the central bank, often with the goal of influencing employment and inflation.

24.5 CONTROLLING THE MONETARY BASE AND BROADER MONEY SUPPLIES

If you create new fiat money, how would you inject it into the economy? Say you have a printer in the basement and (illegally) start printing $20 bills. (Warning: Do not try this at home!) How could you get the money into circulation? Assuming you don't want to give it away, you would basically have two options: (1) You could buy something, or (2) you could lend the money to a person or to your bank. These are basically the two methods most often used by the Fed. Usually, it injects new money by purchasing something—typically, government bonds. It also lends some of the new fiat money, usually to commercial banks.

Tools for Injecting Money into the Economy

The Federal Reserve has four primary tools for controlling base money and broader money supplies—open market operations, discount rate lending, interest on bank reserves, and the required reserve ratio. The most important tool in the Fed's toolbox is to engage in open market operation, and that is where we begin.

Open Market Operations Suppose the Federal Open Market Committee (FOMC) instructs the New York Fed to increase the monetary base by $1 million. The easiest way to increase the money supply is for the Fed to buy $1 million in government bonds. The seller of the bonds receives $1 million in brand-new fiat money created by the Fed, and the Fed receives $1 million in government bonds to add to its balance sheet. Doing so directly increases the monetary base.

This method of increasing the monetary base and the broader money supply is an example of an open market operation. **Open market operations** refers to the sale or purchase of government bonds by the Fed to control the size of the monetary base. When the Fed decides to increase the size of the monetary base, it instructs the New York Fed to do an *open market purchase*—when the Fed buys bonds on Wall Street and pays for the bonds with newly created money. Initially, the money goes into the banking system and becomes a part of reserves. Over time, some of the reserves are paid to bank customers and become part of the cash held by the public.

When the Fed wants to decrease the size of the monetary base, it instructs the New York Fed to do an *open market sale*—when the Fed sells bonds on Wall Street and receives back some of the monetary base that was created earlier. At first, most of the money comes from the banking system, reducing the level of reserves. Over time, banks may try to rebuild their reserves by lending less money and keeping more of the cash that people deposit at the bank. This reduces cash held by the public. Exhibit 5 summarizes open market operations.

Discount Rate The Federal Reserve also can inject new money into the economy by lending it to commercial banks. A loan by the Fed to a commercial bank is called a discount loan. The **discount rate** is the interest rate charged on a loan to commercial banks from the Federal Reserve. If the Fed wishes to lend more money to commercial banks, it can lower the discount rate to make loans more attractive to commercial banks. After the discount loan is made to the commercial bank, it becomes part of the bank's reserves and thus part of the monetary base.

The Fed increases the monetary base by lowering the discount rate. When this is done or when open market purchases are made, some of the increase in the monetary base eventually flows out into cash held by the public. The rest increases bank reserves. To banks, these new reserves are the "raw material" that can be used to expand their balance sheets because banks typically lend out a portion of the extra reserves.

In contrast, if the Fed wishes to reduce discount rate lending, it will raise the discount rate. In turn, banks will borrow less from the Fed, decreasing the amount of discount lending and the monetary base.

open market operations The sale or purchase of government bonds by the Fed to control the size of the monetary base.

discount rate The interest rate charged on a loan to commercial banks from the Federal Reserve.

EXHIBIT 5 An Open Market Purchase and Sale

In Panel A, the Fed makes an open market purchase of bonds. Here, the Fed buys bonds with new money. In Panel B, the Fed makes an open market sale of bonds. Here, the Fed takes existing money out of circulation. Open market operations have traditionally been the most important policy tool of the Fed.

Panel A: Open Market Purchase Increases Money Supply

$ → Public → Bonds → Fed → $

Panel B: Open Market Sale Decreases Money Supply

$ → Public → Bonds → Fed → $

federal funds rate The interest rate that banks pay when borrowing reserves from other banks; also called the *fed funds rate*.

Changes in the money supply and discount rate have a significant impact on another important interest rate—the **federal funds rate** (*fed funds rate*), which is the interest rate that banks pay when borrowing reserves from other banks. As a practical matter, the discount rate is roughly equal to the federal funds rate, although the fed funds rate is market based. Due to the regulatory role of the Fed, banks prefer to borrow from other banks rather than at the discount window. As a consequence, macroeconomists watch the fed funds rate, and the discount rate is often viewed as symbolic. The fed funds rate plays a major role in monetary policy, as is discussed in Chapter 27.

Interest on Bank Reserves The Fed has two other policies in its toolbox that indirectly affect the M1 and M2 money supplies. Instead of changing the size of monetary base, the Fed can indirectly alter bank *demand* for reserves. In general, policies that encourage banks to hold fewer reserves also tend to encourage banks to make more loans, which increases M1 and M2. This is because these policies make the money multiplier larger. In contrast, when banks are encouraged to hold *more* reserves, they tend to make fewer loans.

For instance, the Fed's newest tool—being able to change the interest rate that banks earn on reserves—was introduced in 2008. The Fed can increase the money supply by reducing the interest rate that commercial banks earn on reserves. Doing so decreases banks' demand for reserves and encourages banks to make more loans. Conversely, if the Fed wishes to decrease the money supply, it can do this by raising the interest rate that banks earn on reserves held at the Fed. Doing so encourages banks to make fewer loans, which decreases the broader money supplies.

The Required Reserve Ratio Finally, the Fed also can increase the money supply by reducing the required reserve ratio. This allows banks to hold fewer reserves and make more loans. Alternatively, if the Fed wants to encourage banks to hold more reserves and lend less to the public, it can raise the required reserves ratio. An increase in the money supply results from a decrease in the required reserve ratio, and a decrease in the money supply results from an increase in the required reserve ratio. As a practical matter, however, the Fed seldom changes reserve requirements as a tool of monetary policy. Rather, it is used mostly to ensure bank liquidity.

 POLICY BRIEF The Fed Responds to 9/11

Immediately after the terror attacks in New York, Pennsylvania, and Washington, DC, that occurred on September 11, 2001, much of the U.S. financial system was shut down. Two targets, the Twin Towers in the World Trade Center, were in the financial district of New York City, and transportation and communication were severely disrupted. This turmoil disturbed an economy that already was in recession, and many observers expected a deep contraction in the economy. Some depositors, fearing a disruption in the banking system, wanted cash for safety and suddenly began to withdraw money from their bank accounts.

The Fed responded to the shock with an aggressive policy of discount lending. Prior to the attack, total discount loans were under $100 million. On September 12, 2001, discount loans soared to an unprecedented $45 billion (a number that would be eclipsed during the 2008 financial crisis). This injection of liquidity into the banking system helped stabilize the U.S. financial system. By September 19, 2001, discount lending had dropped off to about $2.5 billion. The financial crisis was mostly over, and the economy began recovering just a few months after 9/11.*

*Christopher J. Neely, 2004. "The Federal Reserve Responds to Crises: September 11th Was Not the First," Federal Reserve Bank of St. Louis *Review*, 86, no. 2 (March–April 2004): 27–42, https://files.stlouisfed.org/files /htdocs/publications/review/04/03/Neely.pdf.

Expansionary and Contractionary Monetary Policy

The four basic tools discussed above—open market operations, discount rate lending, interest on bank reserves, and the required reserve ratio—can be used to expand or contract M1 and M2. Exhibit 6 shows (1) the four ways that the Fed can increase the money supply, which is known as an *expansionary monetary policy*, and (2) the four ways that the Fed can implement a *contractionary monetary policy*, which tends to reduce M1 and M2.

Although the four policy tools look very different, in each case an expansionary policy by the Fed initially causes banks to have more bank reserves than they would prefer to hold. As a result, banks try to reduce their reserve holdings. This is done primarily by lending some of the money, which boosts the total amount of money in circulation. Conversely, a contractionary policy by the Fed initially causes banks to have fewer reserves than they would prefer to hold. In response, banks attempt to increase their reserves by decreasing lending, which reduces the amount of money in circulation.

EXHIBIT 6 Four Tools of Monetary Policy

Monetary Policy	Open Market Operations	Discount Rate	Interest Paid on Reserves	Required Reserve Ratio
Expansionary Monetary Policy (increases M1 and M2)				
Action	Purchases	↓ Discount rate	↓ Interest rate	↓ Required ratio
Direct Impact	Increases the monetary base	Increases the monetary base	Discourages banks from holding reserves	Discourages banks from holding reserves
Contractionary Monetary Policy (decreases M1 and M2)				
Action	Sales	↑ Discount rate	↑ Interest rate	↑ Required ratio
Direct Impact	Decreases the monetary base	Decreases the monetary base	Encourages banks to hold reserves	Encourages banks to hold reserves

The primary policy tool of the Fed is open market operations. In addition, the Fed can change discount rate lending, interest paid on reserves, and the required reserve ratio. Each tool can be employed to have either an expansionary or a contractionary impact on M1 and M2.

The Great Recession and Excess Reserves

In response to the Great Recession of late 2007 to mid-2009, the Fed engaged in massive open market purchases of bonds in an attempt to boost the economy. The potential deposit multiplier analysis shown above suggests that deposits and the overall money supply, measured as M1 and M2, would increase dramatically. They didn't. This faulty prediction was based on the assumption that banks hold very little excess reserves. As can be seen in Exhibit 7, this was the case prior to 2008. But in late 2008, the amount that banks held in excess reserves rose sharply.

Excess reserves and the broader monetary base expanded for two key reasons. First, in late 2008, the Fed changed its policy and began paying interest on reserves held at the Fed. Prior to this change, banks earned no interest on such funds—and so they had an incentive to minimize excess reserves by lending out extra funds (and collecting interest on those loans). The Fed's policy change incentivized banks to hold onto their excess reserves because they would be able to earn interest on reserves without the risks involved in making loans. This lowered the money multiplier and the overall money supply.

More importantly, market interest rates on safe assets fell close to zero in late 2008. This further reduced the incentives of banks to make loans. Banks began to find lending opportunities less attractive, primarily because the interest they could earn on low-risk loans fell to very low levels. The combination of low market interest rates and a positive interest earned on reserves suddenly made holding reserves much more appealing to banks. This dramatically reduced the size of the money multiplier and growth in the overall money supply. In general, the Federal Reserve has much greater control over the monetary base than over the broader money supply (M1 and M2) because it cannot directly control the amount of reserves that banks choose to hold.

EXHIBIT 7   Excess Reserves Held by U.S. Banks

The excess reserve holdings of the Federal Reserve were only a few billion dollars until 2008, when the Fed began paying interest on reserves. By 2015, excess reserves had soared to about $2,500 billion or $2.5 trillion. A higher level of excess reserves will reduce the money multiplier. Shaded areas indicate U.S. recessions.

Data from: Federal Reserve Bank of St. Louis.

CASE STUDY The Banking Crisis of 2008

The 2008 banking crisis dramatically impacted the entire U.S. monetary system. The first signs of trouble appeared in 2007, when increasing numbers of homeowners began defaulting on their home mortgage loans. Over the previous few years, banks had loosened requirements for mortgage loans and offered loans to consumers who had poor credit and lacked a significant down payment. In some cases, banks did not even verify borrowers' incomes. These low-quality, high-risk mortgages were called *subprime mortgages*. Credit was flowing, and people joked that anyone who could "fog a mirror" could get a mortgage. As the crisis intensified and home prices plunged, however, even many people with high-quality mortgages defaulted.

So why were so many subprime mortgages issued in the early 2000s? There are a number of theories:[*]

- *Lax regulation.* Regulators did not prevent banks from making risky loans and sometimes even encouraged this behavior. Banks often were able to package the subprime mortgages into bonds called *mortgage-backed securities* and then sell those bonds to investors. But why would investors buy these risky bonds?

- *The "black swan" theory.* People tend not to worry about events that they have never seen. American investors had never seen a big nationwide crash in the housing market, so they thought mortgage bonds that use homes as collateral would be safe, just as they always had been in the past. In finance, the term *black swan event* means something totally unexpected and refers to the fact up until 1697—when Dutch explorers encountered black swans in Australia—Europeans assumed that all swans were white.[†]

- *Rating agencies.* The companies that rate the quality of bonds, such as Moody's and S&P, did not correctly identify the risk involved in these bonds.

- *Government policies.* The federal government has traditionally encouraged banks to make it easier for people to buy houses and has set up agencies (such as Fannie Mae, Freddie Mac, and the Federal Housing Administration) that encourage mortgage lending. There was political pressure from Washington encouraging these agencies to make it easier for Americans to buy homes.

- *Moral hazard.* Banks may have felt safe in making risky loans if they believed they would be bailed out during a banking crisis, a phenomenon known as *moral hazard*. Although no bank actually wants to make a bad loan (banks did lose quite a bit of money during the crisis), they might not have been as careful as they would have been if they did not expect a bailout.

By the fall of 2008, many banks were in financial trouble. After a Lehman Brothers bank (a large *shadow bank* that was not subject to the strict regulatory oversight of commercial banks) failed in 2008, a severe banking crisis developed. In some ways, this crisis was similar to the early years of the Great Depression but with one important difference. Because ordinary bank deposits were protected by insurance in 2008, the United States did not see the depositor bank runs that plagued the 1930s, when deposits were not protected.[‡]

Unfortunately, other problems emerged. After the failure of Lehman Brothers, major investors began to worry that other big banks might fail. The FDIC insured deposits only up to $250,000—meaning that deposits in excess of that amount were at risk. In addition, deposits at shadow banks were not insured. A modern bank run on these shadow banks ensued as large institutions that had lent vast sums of money quickly withdrew their uninsured funds and sought safety in other assets such as Treasury bonds. Large banks then had trouble attracting enough money to stay in business because they had been relying on loans from wealthy individuals and large institutions such as insurance companies and pension funds. Eventually, the federal government stepped in to stop the bleeding. (We return to this bailout and discuss its effectiveness in Chapter 27.)

Understanding the mortgage crisis requires understanding how mortgages work. The mortgages that banks issue are usually long-term loans. Borrowers typically pay off mortgages in structured payments over 15 to 30 years. After a home loan is issued, banks cannot quickly have their money returned to pay back any individuals who attempt to withdraw their money.

It might help to visualize this at a personal level. Suppose you have a friend who wants to borrow $10,000, which she will pay back at 20% interest over 10 years. In order to obtain the funds to make this loan, you first need to borrow money from your brother, who is willing to lend to you at 12% interest. So you could make an 8% profit by borrowing from your brother and lending to a friend. But your brother is willing to lend for only one month at a time because he feels that a 10-year repayment plan is too risky. After all, he might need the money. You take a chance and hope he'll renew the $10,000 loan after a month has gone by.

Assume that after three consecutive one-month loans, your brother decides not to renew the loan and asks you to repay him. Now you face a liquidity crisis. Your 10-year loan of $10,000 to your friend is still a good long-term loan. She's making her monthly payments, with interest, as planned. But how can you pay your brother back and finance this investment if your brother won't continue the series of one-month loans?

Your dilemma in the previous example is essentially the squeeze that many banks faced during the late 2008 banking crisis. Banks faced a liquidity problem: They had assets (such as home loans) that could not be easily converted into money. In late 2008, many banks could not attract enough deposits to stay in business. Nor could the banks borrow enough money on their own. As a result, the federal government agreed to lend the largest banks enormous sums of money during the crisis, a process often called a *bailout*. Although the bailout came too late to save Lehman Brothers, it partially solved the banking system's liquidity problem.[**]

Many banks also faced solvency problems. Many of the loans they issued were not being repaid due to the housing crash and the steep recession of 2008 and 2009. When a loan is not repaid, the value of the loan to the bank drops significantly. Remember, banks view the loans they have made as an asset: Someone owes the bank money. During the Great Recession, however, some banks ended up owing depositors more than they had in assets. These banks became insolvent and went out of business.

Thus, the banking system is susceptible to two problems—solvency and liquidity. Loans may not be repaid, resulting in insolvent banks. That is a solvency problem. Even if the loans are sound, banks may have trouble attracting enough short-term deposits to stay in business. That is a liquidity problem.

The Fed can provide liquidity during a crisis, but this does not solve the solvency problem. Instead, regulators are increasingly requiring banks to hold more financial capital and make fewer loans. Other things equal, a higher level of financial capital means a safer bank because any loan losses can be absorbed by the bank's owners before the depositors are impacted. Thus, higher minimum levels of capital are the newest trend in bank regulation and represent a response to the crisis of 2008.

*Russell Roberts, "Gambling with Other People's Money: How Perverted Incentives Caused the Financial Crisis," Mercatus Center, George Mason University, April 28, 2010.

†Nassim Nicholas Taleb, *The Black Swan: The Impact of the Highly Improbable*, 2nd ed. (New York: Random House, 2010).

‡James B. Stewart and Peter Eavis, "Revisiting the Lehman Brothers Bailout That Never Was," *New York Times*, September 29, 2014, http://www.nytimes.com/2014/09/30/business/revisiting-the-lehman-brothers-bailout-that-never-was.html?_r=0.

**Ibid.

BUSINESS TAKEAWAY

Much of our monetary system is structured to address the problem of liquidity, an issue that is pertinent to many businesses. Firms may have assets ranging from merchandise in inventory to capital equipment used in production. These assets are relatively illiquid and thus not particularly useful when business owners have a pressing need for cash to pay workers, suppliers, and other bills.

How should businesses respond to the need for liquidity? On the one hand, businesses that hoard large amounts of cash in order to be highly liquid will likely miss out on profit opportunities that could be generated if all that cash were converted to inventories and equipment. On the other hand, a business that overexpands inventory and capital equipment investments may not have enough cash on hand to meet expenses if circumstances change. A firm in such a situation might be forced to sell assets quickly at a loss or perhaps even declare bankruptcy.

The key is to avoid either extreme and maintain a proper balance of risks and rewards—particularly in banking and finance decisions. For example, time deposits involve a *risk* of inadequate liquidity because these deposits must be held for a specified period of time. At the same time, they offer the *reward* of earning greater interest than cash or demand deposits. Firms should hold the mix of bank deposits that meets their need for liquidity in an emergency while also providing as high a return as possible.

CHAPTER STUDY GUIDE

24.1   WHAT IS MONEY?

Money is an asset commonly used in the exchange of goods and services. Money replaced the **barter system**, an economic system where people directly exchange one good for another. Money serves as a **unit of account**, a standard way of measuring prices. Money is also a **medium of exchange**, an asset that is widely used for purchasing other goods and services. Finally, money is a **store of value**, an asset that people can use as a place to put their savings. A **commodity money** is money that has an underlying value apart from its role as money. The most famous example of a commodity money system was the gold standard, where

gold served as money. **Fiat money** is money that is not backed by a commodity and that has little or no underlying value apart from its role as money. Fiat money has value because of network externalities, taxes, and implied backing.

24.2   THE U.S. MONEY SUPPLY

The **money supply** is the total value of financial assets that are considered money. **Liquidity** represents the ease in which an asset can be turned into a medium of exchange. **Demand deposits** are accounts at the bank that are immediately available for spending. They often are called checking accounts. **Time deposits** are accounts that hold money deposited in a bank that cannot be withdrawn for a specified period of time. Demand deposits are more liquid than time deposits. The three main measures of the money supply are M1, M2, and the monetary base. **M1** is a measure of the money supply that includes all cash (including paper money and coins) in circulation, along with demand deposits and traveler's checks. **M2** is a measure of the money supply that includes M1 plus time deposits. The **monetary base** is a measure of the money supply that includes cash held by the general public plus reserves held by commercial banks. It is the money that policymakers have the most direct control over. In total, there is over $4,600 cash in circulation per person in the United States. The large total appears to be the result of dollarization overseas and the U.S. underground economy.

24.3 THE BUSINESS OF FRACTIONAL RESERVE BANKING

Fractional reserve banking is the banking practice of keeping a fraction of deposits available as reserves. This allows banks to provide liquidity services to the public by attracting large numbers of depositors. The **required reserve ratio** is the legally required minimum level of reserves that a bank must hold, expressed as a fraction of deposits. Because many purchases are made with checks, bank deposits are also considered to be a part of the money supply. **Excess reserves** are reserves held above and beyond the legally required minimum level of reserves that a bank must hold. Banks can create money, and the government has the ability to use this to greatly expand the money supply when it increases the monetary base. The **potential deposit multiplier** is the maximum possible change in deposits for each dollar change in bank reserves. It equals 1/Required reserve ratio. The **money multiplier** is the change in the overall money supply resulting from a $1 increase in the monetary base. It is considerably smaller than the potential deposit multiplier due to currency held by the public and excess reserves. A **bank run** (or **banking panic**) is an event that occurs when depositors rush to withdraw money from their bank in fear that the bank may fail. This problem can and often does spread from one bank to another. The Federal Deposit Insurance Corporation was established in 1934 to prevent bank runs and today insures depositors' bank deposits up to $250,000.

24.4 CENTRAL BANKS AND THE FEDERAL RESERVE SYSTEM

A **central bank** is an institution that determines the quantity of fiat money in circulation. In most countries, the central bank also regulates the banking system. The central bank of the United States is formally called the Federal Reserve System (the Fed). The central bank in much of Europe is the European Central Bank (ECB). One of the functions of central banks is to be a lender of last resort. **Monetary policy** is changes in the money supply and interest rates by the central bank, often with the goal of influencing employment and inflation.

24.5 CONTROLLING THE MONETARY BASE AND BROADER MONEY SUPPLIES

The Fed has four monetary policy tools for controlling the monetary base and broader money supplies—open market operations, discount rate lending, interest on bank reserves, and the required reserve ratio. The most important tool is **open market operations**—the sale or purchase of government bonds by the Fed to control the size of the monetary base. New money can be injected into the economy through open purchases of bonds, and money can be withdrawn via open market sales. The money supply also can be increased by decreasing the **discount rate**, which is the interest rate charged on a loan to commercial banks from the Federal Reserve. The **federal funds rate** (or *fed funds rate*) is the interest rate that banks pay when borrowing reserves from other banks. The Fed has two other policies in its toolbox that indirectly affect the M1 and M2 money supplies; changing the interest it pays on reserves and changing the required reserve ratio.

TOP TEN TERMS AND CONCEPTS

1. Money
2. Unit of Account, Medium of Exchange, and Store of Value
3. Commodity and Fiat Money
4. Liquidity of Demand and Time Deposits
5. M1, M2, and Monetary Base
6. Fractional Reserve Banking
7. Potential Deposit Multiplier and Money Multiplier
8. Federal Reserve System
9. Open Market Purchases and Sales
10. Discount Rate, Interest on Reserves, and Required Reserves

STUDY PROBLEMS

1. What are the three roles of money? Describe each.

2. How is money different than wealth?

3. Rank the following items in terms of least liquid to most liquid:

   a. Currency and demand deposits

   b. Gold and silver bars

   c. Time deposits

   d. Valuable paintings by Pablo Picasso

4. State whether each of the following is included as part of M1, M2, the monetary base, or none of the above. Some belong to more than one.

   a. Cash on reserve at the Federal Reserve

   b. Cash in circulation

   c. Demand deposits

   d. Credit cards

   e. Time deposits

5. Name the four tools that the Fed can use to change the money supply. Which tools directly increase the monetary base? Which tools indirectly increase the money supply by encouraging banks to make more loans?

6. After September 11, 2001, the Federal Reserve substantially increased discount lending.[2] Why would the Fed engage in such a policy?

7. Use the Federal Reserve Economic Data (FRED) website to plot the M1 and M2 money supplies over the past 50 years. Why is M2 larger than M1?

8. The required reserve ratio is 10%. If the Fed makes a $1 million open market purchase, what is the potential deposit multiplier? What does the deposit multiplier predict will happen to the money supply? Why is the actual money multiplier considerably smaller than the prediction of the deposit multiplier?

9. Describe the differences between the monetary base, M1, and M2. Why is there more than one measurement of the money supply?

10. Discuss two reasons that the excess reserve ratio rose sharply after 2008. How did this affect the money multiplier? Use the FRED website to plot the reserve ratio over the past 30 years.

11. Why are credit cards not considered money? How does the existence of credit cards affect the public's use of other types of money?

12. College Bank has $100 million dollars in demand deposits and $10 million in reserves and loans out the rest. The required reserve ratio is 10%.

    a. Show the bank's balance sheet.

    b. Suppose a new customer comes in and deposits $10 million dollars. Show the bank's new balance sheet if the bank does not make any new loans.

    c. Now assume the bank loans out the maximum amount possible. Show the bank's balance sheet after the new loan.

    d. What happens to M1 after bank makes the new loan?

13. What changes did the European public have to make in order to adapt to the new euro currency when it was introduced in 2002?

14. Contrast bitcoin and the U.S. dollar. Discuss whether the two types of currency serve the three traditional functions of money (medium of exchange, unit of account, and store of value). Are they fiat or commodity money? Explain.

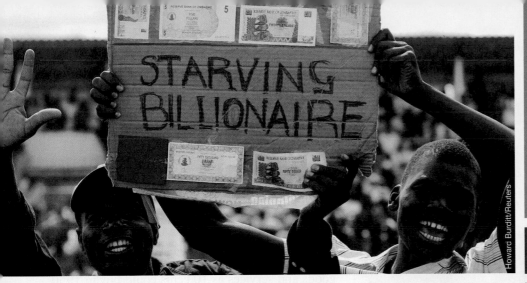

∧ Who needs to be a millionaire when you can be a billionaire? Apparently, not the people of Zimbabwe.

Money and the Price Level in the Long Run

The Quantity Theory and the Fisher Effect

The cost of living in Germany rose by more than a billion-fold between 1920 and 1923. In 2008, Zimbabwe experienced an even more spectacular inflation. In contrast, in recent decades American inflation has averaged about 2% per year, while Japan experienced deflation from the mid-1990s to 2013. What can we make of all these patterns? Why does inflation differ so much over time, and from one country to another?

Changing rates of inflation have an effect on just about every sector of an economy, from individuals and households to multinational corporations and governments. Rapid price increases can devastate savers, unexpected deflation can wipe out borrowers, and both can occasionally lead to political unrest. In this chapter, we focus on the long-run connection between increases in the money supply and the price level. We also examine why people confuse nominal and real variables and the link between the rate of inflation and the nominal interest rate.

Chapter Learning Targets

● Identify the links between the money supply and inflation.

● Explain monetary neutrality and the classical dichotomy.

● Describe the equation of exchange.

● Compare nominal and real interest rates.

● Describe deflation, the gold standard, and the ways that monetarism helped curb inflation.

25.1 INFLATION AS A MONETARY PHENOMENON

In Chapter 20, we showed that **inflation** is an increase in the overall price level that results in a decline in the value or purchasing power of money. Moreover, **deflation** is a decrease in the overall price level that results in an increase in the value or purchasing power of money.

∧ Milton Friedman: "Inflation is always and everywhere a monetary phenomenon."

The **value of money** is the amount of goods and services that can be bought with money—the purchasing power of money, which equals 1/Price level. In the United States, the Consumer Price Index roughly doubled between 1989 and 2017. This means that the lifestyle that could be supported on an income of $50,000 per year in 1989 required an income of $100,000 per year in 2017. The value of each dollar has fallen by half. If you look at prices for 1950, you would find that the same basket of goods costs only $10,000. In other words, each dollar today can purchase about as many goods and services as 10 cents could buy in 1950.

Nobel Prize–winner Milton Friedman (1912–2006) argued that inflation wasn't just a fall in the value of money; it was a "monetary phenomenon," caused by too much money in circulation. Friedman was the leader of the *monetarist* school of economic thought, which is grounded in the belief that inflation is caused by excessive growth in the supply of money. This idea, which goes back hundreds of years, is now called the *quantity theory of money*.

The Quantity Theory of Money

inflation An increase in the overall price level that results in a decline in the value or purchasing power of money.

deflation A decrease in the overall price level that results in an increase in the value or purchasing power of money.

value of money The amount of goods and services that can be bought with money—the purchasing power of money, which equals 1/Price level.

quantity theory of money The theory that a given change in the money supply leads to a proportional change in the price level in the long run.

money demand The amount of money that people want to hold.

excess cash balances The amount by which the supply of money in circulation exceeds the demand for money.

The **quantity theory of money** is the theory that a given change in the money supply leads to a proportional change in the price level in the long run. Recall that the *long run* refers to the time necessary to make all adjustments to economic circumstances. The quantity theory tries to explain changes in the price level *after* individual prices have had time to adjust to changes in the money supply.

Consider this classic thought experiment in economics. A country has 1 million people, citizens typically hold $100 cash in their wallets, and no money is kept in banks. The total supply of cash is $100 million. Suddenly, a helicopter drops an additional $100 million onto the population. After people have rushed about and grabbed all the new money, there is now $200 million in circulation—twice as much as before. So what happens next?

To analyze what happens if the money supply doubles, we must first understand **money demand**—the amount of money that people want to hold. Here, money demand is the amount of cash that people want to carry. Remember that cash and other forms of money are not the same as wealth. Although people want as much wealth as possible, they generally do not want all their assets to be in the form of cash, which does not earn interest and can be stolen or lost.

Most consumers carry a relatively small amount of cash to meet their liquidity needs and occasionally withdraw more from an automatic teller machine. Demand for money is determined by individual preference. You might prefer to hold $120 dollars on an average day, and your neighbor might hold $80 on average. The same is true for every one of the million citizens in our imaginary country. In this example, we know how much they initially chose to hold—an average of $100 per person.

The people living in this country determine how much money they each hold, but after the helicopter drop doubles the supply of money, the population as a whole has more money than they typically prefer to hold. Economists refer to this as **excess cash balances**—the amount by which the supply of money in circulation exceeds the demand for money. If you have ever found yourself with a sudden windfall—or even have just a couple of extra bucks "burning a hole in your pocket"—you have been faced with an excess cash balance. Perhaps you splurged on a dinner out or a new pair of shoes, or maybe you purchased stocks or bonds. People will usually attempt to "get rid of" excess cash balances by spending the money. In the process, someone else receives that money. Now *those* people or businesses are holding more than they prefer. Now, imagine what happens when an entire society has excess cash balances. What happens when society as a whole finds itself with excess cash balances? How can people dispose of that unwanted money?

As people spend their extra money, they drive up demand and increase the prices of goods and services. How high do prices rise? They need to rise high enough so that the public as a whole is comfortable holding the new level of cash balances, which is $200 per person in our example. For this to occur, the basket of goods that used to cost $100 now needs to cost $200. Pizza that used to cost $20 now costs $40. In other words, if society suddenly holds twice as much money but still has the same number of homes, automobiles, and other products, the price of homes, automobiles, and other products will double, *ceteris paribus*. This is the essence of the quantity theory of money.

In real terms, the public's holding of cash has not changed at all after prices double. Relative to what they can purchase, the total value of the public's cash holding is unchanged. The public's wallets and purses have exactly the same *purchasing power* as they did before the money supply and price level doubled. In nominal terms, society has twice as much money, but because prices doubled, the value of each dollar falls in half. Thus, the total purchasing power of the public's cash balances is no greater than before. This increase in the price level is how society as a whole gets rid of excess cash balances: Prices rise enough so that the extra cash is now needed for transactions.

More than 250 years ago, the Scottish philosopher David Hume articulated this basic idea: "If we consider any one Kingdom by itself, it is evident, that the greater or less plenty of money is of no consequence; since the prices of commodities are always proportioned to the plenty of money." Hume is saying that when the government (the "Kingdom") issues more money, it tends to impact only prices and has no impact on *real* variables such as real GDP ("no consequence"). This is the simple intuitive idea underlying the quantity theory of money.

The Long-Run Money Supply and Money Demand Model

Up to this point, we have been discussing the supply of money, the demand for money, and the value of money. That sounds a lot like the familiar supply and demand model. We can demonstrate the helicopter drop thought experiment and the quantity theory of money with a simple money supply and money demand model.

As we begin, we immediately run into a puzzle. An ordinary supply and demand diagram puts the price of the good on the y-axis (vertical axis). But what could it possibly mean to talk about the "price" of money? Isn't a dollar always worth a dollar? In economics, the price of money is measured in terms of its purchasing power.

The Real Value of Money: Its Purchasing Power The real price of an automobile is the amount of goods and services one has to give up to buy the automobile. The same is true for money. The real value of money is its purchasing power—how many goods and services one must forgo to hold an additional dollar. As has been emphasized throughout this text, what really matters is not nominal prices but relative or *real prices*.

In Chapter 20, you learned that an increase in the price level means a decrease in 1/Price level and thus a decline in the value of money. The idea was illustrated with an example of a 10-fold increase in the price of eggs, which can be viewed as either an increase in price (of eggs, in this case) *or* a decline in the value of money.

When drawing the supply and demand curve for eggs, the price (or value) of eggs is placed on the y-axis. Likewise, the value of money is put on the y-axis in the money supply and demand diagram. When you understand this key point, you can see that the diagram works like an ordinary supply and demand curve. The only difference is that a higher value of money represents a lower price level (deflation) and a lower value of money represents a higher price level (inflation).

EXHIBIT 1 The Long-Run Money Supply and Money Demand Model

Increases in the money supply result in a proportional decline in the value of money and an increase in the price level. The value of money is defined as 1/Price level.

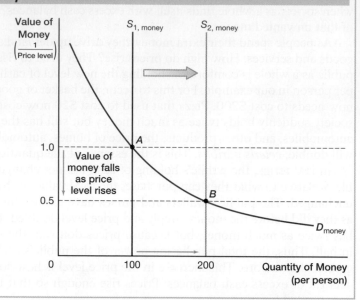

The Long-Run Money Supply and Money Demand Curves For simplicity, we assume that the central bank determines the amount of money in circulation. The *money supply* curve is a vertical line—that is, perfectly inelastic. As is shown in Chapter 24, the Federal Reserve can inject money into the economy with open market purchases or discount loans, shifting the money supply curve to the right. Notice that the equilibrium value of money declines. But the amount of the decline depends on the slope of the demand for money.

According to the quantity theory of money, people care about the *purchasing power* of the money in their wallets, not the nominal value of money. In Exhibit 1, the effect of the helicopter drop is shown when we move from point *A* to point *B*. When the quantity of money supplied doubles from $100 per person to $200, the value of money (1/Price level) falls in half (from 1.0 to 0.5), and the price level doubles. At that new and higher price level, people want to hold twice as many dollars to do their shopping.

The *money demand curve* is downward sloping because when the purchasing power of a dollar falls, people hold more money to make purchases. Just as with any other supply and demand diagram, an increase in the supply of money will reduce its value to the point where the market is again in equilibrium. What makes money special is that the new equilibrium should result in the overall price level rising by the *same proportion* as the money supply.

As discussed in Chapter 24, the central bank determines how much money is in circulation in *nominal* terms. When the central bank increases the quantity of money in circulation, this tends to decrease the purchasing power of *each dollar*, leaving the total purchasing power of the entire money supply unaffected in the long run. In the above example, the money supply and price level doubled thus the value of each dollar was halved; but the total purchasing power of the entire money supply did not change. Central banks cannot change the real value of the public's total money balances.

In real life, there are no helicopter drops. When the Federal Reserve wants to inject money into the economy, it does not simply *give out* money. It purchases Treasury securities through open market purchases. Consequently, when people obtain money by selling Treasury securities to the Fed, they are not significantly better off because they have given up something of roughly equal value. Fortunately, it does not make much difference how the new money is distributed because people would still be left holding excess cash balances. People will still try to get rid of that extra cash by spending *some* of it.

But what if people do not spend *all* of it? What if people save some of it? Do things change if we give people the option of putting the extra cash in the bank?

As is discussed in Chapter 24, cash held by banks is called *reserves*, and banks usually prefer to limit their cash reserves (which earn little or no interest) in favor of higher interest-earning assets, such as loans or Treasury bonds. Like the public, banks want to hold only the cash needed to meet their liquidity needs. In most cases, the money will move into circulation and ultimately be spent. Later we consider the special case that occurs when interest rates are near zero.

25.2 THE NEUTRALITY OF MONEY AND THE CLASSICAL DICHOTOMY

Most economists believe that changes in the money supply have no effect on society's productive capacity, which is impacted by factors such as the amount of physical capital, human capital, and technology. This has important implications for the long-run effects of monetary policy.

Monetary Neutrality

Economic analysis suggests that the only long-run effect of changes in the money supply is a proportionate change in the price level. This concept is known as **monetary neutrality**—the idea that changes in the money supply do not affect real variables in the long run. Monetary neutrality does not imply that changes in the money supply have no effect on the economy; rather, it means there are no *real* effects in the long run. For example, it does not change the number of cars and homes being built. The only long-run effect is proportionately higher prices. Thus, doubling the money supply will not impact real GDP in the long run but will raise nominal GDP, which measures output at the current price level.

The concept of money neutrality is most useful for long-run changes. For example, the cost of living in the United States in 2017 was about 20 times higher than it was in 1917. Over this 100-year period, workers, businesses, savers, and lenders had plenty of time to adjust their behavior to changes in the price level. Thus, the higher price level that resulted from increases in the money supply simply meant a change in the dollar as a measuring stick.

Although this distinction between the real and the nominal sides of the economy is crucial, it can be hard to see in low-inflation countries such as the United States. It is especially important in countries with extremely high rates of inflation. **Hyperinflation** is extremely high rates of inflation and a rapid decline in the value of a nation's currency. The first recorded example of hyperinflation occurred during the French Revolution in December 1795, when prices rose 143% in a single month. Germany experienced a dramatic hyperinflation from 1920 to 1923, with the inflation rate peaking at 29,500% in October 1923 (see **Policy Brief: German Hyperinflation** below). In July 1946, prices tripled every single day in Hungary.

Most recently, Zimbabwe experienced hyperinflation in 2008, when the government printed so much money that it had by far the world's fastest-growing nominal GDP. But all of that "growth" was due to hyperinflation of prices. The country's real GDP was actually declining. In November 2008, prices doubled each day in Zimbabwe, and businesses began to update prices hourly. Most people who received money spent it quickly so that they could exchange it for goods and services before the currency lost even more value, like a child's game of "hot potato." And yet the government kept printing, devaluing its currency to the point where even 100 trillion Zimbabwe dollars could not purchase one meal.

monetary neutrality The idea that changes in the money supply do not affect real variables in the long run.

hyperinflation Extremely high rates of inflation and a rapid decline in the value of a nation's currency.

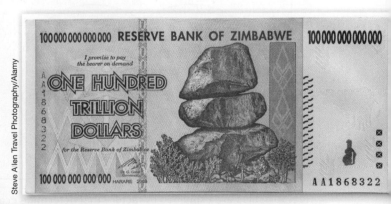

Steve Allen Travel Photography/Alamy

⋀ This $100 trillion dollar bill was printed during the Zimbabwean hyperinflation. The same number of U.S. dollars would be more than enough to buy the entire economy.

POLICY BRIEF German Hyperinflation

One of the most famous examples of hyperinflation occurred in Germany between 1920 and 1923. During that three-year period, the German money supply increased over a billion-fold from 115 million marks (then the currency used in German) in early 1922 to 497 *trillion* million (or 497,000,000,000,000,000,000) marks in 1923. That's a lot of zeros. Prices rose even faster. By late 1923, a billion German marks could not buy a cup of coffee. But what led the German government to print money at such a rapid rate? After all, the quantity theory of money was already well understood by 1920.

When World War I ended in 1918, the victorious powers imposed heavy "reparations" on the defeated powers, including Germany, essentially requiring the losing side to pay for the damage done during the war. At the same time, because Germany's economy was extremely weak, and the German government was virtually bankrupt, the nation fell back on the last resort of printing money to pay its bills.

The consequences were predictable. Prices soared, and savers saw the real value of their bonds or bank accounts fall to almost zero. Even if bondholders were eventually repaid, the money had almost no purchasing power. The rapid pace of price increases led Germans to spend any money they received quickly. In addition, all that extra money tended to raise prices, not output, which is consistent with the concept of monetary neutrality.

Just a few years later, Germany suffered from the opposite problem—deflation. During the severe deflation and depression of 1929 to 1933, the National Socialist German Workers' Party (the Nazis) headed by Adolf Hitler were able to take power in Germany.*

*Liaquat Ahamed, *Lords of Finance: The Bankers Who Broke the World* (New York: Penguin, 2009); Jack Weatherford, *The History of Money* (New York: Three Rivers Press, 1997).

classical dichotomy The division of macroeconomics into two areas—real variables and nominal variables.

EXHIBIT 2 The Classical Dichotomy: Real Variables versus Nominal Variables

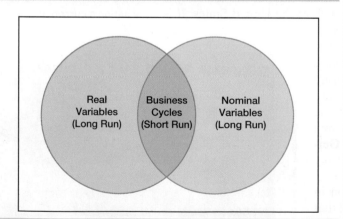

Real variables are explained by factors that determine economic growth, such as innovation and new technology, investments in physical capital, and improvements in human capital. Nominal variables (such as inflation and nominal GDP) are determined by monetary policy in the long run. Both nominal and real variables play roles in the business cycle.

The Classical Dichotomy

There is a world of difference between real variables and nominal variables, and different theories are needed for each. The **classical dichotomy** is the division of macroeconomics into two areas—real variables and nominal variables. The Venn diagram in Exhibit 2 shows how most macroeconomists now think of their field. On the left side of the diagram are real variables in the long run. On the right side are nominal variables (such as inflation and nominal GDP) in the long run, the focus of this chapter. In the middle area is the business cycle, which is affected by both sides of the classical dichotomy.

Monetary Policy Has No Impact on Real GDP in the Long Run On the left side of the Venn diagram in Exhibit 2, we have real variables in the long run. Most economists believe that a change in the money supply can impact real GDP *only* in the short run and that monetary policy has no impact on real GDP in the long run. Instead, long-run sources of economic growth include innovation and new technology, investments in physical capital, and improvements in human capital (see Chapter 22). Simply printing money cannot create economic growth in the long run. If it was effective at boosting real GDP in the long run, then all countries could get rich simply by printing money.

Monetary Policy Does Affect Nominal Variables Nominal variables (such as nominal GDP and inflation) are located on the right side of our Venn diagram. Monetary policy plays an important role in determining the path of nominal variables, especially in the long run. If the Federal Reserve increases the U.S. money supply permanently, the long-run effect is to cause nominal GDP and the price level to rise by the same proportion, leaving real variables unchanged. Hyperinflation is the best example of an almost purely monetary phenomenon.

Monetary Policy Affects Short-Run Business Cycles The spot where long-run real variables overlap with nominal variables captures the most difficult problem in all of macroeconomics—the business cycle. Recall from Chapter 21, that the **business cycle** is short-run alternating periods of economic expansion and recession. In Chapter 26, we will see that both nominal and real variables play a crucial role in the business cycle. This means that changes in the money supply may have real effects on the short-run business cycle.

business cycle Short-run alternating periods of economic expansion and recession.

> ### Think & Speak Like an Economist
>
> Economic outcomes frequently depend on the time frame involved, and the impact of changes in the money supply is no exception. Increases in the money supply impact only nominal variables in the long run, after prices have had time to adjust fully.

Money Illusion

Suppose that a man measures his young son with a yardstick and finds that the boy is 1 yard tall. After 40 years, he measures his son again, this time with a 1-foot ruler, and finds that the boy has grown to be 6-feet tall. The man proudly announces to his friends that the child has grown six-fold. Most people probably would roll their eyes and point out that the man had used two different measuring sticks: 1 yard equals 3 feet.

In the real world, people almost never make this particular mistake. But in the field of economics, finance, and accounting, a similar mistake occurs every day. Suppose that at the end of your career, you claim to be making 6 times as much as you earned 40 years earlier. Most people would not regard this salary claim as being as silly as the man's claim that his son was 6 times taller when he measured him with a 12-inch ruler than he was 40 years earlier when he measured him with a yardstick. With the salary claim, it seems like we have the same "measuring stick" in both cases—U.S. dollars. But a dollar today does not have the same value that a dollar had 40 years ago, and in this example, its purchasing power is only one third as much, as is shown in Exhibit 3.

The change in the price level makes everything we measure with U.S. dollars look three times as big, even if the real value of what we are measuring did not change in 40 years. Recall the previous example of shrinking the yardstick down to the 1-foot ruler, which makes all objects seem three times bigger than when measured with a yardstick.

It is also true that people really can grow taller, and income really can increase in terms of purchasing power. If we divide the 6-foot boy's height by 3 to get 2 yards, we would see that his real height had doubled from 1 yard to 2 yards. Similarly, if we divide the $180,000 annual income by 3 (the new price level), we see that the real purchasing power in terms of 2020 dollars has doubled from $30,000 to $60,000. This person's living standard has doubled.

Because money is neutral in the long run, increasing the money supply simply creates inflation, leaving real economic variables unaffected. All it does is

EXHIBIT 3 A Changing Measuring Stick

Year	Nominal Income	Price Level	Real Income
2020	$30,000	1.0	$30,000
2060	$180,000	3.0	$60,000

If nominal income increases 6-fold while prices triple, real income will only double.

Mike Luckovich/Cartoonist Group

change our measuring stick of value. Many people do not understand this distinction. When people confuse real and nominal variables, economists say that they suffer from **money illusion**—an incorrect assumption that nominal variables represent real variables. Later, we will see that money illusion might be one reason that monetary policy can influence the business cycle. Having a higher nominal income does not always mean you are richer in real terms, but if you feel richer, you might act on that basis.

📊 BUSINESS BRIEF The Money Illusion in Wage Negotiations

In general, workers like to see their wages increase and often object to a cut in wages—by negotiating a better deal, striking, or looking for another job. But economists have found intriguing evidence that people often think in nominal terms, not real terms—especially when it comes to wages. One study looked at thousands of firms and found that most pay increases ranged from 0 to 4% and that very few salaries showed pay reductions (even tiny reductions).

The data suggests that workers are extremely resistant to a pay increase below 0% (that is, a pay cut). But during the same years of the study, inflation averaged about 2%, so *in real terms*, a raise of less than 2% was effectively a *pay cut*. Why did workers often accept a decrease in pay (in real terms) but almost never accept a pay cut (in nominal terms)?[*]

Accepting small nominal pay increases that were below the increase in inflation suggests that the money illusion is real. Those very small nominal pay increases amounted to a real decrease in spending power. Businesses need to account for this sort of money illusion when negotiating wage increases.

Richard Levine/Alamy Stock Photo

∧ No one likes nominal wage cuts, but workers often accept real wage cuts.

[*]Alessandro Barattieri, Susanto Basu, and Peter Gottschalk, "Some Evidence on the Importance of Sticky Wages," NBER Working Paper No. 16130, National Bureau of Economic Research, June 2010, http://www.nber.org/papers/w16130.

Currency Reform

Countries occasionally will replace their existing currency. A **currency reform** is the replacement of one currency by another. In 2002, many European countries replaced their existing currencies with the euro. In this case, the currency reform was designed to help simplify economic transactions between member countries via a single, unified currency.

More often, currency reform is employed to replace a currency that has been devalued by many decades of extremely high inflation. When high inflation causes prices to be measured in the millions, billions, or trillions, a country may do a currency reform to simplify prices. In the early 1990s, the Mexican government determined that currency reform was needed to offset the effects of previous inflation. On January 1, 1993, the "old" Mexican peso was replaced with the "new" peso, and the public exchanged the old currency for new money (at a rate of 1,000 old pesos for one new peso) at commercial banks.

Currency reforms typically work smoothly. These reforms automatically adjust all wage and price contracts, rental agreements, and debt agreements. In Mexico, all nominal prices measured in pesos were instantly reduced by a factor of 1,000. People

money illusion An incorrect assumption that nominal variables represent real variables.

currency reform The replacement of one currency by another.

saw their salaries drop sharply, losing three zeros, but their cost of living fell equally sharply. There was no redistribution of wealth between savers and borrowers because debt contracts were automatically adjusted.

These currency reforms come closest to what economists envision when they discuss monetary neutrality and the idea of money as a measuring stick. Because all wages, prices, and debt contracts are immediately adjusted, there are no real effects on the economy.

If the economy would always adjust as smoothly as it does during a currency reform, then economists would not worry much about inflation and deflation. When more gradual inflation or deflation occurs, however, it takes time for some wages, prices, and debt agreements to adjust, and so there are some short-run effects.

📊 BUSINESS BRIEF Europe Gets a New Currency

Imagine that you wake up one morning and find that the dollar bills in your wallet are no longer used as money. For many European citizens, something like this happened on January 1, 2002. Prior to that date, all European countries had their own currencies (such as the French franc, Italian lira, and German mark), but many agreed to adopt a common currency called the euro. This currency was issued by the European Central Bank and was effective as of January 1, 2002. Here's how the *New York Times* describes the reform:

> In the biggest currency swap in history, more than 300 million Europeans in 12 countries will start using the euro as their day-to-day money Tuesday, irrevocably casting their old marks, francs, lire, pesetas and other national currencies into the trash can of history.*

People holding the old currency notes (such as francs, liras, and marks) brought them to a bank and exchanged them for an equivalent amount of the new euros. The old currency was removed from circulation and eventually destroyed.

Because these countries had previously used their own units of account, the new standardized currency represented a new unit of account. Businesses needed to change prices into the new currency units, and consumers needed to become used to a completely new set of prices. What was once priced at 100 French francs was suddenly priced at 15 euros. If this sounds like a tremendous sale price, it was not. Workers also saw their bank balances and wages adjusted by a similar amount to reflect the new currency.

*Barry James, John Schmid, and International Herald Tribune, "An Extraordinary Moment for Europe as Euro Becomes Everyday," *New York Times*, January 1, 2002, http://www.nytimes.com/2002/01/01/news/01iht-cash .html.

25.3 THE EQUATION OF EXCHANGE AND THE LONG-RUN EFFECTS OF MONEY

Economists have identified two key monetary factors that influence the total amount of spending in the economy. One factor is the amount of money in the economy—the supply of money (discussed above). The other factor is the speed at which money circulates in the economy. This is how often each dollar is spent during a given year. Economists refer to this as the **velocity of money**—the average number of times that money is spent on final goods and services during a year.

Suppose that all transactions for final goods are paid for with money. Further suppose that the average dollar bill is spent once a week on final goods. In this case, the total annual spending on final goods and services or GDP should be about 52 times

velocity of money The average number of times that money is spent on final goods and services during a year.

"SO I HEAR INFLATION IS REALLY RUNNING RAMPANT. SHOULDN'T BE A PROBLEM THOUGH, RIGHT PENNY? COUGH! -- OBSOLETE -- COUGH!"

© Guy & Rodd/Distributed by Universal Uclick via CartoonStock.com

larger than the money supply, reflecting the fact that there are 52 weeks in a year. The velocity of money is captured in the equation of exchange.

The Equation of Exchange

The **equation of exchange** is an economic equation that shows that the quantity of money (M) times the velocity of money (V) equals the price level (P) times real GDP (Y), which also equals nominal GDP (real GDP measured in quantity of goods and services times prices): $M \times V = P \times Y$ = Nominal GDP. The equation of exchange is used to show the relationship between the money supply, velocity, and nominal GDP. The equation of exchange is

$$M \times V = GDP_{nominal}$$

or

$$M \times V = P \times Y_{real\ GDP}$$

In the previous example, if the money supply is $1 billion and each dollar bill is spent once per week on average, then about $52 billion in transactions would occur each year. The velocity is the speed at which money is circulating throughout the economy. In this example, the velocity is 52. If dollars are spent once every two weeks on average, then velocity would be only 26, and GDP would be $26 billion. This helps us to understand how nominal GDP is determined. It is based on both the quantity of money in circulation (which is determined by Federal Reserve policies) and the velocity at which money is spent (which is determined by the public).

To calculate the velocity of money, we divide nominal GDP ($P \times Y_{real\ GDP}$) by the money supply—that is,

$$V = \frac{P \times Y_{real\ GDP}}{M}$$

We can measure M, P, and Y, and we then solve for V. For this reason, the equation of exchange is called an *identity*: It is true by definition.

The Correlation between the Money Supply and the Nominal GDP

Exhibit 4 shows that in the long run there is a clear correlation between changes in the M2 money supply and nominal GDP. The correlation is not perfect because velocity is fairly stable but not precisely constant in the real world. But it is a reasonably close correlation. The data has been *indexed* so that values equal 100 in 1959. Indexing data is done to put each series at the same starting point, which makes it easier to see percentage changes over time.

The economists who developed the quantity theory of money realized that V was determined by the public. We each get to choose how fast we spend the money in our wallets. They assumed that if the central bank increases the money supply, it will not affect velocity in the long run.

It is easy to see that if an increase in M does not affect V, then the right side of the equation, which is nominal GDP (or $P \times Y$), must increase in proportion to the rise in the money supply. Indeed, the correlation between the money supply and nominal GDP is common sense. If printing more money increases *real* GDP in the long run, then a country like

equation of exchange
An economic equation that shows that the quantity of money (M) times the velocity of money (V) equals the price level (P) times real GDP (Y), which also equals nominal GDP (real GDP measured in quantity of goods and services times prices): $M \times V = P \times Y$ = Nominal GDP.

EXHIBIT 4 The Link between the Money Supply and the Nominal GDP

In the long run, there is a clear correlation between changes in the M2 money supply and changes in nominal GDP. The correlation is not perfect because velocity is not precisely constant in the real world. Shaded areas indicate U.S. recessions. Values indexed to equal 100 in 1959.

Data from: Federal Reserve Bank of St. Louis.

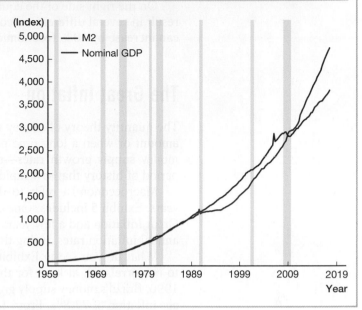

Zimbabwe in the early 2000s or Germany in the early 1920s would have become fabulously wealthy simply by printing lots of cash, especially cash with lots of zeros.

If an increase in *M* does not affect either velocity or real GDP, then it must show up in the form of higher prices. But don't be fooled by the seeming simplicity of the equation of exchange. You will learn that in the short run, changes in the money supply can easily impact any or all of the other three variables (*V*, *P*, and *Y*). This is the all-important business cycle portion of the Venn diagram shown in Exhibit 2.

The Correlation between Money Supply Growth and Inflation

Modern economists are more interested in the rate of inflation than the price level. Therefore, they tend to use a version of the equation of exchange that deals with percentage changes in each variable, not levels. Below, we restate the equation of exchange as percentage rates of change in each of the four variables. Recall that the Greek letter delta (Δ) means "change" and that %Δ means "percentage change." When you have a product of two numbers, such as $M \times V$, the rate of change of the product is approximately the *sum* of the rate of change of each term:*

$$\%\Delta M + \%\Delta V = \%\Delta P + \%\Delta Y$$

If velocity is stable, then the percentage change in velocity is 0%. In that case, the money growth rate equals the inflation rate plus the real GDP growth rate. The sum of inflation and real GDP growth is nominal GDP growth.

The modified version of the equation of exchange shows the link between changes in money, velocity, price levels (that is, inflation), and real GDP. Recall the example where the money supply was $1 billion, each dollar bill was spent once per week on average, and about $52 billion in transactions occurred each year. If the supply of money (*M*) times velocity (*V*) increases by 10% to $57.2 billion ($52 billion + 10% of $52 billion), nominal GDP must increase by 10% to $57.2 billion. If the left side of the equation of exchange ($M \times V$) increases by 10%, the right side (nominal GDP) must do the same.

---

*For those familiar with calculus, the mathematics are a first derivative calculation: $\partial(MV) = \partial M + \partial V + \partial M \partial V$ and $\partial(PY) = \partial P + \partial Y + \partial P \partial Y$. Because $\partial M \partial V$ and $\partial P \partial Y$ are usually very small, they can safely be ignored in most low-inflation examples.

This could occur because the money supply rose by 10% or the velocity of money increased by 10% or some combination of the two.

On the right side of the equation of exchange, a 10% increase in nominal GDP can result in several different outcomes. Prices can increase by 10% (inflation), real GDP can increase by 10% (economic growth), or some combination of the two can occur.

The Great Inflation

The quantity theory of money works best when the money supply changes by a large amount or when a long time period is being looked at. Let's look at some long-term money supply growth rates—real GDP growth rates and inflation rates—during a period of history that saw rapid inflation.

Macroeconomist refer to the years of roughly 1965 to 1982 as Great Inflation years. Exhibit 5 includes some of the lowest- and highest-inflation countries during the Great Inflation and a few years before and after that period. If you look at the average annual inflation rates during this period, you can see why it earned its name.

What do you see in Exhibit 5? The money growth rates and inflation rates seem to be correlated, at least for the high-inflation countries. For example, from 1963 to 1990, Brazil's money supply grew by an average of 77.4% per year and observed average inflation of 77.8%. From 1963 to 1986, Zaire's money supply grew by an average of 29.8% per year while observing an average inflation rate of 30.0%. Real GDP growth rates are usually under 10% per year. Consequently, the link between money

---

EXHIBIT 5   The Great Inflation Period: Evidence of the Equation of Exchange in 14 Countries, 1950 to 1990

Country and Years	Money Growth	GDP Growth	Inflation
Brazil (1963–1990)	77.4%	5.6%	77.8%
Argentina (1952–1990)	72.8	2.1	76.0
Bolivia (1950–1989)	49.0	3.3	48.0
Chile (1960–1990)	47.3	3.1	42.2
Zaire (1963–1986)	29.8	2.4	30.0
Israel (1950–1990)	31.0	6.7	29.4
Iceland (1950–1990)	18.4	4.3	18.8
South Korea (1953–1990)	22.1	7.6	12.8
Portugal (1953–1986)	11.5	4.7	9.9
Great Britain (1951–1990)	6.4	2.4	6.5
United States (1950–1990)	5.7	3.1	4.2
Singapore (1963–1989)	10.8	8.1	3.6
Switzerland (1950–1990)	4.6	3.1	3.2
West Germany (1953–1990)	7.0	4.1	3.0

In high-inflation countries, there is a strong link between growth in the money supply and inflation. In low-inflation countries, the link exists but is weaker because of changes in other variables, such as real GDP and the velocity of money.

Data from: Robert J. Barro, *Macroeconomics* (New York: Wiley, 1993), 167–169.

supply growth rates and inflation is particularly apparent when money supply growth rates are very high, as they were in Brazil and Argentina. In these two countries, both the money supply and the price level doubled about every 15 months.

The correlation is less noticeable for the low-inflation countries. This is because the changes in other variables (velocity and real GDP) also matter. For instance, inflation was significantly less than the money supply growth rate in South Korea and Singapore, partly because their real GDP grew rapidly. In Argentina, inflation was actually higher than money growth because velocity also increased.

Finally, it is often said that *inflation is too much money chasing too few goods*. In fast-growing Singapore and South Korea, there were lots of extra goods, and so the increase in Y (real GDP) on the right side of the equation soaked up some of that extra money, leading to less inflation than one might have expected.

25.4 INFLATION, INTEREST RATES, AND THE FISHER EFFECT

It is often useful to convert nominal variables into a real variable because inflation can distort the meaning of nominal variables. In Chapter 20, you discovered how to convert estimates of nominal GDP into real GDP. Another important example links real interest rates, nominal interest rates, and inflation.

The Fisher Equation

Economist Irving Fisher first explored the differences between real and nominal interest rates. The Fisher equation shows the purchasing power gained from an investment by converting nominal into real interest rates:

$$\text{Real interest rate} = \text{Nominal interest rate} - \text{Inflation}$$

This simple equation allows lenders to calculate the real earnings on their loans. For example, if the interest rate on a bank loan is 4% and inflation is 3%, then the lender will earn a real interest rate of 1%. Suppose that a bank loans $100,000 and the borrower must pay back $104,000 after one year. The nominal interest rate on this loan is 4%. But if inflation is 3%, what used to cost $100,000 now costs $103,000 (on average) when the loan is repaid. Thus, the lender sees a *real* return of only $1,000, or 1% of the $100,000 that was lent. Think of the nominal interest rate as the rate of return in dollars and the real interest rate as the rate of return in purchasing power.

Nominal interest rates cannot fall very far below zero because even cash stored under a mattress earns zero interest. No one would invest in something expected to earn negative 5%. Unlike with nominal interest rates, however, real interest rates can be significantly negative. If inflation is higher than the nominal rate, then the real interest rate is negative. This occurred for some Treasury bonds when the economy was weak during the years following the severe 2008 financial crisis.

The Fisher Effect

Suppose we are not interested in measuring the real rate of return but instead want to understand how the nominal interest rate is determined in the first place. It is then convenient to express the Fisher equation with nominal rates on the left side:

$$\text{Nominal interest rate} = \text{Real interest rate} + \text{Inflation}$$

Fisher effect The idea that a change in expected inflation leads to an equal change in nominal interest rates.

Notice that in this version, we are adding inflation, not subtracting it. This version makes it easier to see how higher inflation can *cause* higher nominal interest rates. In the previous example, the nominal interest rate of 4% equals the real interest rate of 1% plus 3% inflation. In most countries, inflation is positive, and hence the nominal interest rate is higher than the real rate. Moreover, because money is neutral in the long run, an increase in the money supply has no long-run effect on any real variables, including real interest rates.

According to Irving Fisher, higher inflation expectations should affect nominal interest rates and not real rates, at least in the long run. Many factors can influence inflation expectations, but the most important factor is simple—*actual inflation* during recent years. If inflation rises from 2% to 10% and remains at 10% for three or four years in a row, then the public will likely begin to expect 10% inflation going forward.

The **Fisher effect** is the idea that a change in expected inflation leads to an equal change in nominal interest rates (Exhibit 6). In our simple example, if inflation increases to 10%, the nominal interest rate needs to increase to 11% if the real interest rate remains at 1%.

When inflation rises, lenders demand higher nominal interest rates in order to be compensated for the fact that money is losing purchasing power. Borrowers are helped by inflation because it reduces the real burden of their debts. Think about what debtors might do with the money they borrow. If they borrow money to buy a house or business, inflation will tend to cause the value of that asset to rise, which benefits the borrowers, especially because the number of dollars they must repay is generally fixed by the terms of the loan.

Because borrowing and lending are forward-looking transactions, the inflation rate that matters most is the *expected rate of inflation*. Indeed, the Fisher equation is often written with the expected inflation rate and the expected real interest rate. As is discussed after the next business brief, when inflation is unexpected, it redistributes wealth between borrowers and lenders.

Think & Speak Like an Economist

The Fisher equation is often confused with the Fisher effect. The equation is simply a formula showing that the real interest rate equals the nominal interest rate minus inflation. The Fisher effect asserts that a change in inflation or inflation expectations *causes* the nominal interest rate to move by a similar amount and in the same direction.

EXHIBIT 6 The Fisher Effect

Increases in inflation often lead to higher expected inflation, which results in a higher nominal interest rate. Here you see a positive link between the nominal interest rate and inflation.

Data from: Federal Reserve Board.

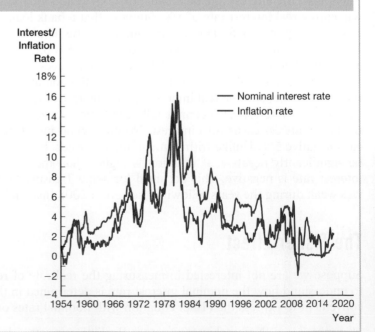

📊 BUSINESS BRIEF The Fisher Effect and the S&L Crisis of the 1980s

As inflation rose during the 1970s, market interest rates also rose due to the Fisher effect. In order to remain competitive, banks increased the interest rates they paid to depositors so that their customers would not seek higher-earning investments elsewhere.

Recall that banks make money by borrowing money from depositors and lending it out at interest rates that are higher than the rates the banks pay to depositors. During a period of high inflation, they can charge high interest on new loans, but they generally cannot raise the interest rate they earn on existing loans.

In the years leading up to the Great Inflation, banks made many 30-year home mortgage loans at low interest rates that were fixed, before double-digit inflation became a problem. When inflation rose, they were stuck with those low-earning mortgages on their balance sheets while they paid higher and higher rates for deposits.

By the early 1980s, many banks began to fail, especially the savings and loan banks (S&Ls) that had concentrated on long-term fixed-rate home mortgage loans. By 1995, nearly one third of S&Ls had gone under. Due to the fixed nature of 30-year loans, banks were unable to realize a positive real return. To be competitive and attract deposits, they needed to pay depositors high interest rates—more than the banks earned on the low-interest mortgage loans that they had made many years earlier. This meant they ended up losing money. In order to make a profit, banks need to earn more on loans than they pay on deposits. During this period, they ended up losing money.

As banks gained a greater understanding of the Fisher effect, they began making more *adjustable-rate mortgages*, which allow the borrower's interest rate to be adjusted up or down automatically any time market interest rates change. When their rates were adjusted upward, however, some homeowners were unable to keep up with their monthly mortgage payments, which contributed to the financial crisis of late 2007 to mid-2009. Sometimes solving one problem creates another one down the road.

Kenneth J. Robinson, "Savings and Loan Crisis: 1980–1990," Federal Reserve History, November 22, 2013, http://www.federalreservehistory.org/Events/DetailView/42.

25.5 SPECIAL TOPICS ON MONEY AND THE PRICE LEVEL

As is shown in Chapter 20, inflation can impose several costs on an economy. The *menu costs* of inflation are the inefficiencies associated with the labor wasted on increasingly frequent price updates during inflationary periods. Inflation can lead to *inflation-induced tax distortions* that raise the effective tax on interest and capital gains and to an *inflation tax* on money as the purchasing power of each dollar falls. Moreover, *unexpected inflation* redistributes wealth and incomes.

Deflation

Given all the costs associated with inflation, you might assume that deflation is a good thing because it brings lower prices for consumers. But many economists are even more worried about deflation than inflation. Deflation occurs when there is a negative inflation rate, which means that prices are declining, on average. Like inflation, deflation can redistribute wealth when it is unexpected. People who are on fixed pensions will

gold standard A system where the value of a currency is set equal to a fixed amount of gold.

benefit because their purchasing power increases. Retirees who receive a fixed payment of $3,000 a month would welcome a decline in prices because the purchasing power of their $3,000 fixed monthly payments would expand. Similarly, deflation may help lenders because it increases the value of the money they get back when a loan is repaid.

Unexpected deflation hurts borrowers because the value of money that needs to be paid back increases in real terms. If deflation is expected, however, borrowers can reasonably require a lower interest rate. As with inflation, many costs and benefits are offset when the deflation is expected.

Japan experienced a very mild deflation from about 1994 to 2013. The United States experienced a brief deflation in 2009 when prices are measured with the Consumer Price Index (but not when inflation is measured using the gross domestic product deflator). A far larger and more damaging deflation occurred in many countries, including the United States, during the Great Depression of the 1930s. The link between deflation and recessions is explored in greater detail in Chapter 26, when we examine the business cycle. Inflation also can lead to zero nominal interest rates, which makes monetary policy less effective.

The Gold Standard

If you went back 100 years in a time machine, you would see consumers buying items with coins and dollar bills that look something like what we use today. One crucial difference between the two eras' currency, however, is that until 1933, all the paper money produced in the United States was a *commodity money* that was "backed" by gold (or sometimes silver). This means that the U.S. government promised to exchange paper money for a specified amount of gold. The **gold standard** is a system where the value of a currency is set equal to a fixed amount of gold.

Deflation was more common in the period prior to 1933, when the United States was on the gold standard. From 1776 to 1933, there was very little change in the average cost of living in the United States. That is quite different from the huge 19-fold increase in price levels during the 84 years after 1933.

The monetary theory of inflation can explain this difference. The money supply increased much faster after 1933, almost certainly because we gradually moved away from the gold standard and adopted a fiat money (see Chapter 24). Globally, the gold standard was common prior to the Great Depression of the 1930s.

Gold is scarce. There is limited supply of it on the planet, and obtaining it is difficult. To increase the money supply under the gold standard, the central bank requires more gold, which is difficult to obtain. Thus, governments adhering to the gold standard are constrained in terms of how much money they can issue. This greatly reduces the growth of the supply of money and in the past kept price levels relatively stable over long periods of time, albeit with frequent year-to-year fluctuations.

Most economists are opposed to a return to the gold standard, even though fiat money is more susceptible to inflation. Although the long-run trend in the price level was flat under the gold standard, the short-run changes were erratic. Years of mild inflation frequently were followed by years of deflation. These year-to-year changes occurred with booms and busts in the discovery of gold, such as the California gold rush of 1849. Changes in money demand were also important. The hoarding of money (and gold) reduced prices during the Great Depression. In fact, the severe deflation of the early 1930s led the United States to start to move away from the gold standard. It left the formal gold standard in 1933, and between 1933 and 1971, only foreigners could convert dollars into gold at the U.S. Treasury. The U.S. dollar's last links with gold ended in 1971.

 POLICY BRIEF Crucified on a Cross of Gold?

Monetary policy is rarely discussed in modern presidential campaigns, but in the late 1800s, it was the number one political issue in the United States. At the Democratic national convention of 1896, William Jennings Bryan delivered what is widely considered to be one of the most powerful political speeches in U.S. history, and it was on the subject monetary policy. At the time, the U.S. dollar was linked to gold, and the country was experiencing deflation, which hurt many people who had borrowed money. Bryan blamed this on the gold standard and proposed adding silver to our monetary system. Bryan argued that adding silver to the monetary system would increase the supply of money and suggested that 16 ounces of silver (a pound) should be treated as the equivalent of an ounce of gold. The boost to the money supply would then be expected to end the deflation that he claimed was hurting key parts of the economy.

In his speech, Bryan used powerful religious symbolism to condemn the deflationary effects of the gold standard:

> Having behind us the producing masses of this nation and the world, supported by the commercial interests, the laboring interests, and the toilers everywhere, we will answer their demand for a gold standard by saying to them: "You shall not press down upon the brow of labor this crown of thorns; you shall not crucify mankind upon a cross of gold."*

A To eliminate the deflation of the 1890s (the "crown of thorns"), William Jennings Bryan proposed adding silver to the gold-backed money supply at the ratio of "16 to 1."

The quote reflects the fact that many workers, farmers, and small business owners had borrowed money that was more difficult to pay back under deflation. Remember that money becomes more valuable during periods of deflation, increasing the burden of a fixed nominal debt. In contrast, bankers who favored the gold standard often benefited from deflation.

Bryan lost the election, but at roughly the same time, major gold discoveries around the world boosted the money supply and ended the deflation. Today, many economists believe that Bryan was correct and that the gold standard led to excessive deflation.

*William Jennings Bryan, "Cross of Gold," *The First Battle: A Story of the Campaign of 1896* (Chicago: W.B. Conkey Company, 1896), 199–206.

Milton Friedman and Monetarism

At the beginning of this chapter, we referenced Milton Friedman, the leader of the *monetarist* school of economic thought, who noted that "[persistent] inflation is always and everywhere a monetary phenomenon." Friedman showed that whenever a country experiences persistent inflation, the root cause is always an excessive increase in the money supply. Friedman focused on many of the key concepts discussed in this chapter, such as the importance of the quantity of money in determining nominal GDP and the link between growth in the money supply and the rate of inflation. He also showed how changes in the quantity of money contributed to the business cycle. In 1976, he was awarded the Nobel Prize in economics for his groundbreaking work in several areas of economics. Perhaps no other economist had as much of an impact on economics in the second half of the 20th century.

Friedman emphasized long-run monetary neutrality—the idea that changes in the money supply do not affect real variables in the long run. But in the short run, an increase in nominal GDP also raises real GDP, and this contributes to the business cycle. In *A Monetary History of the United States, 1867–1960* (1963), Friedman and his coauthor, Anna Jacobson Schwartz, present a wealth of evidence on the link between monetary policy, the money supply, and the business cycle. (These topics are discussed in the next several chapters of this book.)

Friedman also showed that Federal Reserve policy during the early 1930s likely worsened the Great Depression by allowing the money supply to fall sharply. At first, this claim was controversial, but today even the Federal Reserve accepts this view.

Consistent with the concept of monetary neutrality, Friedman showed that in the long run there is no tradeoff between inflation and unemployment, a challenge to the prevailing view at the time that is examined in Chapter 30. Throughout the 1960s, many economists believed that unemployment could be permanently reduced by creating inflation. Friedman showed that people would simply adjust to the changing price level and that unemployment would return to its natural rate. Once higher prices are expected, they are factored into negotiations on wages, rents, and interest rates. The sluggish performance of the economy during the high-inflation 1970s and early 1980s provided strong evidence that Friedman was correct in his view that printing more money would not permanently boost real GDP and reduce unemployment.

After Friedman's death, Paul Samuelson, another Nobel Prize laureate who often disagreed with Friedman, said of his friend and intellectual adversary: "Milton Friedman was a giant. No 20th-century economist had his importance in moving the American economic profession rightward from 1940 to the present."[1]

BUSINESS TAKEAWAY

Businesses must monitor trends in the price level when making decisions on pricing products, negotiating wages, and borrowing money. They need to avoid money illusion and remember that a dollar earned or spent in the future is often worth much less than a dollar today.

High inflation and hyperinflation require businesses to change prices often. When doing business in a country with very high inflation (such as Zimbabwe in 2008), businesses may want to shift their earnings back into dollars as soon as possible to prevent a loss of purchasing power. When inflation is low, businesses can change prices less often. One way for firms to protect themselves against unexpected changes in inflation is to adjust contracts automatically to the price level. This is called indexing. To keep real wages stable, for example, some companies offer pay increases that are indexed to the CPI. Similarly, banks offer adjustable-rate mortgages that are indirectly linked to the inflation rate by being tied to short-term interest rates.

Firms must pay attention to the underlying causes of inflation, especially when doing business internationally. High inflation rates have often occurred in places that have severe government budget problems. A deteriorating budget situation should be viewed as a red flag that high inflation may be on the way, particularly in developing countries.

CHAPTER STUDY GUIDE

25.1 MONEY SUPPLY, INFLATION, AND THE QUANTITY THEORY OF MONEY

Inflation is an increase in the overall price level that results in a decline in the value or purchasing power of money. **Deflation** is a decrease in the overall price level that results in an increase in the value or purchasing power of money. The **value of money** is the amount of

goods and services that can be bought with money—the purchasing power of money, which equals 1/Price level. The **quantity theory of money** is the theory that a given change in the money supply leads to a proportional change in the price level in the long run. The **long run** refers to the time necessary to make all adjustments to economic circumstances. In the long run, it is real prices that matter, and changes in the quantity of money have no impact on real prices. One way to envision the quantity theory of money is to imagine the money supply suddenly doubling without any changes in the amount of goods or services. In this case, the price level would eventually double, as would the nominal demand for money. **Money demand** is the amount of money that people want to hold. It varies directly with the price level. A doubling of the money supply will lead consumers with **excess cash balances** (the amount by which the supply of money in circulation exceeds the demand for money) to get rid of the extra money by spending it. The increase in spending drives up the price level and drives down the value of money, which equals 1/Price level. The value of money is determined by shifts in the supply and demand for money.

25.2 THE NEUTRALITY OF MONEY AND THE CLASSICAL DICHOTOMY

Monetary neutrality is the idea that changes in the money supply do not affect real variables in the long run. Changes in the money supply, for example, do not change the number of cars and homes that are built. The only long-run effect is proportionately higher prices. Excessive increases in the supply of money can result in hyperinflation. **Hyperinflation** is extremely high rates of inflation and a rapid decline in the value of a nation's currency. The **classical dichotomy** is the division of macroeconomics into two areas—real variables and nominal variables. The classical dichotomy suggests that monetary policy affects only nominal variables in the long run, not real variables. The **business cycle** is short-run alternating periods of economic expansion and recession. In the short run, the business cycle is impacted by both nominal and real variables. Changes in the money supply may have real effects on the short-run business cycle but impact inflation only in the long run. **Money illusion** in an incorrect assumption that nominal variables represent real values. A real-world application of the money neutrality concept occurs during a **currency reform**—the replacement of one currency by another. This often is done to bring nominal prices back to a reasonable level.

25.3 THE EQUATION OF EXCHANGE AND THE LONG-RUN EFFECTS OF MONEY

The **velocity of money** is the average number of times that money is spent on final goods and services during a year. The **equation of exchange (quantity equation)** is an equation that shows that the quantity of money (M)

times the velocity of money (V) equals the price level (P) times real GDP (Y), which also equals nominal GDP (real GDP measured in quantity of goods and services times prices): $M \times V = P \times Y$ = Nominal GDP. In the long run, there is a strong correlation between the money supply and nominal GDP.

25.4 INFLATION, INTEREST RATES, AND THE FISHER EFFECT

The Fisher equation defines real interest rates as follows: Real interest rate = Nominal interest rate − Inflation. The **Fisher effect** is the idea that a change in expected inflation leads to an equal change in nominal interest rates. To see this, it is convenient to express the Fisher equation with nominal rates on the left side, so the Nominal interest rate = Real interest rate + Inflation.

25.5 SPECIAL TOPICS ON MONEY AND THE PRICE LEVEL

Deflation redistributes wealth and most notably harms borrowers. The **gold standard** is a system in which the value of a currency is set equal to a fixed amount of gold. Milton Friedman was one of the most influential economists of the second half of the 20th century and is best known as the leader of the monetarist school of thought. He showed that monetary policy has an important impact on both inflation and the business cycle.

TOP TEN TERMS AND CONCEPTS

1. Inflation and Deflation
2. Value of Money
3. Quantity Theory of Money
4. Supply and Demand for Money
5. Monetary Neutrality
6. Hyperinflation
7. Classical Dichotomy
8. Velocity of Money
9. Equation of Exchange (Quantity Equation)
10. Fisher Equation and Fisher Effect

STUDY PROBLEMS

1. According to the quantity theory of money, what would happen to prices when a helicopter drops a large amount of cash on a city? What would happen to the value of money? Demonstrate this using the long-run money supply and money demand model. What impact does such a helicopter drop have on real GDP?

2. ![capitol icon] According to the quantity theory of money, what does a government policy that confiscates half of all money in a society do to consumer prices? What happens to the value of money? Demonstrate this using the long-run money supply and money demand model. What impact does such a policy have on real GDP in the long run?

3. Construct a FRED graph showing the Consumer Price Index and the M2 money supply since 1965. Which increased at a faster rate? What is the most likely explanation for the difference in rate of increase?

4. ![chart icon] Describe the concept of money illusion. What is one piece of evidence that money illusion exists? Describe the concept of indexation. How can indexation help overcome the money illusion problem?

5. Explain the concept of monetary neutrality. Is it a short-run concept or a long-run concept?

6. According to the equation of exchange, when the money supply is $1 billion, nominal GDP equals $4 billion, and the price level equals 2.

   a. What is the velocity of money?

   b. What is real GDP?

   c. What happens to nominal GDP if the money supply doubles while the velocity of money remains unchanged?

7. In the long run, what occurs when the money supply grows faster than real GDP and the velocity of money is constant?

8. ![chart icon] In 1993, Mexico issued a new peso that was equal in value to 1,000 old pesos. This is a modern example of what?[2]

9. During the Great Inflation of roughly 1965 to 1982, what pattern existed between the growth rate of the money supply and inflation? What other factors cause the relationship to be less than perfect?

10. The fallacy of composition says that what is true for the individual may not be true for society as a whole. Apply this fallacy to the concept of excess cash balances. Can individuals get rid of excess cash? How about society as a whole? What happens if people try to do so?

11. Solve each of the following using the Fisher equation:

   a. Nominal interest rates when real interest rates and expected inflation are both 2%

   b. The real interest rate when nominal interest rates are 10% and expected inflation is 5%

   c. Expected inflation when real interest rates are zero and the nominal interest rate is 6%

   d. Nominal interest rates when real interest rates and expected inflation are both 3%

12. In each of the following scenarios, discuss whether the person benefits, is harmed, or is unaffected by unexpected inflation.

   a. A person with a loan with a fixed interest rate

   b. A person with a loan with an interest rate that changes with inflation

   c. A baseball player on a 10-year contract

   d. A mall owner with tenants on 10-year contracts

   e. A retiree who receives a pension with fixed payments

   f. A retiree who receives Social Security payments that are indexed to inflation

13. ![capitol icon] During the 1970s and 1980s, Argentina had very high inflation. How do you think this affected the velocity of money in Argentina during the period when inflation increased? Explain why. Include a discussion of the inflation tax in your answer.

14. Discuss the pros and cons of returning to the gold standard. Do most economists favor the gold standard or a fiat money system?

15. ![capitol icon] What was the direct cause of German hyperinflation from 1920 to 1923? What underlying causes led the German government to adopt policies that led to hyperinflation?

16. ![capitol icon] What economic problem motivated William Jennings Bryan to deliver his famous 1896 "Cross of Gold" speech? How did Bryan propose to solve this problem? (Use the term *money supply* in your answer.)

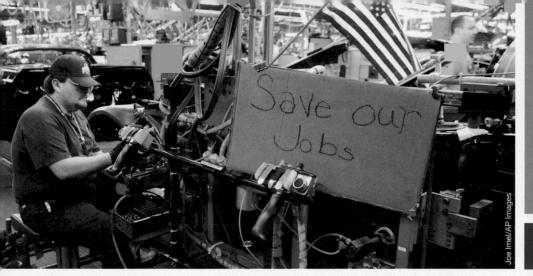

Joe Imel/AP Images

26 CHAPTER

∧ The aggregate supply and demand model can help explain unemployment and the business cycle.

Aggregate Supply and Aggregate Demand

A Model of the Business Cycle

In mid-1929, the U.S. economy seemed to be doing great. Unemployment was low, and prices were stable. New inventions like automobiles, home appliances, and electric power were leading to rapid industrialization and prosperity. The booming economy is one reason that the 1920s were called the "Roaring 20s." Then, in the fall of 1929, the economy suddenly went into a steep nosedive. The U.S. unemployment rate soared to 25% by 1933, and nominal GDP fell by 50%.

Most Americans have heard of the Great Depression of 1929 to 1941, but few understand what caused it. After all, in 1933 the United States had about the same human resources, capital goods, and natural resources as it had in 1929. It seemed as though a mysterious force had suddenly and swiftly crippled the economy. Although many were confused about what went wrong at the time, economists today refer to that mysterious force as *falling aggregate demand*—the total amount of spending on all goods and services in the economy.

Everyone reading this book witnessed the effects of falling aggregate demand during the Great Recession of late 2007 to mid-2009. There was a sizable decline in real GDP during the Great Recession, although it was far less devastating than the one that occurred during the Great Depression. In this chapter, we develop a model that explains why recessions and expansions happen.

Chapter Learning Targets

- Apply the aggregate supply and aggregate demand (AS/AD) model to explain business cycles and the price level.

- Describe what determines aggregate demand and why it shifts.

- Use the AS/AD model to explain how demand and supply shocks create business cycles and inflation.

- Contrast different government economic stabilization policies with the market's long-term ability to self-correct.

- Demonstrate how the AS/AD model can be used to make sense out of a wide variety of economic shocks.

26.1 THE AGGREGATE SUPPLY AND AGGREGATE DEMAND MODEL

After the Great Depression, economists sought to develop an economic model that could explain what had happened to the economy. This proved difficult. Microeconomic theory assumes that wages adjust so that the labor market is in equilibrium, but in the 1930s, many workers were willing to supply labor and yet were unable to find jobs. A new model was required to explain the ups and downs of the business cycle and deep depressions.

The **aggregate supply and aggregate demand (AS/AD) model** is a macroeconomic model that explains major economic changes that impact the entire economy, with a focus on short-run effects. The AS/AD model helps us make sense out of significant macroeconomic events (such as the Great Depression) but also ordinary recessions, booms, inflation, cyclical unemployment, and corrective governmental policies.

The model, which is developed more fully later in the chapter, focuses on the relationship between the price level and real GDP. The basic AS/AD model looks deceptively simple. As you can see in Exhibit 1, the graph looks a lot like ordinary supply and demand. But the aggregate supply and aggregate demand curves differ from ordinary supply and demand curves. In microeconomics, supply and demand curves involve the price and quantity of a single *specific* good or service. In contrast, the AS/AD model involves the *overall price level and total output*. For any single good, consumers can substitute other goods when a relative price changes. Because the AS/AD model covers *aggregate* output, however, there is no longer any substitution effect. Consumers cannot simply switch from relatively high-priced goods to low-priced alternatives when the price level *for all goods* changes.

The AS/AD model was created to explain periods such as the early years of the Great Depression. Between 1929 and 1933, the price level fell by almost 25%, real GDP fell by roughly 30%, and nominal GDP fell by nearly 50%. As you will discover, when both the price level and output are falling, it is a good indication that aggregate demand is declining. **Aggregate demand (AD)** is the total demand for all goods and services at a given price level. Aggregate demand captures total spending in the

aggregate supply and aggregate demand (AS/AD) model A macroeconomic model that explains major economic changes that impact the entire economy, with a focus on short-run effects.

aggregate demand (AD) The total demand for all goods and services at a given price level.

EXHIBIT 1   The Aggregate Supply and Aggregate Demand Model Provides Insights into the Causes of the Great Depression of the 1930s

In 1929, the U.S. economy was booming. The Great Depression of the 1930s was caused by a decline in aggregate demand. During the Depression, both real GDP (Y) and the price level fell. In this graph, the base year for the price index and real GDP is 1929. Real GDP is in billions of dollars.

economy. Economists refer to a sudden and large shift in the aggregate demand curve as a **demand shock**.

Exhibit 1 demonstrates the sharp decline in aggregate demand that occurred during the first four years of the Great Depression. Notice that when aggregate demand declines, the economy experiences a fall in both real GDP and the price level. The short-run aggregate supply (SRAS) curve likely did not decline. A similar but milder pattern occurred in the United States during the Great Recession when real GDP fell by 3% and prices dipped slightly.

In order to understand why aggregate demand declined, we need to first develop the model more fully. We begin by examining **aggregate supply (AS)**, which is the total supply for all goods and services at a given price level. As you have learned, short-run economic outcomes are often very different from long-run outcomes, and this distinction is especially important in analyzing aggregate supply.

> **demand shock** A sudden and large shift in the aggregate demand curve.
>
> **aggregate supply (AS)** The total supply for all goods and services at a given price level.
>
> **long-run aggregate supply (LRAS)** The total supply of all goods and services in the long run after all wages and prices have had time to adjust.
>
> **natural rate of output** The output level where all wages and prices have adjusted and the economy is at full employment.

Long-Run Aggregate Supply

Long-run aggregate supply (LRAS) is the total supply of all goods and services in the long run after all wages and prices have had time to adjust. The long-run aggregate supply curve is vertical, as is shown in Panel A of Exhibit 2. Notice that the natural rate of output can occur at any price level in the long run.

Price-Level Changes Do Not Impact Society's Productive Capacity You might wonder why the long-run aggregate supply curve is vertical when supply curves for individual goods slope upward. In simple terms, this is because in the long run, the size of GDP is determined by the productive capacity of the economy, not by the price level. When the price of a single product rises, firms will respond by producing more of the product to maximize profits. But an increase in the overall price level is very different. If all prices rise by 10% in the long run, then the inputs into the production process also become 10% more costly. In real terms, wages and prices have not changed at all. In Chapter 25, you learned about *monetary neutrality*, which predicts that increases in the money supply will lead to higher prices in the long run but will not lead to higher real GDP.

The Natural Rate of Output Determines the Location of the Long-Run Aggregate Supply The location of the long-run aggregate supply (LRAS) is determined by the same factors that determine a society's productive capacity and economic growth (see Chapter 22). Each country has a different productive capacity. After the productive potential of an economy is determined, that potential becomes the point where the vertical long-run aggregate supply curve intercepts the *x*-axis. The output level associated with the LRAS curve is called the **natural rate of output**—the output level where all wages and prices have adjusted and the economy is at full employment. And this is the output level where unemployment is at its natural rate and the economy is at its long-run equilibrium.

In Chapter 21, we saw that roughly 5% of the U.S. labor force is unemployed when the overall economy is at its long-run equilibrium. At this point, there is no cyclical unemployment, and overall unemployment is at the natural rate. In a recession, however, output is *below* the natural rate, and unemployment is above the natural rate. In 2009, for example, the unemployment rate rose to 10%, and the level of real GDP fell sharply to a point about 5% below the natural rate of output. The economy was operating to the left of the LRAS curve. We were in a recession.

Shifts in the Long-Run Aggregate Supply Curve Fortunately, the basic framework developed for explaining long-run economic growth and productivity also describes factors that shift the long-run aggregate supply curve. If the natural rate

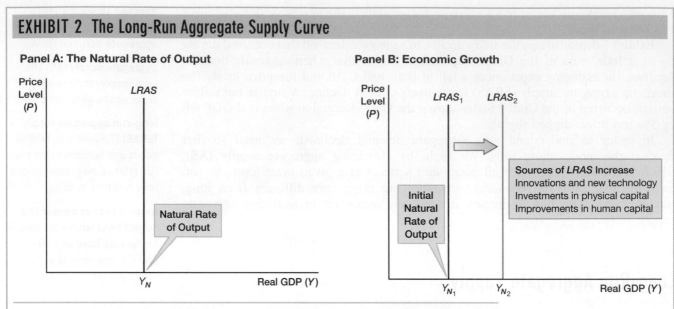

EXHIBIT 2 The Long-Run Aggregate Supply Curve

Panel A: The Natural Rate of Output

Panel B: Economic Growth

The long-run aggregate supply curve is a vertical line at the natural rate of output, as shown in Panel A. This reflects the fact that long-run output is determined by society's productive capacity and not by the price level. Economic growth shifts the long-run aggregate supply curve to the right as the natural rate of output expands, as shown in Panel B. When studying the business cycle, we assume that the LRAS curve does not shift.

of output determines the location of the long-run aggregate supply curve, changes in the natural rate of output will shift the LRAS curve. As is discussed in detail in Chapter 22, the three most important sources of economic growth include innovation and new technology, investments in physical capital, and improvements in human capital. The factors that lead to long-run economic growth also cause the LRAS to shift to the right over time, as is shown in Panel B of Exhibit 2.

A Dilemma: Why Does Aggregate Demand Impact the Business Cycle?

When analyzing booms and recessions, economists hold constant all the factors that cause long-run economic growth. After all, the productive capacity of the U.S. economy in 1933 was probably at least as great as it was during the economic boom in 1929. The real problem was that the economy was operating far below its potential. Therefore, when considering the business cycle, we assume that the long-run aggregate supply does not shift and instead focus on short-run aggregate supply and aggregate demand. This allows us to explain issues such as unemployment, recessions, and changes in inflation.

This short-run focus leads to a dilemma. On the one hand, it appears that a big drop in aggregate demand contributed to the Great Depression. This implies that the aggregate supply curve is not vertical (as shown in Exhibit 2), at least not in the short run. On the other hand, we know that printing lots of money to boost aggregate demand will lead to higher prices in the long run and not lead to economic growth. This dilemma is another example of how long-run economic outcomes are often different from short-run outcomes.

Why the Short-Run Aggregate Supply Curve Is Different

We have seen that the long-run aggregate supply is vertical and therefore is not going to be able to tell us why changes in aggregate demand cause business cycles. Instead, the key to the business cycle seems to be the way that demand shocks interact with the upward-sloping short-run aggregate supply curve. The **short-run aggregate supply (SRAS)** is the total supply of all goods and services in the short run before all wages and prices have had time to adjust. We will not be able to explain why declines in aggregate demand cause recessions unless we can first explain the all-important fact that the SRAS curve seems to have a positive slope, as is shown in Exhibit 3.

Economists have come up with three explanations for the positive slope of the SRAS curve—sticky wages, sticky prices, and money illusion. The key to these explanations is that *in the short run, wages and prices are slow to adjust.*

Sticky Wages The wage rate earned by workers usually changes infrequently, sometimes only once per year. Some workers sign labor contracts that specify their hourly pay rates over the next two or three years. Economists call the slow adjustment in wages *sticky wages* because they tend to stick at one level for an extended period of time.

Because wages are sticky and slow to adjust, an increase in the price level will make it profitable for firms to increase production when the prices of their products increase. Imagine that the price of pizzas goes up by 10% but the wages of workers in the pizza shop stay the same. The shop owner might respond to the higher pizza prices by hiring more workers. Now imagine that thousands of prices rise, all across the economy. When the price level rises and wages are stable, many companies will hire more workers, and real GDP will tend to increase in the short run.

In 2009, just the opposite happened. The average hourly wage rate rose by about 3%, but the price level declined slightly, which led to an increase in real wages. In response, many companies laid off workers, and the unemployment rate rose to a peak of 10% in October 2009. Then wage growth slowed to 2% per year over the next few years, and inflation rose closer to 2%. Unemployment began falling as wages slowly adjusted toward equilibrium.

Sticky Prices In addition to wages being sticky, most prices also are sticky. Imagine a pizza shop that has just spent a lot of money printing a new set of menus. If there is an increase in consumer spending, the shop owner may not want to redo the menus right away. Instead, he or she may increase production rather than prices.

Not all prices need to be sticky for the short-run aggregate supply curve to be upward sloping. Prices may become less sticky as more restaurants and retailers move to electronic pricing systems that allow prices to be changed quickly and easily. But if there are enough sticky prices in an economy, then an increase in total spending often will generate substantially higher output in the short run, with only a relatively small amount of extra inflation. This means the SRAS curve slopes upward with both higher output and higher prices in the short run.

Money Illusion Recall from Chapter 25 that **money illusion** is an incorrect assumption that nominal variables represent real variables. Those suffering from money illusion tend to work harder when inflation pushes up their nominal wages, even if their real wage is falling. Conversely, when the price level declines, workers should be willing to take a corresponding cut

short-run aggregate supply (SRAS) The total supply of all goods and services in the short run before all wages and prices have had time to adjust.

money illusion An incorrect assumption that nominal variables represent real variables.

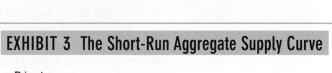

EXHIBIT 3 The Short-Run Aggregate Supply Curve

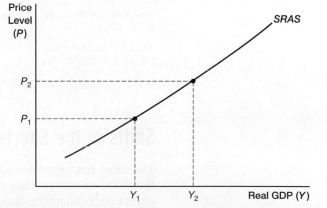

The short-run aggregate supply curve slopes upward, suggesting that increases in the price level result in an increase in real GDP supplied in the short run.

in nominal wages. After all, their cost of living has fallen. But because of money illusion, many workers may not accept a nominal wage cut. Firms respond by reducing hours worked instead.

Periods of *deflation* often lead to lots of unemployment. If prices of finished goods are falling but companies are not able to reduce costs by cutting wages, they may respond by laying off workers. As a result, real GDP declines when a falling price level moves the economy down along the SRAS curve. This is exactly what happened in the 1930s, when prices fell sharply. Workers initially resisted pay cuts, companies responded by reducing their labor force, and unemployment soared to 25%. As the price level continued to fall, unemployed workers eventually accepted lower pay.[1]

The extent of sticky wages, sticky prices, and money illusion is an important unresolved issue in macroeconomics. However, modern economists believe that it is unrealistic to expect *perfect* wage and price flexibility and that the best way to avoid a depression is to prevent the deflation from occurring in the first place

📊 BUSINESS BRIEF Sticky Prices at L.L.Bean

Several economic studies have examined the stickiness of prices for various retailers. One study examined catalog prices over a 35-year period at catalog retailers such as L.L.Bean and Recreational Equipment, Inc. (REI). The study found that the nominal prices of a dozen goods (including shoes, blankets, and a duffle bag) tended to be fixed in excess of a year. Price changes occurred more frequently during periods of high inflation.[*]

A subsequent study looked at over 350 different products covering 70% of consumer spending for a 3-year period and found half of those prices to change less than once every 4.3 months. At one extreme were gasoline stations, which adjusted prices about every 18 days. At the other extreme were coin-operated laundries, which adjusted prices once every 6.6 years. The prices of men's haircuts, newspapers, and taxis changed less than once every 20 months.[†]

What explains these differences? Most of the products that frequently change in price are commodities where supply shifts are common. As with gasoline, very flexible prices were seen with raw food items like tomatoes (adjustments every 24 days) and eggs (every 30 days). In contrast, catalog prices (such as those for L.L.Bean) changed less frequently—partially reflecting menu costs.

Coin-operated laundries have remarkably stable prices for two reasons. First, the supply side of the industry is stable. The biggest cost is rent on the building, a price that generally changes infrequently. In addition, adjusting laundry prices is costly because it requires the physical coin mechanism in washers and dryers to be reengineered, whereas a gas station can change prices digitally.

*Anil Kashyap, "Sticky Prices: New Evidence from Retail Catalogs," *Quarterly Journal of Economics* 110, no. 1 (1995): 245–274.

†Mark Bils and Peter Klenow, "Some Evidence of the Importance of Sticky Price," *Journal of Political Economy* 112, no. 5 (2004): 947–985.

Shifts in the Short-Run Aggregate Supply Curve

The short-run aggregate supply curve will shift when the cost of doing business across the entire economy changes significantly. For example, when oil prices spike upward, costs rise for many businesses, and this decreases aggregate supply, shifting the SRAS curve to the left. Conversely, a decline in wages and rents reduces business costs, increases aggregate supply, and shifts the SRAS curve to the right. These shifts are demonstrated in Exhibit 4. The trick is to think about things that would increase aggregate supply *at any given price level*.

EXHIBIT 4 Shifting the Short-Run Aggregate Supply Curve

Panel A: Decrease in Short-Run Aggregate Supply

Price Level (*P*)

SRAS₂   *SRAS₁*

Sources of Decrease
Increases in wages
Increases in price of raw materials
Decrease in productivity

Real GDP (*Y*)

Panel B: Increase in Short-Run Aggregate Supply

Price Level (*P*)

SRAS₁   *SRAS₂*

Sources of Increase
Decreases in wages
Decreases in price of raw materials
Increase in productivity

Real GDP (*Y*)

A decrease in aggregate supply shifts the short-run aggregate supply curve to the left (Panel A), and an increase in aggregate supply shifts the curve to the right (Panel B).

Changes in Nominal Wages When businesses need to pay workers higher nominal wages, business costs increase, and firms across the economy respond by producing fewer goods and services. In turn, short-run aggregate supply shifts leftward (declines). For example, the supply of pizzas would decline after a massive increase in the minimum wage rate, affecting workers at pizza shops. Conversely, when nominal wages decline, business costs decline, and short-run aggregate supply increases, shifting to the right.

Changes in the Prices of Raw Materials and Resources The cost of raw materials also has a major impact on the cost of doing business across the entire economy. Energy prices are especially volatile. A rise in fuel costs helps firms like Exxon and Shell but hurts the far more numerous firms that use oil and gas. This results in a decline in short-run aggregate supply. In contrast, a decrease in the price of other resources (such as a decline in rents) increases short-run aggregate supply.

Changes in Productivity Increases in productivity often result from technological innovation, which reduces the cost of doing business. For example, when American Telephone and Telegraph replaced human telephone operators with electronic switching, the supply of telephone services increased dramatically, and prices fell sharply. At AT&T's peak in the late 1940s, it employed over 350,000 telephone operators. Today, there are roughly 10,000.[2]

Similarly, long-distance and wireless phone calls went from being a luxury to an everyday occurrence. These sorts of productivity improvements reduce production costs and increase aggregate supply.

26.2 AGGREGATE DEMAND

Most economists agree that both the Great Depression and Great Recession were caused by declines in aggregate demand. We have addressed one part of that explanation—why the short-run aggregate supply curve is positively sloped. Now we need to address the other part of the model—what determines aggregate demand. Recall that aggregate demand is the total demand for all goods and services at a given

EXHIBIT 5   The Aggregate Demand Curve

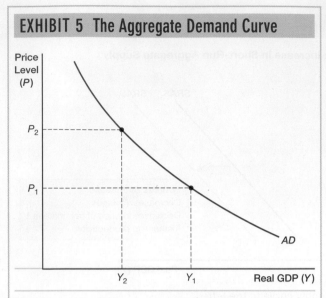

The aggregate demand curve is downward sloping, suggesting that an increase in the price level results in a decrease in the quantity of real GDP demanded.

price level. Aggregate demand captures total spending in the economy. To understand the concept, we need to consider why it slopes downward and what causes it to shift.

Three Reasons That the Aggregate Demand Curve Slopes Downward

Economists generally use an *expenditure approach* to aggregate demand to explain why the aggregate demand curve slopes downward. You may recall that

$$GDP = C + I + G + NX$$

That is, GDP equals consumer spending (C), investment (I), government purchases (G), and net exports (NX). It turns out that total spending is inversely related to the price level because three of the four components of aggregate demand (C, I, and NX) are inversely related to the price level. Consequently, the aggregate demand curve has a negative slope, as is shown in Exhibit 5.

The Wealth Effect and Consumption If the price level increases, you can afford fewer goods. Imagine that you have $20,000 in cash that you plan to use to purchase a car. If the price of a new automobile doubles, you may no longer be able to afford the new car you planned to buy with your existing cash. Similarly, if the prices of *all* goods on average double, you can afford less with your existing $20,000 in cash. This is because the real quantity of consumption spending declines with increases in the price level, *ceteris paribus*. In Exhibit 5, we move along the aggregate demand curve, up and to the left. Under this scenario, the purchasing power of cash is cut in half. In general, an increase in price level decreases the purchasing power of money holdings. Conversely, a decrease in the price level increases the purchasing power of your money: If the price level suddenly drops, you might be able to use your $20,000 to buy a nicer car or even two cars for the family. *Ceteris paribus,*

- ↑Price level → ↓Purchasing power of money and↓Consumption
- ↓Price level → ↑Purchasing power of money and↑Consumption

Think & Speak Like an Economist

Both aggregate demand curves and ordinary demand curves are downward sloping but for different reasons. Ordinary demand curves slope downward primarily because of the ability of consumers to switch to substitute goods. Because aggregate demand includes all goods and services, there can be no substitution effect when the price level changes.

The Interest-Rate Effect and Investment Let's say that you head to the car lot with your $20,000 in cash and find that the car you want now costs only $15,000. Many consumers in this situation will choose to buy the same car and save the $5,000. Other things being equal, when the price level declines, which lowers the cost of living, consumers will increase their saving. In Chapter 23, you learned that an increase in saving (the supply of loanable funds) lowers interest rates. A lower price level allows for more saving, and more saving lowers interest rates.

The final link is between interest rates and investment. When interest rates fall due to more saving, the cost of borrowing declines, and businesses tend to borrow more to invest in new capital equipment. More investment spending on buildings, delivery trucks, machines, and other capital goods occurs when the cost of borrowing declines. For example, if a pizza shop owner can borrow money at 5% instead of 10% or 15%, he or she is more likely to decide to expand to a larger building with new pizza ovens. The reverse is true if the price level rises. *Ceteris paribus,*

- ↑Price level → ↑Interest rates and↓Investment spending
- ↓Price level → ↓Interest rates and↑Investment spending

The Net Export Effect Lower price levels tend to increase net exports. First, when the price level falls in the United States, this *directly* causes U.S. goods to become relatively less expensive for the rest of the world. Other things being equal (including economic conditions in the rest of the world and exchange rates), other countries will wish to purchase more U.S. exports, and the United States will wish to import less from the rest of the world. Recall that net exports equal exports minus imports. In this scenario, net exports will increase. Second, previously we saw that lower prices tend to reduce interest rates. As you will discover in Chapter 32, lower interest rates tend to depreciate the exchange rate, which also tends to increase exports and decrease imports. The end result is that the price level is inversely related to net exports. In summary,

∧ In the United States, consumption is the largest component of aggregate demand.

$$\downarrow \text{Price level} \rightarrow \uparrow \text{Net exports, } ceteris\ paribus$$

$$\uparrow \text{Price level} \rightarrow \downarrow \text{Net exports, } ceteris\ paribus$$

What Causes the Aggregate Demand Curve to Shift?

The wealth effect, interest rate effect, and net export effect explain the negative relationship between total spending and the price level along a *given* aggregate demand curve, holding other things equal. In a dynamic economy, other things often do change, and the AD curve can itself shift. And if the AD curve shifts leftward, as it did during the Great Recession (as shown in Exhibit 1), then falling prices may not increase spending. This leads us to a key problem in business cycle theory: How can we explain the cause of aggregate demand shifts that seem to trigger booms and recessions?

An almost infinite number of factors can cause the aggregate demand curve to shift over time. Here we focus on five key factors—expectations, changes in monetary policy, changes in fiscal policy, financial distress and uncertainty, and global economic conditions. The trick is to think about things that would change aggregate spending *at any given price level*.

Expectations Computer chip maker Intel is less likely to expand if the company expects a recession in the near future. Because most companies feel the same way, pessimistic expectations for the economy's *future* performance often cause a drop in *current* aggregate demand. With more pessimistic expectations, the aggregate demand curve shifts to the left at any given price level.

Conversely, Intel is more likely to decide to expand if the company is optimistic about the economy. When expectations improve, spending on consumer and investment goods tends to increase at any given price level. This shifts the aggregate demand curve to the right, as is shown in Exhibit 6. One popular indicator of public sentiment is the stock market. Stock prices tend to rise when investors feel optimistic. When rapid technological advances at the advent of the Internet age led to extremely high stock market values, consumers and businesses felt more optimistic, which boosted aggregate demand.

Changes in Monetary Policy Central banks such as the Federal Reserve in the United States often adjust the money supply to impact aggregate demand. **Monetary policy** involves changes in the money supply and interest rates by the central bank,

monetary policy Changes in the money supply and interest rates by the central bank, often with the goal of influencing employment and inflation.

EXHIBIT 6 Shifting the Aggregate Demand Curve

Panel A: Decrease in Aggregate Demand

Panel B: Increase in Aggregate Demand

Sources of Decrease
Pessimistic expectations
Decrease in money supply
Decrease in government spending
Increase in taxes
Financial distress and uncertainty
Global stagnation

Sources of Increase
Optimistic expectations
Increase in money supply
Increase in government spending
Decrease in taxes
Financial optimism and clarity
Global growth

A decrease in aggregate demand shifts the curve to the left, and an increase in aggregate demand shifts the curve to the right.

often with the goal of influencing employment and inflation. Monetary policy has an important impact on aggregate demand. When there is an increase in the money supply, the public will have *excess cash balances*. As was discussed in Chapter 25, consumers respond by spending more, reducing their excess cash balances. Higher spending on goods and services directly increases aggregate demand at any given price level. If consumers spend the excess balances on assets such as stocks and bonds, then asset prices rise, which indirectly boosts aggregate demand. In Chapter 27, we will see that an increase in the money supply also can reduce interest rates. This is another mechanism by which an expansionary monetary policy can boost aggregate demand.

Changes in Fiscal Policy Governments impact aggregate demand through changes in taxes and spending. **Fiscal policy** is changes in government spending and taxation by the federal government, often with the goal of influencing employment and inflation. Recall that government spending is one of the four components of GDP (along with consumer spending, investment, and net exports). If government spending increases, it can lead to higher aggregate demand at any given price level, and this shifts the AD curve to the right. Government also can impact aggregate demand through changes in taxes. If the government cuts taxes, people and businesses tend to spend more on consumption and investment. If taxes increase, then consumption and investment tend to fall, *ceteris paribus*, and the AD curve shifts leftward

Financial Distress and Uncertainty Financial distress also impacts aggregate demand. This occurred during both the Great Depression and the Great Recession because many banks and other financial institutions failed due to bad loans. Banks lost enormous amounts of money and responded by setting much tighter lending standards. These restrictions on lending further weakened business conditions and made it especially hard for individuals and small businesses to access credit, reducing aggregate

fiscal policy Changes in government spending and taxation that often are aimed at influencing employment and inflation.

demand. In contrast, when financial distress and uncertainty are reduced, optimism prevails, and investment spending increases. Periods of extremely high optimism and high asset prices are sometimes called "bubbles"—a metaphor suggesting they might not last long.

Global Economic Conditions Global economic conditions have an important impact on aggregate demand in the United States. When the global economy is booming, the demand for exports tends to rise as foreigners spend more on goods and services, including those made in the United States. This leads to an increase in net exports. Conversely, a global recession tends to reduce demand for a country's exports, reducing aggregate demand.

> **Think & Speak Like an Economist**
>
> Many people confuse aggregate demand and consumer spending. U.S. aggregate demand also includes spending on investment, government output, and foreign country spending on U.S. exports.

The global economy is interconnected, so a severe economic recession can spread from one country to another. Most developed countries experienced a recession after the 2008 banking crisis. Small countries such as Singapore and the Netherlands have a high level of international trade relative to their GDP and thus are strongly affected by global economic shocks. Another good example is Canada. The Canadian banking system is more stable than the U.S. system and has not had a major financial crisis in the past 100 years. Nonetheless, because Canada sends over 70% of its exports to the United States, the recession that followed the 2008 U.S. banking crisis led to a sharp drop in demand for Canadian exports such as cars and auto parts made in Ontario, pushing Canada into recession as well.[3]

If Falling Aggregate Demand Caused the Great Depression, What Caused Falling Aggregate Demand?

The negative demand shock of 1929 to 1933 was probably the biggest in U.S. history. But what caused aggregate demand to fall sharply during the early 1930s? It turns out that most of the factors just summarized played a role:

- Consumers and businesses were pessimistic, especially after the stock market crash in October 1929.

- Monetary policy was contractionary. The money supply declined sharply.

- With the economy already in a recession, President Herbert Hoover responded by increasing taxes in 1932 due to concerns about the budget deficit.

- There was a great deal of financial distress as thousands of banks failed, causing many people to lose their life savings.

- Global economic conditions worsened, so demand for exports declined. Lawmakers around the world passed laws to restrict international trade.

Comparing the Great Depression and the Great Recession

The Great Recession of late 2007 to mid-2009 is the closest modern equivalent to the Great Depression of the 1930s. Although not nearly as devastating as the Great Depression of the 1930s, it was an unusually deep and long-lasting recession. Furthermore, it exhibited some important characteristics of the Great Depression, such as a major banking panic and nominal interest rates that fell close to zero, which had not occurred since the 1930s. The European economies were severely impacted, which also occurred in the 1930s.

EXHIBIT 7 Comparing the Great Depression to the Great Recession

	Great Depression (early years, 1929–1933)	Great Recession (2007–2009)
Peak Unemployment Rate	25%	10%
Real GDP	−30%	−3%
Bank Failures	9,000	<100
Stock Price Decline (Dow Jones)	89%	54%

Although a decline in aggregate demand caused both the Great Depression of the 1930s and the Great Recession of late 2007 to mid-2009, the Great Depression was far more severe.

Even though the Great Recession was severe, it pales in comparison to the hardship inflicted on society by the far more severe Great Depression of the 1930s. During the Great Depression, the unemployment rate peaked at 25%. It remained at over 10% for a decade and averaged over 15%. In the Great Recession, the unemployment rate peaked at 10% and then began falling. During the Great Depression, real GDP fell by roughly 30%. During the Great Recession, real GDP fell by roughly 3%. During the Great Depression, roughly 9,000 banks failed (although most were small). Fewer than 100 banks failed during the Great Recession, and depositors were protected by the Federal Deposit Insurance Corporation (FDIC). On the other hand, the so-called shadow banking system discussed in Chapter 24 was hit hard by the Great Recession. Stock prices as measured by the Dow Jones Industrial Average (the Dow) plunged by 89% in the Great Depression. In contrast, stock prices fell by 54% in the Great Recession. These facts are summarized in Exhibit 7, which focuses on the early years of the Great Depression.

BUSINESS BRIEF Car Sales Rocked by Great Depression and Great Recession

Do you dream of driving a Stutz or a Peerless? Would owning a Pierce-Arrow be a signifier of your success? Unless you are an antique car collector, probably not. These three American automobile manufacturers specialized in luxury vehicles that were the height of sophistication in the 1920s. By 1939, all three were defunct. Automobile sales declined by 75% during the Great Depression, and luxury brands took the biggest hit.

During the Great Recession, automobile sales also fell sharply, although by less than during the Great Depression. General Motors, for example, stopped making Pontiac, Hummer, and Saturn brands but continued to sell other models and employ workers. Automobile sales recovered much more quickly after the Great Recession. Less than a decade after U.S. auto sales collapsed in 2008, they were nearing record highs. In contrast, automakers Stutz, Peerless, and Pierce-Arrow never returned to their former glory.

˙G. N. Georgano, ed., *Encyclopedia of American Automobiles*, 2nd ed. (London: Rainbird Reference Books, 1971), 153–154.

∨ Many luxury automakers failed during the Great Depression.

Science History Images/Alamy Stock Photo

26.3 TWO CAUSES OF RECESSIONS AND TWO CAUSES OF INFLATION

The aggregate supply and aggregate demand model is powerful tool for understanding major macroeconomic problems. In this section, we use the model to explain the primary causes of recessions and rising inflation. In the next section and in subsequent chapters, the model is used to demonstrate how an economy might move out of a recession. Because the focus is on short-run effects, we assume that the long-run aggregate supply curve does not shift. Let's begin by examining two possible causes of a recession.

Two Causes of a Recession

Exhibit 8 illustrates two possible causes of a recession. We include the long-run aggregate supply (LRAS) curve as a benchmark that indicates the natural rate of unemployment. Points to the left of the LRAS curve reflect the lower level of output and the higher level of unemployment experienced in a recession.

- *Decline in aggregate demand.* In the United States, the most common cause of a recession is a decline in aggregate demand, shown in Panel A of the exhibit. Notice that both output and prices decline.

- *Decline in aggregate supply.* Less frequently, recessions are caused by a sharp decline in aggregate supply. Notice that output declines but prices increase. In many ways, a decline in aggregate supply is even worse than a decline in aggregate demand because it leads to two problems—higher inflation and higher unemployment.

EXHIBIT 8 Two Causes of a Recession

Most recessions are caused by a decline in aggregate demand (Panel A). This occurred in both the Great Depression and the Great Recession. A recession also can be caused by a decline in short-run aggregate supply (Panel B).

In both of these cases, the economy moves to a point where aggregate demand equals short-run aggregate supply (point E_2) to the left of the long-run aggregate supply. At this short-run equilibrium, the economy is in a recession because real GDP is below the natural rate of output and unemployment is high. A healthy economy will operate at points on the LRAS curve.

Two Causes of Inflation

Inflation can be caused by either an increase in aggregate demand or a decrease in aggregate supply. These two possibilities are shown in Exhibit 9. In both panels, the price level increases, which means inflation.

- *Increase in aggregate demand and demand-pull inflation.* Panel A of the exhibit shows that inflation can occur from an increase (shift) in aggregate demand. When aggregate demand increases, the price level rises. **Demand-pull inflation** is inflation that results from a positive aggregate demand shock. This type of inflation often occurs when large increases in the money supply lead to increases in aggregate demand and higher price levels.

- *Decline in short-run aggregate supply and cost-push inflation.* Panel B demonstrates a decline in aggregate supply. We have just seen that declining aggregate supply can cause a recession. Now we see that it also can cause inflation. Suppose there is a sharp increase in energy prices, wages, or business taxes. A significantly higher cost of doing business pushes the aggregate supply curve up and to the left. Notice that prices rise while output falls and the economy moves into a recession (point E_2). **Cost-push inflation** is inflation that results from a negative aggregate

demand-pull inflation Inflation that results from a positive aggregate demand shock.

cost-push inflation Inflation that results from a negative aggregate supply shock.

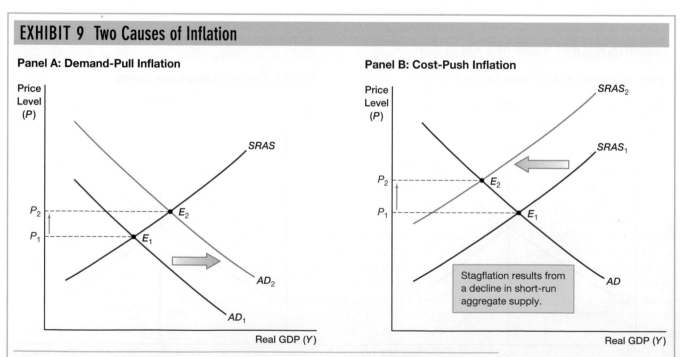

EXHIBIT 9   Two Causes of Inflation

Panel A: Demand-Pull Inflation

Panel B: Cost-Push Inflation

Demand-pull inflation is inflation that results from a positive aggregate demand shock that leads to expanding output (Panel A). Cost-push inflation is inflation that results from a negative aggregate supply shock (Panel B), resulting in stagflation.

supply shock. A **supply shock** is a sudden and large shift in the aggregate supply curve. It reflects significant changes in the economy's ability to produce goods and services. In the United States, the most common cause of supply-side inflation is rising oil prices.

> Never Reason from a Price Change: The AS/AD Model

As has been discussed throughout the book, when examining market outcomes, we never reason from a price change. Instead, we must first consider what caused the price to change. Was there a shift in demand or a shift in supply? For the same reason, we never reason from a change in the overall price level. For instance, suppose that the rate of inflation rises sharply. What does this tell us about the economy? Will output go up or down? As is shown in Exhibit 10, the economy could be in either a recession or a boom, depending on whether the higher inflation was caused by less aggregate supply (stagflation) or more aggregate demand (boom). Conversely, if the price level falls, it does not necessarily mean we are in a recession. It might also be due to strong productivity growth, which shifts the aggregate supply curve to the right.

As with basic supply and demand, we avoid the reasoning from a price change error by first considering what *caused* the price level to change (either a shift in aggregate supply or aggregate demand). However, there is one interesting difference. The biggest mistake in basic supply and demand is to assume that when price is high, quantity will be low. People assume that price changes are due to supply shifts because in many individual markets the supply curve is more volatile. For example, unpredictable weather causes the supply of oranges to change much more than the demand.

In macroeconomics, the opposite occurs. Demand shocks seem to be more important than supply shocks, so many people make the mistake of simply assuming that any price-level change reflects a demand shock. They assume that an economic boom will be associated with high inflation and a recession will be associated with lower inflation. This usually is true but not always. When aggregate supply changes, a boom can see lower inflation, and a recession may see higher inflation.

Stagflation

In the United States, the rate of inflation is usually higher during booms than recessions because its business cycle is dominated by demand shocks. Therefore when the country was hit by sharp declines in aggregate supply in 1973–1974 and 1979–1980, a new term was coined—*stagflation*. **Stagflation** is a decrease in output with rising inflation that generally is associated with high inflation and high unemployment at the same time. In many ways, it is the worst of both worlds. Imagine losing your job while the prices of food, rent, and gasoline are increasing. Stagflation coincides with cost-push inflation, as is shown in Panel B of Exhibit 9.

As is shown in Chapter 3, a major and unexpected disruption in production can cause a supply shock. For instance, a major natural disaster can make production more costly and reduce short-run aggregate supply. In large diversified economies such as the United States and Japan, a supply shock is rarely big enough to create a business cycle. In 2006, for instance, Hurricane Katrina caused severe damage to New Orleans but did not create a recession. In 2011, an even more devastating earthquake and tsunami struck Japan. Certain areas were hit very hard, but the overall economy was not severely affected. In general, declines in one region of a large country are often offset by growth in other areas.

Small economies, however, are more susceptible to supply shocks. Many small developing countries rely heavily on a few agricultural products, and so bad weather or natural disasters can have a major impact on their GDP. In 2010, a major earthquake plunged Haiti into a severe recession. The earthquake damage caused aggregate supply to decline sharply for the entire economy, and output fell by more than 5%.

supply shock A sudden and large shift in the aggregate supply curve.

stagflation A decrease in output with rising inflation that generally is associated with high inflation and high unemployment at the same time.

BUSINESS BRIEF Price of Oil Tripled as OPEC Cut Production

Not all supply shocks are the result of natural disasters. In late 1973, the Organization of the Petroleum Exporting Countries (OPEC) slashed oil production and imposed an oil embargo on the United States and other industrialized countries. Arab and Persian Gulf members of OPEC (including Iran, Iraq, Kuwait, and Saudi Arabia)

cut off oil exports in retaliation for Western support of Israel in its victory in the Yom Kippur War, a part of the on-going Arab-Israeli conflict. Global oil prices soared from $3 to over $10 a barrel as a result of the reduction in supply.*

The cut in production of oil was a negative supply shock that had an immediate impact on the U.S. economy. Stagflation developed as real GDP fell by 0.5% in 1974 and as inflation rose from 6.2% in 1973 to 11% in 1974.† Panel B of Exhibit 10 shows the effect of an adverse supply shock. Note that the aggregate supply curve shifts to the left and the new equilibrium involves higher prices and lower real output.

*Leonard Silk, "Economic Scene; OPEC Failing as Cartel," *New York Times*, March 10, 1983, http://www.nytimes .com/1983/03/11/business/economic-scene-opec-failing-as-cartel.html.

†*Data from:* U.S. Bureau of Economic Analysis and U.S. Bureau of Labor Statistics.

∧ A major disruption in oil supply can result in a supply shock and stagflation.

26.4 STABILIZATION POLICIES AND THE SELF-CORRECTING MECHANISM

Recessions don't last forever. In the United States, the average recession lasts about one year, although unemployment often remains high in the early stages of the recovery. But what causes most recessions to be relatively brief? There are two basic answers—expansionary government policies and the economy's ability to self-correct when something goes wrong.

Two Cures for a Recession

Let's say we have fallen into a recession. What do we do? The economy has two ways out of a recession—by increasing aggregate demand or by increasing short-run aggregate supply. Notice that in Exhibit 10, the economy *starts* in a recession where output is less than society's productive capacity. In order to recover, the short-run equilibrium must move to the right, closer to the long-run aggregate supply.

Stabilizing the Economy by Increasing Aggregate Demand In Panel A of the exhibit, policymakers attempt to boost aggregate demand to move the economy out of a recession, using two primary tools. A central bank (such as the Federal Reserve) can increase the money supply and cut interest rates to stimulate aggregate demand. Fiscal policymakers can increase aggregate demand by lowering taxes or increasing government spending. Because policymakers are given the responsibility of maintaining a healthy economy, stabilization policies are the focus of the next several chapters.

Stabilizing the Economy with an Increase in Aggregate Supply Panel B of the exhibit shows that the economy also can move out of a recession with an increase in

EXHIBIT 10 Two Cures for a Recession

Panel A: Stabilizing the Economy by Increasing Aggregate Demand

Panel B: Stabilizing the Economy with an Increase in Aggregate Supply

In both figures, the economy starts in a recession at point E_1. The economy can move out of a recession by increasing aggregate demand (Panel A) or with an increase in short-run aggregate supply (Panel B).

aggregate supply. Even without government action to boost aggregate demand, aggregate supply will automatically tend to increase over time, and this can help an economy to recover from a recession. Unfortunately for the unemployed, the aggregate supply-side recovery does not happen quickly, as is shown in the next section.

The Self-Correcting Mechanism in a Recession and Inflationary Boom

The economy has a natural tendency to correct itself—particularly in the long run. The **self-correcting mechanism** is the process by which short-run aggregate supply adjusts to return output to the natural rate after either a recession or an inflationary boom. To see how this self-correcting mechanism works, we need to consider what happens to wages and rents when the economy is in a recession. Recall that sticky wages and prices were a big part of the aggregate supply and aggregate demand model, but wages and prices don't stay fixed forever. After they adjust, the short-run aggregate supply curve shifts, and the economy returns to the long-run equilibrium.

Consider a recession caused by a decline in aggregate demand. In Panel A of Exhibit 11, the economy begins at the natural rate of output. We observe a decline in aggregate demand that moves the economy into a recession (E_2). Many workers have lost jobs, and unemployment is above the natural rate. Many offices and storefronts at the mall are unused. After losing their jobs, workers initially are reluctant to take a pay cut. Similarly, when offices or mall stores become empty, landlords initially are reluctant to lower rents.

As time passes, however, unemployed workers and landlords with empty space eventually relent and accept lower wages and rents. When this occurs, the cost of doing business declines, and aggregate supply increases. As the short-run aggregate

self-correcting mechanism
The process by which short-run aggregate supply adjusts to return output to the natural rate after either a recession or an inflationary boom.

EXHIBIT 11 The Impact of Aggregate Demand Shifts in the Short Run and Long Run

Panel A: Self-Correction after a Decrease in Aggregate Demand (Recession)

Panel B: Self-Correction after an Increase in Aggregate Demand (Boom)

In both figures, the economy is initially operating at point E_1. In Panel A, the economy experiences a decline in aggregate demand. In the short run, the economy experiences a recession and moves to point E_2. In the long run, short-run aggregate supply increases due to the self-correcting mechanism moving equilibrium to point E_3. In Panel B, the economy experiences an increase in aggregate demand. In the short run, the economy enters an inflationary boom and moves to point E_2. Wages and rents increase. In the long run, Short-run aggregate supply decreases and the self-correcting mechanism moves equilibrium to point E_3.

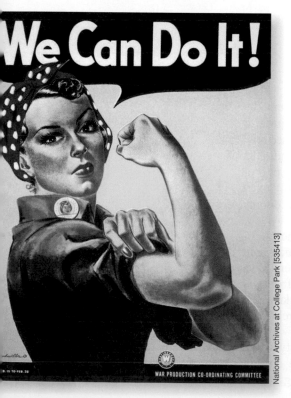

∨ Women like Rosie filled factories during World War II, when unemployment fell to an all-time low.

National Archives at College Park [535413]

supply curve shifts to the right, the economy slowly returns back to the natural rate of output. One example of this process occurred in 2011, well into the Great Recession (which bottomed out in mid-2009). The United Automobile Workers (UAW) union agreed to major wage concessions, including a starting rate of only $14 per hour for new auto workers, which was about half the wage of older workers.[4]

Some economists worry that the self-correcting mechanism takes too long and favor aggressive government policies to boost aggregate demand during a recession. Others prefer that the economy be allowed to adjust naturally to economic shocks, without government intervention. We return to the debate over the role of monetary and fiscal policy in stimulating aggregate demand in the chapters ahead.

Sometimes output moves *beyond* the natural rate. How is this possible? After all, the natural rate of output is sometime described as the economy's "potential." How can an economy produce more than its potential? In the long run, it cannot. But for a short period of time, companies can press employees to work more overtime than usual. They may need to pay higher wages ("overtime pay") to do so. In addition, companies may hire frictionally and structurally unemployed workers who would have trouble finding a job during normal times. In some cases, a booming economy will draw in workers who previously were not in the workforce at all. For example, during World War II, millions of men were drafted into the army, and women were recruited to replace them in factories that produced war materials. Unemployment fell to an all-time low of just over 1% in 1943, and labor force participation rose sharply for women.

Panel B of Exhibit 11 considers the short-run and long-run effects of an increase in aggregate demand that pushes the short-run equilibrium to beyond the natural rate. The economy begins at point E_1 when aggregate demand curve increases. This causes the economy to move to point E_2. At point E_2, two changes have occurred: Output has risen above the natural rate, and the price level has increased. This is an *inflationary boom*.

In the long run, workers and businesses will gradually push wages and prices upward to reflect the higher level of aggregate demand. For instance, when prices start to rise, workers might demand pay increases, and landlords may request higher rents.

As prices begin to rise, companies are willing to pay higher wages in order to ensure they have an adequate workforce to meet the growing level of aggregate demand. As nominal wages and prices adjust upward, the short-run aggregate supply curve shifts leftward, which is a decrease in short-run aggregate supply. Here, the self-correcting mechanism works in the opposite direction from the adjustment during a recession.

26.5 THE AS/AD MODEL: THE BIG PICTURE

In learning all the ways that aggregate supply and demand can interact in both the short run and long run, it's important not to lose sight of the big picture. Try to keep in mind that all the macroeconomic concepts you have learned thus far fit together like pieces of a puzzle. Chapter 22 explains long-run economic growth, which helps us to understand the position of the long-run aggregate supply curve and also the reasons that it shifts. Chapter 21 introduces the natural rate of unemployment, which helps determine the natural rate of output. In contrast, Chapters 24 and 25 discuss the role of money in the economy. Money supply has a tremendous impact on aggregate demand. Furthermore, the neutrality of money helps explain why changes in aggregate demand affect prices only in the long run and thus why the long-run aggregate supply is vertical.

Macroeconomics is easier to learn if you focus on how the pieces fit together and how one chapter of this book relates to another. Consider the variables on each axis of the aggregate supply and aggregate demand model—real GDP (Y) and the price level (P). These two key variables have also been discussed in earlier chapters. You might recall that the identical two variables appear on the right side of the equation of exchange, where the product $P \times Y$ is nominal GDP:

$$M \times V = P \times Y$$

Each change discussed using the equation of exchange also can be described in the AS/AD model. For instance, increases in either M (the money supply) or V (velocity of circulation) will tend to increase aggregate demand for goods and services. When total spending rises, it can increase P (the price level), Y (real output), or both variables.

Now we can see where the AS/AD model comes into the picture. When we studied the quantity theory of money, we learned that an increase in the money supply will boost prices in the long run. But in the short run, output may increase. How much will output rise? That's what the slope of the short-run aggregate supply curve tells us. In the long run, the aggregate supply curve is vertical. This means that when the money supply or velocity increases and aggregate demand shifts to the right, the long-run effect is merely higher prices, with no change in real output. This is the implication of a vertical long-run aggregate supply curve and also the neutrality of money. In contrast, in the short run an increase in spending will lead to *both* increased output and inflation.

One of the best ways to see the big picture is to look at some real-world examples of shifts in aggregate supply or aggregate demand, covering all four possible cases—expansions in aggregate demand and supply and contractions in aggregate demand and supply.

Four Historical Shifts in Aggregate Supply and Aggregate Demand

To understand the AS/AD model, you need to be able to identify four types of shifts and evaluate the ways that each case affects the economy. Here are well-known examples of each type summarized in Exhibit 12.

Expansionary Supply Shock in the Late 1800s Panel A of the exhibit considers the case of a fall in the price level and an increase in real GDP. What sort of shock could cause that pattern? If aggregate supply increases rapidly and aggregate demand is stable, then prices should fall and output should increase. Perhaps the most famous example of this situation occurred during the late 1800s, when the U.S. economy

EXHIBIT 12   Four Shifts in the Aggregate Supply and Aggregate Demand Model

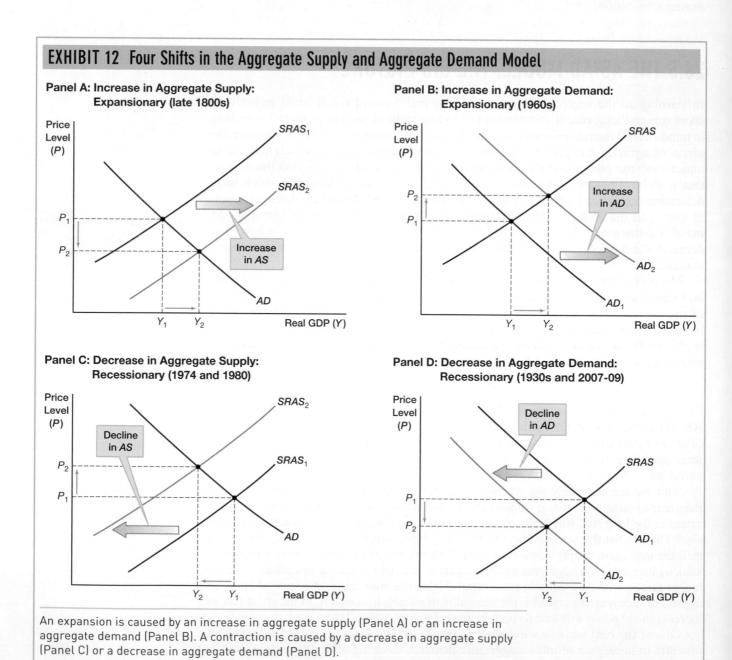

An expansion is caused by an increase in aggregate supply (Panel A) or an increase in aggregate demand (Panel B). A contraction is caused by a decrease in aggregate supply (Panel C) or a decrease in aggregate demand (Panel D).

grew rapidly despite falling prices between 1865 and 1896. Both short- and long-run aggregate supply increased as manufacturing boomed in the United States and immigration led to rapid growth in the labor force. The U.S. economy grew rapidly despite falling prices.

This sort of shock gets less attention for several reasons. First, it leads to higher output and lower inflation, which generally are desirable. In contrast, the other three shifts in aggregate supply and aggregate demand lead to economic problems such as high inflation and recession. Second, it tends to occur gradually. Just as a house can burn down much faster that a house can be built, a negative supply shock (like a war, oil embargo, or natural disaster) can destroy an economy's potential much faster than gradual improvements can boost its potential.

Expansionary Demand Shock in the 1960s Panel B of the exhibit shows the years between 1964 and 1969, when the United States saw a big increase in real GDP, falling unemployment, and higher inflation. What sort of shock could cause this pattern? As can be seen from the graph, an increase in aggregate demand would cause both prices and output to rise at the same time. And that is exactly what happened in the late 1960s.

The primary cause of the increase in aggregate demand was expansionary monetary and fiscal policy. An increase in the money supply combined with increases in government spending on both domestic programs (the Great Society) and military activities (the Vietnam War) caused aggregate demand to increase. At first, wages and prices did not rise rapidly, despite the strong demand. Real GDP growth increased strongly. But inflation also rose somewhat and at an increasing rate as the decade progressed. This was the beginning of the Great Inflation of roughly 1965 to 1982.

Contractionary Supply Shock in the 1970s Panel C of the exhibit shows an increase in the price level (and rate of inflation) in the midst of a contraction. What type of shock could cause this sort of inflation? It happened in the United States in 1973–1974 and 1979–1980. Recall that the problem occurred immediately after the OPEC oil cartel sharply reduced production and boosted oil prices. In 1974 and 1980, the country experienced both a recession and higher inflation at the same time, which is stagflation.

When inflation raises the cost of doing business, companies may respond by reducing output. As a consequence, higher inflation does not necessarily mean that the economy is booming. It depends why the rate of inflation has increased.

Contractionary Demand Shock in the 1930s and 2007–09 Panel D of the exhibit considers the case where both prices and output decrease. What sort of change would produce this combination? At the beginning of this chapter, we discussed the two most famous negative demand shocks: In the Great Depression of the 1930s, the price level sharply decreased, whereas in the Great Recession of 2007–2009, prices fell only slightly.

In Chapter 30 we will see that some contractionary demand shocks lead not to outright deflation but rather to a lower rate of inflation. Recall that the case where prices keep rising but at a slower rate than before is called *disinflation*. For now, just remember that although a negative demand shock can sometimes lead to deflation, often it leads only to disinflation. Later, we explore this distinction in more detail.

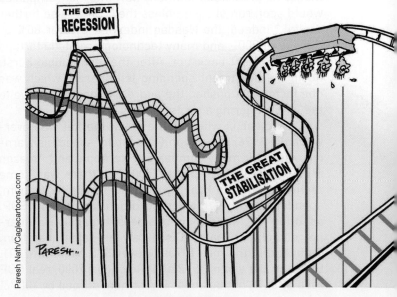

Paresh Nath/Caglecartoons.com

CASE STUDY The 1990s Tech Boom: Irrational Exuberance and a Surge in Productivity

The 1990s was a period of dynamic growth in high tech industries, which caused aggregate supply to grow rapidly. Although home computers were still relatively rare and the Internet was in its infancy, stock market investors were ecstatic about future opportunities. The most speculative part of the market was the Nasdaq stock market, which is dominated by newer companies involved in the Internet and other high tech areas. The Nasdaq quadrupled in price over only a few years. Like the roaring 1920s, the 1990s was a decade of great optimism as entrepreneurs such as Mark Cuban, current owner of the Dallas Mavericks, became rich seemingly overnight. In 1998, Broadcast.com, a company Cuban cofounded, saw its stock price rise nearly 250% on its first day of trading. This made 100 employees instant millionaires. The next year, Yahoo! bought Broadcast.com for $5.7 billion. Stories like this were common during the late 1990s.

In the mid-1990s, Federal Reserve chair Alan Greenspan ominously warned of "irrational exuberance" in the stock market: "Low inflation implies less uncertainty about the future, and lower risk premiums imply higher prices of stocks. . . . But how do we know when irrational exuberance has unduly escalated asset values, which then become subject to unexpected and prolonged contractions?"*

Was Alan Greenspan correct to be concerned over excessively high stock prices? Were stocks overvalued? The answers are unclear. Many people think that the stock market was overvalued in March 2000 when the Nasdaq peaked at over 5,000, nearly four times higher than it had been at the time of Greenspan's comment.

Just a week after the Nasdaq hit its peak, *Barron's* magazine predicted that many new Internet companies would soon run of cash unless they could raise further capital.† Indeed, the Nasdaq index fell by over 80% by the end of 2002, and many technology-related startups eventually went bankrupt. After the tech bubble burst, business investment spending fell sharply, which was one factor that pushed the aggregate demand curve to the left, triggering a recession.

Less clear is whether the stock market was overvalued in 1996, when Alan Greenspan issued his warning. After all, many companies like Apple and Amazon rebounded strongly in the 2000s, so there was some reality behind the hype. During the 1990s tech boom, spending on investment rose much faster than GDP, as often occurs during business expansions. Internet equipment maker Cisco saw its sales soar from $4 billion in the mid-1990s to over $20 billion in 2001. Between the end of 1992 and the end of 2000, real GDP rose by 35%, but business investment surged by 100%.‡

EXHIBIT 13 The Impact of the 1990s Tech Boom on Aggregate Supply and Aggregate Demand

In the 1990s, the dramatic increase in spending on tech investments boosted aggregate demand in the economy. At the same time, improved productivity from tech investments shifted both the short-term aggregate supply and the long-term aggregate supply to the right. Output rose strongly, while prices increased only modestly.

Overall productivity grew at a rate of 2.9% per year between 1995 and 2005, nearly double the rate of the two previous decades. The combination of optimistic expectations and a surge in productivity had two impacts on the economy. First, high stock prices and a genuine sense of optimism stimulated aggregate demand. Second, the gains in productivity resulted in favorable shifts in both the short-run and long-run aggregate supply curves. Exhibit 13 demonstrates the impact of increases in both aggregate supply and aggregate demand during the 1990s. The end result was low inflation, low unemployment, and an economic boom.

Growth in high tech industries slowed sharply after 2000. In the aftermath of the tech bubble, real business investment fell in 2001 and 2002, and stock prices of tech companies fell sharply. Unlike the stock market crash of 1929, which was followed by the Great Depression, the bursting of the tech bubble was followed by a mild recession with the unemployment rate peaking at 6.3%. The mildness of the 2001 recession suggests that the expansionary policies prevented the worst-case outcome. We explore such policies further in later chapters.§

*Alan Greenspan, "The Challenge of Central Banking in a Democratic Society," speech delivered at the American Enterprise Institute for Public Policy Research, Washington, DC, December 5, 1996, http://www.federalreserve.gov/boarddocs/speeches/1996/19961205.htm.

†Jack Willoughby, "Burning Up," *Barron's*, March 20, 2000, http://online.barrons.com/news/articles/SB953335580704470544.

‡James Rogers, "Cisco's Boom and Bust: A History Lesson," *TheStreet*, August 9, 2011, http://www.thestreet.com/story/11212172/1/ciscos-boom-and-bust-a-history-lesson.html.

§Dale W. Jorgenson, Mun S. Ho, and Kevin J. Stiroh, "A Retrospective Look at the U.S. Productivity Growth Resurgence," Staff Report No. 277, Federal Reserve Bank of New York, February 2007, https://www.newyorkfed.org/medialibrary/media/research/staff_reports/sr277.pdf.

BUSINESS TAKEAWAY

Business cycles can have a big impact on a firm's profitability, especially for companies in highly cyclical industries such as housing and automobiles. The aggregate supply and aggregate demand model developed in this chapter can help firms to understand the business cycle better by allowing them to make informed decisions about prices and output. This model shows that a recession can be caused by either a demand shock or a supply shock. Both result in a decline in business conditions, but only a demand shock also reduces inflation. The business cycle also affects investment decisions. Companies need to forecast future growth in GDP in order to make wise choices about how and when to invest in physical capital, human capital, and research and development.

Government policy also affects business cycles, so firms must be clear about what policy steps are being taken to affect aggregate demand. When in a recession, recovery is likely to occur more rapidly when there is expansionary monetary and fiscal policy than it will if the economy relies on the self-correcting mechanism.

The AS/AD model also highlights the role played by wage and price stickiness and by money illusion. Firms must account for the fact that workers have money illusion when negotiating pay rates. Prices also tend to be sticky because they can be costly to change. If prices are too sticky, however, then businesses may lose profits when economic conditions change rapidly. Electronic pricing will be increasingly important in the future, allowing companies to respond to changing market conditions almost instantly.

CHAPTER STUDY GUIDE

26.1 THE AGGREGATE SUPPLY AND AGGREGATE DEMAND MODEL

The **aggregate supply and aggregate demand (AS/AD)** model is a macroeconomic model that explains major economic changes that impact the entire economy, with a focus on short-run effects. The AS/AD model looks at how various economic shocks impact the relationship between the price level and the level of real GDP. The model can be used to show that the Great Depression of the 1930s resulted from a decline in **aggregate demand (AD)**—the total demand for all goods and services at a given price level. Aggregate demand captures total spending in the economy. A **demand shock** is a sudden and large shift in the aggregate demand curve. **Aggregate supply (AS)** is the total supply for all goods and services at a given price level. It turns out that aggregate supply has a very different slope in the long run than in the short run. **Long-run aggregate supply (LRAS)** is the total supply of all goods and services in the long run after all wages and prices have had time to adjust.

The long-run aggregate supply curve is vertical and represents the **natural rate of output**—the output level where all wages and prices have adjusted and the economy is at full employment. The price level and inflation do not impact the long-run aggregate supply curve. Shifts in the LRAS curve reflect changes in society's productive capacity. In contrast, the **short-run** aggregate supply (SRAS) is the total supply of all goods and services in the short run before all wages and prices have had time to adjust. The short-run aggregate supply curve slopes upward because of sticky wages and prices, as well as **money illusion**—an incorrect assumption that nominal variables represent real variables. When the price level rises along a given aggregate supply curve, firms respond by increasing output. SRAS can shift due to changes in wages, the price of raw materials, and productivity.

26.2 AGGREGATE DEMAND

Along a given aggregate demand curve, the price level and real GDP are inversely related due to the wealth effect, the interest rate effect, and the net export effect. The aggregate demand curve can shift due to changes in expectations, **monetary policy** (changes in the money supply and interest rates by the central bank, often with the goal of influencing employment and inflation), **fiscal policy** (changes in government spending and taxation that often are aimed at influencing employment and inflation), financial distress, and global economic conditions.

26.3 TWO CAUSES OF RECESSIONS AND TWO CAUSES OF INFLATION

Most recessions in the United States are caused by a decline in aggregate demand, but they also can be caused by a decline in aggregate supply. **Demand-pull inflation** is inflation that results from a positive aggregate demand shock, and **cost-push inflation** is inflation that results from a negative aggregate supply shock. **Stagflation** is a decrease in output with rising inflation that generally is associated with high inflation and high unemployment at the same time. Stagflation occurs from an adverse **supply shock**, a sudden and large shift in the aggregate supply curve that reflects significant changes in the economy's ability to produce goods and services. This shifts the short-run aggregate supply curve leftward, reduces output, and raises inflation. More commonly, inflation is caused by rising aggregate demand. Thus, a rising price level might be caused by increased aggregate demand (which is expansionary for output) or by falling aggregate supply (which is contractionary for output). Before analyzing the impact of a higher price level, policymakers need to ask why the price level increased and never reason from a price change.

26.4 STABILIZATION POLICIES AND THE SELF-CORRECTING MECHANISM

When an economy is in a recession, aggregate demand can be increased by a central bank (such as the Federal Reserve) increasing the money supply and cutting interest rates and by fiscal policymakers lowering taxes or increasing government spending. Even without government actions, in the long run the economy has an ability to correct itself through an adjustment in short-run aggregate supply. The **self-correcting mechanism** is the process by which short-run aggregate supply adjusts to return output to the natural rate after either a recession or an inflationary boom. This reflects the fact that wages and prices are flexible in the long run and that changes in the price level have no long-run impact on output.

26.5 THE AS/AD MODEL: THE BIG PICTURE

The previous macroeconomic chapters form the building blocks of the aggregate supply and aggregate demand model. The long-run aggregate supply curve is consistent with the natural rate of output. In the equation of exchange, the two variables on the right: P (the price level) and Y (real GDP) are the two axes in the AS/AD model. An adverse demand shock decreases AD and decreases both P and Y. Historical examples show all four of the possible shifts in aggregate supply and aggregate demand curves, illustrating that the AS/AD model can be used to explain any type of macroeconomic shock.

TOP TEN TERMS AND CONCEPTS

(1) Aggregate Supply and Aggregate Demand (AS/AD) Model

(2) Aggregate Demand (AD) and Aggregate Supply (AS)

(3) Long-Run Aggregate Supply (LRAS)

(4) Short-Run Aggregate Supply (SRAS)

(5) What Causes SRAS and LRAS to Shift?

(6) What Causes AD to Shift?

(7) Two Causes of Recessions and Two Causes of Inflation

(8) Demand-Pull Inflation and Cost-Push Inflation

(9) Stabilization Policies

(10) Self-Correcting Mechanism

STUDY PROBLEMS

1. How is the inverse relationship between the price level and real GDP shown in the aggregate demand curve explained by each of the following?

   a. The wealth effect

   b. The interest rate effect

   c. The net export effect

2. Suppose that the economy is operating at equilibrium in the following figure. Describe the four conditions that would cause the economy to move to points A, B, C, and D.

3. According to *The Economist* magazine, "The two nastiest global recessions of recent decades (prior to the Great Recession) were preceded by huge and sudden rises in the price of oil, first in 1973 and then in 1979. These twin spikes, both engineered by the Organization of the Petroleum Exporting Countries limiting its oil shipments, are still the textbook example of an economic "shock"—a sudden change in business conditions."[5] Using an aggregate supply and aggregate demand model, show the impact of these shocks. What type of recession resulted from these shocks?

4. In recent decades, countries such as China and India have grown quickly primarily due to increases in aggregate supply. Model the economy of China as it experienced an increase in aggregate supply.[6] Assume that the economy started at full employment. Explain how this differs from demand-led growth.

5. Suppose that you receive a pay increase of 3% during a year of 4% inflation. In the next year, you receive a 1% raise during a year of 0% inflation. In which year did you receive a larger raise in real terms? Explain why workers might complain more about the 1% raise. This difference in how workers perceive the two raises is an example of what economic phenomenon?

6. Suppose that there is a surge of immigration into the United States. Use an aggregate supply and aggregate demand model to show the impact of this surge. How would this immigration impact real GDP and the price level? Is there any period of U.S. history that matches this example?

7. President Barack H. Obama took office in January 2009, when the economy was in the midst of a deep recession. What would have happened to the economy if policymakers had taken no action to address the recession? Why might President Obama have been reluctant to take a passive approach? What two policies can the government use to impact aggregate demand?

8. Suppose that in the future all price tags are electronic and prices are frequently adjusted to reflect changing conditions of supply and demand. Do you think that the economy would reach long-run equilibrium more quickly or more slowly than today? Explain your answer.

9. In his first inaugural address on March 4, 1933, President Franklin D. Roosevelt said that "the only thing we have to fear is fear . . . fear itself." What was Roosevelt trying to do to the public's expectations? If he had succeeded, would this have affected aggregate supply or aggregate demand? How would output and prices have been impacted by the change in expectations?

10. In 2013, the European economy was suffering from high unemployment. The head of the European Central Bank suggested that falling prices in southern Europe might be good because this would boost the purchasing power of consumers. Explain why this view might or might not be correct. Hint: Consider two reasons that prices in Europe might have been falling.

11. For each of the following events, describe whether it shifts the aggregate supply curve or the aggregate demand curve and in which direction:

    a. A devastating hurricane hits the Gulf Coast.

    b. The minimum wage has a large increase.

    c. The Federal Reserve cuts interest rates by increasing the money supply.

    d. Congress gives every worker a $250 federal income tax cut.

12. Along a given aggregate demand curve, what happens to the quantity demanded as the price level falls? Is this still true if the price level falls due to a *shift* in aggregate demand? Explain.

13. Draw an aggregate supply and aggregate demand graph to show the short- and long-run effects of an increase in aggregate demand. Label the initial short-run equilibrium as point E_1 the new short-run equilibrium E_2 and the long-run equilibrium point as E_3. Which of these points demonstrates the idea of monetary neutrality? Explain briefly.

14. Discuss why the long run aggregate supply curve and the short run aggregate supply curve have different slopes. Which of those two aggregate supply curves explains the business cycle? Which one assumes that wages and prices are sticky? Which one reflects the economy's potential output?

15. Use an aggregate supply and demand diagram to explain how a technological revolution may impact the economy.

16. Suppose that an economy is currently in a recession with high unemployment. Discuss two policies the government could use to restore full employment. Show the impact of these policies using an aggregate supply and aggregate demand diagram. Label the recession point *R* and the full employment point *E*.

17. Use an aggregate supply and demand diagram to show why expansionary monetary and fiscal policies in Argentina did not lead to a long-run increase in real GDP. Which supply curve—a long-run aggregate supply curve or a short-run aggregate supply curve—should be used to illustrate Argentina's growth problem?

18. Why are the prices of some goods stickier than the prices of others?

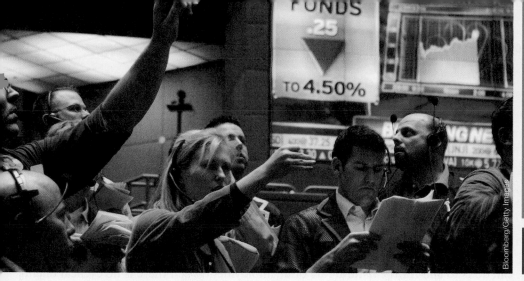

Bloomberg/Getty Images

∧ "The Fed cut less than expected. Sell, sell!"

Monetary Policy

How the Fed Tries to Stabilize the Economy

At 2:14 p.m. on September 18, 2007, traders on Wall Street were sitting on the edge of their seats. One minute later, the Federal Reserve announced a ½% cut in its target interest rate, and stock prices around the globe immediately soared. Three months later, the Fed announced a ¼% rate cut, which was a smaller-than-expected rate cut, and stock prices fell just as sharply on the disappointing news. Fed policy announcements are regular events that occur eight times a year. When the newly announced policy is unexpected by Wall Street traders, it can almost immediately result in hundreds of billions of dollars in paper gains or losses.

The Fed often is viewed as the most powerful economic policymaker in the world because its decisions have a profound impact on the economy, so much so that there are specialists on Wall Street whose only job is to predict and analyze them. The Fed impacts business in many ways, but the easiest one to visualize is interest rates. This is because businesses and consumers alike often use borrowed money to expand, buy new equipment, build homes, and purchase autos. In this chapter, you will learn that the Fed can influence more than just interest rates. It also has an important impact on business conditions such as inflation, unemployment, stock prices, and exchange rates.

27.1 MONEY SUPPLY, MONEY DEMAND, AND INTEREST RATES

Monetary policy refers to changes in the money supply and interest rates by the central bank, often with the goal of influencing employment and inflation. In the United States, monetary policy is set by the Federal Reserve.

Chapter Learning Targets

● Explain the factors determining short-term interest rates.

● Define monetary policy and identify the Fed's dual mandate.

● Describe monetarism, New Keynesian economics, and the historic events that have shaped modern central banking.

● Identify the special problems associated with near zero and very high interest rates.

● Distinguish between alternative transmission mechanisms and monetary policy approaches.

The Dual Mandate of the Federal Reserve

Because monetary policy has such an important effect on the economy, the Federal Reserve has a **dual mandate**—a requirement from Congress to the Federal Reserve to promote the goals of maximum employment and stable prices.

Maximum Employment Taken literally, the term *maximum employment* might suggest that the Fed should aim for the highest possible level of employment. But when aggregate demand pushes the economy past the natural rate of output, inflation will rise. In the long run, aggregate demand has no impact on the natural rate of output or the natural rate of unemployment. For that reason, the Fed has decided that the best it can do is to aim for the natural rate of unemployment when there is no cyclical unemployment (Chapter 21). This rate is believed to be roughly 5% in the United States and is represented by the long-run aggregate supply curve in the aggregate supply and aggregate demand model.

Stable Prices The term *stable prices* does not necessarily mean that prices do not rise. It means that they rise at an acceptable rate. The Federal Reserve has determined that a 2% inflation target is most consistent with its mandate for stable prices. This might seem a bit odd because the phrase *stable prices* taken literally would imply zero percent inflation. The main reason the Fed prefers a slightly positive inflation rate is that the harm to the economy from deflation is believed to be much greater than the harm from a low but positive rate of inflation. The Fed does not have *exact* control of the rate of inflation. Actual inflation rates almost always are a little higher or lower than expected, so targeting zero inflation runs greater risk of actual inflation being negative. Because wages are sticky or hard to reduce, deflation can lead to high unemployment.

In contrast, an inflation rate of 2% does not do much harm if it is anticipated by the public. As long as inflation is relatively *stable and low*, people can factor the 2% inflation rate into decisions such as wage negotiations and interest rates on loans. Workers would know what sort of inflation to expect when they sign a contract to work at a specified wage rate over the next year. Similarly, lenders would know how fast money is likely to lose purchasing power when they set an interest rate on their loans. In contrast, between 1965 and 1981, inflation was very unstable, which made it much harder for lenders and workers to negotiate contracts. Employers, employees, lenders, and borrowers had only a vague idea of how much future monetary payments would be worth.

Interest Rates Affect the Business Environment

In Chapter 24, we describe some of the tools that the Fed uses to manage the money supply. Most often, the Fed will engage in open market operations either to inject new money into the economy or to take money out. As is shown in Chapter 25, in the long run, such a change in the money supply causes a proportionate change in the price level, other things equal.

In this chapter, however, we focus more on the short run, where monetary policy can impact real GDP in addition to prices. One of the most visible short-run effects of monetary policy is the impact on interest rates, which are among the most important prices faced by businesses. When interest rates increase, it is more costly for firms to borrow money to expand their businesses, and consumers pay more interest on car or home mortgage loans (which are typically among the biggest expenses most consumers face).

For example, suppose Monica is seeking a $200,000 mortgage to buy her first home. Because 1% of $200,000 is $2,000, a decrease in mortgage interest rates of one percentage point will reduce the interest cost of Monica's mortgage loan by $2,000 per year in interest alone. That means that a house that is unaffordable for Monica when

monetary policy Changes in the money supply and interest rates by the central bank, often with the goal of influencing employment and inflation.

dual mandate A requirement from Congress to the Federal Reserve to promote the goals of maximum employment and stable prices.

EXHIBIT 1 Borrowing Costs at Three Different Interest Rates

The monthly payment on a 30-year fixed rate mortgage of $200,000 at 18.45% (the average rate in October 1981) is more than three times the cost of a similar loan in at 3.42% (December 2012). Lower rates mean that prospective homeowners today can afford larger mortgages for the same monthly payment.

Monthly Payments on a $200,000 30-Year Mortgage

18.45%	3.99%	3.42%
$3,088	$954	$889
October 1981	January 2018	December 2012

interest rates are 6% might become affordable when rates drop to 5%. This illustrates the impact of a 1% drop in the interest rate on the number of people who are able to buy new homes. It also affects the prices they are willing to pay because lower rates make it possible for people like Monica to buy a more expensive home for the same monthly payment.

Exhibit 1 demonstrates how different interest rates impact monthly mortgage payments at three very different interest rates. In October 1981 (when the prevailing interest rate was about 18.45%), someone who obtained a $200,000 30-year mortgage would have had a monthly payment of $3,088. In December 2012 (when rates were about 3.42%), the monthly payment would have been $889. In January 2018 (when rates for similar loans were about 3.99%), the monthly payment would have been $954.

You also can see how a change in the interest rate affects any industry that finances capital investment. Consider BrightSource Energy's $2 billion solar panel facility in the Mohave Desert. Let's suppose that it can generate $100 million worth of electricity each year. This equates to 5% of the $2 billion investment. If the interest rate on business loans is 6%, the company must pay $120 million in interest payments every year, and the project cannot cover the cost of borrowed money. But if the interest rate is 3%, the company must pay $60 million in interest payments every year, and the project can be profitable. This shows how a project that is unprofitable at a higher interest rate might be undertaken profitably at a lower interest rate.

Understanding Interest Rates in the Short Run

How exactly does the Fed control interest rates? And what factors affect its decision to raise or lower interest rates? To answer these questions, we first need to distinguish between long-term and short-term interest rates:

- *Short-Term Interest Rate.* Monetary policy has a particularly strong effect on short-term interest rates. The **short-term interest rate** is the cost of borrowing money or the reward for saving money for less than one year.

- *Long-Term Interest Rate.* Not all interest rates reflect short-run borrowing costs. The **long-term interest rate** is the cost of borrowing money or the reward for saving money for more than one year. This interest rate applies to many car loans, fixed-rate mortgages, and business loans used for long-term investments (such as corporate bonds).

The Federal Reserve has a much greater influence on short-term interest rates than on long-term interest rates. The impact of monetary policy on long-term interest rates is discussed in later in the chapter. One short-term interest rate that the Federal Reserve focuses on is the federal funds rate. The **federal funds rate** is the interest rate that banks pay when borrowing reserves from other banks; also called

short-term interest rate
The cost of borrowing money or the reward for saving money for less than one year.

long-term interest rate The cost of borrowing money or the reward for saving money for more than one year.

federal funds rate The interest rate that banks pay when borrowing reserves from other banks; also called the *fed funds rate.*

Andrew Harnik/AP Images

∧ In 2018, Jerome Powell
became chair of the
Board of Governors of
the Federal Reserve.

the *fed funds rate*. Because banks often "rent" money from each other on an overnight basis to meet reserve requirements, the fed funds rate is an interest rate that represents the cost of borrowed funds for banks. The fed funds rate should not be confused with the *discount rate*, which applies to loans made directly by the Federal Reserve (see Chapter 24). Even though these two short-term interest rates are usually quite similar, banks generally prefer to borrow from each other in the fed funds market, so the discount rate is largely symbolic.

When the news media discuss monetary policy, they generally focus on how the actions of the Federal Reserve impact the fed funds rate. You can think of it as the "wholesale cost" of credit. When banks loan out money to people or businesses, they must charge a higher interest rate in order to make a profit. As we will see, the fed funds rate is also the short-term interest rate that Federal Reserve officials seek to influence.

📊 BUSINESS BRIEF Low Interest Rates Help Bolster Demand for Autos

You probably have seen ads that say things like "Get this great new car for only $299 per month." Low interest rates lower the monthly payments on car loans and make automobiles more affordable for millions of potential buyers. Consider the following comment from Alec Gutierrez, senior market analyst of automotive insights for Kelley Blue Book, on the recent high numbers of car sales: "Along with an unemployment rate that continues to drop and low interest rates, most signs remain very positive in the automotive market."[*] In 2016, the combination of extremely low interest rates and rapidly rising employment led to the highest number of vehicle sales in the United States ever.[†] When the Fed pushes interest rates lower, one goal is to boost spending on cars by decreasing monthly payments.

[*]Angelo Young, "February 2015 U.S. New-Auto Sales Forecast: Up 8% with Toyota Leading Growth as Corolla Returns as Top-Selling U.S. Car," *International Business Times*, February 26, 2015, http://www.ibtimes.com /february-2015-us-new-auto-sales-forecast-8-toyota-leading-growth-corolla-returns-top-1829868.

[†]Tribune Wire Reports, "Auto Sales Remain Strong Despite Record New Car Prices," *Chicago Tribune*, January 3, 2018, http://www.chicagotribune.com/classified/automotive/ct-auto-sales-strong-record-prices-20180103 -story.html.

The Short-Run Money Market Model

As with goods and services, there is a market for money, and preferences for cash versus other assets reflect the cost of holding money. Exhibit 2 presents the supply and demand for money, with the interest rate being the opportunity cost of holding money. Notice that the money demand curve slopes downward and the money supply curve is vertical.

EXHIBIT 2 The Equilibrium Interest Rate in the Money Market

The money demand curve is downward sloping, reflecting the opportunity cost of holding liquid forms of money such as cash. At low rates of interest, the opportunity cost of holding money is low, and a greater quantity of money is demanded due to the liquidity preference for money. The money supply curve is determined by the Federal Reserve. The equilibrium interest rate is i_e.

The Money Demand Curve Is Downward Sloping The key to understanding the downward-sloping money demand curve is that the interest rate represents the opportunity cost of holding money. Suppose that you hold $100 in cash in your wallet. Also suppose that the market interest rate on assets such as savings accounts and Treasury bills is 5%. If you invest the $100 at 5%, you will earn $5 per year in interest. By keeping $100 in the form of cash, you are forgoing $5 per year in interest. That forgone interest is the opportunity cost of holding cash.

Many individuals do not give much thought to the opportunity cost of cash. But imagine how much cash a big company like Walmart holds in all its cash registers. That cash is not earning any interest for Walmart. So the more quickly Walmart moves the money to a bank in an armored truck, the lower its opportunity cost of holding cash.

In general, both individuals and businesses prefer holding at least some portion of their wealth in the form of cash. They prefer liquidity, which, as is discussed in Chapter 24 is the ease with which an asset can be converted into cash. The demand for highly liquid types of money (such as cash and demand deposits) slopes downward because the nominal interest rate is the opportunity cost of holding money. As interest rates rise, people prefer to hold less cash and put more of their wealth into interest-earning assets such as bonds and bank certificates of deposit. At lower interest rates, people prefer to hold larger cash balances because the opportunity cost of having liquidity is relatively low.

Finally, money often is used to make transactions, so when real GDP increases, the demand for money also tends to increase in order to accommodate additional transactions. This is known as the *transactional demand for money*. This means the demand curve for money shifts to the right, which puts upward pressure on interest rates. During recessions, the transactions demand for money often declines; resulting in a decline in overall money demand and interest rates.

The Money Supply Curve Is Vertical Understanding the vertical money supply curve is easy. Recall that the *monetary base*—that is, the supply of cash in circulation plus bank reserves—is directly controlled by the Federal Reserve and represents the money supply in this graph. Because the Fed is not a profit-maximizing institution, it can set the supply of base money wherever it chooses. The money supply curve is vertical because it represents a given quantity of money, measured on the *x*-axis.

Think & Speak Like an Economist

Recall that economists consider an opportunity cost to be what must be given up in order to acquire or do something else. Money demand is negatively related to interest rates because the opportunity cost of having money that earns zero interest is the forgone interest that could be earned on alternative assets.

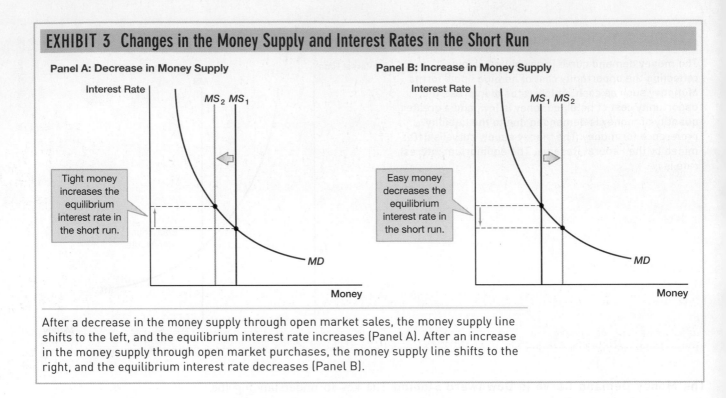

EXHIBIT 3   Changes in the Money Supply and Interest Rates in the Short Run

After a decrease in the money supply through open market sales, the money supply line shifts to the left, and the equilibrium interest rate increases (Panel A). After an increase in the money supply through open market purchases, the money supply line shifts to the right, and the equilibrium interest rate decreases (Panel B).

The Effects of Monetary Policy on Interest Rates

Most people evaluate monetary policy by looking at short-term interest rates. To see why, look at Panel A of Exhibit 3, where we can see the short-run effect of a decrease in the money supply on short-term interest rates. The money supply curve will shift to the left, and the equilibrium interest rate will rise. Because changes in the money supply impact short-term interest rates, the business press usually reports on monetary policy in terms of what the fed funds rate is doing. A decrease in the money supply that reduces interest rates is generally referred to as *tight money*, although a more accurate term for low interest rates might be *tight credit*. Interest rates can also fall due to a drop in money demand.

In contrast, an increase in the money supply shifts the money supply curve to the right, which puts downward pressure on the equilibrium interest rate in the short run (Panel B). An increase in the money supply often is referred to as *easy money*. Although an increase in the money supply will reduce short-term interest rates and vice versa, you cannot simply assume that low interest rates always mean easy money or that high interest rates mean tight money. Monetary policy also impacts inflation, and higher inflation may increase long-term interest rates. Later in the chapter, we revisit the links between inflation and interest rates in the long run.

27.2 UNDERSTANDING MONETARY POLICY

We have seen that an increase in the money supply (easy money) decreases short-run interest rates and that a decrease in the money supply (tight money) does the opposite. Monetary policy also affects aggregate demand, and this is how the Federal Reserve tries to achieve its dual mandate.

The Effects of Monetary Policy on Aggregate Demand

There are at least four reasons why monetary policy impacts aggregate demand—the excess cash balance effect, the interest rate effect, the exchange rate and net export effect, and the asset price effect.

The Excess Cash Balance Effect As is shown in Chapter 25, when money is injected into the economy, businesses and consumers initially have more money than they prefer to hold. In response, the public attempts to reduce their excess cash balances by spending the money on goods, services, and financial assets, which pushes aggregate demand higher.

The Interest Rate Effect In this chapter, we have seen an alternative way that increases in the money supply can boost aggregate demand. When the Fed injects more money into the economy, it reduces interest rates in the short run. This makes consumers more willing to use borrowed money to buy cars and new homes. Businesses will tend to increase investment. Entrepreneurs are more willing to borrow money to finance new office buildings, shopping centers, and factories. A new investment that is not expected to be profitable at 5% interest rates may become profitable if rates are cut to 3%.

The Exchange Rate and Net Export Effect In addition, an increase in the money supply tends to reduce the foreign exchange value of the dollar, so the dollar will tend to depreciate. Recall that an increase in the supply of a product tends to lower its price, and that also applies to money. An increase in the supply of a currency means a lower exchange rate. In addition, an increase in the money supply reduces short-term interest rates. In turn, this reduces the demand for dollar assets (such as Treasury bonds) and the dollar itself. This too can cause the dollar to depreciate. A cheaper dollar that results from changes in the money supply boosts net exports and thus increases aggregate demand.

The Asset Price Effect Finally, excess cash balances lead to more than just increased spending on goods and services. The public also will try to convert this extra money into financial assets. This boosts the price of assets such as stocks and real estate. On several occasions, stock prices rose sharply after just the *announcement* of additional monetary stimulus by the Federal Reserve. For instance, on January 3, 2001, the Fed took the highly unusual step of cutting interest rates about a month prior to the next scheduled meeting. The Standard & Poor's 500 stock index soared by about 5% immediately after the announcement, which was widely unexpected. As is shown in Chapter 26, higher stock and other asset prices can lead to higher consumption and higher investment, thus boosting aggregate demand.

📊 BUSINESS BRIEF Borrow a Million Dollars for Just $25 a Month!

In response to a mild recession in the early 2000s, the Federal Reserve expanded the U.S. money supply, which lowered interest rates. Ordinarily, this stimulus should have encouraged more business investment, but businesses had greatly over-invested during the tech boom of the 1990s. And so the Fed's low interest rate policy impacted mostly residential investment. Between 2000 and 2006, housing construction boomed, and median house prices skyrocketed.* It is unclear, however, exactly how much of the increase in home prices was due to the Fed's easy money policy.

In any case, the soaring house prices led to overconfidence among both home mortgage lenders and borrowers. Both assumed that as long as home values continued to increase—and indeed, housing prices in America had never fallen sharply since record keeping began—real estate would be profitable for home buyers, and real estate loans would be profitable for banks. And so mortgage lending increased

∧ When home prices fall and the economy enters a recession, many homeowners are unable to pay their mortgages.

sharply, with banks offering lenient terms that in retrospect seem mind-boggling. One investment manager framed the terms this way:

> Want to borrow $1,000,000 for just $25 a month? Quicken Loans has now introduced an interest-only adjustable rate mortgage that gives borrowers six months with both zero payments and a 0.03% interest rate.[†]

The excesses that occurred during the period are now the stuff of legend. For example, a Mexican migrant strawberry picker with an income of $14,000 "was lent every penny he needed to buy a house for $724,000."[‡] In the end, real estate prices did collapse—by roughly a third. As a result, many borrowers could no longer refinance, which often resulted in foreclosure for those who could not make the loan payments. More recently, the housing market has recovered in most cities.

[*]David Streitfeld, "Bottom May Be Near for Slide in Housing," *New York Times*, May 31, 2011, http://www.nytimes.com/2011/06/01/business/01housing.html.

[†]Quoted in Michael Lewis, *The Big Short: Inside the Doomsday Machine* (New York: Norton, 2010), 55.

[‡]Ibid., 97.

Fed Monetary Policy and the Business Cycle

The Federal Reserve's ability to influence aggregate demand means that it plays a crucial role in macroeconomic stabilization. An expansionary monetary policy plays an important role in combating recessions, or if high inflation is a problem, the Fed can reduce aggregate demand with a contractionary monetary policy.

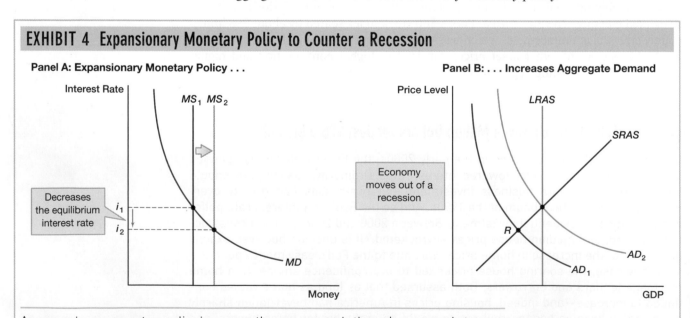

EXHIBIT 4 Expansionary Monetary Policy to Counter a Recession

Panel A: Expansionary Monetary Policy . . .

Panel B: . . . Increases Aggregate Demand

An expansionary monetary policy increases the money supply through open market purchases. The equilibrium interest rate decreases, increasing aggregate demand and moving the economy away from point R (recession).

Expansionary Monetary Policy to Counter a Recession In Exhibit 4, output is at a low level, which implies a high unemployment rate. This is shown as point *R* in Panel B. To counter this, the Fed may engage in an expansionary monetary policy. An **expansionary monetary policy** is a policy that occurs when the central bank increases the money supply and decreases short-term interest rates, often directed at boosting aggregate demand and employment. Panel A shows that in this case the Fed increases the money supply, which reduces the equilibrium interest rate from i_1 to i_2. The lower interest rates boost aggregate demand, which moves the economy out of a recession, as is shown in Panel B.

🏛 POLICY BRIEF The Bank of Japan Adopts an Expansionary Monetary Policy

By the early 1990s, most economists thought that deflation was a relic of the distant past that was associated with the gold standard and the Great Depression of the 1930s. Then Japan slid into a period of deflation that lasted for nearly 20 years. In early 2013, a new government was elected that promised bold reforms to end deflation. One of its policy tools was aggressive monetary stimulus.

In early 2013, the Bank of Japan adopted an expansionary monetary policy to end deflation. According to CNN, the leading policymakers in Japan made "aggressive policy moves to drive down the value of the currency, a trend that will benefit the country's exporters."* Japan sharply increased the Japanese money supply, prompting the depreciation of the Japanese yen in the foreign exchange market. When an expansionary monetary policy pushes the exchange rate lower, one side effect is a boost to exports. By the end of the following year, evidence began to suggest that the policy was working because deflation came to an end. Over the next few years, unemployment in Japan fell sharply.†

*Charles Riley, "Bank of Japan Set to Launch War on Deflation," CNN Money, April 5, 2013, http://money.cnn .com/2013/04/03/news/economy/bank-of-japan/.

†Mitsuru Obe, "Weak Yen Lifts Japan's Exports," *Wall Street Journal*, January 25, 2015, http://www.wsj.com /articles/japan-trade-deficit-halves-in-december-despite-record-annual-shortfall-1422235151.

expansionary monetary policy A policy that occurs when the central bank increases the money supply and decreases short-term interest rates, often directed at boosting aggregate demand and employment.

Contractionary Monetary Policy to Reduce Inflation In Panel B of Exhibit 5, the economy is in a boom and is "overheating." The unemployment rate will be very low. A

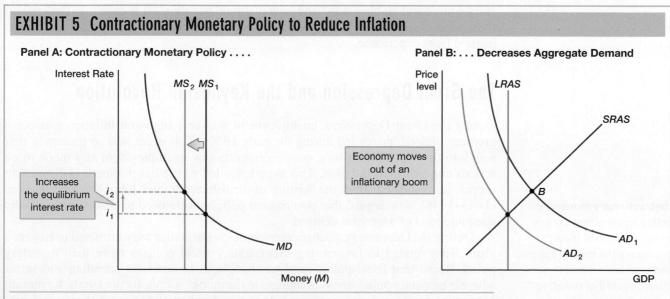

EXHIBIT 5 Contractionary Monetary Policy to Reduce Inflation

Panel A: Contractionary Monetary Policy . . . .

Panel B: . . . Decreases Aggregate Demand

A contractionary monetary policy decreases the money supply through open market sales. The equilibrium interest rate increases, decreasing aggregate demand and moving the economy away from point *B* (inflationary boom).

EXHIBIT 6 Effective Monetary Policy over the Business Cycle

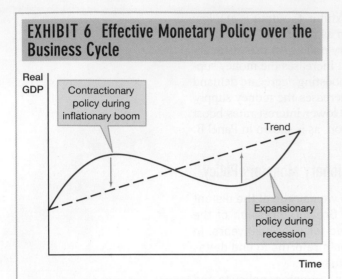

An effective monetary policy will reduce the fluctuations around the long-run growth trend, but it will not change the growth trend overall. This is called a countercyclical policy because it attempts to push back against the business cycle. A countercyclical policy is expansionary during recessions and contractionary during booms.

low unemployment rate sounds good, but if it is below the natural rate of unemployment, then inflation is likely rising because output is above the natural rate of output. Panel A shows that in this case, the Fed decreases the money supply, which increases the equilibrium interest rate from i_1 to i_2. The resulting fall in aggregate demand reduces the price level, as is seen in Panel B. A **contractionary monetary policy** is a policy that occurs when the central bank decreases the money supply and increases interest rates, often directed at reducing aggregate demand and inflation. Without this type of corrective monetary policy, the short-run aggregate supply curve will shift leftward as the economy self-corrects (not shown in this graph for simplicity). However, this would result in an even higher price level.

Monetary Policy and the Business Cycle Exhibit 6 shows a typical business cycle. The arrows indicate what the Fed is trying to achieve. Monetary policy cannot change the long-run trend line. The trend rate of growth is determined by growth in the natural rate of output. We already have seen that factors such as population growth, capital accumulation, and technological progress determine the long-run rate of real GDP growth. However, monetary policy can reduce fluctuations in growth. It can smooth out the business cycle by being expansionary during recessions and contractionary during booms.

27.3 MONETARISM, NEW KEYNESIANISM, AND MODERN CENTRAL BANKING

There are several schools of economic thought regarding which tools the Federal Reserve should use in order to achieve the goals of the dual mandate (maximum employment and stable prices) and how it should use them. It is easiest to understand these ideas if we look at how monetary policy developed over time and how the Fed learned from experience.

The Great Depression and the Keynesian Revolution

During the Great Depression, unemployment was very high and inflation was not a problem. Indeed, prices fell during the early 1930s. This event was so traumatic that well into the mid-20th century, most economists saw unemployment as a much more serious concern than inflation. This experience led to the development of Keynesian economics, modeled after the writing of British economist John Maynard Keynes (1883–1946), who argued that government policymakers need to ensure a continually adequate level of aggregate demand.

During the Depression, younger economists in particular were attracted to Keynes's ideas. They tended to favor using expansionary fiscal policies more than monetary policy. Recall that fiscal policy involves changes in government spending and taxes, whereas monetary policy involves changes in the money supply. By the 1960s, Keynesian economics dominated macroeconomic theory and policy. (For a more thorough examination of Keynesian economics, see Chapter 29.)

contractionary monetary policy A policy that occurs when the central bank decreases the money supply and increases interest rates, often directed at reducing aggregate demand and inflation.

Monetarism: A Focus on the Money Supply to Control Inflation

Due in part to the Fed's focus on expansionary policies in the decades following the Depression, inflation began to rise in the late 1960s. Inflation continued to rise during the 1970s, peaking at 13% in 1980. The high inflation of the 1970s led to a reevaluation of Keynesian ideas and the rise of monetarism. **Monetarism** is a school of economic thought that stresses the role that is played by the money supply in determining nominal GDP and inflation. In other words, the monetarists use the *quantity theory of money* in their analysis. The monetarists argued that monetary policy was more effective than fiscal policy and that the Fed should target the money supply and not interest rates. More specifically, they wanted the Fed to keep the money supply growing at a slow but steady rate, consistent with growth in real GDP. This school of thought is largely associated with Nobel Laureate Milton Friedman.

"I told you the Fed should have tightened."

Bob Mankoff

At the beginning of the 1980s, the Fed began to control the growth rate of the money supply, and this reduced the rate of inflation. This result was seen as supporting the monetarist view that monetary policy is the key to controlling inflation. Recall the equation of exchange from Chapter 25:

$$M \times V = P \times Y$$

The money supply (*M*) times the velocity of money (*V*) (how often money is spent) equals nominal GDP (*P* × *Y*), which is the price level (*P*) times real GDP (*Y*). A change on the left side of the equation must be matched by a corresponding change on the right side.

The monetarists expected stable money growth to be associated with stable velocity of money. However, the velocity of money was somewhat unstable during the early 1980s as money began circulating through the economy at a slower rate. For this reason, the Federal Reserve was reluctant to continue targeting the money supply after inflation had been brought under control. If the money supply grows at a steady rate, as the monetarists recommended, and velocity is *unstable*, then the right side of the equation of exchange will also be unstable. A drop in velocity during 1982 contributed to a severe recession.

Because velocity was unstable, most economists did not fully accept the monetarist theory. However, the Federal Reserve's success in sharply reducing inflation during the 1980s did convince many economists that monetary policy was the government's most powerful tool for reducing inflation. This led to a new school of economic thought— New Keynesian economics, which combined Keynesian and monetarist ideas.

monetarism A school of economic thought that stresses the role that is played by the money supply in determining nominal GDP and inflation.

New Keynesian Economics and the Modern Consensus: Target Short-Term Interest Rates

New Keynesian economics is the view that the central bank should target short-term interest rates, with the goal of keeping inflation low and stable and unemployment close to the natural rate. The New Keynesians agree with the monetarists that sound monetary policy is the key to producing stable growth and low inflation. They do not support the targeting of the money supply, however, but believe that the Fed should target interest rates.

New Keynesian economics The view that the central bank should target short-term interest rates, with the goal of keeping inflation low and stable and unemployment close to the natural rate.

The Federal Reserve and many other central banks around the world accepted this new consensus, leading to a policy that was fairly successful between 1984 and 2007 in producing low inflation and relatively stable employment. Under this new policy, the Federal Reserve targeted the fed funds rate, which is the rate that banks charge when they loan money to each other. The Fed has been able to keep inflation close to 2% since 1990.

New Keynesian economics represents the modern consensus view in central banking. In terms of monetary and fiscal policy, New Keynesians believe the following[1]:

- Interest rate *targets* should be established in conducting monetary policy.
- Monetary policy is usually the most important policy tool for obtaining maximum employment and stable prices.
- Fiscal policy may be more effective than monetary policy at stabilizing the economy when interest rates are stuck near zero. This situation is known as a *liquidity trap* and is discussed shortly.

The Fed Funds Interest Rate Target

Modern central banks generally use interest rate targets in conducting monetary policy. The **fed funds interest rate target** is the fed funds rate that the Federal Reserve believes is most likely to achieve its policy goals. Interest rates are targeted by moving the money supply to a position where it intersects the money demand line at the target interest rate. In Exhibit 7, you can see how the Fed would react to an increase in the demand for money if it were to target interest rates. The demand for money often increases with an expanding economy as the transactional demand for money increases. When the demand for money increases, the Fed has to increase the supply of money by an equal amount in order to keep the interest rate at the target level.

If there were a decrease in the demand for money, the Fed would reduce the money supply in order to stabilize interest rates. So the Fed can target or control short-term interest rates by varying the money supply. But the big issue in monetary policy is *where to set the target.*

The Federal Open Market Committee (FOMC) meets eight times per year to determine monetary policy. At each meeting, members vote on the question of where to set

fed funds interest rate target The fed funds rate that the Federal Reserve believes is most likely to achieve its policy goals.

EXHIBIT 7   Interest Rate Targeting

Initially, the fed funds interest rate equilibrium (E) is the targeted interest rate (i_T). If money demand increases, the Federal Reserve increases the money supply to maintain the interest rate target. If money demand decreases, the Fed does the opposite (not shown).

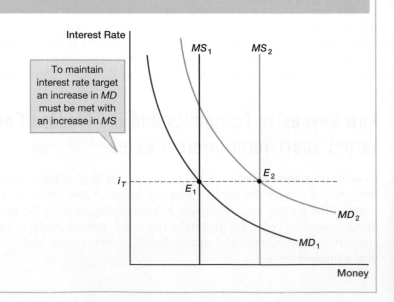

To maintain interest rate target an increase in MD must be met with an increase in MS the fed funds target interest rate. In making these votes, they are guided by the dual mandate (keeping unemployment rate near the natural rate and inflation near 2%). The announcements are typically made in the early afternoon, and traders on Wall Street eagerly await the news, which can immediately impact stock and bond prices. The announcement is televised on financial news networks around the globe.

The key to understanding Federal Reserve monetary policy is to consider how the fed funds interest rate target needs to be adjusted when either inflation or employment are not at the Fed's policy goal. Exhibit 8 shows two important cases—(1) inflation below the goal of 2% or unemployment above the natural rate and (2) inflation above the goal of 2% or unemployment below the natural rate.

The Challenges of Modern Central Banking

It might help to think of the Federal Reserve as like a captain steering a large ocean liner. The captain hopes to end up in New York, but winds and currents can push the ship off course, either toward Boston to the north or Baltimore to the south. When this occurs, the captain needs to make adjustments in the steering.

In a similar way, the Fed frequently makes adjustments to the fed funds rate target to steer the economy toward goals outlined in the dual mandate. When economic forces push the economy toward too much inflation or an unsustainably low unemployment rate, the Fed needs to reduce aggregate demand. It does so by increasing the fed funds rate target. When economic forces push the economy toward too little inflation or excessively high unemployment, the Fed needs to boost aggregate demand. It does so by decreasing the fed funds rate target. The Fed can raise or lower aggregate demand through adjustments in the money supply that affect short-term interest rates. In Chapter 28, we will see that the Fed's job is made more difficult by the fact that the economy often responds slowly to changes in monetary policy—that is, there are policy lags.

If the Fed's only goal were to keep inflation at 2%, then it would be pretty clear how it should adjust the interest rate target. The fact that the Fed has a dual mandate, however, complicates its job. For instance, what should the Fed do in those rare cases where both inflation and unemployment are high at the same time? As is noted in Chapter 26, this problem is called *stagflation*. High inflation calls for tight money, but high unemployment calls for easy money. Should the Fed raise interest rates or lower interest rates? No single monetary policy can address both problems.

EXHIBIT 8 Monetary Policy through Interest Rate Targeting

	Inflation below the Goal of 2% or Unemployment above the Natural Rate	Inflation above the Goal of 2% or Unemployment below the Natural Rate
Monetary Policy	Expansionary	Contractionary
Fed Funds Interest Rate Target	↓	↑
Money Supply	↑	↓
Aggregate Demand	↑	↓

When inflation is below target or unemployment is above the natural rate, the Federal Reserve often conducts an *expansionary* monetary policy by lowering the fed funds rate target. When inflation is above target or unemployment is below the natural rate, the Federal Reserve often conducts a *contractionary* monetary policy by raising the fed funds rate target.

Although the dual mandate occasionally creates a dilemma for policymakers, the economy was relatively stable from 1984 to 2007, with low and stable inflation as well as fairly moderate rates of unemployment. Most economists believed that monetary policy during that period was better than the inflationary policy of the 1970s or the deflationary policy of the 1930s.

Unfortunately, this period of success did not last. In December 2007, the economy went into what is now called the Great Recession and also suffered from a severe financial crisis. The Federal Reserve responded by cutting interest rates to near zero percent and then decided it was unable to cut them further. In the next section, we look at alternative Fed policies for dealing with the Great Recession crisis and especially the problem of zero interest rates.

27.4 MONETARY POLICY AT THE EXTREMES: THE FISHER EFFECT AND LIQUIDITY TRAPS

The New Keynesian model introduced above applies best to situations where interest rates are positive but not too high. But under special circumstances—when interest rates are extremely high and when they are near zero—things become a bit more complicated.

The Fisher Effect and Very High Interest Rates

In Chapter 25, we saw that **Fisher effect** is the idea that a change in expected inflation leads to an equal change in nominal interest rates. Recall that the effect of inflation on interest rates can be explained using the Fisher equation:

Nominal interest rates = Real interest rates + Expected inflation rate

An expansionary monetary policy can cause higher inflation. As expected inflation rises, nominal interest rates tend to rise. In contrast, a contractionary monetary policy that reduces the rate of inflation may reduce nominal interest rates in the long run. Exhibit 9 demonstrates the relationship between the inflation rate (blue line) and short-term interest rates (red line) from 1950 to 2012. The relationship is far from perfect, but there is a clear pattern: Higher inflation often results in higher interest rates in the long run, and low inflation leads to low interest rates.

The Fisher effect largely explains why interest rates fell sharply from 15% in 1981 to 3% by the early 1990s. Inflation is especially important for investors who buy long-term assets (such as 30-year Treasury bonds) and for those who borrow long term (such as those financing houses with 30-year mortgages).

Although a contractionary monetary policy often will raise interest rates in the short run (other things equal), high interest rates do not necessarily imply that monetary policy is "tight" or contractionary. Due to the Fisher effect, an expansionary monetary policy (easy money) can potentially *increase* interest rates in the long run by raising inflation expectations. Once again, the lesson here is that one should *never reason from a price change*. Interest rates are a price, and so we do not know the meaning of high interest rates unless we know whether they are caused by tight money or by high inflation. Exhibit 9 shows that during the 1970s and early 1980s, interest rates rose to very high levels in the United States. This was the result of inflation that ensued from increases in the money supply—that is, easy money.

As you will learn in the next **Policy Brief**, the Fed aggressively fought inflation with a tight money policy in the early 1980s. This resulted in *lower* inflation and eventually also resulted in *lower* interest rates. The bottom line is that one cannot judge whether money is easy or tight merely by looking at interest rates. We must consider other variables, such as inflation and the money supply.

Think & Speak Like an Economist

The *long run* refers to the time that is necessary to make all adjustments to new economic circumstances. In the short run, an increase in the money supply reduces interest rates. In the long run, that same policy may raise inflation and therefore raise interest rates.

Fisher effect The idea that a change in expected inflation leads to an equal change in nominal interest rates.

EXHIBIT 9 The Fisher Effect and the Long-Run Correlation between Inflation and Interest Rates, 1950 to 2020

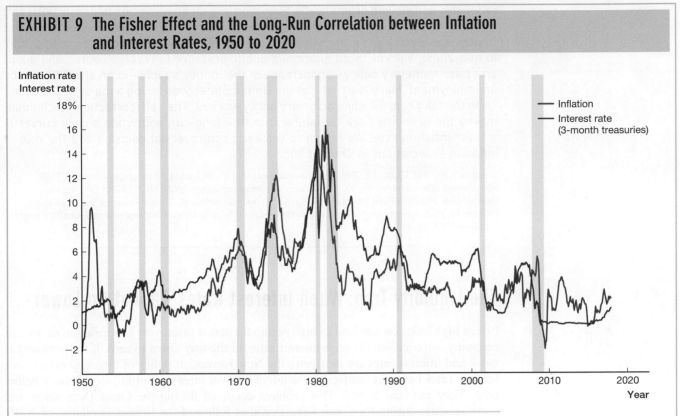

The Fisher effect is an economic theory that says that a change in the expected rate of inflation causes the nominal interest rate to change by the same amount. It is the long-run tendency of nominal interest rates to move one for one with changes in the expected rate of inflation. In the figure, interest rates (red line) are positively correlated to the rate of inflation (blue line). As a consequence, an expansionary monetary policy may lower interest rates in the short run but may increase interest rates in the long run if inflation results.

Data from: Federal Reserve Economic Data (FRED).

Finally, during the Great Depression, *short-term* interest rates were close to zero. That was *not* because money was easy but rather because prices were falling. Deflation usually leads to extremely low interest rates due to the Fisher effect.

 POLICY BRIEF The Fed Tightens Monetary Policy: Interest Rates Soar to 19%

In 1979, when President Jimmy Carter appointed Paul Volcker as chair of the Federal Reserve, the new chair faced a stark policy decision. The nation was suffering from high rates of unemployment, and inflation seemed out of control. Prices had been rising for decades, with inflation reaching 13% in 1979 and 1980.

Controlling inflation should be straightforward: Simply decrease the growth of the money supply. The dilemma that Volcker faced is that fighting inflation requires decreasing aggregate demand, which would lead to much higher interest rates and additional unemployment in the short run. Because of these costs, many naysayers believed that nothing serious would be done.

In the end, Volcker made a highly controversial decision. He focused his efforts on fighting inflation even if they led to higher levels of unemployment in the short run. In this instance, the Fed's independence from the political process proved essential because elected officials tend to avoid policies that they believe will generate higher unemployment. As the money supply growth slowed, interest rates soared to 19%. Borrowing money for home mortgages and business loans became much more expensive and slowed dramatically. Even worse, a steep recession began in 1981, and by the end of 1982 unemployment reached 10.8%, the highest level since the Great Depression (even higher than what occurred during the Great Recession of late 2007 to mid-2009). Volcker faced enormous public pressure to reverse course and adopt an easier monetary policy—an increase in the money supply—in an effort to reduce unemployment. Many worried that the United States was facing a major depression.[*]

In the long run, the contractionary policy worked. The self-correction mechanism moved the economy back to natural rate (the long-run aggregate supply curve) at a *lower* inflation rate. We return to Volcker's controversial decision and the role of inflation expectations in Chapter 30.

[*]Reuters Staff, "FACTBOX: U.S., European Bank Writedowns, Credit Losses," Reuters, November 5, 2009, http://www.reuters.com/article/2009/11/05/banks-writedowns-losses-idCNL554155620091105?rpc=44; International Monetary Fund Monetary and Capital Markets Department, "Global Financial Stability Report, October 29, 2010: Sovereigns, Funding, and Systemic Liquidity," https://www.imf.org/external/pubs/cat/longres .aspx?sk=23543.0.

The Liquidity Trap: When Interest Rates Cannot Go Lower

Just as high inflation can lead to high nominal interest rates, very low inflation or a weak economy can occasionally push interest rates all the way down to zero. If the economy is weak and interest rates are near zero, the New Keynesian policy of targeting even lower interest rates becomes ineffective. Nominal interest rates cannot fall significantly below zero. They are zero bound. This problem occurred during the Great Depression and more recently during the Great Recession that followed the financial collapse of 2008, when *short-term* interest rates fell to near zero and stayed there for seven years.

liquidity trap A situation in which nominal interest rates have fallen close to zero and thus cannot be lowered further by increases in the money supply.

Keynes believed that after interest rates fell to low levels, the central bank could no longer do monetary stimulus because the Federal Reserve cannot cut interest rates below zero. He called the situation a liquidity trap. A **liquidity trap** is a situation in which nominal interest rates have fallen close to zero and thus cannot be lowered further by increases in the money supply. One of the reasons that Keynes favored fiscal policy (in the form of government spending and tax changes) is that he worried that monetary policy might be ineffective during a deep depression.

Cash Is the Reason for the Liquidity Trap In principle, an economy could have sharply negative interest rates except for one problem—cash. The interest rate on currency and coins is always zero. No savers would be willing to accept a negative interest rate as long as they could hold cash. This is why interest rates cannot go meaningfully below zero, at least not while holding cash remains an option.

Zero-interest rates are not low enough to end this recession.

Jason Lutes

There is one minor exception to this rule. Because bank accounts and bonds are more convenient and secure than large piles of cash, a very slightly negative interest rate is possible and occasionally occurs, usually in the form of fees charged on bank accounts. In 2015, Swiss banks began charging depositors a nominal interest rate on large deposits for the privilege of having the bank hold the money. Swiss money was so popular that people were willing to deposit money in Swiss banks even though their bank accounts gradually declined in value.[2] This negative interest rate is essentially a money storage fee. Thus, when economists talk about the "zero lower bound" on interest rates, they actually mean that a slightly negative number (perhaps negative 1% at most) is the lower bound. This explains why a few central banks have set slightly negative interest rate targets in recent years.

The Modern Debate over the Liquidity Trap There is general agreement that if nominal interest rates are near zero, then increasing the money supply cannot meaningfully reduce interest rates. This is demonstrated in Exhibit 10. There is a vigorous debate, however, over the implication of interest rates near zero. The debate centers around one key question: Can monetary stimulus be effective at boosting aggregate demand after interest rates have fallen to zero? Keynesian economists believe that increases

EXHIBIT 10 The Liquidity Trap

A liquidity trap is a situation in which nominal interest rates are close to zero and thus cannot be lowered by increases in the money supply. Increasing the money supply from MS_1 to MS_2 can lower the equilibrium interest rate, but additional increases in the money supply to MS_3 cannot.

in the money supply impact the economy primarily by decreasing interest rates. Under such circumstances, Keynesians believe increasing the money supply when interest rates are near zero is an ineffective monetary policy. Simply put, interest rates cannot go lower.

Some Keynesian economists believe that zero interest rates in economics are similar to a black hole in physics. Many of the laws of economics break down at zero interest rates, just as the ordinary laws of physics breakdown in a black hole. Keynesians believe the following:

- Monetary stimulus is ineffective at zero interest rates.
- Fiscal policy is more effective than monetary policy at zero interest rates.

Not surprisingly, when interest rates fell to zero at the end of 2008, there was revived interest in the ideas of John Maynard Keynes, and lawmakers responded with tax cuts and government spending increases. We consider fiscal policy in detail in the next two chapters.

Pushing a String Is Pointless A tight enough monetary policy can always restrain an economy that is overheating and curtail inflation. That is because there is no upward limit as to how high interest rates can be raised. Just as when a dog strains to run ahead and you pull back strongly enough to stop the dog's progress, there is always some interest rate high enough to reduce aggregate demand and slow the economy.

But there may not be a way to *push* the dog forward if he insists on sitting still. The leash will just go slack. Likewise, at zero interest rates, an injection of new money does not necessarily make people start spending again. Pushing money into circulation may not boost spending if the extra money just sits in banks (or under mattresses) and is not spent. As we will see, this became a problem after 2008.

27.5 ADVANCED TOPIC: ALTERNATIVE APPROACHES TO MONETARY POLICY

In late 2008, the Federal Reserve reduced its fed funds target to close to zero. It also took aggressive steps to rescue several large banks to stabilize the banking system. Despite these actions, the economy continued to worsen. Because the Fed was no longer able to reduce short-term interest rates significantly, some economists believed that monetary policy was no longer effective. The Fed was seen as being stuck in a liquidity trap—as if it was "out of ammunition."

Alternative Transmission Mechanisms

After short-term interest rates fell to zero, Fed officials never accepted the view that they were powerless. Instead, they focused on other transmission mechanisms. The primary **transmission mechanism**—the method by which money affects the economy—discussed in this chapter is short-term interest rates. As has been shown, this mechanism does not work effectively when the economy is in a liquidity trap. Fortunately, economists have identified several other transmission mechanisms through which monetary policy can affect the economy, even when short-term interest rates are zero.

Monetary Stimulus Can Create Excess Cash Balances Monetary policy can affect the economy by creating excess cash balances. In Chapter 25, we discuss the excess cash balance mechanism. When new money is injected into the economy, people temporarily hold more money than they wish to hold. The public may attempt to get rid of these excess balances by spending the money, which tends to push inflation and nominal GDP higher.

Monetary Stimulus Can Lower Long-Term Interest Rates When the Fed purchases long-term bonds, the price of bonds tends to increase. This causes the long-term interest rates to decline, which can encourage business investment. Long-term rates are usually positive, even when short-term rates have fallen to zero. Thus long term rates can be reduced further.

Monetary Stimulus Can Increase Inflation Expectations In the long run, increases in the money supply lead to a higher price level. Because a liquidity trap is not expected to last forever, monetary stimulus could lead the public to expect higher inflation in the future. Higher inflation expectations encourage people to spend more today before prices increase. This can help to boost an economy that is stuck in a liquidity trap. More on the role of inflation expectations can be found in Chapter 30.

Monetary Stimulus Can Boost Asset Prices An easy money policy can boost the price of many different types of assets. One important example is stock prices. Stock prices tend to rise when businesses and investors learn that the Fed is adopting a more expansionary monetary policy. Higher stock prices can encourage business investment and consumption if people feel wealthier.

Monetary Stimulus Can Depreciate a Currency An increase in the supply of nearly anything will tend to lower its value, whether automobiles, pizzas, or currencies. Therefore, monetary stimulus causes the foreign exchange value of the dollar to decrease. The lower value of the dollar tends to boost U.S. exports and reduce U.S. imports. This increases net exports and thus increases aggregate demand. For example, the Fed announced a major expansionary monetary policy on March 19, 2009, when interest rates were zero. That same day, the dollar depreciated 4% relative to the euro as a result of the increase in the money supply. This unusually large change in an exchange rate would tend to stimulate exports. Japan adopted an easy money policy in 2013, which reduced the foreign exchange value of the yen, even though its interest rates were stuck at zero.

Quantitative Easing and Forward Guidance

transmission mechanism
The method by which money affects the economy.

Under the leadership of Ben Bernanke (2006–2014) and Janet Yellen (2014–2018), the Federal Reserve used several unconventional policies to boost the economy during the Great Recession and the subsequent recovery. At the time of the Great Recession, Fed policy was targeting the fed funds rate. After that rate fell close to zero, the Fed could no longer push it significantly lower. In 2009, according to the Federal Reserve Bank of San Francisco, the appropriate fed funds target rate given the high level of unemployment was *minus* 5%. Because the fed funds target rate cannot be that negative, the Fed adopted two alternative policies—quantitative easing and forward guidance.

Quantitative easing is an expansionary monetary policy that involves much larger than normal open market purchases of financial assets and that is intended to increase the size of the money supply and boost spending in the economy. There are three major differences between quantitative easing and ordinary monetary policy. First, quantitative easing generally involves far larger than normal open market purchases, perhaps 100 times larger. Second, the open market purchases may include financial assets not purchased during normal easing. Prior to 2008, the Fed purchased mostly short-term government bonds. After 2008, the Fed also purchased long-term mortgage-backed securities (which help finance home loans) in an attempt to lower mortgage interest rates and stimulate the demand for housing, which was collapsing.

Third, these purchases were no longer done exclusively to target short-term interest rates. During the 2009 to 2014 recovery, there were three separate quantitative easing programs that increased the money supply by utilizing the alternative transmission mechanisms discussed above, including lowering long-term interest rates, increasing inflation expectations, boosting asset prices, and depreciating the dollar.

As is shown in Chapter 26, *expectations* have an important impact on aggregate demand. The Fed may be able use this relationship to influence aggregate demand through a policy of forward guidance. **Forward guidance** is a policy statement issued by the Federal Reserve that signals the future direction of its monetary policy. In 2012, for example, the Fed issued a statement promising to hold interest rates close to zero at least until unemployment fell to 6.5% or inflation rose above 2.5%. This policy of forward guidance was aimed at improving expectations. It was hoped that borrowers (businesses, investors, and homebuyers) would have more confidence if they knew that the Fed would keep interest rates low for an extended period of time. The Fed cannot cut current interest rates below zero, but it can promise not to raise them in the future. Forward guidance can also tend to reduce longer-term interest rates.

Homebuyers and small businesses with adjustable rate loans are especially interested in forward guidance. These loans have interest rates that are adjusted once a year to reflect the current short-term market interest rate. If the Fed promises to keep short-term interest rates low for three years, then businesses know that their borrowing costs will remain low for that period of time. This will make businesses more willing to borrow money and invest, thus boosting aggregate demand. The Fed has continued to use forward guidance in the years since the Great Recession.

Although the Fed believes that both quantitative easing and forward guidance have had some positive effects, they are somewhat experimental policies and remain controversial. A few studies suggest that quantitative easing did have a modest positive effect on growth without triggering high inflation, as some critics had feared.

Should Monetary Policy Attempt to Avoid a Liquidity Trap?

Because there has been a persistent long-run downward trend in real interest rates in many countries, including the United States (Exhibit 11), the Fed might face the same zero interest rate problem the next time the economy is in recession. For this reason, some economists have recently suggested that it would be prudent for policymakers to take steps to try to prevent future liquidity traps.

One option is to set a higher inflation target, perhaps 4% per year. The idea is that higher inflation will lead to higher nominal interest rates, making it less likely that interest rates will fall to zero. This idea is based on the Fisher effect, which says that higher inflation expectations lead to higher nominal interest rates. In high-inflation countries, central banks do not have to worry about what to do when interest rates fall to zero because higher inflation keeps rates well above zero. At the current

quantitative easing An expansionary monetary policy that involves much larger than normal open market purchases of financial assets and that is intended to increase the size of the money supply and boost spending in the economy.

forward guidance A policy statement issued by the Federal Reserve that signals the future direction of its monetary policy.

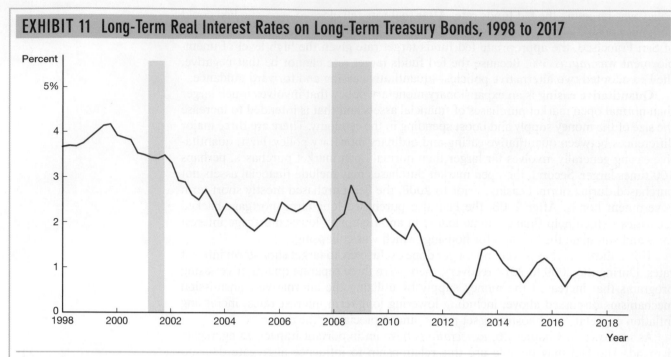

EXHIBIT 11   Long-Term Real Interest Rates on Long-Term Treasury Bonds, 1998 to 2017

The real interest rate on long-term Treasury bonds has fallen from about 4% in the early 2000s to a range of zero to 1% in recent years. Real interest rates on short-term bonds are even lower.

Data from: Federal Reserve Economic Data (FRED); 30 year Treasury Inflation-Indexed Bond, Constant Maturity since 2010 and 30 year Treasury Inflation-Indexed Bond, Due 4/15/2028 prior to 2010.

time, however, the Fed's official inflation rate target remains 2% per year. Fed officials worry that inflation expectations might become unstable if they do not stick to their announced inflation target.

Should Monetary Policy Attempt to Prevent Asset Price Bubbles?

Other economists recommend that the Fed also use monetary policy to prevent large asset price bubbles. Recall from Chapter 10 that a **bubble** is a period of time when prices rise above their true fundamental value as investors get swept up in enthusiasm that prices will rising ever higher. These economists worry that a major bubble in the price of stocks or houses could eventually burst, leading to a severe recession. For example, they claim that a Fed policy of low interest rates in the early 2000s boosted asset prices and contributed to the housing boom, which burst right before the Great Recession.

A major stock market boom also occurred in the 1920s, prior to the Great Depression. At the time, the head of the Federal Reserve was asked to do something about the boom. To paraphrase his response, "If one of my children misbehaves, do I have to spank them all?"[3] In other words, if some Wall Street speculators were taking excessive risks, did the Fed need to restrain them by raising interest rates that also would hurt the rest of society? Eventually, in 1929, the Fed did try to pop the stock bubble with tight money, but today many economists believe that this policy helped trigger the Great Depression.

bubble A period of time when prices rise above their true fundamental value as investors get swept up in enthusiasm that prices will rise ever higher.

The Fed understood this history and argued that if it had not cut interest rates sharply after the tech bubble burst in 2001, the U.S. economy mostly likely would have entered a much deeper recession in the early 2000s. The Fed takes its dual mandate (maximum employment and stable prices) seriously and therefore is reluctant to add a third mandate by trying to pop asset market bubbles.

📊 BUSINESS BRIEF A Collapsing Bubble in the Housing Market

The tech bubble of about 1997 to 2001 burst in the early 2000s, and in its aftermath, low interest rates had a significant impact on the business environment, particularly the housing market. Home builders saw an enormous spike in demand for new homes, building construction boomed, banks were willing to provide mortgage loans without much evidence of ability to repay the loan, and real estate speculators often bought houses and then "flipped" them within a few weeks to another purchaser. Many now view this scenario as a housing bubble.

All of this came to a head in 2006, when real estate prices began declining. The economic fallout from the housing bust and subsequent recession was much bigger than what was seen when the tech bubble burst in the early 2000s. Between 2007 and late 2009, Citigroup had credit losses of over $124 billion as borrowers struggled to pay back their loans. Bank of America, HSBC, Lloyds, Merrill Lynch, the Royal Bank of Scotland, UBS, and Wachovia had losses of over $50 billion. By the end of the crisis, banks lost over $2 trillion dollars globally, an amount roughly equal to one seventh of U.S. GDP. In 2008, the banking crisis helped trigger the Great Recession as banks tightened lending standards. Consumption declined as many homeowners struggled to pay off their mortgages. In response, the Fed lowered interest rates close to zero in December 2008, in an attempt to stimulate aggregate demand.*

*International Monetary Fund. Monetary and Capital Markets Department. "Global Financial Stability Report." Global Financial Stability Report, October 2010 : Sovereigns, Funding, and Systemic Liquidity. Accessed May 26, 2017. https://www.imf.org/external/pubs/cat/longres.aspx?sk=23543.0.

BUSINESS TAKEAWAY

Monetary policy affects all of the key macroeconomic variables that shape the business environment—economic output, the unemployment rate, inflation, and interest rates. Effective business decision-making requires paying attention to how the central bank adjusts its interest rate target. Lower rates give businesses more incentive to borrow for new investment projects. Even more important, the Federal Reserve's forward guidance policy statements on interest rates can influence decisions about whether to borrow money.

Monetary policy affects many other aspects of the economy, including exchange rates. When the first quantitative easing program was announced, for example, the U.S. dollar depreciated sharply against the euro, which lowered the cost of producing goods in the United States relative to Europe. This is the type of development that business managers need to be aware of when deciding where to locate a new factory.

Finally, remember not to reason from a price change. An expansionary monetary policy often leads to lower interest rates, but interest rates sometimes fall because of economic weakness and not because of an expansionary monetary policy. For business decision-making, the distinction is important. Although lower interest rates reduce the interest cost of loans to businesses, borrowing simply because rates are low could be a mistake if rates are low due to a weakening economy. How can a business tell the difference? There is no foolproof indicator, but stock prices usually rise when the Fed employs an expansionary policy and usually fall when the economy is sliding into recession. The bottom line is that businesses cannot focus only on what the central bank is doing to interest rates. They also need to look at exchange rates, stock prices, and the business cycle to form a complete picture of the effects of monetary policy.

CHAPTER STUDY GUIDE

27.1   MONEY SUPPLY, MONEY DEMAND, AND INTEREST RATES

Monetary policy is the actions that a central bank takes to change the money supply and interest rates with the goal of influencing employment and inflation. The **dual mandate** is a requirement from Congress to the Federal Reserve to promote the goals of maximum employment and stable prices. The Fed defines stable prices as roughly 2% inflation and maximum employment as keeping unemployment close to its natural rate. The **short-term interest rate** is the cost of borrowing money or the reward for saving money for less than one year. This interest rate is also the opportunity cost of holding cash and demand deposits that pay no interest. For this reason, the demand for money is negatively related to the short-term interest rate. The **long-term interest rate** is the cost of borrowing money or the reward for saving money for more than one year. These rates are less strongly impacted by monetary policy. Changes in the money supply impact short-term interest rates, particularly the **federal funds rate** which is the interest rate that banks pay when borrowing reserves from other banks.

27.2   UNDERSTANDING MONETARY POLICY

An **expansionary monetary policy** is a policy that occurs when the central bank increases the money supply and decreases short-term interest rates, often directed at boosting aggregate demand and employment. A **contractionary monetary policy** is a policy that occurs when the central bank decreases the money supply and increases short-term interest rates, often directed at reducing aggregate demand and inflation. The Federal Reserve uses expansionary monetary policy to combat a recession and contractionary monetary policy to combat inflation.

27.3   MONETARISM, NEW KEYNESIANISM, AND MODERN CENTRAL BANKING

Monetarism is a school of economic thought that stresses the role that is played by the money supply in determining nominal GDP and inflation. **New Keynesian economics** is the view that the central bank should target short-term interest rates, with the goal of keeping inflation low and stable and unemployment close to the natural rate. New Keynesian economics is the modern consensus. The Federal Reserve usually targets the fed funds rate. The **fed funds interest rate target** is the fed funds rate that the Federal Reserve believes is most likely to achieve its policy goals. The Fed adjusts this target rate as needed to accomplish its dual mandate (maximum employment and stable prices). When the economy is in recession, the Fed usually reduces its fed funds target, and when inflation is too high, the Fed usually raises its fed funds target.

27.4   MONETARY POLICY AT THE EXTREMES: THE FISHER EFFECT AND LIQUIDITY TRAPS

Fisher effect is the idea that a change in expected inflation leads to an equal change in nominal interest rates. An expansionary monetary policy may lower interest rates in the short run but increase interest rates in the long run if it leads to higher inflation expectations. A **liquidity trap** is a situation in which nominal interest rates are close to zero and thus cannot be lowered further by increases in the money supply. This occurred in the United States during both the Great Depression and the Great Recession. Keynesians believe that this prevents monetary policy from impacting aggregate demand.

27.5   ADVANCED TOPIC: ALTERNATIVE APPROACHES TO MONETARY POLICY

A **transmission mechanism** is the method by which money affects the economy. In addition to the interest rate transmission mechanism, there are several alternative transmission mechanisms. Monetary stimulus can create excess cash balances, lower long-term interest rates, increase inflation expectations, boost asset prices, and depreciate a currency. **Quantitative easing** is an expansionary monetary policy that involves much larger than normal open market purchases of financial assets and that is intended to increase the size of the money supply and boost spending in the economy. **Forward guidance** is a policy statement issued by the Federal Reserve that signals the future direction of its monetary policy. Recently, some economists have advocated policies that will decrease the likelihood of a future liquidity trap, and other economists have advocated policies that will make asset bubbles less likely. A **bubble** is a period of time when prices rise above their true fundamental value as investors get swept up in enthusiasm that prices will rise ever higher.

TOP TEN TERMS AND CONCEPTS

(1) Monetary Policy

(2) Dual Mandate

(3) Money Supply Curve and Money Demand Curve

(4) Short- and Long-Term Interest Rates

(5) Fed Funds Rate and Fed Funds Interest Rate Target

(6) Expansionary Monetary Policy and Easy Money

(7) Contractionary Monetary Policy and Tight Money

(8) Monetarism and New Keynesianism

(9) Fisher Effect

(10) Liquidity Trap

STUDY PROBLEMS

1. What is the dual mandate of the Federal Reserve?

2. If the Fed reduces interest rates, how should that affect borrowing activity by businesses and consumers? Briefly explain why.

3. In 2014, the economy of Brazil was at risk of stagflation with high inflation and high unemployment. Explain the complexities of monetary policy during such periods.

4. In recent years, the Federal Reserve has attempted to be more transparent and provide forward guidance. Explain the benefits of greater transparency in monetary policy.[4]

5. Explain the difference between expansionary monetary policy and contractionary monetary policy. Indicate under what economic circumstances each will be applied. Indicate which will decrease the sales of automobiles and houses.

6. Explain why the money demand curve is downward sloping. Draw a money supply curve and a money demand curve. Use the figure to explain why an increase in the money supply will lower interest rates.

7. In 2010, with short-term interest rates near zero, the Federal Reserve announced its intention to purchase $600 billion of long-term Treasury bonds. What new type of policy action is occurring here? Why did the Fed purchase long-term Treasury bonds and not short-term bonds?[5]

8. Draw the money supply and money demand model. Use this model to show the following:

   a. How an expansionary monetary policy changes interest rates

   b. How a contractionary monetary policy changes interest rates

   c. How an increase in money demand changes interest rates

9. Explain the link between fighting deflation with an expansionary monetary policy and seeing changes in exports and exchange rates.

10. When the Fed increases the money supply, interest rates usually decline. And yet studies show that those countries where the money supply grows fastest tend to have the highest rates of interest. Explain this paradox. Consider both the short-run and long-run effects.

11. Suppose that the economy is at risk of falling into recession and the Fed cuts interest rates by more than people were expecting. How do you think the stock market and real estate market would respond? Is the dollar likely to appreciate or depreciate in the foreign exchange markets?

12. During the 1930s, both the money supply and interest rates fell sharply. Which of these two variables did Milton Friedman believe was the best indicator of monetary policy? Explain why.

13. Paul Krugman has argued that interest rates are likely to be lower than normal in the future. Explain why he believes this will make monetary policy more difficult to operate. What two options does the Fed have for dealing with this new environment?

14. Discuss the pros and cons of the claim that the Fed is to blame for the housing bubble. What sort of alternative monetary policy might have prevented the bubble? What sort of alternative *non-monetary* policies might have prevented the bubble? Why do many Fed officials believe that non-monetary policies should be used to prevent excessive asset price bubbles?

> ∧ Fiscal policy such as increased government spending often is used to try to move the economy out of recession.

Fiscal Policy

The Impact of Government Spending and Taxes on GDP

In February 2008, the unemployment rate in the United States was 4.9%. One year later, the unemployment rate reached 8.3% as over 5 million more Americans were no longer employed. The Great Recession was in full effect. That same month, President Barack Obama signed the American Recovery and Reinvestment Act of 2009 (ARRA), aimed at boosting the economy. The ARRA was the second attempt by lawmakers to stimulate the economy in under a year. Initially, the law appeared to have little effect. Factories continued to close, and previously crowded restaurants were half empty on Friday nights. By October 2009, the unemployment rate peaked at 10.0% with an additional 3 million Americans unemployed. Then the unemployment rate began to gradually decline, returning to 4.9% in 2016.

Today, the impact of the ARRA is debated, but most economists believe that it had an expansionary effect. In this chapter, we use an aggregate supply and aggregate demand model to examine how fiscal policy such as the ARRA impacts GDP and the price level.

Chapter Learning Targets

- Define fiscal policy. Distinguish between automatic stabilizers and discretionary spending.

- Describe the fiscal multiplier effect.

- Identify factors that impact the effectiveness of expansionary monetary and fiscal policies.

- Explain how fiscal policy can affect aggregate supply.

28.1 UNDERSTANDING FISCAL POLICY

Fiscal policy refers to changes in government spending and taxation that often are aimed at influencing employment and inflation. The term describes deliberate changes in government spending and taxes at the federal level intended to stabilize the economy, beyond what would occur automatically over a business cycle. Although state governments make policies that impact their local economies, such efforts generally are not referred to as fiscal policy. An overview of government taxes and spending programs can be found in Chapter 7. The focus of this chapter is on how fiscal policy affects the overall economy, especially GDP, unemployment, and other related macro variables. The large size of the federal government in the

United States (currently about 22% of GDP) ensures that changes in federal spending and taxes have a significant impact on our economy.

Expansionary and Contractionary Fiscal Policy

When the economy is in a recession, policymakers often try to stimulate aggregate demand with expansionary fiscal policy. An **expansionary fiscal policy** (commonly referred to as **fiscal stimulus**) is an increase in government spending and/or a decrease in taxes that often is directed at increasing aggregate demand and employment. As you will discover, this policy increases the size of the budget deficit or reduces any budget surplus.

Recall that government purchases is one of the four components of GDP (consumption, investment, government purchases, and net exports): GDP = C + I + G + NX. Thus, an increase in government purchases (G) directly boosts aggregate demand at any given price level. Also recall that by definition, government spending equals government purchases plus transfer payments. Policymakers also can increase aggregate demand by increasing transfer payments (such as unemployment benefits) or by decreasing taxes. These policies encourage greater consumer spending and/or greater investment spending by businesses.

The aggregate supply and aggregate demand model can help us understand how an expansionary fiscal policy moves the economy out of a recession. Exhibit 1 shows the economy operating in a recession (point R). Real GDP at point R is less than real GDP at the natural rate of output and employment, as represented by the long-run aggregate supply curve. This means that there is cyclical unemployment.

Assume that policymakers decide to engage in expansionary fiscal policy in an effort to stimulate employment and output. This entails either lowering taxes to encourage consumption and investment spending, increasing government spending, or doing a combination of the two. In either case, aggregate demand increases, and the aggregate demand curve shifts to the right. If fiscal policy is effective, equilibrium will be established at point E, which is on the long-run aggregate supply curve. Employment is then at the natural rate, and there is no cyclical unemployment.

fiscal policy Changes in government spending and taxation that often are aimed at influencing employment and inflation.

expansionary fiscal policy An increase in government spending and/or a decrease in taxes that often is directed at increasing aggregate demand and employment; also called **fiscal stimulus**.

EXHIBIT 1 Expansionary Fiscal Policy

The economy begins in a recession at point R. An expansionary fiscal policy entails some combination of increases in government spending or lower taxes. This increases aggregate demand and a new equilibrium is established at point E.

On the other hand, a **contractionary fiscal policy** is a decrease in government spending and/or an increase in taxes that often is directed at decreasing aggregate demand and inflation. Graphically, contractionary fiscal policy will shift the aggregate demand curve to the left. This type of policy reduces the budget deficit, perhaps leading to a surplus. In reality, contractionary fiscal policies aimed at decreasing inflation are rare. Most economists believe that monetary policy is more effective at combating inflation. In this chapter, therefore, we focus on expansionary fiscal policy.

How Fiscal Policy Affects the Budget Deficit and National Debt

A budget deficit occurs when there is a negative budget balance. A negative budget balance occurs whenever tax revenue is less than government spending. Specifically,

$$\text{Budget balance} = \text{Taxes} - \text{Government spending}$$

A **budget deficit** is government spending minus net tax revenue, when government spending exceeds net tax revenue. It is simply a negative budget balance, but this negative balance is usually described as a positive number for convenience. Lower taxes and higher government spending decrease the budget balance (often pushing it further into the negative) and thus increase the budget deficit.

The budget deficit needs to be distinguished from the national debt. Recall that the **national debt** is the total amount of money owed by the federal government. It represents budget deficits accumulated over many years and hence is usually much larger than the budget deficit for a single year. Unlike the national debt, which is measured at a point in time, the budget deficit is a flow variable that is measured over a period of time—usually one year. In 2017, the national debt was $20 trillion, which was slightly higher than America's GDP, and the budget deficit for that year was much less than $1 trillion.

Increased deficit spending during tough economic times may seem counterintuitive. After all, when individuals or households suffer a job loss, it would be foolish for them to go on a shopping spree. This is one reason that expansionary fiscal policy is often controversial: It often increases the budget deficit. Even so, many economists believe that budget deficits are sometimes necessary to help move the economy toward full employment by increasing aggregate demand.

During the Great Recession, passage of the American Recovery and Reinvestment Act and other legislation substantially increased the size of the budget deficit and the national debt. Expansionary fiscal policy is sometimes referred to as *deficit spending* because the size of the budget deficit is often used as an indicator of the size of the expansionary fiscal policy. However, this interpretation is too simple. There is a difference between changes in the deficit that occur automatically during a recession and changes in the deficit that occur as part of deliberate actions by lawmakers.

Automatic Stabilizers During a recession, it is common to see the budget deficit increase largely due to automatic declines in tax revenues and increases in government spending. **Automatic stabilizers** are changes in taxes and government spending that occur automatically as a result of changes in the business cycle. Automatic stabilizers require no action by

contractionary fiscal policy A decrease in government spending and/or an increase in taxes that often is directed at decreasing aggregate demand and inflation.

budget deficit Government spending minus net tax revenue, when government spending exceeds net tax revenue.

national debt The total amount of money owed by the federal government.

automatic stabilizers Changes in taxes and government spending that occur automatically as a result of changes in the business cycle.

Fran/Cartoon Stock

current policymakers, which is why they are called "automatic." They occur even if Congress fails to act due to political gridlock.

During a recession, taxes tend to decrease without deliberate action by policymakers for two reasons—the progressive nature of income taxes and lower national income. The tax system is designed to tax those with low incomes at lower rates, which means that the tax system is progressive. This means that when incomes fall during a recession, both tax rates and tax revenues decline automatically. Similarly, corporate profits decline during a recession, automatically resulting in lower corporate income taxes being paid.

In addition, government spending tends to increase during recessions, even without deliberate actions by policymakers. As more people become unemployed, spending on unemployment benefits automatically increase. Federal spending on other social insurance programs (such as housing subsidies and food stamps) also increases automatically during a recession.

Because of automatic stabilizers, economists often look at the budget deficit *adjusted* for the state of the economy. This is known as the *cyclically adjusted budget deficit*, which is an estimate of what the budget deficit would be if the economy was not in a recession and automatic stabilizers were not in effect. During the deep recession of 2009, the budget deficit was $1,413 billion, but the cyclically adjusted deficit is estimated as only $858 billion.[1] The other $555 billion was due to automatic stabilizers.

Discretionary Fiscal Policy In addition to automatic stabilizers, policymakers often feel compelled to help stabilize the economy during a recession with more deliberate actions, such as additional government spending or tax cuts. **Discretionary spending** is government expenditures that are authorized each year by lawmakers in the annual budget. Discretionary spending pays for things like roads, education, job training, and research. In the context of stabilizing the economy, discretionary spending often takes the form of infrastructure projects such as highways and buildings. When discretionary spending is used to stabilize the economy, it is known as *discretionary fiscal policy*. The ARRA of 2009 is an example. Discretionary fiscal policy further increases the deficit beyond what occurs via automatic stabilizers.

🏛 POLICY BRIEF Expansionary Fiscal Policy during the Great Recession

Congress passed two expansionary fiscal policy measures during the Great Recession of late 2007 to mid-2009 in an effort to stimulate the economy. The Housing and Economic Recovery Act of 2008 (HERA) and the American Recovery and Reinvestment Act of 2009 (ARRA) were aimed at boosting aggregate demand by increasing government spending and lowering taxes by a combined total of over a trillion dollars (about 6% of GDP).

HERA was designed to encourage home mortgage lending in response to the subprime mortgage crisis, which had significantly reduced such lending. The act authorized to government to guarantee up to $300 billion in new mortgages if banks and other lenders reduced the loan balances of borrowers. It also provided meaningful tax assistance to first-time homebuyers—effectively providing incentives to people to purchase their first home.[*] The ARRA attempted to stimulate the overall economy via a variety of measures, including roughly $275 billion in targeted tax cuts and roughly $550 billion in increased government spending. The act included new spending on infrastructure, education, and social insurance benefits (particularly unemployment insurance). As you might expect, the combination of tax cuts and spending increases also significantly increased the size of the budget deficit. Although most economists believe that the ARRA helped promote a faster recovery, the precise impact is difficult to measure.[†]

[*]Jeremy Pelofsky, "Bush Signs Housing Bill as Fannie Mae Grows," Reuters, July 30, 2008, http://www.reuters.com/article/us-fannie-freddie-bush-idUSN3042756820080730.

[†]"End-of-Term Report," *The Economist*, September 1, 2012, http://www.economist.com/node/21561909.

discretionary spending
Government expenditures that are authorized each year by lawmakers in the annual budget.

28.2 THE MULTIPLIER EFFECT

Because government purchases are a part of GDP, discretionary spending such as building new infrastructure will directly increase GDP. But many economists believe that the total effect on GDP is even larger than the direct effect because there are indirect effects from the extra spending that affect other industries as well.

For example, consider the effects of $1 billion of government spending on a new highway. The expenditure on the highway itself will directly increase GDP because government expenditures are a part of GDP. But this does not include the indirect effects of the project. Workers and businesses employed on the highway will earn extra income. They will spend part of that extra income on consumer goods. For instance, the construction workers who become employed may then decide to buy a new car, creating more output in the auto industry. This secondary impact on consumption may cause GDP to rise by more than the initial increase in government expenditures.

The **multiplier effect** (sometimes called the **fiscal multiplier** or simply the *multiplier*) is the multiple by which a direct change in fiscal policy will impact aggregate spending. It includes the chain reaction after the initial boost to spending. It is analogous to the ripples observed when a stone is thrown into a pond: The stone initially produces a large wave, but then a series of progressively smaller waves ripple out from the impact. If the workers and businesses that build a new interstate highway spend more on consumption, then workers and businesses selling consumer goods will also earn more income. And they will in turn spend more on consumption.

Mathematically, the effect is similar to the money multiplier discussed in Chapter 24. The multiplier effect for government purchases and for changes in taxes can be expressed as

$$\text{Multiplier effect}_{\text{government purchases}} = \frac{\Delta \text{GDP}}{\Delta G}$$

$$\text{Multiplier effect}_{\text{tax}} = \frac{\Delta \text{GDP}}{\Delta T}$$

Suppose that the government increases purchases by $100 billion. The equilibrium real GDP increases by $120 billion if the multiplier is 1.2. To see this mathematically, we enter the 1.2 and $100 billion in the equation above and simplify:

$$1.2 = \frac{\Delta \text{GDP}}{\$100b}$$

$$\Delta \text{GDP} = 1.2 \times \$100b = \$120b$$

Likewise, a tax cut of $100 billion with a multiplier of negative 1.1 will increase real GDP by $110 billion:

$$-1.1 = \frac{\Delta \text{GDP}}{-\$100b}$$

$$\Delta \text{GDP} = -1.1 \times (-\$100b) = \$110b$$

The negative sign for the multiplier with taxes reflects the fact that a *reduction* in taxes results in an increase in aggregate demand and GDP. A more complete derivation of the multiplier effect is discussed in Chapter 29. For now, it is useful to understand the concept that increases in government expenditures (G) may shift aggregate demand by *more* than the initial increase in G because there may be an indirect effect of the fiscal stimulus boosting consumption. As a consequence, the multiplier may be greater than 1. Exhibit 2 shows the impact of an expansionary fiscal policy on aggregate demand, starting from a position of recession.

How Big Is the Multiplier Effect?

How much does aggregate demand shift after an initial increase in government spending? Hypothetically, the multiplier is unlimited if workers spend *all* of their extra income on domestic consumption: An extra thousand dollars spent by the government

multiplier effect The multiple by which a direct change in fiscal policy will impact aggregate spending; also called **fiscal multiplier**.

EXHIBIT 2 Fiscal Stimulus with the Multiplier Effect (Multiplier >1)

Increased government spending directly boosts aggregate demand, shifting the aggregate demand curve. The extra income earned producing government services then leads to higher consumption, which further boosts aggregate demand when the multiplier is greater than one.

would directly trigger an extra thousand dollars in aggregate income. In turn, this would lead to another extra thousand dollars in spending and even more income in a never-ending cycle.

An infinite multiplier effect might sound too good to be true, and it is. In the real world, not all of the extra income gets spent on the consumption of domestically produced goods. The people who build highways put a part of their extra income into saving, pay another part in taxes, and spend some money on imported goods, which do not directly affect GDP. In fact, if all of the initial thousand dollars in income is placed in savings, goes to taxes, or is spent on imported goods, then there will be no ripple effect at all. In this case, the multiplier would simply be 1—in other words, the original increase in government spending.

Current estimates of the multiplier effect often average somewhat lower than 2.0. Determining the multiplier effect is difficult because economists have identified a myriad of factors that may reduce the size of the multiplier effect. Indeed, the multiplier is not a single number but rather depends on the specific economic situation. As is shown in Exhibit 3, the estimated range of the multiplier varies significantly. Some estimates of the multiplier effect are *less than one*. This implies that an additional $1 billion in government spending increases aggregate demand by *less* than $1 billion. To see why this might be the case, we need to examine factors that weaken the fiscal multiplier effect.

Factors That Weaken the Multiplier Effect

Economists have a variety of factors to consider when analyzing the size of the multiplier. Here we discuss leakages in spending, crowding out of private spending, the permanent income theory, and the monetary offset of fiscal policy.

Leakages in Spending: Savings, Taxes, and Imported Goods Economists have long understood that at least some of the additional income generated by any expenditure will not be spent. Economists use the term **leakage** to describe the portion of income that is not used for the consumption of domestically produced goods but instead goes to taxes, saving, and spending on imported goods. As noted above, if none

leakage The portion of extra income that is not used for the consumption of domestically produced goods but instead goes to taxes, saving, and spending on imported goods.

EXHIBIT 3 Real-World Estimates of the Multiplier Effect in the United States

Fiscal Stimulus	Estimates of Multiplier Effect	
	Low	High
Federal spending on goods and services	0.5	2.5
Transfers to state and local government	0.4	2.2
Transfer payments to individuals	0.5	2.1
Two-year tax cut for low- and middle-income people	0.3	1.5
One-year tax cut for high-income people	0.1	0.6

Estimates of the multiplier effect vary from study to study and vary based on the type of expansionary policy. Note that tax multipliers are technically negative, but usually reported as positive numbers. Tax cuts boost spending.

Data from: Congressional Budget Office, "What Accounts for the Slow Growth of the Economy after the Recession?," November 2012, http://www.cbo.gov/sites/default/files/cbofiles/attachments/43707 -SlowRecovery.pdf.

of the additional income goes to "new" domestic consumption because of savings, taxes, and imports, there is no ripple effect, and the multiplier is 1.

POLICY BRIEF Do Sports Stadiums Boost the Local Economy?

Major sports franchises often pressure local governments to pay part of the cost of new stadiums. In some cases, teams threaten to move to another city if the local government does not provide a new facility. As a result, local governments tend to provide roughly 60% of the money needed for new stadiums, according to one study.

Team owners often use a multiplier argument to try to convince the public to support such subsidies. They claim that the construction of the stadium and the services associated with each game will boost the local economy and provide jobs for the area residents.

Most economists are skeptical of this argument for several reasons. One problem is that spending on sports tends to come out of consumers' limited entertainment budgets. That is, consumers who spend more on baseball or football games often do not spend additional money on other forms of entertainment (like travel, concerts, or dining out). Instead, they spend the money on tickets for games. In addition, a sizable part of the spending goes to wealthy team owners and highly paid athletes, who may save a large share of their income rather than spend it in the local economy. Indeed, some owners and athletes may live most of the year in a different part of the country and spend the dollars that they earn in Cleveland or Buffalo on an expensive home in Miami or Los Angeles.[*]

[*]See Dennis Coates, "A Closer Look at Stadium Subsidies," *The American*, April 29, 2008, https://www.aei.org /publication/a-closer-look-at-stadium-subsidies/.

crowding out The reduction in private spending that occurs in response to increases in government spending.

Crowding Out of Private Spending More spending by one group often means less spending by another group. **Crowding out** refers to the reduction of private spending that occurs in response to increases in government spending. For example, if the government were to provide everyone with free Internet service, then private sector spending on the Internet would decline.

A more important but subtle type of crowding out occurs when increased government spending or tax cuts increase the budget deficit. This requires

Think & Speak Like an Economist

The concept of *opportunity cost*—what must be given up in order to do something else—is applicable for fiscal policymakers. Increased government spending may crowd out private spending.

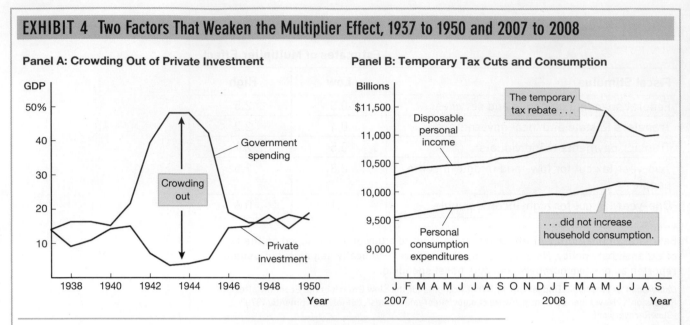

EXHIBIT 4   Two Factors That Weaken the Multiplier Effect, 1937 to 1950 and 2007 to 2008

Panel A: Crowding Out of Private Investment

Panel B: Temporary Tax Cuts and Consumption

Panel A shows that a surge in government spending during World War II crowded out private investment. Panel B shows that a temporary tax cut in 2008 caused disposable income to rise, but it changed consumption relatively little because most of the tax cut was saved.

Data from: Federal Reserve Bank of St. Louis; Congressional Budget Office, "Did the 2008 Tax Rebates Stimulate Short-Term Growth?," June 10, 2009, https://www.cbo.gov/sites/default/files/cbofiles /ftpdocs/96xx/doc9617/06-10-2008stimulus.pdf.

increased borrowing by the government, and the extra demand for loanable funds will tend to push up interest rates—discouraging private investment as well as consumer spending in other areas of the economy.

Imagine a credit market as a large arena where investors have been borrowing funds provided by savers. Now the federal government comes into the arena with hundreds of Treasury agents who are instructed to borrow a significant share of the savings that are available. They will pay whatever interest rate it takes to obtain the funds they need. The federal government's ability to borrow hundreds of billions of dollars would essentially "push aside" some of the private investors who previously had been borrowing money from savers.

There is usually less crowding out when the economy is in recession. In a recession, private investment almost always declines because businesses are reluctant to expand when sales are weak. Thus, it is unlikely that crowding out would completely offset the expansionary effect of fiscal stimulus when in a recession.

A classic example of crowding out occurred in the United States during World War II (1939–1945). When the United States became involved in the war in late 1941, government spending as a share of GDP spiked, primarily due to military spending (see Panel A of Exhibit 4). This crowded out private investment spending (and also consumption).

The Permanent Income Theory The multiplier effect is based on the idea that the public will spend a fairly large share of any increase in *disposable income*, which is the income left over after taxes are paid. In the United States, consumption tends to be about 90% of disposable income in the long run. However, economist Milton Friedman suggested that consumers base their spending decisions on their permanent income and not the income earned during any given year. **Permanent income** is the expected average income over time. **Transitory income** is any temporary increase or decrease in income. The multiplier effect from changes in transitory income is usually

permanent income The expected average income over time.

transitory income Any temporary increase or decrease in income.

much smaller than the effect from changes in permanent income. People tend to save more of temporary increases in income such as from lottery winnings or a gift at graduation.

The Economic Stimulus Act of 2008 provides a classic example of transitory income. It provided taxpayers with temporary rebates, but future tax rates were unchanged. A typical family of four received a rebate check for $1,800, and single taxpayers received a $600 rebate. As shown in Panel B of Exhibit 4, the fiscal stimulus was mostly offset by increases in savings. The Congressional Budget Office found that roughly two thirds of the tax rebate was not spent in the quarter the rebate was issued. This is likely because the tax rebate was viewed as transitory income. Consumers knew it was a one-time windfall and therefore were more inclined to save it than spend it.

∧ An expansionary fiscal policy may have a modest multiplier effect.

This insight has important implications for fiscal policy. If the government cuts taxes and the tax cut is perceived as temporary, then the permanent income theory predicts that the public will treat the extra disposable income as transitory income (money that is not likely to be earned in future years). If so, people will save most of the tax cut. This will reduce the size of the multiplier and is one reason that the one-year tax cut shown in Exhibit 3 has a smaller multiplier effect than the two-year tax cut.

The Monetary Offset of Fiscal Policy Fiscal policy should not be viewed in isolation from its monetary policy counterpart. Rather, the two types of policy should be coordinated. **Monetary offset** is the adjustment of monetary policy by the central bank to offset either a fiscal stimulus or a fiscal austerity. Monetary policy has the *potential* to offset fiscal policy. This is because both monetary policy and fiscal policy impact aggregate demand.

As is shown in Chapter 27, the central bank will adopt the monetary policy that it believes will keep aggregate demand at the appropriate level. If an expansionary or contractionary fiscal policy is adopted, it may push aggregate demand away from the level that the central bank considers appropriate. The central bank will then adjust monetary policy to prevent aggregate demand from being affected. This means that when monetary policy is targeting inflation, fiscal policy changes may be fully offset by changes in monetary policy. This can prevent a fiscal stimulus from having its usual expansionary effect.

Monetary offset is particularly relevant during periods of fiscal austerity. **Fiscal austerity** is a contractionary fiscal policy that is aimed at reducing a budget deficit or national debt. Austerity measures usually are motivated by concerns over an excessive budget deficit and a fast-growing national debt. It is the opposite of fiscal stimulus. Fiscal austerity puts downward pressure on aggregate demand, which could result in a recession, so monetary policymakers attempt to counteract austerity with an offsetting expansionary monetary policy.

Think & Speak Like an Economist

Be sure to understand the difference between *fiscal stimulus* (when the government borrows and spends more existing money) and *monetary stimulus* (when the government creates more new money).

monetary offset The adjustment of monetary policy by the central bank to offset either a fiscal stimulus or a fiscal austerity.

fiscal austerity A contractionary fiscal policy that is aimed at reducing a budget deficit or national debt.

🏛 POLICY BRIEF The Monetary Offset to Fiscal Austerity

In the case of contractionary fiscal policy, such as austerity to reduce the budget deficit or national debt, the monetary offset of fiscal policy may work in reverse. This may have occurred in 2013, when Congress sharply raised taxes and cut spending, in part to reduce the size of the federal budget deficit. The policy was successful in shrinking the budget deficit, which fell from just over a $1 trillion in 2012 to slightly more than $500 billion in 2013.* At the end of 2012, the Federal Reserve anticipated this austerity and adopted a more expansionary monetary policy. This monetary stimulus helped offset the deficit reduction and may have prevented the fiscal austerity from leading to a recession in 2013. For comparison, the European Central Bank failed to do a monetary offset, and Europe suffered from a recession when there was fiscal austerity in 2012.

Commenting on the expected austerity measures in 2012, Charles Evans, Chicago Federal Reserve Bank president, noted that "Such fiscal contraction would be a serious threat to our fragile recovery. And it would be an unusual response to economic weakness. . . . [Therefore,] the FOMC provided a more accommodative monetary policy."[†]

*Note that these deficit figures refer to calendar years, not the more commonly cited fiscal years. The austerity began on January 1, 2013.

[†]Charles Evans, quoted in Joe Weisenthal, "Now That the Fed Has Launched QE Infinity, You Need to Read Every Speech by the Head of the Chicago Fed," *Business Insider*, September 18, 2012, http://www.businessinsider .com/charlie-evans-speech-perspectives-on-current-economic-issues-2012-9.

28.3 THE EFFECTIVENESS OF EXPANSIONARY POLICIES

Economists are concerned with factors that influence the effectiveness of expansionary policies. One goal of an effective stabilization policy (both monetary policy and fiscal policy) is to smooth out the business cycle. Ideally, a policy should be expansionary during the early stages of a recession (to reduce unemployment) and contractionary during an economic boom (to prevent higher inflation). That is, both monetary policy and fiscal policy should be countercyclical. A **countercyclical policy** is a policy that is contractionary during an economic boom and expansionary during a recession. A countercyclical policy will tend to smooth out the business cycle.

However, policies have not always worked out as designed. In some cases, the monetary and fiscal stimulus that is designed to boost the economy during a recession does not kick in right away and actually ends up taking effect during the subsequent expansion. In that case, the policy *unintentionally* ends up being procyclical. A **procyclical policy** is a policy that is expansionary during an economic boom and contractionary during a recession. A procyclical policy makes the business cycle more volatile, which is undesirable. Exhibit 5 demonstrates both procyclical and countercyclical policies over the business cycle.

Policy Lags Weaken the Effectiveness of Expansionary Policies

Sometimes a monetary policy or fiscal policy might end up being procyclical instead of countercyclical. The most important reasons that this occurs have to do with policy lags. A **policy lag** is the delayed effect of policy on the economy. There are three types of policy lags—recognition lag, implementation lag, and impact lag.

Recognition Lag Policymakers seldom know the state of the economy in real time because recognizing major changes in the economy takes time. The *recognition lag* is the time between the beginning of a recession and the point at which the recession is recognized. This lag has two parts. First, it often takes time for policymakers to receive economic data on prices and output. GDP data, for example, comes in with a three-month lag. Second, even after data are available, policymakers commonly require several consecutive periods of data to recognize that a change in the business cycle has occurred. During recent recessions, most economists did not recognize that the recession was occurring until about six months into the recession. The recognition lag impacts both fiscal policymakers and the Federal Reserve.

countercyclical policy A policy that is contractionary during an economic boom and expansionary during a recession.

procyclical policy A policy that is expansionary during an economic boom and contractionary during a recession.

policy lag The delayed effect of policy on the economy.

EXHIBIT 5 Countercyclical and Procyclical Policies

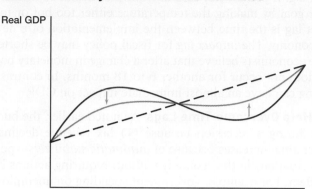

Panel A: Countercyclical Policies Are Well Timed

Real GDP

Time

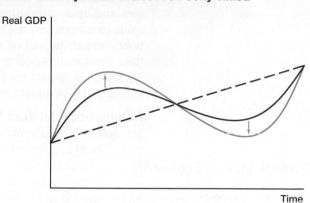

Panel B: Procyclical Policies Are Poorly Timed

Real GDP

Time

A countercyclical policy is a policy that is contractionary during an economic boom and expansionary during a recession. Such policies are ideal because they smooth out the business cycle. A procyclical policy is expansionary during an economic boom and contractionary during a recession. A procyclical policy makes the business cycle more volatile.

Implementation Lag After a recession is recognized, corrective policies are not instantly put into place. The *implementation lag* is the time between the recognition of a recession and the implementation of a policy to address the recession. The implementation lag can vary greatly from one situation to another because the time to implement a new policy depends on the policymaking process. Fiscal stimulus bills are often complex and involve negotiation over changes in government spending and taxes. It is especially difficult to coordinate fiscal policy when different parties have control of different branches of the federal government. In contrast, the implementation lag for monetary policy is relatively short because the Federal Reserve meets every six weeks to make decisions (and sometimes even more often when economic conditions are changing rapidly). The implementation lag also explains why automatic stabilizers are useful.

Recent recessions have seen a relatively slow recovery in the labor market. This gives fiscal policy more time to stimulate the economy before it becomes counterproductive. Unfortunately, the economy has changed in other ways that make timely fiscal stimulus more difficult. During the Great Depression, the U.S. government built many large infrastructure projects, such as roads, bridges, and dams. Today these projects tend to be more complex and require a great deal more planning. For instance, the government today is much more careful about studying the environmental effects of large projects, which can result in long delays between the approval of a project and actual construction. This increases the implementation lag.

In 2009, as part of the American Restoration and Recovery Act, the federal government looked for "shovel ready" projects that had already been studied and approved but that lacked funding. Because it was not possible to begin construction immediately on hundreds of billions of dollars in new infrastructure projects, much of the 2009 fiscal stimulus had to come in the form of tax cuts and increases in government transfer payments.

ʌ To avoid implementation lags, policymakers prefer projects that are "shovel ready."

Impact Lag Have you ever had trouble keeping your home or car at a comfortable temperature? When you raise or lower the heat on the thermostat, the temperature adjusts fairly slowly after the thermostat is changed. There is a delay between your action and your desired result—an impact lag. If you are not careful, your thermostat adjustment may end up overshooting your goal by making the temperature either too hot or too cold. In economics, the impact lag is the time between the implementation of a new policy and its impact on the economy. The *impact lag* for fiscal policy may be shorter than for monetary policy. Some economists believe that after a change in monetary policy, the peak impact on GDP does not occur for another 6 to 18 months. In contrast, changes in government spending can have an almost immediate impact on GDP.

Automatic Stabilizers That Help Overcome Time Lags As noted earlier, the budget deficit typically increases during a recession because (1) tax revenue declines and (2) government spending increases because of *automatic stabilizers*—policies that respond to fluctuations in the economy without requiring actions by Congress and the president. For example, government spending on unemployment benefits increases when unemployment increases. Automatic stabilizers provide policymakers with a tool to overcome problems associated with policy lags. Because of the problems associated with policy lags on discretionary fiscal policy, the single most effective type of fiscal policy may be automatic stabilizers.

> **Think & Speak Like an Economist**
>
> Economists recognize that policy lags can delay the impact of both monetary policy and fiscal policy. This can make stabilization policies less countercyclical and therefore less effective.

Expansionary Policies Are Not Effective at Full Employment

If fiscal and monetary stimulus is capable of increasing GDP, then why aren't expansionary policies always used to stimulate an economy, even when it is at full employment? There are several problems with using fiscal stimulus all the time. First, it eventually would cause the national debt to become unsustainable. But even if debt were not a problem, deficit spending is unlikely to have a simulative effect when the economy is at full employment. If aggregate demand rises when at full employment, the long-run effect will simply be higher prices, not more real output. Recall that the long-run aggregate supply curve is vertical and thus that there is a limit to how much that output can be boosted by increasing demand.

Exhibit 6 uses a production possibility frontier (PPF) (discussed in Chapter 2) to demonstrate the effectiveness of fiscal policy under two possible scenarios. Remember that the PPF represents the limit of what society currently can produce and thus the point where it is at full employment. If the economy is operating within the PPF, such as point *R*, fiscal stimulus may be able to boost output. Notice that the multiplier effect will cause output to rise by more than the increase in government spending because consumption also will increase.

In contrast, if the economy is at full employment on the production possibility frontier, such as point *F*, then any increase in government spending will be offset by lower spending on other goods. This reflects the fact that there is a *resource constraint* at full employment. In other words, when an economy is at full employment, using more workers and other resources in the government sector means that fewer resources are available for the private sector. In this case, an increase in the production of government goods means a reduction in the production of private consumption and investment goods. As a consequence, increases in government spending will fail to boost total employment or total output.

One reason that the military spending of World War II was so effective was that the economy started from a position of being in depression in 1939. But even in that case, which was ideal for fiscal stimulus, consumption declined somewhat during the early 1940s as government spending soared to unprecedented levels.

EXHIBIT 6   Fiscal Policy Is More Effective When Not at Full Employment

Fiscal policy and the multiplier effect can be expressed graphically with the production possibility frontier. At point R (recession), an increase in government spending also can result in an increase in consumption through the multiplier effect. In contrast, if the economy is at point F (full employment), there cannot be an increase in both government spending and consumption. As a consequence, both monetary policy and fiscal policy tend to be more effective when the economy is in a recession and ineffective when it is at full employment.

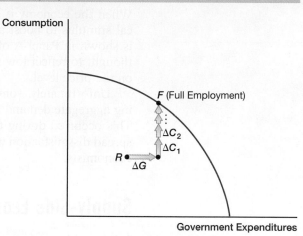

When Are Fiscal and Monetary Policies Most Effective?

Two separate policy options—fiscal policy and monetary policy—are available for combatting a recession and inflation. But which policy is more effective? To combat high inflation, most economists view monetary policy as much more effective than fiscal policy. To combat recessions, the answer is less clear. Here, the relative effectiveness of fiscal policy and monetary policy depends on whether interest rates are near zero.

Fiscal Policy Is More Effective in a Liquidity Trap As is discussed in Chapter 27, nominal interest rates were close to zero in early 2009, a situation that is known as a *liquidity trap.* The Federal Reserve and many private forecasters now believe that low interest rates may be the new normal. Many experts expect interest rates to fall again to zero in the next recession.

This environment of low interest rates has led some policymakers to focus on expansionary fiscal policy for a variety of reasons. First, with interest rates near zero, there is little concern that budget deficits will lead to interest rates high enough to crowd out private investment. Second, with interest rates near zero, there is less concern over an offsetting monetary policy. Finally, the economy is often at less than full employment when interest rates are near zero (as was the case in 2009). In this case, resource constraints that occur at full employment are less of a factor.

Monetary Policy Is More Effective When the Economy Is Not in a Liquidity Trap The modern New Keynesian consensus is that when interest rates are positive and the economy is not in a liquidity trap, central banks are the policymakers that are best able to produce low inflation and output close to the natural rate. During a recession, a monetary stimulus (such as an increase in the money supply) is viewed as more effective when interest rates have room to fall.

Economist and *New York Times* columnist Paul Krugman put it this way: "When there's an ordinary, garden-variety recession, the job of fighting that recession is assigned to the Federal Reserve." Krugman later suggested that expansionary fiscal policy is necessary only "when you're up against the zero lower bound, and conventional monetary policy is useless."[2]

28.4 SUPPLY-SIDE ECONOMICS

When the economy is in a recession, economists usually focus on monetary and fiscal stimulus to boost aggregate demand and move the economy out of recession, as is shown in Panel A of Exhibit 7. In part, this happens because most recessions are thought to reflect low aggregate demand and are associated with downward pressure on the price level.

Unfortunately, some recessions are associated with high inflation, and increasing aggregate demand to reduce unemployment will push the price level even higher. This occurred during the stagflation of the 1970s and early 1980s and led to widespread dissatisfaction with *demand-side* stabilization policies among policymakers and economists.

Supply-Side Economic Policies Increase Aggregate Supply

Is it possible to return to the natural rate of output without generating further inflation? Because demand-side policies do not work well during periods of stagflation, a group of economists began advocating a different type of fiscal policy, called **supply-side economics**—economic policies that are aimed at increasing aggregate supply. Such policies often focus on reducing marginal tax rates to boost people's incentive to work, save, and invest, but also include encouraging the development of new technology and reducing the regulatory burden on the economy. These supply-side policies aim to increase aggregate supply. As shown in Panel B of Exhibit 7, when the economy is experiencing a recession, an increase in short-run aggregate supply can move the economy back to full employment without creating inflation.

supply-side economics
Economic policies that are aimed at increasing aggregate supply.

EXHIBIT 7 Moving Out of a Recession

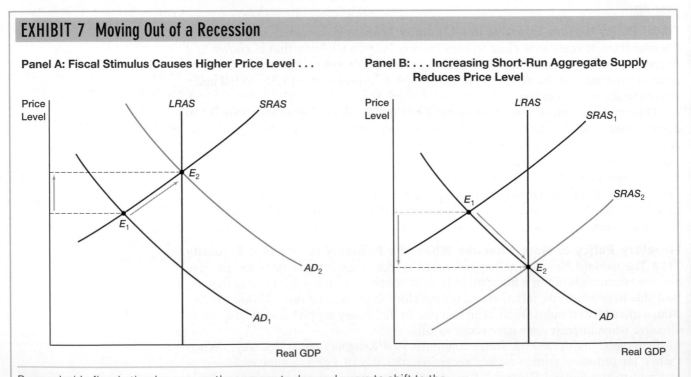

Panel A: Fiscal Stimulus Causes Higher Price Level . . .

Panel B: . . . Increasing Short-Run Aggregate Supply Reduces Price Level

Demand-side fiscal stimulus causes the aggregate demand curve to shift to the right, causing higher inflation and higher output (Panel A). Supply-side policies offer policymakers an alternative approach to moving out of a recession without generating inflation by increasing the short-run aggregate supply (Panel B).

Supply-Side Tax Policies Focus on Lower Marginal Tax Rates and Are Beneficial Even if Total Taxes Paid Are Unchanged As is shown in Chapter 7, taxing any activity tends to reduce the quantity of that activity. Supply-siders are economists who argue that taxes on labor income discourage people from working and that taxes on investment income tend to discourage savings and investment. Supply-siders focus on *marginal tax rates*, which is the tax you pay on additional income.

A cut in marginal tax rates gives workers and firms more incentive to create wealth because they will be able to keep a larger percentage of any additional income they earn. This will shift the short-run aggregate supply curve to the right, lowering inflation and raising output. Supply-siders argue that such tax cuts have additional benefits in the long run because they expand society's productive capacity. Moreover, lower marginal tax rates can boost aggregate supply even if the total tax revenue that is collected does not change.

Supply-siders claim that tax cuts would boost output and employment without any rise in inflation, as can be seen in Panel B of Exhibit 7. This is a radically different way of looking at fiscal policy. Thus, it is helpful to compare two types of tax cuts—a demand-side cut and a supply-side cut:

- *Tax cut A.* Each taxpayer receives a $600 tax rebate similar to the rebate given for the Economic Recovery Act of 2008. Tax rates are unchanged.
- *Tax cut B.* The marginal tax rate is reduced by 2%, and lost tax revenues are offset by closing tax "loopholes" (deductions and exemptions).

In tax cut A, there is no change in marginal tax rates. Taxpayers in the 35% tax bracket continue to pay 35 cents of every extra dollar earned in taxes. However, because of the $600 tax rebate, each taxpayer pays less in total taxes and ends up with more disposable income. This is considered a demand-side tax cut because the extra disposable income should lead to an increase in aggregate demand, especially consumption.

In tax cut B, there is no change in total taxes paid or in disposable income. The marginal tax rate is reduced, but that is offset by fewer tax deductions and exemptions (sometimes called "loopholes"). These include deductions for charitable giving and home mortgage interest, which allow people to pay less in taxes. Eliminating these loopholes allows the government to lower tax *rates* without changing the amount of total taxes paid. Supply-siders argue that the second tax change is more effective than the first, even though it does not cut the total amount of taxes paid. This is because a lower marginal tax rate on an extra dollar earned would increase the *incentive* to work, save, and invest.

Supply-siders claim that cuts in marginal tax rates will boost aggregate supply in the economy even if the amount of total taxes paid remains unchanged. Total taxes paid can remain unchanged by eliminating tax exemptions and tax deductions. Some supply-siders actually prefer a *flat tax*—meaning one low tax rate on all earnings and no tax deductions or exemptions at all. Supply-siders claim that lower marginal tax rates would boost output and employment without any rise in inflation, by shifting the SRAS curve rightward as shown in Panel B of Exhibit 7.

Think & Speak Like an Economist

Remember that marginal analysis involves comparing the additional benefits of an activity with the additional cost. When marginal tax rates are high, the marginal benefit of working additional hours is reduced.

Think & Speak Like an Economist

Economists distinguish between demand-side policies (which encourage people and businesses to spend more money) and supply-side policies (which encourage people and businesses to produce more goods and services).

 POLICY BRIEF Tax Rates and Female Labor Force Participation

The U.S. labor force underwent a dramatic shift in the second half of the twentieth century. From the early 1950s to the early 2000s, women's labor force participation doubled—rising from about 33% to 60%. Many factors encouraged this shift, among them the women's equality movement, the arrival of labor-saving household appliances, the increased availability of birth control, and a subsequent trend toward smaller families. However, tax rates might also have played a role, especially among affluent families.

During the 1950s and early 1960s, it was relatively common for low-income women to work in paid jobs and for women in affluent families to stay home. At that time, the top marginal income tax rate was about 90% for high earners, which meant that the wife of a well-paid business executive who decided to start or return to a career would net very little after-tax income.

The top marginal income tax rate was gradually reduced to 50% and then in 1986 was suddenly reduced all the way down to only 28%. One study found that the 1986 tax cut raised the labor force participation rate for married women in the top 1% earning families by 9 percentage points and for married women in the 75th percentile by 5.3 percentage points. Because the 1986 bill did not significantly reduce marginal tax rates for lower-income families, their labor force participation was not greatly affected.* In the twenty-first century, the typical affluent family now has two professional workers, a reversal of the tradition pattern during the 1950s, when paid work by women was something done mostly by women from lower-income families.

*See Chinhui Juhn and Simon Potter, "Changes in Labor Force Participation in the United States," *Journal of Economic Perspectives* 20, no. 3 (2006): 27–46.

Supply-Side Implications in the Design of Social Insurance Programs
Supply-siders do not focus only on taxes. They also worry that badly designed social insurance programs (such as welfare and food stamps) can discourage people from being more productive. Consider the following example. Suppose that you earn $10,000 per year working part time and receive another $8,000 in government aid for a total of $18,000 per year. Now assume that you are offered a full-time position that pays $20,000 per year (with no additional benefits) but that would require you to lose government aid. In this case, your actual total income, including government aid, would increase by only $2,000 (from $18,000 to $20,000 per year). And that does not even account for the extra costs of working full time, such as increased child-care expenses and commuting costs.

Supply-siders suggest that losing benefits when you work harder has a disincentive effect, much like high marginal tax rates: These disincentive effects from losing benefits are sometimes called *implicit marginal tax rates*. In the above example, the implicit marginal tax rate is 80% because the worker keeps 20% ($2,000) of the $10,000 in additional earnings. Supply-siders tend to prefer social insurance programs that have lower implicit marginal tax rates, such as the Earned Income Tax Credit (EITC). The EITC is a tax benefit for low- to moderate-income working families that reduces the amount of taxes owed and in some cases results in a refund check.

Supply-Side Government Spending Policies Although supply-siders focus on tax cuts, there also may be supply-side effects from some types of government spending. In particular, economists point to three categories of government spending that can make the private sector more productive—infrastructure, research and development, and job training. Notice that these three areas relate to three of the key determinants of long-run growth that are discussed in Chapter 22—physical capital (infrastructure), technology (research and development), and human capital (job training).

The Laffer Curve and U.S. Income Tax Policies

Laffer curve A graph that shows the relationship between tax rates on income and tax revenues.

In Chapter 7, you discovered that higher tax rates on products like pizza and cigarettes *may* reduce total tax revenue when tax rates are relatively high. In the 1980s, Arthur Laffer, a supply-side economist, applied this concept to income taxes. The **Laffer curve** is a graph that shows the relationship between tax rates on income and tax revenues.

EXHIBIT 8 The Laffer Curve

When tax rates on income are zero, the amount of tax revenue collected is zero. Zero tax revenue also is collected when tax rates on income are 100%. Increasing tax rates from zero and decreasing tax rates from 100% both lead to higher tax revenue.

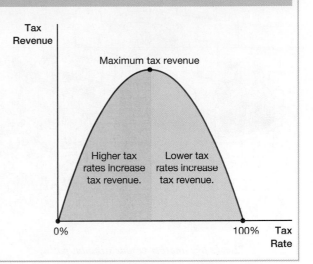

Exhibit 8 shows a Laffer curve. When tax rates on income are zero, the amount of tax revenue collected is zero. Zero tax revenue is also collected when tax rates on income are 100%. This happens because every dollar you earn increases the amount of taxes you pay by one dollar, leaving you with a zero after-tax wage rate and thus no incentive to work. In between these extremes, there was some tax rate that maximized revenue for the government. Increasing tax rates from zero and decreasing tax rates from 100% both lead to higher tax revenue.

Laffer's claim that an income tax cut could yield more revenue for the government underpinned the tax cuts proposed by President Ronald Reagan in 1981. At the time, the top marginal tax rate was 70%, which supply-side economists believed was beyond the peak of the Laffer curve.[3] The tax cuts that followed cemented the association of Reagan's economic policy (sometimes referred to as *Reaganomics*) with the supply-side view. In 2018, the Donald Trump administration cut the corporate tax rate (from 35% to 21%), a move that also was motivated by supply-side arguments that it would boost capital investment in the economy.

The argument for Laffer curve effects is stronger in analyzing the tax reduction that occurred in the early 1960s, when the top federal income tax rate was 90%. In 1962, at the Economics Club of New York, President John F. Kennedy suggested that tax cuts could actually yield more revenue in the long run:

> "It is a paradoxical truth that tax rates are too high today and tax revenues are too low and the soundest way to raise the revenues in the long run is to cut the rates now."[4]

One year later, Congress passed legislation that reduced the top income tax rate from 90% to 70%, and tax revenues increased. The top tax rates remained at 70% until the 1981 Reagan tax cuts.[5]

At today's tax rates, most economists are skeptical that lower tax rates can yield more revenue. In 2012, a survey asked leading economists what would happen to tax revenue if income tax rates were cut. Not a single economist claimed that tax revenue would increase, 91% thought that tax revenue would decrease, and the rest were uncertain or had no opinion.[6] At the time, the top federal tax rate was 35%, and economists widely believed that this tax rate was *not* high enough so that a tax rate cut would increase tax revenue. In other words, we were on the left side of the Laffer curve.

Mick Stevens/Conde Nast

"Looks like another ye olde stimulus package."

Supply-Side versus Demand-Side Views of Fiscal Stimulus

Because demand-side policies are more effective at moving an economy out of a recession than at spurring long-run economic growth, most economists believe that demand-side policies are most effective in the short run. In contrast, supply-siders argue that their preferred policies are more effective in the long run. This is partly because lower tax rates on savings and investment will stimulate capital formation and expand society's productive capacity—a process that takes a fair amount of time. Government spending on infrastructure, research and development, and job training also may encourage long-run economic growth.

There is one important similarity between the supply-side and the demand-side views of fiscal stimulus: Both sides agree that tax cuts are expansionary and should increase real GDP. But they differ about the reasons why. In the demand-side models, the key variable is *disposable income*. Tax cuts give people more disposable income, which encourages consumption and boosts aggregate demand.

Supply-siders view *marginal tax rates* as the key variable. A reduction in marginal tax rates gives people more incentive to work, save, and invest, which boosts aggregate supply. Demand-side models predict that tax cuts should increase aggregate demand and push inflation higher. Supply-side models predict that tax cuts should increase aggregate supply and push inflation lower. As a consequence, supply-side policies will be more effective during stagflation.

Government spending on infrastructure, research and development, and job training also may tend to increase aggregate demand because any increase in government spending can shift aggregate demand rightward. But spending in these areas also can have a favorable impact on aggregate supply by shifting the aggregate supply curve rightward.

Demand-side policies are not very effective during stagflation. If you boost aggregate demand to bring down unemployment, inflation will tend to be pushed even higher. In contrast, supply-side policies may be able to produce the best of both worlds. An increase in aggregate supply will boost real GDP, which increases employment while reducing inflation.

 POLICY BRIEF Supply-Side Tax Policies from around the World

Some supply-siders note that tax rates are considerably higher and labor supply is somewhat lower in most European countries than they are in the United States. In Exhibit 9, the blue line shows average hours worked annually in the United States (roughly 1,700 hours). Note that in Germany (green) and France (red), the hours worked annually used to be higher than the U.S. hours. After the 1960s, however, European tax rates rose to levels well above U.S. tax rates, and this was associated with a decline in hours worked in Western Europe to levels below the hours worked in the United States.

The tax rates in the East Asian countries of South Korea (orange), Singapore (brown), and Hong Kong (purple) are lower than the U.S. rates. Their governments spend only about 18% to 22% of GDP, whereas the U.S. government (local, state, and federal) spends about 35% of GDP, and many European countries spend about 45% to 55% of GDP. People in those East Asian countries work considerably more hours than do people in the United States. Among high-income countries, the international comparisons of hours worked provides additional evidence for the

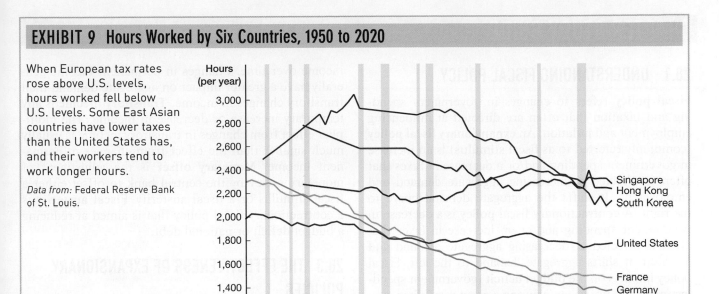

EXHIBIT 9   Hours Worked by Six Countries, 1950 to 2020

When European tax rates rose above U.S. levels, hours worked fell below U.S. levels. Some East Asian countries have lower taxes than the United States has, and their workers tend to work longer hours.

Data from: Federal Reserve Bank of St. Louis.

supply-side effect of taxes that is not picked up in year-to-year changes within the United States. So if taxes do discourage work, saving, and investment, the effect may occur only gradually over time.

BUSINESS TAKEAWAY

Fiscal policy can affect the business environment and subsequent decision-making in two ways—through government spending and through tax changes. Businesses may have an interest in encouraging those types of fiscal stimulus that boost productivity. Airlines and trucking companies are keenly interested in infrastructure improvements.

Although government spending can affect specific sectors of the economy, tax changes can impact all businesses, from the smallest to the largest. One popular antirecession policy is called the *investment tax credit*. This gives companies a tax break (i.e., a subsidy) for making new investments in machines and equipment.

Companies need to pay close attention to the timing of fiscal policy because these tax changes may last for only a year or two. It would be foolish to start an investment project a few weeks before an investment tax credit takes effect, when a brief delay might result in millions of dollars in tax savings.

More broadly, businesses need to pay close attention to fiscal policy because it can impact demand for various products. If Ford Motor Company knows that the government will provide average Americans with a large tax break next year, it may want to gear up now for increased auto production under the assumption that consumers will spend a portion of that tax cut on new cars.

One indicator of the importance of fiscal policy is the enormous growth of lobbying in the Washington, DC, area. Companies and organizations representing specific industries spend a great deal of money trying to ensure that fiscal changes will benefit their particular industries. For example, during the 20-year period ending in 2017, firms in the communication and electronics sector spent more than $6 billion on lobbying activities.[7]

CHAPTER STUDY GUIDE

28.1 UNDERSTANDING FISCAL POLICY

Fiscal policy refers to changes in government spending and taxation that often are directed at influencing employment and inflation. An **expansionary fiscal policy** (commonly referred to as **fiscal stimulus**) is an increase in government spending and/or a decrease in taxes that often is directed at increasing aggregate demand and employment. It shifts the aggregate demand curve to the right. A **contractionary fiscal policy** is a decrease in government spending and/or an increase in taxes that often is directed at decreasing aggregate demand and inflation. It shifts aggregate demand to the left. Fiscal policy impacts on the **budget deficit** (government spending minus net tax revenue during a given year, when government spending exceeds net tax revenue) and **national debt** (the total amount of money owed by the federal government). **Automatic stabilizers** are changes in taxes and government spending that occur automatically as a result of changes in the business cycle. Automatic stabilizers require no action by current policymakers. Because of automatic stabilizers, economists focus on the budget deficit adjusted for the state of the economy. This is known as the cyclically adjusted budget deficit. In addition to automatic stabilizers, policymakers often use discretionary spending (such as additional government spending or tax cuts) to formulate fiscal policies during a recession. **Discretionary spending** is government expenditures that are authorized each year by lawmakers in the annual budget.

28.2 THE MULTIPLIER EFFECT

The **multiplier effect (fiscal multiplier)** is the multiple by which a direct change in fiscal policy will impact aggregate spending. When fiscal policy is the result of an increase in government purchases, the multiplier effect equals $\Delta GDP/\Delta G$. Often this is called simply "the multiplier." Several factors impact the multiplier. Real-world estimates of the multiplier vary due to **leakage**—the portion of income that is not used for the consumption of domestically produced goods but instead goes to taxes, savings, and spending on imported goods. Estimates of the multiplier also are affected by the crowding out of private spending, the permanent income theory, and monetary offset. **Crowding out** refers to the reducing of private spending that occurs in response to increases in government spending. **Permanent income** is the expected average income over time. Changes in permanent income generally have a greater impact on aggregate demand than transitory changes in income. **Transitory income** is any temporary increase or decrease in income. The multiplier effect from changes in transitory income is usually much smaller than the effect from changes in permanent income. **Monetary offset** is the adjustment of monetary policy by the central bank to offset either a fiscal stimulus or a fiscal austerity. **Fiscal austerity** is a contractionary fiscal policy that is aimed at reducing a budget deficit or national debt.

28.3 THE EFFECTIVENESS OF EXPANSIONARY POLICIES

A **countercyclical policy** is a policy that is contractionary during an economic boom and expansionary during a recession. A **procyclical policy** is a policy that is expansionary during an economic boom and contractionary during a recession. Ideally, policy should be countercyclical. A **policy lag** represents the delayed effect of policy on the economy. There are three types of policy lags—recognition lag, implementation lag, and impact lag. The effectiveness of fiscal and monetary policy depends on the state of the economy. At full employment, expansionary fiscal policy tends to be less effective. Fiscal policy is particularly effective in a near-zero interest rate environment (the liquidity trap). In contrast, monetary policy tends to be most effective when interest rates are not near zero.

28.4 SUPPLY-SIDE ECONOMICS

When stagflation is a problem, aggregate demand policies (such as expansionary fiscal and monetary policies) tend to be less effective because increases in aggregate demand further increase inflation. **Supply-side economics** refers to economic policies that are aimed at increasing aggregate supply. Such policies often focus on reducing marginal tax rates to boost people's incentive to work, save, and invest, but also include encouraging the development of new technology and reducing the regulatory burden on the economy. Supply-siders believe that cuts in marginal tax rates will boost aggregate supply in the economy even if the amount of total taxes paid remains unchanged. Moreover, supply-side policies tend to focus on the long run. The Laffer curve is a graph that shows the relationship between tax rates and tax revenues.

TOP TEN TERMS AND CONCEPTS

(1) Expansionary Fiscal Policy (Fiscal Stimulus)

(2) Contractionary Fiscal Policy

(3) Automatic Stabilizers

(4) Multiplier Effect (Fiscal Multiplier)

(5) Crowding Out

(6) Permanent Income and Transitory Income

(7) Monetary Offset

(8) Fiscal Austerity

(9) Policy Effectiveness in a Liquidity Trap

(10) Supply-Side Economics

STUDY PROBLEMS

1. When an economy is in a recession, what is the correct fiscal policy? What will happen to government spending? Taxes? Aggregate demand? Using an aggregate supply and aggregate demand model, graph the impact of the correct fiscal policy.

2. How do taxes act as an automatic stabilizer? Are automatic stabilizers impacted by time lags? Explain.

3. Compare and contrast monetary policy and fiscal policy. Also contrast the goals of both policies.

4. Explain the linkages between the budget deficit and fiscal policy.

5. Explain factors that impact the size of the fiscal multiplier.

6. In the commentary section of the *Wall Street Journal*, Bill Cassidy and Louis Woodhill wrote: "Had GDP grown from 2001 to 2014 at the 3.87% annual rate of 1993 to 2000, the federal government would have had a $500 billion surplus in 2014 instead of a $500 deficit."[8] Explain this quote in the context of cyclical and structural deficits.

7. In 2015, Prime Minister Shinzo Abe of Japan unveiled a plan to balance the budget in five years. Japan's national debt is over twice its GDP. According to Abe, "It's crucial to tackle economic and fiscal overhauls simultaneously and not miss the current opportunity when the economy is progressing toward revival."[9] Explain why it is easier to reduce the national debt in a good economy than during a recession.

8. Compare and contrast supply-side policies with demand-side fiscal policies. Do supply-side policies involve only reducing taxes?

9. In 2012, policymakers were concerned about the budget balance and began engaging in austerity measures. The intended reduction in the deficit was known as the fiscal cliff. Consequently, the Federal Reserve continued to engage in expansionary monetary policy through open market purchases. In late 2012, the president of the Boston Federal Reserve, Charles Rosengren, made the following comment: "In other words, the policy action is open-ended versus time-bound. Should the economy experience another shock—say from a U.S. "fiscal cliff" situation or a shock from abroad, then we could lengthen the period of purchases [quantitative easing] or increase the amounts (or both)."[10] Explain the quote in the context of fiscal austerity and monetary offset.

10. Explain the impact of a temporary tax credit in the context of the permanent income theory.

11. *Forbes* columnist and former Treasury Department economist Bruce Bartlett wrote about a government study that looked at the effectiveness of the 2009 fiscal stimulus. The Congressional Budget Office study found that spending on public works raised GDP by $2.50 for each $1 spent. Spending on transfer payments had a smaller impact than spending on public works but a larger effect than tax cuts. Moreover, "tax cuts for low-income individuals raise GDP by as much as $1.70 for every $1 of revenue loss, while those for the rich and for corporations raised GDP by at most 50 cents for every $1 of revenue loss."[11] What concept is Bartlett describing? Why do estimates vary?

12. Describe how spending on a new sports stadium may crowd out private spending and investment.

13. Explain the link between marginal tax rates and incentives for households and businesses to earn additional income. How do lower marginal tax rates impact the aggregate supply curve?

14. Describe the Laffer curve. Does it suggest that lower tax rates will always increase tax revenue? Explain.

∧ Ideas inspired by John Maynard Keynes led the construction of the Hoover Damn.

The Aggregate Expenditure Model

A Fixed-Price-Level Model of the Economy

"We are all Keynesians now." Those famous words, attributed to President Richard Nixon twenty-five years after the death of John Maynard Keynes (1883–1946), speak to the profound influence that the noted British economist had on economic policy in the twentieth century. His ideas continue to have a major impact on both economics and public policy today. Keynes (pronounced "canes") continued to appear on the covers of magazines like *Time* and *Bloomberg Businessweek* years after his death.

Keynes's landmark theory was developed in the midst of the Great Depression of the 1930s when the economy seemed to be stuck in a period of high unemployment. His most important ideas appear in *The General Theory of Money, Employment, and Income* (1936). In it, Keynes argues that laissez-faire policy approaches were not working and that government needed to actively boost aggregate demand. Keynes became an advocate for using the sort of expansionary fiscal policy covered in Chapter 28 during recessions.

In this chapter, we present Keynes's ideas using the aggregate expenditure model, which assumes a fixed price level when the economy is operating at less than full employment, such as during the Great Depression and Great Recession. The analysis provides insights into Keynes's views and especially the way that his theories shaped the modern view of the multiplier effect.

Chapter Learning Targets

- Summarize how Keynes's economic theories challenged the classical model.

- Describe key components of the aggregate expenditure model.

- Explain equilibrium and the expenditure multiplier effect within the context of the aggregate expenditure model.

- Use the aggregate expenditure model to demonstrate fiscal policy.

- Distinguish key differences between the Keynesian and classical models.

^ John Maynard Keynes was an advocate for using expansionary fiscal policy in a recession.

Bettmann/Getty Images

29.1 KEYNES CHALLENGES THE CLASSICAL VIEW OF ECONOMICS

Prior to John Maynard Keynes, economists largely subscribed to what is now referred to as the classical view, which was the dominant school of economic thought preceding the Great Depression. Classical economists such as Adam Smith argued that free markets were usually optimal for society. In *The Wealth of Nations* (1776), Smith wrote that the free market reaches equilibrium "as if guided by an invisible hand." Although Keynes himself was a highly regarded classically trained economist, the Great Depression led him to reject several key aspects of Smith's classical model.

In order to understand how Keynes changed the field of economics, it is useful first to compare the key differences between Keynesian and classical views.

- *The role of saving.* The classical model reflected traditional ideas such as the notions that saving is virtuous (consider the old saying "A penny saved is a penny earned") and helps an economy to grow over time through capital accumulation. Keynes argued that during a recession, the economy can actually be hurt if society saves more and reduces consumption.

- *The self-correcting mechanism.* The classical economists believed that when an economy temporarily moved away from the natural rate of output and entered a recession, wages and prices would adjust to bring it back to the long-run equilibrium within a year or two. In Keynes's view, an economy may remain in recession indefinitely unless aided by fiscal stimulus.

- *The role of government spending.* The classical view held that an increase in government spending would depress or "crowd out" private-sector spending. This is based on the idea of opportunity cost, which means that if more resources are put into government spending, fewer will be available for other activities. Keynes argued that there are times when more spending on government programs will not involve any opportunity cost because private spending also increases. He convinced most economists that increased government spending can help move an economy out of a recession.

- *The role of money.* The classical view was that increasing the money supply leads to higher prices with no impact on real GDP in the long run. Keynes argued that an increase in the money supply can boost real GDP when the economy is depressed by decreasing interest rates, as long as the economy is not in a liquidity trap with interest rates near zero. When the economy is in a liquidity trap (as was the case during the Great Depression), Keynes argued that increasing the money supply might be ineffective at raising either real GDP or prices.

- *Emphasis on the short run rather than the long run.* The classical view was that the most important factor explaining national income was productivity. As countries become more productive, they become richer. The classical productivity approach is still used to explain long-run economic growth, as is shown in Chapter 22. Keynes understood that productivity is important in the long run but also famously said, "In the long run we are all dead." His focus was on short-run solutions to a lack of aggregate demand.

The Keynesian Short-Run Aggregate Supply Curve

Keynes's most important work focuses on short-run problems, particularly a lack of aggregate demand, which was the major problem during the 1930s. The economy had plenty of capacity to produce goods and services, but the resources were idle. Workers were unemployed, and factories were shut down. Under those conditions, Keynes argued, shifts in aggregate demand are the key to explaining short-run movements in real GDP.

Keynes argued that it is reasonable to treat the price level as fixed when the economy is in a recession. If we think in terms of the aggregate supply and aggregate demand model, then Keynes believed that the economy often operated below its natural rate of output. When output is depressed, he believed that the aggregate supply curve is flat. He also believed that after full employment is reached, the economy is at the natural rate of employment, and additional aggregate demand will lead to higher prices. Thus at full employment his views are similar to the classical theory. Exhibit 1 shows the Keynesian short-run aggregate supply (KSRAS) curve.

In Chapter 28, we assume that fiscal stimulus boosts *both* the price level (creating inflation) and output, a function of an upward-sloping short-run aggregate supply curve. In this chapter, we use the flat portion of the KSRAS to analyze the economy because we now assume less than full employment (the economy is operating below the natural rate at a fixed price level). This means that an increase in aggregate demand will boost *only* real GDP and will have no impact on the price level or inflation. This is most likely to be true when the economy is depressed or in a recession. This stable price level assumption allows us to better understand Keynes's insights into fiscal policy and the multiplier.

The Production Possibility Frontier: Keynesian and Classical Views

If we are operating inside the production possibilities frontier (PPF), then the laws of economics look very different from the classical theories based on opportunity cost. Exhibit 2 demonstrates the difference between the classical view and Keynes's view with two production possibility curves. The classical view of the economy is shown in Panel A, which assumes that the economy is operating on the PPF at the natural rate of output. More spending in one sector of the economy has an *opportunity cost* and

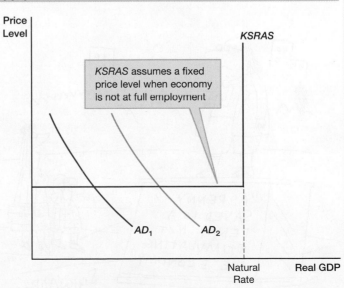

EXHIBIT 1 The Keynesian Short-Run Aggregate Supply (KSRAS) Curve and Fiscal Policy

Keynes viewed the short-run aggregate supply curve as flat for levels of real GDP below the natural rate. As a result, expansionary fiscal policy will stimulate aggregate demand and increase real GDP with no impact on the price level or inflation. Keynes argued that it was reasonable to treat the price level as fixed when the economy is in a recession.

KSRAS assumes a fixed price level when economy is not at full employment

EXHIBIT 2   The Production Possibility Frontier: Keynesian and Classical Views

Panel A: The Classical Opportunity Cost View

Consumption
Goods

More physical capital means less consumption goods

A

B

0   Capital Goods

Panel B: The Keynesian Multiplier View

Consumption
Goods

More physical capital and more consumption goods

B

R

0   Capital Goods

The classical view assumes that the economy is on the production possibility frontier. In Panel A, more investment spending on physical capital has an opportunity cost of fewer consumption goods. In Panel B, the Keynesian view occurs with the economy in a recession (point R). Under such circumstances, both consumption and physical capital can increase.

leads to less spending in other areas. In Exhibit 2, this is demonstrated as a movement from point *A* to point *B*. Producing more capital goods (investment) means that fewer consumption goods can be produced.

In contrast, Panel B shows the PPF during a recession—a Keynesian perspective. Notice that during a recession, spending on both consumer and physical capital can rise at the same time. There is no opportunity cost to more physical capital, which can actually lead to more consumption as well. The increase in physical capital results from investment spending that can come from the private sector (such as when Tesla built a large battery factory in Nevada in 2017) or government spending (such as when the federal government built the Hoover Dam on the Colorado River in the 1930s). Here, more government spending of any type during a recession does not crowd out private spending. This lack of crowding out is one of the most distinctive features of the Keynesian model.

The Paradox of Thrift

Suppose that someone says to you, "More saving is good for the economy. It provides the funds that allow for higher investment." That sounds reasonable, doesn't it? Now suppose that someone says, "If consumers would go shopping and spend more, they would provide a boost to the economy." That also sounds reasonable. But both cannot be true because more spending means less saving. The first statement reflects the classical economists' belief that saving is virtuous, and the second captures Keynes's argument that, during a recession, attempts to increase saving make things worse by decreasing consumption—a phenomenon that Keynes refers to as the paradox of thrift.

The **paradox of thrift** is the economic theory stating that attempts to save more can depress aggregate demand, leaving actual saving no higher than before. Normally, when people save more, the interest rate falls, and this encourages more borrowing for investment. But Keynes suggests another possibility. Suppose that people try to save more by spending less. The lower spending on consumption pushes the economy into a recession. As incomes fall, the public becomes poorer, and this makes people decide not to save more after all. Although we began by assuming that people want to save more, in the end saving and investment may not change because national income falls instead. This is why Keynes calls it a "paradox." The attempt to save more backfires, and we end up in a recession. It is another example of how economic outcomes are often different in the long run than in the short run (Chapter 1). The paradox of thrift is the single best way to understand how Keynes turned the classical model upside down.

In Keynes's view, *national income and expenditures* have a bigger effect on saving and investment than interest rates do. As you will see, national income is the key variable in Keynes's aggregate expenditure model (discussed in the next section). If the economy is depressed, then changes in spending are the key factor driving changes in real GDP.

29.2 THE AGGREGATE EXPENDITURE MODEL

In Chapter 26, we developed the aggregate supply and aggregate demand (AS/AD) model as an all-purpose tool for explaining business cycles and considered both aggregate supply and aggregate demand shocks. In this section, we take a deeper look at the demand side to show how Keynes focuses on explaining changes in aggregate expenditures, which for him is the main factor causing business cycles.

The **aggregate expenditure model** is an economic model that demonstrates the short-run relationship between aggregate expenditures and real GDP, assuming the price level is constant. **Aggregate expenditure** is the level of total spending in the economy at each level of real GDP (income), *ceteris paribus*.

In the following equation (as with aggregate demand), aggregate expenditure (*AE*) equals consumption spending (*C*) plus investment spending (*I*) plus government spending (*G*) and net exports (*NX*):

$$AE = C + I + G + NX$$

For simplicity in this chapter, however, we assume that the economy is not open to international trade and there are no net exports (*NX*):

$$AE = C + I + G$$

The crucial difference between aggregate demand and aggregate expenditure is that aggregate demand depends on the price level whereas the aggregate expenditure model assumes that the price level is fixed. Instead of varying prices, the aggregate expenditure model explains how total expenditures (spending) depend on the level of real aggregate income or real GDP and also how changes in aggregate expenditure affect real GDP. Put simply, how much we spend depends on how much we earn, but it's also true that, in aggregate, how much we earn depends on how much we spend.

There are four key facts to remember about the aggregate expenditure model:

- It is a short-run model.
- It assumes that the price level is fixed.
- It shows the relationship between aggregate expenditures and real GDP.
- It best explains the economy when it is at less than full employment (below the natural rate).

The Consumption Function

We begin by examining consumption, which is the largest share of GDP. Exhibit 3 models the consumption component of aggregate expenditures as a function of real GDP. As with the aggregate supply and aggregate demand model, one axis is labeled "real GDP." Unlike the AS/AD graph, however, the other axis is labeled "expenditures" and not "price level."

paradox of thrift The economic theory stating that attempts to save more can depress aggregate demand, leaving actual saving no higher than before.

aggregate expenditure model An economic model that demonstrates the short-run relationship between aggregate expenditures and real GDP, assuming the price level is constant.

aggregate expenditure The level of total spending in the economy at each level of real GDP (income), *ceteris paribus*.

EXHIBIT 3 The Consumption Function: The Aggregate Expenditure Model

The consumption function shows the relationship between consumption spending and real GDP. The level of autonomous consumption is the level of spending that occurs when income levels are zero. The marginal propensity to consume is the additional consumption from additional income. Here the marginal propensity to consume is 0.75. Data for the graph can be found in Exhibit 4.

Expenditures

$5,000

Marginal propensity to consume (additional income or slope of consumption function) MPC = 0.75

4,000

Consumption

3,000

2,000

1,000

Autonomous consumption = $250

A

0   1,000   2,000   3,000   4,000   5,000

Real GDP

The **consumption function** shows the relationship between consumption spending and real GDP. The function has a positive slope, which is common sense because consumption tends to increase with income. People with high incomes spend more, on average, than people with low incomes. Likewise, spending tends to increase when an individual receives a raise or when a student gets a job after graduation. Also note that in Exhibit 3, there is a positive level of consumption even when income is zero, and consumption tends to rise more slowly than income.

Consumption at Zero Income In the short run, a minimal level of consumption spending occurs regardless of income. The minimum level of consumption is what economists refer to as **autonomous consumption**—the level of expenditure that occurs when income levels are zero.

At the individual level, people can borrow or reduce their savings to survive when they are no longer employed. Think of a college student who has no income but survives by borrowing money or a retired person who no longer earns money but lives by withdrawing from savings. Most people can do this only for short periods of time unless they receive charity or government social welfare benefits. For society, this is possible by reducing **inventory**—a stock of unsold goods and raw materials.

In Exhibit 3, autonomous consumption occurs at the point where the consumption line intercepts the vertical axis and real GDP is zero. This occurs at point A with consumption of $250. Higher income will lead to a higher total level of consumption, but it will not change the level of autonomous consumption that occurs if income is zero.

The Slope of the Consumption Function The second important characteristic of consumption is that it tends to rise more slowly than income. Thus, if someone earns a $1,000 pay raise, he or she might spend an extra $750 on consumption and put an extra $250 into savings. People tend to save part of any increase in income so that they will be able to build up their savings for those periods when they have little or no income.

The **marginal propensity to consume (MPC)** is the additional consumption that occurs from an additional dollar in income. Mathematically, this is shown as

$$MPC = \frac{\Delta \text{Consumption}}{\Delta \text{Income}}$$

consumption function
The relationship between consumption spending and real GDP.

autonomous consumption
The level of expenditure that occurs when income levels are zero.

inventory A stock of unsold goods and raw materials.

marginal propensity to consume (MPC) The additional consumption that occurs from an additional dollar in income.

For example, as real GDP (income) increases from 1,000 to 2,000, consumption spending might increase from 1,000 to 1,750. In this case, the marginal propensity to consume is

$$MPC = \frac{\Delta \text{Consumption}}{\Delta \text{Income}} = \frac{750}{1,000} = 0.75$$

Note that the slope of the consumption function *is* the marginal propensity to consume.

This portion of income that is *not* consumed is saved. The **marginal propensity to save (MPS)** is the additional saving that occurs from an additional dollar in income. Mathematically, this is shown as

$$MPS = \frac{\Delta \text{Saving}}{\Delta \text{Income}}$$

Recall that disposable (after-tax) income can *either* go to consumption or savings. It must be the case that $MPC + MPS = 1$. And thus,

$$MPS = 1 - MPC$$

Notice that each additional $1,000 in income increases saving by $250. The marginal propensity to save is 0.25 in this example, which equals $1 - 0.75$.

> ## Think & Speak Like an Economist
>
> Disposable income is a person's total income plus the value of government benefits minus taxes. A household that earns $100,000 of income, receives no government benefits, and pays $25,000 in taxes has a disposable income of $75,000. This after-tax income can be consumed or saved.

The Aggregate Expenditure Function

Panel A of Exhibit 4 shows the data used to graph the consumption function in Exhibit 3. It also introduces other components of the aggregate expenditure function. The aggregate expenditure function is the sum of the consumption function and the autonomous level of nonconsumption expenditures—investment (I) and government spending (G). Unlike consumption, it is assumed that neither I nor G changes with income—that is, they are fixed. Here, the level of investment is 100, and government spending is 400.

Because it is assumed that I and G do not vary with income, our analysis can be simplified by grouping them together (for now). This is done in Panel B, which graphically presents the data. The level of nonconsumption expenditures ($I + G$) is 500. The total aggregate expenditure line equals the consumption function plus $500.

The Mathematics of the Aggregate Expenditure Model

The aggregate expenditure function also can be expressed mathematically. Businesses and governments spend $500 on $I + G$, and consumers spend

$$C = \$250 + 0.75 \times \text{Income}$$

The $250 represents the level of autonomous consumption, and the 0.75 is the marginal propensity to consume in the preceding example. More generally,

$$C = \text{Autonomous consumption} + MPC \times \text{Income}$$

Total aggregate expenditure is equal to the sum of the three components of GDP (C, I, and G). In a closed economy with no trade, it is

$$AE = C + I + G$$

Using the figures from Exhibit 4,

$$AE = (\$250 + 0.75 \times \text{Income}) + \$100 + \$400$$
$$AE = \$750 + 0.75 \times \text{Income}$$

The $750 represents the level of *autonomous expenditures*. It equals $250 in autonomous consumption plus $100 in investment spending and $400 in government spending.

marginal propensity to save (MPS) The additional saving that occurs from an additional dollar in income.

EXHIBIT 4   The Aggregate Expenditure Model

Panel A: The Aggregate Expenditure Model as a Schedule . . .

Income	Consumption	Investment	Government Spending	Aggregate Spending
$0	$250 (autonomous)	$100	$400	$750
1,000	1,000	100	400	1,500
2,000	1,750	100	400	2,250
3,000	**2,500**	**100**	**400**	**3,000**
4,000	3,250	100	400	3,750
5,000	4,000	100	400	4,500

Panel B: . . . and the Aggregate Expenditure Model as a Graph

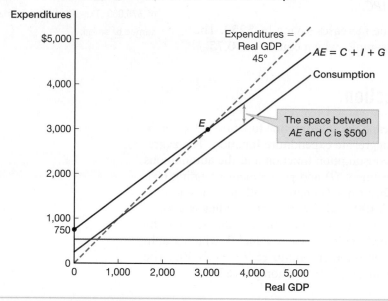

Aggregate expenditure equals spending on consumption goods, investment, and government purchases (net exports are not shown for simplicity)—that is, $AE = C + I + G$.
Equilibrium occurs where aggregate expenditure equals real GDP (income). This is
$3,000 as highlighted in Panel A. Nonconsumption expenditures equal $G + I$ or $500. The
aggregate expenditure function is consumption plus $500. Autonomous expenditures
equal $750, which is autonomous consumption of $250 plus $500. In Panel B, equilibrium
occurs where the aggregate expenditure function intercepts the 45 degree line at point E
($3,000).

29.3 EQUILIBRIUM IN THE AGGREGATE EXPENDITURE MODEL AND THE EXPENDITURE MULTIPLIER

Panel B of Exhibit 4 introduces a 45 degree line, which is used to establish equilibrium.
Points on the 45 degree line represent all points where real GDP equals aggregate
expenditure. This reflects the circular flow model discussed in earlier chapters—that
is, total income in the economy is equal to total expenditure. Equilibrium occurs where
the total amount that various groups choose to spend on consumption, investment and
government output is equal to total national income (GDP.) Equilibrium occurs where

EXHIBIT 5 A Recession in the Aggregate Expenditure Model

The full employment level of output is assumed to be $4,000. At lower levels of output, the economy is in a recession. Equilibrium in the aggregate expenditure model may occur below full employment. In Keynes's view, because the economy is at equilibrium at $3,000, it will remain below full employment absent corrective policy measures.

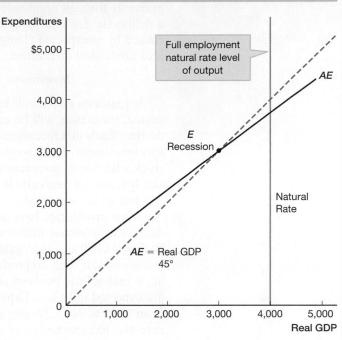

the level of aggregate expenditure is equal to $3,000. In Panel B, this occurs where the aggregate expenditure line intercepts the 45 degree line at point E.

Equilibrium May Not Occur at Full Employment

In the aggregate expenditure model the economy is always operating where the AE line crosses the 45 degree line, because GDP equals both income and expenditure. However, this short-run equilibrium point does not *necessarily* occur at the full employment level of output that occurs at the natural rate. The actual equilibrium output in the economy can be either above or below the natural rate of output.

In Exhibit 5, the aggregate expenditure line intersects the 45 degree line at a level of output below full employment, which is assumed to be at $4,000. This means that there is not enough aggregate expenditure to achieve full employment and that the economy will be in a recession. Because the economy is in equilibrium, there is no inclination to move toward full employment, even if the economy is in a severe recession. In other words, the recession may last for a long time, as did the Great Depression.

Inventories, Planned Investment, and Unplanned Investment

You might wonder what happens when consumer spending suddenly drops sharply, and businesses are not able to sell all the output that they produce. Does that mean that spending falls short of GDP? Actually no. In the short run, the drop in consumption will cause business *inventories* to increase. Recall that additions to inventory count as part of investment (I), as is shown in Chapter 20. Aggregate expenditures (including changes in inventory) still equal real GDP, as the drop in consumer spending is offset by a rise in business spending on inventories, a part of investment.

Keynesians find it useful to distinguish between *planned investment* and *unplanned investment*. **Planned investment** is the amount of investment that businesses intend to do. Planned investment includes the construction of a new factory, the purchase of a new computer system, or any increase in inventories that a firm *schedules* in

planned investment The amount of investment that businesses intend to do.

anticipation of higher sales. These investments reflect deliberate decisions made by businesses. In contrast, **unplanned investment** is unanticipated changes in investment, primarily through unintended changes in inventory. These investments are not part of a deliberate decision. Unplanned investments typically reflect changes in inventories caused by unexpected changes in sales. Actual investment equals planned investment plus unplanned investment:

$$Investment_{actual} = Investment_{planned} + Investment_{unplanned}$$

Inventories are volatile and responsive to the business cycle. If a recession is *unexpected*, businesses will be caught off guard and inventories will initially rise as sales decline. Early in a recession, there will often be an initial increase in *unplanned* inventory investment. For example, a toy retailer that expects large sales in December will be stuck with excess inventory if aggregate expenditures fall sharply just prior to December. Inventories rose early in the Great Recession, reflecting the fact that the recession was not widely expected.

After inventories have unexpectedly increased, businesses eventually respond by decreasing *planned* investment, shifting the aggregate expenditure line downward. Both real GDP and aggregate expenditures decline. Inventories then begin to decline as businesses cut back on production and sales are made from existing inventories. After all, it makes little business sense to expand inventories during a recession, when sales are expected to be low. Exhibit 6 shows total business inventories in the United States from 1992 to 2018. During each recession, inventories eventually decreased sharply in response to expectations of a continuing recession, shifting the aggregate expenditure line downward. This actually made the recession deeper in 2009.

The opposite occurs if sales are higher than expected as unplanned inventories initially decrease. In response, businesses attempt to replenish their inventory, which boosts investment, causing the AE line to shift upwards. This results in an increase in production, and the economy expands. Finally, when sales are equal to what is expected, there will be no unplanned changes in inventory investment. For example, if sales at a pizza restaurant exactly match expectations, managers will maintain their existing inventories by replacing them roughly item for item.

unplanned investment
Unanticipated changes in investment, primarily through unintended changes in inventory.

EXHIBIT 6 Inventories and the Business Cycle

When the economy expands, inventories typically increase. During U.S. recessions (shown as shaded areas in the figure), inventories may rise initially, but eventually decrease sharply as planned inventories decline.

Data from: FRED; Census Bureau, U.S. Department of Commerce, stlouisfed .org.

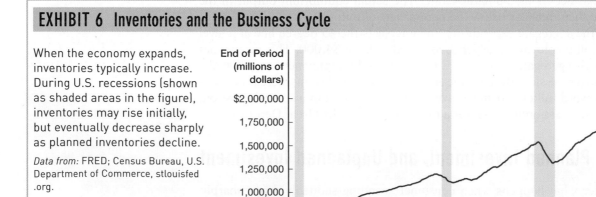

Shifts in Aggregate Expenditures

What causes changes in aggregate expenditures? The aggregate expenditure line can shift for a variety of reasons:

- *Changes in planned investment.* As just noted, when businesses increase planned inventories or investment, aggregate expenditures increase.

- *Changes in expectations.* Businesses and consumers may become *pessimistic* about the economy and reduce consumption and aggregate expenditures. Conversely, if businesses become *optimistic*, they may respond by increasing aggregate expenditures.

- *Changes in government spending.* An increase in government spending increases aggregate expenditures.

- *Changes in taxes.* Increases in taxes reduce consumption, investment, and aggregate expenditures.

- *Changes in real interest rates.* A decline in real interest rates due to an expansionary monetary policy tends to increase investment spending and aggregate expenditures.

- *Changes in wealth.* A decline in the stock market or housing prices decreases aggregate expenditure. An increase in stock or housing prices increases aggregate expenditures.

In this section, we focus on changes in investment spending (I). Later in the chapter, we demonstrate how the outcome is similar when there is an equivalent change in government expenditures (G). Panel A of Exhibit 7 shows the effect of investment spending increasing by $250, from $100 to $350. As a consequence of a $250 increase in investment spending, the equilibrium output rises by $1,000, from $3,000 to $4,000.

Why does output rise by more than the increase in investment? Keynes argued that there is a "multiplier" effect from increased spending, especially when the economy is depressed. This is the same process that applies to fiscal policy in Chapter 28, where the *multiplier effect* shows the impact of increased government expenditure on total expenditure. More generally, the aggregate expenditure model allows us to broaden the multiplier effect to include *any change* in autonomous expenditures, including investment spending (I) and consumption (C), not just fiscal policy.

Panel B graphically displays the effect of this increase in investment on the aggregate expenditure line. Notice that at the new equilibrium (E_2), both expenditure and real GDP have increased by much more than the rise in investment.

The Expenditure Multiplier

Consider the effects of a new investment of $1 billion in an auto factory. The expenditure on the factory itself will directly increase GDP because the construction of new capital goods is a part of GDP. But this does not include the indirect effects of the investment. Workers and businesses employed in building the new factory will earn extra income, and they will spend part of that extra income on consumer goods. How much they spend depends on the marginal propensity to consume (MPC). If the MPC is 0.75, then three fourths of the extra income will be spent on consumer goods, and the other one fourth is saved. An extra $750 million in consumption takes place.

This secondary impact on consumption tends to cause GDP to rise by more than the initial investment expenditure. There are further "ripple effects" even after the initial boost to consumption. If the workers and businesses that build the factory spend more on consumption, then other workers and businesses selling consumer goods will earn more income—an extra $750 million. And they will spend on consumption an

EXHIBIT 7 Changes in Aggregate Expenditure and the Multiplier Effect

Panel A: A $250 Increase in Investment . . .

Income	Consumption	Investment	Government Spending	Aggregate Spending
$0	$250	$350 (up from $100)	$400	$1,000
1,000	1,000	350	400	1,750
2,000	1,750	350	400	2,500
3,000	2,500	350	400	3,250
4,000	**3,250**	**350**	**400**	**4,000**
5,000	4,000	350	400	4,750

Panel B: . . . Shifts the Aggregate Expenditure Function upward by $250

In Panel A, a $250 increase in investment spending to $350 increases equilibrium by $1,000, from $3,000 to $4,000. The size of the increase reflects a multiplier of 4. This also is displayed in Panel B. After the aggregate expenditure function shifts up by $250, the equilibrium goes from point E_1 ($3,000) to E_2 ($4,000).

extra 75% of the $750 million ($562.5 million)—again reflecting the marginal propensity to consume of 0.75. This process continues indefinitely, with each round of increased consumption smaller than the previous round.

The **expenditure multiplier** is the multiple by which changes in autonomous expenditures impact aggregate spending. It is the ratio of the final boost in aggregate spending to the initial increase in investment spending. The fiscal multiplier discussed in Chapter 28 is one application of the expenditure multiplier. In the basic model, the expenditure multiplier effect for changes in *expenditures* will be equal to

$$\text{Expenditure multiplier effect} = \frac{1}{(1 - MPC)}$$

expenditure multiplier effect The multiple by which changes in autonomous expenditures impact aggregate spending.

In this case,

$$\text{Expenditure multiplier effect} = \frac{1}{(1 - 0.75)} = 4$$

The long-run effect of the extra *investment spending* can then be expressed mathematically as

$$\Delta \text{ Aggregate expenditures} = \Delta I \times \text{Expenditure multiplier effect}$$

In Exhibit 7, the change in investment equals $250, the marginal propensity to consumer is 0.75, and the multiplier is 4. In that case,

$$\$1,000 = \Delta \text{ Aggregate expenditures} = \$250 \times 4$$

In this case, a $250 increase in investment *increases* GDP by $1,000. Similarly, if the multiplier is 4, then an increase of $1 billion in investment leads to a $4 billion dollar increase in GDP.

Advanced Topic: The Mathematics of the Expenditure Multiplier

Exhibit 8 demonstrates the impact of a $250 increase in autonomous expenditure (other than consumption) with a marginal propensity to consume of 0.75. Initially, additional expenditure rises directly from the initial additional $250 expenditure. Then, consumption increases by $188 (which equals $250 × 0.75), by $141 ($188 × 0.75), by $105 ($141 × 0.75), by $79 ($105 × 0.75), and by $59 ($79 × 0.75). The process continues indefinitely, eventually resulting in an increase of $1,000 in total additional expenditures ($250 times the multiplier of 4).

This initial autonomous increase in spending of $1,000 with a marginal propensity to consume (MPC) of 0.75 results in the following changes in total expenditures:

- $250 initially.
- $188: This equals $250 × *MPC*.
- $141: This equals $250 × *MPC* × *MPC* (or $250 × *MPC²*).

EXHIBIT 8 The Expenditure Multiplier Step by Step

Consumption Steps	Additional Autonomous Expenditure	Resulting Additional Consumption (Marginal propensity to consume = 0.75)	Total Additional Expenditure (Additional GDP)
—	$250	$0	$250
First	0	188	438
Second	0	141	579
Third	0	105	684
Fourth	0	79	762
Fifth	0	59	822
.	.	.	.
.	.	.	.
.	.	.	.
Final	0	About a penny	1,000

When the marginal propensity to consume is 0.75, the expenditure multiplier is 4. This equals 1/(1 − 0.75). Initially, aggregate expenditure increases by $250. Subsequently, additional increases occur step by step as shown, resulting in an increase of $1,000 in total additional expenditures.

A massive decline in aggregate demand led to the Great Depression. Keynes argued that fiscal stimulus was needed to reverse it.

- $105: This equals $250 × *MPC* × *MPC* × *MPC* (or $250 × *MPC*^{3}).
- $79: This equals $250 × *MPC* × *MPC* × *MPC* × *MPC* (or $250 × *MPC*^{4}).

The result is that the total change in expenditures equals

$$\$250 \times (1 + MPC^1 + MPC^2 + MPC^3 + MPC^4 + \dots)$$

The expression in the parentheses can be simplified to

$$\frac{1}{(1 - MPC)}.$$

This is the expenditure multiplier of 4. So the initial $250 increase in autonomous expenditures increases total expenditures by $1,000.

The multiplier process applies to changes in any component of aggregate expenditures and not just to changes in investment spending. For example, the effect of a change in *government spending* is similar to a change in investment spending:

$$\Delta \text{ Aggregate expenditures} = \Delta G \times \text{Expenditure multiplier effect}$$

The early Keynesians thought that the actual multiplier is quite high when the economy is depressed. That is because most people save only a small percentage of their income and consume the rest. If the marginal propensity to consume is 0.9 (or 90%), then the multiplier will be 10 (= 1/(1 − 0.9)). In that case, a $1 billion investment project would eventually boost GDP by $10 billion!

It is not as easy to estimate the actual multiplier in the real world as it might appear from this simple model. The basic model developed above gives us only the *potential* multiplier. As is shown in Chapter 28, there are several important offsets to this multiplier, such as crowding out and monetary offset. These offsets are relevant particularly when the economy is at full employment or when interest rates are above zero. Due to these offsets, the actual real-world multiplier will be lower than the simple multiplier calculated here. Accounting for these offsets is difficult, but several studies suggest a multiplier of around 1.6 if interest rates are held constant.

📊 BUSINESS BRIEF The Expenditure Multiplier Effect and the Great Depression

Keynes developed the multiplier effect to explain the largest economic disaster in modern history—the Great Depression. In the United States, investment spending by businesses and households was particularly hard hit and declined nearly 90% from $17 billion dollars in 1929 to $2 billion in 1932. Nominal GDP fell over 45% from $105 billion to $57 billion. Businesses across the country suffered as consumption spending was also hard hit.

To see how a decline of this magnitude can occur, first recall that the expenditure multiplier effect can work in reverse as a result of a decline in investment spending. In this case, a decline in investment spending had a negative ripple effect on the overall economy. Most economists believe that the expenditure multiplier effect was somewhat larger than today (perhaps 3) because the economy had far fewer *countercyclical* automatic stabilizers (such as social insurance programs). As such, when investment spending fell by $15 billion, it is not surprising that nominal GDP fell by more than three times this amount ($48 billion).[*]

*Data from: Federal Reserve Board of St. Louis.

---

[*]The expression 1/(1 − *MPC*) is an infinite geometric series.

29.4 FISCAL POLICY IN THE AGGREGATE EXPENDITURE MODEL

As is discussed in the previous chapters, demand-side policies are often used to help stabilize the economy. One option is to use monetary stimulus, at least as long as interest rates are not near zero. However, Keynes is best known for advocating the use of *fiscal policy*. Before considering the role of fiscal policy, let's first think about where we would like to be on the aggregate expenditure diagram.

Comparing the Aggregate Expenditure Model with the Keynes Short-Run AS/AD Model

Unfortunately, equilibrium in the aggregate expenditure model does not always occur at the natural rate of output. Suppose that the natural rate of output is $4,000 on the Keynes short-run aggregate supply and aggregate demand (KSRAS/AD) model shown in Exhibit 9. That is the point where the KSRAS curve becomes vertical and no further increases in output are possible. If aggregate expenditure rises above $4,000, the only effect would be inflation. On the other hand, at a level of aggregate expenditure below $4,000, the economy would be in a recession. Now let's assume that we start from a position where aggregate expenditure and output are at $3,000. Also assume that fiscal spending does not "crowd out" private investment.

The most important problem in a recession is usually unemployment, not inflation. One way that government policymakers can improve the job situation is to increase aggregate expenditure. They can boost total spending with a fiscal policy that increases government spending, lowers taxes, or does a combination of both.

When output is depressed, an increase in aggregate demand should lead to higher real GDP. After full employment is reached, any further increases in aggregate demand merely lead to higher prices, not higher real output. This explains why the vertical part of the KSRAS curve occurs at the natural rate of output.

The next problem is to determine *how much* extra government spending (or how large a tax cut) is needed. Recall that the expenditure multiplier applies to any shift in autonomous spending. In the previous section, we assume the marginal propensity to

---

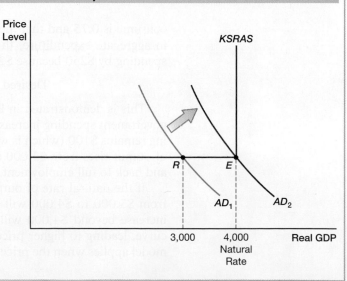

EXHIBIT 9 Fiscal Policy with an Economy in a Recession: The Keynesian Short-Run AS/AD Model

Keynes believed that recessions were the result of inadequate aggregate demand and advocated the use of fiscal policy to stimulate demand. Fiscal policy can move the economy out of a recession by increasing aggregate demand.

EXHIBIT 10 Fiscal Policy and the Multiplier Effect

Panel A: A $250 Increase in Government Expenditures . . .

Income	Consumption	Investment	Government Spending	Aggregate Spending
$0	$250	$100	$650 (up from $400)	$1,000
1,000	1,000	100	650	1,750
2,000	1,750	100	650	2,500
3,000	2,500	100	650	3,250
4,000	**3,250**	**100**	**650**	**4,000**
5,000	4,000	100	650	4,750

Panel B: . . . Shifts the Aggregate Expenditure Function upward by $250

In Panel A, a $250 increase in government expenditures moves the economy to the
natural rate by increasing equilibrium by $1,000, from $3,000 to $4,000. The size of the
increase reflects a multiplier of 4. This is also displayed in Panel B. After the aggregate
expenditure function shifts up by $250, the equilibrium goes from point E_1 ($3,000) to E_2
($4,000).

consume is 0.75 and that the multiplier is 4. In that case, if we need an extra $1,000
in aggregate expenditure, then the government would need to increase government
spending by $250 because $250 times 4 equals $1,000:

$$\text{Desired } \Delta Y = \text{Multiplier} \times \Delta G = 4 \times \$250$$

This is demonstrated in Exhibit 10 using the aggregate expenditure model. Here,
government spending increases by $250 (from $400 to $650), and investment spend-
ing remains $100 (which is what is was in Exhibit 4). As a result, the equilibrium level
of output rises from $3,000 to $4,000. This moves the economy out of the recession
and back to full employment.

If the natural rate of output is $4,000, then an increase in aggregate expenditure
from $3,000 to $4,000 will lead to higher real GDP but no increase in prices. Any
increase beyond $4,000 will push the economy up the vertical part of the KSRAS
curve, leading to higher prices but no increase in output. The aggregate expenditure
model applies when the price level is fixed and the economy is below full employment.

The Tax Multiplier

In contrast with the expenditure multiplier from increases in government purchases, a tax cut or an increase in transfer payments has no direct effect on GDP because taxes and transfers are not a part of GDP. The multiplier process begins with the indirect effects. For example, a $250 tax cut or transfer payment will *initially* increase consumption by only $188 if the marginal propensity to consume is 0.75 ($188 = 0.75 × $250). Thus, the multiplier would be based on a $188 change in autonomous consumption and *not* on the $250 tax cut.

In other words, because there is no direct expenditure effect, the first round of expenditures must be subtracted out of the expenditure effect multiplier to determine the tax multiplier. This means that the tax multiplier will be equal to the expenditure multiplier minus one—in order to remove the direct expenditure effect that occurs with increases in G. In addition, the tax multiplier is a negative number because higher taxes reduce spending:

$$\text{Tax multiplier} = -\left(\frac{MPC}{(1 - MPC)}\right) = -\left(\frac{1}{(1 - MPC)} - 1\right)$$

Thus, if the marginal propensity to consume is 0.75 and the expenditure multiplier is 4, then the tax multiplier will be −3.

In total, the multiplier effect of increasing expenditures is greater than the multiplier effect of tax cuts. This is why Keynesians often favor increases in government expenditures over tax cuts as a way of boosting expenditure during a recession.

 POLICY BRIEF The Multiplier Effect from the American Recovery and Reinvestment Act of 2009

The American Recovery and Reinvestment Act (ARRA) of 2009 is a good example of Keynesian fiscal policy. When President Obama took office in January 2009, the economy was in the midst of the Great Recession that following the housing and banking crisis of 2008. Economists believed that the problem was falling aggregate demand because both prices and output were falling at the same time. The usual remedy for boosting aggregate demand is to adopt a more expansionary monetary policy, but interest rates had already been cut close to zero.

President Obama's key economic advisers were Keynesians, and they believed that a large fiscal stimulus would have a multiplier effect on total aggregate expenditure. In response to the administration's proposals, Congress passed the ARRA, which included a total of nearly $800 billion in increased government spending and tax cuts. Lawmakers frequently change government spending and taxes, but the ARRA provisions were specifically designed to boost aggregate expenditure and hence create more output and employment. The program was spread over several years, with about half of the stimulus occurring in 2010.

It is difficult to know the exact multiplier effect that resulted because we cannot be sure what would have happened without fiscal stimulus. Most economists believe that the program did have a simulative effect and that the slow recovery of the economy was due to the lagged effects of the financial crisis. Some economists are more skeptical and note that the recovery was weaker than predicted, suggesting that the fiscal stimulus discouraged private spending. The precise impact of fiscal stimulus is difficult to determine because many other factors need to be held constant when estimating a multiplier.

In 2015, the Congressional Budget Office analyzed the multiplier effects from major provisions of the act. Exhibit 11 shows that government purchases of goods and

EXHIBIT 11 The Multiplier Effects of Five Provisions of the American Recovery and Reinvestment Act of 2009

Activity	Low Estimate	High Estimate
Purchases of Goods and Services by the Federal Government	0.5	2.5
Transfer Payments to Individuals	0.4	2.1
One-Time Payment to Retirees	0.2	1.0
Two-Year Tax Cuts for Lower- and Middle-Income People	0.3	1.5
One-Year Tax Cut for Higher-Income People	0.1	0.6

These estimates of the multiplier effect of five provisions of the American Recovery and Reinvestment Act (2009) were prepared by the Congressional Budget Office. Note that tax multipliers are technically negative but are usually reported as a positive number. Tax cuts boost spending.

Data from: Congressional Budget Office.

services had an estimated multiplier effect ranging from 0.5 to 2.5. Consistent with economic theory, estimates of the tax cut multipliers were smaller. The multiplier effect of one-year tax cuts for high-income people was particularly small, ranging from 0.1 to 0.6. This is because high-income individuals save more and tend to spend a smaller portion of their marginal income than do low-income individuals. Because high earners have a lower marginal propensity to consume (MPC), the corresponding multiplier effect is somewhat smaller. The one-time cash payment to retirees had a relatively small multiplier effect because it was *not* viewed as permanent income.[*]

[*]"Estimated Impact of the American Recovery and Reinvestment Act on Employment and Economic Output in 2014," Congressional Budget Office, February 2015, https://www.cbo.gov/publication/49958.

No Self-Correcting Mechanism

In the ordinary aggregate supply and aggregate demand model with an upward sloping AS curve, an economy can be moved out of a recession by either increasing aggregate demand or increasing aggregate supply. In that model, you may recall that aggregate supply tends to gradually increase during a recession as unemployed workers and landlords with unused office space slowly begin to accept lower wages and lower rents. This is the essence of the self-correcting mechanism—the process by which the short-run aggregate supply adjusts to return output to the natural rate. Classical economists understood that recessions occasionally occur because wages can be sticky in the short run. They believed that wages and prices adjust over time, allowing the economy to self-correct back to the natural rate of employment within a year or so.

Keynes also believed that wages are sticky, but he disagreed with the classical view that the self-correcting mechanism is sufficient. Keynes saw two problems with the sort of deflation experienced during the Great Depression. First, he worried that workers would be slow to accept wage cuts, even during a period of falling prices. And second, he believed that if wage cuts do occur, this would further depress aggregate expenditures. Thus, the ability of an economy to self-correct is a critical difference between the classical version of the aggregate supply and aggregate demand model and the Keynesian aggregate expenditure model.

In the aggregate expenditure model, self-correction is not possible because the model assumes that prices are fixed. Equilibrium in the aggregate expenditure model may not correspond with the full employment level of output that occurs at the natural rate. Keynes was skeptical of the idea that the economy could self-correct back to full employment, particularly in the short run. Thus, during the Great Depression, Keynes advocated fiscal policy aimed at increasing aggregate expenditures.

There are other key differences between the AS/AD model and the AE model. The ordinary AS/AD model with an upward-sloping AS curve assumes that prices are slow to adjust when output is below equilibrium, not that they are fixed. This long-run wage and price flexibility allows for a self-correcting mechanism. Although many economists now prefer the ordinary AS/AD model, the AE model makes it easier to see the multiplier effect and also does a nice job of explaining how and why fiscal policy can have a multiplier effect on output.

🏛 POLICY BRIEF China's Fiscal Policy in the Great Recession

During the Great Recession, many economies around the world saw a sharp decline in GDP and an increase in unemployment. China was no exception. China's economy observed a 45% decline in exports. In the midst of the Great Recession, China launched a major fiscal stimulus package in late 2008. The package called for a fiscal stimulus of 4 trillion yuan ($586 billion)—roughly the equivalent of 16% of GDP (although part of this spending would have occurred anyway). In comparison, the fiscal stimulus in the United States was roughly 5% of GDP.* China's largest area of spending was on infrastructure, with investments in new rail systems and irrigation. According to one study by the Federal Reserve of St. Louis, China

> implemented bold, decisive fiscal stimulus programs that no other major nations dared to adopt ... to implement its aggressive stimulus program in 2009, consistent with the very Keynesian notion of aggregate demand management through increased government spending and the fiscal multiplier principle.[†]

China's efforts were successful. Over the next few years, its economy grew at a rapid pace, although it is difficult to know exactly how much of that growth was due to the fiscal stimulus.[‡]

*"China Seeks Stimulation," *The Economist*, November 10, 2008, http://www.economist.com/node/12585407.

[†]Yi Wen and Jing Wu, "Withstanding Great Recession Like China," Working Paper 2014-007C, Federal Reserve Bank of St. Louis, October 2017, https://research.stlouisfed.org/wp/more/2014-007.

[‡]Ben Leubsdorf, "'Bold' Chinese Stimulus Eased Recession Pain, Fed Economists Say," *Wall Street Journal*, March 14, 2014, http://blogs.wsj.com/economics/2014/03/14/bold-chinese-stimulus-eased-recession-suffering-fed-economists-say/.

29.5 KEYNESIAN MULTIPLIER EFFECT VERSUS CLASSICAL OPPORTUNITY COST

From its beginning, Keynesian economics has been somewhat controversial. Keynes himself seemed to enjoy overturning conventional wisdom. Recall the "paradox of thrift," which suggests that an activity that traditionally is viewed as virtuous (such as saving) might actually be harmful under certain conditions. Keynes believed that government spending, regardless of whether it is needed or wasteful, can help boost a depressed economy, and many economists now believe that the multiplier effect also provides a strong rationale for extra government spending during a recession.

Consider the popular view that there is an economic benefit from emergency government spending after a natural disaster. Government expenditures on rebuilding efforts might be expansionary, due to the expenditure multiplier effect. Keynesians would point out that this kind of government spending can help an economy recovery *from a recession* (and not just the natural disaster). Thus, in their view, a natural disaster might actually help the economy by leading to fiscal stimulus. This is quite different from the classical view, which would view replacing damaged goods as a wash because the resources used to fix the damage would not be available to produce other goods and services. The classical economists assumed that there was no multiplier effect.

If the two views of the economy were distilled into a quick sound bite, it might be "opportunity cost versus multiplier effect." Classical economists focused on the former, and Keynes emphasizes the latter, arguing that regardless of whether the direct effects of extra government spending are useful, the indirect effects (via the multiplier effect) on consumption are beneficial. Workers building government projects earn more income and then buy other products such as cars and houses. That is the expenditure multiplier effect.

The calls for extra government spending generally have been popular with liberals who favor a larger and more active government. However, this does not mean that Keynesian economics is all about political ideology. For instance, the use of fiscal policy does not necessarily mean bigger government. When the economy is overheating and aggregate expenditure is too high, then a contractionary policy is appropriate. That might involve *less* government spending.

More importantly, taxes also can be used to affect aggregate expenditure. Thus, some conservative economists prefer to use tax cuts (rather than increases in government spending) to increase demand during a recession. Yet there is no doubt that Keynes believed that an active government should spend much more during a depression and that his ideas now have stronger support among economists with similar views of government. Economists who favor smaller government often tend to hold a more classical view of the economy, emphasizing the opportunity cost of increased government spending.

Today, some economists have doubts about the *simple* aggregate expenditure model presented here. For instance, the multiplier might be considerably smaller than the potential multiplier in this chapter, due to offsetting effects. Others worry that Keynes put too much emphasis on the demand side of the economy and not enough on factors that determine aggregate supply and long-run growth. Nonetheless, the simple aggregate expenditure model provides the logic behind Keynesian economics, which even decades after the death of John Maynard Keynes continues to play a major role in modern macroeconomics.

📊 BUSINESS BRIEF The Broken Window Fallacy

The controversy over government spending pre-dates Keynes. In 1850, economist Frédéric Bastiat described what later was called the broken window fallacy. It is a parable of a shopkeeper who must repair a broken window. Because repairing the window involves spending, many view it as helping the economy. Bastiat draws a different conclusion:

> Suppose it cost six francs to repair the damage, and you say that the accident brings six francs to the glazier's trade—that it encourages that trade to the amount of six francs—I grant this. ... ... If you come to the conclusion, as is too often the case, that it is a *good thing to break windows*, that it causes money to circulate, and that the encouragement of industry in general will be the result of it, you will oblige me to call out, "Stop there! Your theory is confined to that which is seen; it takes no account of that which is not seen."*

Bastiat was known for brilliant essays that show how people often overlook the less obvious (or as he said, "not seen") effects of economic activities. In this case, what is not seen is how the shopkeeper would have otherwise spent the money that went toward replacing the broken glass. Even if he had instead saved the money, the bank where he placed his savings might lend it out again for others to use. That is the idea behind opportunity cost. Classical economists did not believe that society benefits from the spending on repairing the broken window, because that spending merely displaces *other* spending that otherwise would have occurred. Keynesians would argue that the window repairs would displace other spending only when the economy is at full employment.

*Frédéric Bastiat, "Essays on Political Economy: Part II, That Which Is Seen, and That Which Is Not Seen" (1848), in *History of Economic Theory: The Selected Essays of T. R. Malthus, David Ricardo, Frédéric Bastiat, and John Stuart Mill*, vol. 1, 127–168 (Dublin, OH: Coventry House, 2013), 128.

BUSINESS TAKEAWAY

When the economy is operating in a depression (such as the Great Depression) or a severe recession (such as the Great Recession), policies that stimulate spending may be helpful in boosting output and reducing unemployment. The aggregate expenditure model shows how increases in aggregate expenditures such as government spending may generate a multiplier effect, which helps move the economy back toward full employment. The model assumes that increases in spending will not generate inflation. Indeed, when the economy is operating well below full employment, businesses may find it difficult to raise prices. In contrast, when the economy is operating at full employment, businesses may be able to respond to a spike in spending by simply raising prices. In turn, this will result in inflation.

Business inventories are volatile and responsive to the business cycle. A recession can impact inventories in two different ways, depending on whether the recession is expected or not expected. Effective decision-making requires understanding this distinction. If a recession is unexpected, businesses will be caught off guard, and inventories will rise as sales decline. This leads to changes in unplanned inventory investment. Effective business decision-making also requires that business expectations change rapidly. When a recession is expected, planned inventory investment declines. For example, a toy retailer that expects large sales in December will be stuck with excess inventory if aggregate expenditures fall sharply just prior to December. But if the sales decline is anticipated several months earlier, the retailer can plan for the decline by ordering fewer toys.

CHAPTER STUDY GUIDE

29.1 KEYNES CHALLENGES THE CLASSICAL VIEW OF ECONOMICS

John Maynard Keynes (1883–1946) challenged many of the assumptions of classical economics. First, he argued that during a recession, the economy could actually be hurt if society tries to save more by reducing consumption. Second, he also challenged the idea that the economy self-corrects. Third, he believed that increased government spending could help move an economy out of a recession. Finally, he argued that when the economy

is in a liquidity trap, monetary policy is ineffective. The **paradox of thrift** is the economic theory stating that attempts to save more can depress aggregate demand, leaving actual saving no higher than before. Keynes believed that increased spending, not saving, is needed to help move an economy out of a recession.

29.2 THE AGGREGATE EXPENDITURE MODEL

The **aggregate expenditure model** is an economic model that demonstrates the short-run relationship between aggregate expenditures and real GDP, assuming the price level is constant. It is best used to model an economy that is at less than full employment. **Aggregate expenditure** is the level of total spending in the economy at each level of real GDP (income), *ceteris paribus*— that is, aggregate expenditure (*AE*) equals consumption (*C*) plus investment (*I*) plus government spending (*G*) plus net exports (*NX*) or $AE = C + I + G + NX$. The **consumption function** is the relationship between consumption spending and real GDP. The function has a positive slope equal to the marginal propensity to consume. **Autonomous consumption** is the level of expenditure that occurs when income levels are zero. **Inventory** is a stock of unsold goods and raw materials. The **marginal propensity to consume (MPC)** is the additional consumption that occurs from an additional dollar in income. Mathematically, this is shown as $MPC = \Delta Consumption / \Delta Income$. The **marginal propensity to save (MPS)** is the additional saving that occurs from an additional dollar in income. Mathematically, this is shown as $MPS = \Delta Savings / \Delta Income = 1 - MPC$.

29.3   EQUILIBRIUM IN THE AGGREGATE EXPENDITURE MODEL AND THE EXPENDITURE MULTIPLIER

Equilibrium in the aggregate expenditure model occurs when aggregate expenditure equals real GDP. At equilibrium, the economy may not be at full employment. In the Keynesian model there is no tendency for the economy to move toward full employment automatically when in a recession. Thus, there is no self-correcting mechanism. **Planned investment** is the amount of investment that businesses intend to do. **Unplanned investment** is unanticipated changes in investment, primarily through unintended changes in inventory. When real GDP exceeds aggregate expenditure, inventories increase, which is an example of an unplanned investment. Investment equals unplanned investment plus planned investment. When the economy expands, inventories typically increase. During a recession, inventories eventually decrease sharply as planned inventories decline. The aggregate expenditure line can shift when the economy experiences changes in expectations, government spending, taxes, real interest rates, or wealth. When there is an increase in aggregate expenditure, equilibrium output will also increase. The size of the increase depends on the expenditure multiplier effect. The **expenditure multiplier effect** is the multiple by which changes in autonomous expenditures impact aggregate spending. Mathematically, this is shown as expenditure multiplier effect $= 1 / (1 / - MPC)$.

29.4   FISCAL POLICY IN THE AGGREGATE EXPENDITURE MODEL

Today, many economists believe that recessions are the result of inadequate demand and advocate the use of fiscal policy to stimulate demand. Fiscal policy can move the economy out of a recession by increasing aggregate expenditures in the aggregate expenditure model and by increasing aggregate demand in the aggregate supply and aggregate demand model. Keynesians tend to prefer increases in government purchases to stabilize the economy, noting the multiplier effect for taxes and transfer payments is smaller because there is no direct effect on GDP. Mathematically, this is shown as tax multiplier $= -MPC/(1 - MPC) = -1/(1 - MPC) - 1$.

29.5   KEYNESIAN MULTIPLIER EFFECT VERSUS CLASSICAL OPPORTUNITY COST

Keynes believed that government spending was needed to stabilize an economy in a recession, in part because the economy does not have an effective self-correcting mechanism In contrast, classical economists assumed that during a recession, wages would decline until full employment was restored. Keynes emphasized the multiplier effect of increased spending, whereas classical economists emphasized the opportunity cost of increased spending.

TOP TEN TERMS AND CONCEPTS

1. Paradox of Thrift
2. Aggregate Expenditure Model
3. Aggregate Expenditure
4. Consumption Function
5. Autonomous Consumption
6. Inventory
7. Marginal Propensity to Consume (MPC)
8. Marginal Propensity to Save (MPS)
9. Planned Investment and Unplanned Investment
10. Expenditure Multiplier Effect

STUDY PROBLEMS

1. Describe four areas where John Maynard Keynes challenged classical economists.

2. ▦ ⊼ Draw a Keynesian aggregate supply curve. What implications does it have for an increase in aggregate demand in the following instances?

   a. When the economy is in a recession

   b. When the economy is at full employment

3. Complete the following table for a closed economy with no taxes.

Real GDP	Consumption	Marginal Propensity to Consume	Marginal Propensity to Save
$100,000	$100,000		0.25
$200,000	$175,000		
$300,000		0.75	
	$325,000	0.75	0.25
$500,000			0.25

4. For the data in question 3, draw the consumption function. What is the level of autonomous consumption? Assume that investment (*I*) plus government spending (*G*) equals $50,000. Draw the aggregate expenditure function. Draw a 45 degree line. What is equilibrium?

5. In questions 3 and 4, what is the expenditure multiplier? If full employment occurs when real GDP is $400,000, how much of a change in government spending (*G*) is required to move the economy to full employment?

6. What is the multiplier for each of the following?

   a. Marginal propensity to consume is 0.5.

   b. Marginal propensity to save is 0.2.

   c. Marginal propensity to consume is 0.9.

   d. Marginal propensity to save is 0.3333.

7. Describe the paradox of thrift. What implications does it have for saving?

8. ⛪ Complete the following table for a closed economy with no taxes.

9. For the data in question 8, draw the consumption function, the aggregate expenditure function, and the 45 degree line.

10. For the data in question 8, answer the following questions.

    a. What is the level of autonomous consumption?

    b. What is the expenditure multiplier?

    c. What is equilibrium?

    d. If full employment occurs at $500,000, what government spending (*G*) or planned investment (*I*) is required to move equilibrium to full employment?

11. ▦ ⊼ Explain the Keynesian view of the correct fiscal policy during a severe recession like the Great Depression or the Great Recession. Provide examples.

12. Compare and contrast the classical view and Keynesian view of saving and investment. Also describe how each group explains how saving and investment reach equilibrium. Which variable does each view think is most important in bringing saving and investment into equilibrium?

13. ▦ ⊼ Breaking windows results in more spending on fixing windows. If this is the case, could an economy grow by breaking every window in a community and then increasing spending to fix them? Discuss the merits of the broken window fallacy.

14. Why is Keynesian economics often more popular with fans of big government? Also describe one Keynesian economic policy that does not lead to bigger government.

Real GDP	Consumption (Marginal propensity to consume = 0.75)	Investment	Government Spending	Aggregate Expenditure
$100,000	$100,000	$25,000	$25,000	$150,000
$200,000		$25,000	$25,000	
$300,000		$25,000	$25,000	
$400,000		$25,000	$25,000	
$500,000		$25,000	$25,000	

∧ Four decades of steering inflation and inflation expectations are represented by Federal Reserve chairs Janet Yellen (2014–2018), Paul Volcker (1979–1987), Alan Greenspan (1987–2006), and Ben Bernanke (2006–2014).

30 CHAPTER

The Role of Expectations in Macroeconomics

Inflation, Unemployment, and Monetary Policy

In 2017, the economy was looking good. A decade after the Great Recession began, unemployment was just 4.4%, and Federal Reserve chair Janet Yellen was anticipating that because of the low unemployment rate, inflation would move up toward the Fed target of 2%.[1] But the latter didn't happen.[2] Why would Yellen—or any economist—assume that low unemployment would lead to higher inflation? And why did this prediction fail to come true in 2017? To answer these questions, we need to understand the Phillips curve model of inflation and unemployment.

In this chapter, we examine how the Phillips curve approach to macroeconomics ultimately led to what now is called the *rational expectations revolution*. Economists gradually realized that *inflation expectations* play a big role in determining the relationship between inflation and unemployment. We will see that before this relationship was well understood, policymakers struggled to keep the economy stable with both low inflation and low unemployment.

Chapter Learning Targets

● Identify the short-run relationship between the inflation rate and the unemployment rate demonstrated in the Phillips curve.

● Discuss the natural rate hypothesis and the long-run Phillips curve.

● Explain how inflation expectations are formed and how they impact policy.

● Describe the expectations-augmented Phillips curve.

● Describe the expectations-augmented Phillips curve using nominal GDP.

30.1 THE RISE AND FALL OF THE SIMPLE PHILLIPS CURVE

In 1958, A. W. H. Phillips startled the economics world with a study of wage inflation and unemployment. Looking at data from United Kingdom from 1861 to 1957, Phillips found that there is an inverse relationship between unemployment and wage inflation. Soon after, economists discovered a similar pattern using price inflation. The **Phillips curve** is a graph that shows the relationship between inflation and

EXHIBIT 1 The Simple Phillips Curve

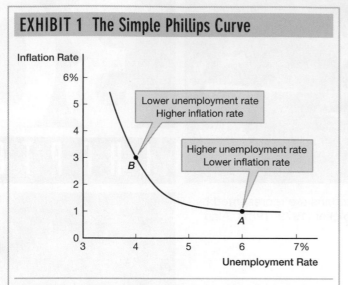

The Phillips curve shows the relationship between the rate of inflation and the rate of unemployment. Inflation tends to be higher when the unemployment rate is lower.

Phillips curve A graph that shows the relationship between inflation and unemployment.

unemployment. According to the Phillips curve, when unemployment is high, inflation tends to be low. When unemployment is extremely low, inflation tends to be high. A simplified version of the Phillips curve is shown in Exhibit 1. At point *A*, the economy has a lower rate of inflation and a higher rate of unemployment than it has at point *B*.

Economists had long understood that inflation tends to be higher during booms, when the rate of unemployment is often low. They assumed that this was because it is easier to negotiate higher wage and prices when the economy is booming. Conversely, recessions are sometimes associated with wage and price cuts. As a consequence, at point *A*, the unemployment rate is higher as the rate of inflation falls. Data from the Phillips curve reinforces this view, although we shall see that things are a bit more complicated.

The Phillips Curve in the United States

Panel A of Exhibit 2 shows the Phillips curve for the United States during the 1960s. Notice how the unemployment rate falls as inflation rises, suggesting a possible tradeoff between the two variables. Problems arose, however, when governments began to rely on the Phillips curve when implementing policy. In the 1960s, the Phillips curve was mistakenly assumed to indicate that there was a *permanent* tradeoff between inflation and

EXHIBIT 2 The Simple Phillips Curve in the United States, 1960 to 2016

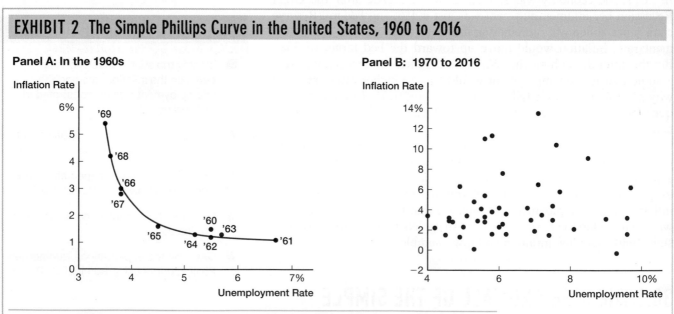

During the 1960s, economic data for the United States suggested there was a tradeoff between inflation and unemployment (Panel A). This data wrongly led some economists to believe that achieving a low unemployment rate was a simple matter of using policy to create high inflation. Since 1970, the relationship between inflation and unemployment is not apparent (Panel B). This is partly the result of shifting inflation expectations that occurred during the period.

Data from: Federal Reserve Bank of St. Louis (FRED).

unemployment. At the time, policymakers were especially worried about unemployment and hence decided to use expansionary monetary and fiscal policies to move the U.S. economy upward and to the left on the Phillips curve diagram. This essentially meant buying lower unemployment at a cost of higher inflation. At first, this is exactly what happened. But beginning around 1970, the negative relationship between inflation and unemployment vanished. The data shown in Panel B shows no apparent relationship between inflation and unemployment between 1970 and 2016.

It is not unusual in science that a discovery fails to hold up under further investigation. But the case of the Phillips curve is especially interesting. Not only does the relationship no longer seem to hold true, but it no longer holds true partly *because* the pattern was discovered and used for policy purposes. Phillips showed that inflation and unemployment are often negatively correlated, but as you will soon discover, the pattern holds *only* if policymakers do nothing to take advantage of that negative relationship.

Shifts in Aggregate Demand and the Simple Phillips Curve

To understand the intuition behind the relationship between inflation and unemployment, it is useful to examine the similarities between the simple Phillips curve and the aggregate supply and aggregate demand model, particularly the short-run aggregate supply curve. A rise in aggregate demand is demonstrated in Panel A of Exhibit 3. For simplicity, we begin with an assumption that the economy expects 0% inflation, but we relax this assumption later in the chapter. The shift in aggregate demand moves us along the short-run aggregate supply curve, which increases the

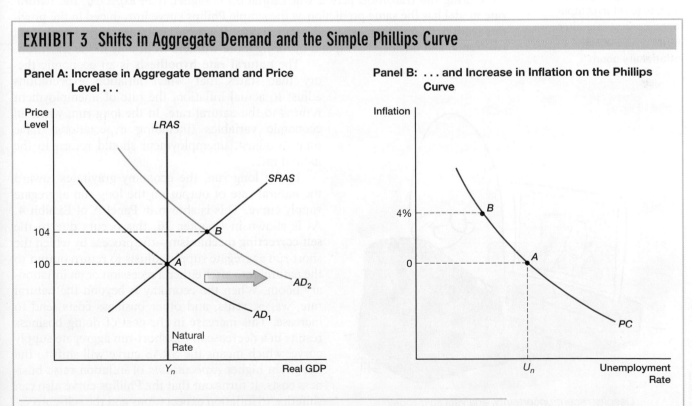

EXHIBIT 3 Shifts in Aggregate Demand and the Simple Phillips Curve

In both panels, higher aggregate demand raises inflation and real GDP. In Panel A, real output rises in the short run. This is consistent with an increase in inflation shown on the simple Phillips curve diagram in Panel B as the unemployment rate falls in the short run.

price level from 100 to 104 and also boosts real GDP. This leads to 4% inflation, and the rising real GDP leads to lower unemployment. Panel B demonstrates a corresponding move along the Phillips curve. Here, as inflation increases the unemployment rate decreases.

30.2 INFLATION EXPECTATIONS AND THE LONG-RUN PHILLIPS CURVE

At first, economists assumed that the Phillips curve allowed us to create a policy that generated a little more inflation as a tradeoff for a little less unemployment. In the late 1960s, economists Edmund Phelps and Milton Friedman independently developed models that exposed a major flaw in the way economists had interpreted the data. Remarkably, they found this flaw when policies based on the Phillips curve still seemed to be working.[3]

The Importance of Inflation Expectations

inflation expectations The amount of inflation that is expected by the public, both businesses and consumers.

natural rate hypothesis An economic theory that states that when inflation expectations adjust, the rate of unemployment returns to the natural rate.

self-correcting mechanism The process by which short-run aggregate supply adjusts to return output to the natural rate after either a recession or an inflationary boom.

The shortcoming of the simple Phillips curve correlation was that it ignored the role of **inflation expectations**, the amount of inflation that is expected by the public, both businesses and consumers. After workers and businesses adjusted their expectations to a higher rate of inflation, both wages and prices adjusted upward, bringing the economy back to the natural rate of unemployment (roughly 5% in the United States).

During the transition period when inflation is higher than *expected*, the natural rate model has the same prediction as the simple Philips curve introduced in the previous section. Higher than expected inflation puts downward pressure on *real* wages and real rents, and businesses respond by hiring more workers—but only in the short run.

The **natural rate hypothesis** is an economic theory that states that when inflation expectations adjust to actual inflation, the rate of unemployment returns to the natural rate. In the long run, when all economic variables (including expectations) have time to adjust, unemployment should return to the natural rate.

In the long run, the economy gravitates toward the natural rate of output on the long-run aggregate supply curve. This is shown in Panel A of Exhibit 4. As is shown in Chapter 26, this occurs due to the **self-correcting mechanism**—the process by which the short-run aggregate supply adjusts to return output to the natural rate after either a recession or an inflationary boom. When the economy is beyond the natural rate, wages, rents, and other business costs tend to increase. This increase in the cost of doing business results in a decrease in the short-run aggregate supply curve, which means the SRAS curve will shift to the left when higher *expectations* of inflation raise business costs. It turns out that the Phillips curve also can shift due to inflation expectations and the self-correcting mechanism.

Despite recent uncertainty, analysts said today they will continue to make predictions.

Mark Dubowski/CartoonStock.com

EXHIBIT 4 The Long-Run Phillips Curve and the Natural Rate Hypothesis

Panel A: Self-Correction in an Aggregate Supply and Aggregate Demand Model

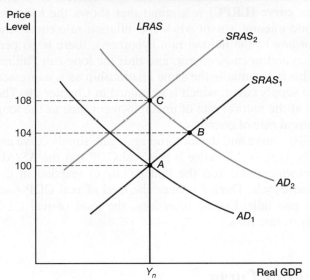

Panel B: Self-Correction and the Long-Run Phillips Curve

In Panel A, due to an increase in aggregate demand, the economy moves from point *A* to point *B*. Due to the self-correction mechanism, the short-run aggregate supply eventually shifts leftward and the economy shifts to the natural rate at point *C*. In Panel B, at point *B* actual inflation (4%) is above expected inflation (0%). Then inflation expectations will start to rise, and the Phillips curve will shift upward, moving the economy to point *C*. According to the natural rate hypothesis, there is no permanent tradeoff between inflation and unemployment, and thus the long-run Phillips curve is a vertical line.

One implication of the natural rate hypothesis is that as the inflation rate rises above zero, there is only a temporary reduction in unemployment. Here are some key implications:

- Actual inflation = Expected inflation → Unemployment rate at the natural rate
- Actual inflation > Expected inflation → Unemployment rate below the natural rate
- Actual inflation < Expected inflation → Unemployment rate above the natural rate

In a nutshell, inflation does not makes unemployment lower: *higher than expected inflation* lowers unemployment. However, when actual inflation is not equal to inflation expectations, the simple Phillips curve will begin to shift. For instance, when actual inflation is greater than expected, people begin to expect higher inflation, and the Phillips curve shifts upward.

This is shown in Panel B of Exhibit 4. At point *A*, actual inflation is 0% and inflation expectations are also 0%. At point *B*, inflation unexpectedly rises to 4%, and unemployment falls to below the natural rate. However, inflation expectations eventually catch up with actual inflation, and the Phillips curve shifts, bringing the economy back to the natural rate at point *C*. Conversely, if inflation is less than expected, the Phillips curve will shift downward.

It was not long before Phelps's and Friedman's natural rate model was confirmed by events in the United States. Inflation rose in the late 1960s and 1970s, but this change did *not* produce a permanent reduction in unemployment. Thus the tradeoff between inflation and unemployment is not stable over time (as shown in Exhibit 2).

Because expected inflation eventually catches up with actual inflation, the Phillips curve tends to be vertical in the long run. Inflation has no long-run effect on unemployment. The **long-run Phillips curve (LRPC)** is a graph that shows the long-run relationship between inflation and unemployment when the inflation rate equals the expected rate of inflation. According to the natural rate hypothesis, there is no permanent tradeoff between inflation and unemployment, and thus the long-run Phillips curve is a vertical line. This is essentially the same relationship as is expressed by the long-run aggregate supply curve, which is examined in Chapter 26. The long-run Phillips curve is at the natural rate of unemployment, just as the long run AS curve is at the natural rate of output.

Both the long-run Phillips curve and the long-run aggregate supply curve are believed to be vertical. The biggest difference is that real GDP (on the AS/AD diagram) and the unemployment rate (on the Phillips curve) respond in the opposite way to the business cycle. During booms, the level of real GDP rises while the unemployment rate falls. During recessions, the level of real GDP falls while the unemployment rate rises.

Flaws in the Simple Phillips Curve

After holding true for nearly a century, why did the relationship that was demonstrated in Phillips's original study suddenly fall apart during the 1970s? Three key factors were overlooked before that time—changes in inflation expectations, aggregate supply shocks, and changes in the natural rate of unemployment.

Changes in Inflation Expectations Perhaps the most important flaw in the simple Phillips curve is that it fails to account for the fact that inflation expectations change. This is shown in Panel B of Exhibit 4. When people saw inflation staying persistently at around 4%, they began to expect inflation at around 4%. When inflation expectations shift, the short-run Phillips curve shifts, and there is no longer a negative relationship between inflation and unemployment. That negative relationship occurs *only* when inflation expectations are stable. During most of the period that Phillips studied, inflation expectations were very stable and close to zero, in part because the gold standard tended to keep prices stable in the long run. With a few notable exceptions (usually during wartime), price level movements were unpredictable, and deflation was almost as common as inflation. When inflation was positive it was higher than expected and when it was negative it was lower than expected.

Aggregate Supply Shocks The simple Phillips curve relies on the assumption that the business cycle was caused solely by demand shocks. If aggregate demand decreases, then inflation will usually fall as unemployment rises, just as the Phillips curve predicts. However, as is noted in Chapter 26, there are two possible causes of a recession—a decline in aggregate demand *or* a decline in aggregate supply.

If a recession is caused by an adverse supply shock, inflation often increases along with unemployment. In that case, there is no negative tradeoff between inflation and unemployment. In the United States, there were two severe supply shocks during the 1970s—as energy prices soared in 1973 and 1974 and again in 1979 and 1980. In both cases, the United States experienced the worst of both worlds—higher than average inflation and unemployment—and the simple Phillips curve worked poorly.

Changes in the Natural Rate of Employment Finally, the simple Phillips curve relationship also requires a stable natural rate of unemployment. As is shown in Chapter 21,

Think & Speak Like an Economist

Economic outcomes are often different in the short run than they are in the long run. In the long run, inflation expectations have time to adjust to changes in inflation, and there is no relationship between the rate of inflation and the rate of unemployment.

long-run Phillips curve (LRPC) A graph that shows the long-run relationship between inflation and unemployment when the inflation rate equals the expected rate of inflation.

EXHIBIT 5 The Natural Rate of Unemployment, 1950 to 2018

Although the unemployment rate can appear volatile, the natural rate of unemployment is relatively stable over time. As a consequence, the long-run Phillips curve is also relatively stable.

Data from: Federal Reserve Bank of St. Louis.

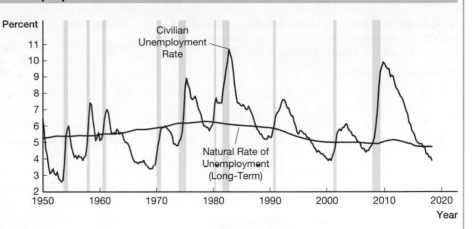

that is approximately true in the United States but not exactly true. Supply-side factors (such as average age of the workforce) can subtly influence the natural rate of unemployment. In Exhibit 5, we can see that even the natural rate of unemployment (blue line) shows some variation over time, although not nearly as much variation as the actual rate of unemployment (red line). For the purposes of this chapter, we assume that the natural rate of unemployment is constant, which means that the long-run Phillips curve is assumed to be stable.

The Phillips Curve and the Great Recession of 2007–2009

It might be expected that with all of its problems the Phillips curve model would be abandoned. Despite the model's shortcomings, however, the relationship between inflation and unemployment remains an important issue. Recently, the United States experienced its first episode of deflation since the 1950s. The inflation rate fell from 3.8% in 2008 to –0.4% in 2009. During the same period, unemployment rose from 5.8% in 2008 to 9.3% in 2009, the largest increase in unemployment since the Great Depression of the 1930s, which is what would be expected from the Phillips curve model. Here are some possible reasons for why the Phillips curve worked in this particular case:

- The sudden fall in inflation was caused by a drop in aggregate demand that was associated with the housing bust and the banking crisis. It was not a supply shock.

- Inflation expectations were stable as the result of the Federal Reserve policy of targeting inflation at 2%. The deflation of 2009 was unexpected.

- The natural rate of unemployment was fairly stable.

The three flaws in the Phillips curve model that were discussed above did not apply in 2008 and 2009, and thus the model worked pretty well during that period.

POLICY BRIEF The Phillips Curve in Hong Kong

Although the Phillips curve model has performed poorly in the United States since 1970, it continues to do well in countries with stable inflation expectations, a stable natural rate of unemployment, and relatively few supply shocks. In Hong Kong, for instance, the Phillips curve continues to show a negative relationship between inflation and unemployment. Hong Kong's currency is fixed to the U.S. dollar. Because the United States kept its expected inflation rate low and stable, inflation expectations

EXHIBIT 6   The Phillips Curve for Hong Kong, 1982 to 2016

Hong Kong had relatively stable inflation expectations, and its economy was hit by substantial demand shocks. This produced the classic Phillips curve pattern.

Data from: World Bank Data.

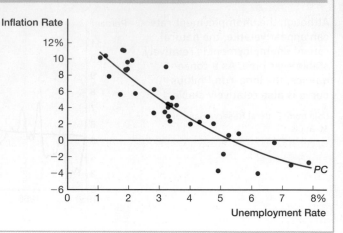

were also relatively stable in Hong Kong. But actual inflation moved around quite a bit due to demand shocks in East Asia. This created a good modern example of the Phillips curve in action, which is demonstrated in Exhibit 6.

30.3 INFLATION EXPECTATIONS AND MACROECONOMIC POLICY

After economists realized that inflation expectations impact the economy, they became increasingly interested how the public forms expectations of variables such as inflation.

How Inflation Expectations Are Formed

The earliest theories of expectations are based on the idea that people look to the past when forecasting the future. Consider the Las Vegas point spread for a sporting event like a football game. If the Chicago Bears are favored by three points over the Denver Broncos, then the average bettor probably expects Chicago to win by about three points. But how do those expectations form? Perhaps they are based on past performance. But which past games?

Expectations Based on the Past The games of the recent past are most likely viewed as providing the best estimate for how a team is likely to perform next week. Sports bettors who use this model are using **adaptive expectations**—the predictions about an economic variable that are based on people's most recent experiences with the variable. For example, the expected rate of inflation might be a weighted average of the past four years of inflation. In that case, people would put more weight on the recent past, just as the recent performance of a football team is viewed as most relevant when making expectations about the next game.

Expectations Based on All Information More recently, economists have concluded that optimal forecasts often involve many factors, not just past performance of the variable being forecast. Consider again the example of the point spread in football. What other factors might come into play when bettors predict the outcome of a game?

adaptive expectations
The predictions about an economic variable that are based on people's most recent experiences with the variable.

In addition to past performance, factors such as key injuries, home field advantage, and weather conditions can influence the outcome of a game.

The theory of rational expectations says that the public considers all relevant factors when making a forecast. **Rational expectations** are the predictions about an economic variable that are based on an optimal forecast using all publicly available information. You may recall that this concept is used in the discussion of efficient financial markets in Chapter 10. A forecast of inflation using rational expectations would take into account not just past inflation rates but also other variables that might affect inflation going forward, such as monetary policy, budget deficits, and disturbances in the supply of oil. Because they include all relevant information, forecasts based on rational expectations are considered superior to those based on adaptive expectations.

▲ Having rational expectations does not mean having a crystal ball—forecasts are not perfect.

Rational expectations should not be confused with perfect foresight. Perfect foresight refers to an ability to predict the future with complete accuracy. The public does not have perfect foresight. When the Chicago Bears are favored by three points over the Denver Broncos, the Bears seldom win by exactly three points.

Likewise, consider the period before the Great Recession of 2007 to 2009. At the time, it might have been rational for the public to expect roughly 2% inflation in 2009 because people were not expecting a deep recession. The actual inflation rate was slightly below zero, but people had no way of knowing that would occur based on the inflation rates and data available beforehand.

POLICY BRIEF A Sudden Change in Inflation Expectations in the United Kingdom

It is often hard to predict changes in the rate of inflation, and the public may often end up using something close to adaptive expectations. If inflation has been running at about 3% for many years, then it seems reasonable to expect more of the same next year. But there are times when rational expectations are a more accurate description of how people think. For instance, in May 1997, the British government suddenly announced a plan to make its central bank, the Bank of England, independent. This meant that the Bank of England could determine monetary policy without interference from government officials who needed to worry about reelection. Many economists believe that independent central banks produce monetary policies that are less expansionary with lower rates of inflation.

On the day the policy was announced, there was no sudden change in the past rates of inflation. So if the public had relied solely on adaptive expectations, people would not have changed their expectations of inflation going forward. But it appears that the British public immediately began to expect less inflation, a sign that they (rationally) concluded that an independent Bank of England would have a less expansionary monetary policy.[*]

You may wonder how we know that inflation expectations fell because of the Bank of England's news. After all, expectations are in the mind, and economists certainly are not mind readers. Instead, economists infer that expectations change by looking at the bond markets. In the United Kingdom (as in the United States), some government bonds pay a nominal interest rate, and others provide inflation "protection" by paying a real interest rate plus actual inflation. The difference between the nominal interest rate on conventional bonds and the real interest rate on inflation protection bonds is (approximately) the expected rate of inflation among investors. When it

rational expectations
The predictions about an economic variable that are based on an optimal forecast using all publicly available information.

was announced that the Bank of England would become independent, that difference narrowed, indicating that investors now expected less inflation.

*Mark M. Spiegel, "British Central Bank Independence and Inflation Expectations," FRBSR Economic Letter 1997-36, Federal Reserve Bank of San Francisco, November 28, 1997, http://www.frbsf.org/economic-research /publications/economic-letter/1997/november/british-central-bank-independence-and-inflation-expectations/.

The Lucas Critique of Macroeconomic Policy

After economists realized that inflation expectations are formed with rational expectations, they saw that policy changes can quickly alter those expectations. As a consequence, policymakers must be careful to consider how policy changes might impact expectations.

In the 1970s, economist Nobel laureate Robert Lucas wrote a paper describing what can go wrong if policymakers ignore the impact of policy on expectations. The ideas in this paper are now called the **Lucas critique**—the observation that past statistical correlations do not provide a reliable guide to policymakers because when a new policy is adopted, the public changes its expectations and therefore the ways that it responds to policy actions. The Lucas critique is an example of the saying *correlation does not mean causation* first discussed in the appendix to Chapter 1, but it also goes a bit further.

The Lucas critique can be illustrated with the Phillips curve example. At the beginning of this chapter, we saw that the original study by Phillips found a relatively stable relationship between inflation and unemployment in the United Kingdom during the period from 1861 to 1957. It should be noted that the price of gold was fixed during that period. Because money was backed by gold, it was not expected to lose much purchasing power over time, so the expected rate of inflation was usually close to zero. As a result, any actual inflation or deflation was largely unanticipated. This partly explains why Phillips found such a strong relationship. He was looking at mostly *unanticipated* moves in inflation, which really do correlate with unemployment.

Soon after the original Phillips study, however, both the United States and the United Kingdom transitioned away from the gold standard and switched to a pure fiat money system where money was *not* backed by gold. This was a major policy change. Under this new system, the expected rate of inflation was no longer close to zero and was heavily influenced by monetary policy. As inflation started rising, expectations began changing. This caused the Phillips curve to begin shifting, and it no longer provided a reliable guide to policymakers.

Robert Lucas was not just saying that the effects of policy are hard to predict. His deeper point is that when a policy changes, the change affects people's expectations. If policymakers do not take the changing expectations into account, then the policy may fail. Indeed, according to the Lucas critique, one reason that the Phillips curve fell apart in the 1970s is that a few years earlier monetary policy had been used to lower unemployment by generating inflation. Using the simple Phillips curve in policymaking eventually shifted inflation expectations and caused it to fail.

Here is an example of how the Lucas critique applies to taxes. Consider these two economic policies:

- *A temporary income tax cut*, sometimes called a *tax rebate*.
- *A temporary cut in a national sales tax*.

Which tax cut will have the greater impact on aggregate demand? The answer depends on expectations. Let us also assume that both tax cuts last for three months and that the two cuts are of roughly equal size. How would their impact differ? Most economists believe that the temporary income tax cut would have only a modest impact on spending. Because consumers know that the income tax rate will go back up in three

Think & Speak Like an Economist

Expectations play a vital role in markets and the economy. Changes in everything from stock prices to the unemployment rate depend not on just the level of an economic variable, but even more so on whether those changes are more or less than expected.

Lucas critique The observation that statistical correlations do not provide a reliable guide to policymakers because when a policy changes, the public changes its expectations and therefore the ways that it responds to policy actions.

months, they will not feel as rich as they would with a permanent tax cut. There might be a bit more consumer spending but not much. Expectations affect how you react to a tax cut.

The sales tax cut is also temporary, but the effect on expectations is very different. Consumers know that the sales tax rate on purchases will rise again in three months. For example, suppose that a family intends to buy a new car in five months. If the family knows that the sales tax rate cut is for only three months, it might make sense to make the car purchase a few months sooner to benefit from the temporarily lower rate. If the tax cut is expected to be temporary, consumers might time their spending to take maximum advantage. In that case, the effect on spending might be surprisingly large. This example shows that policymakers must take expectations into account in order to make sure that policies have the intended effects.

∧ Expectations of higher prices due to a sales tax leads shoppers to stock up before the tax hike.

📊 **BUSINESS BRIEF** Japan Changes Its National Sales Tax Rate; Hits Honda Hard!

On April 1, 2014, Japan raised its national sales tax from 5% to 8%. The national sales tax change was fully anticipated. As expected, consumers rushed to make major purchases on things like Honda automobiles prior to the tax increase. This behavior is consistent with rational expectations because Japanese consumers understood that prices would be higher if they waited until after April 1 to make these purchases.[*] It also illustrates the Lucas critique. Normally, consumer spending would not be much different if sales taxes were 5% or 8%. But when consumers expect a sudden change in tax rates, the effect on spending will be much more pronounced than if the higher rate had always been in effect.

The automobile industry, for example, saw a last-minute surge just prior to the tax hike, as expected. Things changed after the tax hike, when automobile sales across the economy fell sharply. The chair of Honda Motor Company commented in late 2014 that "We thought (sales) would come back after the summer, but it's not coming back at all."[†]

In the first quarter of 2014, Japanese real GDP soared at a 5.1% annual rate as shoppers bought ahead of the tax increase. Then in the second quarter, real GDP fell at an even steeper 6.4% annual rate, which suggests that growth in the first quarter came at the expense of the second.[‡]

[*]"Groundhog Day? Japan's Consumption Tax Hike," *The Economist*, April 5, 2014, https://www.economist.com/blogs/banyan/2014/04/japan-s-consumption-tax-hike.

[†]Kazuaki Nagata, "Sales Tax Hike Stymies Domestic Car Sales: JAMA," *Japan Times*, December 22, 2014, https://www.japantimes.co.jp/news/2014/12/22/business/sales-tax-hike-stymies-domestic-car-sales-jama/#.Wnti9qinGHt.

[‡]Federal Reserve Bank of St. Louis (FRED).

30.4 MODELING THE PHILLIPS CURVE WITH INFLATION EXPECTATIONS

There are two major problems with the simple Phillips curve model—shifting inflation expectation and supply shocks. In this section and the next, we consider more advanced versions of the Phillips curve, which address these two problems one at a time. We begin by addressing the problem of shifting inflation expectations.

The Expectations-Augmented Phillips Curve

The natural rate hypothesis discussed above helps to explain why the Phillips curve shifted over time. Economists eventually realized that inflation was not the best variable to put on the y-axis (vertical axis) on a Phillips curve diagram. Instead, what really matters is the difference between the actual inflation rate and the expected inflation rate.

Exhibit 7 shows an **expectations-augmented Phillips curve**, a graph that shows the relationship between the unexpected inflation rate and the unemployment rate. Because this graph already takes inflation expectations into account, it does not shift when expectations change. It represents a more general model than the previous simple Phillips curve, which held true only when inflation expectations were stable. Point B shows the economy in a boom, when inflation is higher than expected. Point R shows the economy in a recession, when inflation is lower than expected. When the economy is at the natural rate of unemployment, inflation should be roughly equal to expected inflation.

The Role of Credibility in Monetary Policy

This new view of the Phillips curve helps to explain why modern central banks work very hard to maintain credibility—that is, the trust of the public. A *credible policy* is one that the public expects to be carried out. To see why policy credibility is important, consider the following two scenarios:

- The central bank promises to keep inflation at 2% and is believed.

- The central bank fulfills a promise to keep inflation at 2%, but the public expects 5% inflation. In this case, inflation minus expected inflation will be –3% (i.e., 2% actual minus 5% expected).

expectations-augmented Phillips curve A graph that shows the relationship between the unexpected inflation rate and unemployment rate.

Exhibit 7 also can be used to illustrate these two cases, assuming that the central bank does deliver on its promise of 2% inflation. In the first scenario, the economy ends up at the natural rate of unemployment (point U_n) because inflation equals expected inflation. In the second scenario, the economy ends up in recession (point R) because inflation is 3% lower than expected. The first scenario is better in terms of lower unemployment, which explains why central banks try to have credible policies. They would like to have a situation where actual inflation equals expected inflation.

EXHIBIT 7   An Expectations-Augmented Phillips Curve

If inflation is higher than expected, then unemployment is below the natural rate and the economy is at point B (likely a boom). If inflation is lower than expected, then unemployment is higher than the natural rate. For example, if inflation is expected to be 5% but actual inflation is 2%, then the economy will be at point R (likely a recession).

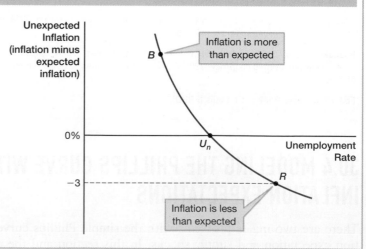

Expectations might seem like a psychological concept, but inflation expectations have real economic consequences for individuals and businesses. An expectation of 5% inflation per year would lead to relatively high nominal interest rates due to the Fisher effect, and workers would demand larger pay increases. High nominal interest rates might seem affordable if 5% inflation is expected, but now suppose that the central bank holds inflation down to its 2% target. Because actual inflation is three percentage points lower than expected, borrowers would find the real burden of their debts to be heavier than they expected when they first borrowed the money. In addition, companies would have difficulty paying the wage contracts that assumed a higher rate of inflation. Workers would be laid off.

∧ Federal Reserve chair Paul Volcker smokes out inflation and inflation expectations.

🏛 POLICY BRIEF Paul Volcker Establishes Fed Credibility

In 1979, the United States was suffering from very high inflation. Prices were rising so fast that many people were losing confidence in the dollar, and financial investments in "inflation hedges" (such as gold and real estate) became very popular. The value of the dollar was also declining in the foreign exchange market as foreign investors lost faith in the U.S. dollar.

President Jimmy Carter turned to economist Paul Volcker, an established monetary expert who was known to favor a "hawkish" or tight money policy, to reduce inflation. Volcker's Federal Reserve established a new policy of reducing the money supply growth rate, which led to sharply higher interest rates in the short run and a decline in aggregate demand. The Fed came under heavy criticism for Volcker's contractionary monetary policy in 1982 as the unemployment rate increased and borrowers had more trouble repaying loans. The disinflation was successful, but there was a very high cost in the short run as unemployment climbed to 10.8%.

Volcker's commitment to a contractionary policy to combat inflation served one particularly useful purpose: It established credibility, which lowered inflation expectations. The move proved effective, inflation fell to about 4% by the end of 1982, and Volcker was able to bring interest rates back down gradually. Years later, Felix Salmon wrote in the *New York Times*:

> In the end, Volcker achieved something genuinely magnificent. They really said it couldn't be done: in 1980, the very deans of the economics profession . . . claimed there was no way the Fed could bring down inflation. . . . But within six years, Volcker had it whipped.*

Volcker's policy did not just control inflation. This policy experiment also changed the way that economists think about monetary policy. Today economists increasingly view the Fed as being responsible for the rate of inflation. The Fed's success at reducing inflation led to the modern era of inflation targeting by the Federal Reserve.

*Felix Salmon, "Central Banker," *New York Times*, October 19, 2012, http://www.nytimes.com/2012/10/21/books/review/volcker-by-william-l-silber.html.

30.5 ADVANCED TOPIC: NOMINAL GDP TARGETING

The simple Phillips curve model does poorly when there are adverse supply shocks during which both inflation and unemployment are high. A recent example occurred during the first half of 2008, when an oil price shock pushed inflation higher even as the economy was falling into recession. This type of event has led some economists to view nominal GDP (NGDP) as a superior guide to monetary policy. **Nominal GDP targeting** is a monetary policy that has a goal of achieving a steady increase in nominal GDP, perhaps something like 4% per year. Proponents of NGDP targeting believe that it is superior to inflation targeting when the economy is hit by supply shocks.

The relationship between unexpected NGDP growth and unemployment is similar to the relationship between unexpected inflation and unemployment. Recall that nominal GDP growth is inflation plus real growth in the economy. To see why it might be preferred to inflation, we need to consider both supply and demand shocks to the economy. In Panel A of Exhibit 8, the economy is hit by a positive demand shock. Both inflation and real GDP increase. This means that inflation and NGDP growth increase at the same time because NGDP growth is the sum of inflation and real growth. With demand shocks, both inflation and NGDP growth respond in the same direction.

In Panel B, we see an important difference between inflation and NGDP as economic indicators. Notice that an adverse supply shock causes higher inflation, even as the economy falls into recession. The adverse supply shock has relatively little impact on NGDP because the higher prices are associated with a lower real GDP. In this case, inflation gives a misleading impression of the strength of the economy.

As noted earlier, the inflation rate was relatively high during the 2008–09 recession (4% in mid-2008). This may have caused policymakers to misjudge the situation by assuming that the economy was strong. In contrast, NGDP growth slowed during 2008, which now seems like the better indicator of what was really going on with the economy. The high inflation caused by rising oil prices quickly ended, and it soon became apparent that a severe recession was a bigger problem than high inflation.

As a result of examples such as this, a number of prominent economists who once favored targeting inflation now argue that the Fed should target the rate of NGDP growth. A target of 4% would be in line with recent trends in NGDP growth. Under this policy, the Fed would tighten policy whenever NGDP growth was expected to exceed 4% and adopt a more expansionary policy when NGDP growth was falling

nominal GDP targeting

A monetary policy that has a goal of achieving a steady increase in nominal GDP, perhaps something like 4% per year.

EXHIBIT 8   Inflation Can Be Caused by Either Demand Shocks or Supply Shocks

Panel A: A Positive Demand Shock

Price Level / Real GDP

SRAS

Nominal GDP and inflation are higher than expected

AD_2

AD_1

Panel B: An Adverse Supply Shock

Price Level / Real GDP

$SRAS_2$

$SRAS_1$

Lower real GDP offset by higher price level

AD

Higher inflation can be caused by either more aggregate demand or less aggregate supply. When AD increases, nominal GDP also tends to increase. However, supply shocks do not have much effect on nominal GDP because prices and output move in opposite directions.

short of 4%. The goal would be to keep NGDP growing along a trend line rising at 4% per year in the hope that this would smooth out the business cycle, while keeping inflation close to 2% in the long run. Targeting nominal GDP allows for year-to-year variations in inflation that result from supply shocks.

Unexpected Nominal GDP and Unemployment

The expectations-augmented Phillips curve improves on the simple Phillips curve by capturing the importance of inflation expectations. Even that model falls short when there is a recession caused by a supply shock. Fortunately, the expectations-augmented Phillips curve can be modified to more narrowly focus on the effect of aggregate demand shocks. As with inflation, what really matters is not what the growth rate of nominal GDP (NGDP) is but whether NGDP growth is higher or lower than expected.

Exhibit 9 shows the relationship between unexpected nominal GDP and unemployment. The relationship looks similar to the expectations-augmented Phillips curve, with unexpected NGDP growth on the y-axis. Once again, point B represents a boom, and point R represents a recession.

The basic idea behind nominal GDP targeting is to keep the growth rate of NGDP fairly stable so that actual NGDP growth will equal expected NGDP growth. In that case, the unemployment rate should stay close to the natural rate of unemployment. In the past, the economy has become unstable when NGDP growth was either too fast or two slow.

In Exhibit 9, point B shows the excessively fast NGDP growth that occurred during the late 1960s. In the short run, both inflation and real GDP growth accelerated during this period, and unemployment declined to low levels, just as the model predicts. But this economic boom occurred at a cost of eventually creating much higher inflation, without boosting employment, especially during the 1970s and early 1980s. Paul Volcker's tight money policy caused NGDP growth to slow in 1982 more sharply than was expected as both inflation and real GDP fell. As a consequence, unemployment rose to over 10%. This is shown as point R.

Point U_n shows the economy during much of the period from 1993 to 2007, when nominal GDP growth averaged about 5%, with roughly 2% inflation and 3% real GDP growth per year. Because nominal GDP growth was fairly close to expectations, the unemployment rate generally remained relatively close to the natural rate. Then, between mid-2008 and mid-2009, NGDP suddenly fell by 3%, which was almost certainly far below what the public had rationally expected based on the previous track

---

EXHIBIT 9 Unexpected Nominal GDP and Unemployment

If nominal GDP is higher than expected, as it was in the late 1960s, then unemployment is below the natural rate (point B). If nominal GDP is lower than expected, as it was in 1982 and 2008–09, then unemployment is higher than the natural rate (point R).

EXHIBIT 10 Nominal Gross Domestic Product, 1991 to 2017

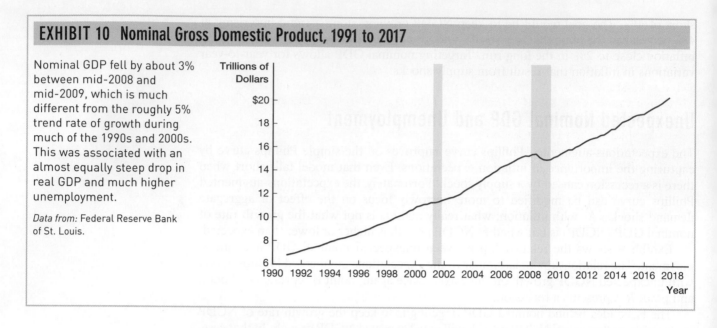

Nominal GDP fell by about 3% between mid-2008 and mid-2009, which is much different from the roughly 5% trend rate of growth during much of the 1990s and 2000s. This was associated with an almost equally steep drop in real GDP and much higher unemployment.

Data from: Federal Reserve Bank of St. Louis.

record of NGDP growth. At this time, the economy entered the Great Recession (point *R* in Exhibit 9). Exhibit 10 shows the unusual drop in NGDP that occurred between 2008 and 2009. Not surprisingly, unemployment rose sharply, peaking at 10% in late 2009.

> Never Reason from a Price Change: Know the Cause of Inflation

The use of inflation as an economic indicator is susceptible to the "Never reason from a price change" problem that is identified in earlier chapters. When looking at a change in the inflation rate, you must first determine the *cause* of the inflation. Changes in inflation can be caused by either supply shocks or demand shocks, which have very different implications for the economy and economic policy. In contrast, nominal GDP (NGDP) growth reflects mostly demand shocks, and some economists believe that it is a better indicator of whether the economy has too little demand or too much. Today, most central banks continue to target inflation and do so with some flexibility when supply shocks hit the economy.

It is too soon to know how the Great Recession will end up impacting future policy, but we do know that the Great Depression and the high inflation of the 1970s both led to significant changes in Federal Reserve policy. Look for more changes ahead.

BUSINESS TAKEAWAY

Imagine that you are a top analyst in a multinational corporation. Your firm's profit depends on the quality of your economic forecast. Where do you start? The simple aggregate supply and aggregate demand model can explain business cycles and the price level. However, you prefer to know the rate of inflation. The Phillips curve model predicts that low rates of unemployment can lead to higher inflation, but only if the economy is being impacted by demand shocks. As a result, some economists suggest that it is better to focus on nominal GDP growth, not inflation.

Understanding the role of inflation and nominal GDP growth expectations is particularly important. Expectations impact all sorts of firms, from tiny businesses to multinational corporations. A small business owner who expects a booming economy is more likely to expand than an owner that sees bad times ahead. In much the same way, expectations of future income and inflation can impact the decision of individuals to buy a new car or home or take a cruise. Workers who expect high inflation will demand bigger pay raises.

It is especially important for businesses to understand the link between inflation and unemployment. Milton Friedman summarized the relationship this way in 1968, although the same sentiment exists among economists today:

> There is always a temporary tradeoff between inflation and unemployment; there is no permanent tradeoff. The temporary tradeoff comes not from inflation per se, but from unanticipated inflation, which generally means, from a rising rate of inflation.*

If a booming economy is accompanied by a rising inflation rate, then firms should not expect the economic boom to last much longer.

*Milton Friedman, "The Role of Monetary Policy," *American Economic Review* 58, no. 1 (1968): 11.

CHAPTER STUDY GUIDE

30.1 THE RISE AND RALL OF THE SIMPLE PHILLIPS CURVE

The simple **Phillips curve** is a graph that shows the relationship between inflation and unemployment. According the Phillips curve, when unemployment is high, inflation is low. When unemployment is extremely low, inflation is high. The correlation existed in the United States throughout the 1960s, but since 1970, the relationship between inflation and unemployment is much less apparent. In the aggregate supply and aggregate demand model, an increase in aggregate demand shifts the aggregate demand curve to the right, resulting in higher inflation and real GDP. In the Phillips curve model, this results in higher inflation and lower unemployment, which is a movement leftward along the curve.

30.2 INFLATION EXPECTATIONS AND THE LONG-RUN PHILLIPS CURVE

The shortcoming of the simple Phillips curve was that it ignored the role of **inflation expectations**—the amount of inflation that is expected by the public, both businesses and consumers. In the long run, the economy gravitates toward the natural rate of output and unemployment. This occurs through the **self-correcting mechanism**—the process by which the short-run aggregate supply curve adjusts to return output to the natural rate after either a recession or an inflationary boom. The

natural rate hypothesis is an economic theory that states that when inflation expectations adjust, the rate of unemployment returns to the natural rate. In the long run, when all economic variables (including expectations) have time to adjust, unemployment should return to the natural rate. The **long-run Phillips curve (LRPC)** is a graph that shows the long-run relationship between inflation and unemployment when the inflation rate equals the expected rate of inflation. There is no permanent tradeoff between inflation and unemployment, and thus the long-run Phillips curve is a vertical line. Flaws in the simple Phillips curve model include shifting inflation expectations, aggregate supply shocks, and an unstable natural rate of unemployment.

30.3 INFLATION EXPECTATIONS AND MACROECONOMIC POLICY

Inflation expectations are formed through adaptive expectations and rational expectations. **Adaptive expectations** are the predictions about an economic variable that are based on people's most recent experiences with the variable. More recently, economists have concluded that optimal inflation forecasts often involve more than just past inflation rates. **Rational expectations** are the predictions about an economic variable that are based on an optimal forecast using all publicly available information. Rational expectations should not be confused with perfect foresight. The **Lucas critique** is the observation that statistical correlations do not provide a reliable guide to policymakers because when a policy changes, the public changes its expectations and therefore the ways that it responds to policy actions. In particular, changes in monetary policy alter inflation expectations.

30.4 MODELING THE PHILLIPS CURVE WITH INFLATION EXPECTATIONS

The **expectations-augmented Phillips curve** is a graph that shows the relationship between the unexpected inflation rate and the unemployment rate. This model incorporates the natural rate hypothesis. The model also illustrates the importance of a credible policy that the public believes will be carried out. It is easier to implement effective monetary policies if the policies are viewed as believable. When policy is credible, the unemployment rate is more likely to stay close to its natural rate.

30.5 ADVANCED TOPIC: NOMINAL GDP TARGETING

Nominal GDP targeting is a monetary policy that has a goal of achieving a steady increase in nominal GDP, perhaps something like 4% per year. Proponents of

NGDP targeting believe that it is superior to inflation targeting when the economy is hit by supply shocks. The relationship between unexpected NGDP growth and unemployment is similar to the relationship between unexpected inflation and unemployment, except it is perhaps even more reliable.

TOP TEN TERMS AND CONCEPTS

(1) Phillips Curve

(2) Inflation Expectations

(3) Self-Correcting Mechanism

(4) Natural Rate Hypothesis

(5) Long-Run Phillips Curve (LRPC)

(6) Adaptive Expectations

(7) Rational Expectations

(8) Lucas Critique

(9) Expectations-Augmented Phillips Curve

(10) Nominal GDP Targeting

STUDY PROBLEMS

1. Draw a short-run Phillips curve. Show how it explains the relationship between inflation and unemployment.

2. Explain the links between the aggregate demand and aggregate supply model and the short-run Phillips curve.

3. Describe the natural rate hypothesis and the long-run Phillips curve.

4. Explain why the short-run Phillips curve relationship held up in the years prior to its discovery in 1958. Explain why the relationship has held up in Hong Kong in recent decades.

5. Rising inflation is sometimes compared to an addictive drug, where the effects are most painful when you try to end the inflation. Do you agree with this analogy? Explain briefly.

6. List three factors that may alter the stability of the short-run tradeoff between inflation and unemployment.

7. During the Great Recession of 2007 to 2009, the short-run Phillips curve held up very well. Explain why.

8. Discuss the difference between the original simple Phillips curve and the expectations-augmented Phillips curve. In which version will the Phillips curve shift if there is an

increase in inflation expectations? In which direction does it shift? Why does the other version of the Phillips curve not shift in that case?

9. Explain why people's inflation expectations changed when the Bank of England gained independence from the political process.

10. Explain the impact of a preannounced increase in a national sales tax, such as that experienced in Japan in 2014. How does it affect the economy before the tax increase occurs, and how does it affect the economy after the increase occurs?

11. Discuss the Lucas critique. How does this idea help explain how the Phillips curve changed after the United States abandoned the gold standard?

12. Discuss why some economists now advocate targeting the nominal GDP growth rate. Why do they believe that this sort of policy is superior to inflation targeting?

13. Explain the importance of having a central bank (such as the Federal Reserve) maintain credibility. How was Paul Volcker able to establish credibility?

14. The "Never reason from a price change" concept is most often used in microeconomics. Explain why it applies not only to the prices of individual goods but also to the overall price level.

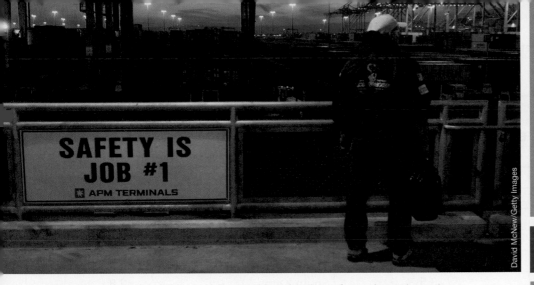

David McNew/Getty Images

31

CHAPTER

∧ Nearly one-fourth of the world's total production of goods and services is exported.

International Trade

Doing Business across Borders

Consider a typical morning. You wake up, check your smartphone (which was designed in California and produced in China or South Korea), and sip your coffee (which was grown in Colombia and roasted in Seattle). You dress in American-branded clothing made in Vietnam and Honduras. As you head off to work or school, you drive a Chevy that contains components made in Mexico.

Nearly a fourth of the world's total production of goods and services is exported. Even businesses that are not directly involved in international trade often have to compete with multinational firms that do business all over the world. In order to be successful, firms need to adapt to an increasingly globalized economy. But the effects of global trade are sometimes controversial. The United States has run a trade deficit every year since 1982, and in recent years, the U.S. trade deficit has averaged about $500 billion—nearly $1,700 per citizen. Is this trade deficit bad for society? Would the United States have more jobs if we imported less? Most economists would say no. In this chapter, we explore why economists generally favor international trade and why some people oppose it.

Chapter Learning Targets

- Apply the concept of comparative advantage in international trade.

- Explain how international trade increases total surplus.

- Identify the economic impact of policies that restrict trade.

- Evaluate arguments about trade policies.

31.1 COMPARATIVE ADVANTAGE AND INTERNATIONAL TRADE

Economists generally agree that trade typically benefits all participants. Because individuals and nations are generally not forced to trade with one another, they presumably do so with the belief that they gain from trade. Economists start from the baseline assumption that both sides gain from trade. In fact, there are no modern examples of a nation that is both isolated from global trade and also prosperous. Exhibit 1 shows the major trading partners of the United States. Through the year ending in January 2018, the top trading partners of the United States include Canada, Mexico, China, Japan, Germany, the United Kingdom, and South Korea.

EXHIBIT 1   The Top Six Trading Partners of the United States, January 2018

U.S. Exports to		U.S. Imports from	
Country	Percentage of Total	Country	Percentage of Total
Canada	18.1%	China	22.5%
Mexico	17.4	Canada	12.9
China	7.8	Mexico	12.7
Japan	4.5	Japan	5.6
United Kingdom	3.8	Germany	4.8
Germany	3.5	South Korea	2.8

The top trading partners of the United States include Canada, Mexico, China, Japan, and Germany.

Data from: United States Census Bureau, Census.gov.

In this section, we return to some of the basic concepts and tools introduced in earlier chapters to show how countries benefit from trade and to examine how international trade increases total surplus. We examine why economists generally favor free trade and then identify some of the reasons that international trade is sometimes controversial.

Determining Comparative Advantage in a Global Context

You already have looked at the concept of **comparative advantage**, which is the ability to produce a product at a lower opportunity cost than a trading partner (Chapter 2). In a global context, a comparative advantage occurs when one country can produce a product at a lower opportunity cost than another country. You also have learned that a *production possibility frontier* (PPF) is an economic model that shows the limit of what an economy can produce when all resources are used efficiently. In this chapter, we use these tools to examine international trade between nations.

Exhibit 2 shows production possibility frontiers for Mexico and the United States, assuming that each country makes only two goods—clothing and trucks. For simplicity, it is assumed that the production possibility frontier is linear (a straight line).

At one extreme, if Mexico devotes its resources to producing four tons of clothing, then it is not able to produce any trucks. This occurs if Mexico completely specializes in clothing. At the other extreme, if Mexico produces no clothing and specializes in trucks, then it can produce 2 trucks. Or Mexico could produce 2 tons of clothing and 1 truck. If the United States produces 6 tons of clothing, it cannot produce any trucks, whereas if it devotes all its resources to producing 12 trucks, then it produces no clothing. Alternatively, the United States could choose to produce somewhere along the frontier, such as 3 tons of clothing and 6 trucks. Recall that points outside the PPF are completely unattainable without trade.

Step One: Compute Opportunity Costs In Exhibit 2, the opportunity cost of producing more trucks is producing less clothing. Similarly, the opportunity of producing more clothing is producing fewer trucks. Note that opportunity cost can be expressed two ways—in terms of trucks and in terms of clothing.

Because nations vary in terms of natural resources, labor, and capital, each nation has a different opportunity cost for producing each product. In this example, the opportunity cost of producing trucks in the United States is different than the opportunity cost of making trucks in Mexico.

comparative advantage The ability to produce a product at a lower opportunity cost than a trading partner.

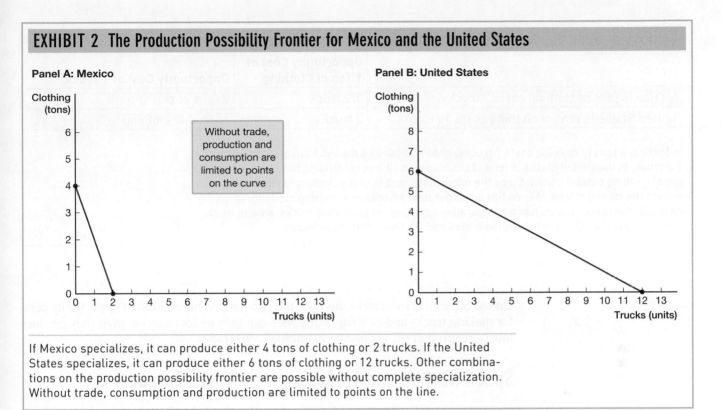

EXHIBIT 2 The Production Possibility Frontier for Mexico and the United States

Panel A: Mexico

Panel B: United States

Without trade, production and consumption are limited to points on the curve

If Mexico specializes, it can produce either 4 tons of clothing or 2 trucks. If the United States specializes, it can produce either 6 tons of clothing or 12 trucks. Other combinations on the production possibility frontier are possible without complete specialization. Without trade, consumption and production are limited to points on the line.

Mathematically, the opportunity cost can be computed by how much less of one good is produced when one more unit of another good is produced. When the production possibility frontier is a straight line, as in the examples above, calculating opportunity costs merely requires a little division. With specialization, Mexico can produce 4 tons of clothing or 2 trucks. This means it gives up 2 tons of clothing for each truck (dividing 4 tons of clothing and 2 trucks each by 2). Likewise, further division shows 1 ton of clothing costs half a truck. Exhibit 3 demonstrates this.

The analysis is similar for the United States, which can produce 6 tons of clothing or 12 trucks. Thus 1 ton of clothing costs 2 trucks (dividing both 6 tons of clothing and 12 trucks by 6), or a half ton of clothing costs one truck (dividing both 6 tons of clothing and 12 trucks by 12 and simplifying).

The opportunity cost of the good on the *x*-axis (horizontal axis; trucks, in this case) is the slope of the production possibility frontier (ignoring the negative sign). For Mexico, the opportunity cost of trucks is 2 tons of clothing because this is the slope of the production possibility frontier. In the United States, the opportunity cost of trucks is half a ton of clothing because this is the slope of the production possibility frontier. Conversely, the opportunity cost of the good on the y-axis (vertical axis; tons of clothing, in this case) is the inverse of the slope (1/slope). For Mexico, the opportunity cost of a ton of clothing is half a truck (inverse of 2), and for the United States, the opportunity cost of a ton of clothing is 2 trucks (the inverse of 1/2).

Think & Speak Like an Economist

Every production decision involves an opportunity cost. If one country can produce a product at a lower opportunity cost relative to another country, it has a comparative advantage over the other country.

Step Two: Compare Opportunity Costs Recall that comparative advantage is a *relative concept* that is measured in terms of opportunity cost. In this example, Mexico is being compared to the United States. The opportunity cost of making 1 truck is 2 tons of clothing in Mexico but only half a ton of clothing in the United States. The United States has the lower opportunity cost of making trucks because is the cheapest place to produce cars in terms of forgone clothing.

Similarly, Mexico is the cheapest place to produce clothing in terms of trucks. In Mexico, the opportunity cost of 1 ton of clothing is only half a truck, whereas in the

EXHIBIT 3   Determining Opportunity Cost and Comparative Advantage

	Opportunity Cost of 1 Ton of Clothing	Opportunity Cost of 1 Truck
Mexico (4 tons of clothing costs 2 trucks)	1/2 truck	2 tons of clothing
United States (6 tons of clothing costs 12 trucks)	2 trucks	1/2 ton of clothing

In Mexico, 4 tons of clothing costs 2 trucks; dividing both by 4 means 1 ton of clothing costs 1/2 truck. In the United States, 6 tons of clothing cost 12 trucks; dividing both by 6 means 1 ton of clothing costs 2 trucks. Since the opportunity cost to make clothing is lower in Mexico than in the United States, Mexico has a comparative advantage in making clothing. In contrast, the United States has a comparative advantage in producing trucks, as one truck costs 1/2 ton of clothing in the United States and 2 tons of clothing in Mexico.

United States it is two trucks. Because the two nations have different opportunity costs for making trucks and clothing, both sides can gain by focusing on what they produce most cheaply and then engaging in international trade.

Specialization and Trade Expands World Output

Countries specialize in the production of goods where they have a comparative advantage. But consumers like to purchase a variety of goods, not just one. Saudi Arabia specializes in oil production because it knows that it can trade that oil for other goods and services. If trade did not exist, Saudi Arabia would be forced to produce far less oil and shift resources to the production of other goods and services, such as food and clothing. That would be less efficient and would reduce its living standards. In a sense, trade makes specialization possible, and specialization makes trade desirable.

In the above example, Mexico has a comparative advantage in the production of clothing: It gives up the production of only half a truck when it produces one additional unit of clothing. In contrast, the United States has a comparative advantage in the production of trucks: It can produce one truck at a cost of half a unit of clothing.

For simplicity, we assume that each nation completely specializes in the product where it has a comparative advantage and trades for the other product. Mexico specializes in clothing, and the United States specializes in trucks. This need not be the case. In more realistic trade models with many different goods, specialization means concentrating on the set of goods for which you have a comparative advantage—that is, producing *more* of the set of goods for which you have a comparative advantage than you would produce without trade.

After specializing in the production of one product, countries trade for the other product. In Exhibit 4, this is accomplished by trading 3 tons of clothing for 3 trucks. In this case, Mexico specializes in clothing, producing 4 tons. In turn, Mexico exports 3 tons of clothing in exchange for the 3 trucks that it imports. Mexico ends up with 3 trucks and 1 ton of clothing. Mexico consumes outside its production limits. In this example, Mexico consumes more trucks than it can possibly produce (although this need not be the case).

Does Mexico's gain somehow harm the United States? Just the opposite happens. The United States specializes in trucks, producing 12. It exports 3 trucks in exchange for the 3 tons of clothing that it imports. The United States ends up with 9 trucks and 3 tons of clothing. The United States, like Mexico, consumes outside its production limits. Specialization and trade allow nations to reach a higher level of consumption—that is, a higher living standard—than they could reach if they were self-sufficient. *Both* nations gain from trade.

In the above example, the two nations traded 3 tons of clothing for 3 trucks. This is referred to as the *terms of trade*, which is another term for *price*. The word *price* is

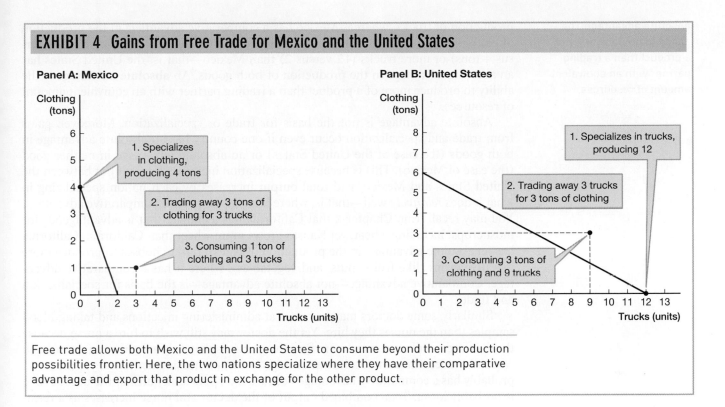

EXHIBIT 4 Gains from Free Trade for Mexico and the United States

Panel A: Mexico

Clothing (tons)

1. Specializes in clothing, producing 4 tons
2. Trading away 3 tons of clothing for 3 trucks
3. Consuming 1 ton of clothing and 3 trucks

Trucks (units)

Panel B: United States

Clothing (tons)

1. Specializes in trucks, producing 12
2. Trading away 3 trucks for 3 tons of clothing
3. Consuming 3 tons of clothing and 9 trucks

Trucks (units)

Free trade allows both Mexico and the United States to consume beyond their production possibilities frontier. Here, the two nations specialize where they have their comparative advantage and export that product in exchange for the other product.

not used because it is not measured in U.S. dollars or Mexican pesos but rather in the number of one good swapped for another. Although money is used in international trade (as is discussed in next chapter), at the most basic level, trade is about swapping one good for another. Money simply facilitates the transactions so that they do not have to occur at the same time. Mexico can sell clothing for money and then later use the U.S. dollars to buy trucks.

For trade to occur, the terms of trade must be beneficial to both sides. Either side can walk away from the deal if the terms are not mutually beneficial. Thus, the terms of trade must lie in between each nation's respective opportunity cost. In Mexico, the opportunity cost of 1 truck is 2 tons of clothing, so Mexico is not willing to export more than 2 tons of clothing for each truck that it imports. Similarly, in the United States, the opportunity cost of 1 truck is half a ton of clothing, so the United States is not willing to accept less than half a ton of clothing for each truck it exports. Therefore, the equilibrium terms of trade must lie between half a ton and 2 tons of clothing for each truck exported.

For simplicity, the exact terms of trade are given to you in this text. But terms of trade must be beneficial to both sides and therefore must be between the two nations opportunity costs. The exact terms of trade are determined by the world price for each item. World prices are determined by the total global market supply and demand for each good. In the previous example, each ton of clothing can be traded for an equal number of trucks, so the world price of one truck equals one ton of clothing. If measured in money terms, these two goods will have the same price.

Although countries gain from specialization and trade in aggregate, not everyone *within* each country is better off. In general, domestic producers of the imported good are made worse off. In Exhibit 4, clothing factory owners and workers in the United States lose if the United States specializes in trucks and imports clothing from Mexico. Likewise, owners and workers at truck factories in Mexico lose from free trade if Mexico specializes in clothing.

Comparative Advantage—Not Absolute Advantage—Is the Basis for Trade In our example, the United States has a comparative advantage in the

Think & Speak Like an Economist

International markets enable countries to specialize and trade, which allows them to consume outside their production possibility frontier. This is why most economists favor free trade: It allows higher living standards.

absolute advantage The ability to produce more of a product than a trading partner with an equivalent amount of resources.

production of trucks, whereas Mexico has a comparative advantage in the production of clothing. But notice that the United States can produce more clothing (6 tons versus 4 tons) or more trucks (12 versus 2) than Mexico—that is, the United States has an absolute advantage in the production of both goods. An **absolute advantage** is the ability to produce more of a product than a trading partner with an equivalent amount of resources.

Absolute advantage is not the basis for trade or specialization. Moreover, gains from trade and specialization occur even if one country has an absolute advantage in both goods (the case of the United States) or an absolute advantage in neither good (the case of Mexico). This is because specialization increases total output between the United States and Mexico, and total output increases by each nation specializing in what it does *relatively* well—that is, where it has its respective comparative advantage. You may recall from Chapter 2 that California has a climate that is advantageous for most crops, including wheat, yet Kansas grows more wheat than California. California has an absolute advantage in the production of wheat, but it chooses to produce more lucrative crops (like fruits, nuts, and vegetables), where it has a comparative advantage. Comparative advantage—not absolute advantage—is the basis for specialization and trade.

Similarly, some doctors may be better at administering injections and taking blood samples than the nurses they hire. Yet the doctor may still wish to hire a nurse because the doctor can bill customers more for other services that only a doctor can do. In such cases, the doctor has an absolute advantage in certain nursing activities, yet the nurse probably has a comparative advantage because the opportunity cost of the nurse's time is probably lower. Total combined output of the doctor and nurse increases as a result of this specialization. Again, comparative advantage—not absolute advantage—is the basis for specialization and trade.

Global Trade Is Not a Zero Sum Game In games like poker, the winnings of one group of players is exactly offset by the losses of another group of players. If the winnings and the losses are added, they sum to zero. It is not uncommon to see politicians or pundits depict trade decisions in the same way—as though gains for one side are matched by equivalent losses on the other. But this is usually not the case. Although tradeoffs and opportunity costs may be involved in a trade, trade generally benefits both sides of the transaction. Otherwise, the trading partners would not engage in it. In the Mexico-U.S. trade example above, both sides win, and neither country loses.

Exhibit 5 provides an alternative example. Suppose that both France and Germany can produce either liters of beer or liters of wine. Each country cannot produce outside its production possibility frontier. The two nations are placed on the same graph to make it easier to see the gains from specialization and trade. For France, the opportunity cost of 1 liter of wine is a quarter liter of beer. This is the slope of the French production possibility frontier (in blue). For Germany, the opportunity cost of 1 liter of wine is 4 liters of beer (in green). France has a comparative advantage in wine and specializes in that product. Germany has a comparative advantage in beer and specializes in that.

Now the nations decide to trade on the basis of comparative advantage. The terms of trade in this example are assumed to be 2 liters of beer for 2 liters of wine. Notice that the terms of trade are favorable to both nations. After trade, both nations end up consuming outside their respective production possibility frontiers. Germany produces 4 liters of beer, exports 2 liters of beer, imports 2 liters of wine, and consumes 2 liters of beer and 2 liters of wine. Germany consumes more than it can produce. France produces 4 liters of wine, exports 2 liters of wine, imports 2 liters of beer, and consumes 2 liters of wine and 2 liters of beer. In the example, France consumes more beer than it can produce. Once again, trade on the basis of comparative advantage benefits both nations.

Think & Speak Like an Economist

Many view trade as a zero sum game with winners and losers. But economists recognize that both sides can gain from trade.

EXHIBIT 5 Comparative Advantages and Gains from Trade for France and Germany

Germany and France have their own production possibility frontiers. For France, the opportunity cost of 1 liter of wine is ¼ liter of beer. This is the slope of the production possibility frontier. For Germany, the opportunity cost of 1 liter of wine is 4 liters of beers. France has a comparative advantage in wine and specializes in that product. Germany has a comparative advantage in beer and specializes in that product. If the terms of trade are 2 beers for 2 wines, each nation will consume outside its PPF. Both sides benefit from trade because trade is not a zero sum game.

1. Each nation specializes
2. Trade 2 liters of wine for 2 liters of beer
3. Consume 2 liters of wine and 2 liters of beer

Sources of Comparative Advantage

Comparative advantage occurs when a nation has a lower opportunity cost than its trade partner. There are many sources of comparative advantage—differences in climate and natural resources, technology and human capital, abundance of labor and physical capital, business environment, and economies of scale—and each can give a nation a slight edge in the production of a specific product.

Differences in Climate and Natural Resources It makes sense for Maine and Alaska to buy orange juice made in Brazil, Florida, and California because the opportunity cost of growing oranges in such cold climates is high. Similarly, it makes sense for Saudi Arabia to produce oil because it can do so cheaply due to plentiful supplies of easy to access crude oil reserves.

Differences in Technological Know-How and Human Capital Some nations know how to mass produce certain products more efficiently than other countries by making better use of technology. The applications of technology are not always universally understood or shared. As a result, different businesses and even different countries may have a technological edge. Likewise, some countries are able to mass produce products more efficiently due to differences in human capital. The United States has relatively more college graduates than many other nations and thus is a hub of innovation in the technology, design, and service industries.

Differences in the Abundance of Labor and Physical Capital Some products require more physical capital in their production than do other products. As such, it makes sense to produce such products where capital is abundant. Products that require more labor in their production are best produced where labor is abundant. India and China, for example, each have populations in excess of 1 billion and a relatively large labor force relative to their capital stock. This is ideally suited for producing products that require a lot of labor.

Differences in the Business Environment Some nations have a business environment that is friendlier toward some industries than others. In an effort to attract businesses, policymakers may lower taxes and offer more favorable regulations for certain industries. For example, France encourages the production of electricity using nuclear

"You drive a Japanese car, drink French wine, eat Chinese food, own an American computer, buy Canadian lumber and vacation in Mexico. How can you be AGAINST free trade?!"

David Brown/Cartoon Stock

power plants, whereas other nations have more restrictive regulations. As a result, France is the world's largest exporter of electricity.

Economies of Scale: The Benefits of Mass Production

Producing some products (such as cars) is often less expensive to do when using mass production techniques such as assembly lines. In economics, this benefit of mass production is known as *economies of scale*. If dozens of countries try to produce the same product in locations around the world, each nation will not be able to utilize the full benefits of mass production. In some instances, economies of scale can be fully utilized only when producing a large share of the world's output. All of the world's large commercial airplanes, for example, are assembled in just two countries, the United States and France, by Boeing and Airbus.

Economies of scale are particularly important in explaining trade between similar economies, such as between the United States and Canada or Japan. It also explains *intra-industry trade*, where similar goods are both imported and exported. One country may have economies of scale in a select niche, and another country may have economies of scale in a different niche. For example, although many countries make automobiles, the United States tends to specialize in trucks, large SUVs, and pickups, Mexico focuses on small cars, and Germany concentrates on luxury automobiles.

📊 **BUSINESS BRIEF** The Comparative Advantage of Chinese Labor

Apple and its various contractors employ a million Chinese workers in the manufacture of its products. In 2015, Apple CEO Tim Cook explained that the reason for locating in China was not cheap labor but rather the specific skill set of the Chinese worker. In China, vocational training is the focus of the education system.[*] This gives China an edge in technological know-how and gives China to a comparative advantage in the production of many products, including Apple's. Cook stated, "You can take every tool and die maker in the United States and probably put them in a room that we're currently sitting in. In China, you would have to have multiple football fields."[†]

He was not exaggerating. Apple has a single factory in Zhengzhou, China, with 350,000 workers in a factory complex sprawling over 2 square miles. Zhengzhou is nicknamed "iPhone City" in part because this factory churns out an astounding 500,000 iPhones per day. Moreover, the factory has developed enormous economies of scale. It would be difficult to recreate that facility anywhere else in the world.[‡]

[*]World Bank, "China: Improving Technical and Vocational Education to Meet the Demand for High-Skilled Workers," World Bank Group, September 14, 2015, http://www.worldbank.org/en/results/2015/09/14/china-improving-technical-and-vocational-education-to-meet-the-demand-for-high-skilled-workers.

[†]Tim Cook, quoted in Charlie Rose, "What's Next for Apple?," CBS News, December 21, 2015, http://www.cbsnews.com/news/60-minutes-apple-tim-cook-charlie-rose.

[‡]David Barboza, "How China Built 'iPhone City' with Billions in Perks for Apple's Partner," *New York Times*, December 29, 2016, https://www.nytimes.com/2016/12/29/technology/apple-iphone-china-foxconn.html?_r=0.

31.2 THE GAINS FROM INTERNATIONAL TRADE

In the previous section we examined how nations gain from trade. Countries export the product that they produce at relatively low opportunity cost, and import the good for which domestic production would have a high opportunity cost. The resulting gain from trade allows nations to consume outside their production possibility frontier.

Next we will see that gains from trade can also increase *total surplus*, which as you'll recall from Chapter 6 is consumer surplus (the buyer's gain from a purchase) plus producer surplus (the seller's gain from a sale). Exhibit 6 shows a domestic market without international trade. The equilibrium price is $20. Consumer surplus is measured as the space between the demand curve and the equilibrium price line (Area *A*); producer surplus is measured as the space between the supply curve and the equilibrium price (Area *Z*). Total surplus is areas *A* + *Z*; it is the total benefit from engaging in domestic trade.

The Gains from Trade with Exports

Assume that a U.S. soybean producer can sell its product in the United States for $20 per bushel or sell to the rest of the world for $25 per bushel. The U.S. producers would clearly prefer to sell the product to the rest of the world for $25. This means that the United States will export soybeans. Conversely, if the rest of the world pays $15 per bushel for bananas and U.S. consumers pay $20 per bushel, then U.S. consumers are better off importing bananas for $15 per bushel rather than paying domestic producers $20.

EXHIBIT 6 Equilibrium without International Trade

Total surplus is consumer surplus (Area *A*) plus producer surplus (Area *Z*).

The *world price* of a good is its prevailing price in international markets. When the world price of an item is different from the domestic (home country) price of an item, imports and exports may occur. To examine this phenomenon, we alter the supply and demand model to show two prices:

- *The domestic (home country) price.* This occurs under self-sufficiency and is where domestic supply (S_{US}) meets domestic demand (D_{US}).

- *The world price.* This price may be higher or lower than the domestic price. It is determined by the global supply and demand for the product.

In Panel A of Exhibit 7, the world price is higher than the domestic equilibrium price. As with soybeans in the example above, domestic businesses wish to export products at the higher world price of $25. In this figure, with no international trade, the U.S. supply and U.S. demand (S_{US} and D_{US}) are in equilibrium at a quantity of 8 and price of $20 ($P_{US}$). As is shown in Chapter 6, consumer surplus consists of areas *A* + *B* and producer surplus is area *Z*.

What happens if free trade is allowed and the world price of $25 is greater than the U.S. price of $20? Businesses begin to export products at the higher world price. This puts upward pressure on the price in the United States until it rises up to the world price. The higher world price lowers the quantity demanded by U.S. consumers from 8 to 4 while increasing the quantity supplied from 8 to 12. Because the quantity supplied in the United States (12) is greater than the quantity demanded (4), the United States will export the excess supply, which is 8 goods in this case.

Notice that U.S. consumers are adversely affected by the higher world price. Consumer surplus declines from *A* + *B* to just area *A*. Exporters benefit from the higher prices. Producer surplus rises from area *Z* to area *Z* + *B* + *G*. Because the gains by producers (*B* + *G*) are greater than the loss to consumers (*B*), total surplus rises by *G*. This is a net *gain* to society. As with the gains from trade shown previously in the production possibility frontier model, society as a whole benefits by exporting its products at the higher world price.

EXHIBIT 7   Gains from Trade: Exports and Imports

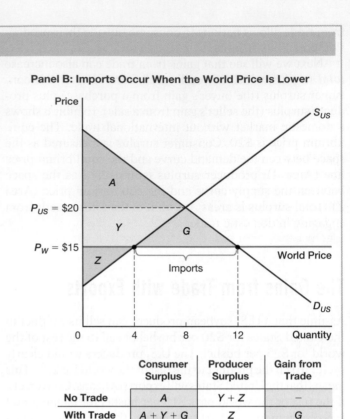

Panel A: Exports Occur When the World Price Is Higher

Panel B: Imports Occur When the World Price Is Lower

	Consumer Surplus	Producer Surplus	Gain from Trade
No Trade	A + B	Z	–
With Trade	A	B + G + Z	G

	Consumer Surplus	Producer Surplus	Gain from Trade
No Trade	A	Y + Z	–
With Trade	A + Y + G	Z	G

The U.S. price of a good is $20. When the world price is higher or lower than this price, international trade occurs. In Panel A, the world price is higher, so U.S. businesses wish to export 8 units (12 minus 4). This raises prices for U.S. consumers to the world price and lowers consumer surplus from $A + B$ to A. The higher price increases producer surplus from Z to $Z + B + G$. Overall society gains area G. In Panel B, the world price is $15, so U.S. consumers wish to import 8 units (12 minus 4). This lowers prices for U.S. consumers to the world prices and increases consumer surplus from A to $A + Y + G$. The lower price decreases producer surplus from $Y + Z$ to Z. Overall, society gains area G.

The Gains from Trade with Imports

We have seen that a society benefits by exporting goods where it has a comparative advantage. This should surprise no one because government policies around the world typically try to boost their country's exports. Thus, it is not surprising to see that an increase in total surplus occurs when products are sold to the rest of the world at higher prices.

Many noneconomists, however, are unaware that the gains from free trade also occur when the world price is lower than the domestic price and the product is imported. Panel B demonstrates. Here, the world price of the good is $15, and the U.S. price remains $20. What happens if free trade is allowed? In that case, society begins to import products at the lower world price. This puts downward pressure on the U.S. price. The lower price raises the quantity demanded by U.S. consumers (from 8 to 12) and decreases the domestic quantity supplied (from 8 to 4). Because the quantity supplied in the United States (4) is less than the quantity demanded (12), the United States will import 8 units.

Who does not like the lower world price of $15? U.S. businesses that compete with the imported goods are hurt by the lower world price. Producer surplus drops from

Y + *Z* to area *Z*. In contrast, U.S. consumers see their consumer surplus rise from area *A* to area *A* + *Y* + *G*. Because the gains to consumers (*Y* + *G*) are greater than the loss to producers (*Y*), total surplus rises by *G*. This may be more surprising because unlike with exports, politicians and pundits often treat imports as hurting an economy. Economists do not agree.

Regardless of whether the world price is above or below the domestic price, free trade is efficient and increases total surplus. However, the gains from free trade are not generally split evenly. In Panel A, the world price ($25) is above the domestic price ($20), total surplus increases as producer surplus increases, but consumer surplus decreases. Recall that consumers are worse off because of the higher world prices. Conversely, in Panel B, the world price ($15) is below the domestic price ($20). Total surplus increases, consumer surplus increases, but producer surplus decreases. Loss in producer surplus often means job losses in specific industries. The fact that not everyone benefits from free trade prompts some individuals to call for barriers to trade, as is discussed later in the chapter.

Free Trade Does Not Mean Complete Specialization

In the previous exhibits, you may have noticed that complete specialization does *not* occur. In Panel A of Exhibit 7, the United States exports the product, but the rest of the world continues to produce the good. But if the United States has a comparative advantage, why does the rest of the world produce anything at all? Similarly, in Panel B of Exhibit 7, the United States imports the product but continues to produce some of the good. This appears to be the case in the real world. The United States produces some cars, buys many imports from Japan and Germany, and also exports cars. So why do we not see complete specialization?

First, complete specialization does not occur because some goods cannot be traded globally. Services such as haircuts and restaurant meals are rarely traded because it would be too costly.

Second, technical skills may vary from country to country. Germany is known for engineering sophisticated cars with good road handling, Italy is good at making exotic sports cars, and Japan excels in producing highly reliable cars for average buyers.

Third, consumers' preferences are often varied. For example, American car buyers can choose between fuel-efficient cars from Japan, exotic sports cars from Europe, or American specialties like muscle cars, pickup trucks, and SUVs. Some prefer to buy an American car made in any of these categories, and others put a premium on Japanese reliability or German engineering. In Europe and Japan, the price of gasoline is substantially higher than in the United States, so many of their consumers prefer fuel-efficient cars. As a consequence, small fuel-efficient cars are often produced in Europe and Japan, and muscle cars, large SUV, and pickups are often produced in the United States, where there is a bigger market for them due to lower gas prices.

Finally, complete specialization often does not occur because of transportation costs, although these costs have declined in recent decades. If the cost of producing cars is fairly similar in the United States and Europe, then it often makes sense to produce cars locally because the lower transportation costs give locally produced cars a slight advantage over imported goods.

▼ An Ohio-made Jeep is sold in China. At the same time, the United States imports many automobiles from around the world.

AFP/Getty Images

📊 BUSINESS BRIEF Containerization Changes the World

Some of the most important technological advances do not seem especially high tech. In 1956, Malcom McLean, founder of the shipping firm Sea-Land Services, revolutionized the shipping industry with the introduction of the standardized shipping container.* These uniform, secure containers can switch seamlessly between shipping goods via trucks, rail, and cargo ships, which greatly reduces shipping costs. The invention changed the nature of global trade, making shipping goods vastly more efficient than it was when goods had to be unloaded from cargo ships manually, one item at time. In 1955, it cost $5.86 per ton to carry cargo. By 2016, the cost had plunged to just $0.16 per ton.†

The process is known as *containerization*. Today, 90% of products purchased have been containerized at some point. The largest container ships can carry nearly 20,000 containers, enough to carry nearly 750 million bananas—one for every person in Europe.‡

*"Malcom McLean: Containerized Shipping," They Made America, PBS, accessed May 30, 2017, http://www.pbs.org/wgbh/theymadeamerica/whomade/mclean_hi.html.

†Marex, "Twenty Ways Shipping Containers Changed the World," *Maritime Executive*, April 30 2015, http://www.maritime-executive.com/article/20-ways-shipping-containers-changed-the-world.

‡Rose George, *Ninety Percent of Everything: Inside Shipping, the Invisible Industry That Puts Clothes on Your Back, Gas in Your Car, and Food on Your Plate* (New York: Metropolitan Books, 2013), 3.

Additional Benefits of International Trade

We have seen that free trade allows the world to produce more total output than would be the case if countries were self-sufficient. But many economists think that it also has other, more subtle benefits:

- *A greater variety of goods.* Free trade enables consumers to buy shoes, wine and beer, automobiles, and countless other products that are made in a wide range of countries.

- *An increased exchange of ideas.* Economists point out that free trade moves more than goods and services across borders. Free trade also means exporting and importing information, ideas, art, and different ways of doing things. For example, as the Internet expanded, individuals in many poor nations where able to learn about improved farming techniques. Likewise, cultural exports are consumed around the globe via a thriving international film and media economy, changing tastes and ideas along the way.

- *Increased competition.* Without trade, Boeing would have no competition when selling jumbo jets to U.S. airlines. Economists typically favor increased competition because it leads to greater innovation and lower prices for consumers. For example, without pressure from Japanese automakers, American automakers might be less likely to pursue electric or hybrid car technology, and the prices of American cars might rise.

∨ Small is beautiful. Global trade has enabled even small countries like Switzerland to prosper.

canadastock/Shutterstock.com

⚜ POLICY BRIEF Free Trade and the Wealth of Small Nations

The World Bank ranks the 10 wealthiest countries in the world in terms of per capita GDP (adjusted for cost of living differences). The United States comes in at number nine on the list. But the other nine nations are quite small: Each has fewer people than the state of New Jersey. Five are major oil exporters and thus rely on a valuable natural resource. But the other four countries—Ireland, Luxembourg, Singapore, and Switzerland—are small nations that do not have a lot of natural resources.* So how did they succeed?

The four countries without a lot of natural resources have pursued policies that encourage trade with other nations. This allows them to specialize in areas in which they are most efficient (such as financial services, technical equipment, and pharmaceuticals) and to take advantage of a thriving import and export sector to trade these highly valued goods and services for a wide range of goods from all over the world. As a result, these relatively small countries can enjoy a higher standard of living than they would if they were self-sufficient.

*"GDP per Capita, PPP (Current International $)," World Development Indicators Database, World Bank, database updated on April 11, 2016.

31.3 INTERNATIONAL TRADE POLICY

Suppose that two children decide to trade snacks from their school lunch boxes. If they agree on a trade (say, two cookies for one cupcake), presumably they both think they will be better off. In this setting, each child's goal is to give up as little as possible and get as much as possible from the other child. In the real world, things can be more complicated than children trading cookies for cupcakes, but this analogy is close to how economists look at trade—swapping one good for another to the benefit of both parties. Economists believe that trade involves countries giving up some goods (exports) so that they will be able to get other goods that they want (imports). Economists believe that exports are the cost that we incur in order to import the goods we want. The whole point of international trade is to import as much as possible and export as little as possible to pay for those exports.

In high-level international trade negotiations, however, countries often do the opposite. Because they often wish to protect domestic industries (and jobs) from import competition, they try to get other countries to take as many of their products as possible and try to receive as few goods as possible in return. They act as if exports are the whole point of trade and imports are a negative. Most economists believe that this misses the point and view trade more like the children in the lunchroom, not like the trade negotiators

As has been shown in this chapter, free trade brings gains in the aggregate. But unfortunately, the gains from free trade are not evenly shared. U.S. clothing companies and workers become worse off as the United States makes less clothing and Mexico makes more. Mexican truck factory owners and workers are worse off if Mexico makes no trucks. These costs are often highly visible and occasionally lead to policies limiting trade.

Protectionist Policies to Limit Imports

In general, when the world price is below the domestic price, free trade makes the domestic producer worse off but benefits society overall. Workers and owners who are hurt by import competition will understandably be passionate about protecting their industry and their jobs. Therefore, it is common for some politicians to promote laws to block free trade, particularly for goods that hurt the businesses in their districts.

Protectionism is the use of government policy to protect domestic businesses from foreign competition. Governments have a variety of protectionist policy options that can be used to reduce imports, including tariffs, quotas, voluntary export restraints, limits on import licenses, and other regulations.

Tariffs: Taxes on Imports One example of a protectionist policy is an import **tariff—** a tax on imports that is imposed by the importing country. Tariffs increase the price of the imported products, lead to fewer imports, and raise the price of similar domestic goods. This helps domestic producers but hurts consumers. For example, if the United States imposes a high tariff on imported clothing, the price of clothing will increase for *all* American clothing because domestic producers will raise their prices in the face of decreased foreign competition. This creates a deadweight loss.

A tariff is sometimes viewed as an indirect subsidy for producers that is paid for by consumers. Exhibit 8 demonstrates. When a tariff of $3 is imposed on sweaters, the price of sweaters increases from the world price of $15 ($P_w$) to the world price *plus* the tariff of $3 to $18 ($P_{W*}$). This hurts consumers. Higher prices increase the domestic quantity supplied (from four to six), which helps explain why domestic businesses lobby for tariffs: The tariffs indirectly subsidize the domestic businesses. Higher prices also reduce the domestic quantity demanded (from 12 to 10) and lower the quantity of imports to 4 (from 10 to 6).

Recall that in Exhibit 7, society goes from no trade to free trade and experiences a net gain. In Exhibit 8, we are now doing the opposite—restricting free trade. Whenever free trade is limited, it reduces the gains from trade, resulting in *deadweight loss*. If the tariff is so high that no goods are imported, then we lose the entire gains from trade.

With free trade, consumer surplus is the area below the demand curve but above the world price of $15. The producer surplus is area Z. Higher prices caused by the tariff lower consumer surplus by $V + W + X + Y$. Higher prices on sweaters raise producer surplus by V. Area $W + X + Y$ is lost from consumer surplus but not captured by producer surplus.

In the case of a tariff, area X represents tariff (tax) revenue that goes to the government. In Exhibit 8, a tax of $3 is paid for each of the imported goods (the tariff is only on the four goods that are now imported, not on the eight that had previously

protectionism The use of government policy to protect domestic businesses from foreign competition.

tariff A tax on imports that is imposed by the importing country.

EXHIBIT 8 Deadweight Loss from a Tariff or Quota

When a tariff or quota is imposed on sweaters, the price of sweaters increases. This lowers the amount of imports from 8 (12 minus 4) to 4 (10 minus 6). The higher price lowers consumer surplus and raises producer surplus from Z to Z + V. Area X is either tariff revenue or foreign producer surplus. Deadweight loss is area W + Y.

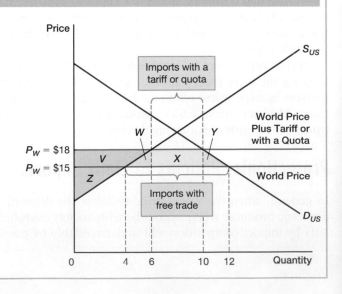

been imported). In this case the tariff revenue is $12 (=$3 × 4 units.) The tariff revenue is not a net loss from society's perspective. Thus, the net deadweight loss is area $W + Y$.

Perhaps the most famous tariff in U.S. history is the Smoot-Hawley Tariff Act of 1930. The law was passed in the wake of the October 1929 stock market crash when lawmakers foolishly tried to protect U.S. industry by blocking imports. Tariffs rose on over 20,000 imported goods to record levels, with an average tariff of 59%. By all counts, the law was a disaster. The day after President Herbert Hoover decided to sign the tariff legislation, the New York stock market saw its biggest losses of the year as traders correctly worried that it would hurt the economy. The law ended up doing more harm than good because U.S. trading partners retaliated with higher tariffs of their own. In the next few years, international trade almost came to a standstill, and the Depression worsened in the United States.

Quotas on Imports There are also nontariff barriers to trade. A **quota** is a quantity restriction on imports that is imposed by the importing country. In Exhibit 8, the government imposes a quota, restricting imports to four units. The effect is generally similar to a tariff. Restricting quantity lowers the combined supply from domestic and foreign sources. And as is shown in Chapter 3, lower supply raises price. Higher prices lower the consumer surplus and also increase the domestic producer surplus to areas $Z + V$. Once again, consumers are made worse off, and producers are made better off.

One difference between a quota and a tariff is who gets area X. With a tariff, the domestic government obtains area X in the form of tariff (tax) revenue. With a quota, area X is often captured by foreign firms that sell fewer units but at a higher price. Area X is foreign producer surplus. Unlike with a tariff, area X is generally *not* captured by the country imposing a quota.

So why not simply impose a tariff and also collect tax revenue? The answer has to do with high-level international trade negotiations. If country A imposes a tariff on products made by country B, country B might retaliate by imposing a tariff on products made by country A (as was done after the passage of Smoot-Hawley). A quota may be perceived as less of a threat because businesses in country B obtain area X, the foreign producer surplus. Although domestic producers are helped by either policy, foreign exporters are hurt less than by a tariff. This makes retaliation less likely.

Voluntary Export Restraints Quotas are often illegal under international trade laws. Therefore, governments sometimes use the power of persuasion to get foreign nations and firms to restrict voluntarily the amount of their products sold in the foreign country. A **voluntary export restraint (VER)** is a quantity restriction on imports that is imposed by negotiating with the foreign exporting country to restrict its exports voluntarily. Foreign countries agree to volunteer to restrict their exports in order to prevent stricter trade policies from being enacted. The effect is identical to a quota, and in most cases the term *voluntary* is a bit misleading. Countries are often strongly pressured to limit exports, often with threats of more restrictive tariffs or quotas by the importing country.

Limits on Import Licenses **Import licenses** are laws requiring importers to obtain a license in order to engage in foreign trade. Governments occasionally limit imports by restricting the number of licenses awarded. In this case, area X is captured by the holder of the import licenses. If governments sell the licenses, then government can collect revenue from the policy, as with a tariff.

Other Regulations Regulations that seem to be unrelated to trade often provide an alternative—and less transparent—approach to restricting imports. For example, governments might use stricter health and safety regulations for imports than for similar products made by domestic firms. The regulations might address legitimate health and

quota A quantity restriction on imports that is imposed by the importing country.

voluntary export restraint (VER) A quantity restriction on imports that is imposed by negotiating with the foreign exporting country to restrict its exports voluntarily.

import licenses Laws requiring importers to obtain a license in order to engage in foreign trade.

Think & Speak Like an Economist

When people consider protectionism, they often think of tariffs and quotas. But economists view protectionism as a wide range of policies that seek to protect domestic industries.

safety concerns, but they also may be an indirect way to reduce the amount of imports without seeming to violate international trade agreements. In Germany, for example, until 1987 brewers had to follow a fifteenth-century "purity law." The law reduced beer imports from foreign nations, which often made beer using less traditional techniques.

Who Bears the Economic Burden of Protectionist Policies?

The implementation of protectionist policies such as tariffs tends to raise the price of imported products, reduce the amount of imports and overall trade, and create a dead-weight loss. This creates an economic burden on three groups—consumers, domestic exporting industries, and poor exporting countries.

First, although the deadweight loss from protectionist policies makes all consumers worse off, the economic burden of a tariff tends to fall especially heavily on the poor. Studies suggest that the United States typically levies higher tariffs on products (such as food and clothing) on which the poor spend a larger share of their income than do the rich. As a result, poor consumers pay tariff rates that are five to ten times larger as a share of their income than higher-income groups pay.

Second, protectionist policies are also likely to burden domestic exporting industries. This is a result of a decline in the amount of overall global trade. Protectionism causes both imports and exports to decline. If, for example, the United States buys fewer goods from the rest of the world, then in the long run, other countries will buy fewer goods from the United States. Sometimes, an exporting business is lost as a consequence of a trade policy. For example, Clarence Crane founded Life Savers in Cleveland in 1912. Today, this iconic American candy is imported to the United States, primarily because sugar prices are considerably higher in the United States than in the rest of the world as a result of government policies, including tariffs and quotas.

Third, poor exporting countries such as Thailand, Cambodia, and Bangladesh are also hurt when the United States places high tariffs on the products they export. Cambodia, for example, paid more in tariffs than Singapore, which has a 100 times higher income per capita. Farm subsidies and import barriers are particularly harmful to low-income countries. High-income countries such as the United States, Japan, and many European nations subsidize agriculture to the tune of nearly $500 billion a year in an attempt to protect their farmers. The benefit of the protectionist subsidy goes to American farmers with average income over $125,000 per year. Who pays for this? Developing countries with a comparative advantage in the production of goods such as cotton. According to one study, if the protectionist subsidies were eliminated an estimated 10 million people in West Africa would see their incomes rise by as much as 5.7% or enough to feed 1 million children.[1]

International Free Trade Agreements

Economic theory suggests that countries would benefit from eliminating trade barriers, even if other countries kept them in place. As a practical matter, however, it is easier for political leaders to remove protectionist policies in their own country when other nations agree to do likewise. In recent decades, countries around the world have promoted free trade and reduced trade barriers. This has been accomplished primarily through regional trade blocs and globally through the World Trade Organization.

World Trade Organization (WTO) An international organization that promotes free trade, supervises the trade policies of member nations, and enforces the trade rules that are agreed to by member nations.

The **World Trade Organization (WTO)** is an international organization that promotes free trade, supervises the trade policies of member nations, and enforces the trade rules that are agreed to by member nations. Over 150 countries have agreed to the rules enforced by the WTO.

Free trade agreements also occur between smaller groups of nations, often known as regional trade blocs. A **regional trade bloc** is an international trade agreement that promotes free trade by reducing trade barriers between participating countries. Lower trade barriers typically exist between member nations within the trade bloc than with nations outside the trade bloc. Regional trade blocs include the following:

- North American Free Trade Agreement (NAFTA) between Mexico, Canada, and the United States
- Central American Free Trade Agreement (CAFTA) between the United States, the Dominican Republic, and smaller countries in Central America
- European Union (EU) between most of the countries in Europe
- Association of Southeast Asian Nations (ASEAN) includes 10 nations in Southeast Asia.

📊 BUSINESS BRIEF   Free Trade Agreements Lure Firms to Mexico

The business decision of where to locate an automobile factory has enormous implications both for the business and the region where the factory is to be located. In Mexico, GM, Chrysler, Ford, and Nissan each have three or four such facilities, and more plants are being planned. In 2016, the country produced 3.5 million lightweight vehicles.*

Discussions of automobile manufacturing in Mexico often focus entirely on the cost of labor, which is cheaper in Mexico than in the United States and many other wealthy countries. But another key factor also plays an important role in a company's decision to open plants in Mexico—Mexico's numerous free trade agreements. Mexico has free trade agreements with over 45 countries, including many countries in Latin America and the Asian Pacific region.† To put this number in perspective, the United States has trade deals with just 20 countries.

Automobiles are an important export industry in many countries. Mexico has been able to use these trade deals to attract automakers that want to sell their products around the globe with the least amount of restrictions, such as tariffs and quotas. Automakers know that if they locate in Mexico, they can export freely to important markets such as the United States, the European Union, and Japan.

*Natalie Kitroeff, "Trump's Threats to Booming Mexico Auto Industry Have Executives' Heads Spinning," *Los Angeles Times*, February 1, 2017, http://www.latimes.com/business/la-fi-mexico-car-trump-20170201-story.html.

†Dudley Althaus and William Boston, "Why Auto Makers Are Building New Factories in Mexico, Not the U.S.," *Wall Street Journal*, March 17, 2015, http://www.wsj.com/articles/why-auto-makers-are-building-new-factories-in-mexico-not-the-u-s-1426645802.

regional trade bloc An international trade agreement that promotes free trade by reducing trade barriers between participating countries.

31.4 WHY ECONOMISTS AND THE PUBLIC OFTEN DISAGREE ON TRADE

Although most economists agree that free trade is mutually beneficial, calls for protectionist policies persist. Widely varying arguments have been offered for restricting trade. Many economists believe that some arguments for protectionism reflect a basic misunderstanding of the nature of trade and that others reflect a desire to protect the groups that lose from free trade.

▼ A 1910 postcard calling for tariffs. Although most economists champion free trade, calls for protectionism do occur.

Michael Nicholson/Getty Images

Protecting Domestic Jobs

The most common complaint levied at free trade is that it costs domestic jobs. Because labor is often cheaper overseas, critics contend that it is difficult for American labor to compete. In Exhibit 2, truck makers in Mexico and clothing makers in the United States experience job losses. Employment often falls in industries as foreign imports increase.

However, free trade creates other jobs as employment increases in the industries that engage in global trade. As shown earlier in the chapter, when the world price is lower than the domestic price (leading to imports), free trade increases the total surplus because the lower price increases the consumer surplus by more than the producer surplus declines. Consumers save money on clothing, autos, and other products and respond by spending part (or all) of these cost savings on other goods. Consumers may eat in restaurants a few more times a year, take longer vacations, or build a bigger house. The increased spending on other things results in additional employment in these other industries. If consumers save part of the gains, that saving tends to boost domestic investment, also creating jobs.

One key issue is the regional impact of trade. Although free trade does not seem to increase the overall unemployment rate, it can sharply increase unemployment in regions where industries hurt by import competition are centered. For example, the booming technology sector has created new jobs in places like San Francisco and Seattle, but areas of the country that focus on traditional manufacturing have suffered as those jobs have been outsourced overseas. In these regions, the job losses due to free trade are highly visible, while the job gains elsewhere are often less apparent. In this sense, trade is sort of like automation—a process that makes the overall economy more productive but at the cost of job loss for specific workers. Economists call this *creative destruction* because the creation of new jobs and industries often comes at the cost of destroying older less efficient industries.

Think & Speak Like an Economist

Economists recognize that although countries as a whole gain from trade, not everyone within each country is better off. In general, domestic producers of goods that are also imported are made worse off by international trade, whereas foreign producers and domestic consumers of imported goods are better off.

Protecting against Dumping and Export Subsidies

When foreign producers flood a market with goods that are priced below cost, it often is viewed as an unfair business practice. Some people worry especially about *predatory dumping*, in which prices are lowered expressly to drive domestic firms out of business, after which they are raised sharply. In response, some call for retaliatory measures known as *countervailing tariffs*.

Many economists are skeptical of this idea. They believe that predatory dumping is not common because it is difficult to make it work in the long run: As soon as prices are raised again, new firms enter the industry, and competition drives prices back down again. To make predatory dumping work would require a global monopoly, but real-world dumping disputes tend to occur in industries such as steel, which involve hundreds of firms in dozens of countries. Economists view countervailing duties as a back-handed method for domestic firms to gain protection from imports. If foreigners lower the price of steel, the U.S. steel industry will likely claim that they must be engaged in dumping. In reality, foreign firms might be utilizing cheaper resources, or they may have developed a more efficient way to produce steel. In addition, many countries (including the United States) engage in the practice of *export subsidies*, which are government policies that are designed to boost exports with low-cost loans and tax benefits.

Some contend that export subsidies provide a case for countervailing tariffs. Just as dumping subsidies can be used to boost exports, countervailing tariffs can be employed to block those exports. Here, too, most economists contend that the case for protectionist policies is weak. If, for example, solar panel exports are being subsidized by the Chinese government, then they would represent a great bargain for U.S. consumers.

What difference does it make to U.S. consumers whether China sells solar panels here at low prices due to subsidies or whether its low prices are due to production efficiencies? Most would prefer to pay the lowest price they can.

To get a sense of why economists are less worried about "unfair competition" than the average person, consider the following parable of trade. Suppose that Americans have been happily buying cheap bananas that they assume are from El Salvador, thinking that they are cheap because of the warm climate in Central America. Then they wake up one day and discover that the bananas actually come from Iceland, where they are produced in expensive greenhouses with huge government subsidies for heating the buildings. At first glance, this seems like "unfair trade" because Icelandic banana producers gain an advantage from government subsidies, which are not available to producers from El Salvador. But should it really matter to the importing country *why* the goods are cheap? Does it matter whether the low prices are due to a natural comparative advantage or to a government subsidy to the foreign producer? Most economists would say that it does not matter. The reason that imported bananas are cheap does not have any impact on whether the cheaper bananas make us better off.

∧ Why would we want to pay more for these solar panels?

📊 BUSINESS BRIEF Antidumping Tariff on Solar Products

In 2014, the United States imposed an antidumping tariff on solar panels and cells produced in Taiwan and China. The tariff exceeded 165%. The U.S. Commerce Department decided that the solar panels and cells were being sold too cheaply, a finding that shocked no one. In fact, the Commerce Department almost always finds that foreign countries are guilty of dumping when U.S. businesses lodge complaints. Meanwhile, India imposed a similar tariff on solar panels from the United States and China, and the European Union set up antidumping measures for Chinese panels and U.S.-made polysilicon, a crucial raw material.[*] If all these various complaints about dumping make your head spin, you are not alone. Remember, just as anti-dumping measures can be enacted for strategic purposes, countervailing tariffs can be imposed for strategic purposes.

In 2018, the United States imposed a smaller tariff of 30% on solar panels. This time, the action came in response to requests from U.S. solar panel manufacturers that were seeing an import surge of panels made in China. But consumers were opposed to the tariff because it would make solar panels more expensive. An association that included solar panel installers estimated that 23,000 Americans employed in their industry would lose their jobs due to the tariff—which, perhaps ironically, was designed in part to save manufacturing jobs.[†]

[*]Krista Hughes, "U.S. Sets Anti-dumping Duties on Solar Imports from China, Taiwan," Reuters, July 25, 2014, https://www.reuters.com/article/us-usa-trade-solar/u-s-sets-anti-dumping-duties-on-solar-imports-from -china-taiwan-idUSKBN0FU29D20140726.

[†]David J. Lynch, "Trump Imposes Tariffs on Solar Panels and Washing Machines in First Major Trade Action of 2018," *Washington Post*, Wonkblog, January 22, 2018, https://www.washingtonpost.com/news/wonk /wp/2018/01/22/trump-imposes-tariffs-on-solar-panels-and-washing-machines-in-first-major-trade -action/?utm_term=.a6b94b32f27c.

Protecting Select Industries

For strategic reasons, governments often try to nurture new industries (commonly referred to as *infant industries*) in areas that they hope will eventually become export industries. They often do so by imposing trade restrictions such as tariffs on imports. For example, after gaining independence from Great Britain, the United States imposed tariffs on imports that competed with domestic businesses. In a somewhat similar vein, products that are made domestically for strategic purposes related to *national defense* are often protected today. For example, a country may wish to make its own tanks, missiles, and jet fighters. Similarly, governments may want to protect their farmers so that they are not dependent on food imports, which could be cut off in times of war.

Most economists believe that these arguments are widely subject to misuse. In the United States, our infant industries are typically in places like Silicon Valley and do very well without any government protection. In contrast, we often protect older industries with no obvious national defense justification. For instance, we protect our farmers in sectors such as sugar, even though overall the United States is a huge food exporter and not in danger of running out of food in wartime.

Deciding which industries to protect is often a political decision that is not based on the economics of an emerging industry or on national defense concerns. In 1954, for example, the U.S. government declared that the mohair fleece of Angora goats was vital for nation security. Moreover, protectionist policies are difficult to remove after they are in place. The much-maligned mohair law was eliminated in 1993, only to be reinstated in 2002. As of 2017, a tariff on mohair still existed.

BUSINESS TAKEAWAY

There is nothing magical about dotted lines on a map: The same concepts of comparative advantage and specialization that apply to individuals and businesses operating across the street from each other also apply to companies that trade across national borders. Countries export products for which they have a comparative advantage, such as wine in France and beer in Germany, and the businesses involved in such exports stand to benefit. Consumers also benefit with lower prices and a wider assortment of product choices. The ability to export goods with ease allows firms to grow, sell more goods abroad, and import cheaper goods to the domestic market (to the benefit of consumers).

Firms can take advantage of a country's comparative advantage in any number of resource markets and especially in the labor market. Workers in countries like India and Mexico are willing to supply labor at a lower cost than American workers are. Firms often respond by outsourcing because locating customer service call centers in India or auto plants in Mexico improves efficiency. Firms in the United States that outsource and the consumers who use their goods and services benefit from free trade, as do workers in Mexico and India.

Firms must pay close attention to government trade policies because changes in foreign trade agreements can open up (or shut down) opportunities to cut costs or reach new markets. For example, prior to 2016, many foreign companies invested in the United Kingdom under the assumption that output could be freely exported to the rest of the European Union without tariffs. With the United Kingdom now in the process of leaving the European Union, that option may be gone. Meanwhile, Mexico's engagement in trade agreements with an unusually large number of countries has incentivized companies to set up manufacturing in Mexico because they know it is a good platform from which to export their products all over the world.

Policies meant to protect some industries can wind up hurting others. In the United States, for example, policies that artificially raise the price of sugar have a negative impact on firms that rely on sugar as an input, driving U.S. candy manufacturers overseas. Recent tariffs placed on solar panels and imported steel may help U.S. producers of those goods but hurt American firms that install solar panels or companies that use steel to make products such as cars.

CHAPTER STUDY GUIDE

31.1 COMPARATIVE ADVANTAGE AND INTERNATIONAL TRADE

Economists generally view trade as beneficial. Today, the top trading partners of the United States include Canada, Mexico, China, Japan, Germany, and the United Kingdom. A production possibility frontier (PPF) can be used to show comparative advantage and the gains from international trade. Begin by determining the opportunity cost of producing an item in various countries. Next, compare the opportunity cost with trading partners. **Comparative advantage** is the ability to produce a product at a lower opportunity cost than a trading partner. Comparative advantage is the basis for specialization and trade. *Specialization* means concentrating on the production of a single good. After specializing in the production of one product, countries will trade for the other product, and gains from trade occur. This increases total global production. The basis for specialization and trade is differences in comparative advantage. In contrast, an **absolute advantage** is the ability to produce more of a product than a trading partner with an equivalent amount of resources. Absolute advantage is not the basis for trade or specialization. Sources of comparative advantage include differences in climate and natural resources, technological know-how and human capital, abundance of labor and physical capital, the business environment, and economies of scale.

31.2 THE GAINS FROM INTERNATIONAL TRADE

Gains from trade also can be shown by examining consumer and producer surplus. In general, international trade increases total surplus. When the world price of an item exceeds the domestic price absent international trade, total surplus will increase as a country increases exports. This occurs as producers benefit from the higher world price. When the world price of an item is less than the domestic price, total surplus will increase as a country increases imports. This occurs as consumers benefit from the lower world price. The model also shows that free trade generally does not result in complete specialization. Other benefits of international trade include a greater variety of goods, an increased exchange of ideas, and increased competition.

31.3 INTERNATIONAL TRADE POLICY

Protectionism is the use of government policy to protect domestic businesses from foreign competition. Protectionist policies result in a loss of society's overall well-being—deadweight loss. One example of protectionism is an import tariff. A **tariff** is a tax on imports that is imposed by the importing country. A **quota** is a quantity restriction on imports that is imposed by the importing country. A

voluntary export restraint (VER) is a quantity restriction on imports that is imposed by negotiating with the foreign exporting country to restrict its exports voluntarily. **Import licenses** are laws requiring importers to obtain a license in order to engage in foreign trade. Protectionism results when import licenses are restricted. Restrictive regulations can also be a form of protectionism. The burden of protectionism falls mainly on the poor, domestic exporting industries, and low-income exporting countries. In recent decades, countries around the world have promoted free trade and reduced trade barriers. This has been accomplished through regional trade blocs and globally through the **World Trade Organization (WTO)**—an international organization that promotes free trade, supervises the trade policies of member nations, and enforces the trade rules that are agreed to by member nations. A **regional trade bloc** is an international trade agreement that promotes free trade by reducing trade barriers between participating countries. Regional trade blocks include the North American Free Trade Agreement (NAFTA), Central American Free Trade Agreement (CAFTA), European Union (EU), and Association of Southeast Asian Nations (ASEAN).

31.4 WHY ECONOMISTS AND THE PUBLIC OFTEN DISAGREE ON TRADE

Calls for protectionism result primarily from the fact that the gains from free trade are not evenly shared. There are several common reasons that some people want protectionism—to protect jobs and employment, to protect against dumping and export subsidies, and to protect infant and defense-related industries. Economist are generally skeptical of such arguments.

TOP TEN TERMS AND CONCEPTS

1. Comparative Advantage
2. Absolute Advantage
3. Sources of Comparative Advantage
4. Gains from Trade with Exports Using the Supply and Demand Model
5. Gains from Trade with Imports Using the Supply and Demand Model
6. Protectionism and Tariffs
7. Quotas and Voluntary Export Restraint
8. Import Licenses
9. World Trade Organization
10. Regional Trade Blocs

STUDY PROBLEMS

1. The states of Maine and Washington want to engage in trade. The following table outlines the maximum output per worker per day for apples and lobster:

	Apples	Lobster
Maine	8	4
Washington	6	2

   a. What is the opportunity cost of one lobster in each state?

   b. Which state has a comparative advantage in lobsters? In apples?

   c. What product should Maine specialize in? Washington?

   d. If Maine and Washington completely specialize and the terms of trade are five apples for two lobsters, what output would each state be able to consume after trade?

2. Using data from the previous question, does Maine benefit from trade? Does Washington benefit from trade? Show your work using a production possibility frontier.

3. A restaurant hires two cooks, Bill and Will. The owner observes their following production levels:

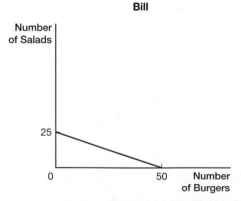

   a. What is the opportunity cost of a burger for Will? For Bill?

   b. Which cook do you suspect that the owner will assign the tasks of making burgers?

   c. Explain your answer using the concept of comparative advantage.

4. Compare and contrast comparative advantage versus absolute advantage.

5. For each of the following, state whether it will increase or decrease total surplus.

   a. A new tariff is imposed.

   b. A voluntary export restraint is reduced.

   c. A new quota is imposed.

   d. Import license requirements are eliminated.

6. List and describe the sources of comparative advantage.

7. Suppose that by allowing imports, the price of sugar falls by $1 per pound. In that case, American consumers gain $1 per pound of sugar they buy, and America producers lose $1 per pound. Do the gains and losses exactly offset? Explain why or why not. What happens to total surplus?

8. Using a supply and demand graph similar to the one presented in the chapter, show how a society gains from trade in the following situations.

   a. The world price is below the domestic price.

   b. The world price is above the domestic price.

9. Using a supply and demand graph similar to the one presented in the chapter, show how a tariff on clothing produces the following results.

   a. The domestic price of clothing increases.

   b. Clothing imports are reduced.

   c. The domestic producer surplus increases.

   d. The consumer surplus is reduced.

   e. The total surplus is reduced.

10. Using a supply and demand graph similar to the one presented in the chapter, explain the how a quota and a tariff are similar and how they are different.

11. Why do protectionist policies exist? Who benefits from such policies? Who suffers from such policies? What is their overall impact?

12. List and explain the rationales for the major types of protectionist policies.

13. What is a regional trade bloc? What are some examples?

14. What is the infant industry argument for protection? Why are many economists skeptical of this argument?

15. What is outsourcing? Does outsourcing increase or decrease economic efficiency? Explain.

16. How does a reduction in shipping cost impact trade? Where would products tend to be produced when shipping costs are high?

17. What are antidumping trade measures? Can such measures be an additional source of protectionism?

18. When was the Smoot-Hawley Tariff Act passed, and what was it intended to do? Many U.S. exporters were opposed to the new tariff. What might they have been afraid of?

∧ The foreign exchange market helps facilitate global trade and travel.

32 CHAPTER

The Foreign Exchange Market

Doing Business in Multiple Currencies

It is spring break, and you are heading to Cancun. After going through customs, you see a sign for CI Banco, a large Mexican bank that will sell you 18.90 pesos for one U.S. dollar and will buy them back at a slightly lower price. At airports, near cruise ship landings, and in many tourism hot spots, travelers rely on local currency dealers to exchange their currency for the currency used by the locals.

Foreign travel is one example of why we need foreign exchange markets, but foreign currency is involved in many more transactions than you may realize. When you buy Turkish towels or handmade Thai jewelry from foreign sellers on Etsy or eBay, your U.S. dollars are converted to Turkish lira or Thai baht somewhere along the line. Likewise, if you purchase a German-made Volkswagen, you probably pay the dealer dollars, but the German workers are ultimately paid in euros.

In Chapter 31, we learned that trade is mutually beneficial, regardless of whether it crosses a street or a dotted line on a map representing an international boundary. International trade, however, often occurs between countries that use different currencies. This means that firms that engage in international trade also must deal with the added complexity of exchanging foreign currencies. In this chapter, we examine a crucial aspect of doing business globally—the roles played by foreign currencies and exchange rates.

Chapter Learning Targets

● Describe currencies, exchange rates, and the effects of changes in the exchange rate.

● Identify how exchange rates are determined.

● Determine the value of payments in a foreign currency.

32.1 CURRENCIES AND EXCHANGE RATES

You don't need to purchase something directly from a foreign vendor to engage in international trade. Many of your everyday transactions have an international component. When you purchase a Japan-made Sony TV at your local Best Buy electronics store, you typically pay for it in U.S. dollars. In the end, however, the Japanese firm must be paid in yen, which is the Japanese currency. You may not play a role in this exchange directly—and nobody at the store probably will either—but at some point, those U.S. dollars will be exchanged for Japanese yen. Such exchanges are made in the **foreign exchange market (FOREX)**—a complex, noncentralized market in which currencies are traded; it is sometimes called the *currency market*. It is not one centralized place but rather a system of international currency brokers and dealers. Although the foreign exchange market is primarily conducted electronically, some exchanges also take place at banks, currency dealers, and other financial firms.

The value of all currency exchanged in one week in the world's foreign currency exchange market exceeds the value of total production of goods and services in the United States (GDP) for an entire year. It dwarfs even the stock market in terms of the dollar value of transactions. Any individual or firm that seeks to do business internationally must understand how currency is exchanged, how exchange rates are expressed, how payments in a foreign currency are calculated, and how best to manage currency risk.

At this time, 180 currencies are in use, ranging from the Afghan afghani to the Zambian kwacha. For simplicity, we focus on three currencies in this chapter:

- U.S. dollar: $ or USD.
- Japanese yen: ¥ or JPY.
- Euro: € or EUR.

The United States and Japan are two of the world's largest economies. Countries that use the euro are collectively referred to as the *eurozone* and are located primarily in continental Europe. Although the euro is widely used in Europe, the United Kingdom uses the British pound sterling (£) and Switzerland uses the Swiss franc. Other major currencies include the Australian dollar ($), Canadian dollar ($), Mexican peso, and Chinese yuan (¥). The FOREX allows for the exchange of all these currencies.

How Exchange Rates Are Expressed

An **exchange rate** is the rate at which one country's currency can be converted into another country's currency. It is basically a price—the price of one currency in terms of another. Financial websites such as CNBC and Bloomberg list exchange rates. Here are two exchange rates listed in August 2016 (the date was chosen for relative mathematical simplicity)—the cost of buying one euro with U.S. dollars and the cost of buying one dollar with Japanese yen:

The cost of one euro

EUR/USD = 1.111

€1 = $1.111

1 euro costs $1.111.

The cost of one dollar

USD/JPY = 100

$1 = ¥100

1 dollar costs ¥100.

Students occasionally are confused by exchange rates. Unlike the money price of goods, an exchange rate is the price of one money in terms of another type of money. What makes exchange rates confusing is the fact that *two* are monies involved. If we talk about the price of apples in the United States, we understand that we are referring to the U.S. dollar price of apples. But if we talk about the EUR/USD exchange rate, we first need to indicate which of the two types of money we are referring to. Is it the U.S. dollar price of euros, or is it the euro price of U.S. dollars?

foreign exchange market (*FOREX*) A complex, noncentralized market in which currencies are traded; also called the *currency market*.

exchange rate The rate at which one country's currency can be converted into another country's currency.

An exchange rate expresses the value of one unit of the *base currency* (in the numerator, which appears in the top or left of the equation) in terms of a specified amount of the *counter currency* (in the denominator, which is in the bottom or right of the equation). For example, EUR/USD shown above is the price of one euro in dollars. How many dollars are needed to buy one euro? In this case, the base currency is the euro, and the counter currency is the dollar. The price of one euro is $1.111. USD/JPY is the price of one dollar in yen. How many yen are needed to buy one dollar? Here, the base currency is the dollar, and the counter currency is the yen. The price of one dollar is ¥100.

This notation is the international standard way of expressing the two currency pairs. In the United States, the international standard notation can cause confusion because the dollar can appear as either the base currency or the counter currency, depending on the exchange rate being considered. Thus, the dollar appears as the numerator in USD/YEN but as the denominator in EUR/USD. The first exchange rate (EUR/USD) is the price of a euro in dollars: It takes $1.111 to buy one euro. It is showing the value of the euro. The second exchange rate (USD/YEN) is the price of a U.S. dollar in yen: It takes ¥100 to buy one dollar. It is showing the value of the dollar.

Students sometimes find this confusing because an exchange rate can be reported in two ways—in terms of one currency or the other currency. Thus, if one dollar costs 100 Japanese yen, then it also is true that one Japanese yen costs 1/100th of a U.S. dollar, or one cent. You can avoid needless confusion if you focus on the currency in the numerator (top or left). That is the one being considered.

Because most people prefer whole numbers to fractions, they find it easier to say that "one dollar equals 100 yen" than to say "one yen equals 0.01 dollars." Therefore in most currency exchange rates the numerator contains the currency with a price greater than 1.0. But even this generalization does not always hold because although one yen is generally far less than one U.S. dollar, some foreign currencies have fluctuated above and below one U.S. dollar.

In the financial media in the United States, the exchange rate often is simplified by eliminating the USD component. Most financial reports simply state "EUR 1.111," assuming that the audience will understand that this is short for EUR/USD (one euro = $1.111). Similarly, the reports state "YEN 100" and assume readers know this is short for USD/YEN (one U.S. dollar = ¥100). Those who follow exchange rates should become familiar with the international standard notation of the currency pair in question. However, examples in this text will *not* use a simplified notation showing just one currency.

Changes in Exchange Rates Represent Currency Appreciation or Depreciation

Most exchange rates are flexible. Each currency has a tendency to change in value over time based on market forces in the FOREX. **Appreciation of a currency** is an adjustment in the exchange rate that makes a country's currency more valuable relative to another country's currency. So if the news media say that the USD/YEN rate increased, it means the dollar appreciated in value. One dollar can be converted into more yen. For example, the USD/YEN exchange rate in August 2016 was roughly 100. Two years later, it was roughly 110. The value of the dollar, which is the currency in the numerator, appreciated: It could be converted into more yen than it could a year earlier. When a country's currency *appreciates*, goods and services produced in

appreciation of a currency An adjustment in the exchange rate that makes a country's currency more valuable relative to another country's currency.

EXHIBIT 1 Currency Appreciation and Depreciation: Dollars, Euros, and Yen, 2016 and 2018

Panel A: Exchange Rates, August 2016

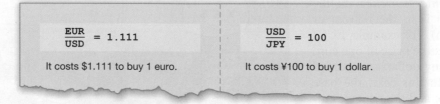

$$\frac{EUR}{USD} = 1.111$$

It costs $1.111 to buy 1 euro.

$$\frac{USD}{JPY} = 100$$

It costs ¥100 to buy 1 dollar.

Panel B: Exchange Rates, April 2018

$$\frac{EUR}{USD} = 1.25$$

It costs $1.25 to buy 1 euro.

$$\frac{USD}{JPY} = 110$$

It costs ¥110 to buy 1 dollar.

EUR appreciates
USD depreciates

USD appreciates
JPY depreciates

Exchange rates reflect the price of a currency. In August 2016, EUR/USD = 1.111, which means it cost $1.111 to buy one euro. In April 2018, EUR/USD = 1.25. This means that the euro appreciated. Simultaneously, the dollar depreciated because it took more dollars to buy one euro. During the same time period, USD/JPY changed from 100 to 110. The dollar appreciated, and the yen depreciated.

depreciation of a currency
An adjustment in the exchange rate that makes a country's currency less valuable relative to another country's currency.

that country are often more expensive to the rest of the world because that country's currency is more expensive.

Conversely, **depreciation of a currency** is an adjustment in the exchange rate that makes a country's currency less valuable relative to another country's currency. So if the news media say that the EUR/USD rate decreased, it means that the euro (the currency in the numerator) depreciated in value. It takes fewer dollars to buy euros. In August 2016, for example, the EUR/USD exchange rate was roughly 1.111, and in December 2016, it was roughly 1.05. The euro depreciated because one euro could be converted into fewer dollars. When a country's currency *depreciates*, goods and services produced in that country are often less expensive to the rest of the world because that country's currency is less expensive. In April 2018, the EUR/USD exchange rate was 1.25 as the euro appreciated.

Finally, when one currency depreciates, the other currency in the currency pair appreciates by the same proportion. Thus, when the value of the euro depreciates, the dollar appreciates. It now takes fewer dollars to buy a euro. Similarly, when one currency appreciates, the other currency in the currency pair depreciates. Exhibit 1 demonstrates how the EUR/USD and the USD/JPY exchange rates changed between August 2016 and April 2018.

Think & Speak Like an Economist

According to the international standard way of expressing exchange rates, the currency being considered is the currency in the numerator (top or left) of a currency pair. For example, EUR/USD is the dollar price of a euro. If that ratio increases, we say that the euro has appreciated.

32.2 CURRENCY SUPPLY AND DEMAND MODELS

Because exchange rates are simply a price of one currency in terms of another, the foreign exchange market can be modeled using a supply and demand framework. This supply and demand model can then be used to explain the depreciation and appreciation of a currency.

EXHIBIT 2 Currency Supply and Demand Model: Dollars Priced in Yen

Exchange rates reflect the price of a currency. Here, the supply and demand for dollars results in an equilibrium USD/JPY exchange rate of ¥100. Japan demands U.S. dollars that are supplied by the United States.

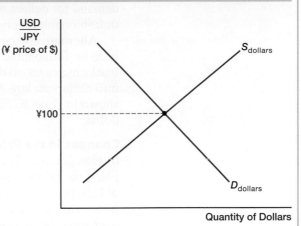

The demand for a currency is derived from the demand for products and financial investments that require that currency. For example, a Japanese business or citizen paying for anything priced in dollars—U.S. labor, capital, stocks, bonds, real estate, autos, pizza, wine, electronics—first needs to buy dollars. And even if the U.S. exporter accepts yen, it would almost certainly want to convert those yen into dollars. The same is true when a Japanese family visits Disney World. The family "converts" Japanese yen in order to buy the U.S. dollars necessary to spend on vacation in the United States. This means that U.S. exports create a demand for dollars. Economists refer to this as *derived demand*. The demand for dollars is derived from the demand for anything priced in U.S. dollars. As you will soon see, the demand curve for a currency has a negative slope. As the price of the dollar falls (depreciates), U.S. products become less expensive, and the Japanese will demand larger quantities of dollars.

Who supplies those U.S. dollars? Primarily Americans. In the FOREX markets, both individuals and large institutions sell dollars in exchange for yen in order to pay for anything priced in that foreign currency. When a U.S. company buys a Sony television or PlayStation, for example, it supplies dollars to the foreign exchange market. The same is true when Americans want to put money into the Japanese stock market or when U.S. families visit Tokyo: They supply dollars in exchange for yen. The supply curve is upward sloping. As the price of the U.S. dollar increases, the Americans will receive more yen for their dollars and are willing to supply a larger quantity, *ceteris paribus*. The demand and supply for yen is shown in Exhibit 2. When the currency being exchanged is dollars priced in yen, it is important to keep the following in mind:

- Japan demands dollars; the demand for dollars ($D_{dollars}$) is negatively sloped.
- The United States supplies dollars; the supply of dollars ($S_{dollars}$) is positively sloped.

As with all supply and demand models, the point where the supply curve intercepts the demand curve is known as *equilibrium*. Here the equilibrium exchange rate is ¥100. Next, we need to explain the forces that cause the supply and demand curves to shift and thus cause the equilibrium exchange rate to change.

Factors That Shift the Currency Demand Curve

The world is always changing. It should be no surprise that the supply and demand curves of currencies are also constantly shifting. For simplicity, we begin by examining factors that shift the demand curve of a currency.

Changes in Foreign Taste for Domestic Products When foreign demand for American goods changes, the demand for U.S. dollars changes as well. For example, the demand for dollars will decline and the dollar will depreciate if U.S. products become unfashionable among foreign consumers, as is shown in Panel A of Exhibit 3.

Alternatively, consider what happens when American pickup trucks suddenly become fashionable in Japan. As the demand for the Ford F150s and Dodge Ram trucks increases, so does the demand for dollars. This is because yen must be converted into dollars to buy American products. The result is an appreciation of the dollar as shown in Panel B. Simultaneously, the yen depreciates, and it takes more yen to buy a dollar.

Changes in the Price of Products and Inflation The actual prices of domestic and foreign goods and serves also impact the supply and demand of a currency. For example, if the prices of goods and services are rising in the United States, then the quantity of U.S. products demanded will fall, and the demand for dollars will decline (Panel A). In general, countries with very high inflation tend to see their currencies depreciate over time. In contrast, if prices are falling in the United States, foreigners will want more U.S.-made goods. As a consequence, the demand for the dollars will increase, and the dollar will appreciate (Panel B).

Changes in International Trade Policy An increase in Japanese tariffs on U.S. products should decrease the demand for U.S. products and the demand for the dollar (Panel A). This causes the dollar to depreciate. Conversely, if tariffs decrease on U.S.-made products, more U.S. products will be demanded, and the demand for the dollar will increase (Panel B). This will likely cause the dollar to appreciate.

Changes in the Interest Rate and the Expected Return on Financial Investments The demand for dollars also will increase if the Japanese can earn a higher return on their savings (bank accounts) from banks in the United States. For instance, if a Japanese bank pays 3% interest and a U.S. bank pays 6% interest, some Japanese

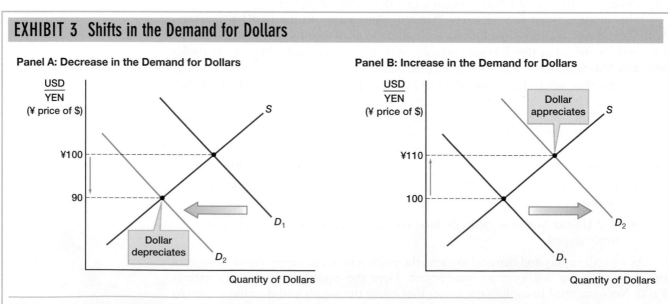

EXHIBIT 3   Shifts in the Demand for Dollars

Panel A: Decrease in the Demand for Dollars

Panel B: Increase in the Demand for Dollars

Changes in exchange rates occur as the result of shifts in the supply and demand for U.S. dollars. A decrease in the demand for dollars, perhaps due to a tariff placed on American-made goods, decreases the demand for dollars, leading the dollar to depreciate (Panel A). An increase in the demand for dollars, perhaps reflective of American products becoming fashionable in Japan, results in the dollar appreciating (Panel B).

may prefer to place their money in a U.S. bank. Thus, if the expected return on stocks and other financial assets in the United States rises above Japanese levels, the demand for dollars will increase (Panel B). At the same time, the United States will supply fewer dollars. Conversely, if U.S. banks begin to pay a lower interest rate or if financial investments in the United States are expected to have a lower return, the demand for dollars will decline. A fall in U.S. interest rates often causes the dollar to depreciate (Panel A). This is especially true when the real interest rate declines.

Factors That Shift the Currency Supply Curve

Suppose that a large institution decreases the supply of dollars on the foreign exchange market. This will cause the total supply of dollars to decrease and the dollar will appreciate. This is shown in Panel A of Exhibit 4. Those studying macroeconomics might recognize that the Federal Reserve has a major impact on the supply of dollars, and thus the exchange rate.

More generally, all of the factors that have been seen to change the demand for a currency can also change the supply of a currency if the two countries involved are reversed. For example, when Japanese products become unfashionable in the United States, the supply of dollars decreases as Americans now supply less dollars in the FOREX market to buy Japanese goods. As a consequence, the dollar appreciates, as is shown in Panel A of Exhibit 4. A U.S. tariff on Japanese goods will also decrease the supply of dollars, causing the dollar to appreciate. If the scenario is reversed and the United States now finds Japanese products to be increasingly fashionable or tariffs are eliminated, then Americans will supply more dollars in exchange for yen. In this case, the increase in the supply of dollars will cause the dollar to depreciate, as shown in Panel B.

EXHIBIT 4   Shifts in the Supply of Dollars

Panel A: Decrease in the Supply for Dollars

Panel B: Increase in the Supply for Dollars

Changes in exchange rates occur as the result of shifts in the supply and demand for dollars. For example, if a large institution such as a central bank decreases the supply of dollars on the foreign exchange market, the dollar will appreciate (Panel A). Conversely, if Americans suddenly want more products made in Japan, this will increase the supply of dollars and cause the dollar to depreciate (Panel B).

> Never Reason from a Price Change: Changes in Exchange Rates and Exports

As is discussed in Chapter 3, one should never reason from a price change when looking at supply and demand. This also applies to the exchange rate, which is the rate at which one country's currency can be converted into another country's currency. You should never begin by drawing conclusions from changes in exchange rates. You should first ask *why* the exchange rate changed.

If the dollar appreciates, then U.S. products become more expensive to the rest of the world. This is why major U.S. exporters such as Boeing and General Electric tend to prefer a weaker dollar. Currency appreciation can *cause* lower exports. However, it is also possible that increases in demand for U.S. exports will cause the dollar to appreciate. This is why we should never reason from a price change. Because higher exports can *cause* the currency to appreciate, a rising currency can be associated with rising exports. Recall that in the appendix to Chapter 1, you learned that the direction of the causation is important in economics. The same applies here. To figure out the impact on the quantity of exports, we first need to consider whether the higher value of the dollar was caused by more demand for U.S. exports or by some other factor. To recap, there are two very different possibilities:

- An increase in the demand for U.S. products (like trucks) increases U.S. exports. This *causes* the dollar to appreciate because the demand for dollars increases.

- The dollar appreciates (due to a lower supply of dollars or more demand for U.S. financial assets). This *causes* U.S. exports to decline.

We cannot simply look at the exchange rate, see that the dollar appreciated, and assume that U.S. exports are declining. Whether exports decline depends on what type of factor caused the original change in the value of the dollar.

Conversely, a depreciated dollar will increase U.S. exports if the depreciation was caused by a decrease in the demand for U.S. financial assets. On the other hand, a depreciated dollar will be associated with fewer exports if the dollar's depreciation was caused by a decreased demand for U.S. products.

📊 BUSINESS BRIEF Iron, Coal, and the Australian Dollar

Although it is often the case that currency appreciation causes lower exports, the reverse can also be true—that is, higher exports can cause a currency to appreciate. A recent example of this can be found in Australia, one of the world's major commodity exporters. A relatively large portion of its economy is in mining (7%). Between 2002 and 2017, developing countries like China dramatically increased their purchases of imported iron ore and coal, two key exports from Australia.

This increase in the demand for Australian exports had two major effects. First, it tended to increase the value of Australian exports, and second, it put upward pressure on the Australian dollar, causing it to appreciate. This is shown in Panel B of Exhibit 3. The net effect of these changes was that Australia's currency appreciated at the same time that its exports were booming.[*]

This is an example of why you should never reason from a price change. One might be tempted to assume that the appreciating Australian dollar might lead to a lower level of exports. But this is not the case if the currency appreciation is *caused by* more demand for Australian exports.

[*]"Australia's Economy," *The Economist*, December 18, 2012, http://www.economist.com/blogs/graphicdetail/2012/12/focus-3.

Advanced Topic: Simultaneous Shifts in Currency Supply and Demand in a Generalized Model

In Exhibits 3 and 4, the dollar is the domestic currency and is priced in yen. The model simplifies things by assuming that only one curve shifts at a time and only two regions or countries exist—the United States and Japan. It often will be useful, however, to explore cases where both the currency supply and demand curves shift and to examine a more generalized model that looks at the value of one currency against a "basket" of other currencies, which is a way of estimating the *average* exchange rate.

What Happens to Exchange Rates When Interest Rates or Price Levels Change? In order to determine whether the supply of a currency shifts or the demand for a currency shifts, we focus on who supplies a currency (in this case, the United States supplies dollars) and who demands it (Japan). As previously explained, changed tastes in *one* country shift one curve, either the currency supply curve or the currency demand curve. A lower Japanese demand for U.S.-made goods, for example, will reduce the demand for dollars.

Things become more complicated, however, when both curves shift. Fortunately, in several important cases, both shifts tend to cause the exchange rate to move *in the same direction*. Consider, for example, what happens if interest rates in the United States rise relative to those in Japan. Some Japanese will wish to place money in U.S. banks, so the demand for dollars will increase. An increase in the demand for dollars tends to cause the dollar to appreciate (as shown Panel B of Exhibit 3). At the same time, however, those from the United States will be less inclined to put money in Japanese banks. This reduces the supply of dollars, also causing the dollar to appreciate (Panel A of Exhibit 4). Both changes impact exchange rates in the same direction, so the dollar will appreciate.

Something similar happens if prices fall in the United States relative to prices in Japan. The demand for dollars will increase because Japan will wish to buy more American goods, which are now cheaper (Panel B of Exhibit 3). At the same time, the supply of dollars will decrease because the United States will likely demand fewer of the now

---

EXHIBIT 5 A Generalized Exchange Rate Model

Panel A: Increase in Supply and Decrease in Demand of a Currency

Panel B: Decrease in Supply and Increase in Demand of a Currency

A generalized exchange rate model allows the domestic currency to be exchanged with any other currency. When the supply of a domestic currency increases while demand simultaneously decreases, that currency tends to depreciate against other currencies (Panel A). When supply decreases while demand of a domestic currency simultaneously increases, that currency tends to appreciate (Panel B).

more expensive Japanese goods (Panel A of Exhibit 4). Once again, both shifts cause the dollar to appreciate.

Conversely, what happens if interest rates become higher in Japan relative to the United States? Or if prices become higher in the United States relative to Japan? In both cases, the demand for dollars will decline, and the dollar will depreciate (Panel A of Exhibit 3). At the same time, the supply of dollars will increase as Americans attempt to put their money in Japanese banks or buy Japanese products. This too causes the dollar to depreciate (Panel B of Exhibit 4).

Generalized Currency Model Exhibit 5 models a domestic currency (home currency) priced in units of a generic foreign currency. Any currency can be the domestic currency. The domestic country supplies its currency while the rest of the world demands it. It also show the case where two curves shift.

Suppose the United States is considered the domestic currency, and interest rates fall in the U.S. This will *simultaneously* increases in the supply of dollars and decrease the demand for dollars as shown in Panel A. This will cause the dollar to depreciate against a basket of other currencies (which means it depreciates against most other currencies). Something similar occurs if prices in the United States increase.

Conversely, if interest rates increase in the United States, Americans will supply fewer dollars while foreigners will simultaneously demand more dollars. As shown in Panel B, this will cause the dollar to appreciate against a basket of other currencies. Something similar occurs if price in the United States decrease.

32.3 DOING BUSINESS IN A FOREIGN CURRENCY

Doing business globally often involves making payments in a foreign currency and managing currency risk. Before we can develop an understanding of these concepts, it is important to understand an alternative way that exchange rates can be expressed.

Understanding Currency Reciprocals

∨ Doing transactions in a foreign currency can be complex. Fortunately, there are ways to simplify things.

Let's review the two exchange rate pairs introduced earlier in the chapter. In August 2016, EUR/USD = 1.111, so one euro cost \$1.111. At the same time USD/YEN = 100, so one U.S. dollar cost ¥100. Businesses need to understand that exchange rates are occasionally expressed as their *reciprocals*—which are obtained by reversing the numerator and denominators. This is because the dollar price of a foreign currency is always the reciprocal or inverse of the foreign currency price of dollars. That is,

$$EUR/USD = \$1.111$$
$$USD/EUR = €(1/1.111)$$
$$= €0.90 \text{ (reciprocal)}$$

The first equation prices euros in U.S. dollars and is the international standard (currency in the numerator). The second equation is the reciprocal—dollars in terms of euros. Specifically, one dollar costs €0.90. Likewise,

$$USD/JPY = ¥100$$
$$JPY/USD = \$(1/100) = \$0.01 \text{ (reciprocal)}$$

EXHIBIT 6   Currency Reciprocals: Dollars, Euros, and Yen

EUR/USD is the standard notation for expressing euros for U.S. dollars, and USD/JPY is the standard notation for expressing dollars for yen. To convert to the nonstandard form of an exchange rate, invert or flip the fraction, and simplify the math.

Convert EUR/USD to USD/EUR

$$\frac{EUR}{USD} = 1.111$$

$$\frac{USD}{EUR} = \frac{1}{1.111}$$

$$\frac{USD}{EUR} = 0.90$$

Convert USD/JPY to JPY/USD

$$\frac{USD}{JPY} = 100$$

$$\frac{JPY}{USD} = \frac{1}{100}$$

$$\frac{JPY}{USD} = 0.01$$

The first equation prices U.S. dollars in terms of yen. The second equation prices Japanese yen in terms of U.S. dollars. One yen costs $0.01. The alternative (non-standard) notations are mathematically equivalent. They are calculated by inverting (flipping) both sides of the equation and simplifying. Exhibit 6 demonstrates how to calculate currency reciprocals.

Paying in a Foreign Currency

Calculating payments in an alternative currency is straightforward after you learn the notation and technique: *Multiply the currency you are swapping out of by the exchange rate or its reciprocal.* For example, an American firm buying products from Japan or Europe would be swapping out of dollars and buying a foreign currency. Ensure that the exchange rate you are converting out of appears in both the numerator and denominator. Assume that USD/YEN remains ¥100. Thus, $1 = ¥100, and its reciprocal is $1 = ¥100/$1 or ¥1/$0.01. Now assume that you are trying to convert $1 million into yen:

$$¥\,100{,}000{,}000 = \$1{,}000{,}000 \times \frac{¥100}{\$1}$$

That is a lot of yen, but it is only the equivalent of $1 million in U.S. dollars.

Likewise, suppose that a eurozone firm owes $1 million and wants to know how many euros it owes. Assuming that EUR/USD = $1.111 and thus that €1/$1.111,

$$€900{,}000 = \$1{,}000{,}000 \times \frac{€1}{\$1.111}$$

It is important to factor out the currency being converted. In both examples the dollar sign factors out because it appears in both the numerator and the denominator. Caution is advised in making such calculations. The most common error is to reverse the exchange rate. For example, it is tempting but inaccurate to multiply by $1.111 and not the reciprocal, but this would *not* factor out dollars.

Alternatively, assume that a U.S. firm owes a Japanese firm ¥112,500,000 for some autos it recently purchased and wants to know how many dollars it owes. The conversion is calculated as follows:

$$\$1{,}125{,}000 = ¥112{,}500{,}000 \times \frac{\$1}{¥100}$$

Because you are converting yen into dollars, you need to factor out yen by having yen appear in both the numerator and denominator.

Consider the following prices in dollars and euros:

- How many euros does a \$20 pizza cost? $€18 = \$20 \times \dfrac{€1}{\$1.111}$

- How many dollars does a €18 product cost? $\$20 = €18 \times \dfrac{\$1.111}{€1}$

In the first equation, we divide by \$1.111 because we are attempting to factor out dollars. The \$20 pizza costs €18. In the second equation, we multiply by \$1.111 and divide by 1 euro because we are attempting to factor out euros. The €18 product costs \$20

Finally, how much does the \$20 pizza cost in yen?

$$¥2000 = \$20 \times \frac{¥100}{\$1}$$

How Firms Can Manage Currency Risk

The value of money is always changing, which can pose a challenge for firms that engage in international trade over time. **Currency risk** is the risk that the values of financial obligations change as the result of currency fluctuations. Suppose that a U.S. business signs a contract to pay ¥100 million to a firm in Japan in two years. This agreement is made at that time the exchange rate is USD/JPY = 111 (the exchange rate in January 2018), and the firm anticipates the exchange rate will stay at this level. In that case, the U.S. firm owes the following in U.S. dollars:

$$\$900,000 = ¥100,000,000 \times \frac{\$1}{¥111}$$

Several years later, the U.S. firm opens up a financial newspaper and sees that USD/JPY = 100. The U.S. firm now owes the following:

$$\$1,000,000 = ¥100,000,000 \times \frac{\$1}{¥100}$$

This is \$100,000 more than expected. Yikes! Fortunately, multinational and smaller businesses have several methods for reducing currency risk.

Have Production and Sales in the Same Currency A simple way to reduce currency risk involves having both production and sales in the same currency. For example, the Japanese automaker Toyota has six major automobile manufacturing plants in the United States, which build cars for sale in the American market. Both costs and revenues from production are measured in U.S. dollars.

Have Assets and Liabilities in the Same Currency In a similar vein, currency risk also can be reduced by offsetting liabilities (money the firm owes) in a particular currency offset by a roughly equal amount of assets (often money the firm is owed) in the *same* currency.

Use Currency Futures and Forwards The exchange rates discussed above are commonly referred to as *spot* exchange rates—shorthand for the exchange rate "on the spot." A **spot exchange rate** is the exchange rate at the current time. Exchange rates also can be expressed for transactions at a future point in time. *Currency futures* and *currency forwards* are agreements to exchange a specified amount of a foreign

currency risk The risk that the values of financial obligations change as the result of currency fluctuations.

spot exchange rate The exchange rate at the current time.

currency at a set price *in the future*. These financial contracts provide businesses with a useful tool to reduce currency risks by essentially locking in a future exchange rate. If a firm knows that it will need ¥100 million six months in the future, it can purchase a forward contract today that will allow it to buy the ¥100 million at a specified price in six months, eliminating the risk of exchange rate changes. There are costs associated with their use, however. The use of currency futures and currency forwards are somewhat limited due to cost, complexity, and minimum required transaction amounts. For this reason, they are typically used by larger businesses and banks, not by tourists.

Partner with a Firm That Can Handle Currency Issues Smaller firms can manage currency risks by partnering with larger institutions. First, they might limit their amount of foreign currency at one point in time. Currency dealers in Mexico, for example, frequently reduce the number of U.S. dollars they have by taking their dollars to a large bank and exchanging them back for Mexican pesos. Similarly, online selling platforms, like Etsy and eBay, enable buyers to pay for foreign goods in their own currency. Banks, credit card companies, and other intermediaries do the currency exchange and manage the risks involved in doing so (sometimes for a fee).

 BUSINESS BRIEF Foreign Loans That Seem Too Good to Be True

European homebuyers in the early 2000s were often tempted to borrow from Swiss banks, which were offering interest rates on mortgage loans as low as 1.5%—which was a great deal at a time when rates in some Eastern European countries were over 10%.

But for borrowers outside of Switzerland, the deal was not as sweet as it looked. Borrowing money in a foreign currency involves currency risk. The Swiss franc is a very strong currency, which tends to appreciate over time. For instance, in 1970, the Swiss franc was worth about 23 cents, and by 2015, its value had risen to roughly one U.S. dollar, which was a more than fourfold increase.

In January 2015, the Swiss franc soared nearly 20% against the euro, and foreign borrowers suddenly found it more difficult to repay their loans. An editor for *The Atlantic* magazine recounted the story of one such borrower, who, despite having made all his payments, suddenly received a demand from his bank requesting a payment of €12,000 (at the time, roughly $14,000): "Although a resident of Austria, he had taken a home mortgage in Swiss francs, which carried a lower interest rate than mortgages in euros. ... That currency appreciation had wiped out his equity in the house. His frightened banker wanted a new infusion of cash to replace the vanished equity."[*]

In total, hundreds of thousands of loans from Swiss banks were issued to households in Austria, Croatia, Poland, Romania, and elsewhere, with Swiss banks holding over $500 billion (half trillion dollars) worth of foreign loans and other assets. Such borrowers could have easily avoided such currency risk by borrowing in their home countries, but they succumbed to the lure of low interest rates in Switzerland. By 2015, European governments were feeling increasing pressure to bail out the borrowers who were unable to repay their Swiss franc loans.[†] But government bailouts do not make the problem go away. Instead, the cost is passed on to taxpayers.

[*]David Frum, "The World's Next Mortgage Crisis?," *The Atlantic*, January 29, 2015, http://www.theatlantic.com /international/archive/2015/01/europe-mortgage-crisis-switzerland-franc/384958/.

[†]"Currency Risk," *The Economist*, January 15, 2015, http://www.economist.com/news/europe/21639760 -poles-were-slow-get-out-swiss-franc-mortgages-now-they-are-paying-price-currency-risk.

BUSINESS TAKEAWAY

Global trade means that transactions continually occur across borders and often involve different currencies. The ability to sell products globally opens up tremendous new opportunities for a business. Businesses that wish to go global need to be aware of two key issues—how to use the foreign exchange market to facilitate transactions in different currencies and how to reduce exchange rate risk.

Technology is helping to make international transactions increasingly simple: E-commerce sites often perform currency conversions for their vendors, enabling international customers on sites like Etsy and eBay to see prices listed in their home currencies. These new technologies can lead to increased sales across borders. When Etsy introduced the option to pay for goods in Japanese yen, sales to customers in Japan increased by 25%.[1]

But things are far more complicated when Ford sells trucks in the United States that it produces at a plant in Mexico with parts produced in China and raw materials from Brazil. Each firm in the supply chain is paid in its domestic currency, regardless of where the final product is sold. Changing exchange rates can significantly alter the cost of doing such business because the value of a foreign payment can change, especially over long periods of time. Thus, it is important for firms engaged in international trade and manufacturing to manage currency risk.

Firms can manage currency risk by locating production and sales in the same country where goods are sold in order to facilitate exchanges in the same currency. It is not a coincidence that the Toyota Camry—the best-selling car in America—is built largely in American factories, primarily from domestic parts, even though Toyota is a Japanese firm.[2]

Currency risk also can be reduced by offsetting liabilities (money the firm owes) in a particular currency, with a roughly equal amount of assets (often money the firm is owed) in the *same* currency. Larger firms often reduce currency risk by utilizing currency futures and forward contracts.

CHAPTER STUDY GUIDE

32.1 CURRENCIES AND EXCHANGE RATES

The **foreign exchange market (FOREX)** is a complex, noncentralized market in which currencies are traded; it is sometimes called the *currency market*. It is not a centralized place but rather a complex system of international currency brokers and dealers. An **exchange rate** is the rate at which one country's currency can be converted into another country's currency. It is basically a price—the price of one currency in terms of another. Exchange rates are the price of one unit of the currency in the numerator (top or left). **Appreciation of a currency** is an adjustment in the exchange rate that makes a country's currency more valuable relative to another country's currency. Conversely, **depreciation of a currency** is an adjustment in the exchange rate that makes a country's currency less valuable relative to another country's currency. When one currency depreciates, the other currency in the currency pair appreciates.

32.2 CURRENCY AND SUPPLY AND DEMAND MODELS

The foreign exchange market can be graphed using the basic currency supply and demand model. Moreover, this supply and demand model can be used to explain the depreciation and appreciation of a currency. The demand for a currency is considered a derived demand. For example, the demand for U.S. dollars is derived from the demand for anything priced in U.S. dollars. Factors that shift currency supply or currency demand include changes in taste for foreign products, changes in the prices of products and inflation, changes in international trade policy, and changes in interest rates. Everything that shifts demand for a currency can also change the supply of a currency if the countries involved are reversed. It is important to never reason from a price change. In general, a depreciated dollar will increase U.S. exports if caused by a decrease in demand for U.S. financial assets.

On the other hand, a depreciated dollar will be associated with fewer exports if the dollar's depreciation was caused by a decreased demand for U.S. products. Finally, it is important to note that changes in price levels and interest rates tend to shift both the supply and demand curves of a currency.

32.3   DOING BUSINESS IN A FOREIGN CURRENCY

Although not standard, exchanges rates also can be expressed as their reciprocals—reversing the numerator and denominator. That is because the dollar price of a foreign currency is always the reciprocal or inverse of the foreign currency price of dollars. Thus if EUR/USD = $1.333, it must be the case that USD/EUR = €(1/1.333) = €0.750 (reciprocal). Calculating payments in an alternative currency is straightforward after you learn the notation and technique. Simply multiply the currency you are swapping out of by the exchange rate or its reciprocal. **Currency risk** is the risk that the values of financial obligations change as the result of currency fluctuations. Currency risk can be managed by having both production and sales in the currency, having assets and liabilities in the same currency, using currency futures and forwards, and partnering with a firm that can handle currency issues. Currency futures and currency forwards are agreements to exchange a specified amount of a foreign currency at a set price in the future. A **spot exchange rate** is the exchange rate at the current time.

TOP TEN TERMS AND CONCEPTS

1. Foreign Exchange Market (FOREX)
2. Exchange Rate
3. USD ($), JPY (¥), and EUR (€)
4. Appreciation of a Currency
5. Depreciation of a Currency
6. Currency Supply and Demand Model
7. Factors That Shift Currency Supply or Currency Demand
8. Currency Reciprocals
9. Currency Risk
10. Spot Exchange Rate

STUDY PROBLEMS

1. Using the U.S. dollar as the base or counter currency, search Bloomberg.com or CNBC.com to find the current exchange rate for the following eight national currencies—the euro, the Japanese yen, the Chinese yuan, the Egyptian and British pounds, and the Australian, Canadian, and New Zealand dollars. In each case, convert $5 U.S. to the equivalent amount of foreign currency.

2. Price each of the following items in U.S. dollars at each exchange rate:

   a. A Sony PlayStation costs ¥40,000 in Japan when USD/YEN = 100.

   b. A pound of German sausage costs €5 when EUR/USD = 1.25.

   c. A Mercedes Benz costs €80,000 when EUR/USD = 1.10.

   d. A Lexus costs ¥3,500,000 when USD/YEN = 100.

3. Use a currency supply and demand model to explain what will happen to the value of the U.S. dollar relative to the Japanese yen in each of the following cases that shift the *demand* for dollars:

   a. The Japanese find U.S. products more fashionable.

   b. Interest rates on Japanese banks decrease relative to U.S. banks.

   c. Japan places a tariff on U.S. products

   d. The price of U.S. products increases.

4. Use a currency supply and demand model to explain what will happen to the value of the U.S. dollar relative to the Japanese yen in each of the following cases that shift the *supply* of dollars:

   a. Americans find Japanese products more fashionable.

   b. Interest rates in Japanese banks decrease relative to rates in U.S. banks.

   c. The United States places a tariff on Japanese products.

   d. The price of Japanese products increases.

5. Why might exporters in the United States oppose trade barriers on imports to the United States? What impact do import trade barriers have on the foreign exchange value of the U.S. dollar?

6. Describe how currency dealers make profits.

7. Discuss whether currency risk exists in each of the following scenarios, and if currency risk exists, explain if the party involved is harmed by or benefits from the change in exchange rates:

   a. A U.S. homebuyer borrows money from Bank of America. The dollar subsequently depreciates relative to other major currencies.

   b. A homeowner in Poland borrows money from a Swiss bank. The Swiss franc appreciates by 20%.

   c. A bank agrees to accept payments in a foreign currency that depreciates.

d. While on an extended vacation, a U.S. traveler borrows €2,000 that he promises to repay when he returns to the United States. The euro appreciates.

8. The United States imports Corona beer from Mexico for $12 per six-pack. The same six-pack costs 120 pesos in Mexico. Assume that there are no transportation costs, taste differences, or trade restrictions, so that the price of beer is the same in either currency. What must the exchange rate be?

9. For each of the following scenarios, use a currency supply and demand framework to state whether the USD will appreciate or depreciate:

a. The price of U.S. goods decreases.

b. The price of foreign-made goods decreases.

c. Interest rates in the United States decrease.

∧ The global economy is interconnected.

33 CHAPTER

International Finance

The Macroeconomics of Exchange Rates and the Balance of Payments

Macroeconomic events in one country can have ramifications in many other parts of the world. News in Asia often has a big effect on stock markets in the United States and Europe, and the reverse is also true. Rising interest rates in the United States impact credit conditions faced by businesses all over the world. Many of the most important recent trends in macroeconomics are global, including the Great Recession, the subsequent period of extremely low interest rates, and a slowdown in the rate of economic growth.

In Chapter 32, we examine how the foreign exchange market facilitates global business transactions. In this chapter, we shift our focus to the ways that economies around the globe are interconnected. First, we examine how a nation's balance of payments provides a summary account of the nation's financial transactions with the rest of the world. We show the forces that impact the balance of payments and the ways that the balance of payments impacts the broader macroeconomy. Second, we return to our analysis of exchange rates and explore the impact of long-run macroeconomic forces such as inflation and interest rates.

Chapter Learning Targets

● Explain the components of the balance of payments.

● Identify the linkages between the current account, saving, and investment.

● Discuss how arbitrage opportunities result in the law of one price in some circumstances.

● Describe purchasing power parity and the ways that it relates to inflation and interest rates.

● Compare alternative exchange rate systems that are used in other countries.

33.1 MEASURING INTERNATIONAL TRANSACTIONS: THE BALANCE OF PAYMENTS

Every year, trillions of dollars of international transactions occur. For the United States, these transactions include everything from buyers who purchase Japanese stocks and Samsung phones to tourists who rent cars in the Bahamas and South Africa. The value of all types of international transactions is captured in a financial statement known as the **balance of payments account**—a summary account of a country's financial transactions with the rest of the world. These transactions

711

balance of payments account A summary account of a country's financial transactions with the rest of the world.

current account The portion of the balance of payments that measures the money flows resulting from exports, imports, international investment income, and transfer payments.

include payments for imports and exports, financial investments, and transfer payments. Every time that a firm or an individual exchanges goods, services, or assets with someone in another country, that transaction becomes part of the balance of payments. This balance contains two major subaccounts—the current account and the capital account.

The Current Account

The first portion of the balance of payments is the **current account**—the portion of the balance of payments that measures the money flows resulting from exports, imports, international investment income, and transfer payments. When a country exports products, it receives money that flows in and is entered as a positive value in the trade balance. When a country imports products, it spends money that flows out and is entered as a negative value in the trade balance.

In Chapter 2, *net exports* are shown to equal a country's exports minus imports. In the current context, we use the term *trade balance*. Exports and imports are the largest categories in the current account. However, although the trade balance and the current account are linked, the trade balance is only a part of the current account.

Money also can flow in or out due to either foreign money transfers or investment earnings. A country's overall current account balance measures the difference between all the money inflows (exports, transfers received, and investment earnings received) and all of the outflows of money (imports, transfers leaving the country, and investment earnings going out to foreigners). The current account balance measures net money *inflows* or *outflows* from trade, transfers, and investment income—that is, all sources *except* the purchase or sale of capital assets (which will be measured in the capital account). It is the sum of the trade balance, net investment income, and net transfers.

EXHIBIT 1 A Simplified Balance of Payments, 2017

The balance of payment statement has two major subaccounts. The current account primarily captures a nation's trade balance. The capital account primarily captures investment flows. Money inflows are entered as positive values, and outflows are entered as negative values. Thus, imports are entered as negative values as money flows out to pay for the imported goods.

Data from: Bureau of Economic Analysis, https://www.bea.gov /international/bp_web/tb_download _type_modern.cfm?list=1&RowID=2.

Simplified U.S. Balance of Payments, 2017 (billions of dollars)

Current Account	
Goods and Services	
Exports	$2331
Imports	−2900
Net Income and Transfer Payments	
Net Income	217
Net Transfer Payments	−115
Current Account Balance	**−467**
Capital Account	
Net Acquisitions of Financial Assets	
U.S.-Owned Assets Abroad	−1212
Foreign-Owned Assets in U.S.	1588
Financial Derivatives	28
Statistical Discrepancy and Adjustments	63
Capital Account Balance	**467**

U.S. Has Trade Balance (Deficit) of −$569 billion NFI = $376 billion

Foreigner Investment Inflows Exceed Outflows

Current Account Offsets Capital Account

EXHIBIT 2 The U.S. Current Account Balance as a Share of GDP, 1982 to 2017

The ratio of the U.S. current account balance to GDP.

Data from: Federal Reserve Bank of St. Louis.

*Two other items are included in the capital account that are not covered in this course. *Financial derivatives* are complex financial instruments that derive their value from other assets. *Statistical discrepancy* captures measurement errors that result from less than perfect data sources. When these values are included, the capital account balance was $467 billion in 2017.

Exhibit 1 shows a simplified balance of payment statement for the United States in 2017. The U.S. trade balance was negative because the country imported more than it exported. As a result, $569 billion flowed out of the United States to finance the trade deficit.

The current account also includes net money flows from income in foreign countries (for example, wages, rents, interest, and profits in foreign countries) and transfers (such as foreign aid and money sent to family members in other countries). For the United States, income received on overseas investments was larger than income paid to foreigners on their investments in the United States Thus, there was a $217 billion surplus in investment income, which was a positive factor in the U.S. current account balance. However, it was partly offset by an outflow of $115 billion in transfers, which refers to the net outflow of foreign aid to other countries and the transfers from foreigners working in the United States who sent money home to their families overseas. In the United States, the current account balance and the trade balance are roughly similar. In the end, the overall current account balance was *negative* $467 billion, which is called a *current account deficit*.

Until the early 1980s, the United States frequently ran current account surpluses, but since then, the country has run a current account deficit every year except 1991. This deficit, currently about 2.5% of GDP, is shown in Exhibit 2. In the next section, we examine the current account deficit, but first we need to understand the other major subaccount of the balance of payments account—the capital account.

The Capital Account

The **capital account** is the portion of the balance of payments that measures the money flows resulting from changes in the international ownership of capital investments. There are two primary types of foreign assets. First, when businesses make physical capital investments in a foreign country (such as by building or buying a facility), it is referred to as *foreign direct investment*. Alternatively, when businesses make financial investments in a foreign country (often by purchasing stocks and bonds), it is referred to as *foreign portfolio investment*.

capital account The portion of the balance of payments that measures the money flows resulting from changes in the international ownership of capital investments.

"I'M AFRAID IN OUR GLOBAL ECONOMY, IT'S NO LONGER POSSIBLE TO GET AWAY FROM IT ALL."

Harley Schwadron/Cartoon Stock

CartoonStock.com

Both foreign direct investment and foreign portfolio investment can involve money inflows or outflows. When BMW builds a factory in the United States, it is considered a foreign direct investment in the United States and a money inflow measured with a positive value. Conversely, when a U.S. firm buys stock in a Mexico-based company, it is a foreign portfolio investment outside the United States and a money outflow measured with a negative value.

Net foreign investment (NFI) is a country's capital investment inflows minus its capital investment outflows; it equals net foreign portfolio investment plus net foreign direct investment. Just as net exports measure the imbalance between exports and imports, net foreign investment measures an imbalance between capital investments into and out of a country.

U.S. investors increased their holdings of foreign assets by $1,212 billion in 2017. Note that this is captured with a negative sign because money flowed out of the United States to buy foreign assets. The capital account also shows that foreign-owned assets in the United States increased by $1,588 billion. By a wide margin, foreigners buy more U.S. assets than the amount of assets bought by the United States in foreign countries. Net foreign investment is *positive* $376 billion. This has been the pattern in recent decades.*

The sum of the balance of payment equals zero. This means that if all transactions were measured perfectly accurately, the current account deficit must exactly offset the capital account surplus. Simply put, the United States sends trillions of dollars to foreigners *primarily* for imports. Much of this money comes back as foreigners buy exported U.S. goods and make income payments on U.S. investments in their own countries. After doing this, foreigners still have money left over. What do they do with this money? They buy U.S. assets! Thus, the current account deficit in the United States is exactly offset by the capital account surplus. The United States sells more assets each year than it buys, offsetting the fact that we buy more goods and services than we sell. One way of looking at it is that the United States sells stocks and bonds to pay for imported cars and TVs.

33.2 SAVING AND THE CURRENT ACCOUNT BALANCE

As shown in Exhibit 2, the United States has run a current account deficit for nearly every year since the 1980s. Not surprisingly, this has become a controversial issue. What causes the current account deficit? And what impact does it have on the economy? Before considering the causes of current account deficits and surpluses, let's look at the current account balance as a share of GDP in some representative nations. This is presented in Exhibit 3. We begin with seven countries with current account surpluses in 2017. Although there are some exceptions, as a general rule the world's current account surpluses are concentrated in countries in northern Europe and East Asia and the major oil producers. Saudi Arabia's surplus is smaller than usual due to low oil prices in 2017.

The world's current account deficits tend to occur in advanced English-speaking countries and also many developing countries. Many people believe that the U.S. current account deficit exists because U.S. companies are unable to compete with workers in low-wage countries, such as China, but the data do not support this claim. Many high-wage countries (such as Japan, Germany, and Switzerland) run surpluses, and many

net foreign investment (NFI) A country's capital investment inflows minus its capital investment outflows; it equals net foreign portfolio investment plus net foreign direct investment.

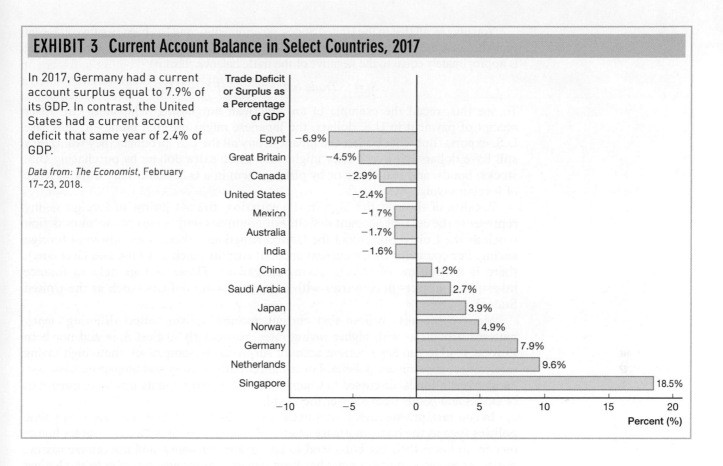

EXHIBIT 3 Current Account Balance in Select Countries, 2017

In 2017, Germany had a current account surplus equal to 7.9% of its GDP. In contrast, the United States had a current account deficit that same year of 2.4% of GDP.

Data from: The Economist, February 17–23, 2018.

Trade Deficit or Surplus as a Percentage of GDP

Country	Percent (%)
Egypt	−6.9%
Great Britain	−4.5%
Canada	−2.9%
United States	−2.4%
Mexico	−1.7%
Australia	−1.7%
India	−1.6%
China	1.2%
Saudi Arabia	2.7%
Japan	3.9%
Norway	4.9%
Germany	7.9%
Netherlands	9.6%
Singapore	18.5%

low-wage developing countries run deficits. South Korea typically ran deficits when it was poor and then began running surpluses as it grew richer and its workers commanded higher wages.

Because the current account deficit is the mirror image of the capital account surplus, there are two ways to analyze the causes of trade deficits:

- *The trade approach.* Why do our imports exceed our exports?
- *The saving and investment approach.* Why does investment exceed domestic saving?

The average person probably thinks about the current account deficit as a trade issue—that we import more than we export. But many economists believe that the more fundamental issue is the shortfall of domestic saving, which leads to an inflow of foreign saving. For instance, the Chinese might buy U.S. mortgage-backed bonds with the money they earn from their trade surplus. This helps to finance the cost of building new homes in the United States. Even if you directly borrow money from a bank in order to buy a new home, your bank may have obtained funding from Chinese or German savers.

The Flow of Foreign Saving Impacts the Current Account

Using a simplified version of the expenditure equation without the government sector or international trade—total output equals consumption plus investment $(Y = C + I)$. You also learned that investment equals saving $(I = S)$ in Chapter 23. When including the government sector and international trade, the saving component is segmented into private saving (S_p), government saving (S_g), and foreign saving (S_f):

$$I = S_p + S_g + S_f$$

You may recall that in the United States, government saving has been negative in recent years because the government has run a budget deficit ($S_g < 0$). Moreover, foreign saving is approximately equal to the negative of the trade balance. That is:

$$S_f = -\,Trade\ balance = -(EX - IM)$$

To see this, recall the example of an American purchasing a Japanese car. After receipt of payment in U.S. dollars, the Japanese might use that money to purchase U.S. exports. But what if after the Japanese buy all the U.S. products they want, they still have dollars left over? They might save those extra dollars by purchasing U.S. stocks, bonds, and real estate or by placing them in a U.S. bank. This is the essence of foreign saving.

Because of the negative sign in the equation, the net inflow of foreign saving represents the current account deficit. For countries with a current account deficit (such as the United States and the United Kingdom), there is an inflow of foreign saving. For countries with a current account surplus (such as China and Germany), there is an outflow of foreign saving (negative). Those savings help to finance investment projects in countries with current account deficits (such as the United States).

Many economists believe that current account deficits reflect differing saving patterns. Countries with higher saving rates, particularly in East Asia and northern Europe, tend to run large current account surpluses. In some cases, these high saving rates reflect government policies. For instance, both Norway and Singapore have sovereign wealth funds, discussed in Chapter 23. Their governments buy large quantities of stocks and bonds from all over the world.

In contrast, private saving rates in the United States are relatively low. U.S. public policies such as the home mortgage interest deduction on taxes (which enables homeowners to lower their tax bills) tend to encourage borrowing and discourage saving. Furthermore, government saving has been negative in recent years due to the budget deficit. As a consequence, a portion of U.S. investment spending is paid for with foreign saving. This results in a current account deficit.

Current account deficits also can reflect a relatively high level of domestic investment, which is often funded with foreign saving. When the U.S. economy is booming, domestic investment tends to rise. This draws in foreign saving, causing the current account deficit to become larger. As shown in Exhibit 2, during a recession, the current account deficit often becomes smaller because investment falls sharply.

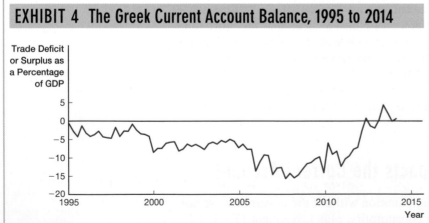

EXHIBIT 4   The Greek Current Account Balance, 1995 to 2014

Trade Deficit or Surplus as a Percentage of GDP

This graph shows the ratio of the Greek current account balance to GDP. In 2007 and 2008, the current account deficit in Greece was almost 15% of GDP.

Data from: Federal Reserve Bank of St. Louis.

 POLICY BRIEF   Greek Deficits and the Eurozone Crisis

After joining the eurozone in 2001, Greeks were able to borrow at lower interest rates than previously. Lenders no longer worried about devaluations of the Greek currency (the drachma), which had occurred frequently before the country joined the euro. As a result, banks in northern Europe lent large sums of money (euros) to the Greek government and to Greek households and businesses. As shown in Exhibit 4, the current account deficit of Greece increased to an astounding 15% of GDP in 2007 and 2008, right before the 2008 global financial crisis.

When Greece fell into a severe recession in 2008, it defaulted on a portion of its debt. Foreign lenders were no longer willing to extend credit, with the exception of a few international organizations that made some emergency loans. The sharp reduction in Greece's capital account surplus corresponds with a reduction in the current account deficit. In the end, the Greeks had to accept much lower living standards, and their access to foreign saving (credit) was cut off.

To understand this on a more personal level, imagine that you were required to boost your personal saving rate at exactly the same time as your income was falling sharply. One of the two wage earners in your household might have lost a job, but you were told to start putting more money into your saving account each month, despite losing one person's income. That is essentially what Greece had to do.

Not all current account deficits lead to a Greek-style crisis. The next example shows that one must consider how foreign savings are used and what type of assets are sold in the capital account.

Is the U.S. Current Account Deficit a Problem?

Just as the causes of current account deficits are somewhat controversial, so are the effects of the deficits. Many people worry about a loss of jobs when imports exceed exports. However, a current account deficit also implies that domestic investment exceeds domestic saving, which means more jobs are available for building houses, factories, and office buildings. Thus, there is no obvious reason why current account deficits should lead to higher unemployment rates. Many countries with current account deficits, such as the United States and the United Kingdom, have lower unemployment rates than areas with current account surpluses, such as the eurozone.

Most economists believe that current account deficits are not necessarily a problem but can become one if they reflect excessive indebtedness. Current account deficits are often financed by borrowing, and when large deficits persist for many years, countries can fall deeply into debt. In many cases, financial crises have been preceded by high levels of borrowing. The previous Policy Brief on Greece is a good example of how large current account deficits can be a warning sign of excessive borrowing. In retrospect, Greek borrowing was certainly excessive. Will the United States meet the same fate? After all, the United States has run a current account deficit almost every year for many decades, and it has a large negative net investment position.

Although some economists are concerned about the U.S. trade deficit, some important differences from Greece need to be accounted for. First, the U.S. current account deficit is generally much smaller (as a share of GDP) than the Greek deficit of the 2000s.

Second, unlike many developing countries and also unlike Greece, the United States generally borrows in a currency it controls, the U.S. dollar. This does not mean that excessive U.S. government borrowing is not a problem, but outright default on

∧ Greece continues to reel from a debt crisis brought on by excessive borrowing in international markets.

Treasury bonds is unlikely. (The bigger risk in the United States is inflation if the public debt becomes too large.)

Third, the United States tends to earn more on its foreign investments than foreigners earn on their investments in the United States This helps to offset the money outflow caused by the large trade deficit. This last point is especially interesting. Because U.S. dollar assets are widely popular all over the world, the United States is able to borrow at lower interest rates than many other countries. This advantage is sometime called the *exorbitant privilege*, which is the advantage of being the world's preeminent economic power. For example, the governments of China and Japan often invest in U.S. Treasury bonds, which have been yielding only 1% or 2% interest. In effect, these governments are lending money to the United States at very low interest rates. In contrast, a U.S. firm like Starbucks or McDonald's might invest in restaurants all over China and Japan and earn a much higher rate of return on that investment, perhaps 5% or 10% per year. This leads to a peculiar situation. Even though the United States is theoretically a "debtor nation" that owes much more to foreigners than it has invested overseas, U.S. inflow of income on foreign investments exceeds the outflow of income to foreigners who invested in the United States.

33.3 ARBITRAGE AND THE LAW OF ONE PRICE

An **exchange rate** is the rate at which one country's currency can be converted into another country's currency. As in Chapter 32, we focus here on two major exchange rates (as of August 2016):[*]

The cost of one euro

EUR/USD = 1.111

€1 = $1.111

1 euro costs $1.111.

The cost of one dollar

USD/JPY = 100

$1 = ¥100

1 dollar costs ¥100.

By convention, an exchange rate expresses the value of one unit of the base currency in the numerator (top or left of the equation) in terms of a specified amount of the counter currency in the denominator (bottom or right of the equation). Thus, one euro costs $1.111, and one dollar costs ¥100.

Exchanges rates are occasionally expressed as their *reciprocals*—the reversal of the numerator and denominator. That is,

The cost of one dollar

USD/EUR = €(1/1.111) = €0.90

1 dollar costs €0.90.

The cost of one yen

JPY/USD = $(1/100) = $0.01

1 yen costs $0.010.

exchange rate The rate at which one country's currency can be converted into another country's currency.

Think & Speak Like an Economist

According to the international standard way of expressing exchange rates, the currency being considered is the currency in the numerator (top or left) of a currency pair. For example, USD/EUR is the yen price of dollar; one dollar costs ¥100.

[*]Reading Chapter 32 is not required to understand this material, but a review of the section "Doing Business in a Foreign Currency" may be helpful.

Calculating payments in an alternative currency is straightforward. Multiply the currency you are swapping out of by the exchange rate or its reciprocal, being careful to include the exchange rate you are converting out of in both the numerator and denominator. For example, suppose that a U.S. firm has a financial asset worth ¥112,500,000 in Japan. The firm wishes to know how many dollars it is worth:

$$\$1,125,000 = ¥112,500,000 \times \frac{\$1}{¥100}$$

The asset is worth an equivalent of $1,125,000. Notice that on the right hand side of the equation, yen appear in both the numerator and in the denominator.

In this section, we begin examining how macroeconomic forces determine exchange rates. The first step is to show how goods and financial assets can be priced in terms of a foreign currency. This framework can then be used to show how prices in different countries are related. From there, we can show that inflation and interest rates are also connected to changes in exchange rates.

Ahn Young-joon/AP Images

∧ Trading of the U.S. dollar (USD) is priced in terms of South Korean won (KRW).

Currency Arbitrage

All exchange rates *must* be related to all other exchange rates. Changes in one pair of exchange rates are quickly reflected in changes in other exchange rate pairs. In time, many other prices and interest rates also will be affected. If this were not the case, individuals could generate enormous profits with very little risk in a process known as *currency arbitrage*. **Arbitrage** is the simultaneous purchase and sale of similar assets in order to profit from price differences with little risk. Exhibit 5 demonstrates a hypothetical example of arbitrage based on the following exchange rates in Tokyo and New York:

$$\text{EUR/YEN} = 120 \ (€1 = ¥120)$$
$$\text{USD/YEN} = 100 \ (\$1 = ¥100)$$
$$\text{EUR/USD} = 1.111 (€1 = \$1.111)$$

EUR/YEN is the yen price of euros. Now suppose that a global firm that engages in arbitrage has $1,000,000. It sees a profit opportunity if it converts dollars into euros, converts euros into yen, and finally converts yen back into dollars:

The firm buys €900,000 $\left(= \$1,000,000 \times \dfrac{€1}{\$1.111}\right)$.

With €900,000, it buys ¥108,000,000 $\left(= €900,000 \times \dfrac{¥120}{€1}\right)$.

Finally, it converts yen back to $1,080,000 $\left(= ¥108,000,000 \times \dfrac{\$1}{¥100}\right)$.

The firm has made an $80,000 profit. Not bad for a few seconds work.

Because speculators are always looking for profit opportunities, prices of similar assets tend to be roughly the same when they can be bought or sold freely all over the world. As a result, the preceding arbitrage example is unlikely to occur in the real world. In the next few sections, we will see that this has important implications for the relationship between exchange rates, the prices of goods, inflation rates, and interest rates in different countries.

arbitrage The simultaneous purchase and sale of similar assets in order to profit from price differences with little risk.

Think & Speak Like an Economist

In the real world, large arbitrage opportunities are rare because the moment that a small arbitrage opportunity opens up, someone takes advantage of it. This action causes the exchange rate to adjust quickly, and the profit opportunity disappears almost immediately.

EXHIBIT 5   A Hypothetical Currency Arbitrage

With any three currencies, knowing two exchange rates implies the third exchange rate. If this were not so, an arbitrage opportunity would exist. Here, $1,000,000 is exchanged for €900,000, then ¥108,000,000, and finally back to $1,080,000. In the real world, currency arbitrage that is this profitable does not occur because the ability to do arbitrage keeps exchange rates interrelated.

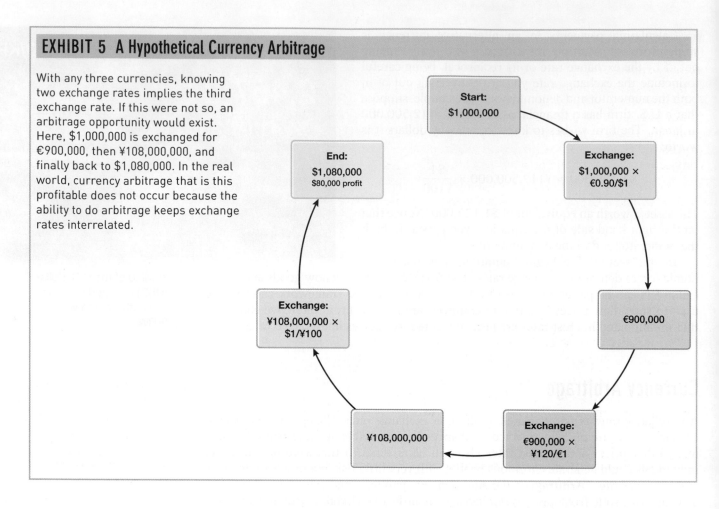

The Law of One Price and Purchasing Power Parity

Large arbitrage opportunities almost never exist in the foreign exchange market. But do they exist with nonfinancial assets such as goods and services? To answer this question, we explore the law of one price and purchasing power parity.

The Law of One Price The **law of one price** is the economic theory that identical products should sell for the same price in separate markets. That is, the price in one market should equal the price in a different market at the current rate of exchange for the two currencies. For example, suppose that one ounce of gold costs $1,200 in New York and ¥100,000 in Tokyo. Also assume that the exchange rate is USD/JPY = 100. How could arbitragers take advantage of the situation?

Because ¥100,000 equals $1,000 in terms of U.S. money ($1,000 = ¥100,000 × $1/¥100), gold is cheaper in Tokyo than in New York, so arbitragers could buy gold in Tokyo for ¥100,000 and sell it in New York for $1,200. Finally, the arbitrager could convert $1,200 back into ¥120,000 (¥120,000 = $1,200 × ¥100/$1) and keep the remaining ¥20,000 as profit.

As more arbitragers buy gold in Tokyo to take advantage of the profit opportunity, the price of gold rises above ¥100,000. As the gold is sold in New York, the price of gold falls below $1,200. Eventually, the price in the two markets equalizes, and the law of one price holds.

The ability to engage in risk-free arbitrage fairly easily tends to equalize asset prices such as gold. Similarly, equilibrium can be reached through changes in the exchange rate. In this case, the exchange rate would need to change so that the $1,200 needed to buy one ounce of gold in New York equals the amount of dollars needed to be converted into enough yen to buy one ounce of gold in Tokyo.

law of one price The economic theory that identical products should sell for the same price in separate markets.

Why the Law of One Price Does Not Always Hold The law of one price is less applicable to products like a Lexus than it is with commodities. Assume that the USD/YEN exchange rate is 100, the price of a Lexus in the United States is $50,000, and the price of the same Lexus in Japan is ¥4 million. An American purchasing a Lexus would pay $50,000 in the United States. In theory, the American could take $40,000 and convert it into ¥4 million ($40,000 = ¥4,000,000 × $1/¥100). The ¥4 million is just enough to buy the Lexus in Japan, and the buyer would have $10,000 left over. As you might expect, this is not as easy as it looks. Economists have identified several obstacles that can prevent the law of one price from occurring, even in the long run:

- *Transportation Costs.* Lexus automobiles are made in Japan. It costs less to ship a Lexus to an auto dealership in Japan than to a dealership in the United States.

- *Goods That Are Not Tradable.* A haircut from a top hair stylist in Milan or Paris cannot be sold in the United States. A luxury apartment in New York City cannot be shipped to the eurozone. Pizza from Mario's is difficult to ship to another country.

- *Taxes, Tariffs, and Nontariff Trade Barriers.* In Europe, gasoline is much more expensive than it is in the United States because European taxes are far higher. In some countries, imported products cost more because of tariffs and other forms of protectionism such as quotas.

- *Goods That Are Not Perfect Substitutes.* Domestic products may not be identical to those made in a foreign country. If this is the case, differences in price may reflect differences in quality and in consumer's preferences. The law of one price tends to hold best for uniform commodities, such as grain, metals, and oil.

- *Rents and Real Estate Costs.* Products usually cost more in regions of the world where real estate is more expensive. Land cannot be traded.

These barriers can prevent prices from equalizing. As an analogy, consider two lakes that are connected by a deep channel. The water flows between the lakes until the level is the same in both bodies of water. That is the idea behind the law of one price. Now assume that a barrier (such as a dam) prevents the free flow of water. The water level in one lake may be higher than the other. That is similar to the impact of the trade obstacles discussed above.

Purchasing Power Parity The law of one price is a microeconomic concept that applies to individual goods. In contrast, **purchasing power parity (PPP)** is the economic theory that exchange rates adjust so that any given amount of currency can buy the same combination or basket of products in another country. Purchasing power parity can be thought of as a macroeconomic counterpart to the law of one price. It occurs when exchange rates adjust to equalize the overall *price level* of a basket of goods in different countries. For instance, if the price of goods in Japan (measured in yen) is on average 100 times higher than the dollar price of goods in the United States, then purchasing power parity holds when the exchange rate (USD/JPY) is equal to 100.

In the next Business Brief, we will discuss an informal and more "digestible" guide to evaluating the purchasing power parity: the Big Mac Index. If the average price of a Big Mac is $5 in the United States, you should be able to exchange $5 into another country's currency and be able to buy the Big Mac in that country. Thus, the Big

purchasing power parity (PPP) The economic theory that exchange rates adjust so that any given amount of currency can buy the same combination or basket of products in another country.

▼ The prices of a Big Mac and other food items shows that purchasing power parity does not always hold true.

Ilya Starikov/Alamy

Mac should cost ¥500 in Japan and €4.50 in the eurozone when exchange rates are USD/JPY = 100 and EUR/USD = 1.111:

$$¥500 = \$5 \times \frac{¥100}{\$1}$$

$$€4.50 = \$5 \times \frac{€1}{\$1.111}$$

Note that on the right side of both equations the dollar sign factors out. As is the case with the law of one price, purchasing power parity does not *always* hold true. In the real world, transport costs and other factors that explain why the law of one price does not hold also prevent price levels from being equalized. Thus, some countries have higher price levels than other countries. Nonetheless, PPP is a useful starting point in understanding how exchange rates are determined, especially in the long run.

BUSINESS BRIEF The Big Mac Index

One interesting test of purchasing power parity, conducted by *The Economist*, compares the price of a Big Mac in many different countries (12 of the countries are shown in Exhibit 6). The Big Mac is a useful comparison because it is a fairly standardized product that consists of several other goods, specifically "two all-beef patties, special sauce, lettuce, cheese, pickles, onions, on a sesame seed bun."

Labor and real estate costs also factor into the price. This makes the Big Mac broadly representative of a modern economy, which features both traded commodities and nontraded labor and real estate.

Although it is not a true price index, the Big Mac index provides some useful insights into purchasing power parity, and *The Economist* regularly updates its Big Mac index. There are some exceptions, but prices tend to be higher in countries that have a high level of real GDP. This probably reflects the fact that wages (a non-traded input) are much higher in places like Norway and Switzerland, as compared to India or South Africa.[*]

[*]"The Big Mac Index: Global Exchange Rates, to Go," *The Economist*, January 17, 2018, http://www.economist.com/content/big-mac-index.

EXHIBIT 6 The Big Mac Index, January 2018

The graph shows the prices of Big Mac hamburgers in various countries in U.S. dollar prices.

Data from: "Our Big Mac Index Shows Fundamentals Now Matter More in Currency Markets," *The Economist*, January 20, 2018, https://www.economist.com/news/finance-and-economics/21735050-last-july-cheap-currencies-have-narrowed-gap-against-dollar-our-big.

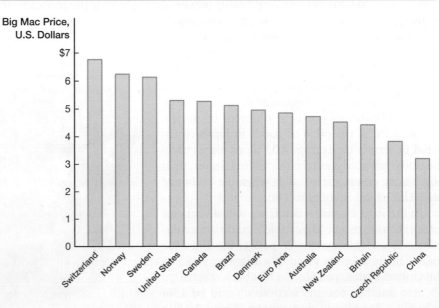

33.4 PURCHASING POWER PARITY AND REAL EXCHANGE RATES

Purchasing power parity (PPP) is a useful starting point for understanding how exchange rates are determined. To see why, imagine that your college roommate tells you that a cup of coffee at Starbucks cost ¥400 in her home country of Japan. That sounds like a lot, but you immediately wonder how much that is in dollars. Now suppose that she asks you to guess the exchange rate: How many yen for one dollar? You know that Starbucks coffee costs about $4 in the United States, so you might guess that if it's ¥400 in Japan, then ¥100 equal $1 in U.S. money. If that is your estimating process, then you would be using the concept of PPP in making your guess. Using PPP will not get you the exact exchange rate, but it will usually get you into the right ballpark. Economists believe that although PPP does not hold exactly true, it is often roughly true. Relative price levels are therefore one of the most important factors in determining exchange rates, especially in the long run.

At the level of individual products, we often take the exchange rate as a given. Thus, if you know the price of gold or copper in the United States, you can figure out the price in Mexico by adjusting for the exchange rate. But when considering the entire price level, things look somewhat different. Exchange rates help us to understand the relationship between the prices of individual goods, but for the overall price level, things work in the opposite direction. The overall price level in any two countries helps *determine* the exchange rate.

Dynamic Purchasing Power Parity: Differences in Inflation Rates

The theory of purchasing power parity also can help us to understand why exchange rates change over time. Economists have long recognized that there is a relationship between inflation rates in two countries and *changes* in exchange rate for the same countries. **Dynamic purchasing power parity (DPPP)** is the economic theory that exchange rates gradually adjust over time in order to offset any differences in inflation rates between two countries. Recall that inflation results in the decline in the value of money; and this also shows up in the currency markets. Thus countries with relatively high inflation have currencies that are losing value in terms of domestic purchasing power, and also in terms of international exchange rate. Using the United States as an example:

- *Higher foreign inflation.* When a country has a higher inflation rate than the United States, the foreign currency will tend to depreciate gradually against the dollar over time.

- *Lower foreign inflation.* When a country has a lower inflation rate than the United States, the foreign currency will tend to appreciate gradually against the dollar over time.

The dynamic purchasing power parity model works particularly well in cases where one country's inflation rate is extremely high—say, over 50% per year—where the currency observes a sharp decline in value. When a country has extremely high inflation rates relative to the U.S. rates, then relative PPP does a pretty good job—*even in the short run*. The law of one price begins to dominate all other factors. Countries suffering from hyperinflation almost always see their currencies depreciate fairly sharply, even in the short run.

Exhibit 7 compares the difference in inflation rates and the change in the exchange rate for 82 countries between 1975 and 2005. On the *y*-axis, higher numbers reflect

dynamic purchasing power parity (DPPP) The economic theory that exchange rates gradually adjust over time in order to offset any differences in inflation rates between two countries.

EXHIBIT 7 Inflation and Purchasing Power Parity, 1975 to 2005

The dynamic purchasing power parity model suggests that relatively high inflation will cause currency depreciation. The figure compares the difference in inflation rates and the change in the exchange rate for 82 countries between 1975 and 2005. In general, currencies depreciate at roughly the rate of their excess inflation.

Data from: Robert C. Feenstra and Alan M. Taylor, *International Economics*, 4th ed. (New York: Worth, 2017), chap. 14.

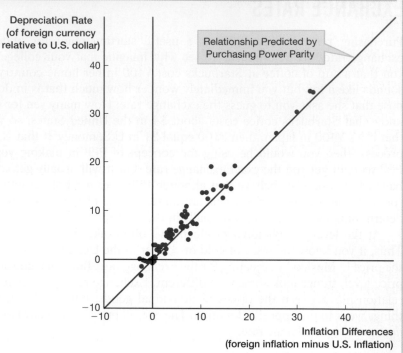

countries with currencies that depreciated more rapidly against the U.S. dollar. Thus, a high number means a country's currency is depreciating rapidly, not appreciating. As you can see, these countries also had inflation rates that were much higher than in the United States, shown on the *x*-axis.

If the dynamic PPP model held perfectly true, then all points would lie along a 45-degree line. In each case, the change in the exchange rate would equal the difference in inflation rates. Thus, countries with inflation rates that are 10% above the U.S. rate would be expected to see their currencies depreciate by about 10% against the dollar. Although this is not exactly true, countries with very high inflation see their currency depreciate sharply against the dollar in the long run, and by a roughly equal amount.

📊 BUSINESS BRIEF Destination Mexico: Tourism in Dollars and Pesos

Between 1988 and 2016, the Consumer Price Index (CPI) in the United States increased by 100%, which means that the cost of living doubled. In Mexico, the CPI increased by 15.6 times between 1988 and 2016, an astounding 1,460% increase in the Mexican cost of living. How have Mexican vacations stayed affordable, despite that high inflation rate?

To find the answer, we need to consider changes in the exchange rate. According to purchasing power parity, the Mexican peso should have lost value, due to Mexico's high rate of inflation. And that is exactly what happened: The peso fell from 2.27 pesos to the dollar in 1988 to 17.6 pesos to the dollar in 2016. A bigger number means that it now takes more pesos to buy one dollar.

Consider the cost of a hypothetical Cancun hotel room. In 1988, the room cost 227 pesos per night, which at that time equaled $100 U.S. dollars.

Now suppose that the price of the hotel room rose along with the Mexican cost of living. To find the cost of the room in 2016, we might multiply 227 pesos times

15.6, which results in a price of 3,541 pesos. But in 2016, the peso is now valued at 17.6 to the dollar. So if we divide 3,541 by 17.6, we get a U.S. dollar price of $201.19.

In terms of U.S. dollars, the price of the hotel room roughly doubled between 1988 and 2016, during a period where the U.S. cost of living also doubled. The increase in prices does not seem very noticeable to American tourists who pay in U.S. dollars because it is roughly equal to the rise in U.S. prices.* Mexican tourism has increased steadily in recent decades, despite Mexico's high inflation rate.

*Data from: World Bank and Federal Reserve Bank of St. Louis.

∧ American tourists don't notice Mexican inflation.

Real Exchange Rates

Thus far, we have been looking at nominal exchange rates—the actual exchange rate that you might see listed in an international airport or on CNBC. Because purchasing power parity does not always hold true, economists use real exchange rates to describe the actual exchange rate relative to the rate that would occur if PPP did hold true. The **real exchange rate (RER)** is the average price of domestic goods and services relative to the average price of the same goods and services in another country, when expressed in a common currency. Thus, when PPP holds exactly true, the real exchange rate is simply one: Prices are equalized. Real exchange rates are actual (nominal) exchange rates times the ratio of domestic and foreign price levels in local currencies. Alternatively, they measure the relative cost of living in different parts of the world. The real exchange rates for the domestic currency relative to a foreign currency can be expressed as follows:

$$\text{RER}_{\text{domestic currency}} = \frac{\text{Price of Domestic Goods (in the domestic currency)}}{\text{Price of Foreign Goods (in the domestic currency)}}$$

If purchasing power parity were exactly true, real exchange rates would be exactly 1.0. Goods and services would cost the same no matter what country you bought them in, but this is not always the case. To get a better understanding of real exchange rates, imagine that you are an American tourist in Japan. At first you see price tags in yen, which look very high. But after you convert the price into U.S. dollars, at the exchange rate of 100 yen per dollar, prices seem about 20% lower than in the United States. In this case, the real exchange rate of the yen is 0.80 because 0.80 is 20% less than 1.00. Alternatively, the value of the yen is 20% less than predicted by the theory of PPP.

Two key aspects of the real exchange rate equation should be kept in mind. First, the price of foreign goods is measured in a common currency (most commonly the domestic currency). Second, the real exchange rate is for the domestic currency relative to the foreign currency, and thus domestic prices are placed in the numerator. In other words, the RER formula always gives you the value of the country's currency that is used in the numerator. If you want the real value of the yen, put Japanese prices in the numerator. If you want the real value of the U.S. dollar, put U.S. prices in the numerator.

Before economists can calculate real exchange rates, they must measure prices in both countries using a common currency. This requires adjusting one of the two price levels by the exchange rate. Recall that calculating payments in an alternative currency simply requires multiplying the currency you are swapping out of by the exchange rate or its reciprocal. Similarly, to

real exchange rate (RER)
The average price of domestic goods and services relative to the average price of the same goods and services in another country, when expressed in a common currency.

Think & Speak Like an Economist

Economic thinking requires focusing on real values, not nominal values, to avoid falling prey to money illusion. A real exchange rate tells how many goods and services in one country can be exchanged for the same goods and services in another country.

calculate real exchange rates, you factor out the currency units by multiplying a ratio of prices in the two countries by either the nominal exchange rate or its reciprocal. You must be careful to ensure that the exchange rate you are converting out of appears in both the numerator and denominator:

$$\text{RER}_{\text{domestic currency}} = e \times \frac{P_{domestic}}{P_{foreign}}$$

$P_{domestic}$ and $P_{foreign}$ are the domestic price level and the foreign price level, measured in each country's currency. The factor e is the nominal (actual) exchange rate or its reciprocal. Multiplying the price ratio by e will give the ratio of prices measured in a common currency unit.

Two Ways to Express Real Exchange Rates Just as with nominal exchange rates, real exchange rates can be expressed two ways. An American tourist in Japan may notice that things cost less than at home and view the yen exchange rate as inexpensive. Conversely, a Japanese tourist in the United States would think the opposite: The dollar would look strong. For any two currencies, the exchange rate can be defined in two different ways. Are you concerned with the value of the dollar in terms of yen or the yen in terms of dollar? In other words, which currency is the domestic currency? Whenever using the real exchange rate formula, always treat the currency you are interested in studying as the domestic country. For example, if you want to determine the real exchange rate for the yen, then the yen is the domestic currency.

Recall that in the previous example, the price of a Lexus was ¥4 million in Japan, which seems very high at first glance. In dollar terms, however, the price in Japan was only $40,000, less than the car's $50,000 price in the United States. When calculating real exchange rates, we need to compare prices using the same currency. This is done in two stages. First, we compute the actual price ratio in each currency, and then we multiply by the nominal exchange rate. In this case, the nominal exchange rate is 100: It costs 100 yen to get one of the domestic currency units. So 100 is the value of the U.S. dollar. A U.S. dollar is worth 100 yen. Computing the real exchange rate for the U.S. dollar relative to the yen is done as follows:

$$\text{RER}_{\text{dollar}} = e \times \frac{P_{dollar}}{P_{yen}}$$

$$\text{RER}_{\text{dollar}} = \left[\frac{¥100}{\$1}\right] \times \frac{\$50,000}{¥4,000,000} = 1.25$$

Notice that currency units (¥ and $) both factor out. The real exchange rate of 1.25 means that that means that goods and services in the United States cost 25% more than in Japan when priced in the same currency. Notice that if purchasing power parity held true, the real exchange rate would be exactly 1.0.

To compute the real exchange rate for the yen in Japan relative to the U.S. dollar, recall that 1/100 is the value of the Japanese yen:

$$\text{RER}_{\text{yen}} = e \times \frac{P_{yen}}{P_{dollar}}$$

$$\text{RER}_{\text{yen}} = \left[\frac{\$1}{¥100}\right] \times \frac{¥4,000,000}{\$50,000} = 0.80$$

The real exchange rate of 0.80 means that prices in Japan are 20% lower than in the United States. Thus, if you take a vacation in Japan, you might notice that prices are (on average) 20% lower than in the United States *after* you convert them into U.S. dollar terms. Just as with nominal exchange rates, the real exchange rate for the yen is the reciprocal of the real exchange rate for the dollar (the reciprocal of 1.25 is 1/1.25, which equals 0.80).

Strong Currencies and Weak Currencies Economists consider the real exchange rate to be a more meaningful indicator of whether a currency is strong or weak. The term *strong currency* usually refers to a real exchange rate that is relatively high (above 1.0) or in some cases a real exchange rate that has been appreciating. The term *weak currency* usually refers to either a low real exchange rate or a real exchange rate that has recently been depreciating.

Purchasing Power Parity and Real Exchange Rates Both Matter If the theory of purchasing power parity worked perfectly, then all real exchange rates would equal 1.0. In practice, real exchange rates often differ from one, but PPP is still important for understanding how exchange rates change over time.

Consider the case of Switzerland, which has had one of the lowest inflation rates in the world for over 50 years. Does hearing that information make you look forward to an inexpensive vacation in Switzerland next summer? If so, you are forgetting to take account of PPP and real exchange rates. Notice that per the Big Mac index, Switzerland is one of the most expensive places to buy hamburgers, and this also is true of many other products. Its real exchange rate is 1.44, indicating a price level that is 44% higher than prices in the United States. So why are things expensive in Switzerland when its inflation has been low?

In the 50 years between 1966 and 2016, the Swiss Consumer Price Index (CPI) rose by 238%, while the U.S. CPI soared by 644%. Both countries had inflation, but the United States had much more. According to PPP, exchange rates should adjust to make prices roughly similar in most countries. If the exchange rate had not changed at all, then Swiss prices would have fallen far below U.S. levels because of low inflation in Switzerland. Instead, the value of the Swiss franc rose from roughly 23 U.S. cents to more than $1.04. That's even more than the inflation differential. This is why prices seem high for tourists visiting Switzerland and why economists regard the Swiss franc as one of the world's strongest currencies.

Economists do not fully understand why real exchange rates vary between countries, but one factor seems to be wages. The price of traded goods gets equalized by arbitrage, whereas nontraded services tend to differ in price. A 30-minute haircut in a high-wage country like Switzerland is much more expensive than a similar haircut in a low-wage country like India. So even if Indian and Swiss consumers pay the same price for imported Toyotas, the overall Swiss cost of living is higher because of expensive nontraded services like haircuts. Thus, Switzerland has a high real exchange rate (a strong currency), and India's real exchange rate is relatively low (a weaker currency).

Interest Rate Parity: Differences in Interest Rates

Just as arbitrage tends to equalize the price of traded goods, it also tends to equalize the rates of return in different countries when measured in the same currency (such as U.S. dollars). This has implications for the way that differences in interest rates impact changes in nominal exchange rates. **Interest rate parity (IRP)** is the economic theory that exchange rates are expected to gradually adjust over time in order to offset any differences in interest rates between two countries. This ensures that the expected net rate of return in both countries is roughly equivalent. More specifically:

- *Higher U.S. interest rate.* When a country's interest rate is lower than the U.S. rate, its currency will be expected to gradually appreciate *going forward* against the dollar over time.

- *Lower U.S. interest rate.* When a country's interest rate is higher than the U.S. rate, its currency will be expected to gradually depreciate *going forward* against the dollar over time.

interest rate parity (IRP)
The economic theory that exchange rates are expected to gradually adjust over time in order to offset any differences in interest rates between two countries.

For example, suppose that the interest rate in the United States is 3% and the interest rate in Canada is 5%. At first glance, it looks like savers would be better off putting their money into Canadian banks, where they would earn a higher interest rate. But we know that arbitrage tends to equalize the rates of return on two similar investments, such as government-insured bank accounts. Arbitragers will move money to Canada to get a higher return, until the Canadian dollar is so high that it is expected to depreciate *going forward*. In this example, if the Canadian dollar is expected to depreciate gradually by 2% over the course of a year (change in nominal exchange rate), then the total return from an investment in Canada will be only 3%. In the United States, investors will be paid a 5% rate by Canadian banks, but they will expect to lose 2% when converting their money back into U.S. dollars after one year. The 5% interest, minus the 2% fall in the exchange rate, yields a 3% rate of return, measured in U.S. dollars.

Interest rate parity is particularly relevant to the *currency futures* and *currency forward* markets discussed in in the last chapter. These markets allow individuals and businesses to lock in a nominal exchange rate for a transaction that will occur several months or years in the future. In the previous example, where interest rates in Canada are 2% higher than in the U.S. rates, the forward market would usually predict that the Canadian dollar will depreciate by 2% over the course of a year. Because investors can move money around the world fairly easily, arbitrage will tend to equalize the total rates of return on similar investments. Interest parity holds more precisely than purchasing power parity.

At first glance, the interest parity condition may seem to conflict with the currency supply and demand model in the last chapter, which notes that a rise in interest rates causes the exchange rate to appreciate immediately. But it does not conflict. The easiest way to see the difference is with an example. Suppose that both the United States and the eurozone have 3% interest rates. Now suppose the U.S. interest rate suddenly rises to 5%. According to the currency supply and demand model, the U.S. dollar should *immediately appreciate* in value. However, because interest rates in the United States would now be higher than in Europe after the initial appreciation, the dollar would be expected to *depreciate gradually* relative to the euro—that is, the initial appreciation would gradually reverse over time.

📊 BUSINESS BRIEF The Interest Rate Parity Condition and the "Carry Trade"

The interest rate parity condition says that exchange rates gradually adjust over time in order to offset any differences in interest rates between two countries. But as with purchasing power parity, the actual nominal exchange rate does not always move as predicted. Sometimes a currency does not depreciate, at least in the short run, despite the higher rates of return that a country offers to investors. And some investors look for these exceptions to interest parity.

One of the most famous examples of these exceptions is the "carry trade" between Japan and Australia. Japan has some of the lowest interest rates in the world, and Australia has relatively high interest rates for a developed country. Investors borrow money at low rates in Japan and invest the money in Australia, hoping to get a higher rate of return. This carry trade was popular in the 1990s and 2000s because for quite some time, the Australian dollar did not depreciate as expected by the interest rate parity theory. This allowed investors to make a profit by borrowing cheaply in Japan and earning higher interest in Australia.* Such an investment strategy is risky, however, because exchange rates can move unpredictably. What worked in one period will not always work in another.

*Andrew Zurawski and Patrick D'Arcy, "Japanese Retail Investors and the Carry Trade," *Reserve Bank of Australia Bulletin*, March 2009, https://www.rba.gov.au/publications/bulletin/2009/mar/pdf/bu-0309-1.pdf.

33.5 ADVANCED TOPIC: ALTERNATIVE FOREIGN EXCHANGE POLICIES

Every nation with its own currency can choose a foreign exchange policy. Most governments allow their currency to be valued primarily by market participants in the foreign exchange market (FOREX). This is known as a **flexible exchange rate**—an exchange rate that is allowed to adjust to changes in supply and demand and is not under the direct control of a government. Because this is now the approach of most major economies, we have assumed a flexible exchange rate policy in our analysis thus far. However, alternative exchange rate policies do exist.

Fixed Exchange Rate Policy

For much of the past 50 years, the Chinese government fixed the prevailing exchange rate. A **fixed (or pegged) exchange rate** is an exchange rate that is determined directly by a government. From 1944 to 1971, most major currencies were fixed to the U.S. dollar, which in turn was fixed to gold (at $35 per ounce). This was called the *Bretton Woods system*, named after the 1944 economic conference at Bretton Woods, New Hampshire (United States), where the policy was developed by 44 allied nations.

A fixed exchange rate does not exempt the currency from the laws of supply and demand. Instead, governments maintain balance with the use of *foreign reserves*—assets held by a central bank and used to support its currency and monetary policy. In order to maintain a fixed exchange rate, a government must have large enough foreign reserves so that it is always able to convert its currency into another currency at the official fixed rate. China was able to fix its exchange rate because the country has sufficient reserves to exchange U.S. dollars for Chinese yuan at a specified rate. In April 2011, China had over $3 trillion on reserve, nearly enough to buy every farm in America, all the real estate in Manhattan, and all shares of stock in Apple, Microsoft, IBM, and Google.[1]

To see why large holdings of foreign exchange are useful, consider what would happen if the demand for the Chinese yuan fell sharply. Normally, a decline in the demand for a currency should cause it to depreciate. Yet if the currency's exchange rate is to remain fixed, the government cannot allow it to depreciate. The fall in demand for yuan would lead to a surplus of Chinese yuan because the supply of currency exceeds the demand. In that case, the official exchange rate can be maintained only if the government buys up enough Chinese yuan to eliminate the surplus. In other words, an increased Chinese government demand for yuan would offset the fall in private demand for yuan.

What would the Chinese government use to buy the yuan? Instead of using Chinese money, it would sell off its holdings of foreign exchange (mostly U.S. dollars), using that money to buy back the surplus yuan. That is why China needs to hold adequate foreign exchange reserves. A government that attempts to maintain a fixed exchange rate is able to do so only as long as it has sufficient reserves to buy back any surplus of its currency that people no longer wish to hold.

One benefit of a fixed exchange rate is that it reduces currency risk for people engaged in trade or investment. For instance, under a fixed exchange rate system, people signing contracts that specify payment in a foreign currency do not have to worry about the exchange rate changing before they actually receive their money.

The major problem with fixed exchange rates is that they often prevent countries from adopting their own macroeconomic policies. Under the Bretton Woods system, countries with currencies that are pegged to the U.S. dollar were forced to have the same level of interest rates as the United States, even if a different interest rate would

flexible exchange rate
An exchange rate that is allowed to adjust to changes in supply and demand and is not under the direct control of a government.

fixed exchange rate An exchange rate that is determined directly by a government; also called **pegged exchange rate**.

have been appropriate. This reflects the interest rate parity condition: Arbitragers equalize rates of return all over the world. If the exchange rate is stable, then the interest rates should be equal, at least on risk-free investments.

When an exchange rate gets out of line with the economic fundamentals in a country, the fixed-rate system may be abandoned. In many cases, these events are traumatic. When a fixed exchange rate *does* change, it often does so abruptly. A currency that was held stable for many years might depreciate 20% or 30% almost overnight. For example, in December 1994, the Mexican peso suddenly plunged by roughly 50% after being fixed to the U.S. dollar for many years. These sudden devaluations may occur when a government runs out of international reserves, but in most cases, the deeper issue is an exchange rate that is out of line with economic fundamentals, such as purchasing power parity.

Flexible exchange rates are increasingly popular, partly because they reduce the risk of a sudden collapse in a currency's value, such as the 1994 plunge in the Mexican peso. Instead, exchange rates adjust a little bit each day, reflecting the forces of supply and demand in the foreign exchange markets.

Managed Exchange Rate Policy

Some currencies have flexible exchange rates with occasional government intervention when their currency is in danger of becoming highly unstable. A **managed exchange rate** is a partially flexible exchange rate that is subject to occasional government intervention designed to offset a rapidly appreciating or depreciating currency (it is sometimes called a *dirty float*). Remember that when a currency appreciates, the country's exports become more expensive. Governments may try to prevent this by increasing their money supply in response to an appreciating currency. By increasing the money supply, governments put downward pressure on the exchange rate. Over the past few years, for example, China has been transitioning from a fixed exchange rate system to a managed exchange rate. The Chinese government now allows some adjustment in the exchange rate but only very gradually.

Exhibit 8 demonstrates such a system. Market forces cause an increase in the demand for the managed currency. This causes the currency to appreciate as equilibrium moves from point *A* to point *B*. In response, the government intervenes by increasing the money supply. The new money is used to purchase international reserves, and this partially offsets the appreciation of the currency. The equilibrium exchange rate ends up at point *C*. The currency appreciates but by a smaller amount.

managed exchange rate A partially flexible exchange rate that is subject to occasional government intervention designed to offset a rapidly appreciating or depreciating currency; also called a *dirty float*.

EXHIBIT 8   A Managed Exchange Rate

Market forces cause an increase in the demand for the dirty float currency. This causes the currency to appreciate as equilibrium moves from point *A* to point *B*. In response, the government intervenes by increasing the money supply, which partially offsets the appreciation of the currency. The equilibrium exchange rate ends up at point *C*. The currency appreciates but by a smaller amount.

Common Currency Policy

As an alternative policy, some countries have found it more useful to adopt the currency of another country or group of countries. The most famous example of this is the eurozone, which now involves 19 of the 28 countries in the European Union. All countries in the eurozone use the same currency, similar to the way that all states in the United States use the U.S. dollar. The euro was created in 1999 and began circulating throughout much of Western Europe in 2002. This system has some similarities to a fixed exchange rate but also some important differences.

A major benefit of the euro is that having a single currency in the eurozone reduces exchange rate risk and currency transactions costs within the eurozone. Prior to the development of the euro, businesses with customers and suppliers in neighboring nations, often only a few miles away, needed to be concerned about currency fluctuations and the costs involved in exchanging currencies. It is commonly believed that this currency risk reduced the eurozone's global competitiveness. Creating a common currency for the region significantly lowered such costs.

The major disadvantage of a single currency is that countries within the eurozone can no longer conduct their own monetary policy to stabilize their economies. If only one or two countries in the eurozone are in a recession when the other countries in the eurozone are not in a recession, the overall eurozone monetary policy may not be appropriate for those countries in recession. In contrast, countries with their own currency can have their own interest rate and monetary policy.

During the Great Recession of 2008 to 2009, some European countries (such as Greece, Italy, and Spain) probably would have liked to devalue their currencies to boost aggregate demand, but because they had adopted the euro, they were unable to do so. Many economists believe that this made their recessions more severe than they would have been under the old system, where each country had its own currency. Within the Eurosystem, all 19 members have a voice in monetary policy, but member countries cannot make their own monetary policy, suited for the needs of their own country.

In other cases, countries have even less of a say in monetary policy. **Currency substitution** is the adoption of a foreign currency by a country along with or in place of its own domestic currency. Because the most frequently substituted currency is the U.S. dollar, the process is often referred to as *dollarization*. Panama, for example, has been using U.S. dollars since 1904, and more recently Ecuador and El Salvador adopted the dollar. Five countries and Vatican City have substituted the euro for their

currency substitution
The adoption of a foreign currency by a country along with or in place of its own domestic currency. Because the most frequently substituted currency is the U.S. dollar, the process is often referred to as *dollarization*.

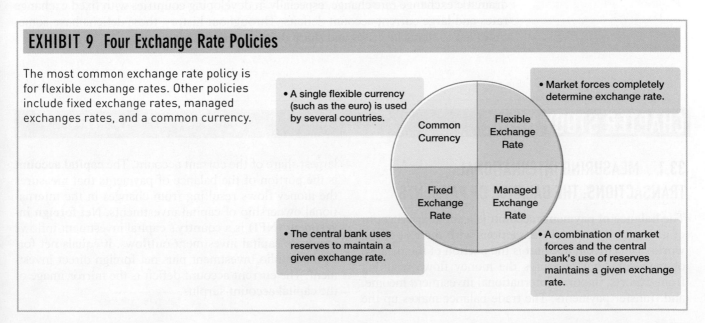

EXHIBIT 9 Four Exchange Rate Policies

The most common exchange rate policy is for flexible exchange rates. Other policies include fixed exchange rates, managed exchanges rates, and a common currency.

- A single flexible currency (such as the euro) is used by several countries.

Common Currency

Flexible Exchange Rate

- Market forces completely determine exchange rate.

Fixed Exchange Rate

Managed Exchange Rate

- The central bank uses reserves to maintain a given exchange rate.

- A combination of market forces and the central bank's use of reserves maintains a given exchange rate.

own currency, even though they are not officially part of the eurozone. The advantage of this approach is that it provides a stable currency for countries, especially small countries that may otherwise not have a stable currency. A disadvantage of currency substitution is that the adopting country is unable to conduct its own monetary policy.

The United States Federal Reserve controls monetary policy for the U.S. dollar, so other dollarized economies (such as Panama's) have no say in the determination of dollar zone monetary policy. Nonetheless, Panama has decided that the advantages of dollarization outweigh the disadvantages, and Panama City has become an important banking center for Latin America.

Exhibit 9 summarizes four exchange rate policies. The most common is flexible exchange rates. Common currencies include the euro and the U.S. dollar, which are used by more than one country.

BUSINESS TAKEAWAY

Exchange rates can have a major effect on any firm doing business internationally. For example, when shipping costs are low, it is difficult to sell a product for higher prices in the United States than in China because Internet platforms such as eBay and Etsy allow buyers to purchase items directly from sellers in India and China.

Firms that sell identical products or services in many different countries offer opportunities to test the law of one price. The price of a Big Mac, for example, can serve as a rough indicator of currency values among countries where McDonald's operates. Likewise, looking at the cost of an Ikea bookcase in a variety of countries could provide a ballpark sense of different currency values.

When purchasing power parity does not hold true, arbitrageurs may be able to take advantage of price differences (at least for a short time). Arbitrage is difficult for many goods (one cannot resell a Big Mac), but it is a powerful force in foreign exchange and other financial markets. As a consequence, interest parity is a considerably more accurate relationship than purchasing power parity.

Some firms (and individuals) might try to take advantage of differences in financing costs by borrowing money from the country with the lowest interest rate. Caution is advised, however, because the countries with low interest rates often see their currency appreciate over time. When it comes time to repay the loan, the currency may be much more expensive to buy in the foreign exchange market.

Firms doing business internationally must bear in mind the risk of a sudden and dramatic exchange rate change, especially in developing countries with fixed exchange rates and large current account deficits. Throughout history, these deficits have sometimes led to financial crises and sharp devaluations in the currency.

CHAPTER STUDY GUIDE

33.1 MEASURING INTERNATIONAL TRANSACTIONS: THE BALANCE OF PAYMENTS

The **balance of payments account** is a summary account of a country's financial transactions with the rest of the world. The **current account** is the portion of the balance of payments that measures the money flows resulting from exports, imports, international investment income, and transfer payments. The trade balance makes up the largest share of the current account. The **capital account** is the portion of the balance of payments that measures the money flows resulting from changes in the international ownership of capital investments. **Net foreign investment (NFI)** is a country's capital investment inflows minus its capital investment outflows; it equals net foreign portfolio investment plus net foreign direct investment. The current account deficit is the mirror image of the capital account surplus.

33.2 UNDERSTANDING THE CURRENT ACCOUNT DEFICIT

There are two ways to analyze the causes of current account deficits. The trade approach analyzes why our imports exceed our exports. The asset market approach analyzes why investment is greater than domestic saving. When investment is greater than private and government saving, it must be financed by foreign saving. Foreign saving (S_f) roughly equals the negative of the trade balance. In the United States, when money flows out to pay for the trade deficit, it returns to the country in the form of foreign saving, which finances U.S. investment. Most economists believe that current account deficits are not necessarily a problem but can be if they are reflective of excessive indebtedness (as in Greece). There are at least three differences between the Greek crisis and the situation in the United States: The U.S. current account deficit is generally smaller than Greece's deficit, the United States borrows in its own currency, and the United States tends to earn more on its foreign investments than foreigners earn on their investments in the United States.

33.3 ARBITRAGE AND THE LAW OF ONE PRICE

An **exchange rate** is the rate at which one country's currency can be converted into another country's currency **Arbitrage** is the simultaneous purchase and sale of similar assets in order to profit from price differences with little risk. Although large currency arbitrage examples almost never occur, the concept helps to explain the law of one price. The **law of one price** is the economic theory that identical products should sell for the same price in separate markets. The law of one price works well with currencies and easily traded commodities like gold. The law of one price does not always hold due to transportation costs, taxes and tariffs, differences in rents and real estate costs, the fact that some goods are not tradeable, and the fact that some goods are not perfect substitutes. **Purchasing power parity (PPP)** is the economic theory that exchange rates adjust so that any given amount of currency can buy the same combination or basket of products in another country.

33.4 PURCHASING POWER PARITY AND REAL EXCHANGE RATES

Dynamic purchasing power parity (DPPP) is the economic theory that exchange rates gradually adjust over time in order to offset any differences in inflation rates between the two countries. The **real exchange rate (RER)** is the average price of domestic goods and services relative to the average price of the same goods and services in another country, when expressed in a common

currency. Real exchange rates are also the actual (nominal) exchange rates times the ratio of domestic and foreign price levels in local currencies. If purchasing power parity held completely true, real exchange rates would be exactly 1.0. The real exchange rate $= e \times P_{domestic}/P_{foreign}$. The term *strong currency* usually refers to a real exchange rate that is relatively high (above 1.0) or in some cases a real exchange rate that has been appreciating. The term *weak currency* usually refers to either a low real exchange rate or a real exchange rate that has recently been depreciating. **Interest rate parity (IRP)** is the economic theory that exchange rates are expected to gradually adjust over time in order to offset any differences in interest rates between two countries. This ensures that the net expected returns in both countries are roughly equivalent.

33.5 ADVANCED TOPIC: ALTERNATIVE FOREIGN EXCHANGE POLICIES

A **flexible exchange rate** is an exchange rate that is allowed to adjust to changes in supply and demand and is not under the direct control of a government. Most major currencies have operated under a system of flexible exchange rates since 1971. A **fixed (or pegged) exchange rate** is an exchange rate that is determined directly by a government. A **managed exchange rate** is a partially flexible exchange rate that is subject to occasional government intervention designed to offset a rapidly appreciating or depreciating currency (it sometimes is referred to as a *dirty float*). **Currency substitution** is the adoption of a foreign currency by a country along with or in place of its own domestic currency. Because the most frequently substituted currency is the U.S. dollar, the process is often referred to as *dollarization*. Several countries have adopted the U.S. dollar or the euro, despite not being part of either the United States or the eurozone. One advantage is that it provides a stable currency for countries, often small, that have a history of unstable currencies. A disadvantage is that dollarization prevents countries from having their own monetary policy.

TOP TEN TERMS AND CONCEPTS

1. Balance of Payments Account
2. Current Account and Capital Account
3. Net foreign investment (NFI)
4. Exchange Rate, Arbitrage, and the Law of One Price
5. Purchasing Power Parity (PPP)
6. Real Exchange Rates

⑦ Dynamic Purchasing Power Parity (DPPP)

⑧ Real Exchange Rate (RER), Interest Rate Parity (IRP), and Flexible Exchange Rate

⑨ Fixed (or Pegged) Exchange Rate and Managed Exchange Rate

⑩ Currency Substitution

STUDY PROBLEMS

1. What are the major components of the current account and capital account?

2. List the balance of payment accounts for five countries for last year.

3. Explain the differences between the trade balance and the current account balance.

4. 🏛 In the decade after the Great Recession, the interest rate on Greek government debt peaked at over 25%. Explain why.

5. Despite running current account deficits for more than 50 years, Australia has avoided a Greek-style debt crisis. Discuss two possible reasons.

6. Explain how purchasing power parity relates to the real exchange rate.

7. Suppose that the EUR/USD exchange rate is $1.10 per euro and that a basket of goods costs $500 in the United States and €600 in the eurozone.

   a. What is the real exchange rate for the dollar relative to the euro?

   b. What is the real exchange rate for the euro relative to the dollar?

   c. Is the dollar a weak or strong currency?

   d. Is the euro a weak or strong currency?

8. Assume that the exchange rate changes to $0.90 per euro. How do your answers to question 7 change?

9. Suppose that the Australian and Canadian dollars have an exchange rate of 1.00. Also suppose that the U.S. dollar price of Australian dollars is 0.80 (80 U.S. cents) and the U.S. dollar price of Canadian dollars is 0.82 (82 U.S. cents). How can arbitrageurs take advantage of this situation? Why is it hard to find these sorts of opportunities in the real world?

10. Explain why the United States has a surplus on investment income, despite being a "debtor nation".

11. Download an up-to-date version of the Big Mac index, and find the weakest and strongest currencies in terms of Big Mac prices.

12. 📊 In recent decades, Mexico has experienced high inflation. Despite this, the price of Mexican vacations in terms of the U.S. dollar has remained relatively stable. How can these two facts coexist?

13. 📊 Explain the link between dynamic purchasing power parity and inflation rates.

14. 📊 In your own words, explain interest rate parity and the carry trade.

15. Describe differences between a flexible exchange rate, a fixed exchange rate, and a managed exchange rate.

16. What is dollarization? Name three countries that engage in dollarization. What is an advantage and disadvantage of dollarization?

17. Many people have argued that Greece would have been better off during the Great Recession if it had never joined the eurozone and instead had kept its own currency (the Greek drachma). Explain why this view is widely held.

18. What is arbitrage? What does it imply about the prices of standardized goods like gold and foreign currency?

19. Assume that currency arbitrage is not currently profitable. What is the USD/YEN exchange rate in each of the following scenarios? (Hint: Convert U.S. dollars into euros and euros into Japanese yen.)

   a. EUR/USD = 1.00 and EUR/YEN = 120

   b. EUR/USD = 1.10 and EUR/YEN = 120

   c. EUR/USD = 1.20 and EUR/YEN = 100

   d. EUR/USD = 1.20 and EUR/YEN = 120

20. What is the law of one price? What are some limitations to the law of one price? How does it compare to purchasing power parity?

Glossary

ability-to-pay principle The belief that taxes should be levied in proportion to taxpayers' wealth and income.

absolute advantage The ability to produce more of a product than a trading partner with an equivalent amount of resources.

accounting costs Explicit costs of production.

accounting profit Total revenue minus accounting costs.

adaptive expectations The predictions about an economic variable that are based on people's most recent experiences with the variable.

advantages of agglomeration The fact that in some industries, productivity is higher when workers are able to interact with others working in the same industry.

adverse selection The tendency of asymmetric information to result in a less desirable selection of goods and services in the marketplace due to uninformed buyers or sellers.

advertising Paid activities that businesses and other organizations use to sell products.

aggregate demand (AD) The total demand for all goods and services at a given price level.

aggregate expenditure The level of total spending in the economy at each level of real GDP (income), *ceteris paribus*.

aggregate expenditure model An economic model that demonstrates the short-run relationship between aggregate expenditures and real GDP, assuming the price level is constant.

aggregate supply (AS) The total supply for all goods and services at a given price level.

aggregate supply and aggregate demand (AS/AD) model A macroeconomic model that explains major economic changes that impact the entire economy, with a focus on short-run effects.

allocative efficiency Obtaining the maximum well-being from producing the right set of goods and services.

anchoring effect The concept of framing economic decisions based on irrelevant information.

antitrust laws Laws designed to limit behavior that substantially lessens competition.

appreciation of a currency An adjustment in the exchange rate that makes a country's currency more valuable relative to another country's currency.

arbitrage The simultaneous purchase and sale of similar assets in order to profit from price differences with little risk.

asymmetric information An exchange where one party has better information than the other.

automatic stabilizers Changes in taxes and government spending that occur automatically as a result of changes in the business cycle.

autonomous consumption The level of expenditure that occurs when income levels are zero.

average cost pricing regulation Policies that require the monopolist to set price equal to ATC ($P = ATC$), resulting in zero economic profit; also called *rate of return regulation*.

average fixed cost (AFC) Fixed costs per unit.

average tax rate Total taxes paid divided by total income.

average total cost (ATC) Total costs per unit; also called *average cost*.

average variable cost (AVC) Variable costs per unit.

balance of payments account A summary account of a country's financial transactions with the rest of the world.

bank run (banking panic) An event that occurs when depositors rush to withdraw money from their bank in fear that the bank may fail. This problem can and often does spread from one bank to another.

barriers to entry Obstacles that prevent other firms from entering an industry.

barter system An economic system where people directly exchange one good for another.

behavioral economics The study of how economic decisions are impacted by psychological factors beyond rational economic self-interest.

benefits-received principle The belief that people should pay taxes in proportion to the benefits they receive from government services.

bond A tradable legally binding obligation to repay borrowed money and interest.

breakeven Occurs when economic profit equals zero.

bubble A period of time when prices rise above their true fundamental value as investors get swept up in enthusiasm that prices will rise ever higher.

budget constraint The limit of all combinations of goods and services that can be afforded within a given budget.

budget constraint line A graphical representation of the limit of all combinations of goods and services that a consumer can afford within a given budget.

budget deficit Government spending minus net tax revenue when government spending exceeds net tax revenue.

budget surplus Net tax revenue minus government spending when net tax revenue exceeds government spending.

business cycle Short-run alternating periods of economic expansion and recession.

capital account The portion of the balance of payments that measures the money flows resulting from changes in the international ownership of capital investments.

cap and trade See **tradable pollution permits**.

capital gain The profit from the sale of a property or financial asset resulting from a price increase between the time of purchase and the time of sale.

cartel An organization of rival firms with agreements among members to collude, often by restricting output and increasing prices.

catch-up effect The theory that nations that start off poor have the potential to grow more rapidly than rich nations.

central bank An institution that determines the quantity of fiat money in circulation. In most countries, the central bank also regulates the banking system.

ceteris paribus The assumption that other economic and business conditions do not change.

circular flow model A simplified diagram that shows how households and businesses interact with one another in the product market and in the resource market.

classical dichotomy The division of macroeconomics into two areas—real variables and nominal variables.

Coase theorem The theory that if property rights are clearly defined and transaction costs are low, then private individuals should be able to negotiate an efficient solution to the problem of external costs (or benefits).

collective bargaining The negotiation of wages, benefits, and working conditions between an employer and a labor union.

collusion An agreement among rivals to cooperate by limiting price and non-price competition.

command-and-control environmental regulations Direct government regulation of business by setting strict pollution limits or requiring the use of pollution-control devices.

commodity money Money that has an underlying value apart from its role as money.

common resource goods Goods that are rival in consumption and non-excludable.

comparative advantage The ability to produce a product at a lower opportunity cost than a trading partner.

compensating differential Additional income given to workers in employment with less desirable job characteristics.

competitive markets Markets that have many buyers and many sellers.

complements Products that are usually consumed together, and for which an increase in the price of one good reduces the demand for another good, and vice versa.

compound interest Interest earned on previously earned and reinvested interest.

concentration ratio The percentage of market sales accounted for by the largest few (usually, 4, 5, or 8) firms in an industry.

conglomerate merger A merger between firms in unrelated industries.

constant cost industry An industry where the entry of new firms does not change average total cost, resulting in a flat long-run supply curve.

constant returns to scale A condition occurring when long-run average total cost does not change as output increases.

consumer price index (CPI) A measure of the average prices paid by a typical urban family of four for a representative basket of goods.

consumer surplus The buyer's gain from a purchase, measured as the difference between the buyer's willingness to pay and the actual price paid.

consumption expenditures Household purchases of goods and services other than new housing.

consumption function The relationship between consumption spending and real GDP.

contestable market A market that is easy for rival firms to enter.

contractionary fiscal policy A decrease in government spending and/or an increase in taxes that often is directed at decreasing aggregate demand and inflation.

contractionary monetary policy A policy that occurs when the central bank decreases the money supply and increases interest rates, often directed at reducing aggregate demand and inflation.

cooperative solution The outcome that occurs when collaboration leads to a situation where both players are better off than under the non-cooperative solution.

copayment An individual's share of the cost on a claim with the insurance provider paying the rest.

copyright The temporary exclusive right to sell books, films, and music.

corporate finance The study of the financial activities of a corporation.

corporate income taxes Taxes on corporate profits.

corporate inversion A tax avoidance strategy whereby a business establishes its corporate headquarters in a low-tax nation, even as a significant part of its operations remains in a nation with very high corporate tax rates; also called **tax inversion**.

corporate social responsibility The idea that corporations have a broader responsibility to society, not just maximizing profits.

corporation A business that exists as a separate legal entity from its owners.

corrective subsidy A subsidy on activities that generate a positive externality or a smaller negative externality than a comparable activity so that the externality is considered in decision making.

corrective tax A tax levied on activities that generate a negative externality so that the externality is considered in decision making.

cost-minimization rule The costs of producing a given level of output are minimized when the marginal physical product per dollar spent on every input is equalized. This occurs when $MPP_L/P_L = MPP_K/P_K$.

cost-push inflation Inflation that results from a negative aggregate supply shock.

countercyclical policy A policy that is contractionary during an economic boom and expansionary during a recession.

country risk The risk that the business environment in a foreign country unexpectedly changes.

coupon The annual interest payment on a bond.

cross-price elasticity of demand A measure of how responsive quantity demanded is to changes in the price of another product; it equals the percentage change in quantity demanded of one product divided by the percentage change in price of another product.

crowding out The reduction in private spending that occurs in response to increases in government spending.

currency reform The replacement of one currency by another.

currency risk The risk that the values of financial obligations change as the result of currency fluctuations.

currency substitution The adoption of a foreign currency by a country along with or in place of its own domestic currency. Because the most frequently substituted currency is the U.S. dollar, the process is often referred to as *dollarization*.

current account The portion of the balance of payments that measures the money flows resulting from exports, imports, international investment income, and transfer payments.

cyclical unemployment Unemployment that results from a recession.

deadweight loss (DWL) The reduction in total surplus that results from a market distortion.

debt ceiling A legal limit on Treasury borrowing set by Congress.

debt ratio The net national debt as a share of GDP.

decision tree A graphical representation of a sequential move game that demonstrates different actions and payoffs.

decreasing cost industry An industry where the entry of new firms decreases average total cost, resulting in a downward-sloping long-run supply curve.

deductible The amount that a consumer must pay before the insurance provider will pay any claims on the policy.

default risk The likelihood that a borrower will fail to make the required payment on debt.

defensive medicine The practice of recommending a diagnostic test or treatment that is not normally required but is done to protect doctors against potential malpractice lawsuits.

deflation A decrease in the overall price level that results in an increase in the value or purchasing power of money.

demand curve A graph showing the quantity demanded of a good at each possible price and is a graphical representation of the demand schedule.

demand deposits Accounts at the bank that are immediately available for spending.

demand schedule A table that shows the quantity demanded of a good at each possible price.

demand shock A sudden and large shift in the aggregate demand curve.

demand-pull inflation Inflation that results from a positive aggregate demand shock.

depreciation of a currency An adjustment in the exchange rate that makes a country's currency less valuable relative to another country's currency.

depreciation of capital The loss of value that occurs when physical capital wears out with use or becomes obsolete.

depression An unusually severe recession.

derived demand A demand for a resource that depends on the demand for the final product.

discount rate The interest rate charged on a loan to commercial banks from the Federal Reserve.

discouraged workers Nonworking individuals who are willing and able to work, have worked or sought employment in the prior 12 months, but currently are not looking for work because they do not believe they will be able to find an appropriate job.

discretionary spending Government expenditures that are authorized each year by lawmakers in the annual budget.

discrimination in labor markets The offering of different opportunities and pay to different employees on the basis of characteristics such as race, age, gender, or sexual orientation.

diseconomies of scale A condition occurring when long-run average total cost increase as output increases.

disposable personal income Earned and unearned income minus taxes.

diversification An investment technique that reduces risk by putting funds into unrelated assets and asset classes.

dividends The portion of profits paid to stockowners per share of stock.

dominant strategy A strategic decision that is best regardless of the strategic decision made by a rival.

dual mandate A requirement from Congress to the Federal Reserve to promote the goals of maximum employment and stable prices.

duopolists' dilemma A condition in which both duopolists are jointly better off under a cooperative solution than the non-cooperative solution, but have difficulties cooperating because individually they gain by cheating.

duopoly An oligopoly with exactly two firms.

dynamic purchasing power parity (DPPP) The economic theory that exchange rates gradually adjust over time in order to offset any differences in inflation rates between two countries.

earned income tax credit (EITC) A tax credit that is designed to supplement the earnings of low-income workers by providing a subsidy for working.

economic costs Explicit costs plus the implicit costs of production.

economic growth A sustained increase in real GDP per capita that occurs over time.

economic profit Total revenue minus economic costs.

economics The study of how individuals, businesses, and governments make decisions on how to use their limited resources.

economies of scale A condition occurring when long-run average total cost declines as output increases.

economies of scope Reductions in costs associated with a business expanding into multiple product lines.

efficiency wages Above-equilibrium wages paid voluntarily by businesses to encourage productivity.

efficiency Getting the most out of available resources.

efficient market hypothesis (EMH) The theory that financial asset prices incorporate all relevant publicly available information.

elasticity A measure of responsiveness to a change in market conditions.

employed Individuals age 16 and over who worked in the past week, even part-time, or are temporarily away from work.

entrepreneurs Individuals who combine various resources into a business in pursuit of profit.

environmental standards Rules to protect the environment through government regulations.

equation of exchange An economic equation that shows that the quantity of money (M) times the velocity of money (V) equals the price level (P) times real GDP (Y), which also equals nominal GDP (real GDP measured in quantity of goods and services times prices): $M \times V = P \times Y =$ Nominal GDP.

equilibrium The quantity and price at which quantity supplied equals quantity demanded, it is the point where the market supply curve intercepts the market demand curve.

equity A general sense of fairness in the distribution of income and output among members of society.

excess capacity The amount by which output would need to increase in order to minimize average total cost.

excess cash balances The amount by which the supply of money in circulation exceeds the demand for money.

excess reserves Reserves held above and beyond the legally required minimum level of reserves that a bank must hold.

exchange rate The rate at which one country's currency can be converted into another country's currency.

exchange trade fund (ETF) A fund that pools money from multiple investors and trades on a stock exchange.

excise tax A tax on the sale of a specific good or service.

excludability Whether it is possible to exclude people who don't pay for a good from benefiting from that good.

expansion A macroeconomic condition associated with rising real GDP and falling unemployment.

expansionary fiscal policy (commonly referred to as **fiscal stimulus**) An increase in government spending and/or a decrease in taxes that often is directed at increasing aggregate demand and employment.

expansionary monetary policy A policy that occurs when the central bank increases the money supply and decreases short-term interest rates, often directed at boosting aggregate demand and employment.

expectations-augmented Phillips curve A graph that shows the relationship between the unexpected inflation rate and unemployment rate.

expenditure approach equation An equation that calculates GDP by adding all expenditures for consumption (C), investment (I), government purchases (G), and exports (NX). Mathematically, this is GDP = $C + I + G + NX$.

expenditure multiplier effect The multiple by which changes in autonomous expenditures impact aggregate spending.

experience rating A method used to determine the price of insurance based on a group's or an individual's history of claims.

explicit costs Input costs that involve actual payments of money.

exports Goods and services produced domestically but sold in a foreign country.

externality A side effect of a transaction that affects someone not directly involved in the transaction.

extractive institutions Laws, practices, or customs that give insiders special rights, allowing them to extract wealth from the general public.

featherbedding The practice of requiring businesses to hire more workers than needed to perform a specific job, which reduces productivity.

fed funds interest rate target The fed funds rate that the Federal Reserve believes is most likely to achieve its policy goals.

federal funds rate The interest rate that banks pay when borrowing reserves from other banks; also called the *fed funds rate*.

fiat money Money that is not backed by a commodity and that has little or no underlying value apart from its role as money.

financial investment A way of employing savings; often refers to the purchase of stocks and bonds.

first-mover advantage Occurs when the first player to act has a strategic advantage.

first-mover disadvantage Occurs when the first player to act has a strategic disadvantage.

fiscal austerity A contractionary fiscal policy that is aimed at reducing a budget deficit or national debt.

fiscal multiplier See **multiplier effect**.

fiscal policy Changes in government spending and taxation that often are aimed at influencing employment and inflation.

fiscal stimulus See **expansionary fiscal policy**.

Fisher effect The idea that a change in expected inflation leads to an equal change in nominal interest rates.

fixed exchange rate An exchange rate that is determined directly by a government; also called **pegged exchange rate**.

fixed costs (FC) Short-run costs that do not change with the quantity of output.

flat tax See **proportional tax**.

flexible exchange rate An exchange rate that is allowed to adjust to changes in supply and demand and is not under the direct control of a government.

foreign aid The transfer of money, food, and other resources, often provided by high-income nations to developing countries.

foreign direct investment The ownership of business activities by an entity based in another country.

foreign exchange market (FOREX) A complex, non-centralized market in which currencies are traded; also called the *currency market*.

foreign saving The saving that foreigners have invested in an economy other than their own.

forward guidance A policy statement issued by the Federal Reserve that signals the future direction of its monetary policy.

fractional reserve banking The banking practice of keeping a fraction of deposits available as reserves.

framing The idea that the way in which a decision is presented to customers often affects their behavior.

franchise A purchased right to operate under an established brand name.

free-rider An individual who receives benefits from a public good without paying for them.

frictional unemployment Unemployment that occurs during the time individuals spend seeking employment that is best suited to their skills.

full employment An economic condition that occurs when cyclical unemployment is at zero and the only remaining unemployment is frictional or structural in nature.

game theory The study of strategic behaviors, and the ways in which individuals (or other entities) make optimal decisions by anticipating how rivals will respond to their actions.

GDP deflator An alternative price index that measures general price levels in the economy in aggregate; also called the **implicit price deflator**.

Gini coefficient A convenient summary measurement of relative income or wealth inequality. It is perhaps the most widely used measure of income inequality.

globalization The opening of markets to foreign trade and financial investment, leading to an increasing interconnectivity of economic transactions across national borders.

gold standard A system where the value of a currency is set equal to a fixed amount of gold.

government purchases Spending by federal, state, and local governments on goods, services, and investments. Government purchases exclude transfer payments.

government saving Saving by the government. It equals net taxes minus government spending.

gross domestic product (GDP) The market value of all final goods and services produced in a country during a given time period.

Herfindahl–Hirschman Index (HHI) A measure of concentration calculated by summing the square of the percentage market share of each and every firm in an industry; $HHI = \sum_{\text{All firms}} (\text{Market share})^2$

horizontal merger A merger between firms in the same industry.

Hotelling's location model An economic model designed to illustrate the optimal location strategy of businesses.

human capital Skills acquired through education, experience, and training that allow labor to be more productive.

hyperinflation Extremely high rates of inflation and a rapid decline in the value of a nation's currency.

imperfect price discrimination A form of price discrimination whereby a firm charges different groups of customers different prices based on either purchasing volume or differences in the price elasticity of demand.

implicit costs Input costs that do not involve payment of money.

implicit price deflator See **GDP deflator**.

import licenses Laws requiring importers to obtain a license in order to engage in foreign trade.

imports Goods and services produced in a foreign country but sold domestically.

inclusive institutions Laws, practices, or customs that allow all members of society the opportunity to create wealth.

income effect The change in the quantity demanded of a good when price changes alter the purchasing power of consumers.

income effect on labor supply An effect that occurs when workers supply less labor at higher wages because the additional income increases the demand for leisure.

income elastic demand An income elasticity of demand that is greater than 1.

income elasticity of demand A measure of how responsive quantity demanded is to changes in consumers' income; it equals the percentage change in quantity demanded divided by the percentage change in income.

income inelastic demand An income elasticity of demand that is between 0 and 1.

income inequality The unequal distribution of income among members of society that occurs when some individuals or households earn more than others.

income mobility The ability of individuals or households to alter their economic status.

increasing cost industry An industry where the entry of new firms increases average total cost, resulting in an upward-sloping long-run supply curve.

index fund A mutual fund or ETF that automatically invests in all of the stocks in a particular stock index.

indifference curve map An infinite set of indifference curves, each depicting a unique level of utility.

indifference curve Shows all the alternative combinations of products that give the consumer the same level of satisfaction.

inferior good A good for which demand decreases as incomes increase, and demand increases as incomes decrease.

inflation An increase in the overall price level that results in a decline in the value or purchasing power of money.

inflation expectations The amount of inflation that is expected by the public, both businesses and consumers.

inflation rate The annual percentage change in average prices.

inflation tax A reduction in the purchasing power of money that occurs with inflation.

interest rate The cost of borrowing money and also the reward for saving money, expressed as a percentage of the amount borrowed or saved.

interest rate parity (IRP) The economic theory that exchange rates are expected to gradually adjust over time in order to offset any differences in interest rates between two countries.

intermediate goods Products used as an input in the production of final goods.

internal rate of return (IRR) The percentage annual rate of return on the amount invested.

internalizing an externality The act of altering private costs or benefits so that they fully account for external effects.

inventory A stock of unsold goods and raw materials.

investment Spending on new capital goods. Investment increases the amount of physical capital in an economy.

labor Human effort used in the production of goods and services.

labor force The number of individuals age 16 and over who are either unemployed or employed.

labor force participation rate (LFPR) The percentage of the adult population that is either employed or unemployed and thus in the labor force.

labor union An organization through which workers bargain collectively for wages, benefits, and work conditions; also called a **union**.

Laffer curve A graph that shows the relationship between tax rates on income and tax revenues.

law of demand The economic principle stating that a negative relationship exists between price and quantity demanded, *ceteris paribus*.

law of diminishing marginal utility The principle that, during a given period of time, increasing consumption of a good decreases marginal utility.

law of diminishing returns Theory stating that in the short run the marginal physical product of labor declines as more labor is employed, with other inputs held fixed.

law of increasing cost Principle stating that the opportunity cost of producing an additional item generally increases as more of the good is produced.

law of one price The economic theory that identical products should sell for the same price in separate markets.

law of supply The economic principle stating that a positive relationship exists between price and quantity supplied, *ceteris paribus*.

leader pricing A strategy whereby businesses reduce the price of a popular item in order to attract customers in an effort to sell other goods.

leading economic indicators Economic statistics that are expected to change before the economy enters or exits a recession.

leakage The portion of extra income that is not used for the consumption of domestically produced goods but instead goes to taxes, saving, and spending on imported goods.

limit pricing A strategic entry deterrence policy of setting price low enough to deter entry while remaining profitable.

limited liability When the owners of a business are not personally responsible for the debt and other financial obligations of a firm beyond what they put into it.

limited liability company (LLC) A partnership whereby some partners enjoy limited liabilities.

liquidity trap A situation in which nominal interest rates have fallen close to zero and thus cannot be lowered further by increases in the money supply.

liquidity The ease with which an asset can be turned into money.

long run The time necessary to make all adjustments to new economic circumstances.

long-run aggregate supply (LRAS) The total supply of all goods and services in the long run after all wages and prices have had time to adjust.

long run average total cost curve (LRATC) Curve that represents the lowest average total cost at which a business can produce various levels of output when all inputs are allowed to vary.

long-run competitive equilibrium Occurs when businesses in a competitive industry have zero economic profit because price equals average total cost at the profit maximizing level of output.

long-run Phillips curve (LRPC) A graph that shows the long-run relationship between inflation and unemployment after the inflation rate equals the expected rate of inflation.

long-term interest rate The cost of borrowing money or the reward for saving money for more than one year.

Lorenz curve A graphical presentation of the cumulative distribution of income or wealth.

Lucas critique The observation that statistical correlations do not provide a reliable guide to policymakers because when a policy changes, the public changes its expectations and therefore the ways that it responds to policy actions.

M1 A measure of the money supply that includes all cash (including paper money and coins) in circulation, along with demand deposits and traveler's checks.

M2 A measure of the money supply that includes M1 plus time deposits.

macroeconomics The branch of economics that focuses on economic issues which impact the overall economy, such as unemployment, inflation, recessions, and economic growth.

managed exchange rate A partially flexible exchange rate that is subject to occasional government intervention designed to offset a rapidly appreciating or depreciating currency; sometimes called a *dirty float*.

marginal analysis The process of comparing the additional benefits of an activity with its additional cost.

marginal cost (MC) The additional costs a business incurs from one additional unit of output.

marginal physical product of labor (MPP_L) The additional output from an additional unit of labor, holding the amount of physical capital and other inputs fixed.

marginal private benefits (MPB) Marginal benefits received by buyers.

marginal private costs (MPC) Marginal costs borne by sellers.

marginal propensity to consume (MPC) The additional consumption that occurs from an additional dollar in income.

marginal propensity to save (MPS) The additional savings that occurs from an additional dollar in income.

marginal rate of substitution The rate at which consumers are willing to exchange one good for another while maintaining the same level of utility.

marginal revenue (MR) The additional revenue a business receives from one additional unit of output.

marginal revenue product of labor (MRP_L) The additional total revenue from an additional unit of labor, holding the amount of physical capital and other inputs fixed.

marginal social benefits (MSB) Marginal private benefits plus additional external benefits.

marginal social costs (MSC) Marginal private costs plus additional external costs.

marginal tax rate The amount of additional taxes one pays from an additional dollar of income.

marginal utility The additional utility gained from consuming an additional unit.

marginal utility per dollar Marginal utility divided by price.

market A means for buyers and sellers to engage in the exchange of a good or service.

market demand The sum of quantity demanded for all buyers, at each price.

market failure A circumstance in which free, unregulated markets fail to maximize economic efficiency.

market structure The business composition of a specific industry or product market, including the size and number of competing firms.

market supply The sum of quantity supplied for all sellers, at each price.

marketing All the activities and strategies that businesses use to sell products. The many decisions involved in marketing products are often referred to as the marketing mix.

medium of exchange An asset that is widely used for purchasing other goods and services.

menu costs Inefficiencies associated with the labor wasted on increasingly frequent price updates during inflationary periods.

merger The combination of two companies into a single firm.

microeconomics The branch of economics that focuses on economic issues faced primarily by individuals and businesses in a particular segment of the overall economy.

minimum efficient scale (MES) The smallest level of output at which all economies of scale have been fully utilized.

monetarism A school of economic thought that stresses the role that is played by the money supply in determining nominal GDP and inflation.

monetary base A measure of the money supply that includes cash held by the general public plus reserves held by commercial banks.

monetary neutrality The idea that changes in the money supply do not affect real variables in the long run.

monetary offset The adjustment of monetary policy by the central bank to offset either a fiscal stimulus or fiscal austerity.

monetary policy Changes in the money supply and interest rates by the central bank, often with the goal of influencing employment and inflation.

money An asset commonly used in the exchange of goods and services.

money demand The amount of money that people want to hold.

money illusion An incorrect assumption that nominal variables represent real variables.

money multiplier The change in the overall money supply resulting from a $1 increase in the monetary base.

money supply The total value of financial assets that are considered money.

monopolistic competition A market structure with many firms selling similar but differentiated products.

monopoly A market structure with a single seller of a product with no close substitutes and high barriers to entry.

monopsony A market with a single buyer.

moral hazard A situation where there is an increased tendency to take risks because some of the potential costs associated with taking such risks will be paid by others.

multinational corporation (MNC) A corporation that produces and sells goods and services in more than one country.

multiplier effect (fiscal multiplier) The multiple by which a direct change in fiscal policy will impact aggregate spending.

mutual fund A financial investment fund that pools money from multiple investors to purchase a portfolio of stocks, bonds, or other financial assets.

Nash equilibrium An outcome in which no player improves through a unilateral change in strategy.

national debt The total amount of money owed by the federal government.

national income Gross domestic product minus depreciation and indirect business taxes.

natural monopoly What occurs when a single firm can supply a product at lower costs than would happen with two or more competing firms.

natural rate hypothesis An economic theory that states that when inflation expectations adjust, the rate of unemployment returns to the natural rate.

natural rate of output The output level where all wages and prices have adjusted and the economy is at full employment.

natural rate of unemployment The unemployment rate that occurs when the economy is at full employment and there is no cyclical unemployment.

natural resources Inputs found in nature that can be used in the production of goods and services.

negative relationship When a decrease in one variable occurs with an increase in another variable, or an increase in one variable occurs with a decrease in the other variable; sometimes called an *inverse relationship*.

net domestic product (NDP) Gross domestic product adjusted for capital depreciation.

net exports Equal a country's exports minus its imports; also referred to as the *trade balance*.

net foreign investment (NFI) A country's capital investment inflows minus its capital investment outflows; it equals net foreign portfolio investment plus net foreign direct investment.

net national debt The total national debt minus debt obligations that the government owes to itself.

net taxes Total taxes paid to the government minus total transfer benefits received from the government.

network externalities The benefits a consumer receives from a good or service as a result of others using the same product.

New Keynesian economics The view that the central bank should target short-term interest rates, with the goal of keeping inflation low and stable and unemployment close to the natural rate.

nominal GDP A measure of GDP using current prices that does not adjust for inflation.

nominal GDP targeting A monetary policy that has a goal of achieving a steady increase in nominal GDP, perhaps something like 4% per year.

nominal values The face values of variables measured in current prices that have not been adjusted for inflation.

non-cooperative solution The outcome that occurs when players do not collaborate, with each pursuing their own self-interest.

non-price competition What occurs when businesses try to distinguish their products from rivals without changing the price.

non-rival private goods Goods that are non-rival in consumption and excludable.

normal good A good for which demand increases as incomes increase, and demand decreases as incomes decrease.

normative analysis Analysis that is subjective and value-based; it considers questions involving goals, values, and ethics.

oligopoly A market structure with a few dominant firms that are highly interdependent.

open market operations The sale or purchase of government bonds by the Fed to control the size of the monetary base.

opportunity cost What must be given up in order to acquire or do something else.

optimal consumption The bundle of goods that maximizes a consumer's utility subject to a budget constraint.

outsourcing When a business obtains products or services from another firm, one frequently located in a foreign country.

P/E ratio The price of a stock divided by its earnings per share; also called the **price /earnings ratio**.

paradox of thrift The economic theory stating that attempts to save more can depress aggregate demand, leaving actual saving no higher than before.

partnership A business owned by more than one individual, not formed as a corporation.

patent The temporary exclusive right to sell a product granted to its inventor.

payoff matrix A graphical representation of a simultaneous move game that demonstrates different actions and their potential payoffs.

pegged exchange rate See **fixed exchange rate.**

perfect competition A market structure in which a very large number of sellers supply a standardized product.

perfect price discrimination A form of price discrimination whereby a firm charges each customer the maximum price the buyer is willing to pay; also called *first-degree price discrimination.*

permanent income The expected average income over time.

personal consumption expenditure price index (PCE) A chain-weighted price index that primarily measures prices of household consumption expenditures.

personal income taxes Taxes on personal and household income.

Phillips curve A graph that shows the relationship between inflation and unemployment.

physical capital Durable equipment and structures used to produce goods and services; sometimes referred to simply as *capital* in economics.

planned investment The amount of investment that businesses intend to do.

policy lag The delayed effect of policy on the economy.

positive analysis Analysis that is objective; it looks at questions involving cause and effect.

positive relationship When an increase in one variable occurs with an increase in another variable, or a decrease in one variable occurs with a decrease in another variable; sometimes called a *direct relationship.*

potential deposit multiplier The maximum possible change in deposits for each dollar change in bank reserves. It equals 1/Required reserve ratio.

poverty line (threshold) The minimum level of income, including certain government benefits, below which an individual, a family, or a household is considered poor.

poverty rate The percentage of the population with incomes below the poverty line.

present value The discounted current value of a future sum of money.

price ceiling A law that sets a maximum price, generally below equilibrium.

price discrimination The business strategy of maximizing profits by selling essentially the same product at different prices to different consumers.

price/earnings ratio See **P/E ratio.**

price elasticity of demand (E_d) A measure of how responsive quantity demanded is to price changes; it equals the percentage change in quantity demanded divided by the percentage change in price.

price elasticity of supply (E_s) A measure of how responsive quantity supplied is to price changes; it equals the percentage change in quantity supplied divided by the percentage change in price.

price fixing Collusion achieved by rivals agreeing to a set price.

price floor A law that sets a minimum price, generally above equilibrium.

price index A measure of average prices of a fixed basket of goods or services.

price leadership An implicit pricing agreement in which one firm in the oligopoly (often the largest) establishes a price that the other firms then adopt.

price of labor (P_l) The total compensation that an employee receives from working. It includes the wages paid to workers, the cost of any benefits the worker receives, and other expenses related to hiring a worker.

price taker A firm that does not have the ability to impact market price.

principal–agent problem The difficulty of making agents act in the best interest of the principals that they serve.

prisoners' dilemma A condition in which two prisoners are jointly better off under a cooperative solution than the non-cooperative solution, but have difficulties cooperating because individually they gain by cheating.

private goods Goods that are rival in consumption and excludable.

procyclical policy A policy that is expansionary during an economic boom and contractionary during a recession.

producer price index (PPI) A price index that measures the price of goods purchased by a typical producer.

producer surplus The seller's gain from a sale, measured as the difference between the seller's willingness to accept and the actual price received.

product differentiation A real or perceived difference among products that are close substitutes.

product mix The assortment of products a business offers its customers.

production function An expression of the technological relationship between different combinations of inputs and maximum output.

production possibility frontier (PPF) An economic model that shows the limit of what an economy can produce when all resources are used efficiently.

productive efficiency (minimum ATC) Obtaining the maximum possible output with a given set of resources or obtaining output for the lowest possible cost.

productivity Output per unit of labor or other production input.

progressive tax A tax that increases as a percentage of income as incomes rise, thus taxing high-income taxpayers at a higher rate than low-income taxpayers.

property taxes Taxes on owners of properties such as real estate and motor vehicles based on the value of such properties.

proportional tax A tax that remains a constant percentage at all levels of income; also called a **flat tax.**

protectionism The use of government policy to protect domestic businesses from foreign competition.

public finance A branch of economics which studies how governments raise and spend money.

public goods Goods that are non-rival in consumption and non-excludable.

purchasing power parity (PPP) The economic theory that exchange rates adjust so that any given amount of currency can buy the same combination or basket of products in another country.

quantitative easing An expansionary monetary policy that involves much larger than normal open market purchases of financial assets and that is intended to increase the size of the money supply and boost spending in the economy.

quantity demanded (Q_d) The amount of a particular good that buyers are willing and able to purchase at a specific price.

quantity supplied (Q_s) The amount of a particular good that sellers are willing and able to supply at a specific price.

quantity theory of money The theory that a given change in the money supply leads to a proportional change in the price level in the long run.

quota A quantity restriction on imports that is imposed by the importing country.

rational expectations The predictions about an economic variable that are based on an optimal forecast using all publicly available information.

real exchange rate (RER) The average price of domestic goods and services relative to the average price of the same goods and services in another country, when expressed in a common currency.

real GDP A measure of GDP using constant prices in order to adjust for inflation.

real GDP per capita A measure of real GDP per person.

real values The values of variables measured in prices that have been adjusted for inflation.

recession A macroeconomic condition associated with falling real GDP and rising unemployment.

regional trade bloc An international trade agreement that promotes free trade by reducing trade barriers between participating countries.

regressive tax A tax that decreases as a percentage of income as incomes rise, thus taxing high-income taxpayers at a lower rate than low-income taxpayers.

rent seeking Activities such as lobbying the government with the goal of obtaining barriers to entry, subsidies, and other special privileges.

required reserve ratio The legally required minimum level of reserves that a bank must hold, expressed as a fraction of deposits.

resources Inputs used in the production of goods and services; they are commonly referred to as *factors of production*.

retained earnings Profits the corporation does not immediately return to stockholders.

rivalry Whether one person's consumption of a good reduces the availability of that good to others.

rule of 70 An estimate of the number of years it takes a variable to double when increasing at a steady percentage rate of growth.

sales taxes Taxes on the sale of goods expressed as a percentage of the selling price of an item.

saving Forgone current consumption, which equals after-tax income minus spending on consumer products.

scarcity A situation that occurs when human wants and needs exceed available resources to meet those wants and needs.

screening The acquisition of reliable information about a product or resource to help make a more informed decision on a purchase or sale.

seasonal adjustment A statistical process based on historic norms that removes seasonal influences in economic data such as GDP, inflation, and the unemployment rate.

self-correcting mechanism The process by which short-run aggregate supply adjusts to return output to the natural rate after either a recession or an inflationary boom.

sequential move game A game that involves all firms making their strategic

decision with full knowledge of the prior actions of their rivals.

sheepskin effect The increase in earnings from obtaining higher credentials as opposed to higher levels of human capital.

shortage An excess of quantity demanded over quantity supplied that occurs at prices below equilibrium, which creates an unstable situation for the market; also called *excess demand*.

short run A time frame that is too short to include all adjustments to new economic circumstances.

short-run aggregate supply (SRAS) The total supply of all goods and services in the short run before all wages and prices have had time to adjust.

short-term interest rate The cost of borrowing money or the reward for saving money for less than one year.

shutdown price The minimum price at which a profit-maximizing firm may choose to operate; this price equals the minimum average variable cost.

signaling The providing of reliable information about a product or resource to help another party make a more informed decision on a purchase or sale.

simultaneous move game A game that involves all firms making their strategic decisions at the same time, without full knowledge of the actions of their rivals.

single-payer health-care system A health-care system where the government pays for the vast majority of health-care costs.

slope Describes how much one variable changes in response to changes in a different variable.

social equilibrium The quantity and price at which quantity supplied equals quantity demanded absent a market failure.

social insurance programs Government programs that provide social insurance against the risk of hardship due to poverty, unemployment, retirement, and health-care expenditures.

social insurance taxes Taxes primarily on wages and salaries paid by employers and employees to fund social insurance programs; also called *payroll taxes*.

sole proprietorship A business owned by one individual.

specialization Concentrating on the production of a single good.

spot exchange rate The exchange rate at the current time.

stagflation A decrease in output with rising inflation that generally is associated with high inflation and high unemployment at the same time.

stakeholders Any group that is impacted by corporate policy decisions.

status quo bias A consumer preference to maintain the current situation.

stock A share of ownership in a corporation.

stock market index An aggregate value of a set of representative stocks.

stockholders The owners of a corporation.

store of value An asset that people can use as a place to put their savings.

strategic entry deterrence An action taken by an existing business that discourages rivals from entering the market.

strike A refusal to work by members of a labor union, which often happens in order to gain some concession from employers.

structural unemployment Unemployment that occurs when workers lack the skills required for available jobs.

substitutes Products that serve the same purpose, and for which an increase in the price of one good increases the demand for another good, and vice versa.

substitution effect The change in the quantity demanded of a good when price changes result in consumers switching from relatively high-priced products to relatively low-priced products.

substitution effect on labor supply An effect that occurs when workers supply more labor at higher wages because the opportunity cost of leisure increases.

sunk costs Costs that are not avoidable, and thus they should not affect economic decision-making.

supply curve A graph showing the quantity supplied of a good at each possible price and is a graphical representation of the supply schedule.

supply schedule A table that shows the quantity supplied of a good at each possible price.

supply shock A sudden and large shift in the aggregate supply curve.

supply side economics Economic policies that are aimed at increasing aggregate supply.

surplus An excess of quantity supplied over quantity demanded that occurs at prices above equilibrium, which creates an unstable situation for the market; also called *excess supply*.

tariff A tax on imports that is imposed by the importing country.

tax avoidance Any effort by taxpayers to legally reduce their tax obligations.

tax credit A tax rule that allows taxpayers to reduce the amount they owe in taxes by exactly the amount of the credit.

tax deduction A tax rule that allows taxpayers to reduce their taxable income by the amount of the deduction.

tax inversion See **corporate inversion**.

tax evasion Any effort by taxpayers to pay fewer taxes by illegal means.

tax incidence A measure of who bears the economic burden of a tax once prices have adjusted.

tax rates The tax per unit, expressed as an exact dollar amount or a percent of sale price or income.

tax revenue The total amount of money the government collects from a tax.

time deposits Accounts that hold money deposited in a bank that cannot be withdrawn for a specified period of time.

time-series graph A graph that shows the relationship between a variable and time.

time value of money The idea that the value of money today is greater than receiving the same amount of money in the future.

tit-for-tat strategy A game theory strategy whereby a player cooperates on the first move and then copies what the other player(s) do on all subsequent moves.

total costs (TC) Cost of all inputs in production, which equals fixed costs plus variable costs.

total revenue The money a business receives from the sale of a product, calculated as the price of the good times the quantity sold; also called *revenue*.

total surplus The sum of consumer surplus and producer surplus, plus any tax revenue.

total utility The overall amount of satisfaction a consumer obtains from consuming a given total of a particular good.

tradable pollution permits A government policy that assigns pollution rights for a strictly limited amount and type of pollution; also called **cap and trade**.

trade deficit An imbalance that occurs when a nation imports more products than it exports, resulting in negative net exports.

trade surplus The imbalance that occurs when a nation exports more products than it imports, resulting in positive net exports.

tragedy of the commons The tendency to overuse common resources.

transfer payments Payments made by a government when no goods and services are currently supplied.

transitory income Any temporary increase or decrease in income.

transmission mechanism The method by which money affects the economy.

trusts Organizations of rival firms that conspired to acquire monopoly power in an industry.

U6 unemployment rate An alternative measure of the unemployment rate that considers both marginally attached and underemployed workers. Mathematically, this is U6 unemployment rate = ((Unemployed + Marginally attached + Underemployed) / (Labor force + Marginally attached)) × 100%.

unemployed Individuals age 16 and over who are available to work, did not work in the past week, and actively looked for work during the previous four weeks.

unemployment insurance Temporary government-provided income to individuals that partially makes up for lost income during periods of involuntary unemployment.

unemployment rate (U3 unemployment rate) The percentage of the labor force that is unemployed. U3 is considered the official unemployment rate.

union See **labor union**.

unit of account A standard way of measuring prices.

universal health coverage A health-care system that ensures that health-care benefits are provided to all citizens.

unplanned investment Unanticipated changes in investment, primarily through unintended changes in inventory.

utility A hypothetic measure of satisfaction experienced by consumers.

value of money The amount of goods and services that can be bought with money—the purchasing power of money, which equals 1/Price level.

variable costs (VC) Short-run costs that change with the quantity of output.

velocity of money The average number of times that money is spent on final goods and services during a year.

vertical merger A merger between firms at different stages of production.

voluntary export restraint (VER) A quantity restriction on imports that is imposed by negotiating with the foreign exporting country to restrict its exports voluntarily.

wage (W) The total payment for labor, which excludes the cost of benefits.

willingness to accept The minimum price a seller is willing to accept for a good or service.

willingness to pay The maximum price a buyer is willing to pay for a good or service.

World Trade Organization (WTO) An international organization that promotes free trade, supervises the trade policies of member nations, and enforces the trade rules that are agreed to by member nations.

Index

Note: Page numbers followed by e indicate exhibits; those followed by n indicate notes; main entries in **boldface** are key terms; main entries in red are business names.

References

Chapter 1

1. Bill Conerly, "Career Advice for Economics Majors," *Forbes,* April 29, 2015, http://www.forbes.com/sites/billconerly/2015/04/29 /career-advice-for-economics-majors/2/#3cc258f31a5c.
2. "How Your Understanding of Economics Can Affect Your Decision Quality," *University of Florida,* n.d., http:// essentialsofbusiness.ufexec.ufl.edu/resources/leadership/ how-your-understanding-of-economics-can-affect-your-decision -quality/#.WC3t3eErLIF.
3. Mike Profita, "Top 10 Jobs for Economics Majors," *The Balance,* July 3, 2017, https://www.thebalance.com/top-jobs -for-economics-majors-2059650.
4. Scott Adams, *Dilbert 2.0: 20 Years of Dilbert* (Kansas, MO: McMeel, 2008).
5. Patricia M. Flynn and Michael A. Quinn, "Economics: A Good Choice of Major for Future CEOs," *SSRN,* November 29, 2006, https://papers.ssrn.com/sol3/papers.cfm?abstract_id=947914.

Chapter 2

1. "Ford's assembly line starts rolling." *History.com*, n.d., accessed April 23, 2017, http://www.history.com/this-day-in-history /fords-assembly-line-starts-rolling.

Chapter 3

1. Michael J. Merced, "Starbucks Announces It Will Close 600 Stores," *The New York Times,* July 1, 2008, http://www.nytimes .com/2008/07/02/business/02sbux.html; and Claire Cain Miller, "Starbucks to Close 300 Stores and Open Fewer New Ones," *The New York Times,* January 28, 2009, http://www.nytimes .com/2009/01/29/business/29sbux.html; and Emily Bryson York, "Where the Hot Spots Are as Eating Moves Back Home," *Ad Age,* August 10, 2009, http://adage.com/article/news /recession-bright-spots-baking-coffee-frozen-pizza/138354/.
2. Jordan Robertson and Technology Writer. "HP Profit Slumps 13% on Weak PC and Ink Sales, Revenue Falls Short," *ABC News,* n.d., accessed May 4, 2017, http://abcnews.go.com /Business/story?id=6910811; and "Gillette's Five-Blade Wonder." *Bloomberg.com,* September 15, 2005, http://www.businessweek .com/stories/2005-09-14/gillettes-five-blade-wonder.
3. Meg LaPorte, "2012 Top 50 Largest Nursing Facility Companies," *Provider: Long Term and Post-Acute Care,* June 1, 2016, http://www.providermagazine.com/reports /Pages/0612/2012-Top-50-Largest-Nursing-Facility-Companies .aspx.
4. "Pocket K No. 5: Documented Benefits of GM Crops," *ISAAA. org,* n.d., accessed May 11, 2017, http://www.isaaa.org /resources/publications/pocketk/5/.
5. "US Shale Spurs Record Foreign Chemical Investment," *Newsmax Finance,* June 27, 2014, . http://www .moneynews.com/InvestingAnalysis/shale-gas-chemical- investment/2014/06/27/id/579712/. "Year-End Chemical Industry Situation and Outlook: American Chemistry Is Back in the Game," *American Chemistry Council,* December 2013, http:// www.americanchemistry.com/Jobs/EconomicStatistics /Year-End-2013-Situation-and-Outlook.pdf.

6. Steve Jones, "Wholesale Seafood Prices Rising as Oil Spill Grows," *Myrtlebeachonline,* May 22, 2010, http://www .myrtlebeachonline.com/2010/05/22/1488631/wholesale -seafood-prices-rising.html.
7. Josh Zumbrun, "Oil's Plunge Could Help Send Its Price Back Up," *The Wall Street Journal,* February 22, 2015, http://www .wsj.com/articles/oils-plunge-could-help-send-its-price-back-up -1424632746?mod=WSJ_hpp_MIDDLENexttoWhatsNewsThird.
8. "China's Auto Retail Market." *China Business Review,* July 1, 2010, http://www.chinabusinessreview.com/chinas-auto-retail -market/.
9. Ellen Huet, "What It Takes to Build the Next Uber." *Forbes* (June 23, 2014).
10. Colleen Schreiber, "With Declining Beef Demand, Prices Not Likely to Improve." *Livestock Weekly,* n.d., http://www .livestockweekly.com.

Chapter 4

1. Timothy J. Richards and Luis Padilla, "Promotion and Fast Food Demand," *American Journal of Agricultural Economics* 91, no. 1 (2009).
2. Timothy Cain. "Hyundai Sonata Sales Figures," *GoodCarBadCar. com,* January 1, 2011, http://www.goodcarbadcar.net/2011/01 /hyundai-sonata-sales-figures.html.
3. "Update Regarding Amazon/Hachette Business Interruption." *Amazon.com* Kindle Forum, July 29, 2014.
4. Bob Evans, "OracleVoice: Data Warehouse 2.0: The 10 Top Trends Driving the Revolution," *Forbes,* February 26, 2013, http://www.forbes.com/sites/oracle/2013/01/14 /data-warehouse-2-0-the-10-top-trends-driving-the-revolution/.
5. "Henry Ford's Business Philosophy," in *American Decades Primary Sources, Vol. 2: 1910–1919,* ed. Cynthia Rose (Detroit: Gale, 2004), 98–102.

Exhibit 2

Patrick L. Anderson, Richard D. McLellan, Joseph P. Overton, and Gary L. Wolfra, *Price Elasticity of Demand* (Midland, MI: MacKinac Center for Public Policy, 1997).

Lesley Chiou, "Empirical Analysis of Competition between Wal-Mart and Other Retail Channels," *Journal of Economics & Management Strategy* 18, no. 2 (2009).

Ronald Cotterill and Ronald Haller, "An Econometric Analysis of the Demand for RTE Cereal: Product Market Definition and Unilateral Market Power Effects," University of Connecticut, Food Marketing Policy Research Rept. No. 35 (1994).

Fabian Duarte, "Price Elasticity of Expenditure Across Health Care Services," *Journal of Health Economics* 31, no. 6 (2012).

Rajeev K. Goel and Michael A. Nelson, "Cigarette Demand and Effectiveness of U.S. Smoking Control Policies: State-Level Evidence for More Than Half a Century," *Empirical Economics* 42 (2012).

Tomas Harvaneka, Zuzana Irsovab, and Karel Jandab, "The Demand for Gasoline Is More Price-Inelastic Than Commonly Thought," *Energy Economics* 34, no. 1 (2012).

C. Y. Cynthia Lin and Lea Prince, "Gasoline Price Volatility and the Elasticity of Demand for Gasoline," *Energy Economics* 38, no. 1 (2013).

Johan Lundberg and Sofia Lundberg, "Distribution Effects of Lower Food Prices in a Rich Country," *Journal of Consumer Policy* 35 (2012).

Levi Perez and David Forrest, "Own- and Cross-Price Elasticities for Games within a State Lottery Portfolio," *Contemporary Economic Policy* 29 (2011).

Christopher Ruhm, "What U.S. Data Should Be Used to Measure the Price Elasticity of Demand for Alcohol?" *Journal of Health Economics* 31, no. 6 (2012).

Henry Saffer and Frank Chaloupka, "The Demand for Illicit Drugs." *Economic Inquiry* 37, no. 3 (1999).

"Price Elasticities of Demand for Passenger Air Travel: A Meta-Analysis," *Journal of Air Transport Management* 8 (2002): 165–175.

Jean-Pierre Dube, "Product Differentiation and Mergers in the Carbonated Soft Drink Industry," *Journal of Economics and Management Strategy* 14, no. 4 (2005): 879–904.

Chapter 6

1. "Rent Control," Chicago Booth School of Business, IGM Economics Experts Panel, February 7, 2012, http://www.igmchicago.org/igm-economic-experts-panel/poll-results?SurveyID=SV_6upyzeUpI73V5k0.

2. Niebanck, cited in Walter Block, "Rent Control," in *Rent Control: The Concise Encyclopedia of Economics*, Indianapolis Library of Economics and Liberty, 2008, http://www.econlib.org/library/Enc/RentControl.html.

3. Sam Bowman, "Only Bombing Would Be Worse Than Rent Control," *Adam Smith Institute*, January 25, 2012, http://www.adamsmith.org/blog/planning-transport/only-bombing-would-be-worse-than-rent-control.

4. http://www.wirelessweek.com/news/2015/05/report-licensed-spectrum-spurs-big-economic-growth.

Chapter 7

1. Paul Krugman, "An Insurance Company with an Army," *The New York Times,* April 27, 2011. (Krugman notes the quote is not original.)

2. Data from the Congressional Budget Office (http://www.CBO.gov).

3. Arnold Harberger, "Tax Lore for Budding Reformers," in *Reform, Recovery, and Growth: Latin America and the Middle East,* eds. Rudiger Dornbusch and Sebastian Edwards (Chicago: University of Chicago Press, 1995), p. 307.

4. Zachary Mider, "Tax Inversion," *Bloomberg View,* March 2, 2017, http://www.bloombergview.com/quicktake/tax-inversion.

5. "Vietnam Considers Increasing Tobacco Tax," *Thanh Nien Daily,* May 31, 2014, http://www.thanhniennews.com/business/vietnam-considers-increasing-tobacco-tax-26677.html.

Chapter 8

1. "Smog Deaths in 1948 Led to Clean Air Laws," *All Things Considered,* April 22, 2009, http://www.npr.org/templates/story/story.php?storyId=103359330.

2. "A Survey of the Future of Energy: The Power and the Glory," *The Economist*, June 19, 2008, http://www.economist.com/node/11565685.

3. Garrett Hardin, "The Tragedy of the Commons," *Science,* vol. 162, December 13, 1968, pp. 1243–1248, http://science.sciencemag.org/content/162/3859/1243.full.

4. IKEA, "No More Plastic Bags: IKEA Led the Movement Back in 2007 to Phase Out All Plastic Bags," 2012, http://www.ikea.com/ms/en_US/img/ad_content/0612_%20REUSABLE_BAGS.pdf.

5. Sherisse Pham, "Why Apple Is Investing in Wind in China," *CNN.com,* December 9, 2016, http://money.cnn.com/2016/12/09/technology/apple-wind-turbine-china-investment/.

Chapter 9

1. Claudia Deutsch, "At Kodak, Some Old Things Are New Again," *The New York Times,* May 2, 2008, http://www.nytimes.com/2008/05/02/technology/02kodak.html.

2. Chunka Mui, "How Kodak Failed," *Forbes,* June 20, 2016, https://www.forbes.com/sites/chunkamui/2012/01/18/how-kodak-failed/#1926ec746f27.

Chapter 10

1. Anita Balakrishnan, "Snap Closes Up 44% After Rollicking IPO," *CNBC,* March 7, 2017, http://www.cnbc.com/2017/03/02/snapchat-snap-open-trading-price-stock-ipo-first-day.html.

2. Burton Gordon Malkiel, *A Random Walk Down Wall Street: Including a Life-Cycle Guide to Personal Investing* (New York: W.W. Norton, 1999).

3. Robert D. Arnott, Jason Hsu, Vitali Kalesnik, and Phil Tindal, "The Surprising Alpha from Malkiel's Monkey and Upside-Down Strategies," *Journal of Portfolio Management* 39, no. 4 (Summer 2013).

4. Michael Cohen and Rene Vollgraaff, "Zuma Takes S. Africa Economy to Brink as Credit Risks Rise," *Bloomberg.com,* December 10, 2015, http://www.bloomberg.com/news/articles/2015-12-10/zuma-takes-south-africa-economy-to-brink-as-credit-risks-rise.

Chapter 11

1. "Tesla Gigafactory," n.d., accessed May 5, 2017, https://www.tesla.com/gigafactory.

2. "How to Lose Half a Trillion Euros," *The Economist,* October 15, 2013, http://www.economist.com/news/briefing/21587782-europes-electricity-providers-face-existential-threat-how-lose-half-trillion-euros.

Chapter 12

1. Hemant K. Sabat, "Why Mobile Wireless Carriers Share Networks and Services Provisioning," *Research, Practice, and Educational Advancements in Telecommunications and Networking,* 178–211, doi:10.4018/978-1-4666-0050-8.ch011.

2. Robert Wright, "GM Hits Accelerator on Strong US Sales," *Financial Times,* July 23, 2015, https://www.ft.com/content/10fdc962-313a-11e5-8873-775ba7c2ea3d.

3. Liezel Hill, "Barrick Gold Closing Mines to Curb Output as Price Drops," *Bloomberg.com,* August 2, 2013, http://www.bloomberg.com/news/articles/2013-08-02/barrick-gold-closing-mines-to-curb-output-as-price-drops.

Chapter 13

1. Quoted in Drake Baer, "Peter Thiel: Google Has Insane Perks Because It's a Monopoly," *Business Insider,* September 16, 2014, http://www.businessinsider.com/peter-thiel-google-monopoly-2014-9.

2. Brent Kendall, "As Mergers Multiply, U.S. Antitrust Cops Raise Their Game," *The Wall Street Journal,* July 2, 2015, http://www.wsj.com/articles/antitrust-enforcers-gain-confidence-1435877627.

3. Kathlyn Stone, "Popular Drugs Going Off-Patent in 2013–2016," *Verywell,* n.d., accessed May 5, 2017, http://pharma.about.com/od/BigPharma/a/Which-Popular-Drugs-Are-Going-Off-Patent-In-2013-2016.htm.

4. Jeff Horwitz and Chris Cumming, "The Taxi Medallion System in New York and Other Cities Raises Fares, Impoverishes Drivers, and Hurts Passengers. So Why Can't We Get Rid of It?," *Slate,* June 6, 2012, http://www.slate.com/articles/business

/moneybox/2012/06/taxi_medallions_how_new_york_s_terrible
_taxi_system_makes_fares_higher_and_drivers_poorer_.html.

Chapter 14

1. N. H. Borden, "The Concept of the Marketing Mix," *Journal of Advertising Research* (1964): 2–7. Jerome E. McCarthy, *Basic Marketing: A Managerial Approach* (Homewood, IL: Irwin, 1964).

2. Jeff Goodby, "20 Years of 'Got Milk?,'" *Adweek*, October 25, 2013, http://www.adweek.com/creativity/20-years-got-milk -153399/.

3. Marlow Stern, "See How Much It'll Cost to Book Your Favorite Musical Act, from Taylor Swift to Phosphorescent," *The Daily Beast*, January 30, 2017, http://www.thedailybeast.com /articles/2014/05/21/see-how-much-it-ll-cost-to-book-your -favorite-musical-act.html.

4. Kristi Palma, "Ski Lift Discounts Across New England," *Boston.com*, January 16, 2015, https://www .boston.com/culture/new-england-travel/2015/01/16 /ski-lift-discounts-across-new-england.

5. Georgia Wells, "The Dating Business: Love on the Rocks," *The Wall Street Journal*, June 10, 2015, http://www.wsj.com/articles /the-dating-business-love-on-the-rocks-1433980637.

Chapter 15

1. Alec Wilkinson, "What Would Jesus Bet?," *The New Yorker*, May 2, 2016, http://www.newyorker.com/magazine/2009/03/30 /what-would-jesus-bet.

2. Sources for Exhibit 11: Anthony DePalma "Ivy Universities Deny Price-Fixing But Agree to Avoid It in the Future," *The New York Times*, May 23, 1991, http://www.nytimes.com/1991/05/23 /us/ivy-universities-deny-price-fixing-but-agree-to-avoid-it-in-the -future.html; press release, "FTC Charges Two Firms That Control the Market for Laser Eye Surgery with Price-Fixing Conspiracy," Federal Trade Commission, September 13, 2006; Ben Popken, "Get Cash Back in Chip Maker Price Fixing Suit," NBCNews.com, March 10, 2014, http://www.nbcnews.com/business/consumer /get-cash-back-chip-maker-price-fixing-suit-n48971; Joan E. Solsman, "LCD Makers Settle Price-Fixing Claims," *The Wall Street Journal*, December 28, 2011, https://www.wsj.com /articles/SB100014240529702034791045771248637693474 98; Brent Kendall, "U.S. to Fine Auto-Parts Makers $740 Million for Price Fixing," *The Wall Street Journal*, September 26, 2013, https://www.wsj.com/articles/us-fines-autoparts-makers-740 -million-for-pricefixing-1380209172?tesla=y; Stephanie Bodoni, "Germans Overpaid for Beer as Brewery Cartel Fined for Price Fix," Bloomberg.com, January 13, 2014, http://www.bloomberg .com/news/2014-01-13/germans-overpaid-for-beer-as-brewery -cartel-fined-for-price-fix.html.

3. Maria Arbatskaya, Morten Hviid, and Greg Shaffer, "On the Use of Low-Price Guarantees to Discourage Price Cutting," *International Journal of Industrial Organization* (November 2006).

4. R. Axelrod and W. Hamilton, "The Evolution of Cooperation," *Science* 211, no. 4489 (1981): 1390–1396, doi:10.1126/ science.7466396.

5. Emily Coyle, "5 Biggest Super Bowl Advertisers Going for It," *USA Today*, January 29, 2016, https://www.usatoday.com/story /money/business/2014/01/25/5-biggest-advertisers-going-for-it -in-super-bowl/4835695/.

6. Andrew R. Johnson, "Banks Plan New Fees for Using Debit Cards," *The Wall Street Journal*, September 30, 2011, http:// online.wsj.com/news/articles/SB100014240529702041382045 76600800330404330.

7. Tara Siegel Bernard, "In Retreat, Bank of America Cancels Debit Card Fee," *The New York Times*, November 1, 2011, http://

www.nytimes.com/2011/11/02/business/bank-of-america-drops -plan-for-debit-card-fee.html?_r=0.

8. Coyle, "5 Biggest Super Bowl Advertisers."

9. "Yankees, Dodgers Are Hit with 2013 Luxury Tax Bill," *The Wall Street Journal*, December 17, 2013, https://www.wsj.com /articles/heard-onthe-field-1387324054?tesla=y.

10. Keitha Nelson, "UF Health Now Able to Open New Hospital in North Jacksonville," *WTLV*, July 30, 2014, http://www .firstcoastnews.com/story/news/local/2014/07/30 /uf-health-open-new-hospital-north-jacksonville/13390667/.

11. "France to Host Airshow-Style Nuclear Exhibition," *Reuters*, June 5, 2014, http://af.reuters.com/article/ idAFL6N0OM5W920140605.

Chapter 16

1. Tversky died in 1996, making him ineligible for the prize. Other behavioral economists to win the Nobel Prize in Economics include George Akerlof (2001), Robert Fogel (1993), Elinor Ostrom (2009), and Richard Thaler (2017).

2. Michael Bourne, "We Didn't Eat the Marshmallow. The Marshmallow Ate Us," *The New York Times*, January 10, 2014, https://www.nytimes.com/2014/01/12/magazine/we-didnt-eat -the-marshmallow-the-marshmallow-ate-us.html?_r=0.

3. Peter Coy, "Why the Price Is Rarely Right," *Bloomberg Businessweek*, January 21, 2010, http://www.businessweek.com /magazine/content/10_05/b4165077443953.htm.

4. "The Jam Study Strikes Back: When Less Choice Does Mean More Sales," *Digital Intelligence Today*, January 19, 2015, http:// digitalintelligencetoday.com/the-jam-study-strikes-back-when -less-choice-does-mean-more-sales/.

5. Brigitte C. Madrian and Dennis F. Shea, "The Power of Suggestion: Inertia in 401(k) Participation and Savings Behavior," *Quarterly Journal of Economics* 116 (November 4, 2001): 1149–1187.

6. Harold Hotelling, "Stability in Competition," *Economic Journal* 39 (1929): 41–57.

7. Hon Hai, "Kicking the Apple Addiction," *The Economist*, September 3, 2015, http://www.economist.com/news /business/21663248-taiwanese-firm-strives-avoid-over -dependence-its-main-client-kicking-apple.

Chapter 17

1. James Bessen, "Toil and Technology," International Monetary Fund: *Finance & Development*, 52, no. 1 (March 25, 2015), https://www.imf.org/external/pubs/ft/fandd/2015/03/pdf /fd0315.pdf.

2. U.S. Bureau of Labor Statistics and Gerald Mayer, "Union Membership Trends in the United States," Cornell University ILR School, August 31, 2004, http://digitalcommons.ilr.cornell.edu /cgi/viewcontent.cgi?article=1176&context=key_workplace.

Chapter 18

1. Anita Manning, "What It Was Like Being Pregnant in 1915," *Maternal & Child Care* (blog), America's Health Rankings, United Health Foundation, http://publichealthlegacy .americashealthrankings.org/being-pregnant-in-1915.

2. George F. Will, "Think You Live in a 'Hellhole' Today? Try Being a Billionaire in 1916," *Washington Post*, May 5, 2017, http://wapo.st/2pPWkn4?tid=ss_tw&utm_ term=.36beee58875e; Don Boudreaux, "Most Ordinary Americans in 2016 Are Richer Than Was John D. Rockefeller in 1916," *Café Hayek*, February 20, 2016, http://cafehayek. com/2016/02/40405.html.

3. Conor Morris, "Report Digs Deep into Poverty in Athens County," *Athens News*, October 2, 2016, https://www .athensnews.com/news/local/report-digs-deep-into-poverty-in

-athens-county/article_74846a0e-88c3-11e6-9a21-6f5abe5c0291.html.

4. Mark R. Rank, "From Rags to Riches to Rags," *New York Times*, April 20, 2014, accessed May 14, 2017, http://www.nytimes.com/2014/04/20/opinion/Sunday/from-rags-to-riches-to-rags.html?_r=0.

5. Ashley N. Edwards, "Dynamics of Economic Well-Being: Poverty, 2009–2011," U.S. Census Bureau, January 2014, https://www.census.gov/prod/2014pubs/p70-137.pdf.

6. Todd Haselton, "Mark Zuckerberg Joins Silicon Valley Bigwigs in Calling for Government to Give Everybody Free Money," CNBC, May 26, 2017, https://www.cnbc.com/2017/05/25/mark-zuckerberg-calls-for-universal-basic-income-at-harvard-speech.html.

Chapter 19

1. "About CarMax," CarMax, https://www.carmax.com/about-carmax.

2. Ayaz Nanji, "World's Smallest Baby Goes Home," CBS News, February 8, 2005, accessed May 7, 2017, https://www.cbsnews.com/news/worlds-smallest-baby-goes-home/.

3. In 2013, the U.S. Census began phrasing questions about health coverage in terms of "at any point during the year" rather than "at the current time." According to the census, "the estimates from the 2013 calendar year and later are not directly comparable to 2012 and prior years." Estimates suggest a similar pattern with a sharp decline in the rate of uninsured in 2014. For more details, see Jessica C. Smith and Carla Medalia, "Health Insurance Coverage in the United States: 2013," Current Population Reports, September 2014, https://census.gov/content/dam/Census/library/publications/2014/demo/p60-250.pdf.

4. "Why Health Insurance Is Important: Protection from High Medical Costs," HealthCare.gov, https://www.healthcare.gov/why-coverage-is-important/protection-from-high-medical-costs.

5. OECD (2017), Health at a Glance 2017: OECD Indicators, OECD Publishing, Paris. http://dx.doi.org/10.1787/health_glance-2017-en.

6. Cheryl Hosmer, "Top Five Most Expensive Medical Devices," Top5.com, August 2, 2013, accessed May 8, 2017, http://random-facts.top5.com/top-5-most-expensive-medical-devices.

7. "The Cost of Dying," produced by Andy Court, CBS News, November 19, 2009, accessed May 7, 2017, http://www.cbsnews.com/news/the-cost-of-dying.

8. Justin E. Bekelman, Scott D. Halpern, Carl Rudolf Blankart, Julie P. Bynum, Joachim Cohen, Robert Fowler, Stein Kaasa, Lukas Kwietniewski, Hans Olav Melberg, Bregje Onwuteaka-Philipsen, Mariska Oosterveld-Vlug, Andrew Pring, Jonas Schreyögg, Connie M. Ulrich, Julia Verne, Hannah Wunsch, Ezekiel J. Emanuel, "Comparison of Site of Death, Health Care Utilization, and Hospital Expenditures for Patients Dying with Cancer in 7 Developed Countries." *JAMA* 315, no. 3 (2016): 272, doi: 10.1001/jama.2015.18603.

Chapter 20

1. Valerie A. Ramey and Neville Francis, "A Century of Work and Leisure," *American Economic Journal: Macroeconomics* 1, no. 2 (2009): 189–224.

2. Paulina Restrepo-Echavarria, "Measuring the Underground Economy Can Be Done, But It Is Difficult," *Regional Economist*, January 2015, Federal Reserve Bank of St. Louis, https://www.stlouisfed.org/publications/regional-economist/january-2015/underground-economy; Matthew Johnson, "How Big Is the Underground Economy in America?," Investopedia, March 29, 2016, http://www.investopedia.com/articles/markets/032916/how-big-underground-economy-america.asp.

Chapter 21

1. C. W., "The Economy Doesn't Matter: Why the American Labour Market Is Still So Slack" (blog), *The Economist*, April 22, 2015,

http://www.economist.com/blogs/freeexchange/2015/04/americas-labour-market.

2. A study by David G. Blanchflower and Alex Bryson estimated the wage premium to be 16.5% in 2002. David G. Blanchflower and Alex Bryson, "The Union Wage Premium in the US and the UK," Centre for Economic Performance, London School of Economics and Political Science, London, February 2004, http://cep.lse.ac.uk/pubs/download/dp0612.pdf.

3. "[Ford] Gives $10,000,000 to 26,000 Employees," *New York Times*, January 5, 1914, http://www.nytimes.com/learning/general/onthisday/big/0105.html#article.

4. Rebecca Rothbaum, "Empire State Building Shoe-Repair Shop to Close after Decades," Wall Street Journal, June 18, 2015, http://www.wsj.com/articles/pitching-it-after-decades-in-business-1434675403.

Chapter 22

1. Hernando De Soto, *The Other Path: The Invisible Revolution in the Third World* (New York: Harper & Row, 1989).

2. Robert J. Gordon, "Is U.S. Economic Growth Over? Faltering Innovation Confronts the Six Headwinds," NBER Working Paper 18315, National Bureau of Economic Research, August 2012.

Chapter 23

1. Min-Jeong Lee, "Samsung to Invest $14.7 Billion in New Chip Plant in South Korea," *Wall Street Journal*, October 6, 2014, http://www.wsj.com/articles/samsung-to-invest-14-7-billion-in-chip-plant-1412559544?cb=logged0.2621279819868505.

Chapter 24

1. Benjamin Wiker, *Ten Books Every Conservative Must Read: Plus Four Not to Miss and One Impostor* (Washington, DC: Regnery, 2010), 180.

2. Christopher J. Neely. "The Federal Reserve Responds to Crises: September 11th Was Not the First," Federal Reserve Bank of St. Louis *Review*, 86, no. 2 (March–April 2004): 27–42, https://ideas.repec.org/a/fip/fedlrv/y2004imarp27-42nv.86no.2.html.

Chapter 25

1. Quoted in Peter Coy, "Milton Friedman: Death of a Giant," *Bloomberg*, November 18, 2006, https://www.bloomberg.com/news/articles/2006-11-17/milton-friedman-death-of-a-giantbusinessweek-business-news-stock-market-and-financial-advice.

Chapter 26

1. Stephen Silver and Scott Sumner, "Nominal and Real Wage Cyclicality During the Interwar Period," *Southern Economic Journal* 61, no. 3 (1995): 588–601.

2. "Telephone Operators," Engineering and Technology History Wiki, accessed May 25, 2017, http://ethw.org/Telephone_Operators; "Occupational Employment and Wages, May 2016, 43-2021 Telephone Operators," Bureau of Labor Statistics, http://www.bls.gov/oes/current/oes432021.htm.

3. "A Look at the Recovery of the Canadian Auto Sector since the 2008–09 Recession," Royal Bank of Canada (RBC), May 2014, http://www.rbc.com/economics/economic-reports/pdf/other-reports/Auto_May_2014.pdf.

4. Bill Vlasic, "Detroit Sets Its Future on a Foundation of Two-Tier Wages," *New York Times*, September 12, 2011, http://www.nytimes.com/2011/09/13/business/in-detroit-two-wage-levels-are-the-new-way-of-work.html?pagewanted=all.

5. "Shock Treatment," *The Economist*, November 15, 2007, http://www.economist.com/node/10130655.

6. Ibid.

Chapter 27

1. N. Gregory Mankiw, "New Keynesian Economics," *The Concise Encyclopedia of Economics*, Library of Economics and Liberty,

accessed May 26, 2017, http://www.econlib.org/library/Enc/NewKeynesianEconomics.html.
2. David Jolly, "Swiss National Bank to Adopt a Negative Interest Rate," *New York Times*, December 18, 2014, http://www.nytimes.com/2014/12/19/business/switzerland-central-bank-interest-rate.html.
3. This anecdote appears in Liaquat Ahamed, *Lords of Finance: The Bankers Who Broke the World* (New York: Penguin Press, 2009), 277.
4. Federal Reserve Bank of New York, "Forward Guidance," Search Results, accessed May 26, 2017, http://search.newyorkfed.org/board_public/search?source=board_pub&text=forward%2Bguidance&submit=Search.
5. Federal Reserve Bank of New York, "FOMC Statement," press release. November 3, 2010, http://www.federalreserve.gov/newsevents/press/monetary/20101103a.htm

Chapter 28

1. Calculated by the authors.
2. Paul Krugman, "The Stimulus Trap," *New York Times*, July 9, 2009, http://www.nytimes.com/2009/07/10/opinion/10krugman.html; Paul Krugman, "On Not Listening," *New York Times*, November 3, 2009, https://krugman.blogs.nytimes.com/2009/11/03/on-not-listening/?_r=0.
3. Eric J. Barr, "The History of Federal Statutory Tax Rates in Maximum Income Brackets and the Evolution of Different Forms of Business Entities," *Valuing Pass-Through Entities* (Hoboken, NJ Wiley, 2014), 11–40.
4. John F. Kennedy, "Address to the Economic Club of New York," December 14, 1962, http://www.americanrhetoric.com/speeches/jfkeconomicclubaddress.html.
5. Barr, "The History of Federal Statutory Tax Rates."
6. "Laffer Curve," survey, IGM Forum, University of Chicago Booth School of Business, June 26, 2012, http://www.igmchicago.org/igm-economic-experts-panel/poll-results?SurveyID=SV_2irlrss5UC27YXi.
7. "Annual Lobbying on Communications/Electronics," Sector Profile: 2017, Communications/Electronics, Center for Responsive Politics, 2017, https://www.opensecrets.org/lobby/indus.php?id=B&year=2017.
8. Bill Cassidy and Louis Woodhill, "Dismal Growth Needs the 3.5% Solution," *Wall Street Journal*, April 30, 2015, http://www.wsj.com/articles/dismal-growth-needs-the-3-5-solution-1430436920.
9. Tatsuo Ito, "Japan Government Takes on Its Deficit-Ridden Finances," *Wall Street Journal*, June 17, 2015, http://www.wsj.com/articles/japan-government-takes-on-its-deficit-ridden-finances-1434569402.
10. Eric Rosengren, "The Economic Outlook and Unconventional Monetary Policy," paper presented at the Stephen D. Cutler Center for Investments for Finance, Babson College, Wellesley, Massachusetts, November 1, 2012, https://www.bostonfed.org/news-and-events/speeches/the-economic-outlook-and-unconventional-monetary-policy.aspx.
11. Bruce Bartlett, "Did the Stimulus Stimulate?," *Forbes*, December 4, 2009, http://www.forbes.com/2009/12/03/tax-cuts-stimulus-jobs-opinions-columnists-bruce-bartlett.html.

Chapter 30

1. Janet Yellen, "Inflation Dynamics and Monetary Policy," Philip Gamble Memorial Lecture, University of Massachusetts, Amherst, Massachusetts, September 24, 2015, https://www.federalreserve.gov/newsevents/speech/yellen20150924a.htm.
2. Greg Ip, "The Fed's Bad Options for Addressing Too-Low Inflation," *Wall Street Journal*, September 13, 2017, https://www.wsj.com/articles/the-feds-awful-options-for-addressing-too-low-inflation-1505313425.
3. See Milton Friedman, "The Role of Monetary Policy," *American Economic Review* 58, no. 1 (March 1968): 1–17; and Edmund S. Phelps, "Money-Wage Dynamics and Labor-Market Equilibrium," *Journal of Political Economy* 76 (1968): 678–711.

Chapter 31

1. Michael Gerson, "Cotton and Conscience," *Washington Post*, November 7, 2007, http://www.washingtonpost.com/wp-dyn/content/article/2007/11/06/AR2007110601808.html.

Chapter 32

1. Cara Waters, "How to Be a Global Business from Day One," *Sydney Morning Herald*, February 16, 2017, http://www.smh.com.au/small-business/startup/etsys-linda-kozlowski-on-how-to-be-a-global-business-from-day-one-20170216-gue7av.html.
2. Chris Woodyard, "Japan's Toyota Has the Most Made-in-the USA Car: Camry," *USA Today*, July 1, 2016, http://www.usatoday.com/story/money/cars/2016/06/29/survey-top-made-usa-cars-toyota-honda/86510052/.

Chapter 33

1. "Who Wants to Be a Triple Trillionnaire? Window Shopping with China's Central Bank," *The Economist*, April 14, 2011, http://www.economist.com/node/18560525.